Social Deviance

Social Deviance

Readings in Theory and Research

Edited by

HENRY N. PONTELL
University of California, Irvine
and
STEPHEN M. ROSOFF
University of Houston–Clear Lake

Mc
Graw
Hill
Connect
Learn
Succeed™

The McGraw·Hill Companies

SOCIAL DEVIANCE: READINGS IN THEORY AND RESEARCH, FIRST EDITION

Published by McGraw-Hill, a business unit of The McGraw-Hill Companies, Inc., 1221 Avenue of the Americas, New York, NY 10020. Copyright © 2011 by The McGraw-Hill Companies, Inc. All rights reserved. No part of this publication may be reproduced or distributed in any form or by any means, or stored in a database or retrieval system, without the prior written consent of The McGraw-Hill Companies, Inc., including, but not limited to, in any network or other electronic storage or transmission, or broadcast for distance learning.

Some ancillaries, including electronic and print components, may not be available to customers outside the United States.

This book is printed on acid-free paper.

1 2 3 4 5 6 7 8 9 0 DOC/DOC 1 0 9 8 7 6 5 4 3 2 1 0

ISBN 978-0-07-340441-7
MHID 0-07-340441-1

Vice President & Editor-in-Chief: *Michael Ryan*
VP EDP/Central Publishing Services: *Kimberly Meriwether David*
Senior Sponsoring Editor: *Gina Boedeker*
Managing Editor: *Meghan Campbell*
Executive Marketing Manager: *Pamela S. Cooper*
Senior Project Manager: *Jane Mohr*
Cover Designer: *Margarite Reynolds*
USE Cover Image Credit: *Chad Baker*
Senior Production Supervisor: *Laura Fuller*
Compositor: *Laserwords Private Limited*
Typeface: *10/12 Perpetua Regular*
Printer: *R.R. Donnelley*

All credits appearing on page or at the end of the book are considered to be an extension of the copyright page.

Library of Congress Cataloging-in-Publication Data

Social deviance : readings in theory and research / edited by Henry N. Pontell and Stephen M. Rosoff. — 1st ed.
   p. cm.
  This work is McGraw-Hill's 1st ed. of: Social deviance/edited by Henry N. Pontell. 5th ed. Upper Saddle River, N.J. : Pearson Prentice Hall, c2005.
   ISBN 978-0-07-340441-7 (alk. paper)
   1. Deviant behavior. I. Pontell, Henry N., 1950– II. Rosoff, Stephen M.
   HM811.S58835 2011
   302.5'42—dc22

2009054447

www.mhhe.com

For our families and friends and in memory of Edwin M. Lemert

Contents

Preface

*S*OCIAL DEVIANCE: READINGS IN THEORY AND *Research* provides a comprehensive source of classic and contemporary selections for students studying deviance. In its first edition with McGraw-Hill, the current volume, now co-edited with Stephen Rosoff of the University of Houston–Clear Lake, builds upon the strengths of past editions. Its contents highlight major sociological and social psychological perspectives that represent the core efforts of the academic field of social deviance, and which describe, explain, and analyze factors related to who becomes deviant, how and why deviant categories arise, and how individual and institutional reactions help define the social reality of deviance (the behavior) and deviants (the persons).

To laypersons, the subject of deviance may appear unusual, exotic, or strange, as it would appear to involve behaviors at the fringes of conventional society. However, it could be reasonably argued that understanding deviance and social control are necessary for understanding society itself. For example, how and why social rules and laws change, how communities adapt or stagnate, how social movements affect our overall values and personal outlooks, why group conflicts are important, how and why punishment operates in the ways that it does, and how the existence of deviance facilitates social change, to name but a few of the most significant general issues raised in this text, are all centrally important to understanding society. The selections in this book address these issues and many more. Moreover, as the field has developed over time, new and important work has emerged in various areas, both theoretical and substantive. The feminist perspective, for example, has added a new and exciting dimension to the field, and we have included classic and contemporary selections that are representative of the best and most interesting work among feminist scholars. Similarly, advances in white-collar theorizing are well represented in this edition, as the topic has become more important in recent years with the major corporate

and accounting meltdowns in the early 1990s, as well as the global economic crisis that has yet to reach its peak at the time of this writing. Throughout the book we have added works that we feel will provide the most enlightening and enriching experiences for students, by providing both a solid grounding in the field, and a means by which to examine more contemporary issues.

We have organized the book in a manner in which we have taught our courses at UC, Irvine and the University of Houston for many years, and which we believe provides an ideal progression of topics and ideas for students who are learning about the subject of social deviance for the first time. After a general introduction to the field (Part I) which includes classic pieces by highly noted authors, the text moves on to the major theoretical perspectives used by researchers and scholars in studying deviance. In this section (Part II) students learn about the various analytical approaches that dominate the academic literature. Most of these pieces are classic works by major figures in the field, and would be discussed at length in most, if not all, college courses on the subject of deviance. The third and final part of the book includes selections that analyze specific forms of deviance. In part III, students can see how the theories and ideas presented earlier in the book can be used to study actual behaviors. Overall, we believe that both the contents and this particular organizational approach provide educational materials appropriate for both undergraduates and graduate student at any college or university who are being introduced to the field of deviance. Moreover, we feel that students who spend time with the materials presented here will become as knowledgeable as those anywhere in the world in terms of a general introduction to the field of deviance. While the organization of topics essentially remains the same as in previous editions, at the suggestion of both colleagues and students we have added new selections throughout the text in addition to new sections on "organized crime" and "physical attributes." Our major objectives in this new edition were: (1) to continue to present both classic theoretical works as well as contemporary substantive research, (2) to provide a broad array of selections representing different perspectives in the field of deviance, and (3) to include readings that would both ignite interest and be suitable for undergraduates.

While some of the older theoretical selections are occasionally more difficult for students to comprehend, they represent major influences in the development of the field of deviance and deserve attention and understanding. In this new edition, we have edited them from their longer versions, reducing the burden of getting through them. In addition, we have included new pedagogical aids at the end of each selection to challenge students to think about what they have just read and to make sure that they have grasped key concepts and information. Each piece is followed by two questions which ask students to analyze what they have just read. Our goal in including them was to provide exercises that allow students to expand upon what they have learned in a creative manner, by using historical examples, the Internet, and experiential knowledge and information. We think that the questions will be of great value, both in igniting classroom discussions and/or providing the basis of more formal written assignments.

This edition has greatly benefited from the work and dedication of our undergraduate research assistants, Giovanni Curcio, Audrey Nguyen, and Reid Whitney of UCI, who helped secure articles and permissions and who sat through numerous meetings where the potential merits of all articles were discussed. We greatly appreciate their efforts and hard work. We also thank Mervyn Vaz in the Department of Criminology, Law and Society at UC, Irvine for his superb support in helping to get the final manuscript off to the publisher. We also thank development editor Lai T. Moy, who helped prepare the manuscript for publication. And to all our editors at McGraw Hill, Meghan Campbell and Gina Boedecker, who have been wonderfully supportive throughout the entire publishing process, we highly value your professional wisdom and friendship and greatly appreciate your faith in our efforts. Finally, we would like to acknowledge and thank the students in our deviance courses for their valuable comments and suggestions regarding past editions that should result in continued improvements to this book.

HENRY N. PONTELL
University of California, Irvine

STEPHEN M. ROSOFF
University of Houston—Clear Lake

Note to the Reader

THE LANGUAGE USED IN SOME OF THESE pieces may be offensive to some readers in that it may reflect insensitivity towards certain social groups. Neither the text author, the publisher nor, for that matter, any of the individual authors to our knowledge, condone or agree with language that could be construed as being racist, sexist, homophobic, or insensitive to the handicapped or other groups. It is the intention of the author and publisher that the chapters be read in the context of the era and theoretical perspective within which they were produced, and valued for their main contributions to the historical development of the field of social deviance.

Understanding Deviance and Conformity: An Introduction

WHAT IS DEVIANCE? THIS IS A DIFFICULT question to answer simply, as the term conjures up many disparate images that take on different meanings to various audiences. Prostitutes, alcoholics, burglars, drug addicts, and transvestites may come to mind. Or, at the other end of the spectrum of respectability, one might think of Michael Milken, Martha Stewart, Enron's Jeffrey Skilling, or others convicted of offenses related to financial activities and who served time in prison. While it may appear that such a wide spectrum of acts has nothing in common, they all represent examples of deviant behavior, in that they involve actions and characteristics that have elicited negative reactions from relatively large or powerful audiences. This is not meant to imply that there is a universal definition of deviance agreed upon by social scientists. On the contrary, those who study the phenomenon are still not in full agreement regarding a precise way to characterize it. The chapters that follow will present these different theoretical concerns and research approaches regarding the study of deviance.

The introductory pieces to this volume provide clear examples of this diversity of thought and represent important contributions to the study of deviance. Howard Becker's classic conception and treatment of "moral entrepreneurs" examines how deviant categories are created and how enforcement of these categories is socially structured. The moral crusader or "rule creator" has a personal stake in the content of social rules and works to change them to fit his and her own world view. The "rule enforcer," on the other hand, takes a detached view of the rule itself and is more interested in work situations involving enforcement. This detachment and concern over job responsibilities leads enforcers to label deviance in a selective manner. Thus, Becker concludes that whether one is actually labeled a deviant depends on factors extraneous to the behavior itself. This idea is central to the labeling perspective on deviance.

Gary Marx's article, "Ironies of Social Control," focuses on a relatively neglected area of study: the interactive context within which deviance occurs. In this important piece, Marx argues that authorities themselves may in fact help deviance and lawbreaking to occur. He classifies those instances where authorities contribute to, or even generate, deviant behavior as including three ideal types. "Escalation" refers to enforcement action that may unintentionally encourage rule breaking. "Nonenforcement" refers to the idea that by not taking action authorities intentionally permit rule breaking. "Covert facilitation" occurs when authorities take deceptive or hidden action that intentionally encourages rule breaking. Marx presents examples of each type of action and shows how more than one may be involved in a given example of rule breaking. His study provides ample evidence that police efforts can positively influence the commission of offenses, a novel idea that appears to fly in the face of both popular and scholarly understandings of deviance and formal social control.

In the "'Discovery' of Child Abuse," Stephen Pfohl examines the social forces that promoted the labeling of child beating as deviant and that produced universal criminal legislation in the 1960s. This is an important work that illustrates how deviant categories are created. Using a historical framework, Pfohl considers the social reaction to child abuse before the formulation of a fixed label and finds that such reactions were sporadic. He shows that the perception of abuse as deviance was not due to any escalation in the behavior itself, but rather to the organizational structure of the medical profession, which led to the "discovery" by pediatric radiologists, who saw

X-rays of broken bones. A new "illness" was created, and the clinical term of "battered child syndrome" was used so that medical practitioners could control the consequences of their diagnoses and prevent management of such cases by extramedical formal social control agents. Pfohl discusses the consequences of this definition for both child abuse legislation and the prosecution of abusers.

In his essay, "Defining Deviancy Down," sociologist and former U.S. Senator from New York, Daniel Patrick Moynihan, laments that more deviance is tolerated in society now than in earlier eras. A judge cited by Moynihan labels this phenomenon "trivializing the lunatic crime rate," whereby citizens become accustomed to an extraordinarily high rate of deviance in society, which appears "normal." Moynihan questions this Durkheimian notion (which is discussed in Section I of this book), asserting that while a certain degree of deviance in society is inevitable and indeed normal, exactly *how much should be tolerated* is a completely separate issue which has not received adequate attention in sociological quarters.

The essay, "Trivializing the Lunatic Crime Rate: Theory Praxis and the Global Economic Meltdown" updates and broadens the scope of Moynihan's analysis by examining how massive amounts of white-collar and corporate crime are tolerated in society, and how this relates to the 2008 U.S. economic crisis that spread to the global financial system. It examines how white-collar crime has been trivialized at both academic and policy levels, and how this results in increasingly severe and widespread financial debacles in which fraud plays a significant, yet still largely unappreciated, role. Moreover, it puts white-collar and corporate crime into theoretical and practical focus as major forms of deviance that continue to have devastating effects on people throughout the world, and whose frequency certainly measures up to—or perhaps far surpasses—the "lunatic crime rate" referred to by Moynihan years ago. ✳

Moral Entrepreneurs
The Creation and Enforcement of Deviant Categories*

Howard S. Becker

Rule Creators

The prototype of the rule creator, but not the only variety, as we shall see, is the crusading reformer. He is interested in the content of rules. The existing rules do not satisfy him because there is some evil which profoundly disturbs him. He feels that nothing can be right in the world until rules are made to correct it. He operates with an absolute ethic; what he sees is truly and totally evil with no qualification. Any means is justified to do away with it. The crusader is fervent and righteous, often self-righteous.

It is appropriate to think of reformers as crusaders because they typically believe that their mission is a holy one. The prohibitionist serves as an excellent example, as does the person who wants to suppress vice and sexual delinquency or the person who wants to do away with gambling.

These examples suggest that the moral crusader is a meddling busybody, interested in forcing his own morals on others. But this is a one-sided view. Many moral crusades have strong humanitarian overtones. The crusader is not only interested in seeing to it that other people do what he thinks [is] right. He believes that if they do what is right it will be good for them. Or he may feel that his reform will prevent certain kinds of exploitation of one person by another. Prohibitionists felt that they were not simply forcing their morals on others, but attempting to provide the conditions for a better way of life for people prevented by drink from realizing a truly good life. Abolitionists were not simply trying to prevent slave owners from doing the wrong thing; they were trying to help slaves achieve a better life. Because of the importance of the humanitarian motive, moral crusaders (despite their

---

relatively single-minded devotion to their particular cause) often lend their support to other humanitarian crusades. Joseph Gusfield has pointed out that:

> The American temperance movement during the 19th century was part of a general effort toward the improvement of the worth of the human being through improved morality as well as economic conditions. The mixture of the religious, the equalitarian, and the humanitarian was an outstanding facet of the moral reformism of many movements. Temperance supporters formed a large segment of movements such as sabbatarianism, abolition, woman's rights, agrarianism, and humanitarian attempts to improve the lot of the poor. . . .
>
> In its auxiliary interests the WCTU revealed a great concern for the improvement of the welfare of the lower classes. It was active in campaigns to secure penal reform, to shorten working hours and raise wages for workers, and to abolish child labor and in a number of other humanitarian and equalitarian activities. In the 1880's the WCTU worked to bring about legislation for the protection of working girls against the exploitation by men.[1]

As Gusfield says,[2] "Moral reformism of this type suggests the approach of a dominant class toward those less favorably situated in the economic and social structure." Moral crusaders typically want to help those beneath them to achieve a better status. That those beneath them do not always like the means proposed for their salvation is another matter. But this fact—that moral crusades are typically dominated by those in the upper levels of the social structure—means that they add to the power they derive from the legitimacy of their moral position, the power they derive from their superior position in society.

Naturally, many moral crusades draw support from people whose motives are less pure than those of the crusader. Thus, some industrialists supported Prohibition because they felt it would provide them with a

---

more manageable labor force.[3] Similarly, it is sometimes rumored that Nevada gambling interests support the opposition to attempts to legalize gambling in California because it would cut so heavily into their business, which depends in substantial measure on the population of Southern California.[4]

The moral crusader, however, is more concerned with ends than with means. When it comes to drawing up specific rules (typically in the form of legislation to be proposed to a state legislature or the federal Congress), he frequently relies on the advice of experts. Lawyers, expert in the drawing of acceptable legislation, often play this role. Government bureaus in whose jurisdiction the problem falls may also have the necessary expertise, as did the Federal Bureau of Narcotics in the case of the marihuana problem.

As psychiatric ideology, however, becomes increasingly acceptable, a new expert has appeared—the psychiatrist. Sutherland, in his discussion of the natural history of sexual psychopath laws, pointed to the psychiatrist's influence.[5] He suggests the following as the conditions under which the sexual psychopath law, which provides that a person "who is diagnosed as a sexual psychopath may be confined for an indefinite period in a state hospital for the insane,"[6] will be passed.

> First, these laws are customarily enacted after a state of fear has been aroused in a community by a few serious sex crimes committed in quick succession. This is illustrated in Indiana, where a law was passed following three or four sexual attacks in Indianapolis, with murder in two. Heads of families bought guns and watch dogs, and the supply of locks and chains in the hardware stores of the city was completely exhausted. . . .
>
> A second element in the process of developing sexual psychopath laws is the agitated activity of the community in connection with the fear. The attention of the community is focused on sex crimes, and people in the most varied situations envisage dangers and see the need of and possibility for their control. . . .
>
> The third phase in the development of those sexual psychopath laws has been the appointment of a committee. The committee gathers the many conflicting recommendations of persons and groups of persons, attempts to determine "facts," studies procedures in other states, and makes recommendations, which generally include bills for the legislature. Although the general fear usually subsides within a few days, a

committee has the formal duty of following through until positive action is taken. Terror which does not result in a committee is much less likely to result in a law.[7]

In the case of sexual psychopath laws, there usually is no government agency charged with dealing in a specialized way with sexual deviations. Therefore, when the need for expert advice in drawing up legislation arises, people frequently turn to the professional group most closely associated with such problems:

> In some states, at the committee stage of the development of a sexual psychopath law, psychiatrists have played an important part. The psychiatrists, more than any others, have been the interest group back of the laws. A committee of psychiatrists and neurologists in Chicago wrote the bill which became the sexual psychopath law of Illinois; the bill was sponsored by the Chicago Bar Association and by the state's attorney of Cook County and was enacted with little opposition in the next session of the State Legislature. In Minnesota all the members of the governor's committee except one were psychiatrists. In Wisconsin the Milwaukee Neuropsychiatric Society shared in pressing the Milwaukee Crime Commission for the enactment of a law. In Indiana the attorney-general's committee received from the American Psychiatric Association copies of all the sexual psychopath laws which had been enacted in other states.[8]

The influence of psychiatrists in other realms of the criminal law has increased in recent years.

In any case, what is important about this example is not that psychiatrists are becoming increasingly influential, but that the moral crusader, at some point in the development of his crusade, often requires the services of a professional who can draw up the appropriate rules in an appropriate form. The crusader himself is often not concerned with such details. Enough for him that the main point has been won; he leaves its implementation to others.

By leaving the drafting of the specific rule in the hands of others, the crusader opens the door for many unforeseen influences. For those who draft legislation for crusaders have their own interest, which may affect the legislation they prepare. It is likely that the sexual psychopath laws drawn by psychiatrists contain many features never intended by the citizens who spearheaded the drives to "do something about sex crimes," features which do however reflect the professional interests of organized psychiatry.

Rule Enforcers

The most obvious consequence of a successful crusade is the creation of a new set of rules. With the creation of a new set of rules we often find that a new set of enforcement agencies and officials is established. Sometimes, of course, existing agencies take over the administration of the new rule, but more frequently a new set of rule enforcers is created. The passage of the Harrison Act presaged the creation of the Federal Narcotics Bureau, just as the passage of the Eighteenth Amendment led to the creation of police agencies charged with enforcing the Prohibition Laws.

With the establishment of organizations of rule enforcers, the crusade becomes institutionalized. What started out as a drive to convince the world of the moral necessity of a new rule finally becomes an organization devoted to the enforcement of the rule. Just as radical political movements turn into organized political parties and lusty evangelical sects become staid religious denominations, the final outcome of the moral crusade is a police force. To understand, therefore, how the rules creating a new class of outsiders are applied to particular people we must understand the motives and interests of police, the rule enforcers.

Although some policemen undoubtedly have a kind of crusading interest in stamping out evil, it is probably much more typical for the policeman to have a certain detached and objective view of his job. He is not so much concerned with the content of any particular rule as he is with the fact that it is his job to enforce the rule. When the rules are changed, he punishes what was once acceptable behavior just as he ceases to punish behavior that has been made legitimate by a change in the rules. The enforcer, then, may not be interested in the content of the rule as such, but only in the fact that the existence of the rule provides him with a job, a profession, and a raison d'être.

Since the enforcement of certain rules provides justification for his way of life, the enforcer has two interests which condition his enforcement activity: first, he must justify the existence of his position and, second, he must win the respect of those he deals with.

These interests are not peculiar to rule enforcer. Members of all occupations feel the need to justify their work and win the respect of others. Musicians would like to do this but have difficulty finding ways of successfully impressing their worth on customers. Janitors fail to win their tenants' respect, but develop an ideology which stresses the quasi-professional responsibility they have to keep confidential the intimate knowledge of tenants they acquire in the course of their work.[9] Physicians, lawyers, and other professionals, more successful in winning the respect of clients, develop elaborate mechanisms for maintaining a properly respectful relationship.

In justifying the existence of his position, the rule enforcer faces a double problem. On the one hand, he must demonstrate to others that the problem still exists: The rules he is supposed to enforce have some point, because infractions occur. On the other hand, he must show that his attempts at enforcement are effective and worthwhile, that the evil he is supposed to deal with is in fact being dealt with adequately. Therefore, enforcement organizations, particularly when they are seeking funds, typically oscillate between two kinds of claims. First, they say that by reason of their efforts the problem they deal with is approaching solution. But, in the same breath, they say the problem is perhaps worse than ever (though through no fault of their own) and requires renewed and increased effort to keep it under control. Enforcement officials can be more vehement than anyone else in their insistence that the problem they are supposed to deal with is still with us, in fact is more with us than ever before. In making these claims, enforcement officials provide good reason for continuing the existence of the position they occupy.

We may also note that enforcement officials and agencies are inclined to take a pessimistic view of human nature. If they do not actually believe in original sin, they at least like to dwell on the difficulties in getting people to abide by rules, on the characteristics of human nature that lead people toward evil. They are skeptical of attempts to reform rule-breakers.

The skeptical and pessimistic outlook of the rule enforcer, of course, is reinforced by his daily experience. He sees, as he goes about his work, the evidence that the problem is still with us. He sees the people who continually repeat offenses, thus definitely branding themselves in his eyes as outsiders. Yet it is not too great a stretch of the imagination to suppose that one of the underlying reasons for the enforcer's pessimism about human nature and the possibilities of reform is that fact that if human nature were perfectible and people could be permanently reformed, his job would come to an end.

In the same way, a rule enforcer is likely to believe that it is necessary for the people he deals with to respect him. If they do not, it will be very difficult to do his job;

his feeling of security in his work will be lost. Therefore, a good deal of enforcement activity is devoted not to the actual enforcement of rules, but to coercing respect from the people the enforcer deals with. This means that one may be labeled as a deviant not because he has actually broken a rule, but because he has shown disrespect to the enforcer of the rule.

Westley's study of policemen in a small industrial city furnishes a good example of this phenomenon. In his interview, he asked policemen, "When do you think a policeman is justified in roughing a man up?" He found that "at least 37% of the men believed that it was legitimate to use violence to coerce respect."[10] He gives some illuminating quotations from his interviews:

> Well, there are cases. For example, when you stop a fellow for a routine questioning, say a wise guy, and he starts talking back to you and telling you you are no good and that sort of thing. You know you can take a man in on a disorderly conduct charge, but you can practically never make it stick. So what you do in a case like that is to egg the guy on until he makes a remark where you can justifiably slap him and, then, if he fights back, you can call it resisting arrest.
>
> Well, a prisoner deserves to be hit when he goes to the point where he tries to put you below him.
>
> You've gotta get rough when a man's language becomes very bad, when he is trying to make a fool of you in front of everybody else. I think most policemen try to treat people in a nice way, but usually you have to talk pretty rough. That's the only way to set a man down, to make him show a little respect.[11]

What Westley describes is the use of an illegal means of coercing respect from others. Clearly, when a rule enforcer has the option of enforcing a rule or not, the difference in what he does may be caused by the attitude of the offender toward him. If the offender is properly respectful, the enforcer may smooth the situation over. If the offender is disrespectful, then sanctions may be visited on him. Westley has shown that this differential tends to operate in the case of traffic offenses, where the policeman's discretion is perhaps at a maximum.[12] But it probably operates in other areas as well.

Ordinarily, the rule enforcer has a great deal of discretion in many areas, if only because his resources are not sufficient to cope with the volume of rule-breaking he is supposed to deal with. This means that he cannot tackle everything at once and to this extent must temporize with evil. He cannot do the whole job and knows it. He takes his time, on the assumption that the problems he deals with will be around for a long while. He establishes priorities, dealing with things in their turn, handling the most pressing problems immediately and leaving others for later. His attitude toward his work, in short, is professional. He lacks the naive moral fervor characteristic of the rule creator.

If the enforcer is not going to tackle every case he knows of at once, he must have a basis for deciding when to enforce the rule, which persons committing which acts to label as deviant. One criterion for selecting people is the "fix." Some people have sufficient political influence or know-how to be able to ward off attempts at enforcement, if not at the time of apprehension then at a later stage in the process. Very often, this function is professionalized; someone performs the job on a full-time basis, available to anyone who wants to hire him. A professional thief described fixers this way:

> There is in every large city a regular fixer for professional thieves. He has no agents and does not solicit and seldom takes any case except that of a professional thief, just as they seldom go to anyone except him. This centralized and monopolized system of fixing for professional thieves is found in practically all of the large cities and many of the small ones.[13]

Since it is mainly professional thieves who know about the fixer and his operations, the consequence of this criterion for selecting people to apply the rules to is that amateurs tend to be caught, convicted, and labeled deviant much more frequently than professionals. As the professional thief notes:

> You can tell by the way the case is handled in court when the fix is in. When the copper is not very certain he has the right man, or the testimony of the copper and the complainant does not agree, or the prosecutor goes easy on the defendant, or the judge is arrogant in his decisions, you can always be sure that someone has got the word in. This does not happen in many cases of theft, for there is one case of a professional to twenty-five or thirty amateurs who know nothing about the fix. These amateurs get the hard end of the deal every time. The coppers bawl out about the thieves, no one holds up his testimony, the judge delivers an oration, and all of them get credit for stopping a crime wave. When the professional hears the case immediately

preceding his own, he will think, "He should have got ninety years. It's the damn amateurs who cause all the heat in the stores." Or else he thinks, "Isn't it a damn shame for that copper to send that kid away for a pair of hose, and in a few minutes he will agree to a small fine for me for stealing a fur coat?" But if the coppers did not send the amateurs away to strengthen their records of convictions, they could not sandwich in the professionals whom they turn loose.[14]

Enforcers of rules, since they have no stake in the content of particular rules themselves, often develop their own private evaluation of the importance of various kinds of rules and infractions of them. This set of priorities may differ considerably from those held by the general public. For instance, drug users typically believe (and a few policemen have personally confirmed it to me) that police do not consider the use of marihuana to be as important a problem or as dangerous a practice as the use of opiate drugs. Police base this conclusion on the fact that, in their experience, opiate users commit other crimes (such as theft or prostitution) in order to get drugs, while marihuana users do not.

Enforcers then, responding to the pressures of their own work situation, enforce rules and create outsiders in a selective way. Whether a person who commits a deviant act is in fact labeled a deviant depends on many things extraneous to his actual behavior: whether the enforcement official feels that at this time he must make some show of doing his job in order to justify his position, whether the misbehaver shows proper deference to the enforcer, whether the "fix" has been put in, and where the kind of act he has committed stands on the enforcer's list of priorities.

The professional enforcer's lack of fervor and routine approach to dealing with evil may get him into trouble with the rule creator. The rule creator, as we have said, is concerned with the content of the rules that interest him. He sees them as the means by which evil can be stamped out. He does not understand the enforcer's long-range approach to the same problems and cannot see why all the evil that is apparent cannot be stamped out at once.

When the person interested in the content of a rule realizes or has called to his attention the fact that enforcers are dealing selectively with the evil that concerns him, his righteous wrath may be aroused. The professional is denounced for viewing the evil too lightly, for failing to do his duty. The moral entrepreneur, at whose instance the rule was made, arises again to say that the outcome of the last crusade has not been satisfactory or that the gains once made have been whittled away and lost.

NOTES

1. Joseph R. Gusfield, "Social Structure and Moral Reform: A Study of the Woman's Christian Temperance Union," *American Journal of Sociology,* LXI (November, 1955), 223.
2. *Ibid.*
3. See Raymond G. McCarthy, editor, *Drinking and Intoxication* (New Haven and New York: Yale Center of Alcohol Studies and The Free Press of Glencoe, 1959), pp. 395–396.
4. This is suggested in Oscar Lewis, *Sagebrush Casinos: The Story of Legal Gambling in Nevada* (New York: Doubleday and Co., 1953), pp. 223–234.
5. Edwin H. Sutherland, "The Diffusion of Sexual Psychopath Laws," *American Journal of Sociology,* LVI (September, 1950), 142–148.
6. *Ibid.*, p. 142.
7. *Ibid.*, pp. 143–145.
8. *Ibid.*, pp. 145–146.
9. See Ray Gold, "Janitors Versus Tenants: A Status-Income Dilemma," *American Journal of Sociology,* LVII (March, 1952), 486–493.
10. William A. Westley, "Violence and the Police," *American Journal of Sociology,* LIX (July, 1953), 39.
11. *Ibid.*
12. See William A. Westley, "The Police: A Sociological Study of Law, Custom, and Morality" (unpublished Ph.D. dissertation, University of Chicago, Department of Sociology, 1951).
13. Edwin H. Sutherland (editor), *The Professional Thief* (Chicago: University of Chicago Press, 1937), pp. 87–88.
14. *Ibid.*, pp. 91–92.

Think Critically

1. Give two contemporary examples of moral entrepreneurs. Describe how they fit with Becker's conceptualization.
2. Can you think of examples where rule enforcers may also be on a "crusade" against deviance and crime? That is, do you feel that they sometimes "cross the line" and become in a sense, "moral entrepreneurs"? Explain.

Ironies of Social Control
Authorities as Contributors to Deviance Through Escalation, Nonenforcement, and Covert Facilitation*

Gary T. Marx

MANY CURRENT THEORETICAL APPROACHES to deviance causation tend to neglect a crucial level of analysis: the specific interactive context within which rule breaking occurs. Anomie (Merton, 1957) and subcultural theorists (Sutherland and Cressey, 1974) and combinations of these approaches (Cloward and Ohlin, 1960) tend to focus on rather abstract initial group properties such as opportunity structures and norms, rather than on the interactive group processes out of which behavior emerges. Those questioning the mechanistic force of such variables nevertheless stress the independence of the deviant as a maker of choices (Matza, 1966) . . .

Whatever merit the above approaches have for dealing with various aspects of deviance, they must be supplemented by a theoretical perspective which focuses on the immediate context of the rule infraction. Such a perspective must at least take as an empirical question the degree of autonomy in the actions of the rule violator, and whether people actually do what they are charged with having done.

In current theories the deviant is seen either as autonomous or as a pawn of broad social and cultural forces. Most interpretations tend to reify the categories of authority and "criminal" and to draw the line between them too sharply. They miss the interdependence that may exist between these groups and the extent to which authorities may induce or help others to break the law, be involved in law breaking themselves, or create false records about others' supposed law breaking. Conversely, the extent to which those engaged in illegal activities may be contributing to social order is also ignored. Here I focus on some neglected aspects of the role of authorities in law violations.

*© 1981 by the Society for the Study of Social Problems. Reprinted from *Social Problems* 28:3 (Feb. 1981), pp. 221–233, by permission of the publisher.

The idea that authorities may play a role in generating deviance is not new. Clearly, the labeling perspective has focused attention on the role of authorities—for example, the work of Tannenbaum (1938), Kitsuse (1962), Becker (1963), Wilkins (1965), Scheff (1966), Lemert (1951, 1972), and Hawkins and Tiedeman (1975). In such work, authorities have been seen to "create" deviance by defining some of a wide range of behavior as illegal, using their discretion about which laws will then be most actively enforced, and singling out some of those who violate these laws for processing by the criminal justice system. Subsequent restrictions on the behavior of those processed as deviants, such as their being singled out for special attention by authorities, and subsequent changes in their self-images, are thought to result in their becoming even more involved in deviant activities.

These are not, however, the roles that authorities play in creating deviance on which I wish to focus. Much of the labeling argument is true by definition; that which isn't seems plausible enough and has the easy virtue of overlapping with the underdog worldview of many who hold it, though systematic research in its support cannot be said to be overwhelming (Manning, 1973; Wellford, 1975; Gove, 1980). Yet if subsequent evidence suggests that labeling as such does not, on balance, amplify deviance and even deters it, I think a strong case can still be made for the important role of authorities.

I do begin at an abstract level with what I see to be a fundamental insight of the labeling perspective: the possible irony of social controllers creating what they set out to control. But then I emphasize a different set of factors. In spite of its calling attention to the role of authorities, the emphasis in the labeling approach is usually placed on what authorities do to others already known or thought to be deviant. Its main concern is with the secondary rather than primary deviance. Its usual focus is not on the behavior of control agents before or during the rule breaking, nor on the degree of autonomy in the actions of the rule breaker. Nor is its usual focus even on whether the deviance actually occurred, preferring instead, in Rains's (1975:10) words, "to describe the full process of imputation without regard for warrant." But here I will deliberately focus on infraction—on some of the ways in which it is shaped or induced by prior or concomitant actions of authorities, and on some of the causes involved.[1]

Situations where social control contributes to, or even generates, rule-breaking behavior include these three ideal types:

A. Escalation (by taking enforcement action, authorities unintentionally encourage rule breaking).
B. Nonenforcement (by strategically taking *no enforcement action,* authorities intentionally permit rule breaking).
C. Covert facilitation (by taking *hidden or deceptive enforcement action,* authorities intentionally encourage rule breaking).

These are analytic distinctions. In a given empirical instance all may be present . . .

Escalation

The clearest cases of authorities contributing to rule breaking involve escalation. As with facilitation, authorities' intervention is conducive to deviance. However, secrecy need not be involved (the facilitation can be overt), and the final consequence is generally not consciously, or at best publicly, sought by controllers when they initially enter the situation.[2] It is not simply that social control has no effect, rather that it can amplify. (In the language of cybernetics, this is a case of deviation amplifying feedback [Cf. Maruyama, 1963]—in everyday language, snowballing or mushrooming). In escalation the very process of social control directly triggers violations. In urging that attention be focused on the deviant act as such, Cohen has written:

> The history of a deviant act is a history of an interaction process. The antecedents of the act are an unfolding sequence of acts contributed by a set of actors (1965:9).

Nowhere is this logic clearer than in the case of escalation. Five major analytic elements of escalation are:

1. An increase in the *frequency* of the original violations.
2. An increase in the *seriousness* of violations, including the greater use of violence.

3. The appearance of *new* categories of violators and/or victims (without a net diminution of those previously present).
4. An increase in the commitment and/or skill and effectiveness of those engaged in the violation.
5. The appearance of violations whose very definition is tied to social control intervention.

Escalation may stem from initial or postapprehension enforcement efforts.

Police involvement in family conflict, crowd, and automobile chase situations can contribute to violations when none were imminent, or it can increase the seriousness of these situations. In responding to challenges to their authority or to interpersonal conflict situations, preemptive police actions (euphemistically called by some with a sardonic smile, "constructive coercion" and "preventive violence") may lead to further violence.

A three-year study of police-citizen incidents in New York City notes "the extent to which the handling of relatively minor incidents such as traffic violations or disorderly disputes between husbands and wives seemed to create a more serious situation than existed prior to the police attempt to control the situation" (McNamara, 1967) . . .

An English policeman characterized the 1960s' riot control behavior of American police in some cities as "oilin' the fire." Police responses to crowd situations offer many examples of escalation (Marx, 1970; Stark, 1972). Provocative overreaction (referred to by another English policeman as "cracking a nut with a sledgehammer") can turn a peaceful crowd into a disorderly one . . .

One consequence of strong enforcement actions can be to change the personnel and social organization of those involved in illegal activities. For example, stepped-up enforcement efforts with respect to heroin and cocaine appear to have moved the drug traffic away from less sophisticated and skilled local, often amateur, groups to more highly skilled, centralized, better organized criminal groups (Young, 1971; Sabbag, 1976; Adler *et al.,* forthcoming). The greater skill and sophistication of those now drawn into the activity may mean the development of new markets. Increased risks may mean greater profits, as well as incentives to develop new consumers and markets. The more professional criminals are more likely to be able to avoid prosecution and are in a better position to induce police corruption.

Increased corruption, a frequent escalatory consequence of stepped-up enforcement efforts, is one of a number of second-order forms of illegality which may indirectly appear. Even attacking corruption may generate other problems. Thus, following reform efforts in one city (Sherman, 1978:257), police morale declined and citizen complaints went up sharply, as did police use of firearms. In Boston a recent increase in high-speed chases and attendant offenses and injuries is directly traceable to an order to enforce traffic laws more stringently. Another second-order effect can be seen in the monopoly profits which may accrue to those who provide vice in a context of strong enforcement pressures. These profits can be invested in still other illegal activities. Thus, some of the tremendous profits earned by organized crime groups that emerged during prohibition, and the skills developed then, went into gambling, labor racketeering, and narcotics. Violence may increase among criminal groups contending for new monopoly profits. Their monopoly may also have been aided by informing on competitors. The increased cost of the product they provide may mean increased illegality on the part of customers facing higher prices (Schur, 1965). A link between drug addiction and street crime, for example, has often been argued.

Authorities may directly provide new resources which have unintended effects. Part of the increased homicide rates in the 1970s, for example, particularly among minority youths, has been attributed to vastly augmented amounts of federal "buy" money for drugs. This increased the opportunity for youths to become informers, and some of them were subsequently killed. The drugs, stolen goods, money, weapons, and tips sometimes given to informers and others who aid police may be used in subsequent crimes. A more benign resource may be the youth workers sent to work with gangs in their environment. Some of the detached street-worker programs, aimed at reducing gang delinquency, may have actually increased it: By strengthening identification with the gang, they made it more cohesive and encouraged new recruits (Klein, 1969). Klein observes that the assumed advantages of group work with gangs are "mythical," and he advocates abandoning standard detached worker programs. In Chicago, anti-poverty funds for self-help programs among gangs offered resources, opportunities and incentives which created a context for fraud, extortion and violence (Short, 1974).

Contemporary American law has evolved an increasing number of crimes which emerge solely as an artifact of social control intervention. These emerge incidentally to efforts to enforce other laws. If authorities had not taken action, the offense would not have been committed. Resisting arrest or assaulting an officer are familiar examples. The prosecution of white-collar crimes offers a different example.

Prosecutors who initially set out to make cases of corruption, fraud, or food and drug violations may be unable to prove the targeted crime, yet still be able to prosecute for perjury or obstruction of justice. The latter violations become possible only after an investigation begins and can exist regardless of the quality of evidence for the case the prosecutor originally hoped to make.

More routine are white-collar offenses involving the violation of requirements imposed on citizens to aid in the investigation of still other crimes. In and of themselves the violations need not produce social harm. In the effort to detect and sanction infractions the criminal justice system can promote crimes because of its own need for information. Failing to file reports or filing a false statement to the U.S. government are examples. Failure to file an income tax form is a crime even if one owes no taxes.[3]

Most of the escalation examples considered here have involved the initial enforcement effort and one point in time. The work of Wilkins (1965) and that of Lemert (1951, 1972) calls attention to postapprehension escalation and a person's "career" as a deviant. Wilkins sees a spiraling interactive process whereby rule breaking leads to sanctioning, which then leads to more serious rule breaking, which in turn leads to more serious sanctioning and so on. Lemert focuses on how people may change their lives and self-conceptions in response to being formally processed, punished, stigmatized, segregated, or isolated. To the extent that their lives and identities come to be organized around the facts of their publicly labeled deviance, they are secondary deviants.

However, postapprehension escalation can occur without an accelerating spiral or changes in self-image. Having been apprehended for one offense, or identified as a rule violator, can set in motion actions by authorities that make additional violations more likely. For one thing, contact with the criminal justice system may alter one's status (e.g., to probationer, inmate, or parolee) so that one is guilty of a misdemeanor or felony for acts that would be legally inoffensive if committed by others. In addition, being placed in such statuses may provide actors with inducements to the commission of a crime, either by way of opportunity or pressure, to which others are not exposed.

Among the most poignant and tragic examples of escalation are those that emerge from the application of the initial sanction. Prisoners, such as George Jackson, who are sent up at a young age for a short term, then who find their sentences continually lengthened because of their behavior in prison, are clear examples. According to one study, only 6 to 40 offenses punishable in one state prison would be misdemeanors or felonies if done outside (Barnes and Teeters, 1959, as cited in Lemert, 1972:81). Similarly, violation of some of the regulations faced by those on parole or probation can send them to prison, but the same acts are not illegal when done by others.

For those not yet in prison, the need to meet bail and expensive legal fees can exert pressure to obtain such funds illegally. Clarence Darrow reported the case of a young thief who wanted the famous lawyer to defend him. Darrow asked if he had any money. The young man said, "No," and then with a smile said he thought he could raise some by that evening. An undercover narcotics detective (more taken by the seeming stupidity of those he arrests than of the system that generates their behavior) reports, "I even make buys again from guys who I've arrested and come right back out to make some fast bread for their expenses in court" (Schiano and Burton, 1974:93). There seems to be the possibility of infinite regress here.

Escalation is of course only one form that the interdependence and reciprocal influences among rule breakers and enforcers can take. It is treated here because of its irony. A more common form is probably displacement (without a significant increase or decrease in infractions). Displacement may occur with respect to other types of rule breaking, rule breakers, victims, place, and procedure (Reppetto, 1976a) . . .

Nonenforcement

In nonenforcement, the contribution of authorities to deviance is more indirect than with escalation or covert facilitation. Rule breaking does not expand unintentionally and authorities do not set people up and covertly facilitate it. Instead, those involved in nonenforcement relationships (e.g., with police) may break rules partly because they believe they will not be appropriately sanctioned. Here we have an exchange relationship between police and offenders. Offenders perform services for police; in return they are allowed to break rules and may receive other benefits.

When it is organized and specialized, non-enforcement is the most difficult of the three forms of interdependence to identify empirically. As a strategy it is often illegal and is more likely to be hidden. One does not find conditions for its use spelled out in policy manuals. Indeed the opposite is more apt to be true. In prohibiting nonenforcement, training and policy guidelines often go to great lengths to point out its dangers. Police are sworn to uphold the law: Not to do so may involve them in malfeasance, aiding and abetting a felon, compounding a felony, perjury, and a host of other violations. Some anticorruption policies are from one perspective antinonenforcement policies. They seek to create conditions that will work against collusive nonenforcement relations; at the same time the realities of the police job are such that it emerges as a major fact of police life . . .

Police may adopt a policy of nonenforcement with respect to (1) informants who give them information about the law breaking of others and/or help in facilitating the controlled commission of a crime; (2) vice entrepreneurs who agree to keep their own illegal behavior within agreed upon bounds; (3) individuals who either directly regulate the behavior of others using resources police lack or means they are denied, or who take actions desired by authorities but considered too politically risky for them to undertake.

A former director of the FBI states, "Without informants we're nothing" (*New York Times,* April 16, 1974). The informant system, central to many types of law enforcement, is a major source of nonenforcement. Informants can offer police a means of getting information and making arrests that cannot come from other sources, given strictures against electronic surveillance, search and seizure, coercion, and the difficulty of infiltration. In return the system can work to the advantage of rule breakers . . .

The system can be used by both police and informants as a form of institutionalized blackmail. Potentially damaging action such as arrest or denouncement of someone as an informant or offender is withheld as long as the cooperation sought is forthcoming.

The tables can also get turned, as the informant manipulates the control agent into corrupt activities (or merely acquiesces in the agent's desire for these). For example, in the case of drugs, the exchange of immunity or drugs for information can, in a series of incremental changes, lead to joint marketing and other criminal ventures (Commission, 1972). The nonenforcement may become mutual and the balance of power shift. The informant not only controls the flow of information but could even threaten exposure, which may entail greater risk for the police officer than for the drug dealer (Moore, 1977; Karchmer, 1979).

Where the informant is involved in the controlled commission of a crime, social control actions may generate rule breaking in two ways. Criminogenic effects may be present because police ignore illegal activities of the informant. But they may also be present because informants covertly facilitate the rule breaking of others. Informants facing charges or desiring drugs, for example, may have strong incentives to facilitate others' deviance.[4] . . .

People often become informants while in jail, or facing arrest. Sentencing may be deferred for a period of time while the informant "works off" the charges (for example, see Cloyd, 1979). In some police circles this is known as "flipping" or "turning" a man. With respect to drug enforcement, in some cities a point system is used whereby the informant receives one point for each marijuana purchase and two points for the purchase of harder drugs. If the informant earns a fixed number of points, such as ten, charges will be dropped. There is no doubt considerable variation among departments and within. Accounts such as that offered by Tackwood are perhaps best treated as ideal-typical illustrations.

The practice of police foregoing prosecution in return for information is more common than granting the informant a wild license to burglarize. Even here, the prior knowledge that one may be able to trade information for leniency can be conducive to law violations. Individuals sometimes manage to avoid arrest by falsely claiming that they are informants . . .

Certain occupational categories such as the fence have historically involved the informant's role (Klockars, 1974). The fence may offer information to the police, can return stolen goods—and in the case of thief takers, such as Jonathan Wild, even directly apprehend thieves, while receiving a degree of immunity and police help in regulating their clientele and employees.

The major vice control strategy at the turn of the century was one of containment, and it is still important. In what would only seem a contradiction to the outside observer, late nineteenth century police in many cities had written rules governing how houses of prostitution and gambling were to be run, though these were clearly illegal. Some vice entrepreneurs took pride in the honest quality of the services they provided. The very extensive Lexow hearings (Senate Committee, 1895) on the New York police show how they systematically licensed gambling, prostitution and police activities (Steffens, 1957, offers a classic discussion).

In return for noninterference from police (often further bought by the payment of bribes), vice entrepreneurs may agree to engage in self-policing and operate with relative honesty (i.e., run orderly disorderly houses), restrict their activities to one type of vice, stay in a given geographical area, and run low-visibility operations. By favoring certain vice operators and cooperating with them to keep others out, police may introduce a degree of control and stability into what would otherwise be a chaotic cutthroat situation. Establishing a peaceful racket organization may also be seen as a way of not alienating a local community that demands vice activities (Whyte, 1967). The goal becomes compromises reached through negotiation and regulation, rather than elimination of the activity.

Instead of being offered as a reward for self-regulation, nonenforcement may also be extended for regulating others. The literature on prisons gives many examples of the role selected prisoners play in maintaining order. Concessions, some clearly illegal, may be given to key prisoners in return for their regulating the behavior of others through questionable means (Sykes, 1958; Cloward *et al.,* 1960).

These represent cases where full control is technically impossible. Authorities need the continuing support of at least some of those they wish to control, and they are willing to pay a price for it. In other cases authorities may be capable of repressive action but prefer to delegate it because it is seen as too risky for them to undertake directly. For example, in 1963 the FBI experienced strong pressure to find the killer of civil rights leader Medgar Evers. They had learned the names of some of those involved and had the murder weapon, but could not obtain evidence on who fired the shot. Under FBI direction, an active burglar and fence kidnapped and threatened to kill a key figure in the plot and was able to obtain a signed statement identifying the murderer. In return, the cooperative burglar was "the beneficiary of the best the Bureau could do for him"—he avoided a long prison sentence for armed robbery and kept $800 in cash stolen from the man's wallet (Villano, 1977).

Vigilante-type groups offer another example. Police may look the other way and essentially delegate certain enforcement rights to a group that wishes to take action that police might like to take but are unwilling to. The summary justice of the southern lynch mob, and group violence against blacks, were often conspicuous because of the lack of a restraining police presence. Until recently in many areas of the South, police (when not themselves members) ignored or gave encouragement to the Klan. The weak, if not openly supportive, attitude of many southern leaders in the face of discrimination and white violence significantly encouraged the Klan. This greatly hampered the federal effort to enforce civil rights laws and protect civil rights workers. With respect to traditional offenses, it has been claimed that in some urban minority areas police have been less than diligent in investigating the murders of drug pushers supposedly carried out by vigilantes seeking to rid their communities of pushers.

Still another type of nonenforcement can originate in some criminals' possession of unique skills, or even in their having the same enemies as authorities do. The fact that organized crime and the United States government have had some common enemies (Mussolini in Italy and Castro in Cuba) has sometimes led to cooperation between them. In Italy local mafiosi were active in the underground and provided the Allies with intelligence for the invasion of Sicily. As the Allies then moved on to the Italian mainland, anti-Fascist mafia were appointed to important positions in many towns and villages. The French liner *Normandie* was burned in New York, just before it was to become an Allied troop ship. Following this incident, the government sought the aid of mob-controlled longshoremen, truckers, and guards as help against waterfront sabotage and infiltration during World War II.[5] Help was received from Joe (Socks) Lanza on the East Side and Lucky Luciano on the West Side. Just what the government offered in return is less clear, although Luciano's cooperation won him, at least, a transfer to more comfortable prison quarters near Albany (Talese, 1972:206) . . .

Still another type of strategic nonenforcement, one not involving exchanges, happens when authorities fail to take action about a violation they know is planned, or in progress, until the violation is carried out. This permits arrest quotas to be met and can lead to heavier charges, greater leverage in negotiations, better evidence, and a higher level of offender arrest . . .

Covert Facilitation

The passive nonenforcement involving exchange relationships described above can be differentiated from a more active surreptitious role authorities may play as they (or

their agents) directly enter into situations in order to facilitate rule breaking by others. The rule breaking that emerges from nonenforcement may be seen by authorities as an undesirable if perhaps necessary side effect. In the case of covert facilitation, authorities consciously seek to encourage rule breaking: Getting someone to break the rule is the major goal. Both law and internal policy are often favorable to police facilitation of crime. This is a very old phenomenon. Eve, after all, was set up by the serpent. In the Bible she says, "The serpent beguiled me and I did eat." Indicating awareness of the paradoxical (provocative yet lawful) nature of the tactic, some police describe it as *lawful* entrapment. A not atypical policy manual of one police department contains a section on "permissible tactics for arranging the controlled commission of an offense." Police are told that they or their agents under appropriate conditions may:

A. affirmatively suggest the commission of the offense to the subject;

B. attempt to form a relationship with the subject of sufficient closeness to overcome the subject's possible apprehension over his trustworthiness;

C. offer the subject more than one opportunity to commit the offense;

D. create a continuing opportunity for the subject to commit the offense;

E. minimize the possibility of being apprehended for committing the offense.

For the purposes of this paper we identify at least three types of covert facilitation:

1. disguised police or their agents cooperating with others in illegal actions;

2. police secretly generating opportunities for rule breaking without being coconspirators;

3. police secretly generating motives for rule breaking without being coconspirators.

With respect to the "controlled commission of an offense," police or their agents may enter into relationships with those who don't know that they are police, to buy or sell illegal goods and services or to victimize others. The former is the most common. Agents of social control may purchase or sell drugs, pose as tourists seeking prostitutes, as prostitutes seeking customers, or as homosexuals seeking partners. They may pose as fences buying or selling stolen goods, as hit men taking a contract, as criminals trying to bribe prosecutors, and as entrepreneurs running pornographic bookstores. They may join groups that are (or become) involved in car theft, burglary, or robbery. They may infiltrate political groups thought to be dangerous. The last decade reveals many examples of covert facilitation as authorities responded to widespread protest (Marx, 1974).

Both of the two other types of covert facilitation (deceptively creating opportunity structures or motives but without collusion) have a "give-them-enough-rope" quality. Police activity here is more passive and the deception is of a greater order from that involved in the "controlled commission of an offense." Police do not directly enter into criminal conspiracies with their targets, and charges of entrapment would not be supported—but they do attempt to structure the world in such a way that violations are made more likely.

The use of decoys to draw street crime is a major form of police creation of opportunity structures. Police anticrime squads, increasingly in vogue, may disguise their members as old women, clerics, derelicts, tennis players, and bike riders; they may use attractive police women in civilian clothes to induce robbery and assault, with other police watching from close by (Halper and Ku, 1976). Private guards posing as inattentive customers paying for small purchases with large bills routinely test cashier honesty. Plain-clothed "security inspectors" may test employee vigilance by seeing if they can get away with shoplifting . . .

Covert facilitation involving the creation of motives can be seen in many counterintelligence activities. Here the goal may be disruption and subversion (rather than strictly law enforcement). In "dirty tricks" campaigns, police may take clandestine actions in the hope of provoking factionalism and violence . . .

In a version of turnabout as fair play (at least to reform police executives), covert facilitation may also be turned inward in efforts to deal with corrupt police and assess police honesty. Tactics recently used by the New York City police include: planting illegally parked cars with money in them to see if police tow truck operators would steal it; planting "lost" wallets near randomly selected police to see if they would be turned in intact; offering bribes to arresting officers; putting through a contrived "open door" call to an apartment where marked money was prominently displayed to see if two officers under suspicion would steal it (they did); establishing phony gambling operations to see if police sought protection money; and having an undercover officer pose as a pusher to see if other undercover narcotics agents paid out the full amount of "buy" money they claimed (*New York Times,* November 29, 1972 and December 28, 1973; Sherman, 1978) . . .

For convenience we have thus far treated three types of interdependence as if they were distinct empirically as well as analytically. However, there are deviance and social control situations in which each or several are present—or where they merge or may be temporally linked. One of the things rule breakers may offer to police in return for nonenforcement is aid in covertly facilitating someone else's rule breaking. The arrest that emerges out of this can involve escalation. For example, a drug informant's petty theft may be ignored (nonenforcement) in return for his making controlled buys (covert facilitation). The arrest growing out of this may lead to additional charges if the suspect is involved in a high-speed chase and fights with the arresting officers after they call him a name. Escalation may lead to a later policy of nonenforcement in those situations where authorities perceive that their intervention would in fact only make matters worse.[6] Stepped-up enforcement may also lead to nonenforcement by increasing opportunities for police corruption.

NOTES

1. Other forms of interdependence treated in the larger work from which this article is drawn, but ignored here, include: (a) "cops as robbers," where authorities are self-interested rule breakers; (b) the falsely accused; (c) the efforts of citizens to provoke, bribe, or otherwise implicate police in their rule breaking.

2. Because of their intentionality, nonenforcement and covert facilitation are social control strategies; this cannot be said of escalation which is defined by its unintended consequences, though these may be present with the former as well. Sometimes, of course, police may follow a policy of deliberate provocation in the hope of encouraging escalation so that they can legally use force, bring heavier charges, or dispense "alley justice."

3. As Jack Katz has pointed out in a private communication, "Such laws reflect the fact that in a way large sections of our society are always under investigation for a crime."

4. A narcotics agent critical of this practice notes: "They put such pressure on the informant that, in effect, you've got him by the nuts. That's even what they call it, 'the nut,' working off the nut, or the violation. The pressure is so great he'll manufacture information, make up some to get off the hook. It's just a perfect example of how law enforcement is maintaining the problem" (Browning, 1976).

5. A more cynical interpretation is that Luciano actually arranged for the destruction of the *Normandie* as the prelude for his subsequently exchanging mob protection against future "foreign" sabotage (Gosch and Hammer, 1975).

6. In the case of civil disorders, however, underreaction as part of a policy of nonenforcement can have the unintended consequence of encouraging the spread of disorder. The three largest civil disorders of the 1960s (Watts, Newark, and Detroit) were all characterized by the initial period of police underreaction. Given the infraction-generating potential of both over- and underreaction, police often find themselves criticized no matter how they respond, and policies are cyclical.

REFERENCES

Adler, P. A., P. Adler and J. Douglas. Forthcoming "Organized crime: Drug dealing for pleasure and profit." In J. Douglas, *Observations of Deviance,* second edition. New York: Random House.

Barnes, H. and N. Teeters. 1959. *New Horizons in Criminology.* Englewood Cliffs, N.J.: Prentice Hall.

Becker, H. 1963. *Outsiders.* Glencoe, Ill.: Free Press.

Browning, F. 1976. "An American gestapo." *Playboy,* February.

Cloward, R. and L. Ohlin. 1960. *Delinquency and Opportunity: A Theory of Delinquent Groups.* Glencoe, Ill.: Free Press.

Cloward, R. *et al.* 1960. *Theoretical Studies in Social Organization of the Prison.* New York: Social Science Research Council.

Cloyd, J. 1979. "Prosecution's power, procedural rights, and pleading guilty: The problem of coercion in plea bargaining cases." *Social Problems* 26(4):452–466.

Cohen, A. 1965. "The sociology of the deviant act." *American Sociological Review* 30:5–14.

Commission to Investigate Allegations of Police Corruption and the City's Anti-Corruption Procedures (1972). *The Knapp Commission Report on Police Corruption.* New York: Braziller.

Gosch, M. and R. Hammer. 1975. *The Last Testament of Lucky Luciano.* Boston: Little, Brown.

Gove, W. R. (ed.). 1980. *The Labeling of Deviance.* Beverly Hills, Calif.: Sage.

Halper, A. and R. Ku. 1976. *New York City Police Department Street Crime Unit.* Washington, D.C.: U.S. Government Printing Office.

Hawkins, R. and G. Tiedeman. 1975. *The Creation of Deviance.* Columbus, Ohio: C. Merrill.

Karchmer, C. 1979. "Corruption towards performance: Goals and operations in proactive law enforcement." Paper presented to Western Political Science Association, Portland, Oregon.

Kitsuse, J. 1962. "Societal reactions to deviant behavior: Problems of theory and method." *Social Problems* 9 (Spring): 247–256.

Klein, M. 1969. "Gang cohesiveness, delinquency and a street work program." *Journal of Research in Crime and Delinquency* 6(1):135–166.

Klockars, C. 1974. *The Professional Fence.* New York: Free Press.

Lardner, J. 1977. "How prosecutors get nabbed." *New Republic,* January 29:22–25.

Lemert, E. 1951. *Social Pathology.* New York: McGraw-Hill.

———. 1972. *Human Deviance, Social Problems and Social Control.* Englewood Cliffs, N.J.: Prentice Hall.

Manning, P. 1973. "On deviance." *Contemporary Sociology: A Journal of Reviews* 2:123–128.

Maruyama, M. 1963. "The second cybernetics: Deviation-amplifying mutual causative processes." *American Scientist* 51:164–179.

Marx, G. 1970. "Civil disorder and the agents of social control." *Journal of Social Issues* 26(1): 19–57.

———. 1974. "Thoughts on a neglected category of social movement participant: Agents provocateurs and informants." *American Journal of Sociology* 80(2):402–442.

———. 1980. "The new police undercover work." *Journal of Urban Life* 8 (4):400–446.

Matza, D. 1966. *Delinquency and Drift.* New York: Wiley.

McNamara, J. H. 1967. "Uncertainty in police work: The relevance of police recruits' background and training." Pp. 163–252 in D. Bordua (ed.). *The Police.* New York: Wiley.

Merton, R. 1957. *Social Theory and Social Structure.* Glencoe, Ill.: Free Press.

Moore, M. 1977. *Buy and Bust.* Lexington, Mass.: Lexington Press.

Plate, N. 1975. *Crime Pays: The Theory and Practice of Professional Crime in the United States.* New York: Simon and Schuster.

Rains, P. 1975. "Imputations of deviance: A retrospective essay on the labeling perspective." *Social Problems* 23(1):1–11.

Reppetto, T. A. 1976a. "Crime prevention and the displacement phenomenon." *Crime and Delinquency* (April):166–177.

Sabbag, R. 1976. *Snow Blind.* New York: Avon.

Scheff, T. 1966. *Being Mentally Ill: A Sociological Theory.* Chicago: Aldine.

Schiano, A. and A. Burton. 1974. *Solo.* New York: Warner.

Schur, E. 1965. *Crimes Without Victims.* Englewood Cliffs, N.J.: Prentice Hall.

Senate Committee Appointed to Investigate the Police Dept. of New York City 1895. Report and Proceedings. Albany, New York.

Sherman, L. 1978. *Scandal and Reform.* Berkeley: University of California Press.

Short, J. F. 1974. "Youth, gangs, and society: Micro- and macrosociological processes." *Sociological Quarterly* 15 (winter): 3–19.

Stark, R. 1972. *Police Riots: Collective Violence and Law Enforcement.* Belmont, Calif.: Wadsworth.

Steffens, L. 1957. *Shame of the Cities.* New York: Hill and Wang.

Sutherland, E. H. and D. Cressey. 1974. *Criminology.* Philadelphia: Lippincott.

Sykes, G. 1958. *The Society of Captives.* Princeton, N.J.: Princeton University Press.

Tannenbaum, F. 1938. *Crime and the Community.* Boston: Ginn.

Villano, A. with G. Astor. 1977. *Brick Agent.* New York: Quadrangle.

Wellford, C. 1975. "Labeling theory and criminology: An assessment." *Social Problems* 22(3):332–345.

Whyte, W. F. 1967. *Street Corner Society.* Chicago: University of Chicago Press.

Wilkins, L. 1965. *Social Deviance.* Englewood Cliffs, N.J.: Prentice Hall.

Young, J. 1971. "The roles of the police as amplifiers of deviancy." Pp. 27–61 in S. Cohen (ed.), *Images of Deviance.* London: Penguin Books.

> ### Think Critically
>
> 1. Think of your own examples of the ironies of social control that Marx describes and how they are tied to escalation, non-enforcement, and covert facilitation. Explain.
> 2. Do you feel that Marx has touched upon an important aspect of the study of deviance? Why or why not?

The "Discovery" of Child Abuse*

Stephen J. Pfohl**

DESPITE DOCUMENTARY EVIDENCE OF CHILD beating throughout the ages, the "discovery" of child abuse as deviance and its subsequent criminalization are recent phenomena. In a four-year period beginning in 1962, the legislatures of all fifty states passed statutes against the caretaker's abuse of children. This paper is a study of the organization of social forces which gave rise to the deviant labeling of child beating and which promoted speedy and universal enactment of criminal legislation. It is an examination of certain organized medical interests, whose concern in the discovery of the "battered child syndrome" manifestly contributed to the advance of humanitarian pursuits while covertly rewarding the groups themselves.

*© 1977 by the Society for the Study of Social Problems. reprinted from *Social Problems,* 24:3 (Feb., 1977), pp. 310–323, by permission of the publisher.

**The author acknowledges the invaluable collaboration of Judith Dilorio of The Ohio State University in bringing this manuscript to its final form. Also acknowledged are the critical comments of John Conrad, Raymond Michalowski, and Dee Roth. Consultation with Simon Dinitz, Gideon Fishman, and Andrew Rutherford on an earlier draft of this paper is likewise appreciated. Gratitude is also expressed to Kathy Delgarn for the preparation of the manuscript.

The structure of the present analysis is fourfold: First, a historical survey of social reaction to abusive behavior prior to the formulation of fixed labels during the early sixties, focussing on the impact of three previous reform movements. These include the nineteenth-century "house-of-refuge" movement, early twentieth century crusades by the Society for the Prevention of Cruelty to Children, and the rise of juvenile courts. The second section concentrates on the web of cultural values related to the protection of children at the time of the "discovery" of abuse as deviance. A third section examines factors associated with the organizational structure of the medical profession conducive to the "discovery" of a particular type of deviant label. The fourth segment discusses social reaction. Finally, the paper provides a sociological interpretation of a particular social-legal development. Generically it gives support for a synthesis of conflict and labeling perspectives in the sociology of deviance and law.

The History of Social Reaction: Preventive Penology and "Society Saving"

Beginning in the early nineteenth century, a series of three reform movements directed attention to the plight of beaten, neglected, and delinquent children. These included the nineteenth century "House of Refuge" movement, the turn of the century crusades by the Society for the Prevention of Cruelty to Children, and the early twentieth century rise of juvenile courts. Social response, however, seldom aimed measures at ameliorating abuse or correcting abusive parents. Instead, the child, rather than his or her guardians, became the object of humanitarian reform.

In each case the primary objective was not to save children from cruel or abusive parents, but to save society from future delinquents. Believing that wicked and irresponsible behavior was engendered by the evils of poverty and city life, these movements sought to curb criminal tendencies in poor, urban youths by removing them from corrupt environments and placing them in institutional settings. There they could learn order, regularity, and obedience (Rothman, 1971). Thus, it was children, not their abusive guardians, who felt the weight of the moral crusade. They, not their parents, were institutionalized.

The "House of Refuge" Movement

Originating in the reformist dreams of the Jacksonian era, the so-called "House of Refuge Movement" sought to stem the social pathologies of an industrializing nation by removing young people endangered by "corrupt urban environments" to institutional settings. Neglect statutes providing for the removal of the young from bad home lives were originally enacted to prevent children from mingling freely with society's dregs in alms houses or on the streets . . .

The constitutionality of the neglect statutes, which formed the basis for the House of Refuge movement, was repeatedly challenged on the grounds that it was really imprisonment without due process. With few exceptions court case after court case upheld the policy of social intervention on the Aristotelian principle of "parens patriae." This principle maintained that the State has the responsibility to defend those who cannot defend themselves, as well as to assert its privilege in compelling infants and their guardians to act in ways most beneficial to the State.

The concept of preventive penology emerged in the wording of these court decisions. A distinction between "deliquency" (the actual violation of criminal codes) and "dependency" (being born into a poor home with neglectful or abusive parents) was considered irrelevant

for "child saving." The two were believed to be intertwined in poverty and desolation. If not stopped, both would perpetuate themselves. For the future good of both child and society, "parens patriae" justified the removal of the young before they became irreparably tainted (Thomas, 1972:322–323).

The underlying concept of the House of Refuge movement was that of preventive penology, not child protection. This crusade registered no real reaction against child beating. The virtue of removing children from their homes was not to point up abuse or neglect and protect its victims, it was to decrease the likelihood that parental inadequacies, the "cause of poverty," would transfer themselves to the child and hence to the next generation of society (Giovannoni, 1971:652). Thus, as indicated by Zalba (1966), the whole nineteenth century movement toward institutionalization actually failed to differentiate between abuse and poverty and therefore registered no social reaction against beating as a form of deviance . . .

Social Reaction at Mid-Century: The Cultural Setting for the "Discovery" of Abuse

The Decline of Preventive Penology

As noted, preventive penology represented the philosophical basis for various voluntary associations and legislative reform efforts resulting in the institutionalization of neglected or abused children. Its primary emphasis was on the protection of society. The decline of preventive penology is partially attributed to three variables: the perceived failure of "institutionalization," the impact of the "Great Depression" of the 1930s, and a change in the cultural meaning of "adult vices."

In the several decades prior to the discovery of abuse, the failure of institutionalization to "reorder" individuals became increasingly apparent. This realization undermined the juvenile courts' role in administering a predelinquency system of crime prevention. Since the rise of juvenile courts historically represented a major structural support for the notion of preventive penology, the lessening of its role removed a significant barrier to concern with abuse as an act of individual victimization. Similarly, the widespread experience of poverty during the Great Depression weakened other beliefs in preventive penology. As impersonal economic factors impoverished a great number of citizens of good moral credentials, the link between poverty and immorality began to weaken.

Another characteristic of the period immediately prior to the discovery of abuse was a changing cultural awareness of the meaning of adult vice as indices of the future character of children. "Parental immoralities that used to be seen as warnings of oncoming criminality in children [became] acceptable factors in a child's homelife" (Fox, 1970:1234). Parental behavior such as drinking, failing to provide a Christian education, and refusing to keep a child busy with useful labor were no longer classified as nonacceptable nor deemed symptoms of immorality transmitted to the young. Hence, the saving of society from the tainted young became less of a mandate, aiding the perception of social harm against children as "beings" in themselves.

Advance of Child Protection

Concurrent with the demise of "society-saving" in the legal sphere, developments in the fields of child welfare and public policy heightened interest in the problems of the child as an individual. The 1909 White House Conference on Children spawned both the "Mother's Aid" movement and the American Association for the Study and Prevention of Infant Mortality. The former group, from 1910 to 1930, drew attention to the benefits of keeping children in the family while pointing out the detrimental effects of dehumanizing institutions. The latter group then, as now, registered concern over the rate of infant deaths.

During the first half of the twentieth century, the Federal Government also met the issue of child protection with legislation that regulated child labor, called for the removal of delinquent youths from adult institutions, and established, in 1930, a bureaucratic structure whose purpose revolved around child protection. The Children's Bureau of HEW immediately adopted a "Children's Charter" promising every child a home with love and security plus full-time public services for protection from abuse, neglect, exploitation or moral hazard (Radbill, 1968:15).

Despite the growth of cultural and structural dispositions favoring the protection and increased rights of children, there was still no significant attention given to perpetrators of abuse, in the courts (Paulsen, 1966:710), in the legislature (DeFrancis, 1967:3), or by child welfare

agencies (Zalba, 1966). While this inactivity may have been partly caused by the lack of effective mechanisms for obtaining data on abuse (Paulsen, 1966:710), these agencies had little social incentive for interfering with an established power set—the parent over the child. As a minority group possessing neither the collective awareness nor the elementary organizational skills necessary to address their grievances to either the courts or to the legislators, abused and neglected children awaited the advocacy of some other organized interest. This outside intervention would not, however, be generated by that sector of "organized helping" most closely associated with the protective needs of children—the growing web of child welfare bureaucracies at state and federal levels. Social work had identified its professional advance with the adoption of the psychoanalytic model of casework (Zalba, 1966). This perspective, rather than generating a concern with political inequities internal to the family, focused instead on psychic disturbances internal to its members. Rather than challenging the strength of parents, this served to reinforce the role of powerful guardians in the rearing of young . . .

While the first half of the twentieth century is characterized by an increasing concern for child welfare, it developed with neither an organizational nor attitudinal reaction against child battering as a specific form of deviance. The "discovery" of abuse, its definition as a social problem and the socio-legal reaction against it, awaited the coalition of organized interests.

The Organization of Social Reaction against the "Battered Child Syndrome"

What organization of social forces gave rise to the discovery of abuse as deviance? The discovery is not attributable to any escalation of abuse itself. Although some authors have recently suggested that the increasing nuclearization of the family may increase the victimization of its offspring (Skolnick & Skolnick, 1971), there has never been any evidence that, aside from reporting inflation due to the impact of new laws, battering behavior was actually increasing (Eads, 1969). The attention here is on the organizational matrix encouraging a recognition of abuse as a social problem. In addressing this issue I will examine factors associated with the organizational structure of the medical profession leading to the discovery of abuse by pediatric radiologists rather than by other medical practitioners.

The "discovery" of abuse by pediatric radiology has often been described chronologically (Radbill, 1968:15; McCoid, 1966:2–5; Thomas, 1972:330). John Caffey (1946) first linked observed series of long bone fractures in children with what he termed some "unspecific origin." Although his assumption was that some physical disturbance would be discovered as the cause of this pattern of "subdural hematoma," Coffey's work prompted a series of further investigations into various bone injuries, skeletal trauma, and multiple fractures in young children. These research efforts lead pediatric radiology gradually to shift its diagnosis away from an internal medical explication toward the ascription of social cause.

In subsequent years it was suggested that what was showing up on x-rays might be the results of various childhood accidents (Barmeyer, *et al.,* 1951), of "parental carelessness" (Silverman, 1953), of "parental conduct" (Bakwin, 1956), and most dramatically, of the "indifference, immaturity and irresponsibility of parents" (Wooley & Evans, 1955). Surveying the progression of this research and reviewing his own investigations, Coffey (1957) later specified "misconduct and deliberate injury" as the primary etiological factors associated with what he had previously labelled "unspecific trauma." The discovery of abuse was on its way. Both in scholarly research (McCoid, 1966:7) and journalist outcry (Radbill, 1968:16), the last years of the fifties showed dramatically increased concern for the beaten child.

Why did pediatric radiologists and not some other group "see" abuse first? Legal and social welfare agents were either outside the scene of abusive behavior or inside the constraining vision of psychoanalytically committed casework. But clinicians, particularly hospital physicians and pediatricians, who encountered abused children more immediately, should have discovered "abuse" before the radiologists.

Four factors impeded the recognition of abuse (as it was later labeled). First, some early research maintained that doctors in emergency room settings were simply unaware of the possibilities of "abuse" as a diagnosis (Bain, 1963; Boardman, 1962). While this may be true, the massive symptoms (blood, burns, bruises) emergency room doctors faced far outweighed the lines appearing on the x-ray screens of radiologic specialists. A second line of evidence contends that many doctors were simply psychologically unwilling to believe that parents would inflict such atrocities on their own children (Elmer, 1960; Fontana, Donovan, Wong, 1963; Kempe *et al.,* 1963). This position is consistent with the existing cultural assumptions pairing parental power with parental wisdom and benevolence. Nonetheless, certain normative and structural elements within professional medicine appear of greater significance in reinforcing the physician's reluctance to get involved, even diagnostically. These factors are the "norm of confidentiality between doctor and client" and the goal of professional autonomy.

The "norm of confidentiality" gives rise to the third obstacle to a diagnosis of abuse: the possibility of legal liability for violating the confidentiality of the physician-patient relationship (Boardman, 1962). Interestingly, although some research connotes doctors' concern over erroneous diagnosis (Braun, Braun & Simonds, 1963), physicians primarily view the parent, rather than the child, as their real patient. On a strictly monetary level, of course, it is the parent who contracts with the doctor. Additional research has indicated that, particularly in the case of pediatricians, the whole family is viewed as one's clinical domain (Bucher & Strauss, 1961:329). It is from this vantage point that the impact of possible liability for a diagnostic disclosure is experienced. Although legal liability for a diagnosis of abuse may or may not have been the risk (Paulsen, 1967b:32), the belief in such liability could itself have contributed to the narrowness of a doctor's diagnostic perceptions (McCoid, 1966:37).

A final deterrent to the physician's "seeing" abuse is the reluctance of doctors to become involved in a criminal justice process that would take both their time (Bain, 1963:895) and ability to guide the consequences of a particular diagnosis (Boardman, 1962:46). This deterrent is particularly related to the traditional success of organized medicine in politically controlling the consequences of its own performance, not just for medical practitioners but for all who come in contact with a medical problem (Freidson, 1969:106; Hyde, *et al.,* 1954).

The political control over the consequences of one's profession would be jeopardized by the medical diagnosis of child abuse. Doctors would be drawn into judicial proceedings and subordinated to a role as witnesses. The outcome of this process would be decided by criminal justice standards rather than those set forth by the medical profession. Combining this relatively unattractive alternative with the obvious and unavoidable drain on a doctor's financial earning time, this fourth obstacle to the clinician's discovery of abuse is substantial.

Factors Conducive to the Discovery of Abuse by Pediatric Radiology

Why didn't the above factors inhibit the discovery of abuse by pediatric radiologists as well as by clinicians? First it must be recognized that the radiologists in question (Caffey, Barmeyer, Silverman, Wooley and Evans) were all researchers of children's x-rays. As such, the initial barrier becomes irrelevant. The development of diagnostic categories was a consequence rather than a precondition of the medical mission. Regarding the psychological denial of parental responsibility for atrocities, it must be remembered that the dramatic character of a beating is greatly reduced by the time it reaches an x-ray laboratory. Taken by technicians and developed as black and white prints, the radiologic remnants of abuse carry with them little of the horror of the bloody assault.

With a considerable distance from the patient and his or her family, radiologists are removed from the third obstacle concerning legal liabilities entailed in violating the doctor-patient relationship. Unlike pediatricians, radiologists do not routinely regard the whole family as their clinical domain. Of primary importance is the individual whose name or number is imprinted on the x-ray frames. As such, fears about legal sanctions instigated by a parent whom one has never seen are less likely to deter the recognition of abuse.

Given the irrelevance of the first three obstacles, what about the last? Pediatric radiologists are physicians and as such would be expected to participate in the "professional control of consequences" ethos. How is it that they negotiate this obstacle in favor of public recognition and labelling of abuse? . . .

The "discovery" of child abuse offered pediatric radiologists an alternative to their marginal medical status. By linking themselves to the problem of abuse, radiologists became indirectly tied into the crucial clinical task of patient diagnosis. In addition, they became a direct source of input concerning the risky "life or death" consequences of child beating. This could represent an advance in status,

a new basis for recognition within the medical profession. Indeed, after initial documentation of abuse, literature in various journals of radiology, roentgenology, and pediatrics, articles on this topic by Wooley and Evans (1955) and Gwinn, Lewin and Peterson (1961) appeared in the *Journal of the American Medical Association*. These were among the very few radiologic research reports published by that prestigious journal during the time period. Hence, the first factor conducive to the radiological discovery of abuse was a potential for intraorganizational advance in prestige.

A second factor encouraging the discovery of abuse by relatively low-status pediatric radiologists concerns the opportunity for a coalition of interests with other more prestigious segments within organized medicine. The two other segments radiologists joined in alliance were pediatrics and psychodynamically oriented psychiatry. By virtue of face-to-face clinical involvements, these specialties were higher ranking than pediatric radiology. Nevertheless each contained a dimension of marginality. Pediatrics had attained valued organizational status several decades prior to the discovery of abuse. Yet, in an age characterized by preventive drugs and treatments for previously dangerous or deadly infant diseases, it was again sliding toward the margins of the profession (Bucher & Strauss, 1961). Psychodynamic psychiatry (as opposed to its psychosomatic cousin) experienced marginality in dealing with non-physical problems.

For both pediatrics and psychodynamic psychiatry, links with the problem of abuse could partially dissipate the respective marginality of each. Assuming a role in combating the "deadly" forces of abuse could enlarge the "risky" part of the pediatric mission. A symbolic alliance of psychodynamic psychiatry with other bodily diagnostic and treatment specialties could also function to advance its status . . .

A crucial impediment to the discovery of abuse by the predominant interests in organized medicine was the norm of controlling the consequences of a particular diagnosis. To diagnose abuse as social deviance might curtail the power of organized medicine. The management of its consequences would fall to the extramedical interests of formal agents of social control. How is it then, that such a diagnosis by pediatric radiology and its endorsement by pediatric and psychiatric specialties is said to have advanced these specialties within the organization of medicine? Wasn't it more likely that they should have received criticism rather than acclaim from the medical profession?

By employing a rather unique labelling process the coalition of discovery interests was able to convert the possible liability into a discernible advantage. The opportunity of generating a medical, rather than socio-legal label for abuse provided the radiologists and their allies with a situation in which they could both reap the rewards associated with the diagnosis and avoid the infringement of extra-medical controls. What was discovered was no ordinary behavior form but a "syndrome." Instead of departing from the tradition of organized medicine, they were able to idealize its most profound mission. Possessing a repertoire of scientific credibility, they were presented with the opportunity "to label as illness what was not previously labeled at all or what was labeled in some other fashion, under some other institutional jurisdiction" (Freidson, 1969:261) . . .

The Generation of the Reporting Movement

The discovery of the "battered child syndrome" was facilitated by the opportunities for various pediatric radiologists to advance in medical prestige, form coalitions with other interests, and invent a professionally acceptable deviant label. The application of this label has been called the child abuse reporting movement. This movement was well underway by the time the 1962 Children's Bureau Conference confirmed the radiological diagnosis of abuse. Besides foreshadowing the acceptance of the sickness label, this meeting was also the basis for a series of articles to be published in *Pediatrics* which would further substantiate the diagnosis of abuse. Soon, however, the reporting movement spread beyond intra-organizational medical maneuvering to incorporate contributions from various voluntary associations, governmental agencies, as well as the media.

Extramedical responses to the newly discovered deviance confirmed the recognition of abuse as an illness. These included reports by various social welfare agencies which underscored the medical roots of the problem. For instance, the earliest investigations of the problem by social service agents resulted in a call for cooperation with the findings of radiologists in deciding the fate of abusers (Elmer, 1960:100). Other studies called for "more comprehensive radiological examinations" (Boardman, 1962:43). That the problem was medical in its roots as well as consequences was reinforced by the frequent referral of caseworkers to themselves as "battered child therapists" whose mission was the "curing" of "patients" (Davoren,

1968). Social welfare organizations, including the Children's Division of the American Humane Association, the Public Welfare Association, and the Child Welfare League, echoed similar concerns in sponsoring research (Children's Division, 1963; De Francis, 1963) and lobbying for "treatment based" legislative provisions (McCoid, 1965).

Not all extramedical interests concurred with treatment of abusers as "sick." Various law enforcement voices argued that the abuse of children was a crime and should be prosecuted. On the other hand, a survey of thirty-one publications in major law journals between 1962–1972 revealed that nearly all legal scholars endorsed treatment rather than punishment to manage abusers. Lawyers disagreed, however, as to whether reports should be mandatory and registered concern over who should report to whom. Yet, all concurred that various forms of immunity should be granted reporters (Paulsen, 1967a; De Francis, 1967). These are all procedural issues. Neither law enforcers nor legal scholars parted from labelling abuse as a problem to be managed. The impact of the acceptable discovery of abuse by a respected knowledge sector (the medical profession) had generated a stigmatizing scrutiny bypassed in previous eras.

The proliferation of the idea of abuse by the media cannot be underestimated. Though its stories were sensational, its credibility went unchallenged. What was publicized was not some amorphous set of muggings but a "syndrome." Titles such as "Cry rises from beaten babies" (*Life,* June 1963), "Parents who beat children" (*Saturday Evening Post,* October 1962), "The shocking price of parental anger" (*Good Housekeeping,* March 1964), and "Terror struck children" (*New Republic,* May 1964) were all buttressed by an awe of scientific objectivity. The problem had become "real" in the imaginations of professionals and laymen alike. It was rediscovered visually by ABC's "Ben Casey," NBC's "Dr. Kildare," and CBS's "The Nurses," as well as in several other television scripts and documentaries (Paulsen, 1967b:488–489).

Discovered by the radiologists, substantiated by their colleagues, and distributed by the media, the label was becoming widespread. Despite this fact, actual reporting laws were said to be the cooperative accomplishments of zealous individuals and voluntary associations (Paulsen, 1967b:491). Who exactly were these "zealous individuals"?

Data on legislative lobbyists reveal that, in almost every state, the civic committee concerned with abuse legislation was chaired by a doctor who "just happened" to be a pediatrician (Paulsen, 1967b:491). Moreover, "the medical doctors who most influenced the legislation frequently were associated with academic medicine" (Paulsen, 1967b:491). This information provides additional evidence of the collaborative role of pediatricians in guiding social reaction to the deviance discovered by their radiological colleagues.

Lack of Resistance to the Label

In addition to the medical interests discussed above, numerous voluntary associations provided support for the movement against child abuse. These included the League of Women Voters, Veterans of Foreign Wars, the Daughters of the American Republic, the District Attorneys Association, Council of Jewish Women, State Federation of Women's Clubs, Public Health Associations, plus various national chapters of social workers (Paulsen, 1967b:495). Two characteristics emerge from an examination of these interests. They either have a professional stake in the problem or represent the civic concerns of certain upper-middle class factions. In either case the labelers were socially and politically removed from the abusers, who in all but one early study (Steele and Pollock), were characterized as lower class and minority group members.

The existence of a wide social distance between those who abuse and those who label facilitates not only the likelihood of labelling but nullifies any organized resistance to the label by the "deviant" group itself. Research findings which describe abusers as belonging to no outside-the-family associations or clubs (Young, 1964) or which portray them as isolates in the community (Giovannoni, 1971) reinforce the conclusion. Labelling was generated by powerful medical interests and perpetuated by organized media, professional and upper-middle class concerns. Its success was enlarged by the relative powerlessness and isolation of abusers, which prevented the possibility of organized resistance to the labelling.

The Shape of Social Reaction

I have argued that the organizational advantages surrounding the discovery of abuse by pediatric radiology set in motion a process of labelling abuse as deviance

and legislating against it. The actual shape of legislative enactments has been discussed elsewhere (De Francis, 1967; Paulsen, 1967a). The passage of the reporting laws encountered virtually no opposition. In Kentucky, for example, no one even appeared to testify for or against the measure (Paulsen, 1967b:502). Any potential opposition from the American Medical Association, whose interests in autonomous control of the consequences of a medical diagnosis might have been threatened, had been undercut by the radiologists' success in defining abuse as a new medical problem. The AMA, unlikely to argue against conquering illness, shifted to support reporting legislation which would maximize a physician's diagnostic options.

The consequences of adopting a "sick" label for abusers is mirrored in two findings: the low rate of prosecution afforded offenders and the modification of reporting statutes so as exclusively to channel reporting toward "helping services." Regarding the first factor, Grumet (1970:306) suggests that despite existing laws and reporting statutes, actual prosecution has not increased since the time of abuse's "discovery." In support is Thomas (1972) who contends that the actual percentage of cases processed by family courts has remained constant during the same period. Even when prosecution does occur, convictions are obtained in only five to ten percent of the cases (Paulsen, 1966b). And even in these cases, sentences are shorter for abusers than for other offenders convicted under the same law of aggravated assault (Grumet, 1970:307).

State statutes have shifted on reporting from an initial adoption of the Children's Bureau model of reporting to law enforcement agents, toward one geared at reporting to child welfare or child protection agencies (De Francis, 1970). In fact, the attention to abuse in the early sixties has been attributed as a factor in the development of specialized "protective interests" in states which had none since the days of the SPCC crusades (Eads, 1969). This event, like the emphasis on abuser treatment, is evidence of the impact of labelling of abuse as an "illness."

REFERENCES

Bain, Katherine. 1963. "The physically abused child." *Pediatrics* 31 (June): 895–897.

Bakwin, Harry. 1956. "Multiple skeletal lesions in young children due to trauma." *Journal of Pediatrics* 49 (July): 7–15.

Barmeyer, G. H., L. R. Anderson and W. B. Cox. 1951. "Traumatic periostitis in young children." *Journal of Pediatrics* 38 (Feb): 184–190.

Becker, Howard S. 1963. *The Outsiders.* New York: The Free Press.

Boardman, Helen. 1962. "A project to rescue children from inflicted injuries." *Journal of Social Work* 7 (January): 43–51.

Braun, Ida G., Edgar J. Braun and Charlotte Simonds. 1963. "The mistreated child." *California Medicine* 99 (August): 98–103.

Bremner, R. 1970. *Children and Youth in America: A Documentary History. Vol. 1.* Cambridge, Mass.: Harvard University Press.

Caffey, John. 1946. "Multiple fractures in the long bones of infants suffering from chronic subdural hematoma." *American Journal of Roentgenology* 56 (August): 163–173.

———. 1957. "Traumatic lesions in growing bones other than fractures and lesions: clinical and radiological features." *British Journal of Radiology* 30 (May): 225–238.

Chambliss, William J. 1964. "A sociological analysis of the law of vagrancy." *Social Problems* 12 (Summer): 67–77.

Children's Division. 1963. *Child Abuse—Preview of a Nationwide Survey.* Denver: American Humane Association (Children's Division).

Davoren, Elizabeth. 1968. "The role of the social worker." Pp. 153–168 in Ray E. Helfer and Henry C. Kempe (eds.), *The Battered Child.* Chicago: University of Chicago Press.

De Francis, Vincent. 1963. "Parents who abuse children." *PTA Magazine* 58 (November): 16–18.

———. 1967. "Child abuse—the legislative response." *Denver Law Journal* 44 (Winter): 3–41.

———. 1970. *Child Abuse Legislation in the 1970's.* Denver: American Humane Association.

Eads, William E. 1969. "Observations on the establishment of child protection services in California." *Stanford Law Review* 21 (May): 1129–1155.

Elmer, Elizabeth. 1960. "Abused young children seen in hospitals." *Journal of Social Work* 3 (October): 98–102.

Folks, Homer. 1902. *The Case of the Destitute, Neglected and Delinquent Children.* New York: Macmillan.

Fontana, V., D. Donovan and R. Wong. 1963. "The maltreatment syndrome in children." *New England Journal of Medicine* 269 (December): 1389–1394.

Fox, Sanford J. 1970. "Juvenile justice reform: an historical perspective." *Stanford Law Review* 22 (June): 1187–1239.

Freidson, Eliot J. 1969. "Medical personnel: physicians." Pp. 105–114 in David L. Sills (ed.), *International Encyclopedia of the Social Sciences.* Vol. 10. New York: Macmillan.

———. 1971. The Profession of Medicine: *A Study in the Sociology of Applied Knowledge.* New York: Dodd, Mead and Co.

Giovannoni, Jeanne. 1971. "Parental mistreatment." *Journal of Marriage and the Family* 33 (November): 649–657.

———. 1971. "Force and violence in the family." *Journal of Marriage and the Family* 33 (November): 424–436.

Grumet, Barbara R. 1970. "The plaintive plaintiffs: victims of the battered child syndrome." *Family Law Quarterly* 4 (September): 296–317.

Gusfield, Joseph R. 1963. *Symbolic Crusades.* Urbana, Ill.: University of Illinois Press.

Gwinn, J.J., K.W. Lewin and H.G. Peterson. 1961. "Roentgenographic manifestations of unsuspected trauma in infancy." *Journal of the American Medical Association* 181 (June): 17–24.

Hall, Jerome. 1952. *Theft, Law and Society.* Indianapolis: Bobbs-Merrill Co.

Hyde, D.R., P. Wolff, A. Gross and E.L. Hoffman. 1954. "The American Medical Association: power, purpose and politics in organized medicine." *Yale Law Journal* 63 (May): 938–1022.

Kempe, C.H., F.N. Silverman, B.F. Steele, W. Droegemuller and H.K. Silver. 1963. "The battered-child syndrome." *Journal of the American Medical Association* 181 (July): 17–24.

Lemert, Edwin M. 1974. "Beyond Mead: the societal reaction to deviance." *Social Problems* 21 (April): 457–467.

McCoid, A.H. 1966. "The battered child syndrome and other assaults upon the family." *Minnesota Law Review* 50 (November): 1–58.

Paulsen, Monrad G. 1966. "The legal framework for child protection." *Columbia Law Review* 66 (April): 679–717.

———. 1967. "Child abuse reporting laws: the shape of the legislation." *Columbia Law Review* 67 (January): 1–49.

Quinney, Richard. 1970. *The Social Reality of Crime.* Boston: Little, Brown.

Radbill, Samuel X. 1968. "A history of child abuse and infanticide." Pp. 3–17 in Ray E. Helfer and Henry C. Kempe (eds.), *The Battered Child.* Chicago: University of Chicago Press.

Rothman, David J. 1971. *The Discovery of the Asylum: Social Order and Disorder in the New Republic.* Boston: Little, Brown.

Silverman, F. N. 1953. "The roentgen manifestations of unrecognized skeletal trauma in infants." *American Journal of Roentgenology, Radium and Nuclear Medicine* 69 (March): 413–426.

Skolnick, Arlene and Jerome H. Skolnick. 1971. *The Family in Transition.* Boston: Little, Brown.

Steele, Brandt and Carl F. Pollock. 1968. "A psychiatric study of parents who abuse infants and small children." Pp. 103–147 in Ray E. Helfer and Henry C. Kempe (eds.), *The Battered Child.* Chicago: University of Chicago Press.

Sutherland, Edwin H. 1950. "The diffusion of sexual psycho-path laws." *American Journal of Sociology* 56 (September): 142–148.

Thomas, Mason P. 1972. "Child abuse and neglect: historical overview, legal matrix and social perspectives." *North Carolina Law Review* 50 (February): 239–249.

Wooley, P. V. and W. A. Evans Jr. 1955. "Significance of skeletal lesions in infants resembling those of traumatic origin." *Journal of the American Medical Association* 158 (June): 539–543.

Young, Leontine. 1964. *Wednesday's Children: A Study of Child Neglect and Abuse.* New York: McGraw-Hill.

Zalba, Serapio R. 1966. "The abused child. I. A survey of the problems." *Social Work* 11 (October): 3–16.

Think Critically

1. What does Pfohl's analysis of the discovery of child abuse as a social problem say about deviance in general? What things appear to be important in this defining process?

2. Give an example of the discovery of another form of deviance. What social factors impeded its social recognition as a social problem? Which ones facilitated it?

Defining Deviance Down

Daniel Patrick Moynihan

IN ONE OF THE FOUNDING TEXTS OF SOCIOLOGY, *The Rules of Sociological Method* (1895), Emile Durkheim set it down that "crime is normal." "It is," he wrote, "completely impossible for any society entirely free of it to exist." By defining what is deviant, we are enabled to know what is not, and hence to live by shared standards. This apercu appears in the chapter entitled "Rules for the Distinction of the Normal from the Pathological" . . .

Durkheim suggests, for example, that "in times of scarcity" crimes of assault drop off. He does not imply that we ought to approve of crime—"plain has likewise nothing desirable about it"—but we need understand its function. He saw religion, in the sociologist Randall Collins's terms, as "fundamentally a set of ceremonial actions, assembling the group, heightening its emotions, and focusing its members on symbols of their common belongingness." In this context "a punishment ceremony creates social solidarity."

The matter was pretty much left at that until seventy years later when, in 1965, Kai T. Erikson published *Wayward Puritans,* a study of "crime rates" in the Massachusetts Bay Colony. The plan behind the hook, as Erikson put it, was "to test [Durkheim's] notion that the number of deviant offenders a community can afford to recognize is likely to remain stable over time." The notion proved out very well indeed.

Despite occasional crime waves, as when itinerant Quakers refused to take off their hats in the presence of magistrates, the amount of deviance in this corner of seventeenth-century New England fitted nicely with the supply of stocks and whipping posts. Erikson remarks:

> It is one of the arguments of the . . . study that the amount of deviation a community encounters is apt to remain fairly constant over time. To start at the beginning, it is a simple logistic fact that the number of deviancies which come to a community's attention are limited by the kinds of equipment it uses to detect and handle them, and to that extent the rate of deviation found in a community is at least in part a function of the size and complexity of its social control apparatus. A community's capacity for handling deviance, let us say, can be roughly estimated by counting its

prison cells and hospital beds, its policemen and psychiatrists, its courts and clinics. Most communities, it would seem, operate with the expectation that a relatively constant number of control agents is necessary to cope with a relatively constant number of offenders. The amount of men, money, and material assigned by society to "do something" about deviant behavior does not vary appreciably over time, and the implicit logic which governs the community's efforts to man a police force or maintain suitable facilities for the mentally ill seems to be that there is a fairly stable quota of trouble which should be anticipated.

In this sense, the agencies of control often seem to define their job as that of keeping deviance within bounds rather than that of obliterating it altogether. Many judges, for example, assume that severe punishments are a greater deterrent to crime than moderate ones, and so it is important to note that many of them are apt to impose harder penalties when crime seems to he on the Increase and more lenient ones when it does not, almost as if the power of the bench were being used to keep the crime rate from getting out of hand. Erikson was taking issue with what he described as "a dominant strain in sociological thinking" that took for granted that a well-structured society "is somehow designed to prevent deviant behavior from occurring." In both authors, Durkheim and Erikson, there is an undertone that suggests that, with deviancy, as with most social goods, there is the continuing problem of demand exceeding supply. Durkheim invites us to imagine a society of saints, a perfect cloister of exemplary individuals. Crimes, properly so called, will there be unknown; but faults which appear venial to the layman will create there the same scandal that the ordinary offense does in ordinary consciousness. If, then, this society has the power to judge and punish, it will define these acts as criminal and will treat them as such. Recall Durkheim's comment that there need be no cause for congratulations should the amount of crime drop "too noticeably below the normal level." It would not appear that Durkheim anywhere contemplates the possibility of too much crime. Clearly his theory would have required him to deplore such a development, but the possibility seems never to have occurred to him.

Erikson, writing much later in the twentieth century, contemplates both possibilities. "Deviant persons can be said to supply needed services to society." There is no doubt a tendency for the supply of any needed thing to run short. But he is consistent. There can, he believes, be too much of a good thing. Hence "the number of deviant offenders a community can afford to recognize is likely to remain stable over time." [My emphasis]

Social scientists are said to he on the lookout for poor fellows getting a bum rap. But here is a theory that clearly implies that there are circumstances in which society will choose not to notice behavior that would be otherwise controlled, or disapproved, or even punished.

It appears to me that this is in fact what we in the United States have been doing of late. I proffer the thesis that, over the past generation, since the time Erikson wrote, the amount of deviant behavior in American society has increased beyond the levels the community can "afford to recognize" and that, accordingly, we have been redefining deviancy so as to exempt much conduct previously stigmatized, and also quietly raising the "normal" level in categories where behavior is now abnormal by any earlier standard. This redefining has evoked fierce resistance from defenders of "old" standards, and accounts for much of the present "cultural war" such as proclaimed by many at the 1992 Republican National Convention.

Let me, then, offer three categories of redefinition in these the *altruistic,* the *opportunistic,* and the *normalizing.*

The first category, the *altruistic,* may be illustrated by the deinstitutionalization movement within the mental health profession that appeared in the 1950s. The second category, the opportunistic, is seen in the interest group rewards derived from the acceptance of "alternative" family structures. The third category, the normalizing, is to be observed in the growing acceptance of unprecedented levels of violent crime.

II

It happens that I was present at the beginning of the deinstitutionalization movement. Early in 1955 Averell Harriman, then the new governor of New York, met with his new commissioner of mental hygiene, Dr. Paul Hoch, who described the development, at one of the state mental hospitals, of a tranquilizer derived from rauwolfia. The medication had been clinically tested and appeared to be an effective treatment for many severely psychotic patients, thus increasing the percentage of patients discharged. Dr. Hoch recommended that it be used systemwide; Harriman found the money. That same year Congress created a Joint Commission on Mental Health and Illness whose mission was to formulate "comprehensive and realistic recommendations" in this area, which was then a matter of considerable public concern. Year after year, the population of mental institutions grew. Year after year, new facilities had to be built. Never mind the complexities: population growth and such like matters. There was a general unease. Durkheim's constant continued to be exceeded. (In *Spanning the Century: The Life I of W. Averell Harriman,* Rudy Abramson writes: "New York's mental hospitals in 1955 were overflowing warehouses, and new patients were being admitted faster than space could be found for them. When he was inaugurated, 94,000 New Yorkers were confined to state hospitals. Admissions were running at more than 2,500 a year and rising, making the Department of Mental Hygiene the fastest-growing, most-expensive, most-hopeless department of state government.")

The discovery of tranquilizers was adventitious. Physicians were seeking cures for disorders that were just beginning to be understood. Even a limited success made it possible to believe that the incidence of this particular range of disorders, which had seemingly required persons to be confined against their will or even awareness, could be greatly reduced. The Congressional Commission submitted its report in 1961; it proposed a nationwide program of deinstitutionalization.

Late in 1961, President Kennedy appointed an inter-agency committee to prepare legislative recommendations based upon the report. I represented Secretary of Labor Arthur J. Goldberg on this committee and drafted its final submission. This included the recommendation of the National Institute of Mental Health that 2,000 community mental health centers (one per 100,000 of population) be built by 1980. A buoyant Presidential Message to Congress followed early in 1963. "If we apply our medical knowledge and social insights fully," President Kennedy pronounced, "all but a small portion of the mentally ill can eventually achieve a wholesome and a constructive social adjustment." A "concerted national attack on mental disorders [was] possible and practical." The President signed the Community Mental Health Centers Construction Act on October 31, 1963, his last public bill-signing ceremony. He gave me a pen.

The mental hospitals emptied out. At the time Governor Harriman met with Dr. Hoch in 1955, there were 93,314 adult residents of mental institutions maintained by New York State. As of August 1992, there were 11,363. This occurred across the nation. However, the number of community mental health centers never came near the goal

of the 2,000 proposed community centers. Only some 482 received federal construction funds between 1963 and 1980. The next year, 1981, the program was folded into the Alcohol and Other Drug Abuse block grant and disappeared from view. Even when centers were built, the results were hardly as hoped for. David F. Musto of Yale writes that the planners had bet on improving national mental health "by improving the quality of general community life through expert knowledge, not merely by more effective treatment of the already ill." There was no such knowledge.

However, worse luck, the belief that there *was* such knowledge took hold within sectors of the profession that saw institutionalization as an unacceptable mode of social control. These activists subscribed to a redefining mode of their own. Mental patients were said to have been "labeled," and were not to be drugged. Musto says of the battles that followed that they were "so intense and dramatic precisely because both sides shared the fantasy of an omnipotent and omniscient mental health technology which could thoroughly reform society; the prize seemed eminently worth fighting for."

But even as the federal government turned to other matters, the mental institutions continued to release inmates. Professor Fred Siegel of Cooper Union observes: "In the great wave of moral deregulation that began in the mid-1960s, the poor and the insane were freed from the fetters of in middle-class u mores." They might henseforth sleep in doorways as often as they chose. The problem of the homeless appeared, characteristically defined as persons who lacked "affordable housing."

The *altruistic* mode of redefinition is just that. There is no reason to believe that there was any real increase in mental illness at the time deinstitutionalization began. Yet there was such a perception, and this enabled good people to try to do good, however unavailing in the end.

III

Our second, or *opportunistic* mode of redefinition, reveals at most a nominal intent to do good. The true object is to do well, a long-established motivation among mortals. In this pattern, a growth in deviancy makes possible a transfer of resources, including prestige, to those who control the deviant population. This control would be jeopardized if any serious effort were made to reduce the deviancy in question. This leads to assorted strategies for redefining the behavior in question as not all that deviant, really.

In the years from 1963 to 1965, the Policy Planning Staff of the U.S. Department of Labor picked up the first tremors of what Samuel H. Preston, in the 1984 Presidential Address to the Population Association of America, would call "the earthquake that shuddered through the American family in the past twenty years." *The New York Times* recently provided a succinct accounting of Preston's point:

> Thirty years ago, 1 in every 40 white children was born to an unmarried mother; today it is 1 in 5, according to Federal data. Among blacks, 2 of 3 children are born to an unmarried mother; 30 years ago the figure was 1 in 5. In 1991, Paul Offner and I published longitudinal data showing that, of children born in the years 1967–69, some 22.1 percent were dependent on welfare—that is to say, Aid to Families with Dependent Children—before reaching age 18. This broke down as 15.7 percent for white children, 72.3 percent for black children. Projections for children born in 1980 gave rates of 22.2 percent and 82.9 percent respectively. A year later, a *New York Times* series on welfare and poverty called this a "startling finding . . . symptom of vast social calamity."

And yet there is little evidence that these facts are regarded as a calamity in municipal government. To the contrary, there is general acceptance of the situation as normal. Political candidates raise the subject, often to the point of dwelling on it. But while there is a good deal of demand for symbolic change, there is none of the marshaling of resources that is associated with significant social action. Nor is there any lack of evidence that there is a serious social problem here.

Richard T. Gill writes of "an accumulation of data showing that intact biological parent families offer children very large advantages compared to any other family or non-family structure one can imagine." Correspondingly, the disadvantages associated with single-parent families spill over into other areas of social policy that now attract great public concern. Leroy L. Schwartz, M.D., and Mark W. Stanton argue that the real quest regarding a government-run health system such as that of Canada or Germany is whether it would work "in a country that has social problems that countries like Canada and Germany don't share to the same extent." Health problems reflect ways of living. The way of life associated with "such social pathologies as the breakdown of the family structure" lead to medical pathologies. Schwartz and Stanton conclude: "The United States is paying dearly for its social and behavioral problems," for they have now become medical problems as well.

To cite another example, there is at present no more vexing problem of social policy in the United States than that posed by education. A generation of ever-more ambitious statutes and reforms have produced weak responses at best and a fair amount of what could more simply be called dishonesty. ("Everyone knows that Head Start works." By the year 2000, American students will "be first in the world in science and mathematics.") None of this should surprise us. The 1966 report *Equality of Educational Opportunity* by James S. Coleman and his associates established that the family background of students played a much stronger role in student achievement relative to variations in the ten (and still standard) measures of school quality.

In a 1992 study entitled *America's Smallest School: The Family,* Paul Barton came up with the elegant and persuasive concept of the parent-pupil ratio as a measure of school quality. Barton, who was on the policy planning staff in the Department of Labor in 1965, noted the great increase in the proportion of children living in single-parent families since then. He further noted that the proportion "varies widely among the states" and is related to "variation in achievement" among them. The correlation between the percentage of eighth graders living in two-parent families and average mathematics proficiency is a solid .74. North Dakota, highest on the math test, is second highest on the family compositions scale—that is, it is second in the percentage of kids coming from two-parent homes. The District of Columbia, lowest on the family scale, is second lowest in the test score . . .

For a period there was some speculation that, if family structure got bad enough, this mode of deviancy would have less punishing effects on children. In 1991 Deborah A. Dawson of the National Institutes of Health, examined the thesis that "the psychological effects of divorce and single parenthood on children were strongly influenced by a sense of shame in being 'different' from the norm." If this were so, the effect should have fallen off in the 1980s, when being from a single-parent home became much more common. It did not. "The problems associated with task overload among single parents are more constant in nature," Dawson wrote, adding that since the adverse effects had not diminished, they were "not based on stigmatization but rather on inherent problems in alternative family structures"—*alternative* here meaning other than two-parent families. We should take note of such candor. Writing in the *Journal of Marriage and the Family* in 1989, Sara McLanahan and Karen Booth noted: "Whereas a decade ago the prevailing view was that single motherhood had no harmful effects on children, recent research is less optimistic."

The year 1990 saw more of this lesson. In a paper prepared for the Progressive Policy Institute, Elaine Ciulla Kamarck and William A. Galston wrote that "if the economic effects of family breakdown are clear, the psychological effects are just now coming into focus" . . .

The life course is full of exciting options. The lifestyle options available to individuals seeking a fulfilling personal relationship include living a heterosexual, homosexual, or bisexual single lifestyle; living in a commune; having a group marriage; beings single parent; or living together. Marriage is yet another lifestyle choice. However, before choosing marriage, individuals should weigh its costs and benefits against other lifestyle options and should consider what they want to get out of their intimate relationships. Even within marriage, different people want different things. For example, some people marry for companionship, some marry in order to have children, some marry for emotional and financial security. Though marriage can offer a rewarding path to personal growth, it is important to remember that it cannot provide a secure or permanent status. Many people will make the decision between marriage and singlehood many times throughout their life.

Divorce represents part of the normal family life cycle. It should not be viewed as either deviant or tragic, as it has been in the past. Rather, it establishes a process for "uncoupling" and thereby serves as the foundation for individual renewal and "new beginnings."

History commences to be rewritten. In 1992, the Select Committee on Children, Youth, and Families of the U.S. House of Representatives held a hearing on "Investing in Families: A Historical Perspective." A fact sheet prepared by committee staff began:

"INVESTING IN FAMILIES: A HISTORICAL PER-SPECTIVE" FACT SHEET
HISTORICAL SHIFTS IN FAMILY COMPOSITION CHALLENGING CONVENTIONAL WISDOM

While in modern times the percentage of children living with one parent has increased, more children lived with just one parent in Colonial America. The fact sheet proceeded to list program on program for which federal funds were allegedly reduced in the 1980s. We then come to a summary. Between 1970 and 1991, the value of AFDC [Aid to Families with Dependent Children] benefits decreased by 41%. In spite of proven success of Head Start, only 28% of eligible children are being served. As of 1990, more than $18 billion in child support went uncollected. At the same time, the poverty rate among single-parent with children under 18 was 44%. Between 1980 and 1990, the rate of growth in the total Federal budget was four times greater than the rate of growth in children's programs. In other words, benefits paid to mothers and children have gone down steadily, as indeed they have done. But no proposal is made to restore benefits to an earlier level, or even to maintain their value, as is the case with other "indexed" Social Security programs. Instead we go directly to the subject of education spending.

Nothing new. In 1969, President Nixon proposed a guaranteed income, the Family Assistance Plan. This was described as an "income strategy" as against a "services strategy." It may or may not have been a good idea, but it was a clear one, and the resistance of service providers to it was equally clear. In the end it was defeated, to the huzzahs of the advocates of "welfare rights." What is going on here is simply that a large increase in what once was seen as deviancy has provided opportunity to a wide spectrum of interest groups that benefit from redefining the problem as essentially normal and doing little to reduce it.

IV

Our normalizing category most directly corresponds to Erikson's proposition that "the number of deviant offenders a community can afford to recognize is likely to remain stable over time." Here we are dealing with the popular psychological notion of "denial." In 1965, having reached the conclusion that there would be a dramatic increase in single-parent families, I reached the further conclusion that this would in turn lead to a dramatic increase in crime. In an article in *America,* I wrote:

> From the wild Irish slums of the 19th century Eastern seaboard to the riot-torn suburbs of Los Angeles, there is one unmistakable lesson in American history: a community that allows a large number of young men to grow up in broken families, dominated by women, never acquiring any stable relationship to male authority, never acquiring any set of rational expectations

about the future—that community asks for and gets chaos. Crime, violence, unrest, unrestrained lashing out at the whole social structure—that is not only to be expected; it is very near to inevitable.

The inevitable, as we now know, has come to pass, but here again our response is curiously passive. Crime is a more or less continuous subject of political pronouncement, and from time to time it will be at or near the top of opinion polls as a matter of public concern. But it never gets much further than that. In the words spoken from the bench, Judge Edwin Torres of the New York State Supreme Court, Twelfth Judicial District, described how "the slaughter of the innocent marches unabated: subway riders, bodega owners, cab drivers, babies; in laundromats, at cash machines, on elevators, in hallways." In personal communication, he writes: "This numbness, this near narcoleptic state can diminish the human condition to the level of combat infantrymen, who, in protracted campaigns, can eat their battlefield rations seated on the bodies of the fallen, friend and foe alike. A society that loses its sense of outrage is doomed to extinction." There is no expectation that this will change, nor any efficacious public insistence that it do so. The crime level has been *normalized* . . .

A Kai Erikson of the future will surely need to know that the Department of justice in 1990 found that Americans reported only about 38 percent of all crimes and 48 percent of violent crimes. This, too, can be seen as a means of normalizing crime. In much the same way, the vocabulary of crime reporting can he seems to move toward the normal-seeming. A teacher is shot on her way to class. The *Times* subhead reads: "Struck in the Shoulder in the Year's First Shooting Inside a School." First of the season.

It is too early, however, to know how to regard the arrival of the doctors on the scene declaring crime a "public health emergency." The June 10, 1992, issue of the *Journal of the American Medical Association* was devoted entirely to papers on the subject of violence, principally violence associated with firearms. An editorial in the issue signed by former Surgeon General C. Everett Koop and Dr. George D. Lundberg is entitled: "Violence in America: A Public Health Emergency." Their proposition is admirably succinct.

> Regarding violence in our society as purely a sociological matter, or one of law enforcement, has led to unmitigated failure. It is time to test further whether violence can be amenable to medical/public health

interventions. We believe violence in America to be a public health emergency, largely unresponsive to methods thus far used in its control. The solutions are very complex, but possible.

The authors cited the relative success of epidemiologists in gaining some jurisdiction in the area of motor vehicle casualties by redefining what had been seen as a law enforcement issue into a public health issue. Again, this process began during the Harriman administration in New York in the 1950s. In the 1960s the morbidity and mortality associated with automobile crashes was, it could be argued, a major public health problem; the public healths strategy, it could also be argued, brought the problem under a measure of control. Not in "the 1970s and 1980s," as the *Journal of the American Medical Association* would have us think: the federal legislation involved was signed in 1965. Such a strategy would surely produce insights into the control of violence that elude law enforcement professionals, but whether it would change anything is another question. For some years now I have had legislation in the Senate that would prohibit the manufacture of .25 and .32 caliber bullets. These are the two calibers most typically used with the guns known as Saturday Night Specials. "Guns don't kill people, I argue, "bullets do."

Moreover, we have a two-century supply of handguns but only a four-year supply of ammunition. A public health official would immediately see the logic of trying to control the supply of bullets rather than of guns.

Even so, now that the doctor has come, it is important that criminal violence not be defined down by epidemiologists. Doctors Koop and Lundberg note that in 1990 in the state of Texas "deaths from firearms, For the first time in many decades, surpassed deaths from motor vehicles, by 3,443 to 3,309." A good comparison. And yet keep in mind that the number of motor vehicle deaths, having leveled off since the 1960s is now pretty well accepted as normal at somewhat less than 50,000 a year, which is somewhat less than the level of the 1960's—the "carnage," as it once was thought to be, is now accepted as normal. This is the price we pay for high-speed transportation: there is a benefit associated with it. But there is no benefit associated with homicide, and no good in getting used to it. Epidemiologists have powerful insights that can contribute to lessening the medical trauma, but they must be wary of normalizing the social pathology that leads to such trauma.

V

The hope—if there be such—of this essay has been two-fold. It is, first, to suggest that the Durkheim constant, as I put it, is maintained by a dynamic process which adjusts upwards and *downwards*. Liberals have traditionally been alert for upward redefining that does injustice to individuals. Conservatives have been correspondingly sensitive to downward redefining that weakens societal standards. Might it not help if we could all agree that there is a dynamic at work here? It is not revealed truth, nor yet a scientifically derived formula. It is simply a pattern we observe in ourselves. Nor is it rigid. There may once have been an unchanging supply of jail cells which more or less determined the number of prisoners. No longer. We are building new prisons at a prodigious rate. Similarly, the executioner is back. There is something of a competition in Congress to think up new offenses for which the death penalty is seemed the only available deterrent. Possibly also modes of execution, as in "fry the kingpins." Even so, we are getting used to a lot of behavior that is not good for us.

As noted earlier, Durkheim states that there is "nothing desirable" about pain. Surely what he meant was that there is nothing pleasurable. Pain, even so, is an indispensable warning signal. But societies under stress, much like individuals, will turn to pain killers of various kinds that end up concealing real damage. There is surely nothing desirable about this. If our analysis wins general acceptance, if, for example, more of us came to share Judge Torres's genuine alarm at "the trivialization of the lunatic crime rate" in his city (and mine), we might surprise ourselves how well we respond to the manifest decline of the American civic order. Might.

Think Critically

1. In his discussion of "defining deviancy down," Moynihan emphasizes how by "lowering" our standards of what we consider conventional behaviors, we have in effect normalized what we once considered deviant. Think of examples of the opposite trend, that is, where we have defined deviancy "up," and cite examples of conventional behaviors that are now considered deviant and/or criminal.

2. What are the implications of Moynihan's thesis for efforts regarding crime control? For white-collar and corporate crime? Explain your response, giving examples that support your claim.

Fraud and Financial Crisis[1]
Trivializing the Lunatic Crime Rate

Henry N. Pontell

THE TITLE OF THIS PAPER REPEATS AN observation by Edwin Torres, a judge on the New York Supreme Court, which was highlighted in an article, "Defining Deviancy Down," by Daniel Patrick Moynihan.[2] Trained as a sociologist, Moynihan would come to serve as a Senator from the state of New York, a post held by, among others, Robert Kennedy and Hillary Rodham Clinton. Torres and Moynihan were expressing their indignation at the way that Americans had come to show a so-what, passive, and shoulder-shrugging indifference about what the two men saw as an intolerable level of criminal behavior. The judge had said that "the slaughter of innocents remains unabated; subway riders, bodega owners, cab drivers, babies; in laundromats, at cash machines, on elevators, in hallways" the victims and these crime sites were being treated with a "near narcoleptic state that could diminish the human condition to the level of combat infantrymen, who, in protracted campaigns, can eat their battlefield rations seated on the bodies of the fallen, friend and foe alike." The grim lesson was that "a country that loses its sense of outrage is doomed to extinction."

Moynihan lamented that Americans had gotten "used to a lot of behavior that is not good for us." True to his disciplinary roots, he harked back to Emile Durkheim to buttress his thesis that crime was being normalized. Durkheim had maintained that every society generates a certain level of waywardness and that this aberrancy serves to notify conformists regarding what constitutes acceptable behavior. In one of his best-known canards, Durkheim insisted that even a society of saints would nonetheless label those somewhat less saintly as deviants, whose actions provided a lesson in how not to behave. Moynihan noted, however, that Durkheim's idea of a "normal" crime rate failed to attend properly to the fact that crime can occur at different rates, and that at some point the "normal" becomes "abnormal" and unacceptable. For Moynihan that level had been reached in the United States.

Expanding on this relativistic principle, Moynihan granted that distinctions must be made between various kinds of acts that are categorized as crime and deviance. Some behaviors, once regarded as wayward, may come to be seen as conventional, no longer objects of social disapproval. He failed to point out that there also was at work a tendency to "define deviancy up," a pattern illustrated by a panoply of new offenses, such as hate crime, child abuse, and marital rape. Moynihan maintained that huge amounts of crime result in only the most dramatic acts getting the public's attention, while the remainder elicit no fanfare, much less any real concern. This results, Moynihan argued, in a process he labeled "defining deviancy down" and Judge Torres tagged as "trivializing the lunatic crime rate."

Evidence supporting Moynihan's observations is all around us. Today, there is no crusade against crime. The subject was totally ignored in the 2008 presidential campaign in the United States. Hot-button issues such as the national and global economic crisis, the war in Iraq, health care, and terrorism pushed the issue of crime to the sidelines. Nonetheless, despite a somewhat declining crime rate, there remain stunningly high rates of serious lawbreaking in the United States. Gene Voegtlin, legislative counsel for the International Organization of Chiefs of Police, points to just one index—the fact that 99,000 people have been murdered in the USA since September 11, 2001 and the fall of 2008. "There is," Voegtlin noted, "a wide level of frustration that this is not a major topic of conversation."[3] Putting the matter another way, Michael Nutter, the mayor of Philadelphia, says: "Fact is, al Qaeda wouldn't last a day in parts of Philadelphia. I've got gangsters with .44s that would run them out of town."[4]

Moynihan's position has not gone without some critical reactions since it was enunciated. Some said that it was no more than political rhetoric directed against "permissiveness" in society and "leniency" in the criminal justice system, views dear to "law-and-order" conservatives. Moynihan was charged with implying that "the problem is public tolerance of intolerable behavior and that the solution is resuming traditional standards by stepping up repression of underclass conduct."[5] In an ironic way that position can be said to reflect poorly on the critics. After all, there are other possible approaches to reducing crime, including most notably altering elements of the social system that correlate with and may be causative of lawbreaking. Moynihan was saying that something ought to be done, not what that something might be.

Trivializing Lunatic White-Collar Crime

One gap in Moynihan's position—or perhaps the need to extend its reach—has not heretofore been noted. The focus in Moynihan's analysis on traditional street crimes constitutes a myopic view of the problem, a kind of astigmatism that characterizes many analysts who pretend that white-collar law-breaking somehow belongs to a realm other than that of crime. C. Wright Mills, the sociologist who earned perhaps the greatest public recognition in the past half-century, wrote, "As news of higher immoralities breaks people often say, 'Well, another one got caught today,'" implying that such cases are not odd events involving occasional characters but indicative of a much broader social phenomenon.

Part of the problem lies in the fact that politicians who set the tone depend very heavily on campaign contributions from people and organizations that supply the corps of white-collar crimes. There is an old folk saying about not biting the hand that feeds you or, in white-collar crime terms, "don't defeat the elite."

Whether called white-collar crime, economic crime, abuse of power, or given some other label, political, professional, and business delicts typically are complex, obscure and somewhat esoteric. Unlike street offenses there never has been, or likely will be, an annual tabulation of the extent of such behavior. As two writers recently noted: "No one can determine or estimate . . . costs with confidence; this would require systematically collected data on the prevalence of white-collar crime, the numbers of victims and their losses. These data do not exist and would be extremely difficult to collect in any case."[6]

Three major problems contribute to the trivializing of white-collar crime. First, white-collar crime is rarely dramatic. Although some white-collar crimes inflict serious physical harm on individuals, much of it is what has been characterized as "diffuse" or affecting large numbers of people indirectly. In addition to the major scandals that reach the headlines, what is likely to be the vast hidden bulk result in financial injuries that are "paper crimes." There is no chalk outline on the sidewalk, no yellow tape sequestering the crime scene, no blood-spattered walls. Of late, in what are referred to as "perp walks," law enforcement personnel have taken to handcuffing persons arrested for white-collar offenses and hustling them between figures with POLICE prominently displayed on their jackets while television cameras record it all. The tactic is an effort to raise the trivialization level a bit.

Second, numerous important but complex cases by sophisticated white-collar offenders and organizations never come before a court. This is unlike the lunatic crime rate that concerned Moynihan where sooner or later the most serious or persistent offenders are likely to be apprehended. In the case of white-collar crime the elements of enforcement resources, power, wealth and corresponding legal resources, politics, and the sometimes extremely complex frauds involved which are designed to hide intent—especially at the heart of many of the largest and most costly crimes—all come into play in determining whether or not criminal charges will result. The social reality of defining such acts as "criminal" is much more difficult and involved than is the case for common crime. Studies of the savings and loan debacle in the United States empirically demonstrated that law enforcement agencies were not able to investigate and assuredly not prosecute offenses that they were aware of because of a shortage of enforcement capacity.[7] Today, offenses associated with the current subprime lending frauds are featured obliquely in political debates but the focus is almost exclusively on the consequent problems for the banking industry and those undergoing or contemplating foreclosure. The word "speculation" sometimes surfaces, and occasionally we hear of high-pressure and misleading sales pitches that induced persons to buy a house they could not truly afford. But the word "crime" is not part of the discussion.

White-collar crimes are very difficult to prove in court, particularly because the requisite element of intent is elusive. "I always intended to sell my options on September first," says the corporate president accused of insider trading. "It just so happened that just before then, I found out that the company anticipated a considerable downturn. That information had nothing to do with the sale of my stock," he says, with the subtext: "And I dare you to prove otherwise beyond a reasonable doubt."

Third, there is a reluctance to define captains of industry as "criminals," perhaps best illustrated by the odd response of Ernest Burgess, one of the most prominent stars in the sociological firmament, to an article on white-collar crime in which he found it *out of order to label as criminals persons who did not see themselves as such.*[8] It also is regarded by some as unpatriotic to label those prominent in their community as law-breakers. Often their illegal behavior inflicted only diffuse injury on a group of anonymous victims. And, besides that, the media often find it difficult to set out the complex details of a white-collar conspiracy in a way that will engage readers and, especially, television viewers who respond to visual imagery: the holdup, the auto chase, the murdered corpse.[9] Filmmaker Michael Moore highlighted this in his Oscar-winning documentary, "Bowling for Columbine," by lampooning the popular U.S. television show "COPS" with another version called "CORPORATE COPS" depicting police catching an executive on a busy New York City street, tackling him, and tearing off his suit jacket and shirt before handcuffing him face down against a parked car.

Moreover, as Tombs and Whyte[10] observe, entrepreneurship and market forces provide inherent hurdles that those seeking information have to overcome to learn important details of white-collar crime. Perpetrators often are protected by a battery of powerful lawyers and public relations specialists. The organization often serves as both a weapon and a shield.[11] The trivialization of white-collar crime also reflects system capacity issues dealing with the allocation of resources and biases in law making and law enforcement.[12]

Re-collaring White-Collar Crime

The revisionist thrust to redefine white-collar crime by elements of the scholarly community offers a particularly stark example of a move that further trivializes the subject and the behavior. The redefinition campaign was inaugurated by Susan Shapiro who argued that the term should be "de-collared."[13] Shapiro cites Merton's claim that the role of conceptual analysis lies in "exposing specious empirical relationships latent in unexamined concepts and in debunking theories based on these relationships."[14] Merton observed that "conceptual language tends to fix our perceptions and, derivatively, our thoughts and behavior" and that sociologists often become "imprisoned in the framework of the (often inherited) concepts they use."[15]

Merton used Sutherland's introduction of the term "white-collar crime" as an illustration of the defining process, and was laudatory of the contribution, noting that it undercut mainstream theories that saw crime as a result of Freudian complexes and other forms of personal and social malaise. Shapiro grants the revolutionary impact of the coining of and concentration on the term, pointing out that "the concept of white-collar crime was thus born of Sutherland's efforts to liberate traditional criminology from the 'cognitive misbehavior' reflected in the spurious correlation between poverty and crime."[16] But now she maintained that the concept had become an "imprisoning framework:" that "causes sociologists to misunderstand the structural impetus for these offenses."[17] The problem she perceives is that the term white-collar crime focuses on "some combination of characteristics of lawbreakers, specifying that they be upper-class, or upper-status individuals, organizations, or corporations, or incumbents of occupations roles, a position that inherently confuses "acts with actors, norms with norm breakers, the modus operandi with the operator."[18]

Neither the reference to Merton's view as adopted by Shapiro nor her own critique is above intellectual rebuttal. That Merton calls for revision of entrenched but outmoded concepts is not the same as a demonstration that his call is relevant to white-collar crime. For her part, Shapiro's concern that acts and actors and other elements of the traditional white-collar crime approach are "confused" is confusing. What is "inherently wrong" with studying and theorizing about acts carried out by specified actors?

Separating the crime from the criminal is more problematic than Shapiro and those who have followed her lead have suggested. The element of power is centrally relevant in analyses of white-collar crime. Among other things, it permits only some types of perpetrators to engage in the act while denying opportunities to others. Separating status from the offense results in operational trivialization. It produces, as we shall see, a portrait of white-collar crime that includes a sizeable percentage of unemployed persons who have passed insufficient funds checks at the local supermarket.

The traditional status-based meaning of white-collar crime raises important empirical and interpretive questions that avoid the definitional trivialization that the revisionist approach encourages. We are led to determine why persons who live otherwise conventional and law-abiding lives commit white-collar crimes, and to consider the role of organizational settings. Removing those concerns denies the significance of privileged contexts and organizational structures in producing illegality. The ethos and curricula of business schools, corporate governance structures, bureaucratic considerations, and political power all become matters of interest when traditional definitions of white-collar crime are in play. Separating the crime from the criminal thrusts these matters into the etiological background or, at worst, eliminates them entirely. The "structural impetus" for these crimes emanates from the very institutions of power and privilege that Sutherland made part of his original definition. Denying the tie between "respectability" and "social status" with the commission of these offenses essentially denies the meaning of the term white-collar crime itself.

High Status and Trivialization

In a major review of the topic, Braithwaite[19] concluded that staying with Sutherland's definition offered the best path to comprehension of an important form of criminal behavior. "This at least excludes welfare cheats and credit card fraud from the domain," Braithwaite observed.[20] Explaining *how* and *why* these acts came about is quite different from identifying *who* engaged in them. Sutherland's approach does not preclude focusing on the relationship between social class and crime and, indeed, may facilitate it. Failure to appreciate that only some persons can engage in certain forms of criminality because of their social position reduces the likelihood of recognizing class considerations in lawbreaking. This was one of Sutherland's seminal points. All persons can engage in crimes that are predominantly committed by those in the lower echelons of society. The pattern, however, is not bi-directional.

Moreover, as Braithwaite and others have emphasized, an integral part of Sutherland's definition—the matter of high social position—if removed, would render the term "white-collar crime" even more trivialized than it is today. Eliminating status from the definition we find white-collar offenders to be middle class, lower class, upper class, and often unemployed.[21]

Finally, Sutherland never conceived of the term white-collar crime as a "legal definition" as some scholars who have challenged the idea maintain.[22] Rather he saw it as a social science construct that would guide research. Sutherland had cooperated with Sellin on his classic, *Culture Conflict and Crime*,[23] in which Sellin argued forcefully that social scientists should not adhere to legal definitions appearing in penal codes. The law, he pointed out, is the product of power, lobbying, whim, and a host of idiosyncratic inputs that often lack logical coherence. Many harmful acts never are outlawed because those who commit them see to it that they are not. He notes: "The unqualified acceptance of the legal definitions of the basic elements of criminological inquiry violates a fundamental criterion of science. The scientist must have freedom to define his own terms based on the intrinsic character of his material and designating properties in that material which are assumed to be universal."[24] The goal was to identify social injury and to examine those who inflict it and, in the course of that enterprise, to determine whether and, if not, why such acts were not forbidden. As Goff and Geis note, "Sellin's revisionist perspective pervades studies of what is called *social deviance.*"[25] For Sutherland, the goal was to shed light on a group of largely overlooked illegal acts that are committed by powerful persons and that generally fall well below the radar of conventional criminological and public attention.

Social Class and the Law in Action

Shapiro's contribution grew out of her connection with a large research grant awarded to a Yale Law School team headed by Stanton Wheeler to study white-collar crime, a particularly unusual funding development tied to the concern in the administration of President Carter with white-collar crime. Driven to a considerable extent by the need to gather information on a readily-discernible cohort of offenders, the Yale group elected to specify selected penal code offenses as constituting the true realm of white-collar crime. Anyone who committed these offenses became by definition a white-collar criminal. The approach ignored regulatory and administrative agencies that deal with episodes that Sutherland regarded as essentially equivalent to acts proscribed by the criminal code. Nor did it attend to accusations of traditional white-collar crime that, research indicates, rarely show up in court statistics because astute and expensive lawyers negotiate compromise settlements for their wealthy and powerful clients. The result is that those tried are the "fish that jumped into the boat."

Goetz's study[26] of arson cases in Boston demonstrated how resource constraints and class bias provided what he labels a "structural cloak" that covers white-collar criminality. The fires were intentionally arranged by landlords in order to collect insurance but were blamed by officials on lower-class occupants of the buildings. By keeping arson-for-profit a non-issue (and arson-for-profit was not one of the Yale categories) a significant aspect of white-collar crime was trivialized.

The Yale researchers concluded that Sutherland was wrong; that white-collar crime was the work of the middle-class, although their sample inevitably included both upper class and lower class representatives. No longer would it be necessary to locate a nexus between status, power and law-breaking.

Unlike Durkheim's thesis regarding traditional crime, there is little doubt white-collar crime visits more harm on our society than those offenses tabulated in official reports. Edwin Sutherland, who coined the term "white-collar crime" in his presidential address in 1939 to the American Sociology Society (riantly known by its acronym) pointed out that, among many other proofs, a great deal more money is embezzled by bank employees than stolen by bank robbers. And while street crimes may reinforce conformity among the citizenry, white-collar crime may be used to justify similar behaviors by persons who had not thought of violating the law. The Internal Revenue Service, for instance, reported that when President Richard Nixon was found to have far overstepped the tax advantage offered for donation of private papers, the number of taxpayers who subsequently tried the same scam rose dramatically.

Sutherland's introduction of the concept of white-collar crime was said to have "altered the study of crime throughout the world in fundamental ways by focusing attention upon a form of law-breaking that had been previously ignored by criminological scholars."[27] That statement in time proved to have a considerable element of hyperbole. White-collar crime became the topic of choice of a rather small cadre of scholars, many of whom cut their teeth on the subject and then, for reasons that have never been clearly determined, moved on to other subjects. The American list includes from earlier days Marshall Clinard, Donald Newman, Richard Quinney, and Donald Cressey and from more recent times Susan Shapiro and David Weisburd.

White-collar crime to a considerable degree suffers not only from trivialization but also to a great extent from a failure of recognition, from invisibility, from its status, in Goetz's term, as a "non-issue." The remainder of this paper will seek to make a logical case for prioritizing the move against trivialization of crime by focusing more strongly on white-collar crime. It does not dispute Moynihan's thesis but rather builds on the anti-Durkheimian theme that white-collar rips at the social fabric by sowing doubt in the integrity of those who hold positions of power and wealth—simply put, by providing poor examples and causing antagonism toward the state and its leaders.

The drift of studies of crime increasingly toward sophisticated statistical analyses and esoteric theoretical interpretation has inevitably exacerbated the trivialization of white-collar crime since its study does not lend itself to the desire by scholarly journal editors and referees for numerical models. Andrew Abbott, a University of Chicago sociologist, speaks not only for his discipline but for criminology as well when he suggests that sociology "is a discipline that is sliding into inconsequence."[28]

Meanwhile, scholarship in the sub-discipline known as "law and society" tends to focus on what is heralded as the "law in action." White-collar crime necessarily gets short shrift, perhaps because so much of it falls under the heading of the "law in inaction."

Many scholars, particularly those who might be regarded as "old-timers" in the field, use Sutherland's definition of white-collar crimes as an illegal act "committed by a person of respectability and high social status in the course of his occupation." The definition obviously contains an element that might reasonably be labeled as propaganda, that is, it focuses attention on wrongdoing by those in prestige positions. In its way it is a corollary of street crime that almost exclusively focuses on wrongdoing by underclass persons. As Anatole France said: "The law in its majestic equality forbids both the poor man and the rich man from sleeping under the bridge."[29] He had no need to mention that rich men are not very likely to need to be sleeping under bridges.

Sutherland's definition of white-collar crime is more precise than many scholars have given it credit for. It emphasizes, for instance, that a common crime committed by a person of high social status is not to be regarded as a white-collar crime since it was not carried out in the course of the person's legitimate occupation. It further identifies crimes that can be committed only by persons of relatively high social status in their occupational roles, so that defining these acts by characteristics of their perpetrators does not result in an "unfortunate mixing of definition as exposition," at least no more than the usual theories of crime that are based entirely on lower-class offending patterns. It puts the crime into an interpretative context. Removing it from that context—"de-collaring" it—leads to trivializing the structural forces that are basic to such crimes and to overlooking policies that best prevent them in the specific context in which they arise. This results in a failure to consider complex social, political, cultural, and economic settings and the emergence of a focus on a heterodox congery of offenders apprehended for breaking an array of rather amorphous laws that are tagged as "white-collar crime."

In a recent essay, Shover and Cullen argue that the two schools of thought regarding the preferable definition of white-collar crime can be seen as a conflict between two positions with ideological underpinnings. There is the "populist" perspective that locates the offenses within the framework of social inequality and what they label the "patrician" perspective that offers a less politicized and more legal-technical perspective. They note that adherents of the "patrician" bloc tend to be characterized by elitist backgrounds and affiliations, such as the Yale Law School. By greatly broadening the embrace of white-collar crime they deflect attention from the wrongdoing of their own kind onto others, those beneath them in the social hierarchy, whose mundane misdeeds are of much less concern to the general public than should be the case with depictions of traditional white-collar crime.

A lunatic rate of white-collar crime is apparent regardless of which prism is used, but the extent of such neglect is a function of the selection of definition. The patrician view minimizes the impact of white-collar crime by considering only those cases found in official statistics. On the other hand, the populist perspective highlights issues of power, of respectability, and privilege as concepts toward understanding the phenomenon.

This theoretical element is not unlike the debate between Sutherland and Tappan, the latter trained in both law and sociology, that took place shortly after Sutherland introduced his concept. Representing patricians, Tappan dubbed the term white-collar crime as loose, derogatory, and doctrinaire, and argued that criminologists should confine themselves to the study of those adjudicated as guilty of certain crime by the legal system.[30] Sutherland, the populist, argued that if criminology confined itself to the well-documented biases that feed into the content of the criminal law researchers would forfeit claims to pursuing a social scientific enterprise.[31]

Revisionist scholars have objected that the Sutherland position is "selectively defined to fit the ideological biases of individual scholars" and that it represents a partisan polemic against corporations and persons of high status.[32] Oddly, while the objection centered solely on individual white-collar crime there was no revisionist drive in regard to corporate crime. Such crime, constituting the largest segment of Sutherland's classic *White Collar Crime,* was first singled out as a separable category of lawbreaking by Clinard and Quinney.[33]

While the overwhelming number of corporate and limited partnership crimes are committed by small businesses (a subject almost totally trivialized), the scandals involving gigantic corporations have increasingly commanded media attention. The roster includes the savings and loan industry collapse in the 1980s, the Enron and Arthur Andersen accounting scandals, and the current economic meltdown of the American economic system that metastasized to the global marketplace.

The 2008 Global Financial Crisis

The current worldwide financial problems have their roots in home mortgage lending practices. Many are part of what have been called "subprime" loans that, at best, are less than prudent, and, at worst, criminally fraudulent.

The bursting of the real estate bubble, which had grown quickly to massive proportions, has resulted in an unprecedented number of foreclosures, a striking collapse in the market value of homes, and heavy losses for those holding investments involving the bundling of loans and debt. Moreover, some of the most sophisticated financial institutions had allowed—and encouraged—practices that were highly imprudent, despite their reputation for expertise in risk management. Well before the bubble burst, William Black noted the danger signs and diagnosed the risks that these companies faced:

> Why? Because their CEOs, acting on the perverse incentives crucial to today's outrageous compensation systems, engaged in practices that vastly increased their corporations' risks in order to drive up corporate income and thereby secure enormous increases in their own individual incomes. And these perverse incomes follow them out the door . . . Pay and productivity (and integrity) have become unhinged in U.S. financial institutions.[34]

Black is perhaps overgenerous in portraying a need to show a particularly healthy balance sheet in order to justify outrageous pay packages for executives. The CEO of AIG, one of the near-bankrupt companies rescued by the U.S. government, saw his company lose $50 billion in the most recent year and his board of directors award him a bonus of $5 million for, well, for what? He also earns a salary of $1 million a month.

The extent of lawbreaking in the world of subprime lending remains to be seen, although enforcement agencies, concentrating their resources on homeland security, will prove to be hard-pressed to satisfactorily investigate and adjudicate this issue. There has been a 36 percent staff reduction since 2001 in FBI agents dealing with white-collar crime and the number of criminal cases brought by the FBI has dropped by slightly more than one quarter during the same period.[35] A Syracuse University study determined that the fall off rate in white-collar crime prosecutions had reached the 50 percent level.[36]

The global financial crisis is inexorably tied to the meltdown of the U.S. economy which was caused by massive fraud in the subprime mortgage industry. Black and others have argued that waves of such "control fraud" or fraud committed by controlling insiders of large organizations, can extend, and hyper-inflate, financial bubbles that eventually result in systemic crises. The late economist whose academic work focused on such matters, Hyman Minsky, used the term "Ponzi" phase to characterize this growth in financial bubbles. It is in fact a descriptive phrase, and not simply metaphorical. The "weapon of choice" in bubbles is accounting and the principal intended victims are the firm, its shareholders, creditors, and customers. Such waves of fraud are neither random nor irrational; they occur when a "criminogenic environment" creates perverse incentives to act unlawfully. The lack of effective financial regulation and enforcement during the Bush administration and policies fostered by former U.S. Federal Reserve Chairman Alan Greenspan allowed such criminogenic environments to flourish in numerous industries related to the origination, sale, and securitization of home loans. Financial instruments based on these "toxic assets" were spread and sold throughout the world.

In terms of the current economic crisis, three major issues stand out. The first is that executive compensation policies turned private market discipline into perverse incentives encouraging massive control fraud even at the most elite firms. The emphasis on short-term results encourages executives to engage in high-risk and illegal practices in order to obtain better compensation packages, while at the same time gambling long-term stability in their companies.

Second, despite accurately warning since September 2004 that mortgage fraud was becoming "epidemic," the FBI reacted to its severe system capacity problems in a manner that failed to challenge Bush administration policies that virtually guaranteed that the FBI would fail to stem the fraud epidemic. The FBI's major strategy was to partner with the Mortgage Bankers Association (MBA). Unfortunately, and most ironically, the MBA is a trade association of mortgage originators representing the worst mortgage control frauds. Mortgage lending personnel are estimated to be complicit in 80% of fraudulent mortgage applications. The FBI began serious investigations of the major mortgage originators only in late 2007, after the major damage had been done. The trivializing of white-collar crime is clearly evident here, not only in terms of the lack of investigative resources and lateness of response, but especially when the MBA touted, as the principal product of its partnership with the FBI, a *poster* warning *customers* not to defraud MBA's members.

Third, and central to the high incidence of subprime fraud, was the fact that no one involved in the process evaluated credit quality. Had they done so they could not have missed—or allowed—the widespread and severe nature of these frauds. This failure to evaluate credit quality was pervasive throughout the industry, and included appraisers, review appraisers, underwriters, loan committee members, purchasers' underwriters, outside auditors at every level, stock analysts, mortgage insurers, and even the credit rating agencies themselves. The trivializing of white-collar crime is evident in the fact that the FBI's 2004 warning of a fraud epidemic due to these practices was ignored by policymakers, and that the mortgage industry's own term for many subprime loans was "liars' loans."

In terms of our theme, it needs to be stressed that except for a regular recourse to "speculators" in the blame game and a not insignificant degree of victim-blaming, the big culprits have escaped condemnation and the only concern is whether they really ought to be given so much taxpayer money to relieve their distress. What we see is the historical record of the trivialization of white-collar crime repeating itself in even grander fashion. That the former U.S. Attorney General declined to create a task force to investigate the roots of the subprime debacle, while likening the problem to "'white-collar street-crime' that could best be handled by individual United States attorneys' offices"[37] is a decision believed to be a reflection of the strong pro-business ideology of the Bush administration.

As former Chairman of the Federal Reserve Alan Greenspan's *mea culpa* made painfully clear, neoclassical economists and those who listen to them are blinded by an ideology that trivializes fraud, proclaims free markets as the panacea, and sees regulation as the bogeyman. Greenspan's "shock" that companies took advantage when they were handed the opportunity to do so, rather than doing the right thing for investors and markets, may appear disingenuous, but it also stems from the refusal to acknowledge that these business contexts constituted what criminologists have for some time noted as "crime-facilitative environments" where white-collar offending can flourish. Economists generally are either unaware or disdainful of the perspectives from other disciplines, and often show contempt for government interventions into the marketplace. They have thus managed to trivialize the matter of fraud in formulating policies that govern banking and finance.

This anti-regulatory, anti-government ideology gained clear expression in the 2008 presidential campaign as the Republicans, in dire straits as the election approached, took to lambasting the Democratic candidates with what they regarded as a powerful curse word: they were "socialists," frightening tools of the Devil. They even had suggested (God forbid), that it might be a good idea to "spread the wealth." European socialist governments might have found this barrage bewildering. It is notable that both the Soviet Union and Nazi Germany felt compelled to insert "Socialism" and "Socialist" in their names in order to lull the populace into believing their motives were decent and benign.

Conclusion

The claim that white-collar crime is primarily a middle class offense and that the status of the offender needs to be separated from the act in order to avoid biased social analysis, implicitly allows the most consequential forms of white-collar and corporate lawbreaking to fly well below the political, academic, and policy radar screens. Put another way, such treatment trivializes the nature and extent of white-collar crime. This trivialization ensures that major white-collar crimes remain largely absent in the development of effective regulatory policies and the law more generally. Nor are they included in what Moynihan described as "a lot of behavior that's not good for us." Trivializing the lunatic white-collar crime rate entails much greater social costs then those related to the crime and deviance considered by Moynihan. The scale of the current global financial crisis is a case in point. Even if one argues that major frauds *weren't* a central underlying component to the meltdown, a little bit of lawbreaking certainly seemed to go a long way.

NOTES

1. I thank Gilbert Geis and William Black for their helpful comments on an earlier draft of this paper.
2. Moynihan, Daniel Patrick (2001). Defining Deviancy Down, *The American Scholar* 62:1.
3. Jones, Ashby (2008). Crime Hasn't Dropped as Much As Our Interest in Talking About It. Wall Street Journal, October 2.
4. Ibid.
5. Karmen, Andrew (1994). "Defining Deviancy Down": How Senator Moynihan's Misleading Phrase About Criminal Justice Is Rapidly Being Incorporated Into Popular Culture, *Journal of Criminal Justice and Popular Culture,* 2(5): 99–112.

6. Shover, Neal and Francis T. Cullen (2008). "Studying and Teaching White-Collar Crime: Populist and Patrician Perspectives." *Journal of Criminal Justice Education* 19:2 (July):155–174. p. 162–163.
7. Pontell, Henry N., Calavita, Kitty and Robert Tillman, "Corporate Crime and Criminal Justice System Capacity: Government Response to Financial Institution Fraud," *Justice Quarterly* 11:3 (September, 1994) pp. 383–410; Kitty Calavita, Kitty, Pontell, Henry N. and Robert Tillman, *Big Money Crime: Fraud and Politics in the Savings and Loan Crisis.* Berkeley: University of California Press, 1997; Tillman, Robert, Pontell, Henry N. and Kitty Calavita, "Criminalizing White-Collar Misconduct: Determinants of Prosecution in Savings and Loan Fraud Cases." *Crime, Law and Social Change* 26:1 (1997) pp. 53–76.
8. Burgess, Ernest W. (1950) "Comment and Concluding Comment." *American Journal of Sociology* 56: 31–34.
9. Rosoff, Stephen M., Pontell, Henry N., and Robert Tillman (2007). *Profit Without Honor: White-Collar Crime and the Looting of America (4th Ed.).* Upper Saddle River, NJ: Prentice Hall.
10. Tombs, Steve and David Whyte, editors (2003). *Unmasking the Crimes of the Powerful: Scrutinizing States and Corporations.* NY: Peter Lang.
11. Wheeler, Stanton, and Michael L. Rothman (1982). "The Organization as Weapon in White-Collar Crime." *Michigan Law Review,* 80:1403–1426.
12. Pontell, Henry N. (1982). "System Capacity and Criminal Justice: Theoretical and Substantive Considerations," in Harold E. Pepinsky (ed.), *Rethinking Criminology.* Beverly Hills: Sage Publications, 131–143; Goetz, Barry (1997) Organization as Class Bias in Local Law Enforcement: Arson-for-Profit as a "Nonissue," *Law & Society Review* 3:557–585; Reiman, Jeffrey. (1998). *The Rich get Richer and the Poor get Prison: Ideology, Class, and Criminal Justice.* Boston: Allyn and Bacon.
13. Shapiro, Susan S. (1990). "Collaring the Crime, not the Criminal: Liberating the Concept of White-Collar Crime. *American Sociological Review* 55:346–365.
14. Ibid., 346
15. Merton, 1949:88–89 in Shapiro.
16. Shapiro, 1990:346
17. Ibid.
18. Ibid., 347.
19. Braithwaite, John (1985). White-Collar Crime. *Annual Review of Sociology* 11:1–25.
20. Ibid., 131.
21. Weisburd, David, Wheeler, Stanton, Waring, Elin, and Nancy Bode (1994). *Crimes of the Middle Classes: White-Collar*

Offenders in the Federal Courts. New Haven, CT: Yale University Press; Daly, Kathleen (1989). "Gender and Varieties of White-Collar Crime." Criminology 27(4):769–794.

22. Shapiro, 1990, op cit.; Zimring, Franklin and David Johnson, (2007). "On the Comparative Study of Corruption." In Henry N. Pontell and Gilbert Geis (eds.) *International Handbook of White-Collar and Corporate Crime.* New York: Springer, pp. 456–473.

23. Sellin, Thorsten (1938). *Culture Conflict and Crime.* NY: Social Science Research Council.

24. Ibid., p. 31.

25. Goff, Colin and Gilbert Geis (2008) The Michael-Adler Report (1933): "Criminology Under the Microscope." *Journal of the History of the Behavioral Sciences* 44(4): 350–363, p. 253.

26. Goetz, 1997, op. cit.

27. Geis, Gilbert, and Colin Goff (1983). Introduction to Edwin H. Sutherland, *White-Collar Crime: The Uncut Version.* New Haven: Yale University Press, pp. ix.

28. Abbott, Andrew (1999). *Department and Discipline: Chicago Sociology at One Hundred.* Chicago: University of Chicago Press, p. 192.

29. France, Anatole (1894). *Le Lys Rouge* [The Red Ruby]. Paris: Calmann-Levy. P. 117.

30. Tappan, Paul W. (1947). "Who is the Criminal?" *American Sociological Review* 12 (February):96–102.

31. Sutherland, Edwin H (1945). "Is 'White-Collar Crime' Crime?" *American Sociological Review* 10 (April):132–139.

32. Johnson, David T. and Leo, Richard A. (1993). "The Yale White-Collar Crime Project: A Review and Critique." *Law and Social Inquiry* 18:63–99, p. 64.

33. Clinard, Marshall and Richard Quinney (1973). *Criminal Behavior Systems: A Typology (2nd ed.).* NY: Holt, Rinehart & Winston.

34. Black, William H. (2007) (Mis)Understanding a Banking Industry in Transition. *Dollars and Sense* No. 273 (Nov/Dec):14–27.

35. Lichtblau, Eric, Johnston, David and Ron Nixon (2008) "FBI Struggles to Handle Financial Fraud Cases." *The New York Times.* Oct. 19. p. A1.

36. Ibid.

37. Ibid.

Think Critically

1. Do you feel that white-collar and corporate crime have been given enough weight by academics, citizens or the government? Why or why not? Explain, and give three reasons that support your answer.

2. What are the impediments to changing how white-collar and corporate crime are viewed, and, correspondingly, what changes do you feel are necessary for these forms of deviance to be "reconstructed" and taken more seriously?"

WHILE IT WOULD STRIKE MOST CASUAL observers as odd, social scientists have noted that deviance can serve positive functions for groups and for society as a whole. Drawing from the classic work of Emile Durkheim, one of the founders of modern sociology, functionalists view deviance as an integral part of healthy societies. Deviance serves to establish group boundaries for acceptable behavior. Punishing violators of group norms can serve to strengthen social rules and sharpen social boundaries by bringing these matters to public attention. Rather than seeing deviance merely as pathological, functionalists focus on the purposes it serves as a normal phenomenon of healthy societies. In fact, they believe that deviance is universal, that it exists in all societies, and that it serves an important role in social life. This position is formulated in Emile Durkheim's classic statement in "The Normal and the Pathological." Durkheim identifies the positive aspects of crime and claims that it is a normal part of society, "a factor in public health, an integral part of all healthy societies."

Anomie is a term used by Durkheim to describe a "lack of norms" in society. This lack of clear rules for behavior can exist at both the societal and individual levels. Rapid social change, for example, may bring new norms to the fore that are neither fully clear nor internalized by all segments of the population. Deviance may arise as persons attempt to adapt to these new situations.

Drawing from this tradition, Robert K. Merton, one of the most famous sociologists of the twentieth century, formulated his classic work, "Social Structure and Anomie." Merton extended Durkheim's insight that deviance arises from social organization, and seeks to examine what processes account for deviance other than biological mechanisms and impulses. His theory centers on the notion that deviance arises from the incongruence between two major elements of social structure: cultural goals and institutionalized norms or means. When these elements are discordant, deviance may result as part of a

THEORIES ~
Functionalism, Anomie, and Strain

normal process of individual adaptation. The typology of adaptations he presents is one of the more famous examples of modern sociology.

Richard Cloward and Lloyd Ohlin's piece extends Merton's formulation by highlighting the notion that adapting in a deviant manner to social strain entails differential access to illegitimate means. In other words, to enact deviance, one must have access to illegitimate groups and structures from which to learn such behavior. Cloward and Ohlin believe that persons have differential opportunities for rule breaking depending on their location in the social structure. When legitimate opportunities are blocked, the extent of deviant behavior will vary according to the availability of illegitimate means.

A more recent perspective that looks at issues related to anomie, and how strain affects deviance and crime, is offered by Robert Agnew. Using ideas from social disorganization and subculture theories, Agnew presents a perspective that offers another explanation for the differences that communities experience in rates of crime. He argues that general strain theory (GST) offers a better model, in that strain or stress in such communities is a major source of criminal motivation. Community differences in crime are explained by community differences in strain, and those factors that condition the effect of strain on crime. Building upon older theories involving relative deprivation and social disorganization, Agnew claims that previous research has not considered fully the different ways in which communities may promote strain, and the ways in which they may condition the effect of strain on crime. Agnew highlights the roles of these GST variables through a review and analysis of past theories and empirical research.

In "Latinos and Lethal Violence: The Impact of Poverty and Inequality," Ramiro Martinez, Jr. examines the relatively understudied area of Latino homicide. He argues that minority groups deprived of economic opportunity, and who are part of a social structure that is characterized by low education, poor wages, impoverished conditions, and less professional status, will tend to have higher levels of frustration and alienation (i.e., strain) that will lead to increased aggression and relatively high rates of homicide. Examining murder rates in 111 cities in 1980, the author finds the most support for the notion that economic inequality leads to violence, leading to the conclusion that socioeconomic conditions are of paramount importance in understanding and ultimately preventing Latino homicides.

In their classic piece, "Broken Windows," James Wilson and George Kelling posit that both untended property and untended behavior lead to a breakdown in community controls, which leads to further lawbreaking. Stopping crimes of vandalism, the authors maintain, is best accomplished when such acts are small, and well before they become a permanent face of the community. Keeping problems from escalating helps keep the community intact by reducing fear of victimization and preventing persons from fleeing the area. Their idea that reducing petty crime and low-level personal crimes will lead to preventing more serious crimes has been criticized in a number of studies including those that show similar reductions in crime in cities without "zero-tolerance" policies. Others have argued that more fundamental social forces were more significant factors responsible for lowering crime rates, including the demographics of young males, and the waning of the crack epidemic, among others. ✳

The Normal and the Pathological*

Emile Durkheim

IF THERE IS ANY FACT WHOSE PATHOLOGICAL character appears incontestable, that fact is crime. All criminologists are agreed on this point. Although they explain this pathology differently, they are unanimous in recognizing it. But let us see if this problem does not demand a more extended consideration.

We shall apply the foregoing rules. Crime is present not only in the majority of societies of one particular species but in all societies of all types. There is no society that is not confronted with the problem of criminality. Its form changes; the acts thus characterized are not the same everywhere; but, everywhere and always, there have been men who have behaved in such a way as to draw upon themselves penal repression. If, in proportion as societies pass from the lower to the higher types, the rate of criminality, i.e., the relation between the yearly number of crimes and the population, tended to decline, it might be believed that crime, while still normal, is tending to lose this character of normality. But we have no reason to believe that such a regression is substantiated. Many facts would seem rather to indicate a movement in the opposite direction. From the beginning of the [nineteenth] century, statistics enable us to follow the course of criminality. It has everywhere increased. In France the increase is nearly 300 percent. There is, then, no phenomenon that presents more indisputably all the symptoms of normality, since it appears closely connected with the conditions of all collective life. To make of crime a form of social morbidity would be to admit that morbidity is not something accidental, but, on the contrary,

---

*Reprinted with the permission of The Free Press, a Division of Simon & Schuster Inc. from *The Rules of Sociological Method* by Emile Durkheim, translated by Sarah A. Solovay and John H. Mueller. Edited by George E. G. Catlin. Copyright © 1938 by George E. G. Catlin; copyright renewed 1966 by S. A. Solovay, J. H. Mueller, and G. E. G. Catlin.

that in certain cases it grows out of the fundamental constitution of the living organism; it would result in wiping out all distinction between the physiological and the pathological. No doubt it is possible that crime itself will have abnormal forms, as, for example, when its rate is unusually high. This excess is, indeed, undoubtedly morbid in nature. What is normal, simply, is the existence of criminality, provided that it attains and does not exceed, for each social type, a certain level, which it is perhaps not impossible to fix in conformity with the preceding rules.[1]

Here we are, then, in the presence of a conclusion in appearance quite paradoxical. Let us make no mistake. To classify crime among the phenomena of normal sociology is not to say merely that it is an inevitable, although regrettable phenomenon, due to the incorrigible wickedness of men; it is to affirm that it is a factor in public health, an integral part of all healthy societies. This result is, at first glance, surprising enough to have puzzled even ourselves for a long time. Once this first surprise has been overcome, however, it is not difficult to find reasons explaining this normality and at the same time confirming it.

In the first place crime is normal because a society exempt from it is utterly impossible. Crime . . . consists of an act that offends certain very strong collective sentiments. In a society in which criminal acts are no longer committed, the sentiments they offend would have to be found without exception in all individual consciousnesses, and they must be found to exist with the same degree as sentiments contrary to them. Assuming that this condition could actually be realized, crime would not thereby disappear; it would only change its form, for the very cause which would thus dry up the sources of criminality would immediately open up new ones.

Indeed, for the collective sentiments which are protected by the penal law of a people at a specified moment of its history to take possession of the public conscience or for them to acquire a stronger hold where they have an insufficient grip, they must acquire an intensity greater than that which they had hitherto had. The community as a whole must experience them more vividly, for it can acquire from no other source the greater force necessary to control these individuals who formerly were the most refractory. For murderers to disappear, the horror of bloodshed must become greater in those social strata from which murderers are recruited; but, first it must become greater throughout the entire society. Moreover, the very absence of crime would directly contribute to produce this horror; because any sentiment seems much more respectable when it is always and uniformly respected.

One easily overlooks the consideration that these strong states of the common consciousness cannot be thus reinforced without reinforcing at the same time the more feeble states, whose violation previously gave birth to mere infraction of convention—since the weaker ones are only the prolongation, the attenuated form, of the stronger. Thus robbery and simple bad taste injure the same single altruistic sentiment, the respect for that which is another's. However, this same sentiment is less grievously offended by bad taste than by robbery; and since, in addition, the average consciousness has not sufficient intensity to react keenly to the bad taste, it is treated with greater tolerance. That is why the person guilty of bad taste is merely blamed, whereas the thief is punished. But, if this sentiment grows stronger, to the point of silencing in all consciousnesses the inclination which disposes man to steal, he will become more sensitive to the offenses which, until then, touched him but lightly. He will react against them, then, with more energy; they will be the object of greater opprobrium, which will transform certain of them from the simple moral faults that they were and give them the quality of crimes. For example, improper contracts, or contracts improperly executed, which only incur public blame or civil damages, will become offenses in law.

Imagine a society of saints, a perfect cloister of exemplary individuals. Crimes, properly so called, will there be unknown; but faults which appear venial to the layman will create there the same scandal that the ordinary offense does in ordinary consciousnesses. If, then, this society has the power to judge and punish,

it will define these acts as criminal and will treat them as such. For the same reason, the perfect and upright man judges his smallest failings with a severity that the majority reserve for acts more truly in the nature of an offense. Formerly, acts of violence against persons were more frequent than they are today, because respect for individual dignity was less strong. As this has increased, these crimes have become more rare; and also, many acts violating this sentiment have been introduced into the penal law which were not included there in primitive times.[2]

In order to exhaust all the hypotheses logically possible, it will perhaps be asked why this unanimity does not extend to all collective sentiments without exception. Why should not even the most feeble sentiment gather enough energy to prevent all dissent? The moral consciousness of the society would be present in its entirety in all the individuals, with a vitality sufficient to prevent all acts offending it—the purely conventional faults as well as the crimes. But a uniformity so universal and absolute is utterly impossible; for the immediate physical milieu in which each one of us is placed, the hereditary antecedents, and the social influences vary from one individual to the next, and consequently diversify consciousnesses. It is impossible for all to be alike, if only because each one has his own organism and that these organisms occupy different areas in space. That is why, even among the lower peoples, where individual originality is very little developed, it nevertheless does exist.

Thus, since there cannot be a society in which the individuals do not differ more or less from the collective type, it is also inevitable that, among these divergences, there are some with a criminal character. What confers this character upon them is not the intrinsic quality of a given act but that definition which the collective conscience lends them. If the collective conscience is stronger, if it has enough authority practically to suppress these divergences, it will also be more sensitive, more exacting; and, reacting against the slightest deviations with the energy it otherwise displays only against more considerable infractions, it will attribute to them the same gravity as formerly to crimes. In other words, it will designate them as criminal.

Crime is, then, necessary; it is bound up with the fundamental conditions of all social life, and by that very fact it is useful, because these conditions of which it is a part are themselves indispensable to the normal evolution of morality and law.

Indeed, it is no longer possible today to dispute the fact that law and morality vary from one social type to the next, nor that they change within the same type if the conditions of life are modified. But, in order that these transformations may be possible, the collective sentiments at the basis of morality must not be hostile to change, and consequently must have but moderate energy. If they were too strong, they would no longer be plastic. Every pattern is an obstacle to new patterns, to the extent that the first pattern is inflexible. The better a structure is articulated, the more it offers a healthy resistance to all modification; and this is equally true of functional, as of anatomical, organization. If there were no crimes, this condition could not have been fulfilled; for such a hypothesis presupposes that collective sentiments have arrived at a degree of intensity unexampled in history. Nothing is good indefinitely and to an unlimited extent. The authority which the moral conscience enjoys must not be excessive; otherwise no one would dare criticize it, and it would too easily congeal into an immutable form. To make progress, individual originality must be able to express itself. In order that the originality of the idealist whose dreams transcend his century may find expression, it is necessary that the originality of the criminal, who is below the level of his time, shall also be possible. One does not occur without the other.

Nor is this all. Aside from this indirect utility, it happens that crime itself plays a useful role in this evolution. Crime implies not only that the way remains open to necessary changes but that in certain cases it directly prepares these changes. Where crime exists, collective sentiments are sufficiently flexible to take on a new form, and crime sometimes helps to determine the form they will take. How many times, indeed, it is only an anticipation of future morality—a step toward what will be! According to Athenian law, Socrates was a criminal, and his condemnation was no more than just. However, his crime, namely, the independence of his thought, rendered a service not only to humanity but to his country. It served to prepare a new morality and faith which the Athenians needed, since the traditions by which they had lived until then were no longer in harmony with the current conditions of life. Nor is the case of Socrates unique; it is reproduced periodically in history. It would never

have been possible to establish the freedom of thought we now enjoy if the regulations prohibiting it had not been violated before being solemnly abrogated. At that time, however, the violation was a crime, since it was an offense against sentiments still very keen in the average conscience. And yet this crime was useful as a prelude to reforms which daily became more necessary. Liberal philosophy had as its precursors the heretics of all kinds who were justly punished by secular authorities during the entire course of the Middle Ages and until the eve of modern times.

From this point of view the fundamental facts of criminality present themselves to us in an entirely new light. Contrary to current ideas, the criminal no longer seems a totally unsociable being, a sort of parasitic element, a strange and unassimilable body, introduced into the midst of society.[3] On the contrary, he plays a definite role in social life. Crime, for its part, must no longer be conceived as an evil that cannot be too much suppressed. There is no occasion for self-congratulation when the crime rate drops noticeably below the average level, for we may be certain that this apparent progress is associated with some social disorder. Thus, the number of assault cases never falls so low as in times of want.[4] With the drop in crime rate, and as a reaction to it, comes a revision, or the need of a revision in the theory of punishment. If, indeed, crime is a disease, its punishment is its remedy and cannot be otherwise conceived; thus, all the discussions it arouses bear on the point of determining what the punishment must be in order to fulfill this role of remedy. If crime is not pathological at all, the objects of punishment cannot be to cure it, and its true function must be sought elsewhere. . . .

NOTES

1. From the fact that crime is a phenomenon of normal sociology, it does not follow that the criminal is an individual normally constituted from the biological and psychological points of view. The two questions are independent of each other. This independence will be better understood when we have shown, later on, the difference between psychological and sociological facts.
2. Calumny, insults, slander, fraud, etc.
3. We have ourselves committed the error of speaking thus of the criminal, because of a failure to apply our rule (*Division du travail social*, pp. 395–96).

4. Although crime is a fact of normal sociology, it does not follow that we must not abhor it. Pain itself has nothing desirable about it; the individual dislikes it as society does crime, and yet it is a function of normal physiology. Not only is it necessarily derived from the very constitution of every living organism, but it plays a useful role in life, for which reason it cannot be replaced. It would, then, be a singular distortion of our thought to present it as an apology for crime. We would not even think of protesting against such an interpretation, did we not know to what strange accusations and misunderstandings one exposes oneself when one undertakes to study moral facts objectively and to speak of them in a different language from that of the layman.

> ## Think Critically
>
> 1. Explain how crime is "normal" in society. In what ways does it improve the functioning of healthy groups?
> 2. According to Durkheim, why is the collective conscience so important in understanding the role of deviance in society, and, in the example given, of a "society of saints?"

Social Structure and Anomie*

Robert K. Merton

THERE PERSISTS A NOTABLE TENDENCY IN sociological theory to attribute the malfunctioning of social structure primarily to those of man's imperious biological drives which are not adequately restrained by social control. In this view, the social order is solely a device for "impulse management" and the "social processing" of tensions. These impulses which break through social control, be it noted, are held to be biologically derived. Nonconformity is assumed to be rooted in original nature.[1] Conformity is by implication the result of a utilitarian calculus or unreasoned conditioning. This point of view, whatever its other deficiencies, clearly begs one question. It provides no basis for determining the nonbiological conditions which induce deviations from prescribed patterns of conduct. In this paper, it will be suggested that certain phases of social structure generate the circumstances in which infringement of social codes constitutes a "normal" response.[2]

The conceptual scheme to be outlined is designed to provide a coherent, systematic approach to the study of sociocultural sources of deviate behavior. Our primary aim lies in discovering how some social structures *exert a definite pressure* upon certain persons in the society to engage in nonconformist rather than conformist conduct. The many ramifications of the scheme cannot all be discussed; the problems mentioned outnumber those explicitly treated.

Among the elements of social and cultural structure, two are important for our purposes. These are analytically separable although they merge imperceptibly in concrete situations. The first consists of culturally defined goals, purposes, and interests. It comprises a frame of aspirational reference. These goals are more or less integrated and involve varying degrees of prestige and sentiment. They constitute a basic, but not the exclusive, component of what Linton aptly has called "designs for group living." Some of these cultural aspirations are related to the original drives of man, but they are not determined by them. The second phase of the social structure defines, regulates, and controls the acceptable modes of achieving these goals. Every social group invariably couples its scale of desired

*"Social Structure and Anomie," by Robert K. Merton. *American Sociological Review,* 3 (1938), pp. 672–682. By permission of the author and The American Sociological Association.

ends with moral or institutional regulation of permissible and required procedures for attaining these ends. These regulatory norms and moral imperatives do not necessarily coincide with technical or efficiency norms. Many procedures which from the standpoint of particular individuals would be most efficient in securing desired values, e.g., illicit oil-stock schemes, theft, fraud, are ruled out of the institutional area of permitted conduct. The choice of expedients is limited by the institutional norms.

To say that these two elements, culture goals and institutional norms, operate jointly is not to say that the ranges of alternative behaviors and aims bear some constant relation to one another. The emphasis upon certain goals may vary independently of the degree of emphasis upon institutional means. There may develop a disproportionate, at times, a virtually exclusive, stress upon the value of specific goals, involving relatively slight concern with the institutionally appropriate modes of attaining these goals. The limiting case in this direction is reached when the range of alternative procedures is limited only by technical rather than institutional considerations. Any and all devices which promise attainment of the all important goal would be permitted in this hypothetical polar case.[3] This constitutes one type of cultural malintegration. A second polar type is found in groups where activities originally conceived as instrumental are transmuted into ends in themselves. The original purposes are forgotten and ritualistic adherence to institutionally prescribed conduct becomes virtually obsessive.[4] Stability is largely ensured while change is flouted. The range of alternative behaviors is severely limited. There develops a tradition-bound, sacred society characterized by neophobia. The occupational psychosis of the bureaucrat may be cited as a case in point. Finally, there are the intermediate types of groups where a balance between culture goals and institutional means is maintained. These are the significantly integrated and relatively stable, though changing, groups.

An effective equilibrium between the two phases of the social structure is maintained as long as satisfactions accrue to individuals who conform to both constraints, viz., satisfactions from the achievement of the goals and satisfactions emerging directly from the institutionally canalized modes of striving to attain these ends. Success, in such equilibrated cases, is twofold. Success is reckoned in terms of the product and in terms of the process, in terms of the outcome and in terms of activities. Continuing satisfactions must derive from sheer *participation* in a competitive order as well as from eclipsing one's competitors if the order itself is to be sustained. The occasional sacrifices involved in institutionalized conduct must be compensated by socialized rewards. The distribution of statuses and roles through competition must be so organized that positive incentives for conformity to roles and adherence to status obligations are provided *for every position* within the distributive order. Aberrant conduct, therefore, may be viewed as a symptom of dissociation between culturally defined aspirations and socially structured means.

Of the types of groups which result from the independent variation of the two phases of the social structure, we shall be primarily concerned with the first, namely, that involving a disproportionate accent on goals. This statement must be recast in a proper perspective. In no group is there an absence of regulatory codes governing conduct, yet groups do vary in the degree to which these folkways, mores, and institutional controls are effectively integrated with the more diffuse goals which are part of the culture matrix. Emotional convictions may cluster about the complex of socially acclaimed ends, meanwhile shifting their support from the culturally defined implementation of these ends. As we shall see, certain aspects of the social structure may generate countermores and antisocial behavior precisely because of differential emphases on goals and regulations. In the extreme case, the latter may be so vitiated by the goal-emphasis that the range of behavior is limited only by considerations of technical expediency. The sole significant question then becomes, Which available means is most efficient in netting the socially approved value?[5] The technically most feasible procedure, whether legitimate or not, is preferred to the institutionally prescribed conduct. As this process continues, the integration of the society becomes tenuous and anomie ensues.

Thus, in competitive athletics, when the aim of victory is shorn of its institutional trappings, and success in contests becomes construed as "winning the game" rather than "winning through circumscribed modes of activity," a premium is implicitly set upon the use of illegitimate but technically efficient means. The star of the opposing football team is surreptitiously slugged; the wrestler furtively incapacitates his opponent through ingenious but illicit techniques; university alumni covertly subsidize "students" whose talents are largely confined to the athletic field. The emphasis on the goal has so attenuated the satisfactions deriving from sheer participation in the competitive activity that these satisfactions are virtually confined to a successful outcome. Through the same process, tension generated by the desire to win in a poker game is relieved by successfully dealing oneself four aces, or, when the cult of success has become completely dominant, by sagaciously shuffling the cards in a game of solitaire. The faint twinge of uneasiness in the last instance and the surreptitious nature of public derelicts indicate clearly that the institutional rules of the game *are known* to those who evade them, but that the emotional supports of these rules are largely vitiated by cultural exaggeration of the success-goal.[6] They are microcosmic images of the social macrocosm.

Of course, this process is not restricted to the realm of sport. The process whereby exaltation of the end generates a *literal demoralization,* i.e., a deinstitutionalization, of the means is one which characterizes many[7] groups in which the two phases of the social structure are not highly integrated. The extreme emphasis upon the accumulation of wealth as a symbol of success[8] in our own society militates against the completely effective control of institutionally regulated modes of acquiring a fortune.[9] Fraud, corruption, vice, crime, in short, the entire catalogue of proscribed behavior becomes increasingly common when the emphasis on the *culturally induced* success-goal becomes divorced from a coordinated institutional emphasis. This observation is of crucial theoretical importance in examining the doctrine that antisocial behavior most frequently derives from biological drives breaking through the restraints imposed by society. The difference is one between a strictly utilitarian interpretation which conceives man's ends as random and an analysis which finds these ends deriving from the basic values of the culture.[10]

Our analysis can scarcely stop at this juncture. We must turn to other aspects of the social structure if we are to deal with the social genesis of the varying rates and types of deviate behavior characteristic of different societies. Thus far, we have sketched three ideal types of social orders constituted by distinctive patterns of relations between culture ends and means. Turning from these types of *culture patterning,* we find five logically possible, alternative modes of adjustment or adaptation *by individuals* within the culture-bearing society or group.[11] These are schematically presented in the following table, where (+) signifies "acceptance," (−) signifies "elimination," and (±) signifies "rejection and substitution of new goals and standards."

Our discussion of the relation between these alternative responses and other phases of the social structure must

	Culture Institutionalized	
	Goals	*Means*
I. Conformity	+	+
II. Innovation	+	−
III. Ritualism	−	+
IV. Retreatism	−	−
V. Rebellion[12]	±	±

be prefaced by the observation that persons may shift from one alternative to another as they engage in different social activities. These categories refer to role adjustments in specific situations, not to personality in toto. To treat the development of this process in various spheres of conduct would introduce a complexity unmanageable within the confines of this paper. For this reason, we shall be concerned primarily with economic activity in the broad sense, "the production, exchange, distribution, and consumption of goods and services" in our competitive society, wherein wealth has taken on a highly symbolic cast. Our task is to search out some of the factors which exert pressure upon individuals to engage in certain of these logically possible alternative responses. This choice, as we shall see, is far from random.

In every society, Adaptation I (conformity to both culture goals and means) is the most common and widely diffused. Were this not so, the stability and continuity of the society could not be maintained. The mesh of expectancies which constitutes every social order is sustained by the modal behavior of its members falling within the first category. Conventional role behavior oriented toward the basic values of the group is the rule rather than the exception. It is this fact alone which permits us to speak of a human aggregate as comprising a group or society.

Conversely, Adaptation IV (rejection of goals and means) is the least common. Persons who "adjust" (or maladjust) in this fashion are, strictly speaking, *in* the society but not *of* it. Sociologically, these constitute the true "aliens." Not sharing the common frame of orientation, they can be included within the societal population merely in a fictional sense. In this category are *some* of the activities of psychotics, psychoneurotics, chronic autists, pariahs, outcasts, vagrants, vagabonds, tramps, chronic drunkards, and drug addicts.[13] These have relinquished, in certain spheres of activity, the culturally defined goals, involving complete aim-inhibition in the polar case, and their adjustments are not in accord with institutional norms. This is not to say that in some cases the source of their behavioral adjustments is not in part the very social structure which they have in effect repudiated nor that their very existence within a social area does not constitute a problem for the socialized population.

This mode of "adjustment" occurs, as far as structural sources are concerned, when both the culture goals and institutionalized procedures have been assimilated thoroughly by the individual and imbued with affect and high positive value, but where those institutional procedures which promise a measure of successful attainment of the goals are not available to the individual. In such instances, there results a twofold mental conflict insofar as the moral obligation for adopting institutional means conflicts with the pressure to resort to illegitimate means (which may attain the goal) and inasmuch as the individual is shut off from means which are both legitimate *and* effective. The competitive order is maintained, but the frustrated and handicapped individual who cannot cope with this order drops out. Defeatism, quietism, and resignation are manifested in escape mechanisms which ultimately lead the individual to "escape" from the requirements of the society. It is an expedient which arises from continued failure to attain the goal by legitimate measures and from an inability to adopt the illegitimate route because of internalized prohibitions and institutionalized compulsives, *during which process the supreme value of the success-goal has as yet not been renounced.* The conflict is resolved by eliminating *both* precipitating elements, the goals and means. The escape is complete, the conflict is eliminated, and the individual is asocialized.

Be it noted that where frustration derives from the inaccessibility of effective institutional means for attaining economic or any other type of highly valued "success," that Adaptations II, III and V (innovation, ritualism, and rebellion) are also possible. The result will be determined by the particular personality, and thus, the *particular* cultural background, involved. Inadequate socialization will result in the innovation response, whereby the conflict and frustration are eliminated by relinquishing the institutional means and retaining the success-aspiration; an extreme assimilation of institutional demands will lead to ritualism, wherein the goal is dropped as beyond one's reach but conformity to the mores persists; and rebellion occurs when emancipation from the reigning standards, due to

frustration or to marginalist perspectives, leads to the attempt to introduce a "new social order."

Our major concern is with the illegitimacy adjustment. This involves the use of conventionally proscribed but frequently effective means of attaining at least the simulacrum of culturally defined success—wealth, power, and the like. As we have seen, this adjustment occurs when the individual has assimilated the cultural emphasis on success without equally internalizing the morally prescribed norms governing means for its attainment. The question arises, Which phases of our social structure predispose toward this mode of adjustment? We may examine a concrete instance, effectively analyzed by Lohman,[14] which provides a clue to the answer. Lohman has shown that specialized areas of vice in the near north side of Chicago constitute a "normal" response to a situation where the cultural emphasis upon pecuniary success has been absorbed, but where there is little access to conventional and legitimate means for attaining such success. The conventional occupational opportunities of persons in this area are almost completely limited to manual labor. Given our cultural stigmatization of manual labor, and its correlate, the prestige of white-collar work, it is clear that the result is a strain toward innovational practices. The limitation of opportunity to unskilled labor and the resultant low income cannot compete *in terms of conventional standards of achievement* with the high income from organized vice.

For our purposes, this situation involves two important features. First, such antisocial behavior is in a sense "called forth" by certain conventional values of the culture *and* by the class structure involving differential access to the approved opportunities for legitimate, prestige-bearing pursuit of the culture goals. The lack of high integration between the means-and-end elements of the cultural pattern and the particular class structure combine to favor a heightened frequency of antisocial conduct in such groups. The second consideration is of equal significance. Recourse to the first of the alternative responses, legitimate effort, is limited by the fact that actual advance toward desired success-symbols through conventional channels is, despite our persisting open-class ideology,[15] relatively rare and difficult for those handicapped by little formal education and few economic resources. The dominant pressure of group standards of success is, therefore, on the gradual attenuation of legitimate, but by and large ineffective, strivings and the increasing use of illegitimate, but more or less effective, expedients of vice and crime. The cultural demands made on persons in this situation are incompatible. On the one hand, they are asked to orient their conduct toward the prospect of accumulating wealth, and on the other, they are largely denied effective opportunities to do so institutionally. The consequences of such structural inconsistency are psychopathological personality, and/or antisocial conduct, and/or revolutionary activities. The equilibrium between culturally designated means and ends becomes highly unstable with the progressive emphasis on attaining the prestige-laden ends by any means whatsoever. Within this context, Capone represents the triumph of amoral intelligence over morally prescribed "failure," when the channels of vertical mobility are closed or narrowed[16] *in a society which places a high premium on economic affluence and social ascent for all its members.*[17]

This last qualification is of primary importance. It suggests that other phases of the social structure besides the extreme emphasis on pecuniary success must be considered if we are to understand the social sources of antisocial behavior. A high frequency of deviate behavior is not generated simply by "lack of opportunity" or by this exaggerated pecuniary emphasis. A comparatively rigidified class structure, a feudalistic or caste order, may limit such opportunities far beyond the point which obtains in our society today. It is only when a system of cultural values extols, virtually above all else, certain *common* symbols of success *for the population at large* while its social structure rigorously restricts or completely eliminates access to approved modes of acquiring these symbols *for a considerable part of the same population* that antisocial behavior ensues on a considerable scale. In other words, our egalitarian ideology denies by implication the existence of noncompeting groups and individuals in the pursuit of pecuniary success. The same body of success-symbols is held to be desirable for all. These goals are held to *transcend class lines,* not to be bounded by them, yet the actual social organization is such that there exist class differentials in the accessibility of these *common* success-symbols. Frustration and thwarted aspiration lead to the search for avenues of escape from a culturally induced intolerable situation; or unrelieved ambition may eventuate in illicit attempts to acquire the dominant values.[18] The American stress on pecuniary success and ambitiousness for all thus invites exaggerated anxieties, hostilities, neuroses, and antisocial behavior.

This theoretical analysis may go far toward explaining the varying correlations between crime and poverty.[19]

Poverty is not an isolated variable. It is one in a complex of interdependent social and cultural variables. When viewed in such a context, it represents quite different states of affairs. Poverty as such, and consequent limitation of opportunity, are not sufficient to induce a conspicuously high rate of criminal behavior. Even the often mentioned "poverty in the midst of plenty" will not necessarily lead to this result. Only insofar as poverty and associated disadvantages in competition for the culture values approved for *all* members of the society are linked with the assimilation of a cultural emphasis on monetary accumulation as a symbol of success is antisocial conduct a "normal" outcome. Thus, poverty is less highly correlated with crime in southeastern Europe than in the United States. The possibilities of vertical mobility in these European areas would seem to be fewer than in this country, so that neither poverty per se nor its association with limited opportunity is sufficient to account for the varying correlations. It is only when the full configuration is considered, poverty, limited opportunity, and a commonly shared system of success symbols, that we can explain the higher association between poverty and crime in our society than in others where rigidified class structure is coupled with *differential class symbols of achievement.*

In societies such as our own, then, the pressure of prestige-bearing success tends to eliminate the effective social constraint over means employed to this end. The "end-justifies-the-means" doctrine becomes a guiding tenet for action when the cultural structure unduly exalts the end and the social organization unduly limits possible recourse to approved means. Otherwise put, this notion and associated behavior reflect a lack of cultural coordination. In international relations, the effects of this lack of integration are notoriously apparent. An emphasis upon national power is not readily coordinated with an inept organization of legitimate, i.e., internationally defined and accepted, means for attaining this goal. The result is a tendency toward the abrogation of international law, treaties become scraps of paper, "undeclared warfare" serves as a technical evasion, the bombing of civilian populations is rationalized,[20] just as the same societal situation induces the same sway of illegitimacy among individuals.

The social order we have described necessarily produces this "strain toward dissolution." The pressure of such an order is upon outdoing one's competitors. The choice of means within the ambit of institutional control will persist as long as the sentiments supporting a competitive system, i.e., deriving from the possibility of outranking competitors and hence enjoying the favorable response of others, are distributed throughout the entire system of activities and are not confined merely to the final result. A stable social structure demands a balanced distribution of affect among its various segments. When there occurs a shift of emphasis from the satisfactions deriving from competition itself to almost exclusive concern with successful competition, the resultant stress leads to the breakdown of the regulatory structure.[21] With the resulting attenuation of the institutional imperatives, there occurs an approximation of the situation erroneously held by utilitarians to be typical of society generally, wherein calculations of advantage and fear of punishment are the sole regulating agencies. In such situations, as Hobbes observed, force and fraud come to constitute the sole virtues in view of their relative efficiency in attaining goals—which were for him, of course, not culturally derived.

It should be apparent that the foregoing discussion is not pitched on a moralistic plane. Whatever the sentiments of the writer or reader concerning the ethical desirability of coordinating the means-and-goals phases of the social structure, one must agree that lack of such coordination leads to anomie. Insofar as one of the most general functions of social organization is to provide a basis for calculability and regularity of behavior, it is increasingly limited in effectiveness as these elements of the structure become dissociated. At the extreme, predictability virtually disappears, and what may be properly termed cultural chaos or anomie intervenes.

This statement, being brief, is also incomplete. It has not included an exhaustive treatment of the various structural elements which predispose toward one rather than another of the alternative responses open to individuals; it has neglected, but not denied the relevance of, the factors determining the specific incidence of these responses; it has not enumerated the various concrete responses which are constituted by combinations of specific values of the analytical variables; it has omitted, or included only by implication, any consideration of the social functions performed by illicit responses; it has not tested the full explanatory power of the analytical scheme by examining a large number of group variations in the frequency of deviate and conformist behavior; it has not adequately dealt with rebellious conduct which seeks to refashion the social framework radically; it has not examined the relevance of cultural conflict for an analysis of culture-goal and institutional-means malintegration. It is suggested that these and related problems may be profitably analyzed by this scheme.

NOTES

1. E.g., Ernest Jones, *Social Aspects of Psychoanalysis*, 28, London, 1924. If the Freudian notion is a variety of the "original sin" dogma, then the interpretation advanced in this paper may be called the doctrine of "socially derived sin."

2. "Normal" in the sense of a culturally oriented, if not approved, response. This statement does not deny the relevance of biological and personality differences which may be significantly involved in the *incidence* of deviate conduct. Our focus of interest is the social and cultural matrix; hence we abstract from other factors. It is in this sense, I take it, that James S. Plant speaks of the "normal reaction of normal people to abnormal conditions." See his *Personality and the Cultural Pattern*, 248, New York, 1937.

3. Contemporary American culture has been said to tend in this direction. See André Siegfried, *America Comes of Age*, 26–37, New York, 1927. The alleged extreme(?) emphasis on the goals of monetary success and material prosperity leads to dominant concern with technological and social instruments designed to produce the desired result, inasmuch as institutional controls become of secondary importance. In such a situation, innovation flourishes as the *range of means* employed is broadened. In a sense, then, there occurs the paradoxical emergence of "materialists" from an "idealistic" orientation. Cf. Durkheim's analysis of the cultural conditions which predispose toward crime and innovation, both of which are aimed toward efficiency, not moral norms. Durkheim was one of the first to see that "contrairement aux idées courantes le criminel n'apparait plus comme un etre radicalement insociable, comme une sort d'element parasitaire, de corps etranger et inassimilable, introduit au sein de la societe; c'est un agent regulier de la vie sociale" (Contrary to common thinking, the criminal no longer appears as a totally unsociable human being, as a sort of parasite, alien and unassimilable, introduced in the midst of society; he is a regular member of social life). See *Les Regles de la Methode Sociologique*, 86–89, Paris, 1927.

4. Such ritualism may be associated with a mythology which rationalizes these actions so that they appear to retain their status as means, but the dominant pressure is in the direction of strict ritualistic conformity, irrespective of such rationalizations. In this sense, ritual has proceeded farthest when such rationalizations are not even called forth.

5. In this connection, one may see the relevance of Elton Mayo's paraphrase of the title of Tawney's well-known book. "Actually the problem *is not that of the sickness of an acquisitive society; it is that of the acquisitiveness of a sick society.*" *Human Problems of an Industrial Civilization*, 153, New York, 1933. Mayo deals with the process through which wealth comes to be a symbol of social achievement. He sees this as arising from a state of anomie. We are considering the unintegrated

monetary-success goal as an element in producing anomie. A complete analysis would involve both phases of this system of interdependent variables.

6. It is unlikely that interiorized norms are completely eliminated. Whatever residuum persists will induce personality tensions and conflict. The process involves a certain degree of ambivalence. A manifest rejection of the institutional norms is coupled with some latent retention of their emotional correlates. "Guilt feelings," "sense of sin," and "pangs of conscience" are obvious manifestations of this unrelieved tension; symbolic adherence to the nominally repudiated values or rationalizations constitute a more subtle variety of tensional release.

7. "Many," and not all, unintegrated groups, for the reason already mentioned. In groups where the primary emphasis shifts to institutional means, i.e., when the range of alternatives is very limited, the outcome is a type of ritualism rather than anomie.

8. Money has several peculiarities which render it particularly apt to become a symbol of prestige divorced from institutional controls. As Simmel emphasized, money is highly abstract and impersonal. However acquired, through fraud or institutionally, it can be used to purchase the same goods and services. The anonymity of metropolitan culture, in conjunction with this peculiarity of money, permits wealth, the sources of which may be unknown to the community in which the plutocrat lives, to serve as a symbol of status.

9. The emphasis upon wealth as a success-symbol is possibly reflected in the use of the term "fortune" to refer to a stock of accumulated wealth. This meaning becomes common in the late sixteenth century (Spenser and Shakespeare). A similar usage of the Latin *fortuna* comes into prominence during the first century B.C. Both these periods were marked by the rise to prestige and power of the "bourgeoisie."

10. See Kingsley Davis, "Mental Hygiene and the Class Structure," *Psychiatry,* 1928, I, esp. 62–63; Talcott Parsons, *The Structure of Social Action,* 59–60, New York, 1937.

11. This is a level intermediate between the two planes distinguished by Edward Sapir; namely, culture patterns and personal habit systems. See his "Contribution of Psychiatry to an Understanding of Behavior in Society," *American Journal of Sociology,* 1937, 42:862–70.

12. This fifth alternative is on a plane clearly different from that of the others. It represents a *transitional* response which seeks to *institutionalize* new procedures oriented toward revamped cultural goals shared by the members of the society. It thus involves efforts to *change* the existing structure rather than to perform accommodative actions *within* this structure, and introduces additional problems with which we are not at the moment concerned.

13. Obviously, this is an elliptical statement. These individuals may maintain some orientation to the values of their particular differentiated groupings within the larger society or, in part, of the conventional society itself. Insofar as they do so, their conduct cannot be classified in the "passive rejection" category (IV). Nels Anderson's description of the behavior and attitudes of the bum, for example, can readily be recast in terms of our analytical scheme. See *The Hobo,* 93–98, et passim, Chicago, 1923.

14. Joseph D. Lohman, "The Participant Observer in Community Studies," *American Sociological Review,* 1937, 2:890–98.

15. The shifting historical role of this ideology is a profitable subject for exploration. The "office-boy-to-president" stereotype was once in approximate accord with the facts. Such vertical mobility was probably more common then than now, when the class structure is more rigid. (See the following note.) The ideology largely persists, however, possibly because it still performs a useful function for maintaining the status quo. For insofar as it is accepted by the "masses," it constitutes a useful sop for those who might rebel against the entire structure, were this consoling hope removed. This ideology now serves to lessen the probability of Adaptation V. In short, the role of this notion has changed from that of an approximately valid empirical theorem to that of an ideology, in Mannheim's sense.

16. There is a growing body of evidence, though none of it is clearly conclusive, to the effect that our class structure is becoming rigidified and that vertical mobility is declining. Taussig and Joslyn found that American business leaders are being *increasingly* recruited from the upper ranks of our society. The Lynds have also found a "diminished chance to get ahead" for the working classes in Middletown. Manifestly, these objective changes are not alone significant; the individual's subjective evaluation of the situation is a major determinant of the response. The extent to which this change in opportunity for social mobility has been recognized by the least advantaged classes is still conjectural, although the Lynds present some suggestive materials. The writer suggests that a case in point is the increasing frequency of cartoons which observe in a tragicomic vein that "my old man says everybody can't be President. He says if ya can get three days a week steady on W.P.A. work ya ain't doin' so bad either." See F. W. Taussig and C. S. Joslyn, *American Business Leaders,* New York, 1932; R. S. and H. M. Lynd, *Middletown in Transition,* 67ff., chap. 12, New York, 1937.

17. The role of the Negro in this respect is of considerable theoretical interest. Certain elements of the Negro population have assimilated the dominant caste's values of pecuniary success and social advancement, but they also recognize that social ascent is at present restricted to their own caste almost exclusively. The pressures upon the Negro which would otherwise derive from the structural inconsistencies we have noticed are hence not identical with those

upon lower class whites. See Kingsley Davis, op. cit., 63; John Dollard, *Caste and Class in a Southern Town,* 66 ff., New Haven, 1936; Donald Young, *American Minority Peoples,* 581, New York, 1932.

18. The psychical coordinates of these processes have been partly established by the experimental evidence concerning *Anspruchsniveaus* and levels of performance. See Kurt Lewin, *Vorsatz, Willie und Bedurfnis,* Berlin, 1926; N. F. Hoppe, "Erfolg und Misserfolg," *Psychologische Forschung,* 1930, 14:1–63; Jerome D. Frank, "Individual Differences in Certain Aspects of the Level of Aspiration," *American Journal of Psychology,* 1935, 47:119–28.

19. Standard criminology texts summarize the data in this field. Our scheme of analysis may serve to resolve some of the theoretical contradictions which P. A. Sorokin indicates. For example, "not everywhere nor always do the poor show a greater proportion of crime . . . many poorer countries have had less crime than the richer countries . . . The [economic] improvement in the second half of the nineteenth century, and the beginning of the twentieth, has not been followed by a decrease of crime." See his *Contemporary Sociological Theories,* 560–61, New York, 1928. The crucial point is, however, that poverty has varying social significance in different social structures, as we shall see. Hence, one would not expect a linear correlation between crime and poverty.

20. See M. W. Royse, *Aerial Bombardment and the International Regulation of War,* New York, 1928.

21. Since our primary concern is with the sociocultural aspects of this problem, the psychological correlates have been only implicitly considered. See Karen Horney, *The Neurotic Personality of Our Time,* New York, 1937, for a psychological discussion of this process.

Think Critically

1. Do you feel that Merton was successful in his approach to finding a theory to the "study of sociocultural sources of deviate behavior?" Explain.
2. Focusing on cultural goals and institutionalized means to attain those goals implies the need for social policies to eradicate crime. Which ones do you feel are most noteworthy?

Illegitimate Means and Delinquent Subcultures*

Richard A. Cloward and Lloyd E. Ohlin

The Availability of Illegitimate Means

Social norms are two-sided. A prescription implies the existence of a prohibition, and vice versa. To advocate honesty is to demarcate and condemn a set of actions which are dishonest. In other words, norms that define legitimate practices also implicitly define illegitimate practices. One purpose of norms, in fact, is to delineate the boundary between legitimate and illegitimate practices. In setting this boundary, in segregating and classifying various types of behavior, they make us aware not only of behavior that is regarded as right and proper but also of behavior that is said to be wrong and improper. Thus the criminal who engages in theft or fraud does not invent a new way of life; the possibility of employing alternative means is acknowledged, tacitly at least, by the norms of the culture.

This tendency for proscribed alternatives to be implicit in every prescription, and vice versa, although widely recognized, is nevertheless a reef upon which many a theory of delinquency has foundered. Much of the criminological literature assumes, for example, that one may explain a criminal act simply by accounting for the individual's readiness to employ illegal alternatives of which his culture, through its norms, has already made him generally aware. Such explanations are quite unsatisfactory, however, for they ignore a host of questions regarding the *relative availability* of illegal alternatives to various potential criminals. The aspiration to be a physician is hardly enough to explain the fact of becoming a physician; there is much that transpires between the aspiration and the achievement. This is no less true of the person who wants to be a successful criminal. Having decided that he "can't make it legitimately," he cannot simply choose among an array of illegitimate means, all equally available to him. . . . It is assumed in the theory of anomie that access to conventional means is differentially distributed, that some individuals, because of their social class, enjoy certain advantages that are denied to those elsewhere in the class structure. For example, there are variations in the degree to which members of various classes are fully exposed to and thus acquire the values, knowledge, and skills that facilitate upward mobility. It should not be starting, therefore, to suggest that there are socially structured variations in the availability of illegitimate means as well. In connection with delinquent subcultures, we shall be concerned principally with differentials in access to illegitimate means within the lower class.

Many sociologists have alluded to differentials in access to illegitimate means without explicitly incorporating this variable into a theory of deviant behavior. This is particularly true of scholars in the "Chicago tradition" of criminology. Two closely related theoretical perspectives emerged from this school. The theory of "cultural transmission," advanced by Clifford R. Shaw and Henry D. McKay, focuses on the development in some urban neighborhoods of a criminal tradition that persists from one generation to another despite constant changes in population.[1] In the theory of "differential association," Edwin H. Sutherland described the processes by which criminal values are taken over by the individual.[2] He asserted that criminal behavior is learned, and that it is learned in interaction with others who have already incorporated criminal values. Thus the first theory stresses the value systems of different areas; the second, the systems of social relationships that facilitate or impede the acquisition of these values.

Scholars in the Chicago tradition, who emphasized the processes involved in learning to be criminal, were actually pointing to differentials in the availability of illegal means— although they did not explicitly recognize this variable in their analysis. This can perhaps best be seen by examining Sutherland's classic work, *The Professional Thief.* "An inclination to steal," according to Sutherland, "is not a sufficient explanation of the genesis of the professional thief."[3] The "self-made" thief, lacking knowledge of the ways of securing immunity from prosecution and similar techniques of defense, "would quickly land in prison; . . . a person can be a professional thief only if he is recognized and received as such by other professional thieves." But recognition is not freely accorded: "Selection and tutelage are the two necessary elements in the process of acquiring recognition as a professional thief . . . A person cannot acquire recognition as a professional thief until he has had tutelage in professional theft, *and tutelage is given only to a few persons selected from the total population.*" For one thing, "the person must be appreciated by the professional thieves. He must be appraised as having an adequate equipment of wits, front, talking ability, honesty, reliability, nerve, and determination." Furthermore, the aspirant is judged by high standards of performance, for only "a very small percentage of those who start on this process ever reach the stage of professional thief . . . . " Thus motivation and pressures toward deviance do not fully account for deviant behavior any more than motivation and pressures toward conformity account for conforming behavior. The individual must have access to a learning environment and, once having been trained, must be allowed to perform his role. Roles, whether conforming or deviant in content, are not necessarily freely available; access to them depends on a variety of factors, such as one's socioeconomic position, age, sex, ethnic affiliation, personality characteristics, and the like. The potential thief, like the potential physician, finds that access to his goal is governed by many criteria other than merit and motivation.

What we are asserting is that access to illegitimate roles is not freely available to all, as is commonly assumed. Only those neighborhoods in which crime flourishes as a stable, indigenous institution are fertile criminal learning environments for the young. Because these environments afford integration of different age-levels of offender, selected young people are exposed to "differential association" through which tutelage is provided and criminal values and skills are acquired. To be prepared for the role may not, however, ensure that the individual will ever discharge it. One important limitation is that more youngsters are recruited into these patterns of differential associations than the adult criminal structure can possibly absorb. Since there is a surplus of contenders for these elite positions, criteria and mechanisms of selection must be evolved. Hence a certain proportion of those who aspire may not be permitted to engage in the behavior for which they have prepared themselves.

Thus we conclude that access to illegitimate roles, no less than access to legitimate roles, is limited by both social and psychological factors. We shall here be concerned primarily with socially structured differentials in illegitimate opportunities. Such differentials, we contend, have much to do with the type of delinquent subculture that develops.

Learning and Performance Structures

Our use of the term "opportunities," legitimate or illegitimate, implies access to both learning and performance structures. That is, the individual must have access to appropriate environments for the acquisition of the values and skills associated with the performance of a particular role, and he must be supported in the performance of the role once he has learned it.

Tannenbaum, several decades ago, vividly expressed the point that criminal role performance, no less than conventional role performance, presupposes a patterned set of relationships through which the requisite values and skills are transmitted by established practitioners to aspiring youth:

> It takes a long time to make a good criminal, many years of specialized training and much preparation. But training is something that is given to people. People learn in a community where the materials and the knowledge are to be had. A craft needs an atmosphere saturated with purpose and promise. The community provides the attitudes, the point of view, the philosophy of life, the example, the motive, the contacts, the friendships, the incentives. No child brings those into the world. He finds them here and available for use and elaboration. The community gives the criminal his materials and habits, just as it gives the doctor, the lawyer, the teacher, and the candlestick-maker theirs.[4]

Sutherland systematized this general point of view, asserting that opportunity consists, at least in part, of learning structures. Thus "criminal behavior is learned" and,

furthermore, it is learned "in interaction with other persons in a process of communication." However, he conceded that the differential-association theory does not constitute a full explanation of criminal behavior. In a paper circulated in 1944, he noted that "criminal behavior is partially a function of opportunities to commit specific classes of crime, such as embezzlement, bank burglary, or illicit heterosexual intercourse." Therefore, "while opportunity may be partially a function of association with criminal patterns and of the specialized techniques thus acquired, it is not determined entirely in that manner, and consequently differential association is not the sufficient cause of criminal behavior."[5]

To Sutherland, then, illegitimate opportunity included conditions favorable to the performance of a criminal role, as well as conditions favorable to the learning of such a role (differential associations). These conditions, we suggest, depend upon certain features of the social structure of the community in which delinquency arises.

Differential Opportunity: A Hypothesis

We believe that each individual occupies a position in both legitimate and illegitimate opportunity structures. This is a new way of defining the situation. The theory of anomie views the individual primarily in terms of the legitimate opportunity structure. It poses questions regarding differentials in access to legitimate routes to success-goals; at the same time it assumes either that illegitimate avenues to success-goals are freely available or that differentials in their availability are of little significance. This tendency may be seen in the following statement by Merton:

> Several researches have shown that specialized areas of vice and crime constitute a "normal" response to a situation where the cultural emphasis upon pecuniary success has been absorbed, but where there is little access to conventional and legitimate means for becoming successful. The occupational opportunities of people in these areas are largely confined to manual labor and the lesser white-collar jobs. Given the American stigmatization of manual labor *which has been found to hold rather uniformly for all social classes,* and the absence of realistic opportunities for advancement beyond this level, the result is a marked tendency toward deviant behavior. The status of unskilled labor and the consequent low income cannot readily compete *in terms of established standards of worth* with the promises of power and high

income from organized vice, rackets, and crime. . . . [Such a situation] leads toward the gradual attenuation of legitimate, but by and large ineffectual, strivings and the increasing use of illegitimate, but more or less effective, expedients.[6]

The cultural-transmission and differential-association tradition, on the other hand, assumes that access to illegitimate means is variable, but it does not recognize the significance of comparable differentials in access to legitimate means. Sutherland's "ninth proposition" in the theory of differential association states:

> *Though criminal behavior is an expression of general needs and values, it is not explained by those general needs and values since non-criminal behavior is an expression of the same needs and values.* Thieves generally steal in order to secure money, but likewise honest laborers work in order to secure money. The attempts by many scholars to explain criminal behavior by general drives and values, such as the happiness principle, striving for social status, the money motive, or frustration, have been and must continue to be futile since they explain lawful behavior as completely as they explain criminal behavior.[7]

In this statement, Sutherland appears to assume that people have equal and free access to legitimate means regardless of their social position. At the very least, he does not treat access to legitimate means as variable. It is, of course, perfectly true that "striving for social status," "the money motive," and other socially approved drives do not fully account for either deviant or conforming behavior. But if goal-oriented behavior occurs under conditions in which there are socially structured obstacles to the satisfaction of these drives by legitimate means, the resulting pressures, we contend, might lead to deviance.

The concept of differential opportunity structures permits us to unite the theory of anomie, which recognizes the concept of differentials in access to legitimate means, and the "Chicago tradition," in which the concept of differentials in access to illegitimate means is implicit. We can now look at the individual, not simply in relation to one or the other system of means, but in relation to both legitimate and illegitimate systems. This approach permits us to ask, for example, how the relative availability of illegitimate opportunities affects the resolution of adjustment problems leading to deviant behavior. We believe that the way in which these problems are resolved may depend upon the kind of support for one or another type of illegitimate

activity that is given at different points in the social structure. If, in a given social location, illegal or criminal means are not readily available, then we should not expect a criminal subculture to develop among adolescents. By the same logic, we should expect the manipulation of violence to become a primary avenue to higher status only in areas where the means of violence are not denied to the young. To give a third example, drug addiction and participation in subcultures organized around the consumption of drugs presuppose that persons can secure access to drugs and knowledge about how to use them. In some parts of the social structure, this would be very difficult; in others, very easy. In short, there are marked differences from one part of the social structure to another in the types of illegitimate adaptation that are available to persons in search of solutions to problems of adjustment arising from the restricted availability of legitimate means.[8] In this sense, then, we can think of individuals as being located in two opportunity structures—one legitimate, the other illegitimate. Given limited access to success-goals by legitimate means, the nature of the delinquent response that may result will vary according to the availability of various illegitimate means.[9]

NOTES

1. See esp. C. R. Shaw, *The Jack-Roller* (Chicago: University of Chicago Press, 1930); Shaw, *The Natural History of a Delinquent Career* (Chicago: University of Chicago Press, 1931); Shaw et al., *Delinquency Areas* (Chicago: University of Chicago Press, 1940); and Shaw and H. D. McKay, *Juvenile Delinquency and Urban Areas* (Chicago: University of Chicago Press, 1942).

2. E. H. Sutherland, ed., *The Professional Thief* (Chicago: University of Chicago Press, 1937); and Sutherland, *Principles of Criminology,* 4th Ed. (Philadelphia: Lippincott, 1947).

3. All quotations on this page are from *The Professional Thief,* pp. 211–13. Emphasis added.

4. Frank Tannenbaum, "The Professional Criminal," *The Century,* Vol. 110 (May–Oct. 1925): p. 577.

5. See A. K. Cohen, Alfred Lindesmith, and Karl Schussler, eds., *The Sutherland Papers* (Bloomington, Ind.: Indiana University Press, 1956), pp. 31–35.

6. R. K. Merton, *Social Theory and Social Structure,* Rev. and Enl. Ed. (Glencoe, Ill.: Free Press, 1957), pp. 145–46.

7. *Principles of Criminology, op. cit.,* pp. 7–8.

8. For an example of restrictions on access to illegitimate roles, note the impact of racial definitions in the following case: "I was greeted by two prisoners who were to be my cell buddies. Ernest was a first offender, charged with being a 'hold-up'

man. Bill, the other buddy, was an old offender, going through the machinery of becoming a habitual criminal, in and out of jail. . . . The first thing they asked me was, 'What are you in for?' I said, 'Jack-rolling.' The hardened one (Bill) looked at me with a superior air and said, 'A hoodlum, eh? An ordinary sneak thief. Not willing to leave jack-rolling to the niggers, eh? That's all they're good for. Kid, jack-rolling's not a white man's job.' I could see that he was disgusted with me, and I was too scared to say anything" (Shaw, *The Jack-Roller, op. cit.,* p. 101).

9. For a discussion of the way in which the availability of illegitimate means influences the adaptations of inmates to prison life, see R. A. Cloward, "Social Control in the Prison," *Theoretical Studies of the Social Organization of the Prison,* Bulletin No. 15 (New York: Social Science Research Council, March 1960), pp. 20–48.

Think Critically

1. In what ways does the theoretical approach expand upon Merton's perspective regarding social structure and anomie?
2. What do the authors mean by "differential opportunity," and how does this relate to the learning approaches they discuss? What types of crime do you feel are better explained by this perspective? Why?

A General Strain Theory of Community Differences in Crime Rates*

Robert Agnew**

SEVERAL MAJOR THEORIES ATTEMPT TO explain community differences in crime rates. Crime rates are an aggregation of individual criminal acts, so these theories essentially describe how community-level variables affect individual criminal behavior. In the words of Coleman (1990), the focus is on the "movement from macro to micro." It is no surprise, then, that these theories explicitly or implicitly draw on microtheories when they explain how community-level variables lead individuals to engage in crime (and thereby produce crime rates). Social disorganization theory draws on social control theory, with disorganization theorists pointing to those community characteristics that ultimately reduce the level

*From Robert Agnew, *Journal of Research in Crime and Delinquency* 36:2 (May 1999), pp. 123–155, copyright © 1999. Reprinted by Permission of Sage Publications, Inc.

**I would like to thank Timothy Brezina, Robert Bursik, Jr., Mitch Chamlin, Frank Cullen, Alex Piquero, and several anonymous reviewers for their comments on earlier drafts of this article.

of social control to which individuals are subject. Subcultural deviance theory draws on differential association/social-learning theory, with subcultural theorists arguing that community values and norms lead some individuals to define crime as a desirable or justifiable response in certain situations. Relative deprivation theory draws on Merton's (1938) version of strain theory, with deprivation theorists arguing that high levels of income or socioeconomic inequality lead some individuals to experience strain or frustration. This article draws on Agnew's (1992) general strain theory (GST) to offer another explanation for community differences in crime rates. This explanation encompasses relative deprivation theory but goes beyond this theory by describing additional ways in which community characteristics may generate strain and foster criminal responses to such strain.

Community is broadly defined to include areas of settlement from the block level to standard metropolitan statistical areas (SMSAs). With certain noted exceptions, the theory is best tested with data from smaller areas, such as "face-blocks" and "nominal communities" (see Bursik and Grasmick 1993). These areas are more homogeneous in terms of most of the independent and intervening variables described in this article. At the same time, there are gross differences in the independent and intervening variables *between* larger aggregates. As such, the theory can also partly explain differences in crime rates across units like cities, SMSAs, and beyond (see Linsky, Bachman, and Straus 1995) . . .

Previous Research and Theory on Community Differences in Crime Rates

There has been much recent research on the determinants of community differences in crime rates. The results of this research are often contradictory, but there are some conclusions that we can draw with confidence.[1] High crime communities tend to be low in economic status, with economic status being measured in terms of such variables as income, poverty, unemployment, welfare, occupation, education, inequality, owner-occupied dwellings, and substandard housing. Economic deprivation, in fact, is perhaps the most distinguishing characteristic of high-crime communities (see, especially, Land, McCall, and Cohen 1990; Sampson, Raudenbush, and Earls 1997). High-crime communities also tend to be large in size and high in population density, over-crowding, residential mobility (particularly poor communities), and percentage non-White. Although these variables usually have significant zero-order correlations with community crime rates, their effect on crime is sometimes reduced to insignificance in multivariate analyses. A key variable that partly mediates the relationship between at least certain of these variables and community crime rates is family disruption, usually measured by divorce/separation rates and/or female-headed households (see Sampson 1995).

Criminologists have offered several explanations for the fact that high-crime communities tend to be poor, urban, dense and overcrowded, transient, and populated by non-Whites and disrupted families. The dominant explanation derives from Shaw and McKay's (1942) social disorganization theory, particularly the reinterpretations and extensions of that theory proposed in recent years (Bursik 1988; Bursik and Grasmik 1993, 1995; Elliott et al. 1996; Kornhauser 1978; Sampson 1995; Sampson

and Groves 1989; Sampson and Wilson 1995). The above factors are said to weaken the ability of local residents to control crime in their communities, which directly causes crime and indirectly causes crime by allowing for the development of delinquent peer groups. Several studies suggest that these factors do, in fact, weaken control at the community level (e.g., Bellair 1997; Elliott et al. 1996; Sampson 1991, 1993; Sampson and Groves 1989; Sampson et al. 1997).

Relative deprivation and subcultural deviance theory have somewhat less support. Relative deprivation theory focuses on the economic plight of high-crime communities, and the theory is usually tested by examining the impact of income or socioeconomic inequality on community crime rates. Inequality has a large direct effect on crime in some studies and an insignificant effect in other studies. Certain methodological and other refinements in recent studies have resulted in more support for the theory (Balkwell 1990; Fowles and Merva 1996; Kovandzic, Vieraitis, and Yeisley 1998; Messner and Golden 1992; Rosenfeld 1986). This article provides further direction for research on relative deprivation and crime rates and extends strain theory so that it can also explain the association between non-economic variables and community crime rates.

Subcultural deviance theory argues that many of the community characteristics listed above contributed to or are associated with the development of subcultures that hold values conducive to crime (Bernard 1990; Curtis 1975; Luckenbill and Doyle 1989; Sutherland, Cressey, and Luckinbill 1992; Wolfgang and Ferracuti 1967). The data on subcultural deviance theory are mixed, although recent studies also hold out some hope for this theory (Anderson 1994; Cao, Adams, and Jensen 1997; Felson et al. 1994; Heimer 1997; Markowitz and Felson 1998; Matsueda et al. 1992). This article builds on previous theory and research and argues that those values conducive to crime are rooted in the "strainful" experiences of community members.

In sum, social disorganization theories now dominate the current research on communities and crime (e.g., Elliott et al. 1996; Sampson et al. 1997; Wilson 1996). It is next argued, however, that community differences in crime rates are a function not only of differences in social control but also of differences in the motivation for crime.

An Overview of the GST of Community Differences in Crime Rates

GST argues that strain or stress is a major source of criminal motivation. The theory explains community differences in crime by community differences in strain and in those factors that condition the effect of strain on crime. In particular, high-crime communities are more likely to select and retain strained individuals, produce strain, and foster criminal responses to strain.

The idea that communities may cause crime through the strain they produce is not new. It is at the heart of relative deprivation theory, and it is a central idea in the theories advanced by Bernard (1990), Hagan (1994), Hagan and McCarthy (1997a), Harvey (1986), Hawkins (1983), Linsky et al. (1995), and numerous conflict theorists. It is also one of the central arguments of Thrasher (1927) and Shaw and McKay (1942; also see Gold 1987), the theorists most closely associated with the development of social disorganization theory. These theorists indicate that slum communities contribute to several types of strain, most notably the failure to achieve economic goals. The strain elements of Shaw and McKay, however, were cut from their theory by Kornhauser (1978) and others in an effort to construct a pure social disorganization theory.

Although a number of researchers have attempted to explain community differences in crime in terms of strain, such attempts have not considered fully the different ways in which communities may promote strain and the ways in which they may condition the effect of strain on crime. This may explain why certain prominent researchers claim that strain theory has little role to play in the explanation of community differences in crime rates (e.g., Sampson and Wilson 1995:45). The GST explanation that follows draws heavily on the work of the above-mentioned theorists and on the communities and crime research to more fully specify the community-level sources of strain and the community-level factors that condition the impact of strain on crime.

A simplified model of the GST explanation is shown in Figure 1. The left side of the model shows those community characteristics that are associated with higher crime rates. These characteristics contribute to strain and the reaction to strain in several ways.

1. Selection and retention of strained individuals. Communities with these characteristics, especially deprived communities, are more likely to select for and retain strained individuals. Strained individuals, especially those experiencing economic strain, are more likely to move into deprived communities because they cannot afford to live elsewhere and because community residents are less able to resist their migration (Reiss 1993). Furthermore, strained individuals are less able to move out of these communities than nonstrained individuals. Nonstrained individuals, in fact, may deliberately migrate to other communities (e.g., Anderson 1990; Bursik, 1986a; Farrington 1993; Liska and Bellair 1995; Morenoff and Sampson 1997; Reiss 1986, 1993; Stark 1987; Wilson 1987, 1996). GST, however, argues that these communities are higher in crime not only because they are more likely to attract and hold strained individuals but also because they cause strain.

2. The failure to achieve positively valued goals. Communities with these characteristics are more likely to cause goal blockage—the first type of strain in GST. In particular, such communities lead individuals to place a strong emphasis on certain goals and make it more difficult for individuals to achieve these goals through legitimate channels. Three goals are emphasized: money, status/respect, and the desire to be treated in a just or nondiscriminatory manner.

3. Relative deprivation. These community characteristics not only increase one's absolute level of goal blockage but also increase one's feeling of relative deprivation. In particular, these and certain other community characteristics influence whether individuals compare themselves to advantaged others, decide that they want and deserve what these others have, and decide that they cannot get what these others have through legitimate channels. An effort is made to extend relative deprivation theory to shed light on the mixed results of past research.

4. The loss of positive stimuli/presentation of negative stimuli. These community characteristics increase the other two types of strain in GST: the loss of positive stimuli and the presentation of negative stimuli. In particular, these community characteristics (1) increase the sensitivity of residents to certain types of aversive stimuli and (2) increase the likelihood that residents will be exposed to aversive stimuli. Several types of aversive stimuli are considered, including economic deprivation, family disruption and its correlates like child abuse, signs of incivility, social cleavages, and "vicarious strain."

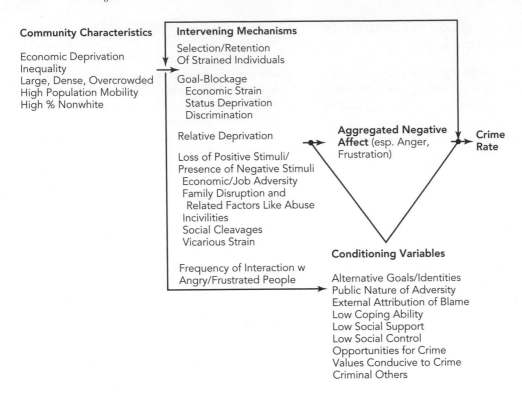

Community Characteristics

Economic Deprivation
Inequality
Large, Dense, Overcrowded
High Population Mobility
High % Nonwhite

Intervening Mechanisms

Selection/Retention
Of Strained Individuals

Goal-Blockage
    Economic Strain
    Status Deprivation
    Discrimination

Relative Deprivation

Loss of Positive Stimuli/
Presence of Negative Stimuli
    Economic/Job Adversity
    Family Disruption and
        Related Factors Like Abuse
    Incivilities
    Social Cleavages
    Vicarious Strain

Frequency of Interaction w
Angry/Frustrated People

Aggregated Negative Affect (esp. Anger, Frustration)

Crime Rate

Conditioning Variables

Alternative Goals/Identities
Public Nature of Adversity
External Attribution of Blame
Low Coping Ability
Low Social Support
Low Social Control
Opportunities for Crime
Values Conducive to Crime
Criminal Others

5. Aggregate levels of negative affect. Goal blockage, relative deprivation, and exposure to aversive stimuli increase the likelihood that community residents will experience a range of negative emotions, including anger and frustration. Aggregated levels of anger/frustration should have a direct effect on crime rates and should *partly* mediate the effect of community characteristics on crime rates (community characteristics may also affect crime rates for reasons related to social control and social learning theories).

6. Increasing the frequency of interaction with angry/frustrated individuals. These community characteristics not only produce angry/frustrated individuals but also increase the likelihood that such individuals will interact with one another. This further increases the level of strain/anger in the community, because these individuals are more likely to mistreat and get into conflicts with one another.

7. Increasing the likelihood of a criminal response to strain. These community characteristics influence several factors that increase the likelihood that individuals will react to strain with anger/frustration

and crime. These factors, in particular, condition the effect of strain on anger/frustration and crime.

8. Community crime rates have a direct and an indirect effect on strain. The high rate of crime that results from the above processes functions as a major source of strain in itself. Criminal victimization, in fact, is one of the most serious types of strain to which individuals are subject, and data suggest that it is a major source of subsequent crime (Dawkins 1997). Furthermore, certain data suggest that high crime rates lead to a further deterioration in community characteristics. Crime prompts many individuals—especially those with economic resources—to flee the community. And crime undermines relationships among those who remain in the community (see Bursik 1986a; Liska and Bellair 1995; Morenoff and Sampson 1997; Reiss 1986, 1993; Sampson and Lauritsen 1993). The result is an amplifying loop. Deprived communities generate strain and crime, whereas crime contributes to a further deterioration in the community and more strain.

The key portions of the GST explanation focus on the effect of community characteristics on individual strain (arguments 2 to 4 and 6). It should be noted that community characteristics might have both a direct and an indirect effect on individual strain. Direct effects are *not* mediated by individual traits or characteristics of the individual's immediate social environment (e.g., family, school, work, peer group). To illustrate, imagine two individuals who are identical in all ways, except that one lives in a deprived community of the type described above and the other does not. The individual in the deprived community will experience more strain. This individual, for example, is more likely to be treated negatively or victimized by others. This argument implies that community characteristics will have a significant direct effect on individual crime after individual-level variables are controlled. Communities also have an indirect effect on strain by influencing individual traits and the individual's immediate social environment. For example, individuals in deprived communities are less likely to develop those skills necessary for successful school and work performance. As a consequence, they are less likely to achieve their economic goals and are more likely to end up in school and work situations that are experienced as aversive. This argument implies that controls for individual-level variables will reduce (but not eliminate) the direct effect of community characteristics on individual crime. The issue of direct versus indirect effects is discussed at certain points in the article.

The GST explanation contributes to the literature on communities and crime in three major ways. First, it integrates much previous theory and research dealing with strain and community crime rates. Second, it extends previous theory by pointing to several new community-level variables that may influence crime, especially intervening and conditioning variables. Third, it offers a new interpretation for the effect of community-level variables on crime. Much data indicate that variables like economic deprivation, mobility, family disruption, and signs of incivility have a large effect on community crime rates. The mechanisms by which these variables affect crime rates, however, are much less clear. GST argues that these variables not only reduce social control but also increase strain. It is important to examine the reasons why community-level variables affect crime rates because these reasons influence the policy recommendations we make. In particular, social disorganization theory suggests that we should help community residents exercise more control over their communities. Strain theorists do not necessarily disagree with

this approach, but they argue that we should also focus on reducing the motivation for crime (see Agnew 1995a, 1995c; Brezina 1995 for a fuller discussion) . . .

The Failure to Achieve Positively Valued Goals

Communities may affect crime rates by influencing the goals that residents pursue and the ability of residents to achieve such goals through legitimate channels. Most research has focused on the inability to achieve the goal of economic success. This source of strain also occupies a central place in GST. GST, however, argues that monetary strain is not the only type of goal blockage experienced by the residents of high-crime communities. GST also focuses on the inability of residents to achieve their status goals and to be treated in a just/fair manner.

Economic Success

Economic status is the factor that most distinguishes high-crime from low-crime communities. GST argues that one reason economically deprived communities are higher in crime is because the residents of such communities have more difficulty achieving their economic goals. This goal blockage creates frustration with one's monetary situation, which, in turn, leads to income-generating crime, aggression, and drug use (see Agnew 1992; Agnew et al. 1996; Wilson 1996) . . .

Status/Respect

Closely related to the desire for money is the desire for status: "achieving respect in the eyes of one's fellows" (Cohen, 1955:65). Individuals may desire status in general as well as particular types of status, with the desire for "masculine" status being especially relevant to crime (see Majors and Billson 1992; Messerschmidt 1993). In the United States, status—including masculine status—is largely a function of income, education, occupation, and race (see Majors and Billson 1992). As a consequence, individuals in deprived communities—especially non-Whites—face status problems more often (see Anderson 1994; Brezina 1995; Cohen 1955; Jankowski 1995; Majors and Billson 1992; Suttles 1968). They may adapt by attempting to achieve status through alternative channels—certain of which involve or are conducive to crime.

One common alternative, particularly among young, African-American males, is described by Anderson (1994) in "The Code of the Streets." People attempt to achieve status/respect through their presentation of self, particularly through the display of certain material possessions (e.g., clothing, jewelry) and the adoption of a tough demeanor—which includes the willingness to respond to even minor shows of disrespect with violence. Individuals who lack material possessions may take them from others, and individuals may actively "campaign for respect" by verbally and physically abusing others (also see Bernard 1990; Majors and Billson 1992) . . .

Class/Race/Ethnic Discrimination

According to GST, individuals not only want to achieve specific goals like monetary success and status/respect; they also have a more general desire to be treated in a just or fair manner. Class, race, and ethnic discrimination represent a fundamental violation of this desire, and for that reason they are discussed as a distinct source of strain. (Such discrimination, of course, also has a major effect on the achievement of the economic and status goals discussed above and on the removal of positive stimuli/presentation of negative stimuli discussed below [e.g., Anderson 1990; Bernard 1990; Hawkins 1983; Mann 1995; Russell 1994; Wilson 1987, 1996].) . . .

Relative Deprivation

As argued above, the residents of deprived communities are more likely to engage in crime because they are more likely to experience goal blockage. But as several strain theorists have argued, individuals do not determine whether they are experiencing goal blockage in isolation from one another. They compare themselves to others; such comparisons influence the goals they pursue and their perceptions about the amount of goal blockage they are experiencing (Cohen 1965, 1997; Passas 1997). In this connection, strain theorists have argued that perceptions of goal blockage should be highest in communities with high levels of income or socioeconomic inequality. In fact, virtually all of the community-level research on strain theory has focused on the relationship between inequality and crime rates. It is assumed that when inequality is high, people compare themselves to advantaged others, decide that they want and deserve what these others have,

and decide that they cannot get what these others have through legitimate channels . . .

Loss of Positive Stimuli/Presentation of Negative Stimuli

Agnew (1992) argues that strain not only results when others prevent you from achieving your goals but also when others present you with negatively valued stimuli (e.g., verbally and physically abuse you) or remove positively valued stimuli you possess (e.g., take your possessions). Communities may contribute to these types of strain by influencing the types of treatment that are defined as aversive and by influencing the exposure of residents to such treatment.

Types of Treatment Defined as Aversive

Some types of treatment—such as physical attack—are defined as negative or aversive across virtually all groups. Other types of treatment, however, are defined differently in different groups. Several theorists have argued that the residents of high-crime communities—especially young, African American males—are more likely to define certain types of treatment as aversive. This is, in fact, a central theme in the leading subcultural theories of violence (Bernard 1990; Luckenbill and Doyle 1989; Wolfgang and Ferracuti 1967; also see Harvey 1986). Luckenbill and Doyle (1989), for example, claim that the subculture of violence "enjoins individuals to be highly sensitive and boldly responsive to affronts"—especially to affronts in which "fundamental properties of the self are attacked." Ethnographic accounts confirm such views. Anderson (1994), for example, states that

> many of the forms that dissing [disrespectful treatment] can take might seem petty to middle-class people (maintaining eye contact for too long, for example), but to those invested in the street code, these actions become serious indications of the other person's intentions. Consequently, such people become very sensitive to advances and slights. (P. 82).

Residents of high-crime communities, then, are more likely to view a range of slights and provocations as aversive. This may partly explain the fact that lower-income individuals are more likely to experience psychological distress in response to a given stressor (e.g., Thoits 1982, 1991) . . .

Summary

The GST described in this article argues that communities differ in their level of crime partly because they differ in the extent to which they produce strain and foster criminal responses to strain.

Communities contribute to strain in several ways. First, they influence the goals that individuals pursue and the ability of individuals to achieve these goals. Economic goals, status goals, and the desire for just/fair treatment occupy a central place in GST. Second, they influence the individual's sense of relative deprivation as well as absolute level of goal blockage. Third, they influence definitions of aversive stimuli and the degree of exposure to such stimuli. A range of aversive stimuli was considered, including economic deprivation, family disruption, child abuse, signs of incivility, social cleavages, and vicarious strains. Fourth, they increase the likelihood that strained and angry/frustrated individuals will interact with one another, which further increases levels of strain and negative affect.

These types of strain, in turn, influence aggregated levels of negative affect in the community—with the emotions of anger/frustration receiving special attention. Aggregated levels of anger/frustration have a direct effect on community crime rates and partly mediate the effect of community characteristics on crime rates. Communities, however, may condition the impact of strain on crime in a number of ways. In particular, communities may make it more difficult for individuals to "define away their strain" through the use of cognitive coping strategies, engage in legitimate behavioral coping, and obtain support from others. Communities may also reduce the costs of criminal coping and increase the disposition to engage in such coping. Relevant community-level variables in these areas were described.

There was a brief overview of the evidence compatible with these arguments, and several strategies for testing these arguments were suggested. At the most general level, it was argued that empirical tests need to devote more attention to intervening processes. With respect to goal blockage, researchers should determine the extent to which the community characteristics in Figure 1 are associated with the experience of monetary strain, status deprivation, and discriminatory treatment by others. These factors influence aggregated levels of negative affect—especially anger and frustration. Negative affect, in turn, influences community crime rates. With respect to relative deprivation, one should examine the extent to which the community characteristics listed in Figure 1 and certain other community characteristics mentioned in the discussion influence perceptions of relative deprivation. Such perceptions, in turn, should influence levels of negative affect. With respect to the loss of positive stimuli/presentation of negative stimuli, one should examine the extent to which the community characteristics in Figure 1 influence exposure to aversive stimuli. Such exposure, in turn, should influence levels of negative affect. With respect to interactional patterns, one should examine the extent to which community characteristics influence the level of interaction with angry/frustrated individuals. Such interaction should influence negative affect.

Finally, one should examine the extent to which community characteristics influence those variables said to condition the effect of strain on anger/frustration and crime. Such variables, however, may not be a complete function of those community characteristics in Figure 1. Therefore, researchers also should obtain independent measures of these variables and examine the extent to which they condition the effect of strain on aggregated levels of negative affect and crime rates.

GST represents a major alternative to those theories that now dominate the research on communities and crime. In particular, GST provides another explanation for the effect of previously examined variables on community crime rates—variables like economic deprivation, mobility, family disruption, and signs of incivility. The effect of these variables is usually explained in terms of social disorganization and, to a lesser extent, subcultural deviance theory. As argued above, one can also explain the effect of these variables in terms of strain theory.

It is important to emphasize, however, that GST is proposed as a supplement rather than as a replacement for social disorganization and subcultural deviance theories. As exemplified in the work of Thrasher (1927) and Shaw and McKay (1942), a full explanation of community differences in crime rates must draw on a range of theories, including those that examine the ways in which communities *motivate* as well as *control* crime.

NOTE

1. For overviews and selected studies, see Bailey 1984; Balkwell 1990; Blau and Blau 1982; Byrne and Sampson 1986; Carroll and Jackson 1983; Crutchfield 1989; Crutchfield,

Geerken, and Gove, 1982; Elliott et al. 1996; Farrington 1993; Golden and Messner 1987; Gottfredson and Taylor 1986; Hagan and Peterson 1995; Harer and Steffensmeier 1992; Hsieh and Pugh 1993; Kornhauser 1978; Kovandzic, Vieraitis, and Yeisley 1998; Krivo and Peterson 1996; Land, McCall, and Cohen 1990; Loftin and Parker 1985; Messner 1982, 1983a, 1983b; Messner and Golden 1992; Messner and South 1986; Messner and Tardiff 1986; Patterson 1991; Rosenfeld 1986; Sampson 1985a, 1985b, 1985c, 1986, 1987, 1995; Sampson and Groves 1989; Sampson and Lauritsen 1993; Sampson, Raudenbush, and Earls 1997; Shihadeh and Steffensmeier 1994; Smith and Jarjoura 1988; Taylor and Covington 1988; Warner and Pierce 1993; Williams 1984; Williams and Flewelling 1988.

REFERENCES

Agnew, Robert. 1992. "Foundation for a General Strain Theory of Crime and Delinquency." *Criminology* 30:47–87.

———. 1995a. "Controlling Delinquency: Recommendations from General Strain Theory." Pp. 43–70 in *Crime and Public Policy,* edited by Hugh D. Barlow. Boulder, CO: Westview.

———. 1995b. "Strain and Subcultural Theories of Criminality." Pp. 305–27 in *Criminology: A Contemporary Handbook,* edited by Joseph F. Sheley. Belmont, CA: Wadsworth.

———. 1995c. "Testing the Leading Crime Theories: An Alternative Strategy Focusing on Motivational Processes." *Journal of Research in Crime and Delinquency* 32:363–98.

Agnew, Robert, Francis T. Cullen, Velmer S. Burton, Jr., T. David Evans and R. Gregory Dunaway. 1996. "A New Test of Classic Strain Theory." *Justice Quarterly* 13:681–704.

Anderson, Elijah. 1990. *Streetwise: Race, Class and Change in an Urban Community.* Chicago: University of Chicago Press.

———. 1994. "The Code of the Streets." *Atlantic Monthly* 273 (May): 81–94.

Balkwell, James W. 1990. "Ethnic Inequality and the Rate of Homicide." *Social Forces* 69:53–70.

Bernard, Thomas J. 1990. "Angry Aggression among the 'Truly Disadvantaged.' " *Criminology* 28:73–96.

Brezina, Timothy. 1995. "Crime, Delinquency, and the Pursuit of Retributive Justice." Paper presented at the annual meeting of the American Society of Criminology, November, Boston.

———. 1996. "Adapting to Strain: An Examination of Delinquent Coping Responses." *Criminology* 34:39–60.

———. 1998. "Maltreatment and Delinquency: The Question of Intervening Processes." *Journal of Research in Crime and Delinquency* 35:71 99.

Bursik, Robert J., Jr. 1986a. "Delinquency Rates as Sources of Ecological Change." Pp. 63–74 in *The Social Ecology of Crime,* edited by James M. Byrne and Robert J. Sampson. New York: Springer-Verlag.

Cao, Liqun, Anthony Adams, and Vickie J. Jensen. 1997. "A Test of the Black Subculture of Violence Thesis: A Research Note." *Criminology* 35:367–79.

Cohen, Albert K. 1965. "The Sociology of the Deviant Act: Anomie Theory and Beyond." *American Sociological Review* 30:5–14.

Curtis, Lynn A. 1975. *Criminal Violence: National Patterns and Behavior.* Lexington, MA: Heath.

Dawkins, Nicola. 1997. "Striking Back: An Empirical Test of the Impact of Victimization on Violent Crime." Paper presented at the annual meeting of the American Society of Criminology, November, San Diego, CA.

Elliott, Delbert S., William Julius Wilson, David Huizinga, Robert J. Sampson, Amanda Elliott, and Bruce Rankin. 1996. "The Effects of Neighborhood Disadvantage on Adolescent Development." *Journal of Research in Crime and Delinquency* 33:389–426.

Farrington, David P. 1993. "Have Any Individual, Family, or Neighborhood Influences on Offending Been Demonstrated Conclusively?" Pp. 7–37 in *Integrating Individual and Ecological Aspects of Crime,* edited by David P. Farrington, Robert J. Sampson, and Per-Olof Wikstrom. Stockholm: National Council for Crime Prevention, Sweden.

Felson, Richard B., Allen E. Liska, Scott J. South, and Thomas L. McNulty. 1994. "The Subculture of Violence and Delinquency: Individual vs. School Context Effects." *Social Forces* 73:155–73.

Fowles, Richard and Mary Merva. 1996. "Wage Inequality and Criminal Activity: An Extreme Bounds Analysis for the United States, 1975–1990." *Criminology* 34:163–82.

Gold, Martin. 1987. "Social Ecology." Pp. 62–105 in *Handbook of Juvenile Delinquency,* edited by Herbert Quay. New York: John Wiley.

Hagan, John. 1994. *Crime and Disrepute.* Thousand Oaks, CA: Pine Forge Press.

Hagan, John and Bill McCarthy. 1997a. *Mean Streets.* Cambridge: UK: Cambridge University Press.

———. 1997b. "Anomie, Social Capital and Street Crime." Pp. 124–41 in *The Future of Anomie Theory,* edited by Nikos Passas and Robert Agnew. Boston: Northeastern University Press.

Harvey, William B. 1986. "Homicide among Young Black Adults: Life in the Subculture of Exasperation." Pp. 153–71 in *Homicide among Black Americans,* edited by Darnell F. Hawkins. Lanham, MD: University Press of America.

Hawkins, Darnell F. 1983. "Black and White Homicide Differentials." *Criminal Justice and Behavior* 10:407–40.

Heimer, Karen. 1997. "Socioeconomic Status, Sub-cultural Definitions, and Violent Delinquency." *Social Forces* 75:799–833.

Kornhauser, Ruth Rosner. 1978. *Social Sources of Delinquency.* Chicago: University of Chicago Press.

Kovandzic, Tomislav V., Lynne M. Vieraitis, and Mark R. Yeisley. 1998. "The Structural Correlates of Urban Homicide: Reassessing the Impact of Income Inequality and Poverty in the Post-Reagan Era." *Criminology* 36:569–600.

Linsky, Arnold S., Ronet Bachman and Murray A. Straus. 1995. *Stress, Culture, and Aggression.* New Haven, CT: Yale University Press.

Liska, Allen E. and Paul E. Bellair. 1995. "Violent-Crime Rates and Racial Composition: Convergence over Time." *American Journal of Sociology* 101:578–610.

Loftin, Colin and Robert Nash Parker. 1985. "An Errors-in-Variable Model of the Effect of Poverty on Urban Homicide Rates." *Criminology* 23:269–87.

Luckenbill, David F. and Daniel P. Doyle. 1989. "Structural Position and Violence: Developing a Cultural Explanation." *Criminology* 27:419–53.

Markowitz, Fred E. and Richard B. Felson. 1998. "Socio-demographic Differences in Attitudes and Violence." *Criminology* 36:117–38.

Matsueda, Ross L., Rosemary Gartner, Irving Pilavin and Michael Polakowski. 1992. "The Prestige of Criminal and Conventional Occupations: A Subcultural Model of Criminal Activity." *American Sociological Review* 57:752–70.

Messner Steven F. and Reid M. Golden. 1992. "Racial Inequality and Racially Disaggregated Homicide Rates: An Assessment of Alternative Theoretical Explanations." *Criminology* 30: 421–47.

Morenoff, Jeffrey D. and Robert J. Sampson. 1997. "Violent Crime and the Spatial Dynamics of Neighborhood Transition: Chicago, 1970–1990." *Social Forces* 76:31–64.

Passas, Nikos. 1997. "Anomie, References Groups and Relative Deprivation." Pp. 62–94 in *The Future of Anomie Theory,* edited by Nikos Passas and Robert Agnew. Boston: Northeastern University Press.

Reiss, Albert J., Jr. 1986. "Why Are Communities Important in Understanding Crime?" Pp. 1–33 in *Crime and Justice,* Vol. 8, *Communities and Crime,* edited by Albert J. Reiss, Jr. and Michael Tonry. Chicago: University of Chicago Press.

———. 1993. "Key Issues in the Integration of Individual and Community Explanations of Crime and Criminality." Pp. 339–56 in *Integrating Individual and Ecological Aspects of Crime,* edited by David P. Farrington, Robert J. Sampson, and Per-Olof H. Wikstrom. Stockholm: National Council for Crime Prevention, Sweden.

Rosenfeld, Richard. 1986. "Urban Crime Rates: Effects of Inequality, Welfare Dependency, Region, and Race." Pp. 116–30 in *The Social Ecology of Crime,* edited by James M. Byrne and Robert J. Sampson. New York: Springer-Verlag.

Ross, Catherine E. and Joan Huber. 1985. "Hardship and Depression." *Journal of Health and Social Behavior* 26:312–27.

Sampson, Robert J. and Janet L. Lauritsen. 1993. "Violent Victimization and Offending: Individual-Situational-, and Community-Level Risk Factors." Pp. 1–114 in *National Research Council, Understanding and Preventing Violence,* Vol. 3, *Social Influences.* Washington, DC: National Research Council.

Sampson, Robert J., Stephen W. Raudenbush, and Felton Earls. 1997. "Neighborhoods and Violent Crime: A Multilevel Study of Collective Efficacy." *Science* 277:918–24.

Sampson, Robert J. and William Julius Wilson. 1995. "Toward a Theory of Race, Crime and Urban Inequality." Pp. 37–54 in *Crime and Inequality,* edited by John Hagan and Ruth Peterson, Stanford, CA: Stanford University Press.

Shaw, Clifford R. and Henry D. Mckay. 1942. *Juvenile Delinquency and Urban Areas.* Chicago: University of Chicago Press.

Stark, Rodney. 1987. "Deviant Places: A Theory of the Ecology of Crime." *Criminology* 25:893–909.

Sutherland, Edwin H., Donald R. Cressey, and David L. Luckenbill. 1992. *Principles of Criminology.* Dix Hills, NY: General Hall.

Thoits, Peggy A. 1982. "Life Stress, Social Support, and Psychological Vulnerability: Epidemiological Considerations." *Journal of Community Psychology* 10:341–62.

———. 1991. "On Merging Identity Theory and Stress Research." *Social Psychology Quarterly* 54:101–12.

Wilson, William J. 1987. *The Truly Disadvantaged.* Chicago: University of Chicago Press.

———. 1996. *When Work Disappears.* Chicago: University of Chicago Press.

Wolfgang, Marvin E. and Franco Ferracuti. 1967. *The Subculture of Violence.* London: Tavistock.

Think Critically

1. How does Agnew's general strain theory (GST) help account for or explain community differences in crime rates?

2. Do you think that GST advances our understanding of community crime rates beyond that offered by social disorganization theories? In what ways does it or does it not?

Latinos and Lethal Violence: The Impact of Poverty and Inequality*

Ramiro Martinez, Jr.

THE LINK BETWEEN ECONOMIC CONDITIONS and homicide has long been a source of controversy among sociologists (see Bonger 1916; Parker 1995). One traditional view holds that increased poverty generates high rates of homicide because deprivation may encourage hostilities that escalate into violence (Bailey 1984; Parker 1989). Others disagree, contending that greater economic inequality is the mechanism whereby conflict and hostilities are reflected in criminal violence (Blau and Blau 1982; Harer and Steffensmeier 1992).

The case of Latinos[1] in the United States provides an opportunity to re-examine the debate. According to researchers on the Latino population, economic conditions rapidly worsened between 1970 and 1980 (Santiago and Wilder 1991). During this period, levels of Latino poverty increased in most metropolitan areas, and more than one-fifth of all Latino families lived below the poverty level (Santiago and Wilder 1991:511). While the highest levels of poverty were concentrated in the Northeast and Midwest—regions hit hard by deindustrialization—many urban areas in the Southwest also experienced high rates of poverty. Though some scholars contend that the economic status of Latinos is improving, Latino families feature prominently among the working poor (Bean and Tienda 1987). As but one example, Latino family income is 25 percent less than that of their Anglo counterparts. Though this difference could be due in part to a number of family characteristics (e.g., family size, levels of education, years of work experience, recency of immigration, etc.), little doubt remains, however, that Latinos are economically disadvantaged when compared to Anglos (Santiago and Wilder 1991).

While this body of research describes the socioeconomic conditions of Latinos, little attention has been paid to its link with violent crime, especially homicide. Thus, Latinos provide a particularly good case for investigating *how* social and economic factors impact homicide. The present study extends our understanding of both the patterns and causes of Latino homicide in the United States. This is accomplished by examining the impact of poverty and economic inequality on Latino homicide victims across 111 U.S. cities. A cross-sectional approach is used because longitudinal data are not presently fully available for Latinos in the United States.

Theoretical Background

Inequitable distribution of economic resources is often thought to encourage high homicide rates in general and high homicide rates among minority groups in the United States in particular (Shihadeh and Steffensmeier 1994). Central to this longstanding subject of inquiry is debate

*An earlier version of this paper was presented at the annual meeting of the American Sociological Association, Miami Beach, Florida, 1993. This research was made possible by a Supplemental Funds Grant from the University of Delaware College of Arts and Sciences and, in part. through a National Institute on Drug Abuse supplemental grant to HHS 2 P50 05313. I thank Kim Shorter, Jamie J. Fader and especially Brian Martin for collecting and coding data. I also thank Larry Hotchkiss for computer assistance. William Bailey provided updated SHR homicide data and suggestions as did Luis Falcon, Richard J. Lundman, Steven S. Martin, Allan McCutcheon, Steven Messner, Amie L. Nielsen, Vilma Ortiz, Ruth Peterson, Leon Pettiway, Mary Romero, Anna M. Santiago, Rogelio Saenz, and Frank Scarpitti. I especially appreciate helpful comments from the editor and anonymous reviewers of *Social Problems*. This paper also benefited from comments during a faculty colloquium at the College of Criminal Justice at Northeastern University. Points of view and errors are, of course, my own. Correspondence to: Department of Sociology and Criminal Justice, 322 Smith Hall, University of Delaware, Newark, DE 19716.

on the impact of poverty versus economic inequality. For example, poverty is at the center of the work on absolute deprivation in the United States (Parker 1989). Low income and educational attainment correspond to higher rates of homicide, especially among minority group members, those most affected by social and economic deprivation (Bailey 1984; Sampson 1987). Parker (1989:986) notes:

> . . . violence is one of the few options available to those without the economic means to deal with problems and crises of everyday life. Absolute deprivation may also produce emotional situations which escalate into violence . . . simply put, the absolute deprivation approach suggests that violence can occur among such individuals because everyday life is difficult.

Others also link various measures of socioeconomic deprivation to high rates of homicides (Bailey 1984).

Still other researchers suggest economic inequality undermines the social status and economic resources of certain groups within the United States, especially minority groups (Blau and Blau 1982; Shihadeh and Steffensmeier 1994). Minority groups deprived of economic opportunity are part of a social structure with low education, poor wages, impoverished conditions, and a diminished professional occupation rate, relative to the dominant group (Anderson 1990). Central to this thesis is that feelings of alienation and frustration are particularly high in the disadvantaged minority group. One suggested response to social and economic deprivation is increased aggression, including high levels of homicide (see Blau and Blau 1982). According to this perspective, economic and racial inequality are viewed as the primary influence on criminal violence in urban areas. High homicide rates correspond to the economic advantage of one racial group over another racial group (Blau and Blau 1982; Land, McCall, and Cohen 1990).

Some researchers contend that the connection between inequality and violent crime is far from clear (Harer and Steffensmeier 1992; Shihadeh and Steffensmeier 1994). Shihadeh and Steffensmeier (1994) propose that a within-group measure of inequality is more consistent with relative deprivation theory, since feelings of deprivation emanate out of comparisons relative to fellow group members when seeking a referent for socioeconomic standings (see Merton 1957; Harer and

Steffensmeier 1992). This approach, building on reference group theory, recognizes that within-group inequality is likely a better predictor of violence than either between-group or absolute measures because group members look internally for standards of comparison (see also Merton and Rossi 1968). Harer and Steffensmeier note:

> People assess how well, or badly, they are faring economically not by comparing themselves with the population as a whole, but with particular reference groups with whom they share some status attribute (1992:1036)

Such is the case for Latinos. Research on youths and gangs demonstrates how Latinos use friends, family, and others in the Latino community as reference points (Horowitz 1983; Moore 1991). Linked to this notion, Moore (1991) notes many young adult gang men refer to other Latinos, including recent immigrants, as standards in economic and occupation comparisons. Youth gang members acknowledge others close by as referents for feelings about themselves, with few comparisons to the Anglo or Black communities (Horowitz 1983). Even research on labor markets shows that Latino workers, disproportionately represented in the secondary labor market, are likely to take other Latino workers close by as their reference point, not Anglos in the primary labor market force (Saenz and Anderson 1994). Therefore, it appears Latinos look within their community for standards of social and economic comparisons.

The Latino Context

Research on the Latino population has only recently emerged. During the 1970s increased demographic trends coupled with pronounced regional concentration heightened awareness of Latinos as a separate and distinct ethnic group in the United States (Bean and Tienda 1987). Rapid growth in population size alerted social scientists to an emerging group and fueled research on the Latino population (Bean and Tienda 1987). Taking advantage of Census Bureau data, scholars identified and examined the Latino population as never before. We now know more about the educational attainment, employment status, and household characteristics of the Latino population (Bean and Tienda 1987).

Unfortunately, owing to a number of difficulties in categorizing Latinos and perhaps biases against recognizing them as a distinct group, answers to seemingly straightforward questions about the incidence of violent crime among Latinos continue to elude researchers (Flowers 1990; Zahn 1987). Though homicide is reported to be the second and third leading cause of death among Mexican and Cuban Latinos respectively (Mercy 1987), little is known about the rate of homicide, our most serious crime, among the Latino population. Few studies examine the extent and causes of Latino killings, even in areas where large numbers of Latinos reside and are clearly identified (Flowers 1990).

This lack of knowledge is the result of the sparse research on Latinos and violence (Zahn 1987). A handful of studies provides comparisons of Black, white, and Latino homicides in specific cities (Beasley and Antunes 1974; Block 1985, 1993; Pokorny 1965). Others focus on Latino homicides in a purely descriptive manner in a single city (Laredo), state (Texas), region (the Southwest), or island (Puerto Rico) and ignore the correlates of Latino killings (see Mercy 1987; Rodriguez 1990; Valdez 1993; Wallace 1964).

Recent homicide research acknowledges the influence of Latinos but such studies are few in number and limited in scope (see Nelsen, Corzine, and Huff-Corzine 1994; Parker and Toth 1990). Though Nelsen and colleagues and Parker and Toth acknowledge the impact of Latinos on homicide in the United States, they restrict themselves to incorporating percent Latino population as one of many control variables shaping overall homicide, and do not directly examine Latino killings. Only Santiago (1986) probed the socioeconomic and sociodemographic factors shaping Latino murder but focused exclusively on the island of Puerto Rico.

Despite these limitations, some have attempted to place research on Latino violence within the general homicide literature (Zahn 1987). In a 1978 nine-cities sample, Zahn discovered the rate of Latino killings fell between Black and white homicide rates. Equally important is Zahn's speculation on the theoretical merits of using relative and absolute deprivation approaches to explain Latino homicide. After examining the socioeconomic characteristics of the Latino population, Zahn stresses absolute poverty does not affect Latino killings and suggests that future researchers pay closer attention to relative deprivation explanations of homicide. Unfortunately she

did not directly test the impact of absolute and/or relative deprivation on Latino violence. Researchers have not yet investigated the social and economic determinants of Latino homicide across the United States.

The present research addresses these limitations by investigating the extent of Latino killings and the effect of several social and economic dimensions, especially poverty and economic inequality, on homicide. In particular, I examine the rate of killings and the socioeconomic determinants of Latino murder.

Data Collection

Data on the 1980 Latino homicide rate were gathered for 111 cities with at least 5,000 Latinos and one reported Latino homicide.[2] These data are drawn from Supplemental Homicide Report (SHR) information. Police agencies provide supplementary information on homicides, including details on victim and offender characteristics. The exact reporting procedures followed by individual agencies in submitting reports vary, depending on how each state processes Uniform Crime Report (UCR) data. In general, agencies submit monthly reports to either their state UCR coordinating agency or directly to the Federal Bureau of Investigation. Though some researchers contend that official police data portray an inaccurate image of crime in the United States, most acknowledge that homicide is the most reliably recorded index crime (Sampson 1987).[3]

A major advantage of the SHR is the detailed city-level information on each reported homicide. The SHR, for the first time in 1980, provided a separate ethnicity category (Hispanic, non-Hispanic, or unknown ethnicity), allowing a distinction by ethnic group in addition to traditional racial categories (white, Black, and Asian). To calculate homicide rates I use victim-level data rather than offender rates, since information on assailant ethnicity is missing for many cases.[4] While it would be desirable to examine Latino subgroups, e.g., Mexican, Puerto Rican, Cuban, and other Latino extractions, homicide data are not available for specific Latino groups, at least not from government statistics.[5]

Data for city characteristics were gathered from the 1980 U.S. Census[6] and merged with the SHR data. Cities are used as units of analyses because they are commonly used in aggregated and disaggregated analyses of homicide. In addition, detailed Latino-specific factors such as income, education, and others are available from published census reports at the city level permitting examination of Latinos across social units. Finally, cities may be considered homogeneous social units compared to SMSAs or states, since the latter encompass areas ranging from sparsely populated rural areas to densely populated cities (see Bailey 1984).

Empirical Model

The model utilized in this study examines measures of social and economic conditions used in previous research (Blau and Blau 1982; Harer and Steffensmeier 1992; Parker 1995; Peterson and Krivo 1993; Shihadeh and Steffensmeier 1994). Although researchers do not agree on what specific variables should be included, the model is essentially that of Peterson and Krivo (1993). Specifically, I use a modified version in which Peterson and Krivo's residential segregation measure is replaced by the immigration index proposed in this article.[7] The present research, also, appropriately employs Latino-specific measures of socioeconomic conditions rather than global indicators of structural conditions. This strategy is important because few scholars have combined group-specific measures of crime with theoretically guided group-specific measures of social and economic conditions (see Shihadeh and Steffensmeier 1994).

This research focuses on the impact of Latino poverty and economic inequality on homicide. Latino homicide rates are expected to change in relation to shifts in the poverty level. Cities with high rates of Latino poverty are hypothesized to also experience increased homicide.

Two measures of economic inequality, based on the distribution of family income, are used in the following analysis. Anglo-Latino income inequality is defined as the ratio of Anglo to Latino median family income. The income ratio allows us to control for differences across cities in average income, providing a measure of economic inequality in dollar figures between Latinos and Anglos. As the gap between Anglo and Latino income increases, the number of killings would be expected to increase. Second, Latino income inequality, as determined by the Gini coefficient, uses other Latinos as the reference point. This variable measures the extent to which Latino median family incomes are dispersed in each city relative to the average Latino income in that city. This objective measure

of income inequality provides a relative interpretation with larger values indicating greater income distribution within our sample of Latinos. Thus, the former inequality income ratio compares Latinos relative to Anglos, and the latter controls for the range of income within the Latino population.

Other Latino economic conditions also are expected to impact homicide rates. Areas with low high school graduation levels would be associated with higher rates of homicide victims. In general, education is included to examine further the range of economic conditions within the Latino population, and it helps extend dimensions of Latino socioeconomic status.

A set of control variables are introduced to address the issue of demographic composition within the Latino population as well as circumstances unique to the Latino community. Percent Latino is included to account for the variation in size of the Latino population in each city. The percent Latino males age 15–24 is used to control for the high-crime prone population. The divorced population is included as a proxy for social disorganization. City population size is included because increases in size of the population increase opportunities for victimization. All four control variables are expected to positively influence the rate of Latino killings.

Two variables were also introduced to capture the unique demographic characteristics of the Latino population. A regional variable (Southwest) was included to distinguish cities in areas formerly belonging to Mexico and located in the southwestern United States. The southwest region is defined as cities in Arizona, California, Colorado, New Mexico, and Texas, an area historically and numerically of Mexican origin. The main consideration is that Latinos, at least in this study, reside primarily in the Southwest and could differ demographically and/or economically from Latinos in other parts of the United States (Nelsen, Corzine, and Huff-Corzine 1994). A second demographic variable was included, as proxy, to account for the impact of Latino immigration on U.S. cities. The immigration index incorporates both percent foreign-born Latinos and proportion of the Latino community residing abroad (in 1975), including Puerto Rico. The rationale is that recent immigration could contribute to the homicide rate in varying ways across the United States. Cities with large influxes of recent Latino immigrants could be more likely to experience growing rates of killings than areas with an older and stable Latino population. In addition, the most recent Latino immigrants, presumably, have a lower socioeconomic status than U.S.-born Latinos.[8] Data for all independent variables were collected from the 1980 U.S. Bureau of the Census Reports.

Operational Definitions of Variables

The Latino homicide rate was estimated as the number of reported Latino homicide victims per 100,000 Latinos in each city. This dependent variable presents for the first time a Latino-specific homicide rate across a large number of U.S cities.

Poverty is measured as the percentage of Latino families living below the federal poverty levels. Economic inequality, as measured by income, was estimated in two measures: Anglo to Latino income is a measure of family income differences of Anglos and Latinos; within-group inequality, Latino to Latino, is defined in terms of the inequality (Gini coefficient) of income among Latino families.

A final indicator of Latinos' varying economic conditions is used: Education, operationalized as the percent of Latino high school graduates, examines the effect of educational attainment.[9] Four control variables were also employed: percent Latinos in each city, percent Latino males age 15–24 years, percent divorced, and city population size (logged). Percent Latino accounts for the size of the Latino population in each city. Percent young Latinos controls for the population at greatest risk of being victimized. The proportion of divorced Latinos in each city is also a commonly used indicator of social disorganization. Population is defined as the population size (logged) in each city. Region was operationalized as a dummy variable coded "1" for cities in the Southwest and "0" for cities in other regions of the United States. Immigration is a z-score index capturing Latinos who are foreign-born or previously resided in Puerto Rico.

Ordinary least squares regression technique (OLS) is employed as the primary analytical tool and to diagnose collinearity among the explanatory variables (see Appendix).[10] Multicollinearity did not emerge as a serious problem in probing Latino homicide. At the bivariate level there was one instance of high correlation (>.60) when Anglo to Latino economic inequality overlapped with Latino poverty (r = .73). Therefore, Latino

homicide was regressed separately on all variables except poverty and again on all variables except Anglo-to-Latino inequality. The results were similar to those in which both poverty and Anglo/Latino inequality are simultaneously entered. An additional test was conducted to test for multicollinearity. Specifically, I regressed each independent variable on all other independent variables. A high degree of collinearity exists if the R^2 is close to 1.0; however, none approached that threshold, thwarting the concern of serious collinearity. Residual plots and partial regression plots were also examined. Three outliers initially appeared (Houston, Miami, and San Antonio). Equations were re-estimated eliminating one of the outliers for each equation. Afterwards, all outliers were deleted. The results were virtually identical. Thus, the regression results that follow are not distorted due to problems of multicollinearity.[11]

Yet another step was taken to address possible data concerns. These data are likely to be heteroscedastic—unequal variances because of the wide variation in rates of Latino homicide. Weighted least squares (WLS) regression corrects for this possibility and yields better estimates with the smallest sampling variance. A two-step weighting procedure provides the efficient estimates presented in the following analysis (see Greene 1993).

Findings

This section begins by briefly highlighting the range of urban Latino homicide. Then, Latino killings are probed by directing initial attention to descriptive analysis. Finally, the full power of the data is harnessed by modeling Latino killings using OLS and WLS regression.

Since one goal of this research is to examine the rate of Latino killings, Table 1 illustrates the clear and dramatic range of urban Latino homicides across the United States. Supplemental Homicide Reports show that for 1980 Latino homicide-victim rates ranged from highs in Dallas (67.87) and Houston (64.13) to lows in Tampa (2.80) and San Francisco (1.19), with an average of 18 Latino killings per 100,000 Latinos in cities such as St. Louis and San Angelo. These initial findings confirm that understanding Latino homicides requires a closer look at the variation within the murder rate. The question is whether and how the range of Latino killings is linked to poverty and inequality.

TABLE 1 Urban Latino Homicide Rates, 1980 (N=111 Cities)

Average Latino homicide rate = 18.407			
Dallas, TX	67.866	Lakewood, CO	15.097
Houston, TX	64.128	McAllen, TX	14.769
Compton, CA	52.442	Worchester, MA	14.373
Hollywood, FL	47.370	San Mateo, CA	13.938
Fort Worth, TX	45.297	Aurora, IL	13.822
Galveston, TX	44.583	Pasadena, CA	13.768
San Bernardino, CA	43.596	Montebello, CA	12.781
Miami, FL	43.260	Ontario, CA	12.451
Chicago, IL	42.309	Irving, TX	12.335
Odessa, TX	38.310	San Diego, CA	12.314
Oceanside, CA	35.653	Whittier, CA	12.296
New York City, NY	35.388	Pico Rivera, CA	12.284
Long Beach, CA	33.697	Costa Mesa, CA	11.799
Lubbock, TX	33.673	San Jose, CA	11.404
Fresno, CA	33.157	Tempe, AZ	11.390
Miami Beach, FL	32.832	Arlington, VA	11.298
Bakersfield, CA	31.341	District of Columbia	11.190
Elgin, IL	30.734	Santa Ana, CA	11.031
Philadelphia, PA	29.617	Providence, RI	10.995
Wichita Falls, TX	27.851	Riverside, CA	10.905
Austin, TX	27.716	El Paso, TX	10.902
Stockton, CA	27.153	Waukegan, IL	10.789
Waco, TX	26.860	Escondido, CA	10.684
Midland, TX	26.826	Wichita, KS	10.231
Corpus Christi, TX	26.795	Laredo, TX	9.405
San Antonio, TX	25.367	Lorain, OH	9.208
Kansas City, KS	25.338	Torrance, CA	9.166
Denver, CO	24.906	Modesto, CA	8.935
Greeley, CO	24.213	Santa Monica, CA	8.717
Phoenix, AZ	23.129	Hialeah, FL	8.341
Albuquerque, NM	22.305	Oxnard, CA	8.338
Ventura, CA	22.297	El Monte, CA	8.213
Amarillo, TX	21.717	Glendale, AZ	8.025
Los Angeles, CA	21.097	Anaheim, CA	7.981
Tucson, AZ	20.684	Las Vegas, NV	7.785
Salinas, CA	19.625	Seattle, WA	7.778
Reno, NV	19.461	Sacramento, CA	7.711
Boston, MA	19.429	Huntington Beach, CA	7.445
Lawrence, MA	19.422	Springfield, MA	7.214
Alameda, CA	19.223	Hartford, CT	7.153
Topeka, KS	18.860	Pomona, CA	7.066
Toledo, OH	18.799	Kansas City, MO	6.762
W. Palm Beach, FL	18.681	Santa Barbara, CA	6.067
St. Louis, MO	18.392	Garden Grove, CA	6.046
San Angelo, TX	17.799	Norwalk, CA	5.846
Victoria, TX	17.582	Inglewood, CA	5.604
Detroit, MI	17.313	Fremont, CA	5.445
Hawthorne, CA	16.988	Pasadena, TX	5.221
Cleveland, OH	16.865	Southgate, CA	5.135
Norfolk, VA	16.285	Monterey Park, CA	4.769
Ft. Lauderdale, FL	15.951	Alhambra, CA	4.116
Carson City, CA	15.779	Milwaukee, WI	3.834
Brownsville, TX	15.446	Oakland, CA	3.112
Arlington, TX	15.340	Tampa, FL	2.795
Chula Vista, CA	15.328	San Francisco, CA	1.188
Joliet, IL	15.271		

TABLE 2   Correlates of Latino Homicide: Descriptions, Means, and Standard Deviations

Variable	Description	Mean	Standard Deviation
Poverty	Percent of Latino families below the poverty line	18.980	9.541
Anglo-Latino income inequality	Ratio of Anglo to Latino median family income	1.387	.314
Latino income inequality	Gini index of family income inequality among Latinos	.377	.556
Education	Percent of Latino population older than 24 that graduated high school	45.453	12.216
Percent Latino	Percent of the total city population that is Latino	20.732	18.994
Percent Latino males, aged 15–24	Percent of Latino males aged 15 to 24	11.750	2.310
Percent Divorced	Percent of the Latino population older than 15 that is currently divorced or separated	6.948	1.819
Population (log)	Natural log of the total city population	5.230	.433
Region	Southwest = 1, Other = 0	.676	.470
Immigration	Index of foreign-born Latinos and Latinos living abroad in 1975	.022	1.820

The descriptive statistics are presented in Table 2. Most notable across the 111 U.S. cities is the high level of poverty and economic inequality. Beginning with the three variables of primary interest, note that urban Latinos in this sample have a substantial rate of poverty (almost 19 percent) and a family income far less than Anglos. On average, Anglos earn $1.39 to every Latino dollar. Latino communities also exhibit strong variability within family income as measured by the Gini coefficient. For Latino inequality, the average income difference among urban Latino families is around two-thirds of the average Latino income. Economic inequality (as measured by income) exists not only relative to Anglos, but within the Latino population as well.

Table 2 further reveals the magnitude of Latino economic conditions. For example, less than half of the Latino population graduated from high school (45 percent). This feature stresses the educational hardship experienced by Latinos in U.S. cities.

Table 3 provides the OLS and WLS estimates for the model probing Latino homicides. I provide the OLS results for comparison but focus attention on the WLS findings.

The WLS results show that absolute deprivation, as measured by poverty, is related to Latino homicide.

However, contrary to expectations, a larger poverty rate is associated with a lower homicide rate. This finding directly contradicts the absolute deprivation interpretation that suggests a larger poverty rate increases Latino homicide. In fact, just the opposite appears to occur for urban Latinos.

Turning to the other variables of theoretical interest, a leading predictor of homicide is Latino income inequality. A one standard deviation increase in Latino-to-Latino inequality is associated with a rise of more than one-third a standard deviation in the rate of Latino killings (b = .354). This finding confirms use of the disaggregation strategy because it captures the uniqueness of the income distribution in Latino areas. As the income gap within the Latino population increases, the rate of killings increases as well. Economic inequality relative to other Latinos, not Anglos, is an important influence on homicide within the Latino community.[12]

One possible explanation for the Latino income inequality effect is that the Gini coefficient is more indicative of unequal resources than other deprivation measures in disaggregated homicide research. To the extent that Latino communities provide limited opportunities to associate with economically well-off Anglos and place

TABLE 3   Regressions of All Cities on Social and Economic Factors, 1980

	OLS		WLS	
Variable	*b*	β	*b*	β
Poverty	−.269	−.199	−.298	−.238***
	(.266)		(.090)	
Latino income inequality	.779	.336**	.806	.354***
	(.315)		(.111)	
Anglo-Latino income inequality	−4.361	−.106	−3.389	−.102
	(6.446)		(2.102)	
Education	−.399	−.379***	−.368	−.386***
	(.146)		(.046)	
Percent Latino	−.140	−.206*	−.125	−.207***
	(.083)		(.026)	
Percent Latino males, aged 15–24	.085	.015	.068	.013
	(.558)		(.173)	
Percent Divorced	−.347	−.049	−.215	−.032
	(.916)		(.287)	
Population (log)	8.469	.285***	7.497	.252***
	(2.843)		(.981)	
Immigration	−.402	−.057	−.286	−.045
	(.735)		(.237)	
Region	6.282	.229*	5.293	.207***
	(3.183)		(1.014)	
Constant	−25.906		−23.654	
R^2	.213		.203	
F	2.708**		21.790***	

Note: Standard errors in parentheses
* $p \leq .05$ ** $p \leq .01$ *** $p \leq .001$

more pressure on associating primarily with other Latinos, this could exert an influence on violence that tends to occur between Latinos.

In particular, note that educational attainment is the strongest predictor of homicide (b = .386). This finding suggests that increased education, as measured by high school graduation, has the most salient effect on decreased killings in the Latino population.

Latino sociodemographic conditions played a significant role in homicide. High rates of Latino killings are more prevalent in cities with increased population size. A larger Latino population is related to less Latino killings. The fact that the Southwest region is positively related to the homicide rates is not surprising given that most Latinos live in this area.

In sum, several clear patterns emerge. Latino income inequality was a significant contributor to homicide. Further, educational attainment played an important role in the level of homicide. City population size also influenced the rate of Latino killings. Region of the country and percent Latino in each city also contributed to Latino homicide. Overall, the findings suggest that though Latino murders are primarily impacted by Latino education and income inequality, demographic factors are also significant contributors to levels of Latino homicide.

I also examined alternative measures of inequality. Balkwell (1990) extended measures of inequality by combining income information on five ethnic groups and weighting by the proportional representation of these groups in 150 SMSAs. As Messner and Golden (1992) and Harer and Steffensmeir (1992) point out, however, there appears to be no need to employ this weighting procedure in disaggregated homicide research because group-specific rates, when serving as the dependent variable, are standardized by the population size of the specific group. Despite this, I tentatively examined the Balkwell thesis. In this study it's plausible that reference points other than Anglos exist for Latinos, especially outside the Southwest. First, other groups (Anglo, Black, Asian, Native Americans) must exist if they are to serve as adequate points of reference. Information was collected on the number of Non-Latino whites, Blacks, Asians, and Native Americans in the present sample of 111 cities. The following distribution was discovered: almost 62 percent of the city population in this sample was white; close to 13 percent was Black; less than 1 percent was Native American, and a little more than 3 percent was Asian. It appears that Anglos are by far the largest group and the primary reference group across the 111 cities.

Indeed, Anglos were the largest group, net of Latinos, in almost every city (n = 107). In addition, recall that one criterion for inclusion in this study was that each city had at least 5,000 Latinos. Applying this same standard to Non-Latino whites, Blacks, Asians, and Native Americans, the following is discovered: In only 1 city did Anglos *not* meet the 5,000 minimum; 39 cities had less than 5,000 Blacks; 38 cities had more than 5,000 Asians; and 5 cities had more than 5,000 Native Americans.

Finally, as a partial test of the Balkwell thesis, I included percent white, Black, Asian, and Native American into the equation and none of the variables was an important indicator of Latino homicide. The model fit, as judged in part by the R-square, was not significantly improved and, in fact, deteriorated. It appears that Anglos are by far the primary reference group across the 111 cities and the most useful point of economic comparison.

Discussion and Conclusions

This paper is the first comprehensive analysis of Latino homicide on a national basis. One purpose of this study is to expand earlier homicide research by examining the variation in Latino homicide-victim rates across U.S. cities. Another is to carefully probe the link between Latino socioeconomic conditions and the incidence of homicide.

Overall, the results in this study reveal that disaggregating the homicide-victim rate and its correlates contributes to our understanding of the sources of killings among urban Latinos. The average Latino homicide rate (almost 20 per 100,000 Latinos) approaches the total African American homicide rate (27 per 100,000 African Americans) reported by Peterson and Krivo (1993:1012) and is twice the total 1980 U.S. homicide rate. This basic, though important, finding, highlights the need for Latino-specific measures in sociological research. Latino homicide is thus an important, largely unstudied, and generally underexamined social problem in contemporary U.S. society.

That economic inequality, not poverty, has a strong effect on Latino homicide is in line with an emerging body of literature (see Harer and Steffensmeier 1992; Shihadeh and Steffensmeier 1994). Steffensmeier and colleagues propose that researchers need to properly assess the effects of race-specific research, especially when conclusions stem from the importance of within-group inequality in explaining minority violence. Researchers should continue to focus attention on the impact of Latino inequality as a source of violence. It is possible that a large income gap within the Latino population creates a milieu in which a need to vent frustration at others results, usually at those in the Latino community, and with deadly consequences. Again, independent of other measures, the effect of Latino inequality, not poverty or inequality relative to Anglos, on homicide was strong and significant across the United States.

Furthermore, this analysis supports Blau and Schwartz's (1984) inequality hypothesis that economic inequality, rather than poverty, is responsible for high homicide rates. However, my findings differ from research proposing that pronounced economic inequalities *between* races leads to other types of conflict across communities (see Balkwell 1990). As demonstrated, intergroup inequality (Anglo-to-Latino) does not influence Latino killings. This finding is particularly noteworthy after taking into consideration prominent work on inequality and homicide (Balkwell 1990; Blau and Schwartz 1984). Note, that the body of research discovering the impact of between-group inequality has typically analyzed total rather than group-specific homicide rates, and has analyzed general rather than group-specific predictors, in SMSAs not cities.

For urban Latinos, emphasizing inequality relative to Anglos provides an incomplete and inaccurate picture of the influences on Latino homicide because aggregate measures would have masked the group-specific sources of violence. Perhaps the varying level of income inequality relative to Anglos is less meaningful since the persistent income gap among Latinos appears more immediate and widespread across the Latino community. This interpretation is speculative, but it highlights how determinants of Latino killings differ from those for total homicides or other group-specific killings (e.g., Black, Asian, Native American).

This is not to say that attention should be taken away from other social or economic sources of Latino homicide. Rather, the deprivation issue for Latinos is different than straight poverty or inequality relative to Anglos. Research by William J. Wilson (1987) provides a possible interpretation; namely, that the changing class structure in some urban areas, resulting from professional flight, followed out by the working class, leaving behind the most economically disadvantaged, is an important factor in understanding urban Latino violence. Alternatively, others argue that the Latino poor are not as concentrated in inner city barrios, relative to the underclass, and that the social structure for Latinos remains secure and stable (Moore and Pinderhughes 1993). Nevertheless, evidence exists that the income gap between middle-class and poor Latinos persists, and perhaps is widening, especially after considering the continuing growth in both classes (see Valdez 1993). As long as Latinos across the United States are concentrated in urban areas, characterized as part of the working poor, and continuously influenced by immigration, it will be difficult to reduce inequality. To illustrate, Perez and Cruz (1994) argue that inadequate levels of education and diminished job markets increase involvement in crime and violence for young urban Latinos. Coupled with the fact that the young and growing Latino population is constantly reinforced by economically and educationally disadvantaged immigrants in search of employment, the chances decline that Latinos will become more integrated, and, possibly, enable the less well-off to compete.

Perhaps enhanced economic opportunities fueled by school reform and greater access to higher education—intertwined with job training programs and economic growth—will reduce the income and educational attainment gap among Latinos. Sampson (1987) suggests that similar policies are more likely in the long run

to reduce violence than alternatives seeking to increase incarceration levels. Unfortunately, legislation such as the recently passed Proposition 187 in California could tend to enhance the marginalization of Latinos by singling them out for discrimination. Such laws will likely decrease education, increase inequality, and make more violence likely.

Naturally, these conclusions are presented with some cautions. This paper encourages scholars to focus attention on a largely underexamined and mostly ignored population in the criminological literature. Clearly, it does not serve as a vehicle to propose or oppose any political agendas. This initial exploration sheds some light on an important social problem and raises questions about the patterns and causes of Latino violence.

In sum, little is known about Latino homicide, and this paper has not addressed every issue associated with Latino killings. It is, however, an important starting point. For the first time, it establishes a national Latino homicide rate and the socioeconomic factors that shape Latino killings. Future analyses will undoubtedly compare these 1980 findings to later time periods for greater clarity on the longitudinal impact of poverty and inequality. Still other studies might extend this area of research by exploring the impact of substance use within the Latino community, clarifying the link between drugs and alcohol to homicide (see Valdez 1993; Parker 1995). All of these issues are worthy of examination and should use this study as a foundation for future research on Latino lethal violence.

NOTES

1. Latinos are defined as persons whose national origin is Mexico, Puerto Rico, Cuba, or any other Spanish-speaking country (See Bean and Tienda 1987; Moore and Pinderhughes 1993). The term Anglo is used in the paper to refer to non-Latino whites (See Santiago and Wilder 1991 for similar usage of both terms).

2. A 5,000 Latino population size was used as a selection criterion (See Peterson and Krivo 1993:1006). Lowering the Latino population threshold led to unreliable homicide rates (e.g., Yakima, Washington, had a homicide rate twice as high as Dallas and Houston, Texas). After application of this criterion the number of Latino areas examined was 111 cities.

3. As best as I can determine, the SHR is the most reliable and consistent source of Latino homicide, although the UCR and Centers for Disease Control (CDC) also provide information on homicide. However, the UCR does not publish ethnic identification data for Latino victims. The SHR data are slightly less complete than the FBI's UCR data, the more

commonly used source. In this analysis total homicide rates from both sources are highly correlated for the 111 cities examined (r = .96). The CDC reports were based on a special study using state-level death certificates in the Southwest and were not broken down beyond that level. Again, the SHR appears to be the only national source of Latino killings.

4. An examination of Anglo-Latino homicide differences, or any other racial/ethnic murder combination, is beyond the scope of this paper. A major reason is that the vast majority of homicides occur within ethnic groups (making the distinction between offender/victim arbitrary), at least in cases cleared with an arrest. In Texas, Rodriguez (1990:98) discovered 86 percent of Latinos were killed by other Latinos. Many other researchers also note the high rate of Latino on Latino murders in urban areas, e.g., Miami, Florida (85 percent); New York City (78 percent); and Chicago, Illinois (82 percent) (See Block 1993:301; Rodriguez 1987:82; Wilbanks 1984:159). Block (1985:112) also notes that from 1965 to 1981 approximately 12,876 homicides were recorded in Chicago. Even though a large number of Latino killings occurred during this time "too few interracial homicides (existed) for an analysis of monthly or even yearly patterns."

5. I thank Orlando Rodriguez at the Fordham University Hispanic Research Center for alerting me to published 1980 New York City Police Department homicide data (See Rodriguez 1987). Unfortunately, the police are not recording victims' ethnicity in the Greater New York-New Jersey metropolitan area (e.g., New Brunswick, Newark, Paterson, Clifton, and Passaic, New Jersey). For example, police agencies in New York and New Jersey failed to report a single Latino homicide victim to the SHR. Public health agencies also report similar missing data problems using death certificates collected at the state level (personal communication October 6, 1993, Lois Fingerhut, National Center of Health Statistics).

6. Census data were gathered from U.S. Bureau of the Census, County and City Data Book, 1988. U.S. Government Printing Office: 1988. U.S. Bureau of the Census, 1980 Census of Population: Volume 1 Characteristics of the Population, Chapter C General Social and Economic Characteristics. U.S. Government Printing Office: 1983. U.S. Bureau of the Census, 1980 Census of Population: Volume 1 Characteristics of the Population, Chapter B General Population Characteristics. U.S. Government Printing Office: 1982. Utilizing data from the 1980 Census establishes a baseline for future analysis of changes occurring in the 1980s.

7. In their original analysis, Peterson and Krivo also employed percent professional. This measure, at least for Latinos, created collinearity problems and other statistical inference problems with the educational deficiency variable. I opted to remove percent professionals because educational attainment is more closely related to homicide rates (See Balkwell 1990).

8. At the city level, data on recency of immigration by country of origin are not readily available (personal communication April 1995, Jorge Del Pinal, U.S. Census Bureau). To estimate a proxy for immigration I did two things. First, I examined a foreign-born variable. The Census Bureau provides data on the number of Latinos in each city born in a foreign country. This variable captures the bulk of Latinos born outside of the United States. However this does not adequately account for "immigration" in the Puerto Rican population. To garner an estimate on the number of Puerto Rican Latinos residing on the island, I incorporated the variable counting the number of Latinos living abroad in 1975, five years before the census was taken. Since both variables were highly correlated (r = .72), I created an index composed of both immigration proxies. The variables were transformed into z-scores and summed to compute the combined variable. This procedure avoids the possibility of counting persons twice. In the analysis that follows, both variables were individually introduced into the models, and then simultaneously incorporated, with similar results as the immigration index. Though not perfect, for the purposes of this paper, immigration is adequately addressed.

9. The unemployment rate was also added but this produced severe collinearity problems with several variables. The reader should note that, with the exception of the Puerto Rican population, Latinos are not characterized by high rates of joblessness but are disproportionately part of the working poor and working class, at least in 1980 (See Bean and Tienda 1987). Similarly, except for New York City and surrounding areas, Latino families are not significantly influenced by large numbers of female-headed households. However I did explore replacing female-headed households with the divorce rate and produced comparable results.

10. The use of OLS on the untransformed homicide rate raises several issues. After examining the skewness of the untransformed and logarithmic transformation homicide rates, and looking at kurtosis tests, several points emerged. First, the homicide distribution is not highly skewed. The natural value was modestly positively skewed, and, when transformed, became moderately negatively skewed. In addition, contrary to usual instance, the transformation seriously eroded the model fit as judged by both the large drop in the R-square and the F-test change from significant to nonsignificant. Based on interpretation ease and superior model fit, the untransformed dependent variable is preferred and used in the following analysis.

11. The issue of multicollinearity is further examined explicitly since it is a common problem inherent to ecological data

(see Land, McCall, and Cohen 1990). First, although bivariate plots were examined and did not suggest that further transformations were necessary, I re-estimated the model by introducing log transformations for each independent variable to check the linear assumption for each regressor. After comparing the kurtosis of each natural expression and log expression, the log expression of each variable was entered individually and in various combinations (e.g., log of A/L inequality and log of Latino poverty, etc). The results did not substantially change.

Next, I examined a number of possible interaction terms. Numerous interactions were looked at, including Anglo-to-Latino inequality, Gini coefficient, poverty, education, divorce rate, and the immigration index in various combinations. None was statistically significant.

Finally, Land and colleagues (1990) stress the need to be sensitive to Gordon's partialling fallacy, a statistical inference problem related to multicollinearity (see also Gordon 1968). Although poverty, Latino income inequality, and Anglo-Latino inequality have some conceptual overlap, each measure has a distinct and intrinsic meaning. To avoid inference problems, each of the three measures of poverty and inequality was individually entered and removed, and again, the following reported results did not appreciably change.

12. The ratio of Anglo-to-Latino median income is a fairly standard measure of intergroup inequality, although it is an imperfect one. Almost without exception, recent disaggregated homicide studies use a similar measure (white-to-Black median income) to, in part, capture majority relative to minority group inequality (see Harer and Steffensmeier 1992; Messner and Golden 1992; Peterson and Krivo 1993; Shihadeh and Steffensmeier 1994). However, I did reestimate the model using an alternative measure of Anglo-to-Latino inequality. A/L inequality was redefined as *relative poverty* by taking percent poor Latinos relative to percent poor Anglos, defined for both groups as those below the poverty line (e.g., percent poor Anglos/percent poor Latinos). This measure is not based on central tendency but rather the lower, deprived end of the income distribution. The results from this alternative specification had no effect on homicide when used in lieu of poverty and/or Anglo to Latino inequality.

REFERENCES

Anderson, Elijah. 1990. *Streetwise*. Chicago: University of Chicago Press.

Bailey, William C. 1984. "Poverty, inequality, and homicide rates." *Criminology* 22:531–550.

Balkwell, James W. 1990. "Ethnic inequality and the rate of homicide." *Social Forces* 69:53–70.

Beasley, Ronald W., and George Antunes. 1974. "The etiology of urban crime: An ecological analysis." *Criminology* 11:439–461.

Bean, Frank, and Marta Tienda. 1987. *The Hispanic Population of the United States*. New York: Russell Sage Foundation.

Blau, Judith R., and Peter M. Blau. 1982. "The cost of inequality: Metropolitan structure and violent crime." *American Sociological Review* 47:114–129.

Blau, Peter M., and Joseph E. Schwartz. 1984. *Crosscutting Social Circles: Testing a Macrostructural Theory of Intergroup Relations*. New York: Academic Press.

Block, Carolyn R. 1985. "Race\ethnicity and patterns of Chicago homicide 1965–1981." *Crime and Delinquency* 31:104–116.

———. 1993. "Lethal violence in the Chicago Latino community." In *Homicide: The Victim/Offender Connection,* ed. Anna Victoria Wilson, 267–342. Cincinnati, Ohio: Anderson Publishing.

Bonger, Wilhelm. 1916. *Criminality and Economic Conditions*. Boston: Little, Brown and Company.

Flowers, Ronald. 1990. *Minorities and Criminality*. New York: Praeger Publishers.

Gordon, Robert A. 1968. "Issues in multiple regression." *American Journal of Sociology* 73:592–616.

Greene, William H. 1993. *Econometric Analysis*. New York: MacMillan Press.

Harer, Miles D., and Darrell Steffensmeier. 1992. "The differing effects of economic inequality on Black and white rates of homicide." *Social Forces* 70:1035–1054.

Horowitz, Ruth. 1983. *Honor and the American Dream*. New Brunswick, N.J.: Rutgers University Press.

Land, Kenneth, Patricia L. McCall, and Lawrence E. Cohen. 1990. "Structural covariates of homicide rates: Are there any invariances across time and social space?" *American Journal of Sociology* 95:922–963.

Mercy, James A. 1987. "Assaultive injury among Hispanics: A public health problem." In *Research Conference on Violence and Homicide in Hispanic Communities,* eds. Jess Kraus, Susan Sorenson, and Paul Juarez, 1–12. Office of Minority Health, U.S. Department of Health and Human Services.

Merton, Robert K. 1957. *Social Theory and Social Structure*. New York: Free Press.

Merton, Robert K., and Alice K. Rossi 1968. "Contributions to the theory of reference group behavior." In *Readings in Reference Group Theory and Research,* eds. Herbert Hyman and Eleanor Singer, 28–68. New York: Free Press.

Messner, Steven, and Reid M. Golden. 1992. "Racial inequality and racially disaggregated homicide rates: An assessment of alternative theoretical explanations." *Criminology* 30:421–445.

Moore, Joan. 1991. *Going Down to the Barrio: Homeboys and Homegirls in Change*. Philadelphia: Temple University Press.

Moore, Joan, and Raquel Pinderhughes, eds. 1993. *In The Barrios: Latinos and the Underclass Debate.* New York: Russell Sage Foundation.

Nelsen, Candace, Jay Corzine, and Lin Huff-Corzine. 1994. "The violent West reexamined: A research note on regional homicide rates." *Criminology* 32:135–148.

Parker, Robert Nash. 1989. "Poverty, subculture of violence, and type of homicide." *Social Forces* 67:983–1007.

———. 1995. *Alcohol and Homicide: A Deadly Combination of Two American Traditions.* Albany, N.Y.: SUNY Press.

Parker, Robert Nash, and Allison M. Toth. 1990. "Family, intimacy, and homicide: A macro-social approach." *Violence and Its Victims* 5:195–210.

Perez, Sonia M., and Steven Cruz. 1994. *Speaking Out Loud: Conversations With Young Puerto Rican Men.* Washington, D.C.: National Council of La Raza.

Peterson, Ruth D., and Lauren J. Krivo. 1993. "Racial segregation and Black urban homicide." *Social Forces* 71:1001–26.

Pokorny, Alex D. 1965. "Human violence: A comparison of homicide, aggravated assault, suicide, and attempted suicide." *Journal of Criminal Law, Criminology and Police Science* 56:488–497.

Rodriguez, Orlando 1987. "Hispanics and homicide in New York City." In *Research Conference on Violence and Homicide in Hispanic Communities,* eds. Jess Kraus, Susan Sorenson, and Paul Juarez, 67–84. Office of Minority Health, U.S. Department of Health and Human Services.

Rodriguez, Salvador F. 1990. "Patterns of homicide in Texas: A descriptive analysis of racial/ethnic involvement by crime-specific categories." Ph.D. dissertation, Ann Arbor, Mich.

Saenz, Rogelio, and Robert N. Anderson. 1994. "The ecology of Chicano interstate net migration, 1975–1980." *Social Science Quarterly* 75:37–52.

Sampson, Robert J. 1987. "Urban Black violence: The effect of male joblessness and family disruption." *American Journal of Sociology* 93:348–382.

Santiago, Anne M. 1986. "Socioedad encarcelada: Lethal violence in Puerto Rico." Report prepared for the Office of Research Coordinator, University of Puerto Rico at Mayaguez.

Santiago, Anne M., and Margaret G. Wilder. 1991. "Residential segregation and the links to minority poverty: The case of Latinos in the United States." *Social Problems* 38:492–515.

Shihadeh, Edward S., and Darrell J. Steffensmeier. 1994. "Economic inequality, family disruption, and urban Black violence: Cities as units of stratification and social control." *Social Forces* 73:729–751.

U.S. Bureau of the Census. 1982. *1980 Census of Population: Volume 1. Characteristics of the Population,* Chapter B. General Population Characteristics. U.S. Government Printing Office.

———. 1983. *1980 Census of Population: Volume 1. Characteristics of the Population,* Chapter C. General Social and Economic Characteristics. U.S. Government Printing Office.

———. 1988. *County and City Data Book.* U.S. Government Printing Office.

Valdez, Avelardo. 1993. "Persistent poverty, crime, and drugs: U.S.-Mexican border region." In *The Barrios: Latinos and the Underclass Debate,* eds. Joan Moore and Raquel Pinderhughes, 173–194. New York: Russell Sage.

Wallace, Samuel E. 1964. "Patterns of violence in San Juan." In *Interdisciplinary Problems in Criminology*, eds. Walter Reckless and Charles J. Newman, 43–48. Columbus, Ohio: Ohio State University Press.

Wilbanks, William. 1984. *Murder in Miami.* Lanham, MD: University Press of America.

Wilson, William J. 1987. *The Truly Disadvantaged.* Chicago: University of Chicago Press.

Zahn, Margaret A. 1987. "Homicide in nine American cities: The Hispanic case." In *Research Conference on Violence and Homicide in Hispanic Communities*, ed. Jess Kraus, Susan Sorenson, and Paul Juarez, 13–30. Office of Minority Health, U.S. Department of Health and Human Services.

Think Critically

1. Martinez supports the theory that socioeconomic inequality versus economic poverty among the Latin community exacerbates conditions of social strain, which thus leads to increased rates of aggression, violent crime, and homicide. Define the difference between socioeconomic inequality and economic poverty as described in this study, then explain to what extent you agree or disagree with its thesis.

2. To address the demographic composition of the Latino population, Martinez introduced two control variables. What were these variables and why did he choose these specific ones? What was he hoping to demonstrate and to what extent did these two variables affect the overall conclusions of his study?

APPENDIX   Zero Order Correlation Matrix (N = 111)

	1	2	3	4	5	6	7	8	9	10	11
Latino Homicide Rate (1)	1.000	.127	.169	.089	−.248	−.082	.026	−.087	.243	−.044	.016
Poverty (2)		1.000	.537	.733	−.586	.087	−.078	−.203	.214	−.013	−.265
Anglo-Latino income inequality (3)			1.000	.509	−.259	−.274	.055	−.054	.287	.047	−.222
Latino income inequality (4)				1.000	−.180	−.032	−.113	.132	.218	.316	−.446
Education (5)					1.000	−.285	.088	.539	−.019	.126	.022
Percent Latino (6)						1.000	−.290	−.331	−.218	.012	.326
Percent Latino males, aged 15–24 (7)							1.000	−.149	−.032	−.032	.074
Percent Divorced (8)								1.000	.144	−.063	−.252
Population* (9)									1.000	.001	−.258
Region (10)										1.000	−.290
Immigration (11)											1.000

*Natural logarithm

Broken Windows

James Q. Wilson and George L. Kelling

IN THE MID-1970S, THE STATE OF NEW JERSEY announced a "Safe and Clean Neighborhoods Program," designed to improve the quality of community life in 28 cities. As part of that program, the state provided money to help cities take police officers out of their patrol cars and assign them to walking beats. The governor and other state officials were enthusiastic about using foot patrol as a way of cutting crime, but many police chiefs were skeptical. Foot patrol, in their eyes, had been pretty much discredited. It reduced the mobility of the police, who thus had difficulty responding to citizen calls for service, and it weakened headquarters control over patrol officers.

Many police officers also disliked foot patrol, but for different reasons: It was hard work, it kept them outside on cold, rainy nights, and it reduced their chances for making a "good pinch." In some departments, assigning officers to foot patrol had been used as a form of punishment. And academic experts on policing doubted that foot patrol would have any impact on crime rates; it was, in the opinion of most, little more than a sop to public opinion. But since the state was paying for it, the local authorities were willing to go along.

Five years after the program started, the Police Foundation, in Washington, D. C., published an evaluation of the foot-patrol project. Based on its analysis of a carefully controlled experiment carried out chiefly in Newark, the foundation concluded, to the surprise of hardly anyone, that foot patrol had not reduced crime rates. But residents of the foot-patrolled neighborhoods seemed to feel more secure than persons in other areas, tended to believe that crime had been reduced, and seemed to take fewer steps to protect themselves from crime (staying at home with the doors locked, for example). Moreover, citizens in the foot patrol areas had a more favorable opinion of the police than did those living elsewhere. And officers walking beats had higher morale, greater job satisfaction, and a more favorable attitude toward citizens in their neighborhoods than did officers assigned to patrol cars.

These findings may be taken as evidence that the skeptics were right—foot patrol has no effect on crime; it merely fools the citizens into thinking that they are safer. But in our view, and in the view of the authors of the Police Foundation study (of whom Kelling was one), the citizens of Newark were not fooled at all. They knew what the foot patrol officers were doing, they knew it was different from what motorized officers do, and they knew that having officers walk beats did in fact make their neighborhoods safer.

But how can a neighborhood be "safer" when the crime rate has not gone down—in fact, may have gone up? Finding the answer requires first that we understand what most often frightens people in public places. Many citizens, of course, are primarily frightened by crime, especially crime involving a sudden, violent attack by a stranger. This risk is very real, in Newark as in many large cities. But we tend to overlook or forget another source of fear—the fear of being bothered by disorderly people. Not violent people, nor, necessarily, criminals, but disreputable or obstreperous or unpredictable people: panhandlers, drunks, addicts, rowdy teenagers, prostitutes, loiterers, the mentally disturbed.

What foot-patrol officers did was to elevate, to the extent they could, the level of public order in these neighborhoods. Though the neighborhoods were predominantly black and the foot patrolmen were mostly white, this "order-maintenance" function of the police was performed to the general satisfaction of both parties.

One of us (Kelling) spent many hours walking with Newark foot-patrol officers to see how they defined "order" and what they did to maintain it. One beat was typical: a busy but dilapidated area in the heart of Newark,

with many abandoned buildings, marginal shops (several of which prominently displayed knives and straight-edged razors in their windows), one large department store, and, most important, a train station and several major bus stops. Though the area was run-down, its streets were filled with people, because it was a major transportation center. The good order of this area was important not only to those who lived and worked there but also to many others, who had to move through it on their way home, to supermarkets, or to factories, etc.

The people on the street were primarily black; the officer who walked the street was white. The people were made up of "regulars" and "strangers." Regulars included both "decent folk" and some drunks and derelicts who were always there but who "knew their place." Strangers were, well, strangers, and viewed suspiciously, sometimes apprehensively. The officer—call him Kelly—knew who the regulars were, and they knew him. As he saw his job, he was to keep an eye on strangers, and make certain that the disreputable regulars observed some informal but widely understood rules. Drunks and addicts could sit on the stoops, but could not lie down. People could drink on side streets, but not at the main intersection. Bottles had to be in paper bags. Talking to, bothering, or begging from people waiting at the bus stop was strictly forbidden. If a dispute erupted between a businessman and a customer, the businessman was assumed to be right, especially if the customer was a stranger. If a stranger loitered, Kelly would ask him if he had any means of support and what his business was; if he gave unsatisfactory answers, he was sent on his way. Persons who broke the informal rules, especially those who bothered people waiting at bus stops, were arrested for vagrancy. Noisy teenagers were told to keep quiet.

These rules were defined and enforced in collaboration with the "regulars" on the street. Another neighborhood might have different rules, but these, everybody understood, were the rules for *this* neighborhood. If someone violated them the regulars not only turned to Kelly for help but also ridiculed the violator. Sometimes what Kelly did could be described as "enforcing the law," but just as often it involved taking informal or extralegal steps to help protect what the neighborhood had decided was the appropriate level of public order. Some of the things he did probably would not withstand a legal challenge.

A determined skeptic might acknowledge that a skilled foot-patrol officer can maintain order but still insist that this sort of "order" has little to do with the real sources of community fear—that is, with violent crime. To a degree, that is true. But two things must be borne in mind. First, outside observers should not assume that they know how much of the anxiety now endemic in many big-city neighborhoods stems from a fear of "real" crime and how much from a sense that the street *is* disorderly, a source of distasteful worrisome encounters. The people of Newark, to judge from their behavior and their remarks to interviewers, apparently assign a high value to public order, and feel relieved and reassured when the police help them maintain that order.

Second, at the community level, disorder and crime are usually inextricably linked, in a kind of developmental sequence. Social psychologists and police officers tend to agree that if a window in a building is broken *and is left unrepaired,* all the rest of the windows will soon be broken. This is as true in nice neighborhoods as in run-down ones. Window-breaking does not necessarily occur on a large scale because some areas are inhabited by determined window-breakers whereas others are populated by window-lovers; rather, one unrepaired broken window is a signal that no one cares, and so breaking more windows costs nothing. (It has always been fun.)

Philip Zimbardo, a Stanford psychologist, reported in 1969 on some experiments testing the broken-window theory. He arranged to have an automobile without license plates parked with its hood up on a street in the Bronx and a comparable automobile on a street in Palo Alto, California. The car in the Bronx was attacked by "vandals" within ten minutes of its "abandonment." The first to arrive were a family—father, mother, and young son—who removed the radiator and battery. Within twenty-four hours, virtually everything of value had been removed. Then random destruction began—windows were smashed, parts torn off, upholstery ripped. Children began to use the car as a playground. Most of the adult "vandals" were well dressed, apparently clean-cut whites. The car in Palo Alto sat untouched for more than a week. Then Zimbardo smashed part of it with a sledgehammer. Soon, passersby were joining in. Within a few hours, the car had been turned upside down and utterly destroyed. Again, the "vandals" appeared to be primarily respectable whites.

Untended property becomes fair game for people out for fun or plunder, and even for people who ordinarily would not dream of doing such things and who probably consider themselves law-abiding. Because of the nature of community life in the Bronx—its anonymity, the frequency with which cars are abandoned and things are stolen or broken, the past experience of "no one caring"—vandalism begins much more quickly than it does in staid Palo Alto, where people have come to believe that private possessions are cared for, and that mischievous behavior is costly. But vandalism can occur anywhere once communal barriers—the sense of mutual regard and the obligations of civility—are lowered by actions that seem to signal that "no one cares."

We suggest that "untended" behavior also leads to the breakdown of community controls. A stable neighborhood of families who care for their homes, mind each other's children, and confidently frown on unwanted intruders can change, in a few years or even a few months, to an inhospitable and frightening jungle. A piece of property is abandoned, weeds grow up, a window is smashed. Adults stop scolding rowdy children; the children, emboldened, become more rowdy. Families move out, unattached adults move in. Teenagers gather in front of the corner store. The merchant asks them to move; they refuse. Fights occur. Litter accumulates. People start drinking in front of the grocery; in time, an inebriate slumps to the sidewalk and is allowed to sleep it off. Pedestrians are approached by panhandlers.

At this point it is not inevitable that serious crime will flourish or violent attacks on strangers will occur. But many residents will think that crime, especially violent crime, is on the rise, and they will modify their behavior accordingly. They will use the streets less often, and when on the streets will stay apart from their fellows, moving with averted eyes, silent lips, and hurried steps. "Don't get involved." For some residents, this growing atomization will matter little, because the neighborhood is not their "home" but "the place where they live." Their interests are elsewhere; they are cosmopolitans. But it will matter greatly to other people, whose lives derive meaning and satisfaction from local attachments rather than worldly involvement; for them, the neighborhood will cease to exist except for a few reliable friends whom they arrange to meet.

Such an area is vulnerable to criminal invasion. Though it is not inevitable, it is more likely that here, rather than in places where people are confident they can regulate public behavior by informal controls, drugs will change hands, prostitutes will solicit, and cars will be stripped. That the drunks will be robbed by boys who do it as a lark and the prostitutes' customers will be robbed by men who do it purposefully and perhaps violently. That muggings will occur.

Among those who often find it difficult to move away from this are the elderly. Surveys of citizens suggest that the elderly are much less likely to be the victims of crime than younger persons, and some have inferred from this that the well-known fear of crime voiced by the elderly' an exaggeration: perhaps we ought not to design special programs to protect older persons; perhaps we should even try to talk them out of their mistaken fears. This argument misses the point. The prospect of a confrontation with an obstreperous teenager or a drunken panhandler can be as fear-inducing for defenseless persons as the prospect of meeting an actual robber; indeed, to a defenseless person, the two kinds of confrontation are often indistinguishable. Moreover, the lower rate at which the elderly are victimized is a measure of the steps they have already taken—chiefly, staying behind locked doors—to minimize the risks they face. Young men are more frequently attacked than older women, not because they are easier or more lucrative targets but because they are on the streets more.

Nor is the connection between disorderliness and fear made only by the elderly. Susan Estrich, of the Harvard Law School, has recently gathered together a number of surveys on the sources of public fear. One, done in Portland, Oregon, indicated that three fourths of the adults interviewed cross to the other side of a street when they see a gang of teenagers; another survey, in Baltimore, discovered that nearly half would cross the street to avoid even a single strange youth. When an interviewer asked people in a housing project where the most dangerous spot was, they mentioned a place where young persons gathered to drink and play music, despite the fact that not a single crime had occurred there. In Boston public housing projects, the greatest fear was expressed by persons living in the buildings where disorderliness and incivility, not crime, were the greatest. Knowing this helps one understand the significance of such otherwise harmless displays, as subway graffiti. As Nathan Glazer has written, the proliferation of graffiti, even when not obscene, confronts the subway rider with the "inescapable knowledge that the environment he must endure for an hour or more a day is uncontrolled and uncontrollable, and that

anyone can invade it to do whatever damage and mischief the mind suggests."

In response to fear, people avoid one another, weakening controls. Sometimes they call the police. Patrol cars arrive, an occasional arrest occurs, but crime continues and disorder is not abated. Citizens complain to the police chief, but he explains that his department is low on personnel and that the courts do not punish petty or first-time offenders. To the residents, the police who arrive in squad cars are either ineffective or uncaring; to the police, the residents are animals who deserve each other. The citizens may soon stop calling the police, because "they can't do anything."

The process we call urban decay has occurred for centuries in every city. But what is happening today is different in at least two important respects. First, in the period before, say, World War II, city dwellers—because of money costs, transportation difficulties, familial and church connections—could rarely move away from neighborhood problems. When movement did occur, it tended to be along public-transit routes. Now mobility has become exceptionally easy for all but the poorest or those who are blocked by racial prejudice. Earlier crime waves had a kind of built-in self-correcting mechanism: the determination of a neighborhood or community to reassert control over its turf. Areas in Chicago, New York, and Boston would experience crime and gang wars, and then normalcy would return, as the families for whom no alternative residences were possible reclaimed their authority over the streets.

Second, the police in this earlier period assisted in that reassertion of authority by acting, sometimes violently, on behalf of the community. Young toughs were roughed up, people were arrested "on suspicion" or for vagrancy, and prostitutes and petty thieves were routed. "Rights" were something enjoyed by decent folk, and perhaps also by the serious professional criminal, who avoided violence and could afford a lawyer.

This pattern of policing was not an aberration or the result of occasional excess. From the earliest days of the nation, the police function was seen primarily as that of a night watchman: to maintain order against the chief threats to order—fire, wild animals, and disreputable behavior. Solving crimes was viewed not as a police responsibility but as a private one. In the March, 1969, *Atlantic,* one of us (Wilson) wrote a brief account of how the police role had slowly changed from maintaining order to fighting crimes. The change began with the creation of private detectives (often ex-criminals), who worked on a contingency-fee basis for individuals who had suffered losses. In time, the detectives were absorbed into municipal police agencies and paid a regular salary; simultaneously, the responsibility for prosecuting thieves was shifted from the aggrieved private citizen to the professional prosecutor. This process was not complete in most places until the twentieth century.

In the 1960s, when urban riots were a major problem, social scientists began to explore carefully the order-maintenance function of the police, and to suggest ways of improving it—not to make streets safer (its original function) but to reduce the incidence of mass violence. Order maintenance became, to a degree, coterminous with "community relations." But, as the crime wave that began in the early 1960s continued without abatement throughout the decade and into the 1970s, attention shifted to the role of the police as crime fighters. Studies of police behavior ceased, by and large, to be accounts of the order-maintenance function and became, instead, efforts to propose and test ways whereby the police could solve more crimes, make more arrests, and gather better evidence. If these things could be done, social scientists assumed, citizens would be less fearful.

A great deal was accomplished during this transition, as both police chiefs and outside experts emphasized the crime-fighting function in their plans, in the allocation of resources, and in deployment of personnel. The police may well have become better crime fighters as a result. And doubtless they remained aware of their responsibility for order. But the link between order maintenance and crime prevention, so obvious to earlier generations, was forgotten.

That link is similar to the process whereby one broken window becomes many. The citizen who fears the ill-smelling drunk, the rowdy teenager, or the importuning beggar is not merely expressing his distaste for unseemly behavior; he is also giving voice to a bit of folk wisdom that happens to be a correct generalization—namely, that serious street crime flourishes in areas in which disorderly behavior goes unchecked. The unchecked panhandler is, in effect, the first broken window. Muggers and robbers, whether opportunistic or professional, believe they reduce their chances of being caught or even identified if

they operate on streets where potential victims are already intimidated by prevailing conditions. If the neighborhood cannot keep a bothersome panhandler from annoying passersby, the thief may reason, it is even less likely to call the police to identify a potential mugger or to interfere if the mugging actually takes place.

Some police administrators concede that this process occurs, but argue that motorized-patrol officers can deal with it as effectively as foot-patrol officers. We are not so sure. In theory, an officer in a squad car can observe as much as an officer on foot; in theory, the former can talk to as many people as the latter. But the reality of police-citizen encounters is powerfully altered by the automobile. An officer on foot cannot separate himself from the street people; if he is approached, only his uniform and his personality can help him manage whatever is about to happen. And he can never be certain what that will be—a request for directions, a plea for help, an angry denunciation, a teasing remark, a confused babble, a threatening gesture.

In a car, an officer is more likely to deal with street people by rolling down the window and looking at them. The door and the window exclude the approaching citizen; they are a barrier. Some officers take advantage of this barrier, perhaps unconsciously, by acting differently if in the car than they would on foot. We have seen this countless times. The police car pulls up to a corner where teenagers are gathered. The window is rolled down. The officer stares at the youths. They stare back. The officer says to one, "C'mere." He saunters over, conveying to his friends by his elaborately casual style the idea that he is not intimidated by authority. "What's your name?" "Chuck." "Chuck who?" "Chuck Jones." "What'ya doing, Chuck?" "Nothin'." "Got a P.O. [parole officer]?" "Nah." "Sure?" "Yeah." "Stay out trouble, Chuckie." Meanwhile, the other boys laugh and exchange comments among themselves, probably at the officer's expense. The officer stares harder. He cannot be certain what is being said, nor can he join in and, by displaying his own skill at street banter, prove that he cannot be "put down." In the process, the officer has learned almost nothing, and the boys have decided the officer is an alien force who can safely be disregarded, even mocked.

Our experience is that most citizens like to talk to a police officer. Such exchanges give them a sense of importance, provide them with the basis for gossip, and allow them to explain to the authorities what is worrying them (whereby they gain a modest but significant sense of having "done something" about the problem). You approach a person on foot more easily, and talk to him more readily than you do a person in a car. Moreover, you can more easily retain some anonymity if you draw an officer aside for a private chat. Suppose you want to pass on a tip about who is stealing handbags, or who offered to sell you a stolen TV. In the inner city, the culprit, in all likelihood, lives nearby. To walk up to a marked patrol car and lean in the window is to convey a visible signal that you are a "fink."

The essence of the police role in maintaining order is to reinforce the informal control mechanisms of the community itself. The police cannot, without committing extraordinary resources, provide a substitute for that informal control. On the other hand, to reinforce those natural forces, the police must accommodate them. And therein lies the problem.

Should police activity on the street be shaped, in important ways, by the standards of the neighborhood rather than by the rules of the state? Over the past two decades, the shift of police from order maintenance to law enforcement has brought them increasingly under the influence of legal restrictions, provoked by media complaints and enforced by court decisions and departmental orders. As a consequence, the order-maintenance functions of the police are now governed by rules developed to control police relations with suspected criminals. This is, we think, an entirely new development. For centuries, the role of the police as watchmen was judged primarily not in terms of its compliance with appropriate procedures, but rather in terms of its attaining a desired objective. The objective was order, an inherently ambiguous term, but a condition that people in a given community recognized when they saw it. The means were the same as those the community itself would employ, if its members were sufficiently determined, courageous, and authoritative. Detecting and apprehending criminals, by contrast, was a means to an end, not an end in itself; a judicial determination of guilt or innocence was the hoped-for result of the law-enforcement mode. From the first, the police were expected to follow rules defining that process, though states differed in how stringent the rules should be. The criminal-apprehension process was always understood to involve individual rights, the violation of which was unacceptable because it meant that the violating officer would

be acting as a judge and jury—and that was not his job. Guilt or innocence was to be determined by universal standards under special procedures.

Ordinarily, no judge or jury ever sees the persons caught up in a dispute over the appropriate level of neighborhood order. That is true not only because most cases are handled informally on the street, but also because no universal standards are available to settle arguments over disorder, and thus a judge may not be any wiser or more effective than a police officer. Until quite recently in many states, and even today in some places, the police make arrests on such charges as "suspicious person" or "vagrancy" or "public drunkenness"—charges with scarcely any legal meaning. These charges exist not because society wants judges to punish vagrants or drunks but because it wants an officer to have the legal tools to remove undesirable persons from a neighborhood when informal efforts to preserve order in the streets have failed.

Once we begin to think of all aspects of police work as involving the application of universal rules under special procedures, we inevitably ask what constitutes an "undesirable person" and why we should "criminalize" vagrancy or drunkenness. A strong and commendable desire to see that people are treated fairly makes us worry about allowing the police to rout persons who are undesirable by some vague or parochial standard. A growing and not-so-commendable utilitarianism leads us to doubt that any behavior that does not "hurt" another person should be made illegal. And thus many of us who watch over the police are reluctant to allow them to perform, in the only way they can, a function that every neighborhood desperately wants them to perform.

This wish to "decriminalize" disreputable behavior that "harms no one"—and thus remove the ultimate sanction the police can employ to maintain neighborhood order—is, we think, a mistake. Arresting a single drunk or a single vagrant who has harmed no identifiable person seems unjust, and in a sense it is. But failing to do anything about a score of drunks or a hundred vagrants may destroy an entire community. A particular rule that seems to make sense in the individual case makes no sense when it is made a universal rule and applied to all cases. It makes no sense because it fails to take into account the connection between one broken window left untended and a thousand broken windows. Of course, agencies other than the police could attend to the problems posed by drunks or the mentally ill, but in most communities—especially where the 'deinstitutionalization' movement has been strong—they do not.

The concern about equity is more serious. We might agree that certain behavior makes one person more undesirable than another, but how do we ensure that age or skin color or national origin or harmless mannerisms will not also become the basis for distinguishing the undesirable from the desirable? How do we ensure, in short, that the police do not become the agents of neighborhood bigotry?

We can offer no wholly satisfactory answer to this important question. We are not confident that there is a satisfactory answer, except to hope that by their selection, training, and supervision, the police will be inculcated with a clear sense of the outer limit of their discretionary authority. That limit, roughly, is this—the police exist to help regulate behavior, not to maintain the racial or ethnic purity of a neighborhood.

Consider the case of the Robert Taylor Homes in Chicago, one of the largest public-housing projects in the country. It is home for nearly 20,000 people, all black, and extends over ninety-two acres along South State Street. It was named after a distinguished black who had been, during the 1940s, chairman of the Chicago Housing Authority. Not long after it opened, in 1962, relations between project residents and the police deteriorated badly. The citizens felt that the police were insensitive or brutal; the police, in turn, complained of unprovoked attacks on them. Some Chicago officers tell of times when they were afraid to enter the homes. Crime rates soared.

Today, the atmosphere has changed. Police-citizen relations have improved—Apparently, both sides learned something from the earlier experience. Recently, a boy stole a purse and ran off. Several young persons who saw the theft voluntarily passed along to the police information on the identity and residence of the thief, and they did this publicly, with friends and neighbors looking on. But problems persist, chief among them the presence of youth gangs that terrorize residents and recruit members in the project. The people expect the police to "do something" about this, and the police are determined to do just that.

But do what? Though the police can obviously make arrests whenever a gang member breaks the law, a gang can form, recruit, and congregate without breaking the law. And only a tiny fraction of gang-related crimes can be solved by an arrest; thus, if an arrest is the only recourse

for the police, the residents' fears will go unassuaged. The police will soon feel helpless, and the residents will again believe that the police "do nothing." What the police in fact do is to chase known gang members out of the project. In the words of one officer, "We kick ass." Project residents both know and approve of this. The tacit police-citizen alliance in the project is reinforced by the police view that the cops and the gangs are the two rival sources of power in the area, and that the gangs are not going to win.

None of this is easily reconciled with any conception of due process or fair treatment. Since both residents and gang members are black, race is not a factor. But it could be. Suppose a white project confronted a black gang, or vice versa. We would be apprehensive about the police taking sides. But the substantive problem remains the same: how can the police strengthen the informal social-control mechanisms of natural communities in order to minimize fear in public places? Law enforcement, per se, is no answer. A gang can weaken or destroy a community by standing about in a menacing fashion and speaking rudely to passersby without breaking the law.

We have difficulty thinking about such matters, not simply because the ethical and legal issues are so complex but because we have become accustomed to thinking of the law in essentially individualistic terms. The law defines *my* rights, punishes *his* behavior, and is applied by *that* officer because of *this* harm. We assume, in thinking this way, that what is good for the individual will be good for the community, and what doesn't matter when it happens to one person won't matter if it happens to many. Ordinarily, those are plausible assumptions. But in cases where behavior that is tolerable to one person is intolerable to many others, the reactions of the others—fear, withdrawal, flight—may ultimately make matters worse for everyone, including the individual who first professed his indifference.

It may be their greater sensitivity to communal as opposed to individual needs that helps explain why the residents of small communities are more satisfied with their police than are the residents of similar neighborhoods in big cities. Elinor Ostrom and her co-workers at Indiana University compared the perception of police services in two poor, all-black Illinois towns—Phoenix and East Chicago Heights—with those of three comparable all-black neighborhoods in Chicago. The level of criminal victimization and the quality of police-community relations appeared to be about the same in the towns and the

Chicago neighborhoods. But the citizens living in their own villages were much more likely than those living in the Chicago neighborhoods to say that they do not stay at home for fear of crime, to agree that the local police have "the right to take any action necessary" to deal with problems, and to agree that the police "look out for the needs of the average citizen." It is possible that the residents and the police of the small towns saw themselves as engaged in a collaborative effort to maintain a certain standard of communal life, whereas those of the big city felt themselves to be simply requesting and supplying particular services on an individual basis.

If this is true, how should a wise police chief deploy his meager forces? The first answer is that nobody knows for certain, and the most prudent course of action would be to try further variations on the Newark experiment, to see more precisely what works in what kinds of neighborhoods. The second answer is also a hedge—many aspects of order-maintenance in neighborhoods can probably best be handled in ways that involve the police minimally, if at all. A busy, bustling shopping center and a quiet, well-tended suburb may need almost no visible police presence. In both cases, the ratio of respectable to disreputable people is ordinarily so high as to make informal social control effective.

Even in areas that are in jeopardy from disorderly elements, citizen action without substantial police involvement may be sufficient. Meetings between teenagers who like to hang out on a particular corner and adults who want to use that corner might well lead to an amicable agreement on a set of rules about how many people can be allowed to congregate, where, and when.

Where no understanding is possible—or if possible, not observed—citizen patrols may be a sufficient response. There are two traditions of communal involvement in maintaining order. One, that of the "community watchmen," is as old as the first settlement of the New World. Until well into the nineteenth century, volunteer watchmen, not policemen, patrolled their communities to keep order. They did so, by and large, without taking the law into their own hands—without, that is, punishing persons or using force. Their presence deterred disorder or alerted the community to disorder that could not be deterred. There are hundreds of such efforts today in communities all across the nation. Perhaps the best known is that of the Guardian Angels, a group of unarmed young persons in distinctive berets and T-shirts, who first came to public attention when they began patrolling the New York City subways but who claim now to have chapters in more than thirty American cities. Unfortunately, we have little information about the effect of these groups on crime. It is possible, however, that whatever their effect on crime, citizens find their presence reassuring, and that they thus contribute to maintaining a sense of order and civility.

The second tradition is that of the "vigilante." Rarely a feature of the settled communities of the East, it was primarily to be found in those frontier towns that grew up in advance of the reach of government. More than 350 vigilante groups are known to have existed; their distinctive feature was that their members did take the law into their own hands, by acting as judge, jury, and often executioner as well as policeman. Today, the vigilante movement is conspicuous by its rarity, despite the great fear expressed by citizens that the older cities are becoming "urban frontiers." But some community-watchmen groups have skirted the line, and others may cross it in the future. An ambiguous case, reported in *The Wall Street Journal,* involved a citizens' patrol in the Silver Lake area of Belleville, New Jersey. A leader told the reporter, "We look for outsiders." If a few teenagers from outside the neighborhood enter it, "we ask them their business," he said. "If they say they're going clown the street to see Mrs. Jones, fine, we let them pass. But then we follow them down the block to make sure they're really going to see Mrs. Jones."

Though citizens can do a great deal, the police are plainly the key to order maintenance. For one thing, many communities, such as the Robert Taylor Homes, cannot do the job by themselves. For another, no citizen in a neighborhood, even an organized one, is likely to feel the sense of responsibility that wearing a badge confers. Psychologists have done many studies on why people fail to go to the aid of persons being attacked or seeking help, and they have learned that the cause is not "apathy" or "selfishness" but the absence of some plausible grounds for feeling that one must personally accept responsibility. Ironically, avoiding responsibility is easier when a lot of people are standing about. On streets and in public places, where order is so important, many people are likely to be "around," a fact that reduces the chance of any one person acting as the agent of the community. The police officer's uniform singles him out as a person who must accept responsibility if asked. In addition, officers, more easily than their fellow citizens, can be expected to distinguish between what is necessary to protect the safety of the street and what merely protects its ethnic purity.

But the police forces of America are losing, not gaining, members. Some cities have suffered substantial cuts in the number of officers available for duty. These cuts are not likely to be reversed in the near future. Therefore, each department must assign its existing officers with great care. Some neighborhoods are so demoralized and crime-ridden as to make foot patrol useless; the best the police can do with limited resources is respond to the enormous number of calls for service. Other neighborhoods are so stable and serene as to make foot patrol unnecessary. The key is to identify neighborhoods at the tipping point—where the public order is deteriorating but not unreclaimable, where the streets are used frequently but by apprehensive people, where a window is likely to be broken at any time, and must quickly be fixed if all are not to be shattered.

Most police departments do not have ways of systematically identifying such areas and assigning officers to them. Officers are assigned on the basis of crime rates (meaning that marginally threatened areas are often stripped so that police can investigate crimes in areas where the situation is hopeless) or on the basis of calls for service (despite the fact that most citizens do not call the police when they are merely frightened or annoyed). To allocate patrol wisely, the department must look at the neighborhoods and decide, from first-hand evidence, where an additional officer will make the greatest difference in promoting a sense of safety.

One way to stretch limited police resources is being tried in some public-housing projects. Tenant organizations hire off-duty police officers for patrol work in their buildings. The costs are not high (at least not per resident), the officer likes the additional income, and the residents feel safer. Such arrangements are probably more successful than hiring private watchmen, and the Newark experiment helps us understand why. A private security guard may deter crime or misconduct by his presence, and he may go to the aid of persons needing help, but he may well not intervene—that is, control or drive away—someone challenging community standards. Being a sworn officer—a "real cop"—seems to give one the confidence, the sense of duty, and the aura of authority necessary to perform this difficult task.

Patrol officers might be encouraged to go to and from duty stations on public transportation and, while on the bus or subway car, enforce rules about smoking, drinking disorderly conduct, and the like. The enforcement need involve nothing more than ejecting the offender (the offense, after all, is not one with which a booking officer or a judge wishes to be bothered). Perhaps the random but relentless maintenance of standards on buses would lead to conditions on buses that approximate the level of civility we now take for granted on airplanes.

But the most important requirement is to think that to maintain order in precarious situations is a vital job. The police know this is one of their functions, and they also believe, correctly, that it cannot be done to the exclusion of criminal investigation and responding to calls. We may have encouraged them to suppose, however, on the basis of our oft-repeated concerns about serious, violent crime, that they will be judged exclusively on their capacity as crime fighters. To the extent that this is the case, police administrators will continue to concentrate police personnel in the highest-crime areas (though not necessarily in the areas most vulnerable to criminal invasion), emphasize their training in the law and criminal apprehension (and not their training in managing street life), and join too quickly in campaigns to decriminalize "harmless" behavior (though public drunkenness, street prostitution, and pornographic displays can destroy a community more quickly than any team of professional burglars).

Above all, we must return to our long-abandoned view that the police ought to protect communities as well as individuals. Our crime statistics and victimization surveys measure individual losses, but they do not measure communal losses. Just as physicians now recognize the importance of fostering health rather than simply treating illness, so the police—and the rest of us—ought to recognize the importance of maintaining intact communities without broken windows.

Think Critically

1. Describe Wilson and Kelling's "broken windows" theory.
2. Do you think that this theory is supported by available evidence? What are some of the potential flaws in it for explaining crime?

SYMBOLIC INTERACTIONISM/ LABELING

LABELING THEORY, OR THE "INTERACTIONIST approach" to deviance, does not focus on the causes of deviance per se, but rather on how certain behaviors come to be labeled as deviant in the first place and how such designations influence future behavior. Whether labeling is actually a "theory" has been debated by sociologists since the term was created. Some have argued that it really isn't a theory since it does not explain the causes of deviance. Rather, it posits a reactive view of deviance, where audience responses are viewed as just as important as the behavior itself. Influenced heavily by the writings of Edwin Lemert, whose initial insights into symbolic interactionism paved the way for future thinking in this area, the labeling approach represents a social-psychological perspective on deviance. A central concept involves what Charles Horton Cooley calls the "social self." Cooley defines the social aspects of the self through his central concept of the "looking-glass self," or how our individual identities revolve around the ways we perceive ourselves. In large part, how we view ourselves (as in a mirror, or looking-glass) depends upon how we think others see us. Our "self feelings" arise from this process, and understanding this dynamic is crucial to understanding how deviant identities are formed.

Edwin Lemert, a preeminent twentieth-century sociologist, had a profound influence on the development of the labeling perspective. In his classic formulation regarding "Primary and Secondary Deviation," Lemert argues that the initial or "primary" causes of deviance were not that important. Of more consequence were the reactions by others to such behaviors. Secondary deviation occurs when the person enacting the deviant behavior organizes his or her identity around these reactions by others.

Stigmatization is a major concept in the sociological study of deviance and refers to a process by which individuals are forced to reconsider their self-identities. In the selection, "Stigma and Social Identity," Erving Goffman describes the concept of stigma and its relevance to the study of deviance. Referring to "an attribute that is deeply discrediting," stigma is a central concept in the labeling approach to deviance. Goffman discusses the different types of stigma and how individuals attempt to manage it in everyday life.

In the article, "On Behalf of Labeling Theory," Erich Goode defends the perspective from critics both within and outside its ranks. Citing the major objections to labeling as a useful perspective in the study of deviance, Goode argues that labeling is important for understanding such behavior even if it isn't a bona fide theory. It is useful, he claims, for examining specific features of deviance, through the introduction of what he identifies as "sensitizing concepts." These ideas can then be used for analyzing the social processes that take place between the commission of a deviant act and the acquisition of a deviant identity.

The Social Self*

Charles Horton Cooley

THE SOCIAL SELF IS SIMPLY ANY IDEA, OR system of ideas, drawn from the communicative life, that the mind cherishes as its own. Self-feeling has its chief scope *within* the general life, not outside of it. . . .

That the "I" of common speech has a meaning which includes some sort of reference to other persons is involved in the very fact that the word and the ideas it stands for are phenomena of language and the communicative life. It is doubtful whether it is possible to use language at all without thinking more or less distinctly of someone else, and certainly the things to which we give names and which have a large place in reflective thought are almost always those which are impressed upon us by our contact with other people. Where there is no communication there can be no nomenclature and no developed thought. What we call "me," "mine," or "myself" is, then, not something separate from the general life, but the most interesting part of it, a part whose interest arises from the very fact that it is both general and individual. That is, we care for it just because it is that phase of the mind that is living and striving in the common life, trying to impress itself upon the minds of others. "I" is a militant social tendency, working to hold and enlarge its place in the general current of tendencies. So far as it can it waxes, as all life does. To think of it as apart from society is a palpable absurdity of which no one could be guilty who really *saw* it as a fact of life. . . .

The reference to other persons involved in the sense of self may be distinct and particular, as when a boy is ashamed to have his mother catch him at something she has forbidden, or it may be vague and general, as when one is ashamed to do something which only his conscience, expressing his sense of social responsibility, detects and disapproves; but it is always there. There is no sense of "I," as in pride or shame, without its correlative sense of you, or he, or they. Even the miser gloating over his hidden gold can feel the "mine" only as he is aware of the world of men over whom he has secret power; and the case is very similar with all kinds of hidden treasure. Many painters, sculptors, and writers have loved to withhold their work from the world, fondling it in seclusion until they were quite done with it; but the delight in this, as in all secrets, depends upon a sense of the value of what is concealed. . . .

We think of the body as "I" when it comes to have social function or significance, as when we say "I am looking well today," or "I am taller than you are." We bring it into the social world, for the time being, and for that reason, put our self-consciousness into it. Now it is curious, though natural, that in precisely the same way we may call any inanimate object "I" with which we are identifying our will and purpose. This is notable in games, like golf or croquet, where the ball is the embodiment of the player's fortunes. You will hear a man say, "I am in the long grass down by the third tee," or "I am in position for the middle arch." So a boy flying a kite will say, "I am higher than you," or one shooting at a mark will declare that he is just below the bullseye.

In a very large and interesting class of cases the social reference takes the form of a somewhat definite imagination of how one's self—that is any idea he appropriates—appears in a particular mind, and the kind of self-feeling one has is determined by the attitude toward this attributed to

*"The Social Self" by Charles H. Cooley, *Human Nature and the Social Order* (New York: Charles Scribner's Sons), 1902, pp. 179–185, 259–260.

that other mind. A social self of this sort might be called the reflected or looking-glass self:

"*Each to each a looking-glass*
Reflects the other that doth pass."

As we see our face, figure, and dress in the glass, and are interested in them because they are ours, and pleased or otherwise with them according as they do or do not answer to what we should like them to be, so in imagination we perceive in another's mind some thought of our appearance, manners, aims, deeds, character, friends, and so on, and are variously affected by it.

A self-idea of this sort seems to have three principal elements: the imagination of our appearance to the other person; the imagination of his judgment of that appearance, and some sort of self-feeling, such as pride or mortification. The comparison with a looking-glass hardly suggests the second element, the imagined judgment, which is quite essential. The thing that moves us to pride or shame is not the mere mechanical reflection of ourselves, but an imputed sentiment, the imagined effect of this reflection upon another's mind. This is evident from the fact that the character and weight of that other, in whose mind we see ourselves, makes all the difference with our feeling. We are ashamed to seem evasive in the presence of a straightforward man, cowardly in the presence of a brave one, gross in the eyes of a refined one, and so on. We always imagine, and in imagining share, the judgments of the other mind. A man will boast to one person of an action—say some sharp transaction in trade—which he would be ashamed to own to another.

It should be evident that the ideas that are associated with self-feeling and form the intellectual content of the self cannot be covered by any simple description, as by saying that the body has such a part in it, friends such a part, plans so much, etc., but will vary indefinitely with particular temperaments and environments. The tendency of the self, like every aspect of personality, is expressive of far-reaching hereditary and social factors, and is not to be understood or predicted except in connection with the general life. Although special, it is in no way separate—speciality and separateness are not only different but contradictory, since the former implies connection with a whole. The object of self-feeling is affected by the general course of history, by the particular development of nations, classes, and professions, and other conditions of this sort.

The truth of this is perhaps most decisively shown in the fact that even those ideas that are most generally associated or colored with the "my" feeling, such as one's idea of his visible person, of his name, his family, his intimate friends, his property, and so on, are not universally so associated, but may be separated from the self by peculiar social conditions. . . .

The peculiar relations to other persons attending any marked personal deficiency or peculiarity are likely to aggravate, if not to produce, abnormal manifestations of self-feeling. Any such trait sufficiently noticeable to interrupt easy and familiar intercourse with others, and make people talk and think *about* a person or *to* him rather than *with* him, can hardly fail to have this effect. If he is naturally inclined to pride or irritability, these tendencies, which depend for correction upon the flow of sympathy, are likely to be increased. One who shows signs of mental aberration is, inevitably perhaps, but cruelly, shut off from familiar, thoughtless intercourse, partly excommunicated; his isolation is unwittingly proclaimed to him on every countenance by curiosity, indifference, aversion, or pity, and insofar as he is human enough to need free and equal communication and feel the lack of it, he suffers pain and loss of a kind and degree which others can only faintly imagine, and for the most part ignore. He finds himself apart, "not in it," and feels chilled, fearful, and suspicious. Thus "queerness" is no sooner perceived than it is multiplied by reflection from other minds. The same is true in some degree of dwarfs, deformed or disfigured persons, even the deaf and those suffering from the infirmities of old age.

Think Critically

1. What are the basic ideas contained in Cooley's explanation of the social self?
2. Why do you think that the social self is an important concept in the study of deviance? Why does it matter?

Primary and Secondary Deviation*

Edwin M. Lemert

Sociopathic Individuation

The deviant person is a product of differentiating and isolating processes. Some persons are individually differentiated from others from the time of birth onward, as in the case of a child born with a congenital physical defect or repulsive appearance, and as in the case of a child born into a minority racial or cultural group. Other persons grow to maturity in a family or in a social class where pauperism, begging, or crime are more or less institutionalized ways of life for the entire group. In these latter instances the person's sociopsychological growth may be normal in every way, his status as a deviant being entirely caused by his maturation within the framework of social organization and culture designated as "pathological" by the larger society. This is true of many delinquent children in our society.[1]

It is a matter of great significance that the delinquent child, growing up in the delinquency areas of the city, has very little access to the cultural heritages of the larger conventional society. His infrequent contacts with this larger society are for the most part formal and external. Quite naturally his conception of moral values is shaped and molded by the moral code prevailing in his play groups and the local community in which he lives . . . the young delinquent has very little appreciation of the meaning of the traditions and formal laws of society. . . . Hence the conflict between the delinquent and the agencies of society is, in its broader aspects, a conflict of divergent cultures.

The same sort of gradual, unconscious process which operates in the socialization of the deviant child may also be recognized in the acquisition of socially unacceptable behavior by persons after having reached adulthood. However, with more verbal and sophisticated adults, step-by-step violations of societal norms tend to be progressively rationalized in the light of what is socially acceptable. Changes of this nature can take place at the level of either overt or covert behavior, but with a greater likelihood that adults will preface overt behavior changes with projective symbolic departures from society's norms. When the latter occur, the subsequent overt changes may appear to be "sudden" personality modifications. However, whether these changes are completely radical ones is to some extent a moot point. One writer holds strongly to the opinion that sudden and dramatic shifts in behavior from normal to abnormal are seldom the case, that a sequence of small preparatory transformations must be the prelude to such apparently sudden behavior changes. This writer is impressed by the day-by-day growth of "reserve potentialities" within personalities of all individuals, and he contends that many normal persons carry potentialities for abnormal behavior, which, given proper conditions, can easily be called into play.[2]

Personality Changes Not Always Gradual

This argument is admittedly sound for most cases, but it must be taken into consideration that traumatic experiences often speed up changes in personality.[3] Nor can the "trauma" in these experiences universally be attributed to the unique way in which the person conceives of the experience subjectively. Cases exist to show that personality modifications can be telescoped or that there can be an acceleration of such changes caused largely by the intensity and variety of the social stimulation. Most soldiers undoubtedly have entirely different conceptions of their roles after intensive combat experience. Many admit to having "lived a lifetime" in a relatively short period of time after they have been under heavy fire in battle for the first time. Many generals have remarked that their men have to be a little "shooted" or "blooded" in order to become good soldiers. In the process of group formation, crises and interactional amplification are vital requisites to forging true, role-oriented group behavior out of individuated behavior.[4]

The importance of the person's conscious symbolic reactions to his or her own behavior cannot be overstressed in explaining the shift from normal to abnormal behavior or from one type of pathological behavior to another, particularly where behavior variations become systematized or structured into pathological roles. This is not to say that conscious choice is a determining factor in the differentiating process. Nor does it mean that the awareness of the self is a purely conscious perception. Much of the process of self-perception is doubtless marginal from the point of view of consciousness.[5] But however it may be perceived, the individual's self-definition is closely connected with such things as self-acceptance, the subordination of minor to major roles, and with the motivation involved in learning the skills, techniques, and values of a new role. *Self-definitions or self-realizations are likely to be the result of sudden perceptions and they are especially significant when they are followed immediately by overt demonstrations of the new role they symbolize.* The self-defining junctures are critical points of personality genesis and in the special case of the atypical person, they mark a division between two different types of deviation.

Primary and Secondary Deviation

There has been an embarrassingly large number of theories, often without any relationship to a general theory, advanced to account for various specific pathologies in human behavior. For certain types of pathology, such as alcoholism, crime, or stuttering, there are almost as many theories as there are writers on these subjects. This has been occasioned in no small way by the preoccupation with the origins of pathological behavior and by the fallacy of confusing *original* causes with *effective* causes. All such theories have elements of truth, and the divergent viewpoints they contain can be reconciled with the general theory here if it is granted that original causes or antecedents of deviant behaviors are many and diversified. This holds especially for

the psychological processes leading to similar pathological behavior, but it also holds for the situational concomitants of the initial aberrant conduct. A person may come to use excessive alcohol not only for a wide variety of subjective reasons, but also because of diversified situational influences, such as the death of a loved one, business failure, or participating in some sort of organized group activity calling for heavy drinking of liquor. Whatever the original reasons for violating the norms of the community, they are important only for certain research purposes, such as assessing the extent of the "social problem" at a given time or determining the requirements for a rational program of social control. From a narrower sociological viewpoint the deviations are not significant until they are organized subjectively and transformed into active roles and become the social criteria for assigning status. The deviant individuals must react symbolically to their own behavior aberrations and fix them in their socio-psychological patterns. The deviations remain primary deviations or symptomatic and situational as long as they are rationalized or otherwise dealt with as functions of a socially acceptable role. Under such conditions normal and pathological behaviors remain strange and somewhat tensional bedfellows in the same person. Undeniably a vast amount of such segmental and partially integrated pathological behavior exists in our society and has impressed many writers in the field of social pathology.

Just how far and for how long a person may go in dissociating his sociopathic tendencies so that they are merely troublesome adjuncts of normally conceived roles is not known. Perhaps it depends upon the number of alternative definitions of the same overt behavior that he can develop; perhaps certain physiological factors (limits) are also involved. However, if the deviant acts are repetitive and have a high visibility, and if there is a severe societal reaction, which, through a process of identification is incorporated as part of the "me" of the individual, the probability is greatly increased that the integration of existing roles will be disrupted and that reorganization based upon a new role or roles will occur. (The "me" in this context is simply the subjective aspect of the societal reaction.) Reorganization may be the adoption of another normal role in which the tendencies previously defined as "pathological" are given a more acceptable social expression. The other general possibility is the assumption of a deviant role, if such exists; or, more rarely, the person may organize an aberrant sect or group in which he creates a special role of his own. *When a person begins to employ his deviant behavior or a role based upon it as a means of defense, attack, or adjustment to the overt and covert problems created by the consequent societal reaction to him, his deviation is secondary.* Objective evidences of this change will be found in the symbolic appurtenances of the new role, in clothes, speech, posture, and mannerisms, which in some cases heighten social visibility, and which in some cases serve as symbolic cues to professionalization.

Role Conceptions of the Individual Must Be Reinforced by Reactions of Others

It is seldom that one deviant act will provoke a sufficiently strong societal reaction to bring about secondary deviation, unless in the process of introjection the individual imputes or projects meanings into the social situation which are not present. In this case anticipatory fears are involved. For example, in a culture where a child is taught sharp distinctions between "good" women and "bad" women, a single act of questionable morality might conceivably have a profound meaning for the girl so indulging. However, in the absence of reactions by the person's family, neighbors, or the larger community, reinforcing the tentative "bad-girl" self-definition, it is questionable whether a transition to secondary deviation would take place. It is also doubtful whether a temporary exposure to a severe punitive reaction by the community will lead a person to identify himself with a pathological role, unless, as we have said, the experience is highly traumatic. Most frequently there is a progressive reciprocal relationship between the deviation of the individual and the societal reaction, with a compounding of the societal reaction out of the minute accretions in the deviant behavior, until a point is reached where ingrouping and outgrouping between society and the deviant is manifest.[6] At this point a stigmatizing of the deviant occurs in the form of name calling, labeling, or stereotyping.

The sequence of interaction leading to secondary deviation is roughly as follows: (1) primary deviation; (2) social penalties; (3) further primary deviation; (4) stronger penalties and rejections; (5) further deviation, perhaps with hostilities and resentment beginning to focus upon those doing the penalizing; (6) crisis reached in the tolerance quotient, expressed in formal action by the community stigmatizing of the deviant; (7) strengthening of the deviant conduct as a reaction to the stigmatizing and penalties; (8) ultimate acceptance of deviant social status and efforts at adjustment on the basis of the associated role.

As an illustration of this sequence the behavior of an errant schoolboy can be cited. For one reason or another, let us say excessive energy, the schoolboy engages in a classroom prank. He is penalized for it by the teacher. Later, due to clumsiness, he creates another disturbance and again he is reprimanded. Then, as something happens, the boy is blamed for something he did not do. When the teacher uses the tag "bad boy" or "mischief maker" or other invidious terms, hostility and resentment are excited in the boy, and he may feel that he is blocked in playing the role expected of him. Thereafter, there may be a strong temptation to assume his role in the class as defined by the teacher, particularly when he discovers that there are rewards as well as penalties deriving from such a role. There is, of course, no implication here that such boys go on to become delinquents or criminals, for the mischief-maker role may later become integrated with or retrospectively rationalized as part of a role more acceptable to school authorities.[7] If such a boy continues this unacceptable role and becomes delinquent, the process must be accounted for in the light of the general theory of this volume. There must be a spreading corroboration of a sociopathic self-conception and societal reinforcement at each step in the process.

The most significant personality changes are manifest when societal definitions and their subjective counterpart become generalized. When this happens, the range of major role choices becomes narrowed to one general class.[8] This was very obvious in the case of a young girl who was the daughter of a paroled convict and who was attending a small Middle Western college. She continually argued with herself and with the author, in whom she had confided, that in reality she belonged on the "other side of the railroad tracks" and that her life could be enormously simplified by acquiescing in this verdict and living accordingly. While in her case there was a tendency to dramatize her conflicts, nevertheless there was enough societal reinforcement of her self-conception by the treatment she received in her relationship with her father and on dates with college boys to lend it a painful reality. Once these boys took her home to the shoddy dwelling in a slum area where she lived with her father, who was often in a drunken condition, they abruptly stopped seeing her again or else became sexually presumptive.

NOTES

1. Shaw, C., *The Natural History of a Delinquent Career,* Chicago, 1941, pp. 75–76. Quoted by permission of the University of Chicago Press, Chicago.
2. Brown, L. Guy, *Social Pathology,* 1942, pp. 44–45.
3. Allport, G., *Personality, A Psychological Interpretation,* 1947, p. 57.
4. Slavson, S. R., *An Introduction to Group Psychotherapy,* 1943, pp. 10, 229ff.
5. Murphy, G., *Personality,* 1947, p. 482.
6. Mead, G., "The Psychology of Punitive Justice," *American Journal of Sociology,* 23 March, 1918, pp. 577–602.
7. Evidence for fixed or inevitable sequences from predelinquency to crime is absent. Sutherland, E. H., *Principles of Criminology,* 1939, 4th ed., p. 202.
8. Sutherland seems to say something of this sort in connection with the development of criminal behavior. *Ibid.,* p. 86.

Think Critically

1. What does Lemert mean by primary and secondary deviation?
2. How does Lemert's analysis contribute to the understanding of deviance? In what ways do you feel it says something important about reactions or labeling?

Stigma and Social Identity*

Erving Goffman

THE GREEKS, WHO WERE APPARENTLY STRONG on visual aids, originated the term *stigma* to refer to bodily signs designed to expose something unusual and bad about the moral status of the signifier. The signs were cut or burnt into the body and advertised that the bearer was a slave, a criminal, or a traitor—a blemished person, ritually polluted, to be avoided, especially in public places. Later, in Christian times, two layers of metaphor were added to the term: the first referred to bodily signs of holy grace that took the form of eruptive blossoms on the skin; the second, a medical allusion to this religious allusion, referred to bodily signs of physical disorder. Today the term is widely used in something like the original literal sense, but is applied more to the disgrace itself than to the bodily evidence of it. Furthermore, shifts have occurred in the kinds of disgrace that arouse concern. Students, however, have made little effort to describe the structural preconditions of stigma, or even to provide a definition of the concept itself. It seems necessary, therefore, to try at the beginning to sketch in some very general assumptions and definitions.

Preliminary Conceptions

Society establishes the means of categorizing persons and the complement of attributes felt to be ordinary and natural for members of each of these categories. Social settings establish the categories of persons likely to be encountered there. The routines of social intercourse in established settings allow us to deal with anticipated others without special attention or thought. When a stranger comes into our presence, then, first appearances are likely to enable us to anticipate his category and attributes, his "social identity"—to use a term that is better than "social status" because personal attributes such as "honesty" are involved, as well as structural ones, like "occupation."

We lean on these anticipations that we have, transforming them into normative expectations into righteously presented demands.

Typically, we do not become aware that we have made these demands or aware of what they are until an active question arises as to whether or not they will be fulfilled. It is then that we are likely to realize that all along we had been making certain assumptions as to what the individual before us ought to be. Thus, the demands we make might better be called demands made "in effect," and the character we impute to the individual might better be seen as an imputation made in potential retrospect—a characterization "in effect," a *virtual social identity*. The category and attributes he could in fact be proved to possess will be called his *actual social identity.*

While the stranger is present before us, evidence can arise of his possessing an attribute that makes him different from others in the category of persons available for him to be, and of a less desirable kind—in the extreme, a person who is quite thoroughly bad, or dangerous, or weak. He is thus reduced in our minds from a whole and usual person to a tainted, discounted one. Such an attribute is a stigma, especially when its discrediting effect is very extensive; sometimes it is also called a failing, a shortcoming, a handicap. It constitutes a special discrepancy between virtual and actual social identity. Note that there are other types of discrepancy between virtual and actual social identity, for example the kind that causes us to reclassify an individual from one socially anticipated category to a different but equally well-anticipated one, and the kind that causes us to alter our estimation of the individual upward. Note, too, that not all undesirable attributes are at issue, but only those which are incongruous with our stereotype of what a given type of individual should be.

The term stigma, then, will be used to refer to an attribute that is deeply discrediting, but it should be seen that a language of relationships, not attributes, is really needed. An attribute that stigmatizes one type of possessor can confirm the usualness of another, and therefore is neither creditable nor discreditable as a thing in itself. For example, some jobs in America cause holders without the expected college education to conceal this fact; other jobs, however, can lead the few of their holders who have a higher education to keep this a secret, lest they be marked as failures and outsiders. Similarly, a middle class

boy may feel no compunction in being seen going to the library; a professional criminal, however, writes:

> I can remember before now on more than one occasion, for instance, going into a public library near where I was living, and looking over my shoulder a couple of times before I actually went in just to make sure no one who knew me was standing about and seeing me do it.[1]

So, too, an individual who desires to fight for his country may conceal a physical defect, lest his claimed physical status be discredited; later, the same individual, embittered and trying to get out of the army, may succeed in gaining admission to the army hospital, where he would be discredited if discovered in not really having an acute sickness.[2] A stigma, then, is really a special kind of relationship between attribute and stereotype, although I don't propose to continue to say so, in part because there are important attributes that almost everywhere in our society are discrediting.

The term stigma and its synonyms conceal a double perspective: Does the stigmatized individual assume his differentness is known about already or is evident on the spot, or does he assume it is neither known about by those present nor immediately perceivable by them? In the first case one deals with the plight of the *discredited,* in the second with that of the *discreditable.* This is an important difference, even though a particular stigmatized individual is likely to have experience with both situations. I will begin with the situation of the discredited and move on to the discreditable but not always separate the two.

Three grossly different types of stigma may be mentioned. First there are abominations of the body—the various physical deformities. Next there are blemishes of individual character perceived as weak will, domineering or unnatural passions, treacherous and rigid beliefs, and dishonesty, these being inferred from a known record of, for example, mental disorder, imprisonment, addiction, alcoholism, homosexuality, unemployment, suicidal attempts, and radical political behavior. Finally there are the tribal stigma of race, nation, and religion, these being stigma that can be transmitted through lineages and equally contaminate all members of a family.[3] In all of these various instances of stigma, however, including those the Greeks had in mind, the same sociological features are found: An individual who might have been received easily in ordinary social intercourse possesses a trait that can obtrude itself upon attention and turn those of us whom he meets away from him, breaking the claim that his other attributes have on us. He possesses a stigma, an undesired differentness from what we had anticipated. We and those who do not depart negatively from the particular expectations at issue I shall call the *normals.*

The attitudes we normals have toward a person with a stigma, and the actions we take in regard to him, are well known, since these responses are what benevolent social action is designed to soften and ameliorate. By definition, of course, we believe the person with a stigma is not quite human. On this assumption we exercise varieties of discrimination, through which we effectively, if often unthinkingly, reduce his life chances. We construct a stigma-theory, an ideology to explain his inferiority and account for the danger he represents, sometimes rationalizing an animosity based on other differences, such as those of social class.[4] We use specific stigma terms such as cripple, bastard, moron in our daily discourse as a source of metaphor and imagery, typically without giving thought to the original meaning.[5] We tend to impute a wide range of imperfections on the basis of the original one,[6] and at the same time to impute some desirable but undesired attributes, often of a supernatural cast, such as "sixth sense," or "understanding":[7]

> For some, there may be a hesitancy about touching or steering the blind, while for others, the perceived failure to see may be generalized into a gestalt of disability, so that the individual shouts at the blind as if they were deaf or attempts to lift them as if they were crippled. Those confronting the blind may have a whole range of belief that is anchored in the stereotype. For instance, they may think they are subject to unique judgment, assuming the blinded individual draws on special channels of information unavailable to others.[8]

Further, we may perceive his defensive response to his situation as a direct expression of his defect, and then see both defect and response as just retribution for something he or his parents or his tribe did, and hence a justification of the way we treat him.[9]

Now turn from the normal to the person he is normal against. It seems generally true that members of a social category may strongly support a standard of judgment that they and others agree does not directly apply to them. Thus it is that a businessman may demand womanly behavior from females or ascetic behavior from monks, and not construe himself as someone who ought to realize either of these styles of conduct. The distinction is between realizing a norm and merely supporting it. The issue of stigma does not arise here, but only where there is some expectation on all sides that those in a given category should not only support a particular norm but also realize it . . .

Moral Career

Persons who have a particular stigma tend to have similar learning experiences regarding their plight, and similar changes in conception of self—a similar "moral career" that is both cause and effect of commitment to a similar sequence of personal adjustments. (The natural history of a category of persons with a stigma must be clearly distinguished from the natural history of the stigma itself—the history of the origins, spread, and decline of the capacity of an attribute to serve as a stigma in a particular society, for example, divorce in American upper middle class society.) One phase of this socialization process is that through which the stigmatized person learns and incorporates the standpoint of the normal, acquiring thereby the identity beliefs of the wider society and a general idea of what it would be like to possess a particular stigma. Another phase is that through which he learns that he possesses a particular stigma and, this time in detail, the consequence of possessing it. The timing and interplay of these two initial phases of the moral career form important patterns, establishing the foundation for later development, and providing a means of distinguishing among the moral careers available to the stigmatized. Four such patterns may be mentioned.

One pattern involves those with an inborn stigma who become socialized into their disadvantageous situation even while they are learning and incorporating the standards against which they fall short.[10] For example, an orphan learns that children naturally and normally have parents, even while he is learning what it means not to have any. After spending the first sixteen years of his life in the institution, he can later still feel that he naturally knows how to be a father to his son.

A second pattern derives from the capacity of a family, and to a much lesser extent a local neighborhood, to constitute itself a protective capsule, for its young. Within such a capsule, a congenitally stigmatized child can be carefully sustained by means of information control.

Self-belittling definitions of him are prevented from entering the charmed circle, while broad access is given to other conceptions held in the wider society, ones that lead the encapsulated child to see himself as a fully qualified ordinary human being, of normal identity in terms of such basic matters as age and sex.

The point in the protected individual's life when the domestic circle can no longer protect him will vary by social class, place of residence, and type of stigma, but in each case will give rise to a moral experience when it occurs. Thus, public school entrance is often reported as the occasion of stigma learning, the experience sometimes coming very precipitously on the first day of school, with taunts, teasing, ostracism, and fights.[11] Interestingly, the more the child is "handicapped" the more likely he is to be sent to a special school for persons of his kind, and the more abruptly he will have to face the view which the public at large takes of him. He will be told that he will have an easier time of it among "his own," and thus learn that the own he thought he possessed was the wrong one, and that this lesser own is really his. It should be added that where the infantilely stigmatized manages to get through his early school years with some illusions left, the onset of dating or job-getting will often introduce the moment of truth. In some cases, merely an increased likelihood of incidental disclosure is involved:

> I think the first realization of my situation, and the first intense grief resulting from this realization, came one day, very casually, when a group of us in our early teens had gone to the beach for the day. I was lying on the sand, and I guess the fellows and girls thought I was asleep. One of the fellows said, "I like Domenica very much, but I would never go out with a blind girl." I cannot think of any prejudice which so completely rejects you.[12]

In other cases, something closer to systematic exposure is involved, as a cerebral palsy victim suggests:

> With one extremely painful exception, as long as I was in the protective custody of family life or college schedules and lived without exercising my rights as an adult citizen, the forces of society were kindly and unruffling. It was after college, business school, and innumerable stretches as a volunteer worker on community projects that I was often bogged down by the medieval prejudices and superstitions of the business world. Looking for a job was like standing before a firing squad. Employers were shocked that I had the gall to apply for a job.[13]

A third pattern of socialization is illustrated by one who becomes stigmatized late in life, or learns late in life that he has always been discreditable—the first involving no radical reorganization of his view of his past, the second involving this factor. Such an individual has thoroughly learned about the normal and the stigmatized long before he must see himself as deficient. Presumably he will have a special problem in reidentifying himself, and a special likelihood of developing disapproval of self:

> When I smelled an odor on the bus or subway before the colostomy I used to feel very annoyed. I'd think that the people were awful, that they didn't take a bath or that they should have gone to the bathroom before traveling. I used to think that they might have odors from what they ate. I used to be terribly annoyed; to me it seemed that they were filthy, dirty. Of course, at the least opportunity I used to change my seat and if I couldn't it used to go against my grain. So naturally, I believe that the young people feel the same way about me if I smell.[14]

While there are certainly cases of individuals discovering only in adult life that they belong to a stigmatized tribal group or that their parents have a contagious moral blemish, the usual case here is that of physical handicaps that "strike" late in life:

> But suddenly I woke up one morning, and found that I could not stand. I had had polio, and polio was as simple as that. I was like a very young child who had been dropped into a big, black hole, and the only thing I was certain of was that I could not get out unless someone helped me. The education, the lectures, and the parental training which I had received for twenty-four years didn't seem to make me the person who could do anything for me now. I was like everyone else—normal, quarrelsome, gay, full of plans, and all of a sudden something happened! Something happened and I became a stranger. I was a greater stranger to myself than to anyone. Even my dreams did not know me. They did not know what they ought to let me do—and when I went to dances or to parties in them, there was always an odd provision or limitation—not spoken of or mentioned, but there just the same. I suddenly had the very confusing mental and emotional conflict of a lady leading a double life. It was unreal and it puzzled me, and I could not help dwelling on it.[15]

Here the medical profession is likely to have the special job of informing the infirm who he is going to have to be.

A fourth pattern is illustrated by those who are initially socialized in an alien community, whether inside or outside the geographical boundaries of the normal society, and who then must learn a second way of being that is felt by those around them to be the real and valid one.

It should be added that when an individual acquires a new stigmatized self late in life, the uneasiness he feels about new associates may slowly give way to uneasiness felt concerning old ones. Post-stigma acquaintances may see him simply as a faulted person; pre-stigma acquaintances, being attached to a conception of what he once was, may be unable to treat him either with formal tact or with familiar full acceptance:

> My task [as a blind writer interviewing prospective clients for his literary product] was to put the men I'd come to see at their ease—the reverse of the usual situation. Curiously, I found it much easier to do with men I'd never met before. Perhaps this was because with strangers there was no body of reminiscences to cover before business could be gotten down to and so there was no unpleasant contrast with the present.[16]

Regardless of which general pattern the moral career of the stigmatized individual illustrates, the phase of experience during which he learns that he possesses a stigma will be especially interesting, for at this time he is likely to be thrown into a new relationship to others who possess the stigma too.

In some cases, the only contact the individual will have with his own is a fleeting one, but sufficient nonetheless to show him that others like himself exist:

> When Tommy came to the clinic the first time, there were two other little boys there, each with a congenital absence of an ear. When Tommy saw them, his right hand went slowly to his own defective ear, and he turned with wide eyes to his father and said, "There's another boy with an ear like mine."[17]

In the case of the individual who has recently become physically handicapped, fellow sufferers more advanced than himself in dealing with the failing are likely to make him a special series of visits to welcome him to the club and to instruct him in how to manage himself physically and psychically:

> Almost my first awareness that there are mechanics of adjustment came to me with the comparison of two fellow patients I had at the Eye and Ear Infirmary. They used to visit me as I lay abed and I came to know them

fairly well. Both had been blind for seven years. They were about the same age—a little past thirty—and both had college educations.[18]

In the many cases where the individual's stigmatization is associated with his admission to a custodial institution such as a jail, sanatorium, or orphanage, much of what he learns about his stigma will be transmitted to him during prolonged intimate contact with those in the process of being transformed into his fellow-sufferers.

As already suggested, when the individual first learns who it is that he must now accept as his own, he is likely, at the very least, to feel some ambivalence; for these others will not only be patently stigmatized, and thus not like the normal person he knows himself to be, but may also have other attributes with which he finds it difficult to associate himself. What may end up as a freemasonry may begin with a shudder. A newly blind girl on a visit to The Lighthouse directly from leaving the hospital provides an illustration:

> My questions about a guide dog were politely turned aside. Another sighted worker took me in tow to show me around. We visited the Braille library; the classrooms; the clubrooms where the blind members of the music and dramatic groups meet; the recreation hall where on festive occasions the blind dance with the blind; the bowling alleys where the blind play together; the cafeteria, where all the blind gather to eat together; the huge workshops where the blind earn a subsistence income by making mops and brooms, weaving rugs, caning chairs. As we moved from room to room, I could hear the shuffling of feet, the muted voices, the tap-tap-tapping of canes. Here was the safe, segregated world of the sightless—a completely different world, I was assured by the social worker, from the one I had just left. . . . I was expected to join this world. To give up my profession and to earn my living making mops. The Lighthouse would be happy to teach me how to make mops. I was to spend the rest of my life making mops with other blind people, eating with other blind people, dancing with other blind people. I became nauseated with fear, as the picture grew in my mind. Never had I come upon such destructive segregation.[19]

Given the ambivalence built into the individual's attachment to his stigmatized category, it is understandable that oscillations may occur in his support of, identification with, and participation among his own. There will be "affiliation cycles" through which he comes to accept the special opportunities for in-group participation or comes to reject them after having accepted them before.[20] There will be corresponding oscillations in belief about the nature of own group and the nature of normals. For example, adolescence (and the high school peer group) can bring a marked decline in own-group identification and a marked increase in identification with normals.[21] The later phases of the individual's moral career are to be found in these shifts of participation and belief.

The relationship of the stigmatized individual to the informal community and formal organizations of his own kind is, then, crucial. This relationship will, for example, mark a great difference between those whose differentness provides them very little of a new "we," and those, such as minority group members, who find themselves a part of a well-organized community with long-standing traditions—a community that makes appreciable claims on loyalty and income, defining the member as someone who should take pride in his illness and not seek to get well. In any case, whether the stigmatized group is an established one or not, it is largely in relation to this own-group that it is possible to discuss the natural history and the moral career of the stigmatized individual.

In reviewing his own moral career, the stigmatized individual may single out and retrospectively elaborate experiences which serve for him to account for his coming to the beliefs and practices that he now has regarding his own kind and normals. A life event can thus have a double bearing on moral career, first as immediate objective grounds for an actual turning point, and later (and easier to demonstrate) as a means of accounting for a position currently taken. One experience often selected for this latter purpose is that through which the newly stigmatized individual learns that full-fledged members of the group are quite like ordinary human beings:

> When I [a young girl turning to a life of vice and first meeting her madam] turned into Fourth Street my courage again failed me, and I was about to beat a retreat when Mamie came out of a restaurant across the street and warmly greeted me. The porter, who came to the door in response to our ring, said that Miss Laura was in her room, and we were shown in. I saw a woman comely and middle-aged, who bore no resemblance to the horrible creature of my imagination. She greeted

me in a soft, well-bred voice, and everything about her so eloquently spoke of her potentialities for motherhood that instinctively I looked around for the children who should have been clinging to her skirts.[22]

Another illustration is provided by a homosexual in regard to his becoming one:

> I met a man with whom I had been at school. . . . He was, of course, gay himself, and took it for granted that I was, too. I was surprised and rather impressed. He did not look in the least like the popular idea of a homosexual, being well-built, masculine, and neatly dressed. This was something new to me. Although I was perfectly prepared to admit that love could exist between men, I had always been slightly repelled by the obvious homosexuals whom I had met because of their vanity, their affected manner, and their ceaseless chatter. These, it now appeared, formed only a small part of the homosexual world, although the most noticeable one. . . .[23]

A cripple provides a similar statement:

> If I had to choose one group of experiences that finally convinced me of the importance of this problem [of self-image] and that I had to fight my own battles of identification, it would be the incidents that made me realize with my heart that cripples could be identified with characteristics other than their physical handicap. I managed to see that cripples could be comely, charming, ugly, lovely, stupid, brilliant—just like all other people, and I discovered that I was able to hate or love a cripple in spite of his handicap.[24]

It may be added that in looking back to the occasion of discovering that persons with his stigma are human beings like everyone else, the individual may bring to bear a later occasion when his pre-stigma friends imputed unhumanness to those he had by then learned to see as full-fledged persons like himself. Thus, in reviewing her experience as a circus worker, a young girl sees first that she had learned her fellow-workers are not freaks, and second that her pre-circus friends fear for her having to travel in a bus along with other members of the troupe.[25]

Another turning point—retrospectively if not originally—is the isolating, incapacitating experience, often a period of hospitalization, which comes later to be seen as the time when the individual was able to think through his problem, learn about himself, sort out his situation, and arrive at a new understanding of what is important and worth seeking in life.

It should be added that not only are personal experiences retrospectively identified as turning points, but experiences once removed may be employed in this way. For example, a reading of the literature of the group may itself provide an experience felt and claimed as reorganizing:

> I do not think it is claiming too much to say that *Uncle Tom's Cabin* was a fair and truthful panorama of slavery; however that may be, it opened my eyes as to who and what I was and what my country considered me; in fact, it gave me my bearing.[26]

NOTES

1. T. Parker and R. Allerton, *The Courage of His Convictions* (London: Hutchinson & Co., 1962), p. 109.

2. In this connection see the review by M. Meltzer, "Countermanipulation through Malingering," in A. Biderman and H. Zimmer, eds., *The Manipulation of Human Behavior* (New York: John Wiley & Sons, 1961), pp. 277–304.

3. In recent history, especially in Britain, low class status functioned as an important tribal stigma, the sins of the parents, or at least their milieu, being visited on the child, should the child rise improperly far above his initial station. The management of class stigma is of course a central theme in the English novel.

4. D. Riseman, "Some Observations Concerning Marginality," *Phylon,* Second Quarter, 1951, 122.

5. The case regarding mental patients is presented by T. J. Scheff in a forthcoming paper.

6. In regard to the blind, see E. Henrich and L. Kriegel, eds., *Experiments in Survival* (New York: Association for the Aid of Crippled Children, 1961), pp. 152 and 186; and H. Chevigny, *My Eyes Have a Cold Nose* (New Haven, Conn.: Yale University Press, paperbound, 1962), p. 201.

7. In the words of one blind woman, "I was asked to endorse a perfume, presumably because being sightless my sense of smell was super-discriminating." See T. Keitlen (with N. Lobsenz), *Farewell to Fear* (New York: Avon, 1962), p. 10.

8. A. G. Gowman, *The War Blind in American Social Structure* (New York: American Foundation for the Blind, 1957), p. 198.

9. For examples, see Macgregor *et al., op. cit.,* throughout.

10. Discussion of this pattern can be found in A. R. Lindesmith and A. L. Strauss, *Social Psychology,* rev. ed. (New York: Holt, Rinehart & Winston, 1956), pp. 180–183.

11. An example from the experience of a blind person may be found in R. Criddle, *Love Is Not Blind* (New York: W. W. Norton & Company, 1953), p. 21; the experience of a dwarfed person is reported in H. Viscardi, Jr., *A Man's Stature* (New York: The John Day Company, 1952), pp. 13–14.

12. Henrich and Kriegel, *op. cit.,* p. 186.

13. *Ibid.,* p. 156.

14. Orbach *et al., op. cit.,* p. 165.

15. N. Linduska, *My Polio Past* (Chicago: Pellegrini and Cudahy, 1947), p. 177.

16. Chevigny, *op. cit.,* p. 136.

17. Macgregor *et al., op. cit.,* pp. 19–20.

18. Chevigny, *op. cit.,* p. 35.

19. Keitlen, *op. cit.,* pp. 37–38. A description of the early vicissitudes of a hospitalized polio patient's identification with fellow-cripples is provided in Linduska, *op. cit.,* pp. 159–165. A fictional account of racial reidentification is provided by J. W. Johnson, *The Autobiography of an Ex-Coloured Man,* rev. ed. (New York: Hill and Wang, American Century Series, 1960), pp. 22–23.

20. A general statement may be found in two of E. C. Hughes' papers, "Social Change and Status Protest," *Phylon,* First Quarter, 1949, 58–65, and "Cycles and Turning Points," in *Men and Their Work* (New York: Free Press of Glencoe, 1958).

21. M. Yarrow, "Personality Development and Minority Group Membership," in M. Sklare, *The Jews* (New York: Free Press of Glencoe, 1960), pp. 468–470.

22. *Madeleine, An Autobiography* (New York: Pyramid Books, 1961), pp. 36–37.

23. P. Wildeblood, *Against the Law* (New York: Julian Messner, 1959), pp. 23–24.

24. Carling, *op. cit.,* p. 21.

25. C. Clausen, *I Love You Honey But the Season's Over* (New York: Holt, Rinehart & Winston, 1961), p. 217.

26. Johnson, *op. cit.,* p. 42. Johnson's novel, like others of its kind, provides a nice instance of myth-making, being a literary organization of many of the crucial moral experiences and crucial turning points retrospectively available to those in a stigmatized category.

Think Critically

1. What are the various components of stigma according to Goffman? Which ones strike you as most useful in understanding the phenomenon? Why?

2. How does the concept of stigma allow a better understanding of deviant behavior? Give some examples.

On Behalf of Labeling Theory*

Erich Goode**

BY THE EARLY 1960S, LABELING THEORY HAD become the major approach in the sociology of deviant behavior. But by the early 1970s, the antilabeling stance became almost as fashionable as labeling had been a decade earlier. The interim witnessed many dozens of critiques. Most—although not all—share three fundamental flaws. First, they tend to be polemical rather than constructive. Instead of urging labeling theorists to sharpen their conceptual tools with the proffered criticisms, their authors seem intent on *extirpating* labeling theory. A second problem with these critiques is that they rarely render a faithful likeness of the original. The perspective has typically been caricatured, made to affirm principles that no labeling theorist has ever written or believed. Third, and most important: Our critics seem incapable of recognizing the crucial difference between what specific labeling theorists have (supposedly) written in specific works and the potential power of the perspective, where future deviance theorists could go with the perspective's root concepts and insights were they to be systematically rethought and developed.

I would like to re-examine a number of key concepts and assertions made both by critics of labeling theory and by authors seen as labeling theorists. I intend to offer a commentary on the validity of these criticisms, a stock-taking of what has and has not been said by the "reactive" perspective, and some thoughts on where a labeling perspective should take us—even if it has not yet done so.

A convincing case could be made for the assertion that labeling theory does not exist in the first place. A field has been fabricated by observers and critics out of the raw material of a few arresting passages, phrases and concepts. Examined carefully, the ideas of the supposed school's adherents sound increasingly less alike, at times revealing more discord than the harmony marking a genuine tradition of thought.

It has been said that the concept of "secondary deviation" is central to labeling theory (Schur, 1971:10). However, the author of this concept, Edwin Lemert, rejects what may be the key idea in any "reactive" perspective in the study of deviance: that the relationship between action and reaction is problematic. Lemert, in counterpoint, invokes "objective aspects of deviance" and "values universal in nature" (1972:22). Consequently, it is difficult to comprehend just what might be meant when it is asserted that Edwin Lemert is a labeling theorist . . .

Howard Becker's work is more frequently cited than that of any other labeling theorist. Yet Becker has written a number of illuminating comments on the "straw theory" nearly everyone takes to be labeling theory (1973). Labeling theory, Becker writes, is, first of all, not a *theory* in the strict sense of the word as it is generally understood. Second, it wasn't meant to "explain" deviant behavior; it is not the literal "cause" of the acts evaluated in the first place. Third: Public stigmatization is neither a necessary nor a sufficient condition for an individual's commitment to a career in deviance. Becker agrees with Cohen (1965) in stating that this is an empirical question; no theory can simply assume it. Last, not only should labeling theory not be called a theory, it probably shouldn't be called "labeling" anything. Since the literal application

*© 1975 by The Society for the Study of Social Problems. Reprinted from *Social Problems*, 22 (June, 1975), pp. 570–583 by permission of the author and the publisher.

**This paper is part of a larger investigation supported by a fellowship from the John Simon Guggenheim Memorial Foundation; I am grateful for its generous support. In addition, the Research Foundation of the State University of New York permitted me a summer unencumbered by teaching responsibilities by awarding me a Faculty Research Fellowship. I would also like to thank Gerald Suttles, Forrest Dill, Robert Stevenson, and Terry J. Rosenberg for critical comments on an earlier draft of this paper; they have been most helpful.

of a negative label to specific individuals committing specific acts is neither the most essential nor even the most fundamental process within the scope of this perspective, perhaps the term "labeling" should be dropped altogether. Becker, along with Rubington and Weinberg (1973), suggests the "interactionist" perspective . . .

This "subjectivistic" view troubles many sociologists. In commenting on the current stress on interpretations of deviant behavior rather than on the behavior itself, Hirschi argues for a return to viewing categories of behavior in terms of objective criteria: "The person may not have committed a 'deviant' act, but he did (in many cases) do *something*. . . And it is just possible that . . . if he were left alone he would *do it again*" (Hirschi, 1973:169). "Extreme relativism," agrees Edwin Lemert, "leaves the unfortunate impression that almost any meaning can be assigned to human attributes and actions."

> Practically all societies in varying degrees and ways disapprove of incest, adultery, promiscuity, cruelty to children, laziness, disrespect for parents and elders, murder, rape, theft, lying and cheating. Perhaps the point to make is that certain kinds of actions are likely to be judged deleterious in any context . . . It is not so much that they violate rules as it is that they destroy, downgrade, or jeopardize values universal in nature (Lemert, 1972:22).

One problem with these assertions is that none of the forms of behavior mentioned comprises a universally agreed-upon category. Just what is regarded as incest isn't the same everywhere; different societies regard different sets of potential sex partners as incestuous. In some civilizations only members of one's immediate family, plus aunts, uncles and grandparents qualify. In others, "the interpretation of incest is so broad as to include as potential sex partners half the available population" (Ford and Beach, 1951:113) . . .

Everything is not relative, of course; the college sophomore's banalization of a basically powerful idea seems to make a travesty of it. (In fact, a diluted "objectivism," if properly understood, can be seen as a kind of relativism, because looking at categories as having universal properties is only one of many viable, available perspectives that could be adopted by an observer—in this case, someone usually called a "social scientist.") There is a definite utility to looking at social behavior in an "objectivistic" fashion. The point is that while adopting subjective categories and realities will yield crucial consequences and payoffs, adopting objective categories and realities constructed by social scientists but not seen by participants also has important consequences and payoffs.

Empathy

Hirschi (1973) is troubled by the use of empathy in the social sciences. He feels that understanding the world through the eyes of the deviant leads the researcher into an empirical blunder: It blinds the sociologist to the less attractive features of deviance.

Being empathetic means that we have to come as close to the behavior under study as we possibly can, given the limitations of our biography, morality, and ideology. Empathy means that the sociologist has mentally, emotionally, and experientially to enter the world of the people he or she wishes to understand. Advocates do not claim that this is the only acceptable means of studying deviance. It does mean that the practitioner of deviant behavior often sees the world in a fairly distinct fashion. It is therefore a crucial and theoretically fruitful dimension of deviance.

This approach has also been called "appreciative" sociology (Matza, 1969:15–40). Perhaps this term is a bit misleading. Deviants may despise what they do or themselves for doing it—witness the child molester (McCaghy, 1967), the stripper (Skipper and McCaghy, 1970), the alcoholic. To assume that prostitutes necessarily enjoy their work would be to fall victim to the "happy hooker" syndrome (Goode and Troiden, 1974:108). In short, deviants may not "appreciate" their own behavior at all. If we were to assume that they do would be anything but empathetic. Their "appreciation" of their deviant behavior is an empirical question.

Empathy does not mean being conned or duped by our subject, by the practitioner of the deviant behavior we study. It does not, above all, indicate a simple-minded gullibility. In fact, it means the reverse: To be conned is to be the victim of an external social facade the deviant presents to the outside world. To empathize is to see the world from a first-hand perspective, to acquire an insider's view, and hence, to recognize the nature of the con job being presented to and believed by those not practiced or adept in the art of empathy. The subject—the deviant—is acutely aware of the fronts he or she presents to the world. Empathy involves knowing just how these fronts operate, not believing in their validity . . .

Empathy does not mean *surrender,* either; it does not mean that the deviant "is always right." Ideological systems describing, explaining and justifying one's own behavior tend to be detailed and subtle. (Although those describing other people's are often shallow and simplified.) Outsiders who are not plugged into what people think and say about what they do, who they are, and what they believe, gloss over the filigree-like fertility of their subjects' worldview. Deviants do not present an "I am always right" impression to one another, nor to themselves. (Perhaps the paranoid is an exception.) But they do to outsiders.

Nuts, Sluts, and Preverts

A sizable proportion of sociological writings on deviance within the labeling tradition has investigated what has come to be called the *nuts, sluts, and deviated preverts* variety of behavior (Liazos, 1972). The study of deviance concentrates on condemned and stigmatized behavior and people; what is studied is specifically only that which is included within these circumscribed boundaries. This means that deviance sociologists have to ignore a great deal of behavior and people that do not fit in with the formal definition, but are similar in interesting ways. This past fascination with dramatic and "immoral" behavior has led to ignoring "the unethical, illegal and destructive actions of powerful individuals, groups and institutions in our society" (Liazos, 1972:111). The "value engaged labelists" express their "class bias" by focusing on the behavior of the powerless and ignoring that of the powerful. In so doing, they avoid examining the workings of the power elite in the drama of deviant behavior, thereby supporting the status quo (Thio, 1973).

This is a valid characterization and criticism of labeling theory as it has been practiced specifically and historically. But critics of this stripe make the assumption that the blunder is inherent to the labeling perspective. In fact, this restriction on what behavior a "reactive" viewpoint can and cannot examine and what levels of society it delves into is entirely self-imposed. I will argue that it is not a logical or a necessary implication of labeling theory. The "interactionist" perspective toward deviance does not automatically restrict our attention to "nuts, sluts, and preverts," to the deviance of the powerless; it can direct our attention to the very phenomena these critics wish to examine. Far from being a kind of ringside seat on a

parade of freaks, weirdos, and colorful characters, our perspective should insist on raising the question why certain kinds of acts tend to be condemned while others are not. Inevitably this leads to an examination of the distribution of power in the society under study.

As sociologists further back than Sutherland have pointed out, the thief in the white collar steals far more from the public pocket than the conventional street criminal. If we were to ask a cross section of the public why crimes such as armed robbery and burglary should receive stiff penalties, the typical reply would be that they represent a great "threat to society." The same public is indifferent toward, fails to condemn—and yet, is being bilked by—the white collar criminal. Why? A recent estimate of bank losses indicated that bank robbers stole approximately 27 million dollars in 1973, while in the same year approximately 150 million was stolen by the bank's own trusted employees. Yet armed robbery was considered significantly more "serious" a crime to a sample of respondents than embezzlement (Rossi, et al., 1974). The public loses incalculably more again from corporate crimes and yet condemns them even less. Which, then, is more deviant? . . .

An adequate understanding of labeling theory demands that damaging but respectable (i.e., non-deviant) behavior be studied. These disjunctions between public condemnation and "objective" social damage should intrigue us. If we define deviance by public condemnation, we have to find out both the "why" of it—why some behavior attracts a label of immorality—was well as the "why not": why other forms of behavior are not considered immoral. We can never fully understand what is deviant until we get a good look at what isn't. By looking at both, we realize that it is not "social cost" nor any "objective threat to society" that accounts for behavior labeled as deviant or crystallized into formal law. We couldn't deal with this issue if we concentrated exclusively on deviant (or criminal) behavior itself . . .

What is Deviance? Who is the Deviant?

Pushed to its logical extreme, the idea of relativity is self-defeating. If what is considered deviant is relative generally to time and place, it is relative even more specifically to each individual instance of time and place. Judgments of the reactions to behavior vary not only across societies and contexts in general, but across specific situations as well. It follows that what is deviance is completely *sui generis* and literally emergent out of actually occurring instances of behavior and reactions to behavior. This is Pollner's "Model II" version of deviance: "the deviant character of the act . . .depends upon, or more emphatically, is constituted by the subsequent response of the community. . . .There is no deviance apart from the response. . . . If the labeling is constitutive of deviance, then the fact that no one reacts to an act as deviant means that it is not deviant" (Pollner, 1974:29, 33).

It becomes impossible, adopting this view, to predict a priori whether a given act will be judged as deviance until we know whether it already has been so judged. Behavior that has escaped the scrutiny and condemnation by alters is not deviant at all. If act A is identical in all respects to act B, differing only in that A has been observed and condemned while B has not, then A is an instance of deviance and B is not. Becker tried to bridge this chasm by introducing the distinction between *deviance* and *rule-breaking* behavior (1963:14), thereby creating a form of behavior that formally breaks the rules but is not perceived as deviance—"secret deviance" (1963:20). But by employing the dimension of literal condemnation "secret deviance" is not deviant at all; it could not exist within Becker's scheme. Of all aspects of his model, perhaps this conceptual difficulty attracted more criticism than any other. It pleased no one, including Becker himself.

Becker's later formulation attempted to resolve this problem. It is not necessary to call behavior deviant if and only if it has already been condemned. Certain acts can be considered deviant "because these acts are likely to be defined as deviant when discovered" (Becker, 1973:181). Referring to his earlier conceptualization of "secret" deviance, Becker comments: "If we begin by saying that an act is deviant when it is so defined, what can it mean to call an act an instance of secret deviance? Since no one has defined it as deviant it cannot, by definition, be deviant; but 'secret' indicates that *we* know it is deviant, even if no one else does" (1973:187). This difficulty forces us to refer to certain acts as *potentially* deviant. Acts have differing degrees of probability attached to them of being condemned. If we knew the situations in which they occurred and the characteristics of the various actors involved, we would have a clearer idea of just what these probabilities

are. This probabilistic conception of deviance permits us to transcend the dilemma that plagued earlier theorists. Behavior is deviant, then, "if it falls within a class of behavior for which there is probability of negative sanctions subsequent to its detection" (Black and Reiss, 1970:63) . . .

If we can determine what deviance is a priori (without turning into a value consensus theorist), does the same hold for identifying the deviant? The word "deviant" is, of course, both an adjective and a noun. Used as an adjective, as in "deviant behavior," it has the same meanings as, but is simply grammatically different from, "deviance." "Deviant" takes on a radically different meaning if it is used as a noun. We all know that *doing* deviance is not the same thing as *being a deviant*. And that one possible avenue to becoming "a" deviant is through the application of a stigmatizing label—Tannenbaum's "dramatization of evil" (1938:19). In this sense to be a deviant is to have one's entire character publicly discredited, tainted, and morally damned. A deviant is one who is widely thought to be routinely immoral by others, who is seen to "belong" to a collectively stigmatized group or category, whose behavior has become so scandalous to others that he or she is thought to be the sort of person who is expected to do immoral, evil, disgraceful, diabolical, irritating things. By this definition, one may be a deviant only if one has, in fact, already been collectively condemned by others.

However, this process of public labeling is atypical. Most of the people who would be considered "deviants" were their behavior to become known to the general public do not conform to this definition. Most people who claim affiliation with a stigmatized group or category never themselves literally become publicly stigmatized as deviants . . .

Some students of behavior are distressed by the fact that the concepts "deviance" and "deviant" are not precisely parallel. By the definitions I proposed here, it is possible to know in advance (roughly, at any rate) what acts stand a high likelihood of being judged as deviant by specific relevant audiences. This is not acceptable for defining individuals as "deviants," however. Acts can be regarded as potentially deviant; people cannot. When we refer to behavior, contingencies *constitute* the character of the act. When we refer to people, contingencies *qualify* their character. When we think of or refer to behavior, ancillary features may or may not render it an instance of a larger, deviant, form of behavior (to a specific audience, of course). "Killing" by itself is not necessarily regarded as deviance; the extenuating circumstances and the contextual features of the act determine whether it is a deviant form of killing, i.e., murder. The many contingencies and auxiliary aspects, its context, the motives regarded as acceptable, are sufficiently qualifying *as to classify it altogether.* These can, however, be spelled out. To cite another instance, one ethnomethodologists are especially fond of, to throw a baby out of a 10-story window is usually taken to be an instance of "insanity." But if the man who does it is a fireman, the building is in flames, and there is a safety net below, it is seen as an instance of "heroism," not madness. The extenuating features of the behavior do not merely qualify it—they constitute it.

It is quite otherwise with the attachment of a deviant label to specific individuals. People can be many more things than a drunk, an adulterer, an embezzler. Conventional audiences are often willing to admit that, yes, he did a horrible thing—but he's not a horrible *man*. The power of ancillary and contingent features of the individuals in question to determine their deviant status is sufficiently great as to demand that we reserve judgment concerning whether or not a given perpetrator of a clearly deviant act is, in fact, *a* deviant until we know his or her relevant qualifying features, and what they mean to relevant audiences. The escalation from deviant acts to deviant character type is sufficiently problematic that the only way of dealing with the problem is to reserve judgment until learning whether a given individual *has already* been regarded as a deviant by relevant audiences—including himself or herself. Specific people live biographical and historical lives; abstract acts are frozen in time. In addition, the passage of time washes many sins away. The compilation of additional features that are conventional or praiseworthy does not render the deviant acts of the past respectable, but they may render the individual respectable.

Conclusion

Labeling theory isn't a theory at all. Perhaps it isn't even as grandiose an edifice as a general perspective. It is merely one way of looking not at deviance in general, but at some specific *features* of deviance. Aspects of labeling theory are relevant for some issues in examining deviant behavior and irrelevant for many others. Some of the basic and fundamental issues raised by labeling theorists—what

something is, what category it "belongs" to, what is deviant, who is a deviant—are always relevant, even when examining deviance in a fairly conventional fashion. But accepting the importance of these issues does not mean, as Hirschi (1973:169–170) seems to have concluded, that this makes deviance "impossible to study." It does mean that the first step in the study of deviance has to be a consideration of these crucial issues. The exquisitely reciprocal relationship between action and reaction makes a simple study of "pure" behavior extremely misleading. Included within the scope of what behavior *is* has to be what it *means*—to the various relevant audiences. Hirschi is incorrect in saying that this makes the study of deviance impossible. But what it does mean is that the issues he takes to be "straightforward empirical questions" quite simply aren't.

Beyond this, a number of critics have pointed out labeling theory's limited scope. The question of etiology, for example (Gibbs, 1966) may very well be beyond the scope of labeling theory; it was never intended to be an explanation of causality. Of course, it would help those studying etiology to specify just what they are trying to find the cause of. But no one would hold that labeling creates a given form of behavior de novo. There may be forms of behavior on which labeling has some etiological impact, but generally, this avenue is unlikely to prove fruitful.

Far from a theory of deviance, the major ideas in labeling theory are at the level of what Herbert Blumer (1969:147–151) calls *sensitizing concepts.* The simple fact of the limitations of the scope of labeling theory is rarely recognized; if it is, it is taken as a devastating defect. Commentators discuss the labeling issue as if different theories are in stiff competition, or locked in mortal combat. "Theoretical" discussions degenerate into polemics; making a point is equated with blasting an opponent's arguments into oblivion. Perhaps if there is anything like a universal rule, I suppose it would be this: The bombardier always attracts more attention than the bricklayer.

REFERENCES

Becker, Howard S. 1963. *Outsiders: Studies in the Sociology of Deviance.* New York: Free Press.

———. 1973. "Labeling theory reconsidered." In *Outsiders,* 2nd edition.

Black, Donald J., and Albert J. Reiss, Jr. 1970. "Police control of juveniles." *American Sociological Review* 35 (February): 63–77.

Blumer, Herbert. 1969. *Symbolic Interactionism: Perspective and Method.* Englewood Cliffs, N.J.: Prentice Hall.

Cohen, Albert K. 1965. "The sociology of the deviant act: anomie theory and beyond." *American Sociological Review* 30 (February): 5–14.

Ford, Clellan S., and Frank A. Beach. 1951. *Patterns of Sexual Behavior.* New York: Harper and Row.

Gibbs, Jack P. 1966. "Conceptions of deviant behavior: the old and the new." *Pacific Sociological Review 9* (Spring): 9–14.

Goode, Erich. 1972. *Drugs in American Society.* New York: Alfred Knopf.

Goode, Erich, and Richard R. Troiden (eds.) 1974. *Sexual Deviance and Sexual Deviants.* New York: William Morrow.

Hirschi, Travis. 1973. "Procedural rules and the study of deviance." *Social Problems* 21 (Fall): 159–173.

Liazos, Alexander. 1972. "The poverty of the sociology of deviance: nuts, sluts, and preverts." *Social Problems 20* (Summer): 103–120.

Matza, David. 1969. *Becoming Deviant.* Englewood Cliffs, N.J.: Prentice Hall.

McCaghy, Charles. 1967. "Child molesters: a study of their careers as deviants." In Marshall B. Clinard and Richard Quinney, *Criminal Behavior Systems: A Typology.* New York: Holt, Rinehart and Winston.

Pollner, Melvin. 1974. "Sociological and common-sense models of the labeling process." In Roy Turner (ed.), *Ethnomethodology: Selected Readings.* Baltimore: Penguin Books.

Rossi, Peter H., et al. 1974. "The seriousness of crimes: normative structure and individual differences." *American Sociological Review* 39 (April): 224–237.

Rubington, Earl, and Martin S. Weinberg (eds.). 1973. *Deviance: The Interactionist Perspective.* New York: Macmillan, 2nd edition.

Schur, Edwin M. 1971. *Labeling Deviant Behavior.* New York: Harper and Row.

Skipper, James K., Jr., and Charles McCaghy. 1970. "Stripteasers: the anatomy and career contingencies of a deviant occupation." *Social Problems* 17 (Winter): 391–405.

Tannenbaum, Frank. 1938. *Crime and the Community.* New York: Columbia University Press.

Thio, Alex. 1973. "Class bias in the sociology of deviance." *The American Sociologist* 8 (February): 1–12.

Think Critically

1. What are some of the shortcomings that Goode notes regarding labeling theory? Which ones do you feel are the most serious? Why?
2. Do you feel that Goode provides reasonable answers to critics of labeling? Why or why not? Give two examples.

CONFLICT THEORY

CONFLICT THEORIES OF DEVIANT BEHAVIOR are of several types, but all of them focus on the central element of power in defining deviance and its social control. Conflict theorists (unlike functionalists) do not believe that societal consensus maintains social order. On the contrary, they assert that most societies are made up of groups with conflicting values, and those with the most power will define certain behaviors of weaker groups as deviant or criminal. Generally, there are cultural, political, economic, and Marxian versions of conflict theory.

In one of the earlier American formulations of the idea of conflict theory as it relates to deviance and crime, Thorsten Sellin introduces the idea of conflicts of cultural codes. Earlier researchers, such as Louis Wirth, had maintained that such conflict was "internal," or that cultural conflict manifested itself as mental conflict in the individual. Wirth postulated that choosing between the norms of divergent cultures led some into lawbreaking. Sellin counters this by arguing that deviance and crime can occur in the absence of any mental conflict whatsoever between norms, and uses an example of a Sicilian father who killed the teenage seducer of his daughter and then expressed surprise at his arrest. He was simply "defending the family's honor" and was behaving in line with norms from the old country. No mental or internal conflict was necessary for the criminal act to occur, but external conflict existed between cultural codes which led to the lawbreaking.

Steven Spitzer's article, "Toward a Marxian Theory of Deviance," lays out the basic tenets of Marxian analysis and applies them to the study of deviance. Marx's writings did not attend much to matters of deviance and crime. Spitzer's analysis draws out the implications of Marxian theory for both the creation and control of deviance and explains how, in a class society, deviance and crime are more likely to be found in the "lowest sediment" of the relative surplus population. Elements of this population may threaten the established order of production, and must be controlled if existing economic relations are to

be preserved. He predicts that as this class is more clearly defined, it becomes more problematic in terms of control, and that more of the state's resources are necessary to effect this end.

Alexander Liazos' piece, "The Poverty of the Sociology of Deviance," provides an important challenge that the field of deviance become more inclusive of forms of deviance in society. Liazos posits in the early 1970s that at that time, the study of deviance largely neglected deviant behaviors of the political and economic elite, and that despite their claims, sociologists had ignored the role of power in defining deviance. Drawing on the work of C. Wright Mills, he argues that while the field had progressed since the 1940s, when Mills wrote, it was still biased in terms of the subjects it chose for study. One neglected area, introduced by Liazos, is what he terms "covert institutional violence," which is built into the social structure itself. Liazos also claims that the effort by some sociologists to show that deviants are not so much different than conformists is defeated by the fact that certain categories of behavior, but not others, are focused on. His forceful argument against the exclusive emphasis on "nuts, sluts, and preverts" (intentionally misspelled in the original) has helped to broaden and diversify the study of deviance over the past two decades.

The classic work by William J. Chambliss, "A Sociological Analysis of the Law of Vagrancy," examines the emergence of vagrancy laws in England, and how they were influenced by political and economic forces of the time. Developed to control labor, vagrancy laws in England (and later in the U.S.) have also been used to control "the undesirable, the criminal and the 'nuisance.'" Equally important, Chambliss provides historical evidence to support class-based explanations for the development of criminal law. The original vagrancy laws, he claims, reflected a socially perceived necessity to provide cheap labor as serfdom was breaking down in Europe and the pool of available labor was low. As feudalism disappeared, however, the laws became dormant. Later, as economic conditions changed and commerce became more important, they were refocused towards "rogues," "vagabonds" and especially "roadmen" who preyed upon citizens transporting goods.

In "Government and State Crime" by Stephen Rosoff, Henry Pontell, and Robert Tillman document how norm— and rule-breaking by government entities themselves have caused widespread damage and harm, not only to individual victims, but to communities, nations, and the world. Among other topics discussed are the use of human guinea pigs in government-sponsored research and dangerous experiments; violations of sovereignty of foreign nations; the infamous "Iran-Contra" scandal involving the highest levels of the U.S. government; various abuses of power by agencies of the federal government, including the recent use of, and official justifications for, torture; and the case that has come to symbolize the abuse of political power and government crime in America: Watergate.

In "Street Crime, Labor Surplus, and Criminal Punishment, 1980–1990," Andrew Hochstetler and Neal Shover find support for the Neo-Marxian idea that the criminal justice system becomes increasingly punitive as surplus labor increases. Using a more theoretically appropriate sample and methodology, they find—independent effects of violent street crime, the proportion of young males in the population, and labor surplus on the use of imprisonment by the state. The study supports Marxian conflict theory in that it provides evidence that the state's punishment mechanism responds not only to levels of actual criminality, but to economic conditions in which certain populations (e.g., the unemployed) need to be controlled as well. They relate these findings to policy concerns regarding punishment and other social problems and the allocation of limited resources to help resolve these issues.

The Conflict of Conduct Norms*

Thorsten Sellin

Culture Conflicts As Conflicts of Cultural Codes

. . . There are social groups on the surface of the earth which possess complexes of conduct norms which, due to differences in the mode of life and the social values evolved by these groups, appear to set them apart from other groups in many or most respects. We may expect conflicts of norms when the rural dweller moves to the city, but we assume that he has absorbed the basic norms of the culture which comprises both town and country. How much greater is not the conflict likely to be when Orient and Occident meet, or when the Corsican mountaineer is transplanted to the

lower East Side of New York. Conflicts of cultures are inevitable when the norms of one cultural or subcultural area migrate to or come in contact with those of another. . . .

Conflicts between the norms of the divergent cultural codes may arise

1. when these codes clash on the border of contiguous culture areas;
2. when, as may be the case with legal norms, the law of one cultural group is extended to cover the territory of another; or
3. when members of one cultural group migrate to another.[1]

Speck, for instance, notes that "where the bands popularly known as Montagnais have come more and more into contact with whites, their reputation has fallen lower among the traders who have known them through

*"The Conflict of Conduct Norms," by Thorsten Sellin. Reprinted from *The Social Science Research Council Bulletin*, 41 (1938), pp. 63–70, by permission of The Social Science Research Council.

commercial relationships within that period. The accusation is made that they have become less honest in connection with their debts, less trustworthy with property, less truthful, and more inclined to alcoholism and sexual freedom as contacts with the frontier towns have become easier for them. Richard White reports in 1933 unusual instances of Naskapi breaking into traders' store houses."[2]

Similar illustrations abound in the works of the cultural anthropologists. We need only to recall the effect on the American Indian of the culture conflicts induced by our policy of acculturation by guile and force. In this instance, it was not merely contact with the white man's culture, his religion, his business methods, and his liquor, which weakened the tribal mores. In addition, the Indian became subject to the white man's law and this brought conflicts as well, as has always been the case when legal norms have been imposed upon a group previously ignorant of them. Maunier,[3] in discussing the diffusion of French law in Algeria, recently stated:

> In introducing the *Code Penal* in our colonies, as we do, we transform into offenses the ancient usages of the inhabitants which their customs permitted or imposed. Thus, among the Khabyles of Algeria, the killing of adulterous wives is ritual murder committed by the father or brother of the wife and not by her husband, as elsewhere. The woman having been sold by her family to her husband's family, the honor of her relatives is soiled by her infidelity. Her father or brother has the right and the duty to kill her in order to cleanse by her blood the honor of her relatives. Murder in revenge is also a duty, from family to family, in case of murder of or even in case of insults to a relative: the vendetta, called the rekba in Khabylian, is imposed by the law of honor. But these are crimes in French law! Murder for revenge, being premeditated and planned, is assassination, punishable by death! . . . What happens, then, often when our authorities pursue the criminal, guilty of an offense against public safety as well as against morality: public enemy of the French order, but who has acted in accord with a respected custom? The witnesses of the assassination, who are his relatives, or neighbors, fail to lay charges against the assassin; when they are questioned, they pretend to know nothing; and the pursuit is therefore useless. A French magistrate has been able to speak of the conspiracy of silence among the Algerians; a conspiracy aiming to preserve traditions, always followed and obeyed, against their violation by our power. This is the tragic aspect of the conflict of laws. A recent decree forbids the husband among the Khabyles to profit arbitrarily by the power given him according to this law to repudiate his wife, demanding that her new husband pay an exorbitant price for her—this is the custom of the lefdi. Earlier, one who married a repudiated wife paid nothing to the former husband. It appears that the first who tried to avail himself of the new law was killed for violating the old custom. The abolition of the ancient law does not always occur without protest or opposition. That which is a crime was a duty; and the order which we cause to reign is sometimes established to the detriment of 'superstition'; it is the gods and the spirits, it is believed, that would punish any one who fails to revenge his honor.

When Soviet law was extended to Siberia, similar effects were observed. Anossow[4] and Wirschubski[5] both relate that women among the Siberian tribes, who in obedience to the law laid aside their veils, were killed by their relatives for violating one of the most sacred norms of their tribes.

We have noted that culture conflicts are the natural outgrowth of processes of social differentiation, which produce an infinity of social groupings, each with its own definitions of life situations, its own interpretations of social relationships, its own ignorance or misunderstanding of the social values of other groups. The transformation of a culture from a homogeneous and well-integrated type to a heterogeneous and dis-integrated type is therefore accompanied by an increase of conflict situations. Conversely, the operation of integrating processes will reduce the number of conflict situations. Such conflicts within a changing culture may be distinguished from those created when different cultural systems come in contact with one another, regardless of the character or stage of development of these systems. In either case, the conduct of members of a group involved in the conflict of codes will in some respects be judged abnormal by the other group.

The Study of Culture Conflicts

In the study of culture conflicts, some scholars have been concerned with the effect of such conflicts on the conduct of specific persons, an approach which is naturally preferred by psychologists and psychiatrists and by sociologists who have used the life history technique. These scholars view the conflict as internal. Wirth[6] states categorically that a culture "conflict can be said to be a factor in delinquency only if the individual feels it or acts as if it were present."

Culture conflict is mental conflict, but the character of this conflict is viewed differently by the various disciplines which use this term. Freudian psychiatrists[7] regard it as a struggle between deeply rooted biological urges which demand expression and the culturally created rules which give rise to inhibitive mechanisms which thwart this expression and drive them below the conscious level of the mind, whence they rise either by ruse in some socially acceptable disguise, as abnormal conduct when the inhibiting mechanism breaks down, or as neuroses when it works too well. The sociologist, on the other hand, thinks of mental conflict as being primarily the clash between antagonistic conduct norms incorporated in personality. "Mental conflict in the person," says Burgess in discussing the case presented by Shaw in *The Jack-Roller*, "may always be explained in terms of the conflict of divergent cultures."[8]

If this view is accepted, sociological research on culture conflict and its relationships to abnormal conduct would have to be strictly limited to a study of the personality of cultural hybrids. Significant studies could be conducted only by the life-history case technique applied to persons in whom the conflict is internalized, appropriate control groups being utilized, of course. . . .

The absence of mental conflict, in the sociological sense, may, however, be well studied in terms of culture conflict. An example may make this clear. A few years ago a Sicilian father in New Jersey killed the sixteen-year-old seducer of his daughter, expressing surprise at his arrest since he had merely defended his family honor in a traditional way. In this case a mental conflict in the sociological sense did not exist. The conflict was external and occurred between cultural codes or norms. We may assume that where such conflicts occur violations of norms will arise merely because persons who have absorbed the norms of one cultural group or area migrate to another and that such conflict will continue so long as the acculturation process has not been completed. . . . Only then may the violations be regarded in terms of mental conflict.

If culture conflict may be regarded as sometimes personalized, or mental, and sometimes as occurring entirely in an impersonal way solely as a conflict of group codes, it is obvious that research should not be confined to the investigation of mental conflicts and that contrary to Wirth's categorical statement that it is impossible to demonstrate the existence of a culture conflict "objectively . . . by a comparison between two cultural codes"[9] this procedure has not

only a definite function, but may be carried out by researches employing techniques which are familiar to the sociologist.

The emphasis on the life history technique has grown out of the assumption that "the experiences of one person at the same time reveals the life activities of his group" and that "habit in the individual is an expression of custom in society."[10] This is undoubtedly one valid approach. Through it we may hope to discover generalizations of a scientific nature by studying persons who (1) have drawn their norms of conduct from a variety of groups with conflicting norms, or (2) who possess norms drawn from a group whose code is in conflict with that of the group which judges the conduct. In the former case alone can we speak of mental or internal culture conflict; in the latter, the conflict is external.

If the conduct norms of a group are, with reference to a given life situation, inconsistent, or if two groups possess inconsistent norms, we may assume that the members of these various groups will individually reflect such group attitudes. Paraphrasing Burgess, the experiences of a group will reveal the life activities of its members. While these norms can, no doubt, be best established by a study of a sufficient number of representative group members, they may for some groups at least be fixed with sufficient certainty to serve research purposes by a study of the social institutions, the administration of justice, the novel, the drama, the press, and other expressions of group attitudes. The identification of the groups in question having been made, it might be possible to determine to what extent such conflicts are reflected in the conduct of their members. Comparative studies based on the violation rates of the members of such groups, the trends of such rates, etc., would dominate this approach to the problem.

In conclusion, then, culture conflict may be studied either as mental conflict or as a conflict of cultural codes. The criminologist will naturally tend to concentrate on such conflicts between legal and nonlegal conduct norms. The concept of conflict fails to give him more than a general framework of reference for research. In practice, it has, however, become nearly synonymous with conflicts between the norms of cultural systems or areas. Most researches which have employed it have been done on immigrant or race groups in the United States, perhaps due to the ease with which such groups may be identified, the existence of more statistical data recognizing such groupings, and the conspicuous differences between some immigrant norms and our norms.

NOTES

1. This is unfortunately not the whole story, for with the rapid growth of impersonal communication, the written (press, literature) and the spoken word (radio, talkie), knowledge concerning divergent conduct norms no longer grows solely out of direct personal contact with their carriers. And out of such conflicts grow some violations of custom and of law which would not have occurred without them.

2. Speck, Frank G. "Ethical Attributes of the Labrador Indians." *American Anthropologist,* n. s. 35:559–94, October–December 1933, p. 559.

3. Maunier, René. "La diffusion du droit francais en Algérie." Harvard Tercentenary Publications, *Independence, Convergence, and Borrowing in Institutions, Thought, and Art.* Cambridge: Harvard University Press, 1937, pp. 84–85.

4. Anossow, J. J. "Die volkstümlichen Verbrechen im Strafkodex der USSR." *Monatsschrift für Kriminalpsychologie und Strafrechtsreform,* 24: 534–37, September 1933.

5. Wirschubski, Gregor. "Der Schutz der Sittlichkeit im Sowjetstrafrecht." *Zeitschrift für die gesamte Strafrechts-wissenschaft,* 51: 317–28, 1931.

6. Wirth, Louis. "Culture Conflict and Misconduct," *Social Forces,* 9: 484–92, June 1931, p. 490. Cf. Allport, Floyd H. "Culture Conflict versus the Individual as Factors in Delinquency." *Ibid.,* pp. 493–97.

7. White, William A., *Crimes and Criminals.* New York: Farrar & Rinehart, 1933. Healy, William, *Mental Conflict and Misconduct.* Boston: Little, Brown & Co., 1917. Alexander, Franz, and Healy, William, *Roots of Crime.* New York: Alfred A. Knopf, 1935.

8. Burgess, Ernest W. in Clifford R. Shaw's *The Jack-Roller.* Chicago: University of Chicago Press, 1930, pp. 184–197, p. 186.

9. Wirth, Louis, *op. cit.,* p. 490. It should be noted that Wirth also states that culture should be studied "on the objective side" and that "the sociologist is not primarily interested in personality but in culture."

10. Burgess, Ernest W., *op. cit.,* p. 186.

> ### Think Critically
>
> 1. Sellin uses cultural conflict to explain deviance. Explain his approach.
> 2. In what regards do you think this approach is useful in explaining deviance? Give some examples.

Toward a Marxian Theory of Deviance*

Steven Spitzer

The Production of Deviance in Capitalist Society

The concept of deviance production offers a starting point for the analysis of both deviance and control. But for such a construct to serve as a critical tool, it must be grounded

*Reprinted from "Toward a Marxian Theory of Deviance," by Steven Spitzer, *Social Problems,* 22 (June, 1975), pp. 641–651. © 1975 by The Society for the Study of Social Problems. Reprinted by permission of the publisher.

in a historical and structural investigation of society. For Marx, the crucial unit of analysis is the mode of production that dominates a given historical period. If we are to have a Marxian theory of deviance, therefore, deviance production must be understood in relationship to specific forms of socio-economic organization. In our society, productive activity is organized capitalistically and it is ultimately defined by "the process that transforms on the one hand, the social means of subsistence and of production into capital, on the other hand the immediate producers into wage labourers" (Marx, 1967:714).

There are two features of the capitalist mode of production important for purposes of this discussion. First, as a mode of production it forms the foundation of infrastructure of our society. This means that the starting point of our analysis must be an understanding of the economic organization of capitalist societies and the impact of that organization on all aspects of social life. But the capitalist mode of production is an important starting point in another sense. It contains contradictions which reflect the internal tendencies of capitalism. These contradictions are important because they explain the changing character of the capitalist system and the nature of its impact on social, political, and intellectual activity. The formulation of a Marxist perspective on deviance requires the interpretation of the process through which the contradictions of capitalism are expressed. In particular, the theory must illustrate the relationship between specific contradictions, the problems of capitalist development, and the production of a deviant class.

The superstructure of society emerges from and reflects the ongoing development of economic forces (the infrastructure). In class societies this superstructure preserves the hegemony of the ruling class through a system of class controls. These controls, which are institutionalized in the family, church, private associations, media, schools, and the state, provide a mechanism for coping with the contradictions and achieving the aims of capitalist development.

Among the most important functions served by the superstructure in capitalist societies is the regulation and management of problem populations. Because deviance processing is only one of the methods available for social control, these groups supply raw material for deviance production, but are by no means synonymous with deviant populations. Problem populations tend to share a number of social characteristics, but most important among these is the fact that their behavior, personal qualities, and/or position threaten the *social relations of production* in capitalist societies. In other words, populations become generally eligible for management as deviant when they disturb, hinder, or call into question any of the following:

1. capitalist modes of appropriating the product of human labor (e.g., when the poor "steal" from the rich);
2. the social conditions under which capitalist production takes place (e.g., those who refuse or are unable to perform wage labor);
3. patterns of distribution and consumption in capitalist society (e.g., those who use drugs for escape and transcendence rather than sociability and adjustment);
4. the process of socialization for productive and nonproductive roles (e.g., youth who refuse to be schooled or those who deny the validity of "family life");[1]
5. the ideology which supports the functioning of capitalist society (e.g., proponents of alternative forms of social organization).

Although problem populations are defined in terms of the threat and costs that they present to the social relations of production in capitalist societies, these populations are far from isomorphic with a revolutionary class. It is certainly true that some members of the problem population may under specific circumstances possess revolutionary potential. But this potential can only be realized if the problematic group is located in a position of functional indispensability within the capitalist system. Historically, capitalist societies have been quite successful in transforming those who are problematic and indispensable (the proto-revolutionary class) into groups who are either problematic and dispensable (candidates for deviance processing) or indispensable but not problematic (supporters of the capitalist order). On the other hand, simply because a group is manageable does not mean that it ceases to be a problem for the capitalist class. Even though dispensable problem populations cannot overturn the capitalist system, they can represent a significant impediment to its maintenance and growth. It is in this sense that they become eligible for management as deviants.

Problem populations are created in two ways—either directly through the expression of fundamental contradictions in the capitalist mode of production or indirectly through disturbances in the system of class rule. An example of the first process is found in Marx's analysis of the "relative surplus-population."

Writing on the "General Law of Capitalist Accumulation" Marx explains how increased social redundance is inherent in the development of the capitalist mode of production.

> With the extension of the scale of production, and the mass of the labourers set in motion, with the greater breadth and fullness of all sources of wealth, there is also an extension of the scale on which greater attraction of labourers by capital is accompanied by their

greater repulsion. . . .The labouring population therefore produces, along with the accumulation of capital produced by it, the means by which itself is made relatively superfluous, . . . and it does this to an always increasing extent (Marx, 1967:631).

In its most limited sense the production of a relative surplus-population involves the creation of a class which is economically redundant. But insofar as the conditions of economic existence determine social existence, this process helps explain the emergence of groups who become both threatening and vulnerable at the same time. The marginal status of these populations reduces their stake in the maintenance of the system while their powerlessness and dispensability renders them increasingly susceptible to the mechanisms of official control.

The paradox surrounding the production of the relative surplus-population is that this population is both useful and menacing to the accumulation of capital. Marx describes how the relative surplus-population "forms a disposable industrial army, that belongs to capital quite as absolutely as if the latter had bred it at its own cost," and how this army, "creates, for the changing needs of the self-expansion of capital, a mass of human material always ready for exploitation" (Marx, 1967:632).

On the other hand, it is apparent that an excessive increase in what Marx called the "lowest sediment" of the relative surplus-population might seriously impair the growth of capital. The social expenses and threat to social harmony created by a large and economically stagnant surplus-population could jeopardize the preconditions for accumulation by undermining the ideology of equality so essential to the legitimation of production relations in bourgeois democracies, diverting revenues away from capital investment toward control and support operations, and providing a basis for political organization of the dispossessed.[2] To the extent that the relative surplus-population confronts the capitalist class as a threat to the social relations of production, it reflects an important contradiction in modern capitalist societies: A surplus-population is a necessary product of and condition for the accumulation of wealth on a capitalist basis, but it also creates a form of social expense which must be neutralized or controlled if production relations and conditions for increased accumulation are to remain unimpaired.

Problem populations are also generated through contradictions which develop in the system of class rule. The

institutions which make up the superstructure of capitalist society originate and are maintained to guarantee the interests of the capitalist class. Yet these institutions necessarily reproduce, rather than resolve, the contradictions of the capitalist order. In a dialectical fashion, arrangements which arise in order to buttress capitalism are transformed into their opposite—structures for the cultivation of internal threats. An instructive example of this process is found in the emergence and transformation of educational institutions in the United States.

The introduction of mass education in the United States can be traced to the developing needs of corporate capitalism (cf. Karier, 1973; Cohen and Lazerson, 1972; Bowles and Gintis, 1972; Spring, 1972). Compulsory education provided a means of training, testing and sorting, and assimilating wage-laborers, as well as withholding certain populations from the labor market. The system was also intended to preserve the values of bourgeois society and operate as an "inexpensive form of police" (Spring, 1973:31). However, as Gintis (1973) and Bowles (1973) have suggested, the internal contradictions of schooling can lead to effects opposite of those intended. For the poor, early schooling can make explicit the oppressiveness and alienating character of capitalist institutions, while higher education can instill critical abilities which lead students to "bite the hand that feeds them." In both cases educational institutions create troublesome populations (i.e., dropouts and student radicals) and contribute to the very problems they were designed to solve. . . .

Two more or less discrete groupings are established through the operations of official control. These groups are a product of different operating assumptions and administrative orientations toward the deviant population. On the one hand, there is *social junk,* which, from the point of view of the dominant class, is a costly yet relatively harmless burden to society. The discreditability of social junk resides in the failure, inability, or refusal of this group to participate in the roles supportive of capitalist society. Social junk is most likely to come to official attention when informal resources have been exhausted or when the magnitude of the problem becomes significant enough to create a basis for "public concern." Since the threat presented by social junk is passive, growing out of its inability to compete and its withdrawal from the prevailing social order, controls are usually designed to regulate and contain rather than eliminate and suppress the problem. Clear-cut examples of social junk in modern capitalist societies might include the officially administered aged, handicapped, mentally ill, and mentally retarded.

In contrast to social junk, there is a category that can be roughly described as *social dynamite*. The essential quality of deviance managed as social dynamite is its potential actively to call into question established relationships, especially relations of production and domination. Generally, therefore, social dynamite tends to be more youthful, alienated, and politically volatile than social junk. The control of social dynamite is usually premised on an assumption that the problem is acute in nature, requiring a rapid and focused expenditure of control resources. This is in contrast to the handling of social junk, frequently based on a belief that the problem is chronic and best controlled through broad reactive rather than intensive and selective measures. Correspondingly, social dynamite is normally processed through the legal system with its capacity for active intervention, while social junk is frequently (but not always)[3] administered by the agencies and agents of the therapeutic and welfare state.

Many varieties of deviant populations are alternatively or simultaneously dealt with as either social junk and/or social dynamite. The welfare poor, homosexuals, alcoholics, and "problem children" are among the categories reflecting the equivocal nature of the control process and its dependence on the political, economic, and ideological priorities of deviance production. The changing nature of these priorities and their implications for the future may be best understood by examining some of the tendencies of modern capitalist systems.

Monopoly Capital and Deviance Production

Marx viewed capitalism as a system constantly transforming itself. He explained these changes in terms of certain tendencies and contradictions immanent within the capitalist mode of production. One of the most important processes identified by Marx was the tendency for the organic composition of capital to rise. Simply stated, capitalism requires increased productivity to survive, and increased productivity is only made possible by raising the ratio of machines (dead labor) to men (living labor). This tendency

is self-reinforcing since, "the further machine production advances, the higher becomes the organic composition of capital needed for an entrepreneur to secure the average profit" (Mandel, 1968:163). This phenomenon helps us explain the course of capitalist development over the last century and the rise of monopoly capital (Baran and Sweezy, 1966).

For the purposes of this analysis there are at least two important consequences of this process. First, the growth of constant capital (machines and raw material) in the production process leads to an expansion in the overall size of the relative surplus-population. The reasons for this are obvious. The increasingly technological character of production removes more and more laborers from productive activity for longer periods of time. Thus, modern capitalist societies have been required progressively to reduce the number of productive years in a worker's life, defining both young and old as economically superfluous. Especially affected are the unskilled, who become more and more expendable as capital expands.

In addition to affecting the general size of the relative surplus-population, the rise of the organic composition of capital leads to an increase in the relative stagnancy of that population. In Marx's original analysis he distinguished between forms of superfluous population that were floating and stagnant. The floating population consists of workers who are "sometimes repelled, sometimes attracted again in greater masses, the number of those employed increasing on the whole, although in a constantly decreasing proportion to the scale of production" (1967:641). From the point of view of capitalist accumulation, the floating population offers the greatest economic flexibility and the fewest problems of social control because they are most effectively tied to capital by the "natural laws of production." Unfortunately (for the capitalist at least), these groups come to comprise a smaller and smaller proportion of the relative surplus-population. The increasing specialization of productive activity raises the cost of reproducing labor and heightens the demand of highly skilled and "internally controlled" forms of wage labor (Gorz, 1970). The process through which unskilled workers are alternatively absorbed and expelled from the labor force is thereby impaired, and the relative surplus-population comes to be made up of increasing numbers of persons who are more or less permanently redundant. The boundaries between the "useful" and the "useless" are more clearly delineated, while standards for social disqualification are more liberally defined.

With the growth of monopoly capital, therefore, the relative surplus-population begins to take on the character of a population which is more and more absolute. At the same time, the market becomes a less reliable means of disciplining these populations, and the "invisible hand" is more frequently replaced by the "visible fist." The implications for deviance production are twofold: (1) problem populations become gradually more problematic—both in terms of their size and their insensitivity to economic controls, and (2) the resources of the state need to be applied in greater proportion to protect capitalist relations of production and ensure the accumulation of capital.

NOTES

1. To the extent that a group (e.g., homosexuals) blatantly and systematically challenges the validity of the bourgeois family, it is likely to become part of the problem population. The family is essential to capitalist society as a unit for consumption, socialization, and the reproduction of the socially necessary labor force (cf. Frankford and Snitow, 1972; Secombe, 1973; Zaretsky, 1973).

2. O'Connor (1973) discusses this problem in terms of the crisis faced by the capitalist state in maintaining conditions for profitable accumulation and social harmony.

3. It has been estimated, for instance, that one-third of all arrests in America are for the offense of public drunkenness. Most of these apparently involve "sick" and destitute "skid-row alcoholics" (Morris and Hawkins, 1969).

REFERENCES

Baran, Paul, and Paul M. Sweezy. 1966. *Monopoly Capital.* New York: Monthly Review Press.

Bowles, Samuel. 1973. "Contradictions in United States higher education." Pp. 165–199 in James H. Weaver (ed.), *Modern Political Economy: Radical Versus Orthodox Approaches.* Boston: Allyn & Bacon.

Bowles, Samuel, and Herbert Gintis. 1972. "I.Q. in the U.S. class structure." *Social Policy* 3 (November/December):65–96.

Cohen, David K., and Marvin Lazerson. 1972. "Education and the corporate order." *Socialist Revolution* (March/April): 48–72.

Frankford, Evenly, and Ann Snitow. 1972. "The trap of domesticity: Notes on the family." *Socialist Revolution* (July/August): 83–94.

Gintis, Herbert. 1973. "Alienation and power." Pp. 431–465 in James H. Weaver (ed.), *Modern Political Economy: Radical Versus Orthodox Approaches.* Boston: Allyn & Bacon.

Gorz, Andre. 1970. "Capitalist relations of production and the socially necessary labor force." Pp. 155–171 in Arthur Lothstein (ed.), *All We Are Saying. . . .* New York: G. P. Putnam.

Karier, Clarence J. 1973. "Business values and the educational state." Pp. 6–29 in Clarence J. Karier, Paul Violas, and Joel Spring (eds.), *Roots of Crisis: American Education in the Twentieth Century.* Chicago: Rand McNally.

Mandel, Ernest. 1968. *Marxist Economic Theory,* Vol. 1. New York: Monthly Review Press.

Marx, Karl. 1964. *Class Struggles in France, 1848– 1850.* New York: International Publishers.

———. 1967. *Capital,* Vol. 1. New York: International Publishers.

Morris, Norval, and Gordon Hawkins. 1969. *The Honest Politician's Guide to Crime Control.* Chicago: University of Chicago Press.

O'Connor, James. 1973. *The Fiscal Crisis of the State.* New York: St. Martin's Press.

Secombe, Wally. 1973. "The housewife and her labour under capitalism." *New Left Review* (January–February): 3–24.

Spring, Joel. 1972. *Education and the Rise of the Corporate State.* Boston: Beacon Press.

———. 1973. "Education as a form of social control." Pp. 30–39 in Clarence J. Karier, Paul Violas, and Joel Spring (eds.), *Roots of Crisis: American Education in the Twentieth Century.* Chicago: Rand McNally.

Zaretsky, Eli. 1973. "Capitalism, the family and personal life: parts 1 & 2." *Socialist Revolution* (January–April/May–June): 69–126, 19–70.

Think Critically

1. Name the major conceptualizations involved in a Marxian approach to deviance, according to Spitzer.

2. What criticisms can be made regarding this approach to deviance? What are its strong points? What do you make of the approach overall? Why do you feel this way?

The Poverty of the Sociology of Deviance
*Nuts, Sluts, and Preverts**

Alexander Liazos**

C. WRIGHT MILLS LEFT A RICH LEGACY TO sociology. One of his earliest, and best, contributions was "The Professional Ideology of Social Pathologists" (1943). In it, Mills argues that the small-town, middle-class background of writers of social problems textbooks blinded them to basic problems of social structure and power, and led them to emphasize melioristic, patchwork types of solutions to America's "problems," ranging from rape in rural districts to public housing, and emphasized the orderly structure of small-town America; anything else was pathology and disorganization. Moreover, these "problems," "ranging from rape in rural districts to public housing," were not explored systematically and theoretically; they were not placed in some larger political, historical, and social context. They were merely listed and decried.[1]

Since Mills wrote his paper, however, the field of social problems, social disorganization, and social pathology has undergone considerable changes. Beginning in the late 1940s and the 1950s, and culminating in the 1960s, the field of "deviance" has largely replaced the social problems orientation. This new field is characterized by a number of features which distinguish it from the older approach.[2]

*© 1972 by the Society for the Study of Social Problems. Reprinted from *Social Problems,* 20 (Summer, 1972), pp. 103–120 by permission of the publisher.
**The subtitle of this paper came from two sources. (a) A Yale undergraduate once told me that the deviance course was known among Yale students as "nuts and sluts." (b) A former colleague of mine at Quinnipiac College, John Bancroft, often told me that the deviance course was "all about those preverts." When I came to write this paper, I discovered that these descriptions were correct, and concise summaries of my argument. I thank both of them. I also want to thank Gordon Fellman for a very careful reading of the first draft of the manuscript, and for discussing with me the general and specific issues I raise here.

First, there is some theoretical framework, even though it is often absent in edited collections (the Rubington and Weinberg (1968) edited book is an outstanding exception). Second, the small-town morality is largely gone. Writers claim they will examine the phenomena at hand—prostitution, juvenile delinquency, mental illness, crime, and others—objectively, not considering them as necessarily harmful and immoral. Third, the statements and theories of the field are based on much more extensive, detailed, and theoretically oriented research than were those of the 1920s and 1930s. Fourth, writers attempt to fit their theories to some central theories, concerns, and problems found in the general field of sociology; they try to transcend mere moralizing.

The "deviant" has been humanized; the moralistic tone is no longer ever-present (although it still lurks underneath the explicit disavowals); and theoretical perspectives have been developed. Nevertheless, all is not well with the field of "deviance." Close examination reveals that writers of this field still do not try to relate the phenomena of "deviance" to larger social, historical, political, and economic contexts. The emphasis is still on the "deviant" and the "problems" *he* presents to himself and others, not on the society within which he emerges and operates.

I examined 16 textbooks in the field of "deviance," eight of them readers, to determine the state of the field. (They are preceded by an asterisk in the references) . . . The field of the sociology of deviance, as exemplified in these books, contains three important theoretical and political biases.

1. All writers, especially those of the labelling school, either state explicitly or imply that one of their main concerns is to *humanize* and *normalize* the "deviant," to show that he is essentially no different from us. But by the very emphasis on the "deviant" and his identity

problems and subculture, the opposite effect may have been achieved. The persisting use of the label "deviant" to refer to the people we are considering is an indication of the feeling that these people are indeed different.

2. By the overwhelming emphasis on the "dramatic" nature of the usual types of "deviance"—prostitution, homosexuality, juvenile delinquency, and others—we have neglected to examine other, more serious and harmful forms of "deviance." I refer to *covert institutional violence* (defined and discussed below) which leads to such things as poverty and exploitation, the war in Vietnam, unjust tax laws, racism and sexism, and so on, which cause psychic and material suffering for many Americans, black and white, men and women.

3. Despite explicit statements by these authors of the importance of *power* in the designation of what is "deviant," in their substantive analyses they show a profound unconcern with power and its implications. The really powerful, the upper classes, and the power elite, those Gouldner (1968) calls the "top dogs," are left essentially unexamined by these sociologists of deviance.

I.

Always implicit, and frequently explicit, is the aim of the labelling school to humanize and normalize the "deviant" . . .

For a number of reasons, however, the opposite effect may have been achieved; and "deviants" still seem different. I began to suspect this reverse effect from the many essays and papers I read while teaching the "deviance" course. The clearest example is the repeated use of the word "tolerate." Students would write that we must not persecute homosexuals, prostitutes, mental patients, and others, that we must be "tolerant" of them. But one tolerates only those one considers less than equal, morally inferior, and weak; those equal to oneself, one accepts and respects; one does not merely allow them to exist, one does not "tolerate" them . . . Moreover, why would we create a separate field of sociology for "deviants" if there were not something different about them? May it be that even we do not believe our statements and protestations?

The continued use of the word "deviant" (and its variants), despite its invidious distinctions and connotations, also belies our explicit statements on the equality of the people under consideration. To be sure, some of the

authors express uneasiness over the term. For example, we are told,

> In our use of this term for the purpose of sociological investigation, we emphasize that we do not attach any value judgement, explicitly or implicitly, either to the word "deviance" or to those describing their behavior or beliefs in this book (McCaghy, *et al.,* 1968:v).

Lofland (1969:2, 9–10) expresses even stronger reservations about the use of the term, and sees clearly the sociological, ethical, and political problems raised by its continued use. Yet, the title of his book is *Deviance and Identity* . . .

Terms like victimization, persecution, and oppression are more accurate descriptions of what is really happening. But even Gouldner (1968), in a masterful critique of the labelling school, while describing social conflict, calls civil-rights and anti-war protesters "political deviants." He points out clearly that these protesters are resisting openly, not slyly, conditions they abhor. Gouldner is discussing political struggles; oppression and resistance to oppression; conflicts over values, morals, interests, and power; and victimization. Naming such protesters "deviants," even if *political* deviants, is an indication of the deep penetration within our minds of certain prejudices and orientations.

Given the use of the term, the definition and examples of "deviant" reveal underlying sentiments and views. Therefore, it is important that we redefine drastically the entire field, especially since it is a flourishing one: "Because younger sociologists have found deviance such a fertile and exciting field for their own work, and because students share these feelings, deviance promises to become an even more important area of sociological research and theory in the coming years" (Douglas, 1970a:3) . . .

Finally, we are told that these are some examples of deviance every society must deal with:

> ". . . .mental illness, violence, theft, and sexual misconduct, as well as . . . other similarly difficult behavior" (Dinitz, *et al.,* 1969:3).

The list stays unchanged with the authors of the labelling school.

> . . . in Part I, "The Deviant Act," I draw rather heavily on certain studies of homicide, embezzlement, "naive" check forgery, suicide and a few other acts . . . in discussing the assumption of deviant identity (Part II) and

the assumption of normal identity (Part III), there is heavy reference to certain studies of paranoia, "mental illness" more generally, and Alcoholics Anonymous and Synanon (Lofland, 1969:34).

Homicide, suicide, alcoholism, mental illness, prostitution, and homosexuality are among the forms of behavior typically called deviant, and they are among the kinds of behavior that will be analyzed (Lofland, 1969:1). Included among my respondents were political radicals of the far left and the far right, homosexuals, militant blacks, convicts and mental hospital patients, mystics, narcotic addicts, LSD and marijuana users, illicit drug dealers, delinquent boys, racially mixed couples, hippies, health-food users, and bohemian artists and village eccentrics (Simmons, 1969:10).

Simmons (1969:27, 29, 31) also informs us that in his study of stereotypes of "deviants" held by the public, these are the types he gave to people: homosexuals, beatniks, adulterers, marijuana smokers, political radicals, alcoholics, prostitutes, lesbians, ex-mental patients, atheists, ex-convicts, intellectuals, and gamblers. In Lemert (1967) we find that except for the three introductory (theoretical) chapters, the substantive chapters cover the following topics: alcohol drinking, four; check forgers, three; stuttering, two; and mental illness, two. Matza (1969) offers the following list of "deviants" and their actions that "must be appreciated if one adheres to a naturalistic perspective:" paupers, robbers, motorcycle gangs, prostitutes, drug addicts, promiscuous homosexuals, thieving Gypsies, and "free love" Bohemians (1969:16). Finally, Douglas' collection (1970a) covers these forms of "deviance": abortion, nudism, topless barmaids, prostitutes, homosexuals, violence (motorcycle and juvenile gangs), shoplifting, and drugs.

The omissions from these lists are staggering. The covert, institutional forms of "deviance" (part II, below) are nowhere to be found. Reading these authors, one would not know that the most destructive use of violence in the last decade has been the war in Vietnam, in which the United States has heaped unprecedented suffering on the people and their land; more bombs have been dropped in Vietnam than in the entire World War II. Moreover, the robbery of the corporate world—through tax breaks, fixed prices, low wages, pollution of the environment, shoddy goods, etc.—is passed over in our fascination with "dramatic and predatory" actions. Therefore, we are told

that "while they certainly are of no greater social importance to us than such subjects as banking and accounting [or military violence], subjects such as marijuana use and motorcycle gangs are of far greater interest to most of us. While it is only a coincidence that our scientific interests correspond with the emotional interest in deviants, it is a happy coincidence and, I believe, one that should be encouraged" (Douglas, 1970a:5). And Matza (1969:17), in commenting on the "appreciative sentiments" of the "naturalistic spirit," elaborates on the same theme: "We do not for a moment wish that we could rid ourselves of deviant phenomena. We are intrigued by them. They are an intrinsic, ineradicable, and vital part of human society."

An effort is made to transcend this limited view and substantive concern with dramatic and predatory forms of "deviance." Becker (1964:3) claims that the new (labelling) deviance no longer studies only "delinquents and drug addicts, though these classical kinds of deviance are still kept under observation." It increases its knowledge "of the processes of deviance by studying physicians, people with physical handicaps, the mentally deficient, and others whose doings were formerly not included in the area." The powerful "deviants" are still left untouched, however. This is still true with another aspect of the new deviance. Becker (1964:4) claims that in the labelling perspective "we focus attention on the other people involved in the process. We pay attention to the role of the non-deviant as well as that of the deviant." But we see that it is the ordinary non-deviants and the low-level agents of social control who receive attention, not the powerful ones (Gouldner, 1968).

In fact, the emphasis is more on the *subculture* and *identity* of the "deviants" themselves rather than on their oppressors and persecutors. To be sure, in varying degrees all authors discuss the agents of social control, but the fascination and emphasis are on the "deviant" himself. Studies of prisons and prisoners, for example, focus on prison subcultures and prisoner rehabilitation; there is little or no consideration of the social, political, economic, and power conditions which consign people to prisons. Only now are we beginning to realize that most prisoners are *political prisoners*—that their "criminal" actions (whether against individuals, such as robbery, or conscious political acts against the state) result largely from current social and political conditions, and are not the work of "disturbed" and "psychopathic" personalities. This realization came about largely because of the writings of political prisoners themselves: Malcolm X (1965), Eldridge Cleaver (1968), and George Jackson (1970), among others.[3]

In all these books, notably those of the labelling school, the concern is with the "deviant's" subculture and identity: his problems, motives, fellow victims, etc. The collection of memoirs and apologies of "deviants" in their own words (McCaghy, *et al.,* 1968) covers the lives and identities of "prevert deviants": prostitutes, nudists, abortionists, criminals, drug users, homosexuals, the mentally ill, alcoholics, and suicides. For good measure, some "militant deviants" are thrown in: Black Muslims, the SDS, and a conscientious objector. But one wonders about other types of "deviants:" how do those who perpetrate the covert institutional violence in our society view themselves? Do they have identity problems? How do they justify their actions? How did the robber barons of the late 19th century steal, fix laws, and buy politicians six days of the week and go to church on Sunday? By what process can people speak of body counts and kill ratios with cool objectivity? On these and similar questions, this book (and all others)[4] provides no answers; indeed, the editors seem unaware that such questions should or could be raised.

Becker (1964), Rubington and Weinberg (1968), Matza (1969), and Bell (1971) also focus on the identity and subculture of "prevert deviants." Matza, in discussing the assumption of "deviant identity," uses as examples, and elaborates upon, thieves and marijuana users. In all these books, there are occasional references to and questions about the larger social and political structure, but these are not explored in any depth; and the emphasis remains on the behavior, identity, and rehabilitation of the "deviant" himself. This bias continues in the latest book which, following the fashions of the times, has chapters on hippies and militant protesters (Bell, 1971) . . .

Because of these biases, there is an implicit, but very clear, acceptance by these authors of the current definitions of "deviance." It comes about because they concentrate their attention on those who have been *successfully labelled as "deviant,"* and not on those who break laws, fix laws, violate ethical and moral standards, harm individuals and groups, etc., but who either are able to hide their actions, or, when known, can deflect criticism, labelling, and punishment . . .

Furthermore, the essence of the labelling school encourages this bias, despite Becker's (1963:14) assertion

that ". . . insofar as a scientist uses "deviant" to refer to any rule-breaking behavior and takes as his subjects of study only those who have been *labelled* deviant, he will be hampered by the disparities between the two categories." But as the following statements from Becker and others show, this is in fact what the labelling school does do.

Deviance is "created by society . . . *social groups create deviance by making the rules whose infraction constitutes deviance,* and by applying those rules to particular people and labelling them as outsiders" (Becker, 1963:8–9). Clearly, according to this view, in cases where no group has labelled another, no matter what the other group or individuals have done, there is nothing for the sociologist to study and dissect . . .

What is important for the social analyst is not what people are by his lights or by his standards, but what it is that people construe one another and themselves to be for what reasons and with what consequences (Lofland, 1969:35).

> . . . deviance is in the eyes of the beholder. For deviance to become a social fact, somebody must perceive an act, person, situation, or event as a departure from social norms, must categorize that perception, must report the perception to others, must get them to accept this definition of the situation, and must obtain a response that conforms to this definition. Unless all these requirements are met, deviance as a social fact does not come into being (Rubington and Weinberg, 1968:v).

The implication of these statements is that the sociologist accepts current, successful definitions of what is "deviant" as the only ones worthy of his attention. To be sure, he may argue that those labelled "deviant" are not really different from the rest of us, or that there is no act intrinsically "deviant," etc. By concentrating on cases of successful labelling, however, he will not penetrate beneath the surface to look for other forms of "deviance"—undetected stealing, violence, and destruction. When people are not powerful enough to make the "deviant" label stick on others, we overlook these cases. But is it not as much a *social fact,* even though few of us pay much attention to it, that the corporate economy kills and maims more, is more violent, than any violence committed by the poor (the usual subjects of studies of violence)? By what reasoning and necessity is the "violence" of the poor in the ghettoes more worthy of our attention than the military bootcamps which numb recruits from the horrors of killing the "enemy" ("Oriental human beings," as we learned during the Calley trial)? But because these acts are not labelled "deviant," because they are covert, institutional, and normal, their "deviant" qualities are overlooked and they do not become part of the province of the sociology of deviance. Despite their best liberal intentions, these sociologists seem to perpetuate the very notions they think they debunk, and others of which they are unaware.

II.

As a result of the fascination with "nuts, sluts, and preverts," and their identities and subcultures, little attention has been paid to the unethical, illegal, and destructive actions of powerful individuals, groups, and institutions in our society. Because these actions are carried out quietly in the normal course of events, the sociology of deviance does not consider them as part of its subject matter. This bias is rooted in the very conception and definition of the field. It is obvious when one examines the treatment, or, just as often, lack of it, of the issues of violence, crime, and white-collar crime.

Discussions of violence treat only one type: the "dramatic and predatory" violence committed by individuals (usually the poor and minorities) against persons and property. For example, we read, "crimes involving violence, such as criminal homicide, assault, and forcible rape, are concentrated in the slums" (Clinard, 1968:123). Wolfgang, an expert on violence, has developed a whole theory on the "subculture of violence" found among the lower classes (e.g., in Rushing, 1969:233–40). And Douglas (1970a:part 4, on violence) includes readings on street gangs and the Hell's Angels. Thompson (1966), in his book on the Hell's Angels, devotes many pages to an exploration of the Angels' social background . . .

In short, violence is presented as the exclusive property of the poor in the slums, the minorities, street gangs, and motorcycle beasts. But if we take the concept *violence* seriously, we see that much of our political and economic system thrives on it. In violence, a person is *violated*—there is harm done to his person, his psyche, his body, his dignity, his ability to govern himself (Garver, in Rose, 1969:6). Seen in this way, a person can be violated in many ways; physical force is only one of them . . .

Moreover, we must see that *covert institutional violence* is much more destructive than overt individual violence. We

must recognize that people's lives are violated by the very normal and everyday workings of institutions. We do not see such events and situations as violent because they are not dramatic and predatory; they do not make for fascinating reading on the lives of preverts; but they kill, maim, and destroy many more lives than do violent individuals . . .

Violence is committed daily by the government, very often by lack of action. The same system that enriches businessmen farmers with billions of dollars through farm subsidies cannot be bothered to appropriate a few millions to deal with lead poisoning in the slums. Young children . . .

> . . . get it by eating the sweet-tasting chips of peeling tenement walls, painted a generation ago with leaded paint.
>
> According to the Department of Health, Education, and Welfare, 400,000 children are poisoned each year, about 30,000 in New York City alone. About 3,200 suffer permanent brain damage, 800 go blind or become so mentally retarded that they require hospitalization for the rest of their lives, and approximately 200 die.
>
> The tragedy is that lead poisoning is totally manmade and totally preventable. It is caused by slum housing. And there are now blood tests that can detect the disease, and medicines to cure it. Only a lack of purpose sentences 200 black children to die each year (Newfield, 1971).[5]

Newfield goes on to report that on May 20, 1971, a Senate-House conference eliminated $5 million from an appropriations budget. In fact, 200 children had been sentenced to death and thousands more to maiming and suffering.

Similar actions of violence are committed daily by the government and corporations; but in these days of misplaced emphasis, ignorance, and manipulation we do not see the destruction inherent in these actions. Instead, we get fascinated, angry, and misled by the violence of the poor and the powerless. We see the violence committed during political rebellions in the ghettos (called "riots" in order to dismiss them), but all along we ignored the daily violence committed against the ghetto residents by the institutions of the society: schools, hospitals, corporations, the government . . .

It may be argued that some of this violence is (implicitly) recognized in discussions of "white-collar" crime. This is not the case, however. Of the 16 books under consideration, only three pay some attention to white-collar crime

(Cohen, 1966; Clinard, 1968; Dinitz, *et al.,* 1969); and of these, only the last covers the issue at some length. Even in these few discussions, however, the focus remains on the *individuals* who commit the actions (on their greediness, lack of morality, etc.), not on the economic and political institutions within which they operate. . . .

The executives convicted in the Electrical Equipment case were respectable citizens. "Several were deacons or vestrymen of their churches." The rest also held prestigious positions: president of the Chamber of Commerce, bank director, little-league organizer, and so on (Dinitz, *et al.* 1969:107). Moreover, "generally . . . in cases of white-collar crime, neither the corporations as entities nor their responsible officers are invested with deviant characters . . ." (Cohen, 1966:30). Once more, there is quiet acquiescence to this state of affairs. There is no attempt to find out why those who steal millions and whose actions violate lives are not "invested with deviant characters." There is no consideration given to the possibility that, as responsible intellectuals, it is our duty to explore and expose the structural causes for corporate and other serious crimes, which make for much more suffering than does armed robbery. We seem satisfied merely to observe what is, and leave the causes unexamined.

In conclusion, let us look at another form of institutional "deviance." The partial publication of the Pentagon papers (June 1971) made public the conscious lying and manipulation by the government to quiet opposition to the Vietnam war. But lying pervades both government and economy. Deceptions and outright lies abound in advertising (see Henry, 1963) . . .

In short, despite the supposedly central position of *social structure* in the sociological enterprise, there is general neglect of it in the field of "deviance." Larger questions, especially if they deal with political and economic issues, are either passed over briefly or overlooked completely. The focus on the actions of "nuts, sluts, and preverts" and the related slight of the criminal and destructive actions of the powerful, are instances of this avoidance.

III.

Most of the authors under discussion mention the importance of *power* in labelling people "deviant." They state that those who label (the victimizers) are more powerful than those they label (the victims). Writers of the labelling school make this point explicitly. According to Becker (1963:17), "who can . . . force others to accept their rules and what are the causes of their success? This is, of course, a question of political and economic power." Simmons (1969:131) comments that historically, "those in power have used their positions largely to perpetuate and enhance their own advantages through coercing and manipulating the rest of the populace." And Lofland (1969:19) makes the same observation in his opening pages:

> It is in the situation of a very powerful party opposing a very weak one that the powerful party sponsors the *idea* that the weak party is breaking the rules of society. The very concepts of "society" and its "rules" are appropriated by powerful parties and made synonymous with their interests (and, of course, believed in by the naive, e.g., the undergraduate penchant for the phrases "society says . . .," "society expects . . .," "society does . . .").

But this insight is not developed. In none of the 16 books is there an extensive discussion of how power operates in the designation of deviance. Instead of a study of power, of its concrete uses in modern, corporate America, we are offered rather fascinating explorations into the identities and subcultures of "deviants," and misplaced emphasis on the middle-level agents of social control. Only Szasz (1961, 1963, and notably 1970) has shown consistently the role of power in one area of "deviance," "mental illness." Through historical and contemporary studies, he has shown that those labelled "mentally ill" (crazy, insane, mad, lunatic) and institutionalized have always been the powerless: women, the poor, peasants, the aged, and others. Moreover, he has exposed repeatedly the means used by powerful individuals and institutions in employing the "mental illness" label to discredit, persecute, and eliminate opponents. In short, he has shown the political element in the "mental illness" game.

In addition, except for Szasz, none of the authors seems to realize that the stigma of prostitution, abortion, and other "deviant" acts unique to women comes about in large part from the powerlessness of women and their status in society. Moreover, to my knowledge, no one has bothered to ask why there have always been women prostitutes for men to satisfy their sexual desires, but very few men prostitutes for women to patronize. The very word *prostitute* we associate with women only, not men. Both men and women have been involved in this "immoral" act, but the stigma has been carried by the women alone . . .

Becker (1963:14) has shown consistent interest in agents of social control. However, a close examination reveals limitations. He discusses "moral crusaders" like those who passed the laws against marijuana. The moral crusader, "the prototype of the rule creator," finds that "the existing rules do not satisfy him because there is some evil which profoundly disturbs him." But the only type of rule creator Becker discusses is the moral crusader, no other. The political manipulators who pass laws to defend their interests and persecute dissenters are not studied. The "unconventional sentimentality," the debunking motif Becker (1964:4–5) sees in the "new deviance" is directed toward the police, the prison officials, the mental hospital personnel, the "average" person and his prejudices. The basic social, political, and economic structure, and those commanding it who guide the labelling and persecution, are left untouched. We have become so accustomed to debunking these low-level agents that we do not even know how to begin to direct our attention to the ruling institutions and groups (for an attempt at such an analysis, see Liazos, 1970) . . .

Discussions of the police reveal the same misplaced emphasis on lower-and middle-level agents of social control. In three of the books (Matza, 1969:182–95; Rubington and Weinberg, 1968: ch. 7; Dinitz, *et al.,* 1969:40–47), we are presented with the biases and prejudices of policemen; their modes of operation in confronting delinquents and others; the pressures on them from various quarters; etc. In short, the focus is on the role and psychology of the policeman.

All these issues about the policeman's situation need to be discussed, of course; but there is an even more important issue which these authors avoid. We must ask, who passes the laws the police enforce? Whose agents are they? Why do the police exist? Three excellent papers (Cook, 1968; A. Silver, in Bordua, 1967; T. Hayden, in Rose, 1969) offer some answers to these questions. They show, through a historical description of the origins of police forces, that they have always been used to defend the status quo, the interests of the ruling powers. When the police force was created in England in the early 1800s, it was meant to defend the propertied classes from the "dangerous classes" and the "mob."[6] With the rise of capitalism and industrialism, there was much unrest from the suffering underclass; the professional police were meant to act as a buffer zone for the capitalist elite . . .

It must be stressed that the police, like all agents of social control, are doing someone else's work. Sometimes they enforce laws and prejudices of "society," the much maligned middle class (on sex, marijuana, etc.); but at other times it is not "society" which gives them their directives, but specific interested groups, even though, often, "society" is manipulated to express its approval of such actions. Above all, we must remember that *"in a fundamentally unjust society, even the most impartial, professional, efficient enforcement of the laws by the police cannot result in justice"* (Cook, 1968:2). More generally, in an unjust and exploitative society, no matter how "humane" agents of social control are, their actions necessarily result in repression.

Broad generalization is another device used by some of these authors to avoid concrete examination of the uses of power in the creation and labelling of "deviance." Clairborne (1971) has called such generalization *"schlock."* The following are some of the tactics he thinks are commonly used in writing popular *schlock* sociology (some sociologists of deviance use similar tactics, as we shall see):

> The Plausible Passive: "New scientific discoveries are being made every day. . . . These new ideas are being put to work more quickly . . ." [Toffler, in *Future Shock,* is] thereby rather neatly obscuring the fact that scientists and engineers (mostly paid by industry) are making the discoveries and industrialists (often with the aid of public funds) are putting them to work. An alternative to the Plausible Passive is the Elusive Impersonal: "Buildings in New York literally disappear overnight." What Toffler is trying to avoid saying is that contractors and real estate speculators *destroy* buildings overnight (Clairborne, 1971:118) . . .

There are parallels in the sociology of deviance. Clinard (1968:ch. 4) argues that urbanization and the slum are breeding grounds for "deviant behavior." But these conditions are reified, not examined concretely. He says about urbanization and social change:

> Rapid social and cultural change, disregard for the importance of stability of generations, and untempered loyalties also generally characterize urban life. New ideas are generally welcome, inventions and mechanical gadgets are encouraged, and new styles in such arts as painting, literature, and music are often approved (1968:90).

But the slum, urbanization, and change are not reified entities working out their independent wills. For example, competition, capitalism, and the profit motive—all encouraged by a government controlled by the upper classes—have had something to do with the rise of slums. There is a general process of urbanization, but at given points in history it is fed by, and gives profits to, specific groups. The following are a few historical examples: the land enclosure policies and practices of the English ruling classes in the 17th and 18th centuries; the building of cheap housing in the 19th century by the owners of factory towns; and the profits it derived from "urban renewal" (which has destroyed neighborhoods, created even more crowded slums, etc.) by the building of highways, luxury apartments, and stores.

Another favorite theme of *schlock* sociology is that "All Men Are Guilty." That means nothing can be done to change things. There is a variation of this theme in the sociology of deviance when we are told that (a) all of us are deviant in some way, (b) all of us label some others deviant, and (c) "society" labels. Such statements preclude asking concrete questions: does the "deviance" of each of us have equal consequences for others? Does the labelling of each of us stick, and with what results? . . .

Another case of *schlock* is found in Matza's discussion (lack of it, really) of "Leviathan" (1969, especially ch. 7). It is mentioned as a potent force in the labelling and handling of "deviance." But, vainly, one keeps looking for some exploration into the workings of "Leviathan." It remains a reified, aloof creature. What is it? Who controls it? How does it label? Why? Matza seems content to try to mesmerize us by mentioning it constantly (Leviathan is capitalized throughout); but we are never shown how it operates. It hovers in the background, it punishes, and its presence somehow cowers us into submission. But it remains a reified force whose presence is accepted without close examination.

The preceding examples typify much of what is wrong with the sociology of deviance: the lack of specific analysis of the role of power in the labelling process; the generalizations which, even when true, explain little; the fascination with "deviants"; the reluctance to study the "deviance" of the powerful.

IV.

I want to start my concluding comments with two disclaimers.

    a. I have tried to provide some balance and perspective in the field of "deviance," and in doing so I have argued against the exclusive emphasis on *nuts, sluts,*

and *preverts* and their identities and subcultures. I do not mean, however, that the usually considered forms of "deviance" are unworthy of our attention. Suicide, prostitution, madness, juvenile delinquency, and others *are* with us; we cannot ignore them. People do suffer when labelled and treated as "deviant" (in *this* sense, "deviants" *are* different from conformists). Rather, I want to draw attention to phenomena which also belong to the field of "deviance."[7]

    b. It is because the sociology of deviance, especially the labelling approach, contains important, exciting, and revealing insights, because it tries to humanize the "deviant," and because it is popular, that it is easy to overlook some of the basic ideological biases still pervading the field. For this reason, I have tried to explore and detail some of these biases. At the same time, however, I do not mean to dismiss the contributions of the field as totally negative and useless. In fact, in my teaching I have been using two of the books discussed here, Simmons (1969) and Rubington and Weinberg (1968).

The argument can be summarized briefly. (1) We should not study only, or predominantly, the popular and dramatic forms of "deviance." Indeed, we should banish the concept of "deviance" and speak of oppression, conflict, persecution, and suffering. By focusing on the dramatic forms, as we do now, we perpetuate most people's beliefs and impressions that such "deviance" is the basic cause of many of our troubles, that these people (criminals, drug addicts, political dissenters, and others) are the real "troublemakers" and, necessarily, we neglect conditions of inequality, powerlessness, institutional violence, and so on, which lie at the bases of our tortured society. (2) Even when we do study the popular forms of "deviance," we do not avoid blaming the victim for his fate; the continued use of the term "deviant" is one clue to this blame. Nor have we succeeded in normalizing him; the focus on the "deviant" himself, on his identity and subculture, has tended to confirm the popular prejudice that he is different.

NOTES

1. Bend and Vogenfanger (1964) examined social problems textbooks of the early 1960s; they found there was little theory or emphasis on social structure in them.

2. What I say below applies to the "labelling-interactionist" school of deviance of Becker, Lemert, Erikson, Matza, and others: to a large degree, however, most of my comments also apply to the other schools.

3. The first draft of this paper was completed in July, 1971. The killing of George Jackson at San Quentin on August 21, 1971, which many people see as a political murder, and the Attica prisoner rebellion of early September, 1971, only strengthen the argument about political prisoners. Two things became clear: (a) Not only a few "radicals," but many prisoners (if not a majority) see their fate as the outcome of political forces and decisions, and themselves as political prisoners (see Fraser, 1971). Robert Chrisman's argument (in Fraser, 1971) points to such a conclusion clearly: "To maintain that all black offenders are, by their actions, politically correct, is dangerous romanticism. Black antisocial behavior must be seen in and of its own terms and corrected for enhancement of the black community." But there is a political aspect, for black prisoners' condition "derives from the political inequity of black people in America. A black prisoner's crime may or may not have been a political action against the state, but the state's action against him is always political." I would stress that the same is true of most white prisoners, for they come mostly from the exploited poorer classes and groups. (b) The state authorities, the political rulers, by their deeds if not their words, see such prisoners as political men and threats. The death of George Jackson, and the brutal crushing of the Attica rebellion, attest to the authorities' realization, and fear, that here were no mere riots with prisoners letting off steam, but authentic political actions, involving groups and individuals conscious of their social position and exploitation.

4. With the exception of E. C. Hughes, in Becker (1964).

5. As Gittlin and Hollander (1970) show, the children of poor whites also suffer from lead poisoning.

6. See Rude (1966) on the role of mobs of poor workers and peasants in 18th and 19th century England and France.

7. The question of "what deviance is to the deviant" (Gordon Fellman, private communication), not what the labelling, anomie, and other schools, or the present radical viewpoint say *about* such a person, is not dealt with here. I avoid this issue not because I think it unimportant, rather because I want to concentrate on the political, moral, and social issues raised by the biases of those presently writing about the "deviant."

REFERENCES

Becker, Howard S. *1963. *Outsiders.* New York: Free Press.

———. *1964. (ed.) *The Other Side.* New York: Free Press.

———.1967. "Whose side are we on?" *Social Problems* 14: 239–247 (reprinted in Douglas, 1970a, 99–111; references to this reprint).

Bell, Robert R. *1971. *Social Deviance: A Substantive Analysis.* Homewood, Illinois: Dorsey.

Bend, Emil and Martin Vogenfanger. 1964. "A new look at Mills' critique," in *Mass Society in Crisis.* Bernard Rosenberg, Israel Gerver, F. William Howton (eds.). New York: Macmillan, 1964, 111–122.

Bordua, David (ed.) 1967. *The Police.* New York: Wiley. Carmichael, Stokeley and Charles V. Hamilton.

———. 1967. *Black Power.* New York: Random House.

Clairborne, Robert. 1971. "Future schlock." *The Nation,* Jan. 25, 117–120.

Cleaver, Eldridge. 1968. *Soul On Ice.* New York: McGraw-Hill.

Clinard, Marshall B. *1968. *Sociology of Deviant Behavior.* (3rd ed.) New York: Holt, Rinehart, and Winston.

Cohen, Albert K. *1966. *Deviance and Control.* Englewood Cliffs, N.J.: Prentice Hall.

Cook, Robert M. 1968. "The police." *The Bulletin of the American Independent Movement* (New Haven, Conn.), 3:6, 1–6.

Dinitz, Simon, Russell R. Dynes, and Alfred C. Clarke (eds.) *1969. *Deviance.* New York: Oxford University Press.

Domhoff, William G. 1967. *Who Rules America?* Englewood Cliffs, N.J.: Prentice Hall.

Douglas, Jack D. *1970a. (ed.) *Observations of Deviance.* New York: Random House.

———. *1970b. (ed.) *Deviance and Respectability: The Social Construction of Moral Meanings.* New York: Basic Books.

Fraser, C. Gerald. 1971. "Black prisoners finding new view of themselves as political prisoners." *New York Times,* Sept. 16.

Gittlin, Todd and Nanci Hollander. 1970. *Uptown: Poor Whites in Chicago.* New York: Harper and Row.

Gouldner, Alvin W. 1968. "The sociologist as partisan: Sociology and the welfare state." *American Sociologist* 3:2, 103–116.

Henry, Jules. 1963. *Culture Against Man.* New York: Random House.

Jackson, George. 1970. *Soledad Brother.* New York: Bantam Books.

Lemert, Edwin M. *1967. *Human Deviance, Social Problems, and Social Control.* Englewood Cliffs, N.J.: Prentice Hall.

Liazos, Alexander. 1970. Processing for Unfitness: socialization of "emotionally disturbed" lower-class boys into the mass society. Ph.D. dissertation, Brandeis University.

Lofland, John. *1969. *Deviance and Identity.* Englewood Cliffs, N.J.: Prentice Hall.

Malcolm X. 1965. *The Autobiography of Malcolm X.* New York: Grove.

Matza, David. *1969. *Becoming Deviant.* Englewood Cliffs, N.J.: Prentice Hall.

McCaghy, Charles H., J. K. Skipper, and M. Lefton (eds.) *1968. In Their Own Behalf: Voices from the Margin.* New York: Appleton-Century-Crofts.

Mills, C. Wright. 1943. "The professional ideology of social pathologists." *American Journal of Sociology* 49: 165–180.

Newfield, Jack. 1971. "Let them eat lead." *New York Times,* June 16, p. 45.

Rose, Thomas (ed.) 1969. *Violence in America.* New York: Random House.

Rubington, Earl and M. S. Weinberg (eds.) *1968. Deviance: The Interactionist Perspective.* New York: Macmillan.

Rude, George. 1966. *The Crowd in History.* New York: Wiley.

Rushing, William A. (ed.) *1969. Deviant Behavior and Social Processes.* Chicago: Rand McNally.

Simmons, J. L. *1969. Deviants.* Berkeley, Cal.: Glendessary.

Szasz, Thomas S. 1961. *The Myth of Mental Illness.* New York: Harper and Row.

———. 1963. *Law, Liberty, and Psychiatry.* New York: Macmillan.

———. 1970. *The Manufacture of Madness.* New York: Harper and Row.

Thompson, Hunter S. 1966. *Hell's Angels.* New York: Ballantine.

Think Critically

1. Comment on the critique that Liazos uses to question major perspectives on deviance, especially those of labeling during the time he wrote this in the early 1970s. What aspects of this critique do you feel are the strongest? Why?

2. What does the phenomenon he conceptualizes as "covert institutional violence" add to our understanding of deviance? Give some concrete examples.

A Sociological Analysis of the Law of Vagrancy

William J. Chambliss

WITH THE OUTSTANDING EXCEPTION OF Jerome Hall's analysis of theft[1] there has been a severe shortage of sociologically relevant analyses of the relationship between particular laws and the social setting in which these laws emerge, are interpreted, and take form. The paucity of such studies is somewhat surprising in view of widespread agreement that such studies are not only desirable but absolutely essential to the development of a mature sociology of law.[2] A fruitful method of establishing the direction and pattern of this mutual influence is to systematically analyze particular legal categories, to observe the changes which take place in the categories and to explain how these changes are themselves related to and stimulate changes in the society. This paper is an attempt to provide such an analysis of the law of vagrancy in Anglo-American Law.

Legal Innovation: The Emergence of the Law of Vagrancy in England

There is general agreement among legal scholars that the first full fledged vagrancy statute was passed in England in 1349. As is generally the case with legislative innovations, however, this statute was preceded by earlier laws which established a climate favorable to such change. The most

---

For a more complete listing of most of the statutes dealt with in this report the reader is referred to Burn, *The History of the Poor Laws.* Citations of English statutes should be read as follows: 3 Ed. 1. c. 1. refers to the third act of Edward the first, chapter one, etc.

significant forerunner to the 1349 vagrancy statute was in 1274 when it was provided:

> Because that abbies and houses of religion have been overcharged and sore grieved, by the resort of great men and other, so that their goods have not been sufficient for themselves, whereby they have been greatly hindered and impoverished, that they cannot maintain themselves, nor such charity as they have been accustomed to do; it is provided, that none shall come to eat or lodge in any house of religion, or any other's foundation than of his own, at the costs of the house, unless he be required by the governor of the house before his coming hither.[3]

Unlike the vagrancy statutes this statute does not intend to curtail the movement of persons from one place to another, but is solely designed to provide the religious houses with some financial relief from the burden of providing food and shelter to travelers.

The philosophy that the religious houses were to give alms to the poor and to the sick and feeble was, however, to undergo drastic change in the next fifty years. The result of this changed attitude was the establishment of the first vagrancy statute in 1349 which made it a crime to give alms to any who were unemployed while being of sound mind and body. To wit:

> Because that many valiant beggars, as long as they may live of begging, do refuse to labor, giving themselves to idleness and vice, and sometimes to theft and other abominations; it is ordained, that none, upon pain of imprisonment shall, under the colour of pity or alms, give anything to such which may labour, or presume to favour them towards their desires; so that thereby they may be compelled to labour for their necessary living.[4]

It was further provided by this statute that:

> . . . every man and woman, of what condition he be, free or bond, able in body, and within the age of threescore years, not living in merchandize nor exercising any craft, nor having of his own whereon to live, nor proper land whereon to occupy himself, and not serving any other, if he in convenient service (his estate considered) be required to serve, shall be bounded to serve him which shall him require . . . And if any refuse, he shall on conviction by two true men, . . . be commited to gaol till he find surety to serve.

> And if any workman or servant, of what estate or condition he be, retained in any man's service, do depart from the said service without reasonable cause or license, before the term agreed on, he shall have pain of imprisonment.[5]

There was also in this statute the stipulation that the workers should receive a standard wage. In 1351 this statute was strengthened by the stipulation:

> An none shall go out of the town where he dwelled in winter, to serve the summer, if he may serve in the same town.[6]

By 34 Ed 3 (1360) the punishment for these acts became imprisonment for fifteen days and if they "do not justify themselves by the end of that time, to be sent to gaol till they do."

A change in official policy so drastic as this did not, of course, occur simply as a matter of whim. The vagrancy statutes emerged as a result of changes in other parts of the social structure. The prime mover for this legislative innovation was the Black Death which struck England about 1348. Among the many disastrous consequences this had upon the social structure was the fact that it decimated the labor force. It is estimated that by the time the pestilence had run its course at least fifty per cent of the population of England had died from the plague. This decimation of the labor force would necessitate rather drastic innovations in any society but its impact was heightened in England where, at this time, the economy was highly dependent upon a ready supply of cheap labor.

Even before the pestilence, however, the availability of an adequate supply of cheap labor was becoming a problem for the landowners. The crusades and various wars had made money necessary to the lords and, as a result, the lord frequently agreed to sell the serfs their freedom in order to obtain the needed funds. The serfs, for their part, were desirous of obtaining their freedom (by "fair means" or "foul") because the larger towns which were becoming more industrialized during this period could offer the serf greater personal freedom as well as a higher standard of living. This process is nicely summarized by Bradshaw:

> By the middle of the 14th century the outward uniformity of the manorial system had become in practice considerably varied . . . for the peasant had begun to drift to the towns and it was unlikely that

the old village life in its unpleasant aspects should not be resented. Moreover the constant wars against France and Scotland were fought mainly with mercenaries after Henry III's time and most villages contributed to the new armies. The bolder serfs either joined the armies or fled to the towns, and even in the villages the free men who held by villein tenure were as eager to commute their services as the serfs were to escape. Only the amount of 'free' labor available enabled the lord to work his demense in many places.[7]

And he says regarding the effect of the Black Death:

> . . . in 1348 the Black Death reached England and the vast mortality that ensued destroyed that reserve of labour which alone had made the manorial system even nominally possible.[8]

The immediate result of these events was of course no surprise: Wages for the "free" man rose considerably and this increased, on the one hand, the landowners problems and, on the other hand, the plight of the unfree tenant. For although wages increased for the personally free laborers, it of course did not necessarily add to the standard of living of the serf, if anything it made his position worse because the landowner would be hard pressed to pay for the personally free labor which he needed and would thus find it more and more difficult to maintain the standard of living for the serf which he had heretofore supplied. Thus the serf had no alternative but flight if he chose to better his position. Furthermore, flight generally meant both freedom and better conditions since the possibility of work in the new weaving industry was great and the chance of being caught small.[9]

It was under these conditions that we find the first vagrancy statutes emerging. There is little question but that these statutes were designed for one express purpose: to force laborers (whether personally free or unfree) to accept employment at a low wage in order to insure the landowner an adequate supply of labor at a price he could afford to pay. Caleb Foote concurs with this interpretation when he notes:

> The anti-migratory policy behind vagrancy legislation began as an essential complement of the wage stabilization legislation which accompanied the break-up of feudalism and the depopulation caused by the Black Death. By the Statutes of Labourers in 1349–1351, every ablebodied person without other means of

support was required to work for wages fixed at the level preceding the Black Death; it was unlawful to accept more, or to refuse an offer to work, or to flee from one county to another to avoid offers of work or to seek higher wages, or go give alms to able-bodied beggars who refused to work.[10]

In short, as Foote says in another place, this was an "attempt to make the vagrancy statutes a substitute for serfdom."[11] This same conclusion is equally apparent from the wording of the statute where it is stated:

> Because great part of the people, and especially of workmen and servants, late died in pestilence; many seeing the necessity of masters, and great scarcity of servants, will not serve without excessive wages, and some rather willing to beg in idleness than by labour to get their living: it is ordained, that every man and woman, of what condition he be, free or bond, able in body and within the age of threescore years, not living in merchandize, (etc.) be required to serve . . .

The innovation in the law, then, was a direct result of the aforementioned changes which had occurred in the social setting. In this case these changes were located for the most part in the economic institution of the society. The vagrancy laws were designed to alleviate a condition defined by the lawmakers as undesirable. The solution was to attempt to force a reversal, as it were, of a social process which was well underway; that is, to curtail mobility of laborers in such a way that labor would not become a commodity for which the landowners would have to compete.

Statutory Dormancy: A Legal Vestige

In time, of course, the curtailment of the geographical mobility of laborers was no longer requisite. One might well expect that when the function served by the statute was no longer an important one for the society, the statutes would be eliminated from the law. In fact, this has not occurred. The vagrancy statutes have remained in effect since 1349. Furthermore, as we shall see in some detail later, they were taken over by the colonies and have remained in effect in the United States as well.

The substance of the vagrancy statutes changed very little for some time after the first ones in 1349–1351 although there was a tendency to make punishments more harsh than originally. For example, in 1360 it was provided that violators of the statute should be imprisoned for fifteen days[12] and in 1388 the punishment was to put the offender in the stocks and to keep him there until "he find surety to return to his service."[13] That there was still, at this time, the intention of providing the landowner with labor is apparent from the fact that this statute provides:

> and he or she which use to labour at the plough and cart, or other labour and service of husbandry, till they be of the age of 12 years, from thenceforth shall abide at the same labour without being put to any mistery or handicraft: and any covenant of apprenticeship to the contrary shall be void.[14]

The next alteration in the statutes occurs in 1495 and is restricted to an increase in punishment. Here it is provided that vagrants shall be "set in stocks, there to remain by the space of three days and three nights, and there to have none other sustenance but bread and water; and after the said three days and nights, to be had out and set at large, and then to be commanded to avoid the town."[15]

The tendency to increase the severity of punishment during this period seems to be the result of a general tendency to make finer distinctions in the criminal law. During this period the vagrancy statutes appear to have been fairly inconsequential in either their effect as a control mechanism or as a generally enforced statute.[16] The processes of social change in the culture generally and the trend away from serfdom and into a "free" economy obviated the utility of these statutes. The result was not unexpected. The judiciary did not apply the law and the legislators did not take it upon themselves to change the law. In short, we have here a period of dormancy in which the statute is neither applied nor altered significantly.

A Shift in Focal Concern

Following the squelching of the Peasant's Revolt in 1381, the services of the serfs to the lord ". . . tended to become less and less exacted, although in certain forms they lingered on till the seventeenth century . . . By the sixteenth century few knew that there were any bondmen in England . . . and in 1575 Queen Elizabeth listened to the prayers of almost the last serfs in England . . . and granted them manumission."[17]

In view of this change we would expect corresponding changes in the vagrancy laws. Beginning with the lessening of punishment in the statute of 1503 we find these changes. However, instead of remaining dormant (or becoming more so) or being negated altogether, the vagrancy statutes experienced a shift in focal concern. With this shift the statutes served a new and equally important function for the social order of England. The first statute which indicates this change was in 1530. In this statute (22 H.8.c. 12 1530) it was stated:

> If any person, being whole and mighty in body, and able to labour, be taken in begging, or be vagrant and can give no reckoning how he lawfully gets his living; . . . and all other idle persons going about, some of them using divers and subtle crafty and unlawful games and plays, and some of them feigning themselves to have knowledge of . . . crafty sciences . . . shall be punished as provided.

What is most significant about this statute is the shift from an earlier concern with laborers to a concern with *criminal* activities. To be sure, the stipulation of persons "being whole and mighty in body, and able to labour, be taken in begging, or be vagrant" sounds very much like the concerns of the earlier statutes. Some important differences are apparent however when the rest of the statute includes those who ". . . can give no reckoning how he lawfully gets his living"; "some of them using divers subtil and unlawful games and plays." This is the first statute which specifically focuses upon these kinds of criteria for adjudging someone a vagrant.

It is significant that in this statute the severity of punishment is increased so as to be greater not only than provided by the 1503 statute but the punishment is more severe than that which had been provided by *any* of the pre-1503 statutes as well. For someone who is merely idle and gives no reckoning of how he makes his living the offender shall be:

> . . . had to the next market town, or other place where they [the constables] shall think most convenient, and there to be tied to the end of a cart naked, and to be beaten with whips throughout the same market town or other place, till his body be bloody by reason of such whipping.[18]

But, for those who use "divers and subtil crafty and unlawful games and plays," etc., the punishment is ". . . whipping at two days together in manner aforesaid."[19] For the second offense, such persons are:

> . . . scourged two days, and the third day to be put upon the pillory from nine of the clock till eleven before noon of the same day and to have one of his ears cut off.[20]

And if he offend the third time ". . . to have like punishment with whipping, standing on the pillory and to have his other ear cut off."

This statute (1) makes a distinction between types of offenders and applies the more severe punishment to those who are clearly engaged in "criminal" activities, (2) mentions a specific concern with categories of "unlawful" behavior, and (3) applies a type of punishment (cutting off the ear) which is generally reserved for offenders who are defined as likely to be a fairly serious criminal.

Only five years later we find for the first time that the punishment of death is applied to the crime of vagrancy. We also note a change in terminology in the statute:

> and if any ruffians . . . after having been once apprehended . . . shall wander, loiter, or idle use themselves and play the vagabonds . . . shall be eftsoons not only whipped again, but shall have the gristle of his right ear clean cut off. And if he shall again offend, he shall be committed to gaol till the next sessions; and being there convicted upon indictment, he shall have judgment to suffer pains and execution of death, as a felon, as an enemy of the commonwealth.[21]

It is significant that the statute now makes persons who repeat the crime of vagrancy a felon. During this period then, the focal concern of the vagrancy statutes becomes a concern for the control of felons and is no longer primarily concerned with the movement of laborers.

These statutory changes were a direct response to changes taking place in England's social structure during this period. We have already pointed out that feudalism was decaying rapidly. Concomitant with the breakup of feudalism was an increased emphasis upon commerce and industry. The commercial emphasis in England at the turn of the sixteenth century is of particular importance in the development of vagrancy laws. With commercialism came considerable traffic bearing valuable items. Where there were 169 important merchants in the middle of the

fourteenth century there were 3,000 merchants engaged in foreign trade alone at the beginning of the sixteenth century.[22] England became highly dependent upon commerce for its economic support. Italians conducted a great deal of the commerce of England during this early period and were held in low repute by the populace. As a result, they were subject to attacks by citizens and, more important, were frequently robbed of their goods while transporting them. "The general insecurity of the times made any transportation hazardous. The special risks to which the alien merchant was subjected gave rise to the royal practice of issuing formally executed covenants of safe conduct through the realm."[23]

Such a situation not only called for the enforcement of existing laws but also called for the creation of new laws which would facilitate the control of persons preying upon merchants transporting goods. The vagrancy statutes were revived in order to fulfill just such a purpose. Persons who had committed no serious felony but who were suspected of being capable of doing so could be apprehended and incapacitated through the application of vagrancy laws once these laws were refocused so as to include ". . . any ruffians . . . [who] shall wander, loiter, or idle use themselves and play the vagabonds . . ."[24]

The new focal concern is continued in 1 Ed. 6. c. 3 (1547) and in fact is made more general so as to include:

> Whoever man or woman, being not lame, impotent, or so aged or diseased that he or she cannot work, not having whereon to live, shall be lurking in any house, or loitering or idle wandering by the highway side, or in streets, cities, towns, or villages, not applying themselves to some honest labour, and so continuing for three days; or running away from their work; every such person shall be taken for a vagabond. And . . . upon conviction of two witnesses . . . the same loiterer (shall) be marked with a hot iron in the breast with the letter V, and adjudged him to the person bringing him, to be his slave for two years . . .

Should the vagabond run away, upon conviction, he was to be branded by a hot iron with the letter S on the forehead and to be thenceforth declared a slave forever. And in 1571 there is modification of the punishment to be inflicted, whereby the offender is to be "branded on the chest with the letter V" (for vagabond). And, if he is convicted the second time, the brand is to be made on the forehead. It is worth noting here that this method of punishment, which first appeared in 1530 and is repeated here with somewhat more force, is also an indication of a change in the type of person to whom the law is intended to apply. For it is likely that nothing so permanent as branding would be applied to someone who was wandering but looking for work, or at worst merely idle and not particularly dangerous *per se*. On the other hand, it could well be applied to someone who was likely to be engaged in other criminal activities in connection with being "vagrant."

By 1571 in the statute of 14 Ed. c. 5 the shift in focal concern is fully developed:

> All rogues, vagabonds, and sturdy beggars shall . . . be committed to the common gaol . . . he shall be grievously whipped, and burnt thro' the gristle of the right ear with a hot iron of the compass of an inch about; . . . And for the second offense, he shall be adjudged a felon, unless some person will take him for two years in to his service. And for the third offense, he shall be adjudged guilty of felony without benefit of clergy.

And there is included a long list of persons who fall within the statute: "proctors, procurators, idle persons going about using subtil, crafty and unlawful games or plays; and some of them feigning themselves to have knowledge of . . . absurd sciences . . . and all fencers, bearwards, common players in interludes, and minstrels . . . all juglers, pedlars, tinkers, petty chapmen . . . and all counterfeiters of licenses, passports and users of the same." The major significance of this statute is that it includes all the previously defined offenders and adds some more. Significantly, those added are more clearly criminal types, counterfeiters, for example. It is also significant that there is the following qualification of this statute: "Provided also, that this act shall not extend to cookers, or harvest folks, that travel for harvest work, corn or hay."

That the changes in this statute were seen as significant is indicated by the following statement which appears in the statute:

> And whereas by reason of this act, the common gaols of every shire are like to be greatly pestered with more number of prisoners than heretofore hath been, for that the said vagabonds and other lewd persons before recited shall upon their apprehension be committed to the said gaols; it is enacted . . .[25]

And a provision is made for giving more money for maintaining the gaols. This seems to add credence to the notion that this statute was seen as being significantly more general than those previously.

It is also of importance to note that this is the first time the term *rogue* has been used to refer to persons included in the vagrancy statutes. It seems, *a priori*, that a "rogue" is a different social type than is a "vagrant" or a "vagabond"; the latter terms implying something more equivalent to the idea of a "tramp" whereas the former (rogue) seems to imply a more disorderly and potentially dangerous person.

The emphasis upon the criminalistic aspect of vagrants continues in Chapter 17 of the same statute:

> Whereas divers *licentious* persons wander up and down in all parts of the realm, to countenance their *wicked behavior;* and do continually assemble themselves armed in the highways, and elsewhere in troops, *to the great terror* of her majesty's true subjects, *the impeachment of her laws,* and the disturbance of the peace and tranquility of the realm; and whereas many outrages are daily committed by these dissolute persons, and more are likely to ensue if speedy remedy be not provided. (Italics added)

With minor variations (*e.g.,* offering a reward for the capture of a vagrant) the statutes remain essentially of this nature until 1743. In 1743 there was once more an expansion of the types of persons included such that "all persons going about as patent gatherers, or gatherers of alms, under pretense of loss by fire or other casualty; or going about as collectors for prisons, gaols, or hospitals; all persons playing of betting at any unlawful games; and all persons who run away and leave their wives or children . . . all persons wandering abroad, and lodging in alehouses, barns, outhouses, or in the open air, not giving good account of themselves," were types of offenders added to those already included.

By 1743 the vagrancy statutes had apparently been sufficiently reconstructed by the shifts of concern so as to be once more a useful instrument in the creation of social solidarity. This function has apparently continued down to the present day in England and the changes from 1743 to the present have been all in the direction of clarifying or expanding the categories covered but little has been introduced to change either the meaning or the impact of this branch of the law.

We can summarize this shift in focal concern by quoting from Halsbury. He has noted that in the vagrancy statutes:

> ". . . elaborate provision is made for the relief and incidental control of destitute wayfarers. These latter, however, form but a small portion of the offenders aimed at by what are known as the Vagrancy Laws, . . . many offenders who are in no ordinary sense of the word vagrants, have been brought under the laws relating to vagrancy, and the great number of the offenses coming within the operation of these laws have little or no relation to the subject of poor relief, but are more properly directed towards the prevention of crime, the preservation of good order, and the promotion of social economy."[26]

Before leaving this section it is perhaps pertinent to make a qualifying remark. We have emphasized throughout this section how the vagrancy statutes underwent a shift in focal concern as the social setting changed. The shift in focal concern is not meant to imply that the later focus of the statutes represents a completely new law. It will be recalled that even in the first vagrancy statute there was reference to those who "do refuse labor, giving themselves to idleness and vice and sometimes to theft and other abominations." Thus the possibility of criminal activities resulting from persons who refuse to labor was recognized even in the earliest statute. The fact remains, however, that the major emphasis in this statute and in the statutes which followed the first one was always upon the "refusal to labor" or "begging." The "criminalistic" aspect of such persons was relatively unimportant. Later, as we have shown, the criminalistic potential becomes of paramount importance. The thread runs back to the earliest statute but the reason for the statutes' existence as well as the focal concern of the statutes is quite different in 1743 than it was in 1349.

Vagrancy Laws in the United States

In general, the vagrancy laws of England, as they stood in the middle eighteenth century, were simply adopted by the states. There were some exceptions to this general trend. For example, Maryland restricted the application of vagrancy laws to "free" Negroes. In addition, for *all* states the vagrancy laws were even more explicitly concerned with the control of criminals and undesirables

than had been the case in England. New York, for example, explicitly defines prostitutes as being a category of vagrants during this period. These exceptions do not, however, change the general picture significantly and it is quite appropriate to consider the U. S. vagrancy laws as following from England's of the middle eighteenth century with relatively minor changes. The control of criminals and undesirables was the *raison d'être* of the vagrancy laws in the U. S. This is as true today as it was in 1750. As Caleb Foote's analysis of the application of vagrancy statutes in the Philadelphia court shows, these laws are presently applied indiscriminately to persons considered a "nuisance." Foote suggests that ". . . the chief significance of this branch of the criminal law lies in its quantitative impact and administrative usefulness."[27] Thus it appears that in America the trend begun in England in the sixteenth, seventeenth and eighteenth centuries has been carried to its logical extreme and the laws are now used principally as a mechanism for "clearing the streets" of the derelicts who inhabit the "skid roads" and "Bowerys" of our large urban areas.

Since the 1800s there has been an abundant source of prospects to which the vagrancy laws have been applied. These have been primarily those persons deemed by the police and the courts to be either actively involved in criminal activities or at least peripherally involved. In this context, then, the statutes have changed very little. The functions served by the statutes in England of the late eighteenth century are still being served today in both England and the United States. The locale has changed somewhat and it appears that the present day application of vagrancy statutes is focused upon the arrest and confinement of the "down and outers" who inhabit certain sections of our larger cities but the impact has remained constant. The lack of change in the vagrancy statutes, then, can be seen as a reflection of the society's perception of a continuing need to control some of its "suspicious" or "undesirable" members.[28]

A word of caution is in order lest we leave the impression that this administrative purpose is the sole function of vagrancy laws in the U.S. today. Although it is our contention that this is generally true it is worth remembering that during certain periods of our recent history, and to some extent today, these laws have also been used to control the movement of workers. This was particularly the case during the depression years and California is of course infamous for its use of vagrancy laws to restrict the admission of migrants from other states.[29] The vagrancy statutes, because of their history, still contain germs within them which make such effects possible. Their main purpose, however, is clearly no longer the control of laborers but rather the control of the undesirable, the criminal and the "nuisance."

Discussion

The foregoing analysis of the vagrancy laws has demonstrated that these laws were a legislative innovation which reflected the socially perceived necessity of providing an abundance of cheap labor to landowners during a period when serfdom was breaking down and when the pool of available labor was depleted. With the eventual breakup of feudalism the need for such laws eventually disappeared and the increased dependence of the economy upon industry and commerce rendered the former use of the vagrancy statutes unnecessary. As a result, for a substantial period the vagrancy statutes were dormant, undergoing only minor changes and, presumably, being applied infrequently. Finally, the vagrancy laws were subjected to considerable alteration through a shift in the focal concern of the statutes. Whereas in their inception the laws focused upon the "idle" and "those refusing to labor" after the turn of the sixteenth century and emphasis came to be upon "rogues," "vagabonds," and others who were suspected of being engaged in criminal activities. During this period the focus was particularly upon "roadmen" who preyed upon citizens who transported goods from one place to another. The increased importance of commerce to England during this period made it necessary that some protection be given persons engaged in this enterprise and the vagrancy statutes provided one source for such protection by refocusing the acts to be included under these statutes.

Comparing the results of this analysis with the findings of Hall's study of theft we see a good deal of correspondence. Of major importance is the fact that both analyses demonstrate the truth of Hall's assertion that "The functioning of courts is significantly related to concomitant cultural needs, and this applies to the law of procedure as well as to substantive law."[30]

Our analysis of the vagrancy laws also indicates that when changed social conditions create a perceived need

for legal changes that these alterations will be effected through the revision and refocusing of existing statutes. This process was demonstrated in Hall's analysis of theft as well as in our analysis of vagrancy. In the case of vagrancy, the laws were dormant when the focal concern of the laws was shifted so as to provide control over potential criminals. In the case of theft the laws were re-interpreted (interestingly, by the courts and not by the legislature) so as to include persons who were transporting goods for a merchant but who absconded with the contents of the packages transported.

It also seems probable that when the social conditions change and previously useful laws are no longer useful there will be long periods when these laws will remain dormant. It is less likely that they will be officially negated. During this period of dormancy it is the judiciary which has principal responsibility for *not* applying the statutes. It is possible that one finds statutes being negated only when the judiciary stubbornly applies laws which do not have substantial public support. An example of such laws in contemporary times would be the "Blue Laws." Most states still have laws prohibiting the sale of retail goods on Sunday yet these laws are rarely applied. The laws are very likely to remain but to be dormant unless a recalcitrant judge or a vocal minority of the population insist that the laws be applied. When this happens we can anticipate that the statutes will be negated.[31] Should there arise a perceived need to curtail retail selling under some special circumstances, then it is likely that these laws will undergo a shift in focal concern much like the shift which characterized the vagrancy laws. Lacking such application the laws will simply remain dormant except for rare instances where they will be negated.

This analysis of the vagrancy statutes (and Hall's analysis of theft as well) has demonstrated the importance of "vested interest" groups in the emergence and/or alteration of laws. The vagrancy laws emerged in order to provide the powerful landowners with a ready supply of cheap labor. When this was no longer seen as necessary and particularly when the landowners were no longer dependent upon cheap labor nor were they a powerful interest group in the society the laws became dormant. Finally a new interest group emerged and was seen as being of great importance to the society and the laws were then altered so as to afford some protection to this group. These findings are thus in agreement with Weber's contention that "status groups" determine the content of the law.[32] The findings are inconsistent, on the other hand, with the perception of the law as simply a reflection of "public opinion" as is sometimes found in the literature.[33] We should be cautious in concluding, however, that either of these positions are necessarily correct. The careful analysis of other laws, and especially of laws which do not focus so specifically upon the "criminal," are necessary before this question can be finally answered.

In conclusion, it is hoped that future analyses of changes within the legal structure will be able to benefit from this study by virtue of (1) the data provided and (2) the utilization of a set of concepts (innovation, dormancy, concern and negation) which have proved useful in the analysis of the vagrancy law. Such analyses should provide us with more substantial grounds for rejecting or accepting as generally valid the description of some of the processes which appear to characterize changes in the legal system.

NOTES

1. Hall, J., *Theft, Law and Society,* Bobbs-Merrill, 1939. See also, Alfred R. Lindesmith, "Federal Law and Drug Addiction," *Social Problems* Vol. 7, No. 1, 1959, p. 48.
2. See, for example, Rose, A., "Some Suggestions for Research in the Sociology of Law," *Social Problems* Vol. 9, No. 3, 1962, pp. 281–283, and Geis, G., "Sociology, Criminology, and Criminal Law," *Social Problems* Vol. 7, No. 1, 1959, pp. 40–47.
3. 3 Ed. 1. c. 1.
4. 35 Ed. 1. c. 1.
5. 23 Ed. 3.
6. 25 Ed. 3 (1351).
7. Bradshaw, F., *A Social History of England,* p. 54.
8. *Ibid.*
9. *Ibid.,* p. 57.
10. Foote, C., "Vagrancy Type Law and Its Administration," *Univ. of Pennsylvania Law Review* (104), 1956, p. 615.
11. *Ibid.*
12. 34 Ed. 3 (1360).
13. 12 R. 2 (1388).
14. *Ibid.*
15. 11 H. & C. 2 (1495).
16. As evidenced for this note the expectation that ". . . the common gaols of every shire are likely to be greatly pestered with more numbers of prisoners than heretofore . . ."

when the statutes were changed by the statute of 14 Ed. c. 5 (1571).
17. Bradshaw, *op. cit.,* p. 61.
18. 22 H. 8. c. 12 (1530).
19. *Ibid.*
20. *Ibid*
21. 27 H. 8. c. 25 (1535).
22. Hall, *op. cit.,* p. 21.
23. *Ibid.,* p. 23.
24. 27 H. 8. c. 25 (1535).
25. 14 Ed. c. 5. (1571).
26. Earl of Halsbury, *The Laws of England,* Butterworth & Co., Bell Yard, Temple Bar, 1912, pp. 606–607.
27. Foote, *op. cit.,* p. 613. Also see in this connection, Irwin Deutscher, "The Petty Offender," *Federal Probation,* XIX, June, 1955.
28. It is on this point that the vagrancy statutes have been subject to criticism. See for example, Lacey, Forrest W., "Vagrancy and Other Crimes of Personal Condition," *Harvard Law Review* (66), p. 1203.
29. Edwards *vs* California. 314 S: 160 (1941).
30. Hall, *op. cit.,* p. XII.
31. Negation, in this instance, is most likely to come about by the repeal of the statute. More generally, however, negation may occur in several ways including the declaration of a statute as unconstitutional. This later mechanism has been used even for laws which have been "on the books" for long periods of time. Repeal is probably the most common, although not the only, procedure by which a law is negated.
32. M. Rheinstein, *Max Weber on Law in Economy and Society,* Harvard University Press, 1954.
33. Friedman, N., *Law in a Changing Society,* Berkeley and Los Angeles: University of California Press, 1959.

Think Critically

1. What do you think are the main reasons why at least some laws are formed, according to Chambliss' socio-historical review of the law of vagrancy?
2. Give examples about how social perceptions of changed social conditions have led to revisions of existing statutes in society.

Governmental and State Crime*

Stephen M. Rosoff, Henry N. Pontell, and Robert H. Tillman

NO AREA OF WHITE-COLLAR CRIME IS MORE infectious than crimes by the government. A government that breaks the law encourages emulation by other elite institutions. In 1928, Justice Louis Brandeis wrote a famous dissent in an early case involving the domestic surveillance of citizens, in which he warned that governmental lawlessness was "contagious." Brandeis further noted that persons in power who disregard or violate the Constitutional tenets upon which the United States was built place our political contract in jeopardy: "In a government of laws, the existence of the government will be imperilled if it fails to observe the law scrupulously."[1]

In this chapter, we will examine how some officials of the American government have discarded fundamental principles of democracy, civil liberty, and morality in the name of expedience. Three illustrative topics will be considered: (1) the use of human "guinea pigs;" (2) violation of sovereignty; and (3) abuse of power.

Use of Human Guinea Pigs

Officially condoned abuses of unknowing or unwilling human subjects immediately suggest the crimes of the Third Reich, where military doctors performed hideous medical experiments on concentration camp prisoners. Without a doubt, no society ever carried human experimentation to such a monstrous extreme; but the United States does have a shameful history of its own.

At the core of the Nazi atrocities was the concept of eugenics—the "improvement" of the human race through such practices as selective breeding and compulsory sterilization. Even before this perverted synthesis of social Darwinism and Mendelian biology was tried in Germany,

the eugenics movement thrived in the U.S. In fact, the United States and Germany remain the only "civilized" Western nations in which sterilization laws were enforced. By the time the infamous Nuremberg Laws were enacted in Germany in 1935, providing for sterilization of those who were considered genetically unfit to propagate the species, an estimated 20,000 Americans deemed feebleminded or morally degenerate already had been sterilized—12,000 in California alone.[2]

In 1933, the *Journal of the American Medical Association* published a report entitled "Sterilization to Improve the Race." Although the subject of the report was Germany's new sterilization laws, the uncritical language helped provide American eugenics statutes with a veneer of scientific respectability:

> Countless individuals of inferior type and possessing serious hereditary defects are propagating unchecked with the result that their diseased progeny becomes a burden to society and is threatening within three generations to overwhelm completely the valuable strata . . . [S]terilization is the only sure means of preventing the further hereditary transmission of mental disease and serious defects.[3]

Between 1924 and 1972, the state of Virginia sterilized over 8,300 mentally retarded citizens.[4] This practice, rooted in what has been called the "biology of stupidity,"[5] was upheld by the U.S. Supreme Court in a landmark 1927 ruling in *Buck v. Bell*.[6] This case involved the first victim of Virginia's Compulsory Sterilization Law—a teenage girl named Carrie Buck, who had been committed to the notorious Lynchburg Colony for Epileptics and the Feebleminded and subsequently was sterilized without her agreement or understanding.[7] Writing for the Court, Justice Oliver Wendell Holmes declared: "Three generations of imbeciles is enough."[8]

---

*Excerpted from Chapter 9 (Crimes by the Government) in *Profit without Honor: White-Collar Crime and the Looting of America* (5th ed.). Upper Saddle River, NJ: Pearson Prentice Hall, 2010, pp. 375–434.

Lamentably, the fate of Carrie Buck was no aberration. The total number of Americans sterilized under eugenics statutes has been estimated at 63,000.[9] Although many of these laws have been repealed, sterilization without a subject's consent still was permitted in 14 states as recently as 1985.[10] In a more modern variation on this theme, a mother, charged in 1991 with beating her children after she caught them smoking, was sentenced by a California court to a year in prison. A condition of her release on probation at the end of that period was that she be given the contraceptive drug Norplant, which must be implanted surgically in a woman's forearm.[11] Civil libertarians have expressed concern that such compulsory contraception violates medical ethics by involving doctors in operations that have nothing to do with medicine, *per se,* and abrogates women's rights to control their procreative capacity. As one observer has noted: "Far from being part of a new trend, these cases hark back to old-fashioned eugenics plans to 'improve' society by ensuring that 'undesirables' do not reproduce."[12]

It also is worth noting that one of the most widely discussed books in recent years is *The Bell Curve*[13] published in 1994, a pseudo-scientific affirmation of racially-based theories of intellectual inferiority. This book has been attacked by some critics as a harbinger of a potential revival of the eugenics movement in the 21st century.

The Tuskegee Syphilis Experiment

The best-documented human guinea pig case in American history is the Tuskegee Study of Untreated Syphilis in the Negro Male.[14] For forty years, between 1932 and 1972, the United States Public Health Service, in cooperation with local health officials, withheld all treatment from more than 400 syphilitic men in an economically depressed, predominantly black county in rural Alabama. The purpose of the Tuskegee study was to compare the incidence of death and debilitation among untreated subjects with a treated sample of syphilitic men, as well as a healthy control group. "[S]yphilis is a highly contagious infection spread by sexual contact, and . . . if untreated, it can lead to blindness; deafness; deterioration of the bones, teeth, and the central nervous system; heart disease; insanity; and even death."[15] Syphilis may be transmitted to a fetus by an infected mother.[16]

All the untreated subjects were uneducated black sharecroppers and laborers. The Tuskegee study thus has to be viewed within the context of the ingrained racist beliefs

permeating the American medical establishment of the time. The social Darwinism that had spurred the eugenics movement had generated a fallacious agreement "that the health of blacks had to be considered separately from the health of whites."[17] Many doctors thought that Africans were genetically predisposed toward sexual promiscuity. "In this atmosphere it was not surprising that physicians depicted syphilis as the quintessential black disease."[18]

The Tuskegee study emerged from a syphilis control survey that had been carried out by Alabama health officials in 1930 at the instigation of a local white plantation owner who had noticed a decline in the live birth rate among his 700 black tenants and had attributed it to syphilis. A curious feature of the program was its avoidance of the word "syphilis." Instead, the health officials told subjects that they had come to test people for "bad blood"—a catchall phrase from the rural black argot, used for everything from indigestion to pellagra.[19]

The survey revealed even a higher incidence of syphilis than had been expected, so, when the program was terminated in 1932, some doctors from the U.S. Public Health Service (PHS) perceived what one termed a "ready-made opportunity"[20] to study untreated syphilis in a living outside the world of modern medicine.

The afflicted men identified by the survey were sent an imposing letter, which invoked the authority of the Macon County Health Department, the Alabama State Board of Health, the U.S. Public Health Service, and even Tuskegee Institute, the eminent college known as the "black Harvard."[21] The opening paragraph read:

> Some time ago you were given a thorough examination and since that time we hope you have gotten a great deal of treatment for bad blood. You will now be given your last chance to get a second examination. This examination is a very special one and after it is finished you will be given a special treatment if it is believed you are in a condition to stand it.[22]

The letter closed with an ominous exhortation, written in capital letters that jumped off the page: "REMEMBER THIS IS YOUR LAST CHANCE FOR SPECIAL TREATMENT."[23] In its skillful exploitation of the subjects' ignorance and desire for medical care, the letter was a "masterpiece of guileful deceit."[24] Among the "special treatments" in store were spinal taps performed without anesthesia.[25]

Participants were not told about the true nature of the experiment. The idea of the study was to observe the subjects over the course of their lives and eventually bring them to autopsy. Burial stipends would be provided to the families of the deceased. Over the next four decades, 161 autopsies were performed.

No therapeutic intervention ever was provided for the subjects, nor for their wives who invariably contracted the disease, nor for their children who subsequently were born with congenital syphilis. Even when antibiotics became available in 1946, and penicillin emerged as an effective drug for syphilis, treatment still was denied.[26] This is particularly troubling, because the advent of penicillin seemingly obviated any rational purpose to the experiment. As one PHS officer finally would acknowledge, 38 years too late: "Nothing learned will prevent, find, or cure a single case of infectious syphilis or bring us closer to our basic mission of controlling venereal disease in the United States."[27] Indeed, the only contribution the Tuskegee study ever made to medical science was keeping laboratories supplied with syphilitic blood samples for testing purposes. "The benefit seems small when one remembers that some of the blood donors later died from syphilis."[28]

In 1965, a young venereal disease investigator employed by the PHS, first heard about the ongoing Tuskegee Study from co-workers. "He had difficulty believing the stories."[29] After reviewing all the articles and official documents on the experiment, he was horrified and began warning his superiors that the ethical and racial aspects of the study were potentially explosive: "The excuses and justifications that might have been offered for starting the study in 1932 were no longer relevant. . . . [Subjects] were nothing more than dupes and were being used as human substitutes for guinea pigs."[30]

Two years after joining the PHS, the investigator resigned. The following year he wrote a letter to the director of the Division of Venereal Diseases, re-expressing grave moral concerns about the experiment. In 1972, he finally told the "bad blood" story to the press. The outrage was predictable. Senator Abraham Ribicoff labeled the Tuskegee study a "frightening instance of bureaucratic arrogance and insensitivity."[31]

Seventy surviving subjects sued the government, and in 1974 an Alabama court awarded each $37,500. When divided by 40 years, that sum worked out to $2.50 a day.[32]

The "bad blood" study was by no means the government's only 40-year excursion into human experimentation. From 1938 to at least 1978, "there was an effort made by the agencies of the U.S. government to develop sophisticated techniques of psycho-politics and mind control."[33] This dangerous research involved tens of thousands of subjects—many of them involuntary.[34] These unwitting human guinea pigs were victimized by an amoral cadre of psychiatrists, psychologists, and chemists under contract to various government agencies, most notably the CIA.[35]

Among the areas under study were: (1) the use of hypnosis to induce amnesia or elicit false confessions;[36] and (2) the refinement of powerful conditioning techniques, such as sensory deprivation, desensitization, and aversion therapy, to control human behavior.[37] In the words of one journalist, these and other methods "were eventually developed and used to reduce some of our own citizens to a zombie state in which they would blindly serve the government."[38] In 1958, the CIA even prepared a report which suggested that the intelligence agencies might control people through drug addiction. "The report went so far as to recommend that wounded GIs who had become addicts to pain-killing drugs be recruited from hospitals"[39] . . .

When the CIA began experimenting with LSD in the early 1950s, it determined that members of the borderline underworld would make the best subjects, because even if they realized that they had been drugged, they would not go to the police. LSD was administered covertly to prostitutes, addicts, and petty criminals. One agent even slipped some LSD to a lieutenant of mob boss Lucky Luciano.[40] "[The CIA] reasoned that if they had to violate the civil rights of anyone, they might as well choose marginal people."[41]

In 1953, the agency decided to test LSD on a group of unsuspecting scientists from the Army Chemical Corps. The drug was mixed into their after-dinner drinks. "The dose pushed one of its victims—Frank Olson—into a psychotic confusion; several days later . . . Olson [apparently] leapt to his death from a New York hotel window."[42] For 26 years, the cause of Olson's death had been concealed from his family, who had been led to believe that he had committed suicide because of an unexplained mental breakdown.[43] When Olson's family finally were told the circumstances of his death, they questioned that he had jumped. On June 2, 1994, more than forty years after Frank Olson's purported leap, his body was exhumed. Forensic remains revealed that "[s]kull injuries and the lack of cuts on the body were inconsistent with the CIA's description of events surrounding his death."[44] Whatever really happened to Frank Olson seems destined to remain a mystery . . .

One of the Army's most brazen experiments took place over a four-day period in 1966. Another microorganism, this one called *Bacillus subtilis,* was dumped into the heart of the New York City subway system. A report on this test, released later under the Freedom of Information Act, described the scene:

> "When the cloud engulfed people," the report says, "they brushed their clothing, looked up at the grating apron and walked on.". . . The experiment was a huge success. Everyone was breathing the bacteria and no one was ever aware of it.[45]

Bacillus subtilis is nearly indestructible, and most of the bacteria dropped in 1966 may remain throughout the 21st century.[46]

> [H]ow dangerous is *Bacillus subtilis?* It is dangerous indeed if one happens to be allergic to it, or is very old, very young, very ill or very anything that classifies a person as a compromised host. Might such people have been riding the subways? Of course. But beyond that, the exposed commuters became carriers, and took the bacteria with them as they traveled to their homes, to their offices or to hospitals to visit elderly relatives."[47]

A spokesperson for the Army's scientific division defended its simulated biological warfare tests by characterizing them as less hazardous than an urban bus ride:

> "[W]hen you get on the bus in Philadelphia or New York, you're going to be riding with a bunch of people—the Chinese, the Vietnamese, the blacks, the lower-class Irish and all these people—that may have tuberculosis and never know it, and be coughing in your face, and end up exposing you to a far more serious type of organism than what was being sprayed into the air."[48]

The bigotry and contempt for humanity that oozes out of every crack in the preceding statement goes a long way toward answering the inevitable "How could they do that?" questions . . .

Prison Experiments: Who Gives a Damn?

Another controversial form of human experimentation is the use of American prisoners as subjects for medical research. In a 1950 memorandum to the Atomic Energy Commission, Dr. Joseph Hamilton of Livermore National

Laboratory in California expressed his concern that "tests aimed at discovering at what level radiation would injure soldiers would conjure up images of Nazi concentration camp experiments if performed on humans."[49] Indeed, after World War II, the issue of experimentation on prisoners was stressed at the Nuremberg War Crimes trials.

Obviously, informed consent had no relevance to the Nazis, but in the United States participation usually is "voluntary," in the technical sense that prisoners must sign consent forms and waivers. However, the psychological defenselessness of a captive role makes genuine consent illusory. "[B]ecause a prisoner has limited choices, his consent to such experimentation cannot be obtained without at least the appearance of coercion."[50] The American Civil Liberties Union has estimated that approximately 10 percent of the American prison population participates in medical and drug experiments.[51]

In 1961, some Harvard University scientists gave a group of inmates at the Concord State Prison in Massachusetts between two and five doses of pellocybin, a dangerous hallucinogenic drug. This research was directed by the flamboyant psychopharmacologist, Timothy Leary.

> He once used Harvard students in some of his drug experiments, and Harvard fired him two years after the Concord experiment when his own drug usage became public . . . Later on, he was imprisoned for smuggling hashish from Afghanistan. President Nixon once described him as "the most dangerous man in America."[52]

The purpose of the Concord prison study was to test whether pellocybin could reduce the high recidivism rate among parolees. All of the participating inmates were chosen because they were scheduled for parole within three months. By 1965, four years after receiving the drug, 59 percent of the subjects were back behind bars.[53]

Between 1963 and 1971, 131 inmates in Washington and Oregon agreed to have their testicles exposed to very high levels of X-rays. This experiment was designed by the government to determine the minimum dose that would cause healthy men to become sterile. While consent forms did indicate some of the risks, no mention was made that radiation could cause testicular cancer. Furthermore, no follow-up studies ever were conducted on the prisoners after the conclusion of the study.[54] A 23-year-old convict, for example, had his testicles bombarded with a dose of radiation equivalent to twenty X-rays in 1965. He had received a stipend of $5 for his participation. Thirty years later, he complained of lumps on his body, along with testicular pain and chronic rashes. Other ex-convicts from similar studies have voiced the same complaints.[55]

At some prisons, pharmaceutical corporations have competed vigorously to purchase exclusive rights to conduct drug toxicity tests on inmates.[56] In 1975, some prisoners testified at a U.S. Senate hearing concerned with human experimentation. One was James Downey, who had been a state prisoner in Oklahoma:

> He told of having participated in a planned thirty-day program to test a potent new drug intended to cure liver ailments. Downey said he was told it was a new "wonder" drug, and was assured it would have no adverse effects.[57]

After 11 days on the "wonder" drug, Downey became very sick. He was denied any medical attention for several days and then was told he had measles. He was assured that his illness was unrelated to the drug; but Downey later learned that he was suffering from drug-induced hepatitis.[58]

From the experimenters' point of view, there are two reasons why prisoners make convenient human subjects. First, because the studies take place in an outcast environment, if prisoners such as James Downey become seriously ill—or even if they happen to die—it is unlikely to generate much public concern.[59] Second, prison studies are economical. Downey told the Senate that he had volunteered in order to earn money for cigarettes. One doctor has remarked that prisoners are ideal for medical experimentation because they are "cheaper than chimpanzees."[60]

Violation of Sovereignty

Most domestic varieties of white-collar crime also have been committed abroad, either by American companies or by the United States government itself. These offenses range from bribery and covert manipulation to outright interference in the affairs of other nations.

Bribery of government officials commonly is used to obtain business contracts in many foreign countries. This practice is often concealed in company books under such euphemistic entries as "facilitating payments."[61] Although bribery violates both American and international law, it has continued for many decades, because the penalties seldom exceed the gains.[62] During the 1970s, nearly 400

American corporations admitted making payments totaling $750 million to foreign officials . . .[63]

American corporations long have insisted that political bribery is a traditional and necessary cost of doing business overseas.[64] This self-serving argument ignores the considerable damage that corporate bribery inflicts on our national image abroad. It also disrespects the principle of national sovereignty, which is the cornerstone of global order. For example, a single corporation—Lockheed—effectively toppled a government in Japan, nearly destroyed the Dutch monarchy, corrupted national elections in Germany, Portugal, and Brazil, and caused the arrest of a former Italian prime minister.[65]

Agencies of the American government have disregarded the sovereignty of other nations even more recklessly than corporations. It is ironic that the United States, which was founded upon the sanctity of self-determination, has such a sorry record of denying that right to others. For example, when the Iranian government attempted to nationalize the properties of American oil companies in the early 1950s, the CIA engineered a coup that restored the dictatorial Shah to the throne.[66] In the 1960s, the CIA financed the overthrow of the left-wing government of Ecuador[67] and played a pivotal role in an Indonesian revolution in which at least 500,000 people were killed.[68]

In fact, it is now acknowledged that the CIA participated in the overthrow or attempted overthrow of numerous regimes around the world, including ones in Syria, Somalia, the Sudan, Angola, Ghana, Guatemala, and Guyana.[69] In each of these countries, "CIA intrusion has left a trail of poverty, social chaos, and political repression."[70]

During the Vietnam War, Congress had by law forbidden the hiring of mercenaries from neighboring countries or the deployment of American troops in those countries. Nevertheless, the CIA organized unlawful secret armies composed of ethnic minorities from Laos and Thailand to fight along the borders of North and South Vietnam.[71] Even more dismaying, when American troops illegally invaded Cambodia, soldiers' death certificates were falsified to read that they had died elsewhere . . .[72]

The Iran-Contra Affair

The Iran Contra affair is a tale of an "invisible government"[73] sustained through deceit and contempt for the rule of law. The roots of this maze of crimes and cover-ups may be traced back to the foreign policy agenda of the new Reagan Administration in 1981. It was President Reagan's announced intention to encourage the removal of the Marxist Sandinista government in Nicaragua. Initially, there was nothing furtive about this policy; the President publicly had supported aid to the Contras, a pro-American rebel army engaged in a guerrilla war against the Sandinistas.

Congress, though, was less willing to authorize funding for an interventionist policy and passed a series of amendments between 1982 and 1986 (known as the Boland Amendments, after their principal author, a Massachusetts congressman), severely limiting or prohibiting the appropriation of funds on behalf of the Contras. By that time, however, the White House had committed itself to backing the Contras at all costs.

> This policy could not be carried out without defying Congress. Open defiance was politically unfeasible. The only other way was to do it covertly.[74]

The administration formulated two types of schemes for circumventing the legally imposed restraints. The first method was to give the task of arming the Contras to the National Security Council (NSC). Congress explicitly had proscribed the use of funds by the Defense Department and the CIA or any other intelligence agency on behalf of the Contras. The NSC was not technically an intelligence agency, so its utilization provided the administration with a way of evading the spirit of the law, if not the letter. The second method was to employ "private" or "third-party" funds, on the assumption that only official United States funds had been prohibited.[75] This plan also would be implemented by the NSC. The NSC was headed by national security adviser Robert McFarlane, who had been instructed by President Reagan to keep the Contras together "body and soul."[76] McFarlane assigned this task to his chief "action officer," Marine Lieutenant Colonel Oliver North.

North, a decorated Vietnam veteran, who reportedly once had suffered a two-year emotional breakdown after the war, became the designated "contact" between the NSC and the Contras. He was appointed Deputy Director for Political Military Affairs, a vague title that removed him from the NSC chain-of-command and made him answerable only to McFarlane. In effect, an obscure soldier became a one-man operation. His job was to recruit others to help fund the Contras.

Foremost among the "others" to whom North turned were a pair of international arms dealers, retired Air Force Major General Richard Secord and his business partner, an Iranian-born American citizen named Albert Hakim. Ultimately, Secord and Hakim sold about $11 million worth of weapons to the Contras.[77] Much of their proceeds were stashed away in Swiss bank accounts. Secord later told Congress that he had been motivated solely by patriotism and would gladly give his share of the profits to the Contras.[78] He never did.

Obviously, the Contras required a large influx of cash in order to pay for weapons and equipment. In order to deceive Congress, millions of dollars had to be raised privately. This was accomplished in part through nonprofit conservative foundations. While private citizens were entitled to raise money for the Contras on their own, official cooperation by the administration entailed a criminal conspiracy—especially when donations were disguised as humanitarian assistance.

The "third-country" strategy began in 1983 when overtures were made to Israel and South Africa regarding aid to the Contras. In 1984, Saudi Arabia agreed to contribute $1 million a month, ostensibly from private funds, to help the Contras survive. The following year, the Saudis' monthly contribution was raised to $2 million. The total Saudi contribution eventually exceeded $30 million.[79] The administration realized that Nicaragua was of no real interest to Saudi Arabia (the two countries did not even have diplomatic relations); thus, the money was solicited as an opportunity for the Saudis to curry personal favor with President Reagan.

The government of Taiwan also contributed $2 million after North promised that Nicaragua would recognize the Taiwanese regime once the Sandinistas were ousted. In addition, President Reagan vetoed a bill which would have placed restrictions on imported Taiwanese textiles.[80]

The "private" and "third-country" contributions enabled the Contras to survive well into 1985. That year, the American ambassador to Costa Rica, Lewis Tambs, was instructed by North to obtain permission from the Costa Rican government for the construction of a "private" airstrip to be used to supply the Contras. When he subsequently was asked if he thought that building a secret pro-Contra military installation in a neutral country violated the Boland Amendments, Tambs replied that he had never read those amendments, since, in his words: "I have difficulty reading a contract for a refrigerator."[81]

The governments of Guatemala, El Salvador, and Honduras also were pressured into cooperation. Honduras was particularly important, because the main Contra force was based there; all supplies had to be brought there for distribution.[82] For example, another arms dealer, retired Major General John Singlaub, purchased weapons from Eastern Europe for $4.8 million, shipped them to Honduras, and sold them to the Contras for $5.3 million.[83]

Concurrent, though seemingly unrelated, events on the other side of the globe were to further complicate an already Byzantine enterprise. Another item on the Reagan foreign policy agenda was the punishment of the Iranian regime led by the ferociously anti-American Ayatollah Khomeini. Khomeini had overthrown the despised Shah in early 1979. The following November, a group of Iranian students had stormed the United States embassy in Tehran on Khomeini's behalf and kidnapped a group of innocent Americans, holding them hostage for 444 days. In 1982, the White House accused Iran of supporting international terrorism and launched a vigorous campaign to block the sale of arms to that nation.

By 1984, however, another group of hostages was being held in Lebanon by Islamic extremists under Khomeini's control. Ronald Reagan looked the American people in the eye and stated his position in resolute terms: "The United States gives terrorists no rewards . . . We make no deals."[84] These words later would come back to haunt the President like Marley's ghost.

On August 6, 1985, McFarlane met with Reagan to discuss a proposal to use Israel for the sale of 100 TOWs (an acronym for Tube-launched Optically-tracked Wire-guided missiles) to Iran, with the deal to be followed by the release of the American hostages. The President later acknowledged that he had authorized the sale, then said that he had *not* authorized the sale, and finally claimed that he had no recollection one way or the other.[85] In any case, two weeks later 96 TOWs were transferred by Israel to Iran. No hostages were released.[86]

Israeli and Iranian negotiators met again in September. The Iranians indicated that one hostage would be released in exchange for an additional 400 TOWs. On September 15, 408 missiles arrived in Tehran, and the first hostage—Presbyterian minister Benjamin Weir—was released.[87] In November, 19 Hawk missiles were delivered from Israel to Iran aboard a CIA plane. No hostages were released.

As 1985 drew to a close, an emotionally exhausted Bud McFarlane resigned as National Security Adviser and

was replaced by his deputy, Vice Admiral John Poindexter.[88] In one of his first acts, Poindexter presented a "finding" to President Reagan. A finding is a written document describing the need for and nature of covert operations and requires the President's signature.[89] Reagan signed that finding, which retroactively authorized the Hawk shipment.[90] A year later, Poindexter destroyed the finding on the ground that it would be politically embarrassing if it ever were revealed publicly. "He could not have realized what a good prophet he was going to be."[91]

Of all the documents written during this period, however, the most notorious was undoubtedly the so-called "diversion memorandum." Drafted by North in April 1986 and forwarded to Reagan and Poindexter, it summarized the Iranian operations and indicated the use of arms sale profits for the Contras in Nicaragua.[92] "Those few lines created more future trouble for North than anything else he ever said or wrote."[93]

On July 26, a second hostage—Father Lawrence Jenko, director of Catholic Relief Services in Beirut—was released. Two weeks later, 240 Hawk missile parts were shipped to Iran.[94]

By the middle of 1986, however, reports were beginning to appear in the press connecting North to fundraising activities on behalf of the Contras. When a supply plane linked to a CIA "front" was shot down over Nicaragua in October, that incident provided an unmistakable disclosure of an illegal, covert American policy. "As might have been expected, a denial reflex took over in official circles."[95] CIA Director William Casey nervously advised North to shut down the operations. North began shredding incriminating documents and destroying ledgers and address books. The spool was starting to unravel. "North was now a man in a hurry."[96]

The news of North's secret role in the arms-for-hostages deals with Iran burst onto the front pages on November 6. When the story broke, North reportedly sat at a computer terminal in his office at the National Security Council and tapped out a weirdly-coded confidential computer memo to a colleague:

> Oh, Lord. I lost the slip and broke one of the high heels. Forgive please. Will return the wig on Monday.[97]

As of this writing, nearly 25 years later, it is still not clear to anybody what this cryptic—and rather kinky—message means.

On November 13, in a speech drafted by North and polished by White House writers, President Reagan addressed the nation and stated: "We did not—repeat—did not trade weapons or anything else for hostages nor will we."[98] A poll in the *Los Angeles Times* reported that only 14 percent of the public believed the President.[99] Even Republican icon Barry Goldwater was skeptical. In his words: "I think President Reagan has gotten his butt in a crack on this Iran thing."[100]

Reagan, unaccustomed to harsh rejection, was shaken.[101] He held a press conference on November 19, which would be remembered as the worst public performance of his presidency. He conceded that a small amount of arms had been sold to Iran, but that he was terminating all such sales. He claimed that he had the legal right not to have informed Congress. When he described the TOW missile as a "shoulder-mounted" weapon, he was corrected by a reporter, who explained to the Commander-in-Chief that TOWs were ground-to-ground weapons fired from tripods.[102]

Reagan's worst blunder occurred when he categorically denied any "third country" involvement. Secretary of State George Schultz already had disclosed to the press that the United States *had* condoned the Israeli shipment of arms to Iran the previous year. Schultz had to meet with Reagan and correct him the day after the press conference. Schultz later testified: "[I]t was not the kind of discussion I ever thought I would have with the President of the United States."[103]

For Reagan, the time had come for damage control. He decided to fire Poindexter and transfer North out of the NSC. But damage control is a two-way street: On November 21, North instructed his young secretary, former fashion model Fawn Hall, to alter a series of NSC documents from his files. She and North also shredded documents until 4:15 a.m.[104] When she later testified before Congress, the intensely loyal Hall was asked whether she had realized that altering these documents was wrong. "Sometimes," she said, "you have to go above the written law."[105]

The next Presidential press conference must have been a painful experience for a politician whose brilliantly successful career had been built upon superb communicative talent. After a few brief remarks, in which he claimed that he had not been fully informed of the Iranian activities, Reagan turned the microphone over to Attorney General Edwin Meese. "After his fiasco on November 19, he could not be trusted—or could not trust himself—to go on the stage and face a disbelieving, tumultuous press conference alone."[106]

Meese acknowledged the diversion of funds from Iranian arms sales to the Contras. He implied that North may have been guilty of violating the law—without presidential authorization. North reportedly was stunned by what he perceived as abandonment by his superiors. He realized that he was in real danger of being convicted of criminal acts. When his office was sealed by NSC security, Fawn Hall smuggled documents out inside her clothing. But surreptitiously removing a few documents, as well as shredding or altering a handful of others, was not going to save Oliver North. "Like many other things North did, this effort to hide the traces of his activity was marked as much by ineptitude as by anything else."[107] A paper trail connecting three continents could not be erased one page at a time.

> So many hundreds of incriminating documents and memoranda were left or recovered that it was possible to reconstruct the course of the Iran and contra affairs in extraordinary detail. Even the diversion, "the deepest, darkest secret of the whole activity," as [North] called it, came to light.[108]

The Iran-Contra Affair effectively was finished. North was not the only figure to be racing ahead of the posse, however. Reagan's friends were urging him to hire a criminal lawyer to defend his position. "[S]ome of those close to Reagan expected him to be one of the prime victims of the scandal."[109] The President immediately appointed a Special Review Board, headed by former Senator John Tower, to study the conduct of the NSC staff. Both houses of Congress created select committees to investigate Iran-Contra. An Independent Counsel also was appointed to prosecute any criminal offenses.[110]

In May 1987, the House and Senate began rare joint hearings on the Iran-Contra Affair. All the major figures testified—with the exception of the President and CIA Director Casey, who died on the second day of the hearings. America heard the feisty Secord explain the logistics of the operation, the contrite McFarlane, three months after a failed suicide attempt, implicate the President in a robotic monotone, and the unrepentant Poindexter blame Congress and the press for distorting the importance of Iran-Contra. Witnesses—from the unscrupulous

Hakim, to the glamorous Hall, to the pugnacious leader of the Contras, Adolfo Calero, to a roll call of supporting players—appeared on millions of American television screens.[111] This cast, however, had to settle for roles in the chorus; center-stage belonged to Oliver North.

North strode into the hearing room in full Marine uniform, complete with six rows of medals. Although he had not worn his uniform in five years at the NSC, it was an effective strategy. North's lawyers had packaged him for the American public as a persecuted patriot. By the time the hearings had concluded, the press had coined the term "Olliemania."

> There were Ollie T-shirts, Ollie bumper stickers, Ollie dolls, Ollie haircuts, Ollieburgers (shredded beef topped with shredded American cheese and shredded lettuce), Ollie recipes, and even Ollie-for-President boomlets.[112]

North presented himself as a defiant hero, an obedient soldier, a blameless scapegoat whose conduct had been dictated or approved by his superiors. He defended the need for covertness and deception, and made clear his low opinion of Congress. With moist eyes, he even spoke of his widowed mother who scrubbed floors to feed her children. It was bathos of Nixonian proportions, executed with far more skill.

> In an astonishing role reversal, North succeeded in transforming the pre-hearings public perception of him as mysterious cowboy run amok—a lone ranger whose horse jumped the fence for a romp through Indian Country without authorization—to persecuted patriotic victim, just following orders. . . He was the Marlboro Man without the Marlboro. The Rebel With a Cause.[113]

The television critic in *The Washington Post* compared North's performance to James Stewart's in the classic movie *Mr. Smith Goes to Washington*. The critic offered a piquant metaphor: "[L]ike they say in pro wrestling, Ollie North is the 'television champion'."[114] Unlike the wrestling arena, however, it was not left to vociferous fans to designate the villains. That responsibility belongs to the courts.

On March 11, 1987, Robert McFarlane pleaded guilty to four misdemeanor counts of withholding information from Congress. He was placed on 2 years probation and fined $20,000. He had avoided a prison sentence

by agreeing to cooperate with the government in its prosecution of the other Iran-Contra cases.[115]

On March 16, a federal grand jury returned criminal indictments against Oliver North, John Poindexter, Richard Secord, and Albert Hakim.[116] Secord made an agreement with the prosecutor in November, under which he pleaded guilty to one felony count and agreed to testify against North and Poindexter in exchange for the dropping of 11 other charges.[117] Like McFarlane, Secord was sentenced to two years probation.[118] Hakim also received 2 years probation (and a $5,000 fine). In an unusual agreement, however, Hakim was allowed to keep a share of the $1.7 million surplus from the arms sales, which was still sitting in Swiss banks.[119] Poindexter became the only Iran-Contra figure to receive a prison term, when he was given a 6-month sentence in 1990 for lying to Congress. Poindexter was the highest White House official since Watergate to be incarcerated for illegal acts committed in office.[120]

As for Oliver North, he worked out an agreement under which he pleaded guilty to three of twelve felony counts, thus avoiding the ignominy of a prison sentence. He was, however, fined $178,785 and ordered to perform 1,200 hours of community service.[121] Many observers considered this a surprisingly light sentence. Not only had North participated in the Iran-Contra cover-up by lying to Congress and shredding key documents, he also had acknowledged using $13,000 of Iran-Contra proceeds to purchase a security system for his home.[122] Moreover, North was accused of cashing $2,000 worth of traveler's checks, part of a $90,000 donation by Contra leader Adolfo Calero meant to help retrieve the hostages from Lebanon. This represented something of a "reverse diversion," with funds going from the Contras to Iran. North's alleged embezzlement was akin, then, to a "diversion of a diversion." North used the siphoned funds to purchase everything from dry cleaning, to groceries, to hosiery, to snow tires. When Calero was shown a chart during the congressional hearings, documenting the dozens of traveler's checks cashed by North, he staunchly defended North's integrity. "He conceded to Senator Rudman that it did not snow in Nicaragua, but he was sure that North could explain the expenditures."[123] On September 16, 1991, a divided appeals court overturned North's conviction on technical grounds regarding the immunity which had been granted to his congressional testimony. A few weeks later, Poindexter's conviction was reversed on the same grounds.[124] North pronounced himself "totally exonerated."[125] Most journalists rejected this claim as a "wild overstatement,"[126] noting that the reversal had nothing to do with the facts of the case.[127] Ironically, North had wriggled off the hook using the very sort of legal loophole which his hardline supporters habitually berate in their "law and order" and "soft on crime" rhetoric.

Oliver North became a luminary on the lecture circuit, commanding $30,000 for an appearance. He was the Republican nominee for a U.S. Senate seat in Virginia in 1994, but was defeated in a very costly and bitterly fought election—the most conspicuous exception to a national Republican landslide. A short time later, he became the host of a nationally syndicated daily radio program.

Abuse of Power

More than 150 years ago, political philosopher John Stuart Mill wrote: "A governing class not accountable to the people are sure, in the main, to sacrifice the people to the pursuit of separate interests and inclinations of their own."[128] Mill's message about the need for accountability has lost none of its timeliness. Even the government of the United States, democratically elected and Constitutionally restrained, has at times been willing to "sacrifice" the rights of its citizens on behalf of some extralegal "higher" purpose. Most of these abuses of power have occurred under the guise of national security.[129]

Consider the ignominious example of the internment of Japanese-American citizens during the Second World War. In 1942, President Roosevelt issued an Executive Order evacuating over 100,000 Japanese-American residents of California, Oregon, and Washington and herding them into barbed wire enclosures under military guard.[130] Victims of racial prejudice and war hysteria, they were branded as traitors and robbed of their businesses and farms. Virtually every one of them, as far as we know, were loyal citizens; most of them were too young or too old to pose any plausible threat.[131]

Moreover, citizens of Japanese ancestry in Central and South American countries were rounded up, handed over to American authorities, transported to the United States, and thrown into concentration camps as well.[132] It is difficult to characterize that abuse of power in any terms other than kidnapping.

In this section, we will analyze the most resonant example in American history of government divorced from accountability: the crimes of Watergate.

Watergate

The cluster of crimes known collectively as "Watergate" has come to symbolize the abuse of political power in America. Richard Nixon, who had won re-election by a huge majority, had to jettison the core of his administrative staff; then, facing certain impeachment, conviction, and removal from office, he himself was forced to resign.[133]

Watergate lies on the cusp between the two types of political crime differentiated by political scientist Theodore Lowi: "Little Corruption," the bribery and individual malfeasance examined in Chapter 8; and "Big Corruption," in which governmental deviance is normalized through political authority.[134] Clearly, Watergate abounded with "Little Corruption." Consider the following examples:

- The Committee to Re-elect the President (known as derisively as CREEP) was indicted for campaign spending violations, following an investigation by the General Accounting Office.[135] It was later revealed that CREEP also had failed to report a secret fund of millions of dollars in campaign contributions.[136]

- The House Banking and Currency Committee reported that CREEP had channeled money through a Luxembourg bank in order to circumvent campaign spending laws.[137]

- John Mitchell and Maurice Stans, former cabinet members, solicited an illegal $200,000 cash contribution to CREEP from Robert Vesco, a financier accused by the Security and Exchange Commission (SEC) of a $244 million stock fraud. Mitchell later arranged a meeting between Vesco and SEC Chairman William Casey after the $200,000 was delivered.[138]

- Illegal campaign contributions were solicited from some of the biggest corporations in America, such as Chrysler, American Airlines, and Ashland Oil. One company, American Motors, was asked for an illegal contribution of $100,000, but rejected the request. It later was given a second chance, at the "bargain" rate of only $50,000.[139] Some corporate executives testified that they were blackmailed by CREEP into giving large donations. For example, the vice president of Gulf Oil maintained that he had been led to believe that a refusal to contribute would have placed his company on a "blacklist" with respect to government contracts.[140]

- "The *Wall Street Journal* [published] documents revealing that President Nixon had been told of the dairy industry's huge campaign contributions, had expressed his gratitude, and two days later had given them highly profitable price-support increases."[141]

- Republican officials donated $50,000 from campaign funds to pay for a 1972 dinner honoring Vice President Spiro Agnew, who would later resign in disgrace (Chapter 8).[142]

- The brother-in-law of White House Chief of Staff H. R. Haldeman received $50,000 in diverted campaign contributions for helping to arrange the purchase of President Nixon's California home.[143]

- Nixon's close friend, banker "Bebe" Rebozo, channeled $50,000 from laundered campaign funds for Nixon's private use. The money had paid for a swimming pool, putting green, and pool table at Nixon's Florida home. "Another $4,562 had gone into the purchase of diamond earrings for the President's wife."[144]

- "[T]he Joint Committee on Internal Revenue Taxation . . . disclosed that [Nixon] used every tax dodge and loophole to escape paying $432,787 in income taxes."[145] The report revealed that the President had grossly underestimated his income and had deducted nearly a half million dollars for donating some of his presidential papers, a vastly inflated figure. Nixon also had charged the government for nearly $100,000 in personal expenses—including $5,000 to throw a lavish party for his daughter.[146]

Outrageous as these offenses were, a review of American history makes clear (and as Chapter 10 will underscore) that corrupt politicians have never been in short supply. Why, then, has the stain of Watergate been so indelible? The naked dishonesty it revealed at the highest level of government is not easily forgotten: campaign contributions illegally donated or extorted, the "skimming" of these funds for gifts to the President's friends and relatives, the purchase of political favors, the sale of ambassadorships, the President's own questionable tax returns.

Beyond all this, however, Watergate was "Big Corruption," a Constitutional crisis of the first magnitude, perhaps America's closest brush with despotism. It revealed the creation of a "shadow government, a secret 'state within a state.'"[147] It signified an attempt to replace a traditional "rule of law" morality with a kind of "new Machiavellianism,"[148] layered with psychopathy and marbled with paranoia.

In the midst of the Senate hearings in 1973, a national poll reported that a majority of the public rated Watergate as the *worst* scandal in American history.[149] Decades later, Watergate remains our transcendent political crime. In perpetual motion, it glides on tightropes of our consciousness; often drifting away, but always coming back.

The scandal began inauspiciously with what President Nixon's Press Secretary dismissed as a "third rate burglary."[150] Early on the morning of June 17, 1972, five men were arrested in national headquarters of the Democratic Party on sixth floor of the swank Watergate Complex in Washington, D.C. The burglars were carrying electronic surveillance equipment.

"Incredulity, sometimes accompanied by cynical laughter, typified the initial public reaction to the bungled break-in."[151] After all, President Nixon's re-election was a virtual certainty; polls put him far ahead of any Democratic rival. Nixon was already on his way to the most smashing presidential landslide in American political history.[152] "One had to suspend logic and belief to link the President or the President's men with the transgressions of Watergate."[153]

Even when it was revealed that the burglars worked for a special "plumbers' unit" of CREEP, the press and public paid scant attention to the incipient scandal. However, from the summer of 1972 through the spring of 1973, a federal grand jury heard testimony in connection with the Watergate burglary. Before too long, the public was not laughing anymore. Stories began to surface about great sums of money allegedly funnelled into Republican intelligence operations. "Bit by bit, the stone wall erected by the White House began to crumble, and the American people learned, not just about the Watergate break-in itself, but about a whole series of related crimes."[154]

On August 1, 1972, journalists Carl Bernstein and Bob Woodward reported in the *Washington Post* that a $25,000 check intended for Nixon's campaign had been deposited in the bank account of one of the Watergate burglars.[155]

Later, CREEP admitted that a $30,000 campaign contribution from the Philippine sugar industry, solicited on behalf of an "urgent White House project,"[156] also had helped pay for the Watergate cover-up.

The FBI reportedly was thwarted in its Watergate investigation by CREEP officials. Acting FBI Director L. Patrick Gray III turned over the bureau's Watergate file to White House Counsel John Dean. On April 27, 1973, the *New York Daily News* further revealed that Gray had destroyed documents belonging to Watergate conspirator E. Howard Hunt. Gray reportedly had been acting under orders from Nixon's chief of domestic affairs, John Ehrlichman.[157] Gray resigned that same day.

A month later, a memorandum was disclosed in which the Deputy Director of the CIA said that H. R. Haldeman, the powerful White House Chief of Staff, told him, "It is the President's wish that the CIA help block an FBI investigation of Nixon campaign money."[158] The money in question had been "laundered" in a Mexican bank. When former CIA Director Richard Helms appeared before the Senate Foreign Relations Committee, he was asked why he had never informed the President of White House efforts to enlist the CIA in a Watergate cover-up. Helms replied: "Frankly, I wanted to stay as head of the agency."[159]

During this same time, all charges were dismissed in the "Pentagon Papers" trial of former Defense Department analyst, Daniel Ellsberg, who had been accused of leaking to the press classified documents that concerned efforts by the Pentagon to deceive Congress into supporting the corrupt regime in South Vietnam. The judge in the Ellsberg case declared that the government had "incurably infected the prosecution."[160] Specifically, it had been revealed that Watergate conspirators E. Howard Hunt and G. Gordon Liddy had carried out a burglary of the office of Ellsberg's former psychiatrist in an effort to uncover discrediting information. In addition, Helms' successor as CIA Director, James Schlessinger, conceded that the CIA had cooperated in the burglary at the instigation of John Ehrlichman.[161] Later testifying before the Watergate Committee, Ehrlichman defended the practice of political espionage and argued that the President had the power to break the law if he believed national security was endangered.[162]

Incredibly, it was also revealed that the judge in the Ellsberg case had been invited to President Nixon's California home where he was asked if he would be interested in becoming the new director of the FBI. This brazen overture later would be characterized by members of the Senate Watergate Committee as attempted bribery.[163]

CREEP used a secret fund to finance intelligence-gathering operations against the Democrats. Democratic presidential contenders and their families were followed, and dossiers were assembled on their personal lives. For example, probes were ordered on close associates of Senator Edward Kennedy, including his mother, Rose.[164] False and defamatory stories about Democratic candidates were leaked to the press, and letters were forged in the name of prominent Democrats. In addition, Republican saboteurs stole Democratic campaign files and hired provocateurs to disrupt the Democratic National convention.[165] When H. R. Haldeman, who controlled the espionage fund, later appeared before the Senate Watergate Committee, he set a new standard for evasive testimony. He responded "I can't remember" or "I don't know" to more than 150 questions.[166]

One of the ringleaders of the Republican political sabotage conspiracy was the President's appointments secretary, Dwight Chapin. He employed a former Treasury Department attorney, Donald Segretti, to engage in a series of "dirty tricks" against the Democrats. In 1972, Segretti distributed a phony letter on the stationery of then-Democratic presidential front-runner, Senator Edmund Muskie, accusing rival presidential aspirants, Senators Henry Jackson and Hubert Humphrey, of sexual misconduct.[167] Segretti later testified before the Senate Committee concerning "all the acts of forgery, libel, burglary, and character assassination he performed to get Nixon re-elected."[168] Patrick Buchanan, Nixon's caustic speech writer, also testified before the committee and admitted participating in the sabotage of the Muskie presidential campaign. Buchanan further admitted to having urged the White House "to use the IRS against . . . Nixon's enemies list."[169]

Richard Nixon, however, did not limit the use of illegal surveillance to his enemies. He once had ordered the Secret Service to wiretap the phone of his brother Donald, out of fear that Donald Nixon's financial dealings might embarrass the re-election campaign.[170] Likewise, on the same day the Senate Watergate Committee began its televised hearings in May of 1973, the *New York Times* reported that the National Security Adviser, Henry Kissinger, had ordered the wiretapping of some of his own aides between 1969 and 1971.[171]

In June, 1973, the *Washington Post* printed a summary that Woodward and Bernstein had obtained of John Dean's testimony at a closed meeting of the Senate Watergate Committee. According to this report, Dean said that Nixon had requested the IRS to stop tax audits of his friends. Dean reportedly also testified that Nixon had ordered him to keep a list of troublesome reporters, so that they could be punished after the 1972 election.[172] In his public testimony, Dean revealed that Nixon's "enemies list" contained hundreds of names singled out for persecution.[173] For example, Daniel Schorr, the CBS White House correspondent and one of the most respected journalists in Washington, had been subjected to an intense FBI investigation.[174]

Dean also maintained that President Nixon had been aware of the Watergate cover-up from the beginning. Nixon denied this and suggested that he had been misled by the unscrupulous Dean. At a televised question-and-answer session before an audience of newspaper editors on November 17, 1973, Richard Nixon delivered the most memorable line of his long political career: "I am not a crook."[175]

During the Watergate hearings, Alexander Butterfield, head of the Federal Aviation Administration and a former Nixon aide, stunned the Committee when he revealed that Nixon secretly had tape recorded all White House conversations, including those relating to Watergate.[176] For the first time in 166 years, a President of the United States was subpoenaed.[177] Nixon refused to cooperate. For months thereafter, the President disobeyed a court order to surrender eight Watergate tapes. Instead he offered special Watergate prosecutor Archibald Cox sanitized written "summaries" of the subpoenaed conversations. When Cox rejected that deal, Nixon ordered Attorney General Elliot Richardson to fire Cox. When Richardson refused, he was fired by Nixon. When Deputy Attorney General William Ruckelshaus also refused, he, too, was fired by Nixon. Finally, Solicitor General Robert Bork agreed to dismiss Cox. An indignant press quickly labeled this remarkable sequence of events the "Saturday Night Massacre."[178] The "third-rate burglary" had become what John Dean would call a "cancer on the Presidency."[179]

While the tapes were being transcribed, Nixon's attorney informed the Watergate court about an unexplainable 18 1/2 minute buzz that "blots out a crucial discussion about Watergate between Nixon and Haldeman on a key tape."[180] The angry judge, John Sirica, demanded an explanation. Rose Mary Woods, the President's longtime secretary, testified that she had been transcribing the tape for the President and accidentally had erased it while answering the telephone. According to her story, while "reaching for [the phone] with one hand, with the other she mistakenly pushed the 'record' instead of the 'stop' button on her recorder, while keeping her foot on the operating treadle."[181] When Woods attempted to demonstrate what allegedly had happened, she resembled a side-show contortionist as she twisted her body into a grotesque posture. Her ludicrous explanation was met with almost universal scorn. In fact, months later a panel of technical experts reported that someone had "made at least five separate, deliberate hand erasures on the tape."[182]

On July 24, 1974, the American people discovered incontrovertibly that their President was indeed a crook. In its decision in *United States v. Richard M. Nixon,* the Supreme Court unanimously ordered that the President surrender the subpoenaed tapes. The most damaging one turned out to be a conversation between Nixon and Haldeman recorded less than a week after the Watergate break-in. On that tape, Haldeman informs Nixon that the burglars had been financed by CREEP campaign funds, and Nixon orders Haldeman to use the CIA to impede the FBI investigation. This tape has become known as the "smoking gun;"[183] it effectively ended the Nixon Presidency. Three days after the tapes were released, the House Judiciary Committee approved a Bill of Impeachment against the President of the United States. Twelve days later, Nixon resigned.

Watergate proved to be a mucilaginous trap; the harder Nixon had tried to extricate himself, the more entangled he had become in crimes, cover-ups, and cover-ups of cover-ups. And like some prehistoric tar pit, Watergate has left a legacy of remains that begs for explanation. Although it obviously was a seminal event, the fundamental meaning of Watergate can be understood in various ways. Interpretation, of course, depends on the perspective of the interpreter.

To many journalists, for example, Watergate was about money. The investigative reports of Bernstein and Woodward, which first revealed the dimensions of the scandal, focused on the illegal contributions, the secret funds, the payoffs and influence peddling. Watergate, however— as we already have observed—transcended "Little Corruption." It must be examined more broadly to grasp its full significance.

To many social psychologists, Watergate was about destructive obedience to a malevolent authority figure, Richard Nixon. Indeed, any retrospective consideration of Watergate must begin with Nixon. Three generations of armchair psychoanalysts have feasted upon the Nixon psyche and its web of contradictions. He has been characterized as a man admired by millions of citizens, who chose to obsess over a relative handful of enemies, real and imagined; a man renowned for his political cunning, yet capable of committing acts of almost unfathomable stupidity; a man seized by a grandiose need for praise, yet filled with petty spite and primal hatred. Columnist Stewart Alsop once said of Nixon: "He behaved as if he were waging war, not politics."[184]

One of Richard Nixon's most striking contradictions was that he could inspire such fierce loyalty in his staff. Given the history of his career, that loyalty could not have been based on any reasonable expectation of reciprocity. His instinct for survival had always been intensely selfish. It was vintage Nixon that he tried to make a scapegoat of the young sycophant, John Dean; or that he retired to opulent exile, pardoned by President Ford for any crimes he might have committed while in office, while some of his closest associates and oldest friends, such as Haldeman, Ehrlichman, and Mitchell, went to prison for crimes committed on his behalf. Nixon's character flaws were nearly as familiar a part of the American landscape as McDonald's arches, so Watergate seems more likely to have been inspired by Nixon the authority figure than by Nixon the inspirational leader.

Whether Nixon personally ordered the burglaries or the extortion of campaign contributions is largely irrelevant. Those acts "were consistent with an operating style that the President himself had followed in the past and was clearly sanctioning, even if he was not familiar with all of the details."[185] It is characteristic of an authoritarian environment that the moral principles which generally govern human relationships cease to apply.

> [W]hen immoral, criminal, or corrupt acts are explicitly ordered, implicitly encouraged, tacitly approved, or at least permitted by legitimate authorities, people's readiness to commit or condone them is considerably enhanced. The fact that such acts are authorized seems to carry automatic justification for them.[186]

"[S]ituational pressures to 'win at all costs' were particularly appealing to the . . . persons who comprised the leadership of the Nixon administration."[187] One merely has to scrutinize the testimony and demeanor of most of the witnesses before the Senate Watergate Committee to discern "an orientation to authority based on unquestioning obedience to superior orders."[188] When one Senator asked John Ehrlichman, for example, whether the President's power to protect national security extended to the commission of murder, Ehrlichman coolly replied: "I do not know where the line is."[189]

To many political sociologists, Watergate was about power.

> Watergate was a scandal motivated by the quest for political power. Although Richard Nixon left the office of the President a far wealthier man than when he entered it, Watergate is not a tale of personal aggrandizement. For the most part, money was simply a means to an end.[190]

Max Weber's early concept of *legitimacy* seems particularly germane to Watergate. A "legitimate" political system is "generally accepted by the populace as ruling in accord with consensual values and norms."[191] In Weber's view, a regime forfeits its legitimacy when it no longer enjoys that acceptance. In other words, "political authorities are [only] legitimate to the extent that the citizens perceive them as holding their positions by right."[192]

When it subverted the 1972 presidential election, the Nixon Administration lost its legitimacy. "Voters who had voted for President Nixon considered their vote to have been fraudulently claimed and felt betrayed."[193] Nixon's "power disease"[194] and its symptomatic intolerance for opposition pulled an unwary nation ever closer to a police state: "The illegal wiretaps [and] political espionage represented, in large part, an attempt to weed out government officials who could not be relied upon to be absolutely loyal to the President."[195]

Also, in the inevitable manner of a police state, the pretext of national security was used to justify every illegal act. Nixon always had both the capacity and the inclination to relegate his opponents to a "less-than-human category, outside of the bounds of human sympathy, and fair game for whatever forms of suppression might be required."[196] Dissenters were persecuted; those citizens consigned to Nixon's "enemies list"—that is, those who opposed the President—were harassed by federal agencies from the IRS to the FBI to the Secret Service to the Post Office.

There were the "Harvards," the Kennedys, the "upper intellectual types," the "establishment," the Jews, the Italians. The famous "enemies list" . . . included such dangerous folk as Carol Channing, Steve McQueen, Barbra Streisand, Gregory Peck, Bill Cosby, Tony Randall, and Joe Namath.[197]

Logic decrees that the hypocrisy of an amoral president, carried to power upon the shoulders of "law and order" rhetoric, would generate profound effects upon a deceived electorate. A president's responsibility, after all, reaches far beyond his role as Commander-in-Chief of the armed forces or administrator of the executive branch. The White House is first and foremost a place of moral leadership. Richard Nixon poisoned the well of political rectitude. His abdication of moral leadership, through his routinization of "Big Corruption," was the ultimate crime of Watergate.

Applying classical sociological theories to Watergate yields some disturbing predictions. For example, the loss of political legitimacy engendered by the scandal might be expected to have produced a general state of normlessness (what Durkheim termed "anomie") or a weakening of the social bonds that tie citizens to critical institutions (what Marx called "alienation"). Did this actually occur? The answer appears to be yes. As one analysis concluded at the time: "Watergate may affect the maintenance of supportive attitudes toward the political system."[198]

A 1976 study reported: "There was a clear and general loss of confidence . . . in the executive branch of the federal government concomitant with the unfolding of the Watergate scandal, and this loss was dispersed or extended to political leaders in general."[199] A 1979 survey revealed that those voters who had misplaced their trust in Richard Nixon, and thus felt most betrayed, became significantly more cynical about people in general than those who had not voted for Nixon.[200]

It is not difficult to understand why Watergate exacerbated public cynicism. For instance, of the twenty-one business executives sanctioned for illegal presidential campaign contributions uncovered by the Watergate Special Prosecutor, just five were convicted of "willful violations" (a felony). Of these, only three officials of the Associated Milk Producers Cooperative were handed short prison terms. The remaining two, Thomas Jones, CEO of the Northrup Corporation, and shipbuilder/ sports mogul George Steinbrenner, were slapped with financially inconsequential fines.[201] Moreover, "with the one exception of campaign financing, no major reforms have been enacted as a direct response to Watergate."[202]

Perhaps most disturbing of all is the effect of Watergate on young Americans of that period. Research on political socialization suggests that "instead of being uninterested in and insulated from political events, children may be one of the more affected segments of the population."[203] Comparative studies of grade-school children's political attitudes in the pre- and post-Watergate era report that children of the post-Watergate era were much more cynical about politics[204] and less respectful of the presidency.[205]

Among college undergraduates, evidence has been presented that Watergate reduced political interest.[206] Moreover, a 1976 study of young voters revealed a negative correlation between support for Richard Nixon and subsequent scores on a moral judgment scale. One implication of this finding is that the cognitive dissonance produced by having voted for a disgraced president may have depressed moral judgment among some young voters.[207] Indeed, CREEP regularly hired undergraduate interns to infiltrate Democratic campaigns and spy for Republicans in exchange for college credits.[208]

Ironically, 1972 was the first presidential election in which 18- to 20-year old voters were allowed to participate. Instead of those new voters making the electoral process more idealistic, the electoral process may have made those new voters less idealistic. One researcher reports that, in the wake of the Watergate scandal, political attitudes of first-time voters became almost indistinguishable from those of their parents.[209] The young subjects of the post-Watergate studies now comprise the dominant demographic segment in the United States. If they are less idealistic, less trusting, and more cynical than they might otherwise have turned out to be, this is indeed a sad legacy of Watergate.

Finally, it is chilling to ponder the "what ifs" of Watergate. What if a night watchman had not stumbled accidentally upon the burglars? What if an obscure White House aide had not off-handedly revealed the existence of the White House tapes? Such questions can only be answered subjunctively, but the crisis of legitimacy created by Nixon's imperious assault on the Constitution may not have occurred without these turns of fate. Democracy often rests at the top and tyranny at the bottom of a slippery slope. Could a second-term Nixon, unable to run again, have shucked any lingering pretense of moral restraint? It is surely fortunate that we will never know . . .

Torture American-Style

The use of torture by governments has a long, ignominious history. For over 2,000 years, from the red-hot irons of ancient Rome to the rack and thumbscrews of the Middle Ages, anyone interrogated by officials of the state could expect to suffer unspeakable cruelty. In the past 200 years or so, from the Age of Enlightenment, when social philosophers like Bentham and Beccaria spoke out against the horrors of torture, to the present time, when organizations like Amnesty International and Human Rights Watch lead sustained anti-torture campaigns, the practice of state-sponsored torture has declined among civilized nations and persons. Nevertheless, it remains a popular method of repression and punishment in totalitarian regimes and terrorist organizations. Philosopher Hannah Arendt regards torture as an indispensible tool of totalitarianism.[210] Moreover, as recent history has revealed, it is still sometimes used by democratic governments as well.

Most formalized definitions of torture are fundamentally similar, though they may differ in the amount of specificity each contains. Some are quite broad:

"Torture" means the intentional infliction of severe pain or suffering, whether physical or mental, upon a person in the custody or under the control of the accused.

Rome Statute of the International Criminal Court

Others are more detailed:

Any act by which severe pain or suffering, whether physical or mental, is intentionally inflicted on a person for such purposes as obtaining from him or a third person information or a confession, punishing him for an act he or a third person has committed or is suspected of having committed, or intimidating or coercing him or a third person . . . when such pain or suffering is inflicted by or at the instigation of or with the consent or acquiescence of a public official or other person acting in an official capacity.

United Nations Convention Against Torture

The Bush administration created a newer and narrower definition:

Physical pain amounting to torture must be equivalent to intensity to the pain accompanying serious physical injury, such as organ failure, impairment of bodily function, or even death.

Justice Department Memorandum, August 1, 2002

The Bush position notwithstanding, official U.S. tolerance of torture has diminished significantly in modern times. Once, the so-called "third degree" was the norm for police interrogation. Consider the opinion rendered by a New York City magistrate in a 1922 investigation of the beating of suspects with wet blackjacks and rubber hoses:

"It is almost impossible to secure evidence in many cases that will result in the conviction of the guilty without obtaining either a confession from the defendant or information from sources hostile to the ends of justice. Hence, when a crime is committed, the custom is to take into custody the suspect and others who are supposed to have knowledge of the occurrence and obtain from them whatever information is possible. It is obvious that, if they are reluctant to speak, they can be induced to do so only by the use of force.[211]

In stark contrast, a New York City judge sentenced an NYPD officer to 30 years in prison for a 1997 interrogation, during which the officer jammed the handle of a plunger into a suspect's rectum. The judge was not the least bit tolerant, condemning the officer's brutality as an "unusually heinous" crime.[212]

While American law enforcement agencies may now eschew torture, the same cannot be said for American intelligence agencies and the U.S. military. Indeed, the use or encouragement of torture by the CIA has a documented history going back nearly 50 years. A now-declassified 1963 CIA training manual, titled *Counterintelligence Interrogation,* describes the torture methods used against prisoners during the Vietnam War.[213] Another declassified document, *Human Resource Exploitation Training Manual—1983,* details techniques of torture used by the CIA against suspected subversives in Central America during the 1980s.[214] Like its 1963 progenitor, the 1983 manual describes stripping suspects naked and keeping them blindfolded. "These interrogation rooms should be windowless, dark and soundproof, with no toilets."[215] According to the manual:

"The 'questioning' room is the battlefield upon which the 'questioner' and the subject meet. . . . However, the 'questioner' has the advantage in that he has total control over the subject and his environment."[216]

Solitary confinement and sensory deprivation are recommended as ways to induce stress and anxiety. "The more complete the deprivation, the more rapidly and deeply the subject is affected."[217] "[P]sychological coercion has been considered effective for most of the life of the agency, and its slippery definition might allow it to squeeze through loopholes in a law that seeks to ban prisoner abuse."[218] The manual cites the results of experiments conducted on volunteers who allowed themselves to be suspended in water while wearing blacked out goggles and ear muffs. "The stress and anxiety became almost unbearable for most subjects."[219]

The manual discourages physical torture, "advising interrogators to use more subtle methods to threaten and frighten the suspect."[220] However, in the shameless manner of O. J. Simpson's notorious "If I Did It" book, the CIA explains—"hypothetically" of course—how to conduct physical torture. The document's introduction states: "While we do not stress the use of coercive techniques, we do want to make you aware of them and the proper way to use them."[221]

Moreover, the manual actually says that such methods are justified when subjects have been trained to resist noncoercive measures.[222]

> "The pain which is being inflicted upon him from outside himself may actually intensify his will to resist. On the other hand, pain which he feels he is inflicting upon himself is more likely to sap his resistance. . . . For example, if he is required to maintain rigid positions such as standing at attention or sitting on a stool for long periods of time, the immediate source of pain is not the 'questioner' but the subject himself. . . . After a period of time the subject is likely to exhaust his internal motivational strength."[223]

A Honduran unit known as Battalion 316 was trained by CIA instructors in the early 1980s, at the height of the Reagan administration's war against communism in Central America. A CIA spokesman later told the Senate Intelligence Committee: "The course consisted of three weeks of classroom instruction, followed by two weeks of practical exercises, which included the questioning of actual prisoners by the students."[224] It was for that purpose the 1983 manual was written.

The manual advises interrogators to "manipulate the subject's environment, to create unpleasant or intolerable situations."[225] In a 1997 interview, a former member of Battalion 316 said that CIA instructors had taught him to discover what his prisoners loved and what they hated: "If a person did not like cockroaches, then that person might

be more cooperative if there were cockroaches running around the room."[226]

The manual also suggests that interrogators show their prisoners letters from home to convey the impression that the prisoners' relatives are suffering or are in danger.[227] Another former member of Battalion 316 recalled using this technique:

> "The first thing we would say is that we know your mother, your younger brother. And better you cooperate, because if you don't, we're going to bring them in and rape them and torture them and kill them."[228]

ABC News has reported that the CIA has a list of six "Enhanced Interrogation Techniques," instituted in 2002.[229] One of them is called "Cold Treatment," in which the prisoner is left to stand naked in a cell kept at 50 degrees and constantly doused with cold water.[230] One detainee reportedly died of hypothermia after he was left to stand naked and wet throughout the harsh Afghanistan night.[231]

According to the *Washington Post,* a CIA detention center in Afghanistan used psychological interrogation techniques known as "stress and duress" tactics, sometimes called "torture lite."[232] Two prisoners died there in 2002. It was initially announced that autopsies had attributed one death to a heart attack and the other to a pulmonary embolism.[233] After a criminal investigation, military pathologists re-classed the modes of death as "homicide," attributing both deaths to "blunt force injuries."[234]

The former section chief of the FBI's International Terrorism Operations has called psychological torture a "voodoo science."[235] The American Medical Association and the American Psychiatric Association have banned their members from participating in interrogations, but the issue has divided the American Psychological Association (APA), which has not forbidden such participation by members. The Army maintains that military psychologists help to make interrogations "safe, legal and effective."[236] In fact, a specially convened APA task force ruled in 2006 that psychologists *could* assist in military interrogations. Critics within the organization believed that the task force had been rigged. Six of the 10 members had ties to the armed services, which ignited conflict of interest charges.[237]

> One theory was that the APA had given its stamp of approval to military interrogations as part of a quid pro quo. In exchange, they suspected the Pentagon

was working to allow psychologists—who, unlike psychiatrists, are not medical doctors—to prescribe medication, dramatically increasing their income. (The military has championed modern-day psychology since World War II, and continues to be one of the largest single employers of psychologists through its network of veterans' hospitals. It also funded a prescription-drug training program for military psychologists in the early 90s.)[238]

In 2007, dozens of angry psychologists wrote a joint letter to the APA's president arguing that abusive interrogations violate the ethics of that organization:

> "We write you as psychologists concerned about the participation of our profession in abusive interrogations of national security detainees. . . . It is now indisputable that psychologists and psychology were directly and officially responsible for the development and migration of abusive interrogation techniques, techniques which the International Committee of the Red Cross has labeled 'tantamount to torture.'"[239]

A few months later, the APA rejected a proposed measure that would have flatly prohibited members from taking any part in interrogations at U.S. military detention centers.[240] The APA, however, did vote to reaffirm its opposition to torture and restricted members from taking part in interrogations involving any of more than a dozen specific practices, including stress positions or sleep deprivation, forced nakedness, hooding, mock executions, simulated drowning (waterboarding), sexual and religious humiliation, the exploitation of phobias, the use of mind-altering drugs, the use of dogs to frighten detainees, exposing prisoners to extreme heat and cold, physical assault, and threats against a prisoner's family.[241] As is now known, most, if not all, of these techniques were utilized in an exotic-sounding place destined to become the symbol of American torture.

During the brutal regime of Iraqi dictator Saddam Hussein, Abu Ghraib, 20 miles outside of Baghdad, was one of the world's most infamous prisons, complete with repulsive living conditions, weekly executions, and routine torture.[242] After Saddam was overthrown by U.S. and coalition military forces in 2003, Abu Ghraib was cleaned up, repaired, and turned into the Baghdad Correctional Facility, a U.S. military prison. While many of the inmates held there were common criminals, some were suspected of being "high value" war criminals and terrorists.[243]

After the Iraqi government fell, Brigadier General Janis Karpinski, an Army reservist, was named commander of the 800th Military Police Brigade and was put in charge of military prisons in Iraq. Karpinski was an experienced intelligence officer, who had served in the Special Forces and in the 1991 Gulf War; but, like most of the 3,400 reservists under her command, she had no training in handling prisoners.[244] In December, 2003, Karpinski described the daily lives of Abu Ghraib prisoners in an interview with the *St. Petersburg Times*: "[L]iving conditions now are better in prison than at home. At one point we were concerned they wouldn't want to leave."[245] But almost right from the start, stories of mistreatment and abuse at Abu Ghraib began quietly circulating. A major investigation of the Army's prison system was undertaken. A month after her rosy interview, Gen. Karpinski was formally admonished and suspended. She would later be demoted to colonel.

In February, 2004 a report written by Major General Antonio M. Taguba, not meant for public release, was completed. "Its conclusions about the institutional failures of the Army prison system were devastating."[246] The report described numerous instances of "sadistic, blatant, and wanton criminal abuses" at Abu Ghraib:[247]

> Breaking chemical lights and pouring the phosforic [sic] liquid on detainees; pouring cold water on naked detainees; beating detainees with a broom handle and a chair; threatening male detainees with rape; allowing a military police guard to stitch the wound of a detainee who was injured after being slammed against the wall of his cell; sodomizing a detainee with a chemical light and perhaps a broom stick, and using military work dogs to frighten and intimidate detainees with threats of attack, and in one instance actually biting a detainee.[248]

Taguba had also collected extremely graphic photographs and video tapes taken by American soldiers as the abuses were occurring—although he did not include this stunning evidence in his report because of their sensitive nature.

> The photographs tell it all. In one, Private England, a cigarette dangling from her mouth, is giving a jaunty thumbs up sign and pointing to the genitals of a young Iraqi, who is naked except for a sandbag over his head, as he masturbates. . . . In another, England stands arm in arm with Specialist Graner; both are grinning and giving the thumbs-up behind a cluster of perhaps seven

naked Iraqis, knees bent, piled clumsily in a pyramid. . . . Then there is another cluster of hooded bodies, with a female soldier standing in front, taking photographs. Yet another photograph shows a kneeling, naked unhooded male prisoner, head momentarily turned away from the camera, posed to make it appear that he is performing oral sex on another male prisoner, who is naked and hooded.[249]

Taguba would later tell reporter Seymour Hersh that a video showing a male American soldier sodomizing a female detainee was too inflammatory to make public. "It's bad enough that there were photographs of Arab men wearing women's panties," Taguba said.[250]

The photos, however, did find their way into the press. In April, 2004, the American public was shocked by televised photographs from Abu Ghraib showing hooded Iraqis stripped naked, posed in contorted positions, and suffering humiliating abuse while American soldiers stood by smiling.[251]

The Taguba report contained quotes from prisoners that added to the horror. Detainee No. 151362 stated:

"They said we will make you wish to die and it will not happen . . . They stripped me naked. One of them told me he would rape me. He drew a picture of a woman to my back and made me stand in a shameful position holding my buttocks.". . . 'Do you pray to Allah?' one asked. I said yes. They said '[expletive] you. And [expletive] him.' One of them said, 'You are not getting out of here health[y], you are getting out of here handicapped.' And he said to me, 'Are you married?' I said, 'Yes.' They said, 'If your wife saw you like this, she will be disappointed.' One of them said, 'But if I saw her now she would not be disappointed now because I would rape her.' . . . They ordered me to thank Jesus that I'm alive. . . . I said to him, 'I believe in Allah.' So he said, 'But I believe in torture and I will torture you.'"[252]

By early 2005, seven members of the 372nd Military Police Company had been charged with various counts of assault, conspiracy, indecent acts, maltreatment, and dereliction of duty.[253] In all, 12 persons were convicted by military courts martial. Most of the sentences were relatively minor, involving a few months of incarceration or, at least in one case, merely a reduction in rank. Three of the sentences, however, were more substantial.

Private First Class Lynndie England, one of the "stars" of the leaked photographs, was sentenced to three years behind bars. She blamed her boyfriend, Specialist Charles Graner, the other notable figure in the original photos, claiming she had been "lured in" by Graner.[254]

Staff Sergeant Ivan Frederick received an eight-year sentence.[255] In a letter to his family, Frederick related a chilling story about an Iraqi prisoner, under the control of what the Abu Ghraib guards called OGA—"Other Government Agencies"—a euphemism for the CIA. The prisoner had been brought to Frederick's unit for questioning. Frederick wrote:

"They stressed him out so bad that the man passed away. They put his body in a body bag and packed him in ice for approximately 24 hours in the shower. . . . The next day the medics came and put his body on a stretcher, placed a fake IV in his arm and took him away."[256]

The prisoner described by Frederick was one of eight so-called "ghost" detainees investigated by the military. They allegedly were incarcerated at Abu Ghraib but kept off the prison's roster at the request of the CIA. According to the investigation, the prisoner observed by Frederick had been detained by Navy Seals, who had hit him in the head with a rifle butt during his arrest, which apparently led to his death. "But the investigation suggested that the detainee might have survived if he had been screened by doctors, as would have been required had he been properly registered with the military."[257]

Army Reserve Specialist Charles Graner, noted earlier, received the harshest of all the Abu Ghraib sentences—10 years in prison. "Led from the courtroom in handcuffs and leg chains, Graner twice answered 'No Ma'am' when asked whether he had any regrets or apologies."[258] He insisted that he had not enjoyed participating in what he called "irregular treatment"[259]—an assertion seemingly belied by his grinning visage in the photos. He also steadfastly claimed that he had been obeying his superiors, following orders from higher-ranking interrogators when he and the other guards abused their prisoners.[260]

Graner's "Nuremberg" defense was self-serving, no doubt; but it did raise disturbing questions about a possible cover-up along the chain of command. There were no officers convicted of any crimes related to Abu Ghraib. Indeed, Sergeant Frederick was the highest-ranking soldier found guilty. The only officer to be charged, Lieutenant Colonel Steven Jordan, was acquitted in 2007 and received a simple reprimand.[261] Colonel Thomas Pappas, the top military intelligence officer stationed at Abu Ghraib, received only a nonjudicial reprimand for two counts of dereliction, including allowing the use of dogs during interrogation.[262]

The most ironic casualty of Abu Ghraib was General Antonio Taguba, whose frank report was the catalyst of the scandal. In 2007, he was forced into retirement by civilian Pentagon officials because he had been too "zealous."[263] Taguba's assignment to investigate Abu Ghraib was a classic no-win predicament. In his words: "If I lie, I lose. And if I tell the truth, I lose."[264]

Indeed, so unpopular was the Taguba report in Pentagon circles that the Army undertook a second investigation of military detention operations in Iraq. This second report reached very different conclusions. Although acknowledging that the soldiers assigned to Abu Ghraib were poorly trained and ineffectively organized, none of these flaws were blamed directly for the abusive treatment. Instead, the report attributed the abuse to the "unauthorized action taken by a few individuals."[265] The report echoed the Pentagon's longstanding argument that a handful of rogue soldiers were responsible for the misconduct at Abu Ghraib.[266]

Likewise, after the shocking photos were revealed on television, Secretary of Defense Donald Rumsfeld quickly assured Congress that the abuses were "perpetrated by a small number of U.S. military."[267] He referred to them as "a few bad apples."[268] But Congress was unconvinced. A report issued by the Senate Armed Services Committee concluded that Rumsfeld and other high-ranking Bush administration officials were responsible for the harsh interrogations that took place at Abu Ghraib. The committee chairman, Senator Carl Levin, stated: "Attempts by senior officials to pass the buck to low-ranking soldiers while avoiding any responsibility for abuses are unconscionable."[269]

According to the Senate report, the prisoner abuses at Abu Ghraib were "not simply the result of a few soldiers acting on their own. . . . [Rumsfeld's] authorization of aggressive interrogation techniques and subsequent interrogation policies and plans approved by senior military and civilian officials conveyed the message that physical pressures and degradation were appropriate treatment for detainees in U.S. military custody."[270]

In 2006, former General Janis Karpinski, who had been in charge of Abu Ghraib until being relieved of her command soon after the scandal broke, told a Spanish newspaper that she had seen a letter signed by Rumsfeld authorizing the mistreatment of detainees and the use of harsh interrogation techniques. According to Karpinski: "The methods consisted of making prisoners stand for long periods, sleep deprivation . . . playing music at full volume, having to sit in uncomfortably [sic] . . . Rumsfeld authorized these things."[271] Karpinski added that a notation in the margin of the letter, in the same handwriting as Rumsfeld's apparent signature, said, "Make sure this is accomplished."[272]

Karpinski's extraordinary allegation was met with understandable skepticism in some quarters, since she had already lied earlier when she described the reluctance of some Iraqi detainees to leave the supposedly comfortable conditions at Abu Ghraib. On the other hand, her story did not conflict with Rumsfeld's hard line image. Indeed, a month before Karpinski's interview with *El Pais,* the increasingly unpopular Rumsfeld had already resigned as Secretary of Defense, largely due to public criticism over the Iraq War.

Historian Alfred W. McCoy, who has written extensively on the practice of torture worldwide, writes that the Abu Ghraib photographs "are snapshots not of simple brutality or even a breakdown in 'military discipline.' What they record are CIA torture techniques that have metastasized like an undetected cancer inside the U.S. intelligence community over the past half century."[273]

> That iconic photo of a hooded Iraqi with fake electrical wires hanging from his arms shows, not the sadism of a few "creeps," but the telltale signs of sophisticated torture. The prisoner is hooded for sensory deprivation. His arms are extended for self-inflicted pain.[274]

McCoy has called the CIA's discovery of psychological torture "The first real revolution in this cruel science since the 17th century."[275]

The Geneva Convention clearly states: "Prisoners of war who refuse to answer may not be threatened, insulted, or exposed to any unpleasant or disadvantageous treatment of any kind."[276] At Abu Ghraib, prisoners were subjected to "unpleasant" treatment of almost *every* kind. Abu Ghraib was the culmination of secret CIA policy begun during the Cold War and formalized in those two infamous torture manuals. Even though Abu Ghraib was a military facility, the fingerprints of the CIA cover its walls.

"The CIA was the lead agency at Abu Ghraib, enlisting Army intelligence to support its mission."[277]

In 2005, yet another military investigation report was released. This one involved a detention camp, half a world away from Iraq, in Cuba. The Guantanamo Bay Naval Base, on the southeastern end of the island, was established in 1898 in the aftermath of the Spanish-American War. Under the 1903 Cuban-American Treaty, the United States was granted a perpetual lease of the area—a lease the Cuban government has long considered illegal. Since 2002, the base has contained a detainment camp for military combatants from Afghanistan and for other suspected terrorists from around the world. Unlike Abu Ghraib, however, Guantanamo does not house Iraqi captives, since they are considered POWs.

The Guantanamo report detailed how Saudi national Mohamed Qahtani, the alleged "20th hijacker" in the 9/11 terrorist attacks, was interrogated in 2002 while being confronted by snarling military dogs. Qahtani also had a leash attached to his chains and was forced to parade around with women's underwear on his head while wearing a bra.[278]

"The military has long contended that abuses at Guantanamo were aberrations for which soldiers have been disciplined."[279] But the 2005 findings presented strong evidence that the abusive practices seen in the photographs from Abu Ghraib were not the invention of a small group of thrill-seeking military police officers. "The report shows that they were used on Qahtani several months before the United States invaded Iraq."[280]

The techniques used on Qahtani were approved by Defense Secretary Rumsfeld as part of a special interrogation plan aimed at breaking down the stubborn detainee. Rumsfeld had approved a list of 16 harsh techniques for use at Guantanamo. Most of these techniques, involving intimidation and humiliation, were described in general terms and were subject to broad interpretation by interrogators.[281] Qahtani endured sleep deprivation and many of the harshest of the approved techniques. The report found that the cumulative effect of those tactics "resulted in degrading and abusive treatment" but stopped short of torture. Moreover, the techniques reportedly forced the silent Qahtani to talk, achieving what were described as "solid intelligence gains."[282] Given the reprehensible nature of Qahtani's alleged complicity in the 9/11 attacks, this can be a tempting neutralization. However, it ignores

a fundamental moral truth: "Torture is defined by what is done to the victim, not by the usefulness of the information obtained."[283]

Furthermore, whether Qahtani's mistreatment reflected a "special plan" for him alone or was standard operating procedure at Guantanamo is, at the very least, debatable. Documents released in 2004 reveal that over a two-year period detainees held at Guantanamo were shackled to the floor in fetal positions for more than 24 hours, left without food and water, and allowed to urinate and defecate on themselves.[284]

According FBI memos, never meant to be disclosed publicly but leaked to the press in late 2004, FBI agents said that they had witnessed detainees subjected to extreme heat and extreme cold, and the routine use of snarling dogs—contrary to previous statements by senior Defense Department officials[285]—and that one detainee was bombarded with ear-splitting rap music and flashing strobe lights while he was wrapped in an Israeli flag. One of the agents alleged that the "softening-up" techniques had been approved by then-Deputy Defense Secretary Paul Wolfowitz.[286] Another agent described a detainee, who was almost unconscious on the floor of an interview room, with a pile of hair next to him. "He had apparently been literally pulling his own hair out throughout the night."[287] One of the memorandums described female interrogators forcibly squeezing male prisoners' genitals and smearing prisoners with red fluid said to be menstrual blood.[288]

When Donald Rumsfeld was asked in 2005 about the force feeding of hunger-striking detainees at Guantanamo—a practice that involved inserting tubes as wide as fingers directly through stomachs and nostrils without anesthesia, as prisoners convulsed and vomited blood—Rumsfeld replied: "I'm not a doctor."[289] It was an interesting comment by Rumsfeld, since actual doctors were among his harshest critics. A report released in 2005 by a Massachusetts-based group of health professionals, Physicians for Human Rights, states that "since at least 2002, the United States has been engaged in systematic psychological torture" of Guantanamo detainees.[290] The group concluded that the interrogation practices at Guantanamo had "led to devastating health consequences for the individuals subjected to them."[291] This was confirmed by a senior Bush administration official in early 2009, when he revealed that the interrogation of Mohammed al-Qahtani was so intense that he had to be hospitalized twice at Guantanamo with bradycardia, a life-threatening condition in which the heart rates drops below 60 beats a minute. "At one point, Qahtani's heart rate dropped to 35 beats a minute, the record shows."[292]

The United States is a signee of the 1984 United Nations Convention against Torture and Other Cruel, Inhuman or Degrading Treatment or Punishment, under which the U.S. agreed to submit to U.N. scrutiny of its compliance with the convention.[293] That agreement was put to the test in 2006, when the United Nations Committee Against Torture released its report on Guantanamo.[294] The report happened to be issued one day after two Guantanamo detainees tried to kill themselves by overdosing on antidepressants. Their attempts brought to 41 the number of inmates who had tried to commit suicide there since 2002.[295] The U.N. panel, comprised of nine international experts, called on the United States to close the detention center at Guantanamo Bay.[296] The report also called for the prosecution of officers and politicians "up to the highest level" who are responsible for the torture of detainees. The Bush administration denounced the report as a "hatchet job."[297]

The State Department's top lawyer told reporters:

"We acknowledge that there were serious incidents of abuse. We've all seen Abu Ghraib. . . . [But] clearly our record has improved over the last few years."[298]

The United Nations report was especially critical of the worst of the CIA's six "Enhanced Interrogation Techniques" practiced at Guantanamo, that of waterboarding—the simulation of the sensation of drowning.[299] After visiting Guantanamo in 2007, a Finnish law professor serving as a U.N. investigator said that he "strongly suspected" the CIA of using torture on terrorism suspects and suggested that many prisoners were not being prosecuted to keep the abuse from emerging at trial. He also accused the CIA of destroying videotapes in 2005 that recorded al-Qaeda suspects undergoing waterboarding.[300]

Waterboarding consists of strapping the person being interrogated onto a board as pints of water are forced into his lungs through a cloth covering on his face. The victim's mouth is forced open in a process of slow-motion suffocation.[301] Dating back to the Spanish Inquisition, the practice was reportedly perfected by Dutch traders in the 17th century for use against their British rivals in the East

Indies.[302] It was banned in Western Europe during the Age of Enlightenment in the early 19th century, when people found it "morally repugnant."[303]

But waterboarding did not disappear by any means and experienced something of a revival in the 20th century. The British used it against both Jews and Arabs in Palestine in the 1930s; the Japanese used it in World War II; The French used it in Algeria in the 1950s; and the Khmer Rouge used it on its own people in Cambodia in the 1970s.[304] Waterboarding also was a favored tool of Latin American dictators in the 1970s and 1980s, particularly in Chile and Argentina, where it was known as *submarino*.[305]

Waterboarding was condemned by the United States in 1901 during the Spanish-American War, when an Army major was sentenced to 10 years of hard labor for waterboarding an insurgent in the Philippines.[306] At the Tokyo War Crimes Trials in the 1940s, several Japanese soldiers were convicted by American-dominated tribunals for waterboarding.[307] It was designated as illegal by American generals in Vietnam in 1965, after a photograph of a U.S. soldier waterboarding a North Vietnamese prisoner appeared in *The Washington Post*. Within a month, the soldier was court-martialed and drummed out of the Army.[308] When it was employed by the Khmer Rouge, the United States again condemned waterboarding as torture. Cases have even been uncovered on U.S. soil. In 1983, Texas Sheriff James Parker was convicted of waterboarding prisoners in order to obtain confessions. He was sentenced to 10 years in prison.[309]

Malcolm Nance, an advisor on terrorism to the U.S. Department of Homeland Security has publicly denounced the practice. He claims to have witnessed "hundreds" of waterboarding training exercises and has concluded that "waterboarding is a torture technique—period."[310] Nance actually allowed himself to experience the waterboarding ordeal when he was chief of training at the U.S. Navy Survival, Evasion, Resistance, and Escape School (SERE) in San Diego, where trainees were taught to endure torture.

"Unless you have been strapped down to the board, have endured the agonizing feeling of water overpowering your gag reflex, and then feel your throat open and allow pint after pint of water to involuntarily fill your lungs, you will not know the meaning of the word. . . . In the media, waterboarding is called 'simulated drowning,' but that's a misnomer. It does not simulate drowning, as the lungs are actually filling with water. There is no way to simulate that. The victim *is* drowning. . . . Call it 'Chinese Water torture,' 'the barrel,' or 'the waterfall,' it is all the same."[311]

According to Nance, waterboarding victims typically go into hysterics as water fills their lungs. "How much the victim is to drown depends on the desired result and the obstinacy of the subject."[312] Moreover, in Nance's words, "The lack of physical scarring allows the victim to recover and be threatened with its use again and again."[313]

In 2006, more than 100 American law professors sent a highly critical open letter to Attorney General Alberto Gonzalez. It read in part:

> We are particularly concerned about your continuing failure to issue clear statements about illegal interrogation techniques, and especially your failure to state that "waterboarding"—a technique that induces the effects of being killed by drowning—constitutes torture, and thus is illegal. We urge you to make such a statement now.[314]

In a 2007 op-ed piece in *Jurist,* one of the signees, Professor Benjamin Davis, went even further. He called for the criminal prosecution of the leaders who put the torture policy in place. He closed with the following:

> "In the military they talk about different spanks for different ranks. It is time for the spanks to be much more severe at the higher level than they have been in the past. Or, in Latin, *refluat stercus*[315] [making "manure" roll uphill]

In another, more surprising, attack from the legal profession, four retired Judge Advocate Generals (JAGs)—two admirals and two generals—wrote to Senate Judiciary Committee Chairman Patrick Leahy in 2007 during the confirmation hearings of Michael Mukasey for the position of Attorney General to replace the departing Alberto Gonzalez:

> In the course of the Senate Judiciary Committee's consideration of President Bush's nominee for the post of Attorney General, there has been much discussion, but little clarity about the legality of "waterboarding" under United States and International law. We write because this issue above all demands clarity: **Waterboarding is inhumane, it is torture, and it is illegal.**[316] [emphasis added]

Mukasey was confirmed, but not before his nomination sparked a heated debate over the legality of waterboarding[317]—especially after Mukasey refused to define it as torture.[318] Three months later, in 2008, Mukasey appeared before the Senate Judiciary Committee and may have set a new Washington standard for hypocrisy. He testified that he could say that waterboarding was always illegal but would consider it torture *if it were done to him.*[319]

A few days later, CIA Director Michael Hayden acknowledged to the Senate Intelligence Committee that three "high value" al-Qaeda suspects had been waterboarded at Guantanamo.[320] It was the first public admission by the CIA that it was using waterboarding on detainees.[321] Hayden also cast doubt on the legality of waterboarding: "[I]n my own view, the view of my lawyers and the Department of Justice, it is not certain that technique would be considered legal under current statutes."[322] That same day, Stephen Bradbury, head of the Justice Department Office of Legal Counsel, told a House Judiciary Committee panel that waterboarding *is* currently illegal. It was the first such outright acknowledgement by a senior Bush administration official.[323]

Congress tried to make it official in March, 2008, when it voted to outlaw waterboarding. President Bush blasted the move, suggesting that those who supported the measure did not "understand the nature of killers."[324] Bush vetoed the legislation, saying in his weekly radio address: "[I]t would take away one of the most valuable tools in the war on terror. . . . This is no time for Congress to abandon practices that have a proven record of keeping America safe."[325] An irate Amnesty International attacked the president's decision: "No one, not even a President, can authorize torture. Anyone who orders, condones or carries out torture exposes themselves to criminal liability under international law."[326]

In the final weeks of the lame-duck Bush administration, Vice President Dick Cheney, long considered the architect of America's war on terror, admitted in an interview that he had personally authorized the waterboarding of the three "high value" suspects at Guantanamo and had also approved the "enhanced interrogation" of 33 other detainees there.[327] Cheney specifically took issue with the notion that waterboarding is torture: "Was it torture? I don't believe it was torture."[328] In another interview, Cheney added: "We don't do torture. We never have."[329] Cheney's "tortured" definition of torture seemed to echo Humpty Dumpty's encounter with Alice in *Through the*

Looking Glass: "When I use a word, it means what I choose it to mean."[330]

Cheney's defense of waterboarding was, of course, no surprise. Two years earlier he had defended the waterboarding of terrorism suspects as a "no brainer."[331] To this, Amnesty International responded:

> "What's really a no-brainer is that no U.S. official, much less a Vice President, should champion torture. Vice President Cheney's advocacy of waterboarding sets a new human rights low at a time when human rights is already scraping the bottom of the Bush administration barrel."[332]

Senator John McCain weighed in on the waterboarding controversy. McCain, a former POW who had endured torture at the hands of his Vietnamese captors, was able to lend a personal insight to the debate that no other major American political figure could provide. In 2005, he wrote:

> [I]f you gave people who have suffered abuse as prisoners a choice between a beating and a mock execution, many, including me, would choose a beating. The effects of most beatings heal. The memory of an execution will haunt someone for a very long time and damage his or her psyche in ways that may never heal. In my view, to make someone believe that you are killing him by drowning is no different than holding a pistol to his head and firing a blank. I believe that it is torture, very exquisite torture.[333]

McCain called on President Bush to ban the torture of detainees in U.S. custody. After months of opposition and attempts to weaken the measure by exempting the CIA, the White House finally agreed in late 2005.[334] McCains's proposal drew overwhelming support from senators and representatives of both parties.[335] McCain said: "We've sent a message to the world that the United States is not like the terrorists. We have no grief for them, but what we are is a nation that upholds values and standards of behavior and treatment of all people, no matter how evil or bad they are."[336]

When President Bush signed the bill outlawing torture, however, he quietly reserved the right to bypass the law under his powers as Commander-in-Chief. After approving the bill, Bush issued a "signing statement"—an official document in which a president lays out his interpretation of a new law. Bush declared that he would view the interrogation limits in the context of his broader powers to protect national security. In other words, Bush believed he could waive the torture restrictions at will.[337] Lost in the shuffle was the unassailable fact that totalitarian regimes around the world—including many governments the United States opposes—almost always sanction torture on the grounds of national security.[338]

Bush's threat to discard the anti-torture law was not empty rhetoric. In 2008, he vetoed the annual intelligence authorization bill, which would have required the CIA to follow the Army Field Manual rules on interrogations, which specifically prohibit torture of suspects, most notably waterboarding. The President said he vetoed the bill because the CIA interrogation program has already prevented a number of terrorist attacks and is vital to making sure that continues.[339] Bush called the CIA's interrogation techniques "safe and lawful."[340] By ignoring inconvenient facts, the President seemed to employ a perverse *Wizard of Oz* strategy—telling the American public to pay no attention to the torture behind the curtain.

Also in 2008, it was revealed that the Bush administration had issued a pair of secret memos to the CIA in 2003 and 2004 that explicitly endorsed the agency's use of waterboarding.[341] In one of the memos, the Justice Department told the CIA that its interrogators would be safe from prosecution for torture if they believed "in good faith" that harsh techniques used to break down prisoners would not cause "prolonged mental harm."[342] The memos were the first—and, for years, the only—actual documentation of the administration's consent for the CIA's use of "Enhanced Interrogation Techniques," such as waterboarding, to extract information from captured al-Qaeda members.[343] The ACLU, which had obtained the heavily censored memos, released the following statement:

> These documents supply further evidence, if any were needed, that the Justice Department authorized the CIA to torture prisoners in its custody. The Justice Department twisted the law, and in some cases ignored it altogether, in order to permit interrogators to use barbaric methods that the U.S. once prosecuted as war crimes.[344]

A few days before assuming office in 2009, President-elect Barack Obama pledged that his administration would not engage in torture. "We will abide by the Geneva Convention. We will uphold our highest ideals."[345] A week later, Obama's Attorney General-nominee, Eric Holder, faced the Senate Judiciary Committee and made an unambiguous statement: "Waterboarding is torture."[346] Holder also asserted that the U.S. detention facility at Guantanamo Bay would be closed as quickly as possible.[347] And the following week Dennis Blair, Obama's National Intelligence Director-nominee, likewise pledged that there would be no torture on his watch. However, to the disappointment of many, he refused to say whether he believes waterboarding is torture.[348]

In February, 2009, Senator Patrick Leahy, chairman of the Senate Judiciary Committee, called for an independent "truth commission" to investigate Bush administration abuses, including its use of torture.[349] President Obama did not embrace Leahy's proposal, saying that backward-looking investigations would be a diversion.[350] In addition, CIA Director-nominee Leon Panetta, has announced that CIA officers who participated in harsh interrogations will not be prosecuted if they had acted on legal orders from the Bush administration.[351] Left unaddressed is the basic question of whether orders to torture can be "legal."

The practice of torture by a government, like that of slavery or genocide, falls under a special legal category known as *jus cogens*—Latin for "higher law." "This means that no country can ever pass a law that allows torture. There can be no immunity from criminal liability for violation of a *jus cogens* prohibition."[352] Under the Eighth Amendment to the U.S. Constitution, which expressly forbids "cruel and unusual punishments," torture is *always* illegal. Moreover, torture is criminalized under several federal statutes, including the Anti-Torture Act, the War Crimes Act (which bans waterboarding), the MCain Amendment to the Detainee Treatment Act, as well as the more generic federal assault laws.[353] The prohibition of torture is also universally accepted under international law; and, for over 100 years, the Supreme Court has held that customary international law is part of U.S. law.[354]

In addition, when the United States ratifies a treaty, that treaty becomes part of the Law of the Land under the Supremacy Clause of the Constitution.[355] Such would be the case with the Senate-ratified Geneva Convention and the Senate-ratified Convention Against Torture.[356] In a 2006 public debate, former Deputy Assistant Attorney General John Yoo, who had authored the Bush administration's shamefully narrow "organ failure or death" definition of torture (noted earlier), claimed that commander-in-chief powers mean that no law can restrict the President's actions in pursuit of war. As an example, Yoo further argued (hypothetically, one hopes) that no treaty can stop the President from torturing someone by crushing the testicles of that person's child.[357]

At the core of the torture debate that has erupted since 9/11 is the basic question of effectiveness. Moral considerations aside, does torture even work? A military intelligence specialist who was sent by the Pentagon to assess interrogations in Iraq—more than a year before the Abu Ghraib scandal—concluded that torture is simply "not a good way to get information."[358] "The intelligence community, including professional interrogators, is virtually unanimous on the point that, as a means of interrogation, torture is effective at one thing-extracting false confessions."[359] Senator John McCain has written: "In my experience, abuse of prisoners often produces bad intelligence because under torture a person will say anything he thinks his captors want to hear—whether it is true or false."[360] According to McCain, when he was a POW he was once physically coerced to provide the names of the members of his flight squadron. He gave them the names of the Green Bay Packers offensive line—and the abuse was suspended.[361]

On the other hand, Bush, Cheney, Rumsfeld, and other former masterminds of the war on terror continue to insist that valuable intelligence and life-saving information has been derived from interrogation tactics that most Americans would consider torture. Pulitzer Prize-winning journalist Diane McWhorter writes that torture represents absolute power when it is imposed without regard to the guilt of its victims.[362] But when some of the victims are actual criminals or undeniable terrorists, this provides the torturers with moral cover. Moments after Attorney General-nominee Eric Holder told the Senate that the use of waterboarding is torture, then-CIA Director Michael Hayden declared: "These techniques worked."[363] Hayden credited waterboarding for the 2007 confession of Guantanamo prisoner Khalid Sheikh Mohammed, who admitted to beheading *Wall Street Journal* reporter Daniel Pearl[364]—a gruesome crime that was widely disseminated on the Internet in 2002.[365] In the turbulent post-9/11 era, tales of "fruitful" torture are seductive and have found a receptive audience in some unexpected quarters. For example, Harvard Law Professor Alan Dershowitz, a stalwart civil libertarian, has proposed the use of "torture warrants" in emergency situations.[366] Dershowitz argues that placing torture under strict judicial guidelines would help keep it from sliding down a slippery slope into non-emergency usage.[367]

Arguments supporting the torture of suspected terrorists have been raised even by some who doubt its value in the acquisition of good intelligence. They assert that torture is not just about extracting information. It is also designed to break the victim's will and deter others in his social surroundings. "As an interrogation tool, torture is a bust. But when it comes to social control, nothing works quite like torture."[368]

Of course, torture cannot be analyzed in a morally detached vacuum, so removing moral considerations from the debate is impossible. Susan J. Crawford is a staunch Republican, a retired judge who served as general counsel for the Army during the Reagan administration and as Pentagon inspector general when Dick Cheney was Secretary of Defense. In 2007, she was named convening authority of military commissions by the Defense Department. Just days before President Bush left office in 2009, she became the first senior administration official responsible for reviewing the practices at Guantanamo to state publicly that Mohamed Qahtani was tortured:

> "I sympathize with the intelligence gatherers in those days after 9/11, not knowing what was coming next and trying to gain information to keep us safe. . . . But there still has to be a line that we should not cross. And unfortunately what this has done, I think, has tainted everything going forward."[369]

The line Susan Crawford warns of crossing is also the *bottom line* of the torture issue. It is indisputable that the worst American excesses pale in comparison to the bestial crimes committed by 21st-century jihadists, who seem determined to drench the world in blood. However, as Crawford appears to recognize, if the United States aspires to lead the war against terrorism, it must do so not only through its military might but through the example set by its principles and ideals. Otherwise, a war between good and evil becomes a war between bad and worse.

Despite the Bush administration's efforts to minimize it and rename it, almost everyone understands that prisoners at Abu Ghraib and Guantanamo were tortured. What is far more polarizing is whether such exigent practices may be justified in the post-9/11 era. Many Americans insist that the war against terrorism is a literal battle for survival and not an abstract law school debate. In their view, if laws against torture need to be bent a little—or even a lot—that is an unfortunate but necessary cost of victory. But many other Americans—no less patriotic—cannot accept torture as a defensible policy. Their arguments have little to do with terrorists, who have forfeited any decent claim to sympathy. It is not about them; it is about *us*. If we allow ourselves to sink to the level of our enemies, they win.

NOTES

1. *Olmstead v. United States,* 277 U.S. 438 (1928).
2. Allen, Garland E. "The Misuse of Biological Hierarchies: The American Eugenics Movement, 1900–1940." *History and Philosophy of the Life Sciences* 5, 1983: 105–128.
3. *Journal of the American Medical Association.* "Sterilization to Improve the Race." September 9, 1933: p. 866.
4. Reinhold, Robert. "Some Unfortunate Verdicts on Writing Science into the Law." *New York Times,* March 9, 1980: p. 8E. For a historical review of the American eugenics movement, see also: Rafter, Nicole H. "Claims-Making and Socio-Cultural Context in the First U.S. Eugenics Campaign." *Social Problems* 39, 1992: 17 35.
5. Barker, David. "The Biology of Stupidity: Genetics, Eugenics and Mental Deficiency in the Inter-War Years." *British Journal of Health Science* 22, 1989: 347–375.
6. Leonard, Arthur S. *Sexuality and the Law: An Encyclopedia of Major Legal Cases.* New York: Garland Publishing, 1993.
7. Smith, J. David, and Nelson, K. Ray. *The Sterilization of Carrie Buck.* Far Hills, NJ: New Horizon Press, 1989.
8. *Buck v. Bell,* 274 U.S. 200 (1927).
9. Reinhold, Robert. "Virginia Hospital's Chief Traces 50 Years of Sterilizing the 'Retarded'." *New York Times,* February 23, 1980: p. 6.
10. Stroman, Duane F. *Mental Retardation in Social Context.* Lanham, MD: University Press of America, 1989.
11. Platt, Steve. "Fertility Control." *New Statesman and Society* 4, 1991: 11.
12. *Ibid.* p. 7
13. Herrnstein, Richard J. and Murray, Charles. *The Bell Curve.* New York: Free Press, 1994.
14. Jones, James H. *Bad Blood: The Tuskegee Syphilis Experiment—A Tragedy of Race and Medicine.* New York: The Free Press, 1981; p. 91.
15. Mintz, Morton and Cohen, Jerry. *Power, Inc.: Public and Private Rulers and How to Make Them Accountable.* New York: Viking, 1976; p. 477.

16. Jones, *op. cit.*

17. *Ibid.*, p. 16

18. *Ibid.*, p. 24

19. *Ibid.*

20. Quoted in *Ibid.*, p. 44

21. *Ibid.*

22. *Ibid.*, p. 127

23. *Ibid.*, p. 127

24. *Ibid.*, p. 126

25. Stolberg, *op. cit.*

26. Mintz and Cohen, *op. cit.*

27. Jones, *op. cit.*, p. 202

28. *Ibid.*, p. 202

29. *Ibid.*, p. 191

30. *Ibid.*, pp. 193, 192

31. Quoted in Mintz and Cohen, *op. cit.*, p. 478

32. Cohn, Victor. "Experiment Settlement is Faulted." *Washington Post,* December 18, 1974: p. 6a.

33. Bowart, Walter. *Operation Mind Control.* New York: Dell, 1978; p. 23.

34. Eitzen, D. Stanley and Timmer, Doug A. *Criminology: Crime and Criminal Justice.* New York: John Wiley & Sons, 1985.

35. Bowart, *op. cit.*

36. *Ibid.*

37. *Ibid.*

38. *Ibid.*, p. 73

39. *Ibid.*, p. 81

40. *Ibid.*

41. *Ibid.*, p. 14

42. *Ibid.*, p. 13

43. Bowart, *op. cit.*

44. *Houston Post.* "LSD Death Inquiry." July 13, 1994: p. A16.

45. *Ibid.*, p. 398

46. *Ibid.*

47. *Ibid.*, 398–399

48. Quoted in *Ibid.*, p. 399

49. Allen, Scott and Kong, Dolores. "'50 Memo Warned Radiation Tests Would Suggest Nazism." *Boston Globe,* December 28, 1993: p. 1.

50. Mintz and Cohen, *op. cit.*, p. 480

51. Mitford, Jessica. *Kind and Usual Punishment: The Prison Business.* New York: Knopf, 1973.

52. McGrory, Brian and Murphy, Sean. "Inmates Used in '60s Drug Tests." *Boston Globe,* January 1, 1994: p. 16.

53. *Ibid.*

54. Schneider, December 17, 1993, *op. cit.*

55. Hoversten, *op. cit.*, p. 10A

56. Mitford, *op. cit.*

57. Mintz and Cohen, *op. cit.*, p. 479

58. *Ibid.*

59. Mitford, *op. cit.*

60. *Ibid.*, p.139–140

61. Rakstis, Ted J. "The Business Challenge: Confronting the Ethics Issue." *Kiwanis Magazine,* September 1990: p. 30.

62. Beck, Paul J. and Maher, Michael W. "Competition, Regulation and Bribery." *Managerial and Decision Economics* 10, 1989: 1–12.

63. Roebuck, Julian, and Weeber, Stanley C. *Political Crime in the U.S.: Analyzing Crime By and Against Government.* New York: Praeger, 1978.

64. Hershey, Robert D. "Payoffs: Are They Stopped or Just Better Hidden?" *New York Times,* January 29, 1978: p. 23.

65. Sampson, Anthony T. *The Arms Bazaar.* New York: Viking Press, 1977.

66. Eitzen and Timmer, *op. cit.*

67. Roebuck and Weeber, *op. cit.*

68. Agee, Phillip. *Inside the Company: CIA Diary.* New York: Stonehill Publishing, 1975.

69. Roebuck and Weeber, *op. cit.*

70. *Ibid.*

71. Halperin, *op. cit.*

72. Wise, David. *The Politics of Lying.* New York: Vantage, 1973.

73. Bradlee, Jr., Ben. *Guts and Glory: The Rise and Fall of Oliver North.* New York: Donald Fine, 1988.

74. Draper, Theodore. *A Very Thin Line: The Iran-Contra Affairs.* New York: Hill and Wang, 1991; p. 27.

75. *Ibid.*

76. Bradlee, *op. cit.*

77. Draper, *op. cit.*

78. Magnuson, Ed. "Patriots Pursuing Profits." *Time,* June 8, 1987: 24–25.

79. Draper, *op. cit.*

80. Bradlee, *op. cit.*

81. Quoted by Draper, *op. cit.*, p. 98

82. Draper, *op. cit.*

83. *Ibid.*

84. *New York Times.* "Transcript of Reagan's Remarks on the Hostages." July 1, 1985: p. 10a.

85. Cohen, William S. and Mitchell, George J. *Men of Zeal: A Candid Inside Story of the Iran-Contra Hearings.* New York: Viking, 1988.

86. *Ibid.*

87. *Ibid.*

88. Bradlee, *op. cit.*

89. Draper, *op. cit.*

90. Cohen and Mitchell, *op. cit.*

91. Draper, *op. cit., p. 216*

92. Cohen and Mitchell, *op. cit.*

93. Draper, *op. cit., p. 302*

94. Cohen and Mitchell, *op. cit.*

95. Draper, *op. cit., p. 355*

96. *Ibid., p. 417*

97. Quoted in: Wine, Michael."White House E-Mail Gives Peek at Hi-Jinks During Iran-Contra." *Houston Chronicle,* November 26, 1995: p. 2A.

98. *New York Times.*"Transcript of Remarks by Reagan About Iran." November 14, 1986: p. A8.

99. Reagan, Ronald. *An American Life.* New York: Simon and Schuster, 1990.

100. Draper, *op. cit., p. 475*

101. Reagan, Ronald. *An American Life.* New York:

102. Draper, *op. cit.*

103. Cohen and Mitchell, *op. cit., p. xxviii*

104. *Ibid.*

105. Bradlee, *op. cit., p. 491*

106. Draper, *op. cit., 541–542*

107. *Ibid., p. 551*

108. *Ibid., p. 551*

109. *Ibid., p. 552*

110. Morganthau, Tom."Ollie North's Secret Network." *Newsweek,* March 9, 1987: 32–37.

111. Bradlee, *op. cit.*

112. *Ibid., p. 538*

113. *Ibid., p. 538*

114. Shales, Tom."On the Air: The High Drama of a Duel." *Washington Post,* July 8, 1987: p. B2.

115. Kaplan, Fred."Judge Gives McFarlane $20K Fine." *Boston Globe,* March 4, 1989: pp. 1, 4.

116. Dellinger, Walter."Case Closed." *The New Republic,* January 9 & 16, 1989: 15–16.

117. Kaplan, Fred."Secord Guilty Plea Avoids Trial." *Boston Globe,* November 5, 1989: p. 3.

118. Yost, Peter."Secord, Iran-Contra Figure, Gets 2 Years' Probation." *Boston Globe,* January 26, 1990: p. 5.

119. Wines, Michael."Hakim on Probation in Iran-Contra Deal but Shares Proceeds." *New York Times,* February 2, 1990: pp. A1, A18.

120. Johnston, David. "Iran-Contra Role Brings Pondexter 6 Months in Prison." *New York Times,* June 12, 1990: pp. A1, A19.

121. Lowther, William."A Forgiving Sentence." *Maclean's* July 17, 1989: p. 23.

122. Lamar, *op. cit.*

123. Cohen and Mitchell, *op. cit., p. 97*

124. Johnston, September 17, 1991, *op. cit.*

125. Johnston, David."Judge in Iran-Contra Trial Drops Case Against North After Prosecutor Gives Up." *New York Times,* September 17, 1991: pp. A1, A19.

126. *New York Times.*"Oliver North Beats the Rap." [Editorial], September 17, 1991: p. A20.

127. Gartner, Michael."Oliver North's Disloyalty." *USA Today,* October 18, 1994: p. 11A.

128. Mill, John Stuart. *Dissertations and Discussions: Political, Philosophical, and Historical.* New York: Haskell House, 1975.

129. Eitzen and Timmer, *op. cit.*

130. Daniels, Roger. *Concentration Camps USA: Japanese-Americans and World War II.* New York: Holt, Rinehart, and Winston, 1972.

131. Girdner, Audrie and Loftis, Anne. *The Great Betrayal: The Evacuation of the Japanese-Americans During World War II.* London: MacMillan, 1969.

132. Weglyn, Micki. *Years of Infamy: The Untold Story of American Concentration Camps.* New York: William Morrow and Company, 1976.

133. Archer, Jules. *Watergate: America in Crisis.* New York: Thomas Y. Crowell, 1975: p. 270.

134. Lowi, Theodore."The Intelligent Person's Guide to Political Corruption." *Public Affairs* 82, 1981: 1–8.

135. Congressional Quarterly. *Watergate: Chronology of a Crisis.* Washington, D.C.: Congressional Quarterly, Inc., 1974.

136. *Ibid.*

137. *Ibid.*

138. *Ibid.*

139. *Ibid.*

140. Cook, Fred J. *The Crimes of Watergate.* New York: Franklin Watts, 1981.

141. *Ibid., p. 112*

142. Congressional Quarterly, *op. cit.*

143. Archer, Jules. *Watergate: America in Crisis.* New York: Thomas Y. Crowell, 1975,

144. *Ibid., p. 236*

145. *Ibid., p. 224*

146. *Ibid.*

147. Wrong, Dennis H."Watergate: Symptom of What Sickness?" *Dissent* 23, 1974: p. 502.

148. Brown, Bruce."Watergate: Business as Usual." *Liberation* July/August 1974, p. 22.

149. Erskine, Hazel."The Polls: Corruption in Government." *Public Opinion Quarterly* 37, 1973: 628–644.

150. Quoted in Silverstein, Mark. "Watergate and the American Political System." In Markovits, Andrei S. and Silverstein, Mark (Eds.), *The Politics of Scandal: Power and Process in Liberal Democracies.* New York: Holmes & Meier, 1988; 15–37.

151. Cook, *op. cit.,* p. 2

152. *Ibid.*

153. Silverstein, *op. cit.,* p. 15

154. Cook, *op. cit.,* p. 2

155. Bernstein, Carl and Woodward, Bob. *All the President's Men.* New York: Simon and Schuster, 1974.

156. Congressional Quarterly, *op. cit.,* p. 139

157. Wieghart, James. "FBI Chief to Tell of Burning Hunt File." *New York Daily News,* April 27, 1973: pp. 1, 81.

158. Congressional Quarterly, *op. cit.,* p. 149

159. *Ibid.,* p.150

160. Bernstein and Woodward, *op. cit.,* p. 313

161. Congressional Quarterly, *op. cit.*

162. Ehrlichman, John. *Witness to Power.* New York: Simon and Schuster, 1982.

163. *Ibid.*

164. Congressional Quarterly, *op. cit.*

165. Bernstein and Woodward, *op. cit.*

166. Archer, *op. cit.*

167. Congressional Quarterly, *op. cit.*

168. Archer, *op. cit.,* p. 200

169. *Ibid.,* p. 200

170. Archer, *op. cit.*

171. Hersh, Seymour M. "Kissinger Said to Have Asked F.B.I. to Wiretap a Number of His Aides." *New York Times,* May 17, 1973: pp. 1, 35.

172. Woodward, Bob and Bernstein, Carl. "Dean: Nixon Asked IRS to Stop Audits." *Washington Post,* June 20, 1973: pp. A1, A7.

173. Dean, John. *Blind Ambition: The White House Years.* New York: Simon and Schuster, 1976.

174. Cook, *op. cit.*

175. Feinberg, Barbara S. *Watergate: Scandal in the White House.* New York: Franklin Watts, 1990.

176. Congressional Quarterly, *op. cit.*

177. Barker, Karlyn and Pincus, Walter. "Watergate Revisited." *Washington Post,* June 14, 1992: p. A1.

178. Cook, *op. cit.*

179. *Ibid.,* p. 112

180. Feinberg, *op. cit.,* p. 216

181. Archer, *op. cit.,* p. 216

182. *Ibid.,* p. 216

183. Archer, *op. cit.*

184. Quoted in *Ibid.,* p. 271

185. Kelman, *op. cit.,* p. 307

186. Kelman, Herbert C. "Some Reflections on Authority, Corruption, and Punishment: The Social-Psychological Context of Watergate." *Psychiatry* 39, 1976: 303–317.

187. Candee, Dan. "The Moral Psychology of Watergate." *Journal of Social Issues* 21, 1975: p. 183.

188. Kelman, *op. cit.,* p. 307

189. Cook, *op. cit.,* p. 139

190. Silverstein, *op. cit.,* p. 33

191. Dunham, Roger G. and Mauss, Armand L. "Waves from Watergate: Evidence Concerning the Impact of the Watergate Scandal upon Political Legitimacy and Social Control." *Pacific Sociological Review* 19, 1976: p. 470.

192. Kelman, *op. cit.,* p. 304

193. Vidich, Arthur J. "Political Legitimacy in Bureaucratic Society: An Analysis of Watergate." *Social Research*

194. Barber, James D. "The Nixon Brush with Tyranny." *Political Science Quarterly* 92, 1977: p. 594.

195. Archer, *op. cit.,* p. 274

196. Kelman, *op. cit.,* p. 311

197. *Ibid.,* p. 603

198. Hershey, Marjorie R. and Hill, David B. "Watergate and Preadults' Attitudes Toward the President." *American Journal of Political Science* 19, 1975: 703–726.

199. Dunham and Mauss, *op. cit.,* p. 485

200. Zimmer, Troy. "The Impact of Watergate on the Public's Trust in People and Confidence in the Mass Media." *Social Science Quarterly* 59, 1979: 743–751.

201. Jensen, Michael C. "Watergate Donors Still Riding High." *New York Times,* August 24, 1978: pp. 1, 7.

202. Hedlo, Hugh, Brown, Fred R., and Dillon, Conley. "Watergate in Retrospect: The Forgotten Agenda." *Public Administration Review* 36, 1976: p. 306.

203. Hawkins, Robert P., Pingree, Suzanne, and Roberts, Donald F. "Watergate and Political Socialization: The Inescapable Event." *American Politics Quarterly* 3, 1975: p. 406.

204. Arterton, F. Christopher. "The Impact of Watergate on Children's Attitudes toward Political Authority." *Political Science Quarterly* 89, 1974: 269–288.

205. Dennis, Jack and Webster, Carol. "Children's Images of the President and of Government in 1962 and 1974." *American Politics Quarterly* 3, 1974: 386–405.

206. Fowlkes, Diane L. "Realpolitik and Play Politics: The Effects of Watergate and Political Gaming on Undergraduate Students' Political Interest and Political Trust." *Simulation & Games* 8, 1977: 419–438.

207. Garrett, James B. and Wallace, Benjamin. "Cognitive Consistency, Repression-Sensitization, and Level of Moral Judgment: Reactions of College Students to the Watergate Scandals." *Journal of Social Psychology* 98, 1976: 69–76.

208. Congressional Quarterly, *op. cit.*

209. Chaffee, Steven H. and Becker, Lee B. "Young Voters' Reactions to Early Watergate Issues." *American Politics Quarterly* 3, 1975: 360–386.

210. Arendt, Hannah. *The Origins of Totalitarianism.* NY: Schocken Books, 2004 (originally published 1951).

211. *New York Times* (online). "Says Usual Police Practice Is to Club," January 29, 1922.

212. Fried, Joseph R. "Volpe Sentenced to a 30-Year Term in Louima Torture." nytimes.com, December 14, 1999.

213. Central Intelligence Agency. *KUBARK: Counterintelligence Interrogation,* July 1963. KUBARK is a code name for the CIA.

214. Central Intelligence Agency, *Human Resources Exploitation Training Manual*—1983.

215. Cohn, Gary, Thompson, Ginger, and Matthews Mark. "Torture Was Taught by CIA; Declassified Manual Details the Methods Used in Honduras; Agency Denials Refuted." *Baltimore Sun* (online), January 27, 1997.

216. Quoted in CIA, 1983, *op. cit.* [The manual is not paginated.]

217. *Ibid.*

218. Benjamin, Mark. "The CIA's Favorite Form of Torture." salon.com, June 7, 2007.

219. Cohn et al., *op. cit.*

220. Cohn et al., *op. cit.*

221. CIA, 1983, *op. cit.*

222. Cohn et al., *op. cit.*

223. CIA, 1983, *op. cit.*

224. Quoted in Cohn, et al., *op. cit.*

225. CIA, 1983, *op. cit.*

226. Quoted in *Ibid.*

227. *Ibid.*

228. Quoted in *Ibid.*

229. Ross, Brian and Esposito, Richard. "CIA's Harsh Interrogation Techniques Described." abcnews.com, November 28, 2005.

230. Whitaker, Raymond. "The Torture Files." president-bush. com, December 4, 2005.

231. Ross and Esposito, *op. cit.*

232. Ladisch, Virginie. "'Stress and Duress:' Drawing the Line Between Interrogation and Torture." crimesofwar.com, April 24, 2003.

233. Priest, Dana and Gellman, Barton. "'Stress and Duress' Tactics Used on Terrorism Suspects Held in Secret Overseas Facilities." *Washington Post* (online), December 26, 2002.

234. Ladisch, *op. cit.*

235. Eban, Katherine. "The Psychology-Torture Connection." vanityfair.com, June 18, 2008.

236. Eban, Katherine. "Rorschach and Awe." vanityfair.com, July 17, 2007.

237. *Ibid.*

238. *Ibid.*

239. Benjamin, Mark. "The CIA's Torture Teachers." salon.com, June 21, 2007.

240. Thanawala, Sudhin. "US Psychologists Scrap Interrogation Ban." washingtonpost.com, August 20, 2007.

241. Vedantam, Shankar. "APA Rules on Interrogation Abuse." *Washington Post,* August 20, 2007: A3.

242. Hersh, Seymour M. "Torture at Abu Ghraib." newyorker. com, May 10, 2004.

243. *Ibid.*

244. *Ibid.*

245. Martin, Susan Taylor. "Her Job: Lock Up Iraq's Bad Guys." sptimes.com, December 14, 2003.

246. Hersh, 2004, *op. cit.*

247. ARTICLE 15-6 INVESTIGATION OF THE 800TH MILITARY POLICE BRIGADE.

248. *Ibid.*

249. Hersh, 2004, *op. cit.*

250. Quoted in Hersh, Seymour M. "The General's Report." newyorker.com, June 25, 2007.

251. McCoy, Alfred W. "The Hidden History of CIA Torture: America's Road to Abu Ghraib." *commondreams.org,* September 9, 2004.

252. ARTICLE 15-6 INVESTIGATION OF THE 800TH MILITARY POLICE BRIGADE, *op. cit.*

253. Zernike, Kate. "Detainees Describe Abuses by Guard in Iraq Prison." nytimes.com, January 13, 2005.

254. MSNBC.com. "England Gets 3 Years For Prison Abuse," September 28, 2005.

255. Wong, Edward. "Trial Date Set For Another Reservist in Prison Abuse Case." nytimes.com, October 22, 2004.

256. Quoted in Hersh, 2004, *op. cit.*

257. Jehl, Douglas and Johnston, David. "C.I.A. Expands Its Inquiry Into Interrogation Tactics." nytimes.com, August 29, 2004.

258. CNN.com. "Graner Sentenced to 10 Years For Abuses," January 15, 2005.

259. *Ibid.*

260. MSNBC.com. "Graner to Testify at Lynndie England's Sentencing," May 4, 2005.

261. Dishneau, David. "Abu Ghraib Officer's Sentence: Reprimand." uUSAToday.com, August 28, 2007.

262. Smith, R. Jeffrey. "Abu Ghraib Officer Gets Reprimand." *Washington Post,* May 12, 2005: A 16.

263. Cloud, David S. "General Says Prison Inquiry Led to His Forced Retirement." nytimes.com, June 17, 2007.

264. Quoted in Hersh, 2007, *op. cit.*

265. Schmitt, Eric. "Army Report Says Flaws in Detention Didn't Cause Abuse." nytimes.com, July 23, 2004.

266. *Ibid.*

267. Quoted in McCoy, *op. cit.*

268. Quoted in Fisher, William. "Rumsfeld's 'Bad Apples' Didn't Fall Far From the Tree." *commondreams.org,* December 20, 2008.

269. Quoted in *Ibid.*

270. *Ibid.*

271. Quoted in *commondreams.org.* "Rumsfeld Okayed Abuses Says Former U.S. General," August 25, 2006.

272. *Ibid.*

273. McCoy, 2004, *op. cit.*

274. *Ibid.*

275. *Ibid.*

276. *Ibid.*

277. Quoted in McCoy, Alfred W. "Torture at Abu Ghraib Followed CIA's Manual." *commonsdreams.org,* May 14, 2004.

278. White, Josh. "Abu Ghraib Tactics Were First Used at Guantanamo." *Washington Post,* July 14, 2005: A1.

279. Lewis, Neil A. and Schmitt, Eric. "Inquiry Finds Abuses at Guantanamo Bay." nytimes.com, May 1, 2005.

280. *Ibid.*

281. *Ibid.*

282. *Ibid.*

283. *Los Angeles Times.* "It's Torture; It's Illegal," February 2, 2008: A20.

284. Eggen, Dan and Smith, R. Jeffrey. "FBI Agents Allege Abuse of Detainees at Guantanamo Bay." *Washington Post,* December 21, 2004: A1.

285. washingtonpost.com. "The Truth About Abu Ghraib," July 29, 2005.

286. Eggen and Smith, *op. cit.*

287. Quoted in *Ibid.*

288. Lewis and Schmitt, *op. cit.*

289. Quoted in Watson, Paul Joseph. "Rumsfeld Openly Admits Guantanamo Torture." infowars.com, November 3, 2005.

290. Quoted in *Ibid.*

291. Quoted in *Ibid.*

292. Woodward, Bob. "Detainee Tortured Says U.S. Official." *Washington Post,* January 14, 2009: A1.

293. forbes.com. "US Acknowledges Torture at Guantanamo; in Iraq, Afghanistan—UN," June 24, 2005.

294. United Nations Committee Against Torture. "Consideration of Reports Submitted by States Parties Under Article 19 of the Convention." May 18, 2006.

295. Lynch, Colum. "Military Prison's Closure Is Urged." *Washington Post.* May 20, 2006: A1.

296. Wright, Tom. "Close Guantanamo, UN Panel Urges." iht. com, May 19, 2006.

297. Coughlin, Con. "UN Inquiry Demands Immediate Closure of Guantanamo." *telegraph.co.uk,* February 13, 2006.

298. Quoted in Lynch, *op. cit.*

299. Lynch, *op. cit.*

300. Nebehay, Stephanie. "U.N. Rights Envoy Suspects CIA of Guantanamo Torture." reuters.com, December 13, 2007.

301. Doyle, Leonard. "Waterboarding Is Torture—I Did It Myself, Says US Advisor." *The Independent* (online), November 1, 2007.

302. Weiner, Eric. "Waterboarding: A Tortured History." npr. com, February 4, 2007.

303. *Ibid.*

304. *Ibid.*

305. *hrw.org.* "CIA Whitewashing Torture," November 20, 2005.

306. abcnews.com. "History of an Interrogation Technique: Water Boarding," November 29, 2005.

307. Weiner, *op. cit.*

308. *Ibid.*

309. Wallach, Evan. "Waterboarding Used to Be a Crime." *Washington Post,* November 4, 2007: B1.

310. Quoted in abcnews.com, November 29, 2005, *op. cit.*

311. Nance, Malcolm. "I Know Waterboarding Is Torture—Because I Did It Myself." nydailynews.com, October 31, 2007.

312. Quoted in Doyle, *op. cit.*

313. Nance, *op. cit.*

314. Human Rights Watch. "Open Letter to Attorney General Alberto Gonzalez." *hrw.org,* April 5, 2006.

315. Davis, Benjamin. "Endgame on Torture: Time to Call the Bluff." *Jurist* (online), October, 2007.

316. Quoted in Belle, Nicole. "Retired JAGs Send Letter to Leahy: *"Waterboarding Is Inhumane, It Is Torture, and It Is Illegal."* crooksandliars.com, November 2, 2007.

317. Shane, Scott. "A Firsthand Experience Before Decision to Torture." nytimes.com, November 7, 2007.

318. *democracynow.org.* "Despite Waterboarding Stance, Senate Committee Approves Mukassey's Attorney General Nomination," November 7, 2008.

319. *Los Angeles Times,* February 2, 2008, *op. cit.*

320. Tran, Mark. "CIA Admit 'Waterboarding' al-Qaida Suspects." *guardian.co.uk,* February 9, 2008.

321. *bbc.co.uk.* "CIA Admits Waterboarding Inmates," February 5, 2008.

322. Quoted in military.com. "Hayden: Waterboarding May Be Illegal," February 8, 2008.

323. Schor, Elana. "US Official Admits Waterboarding Presently Illegal." *guardian.co.uk,* February 14, 2008. Another administration heavyweight, Secretary of State Condoleezza Rice, admitted for the first time in late 2008 that, as early as 2002, when she was national security advisor, she had led high-level discussions about subjecting suspected al-Qaeda terrorists detained at military installations to waterboarding. (Fisher, William. "Rumsfeld's 'Bad Apples Didn't Fall Far From the Tree." *commondreams.org,* December 20, 2008.)

324. Quoted in newser.com. "Bush Rips Congress on Waterboarding Ban," February 15, 2008.

325. Quoted in Eggen, Dan. "Bush Announces Veto of Waterboarding Ban." washingtonpost.com, March 8, 2008.

326. Amnesty International (press release). "USA: Water Torture is Always Illegal." February 15, 2008.

327. Leopold, Jason. "Cheney Admits He 'Signed Off' on Waterboarding of Three Guantanamo Prisoners." onlinejournal. com, December 29, 2008.

328. Quoted in *Ibid.*

329. Quoted in Duss, Matthew. "Cheney the Failed Architect." *guardian.co.uk,* December 17, 2008.

330. Carroll, Lewis. *Alice's Adventures in Wonderland and Through the Looking Glass.* NY: Signet Classics, 2000. [originally published 1899]

331. Quoted in Eggen, Dan. "Chaney's Remarks Fuel Torture Debate." *Washington Post,* October 27, 2006.

332. Amnesty International (press release). "Amnesty International's Response to Cheney's 'No-Brainer' Comment." October 26, 2006.

333. McCain, John. "Torture's Terrible Toll." Newsweek.com, November 21, 2005.

334. White, Josh. "President Relents, Backs Torture Ban." *Washington Post,* December 16, 2005: A1.

335. Miller, Greg and Reynolds, Maura. "McCain Wins Agreement From Bush on Torture Ban." *Los Angeles Times,* December 16, 2005: A1.

336. CNN.com. "McCain, Bush Agree on Torture Ban," December 15, 2005.

337. Savage, Charlie. "Bush Could Bypass New Torture Ban." boston.com, January 4, 2006.

338. *Washington Post.* "Legalizing Torture," June 9, 2004: A20.

339. Landers, Ken. "Bush Veto Allows CIA Torture to Continue." *abc.net.au,* March 10, 2008.

340. Quoted in *Ibid.*

341. Warrick, Joby. "CIA Tactics Endorsed in Secret Memos." *Washington Post,* October 15, 2008: A1.

342. Hess, Pamela and Jordan, Lara Jakes. "CIA Torture Memo: Harsh Interrogation Legal If It's in 'Good Faith'." huffingtonpost.com, July 25, 2008.

343. Warrick, *op. cit.*

344. American Civil Liberties Union (press release). "ACLU Obtains Key Memos Authorizing CIA Torture Methods," July 24, 2008.

345. Quoted in MSNBC.com. "Obama: U.S. Will Not Torture," January 9, 2009.

346. Quoted in Margasak, Larry. "Holder: Waterboarding Is Torture." usnews.com, January 15, 2009.

347. Bresnahan, John. "'Waterboarding Is Torture,' Says Holder." politico.com, January 16, 2009.

348. Hess, Pamela. "Obama Intel Nominee Says No Torture on His Watch." Associated Press (online), January 22, 2009.

349. Phillips, Kate. "Judiciary Chairman Calls For Commission to Delve into Bush Practices." nytimes.com, February 9, 2009.

350. Leopold, Jason. "Obama Signals He Doesn't Back Leahy's Plan to Probe Bush Abuses." onlinejournal.com, February 10, 2009.

351. Hess, Pamela. "No Punishment Planned for CIA Interrogators." *Houston Chronicle,* February 7, 2009: A10.

352. Cohn, Marjorie. "Under U.S. Law Torture Is Always Illegal." *counterpunch.org,* May 6, 2008.

353. American Civil Liberties Union (press release). "Is Torture Illegal? Let Us Count the Ways." November 8, 2007.

354. *The Paquete Habana,* 175 U.S. 677 (1900).

355. This principle was established by the United States Supreme Court in one of its earliest landmark decisions in *Martin v. Hunter's Lessee,* 14 U.S. 304 (1816).

356. American Civil Liberties Union, May 8, 2007, *op. cit.*

357. Watts, Philip. "Bush Advisor Says President Has Legal Power to Torture Children." *informationclearinghouse.info,* January 8, 2006.

358. Quoted in Applebaum, Anne. "The Torture Myth." *Washington Post,* January 12, 2003: A21.

359. Duss, *op. cit.*

360. McCain, *op. cit.*

361. *Ibid.*

362. McWhoter, Dianne. "Don't Punt on Torture" *USA Today,* February 11, 2009: 11A.

363. cbsnews.com. "CIA Director: Harsh Interrogations Were Effective," January 15, 2009.

364. Murdock, Deroy. "Waterboarding Has Its Benefits." nationalreview.com, November 5, 2007. abcnews.com. "CIA Director's Strong Defense of Interrogation Techniques," January 15, 2009.

365. Burger, Timothy J. and Zagrin, Adam. "Fingering Danny Pearl's Killer." time.com, October 12, 2006.

366. Dershowitz, Alan M. *Shouting Fire: Civil Liberties in a Turbulent Age.* NY: Little, Brown, 2002.

367. Dershowitz, Alan M. "Want to Torture? Get a Warrant." sfgate.com, January 22, 2002.

368. Klein, Naomi. "Torture's Dirty Secret: It Works." thenation.com, May 12, 2005.

369. Quoted in Woodward, *op. cit.*

> ## Think Critically
>
> 1. How does the general phenomenon of government and state crime relate to conflict theory? Give some major theoretical connections.
> 2. Which examples of government crime described by Rosoff, Pontell, and Tillman best illustrate the conflict perspective? Describe both the examples and the reasons you feel this way.

Street Crime, Labor Surplus, and Criminal Punishment, 1980–1990*

Andrew L. Hochstetler and Neal Shover

THERE IS ENORMOUS GEOGRAPHIC AND temporal variation in state use of punishment. In the United States, for example, there is well-documented regional and state-level variation in the use of imprisonment; in 1994, the incarceration rate (the number of imprisoned adults per 100,000 total population) was 462 for southern states but only 291 for the northeastern states (United States Bureau of Justice Statistics 1996). Geographic variation is apparent also in use of the death penalty; whereas some states do not permit capital punishment, others routinely and regularly execute offenders. As for evidence of temporal variation in punishment, we need look no farther than recent history. In the years after 1973, America's training school, jail and prison populations climbed to historically unprecedented levels. The adult imprisoned population alone grew by more than 300 percent between 1975 and 1994 (United States

Bureau of Justice Statistics 1996). Explaining geographic and temporal variation in official use of imprisonment and other forms of punishment is a long-standing focal point of social problems theory and research. We continue this line of investigation by examining community-level determinants of change in the use of imprisonment by local courts in the United States during the 1980s.

Background

In conflict-theoretical explanations, crime control is portrayed as a process unusually sensitive to the interests and machinations of dominant classes and elites. Grounded in neo-Marxism, analysts sketch criminal punishment as a strategy and mechanism employed by the state to control a class whose interests potentially are threatening to capitalist structures and elites. Viewed in this way, the use of punishment may fluctuate with levels of street crime, but it also varies with prevailing economic conditions. When the economy is strong and the labor surplus shrinks, punishment is relaxed; in times of economic stagnation or crisis,

*We are grateful to Mitchell B. Chamlin for statistical assistance and to anonymous reviewers. Correspondence: Department of Sociology, University of Tennessee, Knoxville, TN 37996-0490.

when the labor surplus grows larger, official use of punishment rises. It is during these times that the structures of criminal justice draw off increasing numbers of those now rendered superfluous for production. This means that:

> increased use of imprisonment is not a direct response to any rise in crime, but is an ideologically motivated response to the perceived threat of crime posed by the swelling population of economically marginalized persons. This position does not deny the possibility of increasing crime accompanying unemployment, but states instead that unemployment levels have an effect on the rate and severity of imprisonment *over and above* the changes in the volume and pattern of crime. (Box and Hale 1982:22)

With roots in pioneering work by Rusche and Kirchheimer (1939), there are several complementary theoretical explanations for the link between surplus labor and punishment. They variously emphasize economic, political and ideological forces, and they impute a variety of motives to elites and to criminal justice managers (Chiricos and Delone, 1992). Our theoretical point of departure is the general proposition that the unemployed are a threat or source of concern for dominant groups which is alleviated or otherwise managed by increased punishment. It is their presumed declining stake in conformity and their mounting desperation that make the unemployed the primary target of intensified punishment initiatives. Behind these crackdowns is elite anxiety, perhaps over potentially increasing political consciousness (Adamson 1984; Wallace 1980), class conflict (Melossi 1989), or rising levels of violent, expropriative street crime (Box and Hale 1982). A swelling mass of the unemployed is "social dynamite" (Spitzer 1975).

The structure of the American economy and the nature of American politics insure that both the shape and the dynamics of criminal justice reflect elite interests (Jacobs 1979). This requires neither the assumption that they conspire in the process or that they orchestrate the actions of criminal justice managers. The aggregate objective consequences of their anxiety are one thing; institutional dynamics and the motives of criminal justice practitioners are another. Remarkably little is known, however, about mechanisms and processes by which elite concerns may be communicated to and acted upon by control managers and apparatchiks. This is an area in which Marxist theories of social control lack specificity and precision.

Increasing anxiety and resentment in the ranks of criminal justice may also contribute to harsher punishment during economic downturns and times of rising unemployment. Squeezed fiscally between increases in the cost of living and their marginal, stagnant salaries, functionaries find new merit in the notion that severe penalties are needed to counteract the heightened temptations of illicit activity caused by hard times. The widespread belief that unemployment causes crime and that severe punishment deters underlies an increasing proportion of their decisions. Day-to-day they do what they can to increase the odds that crime does not become an alternative to economic hardship. The end result of their countless individual decisions is increased severity of punishment. Thus, part of the aggregate-level escalation of punishment may be an unintended consequence of employees in control bureaucracies applying conventional assumptions to crime control. Evidence suggests that for individual defendants, judicial decisions to incarcerate vary significantly by employment status (Chiricos and Bales 1991). Judges apparently view steady employment as an indicator of stability and unemployment as a sign of potential future trouble. Their actions may reassure elites even if this is not their intent. The relationship between labor surplus and penal sanctions requires assumptions about neither conspiracy nor specific direction.

The expanding crime-control apparatus that often accompanies the transformation and growth of punishment aids in the maintenance of stability and social order by providing jobs and a secure legitimate income for increasing numbers of the economically marginalized (Christie 1994). The criminal justice system, therefore, plays a dual role in managing the disadvantaged, desperate, and potentially lawless; in addition to incapacitation, employment opportunities provided by the expansion of criminal justice function as a relief valve for social discontent.

When the economy is strong and unemployment is low, institutional growth in crime control may level off, use of punishment is relaxed, and inclusionary crime-control approaches gain support from elected officials and state managers (Cohen 1985). This explanation for the changing use of punishment is consistent with the growth of rehabilitative ideologies and strategies in the United States during the years of post-World War II prosperity. It also helps explain why economic and structural transformations accompanying growth of the global economy, and the generalized anxiety they produce, has all but ended elected officials' public support for these "softer" crime-control approaches.

The preponderance of evidence from studies of the labor-surplus/punishment nexus supports conflict-theoretical explanations, even when fluctuation in street crime is controlled (Chiricos and Delone 1992). Supportive evidence is provided, first, by nation-level studies both in Europe and in the United States which operationalize punishment as the rate of imprisonment (Box and Hale 1982; 1985; Jankovic 1977; Laffargue and Godefroy 1989; Wallace 1980). Not all investigators report a significant relationship between unemployment and imprisonment (Jacobs and Helms 1996), but a substantial majority do. Results from state-level studies of the unemployment/imprisonment nexus are mixed; studies that employ longitudinal methods generally find the strongest support for the hypothesized relationship, while cross-sectional studies report more contradictory findings (Chiricos and Delone 1992).

Despite the generally confirmatory results of past research, there are reasons to question the labor-surplus/punishment relationship. To begin, methodological considerations suggest that nations and states may not be optimal units of analysis for investigating it. Since larger geographic units generally are more heterogeneous than smaller ones, national-level data are particularly likely to aggregate heterogeneity and mask substantial regional variation. This can confound and obscure empirical relationships of theoretical interest. In the United States, there is considerable intra-state variation in economic, demographic, crime and punishment variables. Analytically, state-level studies usually regress prison population variables on state demographic indicators despite the fact that inmates are not drawn randomly from its population, but largely from urbanized areas.

There is a theoretical reason as well for questioning the use of nations and states as units of analysis. Punishment policies generally are made at federal and state levels, but punishment is dispensed normally by *local* prosecutors and judges. Most serve local constituencies, and local political, structural and labor-market conditions likely constrain their decisions. Investigators are correct to use state-level data to examine variation in punishment policy (Link and Shover 1986; Barlow, Barlow, and

Johnson 1996). Counties or SMSAs, however, may be a more appropriate unit of analysis for examining the relationship between labor surplus and punishment (Colvin 1990; Jankovic 1977; McCarthy 1990). Consistent with findings from national- and many state-level investigations, the small number of county-level studies published thus far report a positive relationship between unemployment and the use of imprisonment (Chiricos and Delone 1992).

Past county-level studies unfortunately are flawed by methodological shortcomings that limit confidence in theoretical understanding of the labor-surplus/punishment nexus. The theory linking historical change in punishment with change in the economy is a temporally dynamic one: as labor surplus increases criminal justice cracks down. Past county-level examinations of variation in use of imprisonment have employed cross-sectional analytic techniques that cannot assess these dynamic effects. Longitudinal techniques are required. Historically, problems of missing, inaccurate or inconsistently recorded information plagued county-level data. These shortcomings made investigators slow to use county-level data to examine justice issues. Complete and reliable county-level data became available in manageable format only recently. Despite an abundance of longitudinal national- and state-level studies of labor surplus and imprisonment, there are no dynamic spatial investigations at the county level.

The shortcomings of previous research diminish confidence in the underlying theoretical construction of the link between economic conditions and punishment. The present longitudinal study may help to rectify this. We test for a direct effect of *change* in the size of the labor surplus on *change* in the use of punishment while controlling for fluctuation in street crime and other variables. Thus, our methodology enables us to examine temporally dynamic causal relationships, and our use of counties as the units of analysis permits a test of the theoretical problem at the most appropriate aggregation.

Data and Methods

From correspondence with top-level criminal justice managers in the 50 states, we learned that 16 states could provide the requisite annual county-level prison commitment data. We began by selecting ten of these for inclusion in our state sample. We chose states from all regions

TABLE 1   Comparison of Sample and All Counties with Populations 25,000 and Over

Variable	Sample	Population
Mean Population Size	134,266	120,868
Proportion White	.86	.88
Proportion Unemployed	.08	.08
Poverty Rate	13	.14
Income per capita 1989	$12,689	$12,367

of the United States, including only states with complete and apparently accurate data, and that would not require potentially time-consuming additional requirements to secure the needed data. The sample of states includes California, New Jersey, Ohio, Nebraska, Wisconsin, Illinois, Michigan, Mississippi, North Carolina and South Carolina. For each state, we then selected from the listing of counties published in the *Uniform Crime Reports* all counties within designated Standard Metropolitan Statistical Areas and all counties with a 1980 total population of more than 25,000 (United States Department of Justice 1980). Because we are interested in how closely our resulting sample of 269 counties approximates characteristics of United States counties, we compared them to all 1,409 counties of similar size in the United States in 1980 (United States Bureau of the Census 1994c). As Table 1 shows, we found that, save for population size (sample counties were somewhat larger than the population), the sample compares closely with the population.

Nevertheless, the fact that the relationship between our sample of 269 counties and populations of theoretical or policy significance is unknown mandates caution in generalizing from the findings. Data were collected for the years 1980 and 1990, principally from official state and federal records. Sources of data are noted and discussed in the Appendix.

As most investigators have done, we use the official rate of unemployment as our measure of labor surplus. In doing so, we are not unmindful of the belief that it is an unsatisfactory measure of the true level of unemployment in a community. It does not, for example, include unemployed men and women who have ceased searching actively for a job. The limitations of our data, however, do not permit us to construct an alternative measure of the size of the labor surplus.

Since variation in state use of punishment generally is attributed to variation in street crime, we included in the analysis measures of both violent and nonviolent crimes known to the police. We also included as control variables socio-demographic characteristics that may contribute to the rate of prison commitments, chief among them the proportion of young adult males in the population (Cohen and Land 1987; Inverarity and McCarthy 1988). Since crime and imprisonment are experiences disproportionately characteristic of young males, counties with a high percentage of young men in their population generally have higher crime rates and, consequently, more imprisonment (Blumstein 1983).

One of the most important changes in America's response to crime in the past 15 years is the dramatic increase of attention and resources devoted to drug-law enforcement. One indicator of this is a sharp increase in the proportion of the imprisoned population serving time for drug offenses (United States Bureau of Justice Statistics 1996). In light of this development, it would be useful to include as controls county-level arrests and prison commitments for drug crimes. The necessary data are not available. Myers and Inverarity (1992) show, however, that increasing arrests from drug crimes do not mediate unemployment's relationship to or explain changing rates in state-level imprisonment.

Inclusion of crime rates in our analysis controls for the effect of age on imprisonment that is mediated by the crime rate. The effect of age on imprisonment should be minimal if the conventional assumption that the age of the population affects imprisonment via crime is true. But age structure also may influence imprisonment directly, particularly if, as seems likely, the population perceived as most dangerous by political-economic elites is young males with restricted access to legitimate labor markets

(Box and Hale 1982). Apart from any real threat from crime, large numbers of young males in a county may effect imprisonment by creating the perception of a threat from a population believed to be aggressive and difficult to control (Tittle and Curran 1988). The effect of a county's age structure on imprisonment after controlling for crime is interpreted as a reflection of this age-threat process. We used age data both to control for the proportion of the population composed of males ages 20–34 and to test for this direct effect.

The use of imprisonment varies directly with the size of the non-white population (Carroll and Doubet 1983; Joubert, Picou, and MacIntosh 1981). Like the young and the unemployed, non-whites may be perceived as particularly threatening, restive and potentially criminal. The presence of non-whites is viewed by some criminal justice officials as an indicator of a crime problem and, therefore, increases the use of crime control and imprisonment. Although there is some evidence that blacks receive longer sentences than whites for similar offenses (e.g., Spohn 1994), other studies suggest that the degree of discrimination against non-whites in sentencing and incarceration varies by social and economic context (Myers and Sabol 1987; Myers and Talarico 1986). For these reasons, we also controlled for the proportionate size of the non-white population.

Other measures of the economic health of a community may influence the use of imprisonment. Marxist theorists suggest that the poor are perceived to be a potential threat to social order. The effect of the impoverished working population on imprisonment is not reflected in unemployment rates. Increases in the proportionate size of the impoverished population may have an effect on change in imprisonment similar to unemployment. Consequently, poverty rates are included as a control variable, principally because they are a reasonable measure of an employed underclass. Poverty rates, however, represent only the percentage of a county's population who are officially poor and are not an indicator of the amount of wealth available to its families. Income is a better measure than poverty of the economic situation faced by them. A county's average personal income in 1980 dollars is included as a control variable to measure each county's economic health.

Given the methodological shortcomings of previous studies, we opted for statistical procedures that permit examination of changes in multiple cases at a few points in time. We used a panel design and analytic technique. Community values, traditions, cultures and institutional inertia all have an impact on both types and amounts of punishment employed against convicted offenders. Panel designs can account for both temporal and geographic variation. By observing the same counties at two points in time we insure that similar extraneous variables are in play in both time periods. We also can observe and analyze how change in some variables contributes to change in others and can even control for ongoing patterns of change common to all counties. A panel design permits us to investigate the effects of change in independent variables on change in imprisonment over the decade.

We used residual-change regression analysis to estimate changes in the level of variables in the panel from 1980 to 1990. This technique, which makes use of residual-change scores, has been employed to examine a variety of social problems (Bursik and Webb 1982; Chamlin 1992; Elliott and Voss 1974). To derive a residual-change score, the level of a variable in 1990 is regressed on its level in 1980. The equation then is used to predict the level of each variable in 1990. Subtracting the predicted value from the observed value in 1990 yields a measure of residual change. Residual-change scores have two properties useful for this research. First, they provide a measure of change that is statistically independent of a variable's initial levels, removing a variables initial level's effect on the subsequent level of that same variable. The result represents change that is not expected on the basis of the variable's initial level alone (Bohrnstedt 1969). Residual-change regression permits an examination of how change in the levels of independent variables affect change in imprisonment.

Second, residual-change scores adjust for changes that other counties have undergone. They control the effects of trends common to all counties to determine change attributable to the variables of interest in a particular county. Since all 269 counties are used to estimate the regression equation which predicts the levels in 1990, the predicted values are automatically adjusted for change that other counties have undergone during the decade. Changes that occur across counties are controlled, leaving each county's unique change. We examine change by using two waves of data from 1980 and 1990 to determine change in socio-economic variable's contribution to change in imprisonment This involves regressing the

TABLE 2   Summary Table for Regression of Changes in Imprisonment on Changes in Independent Variables, 1980-1990

Variable	*B*	*Beta*
Unemployment	.010	.169**
Violent Crime	.054	.147*
Property Crime	−.003	−.035
Males 20-34	.013	.267***
Non-white	.002	.051
Poverty	−.004	−.102
Income	0.000	.034
$R^2 = .139$		Constant = .084*

*p ≤ .05
**p ≤ .01
***p ≤ .005

residual-change scores for imprisonment on the residual-change scores of the other variables. Changes in the independent variables, theoretically, should find expression in changes in imprisonment. This equation takes the form:

$$\text{Imprisonment}_{res:t,t\text{-}10} = f(\text{unemployment}_{res:t,t\text{-}10}, \text{violent crime}_{res:t,t\text{-}10}, \text{property crime}_{res:t,t\text{-}10}, \text{percent non-white}_{res:t,t\text{-}10}, \text{age}_{res:t,t\text{-}10}, \text{income}_{res:t,t\text{-}10}, \text{poverty}_{res:t,t\text{-}10}).$$

The subscripts for independent variables indicate that they are residual-change transformations. Imprisonment $_{res:t,t\text{-}10}$ is the residual-change score of prison commitments during the 10-year period.

Failure to find a positive, significant contribution of unemployment to county prison commitments would cast doubt on the notion of imprisonment as a response to the unemployed's threats to elites. The presence of significant effects for crime in the absence of significance for unemployment will not support the hypothesis of an independent effect of unemployment on imprisonment.

Results

Recall that we expect imprisonment to covary positively with all the independent variables. To test this, we begin by examining the relationships between change in the rate of prison commitments, in unemployment, in crime, and in the other control variables between 1980 and 1990. As predicted, the results reported in Table 2 show that change in

the rate of unemployment (b = .169), violent crime rates (b = .147), and the proportion of males age 20-34 in counties' population (b = .267) are related positively to change in imprisonment rates. The finding which has the greatest bearing on our research question, of course, is that change in unemployment is an independently significant predictor of change in imprisonment. Change in unemployment is related to change in use of imprisonment over and above the effects of crime and the other control variables. Change in property crime, percent non-white, poverty rates, and average income do not produce change in imprisonment. Because some evidence suggests very high non-white population rates may decrease crime control aimed at minorities (Liska and Chamlin 1984), we also tested for a curvilinear effect for non-white. None was found.

To determine if our results were biased by collinearity, a common problem in research using economic predictors, we examined zero-order correlations and performed standard regression diagnostics (Belsley, Kuh, and Welsh 1980). Some high zero-order correlations between predictor variables were identified, particularly between violent and property crime (r = .45) and between poverty and income (r = .49). These correlations do not necessarily indicate the presence of collinearity, but they did warrant further investigation. Subsequent collinearity diagnostics yielded low VIF values and low condition indices, which indicates multicollinearity is not a concern in this equation.

The explained variance of our model is low ($R^2 = .14$). One possible explanation of this is that there is little change left to explain because imprisonment levels in 1980 explain most of the variation in 1990. We checked to see if this was the source of our small R^2 by regressing 1990 imprisonment on the full set of predictors and on 1980 imprisonment. The results were clear; the single best predictor by far was 1980 imprisonment ($R^2 = .74$). By comparison, other effects were negligible. This suggests either that there is very little change from 1980 to 1990 or that the pattern of change is similar across counties. Since 1990 imprisonment levels are accounted for by 1980 levels, only a small amount of change remains unexplained, and the low explained variance in our results can still be viewed as substantively important.

Conclusions and Implications

Our findings can be summarized briefly. Change in violent street crime, in the proportionate size of the young male population, and in labor surplus contribute to change in the use of imprisonment while changing levels of property crime do not. These relationships persist even when street-crime rates and other presumed correlates of imprisonment are controlled. Our analysis, therefore, confirms findings from earlier investigations of the relationship between labor surplus and punishment. The criminal justice system grows increasingly punitive as labor surplus increases. The fact that our findings were achieved using both a unit of analysis more appropriate theoretically than measures employed by most investigators and a longitudinal design only strengthen confidence in them.

The observed relationship between violent street crime and punishment is consistent with results obtained by other investigators (e.g., Inverarity and McCarthy 1988). That our findings differed for violent crime and property crime reinforces the importance of disaggregating crime rates in macro-level research. The relationship between the proportionate size of the young male population and punishment is not surprising. The fact that young males commit the majority of street crime means that in the aggregate they probably symbolize the threat of crime and disorder.

Although our principal objective has been a conflict interpretation of the relationship among street crime,

labor surplus and punishment, the significance of our investigation is more than theoretical. At a time when public schools in many regions of the United States are under severe budgetary constraints, when major components of the nation's infrastructure have eroded, and millions of citizens cannot secure quality health care, expenditure of tax revenues for crime control has skyrocketed. It is only through a better understanding of the sources of these changes that we can predict their likely development or have any hope of controlling them. The findings of this study and others like it suggest an explanation for why past predictions about fluctuations in punishment that failed to include projected rates of unemployment or other economic measures have proven inaccurate.

REFERENCES

Adamson, Christopher. 1984. "Toward a Marxian penology: Captive criminal populations as economic threats and resources." *Social Problems* 31:435–458.

Barlow, David E., Melissa Hickman Barlow, and W. Wesley Johnson. 1996. "The political economy of criminal justice policy: A time-series analysis of economic conditions, crime and federal criminal justice legislation, 1948–1987." *Justice Quarterly* 13:223–242.

Belsley, David A., Edwin Kuh, and Roy E. Welsh. 1980. *Regression Diagnostics: Identifying Influential Data and Sources of Collinearity.* New York: John Wiley & Sons.

Blumstein, Alfred. 1983. "Prisons: Population, capacity, and alternatives." In *Crime and Public Policy,* J. Q. Wilson (ed.), 229–250. San Francisco: ICS.

Bohrnstedt, George W. 1969. "Observations on the measurement of change." In *Sociological Methodology* 1969, E. F. Borgata and G. W. Bohrnstedt (eds.), 113–136. San Francisco: Jossey-Bass.

Box, Steven, and Chris Hale. 1982. "Economic crisis and the rising prisoner population in England and Wales." *Crime and Social Justice* 17:20–35.

———. 1985 "Unemployment, imprisonment and prison overcrowding." *Contemporary Crises* 9:209–228.

Bursik, Robert J., and Jim Webb. 1982. "Community change and patterns of delinquency." *American Journal of Sociology* 88:24–42.

Carroll, Leo, and Mary Beth Doubet. 1983. "U.S. social structure and imprisonment." *Criminology* 21:449–456.

Chamlin, Mitchell B. 1992. "Intergroup threat and social control: Welfare expansion among states during the 1960s and 1970s." In *Social Threat and Social Control,* A.E. Liska (ed.), 151–164. Albany: State University of New York Press.

Chiricos, Theodore G., and William D. Bales. 1991. "Unemployment and punishment: An empirical assessment." *Criminology* 29:701–724.

Chiricos, Theodore G., and Miriam A. Delone. 1992. "Labor surplus and punishment: A review and assessment of theory and evidence." *Social Problems* 39:421–446.

Christie, Nils. 1994. *Crime Control as Industry: Toward GULAGS Western Style.* New York: Routledge.

Cohen, Stanley. 1985. *Visions of Social Control.* Cambridge, U.K.: Polity.

Cohen, Lawrence E., and Kenneth L. Land. 1987. "Age structure and crime: Symmetry versus asymmetry and the projection of crime rates through the 1990s." *American Sociological Review* 52:170–183.

Colvin, Mark. 1990. "Labor markets, industrial monopolization, welfare and imprisonment: Evidence from a cross section of U.S. counties." *Sociological Quarterly* 31:440–456.

Elliot, Delbert S., and Harwin L. Voss. 1974. *Delinquency and Dropout.* Lexington, Mass.: Heath.

Inter-university Consortium for Political and Social Research. 1991. *Uniform Crime Report: County Level Arrest and Offenses Data.* Ann Arbor: University of Michigan.

Inverarity, James, and Daniel McCarthy. 1988. "Punishment and social structure revisited: Unemployment and imprisonment in the U.S., 1948–1984." *Sociological Quarterly* 29:263–279.

Jacobs, David. 1979. "Inequality and police force strength: Conflict theory and coercive control in metropolitan areas." *American Sociological Review* 44:913–925.

Jacobs, David, and Ronald E. Helms. 1996. "Toward a political model of incarceration: A time-series examination of multiple explanations for prison admission rates." *American Journal of Sociology* 102:323–357.

Jankovic, Ivan. 1977. "Labor market and imprisonment." *Crime and Social Justice* 8:17–31.

Joubert, Paul E., J. Steven Picou, and Alex McIntosh. 1981. "U.S. social structure, crime, and imprisonment." *Criminology* 19:344–359.

Laffargue, Bernard, and Thiery Godefroy. 1989. "Economic cycles and punishment." *Contemporary Crises* 13:371–404.

Link, Christopher T., and Neal Shover. 1986. "The origins of criminal sentencing reforms." *Justice Quarterly* 3:329–341.

Liska, Allen E., and Mitchell B. Chamlin. 1984. "Social structure and crime control among macrosocial units." *American Journal of Sociology* 90:383–395.

McCarthy, Belinda. 1990. "A micro-level analysis of social structure and social control: Intrastate use of jail and prison confinement." *Justice Quarterly* 7:325–340.

Melossi, Dario. 1989. "An introduction: Fifty years later, Punishment and Social Structure in comparative analysis." *Contemporary Crises* 13:311–326.

Myers, Greg, and James Inverarity. 1992. "Strategies of disaggregation in imprisonment rate research." Presented at the annual meeting of the American Society of Criminology.

Myers, Martha A., and Susette M. Talarico. 1986. "The social context of racial discrimination in sentencing." *Social Problems* 33:236–251.

Myers, Samuel L., Jr., and William J. Sabol. 1987. "Business cycles and racial disparities in punishment." *Contemporary Policy Issues* 5:46–58.

Rusche, Georg, and Otto Kirchheimer. 1939. *Punishment and Social Structure.* New York: Columbia University Press.

Spitzer, Steven. 1975. "Toward a Marxian theory of deviance." *Social Problems* 22:638–651.

Spohn, Cassia. 1994. "Crime and the social control of blacks: Offender/victim race and the sentencing of violent offenders." In *Inequality, Crime, and Social Control,* G. S. Bridges and M. Myers (eds.), 249–268. Boulder, Colo.: Westview.

Tittle, Charles R., and Debra A. Curran. 1988. "Contingencies for dispositional disparities in juvenile justice." *Social Forces* 67:23–58.

U.S. Bureau of the Census. 1994a. *Revised Estimates of County Population Characteristics 1980–1989.* Washington, D.C.: Estimates Division, U.S. Bureau of the Census.

———. 1994b *Modified Age, Race and Sex.* Washington, D.C.: Estimates Division, U.S. Bureau of the Census.

———. 1994c *County and City Data Book: U.S.A. Counties.* (CD-ROM). Washington, D.C.: U.S. Government Printing Office.

U.S. Bureau of Economic Analysis. 1994. *Regional Economic Information System 1969–1993.* (CD-ROM). Washington, D.C.: U.S. Government Printing Office.

U.S. Bureau of Justice Statistics. 1996. *Correctional Populations in the United States 1994.* Washington, D.C.: U.S. Government Printing Office.

U.S. Bureau of Labor Statistics. 1992. *The Consumer Price Index: Questions and Answers.* Washington, D.C.: U.S. Government Printing Office.

U.S. Department of Justice. 1980. *Uniform Crime Reports for the United States.* Washington, D.C.: U.S. Government Printing Office.

Wallace, Don. 1980. "The political economy of incarceration trends in late U.S. capitalism." *Insurgent Sociologist* 9:59–65.

APPENDIX

Imprisonment

Annual number of new prison commitments from each county (per 100,000 population). These data were provided by each state's Department of Corrections.

Unemployment

Annual mean monthly rate of unemployment. The source is each state's Department of Employment Security.

Violent Crime

The number of murders, manslaughters, rapes, robberies and aggravated assaults reported annually to police (per 100,000 population). Initially compiled by the Federal Bureau of Investigation for its uniform crime reporting program, these data are aggregated to the county-level in *Uniform Crime Report: County Level Arrest and Offenses Data*. (Inter-university Consortium for Political and Social Research 1991)

Property Crime

The number of burglaries, larcenies and motor vehicle thefts reported to the police (per 100,000 population). Same source as Violent Crime.

Males 20–34

Number of males ages 20–34 divided by each county's total population. These data are adjusted by the United States Bureau of the Census to correct for reporting problems and changes in county boundaries. (United States Bureau of the Census 1994a; 1994b)

Non-White

The proportion of a county's population composed of non-whites. Before publication, these data are corrected by the Bureau of the Census for reporting problems and changes in county boundaries (United States Bureau of the Census 1994a; 1994b).

Poverty Rate

The proportion of families with an income below the official poverty line (*County and City Data Book: U.S.A. Counties—U.S. Bureau of the Census, 1994c*).

Income

Source is United States Bureau of Economic Analysis (1994). Data for 1980 are average county income in 1980 dollars while 1990 income was converted to 1980 dollars using the consumer price index (United States Bureau of Labor Statistics 1992).

Think Critically

1. What does this study by Hochstetler and Shover say about economic conditions, crime, and punishment in society? What issues are important in examining these from a conflict-theoretical perspective?

2. Do you think that the American economy and nature of its politics results in the reflection of elite interests in the criminal justice system? Give 3 reasons for your position.

LEARNING

ANOTHER USEFUL PERSPECTIVE FOR understanding deviance is that of learning theory. In general, such theories examine the processes by which deviant behavior and values are learned through group interaction. Learning theorists focus on group behavior, affiliation, and how individuals internalize norms associated with such groups.

Gresham Sykes and David Matza's classic article, "Techniques of Neutralization," describes the rationalizations that juveniles offer for their deviant and criminal behavior. Such rationalizations are learned through group interaction and allow for one to engage in deviant behavior by suspending conventional norms that generally control behavior. Elaborating upon Sutherland's work (discussed below), they argue that techniques of neutralization make up a significant component of the definitions favorable to law violation, and must be learned and accepted before one is able to engage in deviance. These techniques allow one to drift in and out of law-abiding behavior and are learned in group interaction. Sykes and Matza classify five major types of neutralization techniques, and later theorists have added others. The five techniques they describe are: the denial of responsibility, the denial of injury, the denial of victim, the condemnation of condemners, and the appeal to higher loyalties. All of these learned techniques allow the enactment of deviance and are part of a larger system of attitudes and beliefs that are important for understanding delinquency and other acts of lawbreaking.

In "Becoming a Marihuana User," Howard Becker argues that this form of drug use can best be understood not by theories that focus on traits which predispose one to engage in the behavior, but rather by the sequence of learning that leads to "the use of marihuana for pleasure." Using personal accounts of users, Becker shows that people "learn" the technique of using marihuana to produce this effect, as well as learning to perceive certain effects through experimentation, which usually occurs in a social context. Finally, learning to enjoy the effects of the drug allows for possible continued use. Conceptions of the drug change during this

learning process, which helps the user develop motivations or dispositions to use marihuana that could not have been present before actually experiencing its effects.

One of the more famous learning theories is Edwin Sutherland's theory of "differential association." Sutherland attempted to create a theory that would account for all criminal behavior, including what he termed "white-collar crime." He maintained that crime was learned, just as anything else is learned by members of society. That is, the knowledge necessary to commit deviant acts, along with the motives, values, and skills, are acquired through personal interactions that take place in groups. Deviant groups are those where there is "an excess of definitions favorable to law violation over those favorable to conformity." The theory has been criticized on the grounds that it is too vague and untestable. Also, some crimes, such as check forgery and embezzlement, do not fit the differential association model. Despite these limitations, many forms of deviant and criminal behavior do fit Sutherland's model, and it has had a major impact on the field of deviance theory.

One of the variations on Sutherland's theory of differential association is found in Daniel Glaser's formulation of "differential identification." According to Glaser, it is not always necessary to have direct group interaction to acquire the values and knowledge to commit acts of deviance and crime. A person may simply identify with a real or imaginary group or persons from whose perspective deviance is acceptable. Here the emphasis is on the choice of models, rather than the direct interaction with deviant subgroups.

Some 59 years after the publication of his seminal article, "Social Structure and Anomie," Robert Merton addressed the evolution of anomie theory in the study of deviance and crime, and its relationship to learning approaches to deviance from the perspective of the sociology of science. The article, published in *Criminology*, is the text of Merton's Edwin H. Sutherland Award speech which he delivered at the annual meetings of the American Society of Criminology. Merton reflects on the strengths and weaknesses of both anomie theory, which he brought to the sociological forefront, and Sutherland's classic differential association theory, and how the two are complementary approaches in the study of deviant and criminal behavior. He discusses the evolving synthesis and extensions in both schools of thought over the decades in social scientific work, culminating in the theoretical work of Cloward and Ohlin (see earlier in this text) which *combines both learning and social structural approaches* and focuses on the role of "differential opportunity structures" in producing deviance and criminality.

Techniques of Neutralization
A Theory of Delinquency*

Gresham M. Sykes and David Matza

AS MORRIS COHEN ONCE SAID, ONE OF THE most fascinating problems about human behavior is why men violate the laws in which they believe. This is the problem that confronts us when we attempt to explain why delinquency occurs despite a greater or lesser commitment to the usages of conformity. A basic clue is offered by the fact that social rules or norms calling for valued behavior seldom if ever take the form of categorical imperatives. Rather, values or norms appear as *qualified* guides for action, limited in their applicability in terms of time, place, persons, and social circumstances. The moral injunction against killing, for example, does not apply to the enemy during combat in time of war, although a captured enemy comes once again under the prohibition. Similarly, the taking and distributing of scarce goods in a time of acute social need is felt by many to be right, although under other circumstances private property is held inviolable. The normative system of a society, then, is marked by what Williams has termed *flexibility;* it does not consist of a body of rules held to be binding under all conditions.[1]

This flexibility is, in fact, an integral part of the criminal law in that measures for "defenses to crimes" are provided in pleas such as non-age, necessity, insanity, drunkenness, compulsion, self-defense, and so on. The individual can avoid moral culpability for his criminal action—and thus avoid the negative sanctions of society—if he can prove that criminal intent was lacking. *It is our argument that much delinquency is based on what is essentially an unrecognized extension of defenses to crimes, in the form of justifications for deviance that are seen as valid by the delinquent but not by the legal system or society at large.*

These justifications are commonly described as rationalizations. They are viewed as following deviant behavior and as protecting the individual from self-blame and the blame of others after the act. But there is also reason to believe that they precede deviant behavior and make deviant behavior possible. It is this possibility that Sutherland mentioned only in passing and that other writers have failed to exploit from the viewpoint of sociological theory. Disapproval flowing from internalized norms and conforming others in the social environment is neutralized, turned back, or deflected in advance. Social controls that serve to check or inhibit deviant motivational patterns are rendered inoperative, and the individual is freed to engage in delinquency without serious damage to his self-image. In this sense, the delinquent both has his cake and eats it too, for he remains committed to the dominant normative system and yet so qualifies its imperatives that violations are "acceptable" if not "right." Thus the delinquent represents not a radical opposition to law-abiding society but something more like an apologetic failure, often more sinned against than sinning in his own eyes. We call these justifications of deviant behavior techniques of neutralization; and we believe these techniques make up a crucial component of Sutherland's "definitions favorable to the violation of law."

*"Techniques of Neutralization: Theory of Delinquency" by Gresham M. Sykes and David Matza. *American Sociological Review,* 22 (Dec., 1957).

It is by learning these techniques that the juvenile becomes delinquent, rather than by learning moral imperatives, values, or attitudes standing in direct contradiction to those of the dominant society. In analyzing these techniques, we have found it convenient to divide them into five major types.

The Denial of Responsibility

Insofar as the delinquent can define himself as lacking responsibility for his deviant actions, the disapproval of self or others is sharply reduced in effectiveness as a restraining influence. As Justice Holmes has said, even a dog distinguishes between being stumbled over and being kicked, and modern society is no less careful to draw a line between injuries that are unintentional, i.e., where responsibility is lacking, and those that are intentional. As a technique of neutralization, however, the denial of responsibility extends much further than the claim that deviant acts are an "accident" or some similar negation of personal accountability. It may also be asserted that delinquent acts are due to forces outside of the individual and beyond his control such as unloving parents, bad companions, or a slum neighborhood. In effect, the delinquent approaches a "billiard ball" conception of himself in which he sees himself as helplessly propelled into new situations. From a psychodynamic viewpoint, this orientation toward one's own actions may represent a profound alienation from self, but it is important to stress the fact that interpretations of responsibility are cultural constructs and not merely idiosyncratic beliefs. The similarity between this mode of justifying illegal behavior assumed by the delinquent and the implications of a "sociological" frame of reference or a "humane" jurisprudence is readily apparent.[2] It is not the validity of this orientation that concerns us here, but its function of deflecting blame attached to violations of social norms and its relative independence of a particular personality structure.[3] By learning to view himself as more acted upon than acting, the delinquent prepares the way for deviance from the dominant normative system without the necessity of a frontal assault on the norms themselves.

The Denial of Injury

A second major technique of neutralization centers on the injury or harm involved in the delinquent act. The criminal law has long made a distinction between crimes which are *mala in se* and *mala prohibita*—that is, between

acts that are wrong in themselves and acts that are illegal but not immoral—and the delinquent can make the same kind of distinction in evaluating the wrongfulness of his behavior. For the delinquent, however, wrongfulness may turn on the question of whether or not anyone has clearly been hurt by his deviance, and this matter is open to a variety of interpretations. Vandalism, for example, may be defined by the delinquent simply as "mischief"—after all, it may be claimed, the persons whose property has been destroyed can well afford it. Similarly, auto theft may be viewed as "borrowing," and gang fighting may be seen as a private quarrel, an agreed-upon duel between two willing parties, and thus of no concern to the community at large. We are not suggesting that this technique of neutralization, labeled the denial of injury, involves an explicit dialectic. Rather, we are arguing that the delinquent frequently, and in a hazy fashion, feels that his behavior does not really cause any great harm despite the fact that it runs counter to law. Just as the link between the individual and his acts may be broken by the denial of responsibility, so may the link between acts and their consequences be broken by the denial of injury. Since society sometimes agrees with the delinquent, e.g., in matters such as truancy, "pranks," and so on, it merely reaffirms the idea that the delinquent's neutralization of social controls by means of qualifying the norms is an extension of common practice rather than a gesture of complete opposition.

The Denial of the Victim

Even if the delinquent accepts the responsibility for his deviant actions and is willing to admit that his deviant actions involve an injury or hurt, the moral indignation of self and others may be neutralized by an insistence that the injury is not wrong in light of the circumstances. The injury, it may be claimed, is not really an injury; rather, it is a form of rightful retaliation or punishment. By a subtle alchemy the delinquent moves himself into the position of an avenger and the victim is transformed into a wrongdoer. Assaults on homosexuals or suspected homosexuals, attacks on members of minority groups who are said to have gotten "out of place," vandalism as revenge on an unfair teacher or school official, thefts from a "crooked" store owner—all may be hurts inflicted on a transgressor, in the eyes of the delinquent. As Orwell has pointed out, the type of criminal admired by the general public has probably changed over the course of years and Raffles no longer serves as a hero;[4] but Robin Hood, and his latter-day derivatives such as the tough detective seeking justice outside the law, still capture the popular imagination, and the delinquent may view his acts as part of a similar role.

To deny the existence of the victim, then, by transforming him into a person deserving injury is an extreme form of a phenomenon we have mentioned before, namely, the delinquent's recognition of appropriate and inappropriate targets for his delinquent acts. In addition, however, the existence of the victim may be denied for the delinquent, in a somewhat different sense, by the circumstances of the delinquent act itself. Insofar as the victim is physically absent, unknown, or a vague abstraction (as is often the case in delinquent acts committed against property), the awareness of the victim's existence is weakened. Internalized norms and anticipations of the reactions of others must somehow be activated if they are to serve as guides for behavior; and it is possible that a diminished awareness of the victim plays an important part of determining whether or not this process is set in motion.

The Condemnation of the Condemners

A fourth technique of neutralization would appear to involve a condemnation of the condemners or, as McCorkle and Korn have phrased it, a rejection of the rejectors.[5] The delinquent shifts the focus of attention from his own deviant acts to the motives and behavior of those who disapprove of his violations. His condemners, he may claim, are hypocrites, deviants in disguise, or impelled by personal spite. This orientation toward the conforming world may be of particular importance when it hardens into a bitter cynicism directed against those assigned the task of enforcing or expressing the norms of the dominant society. Police, it may be said, are corrupt, stupid, and brutal. Teachers always show favoritism and parents always "take it out" on their children. By a slight extension, the rewards of conformity—such as material success—become a matter of pull or luck, thus decreasing still further the stature of those who stand on the side of the law-abiding. The validity of this jaundiced viewpoint is not so important as its function in turning back or deflecting the negative sanctions attached to violations of the norms. The delinquent,

in effect, has changed the subject of the conversation in the dialogue between his own deviant impulses and the reactions of others; and by attacking others, the wrongfulness of his own behavior is more easily repressed or lost to view.

The Appeal to Higher Loyalties

Fifth, and last, internal and external social controls may be neutralized by sacrificing the demands of the larger society for the demands of the smaller social groups to which the delinquent belongs, such as the sibling pair, the gang, or the friendship clique. It is important to note that the delinquent does not necessarily repudiate the imperatives of the dominant normative system, despite his failure to follow them. Rather, the delinquent may see himself as caught up in a dilemma that must be resolved, unfortunately, at the cost of violating the law. One aspect of this situation has been studied by Stouffer and Toby in their research on the conflict between particularistic and universalistic demands, between the claims of friendship and general social obligations, and their results suggest that "it is possible to classify people according to a predisposition to select one or the other horn of a dilemma in role conflict."[6] For our purposes, however, the most important point is that deviation from certain norms may occur not because the norms are rejected but because others' norms, held to be more pressing or involving a higher loyalty, are accorded precedence. Indeed, it is the fact that both sets of norms are believed in that gives meaning to our concepts of dilemma and role conflict.

The conflict between the claims of friendship and the claims of law, or a similar dilemma, has of course long been recognized by the social scientist (and the novelist) as a common human problem. If the juvenile delinquent frequently resolves his dilemma by insisting that he must "always help a buddy" or "never squeal on a friend," even when it throws him into serious difficulties with the dominant social order, his choice remains familiar to the supposedly law-abiding. The delinquent is unusual, perhaps, in the extent to which he is able to see the fact that he acts in behalf of the smaller social groups to which he belongs as a justification for violations of society's norms, but it is a matter of degree rather than of kind.

"I didn't mean it." "I didn't really hurt anybody." "They had it coming to them." "Everybody's picking on me." "I didn't do it for myself." These slogans or their variants, we hypothesize, prepare the juvenile for delinquent acts.

These "definitions of the situation" represent tangential or glancing blows at the dominant normative system rather than the creation of an opposing ideology; and they are extensions of patterns of thought prevalent in society rather than something created *de novo*.

Techniques of neutralization may not be powerful enough to fully shield the individual from the force of his own internalized values and the reactions of conforming others, for as we have pointed out, juvenile delinquents often appear to suffer from feelings of guilt and shame when called into account for their deviant behavior. And some delinquents may be so isolated from the world of conformity that techniques of neutralization need not be called into play. Nonetheless, we would argue that techniques of neutralization are critical in lessening the effectiveness of social controls and that they lie behind a large share of delinquent behavior. Empirical research in this area is scattered and fragmentary at the present time, but the work of Redl,[7] Cressey,[8] and others has supplied a body of significant data that has done much to clarify the theoretical issues and enlarge the fund of supporting evidence. Two lines of investigation seem to be critical at this stage. First, there is need for more knowledge concerning the differential distribution of techniques of neutralization, as operative patterns of thought, by age, sex, social class, ethnic group, etc. On a priori grounds it might be assumed that these justifications for deviance will be more readily seized by segments of society for whom a discrepancy between common social ideals and social practice is most apparent. It is also possible, however, that the habit of "bending" the dominant normative system—if not "breaking" it—cuts across our cruder social categories and is to be traced primarily to patterns of social interaction within the familial circle. Second, there is need for a greater understanding of the internal structure of techniques of neutralization, as a system of beliefs and attitudes, and its relationship to various types of delinquent behavior. Certain techniques of neutralization would appear to be better adapted to particular deviant acts than to others, as we have suggested, for example, in the case of offenses against property and the denial of the victim. But the issue remains far from clear and stands in need of more information.

In any case, techniques of neutralization appear to offer a promising line of research in enlarging and systematizing the theoretical grasp of juvenile delinquency. As more information is uncovered concerning techniques of neutralization, their origins, and their consequences, both juvenile delinquency in particular and deviation from normative systems in general may be illuminated.

NOTES

1. Cf. Robin Williams, Jr., *American Society,* New York: Knopf, 1951, p. 28.
2. A number of observers have wryly noted that many delinquents seem to show a surprising awareness of sociological and psychological explanations for their behavior and are quick to point out the causal role of their poor environment.
3. It is possible, of course, that certain personality structures can accept some techniques of neutralization more readily than others, but this question remains largely unexplored.
4. George Orwell, *Dickens, Dali, and Others,* New York: Reynal, 1946.
5. Lloyd W. McCorkle and Richard Korn, "Resocialization Within Walls," *The Annals of the American Academy of Political and Social Science,* 293 (May, 1954), pp. 88–98.
6. See Samuel A. Stouffer and Jackson Toby, "Role Conflict and Personality," in *Toward a General Theory of Action,* edited by Talcott Parsons and Edward A. Shils, Cambridge, Mass.: Harvard University Press, 1951, p. 494.
7. See Fritz Redl and David Wineman, *Children Who Hate,* Glencoe, Ill.: The Free Press, 1956.
8. See D. R. Cressey, *Other People's Money,* Glencoe, Ill.: The Free Press, 1953.

Think Critically

1. Give three specific examples of deviance in which neutralization techniques could be used, and identify the form(s) of neutralization for each example.
2. Since Sykes and Matza first published their classic article, there have been many attempts to expand upon the list of neutralization techniques employed by deviants. Can you think of any new forms? Look up some of these new forms and the later studies in which they appear. Briefly summarize each theory to the best of your ability.

Becoming a Marihuana User*

Howard S. Becker

AN UNKNOWN, BUT PROBABLY QUITE LARGE, number of people in the United States use marihuana. They do this in spite of the fact that it is both illegal and disapproved.

The phenomenon of marihuana use has received much attention, particularly from psychiatrists and law enforcement officials. The research that has been done, as is often the case with research on behavior that is viewed as deviant, is mainly concerned with the question: why do they do it? Attempts to account for the use of marihuana lean heavily on the premise that the presence of any particular kind of behavior in an individual can best be explained as the result of some trait which predisposes or motivates him to engage in that behavior. In the case of marihuana use, this trait is usually identified as psychological, as a need for fantasy and escape from psychological problems the individual cannot face.[1]

I do not think such theories can adequately account for marihuana use. In fact, marihuana use is an interesting case for theories of deviance, because it illustrates the way deviant motives actually develop in the course of experience with the deviant activity. To put a complex argument in a few words: Instead of the deviant motives leading to the deviant behavior, it is the other way around; the deviant behavior in time produces the deviant motivation. Vague impulses and desires—in this case, probably most frequently a curiosity about the kind of experience the drug will produce—are transformed into definite patterns of action through the social interpretation of a physical experience which is in itself ambiguous. Marihuana use is a function of the individual's conception of

marihuana and of the uses to which it can be put, and this conception develops as the individual's experience with the drug increases.[2]

The research reported [here] deals with the career of the marihuana user, [specifically, with] the development of the individual's immediate physical experience with marihuana . . . What we are trying to understand here is the sequence of changes in attitude and experience which lead to the use of marihuana for pleasure. This way of phrasing the problem requires a little explanation. Marihuana does not produce addiction, at least in the sense that alcohol and the opiate drugs do. The user experiences no withdrawal sickness and exhibits no ineradicable craving for the drug.[3] The most frequent pattern of use might be termed "recreational." The drug is used occasionally for the pleasure the user finds in it, a relatively casual kind of behavior in comparison with that connected with the use of addicting drugs. The report of the New York City Mayor's Committee on Marihuana emphasizes this point:

> A person may be a confirmed smoker for a prolonged period, and give up the drug voluntarily without experiencing any craving for it or exhibiting withdrawal symptoms. He may, at some time later on, go back to its use. Others may remain infrequent users of the cigarette, taking one or two a week, or only when the "social setting" calls for participation. From time to time we had one of our investigators associate with a marihuana user. The investigator would bring up the subject of smoking. This would invariably lead to the suggestion that they obtain some marihuana cigarettes. They would seek a "tea-pad," and if it was closed the smoker and our investigator would calmly resume their previous activity, such as the discussion of life in general or the playing of pool. There were apparently no signs indicative of frustration in the smoker

*"Becoming a Marihuana User" by Howard S. Becker. *American Journal of Sociology*, 59 (Nov., 1953), pp. 235–242. Reprinted by permission of the author and the University of Chicago Press.

at not being able to gratify the desire for the drug. We consider this point highly significant since it is so contrary to the experience of users of other narcotics. A similar situation occurring in one addicted to the use of morphine, cocaine or heroin would result in a compulsive attitude on the part of the addict to obtain the drug. If unable to secure it, there would be obvious physical and mental manifestations of frustration. This may be considered presumptive evidence that there is no true addiction in the medical sense associated with the use of marihuana.[4]

In using the phrase "use for pleasure," I mean to emphasize the noncompulsive and casual character of the behavior. (I also mean to eliminate from consideration here those few cases in which marihuana is used for its prestige value only, as a symbol that one is a certain kind of person, with no pleasure at all being derived from its use) . . .

In doing the study, I used the method of analytic induction. I tried to arrive at a general statement of the sequence of changes in individual attitude and experience which always occurred when the individual became willing and able to use marihuana for pleasure, and never occurred or had not been permanently maintained when the person was unwilling to use marihuana for pleasure. The method requires that *every* case collected in the research substantiate the hypothesis. If one case is encountered which does not substantiate it, the researcher is required to change the hypothesis to fit the case which has proven his original idea wrong.[5]

To develop and test my hypothesis about the genesis of marihuana use for pleasure, I conducted fifty interviews with marihuana users. I had been a professional dance musician for some years when I conducted this study and my first interviews were with people I had met in the music business. I asked them to put me in contact with other users who would be willing to discuss their experiences with me. Colleagues working on a study of users of opiate drugs made a few interviews available to me which contained, in addition to material on opiate drugs, sufficient material on the use of marihuana to furnish a test of my hypothesis.[6] Although in the end half of the fifty interviews were conducted with musicians, the other half covered a wide range of people, including laborers, machinists, and people in the professions. The sample is, of course, in no sense "random"; it would not be possible to draw a random sample, since no one knows the nature of the universe from which it would have to be drawn . . .

Learning the Technique

The novice does not ordinarily get high the first time he smokes marihuana, and several attempts are usually necessary to induce this state. One explanation of this may be that the drug is not smoked "properly," that is, in a way that insures sufficient dosage to produce real symptoms of intoxication. Most users agree that it cannot be smoked like tobacco if one is to get high:

> Take in a lot of air, you know, and . . . I don't know how to describe it, you don't smoke it like a cigarette, you draw in a lot of air and get it deep down in your system and then keep it there. Keep it there as long as you can.

Without the use of some such technique,[7] the drug will produce no effects, and the user will be unable to get high:

> The trouble with people like that [who are not able to get high] is that they're just not smoking it right, that's all there is to it. Either they're not holding it down long enough, or they're getting too much air and not enough smoke, or the other way around or something like that. A lot of people just don't smoke it right, so naturally nothing's gonna happen.

If nothing happens, it is manifestly impossible for the user to develop a conception of the drug as an object which can be used for pleasure, and use will therefore not continue. The first step in the sequence of events that must occur if the person is to become a user is that he must learn to use the proper smoking technique so that his use of the drug will produce effects in terms of which his conception of it can change.

Such a change is, as might be expected, a result of the individual's participation in groups in which marihuana is used. In them the individual learns the proper way to smoke the drug. This may occur through direct teaching:

> I was smoking like I did an ordinary cigarette. He said, "No, don't do it like that." He said, "Suck it, you know, draw in and hold it in your lungs till you . . . for a period of time."

I said, "Is there any limit of time to hold it?"

He said, "No, just till you feel that you want to let it out, let it out." So I did that three or four times.

Many new users are ashamed to admit ignorance and, pretending to know already, must learn through the more indirect means of observation and imitation:

I came on like I had turned on many times before, you know. I didn't want to seem like a punk to this cat. See, like I didn't know the first thing about it—how to smoke it, or what was going to happen, or what. I just watched him like a hawk—I didn't take my eyes off him for a second, because I wanted to do everything just as he did it. I watched how he held it, how he smoked it, and everything. Then when he gave it to me I just came on cool, as though I knew exactly what the score was. I held it like he did and took a poke just the way he did.

No one I interviewed continued marihuana use for pleasure without learning a technique that supplied sufficient dosage for the effects of the drug to appear. Only when this was learned was it possible for a conception of the drug as an object which could be used for pleasure to emerge. Without such a conception marihuana use was considered meaningless and did not continue.

Learning to Perceive the Effects

Even after he learns the proper smoking technique, the new user may not get high and thus not form a conception of the drug as something which can be used for pleasure. A remark made by a user suggested the reason for this difficulty in getting high and pointed to the next necessary step on the road to being a user:

As a matter of fact, I've seen a guy who was high out of his mind and didn't know it.

[How can that be, man?]

Well, it's pretty strange, I'll grant you that, but I've seen it. This guy got on with me, claiming that he'd never got high, one of those guys, and he got completely stoned. And he kept insisting that he wasn't high. So I had to prove to him that he was.

What does this mean? It suggests that being high consists of two elements: the presence of symptoms caused by marihuana use and the recognition of these symptoms and their connection by the user with his use

of the drug. It is not enough, that is, that the effects be present; alone, they do not automatically provide the experience of being high. The user must be able to point them out to himself and consciously connect them with having smoked marihuana before he can have this experience. Otherwise, no matter what actual effects are produced, he considers that the drug has had no effect on him: "I figured it either had no effect on me or other people were exaggerating its effect on them, you know. I thought it was probably psychological, see." Such persons believe the whole thing is an illusion and that the wish to be high leads the user to deceive himself into believing that something is happening when, in fact, nothing is. They do not continue marihuana use, feeling that "it does nothing" for them.

Typically, however, the novice has faith (developed from his observation of users who do get high) that the drug actually will produce some new experience and continues to experiment with it until it does. His failure to get high worries him, and he is likely to ask more experienced users or provoke comments from them about it. In such conversations he is made aware of specific details of his experience which he may not have noticed or may have noticed but failed to identify as symptoms of being high:

I didn't get high the first time. . . . I don't think I held it in long enough. I probably let it out, you know, you're a little afraid. The second time I wasn't sure, and he [smoking companion] told me, like I asked him for some of the symptoms or something, how would I know, you know. . . . So he told me to sit on a stool. I sat on—I think I sat on a bar stool—and he said, "Let your feet hang," and then when I got down my feet were real cold, you know.

And I started feeling it, you know. That was the first time. And then about a week after that, sometime pretty close to it, I really got on. That was the first time I got on a big laughing kick, you know. Then I really knew I was on.

One symptom of being high is an intense hunger. In the next case the novice becomes aware of this and gets high for the first time:

They were just laughing the hell out of me because like I was eating so much. I just scoffed [ate] so much food, and they were just laughing at me, you know. Sometimes I'd be looking at them, you know, wondering why they're laughing, you know, not knowing what I was doing. [Well, did they tell you why they were laughing eventually?] Yeah, yeah, I come back, "Hey, man, what's happening?" Like, you know, like I'd ask, "What's happening?" and all of a sudden I feel weird, you know. "Man, you're on, you know. You're on pot [high on marihuana]." I said, "No, am I?" Like I don't know what's happening.

The learning may occur in more indirect ways:

I heard little remarks that were made by other people. Somebody said, "My legs are rubbery," and I can't remember all the remarks that were made because I was very attentively listening for all these cues for what I was supposed to feel like.

The novice, then, eager to have this feeling, picks up from other users some concrete referents of the term "high" and applies these notions to his own experience. The new concepts make it possible for him to locate these symptoms among his own sensations and to point out to himself a "something different" in his experience that he connects with drug use. It is only when he can do this that he is high . . .

With increasing experience the user develops a greater appreciation of the drug's effects; he continues to learn to get high. He examines succeeding experiences closely, looking for new effects, making sure the old ones are still there. Out of this there grows a stable set of categories for experiencing the drug's effects whose presence enables the user to get high with ease.

The ability to perceive the drug's effects must be maintained if use is to continue; if it is lost, marihuana use ceases. Two kinds of evidence support this statement. First, people who become heavy users of alcohol, barbiturates, or opiates do not continue to smoke marihuana, largely because they lose the ability to distinguish between its effects and those of the other drugs.[8] They no longer know whether the marihuana gets them high. Second, in those few cases in which an individual uses marihuana in such quantities that he is always high, he is apt to feel the drug has no effect on him, since the essential element of a noticeable difference between feeling high and feeling normal is missing. In such a situation, use is likely to be given up completely, but temporarily, in order that the user may once again be able to perceive the difference.

Learning to Enjoy the Effects

One more step is necessary if the user who has now learned to get high is to continue use. He must learn to enjoy the effects he has just learned to experience. Marihuana-produced sensations are not automatically or necessarily pleasurable. The taste for such experience is a socially acquired one, not different in kind from acquired tastes for oysters or dry martinis. The user feels dizzy, thirsty; his scalp tingles; he misjudges time and distances. Are these things pleasurable? He isn't sure. If he is to continue marihuana use, he must decide that they are. Otherwise, getting high, while a real enough experience, will be an unpleasant one he would rather avoid.

The effects of the drug, when first perceived, may be physically unpleasant or at least ambiguous:

It started taking effect, and I didn't know what was happening, you know, what it was, and I was very sick. I walked around the room, walking around the room trying to get off, you know; it just scared me at first, you know. I wasn't used to that kind of feeling.

In addition, the novice's naïve interpretation of what is happening to him may further confuse and frighten him, particularly if he decides, as many do, that he is going insane:

I felt I was insane, you know. Everything people done to me just wigged me. I couldn't hold a conversation, and my mind would be wandering, and I was always thinking, oh, I don't know, weird things, like hearing music different. . . . I get the feeling that I can't talk to anyone. I'll goof completely.

Given these typically frightening and unpleasant first experiences, the beginner will not continue use unless he learns to redefine the sensations as pleasurable:

It was offered to me, and I tried it. I'll tell you one thing. I never did enjoy it at all. I mean it was just nothing that I could enjoy. [Well, did you get high when you turned on?] Oh, yeah, I got definite feelings from it. But I didn't enjoy them. I mean I got plenty of reactions, but they were mostly reactions of fear. [You were frightened?] Yes. I didn't enjoy it. I couldn't seem to relax with it, you know. If you can't relax with a thing, you can't enjoy it, I don't think . . .

The more experienced user may also teach the novice to regulate the amount he smokes more carefully, so as to avoid any severely uncomfortable symptoms while retaining the pleasant ones. Finally, he teaches the new user that he can "get to like it after awhile." He teaches him to regard those ambiguous experiences formerly defined as unpleasant as enjoyable. The older user in the following incident is a person whose tastes have shifted in this way, and his remarks have the effect of helping others to make a similar redefinition:

> A new user had her first experience of the effects of marihuana and became frightened and hysterical. She "felt like she was half in and half out of the room" and experienced a number of alarming physical symptoms. One of the more experienced users present said, "She's dragged because she's high like that. I'd give anything to get that high myself. I haven't been that high in years."

In short, what was once frightening and distasteful becomes, after a taste for it is built up, pleasant, desired, and sought after. Enjoyment is introduced by the favorable definition of the experience that one acquires from others. Without this, use will not continue, for marihuana will not be for the user an object he can use for pleasure.

In addition to being a necessary step in becoming a user, this represents an important condition for continued use. It is quite common for experienced users suddenly to have an unpleasant or frightening experience, which they cannot define as pleasurable, either because they have used a larger amount of marihuana than usual or because the marihuana they have used turns out to be of a higher quality than they expected. The user has sensations which go beyond any conception he has of what being high is and is in much the same situation as the novice, uncomfortable and frightened. He may blame it on an overdose and simply be more careful in the future. But he may make this the occasion for a rethinking of his attitude toward the drug and decide that it no longer can give him pleasure. When this occurs and is not followed by a redefinition of the drug as capable of producing pleasure, use will cease . . .

In summary, an individual will be able to use marihuana for pleasure only when he goes through a process of learning to conceive of it as an object which can be used in this way. No one becomes a user without (1) learning to smoke the drug in a way which will produce real effects; (2) learning to recognize the effects and connect them with drug use (learning, in other words, to get high); and (3) learning to enjoy the sensations he perceives. In the course of this process he develops a disposition or motivation to use marihuana which was not and could not have been present when he began use, for it involves and depends on conceptions of the drug which could only grow out of the kind of actual experience detailed above. On completion of this process he is willing and able to use marihuana for pleasure.

He has learned, in short, to answer "Yes" to the question: "Is it fun?" The direction his further use of the drug takes depends on his being able to continue to answer "Yes" to this question and, in addition, on his being able to answer "Yes" to other questions which arise as he becomes aware of the implications of the fact that society disapproves of the practice: "Is it expedient?" "Is it moral?" Once he has acquired the ability to get enjoyment by using the drug, use will continue to be possible for him. Considerations of morality and expediency, occasioned by the reactions of society, may interfere and inhibit use, but use continues to be a possibility in terms of his conception of the drug. The act becomes impossible only when the ability to enjoy the experience of being high is lost, through a change in the user's conception of the drug occasioned by certain kinds of experience with it.

NOTES

1. See, as examples of this approach, the following: Eli Marcovitz and Henry J. Meyers, "The Marihuana Addict in the Army," *War Medicine,* VI (December, 1944), 382–391; Herbert S. Gaskill, "Marihuana, an Intoxicant," *American Journal of Psychiatry,* CII (September, 1945), 202–204; Sol Charen and Luis Perelman, "Personality Studies of Marihuana Addicts," *American Journal of Psychiatry,* CII (March, 1946), 674–682.

2. This theoretical point of view stems from George Herbert Mead's discussion of objects in *Mind, Self, and Society* (Chicago: University of Chicago Press, 1934), pp. 277–280.

3. Cf. Rogers Adams, "Marihuana," *Bulletin of the New York Academy of Medicine,* XVIII (November, 1942), 705–730.

4. The New York City Mayor's Committee on Marihuana, *The Marihuana Problem in the City of New York* (Lancaster, Pennsylvania: Jacques Cattell Press, 1944), pp. 12–13.

5. The method is described in Alfred R. Lindesmith, *Opiate Addiction* (Bloomington, Indiana: Principia Press, 1947), chap. 1. There has been considerable discussion of this method in the literature. See, particularly, Ralph H. Turner, "The Quest for Universals in Sociological Research," *American Sociological Review*, 18 (December, 1953), 604–611, and the literature cited there.

6. I wish to thank Solomon Kobrin and Harold Finestone for making these interviews available to me.

7. A pharmacologist notes that this ritual is in fact an extremely efficient way of getting the drug into the blood stream. See R. P. Walton, *Marihuana: America's New Drug Problem* (Philadelphia: J. B. Lippincott, 1938), p. 48.

8. "Smokers have repeatedly stated that the consumption of whiskey while smoking negates the potency of the drug. They find it very difficult to get 'high' while drinking whiskey and because of that smokers will not drink while using the 'weed.'" (New York City Mayor's Committee on Marihuana, *The Marihuana Problem in the City of New York, op. cit.*, p. 13.)

Think Critically

1. Becker argues against the stance that the "presence of any particular kind of behavior in an individual can best be explained as the result of some trait which predisposes or motivates him to engage in that behavior." Do you feel that his analysis of marihuana use supports his argument? Why or why not? Explain.

2. Do you feel that the learning techniques described by Becker can be generalized to other forms of drug use? Explain why it would or wouldn't be applicable to at least two specific forms of drug use.

Differential Association*

Edwin H. Sutherland

THE SCIENTIFIC EXPLANATION OF A phenomenon may be stated either in terms of the factors which are operating at the moment of the occurrence of a phenomenon or in terms of the processes operating in the earlier history of that phenomenon. In the first case the explanation is mechanistic, in the second historical or genetic; both are desirable. The physical and biological scientists favor the first of these methods and it would probably be superior as an explanation of criminal behavior. Efforts at explanations of the mechanistic type have been notably unsuccessful, perhaps largely because they have been concentrated on the attempt to isolate personal

*Selections from *Principles of Criminology* by Edwin H. Sutherland. (Philadelphia: J. B. Lippincott Co.), 1947, pp. 5–9.

and social pathologies. Work from this point of view has, at least, resulted in the conclusion that the immediate factors in criminal behavior lie in the person-situation complex. Person and situation are not factors exclusive of each other, for the situation which is important is the situation as defined by the person who is involved. The tendencies and inhibitions at the moment of the criminal behavior are, to be sure, largely a product of the earlier history of the person, but the expression of these tendencies and inhibitions is a reaction to the immediate situation as defined by the person. The situation operates in many ways, of which perhaps the least important is the provision of an opportunity for a criminal act. A thief may steal from a fruit stand when the owner is not in sight but refrain when the owner is in sight; a bank burglar may attack a bank which is poorly protected but refrain from attacking a bank protected by watchmen and burglar alarms. A corporation which manufactures automobiles seldom or never violates the Pure Food and Drug Law but a meat-packing corporation violates this law with great frequency.

The second type of explanation of criminal behavior is made in terms of the life experience of a person. This is an historical or genetic explanation of criminal behavior. This, to be sure, assumes a situation to be defined by the person in terms of the inclinations and abilities which the person has acquired up to that date. The following paragraphs state such a genetic theory of criminal behavior on the assumption that a criminal act occurs when a situation appropriate for it, as defined by a person, is present.

Genetic Explanation of Criminal Behavior

The following statement refers to the process by which a particular person comes to engage in criminal behavior.

1. *Criminal behavior is learned.* Negatively, this means that criminal behavior is not inherited, as such; also, the person who is not already trained in crime does not invent criminal behavior, just as a person does not make mechanical inventions unless he has had training in mechanics.

2. *Criminal behavior is learned in interaction with other persons in a process of communication.* This communication is verbal in many respects but includes also "the communication of gestures."

3. *The principal part of the learning of criminal behavior occurs within intimate personal groups.* Negatively, this means that the impersonal agencies of communication, such as picture shows and newspapers, play a relatively unimportant part in the genesis of criminal behavior.

4. *When criminal behavior is learned, the learning includes (a) techniques of committing the crime, which are sometimes very complicated, sometimes very simple; (b) the specific direction of motives, drives, rationalizations, and attitudes.*

5. *The specific direction of motives and drives is learned from definitions of the legal codes as favorable or unfavorable.* In some societies an individual is surrounded by persons who invariably define the legal codes as rules to be observed, while in others he is surrounded by persons whose definitions are favorable to the violation of the legal codes. In our American society these definitions are almost always mixed and consequently we have culture conflict in relation to the legal codes.

6. *A person becomes delinquent because of an excess of definitions favorable to violation of law over definitions unfavorable to violation of law.* This is the principle of differential association. It refers to both criminal and anti-criminal associations and has to do with counteracting forces. When persons become criminal, they do so because of contacts with criminal patterns and also because of isolation from anti-criminal patterns. Any person inevitably assimilates the surrounding culture unless other patterns are in conflict; a Southerner does not pronounce "r" because other Southerners do not pronounce "r." Negatively, this proposition of differential association means that associations which are neutral so far as crime is concerned have little or no effect on the genesis of criminal behavior. Much of the experience of a person is neutral in this sense, e.g., learning to brush one's teeth. This behavior has no negative or positive effect on criminal behavior except as it may be related to associations which are concerned with the legal codes. This neutral behavior is important especially as an occupier of the time of a child so that he is not in contact with criminal behavior during the time he is so engaged in the neutral behavior.

7. *Differential associations may vary in frequency, duration, priority, and intensity.* This means that associations with criminal behavior and also associations with anti-criminal behavior vary in those respects. "Frequency" and "duration" as modalities of associations are obvious and need no explanation. "Priority" is assumed to be important in the sense that lawful behavior developed in early childhood may persist throughout life, and also that delinquent behavior developed in early childhood may persist throughout life. This tendency, however, has not been adequately demonstrated, and priority seems to be important principally through its selective influence. "Intensity" is not precisely defined but it has to do with such things as the prestige of the source of a criminal or anti-criminal pattern and with emotional reactions related to the associations. In a precise description of the criminal behavior of

a person these modalities would be stated in quantitative form and a mathematical ratio be reached. A formula in this sense has not been developed and the development of such a formula would be extremely difficult.

8. *The process of learning criminal behavior by association with criminal and anti-criminal patterns involves all of the mechanisms that are involved in any other learning.* Negatively, this means that the learning of criminal behavior is not restricted to the process of imitation. A person who is seduced, for instance, learns criminal behavior by association but this process would not ordinarily be described as imitation.

9. *While criminal behavior is an expression of general needs and values, it is not explained by those general needs and values since non-criminal behavior is an expression of the same needs and values.* Thieves generally steal in order to secure money, but likewise honest laborers work in order to secure money. The attempts by many scholars to explain criminal behavior by general drives and values, such as the happiness principle, striving for social status, the money motive, or frustration, have been and must continue to be futile since they explain lawful behavior as completely as they explain criminal behavior. They are similar to respiration, which is necessary for any behavior but which does not differentiate criminal from non-criminal behavior.

It is not necessary, at this level of explanation, to explain why a person has the associations which he has; this certainly involves a complex of many things. In an area where the delinquency rate is high a boy who is sociable, gregarious, active, and athletic is very likely to come in contact with the other boys in the neighborhood, learn delinquent behavior from them, and become a gangster; in the same neighborhood the psychopathic boy who is isolated, introvert, and inert may remain at home, not become acquainted with the other boys in the neighborhood, and not become delinquent. In another situation, the sociable, athletic, aggressive boy may become a member of a scout troop and not become involved in delinquent behavior. The person's associations are determined in a general context of social organization. A child is ordinarily reared in a family; the place of residence of the family is determined largely by family income; and the delinquency rate is in many respects related to the rental

value of the houses. Many other factors enter into this social organization, including many of the small personal group relationships.

The preceding explanation of criminal behavior was stated from the point of view of the person who engages in criminal behavior. It is possible, also, to state theories of criminal behavior from the point of view of the community, nation, or other group. The problem, when thus stated, is generally concerned with crime rates and involves a comparison of the crime rates of various groups or the crime rates of a particular group at different times. One of the best explanations of crime rates from this point of view is that a high crime rate is due to social disorganization. The term "social disorganization" is not entirely satisfactory and it seems preferable to substitute for it the term "differential social organization." The postulate on which this theory is based, regardless of the name, is that crime is rooted in the social organization and is an expression of that social organization. A group may be organized for criminal behavior or organized against criminal behavior. Most communities are organized both for criminal and anti-criminal behavior and in that sense the crime rate is an expression of the differential group organization. Differential group organization as an explanation of a crime rate must be consistent with the explanation of the criminal behavior of the person, since the crime rate is a summary statement of the number of persons in the group who commit crimes and the frequency with which they commit crimes.

Think Critically

1. Sutherland's contention that all criminal behavior is learned has come under close scrutiny by researchers throughout the years. What do you make of his theory of differential association? Locate one study that critiques the theory, and discuss the findings.

2. How does Sutherland's work relate to the notion of differential opportunity discussed by Cloward and Ohlin covered in the earlier reading?

Differential Identification*

Daniel Glaser

WE DESCRIBED IDENTIFICATION SOMEWHAT unconventionally as "the choice of another, from whose perspective we view our own behavior." What we have called "differential identification" reconceptualizes Sutherland's theory in role-taking imagery, drawing heavily on Mead as well as on later refinements of role theory."[1] Most persons in our society are believed to identify themselves with both criminal and non-criminal persons in the course of their lives. Criminal identification may occur, for example, during direct experience in delinquent membership groups, through positive reference to criminal roles portrayed in mass media, or as a negative reaction to forces opposed to crime. The family probably is the principal non-criminal reference group, even for criminals. It is supplemented by many other groups of anti-criminal "generalized others."

The theory of differential identification, in essence, is that *a person pursues criminal behavior to the extent that he identifies himself with real or imaginary persons from whose perspective his criminal behavior seems acceptable.* Such a theory focuses attention on the interaction in which choice of models occurs, including the individual's interaction with himself in rationalizing his conduct. This focus makes differential identification theory integrative, in that it provides a criterion of the relevance, for each individual case of criminality, of economic conditions, prior frustrations, learned moral creeds, group participation, or other features of an individual's life. These features are relevant to the extent that they can be shown to affect the choice of the other from whose perspective the individual views

his own behavior. The explanation of criminal behavior on the basis of its imperfect correlation with any single variable of life-situations, if presented without specifying the intervening identification, evokes only a disconnected image of the relationship between the life-situation and the criminal behavior.

Sutherland supported the differential association theory by evidence that a major portion of criminality is learned through participation in criminal groups. Differential identification is a less disconnected explanation for such learning, and it also does not seem vulnerable to most of the objections to differential association. Because opposing and divisive roles frequently develop within groups, because our identification may be with remote reference groups or with imaginary or highly generalized others, and because identifications may shift rapidly with dialectical processes of role change and rationalization during social interaction, differential association, as ordinarily conceived, is insufficient to account for all differential identification.

In practice, the use of differential identification to explain lone crimes where the source of learning is not readily apparent (such as extremes of brutality or other abnormality in sex crimes) gives rise to speculation as to the "others" involved in the identification. The use of this theory to explain a gang member's participation in a professional crime against property presents fewer difficulties. Insofar as the former types of offense are explained by psychiatrists without invoking instincts or other mystical forces, they usually are interpreted, on a necessarily speculative basis, in terms of the self-conception which the offender develops in supporting his behavior and the sources of that self-conception. Such differential identification, in the case of most unusual and compulsive crimes, offers a less disconnected explanation than explanations derived from the alternative theories.[2]

*"Criminality Theories and Behavioral Images" by Daniel Glaser. *The American Journal of Sociology,* 61 (March, 1956), pp. 440–441. Reprinted by permission of the author and the University of Chicago Press.

The one objection to the theory of differential association which cannot be met by differential identification is that it does not account for "accidental" crimes. Differential identification treats crime as a form of voluntary (i.e., anticipatory) behavior, rather than as an accident. Indeed, both legal and popular conceptions of "crime" exclude acts which are purely accidental, except for some legislation on felonious negligence, to which our discussion of criminality must be considered inapplicable. Even for the latter offenses, however, it is noteworthy that the consequences of accidentally committing a crime may be such as to foster identification with criminal-role models (whether one is apprehended for the accidental crime or not).

During any period, *prior identifications* and *present circumstances* dictate the selection of the persons with whom we identify ourselves. Prior identifications which have been pleasing tend to persist, but at any time the immediate circumstances affect the relative ease (or salience) of alternative identifications. That is why membership groups so frequently are the reference groups, although they need not be. That, too, is why those inclined to crime usually refrain from it in situations where they play satisfying conventional roles in which crime would threaten their acceptance. From the latter situations their identification with non-criminal others may eventually make them anticriminal. This is the essence of rehabilitation.[3]

There is evidence that, with the spread of urban secularism, social situations are becoming more and more deliberately rather than traditionally organized. Concurrently, roles are increasingly adjusted on the basis of the apparent authority or social pressure in each situation.[4] Our culture is said to give a common level of aspiration but different capacities of attainment according to socioeconomic class. At the same time, it is suggested, economic sources of status are becoming stronger while non-economic sources are becoming weaker. Therefore, when conventional occupational avenues of upward mobility are denied, people are more and more willing to seek the economic gains anticipated in crime, even at the risk of losing such non-economic sources of status as acceptance by non-criminal groups.[5] All these alleged features of urbanism suggest a considerable applicability of differential identification to "situational" and "incidental" crimes; focus on differential identification with alternative reference groups may reveal "situational imperatives" in individual life histories.

Differential identification may be considered tautological, in that it may seem merely to make "crime" synonymous with "criminal identification." It is more than a tautology, however, if it directs one to observations beyond those necessary merely for the classification of behavior as criminal or non-criminal. It is a fruitful empirical theory leading one to proceed from the legalistic classification to the analysis of behavior as identification and role-playing.[6]

NOTES

1. Cf. D. Glaser, "A Reconsideration of Some Parole Prediction Factors," *American Sociological Review,* XIX (June, 1954), 335–41; G. H. Mead, *Mind, Self, and Society* (Chicago: University of Chicago Press, 1934); N. N. Foote, "Identification as the Basis for a Theory of Motivation," *American Sociological Review,* XVI (February, 1951), 14–22; C. W. Mills, "Situated Actions and Vocabularies of Motive," *American Sociological Review,* V (December, 1940), 904–913; T. Shibutani, "Reference Groups as Perspectives," *American Journal of Sociology,* LX (May, 1955), 562–69.

2. For an outstanding illustration of what becomes differential identification rather than the usual conception of differential association, applied to compulsive crimes, see Donald R. Cressey, "Differential Association and Compulsive Crimes," *Journal of Criminal Law, Criminology, and Police Science,* XLV (May–June, 1954), 29–40.

3. Cf. Donald R. Cressey, "Contradictory Theories in Correctional Group Therapy Programs," *Federal Probation,* XVIII (June, 1954), 20–26.

4. This evidence has come most dramatically from recent studies of race relations. Cf. Joseph D. Lohman and Dietrich C. Reitzes, "Note on Race Relations in Mass Society," *American Journal of Sociology,* LVIII (November, 1952), 240–46; Dietrich C. Reitzes, "The Role of Organizational Structures," *Journal of Social Issues,* IX, No. 1 (1953), 37–44; William C. Bradbury, "Evaluation of Research in Race Relations," *Inventory of Research in Racial and Cultural Relations,* V (winter–spring, 1953), 99–133.

5. Cf. Merton, *Social Theory and Social Structure* (Glencoe, Ill.: Free Press, 1949), chap. IV. It may be noteworthy here that classification of Illinois parolees by status ratings of the jobs to which they were going was more predictive than classification by the status of their father's occupation or by whether their job was of higher, lower, or equal status than their father's occupation. Regardless of their class background, the parolees' infractions seemed primarily to be a function of their failure to approach middle-class status

(cf. Daniel Glaser, "A Reformulation and Testing of Parole Prediction Factors" [unpublished Ph.D. dissertation, University of Chicago, 1954], pp. 253–59).

6. A number of examples of useful tautologies in social science are presented in Arnold Rose, *Theory and Method in the Social Sciences* (Minneapolis: University of Minnesota Press, 1954), pp. 328–38. Insofar as a proposition is of heuristic use, however, one may question whether it is appropriately designated a "tautology."

Think Critically

1. Describe the ways in which Glaser's work builds upon Sutherland's.
2. Give two examples of the way that differential identification could produce actual deviant behaviors.

On the Evolving Synthesis of Differential Association and Anomie Theory[1]:
A Perspective from the Sociology of Science

Robert K. Merton

IT WAS WITH GREAT PLEASURE AND, I CONFESS, with no little pride that I learned from your president, Charles F. Wellford, and your president-elect, James F. Short, Jr., that the American Society of Criminology had granted me the Edwin H. Sutherland Award. In all innocence, I had intended to limit myself this evening to just a few words of deep-felt appreciation, but then Professor Wellford let me know that 20 minutes or so are usually set aside for recipients of the award and that I, too, was expected to fill that cognitive space. And so I continue with a scattering of reminiscent observations linking Edwin Sutherland's and my own theoretical work.

The Sutherland Award holds much special meaning for me. After all, it is notorious that I am not a full-fledged criminologist. However, it happens that some two-thirds of a century ago I became persuaded that theoretical sociology was too sharply focussed on social patterns of conforming behavior and so I turned to the task of trying to develop a sociological theory of deviant behavior. And, of course, deviant behavior notably includes crime and delinquency. You will understand, then, that it means much to a disciplinary outsider like myself to have your society of specialists in the science, art, and craft of criminology

grant this fine recognition to the stubborn efforts of a generalist.

It also means much to me that yours is the *Sutherland* Award. For I have long admired the exercises in metatheorizing that were often implicit in Edwin Sutherland's explicit contributions to criminology. Thus, back in 1945, a few years after his paper on "white-collar criminality" had appeared, I took occasion to observe that a major

> function of conceptual clarification [is] to make explicit the character of data subsumed under a concept. It serves to reduce the likelihood that spurious empirical findings will be couched in terms of given concepts. Thus, Sutherland's re-examination of the received concept of "crime" provides an instructive instance of how such clarification induces a revision of hypotheses concerning the data organized in terms of the concept [Sutherland, 1940]. He demonstrates an equivocation implicit in criminological theories which seek to account for the fact that there is a much higher rate of crime, as "officially measured," in the lower than in the upper social classes. These crime "data" (organized in terms of a particular operational concept and measure of crime) have led to a series of hypotheses which

view poverty, slum conditions, feeblemindedness, and other characteristics held to be highly associated with low[er]-class status as the [so-called] "causes" of criminal behavior. [However,] once the concept of crime is clarified to refer to the violation of criminal law and is thus extended to include "white-collar criminality" in business and the professions—violations which are less often reflected in official crime statistics than are lower-class violations—the presumptive [strong] association between low social status and crime may no longer [be as strong as it seemed]. We need not pursue Sutherland's analysis further to detect the function of conceptual clarification in this instance. It provides for a *reconstruction of data* by indicating more precisely just what they include and what they exclude. In doing so, it leads to a liquidation of hypotheses set up to account for spurious data by questioning the assumptions on which the statistical data were based. By hanging a question mark on an implicit assumption underlying the research definition of crime—the assumption that violations of the criminal code by members of the several social classes are representatively registered in the official statistics—this conceptual clarification had direct implications for a nucleus of theories (Merton, 1945:465–466).

I have quoted at length from that paper of half a century ago only to indicate that my appreciation of Sutherland's foundational work in criminology is of long standing rather than being newly evoked by this special occasion. And now, at my improbably advanced age, I am also prepared to say, as I obviously could not say when still in my 20s, that when it comes to the study of deviant behavior, I regard Sutherland's evolving idea of differential association and my evolving idea of anomie-and-opportunity-structures as definite complementarities. They are complementary in several respects.

To begin with, as implied by that long quotation, it can be argued that, rightly understood, Sutherland's specialized theorizing in criminology has contributed to general theorizing in sociology, just as the Sutherland Award now confirms the hope that my general theorizing in sociology may have contributed to specialized theorizing in criminology.

Further, as I have also observed in print—this, a mere 20 years ago,[2] our sociological ideas are complementary in their problematics and key questions: Put in overly compressed terms, the theory of differential association holds that individuals learn to engage in criminal behavior by associating with others, principally in face-to-face groups, who prefer and practice such behavior. Thus, the key question in this theory centers on the sociocultural transmission of criminal patterns: It inquires into the processes of socialization and social learning through which such patterns are learned from significant others. With its focus on this key question, the theory has little to say about how those patterns of criminal preferences and behavior emerged in the first place.

Correlatively, the theory of anomie-and-opportunity-structures also has a delimited problematics. It holds that rates of various types of deviant behavior (not only crime) are high in a society where, as with the American Dream, the culture places a high premium on economic success and upward mobility for *all* its members, although in brute social fact large numbers of people located in the lower reaches of the social structure have severely limited access to legitimate resources for achieving those culturally induced or reinforced goals. Since the key question in this theory focusses on the socially structured sources and consequences of deviant behavior, it says next to nothing about the social mechanisms for transmitting such patterns of behavior or about the ways in which individuals' initial departures from the norms crystallize into deviant careers. In short, the two theories focus on complementary problematics and seek to provide complementary solutions of those problems.

As I now learn, thanks to the recent scholarship of Elin Waring, David Weisburd, and Ellen Chayet, Sutherland himself indicated that, to his mind, anomie theory and his theory of differential association "are consistent with each other and one is the counterpart of the other. Both apply to ordinary crime as well as to white-collar crime" (Waring et al., 1995:208, quoting Sutherland, 1949b:255).

Early compelling evidence of the complementarity of the two theories was provided by their syntheses and extensions that started with the pioneering work of Albert K. Cohen, Lloyd E. Ohlin, and Richard A. Cloward in the 1950s and continue on an enlarged scale to the present day. It would make no more sense to bring a detailed account of those enduring contributions to *this* company than to bring coals to Newcastle or timber into the woods. But I can point out that those still consequential synthesis plainly presuppose an underlying complementarity; they are not would-be Hegelian syntheses of thesis and antithesis—as those three pioneering criminologists were of course abundantly aware. Thus, Cohen has repeatedly observed that his 1955 monograph *Delinquent Boys: The Culture of the Gang,* which introduced the concept of "delinquent subcultures," represented "a fusion of the Chicago and anomie tradition" (Cohen, 1968:IV–152). (And of course, the Chicago tradition eminently includes Sutherland as well as Clifford Shaw and Henry McKay.) A few years later, the complementarity of those two traditions was further demonstrated by their major fusion and extension in the Cloward and Ohlin (1960) monograph *Delinquency and Opportunity* as was crisply symbolized by its joint dedication "To Robert K. Merton and Edwin H. Sutherland."

Shifting gears for a moment to the perspective of the sociology of science, one notes that these early extenders of the two traditions were Sutherland's and my students or associates. That is to say, they came from one or both of our cognitive micro-environments. As an undergraduate at Harvard in the late 1930s, Albert Cohen had been subjected to an oral as well as a printed publication of "Social Structure and Anomie" (Merton, 1938) in a course he happened to take with me. He then went on to Indiana University for graduate study with Sutherland in 1939, where, after a three-year stint in the armed forces, he returned in due course as Sutherland's associate on the faculty. As once before, I hazard the conjecture that Cohen's experience in those two micro-environments may have facilitated, though it did not of course determine, his blending and notable development of the two theoretical traditions.

In like fashion, Lloyd Ohlin had found his way in the mid-1950s to the Columbia micro-environment as a faculty member of its School of Social Work after having studied with Sutherland at Indiana and taken his doctorate at the University of Chicago. Thus, he had had firsthand exposure to the cultural transmission and differential association traditions in both micro-environments where they had originated and had been substantially developed. At Columbia, Ohlin encountered Dick Cloward, who was then at work on his dissertation "Social Control and Anomie: A Study of the Prison Community," which as it happens, he was writing largely under my direction. And

again, we notice that their early blending and considerable extension of the two traditions followed upon direct or vicarious involvement in the two cognitive micro-environments.

The cognitive process involved in the syntheses and extensions of those traditions holds further interest for the sociology of science. In both cases, it involved a process recurrent in the selective accumulation of scientific knowledge: the successive *explicit* identification of theoretical problems and the emergence of consequential concepts that had remained *implicit* in prior formulations. Thus, Albert Cohen had identified a sociological gap in the problematics of Sutherland's basically sociopsychological paradigm of differential association as well as a gap in the problematics of "social structure and anomie" that ignored the social interactions influencing individuals' choices of solutions to structurally induced strains. It was that double specification of theoretical ignorance which helped lead him to the important sociological concept of "delinquent subcultures." So, too, we find Cloward and Ohlin specifying a conceptual gap in the anomie-and-opportunity-structure paradigm and developing a subsequent idea in Sutherland's paradigm by adding the important parallel concept of "illegitimate opportunity structure" to the received concept of "legitimate opportunity structure."

Although those early extensions of the two theoretical traditions derived from colleagues in local cognitive environments, here as with scientific knowledge generally, further developments derived largely from those colleagues-at-a-distance who constitute what the historian of science, Derek de Solla Price, described as "invisible colleges": informal collectives of scientists interacting at the same research fronts and generally limited to a size "that can be handled by interpersonal relationships" (Price, 1963:ch. 3; see also Crane, 1972; Chubin, 1983). So far as I know, no sociologist of science has yet begun to study the invisible colleges at work on the various research fronts in criminology, past and present. It should be enlightening to examine the diffusion and differentiation of criminological knowledge as it moved from local micro-environments to cosmopolitan macro-environments.

Having noted the substantive complementarity of Sutherland's and my ideas, I now note formal similarities and differences in our styles of work. By way of similarity, we both made a practice of tenaciously following up our ideas, Sutherland continuously and I intermittently. As you know, the first formulations of the two theories appeared at almost the same time, differential association in 1939 and anomie-and-structurally-differentiated-access-to-opportunity in 1938. We then worked, each in our own way, to *evolve* those ideas by reflecting critically on them over the years. Sutherland extended the first formulation of his theory in the 1947 (fourth) edition of his still enduring textbook *Principles of Criminology,* and he dealt with it further in the monograph *White Collar Crime* (1949a) published shortly before his death. His other severely critical reflections on the theory appear in the *Sutherland Papers,* which were put together after his death by the benign editorial hands of Albert Cohen, Alfred Lindesmith, and Karl Schuessler (1956). That critique, the editors tell us, "was intended only for circulation among Sutherland's associates" and was titled, with almost masochistic detachment, "The Swan Song of Differential Association." Most in point for present purposes, this reflective self-critique, written in 1944 and unpublished in Sutherland's lifetime, introduced a fundamental new ingredient, the concept of "opportunity":

> One factor in criminal behavior that is at least partially extraneous to differential association is opportunity. Criminal behavior is partially a function of opportunities to commit specific classes of crime, such as embezzlement, bank burglary or illicit heterosexual intercourse. Opportunities to commit crimes of these classes are partially a function of physical factors and of cultures which are neutral as to crime. Consequently, criminal behavior is not caused entirely by association with criminal and anti-criminal patterns, and differential association is not a sufficient cause of criminal behavior (Cohen et al., 1956:31).

Thus, Sutherland had himself moved toward a convergence between the two theories and, as I've intimated, partly anticipated in undeveloped sociological form the clear-cut Cloward and Ohlin theoretical advance of supplementing the concept of differential access to the *legitimate* opportunity structure with the concept of differential access to the *illegitimate* opportunity structure.

As Sutherland tried in his way to extend the first formulation of differential association theory of 1939, so I have tried in my way to extend the first formulation of anomie-and-opportunity-structure theory of 1938. This

I undertook in a half dozen papers appearing between 1949 and 1976 and in another appearing most recently in 1995.[3] However, when witnessed from the perspective of the sociology of scientific knowledge, it is clear that both theoretical traditions have evolved principally through the work still being carried forward by the various invisible colleges. So far as I know, the most recent works are the volume edited by Freda Adler and William S. Laufer, which appeared in 1995 under the telling title *The* Legacy *of Anomie Theory,* and the volume edited by Nikos Passas and Robert Agnew, which is to appear in 1997 under the telling correlative title *The* Future *of Anomie Theory.* Various papers in both volumes contribute to the evolving synthesis of the two theoretical orientations.

So much for the similarity in Sutherland's and my styles of work: Both of us have engaged in a pattern of iterative critical examination of our ideas over extended periods of time in an effort to develop better approximations to a workable theory.

Now, a few concluding words about a distinct difference in our work styles: Sutherland worked *continuously* toward that objective by focussing on the evolving idea of differential association, while I worked *discontinuously* on the evolving idea of anomie-and-opportunity structures when turning temporarily from diverse other problems in the sociology of science, structural sociology, mass communications, reference group theory, the focussed group interview (whence, the widely used and often-abused "focus group"), the accumulation of advantage and disadvantage involving the Matthew effect, and the dynamics of unintended consequences and the self-fulfilling prophecy. What one can see exemplified in our respective work styles is, I believe, the metaphorical contrast between *The Hedgehog and the Fox,* a contrast brought to contemporary attention by the social philosopher Isaiah Berlin (1953), who quotes the ancient Greek poet Archilochus as saying, "The fox knows many things, but the hedgehog knows one big thing." Otherwise put, this is the contrast between the pluralist and the monist. As a consummate monist, Sutherland was definitely a hedgehog, just as, in effect, he once declared my pluralist self to be a fox—this, in the only note I still have from him, written better than half a century ago, which closes by remarking that "I marvel at your ability to write so much on such varied topics."

As you see, the Sutherland Award has evoked a scattering of reminiscent reflections on the evolving synthesis of the two theoretical traditions. I suspect that one unintended consequence of that award will be my further pondering on that still consequential development in criminological inquiry.

NOTES

1. Since the term *theory* has been historically adopted for these ideas for better than half a century, I adopt it here as well, not pausing for metatheorizing designed to distinguish *theory* from *pre-Kuhnian paradigm* and *model*.

2. Continuing with this retrospective, I barely paraphrase page 32 from the opening chapter, "The Sociology of Social Problems," of *Contemporary Social Problems* (Merton and Nisbet, 1976).

3. That evolution of anomie theory was emphatically and critically noted in finegrained detail by Stephen Cole (1975:175–220). Drawing upon my "Social Structure and Anomie" (1938:672–682), Cole also draws upon most of my further efforts at extensions and continuities: "Social Structure and Anomie: Revisions and Extensions" (1949:226–257); "The Socio-Cultural Environment and Anomie" (1955:24–50); "Continuities in the Theory of Social Structure and Anomie" (1957a:161–194); "Priorities in Scientific Discovery: A Chapter in the Sociology of Science" (1957b:635–649), an application of anomie theory to deviant behavior in science; "Social Conformity, Deviation, and Opportunity Structures" (1959:177–189); and "Anomie, Anomia, and Social Interaction: Contexts of Deviant Behavior" (1964:213–242). Writing in 1975, Cole could not draw upon two further cases in point of what I have taken to be complementarity: "The Sociology of Social Problems" (1976, esp. at pp. 31–37); and "Opportunity Structure: The Emergence, Diffusion, and Differentiation of a Sociological Concept, 1930s–1950s" (1995:3–78).

REFERENCES

Adler, Freda and William S. Laufer (eds.). 1995. *The Legacy of Anomie Theory.* New Brunswick, N.J.: Transaction.

Berlin, Isaiah. 1953. *The Hedgehog and the Fox: An Essay on Tolstoy's View of History.* 1986. New York: Simon & Schuster.

Chubin, Daryl E. 1983. *Sociology of Sciences: An Annotated Bibliography on Invisible Colleges.* New York: Garland.

Cloward, Richard A. and Lloyd E. Ohlin. 1960. *Delinquency and Opportunity.* New York: Free Press.

Cohen, Albert K. 1955. *Delinquent Boys: Culture of the Gang.* 1963. New York: Free Press.

———. 1968. Deviant behavior. In David L. Sills (ed.), *International Encyclopedia of the Social Sciences.* Vol. IV. New York: Macmillan-Free Press.

Cohen, Albert K., Alfred Lindesmith, and Karl Schuessler (eds.) 1956. *The Sutherland Papers.* Bloomington: University of Indiana Press.

Cole, Stephen. 1975. The growth of scientific knowledge: Theories of deviance as a case study. In Lewis A. Coser (ed.)., *The Idea of Social Structure.* New York: Harcourt Brace Jovanovich.

Crane, Diana. 1972. *Invisible Colleges.* Chicago: University of Chicago Press.

Merton, Robert K. 1938. Social structure and anomie. *American Sociological Review* 3:672–682.

———. 1945. Sociological theory. *American Journal of Sociology* 50:462–473.

———. 1949. Social structure and anomie: Revisions and extensions. In Ruth N. Anshen (ed.), *The Family: Its Functions and Destiny.* New York: Harper & Brothers.

———. 1955. The socio-cultural environment and anomie. In Helen L. Witmer and Ruth Kotinsky (eds.), *New Perspectives for Research on Juvenile Delinquency.* Washington, D.C.: U.S. Government Printing Office.

———. 1957a. Continuities in the theory of social structure and anomie. In Robert K. Merton, *Social Theory and Social Structure.* Rev. ed. New York: Free Press.

———. 1957b. Priorities in scientific discovery: A chapter in the sociology of science. *American Sociological Review* 22:635–659.

———. 1959. Social conformity, deviation, and opportunity structures. *American Sociological Review* 24:177–189.

———. 1964. Anomie, anomia, and social interaction: Contexts of deviant behavior. In Marshall Clinard (ed.), *Anomie and Deviant Behavior.* New York: Free Press.

———. 1976. The sociology of social problems. In Robert K. Merton and Robert Nisbet (eds.), *Contemporary Social Problems.* New York: Harcourt Brace Jovanovich.

———. 1995. Opportunity structure: The emergence, diffusion and differentiation of a sociological concept, 1930s–1950s. In Freda Adler and William S. Laufer (eds.), *The Legacy of Anomie Theory.* New Brunswick, N.J.: Transaction.

Merton, Robert K. and Robert Nisbet (eds.). 1976. *Contemporary Social Problems.* New York: Harcourt Brace Jovanovich.

Passas, Nikos and Robert Agnew (eds.). 1997. *The Future of Anomie Theory.* Boston: Northeastern University Press.

Price, Derek J. de Solla. 1963. *Little Science, Big Science . . . and Beyond.* 1986. New York: Columbia University Press.

Sutherland, Edwin H. 1940. White-collar criminality. *American Sociological Review* 5:1–12.

————. 1947. *Principles of Criminology.* New York: Lippincott.

————. 1949a. *White Collar Crime.* New York: Holt, Rinehart & Winston.

————. 1949b. *White Collar Crime: The Uncut Version.* 1983. New Haven: Yale University Press.

Waring, Elin, David Weisburd, and Ellen Chayet. 1995. White-collar crime and anomie. In Freda Adler and William S. Laufer (eds.), *The Legacy of Anomie Theory.* New Brunswick, N.J.: Transaction.

Think Critically

1. What does Merton have to say about Sutherland's conceptualization of white-collar crime, and why does he see it as so important for theory development in criminology?

2. Anomie and differential association perspectives on criminality grew out of two distinct traditions. How are the two complementary according to Merton?

SELF-CONTROL THEORY

ONE OF THE MOST RECENT CONTROVERSIAL areas of deviance and criminological theory involves self-control theory. This perspective emanates from the earlier work of Hirschi and Gottfredson on control theory, and is fully expounded upon in their book, *A General Theory of Crime*. The authors elaborate on classical theories of crime, from which Hirschi's writings on control theory were born. They note that classical theory concerns *external* social controls involving the costs of crime, which depend on an individual's current location in or bond to society. The theory, they argue, is therefore incomplete. That is, it does not account for *internal* controls, or "the idea that people also differ in the extent to which they are vulnerable to the temptations of the moment." Combining these two elements "recognizes the simultaneous existence of social and individual restraints on behavior." In this passage from their book, Gottfredson and Hirschi describe the elements of self-control, how they are related to criminality, the manifestations of low self-control, and the causes of self-control which are rooted in family child-rearing practices. As they see it, the major "cause" of low self-control is found in ineffective child-rearing practices. Gottfredson and Hirschi's self-control theory is clearly a highly sophisticated treatment and synthesis of many ideas regarding the etiology of crime and deviance.

The response to this theoretical perspective has been mixed. While the theory may have value in explaining some criminality, it is certainly not without fault. First and foremost, as a general theory meant to explain "all" criminality, it suffers from the usual gamut of shortcomings common to all "grand theorizing" in the social sciences, in which an attempt is made to account for a phenomenon in its entirety. The preeminent criminologist, Gilbert Geis, offers a detailed critique of self-control theory in his piece, "On the Absence of Self-Control as the Basis for a General Theory of Crime." Geis meticulously dissects the theory and its assumptions and finds numerous deficiencies regarding its applicability to all crime. He provides numerous examples of crime that appear to fall outside of Gottfredson and Hirschi's model, and refers to the common criticism that the theory itself may be tautological (explaining the propensity to commit crime by low self-control). He also takes the authors to task on issues related to criminal law, other acts they claim are explained by the theory, exceptions to their model, the idea of "opportunity," aging and self-control, white-collar crime, methodological and research issues, and child raising. The criticisms that Geis raises are important in assessing self-control as a "general theory" and provide major support to a growing chorus of researchers who have argued that "it is a general theory of some instances of some forms of crime."

Low Self-Control and Crime*

Michael R. Gottfredson and Travis Hirschi

THEORIES OF CRIME LEAD NATURALLY TO interest in the propensities of individuals committing criminal acts. These propensities are often labeled "criminality." In pure classical theory, people committing criminal acts had no special propensities. They merely followed the universal tendency to enhance their own pleasure. If they differed from noncriminals, it was with respect to their location in or comprehension of relevant sanction systems. For example, the individual cut off from the community will suffer less than others from the ostracism that follows crime; the individual unaware of the natural or legal consequences of criminal behavior cannot be controlled by these consequences to the degree that people aware of them are controlled; the atheist will not be as concerned as the believer about penalties to be exacted in a life beyond death. Classical theories on the whole, then, are today called *control* theories, theories emphasizing the prevention of crime through consequences painful to the individual.

Although, for policy purposes, classical theorists emphasized legal consequences, the importance to them of moral sanctions is so obvious that their theories might well be called underdeveloped *social control* theories. In fact, Bentham's list of the major restraining motives— motives acting to prevent mischievous acts—begins with goodwill, love of reputation, and the desire for amity (1970: 134–36). He goes on to say that fear of detection prevents crime in large part because of detection's consequences for "reputation, and the desire for amity" (p. 138). Put another way, in Bentham's view, the restraining power

of legal sanctions in large part stems from their connection to social sanctions.

If crime is evidence of the weakness of social motives, it follows that criminals are less social than noncriminals and that the extent of their asociality may be determined by the nature and number of their crimes. Calculation of the extent of an individual's mischievousness is a complex affair, but in general the more mischievous or depraved the offenses, and the greater their number, the more mischievous or depraved the offender (Bentham 1970: 134–42). (Classical theorists thus had reason to be interested in the seriousness of the offense. The relevance of seriousness to current theories of crime is not so clear.)

Because classical or control theories infer that offenders are not restrained by social motives, it is common to think of them as emphasizing an asocial human nature. Actually, such theories make people only as asocial as their acts require. Pure or consistent control theories do not add criminality (i.e., personality concepts or attributes such as "aggressiveness" or "extraversion") to individuals beyond that found in their criminal acts. As a result, control theories are suspicious of images of an antisocial, psychopathic, or career offender, or of an offender whose motives to crime are somehow larger than those given in the crimes themselves. Indeed, control theories are compatible with the view that the balance of the total control structure favors conformity, even among offenders:

> For in every man, be his disposition ever so depraved, the social motives are those which . . . regulate and determine the general tenor of his life. . . . The general and standing bias of every man's nature is, therefore, towards that side to which the force of the social motives would determine him to adhere. This being the case, the force of the social motives tends continually to put an end to that of the dissocial ones; as, in natural bodies, the force of friction tends to put an end to

that which is generated by impulse. Time, then, which wears away the force of the dissocial motives, adds to that of the social. [Bentham 1970: 141]

. . . If individual differences in the tendency to commit criminal acts (within an overall tendency for crime to decline with age) are at least potentially explicable within classical theory by reference to the social location of individuals and their comprehension of how the world works, the fact remains that classical theory cannot shed much light on the positivistic finding (denied by most positivistic theories . . . that these differences *remain reasonably stable with change in the social location of individuals and change in their knowledge of the operation of sanction systems.* This is the problem of self-control, the differential tendency of people to avoid criminal acts whatever the circumstances in which they find themselves. Since this difference among people has attracted a variety of names, we begin by arguing the merits of the concept of self-control.

Self-Control and Alternative Concepts

Our decision to ascribe stable individual differences in criminal behavior to self-control was made only after considering several alternatives, one of which (criminality) we had used before (Hirschi and Gottfredson 1986). A major consideration was consistency between the classical conception of crime and our conception of the criminal. It seemed unwise to try to integrate a choice theory of crime with a deterministic image of the offender, especially when such integration was unnecessary. In fact, the compatibility of the classical view of crime and the idea that people differ in self-control is, in our view, remarkable. As we have seen, classical theory is a theory of social or external control, a theory based on the idea that the costs of crime depend on the individual's current location in or bond to society. What classical theory lacks is an explicit idea of self-control, the idea that people also differ in the extent to which they are vulnerable to the temptations of the moment. Combining the two ideas thus merely recognizes the simultaneous existence of social and individual restraints on behavior.

An obvious alternative is the concept of criminality. The disadvantages of that concept, however, are numerous. First, it connotes causation or determinism, a positive tendency to crime that is contrary to the classical model and, in our view, contrary to the facts. Whereas self-control suggests that people differ in the extent to which they are restrained from criminal acts, criminality suggests that people differ in the extent to which they are compelled to crime. The concept of self-control is thus consistent with the observation that criminals do not require or need crime, and the concept of criminality is inconsistent with this observation. By the same token, the idea of low self-control is compatible with the observation that criminal acts require no special capabilities, needs, or motivation; they are, in this sense, available to everyone. In contrast, the idea of criminality as a special tendency suggests that criminal acts require special people for their performance and enjoyment. Finally, lack of restraint or low self-control allows almost any deviant, criminal, exciting, or dangerous act; in contrast, the idea of criminality covers only a narrow portion of the apparently diverse acts engaged in by people at one end of the dimension we are now discussing.

The concept of conscience comes closer than criminality to self-control, and is harder to distinguish from it. Unfortunately, that concept has connotations of compulsion (to conformity) not, strictly speaking, consistent with a choice model (or with the operation of conscience). It does not seem to cover the behaviors analogous to crime that appear to be controlled by natural sanctions rather than social or moral sanctions, and in the end it typically refers to how people feel about their acts rather than to the likelihood that they will or will not commit them. Thus accidents and employment instability are not usually seen as produced by failures of conscience, and writers in the conscience tradition do not typically make the connection between moral and prudent behavior. Finally, conscience is used primarily to summarize the results of learning via negative reinforcement, and even those favorably disposed to its use have little more to say about it (see, e.g., Eysenck 1977; Wilson and Herrnstein 1985) . . .

The Elements of Self-Control

Criminal acts provide *immediate* gratification of desires. A major characteristic of people with low self-control is therefore a tendency to respond to tangible stimuli in the immediate environment, to have a concrete "here and now" orientation. People with high self-control, in contrast, tend to defer gratification.

Criminal acts provide *easy or simple* gratification of desires. They provide money without work, sex without courtship, revenge without court delays. People lacking self-control also tend to lack diligence, tenacity, or persistence in a course of action.

Criminal acts are *exciting, risky, or thrilling.* They involve stealth, danger, speed, agility, deception, or power. People lacking self-control therefore tend to be adventuresome, active, and physical. Those with high levels of self-control tend to be cautious, cognitive, and verbal.

Crimes provide *few or meager long-term benefits.* They are not equivalent to a job or a career. On the contrary, crimes interfere with long-term commitments to jobs, marriages, family, or friends. People with low self-control thus tend to have unstable marriages, friendships, and job profiles. They tend to be little interested in and unprepared for long-term occupational pursuits.

Crimes require *little skill or planning.* The cognitive requirements for most crimes are minimal. It follows that people lacking self-control need not possess or value cognitive or academic skills. The manual skills required for most crimes are minimal. It follows that people lacking self-control need not possess manual skills that require training or apprenticeship.

Crimes often result in *pain or discomfort for the victim.* Property is lost, bodies are injured, privacy is violated, trust is broken. It follows that people with low self-control tend to be self-centered, indifferent, or insensitive to the suffering and needs of others. It does not follow, however, that people with low self-control are routinely unkind or antisocial. On the contrary, they may discover the immediate and easy rewards of charm and generosity.

Recall that crime involves the pursuit of immediate pleasure. It follows that people lacking self-control will also tend to pursue immediate pleasures that are *not* criminal: they will tend to smoke, drink, use drugs, gamble, have children out of wedlock, and engage in illicit sex.

Crimes require the interaction of an offender with people or their property. It does not follow that people lacking self-control will tend to be gregarious or social. However, it does follow that, other things being equal, gregarious or social people are more likely to be involved in criminal acts.

The major benefit of many crimes is not pleasure but relief from momentary irritation. The irritation caused by a crying child is often the stimulus for physical abuse. That caused by a taunting stranger in a bar is often the stimulus for aggravated assault. It follows that people with low self-control tend to have minimal tolerance for frustration and little ability to respond to conflict through verbal rather than physical means.

Crimes involve the risk of violence and physical injury, of pain and suffering on the part of the offender. It does not follow that people with low self-control will tend to be tolerant of physical pain or to be indifferent to physical discomfort. It does follow that people tolerant of physical pain or indifferent to physical discomfort will be more likely to engage in criminal acts whatever their level of self-control . . .

In sum, people who lack self-control will tend to be impulsive, insensitive, physical (as opposed to mental), risk-taking, short-sighted, and non-verbal, and they will tend therefore to engage in criminal and analogous acts. Since these traits can be identified prior to the age of responsibility for crime, since there is considerable tendency for these traits to come together in the same people, and since the traits tend to persist through life, it seems reasonable to consider them as comprising a stable construct useful in the explanation of crime.

The Many Manifestations of Low Self-Control

Our image of the "offender" suggests that crime is not an automatic or necessary consequence of low self-control. It suggests that many noncriminal acts analogous to crime (such as accidents, smoking, and alcohol use) are also manifestations of low self-control. Our image therefore implies that no specific act, type of crime, or form of deviance is uniquely required by the absence of self-control.

Because both crime and analogous behaviors stem from low self-control (that is, both are manifestations of low self-control), they will all be engaged in at a relatively high rate by people with low self-control. Within the domain of crime, then, there will be much versatility among offenders in the criminal acts in which they engage.

Research on the versatility of deviant acts supports these predictions in the strongest possible way. The variety of manifestations of low self-control is immense. In spite of years of tireless research motivated by a belief in specialization, no credible evidence of specialization has been reported. In fact, the evidence of offender versatility is overwhelming (Hirschi 1969; Hindelang 1971; Wolfgang,

Figlio, and Sellin 1972; Petersilia 1980; Hindelang, Hirschi, and Weis 1981; Rojek and Erickson 1982; Klein 1984).

By versatility we mean that offenders commit a wide variety of criminal acts, with no strong inclination to pursue a specific criminal act or a pattern of criminal acts to the exclusion of others. Most theories suggest that offenders tend to specialize, whereby such terms as robber, burglar, drug dealer, rapist, and murderer have predictive or descriptive import. In fact, some theories create offender specialization as part of their explanation of crime. For example, Cloward and Ohlin (1960) create distinctive subcultures of delinquency around particular forms of criminal behavior, identifying subcultures specializing in theft, violence, or drugs. In a related way, books are written about white-collar crime as though it were a clearly distinct specialty requiring a unique explanation. Research projects are undertaken for the study of drug use, or vandalism, or teen pregnancy (as though every study of delinquency were not a study of drug use and vandalism and teenage sexual behavior). Entire schools of criminology emerge to pursue patterning, sequencing, progression, escalation, onset, persistence, and desistance in the career of offenses or offenders. These efforts survive largely because their proponents fail to consider or acknowledge the clear evidence to the contrary. Other reasons for survival of such ideas may be found in the interest of politicians and members of the law enforcement community who see policy potential in criminal careers or "career criminals" (see, e.g., Blumstein et al. 1986).

Occasional reports of specialization seem to contradict this point, as do everyday observations of repetitive misbehavior by particular offenders. Some offenders rob the same store repeatedly over a period of years, or an offender commits several rapes over a (brief) period of time. Such offenders may be called "robbers" or "rapists." However, it should be noted that such labels are retrospective rather than predictive and that they typically ignore a large amount of delinquent or criminal behavior by the same offenders that is inconsistent with their alleged specialty. Thus, for example, the "rapist" will tend also to use drugs, to commit robberies and burglaries (often in concert with the rape), and to have a record for violent offenses other than rape. There is a perhaps natural tendency on the part of observers (and in official accounts) to focus on the most serious crimes in a series of events, but this tendency should not be confused with a tendency on the part of the offender to specialize in one kind of crime.

Recall that one of the defining features of crime is that it is simple and easy. Some apparent specialization will therefore occur because obvious opportunities for an easy score will tend to repeat themselves. An offender who lives next to a shopping area that is approached by pedestrians will have repeat opportunities for purse snatching, and this may show in his arrest record. But even here the specific "criminal career" will tend to quickly run its course and to be followed by offenses whose content and character is likewise determined by convenience and opportunity (which is the reason why some form of theft is always the best bet about what a person is likely to do next).

The evidence that offenders are likely to engage in noncriminal acts psychologically or theoretically equivalent to crime is, because of the relatively high rates of these "noncriminal" acts, even easier to document. Thieves are likely to smoke, drink, and skip school at considerably higher rates than nonthieves. Offenders are considerably more likely than nonoffenders to be involved in most types of accidents, including household fires, auto crashes, and unwanted pregnancies. They are also considerably more likely to die at an early age (see, e.g., Robins 1966; Eysenck 1977; Gottfredson 1984).

Good research on drug use and abuse routinely reveals that the correlates of delinquency and drug use are the same. As Akers (1984) has noted, "compared to the abstaining teenager, the drinking, smoking, and drug-taking teen is much more likely to be getting into fights, stealing, hurting other people, and committing other delinquencies." Akers goes on to say, "but the variation in the order in which they take up these things leaves little basis for proposing the causation of one by the other." In our view, the relation between drug use and delinquency is not a causal question. The correlates are the same because drug use and delinquency are both manifestations of an underlying tendency to pursue short-term, immediate pleasure. This underlying tendency (i.e., lack of self-control) has many manifestations, as listed by Harrison Gough (1948):

> unconcern over the rights and privileges of others when recognizing them would interfere with personal satisfaction in any way; impulsive behavior, or apparent incongruity between the strength of the stimulus and the magnitude of the behavioral response; inability to form deep or persistent attachments to other persons or to identify in interpersonal relationships; poor judgment and planning in attaining defined goals; apparent

lack of anxiety and distress over social maladjustment and unwillingness or inability to consider maladjustment qua maladjustment; a tendency to project blame onto others and to take no responsibility for failures; meaningless prevarication, often about trivial matters in situations where detection is inevitable; almost complete lack of dependability . . . and willingness to assume responsibility; and, finally, emotional poverty. [p. 362]

This combination of characteristics has been revealed in the life histories of the subjects in the famous studies by Lee Robins. Robins is one of the few researchers to focus on the varieties of deviance and the way they tend to go together in the lives of those she designates as having "antisocial personalities." In her words: "We refer to someone who fails to maintain close personal relationships with anyone else, [who] performs poorly on the job, who is involved in illegal behaviors (whether or not apprehended), who fails to support himself and his dependents without outside aid, and who is given to sudden changes of plan and loss of temper in response to what appear to others as minor frustrations" (1978: 255) . . .

Note that these outcomes are consistent with four general elements of our notion of low self-control: basic stability of individual differences over a long period of time; great variability in the kinds of criminal acts engaged in; conceptual or causal equivalence of criminal and non-criminal acts; and inability to predict the specific forms of deviance engaged in, whether criminal or non-criminal. In our view, the idea of an antisocial personality defined by certain behavioral consequences is too positivistic or deterministic, suggesting that the offender must do certain things given his antisocial personality. Thus we would say only that the subjects in question are *more likely* to commit criminal acts (as the data indicate they are). We do not make commission of criminal acts part of the definition of the individual with low self-control . . .

The Causes of Self-Control

We know better what deficiencies in self-control lead to than where they come from. One thing is, however, clear: low self-control is not produced by training, tutelage, or socialization. As a matter of fact, all of the characteristics associated with low self-control tend to show themselves in the absence of nurturance, discipline, or training. Given

the classical appreciation of the causes of human behavior, the implications of this fact are straightforward: the causes of low self-control are negative rather than positive; self-control is unlikely in the absence of effort, intended or unintended, to create it. (This assumption separates the present theory from most modern theories of crime, where the offender is automatically seen as a product of positive forces, a creature of learning, particular pressures, or specific defect. We will return to this comparison once our theory has been fully explicated.)

At this point it would be easy to construct a theory of crime causation, according to which characteristics of potential offenders lead them ineluctably to the commission of criminal acts. Our task at this point would simply be to identify the likely sources of impulsiveness, intelligence, risk-taking, and the like. But to do so would be to follow the path that has proven so unproductive in the past, the path according to which criminals commit crimes irrespective of the characteristics of the setting or situation.

We can avoid this pitfall by recalling the elements inherent in the decision to commit a criminal act. The object of the offense is clearly pleasurable, and universally so. Engaging in the act, however, entails some risk of social, legal, and/or natural sanctions. Whereas the pleasure attained by the act is direct, obvious, and immediate, the pains risked by it are not obvious, or direct, and are in any event at greater remove from it. It follows that, though there will be little variability among people in their ability to see the pleasures of crime, there will be considerable variability in their ability to calculate potential pains. But the problem goes further than this: whereas the pleasures of crime are reasonably equally distributed over the population, this is not true for the pains. Everyone appreciates money; not everyone dreads parental anger or disappointment upon learning that the money was stolen.

So, the dimensions of self-control are, in our view, factors affecting calculation of the consequences of one's acts. The impulsive or short-sighted person fails to consider the negative or painful consequences of his acts; the insensitive person has fewer negative consequences to consider; the less intelligent person also has fewer negative consequences to consider (has less to lose).

No known social group, whether criminal or noncriminal, actively or purposefully attempts to reduce the self-control of its members. Social life is not enhanced by low self-control and its consequences. On the contrary, the exhibition of these tendencies undermines harmonious group relations and the ability to achieve collective ends. These facts explicitly deny that a tendency to crime is a product of socialization, culture, or positive learning of any sort.

The traits composing low self-control are also not conducive to the achievement of long-term individual goals. On the contrary, they impede educational and occupational achievement, destroy interpersonal relations, and undermine physical health and economic well-being. Such facts explicitly deny the notion that criminality is an alternative route to the goals otherwise obtainable through legitimate avenues. It follows that people who care about the interpersonal skill, educational and occupational achievement, and physical and economic well-being of those in their care will seek to rid them of these traits.

Two general sources of variation are immediately apparent in this scheme. The first is the variation among children in the degree to which they manifest such traits to begin with. The second is the variation among caretakers in the degree to which they recognize low self-control and its consequences and the degree to which they are willing and able to correct it. Obviously, therefore, even at this threshold level the sources of low self-control are complex.

There is good evidence that some of the traits predicting subsequent involvement in crime appear as early as they can be reliably measured, including low intelligence, high activity level, physical strength, and adventuresomeness (Glueck and Glueck 1950; West and Farrington 1973). The evidence suggests that the connection between these traits and commission of criminal acts ranges from weak to moderate. Obviously, we do not suggest that people are born criminals, inherit a gene for criminality, or anything of the sort. In fact, we explicitly deny such notions. . . . What we do suggest is that individual differences may have an impact on the prospects for effective socialization (or adequate control). Effective socialization is, however, always possible whatever the configuration of individual traits.

Other traits affecting crime appear later and seem to be largely products of ineffective or incomplete socialization. For example, differences in impulsivity and insensitivity become noticeable later in childhood when they are no longer common to all children. The ability and willingness to delay immediate gratification for some larger purpose may therefore be assumed to be a consequence of training. Much parental action is in fact geared toward suppression

of impulsive behavior, toward making the child consider the long-range consequences of acts. Consistent sensitivity to the needs and feelings of others may also be assumed to be a consequence of training. Indeed, much parental behavior is directed toward teaching the child about the rights and feelings of others, and of how these rights and feelings ought to constrain the child's behavior. All of these points focus our attention on child-rearing.

Child-Rearing and Self-Control: The Family

The major "cause" of low self-control thus appears to be ineffective child-rearing. Put in positive terms, several conditions appear necessary to produce a socialized child. Perhaps the place to begin looking for these conditions is the research literature on the relation between family conditions and delinquency. This research (e.g., Glueck and Glueck 1950; McCord and McCord 1959) has examined the connection between many family factors and delinquency. It reports that discipline, supervision, and affection tend to be missing in the homes of delinquents, that the behavior of the parents is often "poor" (e.g., excessive drinking and poor supervision [Glueck and Glueck 1950: 110–11]); and that the parents of delinquents are unusually likely to have criminal records themselves. Indeed, according to Michael Rutter and Henri Giller, "of the parental characteristics associated with delinquency, criminality is the most striking and most consistent" 1984: 182).

Such information undermines the many explanations of crime that ignore the family, but in this form it does not represent much of an advance over the belief of the general public (and those who deal with offenders in the criminal justice system) that "defective upbringing" or "neglect" in the home is the primary cause of crime.

To put these standard research findings in perspective, we think it necessary to define the conditions necessary for adequate child-rearing to occur. The minimum conditions seem to be these: in order to teach the child self-control, someone must (1) monitor the child's behavior; (2) recognize deviant behavior when it occurs; and (3) punish such behavior. This seems simple and obvious enough. All that is required to activate the system is affection for *or* investment in the child. The person who cares for the child will watch his behavior, see him doing things he should not do, and correct him. The result may be a child more capable of delaying gratification, more sensitive to the interests and desires of others, more independent, more willing to accept restraints on his activity, and more unlikely to use force or violence to attain his ends.

When we seek the causes of low self-control, we ask where this system can go wrong. Obviously, parents do not prefer their children to be unsocialized in the terms described. We can therefore rule out in advance the possibility of positive socialization to unsocialized behavior (as cultural or subcultural deviance theories suggest). Still, the system can go wrong at any one of four places. First, the parents may not care for the child (in which case none of the other conditions would be met); second, the parents, even if they care, may not have the time or energy to monitor the child's behavior; third, the parents, even if they care *and* monitor, may not see anything wrong with the child's behavior; finally, even if everything else is in place, the parents may not have the inclination or the means to punish the child. So, what may appear at first glance to be nonproblematic turns out to be problematic indeed. Many things can go wrong. According to much research in crime and delinquency, in the homes of problem children many things have gone wrong: "Parents of stealers do not track ([they] do not interpret stealing . . . as 'deviant'); they do not punish; and they do not care" (Patterson 1980: 88–89; see also Glueck and Glueck 1950; McCord and McCord 1959; West and Farrington 1977).

Let us apply this scheme to some of the facts about the connection between child socialization and crime, beginning with the elements of the child-rearing model.

The Attachment of the Parent to the Child

Our model states that parental concern for the welfare or behavior of the child is a necessary condition for successful child-rearing. Because it is too often assumed that all parents are alike in their love for their children, the evidence directly on this point is not as good or extensive as it could be. However, what exists is clearly consistent with the model. Glueck and Glueck (1950: 125–28) report that, compared to the fathers of delinquents, fathers of non-delinquents were twice as likely to be warmly disposed toward their sons and one-fifth as likely to be hostile toward them. In the same sample, 28 percent of the mothers of delinquents were characterized as "indifferent or hostile" toward the child as compared to 4 percent of

the mothers of nondelinquents. The evidence suggests that stepparents are especially unlikely to have feelings of affection toward their stepchildren (Burgess 1980), adding in contemporary society to the likelihood that children will be "reared" by people who do not especially care for them.

Parental Supervision

The connection between social control and self-control could not be more direct than in the case of parental supervision of the child. Such supervision presumably prevents criminal or analogous acts and at the same time trains the child to avoid them on his own. Consistent with this assumption, supervision tends to be a major predictor of delinquency, however supervision or delinquency is measured (Glueck and Glueck 1950; Hirschi 1969; West and Farrington 1977; Riley and Shaw 1985).

Our general theory in principle provides a method of separating supervision as external control from supervision as internal control. For one thing, offenses differ in the degree to which they can be prevented through monitoring; children at one age are monitored much more closely than children at other ages; girls are supervised more closely than boys. In some situations, monitoring is universal or nearly constant; in other situations monitoring for some offenses is virtually absent. In the present context, however, the concern is with the connection between supervision and self-control, a connection established by the stronger tendency of those poorly supervised when young to commit crimes as adults (McCord 1979).

Recognition of Deviant Behavior

In order for supervision to have an impact on self-control, the supervisor must perceive deviant behavior when it occurs. Remarkably, not all parents are adept at recognizing lack of self-control. Some parents allow the child to do pretty much as he pleases without interference. Extensive television-viewing is one modern example, as is the failure to require completion of homework, to prohibit smoking, to curtail the use of physical force, or to see to it that the child actually attends school. (As noted, truancy among second-graders presumably reflects on the adequacy of parental awareness of the child's misbehavior.) Again, the research is not as good as it should be, but evidence of "poor conduct standards" in the homes of delinquents is common.

Punishment of Deviant Acts

Control theories explicitly acknowledge the necessity of sanctions in preventing criminal behavior. They do not suggest that the major sanctions are legal or corporal. On the contrary, as we have seen, they suggest that disapproval by people one cares about is the most powerful of sanctions. Effective punishment by the parent or major caretaker therefore usually entails nothing more than explicit disapproval of unwanted behavior. The criticism of control theories that dwells on their alleged cruelty is therefore simply misguided or ill informed (see, e.g., Currie 1985).

Not all caretakers punish effectively. In fact, some are too harsh and some are too lenient (Glueck and Glueck 1950; McCord and McCord 1959; West and Farrington 1977; see generally Loeber and Stouthamer-Loeber 1986). Given our model, however, rewarding good behavior cannot compensate for failure to correct deviant behavior. (Recall that, in our view, deviant acts carry with them their own rewards. . . .)

Given the consistency of the child-rearing model with our general theory and with the research literature, it should be possible to use it to explain other family correlates of criminal and otherwise deviant behavior.

Parental Criminality

Our theory focuses on the connection between the self-control of the parent and the subsequent self-control of the child. There is good reason to expect, and the data confirm, that people lacking self-control do not socialize their children well. According to Donald West and David Farrington, "the fact that delinquency is transmitted from one generation to the next is indisputable" (1977: 109; see also Robins 1966). Of course our theory does not allow transmission of criminality, genetic or otherwise. However, it does allow us to predict that some people are more likely than others to fail to socialize their children and that this will be a consequence of their own inadequate socialization. The extent of this connection between parent and child socialization is revealed by the fact that in the West and Farrington study fewer than 5 percent of the families accounted for almost half of the criminal convictions in the entire sample. (In our view, this finding is more important for the theory of crime, and for public policy, than the much better-known finding of Wolfgang and his colleagues [1972] that something like 6 percent of

individual offenders account for about half of all criminal acts.) In order to achieve such concentration of crime in a small number of families, it is necessary that the parents and the brothers and sisters of offenders also be unusually likely to commit criminal acts.[1]

Why should the children of offenders be unusually vulnerable to crime? Recall that our theory assumes that criminality is not something the parents have to work to produce; on the contrary, it assumes that criminality is something they have to work to avoid. Consistent with this view, parents with criminal records do *not* encourage crime in their children and are in fact as disapproving of it as parents with no record of criminal involvement (West and Farrington 1977). Of course, not wanting criminal behavior in one's children and being upset when it occurs do not necessarily imply that great effort has been expended to prevent it. If criminal behavior is oriented toward short-term rewards, and if child-rearing is oriented toward long-term rewards, there is little reason to expect parents themselves lacking self-control to be particularly adept at instilling self-control in their children.

Consistent with this expectation, research consistently indicates that the supervision of delinquents in families where parents have criminal records tends to be "lax," "inadequate," or "poor." Punishment in these families also tends to be easy, short-term, and insensitive—that is, yelling and screaming, slapping and hitting, with threats that are not carried out.

Such facts do not, however, completely account for the concentration of criminality among some families. A major reason for this failure is probably that the most subtle element of child-rearing is not included in the analysis. This is the element of *recognition* of deviant behavior. According to Gerald Patterson (1980), many parents do not even recognize *criminal* behavior in their children, let alone the minor forms of deviance whose punishment is necessary for effective child-rearing. For example, when children steal outside the home, some parents discount reports that they have done so on the grounds that the charges are unproved and cannot therefore be used to justify punishment. By the same token, when children are suspended for misbehavior at school, some parents side with the child and blame the episode on prejudicial mistreatment by teachers. Obviously, parents who cannot see the misbehavior of their children are in no position to correct it, even if they are inclined to do so.

Given that recognition of deviant acts is a necessary component of the child-rearing model, research is needed on the question of what parents should and should not recognize as deviant behavior if they are to prevent criminality. To the extent our theory is correct, parents need to know behaviors that reflect low self-control. That many parents are not now attentive to such behaviors should come as no surprise. The idea that criminal behavior is the product of deprivation or positive learning dominates modern theory. As a consequence, most influential social scientific theories of crime and delinquency ignore or deny the connection between crime and talking back, yelling, pushing and shoving, insisting on getting one's way, trouble in school, and poor school performance. Little wonder, then, that some parents do not see the significance of such acts. Research now makes it clear that parents differ in their reaction to these behaviors, with some parents attempting to correct behaviors that others ignore or even defend (Patterson 1980). Because social science in general sees little connection between these acts and crime, there has been little systematic integration of the child development and criminological literatures. Furthermore, because the conventional wisdom disputes the connection between child training and crime, public policy has not focused on it. We do not argue that crime is caused by these early misbehaviors. Instead, we argue that such behaviors indicate the presence of the major individual-level cause of crime, a cause that in principle may be attacked by punishing these early manifestations. Nor do we argue that criminal acts automatically follow early evidence of low self-control. Because crime requires more than low self-control, some parents are lucky and have children with low self-control who still manage to avoid acts that would bring them to the attention of the criminal justice system. It is less likely (in fact unlikely), however, that such children will avoid altogether behavior indicative of low self-control. Put another way, low self-control predicts low self-control better than it predicts any of its specific manifestations, such as crime.

Family Size

One of the most consistent findings of delinquency research is that the larger the number of children in the family, the greater the likelihood that each of them will be delinquent. This finding, too, is perfectly explicable from a child-rearing model. Affection for the individual child may be unaffected by numbers, and parents with large families may be as able as anyone else to recognize deviant behavior, but monitoring and punishment are probably more difficult the greater the number of children in the family. Greater numbers strain parental resources of time and energy. For this reason, the child in the large family is likely to spend more time with other children and less time with adults. Children are not as likely as adults to be effective trainers. They have less investment in the outcome, are more likely to be tolerant of deviant behavior, and do not have the power to enforce their edicts.

If the analysis of criminality of parents and size of family is sufficient to establish the plausibility of our child-rearing explanation, we can now attempt to apply it to some of the more problematic issues in the connection between the family and crime.

The Single-Parent Family

Such family measures as the percentage of the population divorced, the percentage of households headed by women, and the percentage of unattached individuals in the community are among the most powerful predictors of crime rates (Sampson 1987). Consistent with these findings, in most (but not all) studies that directly compare children living with both biological parents with children living in "broken" or reconstituted homes, the children from intact homes have lower rates of crime.

If the fact of a difference between single-and two-parent families is reasonably well established, the mechanisms by which it is produced are not adequately understood. It was once common in the delinquency literature to distinguish between homes broken by divorce and those broken by death. This distinction recognized the difficulty of separating the effects of the people involved in divorce from the effects of divorce itself. Indeed, it is common to find that involuntarily broken homes are less conducive to delinquency than homes in which the parent was a party to the decision to separate.

With the continued popularity of marriage, a possible complication enters the picture. The missing biological parent (in the overwhelming majority of cases, the father) is often replaced at some point by a stepparent. Is the child better or worse off as a result of the presence of an "unrelated" adult in the house?

The model we are using suggests that, *all else being equal,* one parent is sufficient. We could substitute "mother" or "father" for "parents" without any obvious loss in child-rearing ability. Husbands and wives tend to be sufficiently alike on such things as values, attitudes, and skills that for many purposes they may be treated as a unit. For that matter, our scheme does not even require that the adult involved in training the child be his or her guardian, let alone a biological parent. Proper training can be accomplished outside the confines of the two-parent home.

But all else is rarely equal. The single parent (usually a woman) must devote a good deal to support and maintenance activities that are at least to some extent shared in the two-parent family. Further, she must often do so in the absence of psychological or social support. As a result, she is less able to devote time to monitoring and punishment and is more likely to be involved in negative, abusive contacts with her children.

Remarriage is by no means a complete solution to these problems. As compared to natural parents, stepparents are likely to report that they have no "parental feelings" toward their stepchildren, and they are unusually likely to be involved in cases of child abuse (Burgess 1980). The other side of the coin is the affection of the child for the parent. Such affection is conducive to non-delinquency in its own right and clearly eases the task of child-rearing. Affection is, for obvious reasons, less likely to be felt toward the new parent in a reconstituted family than toward a biological parent in a continuously intact family.

The Mother Who Works Outside the Home

The increase in the number of women in the labor force has several implications for the crime rate. To the extent this increase contributes to the instability of marriage, it will have the consequences for crime just discussed. Traditionally, however, the major concern was that the mother working outside the home would be unable to supervise or effectively rear her children. Sheldon and Eleanor Glueck (1950) found that the children of women who work, especially the children of those who work "occasionally" or "sporadically," were more likely to be delinquent. They also showed that the effect on delinquency of the mother's working was *completely* accounted for by the quality of supervision provided by the mother. (Such complete explanations of one factor by another are extremely rare in social

science.) When the mother was able to arrange supervision for the child, her employment had no effect on the likelihood of delinquency. In fact, in this particular study, the children of regularly employed women were least likely to be delinquent when supervision was taken into account. This does not mean, however, that the employment of the mother had no effect. It did have an effect, at least among those in relatively deprived circumstances: the children of employed women were more likely to be delinquent.

More commonly, research reports a small effect of mother's employment that it is unable to explain. The advantage of the nonemployed mother over the employed mother in child-rearing remains when supervision and other characteristics of the mother, the family, and the child are taken into account. One possible implication of this explanatory failure is that the effects of employment influence children in ways not measurable except through their delinquency. One way of addressing this question would be to examine the effect of mother's employment on measures of inadequate self-control other than the commission of criminal acts—such as on accidents or school failure. If we are dealing with a social-control effect rather than a socialization effect, it should be possible to find a subset of deviant behaviors that are more affected than others by mother's employment. Although our scheme does not allow us *a priori* to separate the enduring effects of child "rearing" from the temporary effects of child "control," it alerts us to the fact that self-control and supervision can be the result of a single parental act.

Another consequence of female labor-force participation is that it leaves the house unguarded for large portions of the day. The unoccupied house is less attractive to adolescent members of the family and more attractive to other adolescents interested only in its contents. As we indicated earlier, research shows that the absence of guardians in the home is a good predictor of residential burglary.

Child Rearing and Self-Control: The School

Most people are sufficiently socialized by familial institutions to avoid involvement in criminal acts. Those not socialized sufficiently by the family may eventually learn self-control through the operation of other sanctioning systems or institutions. The institution given principal responsibility for this task in modern society is the school. As compared to the family, the school has several advantages as a socializing institution. First, it can more effectively monitor behavior than the family, with one teacher overseeing many children at a time. Second, as compared to most parents, teachers generally have no difficulty recognizing deviant or disruptive behavior. Third, as compared to the family, the school has such a clear interest in maintaining order and discipline that it can be expected to do what it can to control disruptive behavior. Finally, like the family, the school in theory has the authority and the means to punish lapses in self-control.

All else being equal, it would appear that the school could be an effective socializing agency. The evidence suggests, however, that in contemporary American society the school has a difficult time teaching self-control. A major reason for this limited success of the modern school appears to stem from the lack of cooperation and support it receives from families that have already failed in the socialization task. When the family does not see to it that the child is in school doing what he or she should be doing, the child's problems in school are often directly traceable to the parents. For example, according to Robins (1966), truancy begins in the first and second grades (and is not, as some assume, solely an adolescent problem). Truancy or absence in the first and second grades can hardly be attributed to the child alone. Whatever the source of such truancy, it is highly predictive of low self-control later in life.

The question, then, is whether inadequate socialization by the family could be corrected by the school if it were given the chance—that is, if the family were cooperative. Robins, whose analyses of the stability of the antisocial personality are not ordinarily optimistic, notes that the school could be used to locate preadolescents with low self-control and that it might be effective in doing what the family has failed to do: "Since truancy and poor school performance are nearly universally present in pre-sociopaths, it should be possible to identify children requiring treatment through their school records. . . . [T]he fact that a gross lack of discipline in the home predicted long-term difficulties suggests trying a program in which the schools attempt to substitute for the missing parental discipline in acting to prevent truancy and school failures" (1966: 306–7).[2]

Even without parental support, in our view, the net effect of the school must be positive. As a result of the school experience, some students learn better to appreciate the advantages and opportunities associated with self-control and are thus effectively socialized regardless of their familial experiences. One of the major school correlates of crime has always been the mundane homework. Those who do it are by definition thinking about tomorrow. Those who do not do it have a shorter time frame. One mark of socialization is considering the consequences of today's activities for tomorrow. Homework thus indexes and perhaps contributes to socialization.

Another major predictor of crime is not liking school. This connection is so strong that the statement "delinquents do not like school" does not require much in the way of qualification (Glueck and Glueck 1950: 144). The connection speaks well for the school as a socializing institution. Socializing institutions impose restraints; they do not allow unfettered pursuit of self-interest; they require accomplishment. Lack of self-control activates external controls, controls that are not applied to or felt by everyone, thus resulting in differences in attitude toward the school.

School performance also strongly predicts involvement in delinquent and criminal activities. Those who do well in school are unlikely to get into trouble with the law. This, too, supports the view of the school as a potentially successful training ground for the development of self-control. Students who like school and do well in it are likely to perceive a successful future and are thus susceptible to school sanctions (Stinchcombe 1964).

The crime and low self-control perspective organizes and explains most facts about the relation between schooling and crime, one of the staples of delinquency research. . . . For now, suffice it to say that self-control differences seem primarily attributable to family socialization practices. It is difficult for subsequent institutions to make up for deficiencies, but socialization is a task that, once successfully accomplished, appears to be largely irreversible.

The Stability Problem

Competent research regularly shows that the best predictor of crime is prior criminal behavior. In other words, research shows that differences between people in the likelihood that they will commit criminal acts persist over time.[3] This fact is central to our conception of criminality. In the next chapter we show how it calls into question the many theories of crime that depend on social institutions to create criminals from previously law-abiding citizens. For now, we briefly reconcile the fact of stability with the idea that desocialization is rare.

Combining little or no movement from high self-control to low self-control with the fact that socialization continues to occur throughout life produces the conclusion that the proportion of the population in the potential offender pool should tend to decline as cohorts age. This conclusion is consistent with research. Even the most active offenders burn out with time, and the documented number of "late-comers" to crime, or "good boys gone bad," is sufficiently small to suggest that they may be accounted for in large part by misidentification or measurement error. (This result is also consistent with Bentham's theory in that all sanction systems work against the possibility of lengthy careers in crime.) Put another way, the low self-control group continues over time to exhibit low self-control. Its size, however, declines.

Such stability of criminality is a staple of pragmatic criminology. The criminal justice system uses this fact in much the same way that educational institutions use prior academic performance to sort students and select personnel—that is, without much concern for the meaning of the variable. (A variant of the pragmatic response seeks to identify career criminals or high-rate offenders and thereby refine selection decisions, but here too nothing is usually said about what it is that produces long-standing differences in the level of involvement in crime [Blumstein et al. 1986].)

The traditional theoretical response denies stability and constructs theories that do not deal with "individual-level" variables. These theories automatically suggest that the causes of the "onset" of crime are not the same as the causes of "persistence" in crime. They also suggest that "desistance" from crime has unique causes. On analysis, however, most criminological theories appear to deal with onset and remain agnostic or silent on the persistence and desistence issues.

Thus no currently popular criminological theory attends to the stability of differences in offending over the life course. We are left with a paradoxical situation: a major finding of criminological research is routinely ignored or denied by criminological theory. After a century of research, crime theories remain inattentive to the fact that people differ in the likelihood that they will commit crimes and that these differences appear early and remain stable over much of the life course. Perhaps a major reason for ignoring the stability of low self-control is the assumption that other individual traits are stable and thereby account for apparently stable differences in criminal behavior. These are the so-called personality explanations of crime.

Personality and Criminality

Sociological criminology takes the position that no trait of personality has been shown to characterize criminals more than noncriminals (Sutherland and Cressey 1978: ch. 8). Psychological criminology takes the position that many personality traits have been shown to characterize criminals more than noncriminals (Wilson and Herrnstein 1985: ch. 7). We take the position that both views are wrong. The level of self-control, or criminality, distinguishes offenders from nonoffenders, and the degree of its presence or absence can be established before (and after) criminal acts have been committed. This enduring tendency is well within the meaning of "personality trait" and is thus contrary to the sociological view. Contrary to the psychological view, the evidence for personality differences between offenders and nonoffenders beyond self-control is, at best, unimpressive. Most of this evidence is produced by attaching personality labels to differences in rates of offending between offenders and nonoffenders—that is, by turning one difference into many.

For example, Wilson and Herrnstein (1985: ch. 7) report that delinquents score higher than nondelinquents on the following dimensions of personality (see also Herrnstein 1983):

1. "Q" scores on the Porteus Maze Tests.
2. Assertiveness.
3. Fearlessness.
4. Aggressiveness.
5. Unconventionality.
6. Extroversion.
7. Poor socialization.
8. Psychopathy.
9. Schizophrenia.
10. Hypomania.
11. Hyperactivity.
12. Poor conditionability.
13. Impulsiveness.
14. Lefthandedness.

All of these "personality" traits can be explained without abandoning the conclusion that offenders differ from nonoffenders only in their tendency to offend. One problem that has historically plagued personality research is the failure of its practitioners to report the content of their measuring instruments. This failure may be justified by the fact that the tests have commercial value, but the scientific result is the reporting of what are rightly considered "empirical tautologies," the discovery that two measures of the same thing are correlated with each other. In the present case, it seems fair to say that no one has found an independently measured personality trait substantially correlated with criminality. For example, the Minnesota Multiphasic Personality Inventory has three subscales said to distinguish between delinquents and nondelinquents. The major discriminator is the Psychopathic Deviate subscale. As Wilson and Herrnstein note, this subscale includes "questions about a respondent's past criminal behavior" (1985: 187). But if this is so, then scale scores obviously cannot be used to establish the existence of a trait of personality independent of the tendency to commit criminal acts.

The situation is the same with the socialization subscale of the California Personality Inventory. This subscale contains items indistinguishable from standard self-report delinquency items. That it is correlated with other measures of delinquency supports the unremarkable conclusion that measures of delinquency tend to correlate with one another. By the same token, a high score on the Q scale of the Porteus Maze Tests indicates subjects who frequently "break the rules by lifting his or her pencil from the paper, by cutting corners, or by allowing the pencil to drift out of the maze channels" (Wilson and Herrnstein 1985: 174). This measure is reminiscent of the measure of cheating developed by Hugh Hartshorne and Mark May (1928). That people who lie, cheat, and steal are more likely to cheat is not particularly instructive.

Earlier we examined the misleading suggestion that offenders can be usefully characterized as highly aggressive. Because measures of aggressiveness include many criminal acts, it is impossible to distinguish aggressiveness from criminality. . . . And so on through the list above. The measures of personality are either direct indicators of crime or conceptually indistinguishable from low self-control. Some, of course, are simply not supported by credible research (such as lefthandedness), and their continual reappearance should by now begin to undermine the credibility of psychological positivism.

The limited life of personality-based theories of crime is illustrated by the work of Hans Eysenck. He concluded that "persons with strong antisocial inclinations

[should] have high P, high E, and high N scores," where P is psychoticism, E is extraversion, and N is neuroticism (1964: 58). Eysenck provided detailed descriptions of persons scoring high on extraversion and psychoticism. For example, the extravert is "sociable, likes parties, has many friends, needs to have people to talk to, and does not like reading and studying by himself. . . . He prefers to keep moving and doing things, tends to be aggressive and loses his temper quickly; his feelings are not kept under tight control and he is not always a reliable person" (pp. 50–51). In contrast, the person scoring high on the P factor is "(1) solitary, not caring for other people; (2) troublesome, not fitting in; (3) cruel, inhumane; (4) lack of feeling, insensitive; (5) lacking in empathy; (6) sensation-seeking, avid for strong sensory stimuli; (7) hostile to others, aggressive; (8) [has a] liking for odd and unusual things; (9) disregard for dangers, foolhardy; (10) likes to make fools of other people and to upset them" (p. 58).

Although Eysenck is satisfied that research supports the existence of these dimensions and the tendency of offenders to score high on them (Eysenck 1989), many scholars (e.g., Rutter and Giller 1984) have not been convinced of the utility of Eysenck's personality scheme. (Wilson and Herrnstein do not include Eysenck's dimensions among the many personality traits they list.) In the current context, this scheme epitomizes the difficulties of the personality perspective (whatever the assumed source of personality differences) when applied to criminal behavior. In Eysenck's case, these difficulties are manifest in the obvious conceptual overlap of the personality dimensions and in the inability to measure them independently of the acts they are meant to produce.

The search for personality characteristics common to offenders has thus produced nothing contrary to the use of low self-control as the primary individual characteristic causing criminal behavior. People who develop strong self-control are unlikely to commit criminal acts throughout their lives, regardless of their other personality characteristics. In this sense, self-control is the only enduring personal characteristic predictive of criminal (and related) behavior. People who do not develop strong self-control are more likely to commit criminal acts, whatever the other dimensions of their personality. As people with low self-control age, they tend less and less to commit crimes; this decline is probably not entirely due to increasing self-control, but to age as well. . . .

NOTES

1. It is commonly observed (in an unsystematic way) that in an otherwise law-abiding family individual children are seriously delinquent. This observation is taken as evidence against family or child-rearing explanations of crime. (If the parents reared most of their children properly, how can their child-rearing practices be responsible for their delinquent children as well?) Such observations do not dispute the strong tendencies toward consistency within families mentioned in the text. They do suggest that family child-rearing practices are not the only causes of crime.

2. In subsequent chapters we emphasize the limited power of institutions to create self-control later in life when it has been therefore lacking. Our theory clearly argues, however, that it is easier to develop self-control among people lacking it than to undermine or destroy self-control among those possessing it. Consistent with this position, the data routinely show that preadolescents without behavior problems rarely end up with significant problems as adults (see, e.g., Robins 1966; Glueck and Glueck 1968).

3. We described the research documenting the stability of "aggression" in Chapter 3 [not reprinted here], and the research documenting the stability of "criminality" is discussed at length in Chapter 11 [not reprinted here] in reference to methodologies for studying crime and criminality.

REFERENCES

Bentham, Jeremy. 1970 [1789]. *An Introduction to the Principles of Morals and Legislation.* London: The Athlone Press.

Blumstein, Alfred, Jacqueline Cohen, Jeffery Roth, and Christy Visher. 1986. *Criminal Careers and "Career Criminals."* Washington, D.C.: National Academy Press.

Burgess, Robert L. 1980. "Family Violence: Implications from Evolutionary Biology." In *Understanding Crime,* edited by T. Hirschi and M. Gottfredson (pp. 91–101). Beverly Hills, Calif.: Sage.

Cloward, Richard, and Lloyd Ohlin. 1960. *Delinquency and Opportunity.* New York: The Free Press.

Eysenck, Hans. 1964. *Crime and Personality.* London: Routledge and Kegan Paul.

———. 1977. *Crime and Personality.* Rev. ed. London: Paladin.

———. 1989. "Personality and Criminality: A Dispositional Analysis." In *Advances in Criminological Theory,* edited by W. S. Laufer and F. Adler (pp. 89–110). New Brunswick, N.J.: Transaction.

Glueck, Sheldon, and Eleanor Glueck. 1950. *Unraveling Juvenile Delinquency.* Cambridge, Mass.: Harvard University Press.

———. 1968. *Delinquents and Nondelinquents in Perspective.* Cambridge, Mass.: Harvard University Press.

Gottfredson, Michael. 1984. *Victims of Crime: The Dimensions of Risk.* London: HMSO.

Gough, Harrison G. 1948. "A Sociological Theory of Psychopathy." *American Journal of Sociology,* 53: 359–66.

Hartshorne, Hugh, and Mark May. 1928. *Studies in the Nature of Character.* New York: Macmillan.

Herrnstein, Richard. 1983. "Some Criminogenic Traits of Offenders." In *Crime and Public Policy,* edited by J. Q. Wilson (pp. 31–52). San Francisco: Institute for Contemporary Studies.

Hindelang, Michael J. 1971. "Age, Sex, and the Versatility of Delinquent Involvements." *Social Problems,* 18: 522–35.

Hindelang, Michael, Travis Hirschi, and Joseph Weis. 1981. *Measuring Delinquency.* Beverly Hills, Calif.: Sage.

Hirschi, Travis. 1969. *Causes of Delinquency.* Berkeley: University of California Press.

Hirschi, Travis, and Michael. Gottfredson. 1986. "The Distinction Between Crime and Criminality." In *Critique and Explanation: Essays in Honor of Gwynne Nettler,* edited by T. F. Hartnagel and R. Silverman (pp. 55–69). New Brunswick, N.J.: Transaction.

Klein, Malcolm. 1984. "Offense Specialization and Versatility Among Juveniles." *British Journal of Criminology,* 24: 185–94.

Loeber, Rolf, and Magda Stouthamer-Loeber. 1986. "Family Factors as Correlates and Predictors of Juvenile Conduct Problems and Delinquency." In *Crime and Justice: An Annual Review of Research,* vol. 7, edited by M. Tonry and N. Morris (pp. 29–149). Chicago: University of Chicago Press.

McCord, Joan. 1979. "Some Child-Rearing Antecedents of Criminal Behavior in Adult Men." *Journal of Personality and Social Psychology,* 37: 1477–86.

McCord, William, and Joan McCord. 1959. *Origins of Crime: A New Evaluation of the Cambridge-Somerville Study.* New York: Columbia University Press.

Mednick, Sarnoff. 1977. "A Bio-social Theory of the Learning of Law-Abiding Behavior." In *Biosocial Bases of Criminal Behavior,* edited by S. Mednick and K. O. Christiansen (pp. 1–8). New York: Gardner.

Patterson, Gerald R. 1980. "Children Who Steal." In *Understanding Crime,* edited by T. Hirschi and M. Gottfredson (pp. 73–90). Beverly Hills, Calif.: Sage.

Petersilia, Joan. 1980. "Criminal Career Research: A Review of Recent Evidence." In *Crime and Justice: An Annual Review of Research,* vol. 2, edited by M. Tonry and N. Morris (pp. 321–79). Chicago: University of Chicago Press.

Riley, David, and Margaret Shaw. 1985. *Parental Supervision and Juvenile Delinquency.* Home Office Research Study no. 83. London: HMSO.

Robins, Lee. 1966. *Deviant Children Grown Up.* Baltimore: Williams and Wilkins.

Robins, Lee. 1978. "Aetiological Implications in Studies of Childhood Histories Relating to Antisocial Personality." In *Psychopathic Behavior,* edited by R. Hare and D. Schalling (pp. 255–71). New York: Wiley.

Rojek, Dean, and Maynard Erickson. 1982. "Delinquent Careers." *Criminology,* 20: 5–28.

Rutter, Michael, and Henri Giller. 1984. *Juvenile Delinquency: Trends and Perspectives.* New York: Guilford.

Sampson, Robert J. 1987. "Urban Black Violence: The Effect of Male Joblessness and Family Disruption." *American Journal of Sociology,* 93: 348–82.

Stinchcombe, Arthur. 1964. *Rebellion in a High School.* Chicago: Quadrangle.

Sutherland, Edwin, and Donald Cressey. 1978. *Principles of Criminology.* 10th ed. Philadelphia: Lippincott.

West, Donald, and David Farrington. 1973. *Who Becomes Delinquent?* London: Heinemann.

———. 1977. *The Delinquent Way of Life.* London: Heinemann.

Wilson, James Q., and Richard Herrnstein. 1985. *Crime and Human Nature.* New York: Simon and Schuster.

Wolfgang, Marvin, Robert Figlio, and Thorsten Sellin. 1972. *Delinquency in a Birth Cohort.* Chicago: University of Chicago Press.

Think Critically

1. Why is self-control so important in explaining criminality according to Gottfredson and Hirschi?
2. This theory purports, "all crime, at all times and in all places." That said, how does this theory explain the importance or effect of child-rearing in producing self control?

On the Absence of Self-Control as the Basis for a General Theory of Crime
A Critique*

Gilbert Geis**

IN THE FINAL SENTENCE OF *A GENERAL THEORY OF Crime,* Michael R. Gottfredson and Travis Hirschi note that they 'will be happy if our theory helps renew some intellectual interest in criminology, a field that once engaged the finest minds in the community' (Gottfredson and Hirschi, 1990: 275). Putting aside the arguable proposition that minds currently grappling with the subject of crime are less keen than those that tackled the subject in earlier years, the present critique of Gottfredson and Hirschi's work, seen beneficently, seeks to contribute to the ultimate happiness of the progenitors of what in disciplinary shorthand has come to be known as 'self-control theory.' Seen less benignly, this article raises a number of issues that, if I am correct, fatally undermine the logic and implications and, more specifically, the value of self-control theory.

For starters, we can juxtapose the dictum about theorizing by Richard Feynman, a Nobel Prize physicist, to the position taken by Hirschi on the same issue. Feynman insists that full disclosure is a prerequisite for the responsible promulgation of a theory:

> Details that could throw doubt upon your interpretation must be given, if you know them. You must do the best you can—if you know anything at all wrong, or

*From Gilbert Geis, *Theoretical Criminology* 4:1, pp. 35–53, copyright © 2000. Reprinted by permission of Sage Publications, Inc.
**I want to thank the following for their reviews of an earlier version of this article and to indicate that in no regard do they necessarily agree with the views I express: John Braithwaite, Frank Cullen, Gary Green, Ted Huston, Val Jenness, and Bob Meier. Richard Perry was instrumental in convincing me to turn a brief satire into a longer and more serious review of self-control theory.

possibly wrong—to explain it. If you make a theory
. . . then you must put down all the facts that disagree
with it.

(Feynman, 1985: 341)[1]

Compare this with Hirschi's position on the same matter:

A major mistake in my original oppositional comparison
of social control and social learning theory was to grant
a gap in control theory that might possibly be filled
by social learning theory. Almost immediately, hordes
of integrationist and social learning theorists began
to pour through the hole I had pointed out to them,
and control theory was to that extent subsequently
ignored. It was there that I learned the lesson . . . the
first purpose of oppositional theory construction is to
make the world safe for a theory contrary to currently
accepted views. Unless this task is accomplished, there
will be little hope for the survival of the theory and
less hope for its development. Therefore, oppositional
theories should not make life easy for those interested
in preserving the status quo. They should at all times
remain blind to the weaknesses of their own position
and stubborn in its defense.

(Hirschi, 1989: 45)

Hirschi's position lays a particular burden on critics that
the originators of self-control theory evade: to find, if
they exist, flaws in the formulation. We shall look at self-
control theory in regard to:

A. its definition of crime;

B. the matter of tautology;

C. its discussion of criminal law;

D. its inclusion of acts analogous to crimes;

E. exceptions to the theory;

F. the role played in the theory by the concept of
opportunity;

G. its views about specialization in criminal behavior;

H. its handling of the matter of aging;

 I. how it deals with white-collar crime;

J. research on the theory;

K. ideological issues; and

L. child-rearing and the theory.

Defining Crime

Gottfredson and Hirschi note that 'no theory of criminality has taken as its starting point a thorough examination
of the concept of crime' (1990: 23). They quote, only to
reject, the position of Wilson and Herrnstein, who have
written:

The word 'crime' can be applied to such varied
behavior that it is not clear that it is a meaningful
category of analysis. Stealing a comic book, punching
a friend, cheating on a tax return, murdering a wife,
robbing a bank, bribing a politician, hijacking an air-
plane—these and countless other acts are all crimes.
Crime is as broad a category as disease, and perhaps as
useless.

(Wilson and Herrnstein, 1985: 21)

For their part, Gottfredson and Hirschi say that 'we
intend our theory to apply to all these cases, and more. It is
meant to explain *all* crime, at all times, and, for that matter, many forms of behavior that are not sanctioned by the
state' (1990: 116; my italics). But only a few pages later
we are informed that there are crimes that are 'rare,' and
'complex,' and 'difficult,' and that therefore they offer 'an
inadequate basis for theory and policy' (1990: 119). So
much for the earlier idea that self-control theory explains
'all crime, at all times.' Nor is it accurate that only 'rare,'
'complex,' and 'difficult' (what precisely does 'difficult'
mean?) crimes fail to come within the theoretical embrace
of self-control theory. As I proceed I will offer samples of
a considerable roster of proscribed acts that are neither
complex nor difficult nor rare and yet which seem to have
little relationship to either the presence or the absence of
self-control.

Crime for Gottfredson and Hirschi is not to be
defined in strictly behavioral or legalistic terms because
one and the same act may be criminal in some contexts
and not in others (1990: 175). But research in Nigeria
would point out that self-control theory does not travel
well because it contains 'unacknowledged value assumptions' that 'undermine its claim to universality' (Marenin
and Reisig, 1995: 501).

There is also the interesting observation by Gottfredson and Hirschi that 'if a society defines an act as
criminal, our definition should be able to comprehend
the basis for that society's definition' (1990: 175). How,
for example, does self-control theory advance our understanding of legislative enactments that penalize some
drug usages and ignore others? Does the answer lie in the
Hirschi–Gottfredson formulation or is a more adequate
comprehension likely to emerge from a focus on power
relationships?

Gottfredson and Hirschi decide that the core characteristic of criminal behavior—its 'essential nature' (1990: xiv)—is that nearly all crimes are 'mundane, simple, trivial, easy acts aimed at satisfying desires of the moment' (1990: xiv–xv). They also insist that modern criminologists have rarely appreciated that 'various types of behavior—some criminal, some noncriminal—may have enough in common to justify treating them as the same thing' (1990: 53). While some crimes do appear to possess etiological similarities, many of the behaviors that Goffredson and Hirschi force under one rubric appear distinctive enough to require other kinds of explanations if we expect to be able to understand them and to predict their occurrence with some accuracy.

Gottfredson and Hirschi see criminal behavior as involving 'acts of force or fraud undertaken in the pursuit of self-interest' (1990: 14). This embraces an enormous spread of human activity, particularly if 'fraud' is viewed as the tendency to twist the truth to serve our own purposes. It seems reasonable to conclude that all human activity has self-interest at its base. Presumably any path in pursuit of our self-interest that is not absolutely honest is fraud.

Then Gottfredson and Hirschi add that criminal behaviors also provide 'immediate, easy, and certain short-term pleasure' (1990: 41). 'We are careful,' the authors note, 'to avoid an image of crime as a long-term, difficult, or drawn-out endeavor' (1990: 115). But what about law-breaking, such as many acts of kidnapping for ransom, that do not manifest these latter elements? Also, the 'certain' tag that they attach to short-term pleasure is puzzling. Few of us know with assurance the outcomes of many of our endeavors, short or long term. Is an act to be excluded from the theory's embrace if the pleasure it promises is not 'certain' or if the long-term consequences are far from assured, and, indeed, may never ensue?

Criminal acts are said to be 'exciting, risky or thrilling' (1990: 89), with the first and third conditions rather difficult to distinguish from each other. Presumably these characteristics of crime may be juxtaposed to the uneventful, safe, and boring behavior that denotes the acts of choice for those who demonstrate self-control. Criminal acts are also said often to produce 'pain or discomfort for the victim' (1990: 89). Such harmful consequences are believed by Gottfredson and Hirschi to be a matter of indifference to those with low self-control since they tend to be self-centered and insensitive to the needs of others.

But there are legions of noncriminal acts, beyond those casually listed by Gottfredson and Hirschi, in which such harm-inflicting indifference is manifest. Essentially what Gottfredson and Hirschi do is to list what they believe are the elements of criminal activity as well as the elements of low self-control and then to insist that the second causes the first—or, rather, that it tends to cause the first.

Some other criminological theories are critiqued by Gottfredson and Hirschi on the ground that they 'are betrayed by the assumption that crime is analogous to an occupation, a career, or an organized way of life' (1990: 161). Crime, it is said, is not a full-time job and takes little in the way of time and energy. Were crime to require such dedication, it would not be attractive to offenders (1990: 63). Tell that to, among others, embezzlers who refuse to take vacation time out of fear that their cooking of the books will be discovered.

Tautology and Self-Control Theory

Probably the most common criticism of Gottfredson and Hirschi's self-control theory is that it is tautological (see, for example, Akers, 1991; Meier, 1995), that is, to use a dictionary definition, it is characterized by a 'needless repetition of an idea . . . without imparting additional force or clearness' (Stein, 1969: 1456). '[I]t would appear to be tautological to explain the propensity to commit crime by low self-control,' Akers (1991: 204) observes. 'They are one and the same, and such assertions about them are true by definition. The assertion means that low self control causes low self control.' The tautological underpinning of self-control theory surfaces in statements by Gottfredson and Hirschi (1990: 87) such as their depiction of self-control as 'the differential tendency of people to avoid criminal acts whatever the circumstances in which they find themselves.'

Hirschi and Gottfredson (1993: 54), maintain, slyly, that this criticism is 'a compliment,' because it demonstrates that they 'followed the path of logic in producing an internally consistent result' (Hirschi and Gottfredson, 1993: 52). One can only hope that the authors allowed themselves a bit of a smile here, well aware of the taradillic nature of their position. A similar hope attaches to their observation that the fact that the 'apparently modest results' achieved in tests of their position 'may in fact be highly supportive of the validity of the theory' (Hirschi and Gottfredson, 1993: 48).

Criminal Law and Self-Control Theory

Disconcerting issues arise from the Gottfredson and Hirschi pronouncement that self-control theory stems from the 'essential nature' of criminal behavior (1990: xii). The most (and perhaps the only) common element of all criminal acts is that they are in violation of the law. Gottfredson and Hirschi maintain that law is but one of the many forces that inhibit or fail to inhibit criminal activity (1990: xv), and one that is no more and often less important than an array of other items, such as social values, moral codes, and the anticipated displeasure of family and friends. There is some wisdom in this position, but it falls short when what the law is proscribing is not a behavior that requires self-control to avoid but rather one rooted in morality.

The Gottfredson and Hirschi position also cannot explain satisfactorily significant hunks of human activity that are proscribed by penal codes. To cheat on income taxes is most unlikely to have long-term harmful consequences and will likely produce short-term gains. Crimes of omission (such as not registering for selective service during the war or failing to install safety equipment in a workplace) and those imposing strict liability also are an unmanageable explanatory fit with self-control theory. Other serious criminal acts that at best are arguably tied to an absence of self-control include terrorism conducted for political ends, campaign finance finagling, and call-girl prostitution to earn a satisfying livelihood. Note, for instance, Hoffman's (1998: 157) summary of the roots of terrorism in regard to matters of self-control: 'The wrath of the terrorist is rarely uncontrolled. Contrary to popular belief and media depiction, most terrorism is neither crazed nor capricious. Rather, terrorist attacks are generally both premeditated and carefully planned.'

Acts Analogous to Crimes

Crime, as we noted briefly earlier, is but one of a number of behaviors that Gottfredson and Hirschi attest can be explained satisfactorily by their theory. The theory is said to embrace events such as 'accidents, victimizations, truancies from home, school, and work, substance abuse, family problems, and disease' (1990: ix). Disease? Tell that to cancer victims with no history of smoking or other

apparent etiological precursors that reasonably can be tied to their own actions.

Empirical work also challenges the noncrime reach of Gottfredson and Hirschi's general theory when it departs from the penal codes. While lack of self-control was found to be related to gambling and drinking, it failed to differentiate smokers and nonsmokers. This result led Arneklev and his colleagues to suggest that 'the theory may not be as general as the authors think' (Arneklev et al., 1993: 244).

In the context of its excursion into acts said to be analogous to crime, Marenin and Reisig offer a particularly sage observation on self-control theory:

> Of course, this is not a theory of crime, but of imprudent or risk-taking behaviors. The theory explains bungee-jumping or skydiving as much as theft or rape. Whether behavior is criminal and condemned, or simply imprudent but admired is determined by social conventions and law.
>
> (Marenin and Reisig, 1995: 516)

There are other perplexing aspects of this extension of Gottfredson and Hirschi's formulation beyond crime. For one thing, it totally neglects what, for a very large number of persons, at least in the US, represents the quintessential absence of self-control: overeating. Should not overeaters be placed on the same short-term pleasure/long-term pain roster that is said to include both criminal acts and also a variety of noncriminal behaviors 'such as gambling, having sex, drinking alcohol, smoking cigarettes, and quitting a job' (1990: 178)? Moreover, how can the theory incorporate the uncounted number of criminal abortions undergone by women before the procedure was legalized by *Roe* v. *Wade* in 1973? (Reagan, 1993). Surely, it would be stretching matters greatly to maintain that the actions of women who opted for illegal abortions could be understood in terms of an absence of sufficient self-control.

Take another item on this roster of noncriminal matters. One of the entries is 'having sex.' In his earlier days Hirschi criticized Kingsley Davis for using the term 'sexual irregularities' (Davis, 1961: 284), a descriptor Hirschi found 'new and strangely vague' (Hirschi, 1973: 162). He and Gottfredson apparently intend 'having sex' to mean intercourse or a reasonable facsimile thereof, without the sanction of the state. But there must be a very large number of very passionate marital interludes that might be seen to demonstrate inadequate self-control. Are the marital orgies differentiated from nonmarital forms of 'having sex?' Or are we faced with a moral rather than a social scientific judgment? And is the singling out of 'the wife who has love affairs' to illustrate behavior engaged in without satisfactory consideration of long-term interests merely illustrative or is it meant to differentiate her situation from that of her mate?

Self-Control Theory and Its Exceptions

Gottfredson and Hirschi's self-control theory, as Reed and Yeager (1996: 359) observe, is probabilistic rather than deterministic. But how much need there be of a sometimes-result to justify treating diverse behaviors as the same?

The 'nearly' in the definition of crime by Gottfredson and Hirschi is a tactic that allows the authors a great deal of room to maneuver. They tend to have a strong tendency to employ the word 'tend' for the same purpose; thus, among innumerable other examples: '[O]ffenders . . . tend to be involved in accidents, illness, and death at higher rates than the general population; they tend to have difficulty persisting in a job regardless of the particular characteristics of the job' (1990: 94).

The difficulty with these equivocations lies in determining the tolerance to be allowed a theory that insists it has the right to claim that it is a 'general theory.' How many exceptions are to be permitted before the theory can be said to have been disconfirmed or falsified? Observe, in this regard, satirist Jonathan Swift's 18th-century depiction of how Brobdingnagian pedants resolved the question of a human exemplar who did not mesh with the regnant theoretical construct:

> He was then handed over for examination by the great scholars attending the court, who eventually agreed that he must be a '*lusus naturae*'—a freak of nature. Such a conclusion, reached after extensive empirical observation, mocks the pretensions of scientists who seek to explain the workings of the natural world. For in the face of a phenomenon that does not fit in with their preconceived ideas, the scholars make no attempt to revise their thinking, but only produce a meaningless formula that dismisses the phenomenon as an exception. The professors of Europe no longer rely on the supernatural to explain the apparently inexplicable,

but this does not mean that the theories they advance are any more logical or scientific than those of their forebears. They, like the Brobdingnagians, have developed the concept of the '*lusus naturae*' as a wonderful solution to all difficulties, to the unspeakable advancement of human knowledge.

(Swift, 1726: 143)[2]

The Opportunistic Use of 'Opportunity'

Gottfredson and Hirschi not only exempt from their general theory 'rare' matters that do not fit, they also include a variable of basic importance that they hardly make any effort to address systematically, but rather they use as a catchall refuge to explain what otherwise might be inexplicable. Their contemporary *lusus naturae*—the idea of opportunity—is employed to account for predictions based on their formulation that might fall short. To be useful a theory ought to be able to specify with some precision those 'opportunities' that will or will not trigger the allegedly latent trait that is claimed to 'cause' the criminal behavior. Opportunity apparently refers to the availability of a target and the possibility of criminally taking advantage of that availability. Admittedly, those without fingers will find it difficult to pick pockets and those without jobs will be unable to violate the antitrust laws. But the opportunity to steal, rape, and murder seems virtually ubiquitous: it is about as unproblematic as the ability to smoke or overeat. Gottfredson and Hirschi grant as much: 'criminal acts,' they note, 'require no special capabilities, needs or motivation; they are, in this sense, available to everyone' (1990: 88). They use this point to oppose learning theories: 'There is nothing in crime that requires the transmission of values or the support of other people . . . [or] the transmission of skills, or techniques, or knowledge from other people' (1990: 151), a statement followed a few pages later with the comment that 'some acts will be outside the repertoire of some offenders (since no direct learning of those acts has been available)' (1990: 156).

Note in this context the following observation:

> criminal acts are problematically related to the self-control of the actor: under some conditions people with low self-control may have few opportunities to commit crimes, and under other conditions people with high self-control may have many opportunities to commit them. If such people are mixed together in

the same sample, differences in opportunities to commit crime will be confounded with differences of self-control such that the researcher may mistake the influence of one for the effects of the other.

(1990: 219–20)

After this is the statement that '[t]he fact that crime is by all odds the major predictor of crime is central to our theory' (1990: 232). This fact somehow tells Gottfredson and Hirschi that low self-control is a 'unitary phenomenon that absorbs its causes' and that therefore 'the search for personality correlates of crime other than self-control is unlikely to bear fruit' (1990: 232). These remarks segue into the determination that short-term institutional experience (why only short-term?) such as treatment programs as well as jobs 'are incapable of producing any meaningful change in criminality' (1990: 232).

'In our view,' Gottfredson and Hirschi observe, 'lack of self-control does not require crime and can be counteracted by situational characteristics or other properties of the individual' (1990: 89). This is saying, in essence, that absence of self-control causes all crimes except those that it does not cause. And that the exceptions may be regarded as lying in a quite amorphous range of possibilities either within the social setting or within the person.

Are Criminals Polymorphously Perverse?

Gottfredson and Hirschi maintain that 'specialization in particular criminal acts' is 'contrary to fact' (1990: 77, 266) and that the forms that illegal acts take are interchangeable (1990: 21–2). Research indicates, however, that criminal offenders are not necessarily polymorphously perverse. It shows that the nature of their lawbreaking at any given time is not only a response to what is available when the self-control they allegedly failed to acquire before around the age of six or eight or so (1990: 272) (suddenly) prompts them into illegal action. Offenders often specialize.

The Gottfredson and Hirschi stress on the ubiquity of offending forms for all offenders again raises the question of how much specialization is necessary to render their categoric observation incorrect. 'Our portrait of the burglar applies equally well to the white-collar offender, the organized-crime offender, the dope dealer, and the assaulter; they are, after all, the *same* people,' Gottfredson

and Hirschi insist (1990: 74). 'They *seem* to do just *about* everything they can do: they do not specialize' (1990: 190; my italics). Benson and Moore (1992: 252) note that '[c]ontrary to the claim of Gottfredson and Hirschi, we find that those who commit even run-of-the-mill, garden-variety white-collar offenses, can, as a group, be distinguished from those who commit "ordinary street offenses".' Similarly, Wright et al. (1995) have argued that burglars are likely to *specialize* in that offense because they acquire expertise. Wright et al.'s (1995: 40) interviews with 47 active residential burglars showed 'strong evidence of technical and interpersonal skill and knowledge relevant to specific crime opportunities.'

Aging and Self-Control

Gottfredson and Hirschi scoff at the idea that 'maturational reform' lies at the heart of desistance from criminal activity as people age, calling it and other such concepts an 'unexplained process.' But one can search their writing in vain for a clear and convincing alternative explanation for why people learn to control their 'stable' absence of self-control. They maintain that other writers have 'confuse[d] change in crime (which declines [with age] with change in tendency to commit crime (which may not change at all)' (1990: 137, 144). But research findings advance the view that as they grow up some antisocial children strengthen their prosocial ties. Researchers also maintain that poor early behavior triggers hostile responses that feed into subsequent wrongdoing and that it is not the absence of self-control that is causative (Simons et al., 1998). '[Other theorists] are reluctant to acknowledge the idea of stable characteristics of the individual bearing on criminal behavior,' Gottfredson and Hirschi note critically (1990: 114). But how do you prove the existence of a trait that lies dormant?

Self-Control and White-Collar Crime

Theories such as that proposed by Gottfredson and Hirschi often have fallen prey to behavior that is defined as white-collar crime, namely, 'a crime committed by a person of respectability and high social status in the course of his occupation' (Sutherland, 1949: 9). Gottfredson and Hirschi sought to overcome this obstacle by insisting that white-collar crime is no different from any other form of crime and that its perpetrators also are marked by an absence of self-control (1990: 180–201; see also Hirschi and Gottfredson, 1987). They rely on the definition of the Yale studies of white-collar crime (see, for example, Weisburd et al., 1991) which examined a sample of 'white-collar criminals' that included, for instance, a female population in which one-third of the persons was unemployed (Daly, 1989).

Several major reviews of self-control theory and white-collar crime have demonstrated that its application to white-collar crime, defined as it traditionally has been, shows gaping holes. Reed and Yeager (1996: 359) point out that Gottfredson and Hirschi rely upon the Uniform Crime Reports (UCR), which provide what they regard as a faulty measure of white-collar crime, since it focuses only on acts that most resemble conventional law-breaking (see also Steffensmeier, 1989; Benson and Moore, 1992; Curran and Renzetti, 1994: 216–18) for a differing view on corporate crime and self-control (see Herbert et al., 1998). To say that an absence of self-control prods the decisions of top-level business officers who violate the law is to trivialize the roots of their actions. As Jamieson (1994: 216–18) has observed: 'The complexities behind decisions of corporate executives to engage in illegal behaviors cannot be overestimated.' But they may be underestimated.

Finally, we might note a study of savings and loan swindles that concluded that what it learned 'moves in exactly the opposite direction to Gottfredson and Hirschi's theoretical position by suggesting that many forms of white-collar crime are not reducible to individuals and their characteristics, but are embedded in large institutional and organizational arrangements' (Tillman and Pontell, 1995: 1459).

Research on Self-Control Theory

There has emerged a flourishing criminological cottage industry that has seized upon self-control theory as a research topic. A researcher defines self-control, locates this or that sample, and then determines the relationship between self-control and criminal activity and/or some of the cognate behaviors specified in the general theory.

The research that has been published to date on social control theory finds pretty much what the initial reviewers of the Gottfredson and Hirschi book presumed they would find. Grasmick et al. (1993), for instance, used a survey instrument on Oklahoma City adults to measure self-control, found 'inconsistencies,' and noted that 'criminal opportunity has a significant main effect.' 'The [self-control] theory,' they concluded 'is in need of modification and expansion' (Grasmick et al., 1993: 22). A notably sophisticated analysis of National Youth Survey data by Greenberg et al. (forthcoming) found that the results suggested that, contrary to Gottfredson and Hirschi's thesis, 'different kinds of delinquent/criminal or risky behaviors have distinct causes.'

To determine whether self-control relates to differences in crime by gender, Burton et al. (1998) introduced a curious measure of opportunity—'the number of evenings per week you go out for recreation activities.' Though they find their results 'largely consistent' with self-control theory, they grant that their measure of opportunity is at best 'limited' and probably has little to do with, say, work-related crimes and income tax evasions. They conclude, inconclusively, that the theory has 'implications' for understanding gender-related differentials (see also Cochran et al., 1998; LaGrange and Silverman, 1999). It seems a rather long stretch to self-control from evenings out; and in many ways the Burton et al. (1998) research illustrates the problems likely to arise in an attempt to prove or disprove the Gottfredson and Hirschi postulates.

There also have been attempts to determine through questionnaires given to university students whether parental behavior is a 'primary' influence on the development of a child's self-control, using self-report data on class absenteeism, academic cheating, and alcohol consumption as the measures of aberrance. The results offer 'modest support.' That the support is not stronger is self-effacingly credited by the authors to the fact that 'our particular methods may be a source of particular error' (Gibbs et al., 1998: 40, 65; see also Longshore, 1998).

The research reports almost invariably include disclaimers that are strikingly similar. Typically, the authors apologize for the shortcomings of their measurement items (e.g. Arneklev et al., 1993), and include a caveat about their results: (my research 'should in no way be regarded as a complete and definitive test' [Brownfield and Sorenson, 1993: 259]), and then point out that, just because they found the theory wanting, the reader should not conclude that it truly lacks scientific strength. They then offer a boilerplate observation that more and better research is essential before the truth of the matter can be ascertained.

Gottfredson and Hirschi offer one of many hypotheses that might be tested: 'Holding propensity constant,' they write, 'communities in which schools enforce attendance rules would be expected to have lower crime rates than communities in which such rules were ignored' (1990: 252). It is not clear how one goes about 'holding propensity constant.' There also are many alternative plausible hypotheses that might well explain why one school and not another enforces its truancy rules. Many of these other explanations could provide an understanding of what we can presume will be slight variations in crime rates, if all other matters are similar, the last a most unlikely condition. Apparently no one, including Gottfredson and Hirschi, has seized upon this research suggestion.

The body of research about self-control theory can be summarized rather readily by noting that researchers typically find that there is a better-than-average chance that persons who commit traditional kinds of criminal acts lack self-control, however defined. They also find that there are many persons who do not fit the criteria that have been used to determine low self-control but who violate the law, and smoke, gamble, and have illicit sex as well as having children out of wedlock (see, for example, Burton, Jr, et al., 1999). The published articles lustily debate the adequacy of diverse measures of self-control and other inquiry tactics, but nobody bothers to examine the theory in terms of logic and commonsense before launching upon the operationalization of the concepts and the testing. What we see going on in regard to self-control theory today meshes with the title of an article bearing on an altogether different subject: 'Ours is Not to Question Why, Ours is to Quantify' (Heiman, 1997).

Gottfredson and Hirschi's main reservation about studies that seek empirical data on their theory seems to involve the manner in which the investigators define self-control. Their preference, they observe, would be for behavioral measures, such as whether persons fasten their seat belts (Keane et al., 1993), rather than responses to personality and attitudinal surveys. But Evans et al. (1997: 495) note of such measures that it would not be clear 'whether self-control is predicting crime or whether behaviors similar in nature (analogous and criminal) are merely predicting each other.'

'Fads and fashions of research design in criminology come and go,' Gottfredson and Hirschi point out in their critique of longitudinal methods (1990: 252). The same observation can be made in regard to theoretical statements. Typically, the deteriorating fate of a theory once regnant is not the product of falsification by research: that the theory falls far short of its grandiose claims is usually evident from the beginning. In time, there develops an element of weariness, a kind of ennui, that begins to descend upon the threshers in the subdisciplinary field, often accompanied by the appearance of another theoretical contender. Attention then turns to the newcomer, an entrant that traditionally either seeks to amalgamate earlier views or to set off on a totally different path. Cumulative refinement of earlier positions has been markedly absent from criminological theorizing.

Ideological Issues in Self-Control Theory

Notice also might be taken of elements in the Gottfredson—Hirschi presentation that seem to sacrifice logic at the altar of ideology. All theories, of course, carry with them implicit or explicit ideological offspring, but it is essential that the ideological and the policy recommendations be tied in a reasonable fashion to the theory. So unanchored at times is its ideological element that adherents to the full sweep of the Gottfredson and Hirschi presentation might well be positioned in that cadre demarcated by Justice Holmes: 'Proper geese following their propaganda' (Howe, 1957: 25).

Note, for instance, the following statement:

> We see little hope for important reductions in crime through modification of the criminal justice system. We see considerable hope in policies that would reduce the role of the state and return responsibility for crime control to ordinary citizens.
>
> (Gottfredson and Hirschi, 1990: xvi)

First, let us attend to the phrase 'important reductions.' How 'important' are the decreases that now *keep* showing up in UCR-reported offenses. While they may not altogether represent the efforts of the criminal justice system, they are inordinately unlikely to be the product of the inculcation of additional self-control in their children by parents. The 'ordinary' in 'ordinary citizens' (who exactly are the extraordinary citizens?) in the quotation is, of course, an ideological buzz-word (see Geis, 1994). How such ordinary citizens would exercise their crime control responsibility, considered in terms of public opinion today regarding issues such as the death penalty, Megan's law, and three-strikes, would seem to suggest at least some deeper soul-searching before such uninflected pronouncements are placed into a scientific treatise. Equally ideological and disturbing is the 'theoretically derived' insistence that 'policies that seek to reduce crime by the satisfaction of theoretically derived wants (e.g. equality, adequate housing, good jobs, self-esteem) are likely to be unsuccessful' (1990: 256). Even if self-control were at the root of criminal acts, it would seem much more sensible to view such things as a lousy job and inadequate housing as conditions that would bear upon frustration and absence of self-control.

In addition, scholars seeking explanations for variations in racial differences in rates of crime, Gottfredson and Hirschi maintain, should not pursue 'fruitless' paths that ascribe such differences to culture or strain but should focus on 'differential child-rearing practices' (1990: 153). It is not poverty, not discrimination, not absence of equal opportunity, but poor parenting that must bear the blame for the striking distinction in levels of criminal behavior when looked at in terms of the perpetrators' race. To test the theory, they suggest, efforts need to be made to relate such behaviors as 'whining, pushing, and shoving (as a child)' to later criminal acts, a strange task at best and a curious one given the authors' intellectual antagonism to longitudinal inquiries (1990: 220–40).

Child-Rearing and Self-Control

For Gottfredson and Hirschi '[t]he major cause of low self-control . . . appears to be ineffective child-rearing' (1990: 97), though an escape hatch is opened thereafter: 'family child-rearing practices are not the only causes of crime' (1990: 101).

The cure for crime involves training adults, though 'not . . . in one or another of the various academic treatment disciplines' (an odd aside). The adults 'need only learn the requirements of early childhood socialization, namely to watch for and recognize signs of low self-control and to punish them' (1990: 269). To produce 'enduring consequences' the focus of crime control must be on 'parents or adults with responsibilities for child-rearing' (1990: 269).

We learn that some parents of children with low self-control are 'lucky,' that their children will not turn into criminals, though it is likely that such children will do something else indicative of low self-control. 'Put another way,' the authors observe sagely, 'low self-control predicts low self-control better than it predicts any of its specific manifestations' (1990: 102). There will be few who will argue with this statement, though they might regard it as somewhat less than altogether profound.

Conclusion

A famous scientist once observed that nothing is more tragic than the murder of a grand theory by a little fact. But he hastened to add that nothing is more surprising than the way in which a theory will continue to survive long after its brains have been knocked out (Thomas, 1960). Palumbo (1992: 538), writing about the considerable number of studies seeking to examine self-control theory, notes that their authors often feel pressed 'to perform wondrous mental gymnastics' (or, in Tittle's (1991: 1610) phrase, 'intellectual contortions') to reconcile theory and reality, 'to explain away much of the research that is incompatible with their theory.' Tittle (1991: 1611), in fact, quite correctly maintains that 'with a little modification, the self-control theory could readily accommodate the idea that strong, as well as weak, self-control can lead to force and fraud in the service of self-interest.' Gibbons (1994: 194) believes that self-control is 'a general theory of some instances of some forms of crime,' a view shared by Polk (1991: 576) who concluded that 'too much of crime falls outside the boundaries of their definition for this theory to be of much use' and that there is a 'general tendency that is true throughout the book for the authors to shape the facts of crime so that these fit conveniently into the patterns consistent with the theory' (Polk, 1991: 577). Perhaps this is why the eminent physical anthropologist Mary Leakey preferred field work in the hot African sun to theorizing in the shade. 'Theories come and go,' she maintained, 'but fundamental data always remain the same' (Golden, 1996: 33).

General theorizing, as represented by the social control concept, faces a basic question: How much variance can the theory explain? Longshore (1998: 102) observes, for instance, that research testing self-control theory shows the variance explained to be 'modest'—between 3 and 11 percent.

We would endorse Gibbs' (1987: 830) observation that '[e]ach theory should be limited to one type of crime if only because it is unlikely that any etiological or reactive variable is relevant for all crimes'. Gibbons (1994: 196–7) echoes this observation: 'If we take seriously the claim that criminology deals with lawbreaking in all of its forms, we may well discover that the more modest goal of developing a "family of theories" makes the greatest sense for the criminological enterprise.'

Some shrewd observers of social behavior have concluded that a general theory is possible neither in regard to human acts nor to so broad a category as criminal behavior. 'The wish to establish a natural science of society, which would possess the same sort of logical structure and pursue the same achievements as the science of nature probably remains, in the English-speaking world at least, the dominant standpoint today,' Giddens (1976: 13) has observed. 'But those who are waiting for a [social science] Newton are not only waiting for a train that won't arrive; they're in the wrong station altogether' (1976: 13).

I presume that self-control theory in due time will join the now-crowded cohort of vainglorious efforts in whatever place is reserved for such endeavors. Let it be noted, in conclusion, that while Gottfredson and Hirschi adhere admirably to Einstein's dictum that 'the supreme goal of all theory is to make the irreducible basic elements as simple and as few as possible,' they fail to come anywhere near meeting the second element of Einstein's blueprint for a satisfactory theory: the simple and few elements of the theoretical construct, he observed, must be enunciated 'without having to surrender the adequate representation of a single datum of experience' (Einstein, 1933: 10–11).

NOTES

1. Complementing Feynman's view is that of Charles Darwin who noted how quickly he tended to forget any fact that seemed to contradict his theories. Darwin therefore made it a 'golden rule' to write down such information so that he would not later overlook it (Darwin, 1958/1856: 123).

2. Swift was not alone in addressing this issue satirically. The Frenchman Alfred Jarry (1923), an "extremely odd character" (Tomkins, 1996: 70), in a posthumously published book, has a Dr Faustroll invent "pataphysics," a new science dealing with the laws that govern exceptions. Science's so called laws, Jarry proclaimed, are simply exceptions that occur more frequently than others.

REFERENCES

Akers, Ronald L. (1991) 'Self-Control as a General Theory of Crime,' *Journal of Quantitative Criminology* 7(2): 201–11.

Arneklev, Bruce J., Harold G. Grasmick, Charles R. Tittle and Robert J. Bursik, Jr. (1993) 'Low Self-Control and Imprudent Behavior,' *Journal of Quantitative Criminology* 9(3): 225–47.

Benson, Michael L. and Elizabeth Moore (1992) 'Are White-Collar and Common Offenders the Same? An Empirical and Theoretical Critique of a Recently Proposed General Theory of Crime,' *Journal of Research in Crime and Delinquency* 29(2): 251–72.

Brownfield, David and Ann-Marie Sorenson (1993) 'Self-Control and Juvenile Delinquency: Theoretical Issues and an Empirical Assessment of Selected Elements of a General Theory of Crime,' *Deviant Behavior* 14(3): 243–64.

Burton, Velmer S., Jr, Francis T. Cullen, T. David Evans, Leanne Fiftal Alarid and R. Gregory Dunaway (1998) 'Gender, Self-Control, and Crime,' *Journal of Research in Crime and Delinquency* 35(2): 123–47.

Burton, Velmer S., Jr, T. David Evans, Francis T. Cullen, Kathleen M. Olivares and R. Gregory Dunaway (1999) 'Age, Self-Control, and Adults' Offending Behaviors: A Research Note Assessing *A General Theory of Crime,' *Journal of Criminal Justice* 27(1): 45–54.

Cochran, John K., Peter B. Wood, Christine S. Sellers, Wendy Wilkerson and Michelle B. Chamlin (1998) 'Academic Dishonesty and Low Self-Control: An Empirical Test of General Theory of Crime,' *Deviant Behavior* 19(3): 227–55.

Curran, Daniel J. and Claire M. Renzetti (1994) *Theories of Crime.* Boston, MA: Allyn & Bacon.

Daly, Kathleen (1989) 'Gender and Varieties of White-Collar Crime,' *Criminology* 27(4): 769–93.

Darwin, Charles (1856)/(1958) *The Autobiography of Charles Darwin, 1809–1882,* edited by Nora Barlow. London: Collins.

Davis, Kingsley (1961) 'Prostitution,' in Robert K. Merton and Robert A. Nisbet (eds) *Contemporary Social Problems,* pp. 262–88. New York: Harcourt, Brace & World.

Einstein, Albert (1933) *On the Method of Theoretical Physics.* New York: Oxford University Press.

Evans, T. David, Francis T. Cullen, Velmer E. Burton, Jr, R. Gregory Dunaway and Michael L. Benson (1997) 'The Social Consequences of Self-Control Theory,' *Criminology* 35(3): 475–501.

Feynman, Richard (1985) *'Surely You're Joking, Mr Feynman?': Adventures of a Curious Character.* New York: W.W. Norton.

Geis, Gilbert (1994) 'Moral Innatism, Connatural Ideas, and Impuissance in Daily Affairs: James Q. Wilson's Acrobatic Dive into an Empty Pool,' *Criminal Justice Ethics* 13(2): 78–82.

Gibbons, Don C. (1994) *Talking About Crime and Criminals: Problems and Issues in Theory Development in Criminology.* Englewood Cliffs, NJ: Prentice-Hall.

Gibbs, Jack (1987) 'The State of Criminological Theory,' *Criminology* 25(4): 821–40.

Gibbs, John J., Dennis Giever and James S. Martin (1998) 'Parental Management and Self-Control: An Empirical Test of Gottfredson and Hirschi's General Theory,' *Journal of Research in Crime and Delinquency* 35(1): 40–70.

Giddens, Anthony (1976) *New Rules of Sociological Method: A Positive Critique of Interpretative Sociologies.* London: Hutchinson.

Golden, Frederic (1996) 'First Lady of Fossils,' *Time* (23 December): 33.

Gottfredson, Michael R. and Travis Hirschi (1990) *A General Theory of Crime.* Stanford, CA: Stanford University Press.

Grasmick, Harold G., Charles R. Tittle, Robert J. Bursik, Jr. and Bruce J. Arneklev (1993) 'Testing the Core Empirical Implications of Gottfredson and Hirschi's General Theory of Crime,' *Journal of Research in Crime and Delinquency* 30(1): 5–29.

Greenberg, David F., Robin Tamarelli and Margaret Kelley (forthcoming) 'The Generality of the Gottfredson–Hirschi *General Theory of Crime,' Advances in Criminological Theory.*

Heiman, Michael K. (1997) 'Ours is Not to Question Why, Ours is to Quantify,' *Journal of Planning Education and Research* 16(4): 301–3.

Herbert, Carey L., Gary S. Green and Victor Larragoite (1998) 'Clarifying the Reach of *A General Theory of Crime* for Organizational Offenders: A Comment on Reed and Yeager,' *Criminology* 36(1): 101–17.

Hirschi, Travis (1973) 'Procedural Rules and the Study of Deviant Behavior,' *Social Problems* 21(2): 159–73.

Hirschi, Travis (1989) 'Exploring Alternatives to Integrated Theory,' in Steven E. Messner, Marvin D. Krohn, and Allen E. Liska (eds) *Theoretical Integration in the Study of Deviance and Crime: Problems and Perspectives,* pp. 37–49. Albany, NY: State University of New York Press.

Hirschi, Travis and Michael Gottfredson (1987) 'Causes of White-Collar Crime,' *Criminology* 25(1): 949–74.

Hirschi, Travis and Michael Gottfredson (1993) 'Commentary: Testing the General Theory of Crime,' *Journal of Research on Crime and Delinquency.* 30: 47–54.

Hirschi, Travis and Michael Gottfredson (1995) 'Control Theory and the Life-Course Perspective,' *Studies on Crime and Crime Prevention: Annual Review* 4: 131–42.

Hoffman, Bruce (1998) *Inside Terrorism.* New York: Columbia University Press.

Howe, Mark DeWolfe (1957) *Justice Oliver Wendell Holmes: The Shaping Years, 1841–1870.* Cambridge: Harvard University Press.

Jamieson, Katherine M. (1994) *The Organization of Corporate Crime: Dynamics of Antitrust Violations.* Thousand Oaks, CA: Sage.

Jarry, Alfred (1923) *Gestes et Opinions du Docteur Faustroll Pataphysicien.* Paris: Stock.

Keane, Carl, Paul S. Maxim and James J. Teevan (1993) 'Drinking and Driving, Self-Control and Gender: Testing a General Theory of Crime,' *Journal of Research in Crime and Delinquency* 30(1): 30–46.

LaGrange, Teresa C. and Robert A. Silverman (1999) 'Low Self-Control and Opportunity: Testing the General Theory of Crime as an Explanation for Gender Differences in Delinquency,' *Criminology* 37(1): 41–72.

Lilly, J. Robert, Francis T. Cullen and Richard A. Ball (1995) *Criminological Theory: Context and Consequences,* 2nd edn. Thousand Oaks, CA: Sage.

Longshore, Douglas (1998) 'Self-Control and Criminal Opportunity: A Prospective Test of the General Theory of Crime,' *Social Problems* 45(1): 102–13.

Marenin, Otwin and Michael D. Reisig (1995) '*A General Theory of Crime:* Patterns of Crime in Nigeria: An Explanation of Methodological Assumptions,' *Journal of Criminal Justice* 23(6): 501–18.

Meier, Robert F. (1995) 'Book Review,' *Social Forces* 73: 1627–9.

Palumbo, Dennis (1992) 'Review of *A General Theory of Crime,*' *American Political Science Review* 86(2): 537–8.

Polk, Kenneth (1991) '*A General Theory of Crime* by Michael R. Gottfredson and Travis Hirschi,' *Crime and Delinquency* 37(4): 575–9.

Reagan, Leslie J. (1993) *When Abortion Was a Crime: Women, Medicine, and Law in the United States, 1867–1973.* Berkeley, CA: University of California Press.

Reed, Gary E. and Peter C. Yeager (1996) 'Organizational Offending and Neoclassical Criminology: Challenging the Reach of *A General Theory of Crime,*' *Criminology* 34(3): 357–82.

Simons, Ronald L., Christine Johnson, Rand D. Conger and Glen Elder, Jr (1998) 'A Test of Latent Traits Versus Life-Course Perspectives on the Stability of Adolescent Antisocial Behavior,' *Criminology* 36: 217–43.

Steffensmeier, Darrell (1989) 'On the Causes of "White-Collar Crime": An Assessment of Hirschi and Gottfredson's Claims,' *Criminology* 27(2): 345–58.

Stein, Jess (ed.) (1969) *Random House Dictionary of the English Language: The Unabridged Edition.* New York: Random House.

Sutherland, Edwin H. (1949) *White Collar Crime.* New York: Dryden.

Swift, Jonathan (1726)/(1967) *Gulliver's Travels*. Baltimore, MD: Penguin.

Thomas, Helen (1960) *Felix Frankfurter: Scholar on the Bench*. Baltimore, MD: Johns Hopkins University Press.

Tillman, Robert and Henry Pontell (1995) 'Organizations and Fraud in the Savings and Loan Industry,' *Social Forces* 73(4): 1439–63.

Tittle, Charles R. (1991) 'Book Review,' *American Journal of Sociology* 96(6): 1609–11.

Tomkins, Calvin (1996) *Duchamp: A Biography*. New York: Holt.

Weisburd, David, Stanton Wheeler, Elin Waring and Nancy Bode (1991) *Crimes of the Middle Class: White-Collar Offending in the Federal Courts*. New Haven, CT: Yale University Press.

Wilson, James Q. and Richard J. Herrnstein (1985) *Crime and Human Nature*. New York: Simon & Schuster.

Wright, Richard, Robert H. Logie and Scott Decker (1995) 'Criminal Expertise and Offender Decision Making: An Experimental Study of the Target Selection Process in Residential Burglary,' *Journal of Research in Crime and Delinquency* 32(1): 39–53.

Think Critically

1. One of the most common criticisms of self-control theory is that it is tautological in nature. That is, it involves "the needless repetition of an idea." How do Geis and others relate this idea to the theory, and do you think that they are correct? Explain why or why not.

2. Grand theorizing in the social sciences almost invariably has conceptual weaknesses. Do you feel that the criticisms noted by Geis are fair? Are his conclusions justified by the various points he raises as to the shortcomings he claims are inherent to the self-control theory of criminality?

FEMINISM

DURING THE LAST DECADE, FEMINIST scholarship has expanded throughout many disciplines, including the areas of criminology and deviance theory. Feminism generally refers to the idea that women experience subordination on the basis of their sex. Feminist scholars are interested in understanding the origins and ramifications of this inequality. While there are different strains of feminist theory found in the literature, researchers usually relate their work to male-dominated institutions in order to discover patterns of sexual bias. As far as deviance theory is concerned, women have been largely ignored, both in past theorizing and research. When they were included, their importance and roles were essentially trivialized. This situation is changing as scholars turn their attention to issues of female deviance and crime, victimization, and the treatment of women by formal institutions of social control.

In "Girls' Crime and Woman's Place," Meda Chesney-Lind, a leading feminist scholar in the field of deviance and crime, argues that existing theories of deviance and delinquency are inadequate for explaining female delinquency and official reactions to girls' deviance. By reviewing the available evidence on female offending, she cites the need for a feminist model of female delinquency. The juvenile justice system is found to be a major force in women's oppression, as it has historically served to reinforce obedience to the demands of patriarchal authority. Chesney-Lind calls for increased research into female delinquency and the reactions of social control institutions to such behavior in order to develop theories that are sensitive to the context of patriarchy.

Ryan Bishop and Lillian S. Robinson discuss the nature of international commercial sex in Thailand in their piece, "In the Night Market." Taken from a book on the topic, the authors conducted extensive fieldwork to examine the structural and personal dimensions of the profitable and popular sex tourist industry. They characterize the experiences of customers and workers in terms of "international sexual alienation," which is part of a larger system of "totalizing alienation," under which both industrialized sexuality and industrialized leisure exist. They conclude that understanding sexual alienation as a system helps explain the purchase of sex as a commodity, including both the appeal and popularity of such activity.

In the article, "On the Backs of Working Prostitutes," Annette Jolin uses feminist theory to examine major issues related to prostitution policy. Her analysis explores why prostitution remains as controversial as it was 4000 years ago, why feminists are involved in the controversy, and what effects this controversy has on working prostitutes. Looking at the historical record, Jolin argues that answers can be found in the institutionalized sexual double standard of Western patriarchal societies and economic arrangements involving promiscuity, chastity, and inequality. She concludes that prostitution theories do not adequately address the actual problems experienced by prostitutes and calls for a new feminist synthesis that addresses both rights to choose and rights to protection.

"Appearance and Delinquency" by Jill Leslie Rosenbaum and Meda Chesney-Lind, is another example of the new feminist scholarship in the field of deviance. Focusing on official reactions to female deviants, this novel study finds that culturally derived standards of attractiveness are used in determining the treatment women receive in the criminal justice system. Using data from the California Youth Authority, Rosenbaum and Chesney-Lind find that a variety of physical descriptions regarding appearance and attractiveness was mentioned in official files. This was more likely to be the case for those charged with immorality. The study provides an interesting glimpse of the world view of those who process female offenders and presents evidence that officials may look upon attractive girls who engage in sexual "immorality" more harshly.

In the article "Identity, Strategy, and Feminist Politics," Patricia Gagné examines the impact of feminist activism on the decision to grant clemency to women incarcerated for killing or assaulting abusive intimate partners or stepfathers. Identifying the tactics and strategies employed by the feminist battered women's movement, she finds that incarcerated battered women used their careers and personal relationships to form consciousness-raising groups in prison that established a social movement community that gained access to authorities and the public. Gagne discusses how feminists created an opportunity structure resulting in clemency, as well as what strategies and tactics other social movements need to consider in hostile cultural and political environments.

Girls' Crime and Woman's Place
Toward a Feminist Model of Female Delinquency*

Meda Chesney-Lind

I ran away so many times. I tried anything, man, and they wouldn't believe me. . . . As far as they are concerned they think I'm the problem. You know, runaway, bad label. (Statement of a 16-year-old girl who, after having been physically and sexually assaulted, started running away from home and was arrested as a "runaway" in Hawaii.)

You know, one of these days I'm going to have to kill myself before you guys are gonna listen to me. I can't stay at home. (Statement of a 16-year-old Tucson runaway with a long history of physical abuse [Davidson, 1982, p. 26].)

Who is the typical female delinquent? What causes her to get into trouble? What happens to her if she is caught? These are questions that few members of the general public could answer quickly. By contrast, almost every citizen can talk about "delinquency," by which they generally mean male delinquency, and can even generate some fairly specific complaints about, for example, the failure of the juvenile justice system to deal with such problems as "the alarming increase in the rate of serious juvenile crime" and the fact that the juvenile courts are too lenient on juveniles found guilty of these offenses (Opinion Research Corporation, 1982).

This situation should come as no surprise since even the academic study of delinquent behavior has, for all intents and purposes, been the study of male delinquency. "The delinquent is a rogue male" declared Albert Cohen

(1955, p. 140) in his influential book on gang delinquency. More than a decade later, Travis Hirschi, in his equally important book entitled *The Causes of Delinquency,* relegated women to a footnote that suggested, somewhat apologetically, that "in the analysis that follows, the 'non-Negro' becomes 'white,' and the girls disappear."

This pattern of neglect is not all that unusual. All areas of social inquiry have been notoriously gender-blind. What is perhaps less well understood is that theories developed to describe the misbehavior of working- or lower-class male youth fail to capture the full nature of delinquency in America; and, more to the point, are woefully inadequate when it comes to explaining female misbehavior and official reactions to girls' deviance.

To be specific, delinquent behavior involves a range of activities far broader than those committed by the stereotypical street gang. Moreover, many more young people than the small visible group of "troublemakers" that exist on every intermediate and high school campus commit some sort of juvenile offense and many of these youth have brushes with the law. One study revealed, for example, that 33% of all the boys and 14% of the girls born in 1958 had at least one contact with the police before reaching their 18th birthday (Tracy Wolfgang, and Figlio, 1985, p. 5). Studies that solicit from youth themselves the volume of their delinquent behavior consistently confirm that large numbers of adolescents engage in at least some form of misbehavior that could result in their arrest. As a consequence, it is largely trivial misconduct, rather than the

*From Meda Chesney-Lind, *Crime and Delinquency,* vol. 35, No. 1, pp. 5–29, copyright © 1989 by Sage Publications, Inc. Reprinted by permission of Sage Publications, Inc.

commission of serious crime, that shapes the actual nature of juvenile delinquency. One national study of youth aged 15–21, for example, noted that only 5% reported involvement in a serious assault, and only 6% reported having participated in a gang fight. In contrast, 81% admitted to having used alcohol, 44% admitted to having used marijuana, 37% admitted to having been publicly drunk, 42% admitted to having skipped classes (truancy), 44% admitted having had sexual intercourse, and 15% admitted to having stolen from the family (McGarrell and Flanagan, 1985, p. 363). Clearly, not all of these activities are as serious as the others. It is important to remember that young people can be arrested for all of these behaviors . . .

Examining the types of offenses for which youth are actually arrested, it is clear that again most are arrested for the less serious criminal acts and status offenses. Of the one and a half million youth arrested in 1983, for example, only 4.5% of these arrests were for such serious violent offenses as murder, rape, robbery, or aggravated assault (McGarrell and Flanagan, 1985, p. 479). In contrast, 21% were arrested for a single offense (larceny theft) much of which, particularly for girls, is shoplifting (Shelden and Horvath, 1986).

Table 1 presents the five most frequent offenses for which male and female youth are arrested, and from this it can be seen that while trivial offenses dominate both male and female delinquency, trivial offenses, particularly status offenses, are more significant in the case of girls' arrests; for example, the five offenses listed in Table 1 account for nearly three-quarters of female offenses and only slightly more than half of male offenses.

More to the point, it is clear that, though routinely neglected in most delinquency research, status offenses play a significant role in girls' official delinquency. Status offenses accounted for about 25.2% of all girls' arrests in 1986 (as compared to 26.9% in 1977) and only about 8.3% of boys' arrests (compared to 8.8% in 1977). These figures are somewhat surprising since dramatic declines in arrests of youth for these offenses might have been expected as a result of the passage of the Juvenile Justice and Delinquency Prevention Act in 1974, which, among other things, encouraged jurisdictions to divert and deinstitutionalize youth charged with noncriminal offenses. While the figures in Table 1 do show a decline in these arrests, virtually all of this decline occurred in the 1970s. Between 1982 and 1986 girls' curfew arrests increased by 5.1% and runaway arrests increased by a striking 24.5%.

And the upward trend continues; arrests of girls for running away increased by 3% between 1985 and 1986 and arrests of girls for curfew violations increased by 12.4% (Federal Bureau of Investigation, 1987, p. 171).

Looking at girls who find their way into juvenile court populations, it is apparent that status offenses continue to play an important role in the character of girls' official delinquency. In total, 34% of the girls, but only 12% of the boys, were referred to court in 1983 for these offenses (Snyder and Finnegan, 1987, pp. 6–20). Stating these figures differently, they mean that while males constituted about 81% of all delinquency referrals, females constituted 46% of all status offenders in courts (Snyder and Finnegan, 1987, p. 20). Similar figures were reported for 1977 by Black and Smith (1981). Fifteen years earlier, about half of the girls and about 20% of the boys were referred to court for these offenses (Children's Bureau, 1965). These data do seem to signal a drop in female status offense referrals, though not as dramatic a decline as might have been expected.

For many years statistics showing large numbers of girls arrested and referred for status offenses were taken to be representative of the different types of male and female delinquency. However, self-report studies of male and female delinquency do not reflect the dramatic differences in misbehavior found in official statistics. Specifically, it appears that girls charged with these noncriminal status offenses have been and continue to be significantly overrepresented in court populations . . .

Delinquency theory, because it has virtually ignored female delinquency, failed to pursue anomalies such as those found in the few early studies examining gender differences in delinquent behavior. Indeed, most delinquency theories have ignored status offenses. As a consequence, there is considerable question as to whether existing theories that were admittedly developed to explain male delinquency can adequately explain female delinquency. Clearly, these theories were much influenced by the notion that class and protest masculinity were at the core of delinquency. Will the "add women and stir approach" be sufficient? Are these really theories of delinquent behavior as some (Simons, Miller, and Aigner, 1980) have argued?

This article will suggest that they are not. The extensive focus on male delinquency and the inattention to the role played by patriarchal arrangements in the generation of adolescent delinquency and conformity has rendered the major delinquency theories fundamentally inadequate to the task of explaining female behavior. There is, in short, an urgent need to rethink current models in light of girls' situation in patriarchal society . . .

The Romance of the Gang or the "West Side Story" Syndrome

From the start, the field of delinquency research focused on visible lower-class male delinquency, often justifying the neglect of girls in the most cavalier of terms. Take, for example, the extremely important and influential work of Clifford R. Shaw and Henry D. McKay who, beginning in 1929, utilized an ecological approach to the study of juvenile delinquency. Their impressive work, particularly *Juvenile Delinquency in Urban Areas* (1942) and intensive biographical case studies such as Shaw's *Brothers in Crime* (1938) and *The Jack-Roller* (1930), set the stage for much of the subcultural research on gang delinquency. In their ecological work, however, Shaw and McKay analyzed only the official arrest data on male delinquents in Chicago and repeatedly referred to these rates as "delinquency rates" (though they occasionally made parenthetical reference to data on female delinquency) (see Shaw and McKay, 1942, p. 356). Similarly, their biographical work traced only male experiences with the law; in *Brothers in Crime,* for example, the delinquent and criminal careers of five brothers were followed for fifteen years. In none of these works was any justification given for the equation of male delinquency with delinquency.

Early fieldwork on delinquent gangs in Chicago set the stage for another style of delinquency research. Yet here too researchers were interested only in talking to and following the boys. Thrasher studied over a thousand juvenile gangs in Chicago during roughly the same period as Shaw and McKay's more quantitative work was being done. He spent approximately one page out of 600 on the five of six female gangs he encountered in his field observation of juvenile gangs. Thrasher (1927, p. 228) did mention, in passing, two factors he felt accounted for the lower number of girl gangs: "First, the social patterns for the behavior of girls, powerfully backed by the great weight of tradition and custom, are contrary to the gang and its activities; and secondly, girls, even in urban disorganized areas, are much more closely supervised and guarded than boys and usually well incorporated into the family groups or some other social structure."

Another major theoretical approach to delinquency focuses on the subculture of lower-class communities as a generating milieu for delinquent behavior. Here again, noted delinquency researchers concentrated either exclusively or nearly exclusively on male lower-class culture. For example, Cohen's work on the subculture of delinquent gangs, which was written nearly twenty years after Thrasher's, deliberately considers only boys' delinquency. His justification for the exclusion of the girls is quite illuminating:

> My skin has nothing of the quality of down or silk, there is nothing limpid or flute-like about my voice, I am a total loss with needle and thread, my posture and carriage are wholly lacking in grace. These imperfections cause me no distress—if anything, they are gratifying—because I conceive myself to be a man and want people to recognize me as a full-fledged, unequivocal representative of my sex. My wife, on the other hand, is not greatly embarrassed by her inability to tinker with or talk about the internal organs of a car, by her modest attainments in arithmetic or by her inability to lift heavy objects. Indeed, I am reliably informed that many women—I do not suggest that my wife is among them—often affect ignorance, frailty and emotional instability because to do otherwise would be out of keeping with a reputation for indubitable femininity. In short, people do not simply want to excel; they want to excel as a man or as a woman [Cohen, 1955, p. 138].

From this Cohen (1955, p. 140) concludes that the delinquent response, "however it may be condemned by others on moral grounds, has at least one virtue: it incontestably confirms, in the eyes of all concerned, his essential masculinity." Much the same line of argument appears in Miller's influential paper on the "focal concerns" of lower-class life with its emphasis on importance of trouble, toughness, excitement, and so on. These, the author concludes, predispose poor youth (particularly male youth) to criminal misconduct. However, Cohen's comments are notable in their candor and probably capture both the allure that male delinquency has had for at least some male theorists, as well as the fact that sexism has rendered the female delinquent as irrelevant to their work.

Emphasis on blocked opportunities (sometimes the "strain" theories) emerged out of the work of Robert K. Merton (1938) who stressed the need to consider how some social structures exert a definite pressure upon certain persons in the society to engage in nonconformist rather than conformist conduct. His work influenced research largely through the efforts of Cloward and Ohlin who discussed access to "legitimate" and "illegitimate" opportunities for male youth. No mention of female delinquency can be found in their *Delinquency and Opportunity* except that women are blamed for male delinquency. Here, the familiar notion is that boys, "engulfed by a feminine world and uncertain of their own identification . . . tend to 'protest' against femininity" (Cloward and Ohlin, 1960, p. 49). Early efforts by Ruth Morris to test this hypothesis utilizing different definitions of success based on the gender of respondents met with mixed success. Attempting to assess boys' perceptions about access to economic power status while for girls the variable concerned itself with the ability or inability of girls to maintain effective relationships, Morris was unable to find a clear relationship between "female" goals and delinquency (Morris, 1964).

The work of Edwin Sutherland emphasized the fact that criminal behavior was learned in intimate personal groups. His work, particularly the notion of differential association, which also influenced Cloward and Ohlin's work, was similarly male oriented as much of his work was affected by case studies he conducted of male criminals. Indeed, in describing his notion of how differential association works, he utilized male examples (e.g., "In an area where the delinquency rate is high a boy who is sociable, gregarious, active, and athletic is very likely to come in contact with the other boys, in the neighborhood, learn delinquent behavior from them, and become a gangster" [Sutherland, 1978, p. 131]). Finally, the work of Travis Hirschi on the social bonds that control delinquency ("social control theory") was, as was stated earlier, derived out of research on male delinquents (though he, at least, studied delinquent behavior as reported by youth themselves rather than studying only those who were arrested).

Such a persistent focus on social class and such an absence of interest in gender in delinquency is ironic for two reasons. As even the work of Hirschi demonstrated, and as later studies would validate, a clear relationship between social class position and delinquency is problematic, while it is clear that gender has a dramatic and consistent effect on delinquency causation (Hagan, Gillis, and Simpson, 1985). The second irony, and one that consistently eludes even contemporary delinquency theorists, is the fact that while the academics had little interest in female delinquents, the same could not be said for the juvenile justice system. Indeed, work on the early history of the separate system for youth, reveals that concerns about girls' immoral conduct were really at the center of what some have called the "childsaving movement" (Platt, 1969) that set up the juvenile justice system.

"The Best Place to Conquer Girls"

The movement to establish separate institutions for youthful offenders was part of the larger Progressive movement, which among other things was keenly concerned about prostitution and other "social evils" (white slavery and the like) (Schlossman and Wallach, 1978; Rafter, 1985, p. 54). Childsaving was also a celebration of women's domesticity, though ironically women were influential in the movement (Platt, 1969; Rafter, 1985). In a sense, privileged women found, in the moral purity crusades and the establishment of family courts, a safe outlet for their energies. As the legitimate guardians of the moral sphere, women were seen as uniquely suited to patrol the normative boundaries of the social order. Embracing rather than challenging these stereotypes, women carved out for themselves a role in the policing of women and girls (Feinman, 1980; Freedman, 1981; Messerschmidt, 1987). Ultimately, many of the early childsavers' activities revolved around the monitoring of young girls', particularly immigrant girls', behavior to prevent their straying from the path.

This state of affairs was the direct consequence of a disturbing coalition between some feminists and the more conservative social purity movement. Concerned about female victimization and distrustful of male (and to some degree female) sexuality, notable women leaders, including Susan B. Anthony, found common cause with the social purists around such issues as opposing the regulation of prostitution and raising the age of consent (see Messerschmidt, 1987). The consequences of such a partnership are an important lesson for contemporary feminist movements that are, to some extent, faced with the same possible coalitions.

Girls were the clear losers in this reform effort. Studies of early family court activity reveal that virtually all the girls who appeared in these courts were charged for immorality or waywardness (Chesney-Lind, 1971; Schlossman and Wallach, 1978; Shelden, 1981). More to the point, the sanctions for such misbehavior were extremely severe. For example, in Chicago (where the first family court was founded), one-half of the girl delinquents, but only one-fifth of the boy delinquents, were sent to reformatories between 1899–1909. In Milwaukee, twice as many girls as boys were committed to training schools (Schlossman and Wallach, 1978, p. 72); and in Memphis females were twice as likely as males to be committed to training schools (Shelden, 1981, p. 70) . . .

Not surprisingly, large numbers of girl's reformatories and training schools were established during this period as well as places of "rescue and reform." For example, Schlossman and Wallach note that 23 facilities for girls were opened during the 1910–1920 decade (in contrast to the 1850–1910 period where the average was 5 reformatories per decade [Schlossman and Wallach, 1985, p. 70]), and these institutions did much to set the tone of official response to female delinquency. Obsessed with precocious female sexuality, the institutions set about to isolate the females from all contact with males while housing them in bucolic settings. The intention was to hold the girls until marriageable age and to occupy them in domestic pursuits during their sometimes lengthy incarceration . . .

In their historic obsession about precocious female sexuality, juvenile justice workers rarely reflected on the broader nature of female misbehavior or on the sources of this misbehavior. It was enough for them that girls' parents reported them out of control. Indeed, court personnel tended to "sexualize" virtually all female defiance that lent itself to that construction and ignore other misbehavior (Chesney-Lind, 1973, 1977; Smith, 1978). For their part, academic students of delinquency were so entranced with the notion of the delinquent as a romantic rogue male challenging a rigid and unequal class structure, that they spent little time on middle-class delinquency, trivial offenders, or status offenders. Yet it is clear that the vast bulk of delinquent behavior is of this type.

Some have argued that such an imbalance in theoretical work is appropriate as minor misconduct, while troublesome, is not a threat to the safety and well-being of the community. This argument might be persuasive if two additional points could be established. One, that some small number of youth "specialize" in serious criminal behavior while the rest commit only minor acts, and, two, that the juvenile court rapidly releases those youth that come into its purview for these minor offenses, thus reserving resources for the most serious youthful offenders.

The evidence is mixed on both of these points. Determined efforts to locate the "serious juvenile offender" have failed to locate a group of offenders who specialize only in serious violent offenses. For example, in a recent analysis of a national self-report data set, Elliott and his associates noted "there is little evidence for specialization in serious violent offending; to the contrary, serious violent offending appears to be embedded in a more general involvement in a wide range of serious and non-serious offenses" (Elliott, Huizinga, and Morse, 1987). Indeed, they went so far as to speculate that arrest histories that tend to highlight particular types of offenders reflect variations in police policy, practices, and processes of uncovering crime as well as underlying offending patterns.

More to the point, police and court personnel are, it turns out, far more interested in youth they charge with trivial or status offenses than anyone imagined. Efforts to deinstitutionalize "status offenders," for example, ran afoul of juvenile justice personnel who had little interest in releasing youth guilty of noncriminal offenses (Chesney-Lind, 1988). As has been established, much of this is a product of the system's history that encouraged court officers to involve themselves in the noncriminal behavior of youth in order to "save" them from a variety of social ills . . .

The most influential delinquency theories, however, have largely ducked the issue of status and trivial offenses and, as a consequence, neglected the role played by the agencies of official control (police, probation officers, juvenile court judges, detention home workers, and training school personnel) in the shaping of the "delinquency problem." When confronting the less than distinct picture that emerges from the actual distribution of delinquent behavior, however, the conclusion that agents of social control have considerable discretion in labeling or choosing not to label particular behavior as "delinquent" is inescapable. This symbiotic relationship between delinquent behavior and the official response to that behavior is particularly critical when the question of female delinquency is considered.

Toward a Feminist Theory of Delinquency

To sketch out completely a feminist theory of delinquency is a task beyond the scope of this article. It may be sufficient, at this point, simply to identify a few of the most obvious problems with attempts to adapt male-oriented theory to explain female conformity and deviance. Most significant of these is the fact that all existing theories were developed with no concern about gender stratification.

Note that this is not simply an observation about the power of gender roles (though this power is undeniable). It is increasingly clear that gender stratification in patriarchal society is as powerful a system as is class. A feminist approach to delinquency means construction of explanations of female behavior that are sensitive to its patriarchal context. Feminist analysis of delinquency would also examine ways in which agencies of social control—the police, the courts, and the prisons—act in ways to reinforce woman's place in male society (Harris, 1977; Chesney-Lind, 1986). Efforts to construct a feminist model of delinquency must first and foremost be sensitive to the situations of girls. Failure to consider the existing empirical evidence on girls' lives and behavior can quickly lead to stereotypical thinking and theoretical dead ends.

An example of this sort of flawed theory building was the early fascination with the notion that the women's movement was causing an increase in women's crime; a notion that is now more or less discredited (Steffensmeier, 1980; Gora, 1982). A more recent example of the same sort of thinking can be found in recent work on the "power-control" model of delinquency (Hagan, Simpson, and Gillis, 1987). Here, the authors speculate that girls commit less delinquency in part because their behavior is more closely controlled by the patriarchal family. The authors' promising beginning quickly gets bogged down in a very limited definition of patriarchal control (focusing on parental supervision and variations in power within the family). Ultimately, the authors' narrow formulation of patriarchal control results in their arguing that mother's work force participation (particularly in high status occupations) leads to increases in daughters' delinquency since these girls find themselves in more "egalitarian families."

This is essentially a not-too-subtle variation on the earlier "liberation" hypothesis. Now, mother's liberation causes daughter's crime. Aside from the methodological problems with the study (e.g., the authors argue that female-headed households are equivalent to upper-status "egalitarian" families where both parents work, and they measure delinquency using a six-item scale that contains no status offense items), there is a more fundamental problem with the hypothesis. There is no evidence to suggest that as women's labor force participation has increased, girls' delinquency has increased. Indeed, during the last decade when both women's labor force participation accelerated and the number of female-headed households

soared, aggregate female delinquency measured both by self-report and official statistics either declined or remained stable (Ageton, 1983; Chilton and Datesman, 1987; Federal Bureau of Investigation, 1987).

By contrast, a feminist model of delinquency would focus more extensively on the few pieces of information about girls' actual lives and the role played by girls' problems, including those caused by racism and poverty, in their delinquency behavior. Fortunately, a considerable literature is now developing on girls' lives and much of it bears directly on girls' crime.

Criminalizing Girls' Survival

It has long been understood that a major reason for girls' presence in juvenile courts was the fact that their parents insisted on their arrest. In the early years, conflicts with parents were by far the most significant referral source; in Honolulu 44% of the girls who appeared in court in 1929 through 1930 were referred by parents.

Recent national data, while slightly less explicit, also show that girls are more likely to be referred to court by "sources other than law enforcement agencies" (which would include parents). In 1983, nearly a quarter (23%) of all girls but only 16% of boys charged with delinquent offenses were referred to court by non-law enforcement agencies. The pattern among youth referred for status offenses (for which girls are overrepresented) was even more pronounced. Well over half (56%) of the girls charged with these offenses and 45% of the boys were referred by sources other than law enforcement (Snyder and Finnegan, 1987, p. 21; see also Pope and Feyerherm, 1982).

The fact that parents are often committed to two standards of adolescent behavior is one explanation for such a disparity—and one that should not be discounted as a major source of tension even in modern families. Despite expectations to the contrary, gender-specific socialization patterns have not changed very much and this is especially true for parents' relationships with their daughters (Katz, 1979). It appears that even parents who oppose sexism in general feel "uncomfortable tampering with existing traditions" and "do not want to risk their children becoming misfits" (Katz, 1979, p. 24). Clearly, parental attempts to adhere to and enforce these traditional notions will continue to be a source of conflict between girls and their elders. Another important explanation for girls' problems with their parents, which has received attention only in more recent years, is the problem of physical and sexual abuse. Looking specifically at the problem of childhood sexual abuse, it is increasingly clear that this form of abuse is a particular problem for girls . . .

Not surprisingly, then, studies of girls on the streets or in court populations are showing high rates of both physical and sexual abuse. Silbert and Pines (1981, p. 409) found, for example, that 60% of the street prostitutes they interviewed had been sexually abused as juveniles. Girls at an Arkansas diagnostic unit and school who had been adjudicated for either status or delinquent offenses reported similarly high levels of sexual abuse as well as high levels of physical abuse; 53% indicated they had been sexually abused, 25% recalled scars, 38% recalled bleeding from abuse, and 51% recalled bruises (Mouzakitas, 1981) . . .

Many young women, then, are running away from profound sexual victimization at home, and once on the streets they are forced further into crime in order to survive. Interviews with girls who have run away from home show, very clearly, that they do not have a lot of attachment to their delinquent activities. In fact, they are angry about being labeled as delinquent, yet all engaged in illegal acts (Koroki and Chesney-Lind, 1985). The Wisconsin study found that 54% of the girls who ran away found it necessary to steal money, food, and clothing in order to survive. A few exchanged sexual contact for money, food, and/or shelter (Phelps et al., 1982, p. 67). In their study of runaway youth, McCormack, Janus, and Burgess (1986, pp. 392–393) found that sexually abused female runaways were significantly more likely than their nonabused counterparts to engage in delinquent or criminal activities such as substance abuse, petty theft, and prostitution. No such pattern was found among male runaways.

Research (Chesney-Lind and Rodriguez, 1983) on the backgrounds of adult women in prison underscores the important links between women's childhood victimizations and their later criminal careers. The interviews revealed that virtually all of this sample were the victims of physical and/or sexual abuse as youngsters; over 60% had been sexually abused and about half had been raped as young women. This situation prompted these women to run away from home (three-quarters had been arrested for status offenses) where once on the streets they began engaging in prostitution and other forms of petty property crime. They also begin what becomes a lifetime problem with drugs. As adults, the women continue in these activities since they

possess truncated educational backgrounds and virtually no marketable occupational skills (see also Miller, 1986).

Confirmation of the consequences of childhood sexual and physical abuse on adult female criminal behavior has also recently come from a large quantitative study of 908 individuals with substantiated and validated histories of these victimizations. Widom (1988) found that abused or neglected females were twice as likely as a matched group of controls to have an adult record (16% compared to 7.5). The difference was also found among men, but it was not as dramatic (42% compared to 33%). Men with abuse backgrounds were also more likely to contribute to the "cycle of violence" with more arrest for violent offenses as adult offenders than the control group. In contrast, when women with abuse backgrounds did become involved with the criminal justice system, their arrests tended to involve property and order offenses (such as disorderly conduct, curfew, and loitering violations) (Widom, 1988, p. 17).

Given this information, a brief example of how a feminist perspective on the causes of female delinquency might look seems appropriate. First, like young men, girls are frequently the recipients of violence and sexual abuse. But unlike boys, girls' victimization and their response to that victimization is specifically shaped by their status as young women. Perhaps because of the gender and sexual scripts found in patriarchal families, girls are much more likely than boys to be victim of family related sexual abuse. Men, particularly men with traditional attitudes toward women, are likely to define their daughters or stepdaughters as their sexual property (Finkelhor, 1982). In a society that idealizes inequality in male/female relationships and venerates youth in women, girls are easily defined as sexually attractive by older men (Bell, 1984). In addition, girls' vulnerability to both physical and sexual abuse is heightened by norms that require that they stay at home where their victimizers have access to them.

Moreover, their victimizers (usually males) have the ability to invoke official agencies of social control in their efforts to keep young women at home and vulnerable. That is to say, abusers have traditionally been able to utilize the uncritical commitment of the juvenile justice system toward parental authority to force girls to obey them. Girls' complaints about abuse were, until recently, routinely ignored. For this reason, statutes that were originally placed in law to "protect" young people have, in the case of girls' delinquency, criminalized their survival strategies. As they run away from abusive homes, parents have been able to employ agencies to enforce their return. If they persisted in their refusal to stay in that home, however intolerable, they were incarcerated . . .

Female Delinquency, Patriarchal Authority, and Family Courts

The early insights into male delinquency were largely gleaned by intensive field observation of delinquent boys. Very little of this sort of work has been done in the case of girls' delinquency, though it is vital to an understanding of girls' definitions of their own situations, choices, and behavior (for exceptions to this see Campbell, 1984; Peacock, 1981; Miller, 1986; Rosenberg and Zimmerman, 1977). Time must be spent listening to girls. Fuller research on the settings, such as families and schools, that girls find themselves in and the impact of variations in those settings should also be undertaken (see Figueira-McDonough, 1986). A more complete understanding of how poverty and racism shape girls' lives is also vital (see Messerschmidt, 1986; Campbell, 1984). Finally, current qualitative research on the reaction of official agencies to girls' delinquency must be conducted. This latter task, admittedly more difficult, is particularly critical to the development of delinquency theory that is as sensitive to gender as it is to race and class.

It is clear that throughout most of the court's history, virtually all female delinquency has been placed within the larger context of girls' sexual behavior. One explanation for this pattern is that familial control over girls' sexual capital has historically been central to the maintenance of patriarchy (Lerner, 1986). The fact that young women have relatively more of this capital has been one reason for the excessive concern that both families and official agencies of social control have expressed about youthful female defiance (otherwise much of the behavior of criminal justice personnel makes virtually no sense). Only if one considers the role of women's control over their sexuality at the point in their lives that their value to patriarchal society is so pronounced, does the historic pattern of jailing of huge numbers of girls guilty of minor misconduct make sense.

This framework also explains the enormous resistance that the movement to curb the juvenile justice system's authority over status offenders encountered. Supporters of the change were not really prepared for the political significance of giving youth the freedom to run. Horror stories told by the opponents of deinstitutionalization about victimized youth, youthful prostitution, and youthful involvement in pornography (Office of Juvenile Justice and Delinquency Prevention, 1985) all neglect the unpleasant reality that most of these behaviors were often in direct response to earlier victimization, frequently by parents, that officials had, for years, routinely ignored. What may be at stake in efforts to roll back deinstitutionalization efforts is not so much "protection" of youth as it is curbing the right of young women to defy patriarchy.

In sum, research in both the dynamics of girls' delinquency and official reactions to that behavior is essential to the development of theories of delinquency that are sensitive to its patriarchal as well as class and racial context.

REFERENCES

Ageton, Suzanne S. 1983. "The Dynamics of Female Delinquency, 1976–1980." *Criminology* 21:555–584.

Bell, Inge Powell. 1984. "The Double Standard: Age." In *Women: A Feminist Perspective,* edited by Jo Freeman. Palo Alto, CA: Mayfield.

Black, T. Edwin and Charles P. Smith. 1981. *A Preliminary National Assessment of the Number and Characteristics of Juveniles Processed in the Juvenile Justice System.* Washington, DC: Government Printing Office.

Campbell, Ann. 1984. *The Girls in the Gang.* Oxford: Basil Blackwell.

Chesney-Lind, Meda. 1973. "Judicial Enforcement of the Female Sex Role." *Issues in Criminology* 3:51–71.

———— 1978. "Young Women in the Arms of the Law." In *Women, Crime and the Criminal Justice System,* edited by Lee H. Bowker. Boston: Lexington.

———— 1986. "Women and Crime: The Female Offender." *Signs* 12:78–96.

———— 1988. "Girls and Deinstitutionalization: Is Juvenile Justice Still Sexist?" *Journal of Criminal Justice Abstracts* 20:144–165.

———— and Noelie Rodriguez. 1983. "Women Under Lock and Key." *Prison Journal* 63:47–65.

Children's Bureau, Department of Health, Education and Welfare. 1965. *1964 Statistics on Public Institutions for Delinquent Children.* Washington, DC: Government Printing Office.

Chilton, Roland and Susan K. Datesman. 1987. "Gender, Race and Crime: An Analysis of Urban Arrest Trends, 1960–1980." *Gender and Society* 1:152–171.

Cloward, Richard A. and Lloyd E. Ohlin. 1960. *Delinquency and Opportunity.* New York: Free Press.

Cohen, Albert K. 1955. *Delinquent Boys: The Culture of the Gang.* New York: Free Press.

Davidson, Sue, ed. 1982. *Justice for Young Women.* Tucson, AZ: New Directions for Young Women.

Elliott, Delbert, David Huizinga, and Barbara Morse. 1987. "A Career Analysis of Serious Violent Offenders." In *Violent Juvenile Crime: What Can We Do About It?* edited by Ira Schwartz. Minneapolis, MN: Hubert Humphrey Institute.

Federal Bureau of Investigation. 1987. *Crime in the United States 1986.* Washington, DC: Government Printing Office.

Feinman, Clarice. 1980. *Women in the Criminal Justice System.* New York: Praeger.

Figueira-McDonough, Jose Fina. 1986. "School Context, Gender, and Delinquency." *Journal of Youth and Adolescence* 15:79–98.

Finkelhor, David. 1982. "Sexual Abuse: A Sociological Perspective." *Child Abuse and Neglect* 6:95–102.

Freedman, Estelle. 1981. *Their Sisters' Keepers.* Ann Arbor: University of Michigan Press.

Gora, JoAnn. 1982. *The New Female Criminal: Empirical Reality or Social Myth.* New York: Praeger.

Hagan, John, A. R. Gillis, and John Simpson. 1985. "The Class Structure of Gender and Delinquency: Toward a Power-Control Theory of Common Delinquent Behavior." *American Journal of Sociology* 90:1151–1178.

Hagan, John, John Simpson, and A. R. Gillis. 1987. "Class in the Household: A Power-Control Theory of Gender and Delinquency." *American Journal of Sociology* 92:788–816.

Harris, Anthony. 1977. "Sex and Theories of Deviance." *American Sociological Review* 42:3–16.

Herman, Julia L. 1981. *Father-Daughter Incest.* Cambridge, MA: Harvard University Press.

Katz, Phyllis A. 1979. "The Development of Female Identity." In *Becoming Female: Perspectives on Development,* edited by Claire B. Kopp. New York: Plenum.

Koroki, Jan and Meda Chesney-Lind. 1985. *Everything Just Going Down the Drain.* Hawaii: Youth Development and Research Center.

Lerner, Gerda. 1986. *The Creation of Patriarchy.* New York: Oxford.

McCormack, Arlene, Mark-David Janus, and Ann Wolbert Burgess. 1986. "Runaway Youths and Sexual Victimization: Gender Differences in an Adolescent Runaway Population." *Child Abuse and Neglect* 10:387–395.

McGarrell, Edmund F. and Timothy J. Flanagan, eds. 1985. *Sourcebook of Criminal Justice Statistics—1984.* Washington, DC: Government Printing Office.

Merton, Robert K. 1938. "Social Structure and Anomie." *American Sociological Review* 3(October):672–682.

Messerschmidt, James. 1986. *Capitalism, Patriarchy, and Crime: Toward a Socialist Feminist Criminology.* Totowa, NJ: Rowman & Littlefield.

———— 1987. "Feminism, Criminology, and the Rise of the Female Sex Delinquent, 1880–1930." *Contemporary Crises* 11:243–263.

Miller, Walter B. 1958. "Lower Class Culture as the Generating Milieu of Gang Delinquency." *Journal of Social Issues* 14:5–19.

Morris, Ruth. 1964. "Female Delinquency and Relational Problems." *Social Forces* 43:82–89.

Mouzakitas, C. M. 1981. "An Inquiry into the Problem of Child Abuse and Juvenile Delinquency." In *Exploring the Relationship Between Child Abuse and Delinquency,* edited by R. J. Hunner and Y. E. Walkers. Montclair, NJ: Allanheld, Osmun.

National Female Advocacy Project. 1981. *Young Women and the Justice System: Basic Facts and Issues.* Tucson, AZ: New Directions for Young Women.

Office of Juvenile Justice and Delinquency Prevention. 1985. *Runaway Children and the Juvenile Justice and Delinquency Prevention Act: What is the Impact?* Washington, DC: Government Printing Office.

Opinion Research Corporation. 1982. "Public Attitudes Toward Youth Crime: National Public Opinion Poll." Mimeographed. Minnesota: Hubert Humphrey Institute of Public Affairs, University of Minnesota.

Peacock, Carol. 1981. *Hand Me Down Dreams.* New York: Schocken.

Phelps, R. J. et al. 1982. *Wisconsin Female Juvenile Offender Study Project Summary Report.* Wisconsin: Youth Policy and Law Center, Wisconsin Council on Juvenile Justice.

Platt, Anthony M. 1969. *The Childsavers.* Chicago: University of Chicago Press.

Pope, Carl and William H. Feyerherm. 1982. "Gender Bias in Juvenile Court Dispositions." *Social Service Review* 6:1–17.

Rafter, Nicole Hahn. 1985. *Partial Justice.* Boston: Northeastern University Press.

Rosenberg, Debby and Carol Zimmerman. 1977. *Are My Dreams Too Much To Ask For?* Tucson, AZ: New Directions for Young Women.

Russell, Diana E. 1986. *The Secret Trauma: Incest in the Lives of Girls and Women.* New York: Basic Books.

Schlossman, Steven and Stephanie Wallach. 1978. "The Crime of Precocious Sexuality: Female Juvenile Delinquency in the Progressive Era." *Harvard Educational Review* 48:65–94.

Shaw, Clifford R. 1930. *The Jack-Roller.* Chicago: University of Chicago Press.

———— 1938. *Brothers in Crime.* Chicago: University of Chicago Press.

———— and Henry D. McKay. 1942. *Juvenile Delinquency in Urban Areas.* Chicago: University of Chicago Press.

Shelden, Randall. 1981. "Sex Discrimination in the Juvenile Justice System: Memphis, Tennessee, 1900–1917." In *Comparing Female and Male Offenders,* edited by Marguerite Q. Warren. Beverly Hills, CA: Sage.

————— and John Horvath. 1986. "Processing Offenders in a Juvenile Court: A Comparison of Males and Females." Paper presented at the annual meeting of the Western Society of Criminology, Newport Beach, CA, February 27–March 2.

Silbert, Mimi and Ayala M. Pines. 1981. "Sexual Child Abuse as an Antecedent to Prostitution." *Child Abuse and Neglect* 5:407–411.

Simons, Ronald L., Martin G. Miller, and Stephen M. Aigner. 1980. "Contemporary Theories of Deviance and Female Delinquency: An Empirical Test." *Journal of Research in Crime and Delinquency* 17:42–57.

Smith, Lesley Shacklady. 1978. "Sexist Assumptions and Female Delinquency." In *Women, Sexuality and Social Control,* edited by Carol Smart and Barry Smart. London: Routledge & Kegan Paul.

Snyder, Howard N. and Terrence A. Finnegan. 1987. *Delinquency in the United States.* Washington, DC: Department of Justice.

Steffensmeier, Darrell J. 1980. "Sex Differences in Patterns of Adult Crime, 1965–1977." *Social Forces* 58:1080–1109.

Sutherland, Edwin. 1978. "Differential Association." In *Children of Ishmael: Critical Perspectives on Juvenile Justice,*

edited by Barry Krisberg and James Austin. Palo Alto, CA: Mayfield.

Thrasher, Frederic M. 1927. *The Gang.* Chicago: University of Chicago Press.

Tracy, Paul E., Marvin E. Wolfgang, and Robert M. Figlio. 1985. *Delinquency in Two Birth Cohorts: Executive Summary.* Washington, DC: Department of Justice.

Widom, Cathy Spatz. 1988. "Child Abuse, Neglect, and Violent Criminal Behavior." Unpublished manuscript.

Think Critically

1. Discuss the ways that traditional criminology theories have neglected female deviance and crime.
2. Which aspect(s) of Chesney-Lind's critique do you feel are most important in her discussion? Why?

On the Backs of Working Prostitutes

*Feminist Theory and Prostitution Policy**

Annette Jolin

W HY IS PROSTITUTION AS CONTROVERSIAL today as it was 4000 years ago? Why are feminists embroiled in the prostitution controversy? And what is it about prostitution that defies resolution? I argue that the answers to these questions can be found in a fundamental contradiction in Western culture, a contradiction that arises from the institutionalization of a sexual double standard in patriarchal societies, wherein prostitution owes its existence to an interplay of social and economic arrangements that involve promiscuity, chastity, and inequality.

Throughout its long history, prostitution has neither enjoyed uncontested acceptance nor endured total condemnation. In times of acceptance, as in times of condemnation, prostitution was always controversial. That conflict has always involved one or more of the elements in the promiscuity-chastity-inequality model of prostitution. Whatever form this conflict takes, however, it is always the women[1] who work as prostitutes who suffer. This is perhaps easier to understand in times when men, rather than women, dominate the prostitution debate, but even today when the prostitution controversy largely involves a debate *between* women and ending male dominance— about ending inequality, it is still the prostitute who suffers. The schism between women is deep. This divisiveness among women, as we shall see, exists for good reason, but it is also the case that today, after more than a century of feminism, the United States is one of the few industrial societies where prostitutes are defined as criminals.

The Promiscuity-Chastity-Inequality Model of Prostitution

Prostitution is an activity, which in broad terms can be identified as the exchange of sex for money: Women typically provide the sex and men the money (Lerner 1986, p. 131).

The controversial character of prostitution, and the often bitter social conflicts arising from disagreements about it, are the result of a profound cultural contradiction, which originates in the desire of men to ensure promiscuity for themselves and chastity for women. Men want sex with different women and they want women who have sex with only one man, a theoretical impossibility to which men have found a practical, albeit controversial, solution, one that requires "setting aside" a few women to meet the needs of men without substantially reducing the availability of chaste women or threatening the chastity of wives.

Historically, the process of "setting aside" a group of women and keeping them there succeeded because men had the power to overcome the resistance of women to being set aside. Voluntary entrance of women into prostitution seems highly unlikely, given a social order that linked female worth and economic survival to marriage, and marriageability to chastity.

In summary, prostitution in patriarchal society resulted from the following arrangements:

1. Male sexuality was defined to include promiscuity.
2. Female sexuality was defined to dictate chastity.
3. Men had the power to enforce both.

I refer to these arrangements as the promiscuity-chastity-inequality model of prostitution etiology. The term *inequality* is used to reflect men's social and economic dominance over women. The term *equality* refers to the social and economic equality of women with men.[2]

As the model suggests, prostitution owes its existence to a sexual double standard, the implementation of which is predicated on the economic and social dominance of men over women. It is not surprising that prostitution,

which incorporates male sexual duplicity and inequality between the sexes, has inspired moral crusaders and social reformers to speak out against it. Until the mid-19th century, those who spoke out against prostitution were almost exclusively men. Only since then have women become involved in the public debate.

Historical Controversies

The following discussion of prostitution controversies makes use of only a few of the examples that have been documented over the course of nearly 4000 years. History is replete with challenges to prostitution, followed by decades, even centuries, of relatively quiet tolerance. Yet neither support nor challenges have ever succeeded in freeing prostitution from controversy. For example, it rarely enjoyed greater social acceptance than it did among ancient Greeks, where all forms of prostitution flourished, and where upper-class prostitutes frequently attained prominence as highly cultured companions of powerful Greek citizens (for detailed discussions of prostitution in history, see Roberts 1992; Bullough and Bullough 1987; Henriques 1962). But despite public admiration and the association with powerful men, even these prostitutes were refused the status of wife and with it, the ultimate affirmation of legitimacy for women in Greek society, thus ensuring that the bad woman-good woman, today more popularly known as the whore-Madonna, dichotomy remains intact.

Once Christianity was firmly established, tolerance for prostitution took on a functionalist character. Religious leaders such as Augustine and St. Thomas Aquinas urged tolerance on the grounds that prostitution, an admittedly troublesome social phenomenon, nonetheless served a basic need, which if left unmet would lead to greater harm than prostitution itself. St. Thomas Aquinas, for example, compared the function of prostitution to that of a sewer in a palace: "If the sewer were removed, the palace would be filled with pollution; similarly if prostitution was removed the world would be filled with sodomy and other crimes" (Bullough and Bullough 1987, p. 120). Although Aquinas presented an argument in support of tolerance for prostitution, he clearly viewed it as an evil, albeit the lesser of two evils. This line of reasoning is as old as prostitution itself and, through the years, has taken a variety of forms (Davis 1937; Schreiber 1986;

Sieverts and Schneider 1977; Middendorf 1959; Simmel 1971; Kahmann and Lanzerath 1981; Otis 1985; Roberts 1992).

But tolerance, not infrequently, was replaced by movements to abolish prostitution. For instance, when Lutheran thinking came to prevail in 16th-century Europe, all pretense of tolerance disappeared. Martin Luther advocated the abolition of prostitution on moral grounds. He pointed to the moral reprehensiveness of promiscuity (Otis 1985, p. 41) and depicted prostitutes as emissaries of the devil who were sent to destroy faith (Bullough and Bullough 1978, p. 142). Lutheran sexual morality decreed chastity for all, promiscuity for none . . .

It is not until the middle of the 19th century that we find concerns about prostitution linked to either inequality—setting women aside, or chastity—as the norm for female sexuality.

Prostitution and 19th-Century Feminism

The 19th-century feminist movement in the United States gave women an opportunity to voice their opinions about prostitution. Then, as now, their voices were not in harmony. Some activist women called for the eradication of prostitution by citing the moral degeneracy of male promiscuity, whereas others urged that society give prostitution legitimacy as an expression of female sexuality outside of marriage. Representatives of the former view included eminent feminists Elizabeth Cady Stanton and Susan B. Anthony. In 1871, they successfully fought government proposals to legalize prostitution. Legitimizing prostitution, they argued along with social purity reformers, was nothing less than capitulating "to the morality of Sodom and Gomorrah" (Pleck 1987, pp. 89–90). Social purity reformers viewed male sexuality in general, and promiscuity in particular, as the source of a variety of social ills, among them prostitution. Prostitutes were cast as being among the "innocents," like many wives and children, victims of licentious men (Pleck 1987; Jenness 1993).

Other feminists regarded stanton and Anthony's victory as a disaster. They felt that suppressing prostitution was a threat to free love and to a woman's ability to exercise sexual and economic choice . . .

Free love advocates clearly questioned the traditional view of chastity—the one man-one *pure* woman rule—in the prostitution debate. If the lives of chaste wives are no better, and in some ways conceivably worse than those of promiscuous women, what is the value of chastity? And free love advocates were not alone in questioning marriage as the "naturally" superior social arrangement for women. Engels ([1884] 1942), for example, wrote that bourgeois marriage

> turns often enough into crassest prostitution—sometimes of both partners, but far more commonly of the woman, who only differs from the ordinary courtesan in that she does not let out her body on piece-work as a wage-worker, but sells it once and for all into slavery. (p. 63)

This is one of the first times that the institution of marriage was portrayed as potentially less acceptable than prostitution. And with it, chastity, as it is originally defined in the promiscuity-chastity-inequality model, becomes the focus of the attack on prostitution.

All 19th-century feminists agreed, however, that inequality was bad for women, that the social and economic forces that permitted setting women aside for prostitution (i.e., inequality) were indeed a problem. What divided them were different conceptions about the role of prostitution in women's struggle for equality. Social purity feminists like Stanton and Anthony saw prostitution as the embodiment of female *inequality,* and free love feminists like Woodhull saw prostitution as the embodiment of female *equality.* For Stanton and Anthony, the prostitute represented the victim of male sexuality and dominance; for Woodhull she represented an empowered woman who had cast aside the shackles of chastity and marriage. In its fundamental form, this describes the polar positions in the ideological divide among contemporary feminists as well (Tong 1984). And not even today, more than a century later, according to Barbara Meil-Hobson (1987), "neither those who cast the prostitute as victim or those who viewed her as empowered could create an ideological consensus" (p. 223).

The Prostitution Controversy Among Contemporary Feminists

. . . The 20th-century prostitution debate has its origins in the civil rights and feminist movements of the 1960s (Meil-Hobson 1987; Daly and Chesney-Lind 1988). In its fundamental form, the modern framework for discussing prostitution echoes that of the preceding century (Tong 1984; Jenness 1993). Thus contemporary feminist perspectives, philosophies, and language cast prostitution as a civil rights issue involving either the right to free sexual expression or the right to be protected from male sexual exploitation (the male sexual brute in 19th-century language) . . .

Contemporary feminists are in full agreement that the social and economic forces that allow men to set aside women, that is, inequality, are bad for all women and must be changed, but how to bring about these changes continues to be a deeply divisive issue for contemporary feminists[3] (Davis 1993; Meil-Hobson 1987; Tong 1984; Schur 1984; Jenness 1993; Bell 1987; Pheterson 1989; Roberts 1992; Hydra 1988; Alexander 1987). Modern feminists have been unable to resolve questions of this sort: Is it sexual or economic inequality that keeps women from attaining equality? Should protecting women from male sexual subjugation entail restricting women's ability to make choices? Are women victims or entrepreneurs? . . .

Those feminists who stress freedom of choice as the primary element in the struggle to overcome women's inequality assert that all steps toward equality must be accompanied by women's freedom to choose even when it involves prostitution. They further maintain that, given the social changes of the last century and a half, choice is eminently relevant in the inequality-equality debate, whether it involves attempts to gain social and economic or sexual equality. Insofar as women today are no longer bound by earlier definitions of promiscuity and marriage no longer represents their only path to social standing and economic security, freedom of choice becomes the central issue in debates about women's equality. Choice in sexual matters is as much as equality issue for women as is choice in the economic, social, or political arenas.

The Sexual Equality First (SEF) Approach

This argument asserts that equality for women depends directly on their ability to eliminate male sexual oppression. Although proponents of this view do not deny the importance of choice in the fight for equality, they contend that until women are equal members of society, free

choice is essentially illusionary. To attain equality, and with it, genuine freedom of choice, choices that involve male sexual dominance undermine the pursuit of equality and must therefore be restricted.

Two prominent representatives of this approach are radical feminist theorists Catherine MacKinnon (1987) and Andrea Dworkin (1989). They talk about the power-sex nexus in patriarchal societies, where male power is inextricably linked with female sexual subjugation. Women's equality, their argument asserts, sexual and otherwise, cannot be achieved so long as prostitution, which is predicated on the sexual subordination of women to men, continues to exist . . .

The Free Choice First (FCF) Approach

For freedom of choice proponents, the freedom to choose must accompany the pursuit of equality in all of its phases. Choice is at all times linked to full and equal personhood. Restricting choice for a woman, for any reason, reduces her status as a full and equal human being.

For feminists of this persuasion, the fight for women's equality depends on the rejection of *all* attempts *by men or women* to forcibly impose their will on women. Taking away a woman's choice by forcibly imposing one's will on her requires that the person whose will prevails has greater power than the person whose choice is preempted. As long as men have the ability to impose their will by overcoming women's resistance, the power balance between men and women is weighted in favor of men . . .

Prostitution Policy and the Sexual Equality First Perspective

For SEF feminists, the existence of prostitution presents a priori proof of women's inequality. To achieve true equality therefore requires that prostitution must cease to exist. Appropriately translated into 20th-century prostitution policy, this means criminalizing prostitution.[4] But endorsing criminalization puts SEF feminists in the untenable position of supporting fundamentally contradictory approaches: As feminists in general, they work to liberate women from sexual restrictions, but as feminists in the prostitution debate, they work to impose restrictions on women's sexuality. In other words, SEF feminists advocate women's sexual freedom unless it occurs in exchange for money. This makes it hard to dismiss critics such as Walkowitz (1982) and Coles and Coles (1978), who suggest that these feminists fail to recognize the difference of their middle-class interests from those of the women involved in prostitution, for whom sex is an economic issue first and an equality issue second, if at all. In other words, giving priority to issues of sexuality over issues of economic survival is a luxury in which many women cannot indulge. When the availability of choosing prostitution as an income-producing activity is eliminated, the economic impact will be felt by some women more so than others. It will further curtail economic options for lower-class women because most prostitutes come from that class (Alexander 1987). And as critics suggest, SEF feminists will not be the ones to suffer economic setbacks from the abolition of prostitution. In response to such criticism, proponents of the SEF perspective, except for a very small minority, are tentative in their support of criminalization and have instead aligned themselves most closely, but not without reservation with what Tong (1984, p. 58) calls laissez-faire decriminalization. This form of decriminalization involves repealing all laws and regulations that impinge on prostitution (City Club of Portland 1984, p. 54). But SEF feminists are uneasy and, at most, are willing to endorse decriminalization as a short-term strategy (Schur 1984, p. 172). In the long run, they insist, the continued existence of prostitution is irreconcilable with women's equality. Such ambivalent attitudes "may explain why no campaign around prostitution has materialized within the American feminist movement" (Meil-Hobson 1987, p. 220).

Prostitution Policy and the Free Choice First Perspective

For FCF proponents, choice is inalienably linked to full and equal personhood. Restricting a woman's choice or right to engage in prostitution denies her equality and with it, her status as a full and equal human being. Prostitution, as an act of sexual self-determination, becomes an expression of women's status as an equal, not a symptom of woman's subjugation. This view is most vigorously supported by feminist sex workers and feminist prostitutes' rights groups, which include Call Off Your Old Tired Ethics (COYOTE) in San Francisco, Hooking

is Real Employment (HIRE) in Atlanta, the Canadian Organization for the Rights of Prostitutes (CORP), Projekt Hydra in Germany, and the International Committee for Prostitutes' Rights (ICPR), which was organized during the Second World Whores' Congress in 1986 in Brussels.

For many of the FCF or prostitute rights proponents, prostitution is seen first and foremost as an economic issue. This perspective was colorfully expressed by Margo St. James (1989): "A blow job is better than no job" (p. 21). For these feminists, women's inequality rests as much, if not more, in economic and social inequality as it does in sexual inequality. Mariana Valverde (1987), a feminist freedom of choice proponent, accuses MacKinnon and Dworkin of doing a "disservice to the women's movement by claiming sexuality as the site of women's oppression" (p. 30). Valverde sees this as a dangerous reduction of the many complex social and economic factors involved in women's inequality. What is needed instead, according to Gail Pheterson (1989), is "the recognition of prostitutes' rights as an emancipation and labor issue rather than as an issue of criminality, immorality or disease" (p. 26) . . .

Despite their profound disagreements, both groups of feminists proclaim decriminalization as their prostitution policy of choice. While SEF proponents, as we noted above, are ambivalent in their endorsement of decriminalization, FCF advocates give it their unqualified, enthusiastic support. Yet neither ambivalence nor unqualified support have had much of an impact on prostitution policy in the United States. Prostitution, to this day, remains a criminal act in all but a few jurisdictions.

Although prostitution policies are not limited to criminalization and decriminalization, the feminist debate has virtually ignored the other primary approach to prostitution policy: legalization. Neither SEF nor FCF feminists appear to regard legalization as a policy worth considering. This stance seems to be largely based on a general distrust, by both groups, that a male-dominated state system could develop "women-centered systems of state licensing" (Tong 1984, p. 58). Instead, most feminists foresee that legalization strategies would lead to the expansion of state control in women's lives. For example, mandatory medical examinations for prostitutes would mean "increased male control of women's bodies," and as such would do little more than further "highlight the gender and class bias in prostitution policy" (Meil-Hobson 1987, p. 217). Insofar as most legalization policies enable the state to determine where, when, and how prostitution can be pursued, legalization allows the state—a predominantly male institution—to regulate female sexual conduct, and, as such, represents yet another form of male sexual domination for women. Legalization, therefore, presents an obstacle to both sexual equality and free choice.

The Working Prostitute as Criminal

Criminalizing prostitution has been dismissed by feminists of both perspectives on the grounds that it intensifies female inequality and furthers discrimination against women. In addition to all other inequities, this policy means that prostitutes bear the additional physical, psychological, and economic burdens of being identified as criminals (Tong 1984; Schur 1984; City Club of Portland 1984; Millett 1970; Jenness 1993) . . .

Prostitution theories, it has become clear, do not address that actual problems experienced by prostitutes, and neither do the strategies that flow from these theories. The fact that, despite feminists' advocacy of decriminalization, prostitution in 1993 continues to be a crime underscores this point. And, for the street prostitute, criminalization translates into a very real, very long, and very painful list of daily victimizations and indignities, to which she can add the further burden of becoming the victim of feminist prostitution ideology. This is a cruel irony, when one considers that much of the motivation, especially among SEF feminists, stems from the wish to protect women from victimization.

The fact that criminalization has prevailed as prostitution policy in the United States could mean that SEF feminists did little more than pay lip service in their endorsement of decriminalization, which undermined the efforts of FCF feminists and, as a consequence, preserved the status quo. It could also mean that longstanding cultural values that are not central to the contemporary feminist debate, such as concerns about the moral reprehensibility of promiscuity, present greater obstacles to change than feminists anticipated.

However, as the central argument in this discussion of prostitution and prostitution-associated controversies maintains, the cultural origins of prostitution have exposed in the past, and will continue to expose, prostitution to a variety of legitimate challenges. Until such time as a woman's sexual conduct is of her choice (equality), and neither detracts from (promiscuity) nor enhances (chastity) her worth, prostitution will continue to exist and it will continue to be fraught with controversy.

But because in the meantime real women live real lives as prostitutes, and some prostitution policies are less harmful to women than others, it is incumbent upon feminists to create a synthesis in the dialectic of the rights to choose and the rights to protections. Both depictions, of the prostitute as a woman empowered and of the prostitute as a woman enslaved, capture but a fraction of the women who work as prostitutes. After 150 years of feminism—of women working with women—we as feminists must work with all women.

NOTES

1. For purposes of this article, prostitution will be defined as an activity wherein women provide the sex and men provide the money—commonly known as female prostitution. The scope of this article is purposely limited to the discussion of female prostitution. Male prostitution, which has its own long-standing history (Roberts 1992) and shares many of the economic, social class, and stigmatization issues with female prostitution, is therefore not reflected in any of the subsequent discussion.

2. Lerner (1986, p. 236) notes that a distinction must be made between equality and emancipation. The former refers to obtaining equality with men and the latter refers to gaining freedom from restrictions. Equality as it is used here leads to emancipation, and inequality to lack thereof. In patriarchal societies, social and economic inequality or dominance is associated with sexual emancipation, whereas the lack of social and economic dominance is associated with sexual restrictions (chastity) or forced sexual activities (prostitution). Thus, in the context of the present discussion, the terms equality and inequality are causally related to emancipation.

3. According to Daly and Chesney-Lind (1988, p. 502), some of the divisiveness is related to difficulties with the definition of feminism itself. Feminists confront a variety of difficulties when they try to define feminism. Delmar (1986), for example, offers what she thinks might be a baseline definition, with which she hopes most women might be able to agree. Feminism, she suggests, accepts that women experience discrimination because of their sex,

and that due to this discrimination, they have needs that are negated and unsatisfied, and that the satisfaction of these needs requires a radical change. Beyond that, Delmar says, "things immediately become more complicated" (p. 8). And indeed, the contemporary prostitution debate takes place in Delmar's "beyond."

4. There are private nonprofit groups, such as the Portland, Oregon-based Council for Prostitution Alternatives, that provide broad-based support for women who wish to leave prostitution. Despite these efforts, the dominant social response to prostitution remains treating prostitutes as criminals.

REFERENCES

Alexander, Priscilla. 1987. "Prostitution: A Difficult Issue for Feminists." Pp. 184–214 in *Sex Work Writing by Women in the Sex Industry,* edited by F. Delacoste and P. Alexander. Pittsburgh, PA: Cleis Press.

Bell, Laurie. 1987. *Good Girls/Bad Girls.* Seattle: Seal Press.

Bullough, Vern and Bonnie Bullough. 1978. *Prostitution: An Illustrated Social History.* New York: Crown.

———. 1987. *Women and Prostitution: A Social History.* Buffalo, NY: Prometheus.

City Club of Portland. 1984. "Report on Adult Prostitution in Portland." Special Issue. *Bulletin* 65(August 31).

Coles, Robert and Jane Hallowell Coles. 1978. *Women of Crisis.* New York: Dell.

Daly, Kathleen and Meda Chesney-Lind. 1988. "Feminism and Criminology." *Justice Quarterly* 5:497–98.

Davis, Nanette J. 1993. *Prostitution: An International Handbook on Trends, Problems, and Policies.* Westport, CT: Greenwood.

Delmar, Rosalind. 1986. "What Is Feminism?" Pp. 8–33 in *What is Feminism?* edited by J. Mitchell and A. Oakley. New York: Pantheon.

Dworkin, Andrea. 1989. *Pornography.* New York: Dutton.

Engels, Friederich. [1884] 1942. *The Origin of the Family, Private Property, and the State.* New York: International.

Henriques, Fernando. 1962. *Prostitution and Society.* New York: Grove Press.

Hydra, Prostituiertenprojekt. 1988. *Beruf Hure.* Hamburg: Verlag am Galgenberg.

Jenness, Valerie. 1993. *Making It Work: The Prostitutes' Rights Movement in Perspective.* New York: de Gruyter.

Kahmann, Jurgen and Hubert Lanzerath. 1981. *Weibliche Prostitution in Hamburg.* Heidelberg: Kriminalistik.

Lerner, Gerda. 1986. *The Creation of Patriarchy.* New York: Oxford University Press.

MacKinnon, Catherine A. 1987. *Feminism Unmodified: Discourses on Life and Law.* Cambridge, MA: Harvard University Press.

Meil-Hobson, Barbara. 1987. *Uneasy Virtue.* New York: Basic Books.

Middendorf, D. 1959. "Die Sittlichkeitsdelikte in historischer und internationaler Sicht." In *Bekampfung der Sittlichkeitsdelikte.* Wiesbaden: Bundeskriminalamt.

Millett, Kate. 1970. *Sexual Politics.* Garden City, NY: Doubleday.

Otis, Leah. 1985. *Prostitution in Medieval Society.* Chicago: University of Chicago Press.

Pheterson, Gail. 1989. *A Vindication of the Rights of Whores.* Seattle: Seal Press.

Pleck, Elizabeth. 1987. *Domestic Tyranny.* New York: Oxford University Press.

St. James, Margo. 1987. "The Reclamation of Whores." Pp. 81–87 in *Good Girls/Bad Girls,* edited by L. Bell. Seattle: Seal Press.

Schreiber, Manfred. 1986. "Prostitution und Kriminalpolitik." Unpublished lecture, University of Munich.

Schur, Edwin M. 1984. *Labeling Women Deviant: Gender, Stigma, and Social Control.* Philadelphia: Temple University Press.

Sieverts, Rudolph and Hans Schneider. 1977. *Handwörterbuch der Kriminologie.* Berlin: de Gruyter.

Tong, Rosemary. 1984. *Women, Sex, and the Law.* Totowa, NJ: Rowman and Allanheld.

Tubinger Projektgruppe Fraunhandel. 1989. *Frauenhandel in Deutschland.* Bonn: J. H. W. Dietz.

Valverde, Mariana. 1987. "Too Much Heat, Not Enough Light." Pp. 27–33 in *Good Girls/Bad Girls,* edited by L. Bell. Seattle: Seal Press.

Walkowitz, Judith. 1982. "Male Vice and Feminist Virtue: Feminism and the Politics of Prostitution in Nineteenth Century Britain." *History Workshop* 13:79–83.

Think Critically

1. Discuss two major ways, according to Jolin, that feminism is related to views regarding prostitution.

2. How do present debates among feminists relate to both the criminalization of prostitution and to policies regarding prostitution? Explain.

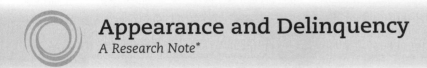

Appearance and Delinquency
A Research Note*

Jill Leslie Rosenbaum and Meda Chesney-Lind

WOMEN ARE JUDGED BY CULTURALLY derived standards of attractiveness. These culturally created standards affect women in all walks of life, including it appears, the way they are treated by the criminal justice system. Research has shown that perception of physical appearance can have a significant impact on an individual's success in a variety of endeavors. These endeavors include dating opportunities (Crause and Mehrabian 1977; Stretch and Figley 1980; Walster, Aronson, Abrahams, and Rottman 1966), the initiation of relationships (Murstein and Christy 1976; Price and Vandenberg 1979; White 1980), teachers' evaluations of students (Clifford and Walster 1973; Dion 1973), and corporate success (Heilman and Stopeck 1985; Heilman and Sarawatari 1979).

The role of appearance in judgments of criminal responsibility and the punishment of such behavior have also been the focus of a variety of psychological studies (Efran 1974; Sigall and Ostrove 1975; Stewart 1980). These studies consistently indicate that physical attractiveness influences judgments of wrongdoing. Dion (1973) found that adult judgments of children's transgressions were affected by the attractiveness of the child. Transgressions, both mild and severe, were perceived to be less undesirable when committed by an attractive child than an unattractive child. Furthermore, subjects were less likely to attribute chronic antisocial behavior to attractive than to unattractive children.

The work of Sigall and Ostrove (1975) suggests that the sentences given to offenders are often conditioned by the appearance of the offender. Attractive female offenders, whose offense was not appearance-related (burglary),

received greater leniency than unattractive offenders. However, when the offense was attractiveness-related (swindle), attractive offenders received harsher sentences than their unattractive counterparts. These findings are consistent with those of Efran (1974), whose work has shown that attractive defendants are much less likely to be found guilty than unattractive defendants. This becomes especially pronounced when males are judging the culpability of females. Sigall and Ostrove (1975) and Efran (1974) also indicate that when a female offender is seen as using her attractiveness to assist in the commission of a crime, attractive defendants were more likely to be found guilty.

Studies of appearance also demonstrate that society has higher expectations for attractive individuals; some of these expectations pertain exclusively to women. For instance, attractive women are assumed to be more feminine and have a more socially desirable personality, and as a result, they are assumed to have greater overall happiness in their personal, social, and professional lives (Dion, Berscheid, and Walster 1973). It is also assumed that they are less likely to remain single, more likely to marry earlier, be better spouses, and be better sexual partners as well.

Although the lives of attractive women are assumed to be far superior to those of less attractive women, some believe that attractive women have less integrity, and thus managerial opportunities for them may be hindered. In fact, Heilman and Sarawatari (1979) concluded that women with more masculine characteristics are believed to have greater ability than women with feminine characteristics. Thus, although attractive women are thought to be more feminine, they are also thought to be less well-suited for nontraditional female roles.

Finally, Emerson (1969) noted that judges and other juvenile court personnel often expressed considerable

*From Jill Leslie Rosenbaum and Meda Chesney-Lind, *Crime and Delinquency*, vol. 40, No. 2, pp. 250–261, copyright © 1994 by Sage Publications, Inc. Reprinted by permission of Sage Publications, Inc.

interest in the appearance of girls appearing before the court he observed. He noted a judge's interest in whether runaway girls were "clean" after having been away from home for more than a day or two; the assumption was that if they were clean and/or heavily made up, they might be engaging in prostitution (Emerson 1969, p. 112). Emerson observed that appearance was taken as an indication of sexual morality or immorality. Numerous notations on the sexual and moral activities of girls, but not of boys, were also noted by Hancock (1981) in her study of police records in Victoria, Australia.

Attractiveness can be somewhat of a double-edged sword. The situation becomes all the more complex for girls and women who find their way into the criminal justice system for offenses either directly or indirectly related to their sexuality and sexual deportment (Schlossman and Wallach 1978; Rafter 1990). This pattern has been especially marked in the case of young women coming into the juvenile justice system.

Since the establishment of the first juvenile court, there has been ongoing interest by judges and other court workers in the sexual activity of girls. In the early days of the court (1899–1920), there was a clear bias against girls deemed sexually active and a harsh official response to their misbehavior. Virtually all of the girls who appeared before the first juvenile courts were charged with immorality or waywardness (Chesney-Lind 1971; Schlossman and Wallach 1978; Shelden 1981; Rafter 1990), and the response of the courts to this noncriminal behavior frequently was incarceration. For example, between 1899–1909 in Chicago (where the first family court was founded), one-half of the female delinquents, but only one-fifth of the male delinquents, were sent to reformatories. In Milwaukee, twice as many girls as boys were committed to training schools (Schlossman and Wallach 1978, p. 72), and in Memphis, females were twice as likely as males to be committed to training schools (Shelden 1981, p. 70) . . .

National statistics reflect the official enthusiasm for the incarceration of girls during the early part of this century; their share of the population of juvenile correctional facilities increased from 1880 (when girls were 19% of the population) to 1923 (when girls were 28%). By 1950, girls had climbed to 34% of the total and in 1960 they were still 27% of those in correctional facilities. By 1980, this pattern appeared to be reversed and girls were again 19% of those in correctional facilities (Calahan 1986,

p. 130) and in 1989, girls accounted for 11.9% of those held in public detention centers and training schools (Allen-Hagen 1991, p. 4).

The decline in incarceration of juvenile females in public facilities run by the juvenile justice system is directly linked to an intense debate on the issue of the institutionalization of young people, especially youth charged with noncriminal status offenses (e.g., running away from home, being incorrigible, truant, or in danger of leading a lewd and lascivious lifestyle). In particular, the Juvenile Justice and Delinquency Prevention Act (JJDPA) of 1974 stressed the need to divert and deinstitutionalize youth charged with status offenses and provided states with a number of incentives to achieve this goal.

These figures, then, represent some very good news to those concerned with the court's sexual policing of girls. Prior to the passage of the JJDPA of 1974, nearly three quarters (71%) of the girls and 23% of the boys in the nation's training schools were incarcerated for status offenses (Schwartz, Stekette, and Schneider 1990). Between 1974 and 1979, the number of girls admitted to public detention facilities and training schools dropped by 40%. Since then, however, the deinstitutionalization trend has slowed in some areas of the country, particularly at the detention level. Between 1979 and 1989, for example, the number of girls held in these same public facilities actually increased by 10% (Jamieson and Flanagan 1987; Flanagan and McGarrell 1986; Allen-Hagen 1991). These figures have also been accompanied by sharp increases in the last decade (1981–1990) of arrests of girls for running away (up 19%) and curfew violation (up 36.6%). Again, these figures represent a shift away from the decline in arrests of youth for status offenses that was seen in the late 1970s.

Critical to any understanding of the dynamics of gender bias in the juvenile justice system, then, is an appreciation of the gendered nature of delinquency, and particularly status offenses. It should be understood that status offenses have also served as "buffer charges" for the court's historic, but now implicit interest in monitoring girls' sexual activities and their obedience to parental authority (Gold 1971, p. 571). In essence, modern status offense charges mask the court's historic interest in girls' propriety and obedience to parental authority (Chesney-Lind and Shelden 1992).

Because of the recent but eroding success of the JJDPA of 1974, it is perhaps essential to review the dynamics of sexism within the juvenile justice system immediately prior to the passage of this act. The study reported here, although relatively modest, documents one aspect of the sexism that girls encountered as they entered institutions in the 1960s: the interest of criminal justice professionals in the physical appearance of girls.

Data and Methods

This analysis is based on the records of 159 women who, as juveniles, were committed to the California Youth Authority (CYA) during the 1960s. Records were requested on all 240 of the girls who were sentenced to the CYA between 1961 and 1965 from San Francisco and the Sacramento Valley. There were 59 cases unavailable because the juvenile records had been purged and another 22 cases could not be located. For the 159 cases where data was available, the records included the complete CYA files containing all comments/reports regarding the ward and the case by CYA intake workers, counselors, teachers, living unit personnel, chaplains, social workers, and psychologists (for more information regarding data collection, see Warren and Rosenbaum 1986).

The racial composition of these 159 cases was 51% Caucasian, 30% African American, 9% Latino, and the remaining 10% were Asian or Native American. Two-thirds of the girls had been committed to the CYA for status offenses and, more specifically, 49% were charged with running away from home, 28% for being "beyond control," 12% for "being in danger of a lewd and lascivious lifestyle," 7% for truancy, and 4% curfew. To say that these girls were committed for status offenses actually understates the role of status offenses in their delinquency records; this group of girls committed 698 offenses prior to their commitment to the CYA. The average number of arrests was six, and over 90% of these were status offenses. There were no racial differences observed in the distribution of these offenses . . .

Findings

A variety of physical descriptions were recorded for the 75 wards whose appearance was mentioned in the files. These show male staff concern with the physical maturity of the girls, as well as some evidence of racial stereotyping; indeed, of those where evaluative judgments

about appearance were made, 60% were made about minority-group females. Moreover, those viewing these young women of color adhered to "representations of race" (Hooks 1992) that negate any beauty that does not conform to white standards of appearance, while celebrating those images that mimic white appearance . . .

From the descriptions of the girls' appearance, four general categories emerged: attractive, unattractive, plain/wholesome, and "well-built."[1] Of the wards whose appearance was mentioned, 26% (19) were described as attractive (e.g., "the ward is an attractive, physically mature 13-year-old"), whereas 38% (27) were described as unattractive (e.g., "Her appearance is rather uninteresting and unattractive"); 19% as plain or wholesome; and 17% (14) were described as well-built.

Differences emerged when the relationship between the type of offense and the mention of appearance in the intake evaluations was examined. About 50% (56) of the girls who had been evaluated by a male had at least one immorality charge against them. When females who had been charged with immorality offenses (being in danger of leading a lewd and lascivious life and prostitution) were compared with those who had no such charge, differences in the mention of appearance became especially pronounced. For instance, for those charged with one or more counts of immorality, a physical description was present in 93% (55) of the cases. However, when no immorality charges were present, a physical description was included in only 37% (20) of the cases. Looking at the data from another perspective, in cases where no description of the girl's appearance was present, 89% (34) had no charges of immorality. A significant relationship ($X^2 = 37.5$) was found between having at least one immorality charge and having mention made of the girl's appearance in her file.

Differences also existed with respect to the type of offenses present and the description given. All of the girls who were described as attractive and all of the girls who were described as well-built had been charged with at least one immorality offense. However, only 26% of the girls described as plain/wholesome and 34% of those described as unattractive had similar charges against them. Although these numbers are small, the magnitude of the difference is clearly significant.

More Recent Data

To assess whether or not appearance remains an issue today, more recent data from the CYA and also Hawaii were examined. In the process of collecting data from the CYA files of all girls who were wards of the CYA in 1990, close attention was paid to any mention of the girl's appearance. Similar attention was paid in a separate examination of the case files of all boys and girls who were confined in the Hawaii Youth Correctional Facility in 1989.

Although there were 214 girls who were wards of the CYA in 1990, comments regarding appearance were found in only eight files. All, except one who was described as slovenly and unattractive, were simply described as attractive. Five of the eight had arrests for violent crime, the other three had long records for property and drug offenses. Although the vast majority of the girls' arrests during the 1960s were for status offenses, only 4% of their 1990 counterparts' arrests were for status offenses.

In Hawaii, however, comments such as the following were still found in girls' files in 1990:

> [Minor is] highly sexual and very seductive . . . she is thought to be sexually active.

> [Minor's] neck was loaded with hickies . . .

Discussion

The emphasis on physical appearance found in this small study, and the link between this interest in girls' appearance and their noncriminal delinquent behavior is more important than it might first seem. In essence, these observations provide a window into the worldview of the keepers of young women during the years prior to the passage of the JJDPA of 1974; sadly, they may also reflect a bias that remains in the states that have been resistant to the deinstitutionalization efforts signaled by the passage of that act. Like earlier studies, which found a large number of girls in institutions subjected to physical examinations to determine if they were virgins (see Chesney-Lind and Shelden 1992), interest in the physical appearance of girls, and particularly their physical maturity, indicates substantial interest in the sexual behavior of girls and illuminates another important dimension of the sexual policing of girls (Cain 1989).

Particularly troubling are the comments which indicate a presumed association between "beauty," specifically male Caucasian standards of beauty, and sexual behavior.

Certainly the fact that these girls were incarcerated for noncriminal offenses indicates the seriousness with which the criminal justice system viewed their transgressions. In short, these data provide some support for the notion, suggested by Sigall and Ostrove (1975), as well as that by Efran (1974), that judges, social workers, and other criminal justice professionals (particularly if they are male) may look upon attractive girls who engage in sexual "immorality" more harshly. They may also overlook some of the same behaviors in less attractive girls.

Such a fascination with appearance is also at odds with the literature on street prostitutes. These studies indicate that the pace and pressure of this life does not produce "attractive" young women, but instead tends to take a physical toll on the girls engaged in the behavior (Weisberg 1985, p. 116). Indeed, some descriptions of prostitutes describe them as unattractive, overweight, with poor complexions and bad teeth (Winick and Kinsie 1972, p. 35).

The remarks found in the files, which were made by male intake workers, suggest a fascination with the appearance of the girls who were charged with immorality. Clearly there was considerable concern with their physical maturity and physical attraction. The comments regarding the girls' appearance suggest that status offenses may have functioned as buffer charges for suspected sexual behavior. Although it appears that at least in California, where girls are no longer incarcerated for noncriminal offenses, this no longer seems to be a problem, national data suggest that in some states, like Hawaii, the detention and incarceration of girls for noncriminal status offenses persists; thus the concerns raised by this article may, sadly, not be of simply historic interest.

NOTE

1. These categories are broad and somewhat evasive; however, they were the factors that emerged during this analysis. It is important to remember that attractiveness is in the eye of the beholder and we, as researchers, are merely reporting the subjective assessments that we found.

REFERENCES

Allen-Hagen, Barbara. 1991. *Children in Custody 1989*. Washington, DC: Bureau of Justice Statistics.

Cain, Maureen. 1989. *Growing Up Good: Policing the Behavior of Girls in Europe*. London: Sage.

Calahan, M. W. 1986. *Historical Corrections Statistics in the United States 1950–1984*. Washington, DC: U.S. Department of Justice.

Chesney-Lind, Meda. 1971. *Female Juvenile Delinquency in Hawaii.* Master's thesis, University of Hawaii at Manoa.

Chesney-Lind, Meda and Randall Shelden. 1992. *Girls, Delinquency, and the Juvenile Justice System.* Pacific Grove, CA: Brooks/Cole.

Clifford, Mark and Elaine Walster. 1973. "The Effect of Physical Attractiveness on Teacher Expectations." *Sociology of Education* 46:248–58.

Crause, Bryant B. and Albert Mehrabian. 1977. "Affiliation of Opposite-Sexed Strangers." *Journal of Research in Personality* 11:38–47.

Dion, Karen. 1973. "Physical Attractiveness and Evaluation of Children's Transgressions." *Journal of Personality and Social Psychology* 24:207–18.

Dion, Karen, Ellen Berscheid, and Elaine Walster. 1973. "What Is Beautiful Is Good." *Journal of Personality and Social Psychology* 24:285–90.

Efran, Michael. 1974. "The Effect of Physical Appearance on the Judgement of Guilt, Interpersonal Attraction, and Severity of Recommended Punishment." *Journal of Experimental Research in Personality* 8:45–54.

Emerson, Robert. 1969. *Judging Delinquents.* Chicago: Aldine.

Flanagan, Timothy J. and Edmund F. McGarrell, eds. 1986. *Sourcebook of Criminal Justice Statistics—1985.* Washington, DC: U.S. Department of Justice.

Gold, Steven. 1971. "Equal Protection for Girls in Need of Supervision in New York State." *New York Law Forum* 17:570–91.

Hancock, L. 1981. "The Myth That Females Are Treated More Leniently Than Males in the Juvenile Justice System." *Australian and New Zealand Journal of Sociology* 16:4–14.

Heilman, Madeline and Lois Sarawatari. 1979. "When Beauty Is Beastly: The Effects of Appearance and Sex on Evaluations of Job Applicants for Managerial and Nonmanagerial Jobs." *Organizational Behavior and Human Performance* 23: 360–72.

Heilman, Madeline and Melanie Stopeck. 1985. "Attractiveness and Corporate Success: Different Causal Attributions for Males and Females." *Journal of Applied Psychology* 70:379–88.

Hooks, Bell. 1992. *Black Looks.* Boston: South End Press.

Jamieson, Katherine M. and Timothy Flanagan, eds. 1987. *Sourcebook of Criminal Justice Statistics—1986.* Washington, DC: U.S. Department of Justice, Bureau of Justice Statistics.

Murstein, B. and P. Christy. 1976. "Physical Attractiveness and Marriage Adjustment in Middle Aged Couples." *Journal of Personality and Social Psychology* 34:537–42.

Price, Richard and Steven Vandenberg. 1979. "Matching for Physical Attractiveness in Married Couples." *Personality and Social Psychology Bulletin* 5:398–99.

Rafter, Nicole. 1990. *Partial Justice: Women, Prisons and Social Control.* New Brunswick, NJ: Transaction Books.

Schwartz, Ira M., M. Stekette, and V. Schneider. 1990. "Federal Juvenile Justice Policy and the Incarceration of Girls." *Crime & Delinquency* 36:503–20.

Shelden, Randall. 1981. "Sex Discrimination in the Juvenile Justice System: Memphis, Tennessee, 1900–1971." In *Comparing Male and Female Offenders,* edited by M. Q. Warren. Beverly Hills, CA: Sage.

Sigall, Harold and Nancy Ostrove. 1975. "Beautiful But Dangerous: Effects of Offender Attractiveness and Nature of Crime on Juridic Judgement." *Journal of Personality and Social Psychology* 31:410–14.

Stewart, John. 1980. "Defendant's Attraction as a Factor in the Outcome of Criminal Trials: An Observational Study." *Journal of Applied Social Psychology* 10:348–61.

Stretch, Richard and Charles Figley. 1980. "Beauty and the Beast: Predictions of Interpersonal Attraction in a Dating Experiment." *Psychology, a Quarterly Journal of Human Behavior* 17:34–43.

Walster, Elaine, E. Aronson, D. Abrahams, and L. Rottman. 1966. "Importance of Physical Attractiveness in Dating Behavior." *Journal of Personality and Social Psychology* 4:508–16.

Warren, Marguerite Q. and Jill Rosenbaum. 1986. "Criminal Careers of Female Offenders." *Criminal Justice and Behavior* 13:393–418.

Weisberg, D. Kelly. 1985. *Children of the Night: A Study of Adolescent Prostitution.* Lexington, MA: Lexington Books.

White, Gregory. 1980. "Physical Attractiveness and Courtship Progress." *Journal of Personality and Social Psychology* 39:660–68.

Winick, Charles and Paul M. Kinsie. 1972. *The Lively Commerce.* New York: Signet.

Think Critically

1. What do you make of the role of appearance judgments that are made regarding attractive women who come before the criminal justice system? Give examples to support your viewpoint.

2. Rosenbaum and Chesney-Lind's findings on the emphasis on physical appearance and its link to non-delinquent behavior indicates how sexism enters into criminal justice decision making. In what other ways might sexism manifest itself in the justice system? Give some examples.

Identity, Strategy, and Feminist Politics
Clemency for Battered Women Who Kill*

Patricia Gagné**

THE FEMINIST BATTERED WOMEN'S movement has been widely credited with creating public awareness of wife abuse as a social problem, establishing safe places for victims of intimate violence, working to eliminate gender bias in the law, and creating equal protection for battered women (Davis 1988; Dobash and Dobash 1992; Schechter 1982; Tierney 1982). Most studies of the battered women's movement of the 1970s and 1980s were grounded in resource mobilization theory (see McCarthy and Zald 1973, 1977). While the early developments in resource mobilization focused on availability of resources and the ability of activists to organize them, a subsequent strand focused on the social and political context as an opportunity for action (Jenkins 1983). Most analyses of the battered women's movement have taken the first approach, focusing on shelters as social movement organizations (but see Schechter 1982). As a result of the focus on shelters, as opposed to an examination of activists agitating for change in other arenas, analysts have argued that the movement has been, or is in danger of being, co-opted (Ferraro 1983; Johnson 1981; Schechter 1982).[1]

*© 1996 by the Society for the Study of Social Problems. Reprinted from *Social Problems*, 43:1 (February 1996), pp. 77–93 by permission of the author and publisher.
**My thanks to Angela Browne, Ann Goetting, J. Craig Jenkins, Mark Richard, Joseph Scott, Verta Taylor, Richard Tewksbury, and three anonymous reviewers for their comments on this work, This research was funded by a grant from the Elizabeth Gee Fund for Research on Women from the Center for Women's Studies and a Research Intense Summer Fellowship from the Department of Sociology, both at The Ohio State University, and by a Project Completion Grant from the College of Arts and Sciences at the University of Louisville. Correspondence: Department of Sociology, University of Louisville, Louisville, KY 40292.

Resource mobilization theory is grounded in theories of liberal democracy, which narrowly define politics as separate from civic society, personal life, and social movements (Acklesberg 1988; Ferree 1992). With its narrow and rigidly defined conceptualization of social movements, resource mobilization theory is problematic in the examination of women's movements, primarily because it is based upon a white, middle class, masculine (or liberal democratic) tradition of personal and civic life and participation in politics (Ferree 1992). That is, it assumes that activists are people outside of institutionalized positions of authority. It overlooks the liberal feminist goal of placing women in key political positions and other careers where they will work to create social change, excludes the radical feminist concept that the personal is political, and obviates an examination of acts of "everyday resistance" (Collins 1990).

Feminists have challenged the tenet that institutionalized politics are separable from personal life or activism (Acklesberg 1988; Alonso 1992; Cassell 1977; Elshtain 1981; Evans 1979; Kauffman 1989; Morgen and Bookman 1988; Mouffe 1992). Similarly, post-modern, critical, feminist, and new social movement theorists have argued that a merging of political and non-political spheres of life has taken place in post-industrial societies (Acklesberg 1988; Alonso 1992; Bernstein 1985; Elshtain 1981; Foucault 1979; Habermas 1985; Melucci 1980; Morgen and Bookman 1988; Mouffe 1992; Offe 1985; Taylor and Whittier 1992; Touraine 1985). Therefore, an examination of the feminist battered women's movement that-is based upon liberal democratic assumptions will overlook the activism that has taken place in non-traditional arenas (such as the work place), institutional politics, or personal relationships and will obscure examinations of activists' efforts to create a political and cultural context conducive to movement success.

Drawing on a case study of the 1990 decision by then-Ohio Governor Richard Celeste to grant clemency to 26 women who were incarcerated for killing or assaulting abusive intimate partners or stepfathers, this paper examines the strategies and tactics used by feminists in the battered women's movement to lay the groundwork for and establish a clemency review process. I have chosen to focus on the Ohio movement for the following reasons: It was the first multiple clemency decision of its type; it was directly influenced by feminists in the women's and battered women's movements; to date, it has resulted in the largest number of women being released from prison at one time; and finally, it appears to have set a precedent that was followed by similar decisions by three other governors, and by feminist organizing efforts in 17 other states. By examining this event in light of social movement and political theories that challenge the assumptions of liberal democratic theories, my goals are to: (1) document an historical event that might otherwise be lost; (2) challenge the notion that the battered women's movement was co-opted in the 1980s; (3) identify movement tactics that worked in an environment relatively conducive to change; (4) hypothesize about strategies and tactics that might work in a less hospitable era; and (5) conceptually expand our understanding of what constitutes activism.

Methods

The data for this article come from 45 intensive, semi-structured, tape recorded interviews with members of the Ohio battered women's movement and key informants in state government.[2] I used a snowball sampling method, beginning with First Lady Dagmar Celeste, who was involved in the women's and battered women's movements from the 1960s and who was influential in promoting women's prison reform and the clemency review. In addition to Dagmar Celeste, my sample included members of her staff, many of the founders of the battered women's movement, the governor, cabinet members, aides to the governor and cabinet, employees of the Ohio Department of Rehabilitation and Correction, members of a statewide network of direct service providers, former members of three support groups for incarcerated battered women, defense attorneys, judges, feminist and pro-feminist Ohio legislators, and 12 of the 26 women who were granted clemency[3] . . .

The Context

In 1982 Richard Celeste was elected governor by a decisive majority. His success was due, in part, to the recession and high unemployment that had hit the state, particularly in the "rust belt," and to a strong anti-Republican sentiment. Voters were liberal on economic, but not social, issues. To fight against further erosion of jobs and the decline of schools, voters elected Democrats to office across the board. In 1986 Celeste ran for re-election against James Rhodes, a candidate who had already served four terms as governor (in two, two-term periods). At that time, Ohio's economy was on the rebound, and again voters elected Celeste to office by a decisive margin. In neither term was Celeste elected on social issues, nor did he campaign on them strongly. While he had the legal authority to grant clemency to whomever he chose, he lacked a political mandate on left wing or feminist social issues. Although he had received the backing of activists advocating for social change, his staff understood the political risks of being too socially progressive, and they worked to protect him from such demands.

When he took office in 1983, the governor provided Dagmar Celeste with a staff and office space in the State House and depended on her to get involved with many of the issues affecting Ohio citizens. She called upon feminist colleagues and friends, many of whom had helped found the women's and battered women's movements, to help her create a "First Lady's Agenda." Some of those women served in the "First Lady's Unit," but more were selected by the governor to serve in cabinet and sub-cabinet level positions as directors of government agencies and in a variety of other positions. During the second term, these women organized the Women's Interagency Task Force, a network of feminists representing governmental departments and agencies. The Task Force met on a regular basis to discuss social policy as it related to women, review what agencies were doing about women's issues, provide an annual review of the governor's budget from a feminist perspective, and coordinate efforts on behalf of women throughout the state. The result was more efficient mobilization of a feminist community, which increased its influence throughout the state. With backing from the Task Force, as the term progressed, the First Lady's Unit increased pressure on members of the governor's staff who thought certain issues "too controversial" for the governor to address.

Feminists created support for clemency by raising public, judicial, and legislative awareness of gender biases in self-defense law and by pressing for change. In 1989 the Ohio Domestic Violence Network (ODVN) and feminists in the legislature pressed the passage of HB 484, despite well-organized opposition from conservative legislators and prosecutors. At the same time, feminist therapists, expert witnesses, and advocates worked to educate judges and Supreme Court justices about battered woman syndrome and its role in domestic homicides. By passing HB 484 and doing the background work that led to the *Koss* decision, they helped to create a context in which clemency reviews could be justified, particularly for women who, according to the law in 1990, had not received fair trials. Feminists developed the context of opportunity the governor needed, but more work had to be done to put the review process in place.

Emergent Frames and the Rhetoric of Wife Abuse

Collective action frames are dynamic efforts by movements to "package" an issue by creating a sense of injustice and attributing blame for it to a particular social group or agent (Snow and Benford 1992). In an informal sense, the movement creates a theory about the source and solutions to the problem and presents it to the public and/or authorities. On a larger scale, master frames are more abstract theories that guide the discourse of movements within the social movement sector (Snow and Benford 1992). Like theories to a paradigm, the collective action frames of individual movements are likely to adhere to the discourse of the larger master frame.

The master frame of the movements of the 1960s and early 1970s focused on structural and cultural inequality, with goals such as equal rights, justice, and freedom from oppression. When the battered women's movement first emerged in the mid-1970s, the cycle of protest that had begun in the 1950s was reaching the end of its heyday (Jenkins 1987). When the battered women's movement became well established in the late 1970s the cycle of protest was in decline (Jenkins 1987) and the anti-feminist, pro-family backlash was gaining momentum (Crawford 1980; Faludi 1991). At the same time, mental health professionals began to reframe battered women's issues in non-oppositional terms and to encroach on the movement

(Johnson 1981; Schechter 1982). By the end of the 1970s, the majority of shelters were non-feminist in orientation (Ferraro 1983; Johnson 1981). At the same time, the master frame of that cycle of protest had begun to shift toward personal development, and many radical feminists began to turn toward a cultural or eco-feminist analysis. Whereas radicals were social constructionist in orientation and sought to eliminate the sex-class system, cultural and eco-feminists based their discourse on essentialist premises, with a focus on elevating women's inherent virtues and putting greater emphasis on women's spiritual growth (Echols 1989). In Ohio, the battered women's movement shifted from a focus on gender equality to one of difference, incorporating elements of a debate that has been going on for more than a century . . .

Framing Demands for Prison Reform

Had the first lady and members of the network advocated the formation of feminist consciousness-raising groups for incarcerated women, it is likely the governor's staff and prison authorities would have resisted their efforts. However, by focusing on "recovery" services they were able to establish groups that became a key factor in creating a social movement community within the women's prison.

Consciousness Raising and the Politicization of Identity

The central task of the Ohio battered women's movement in achieving clemency was to create a collective identity among women inmates (see Melucci 1989). All the women I met who had attended educational or support groups for battered women talked about realizing they were not alone in their experiences. They explained how other women in their groups helped them understand how they had been dominated and controlled and how society had failed to help them.

In time women began to see themselves as survivors, rather than perpetual victims, and to understand how they came to be controlled, abused, and ultimately trapped in violent relationships.

Talking about their experiences was central in helping the women "reclaim" their definition of self, a step central to the politicization of identity (see D'Emilio 1983; Herman and Miall 1990). Based on my interviews with clemency recipients, activists, and authorities, I found that the importance of reclaiming identity is threefold. First, privately discussing the violent relationship with women who have claimed the identity "survivor" helps the "victim" reinterpret her experiences within the social context and begin to redefine herself.[4] As the victim redefines herself as a survivor, she realizes her strengths and how society has socialized her to be weak, failed to protect her, and blamed her for her own victimization. Second, as the public witnesses the reclaiming and public identification with a previously stigmatized status, old stereotypes and definitions are challenged and the identity is publicly renegotiated and redefined. Third, by publicly discussing and redefining the issues, their private nature is challenged and transformed from a personal to a social problem, deserving of social recompense.

From prison the women carried on a campaign to educate authorities and the public about Battered Woman Syndrome. They told about their experiences with violent and abusive spouses and parents and the injustices they had endured in the criminal justice system. For most, these efforts involved letter-writing campaigns and meeting with public officials who were frequently brought to the prison by the first lady or feminist legislators. They met with legislators to talk about their experiences, their reactions to abuse, Battered Woman Syndrome, and the need for laws recognizing it. They shared their experiences in closed meetings with the governor's staff and in groups organized to garner media attention, such as a meeting Dagmar Celeste's staff arranged with Miss America. They told their stories on television news magazines and to anyone else who would listen. Their goals were to educate government officials and the public about wife abuse and build public sympathy for their cases. One legislator explained how meeting with the women helped him understand what battered women endure and why it was necessary to change the law and remedy past inequities. He said:

> I wanted to really talk to a real person who's been through this. . . . One woman told me how the windows were nailed shut. When the guy left . . . he took the phone with him and warned her that if she left the house . . . or contacted the authorities, that her children were going to be in serious harm's way. . . . And this had gone on for a decade. So one day, he came home and that was it. . . . He was going to abuse her physically, sexually, too. . . . She shot him dead with a shotgun. And she was in her . . . ninth year of incarceration.

The women's stories matched real lives with the theories and put faces on the statistics. With what they learned in prison, the governor's aides and supporters of HB 484 were able to win the votes of those who opposed the legislation . . .

Only three of the women I talked with had had problems with men since being released. One, whose entire family was abusive, tolerated the violence because, as she explained, "I know he loves me." A second left a man she had met who had become abusive. The third was very assertive in communicating that she would not tolerate abuse. When her partner pushed her, she had him arrested and pressed charges. When I talked to her, the two were in couples' counseling and recovery groups and were trying to "work things out." Still, she was adamant that although she loved him, she knew she "deserved better than that." These forms of everyday resistance were made possible because women acknowledged that they had been abused and, in the process, learned to protect themselves and help others.

While inmates' actions were central in the transformation of identity, their voices alone were not enough to result in clemency. That goal required activism outside the prison. To accomplish that, the systems by which women had been dominated had to be appropriated and used to their own benefit.

Appropriating and Career Activism

One outcome of many of the social movements of the 1960s and 1970s was the creation of job opportunities for activists (McAdam 1988; McCarthy and Zald 1973). However, as the "cycle of protest" (Tarrow 1991) wound down for many movements of the period, activists found themselves in an increasingly tight activist job market (McAdam 1988). Nonetheless, the presence of the growing women's movement gave women expanding career outlets for their activism (McAdam 1988). A major distinction between the experiences of men in the new left and feminists is that the former eschew participation in "the establishment," while many feminists have looked upon career success as one potential means of addressing the economic and power inequities between women and men. For example, a 1960s student radical would look upon the offer of a position as judge as an effort at co-optation, while feminists have sought such positions as avenues to reinterpret or change the law.

Feminist activism on the job entails working to advance the goals of the women's movement as part of one's career. Within the Ohio battered women's movement, efforts to institutionalize change ranged from municipal court systems to the Supreme Court, the state legislature, and the Celeste Administration. At the municipal level, feminist judges, attorneys, shelter directors, and other direct service providers worked together to coordinate the police and judicial response to battering. Throughout the state the Governor's Task Force on Family Violence endeavored to understand and coordinate services for battered women and other victims of family violence. Feminist doctors worked to train their colleagues about family violence. Feminists in the Ohio Public Defender's Office were active in supporting legislation and working to educate their colleagues about battered woman syndrome. After *State v. Koss,* the Supreme Court created a task force to educate judges about domestic violence and battered woman syndrome and called upon movement founders who had established themselves in government careers to work with them. Feminist researchers and correctional staff, working to document the presence of battered woman syndrome among Ohio's female inmate population, stood their ground as the integrity of their work was challenged by their supervisors, and they ensured that the cases of all women who were eligible for review made it to the governor's office. Feminists within the First Lady's Unit and in the cabinet worked to educate the governor and his staff about wife abuse . . .

Conclusion

Previous examinations of the battered women's movement have focused primarily on shelters as social movement organizations and have concluded that the feminist principles of the movement have been co-opted by mental health professionals. In Ohio I found a well-organized network of feminist shelters that worked toward social change on the local and state levels, despite an anti-feminist/pro-family cultural backlash, an increasingly conservative political environment, and efforts by mental health professionals to redefine the issues. While they staffed the "front lines," the majority of activism that made the clemencies possible occurred in arenas traditionally considered outside the domain of social movements.

Because they did not respect the boundaries between public and private, feminists successfully forced a recognition

of the social factors that frequently entrap women in violent relationships. As ideological outsiders within the systems they wanted to change, they created a climate more favorable to clemency by framing issues in terms authorities were likely to understand and accept. This rhetorical compromise helped feminists establish a social movement community within the prison. In Ohio, feminists achieved their goals by carrying their activism into their careers and personal lives and by recognizing that political change occurs at the level of individual identity, as it did when women inmates began to advocate for their own clemencies. Feminists could only achieve these goals by resisting individual explanations of wife abuse, focusing on the need for personal transformation and social change, and remaining ideologically outside the systems they wanted to appropriate and change.

In periods that are inhospitable to movement goals, activists must identify strategies and tactics that are most likely to result in the achievement of movement goals. Based on the success of the Ohio battered women's movement, I have identified six tactics that may assist other movements during inhospitable or hostile cycles. First, movements can elect public officials sympathetic to their views and infiltrate positions of authority in order to swing the political pendulum in their favor. Along these lines, they must recognize the increasingly important role of political spouses in providing or denying access to political decision makers and other authorities. Second, movements can work toward social change in every aspect of their personal and public lives, bearing in mind that identity transformation among nonactivists is a powerful potential source of movement growth. Third, movements can work to create democratic spaces in previously private or non-democratic arenas. Fourth, unless they are able to build a powerful coalition, strong enough to challenge authorities and sway public opinion, movements can engage in rhetorical compromise by framing their demands in terms more likely to resonate with authorities and the public. Fifth, movements can work to create coalitions with activists from across the ideological spectrum, finding a role for all groups and coordinating their activities. Sixth, movements can work from within and outside the system, exerting influence on every pressure point and providing access to, and on behalf of, already marginalized groups. If social scientists are to understand the dynamics of social change, we must continue to examine social movements. However, as I have demonstrated in this paper, an examination of outsider challengers or activism that takes place through social movement organizations or in "public" places gives us only a partial understanding of how change occurs, how demands become institutionalized, and how new challengers arise and infiltrate the systems they wish to change. Further research is needed to examine to what extent these tactics have been used by other activists, in both left and right wing movements.

NOTES

1. Within the majority of articles arguing that the movement has been co-opted, the term is generally poorly defined. However, co-optation, as it is discussed in the context of the battered women's movement, generally refers to a shift away from feminist principles of pragmatic assistance, self-help, consciousness raising, empowerment, and non-hierarchical organization to a mental health or social welfare model that relies heavily on counseling, rigid rules, and bureaucratic organization, and that assumes that the problem is rooted in individual pathology or within a dysfunctional family system (see Davis 1988).

2. Although it may appear that part of my research was ethnographic in nature, I was not involved in activism or decision making during any stage of the organizing or clemency review process. My involvement in this project began when then former First Lady Dagmar Celeste suggested to my advisor that someone needed to research the clemency decisions.

3. One of the women died shortly after being released and another has returned to prison. Of the remainder, five did not respond to telephone calls and letters, and four refused to be interviewed, saying they wanted to put the past behind them and get on with their lives. I was unable to locate three.

4. In groups open only to inmates, women varied in their degree of reclaiming identity, with each helping the others at various stages of the consciousness raising process. In addition to these private group sessions, a seminar was developed by an organization of inmates serving life sentences. At that seminar, formerly incarcerated battered women who killed abusers shared their life experiences with clemency applicants. The overwhelming response from inmates who attended was that the seminar was empowering and that more opportunities like it should be made available to women in prison. (This response is based on program evaluation forms filled out by all inmates who attended the seminar) . . .

REFERENCES

Acklesberg, Martha A. 1988. "Communities, resistance, and women's activism: Some implications for a democratic polity." In *Women and the Politics of Empowerment,* eds. Ann Bookman and Sandra Morgen, 297–313. Philadelphia: Temple University Press.

Alonso, Ana María 1992. "Gender, power, and historical memory: Discourses of Serrano resistance." In *Feminists Theorize the Political,* eds. Judith Butler and Joan W. Scott, 404–425. New York: Routledge.

Bernstein, Richard J. 1985. "Introduction." In *Habermas and Modernity,* ed. Richard J. Bernstein, 1–32. Cambridge: The MIT Press.

Black, Maureen 1990. "Battered Spousal/Woman Syndrome Project: Report." Columbus: Ohio Department of Rehabilitation and Correction.

Cassell, Joan 1977. *A Group Called Women: Sisterhood and Symbolism in the Feminist Movement.* Prospect Heights, Ill.: Waveland Press.

1990. *Black Feminist Thought: Knowledge, Consciousness, and the Politics of Empowerment.* London: HarperCollins Academic.

Crawford, Alan 1980. *Thunder on the Right: The "New Right" and the Politics of Resentment.* New York: Pantheon Books.

D'Emilio, John 1983. *Sexual Politics, Sexual Communities: The Making of a Homosexual Minority in the United States, 1940–1970.* Chicago: University of Chicago Press.

Dobash, R. Emerson, and Russell P. Dobash 1992. *Women, Violence and Social Change.* New York: Routledge.

Echols, Alice 1989. *Daring to Be Bad: Radical Feminism in America 1967–1975.* Minneapolis: University of Minnesota Press.

Elshtain, Jean Bethke 1981. *Public Man, Private Woman: Women in Social and Political Thought.* Princeton: Princeton University Press.

Evans, Sara 1979. *Personal Politics.* New York: Vintage Books.

Faludi, Susan 1991. *Backlash: The Undeclared War Against American Women.* New York: Crown Publishers, Inc.

Ferraro, Kathleen J. 1983. "Negotiating trouble in a battered women's shelter," *Urban Life* 12:287–306.

Ferree, Myra Marx 1992. "The political context of rationality: Rational choice theory and resource mobilization." In *Frontiers in Social Movement Theory,* eds. Aldon D. Morris and Carol McClurg Mueller, 29–52. New Haven, Conn.: Yale University Press.

Ferree, Myra Marx, and Beth B. Hess 1985. *Controversy and Coalition: The New Feminist Movement.* Boston: Twayne Publishers.

Foucault, Michel 1979. *Discipline and Punish: The Birth of the Prison.* New York: Random House.

Habermas, Jürgen 1985. "Neoconservative culture criticism in the United States and West Germany: An intellectual movement in two political cultures." In *Habermas and Modernity,* ed. Richard J. Bernstein, 78–94. Cambridge: The MIT Press.

Herman, Nancy J., and Charlene E. Miall 1990. "The positive consequences of stigma: Two case studies in mental and physical disability." *Qualitative Sociology* 13:251–269.

Jenkins, J. Craig 1983. "Resource mobilization theory and the study of social movements." *Annual Review of Sociology* 9:527–553.

———. 1987. "Interpreting the story 1960s: Three theories in search of a political age." *Research in Political Sociology* 3:269–303.

Johnson, John M. 1981. "Program enterprise and official co-optation in the battered women's shelter movement. *American Behavioral Scientist* 24: 827–842.

Kauffman, L. A. 1989. "The anti-politics of identity." *Socialist Review* 20:67–80.

McAdam, Doug 1988. *Freedom Summer.* New York: Oxford University Press.

McCarthy, John D., and Mayer N. Zald 1973. *The Trend of Social Movements in America: Professionalization and Resource Mobilization.* Morristown, N. J.: General Learning Corporation.

———. 1977. "Resource mobilization and social movements: A partial theory." *American Journal of Sociology* 82:1212–1240.

Melucci, Alberto 1980. "The new social movements: A theoretical approach." *Social Science Information* 19:199–226.

———. 1989. *Nomads of the Present: Social Movements and Individual Needs in Contemporary Society.* Philadelphia: Temple University Press.

Morgen, Sandra, and Ann Bookman 1988. "Rethinking women and politics: An introductory essay." In *Women and the Politics of Empowerment,* eds. Ann Bookman and Sandra Morgen, 3–29. Philadelphia: Temple University Press.

Mouffe, Chantal 1992. "Feminism, citizenship, and radical democratic politics." In *Feminists Theorize the Political,* eds. Judith Butler and Joan W. Scott, 369–384. New York: Routledge.

Offe, Claus 1985. "New social movements; Challenging the boundaries of institutional politics." *Social Research* 52:817–868.

Schechter, Susan 1982. *Women and Violence: The Visions and Struggles of the Battered Women's Movement.* Boston: South End Press.

Snow, David A., and Robert D. Benford 1992. "Master frames and cycles of protest." In *Frontiers in Social Movement Theory,* eds. Aldon D. Morris and Carol McClurg Mueller, 133–155. New Haven, Conn.: Yale University Press.

Sussman, Vicki 1990. "Battered women who commit violent offenses: A study of battered women incarcerated at the Ohio Reformatory for Women." Columbus, Ohio: Bureau of Planning and Research, Ohio Department of Rehabilitation and Correction.

Tarrow, Sidney 1991. *Struggle, Politics, and Reform: Collective Action, Social Movements, and Cycles of Protest.* Ithaca, N.Y.: Center for International Studies, Cornell University.

Taylor, Verta, and Nancy Whittier 1992. "Collective identity in social movement communities: Lesbian feminist mobilization." In *Frontiers in Social Movement Theory,* eds. Aldon D. Morris and Carol McClurg Mueller, 104–129. New Haven, Conn.: Yale University Press.

Tierney, Kathleen J. 1982. "The battered women movement and the creation of the wife beating problem." *Social Problems* 29:207–220.

Touraine, Alain 1985. "An introduction to the study of social movements." *Social Research* 52: 749–787.

Think Critically

1. How are social movement theories applied to the situation of wife battering described by Gagne? In your response, discuss some of the processes that are highlighted by such theories.

2. Do you feel that such theories are valuable in understanding other social problems more generally? Give examples to support your viewpoint.

IN JOSEPH GUSFIELD'S CLASSIC WORK, "Moral Passage," an account is given as to how deviant behavior regarding drinking was defined in the United States. Using an interactionist approach, Gusfield examines how symbolic processes helped shape the movement to limit and control the personal consumption of alcohol. His analysis shows how deviant categories have distinct social histories, and how the reactions of specific groups provided the grounds for a "moral passage" of the act of drinking from one status (conventional) to another (deviant).

Howard Becker's piece, "Marihuana Use and Social Control," examines factors that both encourage and limit the use of marihuana as a recreational drug. Becker's analysis focuses on issues such as supply, secrecy, and morality in explaining the use of marihuana, and how social controls that limit its use are broken down, allowing individuals to become marihuana users more easily.

DEVIANT BEHAVIORS ~
Alcohol and Drug Use

In "Deviance as a Situated Phenomenon," James Orcutt uses questionnaires administered to a sample of students to examine their interpretations of marihuana and alcohol use in eight different social situations. He finds that the interpretations of the use of marihuana and alcohol as "deviant" vary depending on the situation in which they occur, but notes that the nature of the act itself also influences reactions. His study supports the idea that deviance is neither a totally relativistic concept nor a concrete thing, but rather lies somewhere in between.

Moral Passage
*The Symbolic Process in Public Designations of Deviance**

Joseph R. Gusfield

RECENT PERSPECTIVES ON DEVIANT BEHAVIOR have focused attention away from the actor and his acts and placed it on the analysis of public reactions in labelling deviants as "outsiders."[1] This perspective forms the background for the present paper. In it I will analyze the implications which defining behavior as deviant has for the public designators. Several forms of deviance will be distinguished, each of which has a different kind of significance for the designators. The symbolic import of each type, I argue, leads to different public responses toward the deviant and helps account for the historical changes often found in treatment of such delinquents as alcoholics, drug addicts, and other "criminals," changes which involve a passage from one moral status to another.

Instrumental and Symbolic Functions of Law[2]

Agents of government are the only persons in modern societies who can legitimately claim to represent the total society. In support of their acts, limited and specific group interests are denied while a public and societal interest is claimed.[3] Acts of government "commit the group to action or to perform coordinated acts for general welfare."[4] This representational character of governmental officials and their acts makes it possible for them not only to influence the allocation of resources but also to define the public norms of morality and to designate which acts violate them. In a pluralistic society these defining and designating acts can become matters of political issue because they support or reject one or another of the competing and conflicting cultural groups in the society.

Let us begin with a distinction between *instrumental* and *symbolic* functions of legal and governmental acts. We readily perceive that acts of officials, legislative enactments, and court decisions often affect behavior in an instrumental manner through a direct influence on the actions of people. The Wagner Labor Relations Act and the Taft-Hartley Act have had considerable impact on the conditions of collective bargaining in the United States. Tariff legislation directly affects the prices of import commodities. The instrumental function of such laws lies in their enforcement; unenforced they have little effect.

Symbolic aspects of law and government do not depend on enforcement for their effect. They are symbolic in a sense close to that used in literary analysis. The symbolic act "invites consideration rather than overt reaction."[5] There is a dimension of meaning in symbolic behavior which is not given in its immediate and manifest significance but in what the action connotes for the audience that views it. The symbol "has acquired a meaning which is added to its immediate intrinsic significance."[6] The use of the wine and wafer in the Mass or the importance of the national flag cannot be appreciated without knowing their symbolic meaning for the users. In analyzing law as symbolic we are oriented less to behavioral consequences as a means to a fixed end; more to meaning as an act, a decision, a gesture important in itself.

An action of a governmental agent takes on symbolic import as it affects the designation of public norms. A courtroom decision or a legislative act is a gesture which often glorifies the values of one group and demeans those of another. In their representational character, governmental actions can be seen as ceremonial and ritual performances, designating the content of public morality. They are the statement of what is acceptable in the public interest. Law can thus be seen as symbolizing the public affirmation of social ideals and norms as well as a means of direct social control. This symbolic dimension is given in the statement, promulgation, or announcement of law unrelated to its function in influencing behavior through enforcement.

It has long been evident to students of government and law that these two functions, instrumental and symbolic, may often be separated in more than an analytical sense. Many laws are honored as much in the breach as in performance.[7] Robin Williams has labelled such institutionalized yet illegal and deviant behavior the "patterned evasion of norms." Such evasion occurs when law proscribes behavior which nevertheless occurs in a recurrent socially organized manner and is seldom punished.[8] The kinds of crimes we are concerned with here quite clearly fall into this category. Gambling, prostitution, abortion, and public drunkenness are all common modes of behavior although laws exist designating them as prohibited. It is possible to see such systematic evasion as functioning to minimize conflicts between cultures by utilizing law to proclaim one set of norms as public morality and to use another set of norms in actually controlling that behavior.

While patterned evasion may perform such harmonizing functions, the passage of legislation, the acts of officials, and decisions of judges nevertheless have a significance as gestures of public affirmation. First, the act of public affirmation of a norm often persuades listeners that behavior and norm are consistent. The existence of law quiets and comforts those whose interests and sentiments are embodied in it.[9] Second, public affirmation of a moral norm directs the major institutions of the society to its support. Despite patterned practices of abortion in the United States, obtaining abortions does require access to a subterranean social structure and is much more difficult than obtaining an appendectomy. There are instrumental functions to law even where there is patterned evasion.

A third impact of public affirmation is the one that most interests us here. The fact of affirmation through acts of law and government expresses the public worth of one set of norms, of one subculture vis-à-vis those of others. It demonstrates which cultures have legitimacy and public domination, and which do not. Accordingly it enhances the social status of groups carrying the affirmed culture and degrades groups carrying that which is condemned as deviant. We have argued elsewhere that the significance

of Prohibition in the United States lay less in its enforcement than in the fact that it occurred.[10] Analysis of the enforcement of Prohibition law indicates that it was often limited by the unwillingness of Dry forces to utilize all their political strength for fear of stirring intensive opposition. Great satisfaction was gained from the passage and maintenance of the legislation itself.[11]

Irrespective of its instrumental effects, public designation of morality is itself an issue generative of deep conflict. The designating gestures are dramatistic events, "since it invites one to consider the matter of motives in a perspective that, being developed in the analysis of drama, treats language and thought primarily as modes of action."[12] For this reason the designation of a way of behavior as violating public norms confers status and honor on those groups whose cultures are followed as the standard of conventionality, and derogates those whose cultures are considered deviant. My analysis of the American Temperance movement has shown how the issue of drinking and abstinence became a politically significant focus for the conflicts between Protestant and Catholic, rural and urban, native and immigrant, middle class and lower class in American society. The political conflict lay in the efforts of an abstinent Protestant middle class to control the public affirmation of morality in drinking. Victory or defeat were consequently symbolic of the status and power of the cultures opposing each other.[13] Legal affirmation or rejection is thus important in what it symbolizes as well or instead of what it controls. Even if the law was broken, it was clear whose law it was.

Deviant Nonconformity and Designator Reaction

In Durkheim's analysis of the indignant and hostile response to norm-violation, all proscribed actions are threats to the existence of the norm.[14] Once we separate the instrumental from the symbolic functions of legal and governmental designation of deviants, however, we can question this assumption. We can look at norm-violation from the standpoint of its effects on the symbolic rather than the instrumental character of the norm. Our analysis of patterned evasion of norms has suggested that a law weak in its instrumental functions may nevertheless perform significant symbolic functions. Unlike human limbs, norms do not necessarily atrophy through disuse.

Standards of charity, mercy, and justice may be dishonored every day yet remain important statements of what is publicly approved as virtue. The sexual behavior of the human male and the human female need not be a copy of the socially sanctioned rules. Those rules remain as important affirmations of an acceptable code, even though they are regularly breached. Their roles as ideals are not threatened by daily behavior. In analyzing the violation of norms we will look at the implications of different forms of deviance on the symbolic character of the norm itself. *The point here is that the designators of deviant behavior react differently to different norm-sustaining implications of an act.* We can classify deviant behavior from this standpoint.

The Repentant Deviant

The reckless motorist often admits the legitimacy of traffic laws, even though he has broken them. The chronic alcoholic may well agree that both he and his society would be better if he could stay sober. In both cases the norm they have violated is itself unquestioned. Their deviation is a moral lapse, a fall from a grace to which they aspire. The homosexual who seeks a psychiatrist to rid himself of his habit has defined his actions similarly to those who have designated him as a deviant. There is a consensus between the designator and the deviant; his repentance confirms the norm.

Repentance and redemption seem to go hand-in-hand in court and church. Sykes and Matza have described techniques of neutralization which juvenile delinquents often use with enforcement agencies . . .

A show of repentance is also used, say Sykes and Matza, to soften the indignation of law enforcement agents. A recent study of police behavior lends support to this. Juveniles apprehended by the police received more lenient treatment, including dismissal, if they appeared contrite and remorseful about their violations than if they did not. This difference in the posture of the deviant accounted for much of the differential treatment favoring middle-class "youngsters" as against lower-class "delinquents."[15]

The Sick Deviant

Acts which represent an attack upon a norm are neutralized by repentance. The open admission of repentance confirms the sinner's belief in the sin. His threat to the norm is removed and his violation has left the norm intact. Acts which we can perceive as those of sick and diseased people are irrelevant to the norm; they neither attack nor defend it. The use of morphine by hospital patients in severe pain is not designated as deviant behavior. Sentiments of public hostility and the apparatus of enforcement agencies are not mobilized toward the morphine-user. His use is not perceived as a violation of the norm against drug use, but as an uncontrolled act, not likely to be recurrent[16] . . .

The Enemy Deviant

Writing about a Boston slum in the 1930s, William F. Whyte remarks:

> The policeman is subject to sharply conflicting pressures. On one side are the "good people" of Eastern City, who have written their moral judgments into law and demand through their newspapers that the law be enforced. On the other side are the people of Cornerville, who have different standards and have built up an organization whose perpetuation depends upon the freedom to violate the law.[17]

Whyte's is one of several studies that have pointed out the discrepancies between middle-class moralities embodied in law and lower-class moralities which differ sharply from them.[18] In Cornerville, gambling was seen as a "respectable" crime, just as antitrust behavior may be in other levels of the social structure. In American society, conflicts between social classes are often also cultural conflicts reflecting moral differences. Coincidence of ethnic and religious distinctions with class differences accentuates such conflicts between group values.

In these cases, the validity of the public designation is itself at issue. The publicly defined deviant is neither repentant nor sick, but is instead an upholder of an opposite norm. He accepts his behavior as proper and derogates the public norm as illegitimate. He refuses to internalize the public norm into his self-definition. This is especially likely to occur in instances of "business crimes." The buyer sees his action as legitimate economic behavior and resists a definition of it as immoral and thus prohibitable. The issue of "off-track" betting illustrates one area in which clashes of culture have been salient . . .

It is when the deviant is also an enemy and his deviance is an aspect of group culture that the conventional norm is most explicitly and energetically attacked. When those once designated as deviant have achieved enough political power they may shift from disobedience to an effort to change the designation itself. This has certainly happened in the civil rights movement. Behavior viewed as deviant in the segregationist society has in many instances been moved into the realm of the problematic, now subject to political processes of conflict and compromise.

When the deviant and the designator perceive each other as enemies, and the designator's power is superior to that of the deviant, we have domination without a corresponding legitimacy. Anything which increases the power of the deviant to organize and attack the norm is thus a threat to the social dominance symbolized in the affirmation of the norm. Under such conditions the need of the designators to strengthen and enforce the norms is great. The struggle over the symbol of social power and status is focused on the question of the maintenance or change of the legal norm. The threat to the middle class in the increased political power of Cornerville is not that the Cornerville resident will gamble more; he already does gamble with great frequency. The threat is that the law will come to accept the morality of gambling and treat it as a legitimate business. If this happens, Boston is no longer a city dominated by middle-class Yankees but becomes one dominated by lower-class immigrants, as many think has actually happened in Boston. The maintenance of a norm which defines gambling as deviant behavior thus symbolizes the maintenance of Yankee social and political superiority. Its disappearance as a public commitment would symbolize the loss of that superiority.

The Cynical Deviant

The professional criminal commits acts whose designation as deviant is supported by wide social consensus. The burglar, the hired murderer, the arsonist, the kidnapper all prey on victims. While they may use repentance or illness as strategies to manage the impressions of enforcers, their basic orientation is self-seeking, to get around the rules. It is for this reason that their behavior is not a great threat to the norms although it calls for social management and repression. It does not threaten the legitimacy of the normative order.

Drinking as a Changing Form of Deviance

Analysis of efforts to define drinking as deviant in the United States will illustrate the process by which designations shift. The legal embodiment of attitudes toward drinking shows how cultural conflicts find their expression in the symbolic functions of law. In the 160 years since 1800, we see all our suggested types of non-conforming behavior and all the forms of reaction among the conventional segments of the society.

The movement to limit and control personal consumption of alcohol began in the early nineteenth century, although some scattered attempts were made earlier.[19] Colonial legislation was aimed mainly at controlling the inn through licensing systems. While drunkenness occurred, and drinking was frequent, the rigid nature of the colonial society, in both North and South, kept drinking from becoming an important social issue.[20]

The Repentant Drinker

The definition of the drinker as an object of social shame begins in the early nineteenth century and reaches full development in the late 1820s and early 1830s. A wave of growth in Temperance organizations in this period was sparked by the conversion of drinking men to abstinence under the stimulus of evangelical revivalism.[21] Through drinking men joining together to take the pledge, a norm of abstinence and sobriety emerged as a definition of conventional respectability. They sought to control themselves and their neighbors.

The norm of abstinence and sobriety replaced the accepted patterns of heavy drinking countenanced in the late eighteenth and early nineteenth century. By the 1870s rural and small-town America had defined middle-class morals to include the Dry attitude. This definition had little need for legal embodiment. It could be enunciated in attacks on the drunkard which assumed that he shared the normative pattern of those who exhorted him to be better and to do better. He was a repentant deviant, someone to be brought back into the fold by moral persuasion and the techniques of religious revivalism.[22] His error was the sin of lapse from a shared standard of virtue. "The Holy Spirit will not visit, much less will He dwell within he who is under the polluting, debasing effects of intoxicating drink.

The state of heart and mind which this occasions to him is loathsome and an abomination."[23]

Moral persuasion thus rests on the conviction of a consensus between the deviant and the designators. As long as the object of attack and conversion is isolated in individual terms, rather than perceived as a group, there is no sense of his deviant act as part of a shared culture. What is shared is the norm of conventionality; the appeal to the drinker and the chronic alcoholic is to repent. When the Woman's Anti-Whiskey Crusade of 1873–1874 broke out in Ohio, church women placed their attention on the taverns. In many Ohio towns these respectable ladies set up vigils in front of the tavern and attempted to prevent men from entering just by the fear that they would be observed.[24] In keeping with the evangelical motif in the Temperance movement, the Washingtonians, founded in 1848, appealed to drinkers and chronic alcoholics with the emotional trappings and oratory of religious meetings, even though devoid of pastors.[25]

Moral persuasion, rather than legislation, has been one persistent theme in the designation of the drinker as deviant and the alcoholic as depraved. Even in the depictions of the miseries and poverty of the chronic alcoholic, there is a decided moral condemnation which has been the hallmark of the American Temperance movement. Moral persuasion was ineffective as a device to wipe out drinking and drunkenness. Heavy drinking persisted through the nineteenth century and the organized attempts to convert the drunkard experienced much backsliding.[26] Nevertheless, defections from the standard did not threaten the standard. The public definition of respectability matched the ideal of the sober and abstaining people who dominated those parts of the society where moral suasion was effective. In the late nineteenth century those areas in the which temperance sentiment was strongest were also those in which legislation was most easily enforceable.[27]

The Enemy Drinker

The demand for laws to limit alcoholic consumption appears to arise from situations in which the drinkers possess power as a definitive social and political group and, in their customary habits and beliefs, deny the validity of abstinence norms. The persistence of areas in which Temperance norms were least controlling led to the emergence of attempts to embody control in legal measures. The drinker as enemy seems to be the greatest stimulus to efforts to designate his act as publicly defined deviance.

In its early phase the American Temperance movement was committed chiefly to moral persuasion. Efforts to achieve legislation governing the sale and use of alcohol do not appear until the 1840s. This legislative movement had a close relationship to the immigration of Irish Catholics and German Lutherans into the United States in this period. These non-evangelical and/or non-Protestant people made up a large proportion of the urban poor in the 1840s and 1850s. They brought with them a far more accepting evaluation of drinking than had yet existed in the United States. The tavern and the beer parlor had a distinct place in the leisure of the Germans and the Irish. The prominence of this place was intensified by the stark character of the developing American slum.[28] These immigrant cultures did not contain a strong tradition of Temperance norms which might have made an effective appeal to a sense of sin. To be sure, excessive drunkenness was scorned, but neither abstinence nor constant sobriety were supported by the cultural codes.

Between these two groups—the native American, middle-class evangelical Protestant and the immigrant European Catholic or Lutheran occupying the urban lower class—there was little room for repentance. By the 1850s the issue of drinking reflected a general clash over cultural values. The Temperance movement found allies in its political efforts among the nativist movements.[29] The force and power of the anti-alcohol movements, however, were limited greatly by the political composition of the urban electorate, with its high proportion of immigrants. Thus the movement to develop legislation emerged in reaction to the appearance of cultural groups least responsive to the norms of abstinence and sobriety. The very effort to turn such informal norms into legal standards polarized the opposing forces and accentuated the symbolic import of the movement. Now that the issue had been joined, defeat or victory was a clear-cut statement of public dominance.

It is a paradox that the most successful move to eradicate alcohol emerged in a period when America was shifting from a heavy-drinking society, in which whiskey was the leading form of alcohol, to a moderate one, in which beer was replacing whiskey. Prohibition came as the culmination of the movement to reform the immigrant cultures and at the height of the immigrant influx into the United States . . .

The symbolic effect of Prohibition legislation must be kept analytically separate from its instrumental, enforcement side. While the urban middle class did provide much of the organizational leadership to the Temperance and Prohibition movements, the political strength of the movement in its legislative drives was in the rural areas of the United States. Here, where the problems of drinking were most under control, where the norm was relatively intact, the appeal to a struggle against foreign invasion was the most potent. In these areas, passage of legislation was likely to make small difference in behavior. The continuing polarization of political forces into those of cultural opposition and cultural acceptance during the Prohibition campaigns (1906–1919), and during the drive to Repeal (1926–1933), greatly intensified the symbolic significance of victory and defeat.[30] Even if the Prohibition measures were limited in their enforceability in the metropolis, there was no doubt about whose law was public and what way of life was being labeled as opprobrious.

After Repeal, as Dry power in American politics subsided, the designation of the drinker as deviant also receded. Public affirmation of the temperance norm had changed and with it the definition of the deviant had changed. Abstinence was itself less acceptable. In the 1950s the Temperance movement, faced with this change in public norms, even introduced a series of placards with the slogan, "It's Smart *Not* to Drink."

Despite this normative change in the public designation of drinking deviance, there has not been much change in American drinking patterns. Following the Prohibition period the consumption of alcohol has not returned to its pre-1915 high. Beer has continued to occupy a more important place as a source of alcohol consumption. "Hard drinkers" are not as common in America today as they were in the nineteenth century. While there has been some increase in moderate drinking, the percentage of adults who are abstainers has remained approximately the same (one-third) for the past 30 years. Similarly, Dry sentiment has remained stable, as measured by local opinion results.[31] In short, the argument over deviance designation has been largely one of normative dominance, not of instrumental social control. The process of deviance

designation in drinking needs to be understood in terms of symbols of cultural dominance rather than in the activities of social control.

The Sick Drinker

For most of the nineteenth century, the chronic alcoholic as well as the less compulsive drinker was viewed as a sinner. It was not until after Repeal (1933) that chronic alcoholism became defined as illness in the United States. Earlier actions taken toward promotion of the welfare of drinkers and alcoholics through Temperance measures rested on the moral supremacy of abstinence and the demand for repentance. The user of alcohol could be an object of sympathy, but his social salvation depended on a willingness to embrace the norm of his exhorters. The designation of alcoholism as sickness has a different bearing on the question of normative superiority. It renders the behavior of the deviant indifferent to the status of norms enforcing abstinence.

This realization appears to have made supporters of Temperance and Prohibition hostile to efforts to redefine the deviant character of alcoholism. They deeply opposed the reports of the Committee of Fifty in the late nineteenth century.[32] These volumes of reports by scholars and prominent men took a less moralistic and a more sociological and functional view of the saloon and drinking than did the Temperance movement.

The soundness of these fears is shown by what did happen to the Temperance movement with the rise of the view that alcoholism is illness. It led to new agencies concerned with drinking problems. These excluded Temperance people from the circle of those who now define what is deviant in drinking habits. The National Commission on Alcoholism was formed in 1941 and the Yale School of Alcoholic Studies formed in 1940. They were manned by medical personnel, social workers, and social scientists, people now alien to the spirit of the abstainer. Problems of drinking were removed from the church and placed in the hands of the universities and the medical clinics. The tendency to handle drinkers through protective and welfare agencies rather than through police or clergy has become more frequent.

"The bare statement that 'alcoholism is a disease' is most misleading since . . . it conceals what is essential— that a step in public policy is being recommended, not a scientific discovery announced."[33] John Seeley's remark is an apt one. Replacement of the norm of sin and repentance by that of illness and therapy removes the onus of guilt and immorality from the act of drinking and the state of chronic alcoholism. It replaces the image of the sinner with that of a patient, a person to be helped rather than to be exhorted. No wonder that the Temperance movement has found the work of the Yale School, and often even the work of Alcoholics Anonymous, a threat to its own movement. It has been most limited in its cooperation with these organizations and has attempted to set up other organizations which might provide the face of Science in league with the tone of the movement.[34]

The redefinition of the alcoholic as sick thus brought into power both ideas and organizations antithetical to the Temperance movement. The norm protected by law and government was no longer the one held by the people who had supported Temperance and Prohibition. The hostility of Temperance people is readily understandable; their relative political unimportance is crucial to their present inability to make that hostility effective.

Movements of Moral Passage

In this paper we have called attention to the fact that deviance designations have histories; the public definition of behavior as deviant is itself changeable. It is open to reversals of political power, twists of public opinion, and the development of social movements and moral crusades. What is attacked as criminal today may be seen as sick next year and fought over as possibly legitimate by the next generation.

Movements to redefine behavior may eventuate in a moral passage, a transition of the behavior from one moral status to another. In analyzing movements toward the redefinition of alcohol use, we have dealt with moral crusades which were restrictive and others which were permissive toward drinking and toward "drunkards." (We might have also used the word "alcoholics," suggesting a less disapproving and more medical perspective.) In both cases, however, the movements sought to change the public designation. While we are familiar with the restrictive or enforcing movements, the permissive or legitimizing movement must also be seen as a prevalent way in which deviants throw off the onus of their actions and avoid the sanctions associated with immoral activities.

Even where the deviants are a small and politically powerless group they may nevertheless attempt to protect themselves by influence over the process of designation. The effort to define themselves as ill is one plausible means to this end. Drug addiction as well as drunkenness is partially undergoing a change toward such redefinition.[35] This occurs in league with powerful groups in society, such as social workers, medical professionals, or university professors. The moral passage achieved here reduces the sanctions imposed by criminal law and the public acceptance of the deviant designation.

The "lifting" of a deviant activity to the level of a political, public issue is thus a sign that its moral status is at stake, that legitimacy is a possibility. Today the moral acceptance of drinking, marijuana and LSD use, homosexuality, abortion, and other "vices" is being publicly discussed, and movements championing them have emerged. Such movements draw into them far more than the deviants themselves. Because they become symbols of general cultural attitudes they call out partisans for both repression and permission. The present debate over drug addiction laws in the United States, for example, is carried out between defenders and opposers of the norm rather than between users and non-users of the drugs involved.

As the movement for redefinition of the addict as sick has grown, the movement to strengthen the definition of addiction as criminal has responded with increased legal severity. To classify drug users as sick and the victims or clients as suffering from "disease" would mean a change in the agencies responsible for reaction from police enforcement to medical authorities. Further, it might diminish the moral disapproval with which drug use, and the reputed euphoric effects connected with it, are viewed by supporters of present legislation. Commenting on the clinic plan to permit medical dispensing of narcotics to licensed addicts, U.S. Commissioner of Narcotics Anslinger wrote:

> This plan would elevate a most despicable trade to the avowed status of an honorable business, nay, to the status of practice of a time-honored profession; and drug addicts would multiply unrestrained, to the irrevocable impairment of the moral fiber and physical welfare of the American people.[36]

In this paper we have seen that redefining moral crusades tends to generate strong counter-movements. The deviant as a cultural opponent is a more potent threat to the norm than is the repentant, or even the sick, deviant. The threat to the legitimacy of the norm is a spur to the need for symbolic restatement in legal terms. In these instances of "crimes without victims" the legal norm is *not* the enunciator of a consensus within the community. On the contrary, it is when consensus is least attainable that the pressure to establish legal norms appears to be greatest.

NOTES

1. Howard S. Becker, *Outsiders: Studies in the Sociology of Deviance,* Glencoe: The Free Press, 1963, Chap. 1. A similar view is presented in John Kitsuse, "Societal Reaction to Deviant Behavior," *Social Problems,* 9 (Winter, 1962), pp. 247–256; Kai Erikson, "Sociology of Deviance," in E. McDonagh and J. Simpson, editors, *Social Problems,* New York: Holt, Rinehart and Winston, Inc., 1965, pp. 457–464, p. 458.

2. The material of this section is more fully discussed in my book *Symbolic Crusade: Status Politics and the American Temperance Movement,* Urbana: University of Illinois Press, 1963, esp. Chap. 7.

3. See the analysis of power as infused with collective goals in Parsons's criticism of C. Wright Mills, *The Power Elite:* Talcott Parsons, "The Distribution of Power in American Society," *World Politics,* 10 (October, 1957), p. 123, 144.

4. Francis X. Sutton, "Representation and the Nature of Political Systems," *Comparative Studies in Society and History,* 2 (October, 1959), pp. 1–10. In this paper Sutton shows that in some primitive societies, political officials function chiefly as representatives to other tribes rather than as law enforcers or policy makers.

5. Phillip Wheelwright, *The Burning Fountain,* Bloomington: Indiana University Press, 1964, p. 23.

6. Talcott Parsons, *The Social System,* Glencoe: The Free Press, 1954, p. 286.

7. Murray Edelman has shown this in his analysis of the discrepancy between legislative action and administrative agency operation. Murray Edelman, *The Symbolic Uses of Politics,* Urbana: University of Illinois Press, 1964.

8. Robin Williams, *American Society,* New York: A. A. Knopf, 1960, pp. 372–396. Hyman Rodman's analysis of "lower-class value stretch" suggests yet another ambiguity in the concept of norm. He found that in Trinidad, among lower-class respondents, *both* marriage and non-legal marital union are normatively accepted, although marriage is preferred. Hyman Rodman, "Illegitimacy in the Caribbean Social Structure," *American Sociological Review,* 31 (October, 1966), pp. 673–683.

9. Edelman, *op. cit.,* Chap. 2. The author refers to this as a process of political quiescence. While Edelman's symbolic analysis is close to mine, his emphasis is on the reassurance function of symbols in relation to presumed instrumental affects. My analysis stresses the conflict over symbols as a process of importance apart from instrumental effects.

10. Gusfield, *op. cit.,* pp. 117–126.

11. Joseph Gusfield, "Prohibition: The Impact of Political Utopianism," in John Braeman, editor, *The 1920's Revisited,* Columbus: Ohio State University Press, forthcoming; Andrew Sinclair, *The Era of Excess,* New York: Harper Colophon Books, 1964, Chap. 10, pp. 13–14.

12. Kenneth Burke, *A Grammar of Motives,* New York: Prentice Hall, 1945, p. 393. Burke's writings have been the strongest influence on the mode of analysis presented here. Two other writers, whose works have been influential, themselves influenced by Burke, are Erving Goffman and Hugh D. Duncan.

13. Gusfield, *Symbolic Crusade, op. cit.,* Chap. 5.

14. Emile Durkheim, *The Division of Labor in Society,* trans. George Simpson, Glencoe: The Free Press, 1947, especially at pp. 96–103. For a similar view see Lewis Coser, "Some Functions of Deviant Behavior and Normative Flexibility," *American Journal of Sociology,* 68 (September, 1962), pp. 172–182.

15. Irving Piliavin and Scott Briar, "Police Encounters with Juveniles," *American Journal of Sociology,* 70 (September, 1964), pp. 206–214.

16. This of course does not mean that the patient using morphine may not become an addict.

17. William F. Whyte, *Street-Corner Society,* Chicago: University of Chicago Press, 2nd edition, 1955, p. 138.

18. See William Westley's analysis of the differences between the morality shared by the lower class and the police in contrast to that of the courts over such matters as gambling, prostitution, and sexual perversion. The courts take a sterner view of gamblers and prostitutes than do the police, who take a sterner view of the sexual offender. William Westley, "Violence and the Police," *American Journal of Sociology,* 59 (July, 1953), pp. 34–42.

19. The best single account of Temperance activities before the Civil War is that of John Krout, *The Origins of Prohibition,* New York: A. A. Knopf, 1925.

20. *Ibid.,* Chapters 1 and 2; also see Alice Earle, *Home Life in Colonial Days,* New York: Macmillan and Co., 1937, pp. 148–149; 156–165.

21. Gusfield, *Symbolic Crusade, op. cit.,* pp. 44–51.

22. *Ibid.,* pp. 69–86.

23. *Temperance Manual* (no publisher listed, 1836), p. 46.

24. See the typical account by Mother Stewart, one of the leaders in the 1873–74 Woman's War on Whiskey, in Eliza D. Steward, *Memories of the Crusade,* Columbus, Ohio: W. G. Hibbard, 2nd edition, 1889, pp. 139–143; also see *Standard Encyclopedia of the Alcohol Problem,* 6 (Westerville, Ohio: American Issue Publishing Co., 1930), pp. 2902–2905.

25. Krout, *op. cit.,* Chap. 9.

26. See the table of consumption of alcoholic beverages, 1850–1957, in Mark Keller and Vera Efron, "Selected Statistics on Alcoholic Beverage," reprinted in Raymond McCarthy, editor, *Drinking and Intoxication,* Glencoe: The Free Press, 1959, p. 180.

27. Joseph Rowntree and Arthur Sherwell, *State Prohibition and Local Option,* London: Hodden and Stoughton, 1900, using both systematic observation and analysis of Federal tax payments, concluded (p. 253) that ". . . local veto in America has only been found operative outside the larger towns and cities."

28. See the accounts of drinking habits among Irish and German immigrants in Oscar Handlin, *Boston's Immigrants,* Cambridge, Massachusetts: Harvard University Press, 1941, pp. 191–192, 201–209; Marcus Hansen, *The Immigrant in American History,* Cambridge, Massachusetts: Harvard University Press, 1940.

29. Ray Billington, *The Protestant Crusade,* 1800–1860, New York: Macmillan, 1938, Chap. 15; Gusfield, *Symbolic Crusade, op. cit.,* pp. 55–57.

30. Although a well-organized Temperance movement existed among Catholics, it was weakened by the Protestant drive for Prohibition: See Joan Bland, *Hibernian Crusade,* Washington, D.C.: Catholic University Press, 1951.

31. See my analysis of American drinking in the post-Repeal era. Gusfield, "Prohibition: The Impact of Political Utopianism," *op. cit.*

32. The Committee of Fifty, a group of prominent educators, scientists, and clergymen sponsored and directed several studies of drinking and the saloon. Their position as men unaffiliated to temperance organizations was intended to introduce unbiased investigation, often critical of Temperance doctrine. For two of the leading volumes see John Shaw Billing's, *The Physiological Aspects of the Liquor Problem,* Boston and New York: Houghton, Mifflin and Co., 1903; Raymond Calkins, *Substitutes for the Saloon,* Boston and New York: Houghton, Mifflin and Co., 1903.

33. John Seeley, "Alcoholism Is a Disease: Implications for Social Policy," in D. Pittman and C. Snyder, editors, *Society, Culture and Drinking Patterns,* New York: John Wiley and Sons, 1962, pp. 586–593, at p. 593. For a description of the variety of definitions of alcoholism and drunkenness, as deviant and non-deviant, see the papers by Edwin Lemert, "Alcohol, Values and Social Control" and by Archer Tongue, "What the State Does About Alcohol and Alcoholism," both in the same volume.

34. The WCTU, during the 1950s, persistently avoided support to Alcoholics Anonymous. The Yale School of Alcohol Studies was attacked and derogated in Temperance literature. A counter-organization, with several prominent pro-Dry scientists, developed, held seminars, and issued statements in opposition to Yale School publications.

35. Many of the writings of sociologists interested in drug addiction have contained explicit demands for such redefinitions. See Becker, *op. cit.;* Alfred Lindesmith, *The Addict and the Law,* Bloomington: Indiana University Press, 1965, and David Ausubel, *Drug Addiction,* New York: Random House, 1958. The recent movement to redefine marijuana and LSD as legitimate is partially supported by such writings but is more saliently a movement of enemy deviants. The activities of Timothy Leary, Allen Ginsberg, and the "hipsters" is the most vocal expression of this movement.

36. Harry Anslinger and William Tompkins, *The Traffic in Narcotics,* New York: Funk and Wagnalls Co., Inc., 1953, p. 186.

Think Critically

1. Gusfield examines "symbolic processes" and "moral passage" in defining the use of alcohol as deviant. What does he mean by these terms, and how are they tied more generally to the symbolic interactionist/labeling perspective of deviance?

2. Gusfield explains that the "enemy deviant" is of more general social concern than other types of deviants. In what way(s) is this accurate? How are the deviants fundamentally different? Why is this important theoretically?

Marihuana Use and Social Control*

Howard S. Becker**

WHEN DEVIANT BEHAVIOR OCCURS IN A society—behavior which flouts its basic values and norms—one element in its coming into being is a breakdown in social controls, those mechanisms which ordinarily operate to maintain valued forms of behavior. In complex societies, the process is somewhat more complicated since breakdowns in social control are often the consequences of the person becoming a participant in a subculture whose controls operate at cross-purposes to those of the larger society. Important factors in the genesis of deviant behavior, then, may be sought in those processes by which people are emancipated from the larger set of controls and become responsive to those of the subculture.

Social controls affect individual behavior, in the first instance, through the use of power, the application of sanctions. Valued behavior is rewarded and negatively valued behavior is punished. Control would be difficult to maintain if such enforcement were always needed, so that more subtle mechanisms performing the same function arise. Among these is the control of behavior achieved by affecting the conceptions persons have of the to-be-controlled activity, and of the possibility or feasibility of engaging in it. These conceptions arise in social situations in which they are communicated by persons regarded as reputable and validated in experience. Such situations may be so ordered that individuals come to conceive of the activity as distasteful, inexpedient, or immoral, and therefore do not engage in it.

Such a perspective invites us to analyze the genesis of deviant behavior in terms of events which render sanctions ineffective and experiences which shift conceptions so that the behavior becomes a conceivable possibility to the person. This paper is devoted to an analysis of this process in the instance of marihuana use. Its basic question is: what is the sequence of events and experiences by which a person comes to be able to carry on the use of marihuana, in spite of the elaborate social controls functioning to prevent such behavior?

A number of potent forces operate to control the use of marihuana in this country. The act is illegal and punishable by severe penalties. Its illegality makes access to the drug difficult, placing immediate obstacles before anyone who wishes to use it. Actual use can be dangerous, for arrest and imprisonment are always possible consequences. In addition, those who are discovered in their use of the drug by family, friends, or employers may be subject to various kinds of informal but highly effective sanctions and social punishments; ostracism, withdrawal of affection, etc. Finally, a set of traditional views has grown up, defining the practice as a violation of basic moral imperatives, as an act leading to loss of self-control, paralysis of the will, and eventual slavery to the drug. Such views are commonplace and are an effective force preventing marihuana use.

The development of marihuana-using activity in an individual may be divided into three stages, each representing a distinct shift in the person's relations to these social controls of the larger society and those of the subculture in which marihuana use is found. The first stage is represented by the *beginner,* the person smoking marihuana for the first time; the second, by the *occasional user,* whose use is sporadic and dependent on chance factors; and the third, by the *regular user,* for whom use becomes a systematic daily routine.

*© 1955 by the Society for the Study of Social Problems. Reprinted from *Social Problems,* 54 (July, 1955), pp. 35–44 by permission of the author and the publisher.

**The research on which this paper is based was done while I was a member of the staff of the Chicago Narcotics Survey, a project done by the Chicago Area Project, Inc., under a grant from the National Mental Health Institute. I wish to thank Eliot Freidson, Erving Goffman, Anselm Strauss, and R. Richard Wohl for reading and commenting on an earlier version.

The analysis will be pursued in terms of the processes by which the various kinds of social controls become progressively less effective as the user moves from level to level of use or, alternatively, the ways in which they prevent such movement by remaining effective. The major kinds of controls to be considered are: (a) control through limiting of supply and access to the drug; (b) control through the necessity of keeping non-users from discovering that one is a user; (c) control through definition of the act as immoral. The rendering ineffective of these controls, at the levels and in the combinations to be described, may be taken as an essential condition for continued and increased marihuana use . . .

Supply

Marihuana use is limited, in the first instance, by laws making possession or sale of drugs punishable by severe penalties. This confines its distribution to illicit sources which are not available to the ordinary person. In order for a person to begin marihuana use, he must begin participation in some group through which these sources of supply become available to him, ordinarily a group organized around values and activities opposing those of the larger conventional society . . .

If an occasional user begins to move on toward a more regularized and systematic mode of use, he can do it only by finding some more stable source of supply than more-or-less chance encounters with other users, and this means establishing connections with persons who make a business of dealing in narcotics. Although purchases in large quantities are necessary for regular use, they are not ordinarily made with that intent; but, once made, they do render such use possible, as it was not before. Such purchases tend to be made as the user becomes more responsive to the controls of the drug-using group:

> I was running around with this whole crowd of people who turned on then. And they were always turning me on, you know, until it got embarrassing. I was really embarrassed that I never had any, that I couldn't reciprocate. . . . So I asked around where I could get some and picked up for the first time.

Also, purchasing from a dealer is more economical, since there are no middlemen and the purchaser of larger quantities receives, as in the ordinary business world, a lower price.

However, in order to make these purchases, the user must have a "connection"—know someone who makes a business of selling drugs. These dealers operate illicitly, and in order to do business with them one must know where to find them and be identified to them in such a way that they will not hesitate to make a sale. This is quite difficult for persons who are very casually involved in drug-using groups. But as a person becomes more identified with these groups, and is considered more trustworthy, the necessary knowledge and introductions to dealers become available to him. In becoming defined as a member, one is also defined as a person who can safely be trusted to buy drugs without endangering anyone else . . .

Each level of use, from beginning to routine, thus has its typical mode of supply, which must be present for such use to occur. In this sense, the social mechanisms which operate to limit availability of the drug limit its use. However, participation in groups in which marihuana is used creates the conditions under which these controls which limit access to it no longer operate. Such participation also involves increased sensitivity to the controls of the drug-using group, so that there are forces pressing toward use of the new sources of supply. Changes in the mode of supply in turn create the conditions for movement to a new level of use. Consequently, it may be said that changes in group participation and membership lead to changes in level of use by affecting the individual's access to marihuana under present conditions in which the drug is available only through illicit outlets.

Secrecy

Marihuana use is limited also to the extent that individuals actually find it inexpedient or believe that they will find it so. This inexpediency, real or presumed, arises from the fact or belief that if non-users discover that one uses the drug, sanctions of some important kind will be applied. The user's conception of these sanctions is vague, because few of them seem ever to have had such an experience or to have known anyone who did. Although he does not know what specifically to expect in the way of punishments, the outlines are clear: He fears repudiation by people whose respect and acceptance he requires both practically and emotionally. That is, he expects that his relationships with non-users will be disturbed and disrupted if they should find out, and limits and controls his behavior accordingly.

This kind of control breaks down in the course of the user's participation with other users and in the development of his experience with the drug, as he comes to realize that, though it might be true that sanctions would be applied if non-users found out, they need never find out. At each level of use, there is a growth in this realization which makes the new level possible.

For the beginner, these considerations are very important and must be overcome if use is to be undertaken at all. These fears are challenged by the sight of others—more experienced users—who apparently feel there is little or no danger and appear to engage in the activity with impunity. If one does "try it once," he may still his fears by observations of this kind. Participation with other users thus furnishes the beginner with the rationalizations with which first to attempt the act.

Further participation in the marihuana use of these groups allows the novice to draw the further conclusion that the act can be safe no matter how often indulged in, as long as one is careful and makes sure that non-users are not present or likely to intrude. This kind of perspective is a necessary prerequisite for occasional use, in which the drug is used when other users invite one to join them. While it permits this level of use, such a perspective does not allow regular use to occur for the worlds of user and non-user, while separate to a degree allowing the occasional use pattern to persist, are not completely segregated. The points where these worlds meet appear dangerous to the occasional user who must, therefore, confine his use to those occasions on which such meeting does not seem likely.

Regular use, on the other hand, implies a systematic and routine use of the drug which does not take into account such possibilities and plan periods of "getting high" around them. It is a mode of use which depends on another kind of attitude toward the possibility of non-users finding out, the attitude that marihuana use can be carried on under the noses of non-users, or, alternatively, on the living of a pattern of social participation which reduces contacts with non-users almost to the zero point. Without this adjustment in attitude, participation, or both, the user is forced to remain at the level of occasional use. These adjustments take place in terms of two categories or risks involved: First, that non-users will discover marihuana in one's possession and second, that one will be unable to hide the effects of the drug when he is "high" while with non-users . . .

If a person uses marihuana regularly and routinely it is almost inevitable—since even in urban society such roles cannot be kept completely separate—that he one day find himself "high" while in the company of non-users from whom he wishes to keep his marihuana use secret. Given the variety of symptoms the drug may produce, it is natural for the user to fear that he might reveal through his behavior that he is "high," that he might be unable to control the symptoms and thus give away his own secret. Such phenomena as difficulty in focusing one's attention and in carrying on normal conversation create a fear that everyone will know exactly why one is behaving in this way, that the behavior will be interpreted automatically as a sign of drug use.

Those who progress to regular use manage to avoid this dilemma. It may happen, as noted above, that they come to participate almost completely in the subcultural group in which the practice is carried on, so that they simply have a minimal amount of contact with non-users about whose opinions they care. Since this isolation from conventional society is seldom complete, the user must learn another method of avoiding the dilemma, one which is the most important method for those whose participation is never so completely segregated. This consists of learning to control the drug's effects while in the company of non-users, so that they can be fooled and the secret successfully kept even though one continues participation with them . . .

In short, persons limit their use of marihuana in proportion to the degree of their fear, realistic or otherwise, that non-users who are important to them will discover that they use drugs and react in some punishing way. This kind of control breaks down as the user discovers that his fears are excessive and unrealistic, as he comes to conceive of the practice as one which can be kept secret with relative ease. Each level of use can occur only when the person has revised his conception of the dangers involved in such a way as to allow it.

Morality

This section discusses the role of conventional notions of morality as a means through which marihuana use is controlled. The basic moral imperatives which operate here are those which require the individual to be responsible for his own welfare, and to be able to control his behavior rationally. The stereotype of the dope fiend portrays a person who violates these imperatives. A recent description of the marihuana user illustrates the principal features of this stereotype:

> In the earliest stages of intoxication the willpower is destroyed and inhibitions and restraints are released; the moral barricades are broken down and often debauchery and sexuality result. Where mental instability is inherent, the behavior is generally violent. An egotist will enjoy delusions of grandeur, the timid individual will suffer anxiety, and the aggressive one often will resort to acts of violence and crime. Dormant tendencies are released and while the subject may know what is happening, he has become powerless to prevent it. Constant use produces an incapacity for work and a disorientation of purpose.

One must add to this, of course, the notion that the user becomes a slave to the drug, that he voluntarily surrenders himself to a habit from which there is no escape. The person who takes such a stereotype seriously is presented with a serious obstacle to drug use. Use will ordinarily be begun, maintained and increased only when some other way of viewing the practice is accepted by the individual.

The beginner has at some time shared these views. In the course of his participation in some unconventional segment of society, however, he is likely to acquire a more "emancipated" view of the moral standards implicit in this characterization of the drug user, at least to the point that he will not reject activities out of hand simply because they are conventionally condemned. The observation of others using the drug may further tempt him to apply his rejection of conventional standards to the specific instance of marihuana use. Such participation, then, tends to provide the conditions under which these controls can be circumvented at least sufficiently for first use to be attempted.

In the course of further experience in these groups, the novice acquires a whole series of rationalizations and justifications with which he may answer objections to occasional use if he decides to engage in it. If he should raise himself the objections of conventional morality he finds ready answers available in the folklore of marihuana using groups.

One of the most common rationalizations is that conventional persons indulge in much more harmful practices and that a comparatively minor vice like marihuana smoking cannot really be wrong when such things as the use of alcohol are so commonly accepted:

> (You don't dig (like) alcohol then?) No, I don't dig it at all. (Why not?) I don't know. I just don't. Well, see,

here's the thing. Before I was at the age where kids start drinking I was already getting on (using marihuana) and I saw the advantages of getting on, you know, I mean there was no sickness and it was much cheaper. That was one of the first things I learned, man. Why do you want to drink? Drinking is dumb, you know. It's so much cheaper to get on and you don't get sick, and it's not sloppy and takes less time. And it just grew to be the thing, you know. So I got on before I drank, you know. . . .

Additional rationalizations enable the user to suggest to himself that the drug's effects, rather than being harmful, are in fact beneficial:

> I have had some that made me feel like . . . very invigorated and also it gives a very strong appetite. It makes you very hungry. That's probably good for some people who are underweight.

Finally, the user, at this point, is not using the drug all the time. His use is scheduled, there being times when he considers it appropriate and times when he does not. The fact of this schedule allows him to assure himself that he controls the drug, rather than the drug controlling him, and becomes a symbol of the harmlessness of the practice. He does not consider himself a slave to the drug, because he can and does abide by this schedule, regardless of the amount of use the particular schedule may allow. The fact that there are times when he does not, on principle, use the drug, can be used as proof to himself of his freedom with respect to it . . .

Occasional use can occur in an individual who accepts these views, for he has reorganized his moral notions in such a way as to permit it, primarily by acquiring the conceptions that conventional moral notions about drugs do not apply to this drug and that, in any case, his use of it has not become excessive.

If use progresses to the point of becoming regular and systematic, these questions may again be raised for the user, for he begins now to look, to himself as well as others, like the uncontrolled "dope fiend" of popular mythology. He must convince himself again, if use is to continue at this level, that he has not crossed this line . . .

The earlier rationalization with regard to the beneficial effects of the drug remain unchanged and may even undergo a considerable elaboration. But the question raised in the last quotation proves more troublesome. In view of his increased and regularized consumption of the drug, the user is not sure that he is really able to control, that he has not possibly become the slave of a vicious habit. Tests are made—use is given up and the consequences awaited—and when nothing untoward occurs, the user is able to draw the conclusion that there is nothing to fear.

The problem is, however, more difficult for some of the more sophisticated users who derive their moral directives not so much from conventional thinking as from popular psychiatric "theory." Their use troubles them, not in conventional terms, but because of what it may indicate about their mental health. Accepting current thinking about the causes of drug use, they reason that no one would use drugs in any large amounts unless "something" were "wrong" with him, unless there were some neurotic maladjustment which made drugs necessary. The fact of marihuana smoking becomes a symbol of psychic weakness and, ultimately, moral weakness . . .

Certain morally toned conceptions about the nature of drug use and drug users thus influence the marihuana user. If he is unable to explain away or ignore these conceptions, use will not occur at all, and the degree of use appears to be related to the degree to which these conceptions no longer are influential, having been replaced by rationalizations and justifications current among users.

Discussion

The extent of an individual's use of marihuana is at least partly dependent on the degree to which conventional social controls fail to prevent his engaging in the activity. Apart from other possible necessary conditions, it may be said that marihuana use can occur at the various levels described only when the necessary events and shifts in conception of the activity have removed the individual from the influence of these controls and substituted for them the controls of the subcultural group.

This kind of analysis seems to put some experiential flesh on the bare bones of the contention that the assumption of roles in a deviant subculture accounts for deviant behavior. There is, of course, a close relationship between the two. But a good deal of theoretical and practical difficulty is avoided by introducing an intervening process of change in social participation and individual conception made possible, but not inevitable by subcultural membership, and which becomes itself the explanatory factor. In this way, the element of truth in the simpler statement is conserved while the difficulties posed by those who

participate in such groups without engaging in the deviant behavior are obviated. Such membership only provides the possibility, not the necessity, of having those experiences which will produce the behavior. The analysis may be made finer by then considering those contingencies which tend to determine whether or not the member of such a group actually has the necessary experiences.

Such a view necessarily implies the general hypothesis, of some interest to students of culture and personality, that the holding of a social position, in and of itself, cannot be considered to explain an individual's behavior. Rather, the analysis of behavior must take account of social roles in a more subtle fashion, by asking what possibilities of action and what experiences which might shape the individual's appreciation and tendency to make use of those possibilities are provided by a given role. Such a viewpoint continues to insist on the analytic importance of the role concept, which calls our attention to the patterning of an individual's experience by the position which he holds in an organized social group, but adds to this an emphasis on the experience itself as it shapes conduct and the process by which this shaping occurs.

REFERENCES

H. J. Anslinger and William F. Tompkins. *The Traffic in Narcotics,* New York: Funk and Wagnalls Company, 1953, pp. 21–2.

Howard S. Becker. "Becoming a Marihuana User," *American Journal of Sociology,* LIX (November, 1953), 235–42.

Alfred R. Lindesmith. *Opiate Addiction,* Bloomington: Principia Press, 1947.

Think Critically

1. Discuss the stages that marijuana users go through in terms of negotiating the social controls that exist against their behavior. Do you feel that the process Becker identifies is useful in understanding other drug use? Explain why or why not.
2. Describe the ways in which marijuana use is limited according to Becker. How might this help in understanding drug use more generally?

Deviance as a Situated Phenomenon
*Variations in the Social Interpretation of Marijuana and Alcohol Use**

James D. Orcutt**

Introduction

A relativistic orientation has become preeminent in recent theoretical work in the field of deviance (Douglas, 1971; Rubington and Weinberg, 1973; Davis, 1972; Matza, 1969; Schur, 1971). In contrast to earlier structural or normative theories of deviant behavior, relativistic theories do not treat deviance as an objectively given quality of certain acts or actors. Rather, deviance is viewed as analytically identifiable only *in relation to* interpretational and interactional processes through which acts and actors are *socially defined* as deviant. Erikson (1966:11), for example, states: "Deviance is not a property *inherent in* certain forms of behavior; it is a property *conferred upon* these forms by the audiences which directly or indirectly witness them" (emphasis in original). Assignment of this symbolic property to a certain act may depend as much or more on various characteristics of the actors, audiences, and situations involved than on the nature of the act itself. Thus, an actor's behavior is but one of a number of contingencies which must be considered in relativistic analyses of social definitions of deviance.

Unfortunately, this relativistic orientation has served more as a focal point for critique, debate, and speculation than as a heuristic stimulus for empirical research (see Gibbs, 1966; 1972; Schur, 1971: 7–36; Davis, 1972). In particular, few studies have dealt with the relativistic

argument that social interpretations of "deviant behavior" are situationally problematic. Audience interpretations of a given act as deviant or nondeviant are taken to be highly dependent upon the social circumstances within which that act is embedded. The same act interpreted as deviant under one set of circumstances might be seen as quite acceptable under other circumstances. As an illustration of this argument, Douglas (1971:139) cites the following example adapted from Blum (1970):

> . . . a woman observed on the streets of a city to be wailing might well be thought to be "mentally ill." Yet once we know that she has just been in an automobile accident in which a loved one has been killed, her behavior can be seen to be "normal grief" and not "mental illness." Only the situational context makes this clear to us.

Deviance theorists in the "ethnomethodological" tradition, such as Douglas, Blum, and McHugh (1970) have been especially insistent on treating deviance as a "situated" phenomenon. However, a concern with situational variations in interpretational processes is also evident in more conventional theories of societal reaction and labeling (Kitsuse, 1962; Rubington and Weinberg, 1973: 1–10). Yet with the exception of several studies on police work (Piliavin and Briar, 1964; Bittner, 1967a; 1967b; Black and Reiss, 1970; Black, 1970), deviance research has overlooked this problem.

Previous theoretical discussions of situated interpretations of deviance have been rather abstract and have not provided systematic guidelines for research. This study will attempt to specify several situational factors which influence the interpretational process. The influences of these factors will be examined empirically, using survey data which compare interpretive reactions to marijuana use and alcohol use in various situations.

*© 1978 by the Society for the Study of Social Problems.
Reprinted from *Social Problems,* 22 (February 1975), pp. 346–356 by permission of the author and publisher.
**Presented at the 1974 Annual Meeting of the Southern Sociological Society, Atlanta. The author wishes to thank Donald A. Biggs for facilitating this research and to acknowledge the support of a grant from the Office for Student Affairs, University of Minn.

Situational Variations in the Interpretational Process

One of the earliest and clearest statements of the relativistic orientation is Kitsuse's (1962) analysis of societal reactions to deviance. Deviance, for Kitsuse, must be defined and analyzed from the point of view of those who interpret and react to behavior as deviant. Accordingly, he conceptualizes "deviance" as a three-stage process "by which the members of a group, community, or society (1) interpret behavior as deviant, (2) define persons who so behave as a certain kind of deviant, and (3) accord them the treatment considered appropriate to such deviants" (Kitsuse, 1962:248). These stages represent empirically related, but analytically distinct sources of variation in social definitions of deviance. The initiating stage in Kitsuse's formulation—interpretations of behavior as deviant—is of primary interest here.[1] Although Kitsuse (1962:255) indicates that the "interpretational process may be activated by a wide range of situational behavior," he does not present a detailed analysis of these situational variations.

In a recent paper, Orcutt (1973) attempts to extend Kitsuse's work by relating it to laboratory studies of deviation in small groups. On the basis of a reanalysis of two small group studies, he identifies three situational conditions which appear to influence naïve group members' interpretations of "deviation" performed by experimental confederates during group discussions. Group members' attitudinal hostility toward a confederate tends to increase to the extent that the confederate's behavior is perceived (1) to interfere with central situational goals, (2) to be stable, i.e., unresponsive to social influence and situational change, and (3) to be motivated by pervasive personal dispositions of the confederate rather than by immediate social events in the situation. These three conditions refer to joint perceptual relationships between the confederate's actions and the situational context from which interpretations of deviant behavior are derived. Cumulative combinations of these perceptual conditions are used by group members as grounds for assigning "deviance" as a situated meaning to the confederate's actions. Consistent with Kitsuse's formulation, Orcutt argues that such interpretations subsequently provide members with evidence for defining the confederate as deviant *in character* and with justification for reacting to him accordingly.

Orcutt's (1973) analysis of situational contingencies in the interpretational process is limited by its reliance on indirect inference from previously published research. A more adequate analysis of these conditional factors would require that the situational context be systematically varied while holding the actor's behavior constant. The present study attempts such an analysis. Respondents in the investigation reported here were asked to interpret the acceptability or unacceptability of marijuana use or alcohol use in various hypothetical situations. Situational circumstances were systematically varied according to three conditions suggested by Orcutt's reanalysis of small group studies.

The first of these conditions relates to *situational goals* and varies according to whether drug use occurs in a *task* situation or in a *socioemotional* situation. The use of either marijuana or alcohol should generally be perceived as consistent with the goals of a socioemotional situation, such as a party, but as a potential source of interference with goal-attainment in a task situation. Therefore, the acts of marijuana use or alcohol use will tend to be interpreted as deviant when situated in a task setting.

The situational *stability* of marijuana or alcohol use is also varied. In some of the items presented to respondents, drug-using behavior was described as *intra*-situational, i.e., a single, situationally circumscribed occurrence. Other items described marijuana or alcohol use as *inter*-situational, i.e., the act of drug use was presented as a stable pattern of repeated occurrences across several situations. Attribution theorists (Heider, 1958; Kelley, 1967) argue that the certainty with which inferences or interpretations can be made regarding an act will be an increasing function of the consistency of the act's occurrence across situations. When drug use is perceived as a stable *inter*-situational pattern, it will be more likely to be interpreted as deviant. Some support for this hypothesis is supplied by Johnston's (1973:74) recent study of attitudes toward drug use.

The third and final situational variation considered in this study relates to *motivations* attributed to the marijuana or alcohol user. A central issue for attribution theories in social psychology (Heider, 1958; Kelley, 1967), as well as for relativistic theories of deviance (McHugh, 1970), is whether situational circumstances or personal motives of the actor are perceived to be responsible for the occurrence of an act. Situational causes are frequently viewed as legitimate "excuses" for a deviant act (Scott and Lyman, 1963).

An attempt is made to tap this aspect of situational interpretations in the present study by varying drug-using situations according to a distinction between *social* and *personal* motivations for use. Social motivations were depicted in situations which reflect mutual social participation in marijuana or alcohol use. Personal motivations were implied where drug use is presented as an individualistic attempt to cope with the situation. Interpretations of deviance should be more likely under the latter condition.

In addition to its focus on these three situational variations, the present study also attempts to take into consideration recent criticism advanced by Lemert (1972) of relativistic theories of deviance. Lemert cautions against the tendency of some theorists to overemphasize subjective social definitions and to ignore the objective nature of the deviant act itself. He argues that "(t)he extreme relativism in some statements of labeling theory leaves the unfortunate impression that almost any meaning can be assigned to human attributes and actions" (1972:22). Deviance research should attend both to objective factors and to subjective factors and "it has to be heeded continually that deviance outcomes flow from interaction between the two sets of factors . . ." (1972:21).

In order to deal empirically with Lemert's arguments, the research reported here incorporates comparisons between two objectively different acts, marijuana use and alcohol use. Half of the respondents in this study were presented with situational variations in marijuana use, while the other half were asked to interpret alcohol use in the same situations. These two acts are similar enough to permit standardization of situational variations, but sufficiently different to permit comparative assessment of unique effects of an act upon respondents' interpretations. For example, is marijuana use *generally* interpreted as more deviant than alcohol use, irrespective of situational contexts? Also, does the nature of these acts "interact," in Lemert's words, with certain situational features to produce unique interpretations of deviance? This analysis will focus on these substantive questions as well as on the relativistic problem of situated deviance . . .

Discussion

The situational variations examined in this analysis do produce substantial and predictable changes in respondents' interpretations of marijuana and alcohol use. Each of the three situational conditions has at least some effect on respondents' interpretations and the cumulative effects of these variations are dramatic. This is particularly so in the case of alcohol use, where interpretations vary from almost unanimous acceptance to unanimous nonacceptance. In short, what is nondeviant in some situations is deviant in others. These data generally lend empirical substance to relativistic discussions of deviance as a situated phenomenon.

However, Lemert's caution against "radical" relativism also finds justification in these data. Several findings indicate that the nature of the act itself has important influences on respondents' interpretations. In contrast to marijuana use, alcohol use tends to receive substantial disapproval only after personal motivations are situationally attributed to the act. Once alcohol use is perceived to be associated with personal motivations, interpretive differences between this act and the act of marijuana use diminish considerably. On the other hand, marijuana use is clearly viewed as deviant in a typical task situation where alcohol use is overwhelmingly accepted by the respondents. An understanding of these results requires analysis of differences between the acts themselves.

Respondents may view marijuana use and alcohol use differently in terms of *typical* motivations for these acts. Respondents seem tacitly to assume that alcohol use is socially motivated, unless notified otherwise by situational circumstances. It is likely that a similar tacit assumption is not made with regard to marijuana use. Given the typical nature of marijuana use among American college students, the act itself might imply some degree of personal motivation in any situation. These observations are consistent with research and theory which documents the general motivational and functional importance of alcohol as a "social mixer" and the more personalized, experiential motivations associated with marijuana use (Orcutt, 1972; Cahalan *et al.,* 1969; Goode, 1972).

These remarks suggest that respondents may use *either the situational context of the act or the act itself* as sources of evidence for motivational attributions. Even when marijuana is used in a situation that does not present explicit evidence of personal motivation, the act *per se* will still serve as an alternative source which carries this information. In the case of alcohol use, however, the situation must explicitly imply personal motivations, since the act *per se* does not.

This explanation helps to account for the responsiveness of interpretations of alcohol use to situational perceptions of personal motivation. The situation, and not the act, is the primary source of motivational evidence. Insight is also gained into the markedly discrepant interpretations of marijuana use and alcohol use in the "salesman-client" task situation. If alcohol use is assumed to be socially motivated, it can be accepted as an activity which facilitates interpersonal interaction and the attainment of task goals. On the other hand, if marijuana use is assumed to be personally motivated, it will tend to be viewed as a potential impediment to the attainment of task goals. Task activities require focused involvement in and attention to the *interpersonal* situation. The act of marijuana use instead implies a motivation to focus inward on *interpersonal* experience. In the task situation, then, marijuana use will be perceived as motivationally inconsistent with task requirements and interpreted as deviant.

Conclusion

The results of this study indicate the usefulness of relativistic conceptions of situated deviance. Situational circumstances appear to account for a considerable degree of the perceptual variance in respondents' interpretations of marijuana and alcohol use as deviant acts. At the same time, the findings caution against a radical relativism which would deny interpretive significance to the nature of the act itself.

Unfortunately, this study fails to come to grips with the interactional implications of relativistic theorizing, a weakness it shares with most of the research literature on deviance (Orcutt, 1973). The relationship between subjective interpretations of deviant acts and overt reactions to such acts by social audiences remains conceptually and empirically problematic. The kinds of situational conditions hypothetically varied in this survey investigation could conceivably be manipulated in experimental and quasi-experimental designs which focus on behavioral reactions to situated deviance.

Relativistic theories have raised new and important problems for the field of deviance. But it is time attention was shifted from the endless round of critique and debate of these ideas to the more crucial task of empirical evaluation.

NOTE

1. Behavioral evidence is not a necessary condition for imputations of deviance to an actor (Katz, 1972). In most empirical instances, however, definitions of an actor as deviant and reactions to the actor's deviance are based on interpretations of behavior as deviant.

REFERENCES

Bittner, E. 1967a. "The police on skid-row: A study of peace keeping." *American Sociological Review* 32(October): 699–715.

———.1967b. "Police discretion in emergency apprehension of mentally ill persons." *Social Problems* 14(Winter): 278–292.

Black, D. J. 1970. "Production of crime rates." *American Sociological Review* 35(August): 733–748.

Black, D. J. and A. J. Reiss, Jr. 1970. "Police control of juveniles." *American Sociological Review* 35 (February): 63–77.

Blum, A. F. 1970. "The sociology of mental illness," pp. 31–60 in Jack D. Douglas (ed.), *Deviance and Respectability: The Social Construction of Moral Meanings.* New York: Basic Books.

Cahalan, Don, Ira H. Cisin, and Helen M. Crossley. 1969. *American Drinking Practices.* New Brunswick: Rutgers Center of Alcohol Studies.

Davis, N. J. 1972. "Labeling theory in deviance research: A critique and reconsideration." *Sociological Quarterly* 13(Autumn): 447–474.

Douglas, Jack D. 1971. *Deviance and Respectability.* New York: Basic Books.

Douglas, Jack D. 1971. *American Social Order: Social Rules in a Pluralistic Society.* New York: The Free Press.

Gibbs, J. 1972. "Issues in defining deviant behavior," pp. 39–68 in Robert A. Scott and Jack D. Douglas (eds.), *Theoretical Perspectives on Deviance.* New York: Basic Books.

———. 1966. "Conceptions of deviant behavior: The old and the new." *Pacific Sociological Review* 9(Spring): 9–14.

Goode, Erich. 1972. *Drugs in American Society.* New York: Knopf.

Heider, Fritz. 1958. *The Psychology of Interpersonal Relations.* New York: Wiley.

Johnston, Lloyd. 1973. *Drugs and American Youth.* Ann Arbor: Institute for Social Research.

Katz, J. 1972. "Deviance, charisma, and rule-defined behavior." *Social Problems* 20(Fall): 186–202.

Kelley, H. H. 1967. "Attribution theory in social psychology," pp. 192–240 in David Levine (ed.), *Nebraska Symposium on Motivation, 1967.* Lincoln: University of Nebraska Press.

Kitsuse, J. I. 1962. "Societal reaction to deviant behavior: Problems of theory and method." *Social Problems* 9(Winter): 247–256.

Lemert, Edwin M. 1972. *Human Deviance, Social Problems, and Social Control* (2nd ed.). Englewood Cliffs, NJ: Prentice Hall.

Matza, David. 1969. *Becoming Deviant.* Englewood Cliffs, NJ: Prentice Hall.

McHugh, P. 1970. "A common-sense conception of deviance." Pp. 61–88 in Jack D. Douglas (ed.), *Deviance and Respectability: The Social Construction of Moral Meanings.* New York: Basic Books.

Orcutt, J. D. 1973. "Societal reaction and the response to deviation in small groups." *Social Forces* 52(December): 259–267.

———. 1972. "Toward a sociological theory of drug effects: A comparison of marijuana and alcohol." *Sociology and Social Research* 56(January): 242–253.

Piliavin, I. and S. Briar. 1964. "Police encounters with juveniles." *American Journal of Sociology* 69(September): 206–214.

Rubington, Earl and Martin S. Weinberg. 1973. *Deviance: The Interactionist Perspective* (2nd ed.). New York: Macmillan.

Schur, Edwin M. 1971. *Labeling Deviant Behavior: Its Sociological Implications.* New York: Harper and Row.

Scott, M. B. and S. M. Lyman 1963. "Accounts." *American Sociological Review* 33(February): 46–62.

Think Critically

1. What does Orcutt mean by the phrase, "deviance as a situated phenomenon?"
2. What does this imply about our understanding of the social reactions to marijuana and alcohol use? Explain.

SEXUAL DEVIANCE

WHEN ASKED TO GIVE EXAMPLES OF DEVIANT behavior, *sexual deviance is one of the categories that people most frequently choose.* Acts of violence such as rape and child molestation may be cited, along with prostitution, incest, and various fetishes. Some people will still cite homosexuality, despite the fact that it has been increasingly accepted as a conventional behavior over the past few decades. Of all sexual acts, pornography and prostitution are widely condemned and yet commonly practiced. This is interesting sociologically, since there are wide numbers of people acting to keep these institutions as a viable part of the social structure, while at the same time those institutions are widely socially disvalued and condemned, sometimes by those same people.

Laud Humphreys' study of what he termed the "Tearoom Trade" is a classic and controversial study of homosexual relations that take place in public restrooms. The study has been harshly criticized for the unethical research techniques employed (the study was conducted before the existence of "human subjects" review boards) regarding the treatment of subjects who were observed undercover and misled during later interviews. Humphreys' defense of such tactics was not accepted by large portions of the scientific community. However, the findings of his study stand as an important contribution to the understanding of homosexuality as a social phenomenon. The selection from his book of the same title focuses on the social organization of the sexual encounters themselves. What is perhaps more important in terms of the overall understanding of such relations is that when interviewed later, it was found that most of the individuals involved in tearoom encounters were married men with heterosexual self-identities who had no interest or identification with the homosexual subculture other than engaging in the sexual acts described in this chapter.

Rape constitutes an act of violence as well as the sexual abuse of women. How rape is considered by rapists themselves is the topic of Diana Scully and Joseph Marolla's research entitled, "Convicted Rapists' Vocabulary of Motive." Using personal interviews with rapists, the authors attempt to understand the ways in which perpetrators of such acts employ techniques that allow them to excuse and justify their violent sexual acts against women. Contrasting the "admitters" to "deniers," the authors find that the former are more prone to excuse rape while the latter tend to justify it. Sexist images and stereotypes are used by both groups in providing a "vocabulary of motive" for rape.

Jacqueline Lewis examines the world of strippers in her work, "Learning to Strip." In studying the socialization experiences of exotic dancers, she examines the differences in this sex-related job which requires that women manipulate clients for money while rationalizing their participation in a deviant occupation. Lewis finds that some women had at least anticipated what the job entailed, although for most, the process of socialization occurred after they had begun working in clubs. How women enter the occupation, become socialized and obtain job competence are the subjects of her research.

"From Sex as Sin to Sex as Work," by Valerie Jenness, examines a number of social issues that form the foundation of the prostitution social movement known as COYOTE ("Call Off Your Tired Old Ethics"). Using historical documents, Jenness focuses on the campaign to socially redefine prostitution by separating it from its historical roots in sin, crime and illicit sex, and placing it instead within the realm of work, free choice, and civil rights. Any success in these efforts was gained through COYOTE's extended debates with law enforcement officials over discrimination and selective enforcement of the law, with the feminist movement over the freedom of women to control and use their bodies as they see fit, and with public health officials regarding the role of prostitutes in the AIDS epidemic. Jenness vividly portrays the inherent problems faced by those wishing to redefine deviant behavior and social problems in society, and the practical and political struggles that are part of that process.

In a piece which considers deviance in international and global perspectives, Nancy Wonders and Raymond Michalowski examine how forces associated with an increase in tourism by the relatively well-heeled, as well as migrations of the poor in search of work or safety, have affected the production and consumption of sex tourism in two very different cities: Amsterdam and Havana. Through a combination of theoretical perspectives, and using global ethnographic methods and data, the authors argue that these abstract global forces find concrete expression in specific sex tourism practices. Mediating factors between global and local factors in each city include the influence of four basic institutions: the tourism industry, labor markets, the sex industry, and law and policy. The authors conclude that global economic forces increasingly affect the practice of sex work in each city through the broader phenomenon of globalized sex tourism.

Tearoom Trade*

Laud Humphreys

While the agreements resulting in "one-night-stands" occur in many settings—the bath, the street, the public toilet—and may vary greatly in the elaborateness or simplicity of the interaction preceding culmination in the sexual act, their essential feature is the expectation that sex can be had without obligation or commitment.[1]

AT SHORTLY AFTER FIVE O'CLOCK ON A WEEKDAY evening, four men enter a public restroom in the city park. One wears a well-tailored business suit; another wears tennis shoes, shorts, and T-shirt; the third man is still clad in the khaki uniform of his filling station; the last, a salesman, has loosened his tie and left his sports coat in the car. What has caused these men to leave the company of other homeward-bound commuters on the freeway? What common interest brings these men, with their divergent backgrounds, to this public facility?

They have come here not for the obvious reason, but in a search for "instant sex." Many men—married and unmarried, those with heterosexual identities and those whose self-image is a homosexual one—seek such impersonal sex, shunning involvement, desiring kicks without commitment. Whatever reasons—social, physiological, or psychological—might be postulated for this search, the phenomenon of impersonal sex persists as a widespread but rarely studied form of human interaction.

There are several settings for this type of deviant activity—the balconies of movie theaters, automobiles, behind bushes—but few offer the advantages for these men that public restrooms provide. "Tearooms," as these facilities are called in the language of the homosexual subculture,[2] have several characteristics that make them attractive as locales for sexual encounters without involvement.

According to its most precise meaning in the argot, the only "true" tearoom is one that gains a reputation as a place where homosexual encounters occur. Presumably, any restroom could qualify for this distinction, but comparatively few are singled out for this function at any one time. For instance, I have researched a metropolitan area with more than ninety public toilets in its parks, only twenty of which are in regular use as locales for sexual games. Restrooms thus designated join the company of automobiles and bathhouses as places for deviant sexual activity second only to private bedrooms in popularity.[3] During certain seasons of the year—roughly, that period from April through October that midwestern homosexuals call "the hunting season"—tearooms may surpass any other locale of homoerotic enterprise in volume of activity.

Public restrooms are chosen by those who want homoerotic activity without commitment for a number of reasons. *They are accessible, easily recognized by the initiate, and provide little public visibility.* Tearooms thus offer the advantages of both public and private settings. They are available and recognizable enough to attract a large volume of potential sexual partners, providing an opportunity for rapid action with a variety of men. When added to the relative privacy of these settings, such features enhance the impersonality of the sheltered interaction.

Availability

In the first place, tearooms are readily accessible to the male population. They may be located in any sort of public gathering place: department stores, bus stations, libraries, hotels, YMCAs, or courthouses. In keeping with the drive-in craze of American society, however, the more popular facilities are those readily accessible to the roadways. The restrooms of public parks and beaches—and, more recently, the rest stops set at programmed intervals along superhighways—are now attracting the clientele that, in a more pedestrian age, frequented great buildings of the inner cities. . . . [M]y research is focused on the activity that takes place in the restrooms of public parks, not only because (with some seasonal variation) they provide the most action but also because of other factors that make them suitable for sociological study.

It is a function of some societies to make these facilities for elimination available to the public. Perhaps the public toilet is one of the marks of "civilization," at least as perceived by European and post-European culture. I recall a letter from a sailor stationed in North Africa during World War II in which he called the people "uncivilized" because they had no public restrooms and used streets and gutters for the purpose of elimination.

For the cultural historian, American park restrooms merit study as physical traces of modern civilization. The older ones are often appended to pavilions or concealed beneath the paving of graceful colonnades. One marble-lined room in which I have done research occupies half of a Greek temple-like structure, a building of beautiful lines

and proportions. A second type, built before the Great Depression, are the toilet facilities located in park administration buildings, maintenance shops, or garages. For the most part, these lack the artistic qualities of the first type. Partly because they are not as accessible from the roads and partly because they are too easily approached by supervisory personnel and other interfering "straights," these restrooms enjoy homosexual popularity only during the months when other outlets are closed.

With the Depression of the 1930s, a new variety of public toilet appeared on the park scene. Ten of the twelve tearooms in which I made systematic observations . . . were of this category. Although the floor plans and building materials used vary from city to city, the majority of restrooms I have seen were constructed during this period. These have been built by the Work Projects Administration and, in any one community, seem to have been stamped from the same die. In the city where most of my research took place, they are constructed of a native white stone with men's and women's facilities back-to-back under one red roof. They have heavy wooden doors, usually screened from public view by a latticework partition attached to the building's exterior. In most of these doors, there is an inset of opaque French panes.

Each of the toilet facilities in the building has two windows of the same opaque glass, situated at either side of the room. The outside of these apertures is always covered with heavy screen. Against the blank wall opposite the door there are (from left to right) three urinals and two stalls, although smaller restrooms may provide only two urinals and one stall. Some of the facilities still have wash basins intact, situated in the corner to the left as one enters the door, but few of these are in working order. There is an occasional wastebasket. Paper towels are seldom provided, and there are no other furnishings in the rooms (see Figure 1).

Few park restrooms date back to the 1940s, when the nation was concerned with building those other major outlets for homosexual activity, the military posts. Apparently, most public construction in the 1950s was connected with the rush to provide more athletic facilities—swimming pools, golf courses, skating rinks, and the like.

The past decade has witnessed the construction of new, functional, cement-block facilities. Most of these structures are located along the expressways, but a

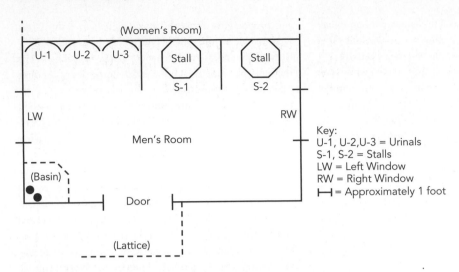

FIGURE 1   Diagram of Typical Public Park Restroom.

number are appearing in the parks and playgrounds of our cities. These relief stations may be viewed as an expression of the current interest in urban planning: some replace buildings no longer fit for use; others are located on the newly created urban playgrounds; and the bulk accompany the nation's answer to problems of mass transportation. However one may interpret the new construction as a reflection of the course of American history, it should be a boon to the tearoom customers. Most of the newly built restrooms are isolated structures with ready access to the roads and thus meet the prime requisites of tearoom activity.

According to some older respondents, the real turning point for the tearoom trade arrived with the WPA. One man, who has been active in the homosexual subculture for more than forty years, puts it this way:

> I suppose there has been such activity since the invention of plumbing. I first started out in one of those pavilion places. But the real fun began during the Depression. There were all those new buildings, easy to reach, and the automobile was really getting popular about then. . . . Suddenly, it just seemed like half the men in town met in the tearooms.

Not all of the new buildings were easy to reach, but those that were soon found popularity for homosexual activity. Tearoom ecology, like that of society at large, is highly affected by the location of transportation routes. Whether by accident or design, most large city parks

are located close to major thoroughfares and freeways. Because the activity in tearooms reaches its peak at the close of the workday, restrooms will draw more customers if located near principal commuting routes of the metropolitan area. The two facilities that I found to attract the greatest numbers for homosexual relations were adjacent to four-lane traffic arteries. All others in which any noteworthy amount of activity was observed were located within five minutes' driving time of the expressways that circle and cross the city.

Locating the Action

There is a great deal of difference in the volumes of homosexual activity that these accommodations shelter. In some, one might wait for months before observing a deviant act (unless solitary masturbation is considered deviant). In others, the volume approaches orgiastic dimensions. One summer afternoon, for instance, I witnessed twenty acts of fellatio in the course of an hour while waiting out a thunderstorm in a tearoom. For one who wishes to participate in (or study) such activity, the primary consideration is one of finding where the action is.

Occasionally, tips about the more active places may be gained from unexpected sources. Early in my research, I was approached by a man (whom I later surmised to be a park patrolman in plain clothes) while waiting at the window of a tearoom for some patrons to arrive. After finishing his business at the urinal and exchanging some remarks about the weather (it had been raining), the man came abruptly to the point: "Look, fellow, if you're looking for sex, this isn't the place. We're clamping down on this park because of trouble with the niggers. Try the john at the northeast corner of [Reagan] Park. You'll find plenty of action there." He was right. Some of my best observations were made at the spot he recommended. In most cases, however, I could only enter, wait, and watch—a method that was costly in both time and gasoline. After surveying a couple of dozen such rooms in this way, however, I became able to identify the more popular tearooms by observing certain physical evidence, the most obvious of which is the location of the facility. During the warm seasons, those restrooms that are isolated from other park facilities, such as administration buildings, shops, tennis courts, playgrounds, and picnic areas, are the more popular for deviant activity. The most active tearooms studied were all isolated from recreational areas, cut off by drives or lakes from baseball diamonds and picnic tables.

I have chosen the term "purlieu" (with its ancient meaning of land severed from a royal forest by perambulation) to describe the immediate environs best suited to the tearoom trade. Drives and walks that separate a public toilet from the rest of the park are almost certain guides to deviant sex. The ideal setting for homosexual activity is a tearoom situated on an island of grass, with roads close by on every side. The getaway car is just a few steps away; children are not apt to wander over from the playground; no one can surprise the participants by walking in from the woods or from over a hill; it is not likely that straight people will stop there at all. According to my observations, the women's side of these buildings is seldom used.

Active tearooms are also identifiable by the number of automobiles parked nearby. If two or more cars remain in front of a relatively isolated restroom for more than ten minutes, one may be reasonably certain that homosexual activity is in progress inside. This sign that the sexual market is in operation is an important one to the participants, who seldom enter a park restroom unless the presence of other unoccupied cars indicates that potential partners are inside. A lone arriver will usually wait in his auto until at least one other has parked nearby. That this signal is obscured when a golf course, zoo, or other facility that draws automobiles is located in close proximity may help explain the popularity of the isolated restroom.

Another means of recognizing the active tearoom requires closer inspection. Here, I refer to the condition of the windows and doors. Men who play the tearoom game must be able to know when someone is approaching. A door that squeaks or sticks is of great assistance; however, the condition of the windows is even more important. If they are of opaque glass, are nailed shut, or have no broken panes, the researcher may presume that the facility is seldom used for homosexual encounters.

In a western city, I have observed an exception to this rule. One of the popular meeting places there was a restroom located beneath the pavement of a colonnade. There were vents but no windows. The only access to this tearoom, however, was by means of a circular, metal stairway, and clanging footfalls could be heard well before the intruder was far enough down to see into the room. Normally, popular tearooms have at least one pane broken from each window, unless the windows have been opened. Fragments of glass that remain between the window frame and an outside screen are indicative of destruction that was initiated from within the restroom rather than by outside vandals. As [one] account of a teenage attack . . . indicates, occasional damage to the buildings comes from outside. But one of the first acts of participants after the spring opening or renovation of a facility is to break out a few carefully selected panes so that insiders can see who is approaching . . .

Volume and Variety

The availability of facilities they can recognize attracts a great number of men who wish, for whatever reason, to engage in impersonal homoerotic activity. Simple observation is enough to guide these participants, the researcher, and, perhaps, the police to active tearooms. It is much more difficult to make an accurate appraisal of the proportion of the male population who engage in such activity over a representative length of time. Even with good sampling procedures, a large staff of assistants would be needed to make the observations necessary for an adequate census of this mobile population.[4] All that may be said with some degree of certainty is that the percentage of the male population who participate in tearoom sex in the United States is somewhat less than the 16 percent of the adult white male population Kinsey found to have "at least as much of the homosexual as the heterosexual in their histories."[5]

Participants assure me that it is not uncommon in tea-rooms for one man to fellate as many as ten others in a day. I have personally watched a fellator take on three men in succession in a half hour of observation. One respondent, who has cooperated with the researcher in a number of taped interviews, claims to average three men each day during the busy seasons.

I have seen some wait in turn for this type of service. Leaving one such scene on a warm September Saturday, I remarked to a man who left close behind me: "Kind of crowded in there, isn't it?" "Hell, yes," he answered. "It's getting so you have to take a number and wait in line in these places!"

There are many who frequent the same facility repeatedly. Men will come to be known as regular, even daily, participants, stopping off at the same tearoom on the way to or from work. One physician in his late fifties was so punctual in his appearance at a particular restroom that I began to look forward to our daily chats. This robust, affable respondent said he had stopped at this tearoom every evening of the week (except Wednesday, his day off) for years "for a blow-job." Another respondent, a salesman whose schedule is flexible, may "make the scene" more than once a day—usually at his favorite men's room. At the time of our formal interview, this man claimed to have had four orgasms in the past twenty-four hours . . .

Of the bar crowd in gay (homosexual) society, only a small percentage would be found in park restrooms. But this more overt, gay bar clientele constitutes a minor part of those in any American city who follow a predominantly homosexual pattern. The so-called closet queens and other types of covert deviants make up the vast majority of those who engage in homosexual acts—and these are the persons most attracted to tearoom encounters. . . .

Tearooms are popular, not because they serve as gathering places for homosexuals but because they attract a variety of men, a *minority* of whom are active in the homosexual subculture. When we consider the types of participants, it will be seen that a large group of them have no homosexual self-identity. For various reasons, they do not want to be seen with those who might be identified as such or to become involved with them on a "social" basis.

Privacy in Public

I have mentioned that one of the distinguishing traits of an active tearoom is its isolation from other facilities in a park. The addition of four picnic tables close to a once popular restroom all but eliminated that facility for research purposes. This portion of a tape, made as I toured the parks in search of action one April Sunday, is indicative of this ecological pattern:

> This [park] is really dead! The tremendous volume of picnickers in all of the parks. . . . It seems like every family in the city is out today. It is a beautiful day, very warm, very pleasant. And everyone is out with their children. . . . The one facility in this park which is most active consistently is just completely surrounded by picnickers, and this would kill any gay activity. . . .

At this stage in the development of American culture, at least, some sort of privacy is requisite for sex. Whether deviant or "normal," sexual activity demands a degree of seclusion. Even orgies, I am told, require darkness or a minimum of light. When, as is the case with fellatio, the form of sexual engagement is prohibited, privacy decreases risk and is even more valued.

This constitutes a dilemma for those who would engage in impersonal sex of this type: how to find a setting that is accessible and identifiable, that will provide the necessary volume and variety of participants, while preserving at least a minimum of privacy? The trysting place must not be too available for the undesired. It must not be identifiable by the uninitiated. The potential participant passing by should be able to perceive what is taking place inside, while those playing baseball across the way should remain ignorant of the sexual game behind tearoom walls.

Ecological factors, the tearoom purlieu, that separate these facilities from other activity in the public park, have already been discussed. The presence of walls and stalls and opaque windows also help preserve the needed privacy. But there is another aspect of the tearoom encounters that is crucial to the maintenance of privacy in public settings. I refer to the silence of the interaction.

Throughout most homosexual encounters in public restrooms, nothing is spoken. One may spend many hours in these buildings and witness dozens of sexual acts without hearing a word. Of fifty encounters on which I made extensive notes,[6] only fifteen included vocal utterances.

The fifteen instances of speech break down as follows: Two were encounters in which I sought to ease the strain of legitimizing myself as lookout by saying, "You go ahead—I'll watch." Four were whispered remarks between sexual partners, such as, "Not so hard!" or "Thanks." One was an exchange of greetings between friends.

The other eight verbal exchanges were in full voice and more extensive, but they reflected an attendant circumstance that was exceptional. When a group of us were locked in a restroom and attacked by several youths, we spoke for defense and out of fear. . . . This event ruptured the reserve among us and resulted in a series of conversations among those who shared this adventure for several days afterward. Gradually, this sudden unity subsided, and the encounters drifted back into silence.

Barring such unusual events, an occasionally whispered "thanks" at the conclusion of the act constitutes the bulk of even whispered communication. At first, I presumed that speech was avoided for fear of incrimination. The excuse that intentions have been misunderstood is much weaker when those proposals are expressed in words rather than signalled by body movements. As research progressed, however, it became evident that the privacy of silent interaction accomplishes much more than mere defense against exposure to a hostile world. Even when a careful lookout is maintaining the boundaries of an encounter against intrusion, the sexual participants tend to be silent. The mechanism of silence goes beyond satisfying the demand for privacy. Like all other characteristics of the tearoom setting, it serves to guarantee anonymity, to assure the impersonality of the sexual liaison.

Tearoom sex is distinctly less personal than any other form of sexual activity, with the single exception of solitary masturbation. . . . For now, let me indicate only what I mean by "less personal": simply, that there is less emotional and physical involvement in restroom fellatio—less, even, than in the furtive action that takes place in autos and behind bushes. In those instances, at least, there is generally some verbal involvement. Often, in tearoom stalls, the only portions of the players' bodies that touch are the mouth of the insertee and the penis of the insertor; and the mouths of these partners seldom open for speech.

Only a public place, such as a park restroom, could provide the lack of personal involvement in sex that certain men desire. The setting fosters the necessary turnover in participants by its accessibility and visibility to the "right" men. In these public settings, too, there exists a sort of democracy that is endemic to impersonal sex. Men of all racial, social, educational, and physical characteristics meet in these places for sexual union. With the lack of involvement, personal preferences tend to be minimized.

If a person is going to entangle his body with another's in bed—or allow his mind to become involved with another mind—he will have certain standards of appearance, cleanliness, personality, or age that the prospective partner must meet. Age, looks, and other external variables are germane to the sexual action. As the amount of anticipated contact of body and mind in the sex act decreases, so do the standards expected of the partner . . .

NOTES

1. Evelyn Hooker, "Male Homosexuals and Their 'Worlds,'" in Judd Marmor, ed., *Sexual Inversion* (New York: Basic Books, 1965), p. 97.

2. Like most other words in the homosexual vocabulary, the origin of *tearoom* is unknown. British slang has used "tea" to denote "urine." Another British usage is as a verb, meaning "to engage with, encounter, go in against." See John S. Farmer and W. E. Henley, *A Dictionary of Slang and Colloquial English* (London: George Rutledge & Sons, 1921).

3. It is not possible to know how many sexual acts are performed in the various types of settings. Writers on the homosexual subculture agree, in general, on the relative popularity of these locales. For general surveys of the homosexual scene, see especially Evelyn Hooker, "The Homosexual Community," in *Personality Research* (Copenhagen: Monksgaard, 1962), pp. 40–59; and Maurice Leznoff and William A. Westley, "The Homosexual Community," *Social Problems*, Vol. 3, No. 4 (April, 1965), pp. 257–263.

4. By estimating (a) the average daily frequency of sex acts in each of twenty restrooms observed and (b) the average number of automobiles suspected of having been parked by participants near restrooms in five different parks, I have concluded that approximately five percent of the adult male population of the metropolitan area under study are involved in these encounters in a year's time. The imprecision of the methods used in obtaining this "guesstimate" does not warrant elaboration.

5. Alfred C. Kinsey and others, *Sexual Behavior in the Human Male* (Philadelphia: Saunders, 1948), pp. 650–651. See also

William Simon and John H. Gagnon, "Homosexuality: The Formulation of a Sociological Perspective," *Journal of Health and Social Behavior,* Vol. 8, No. 3 (September, 1967), p. 180: "About one half [of the male homosexuals studied] reported that sixty percent or more of their sexual partners were persons with whom they had sex only one time. Between ten and twenty percent report that they often picked up their sexual partners in public terminals, and an even larger proportion reported similar contacts in other public or semipublic locations."

6. Although I made fifty systematic observations of tearoom encounters, fifty-three acts of fellatio were observed at those times. The sexual acts sometimes occur in such rapid succession that it is impossible to report them as involving separate encounters. . . .

> ### Think Critically
> 1. Describe what Humphreys refers to as the "tearoom trade." What are the major social components; that is, how and why does it "work" for participants?
> 2. In the time this article was published, what aspects of it were most likely to be seen by readers as most relevant or salient? Do you feel that today people would read this study the same way? Explain your reasoning.

Convicted Rapists' Vocabulary of Motive
Excuses and Justifications*

Diana Scully and Joseph Marolla**

PSYCHIATRY HAS DOMINATED THE LITERATURE on rapists since "irresistible impulse" (Glueck, 1925:323) and "disease of the mind" (Glueck, 1925:243) were introduced as the causes of rape. Research has been based on small samples of men, frequently the clinicians' own patient population. Not surprisingly, the medical model has predominated: Rape is viewed as an individualistic, idiosyncratic symptom of a disordered personality. That is, rape is assumed to be a psychopathologic problem and individual rapists are assumed to be "sick." However,

*© 1984 by The Society for the Study of Social Problems. Reprinted from *Social Problems,* 31:5 (June, 1984), pp. 530–544 by permission of the authors and the publisher.

**This research was supported by a grant (RO 1 MH33013) from the National Center For the Prevention and Control of Rape, National Institute of Mental Health. The authors thank the Virginia Department of Corrections for their cooperation and assistance in this research. Correspondence to: Department of Sociology and Anthropology, Virginia Commonwealth University, 312 Shafer Court, Richmond, VA 23284.

advocates of this model have been unable to isolate a typical or even predictable pattern of symptoms that are causally linked to rape. Additionally, research has demonstrated that fewer than 5 percent of rapists were psychotic at the time of the rape (Abel et al., 1980).

We view rape as behavior learned socially through interaction with others; convicted rapists have learned the attitudes and actions consistent with sexual aggression against women. Learning also includes the acquisition of culturally derived vocabularies of motive, which can be used to diminish responsibility and to negotiate a non-deviant identity.

Sociologists have long noted that people can, and do, commit acts they define as wrong and, having done so, engage various techniques to disavow deviance and present themselves as normal. Through the concept of "vocabulary of motive," Mills (1940:904) was among the first to shed light on this seemingly perplexing contradiction. Wrongdoers attempt to reinterpret their actions through the use of a linguistic device by which norm-breaking conduct is socially interpreted. That is, anticipating the negative consequences of their behavior, wrongdoers attempt to present the act in terms that are both culturally appropriate and acceptable.

Following Mills, a number of sociologists have focused on the types of techniques employed by actors in problematic situations (Hall and Hewitt, 1970; Hewitt and Hall, 1973; Hewitt and Stokes, 1975; Sykes and Matza, 1957). Scott and Lyman (1968) describe excuses and justifications, linguistic "accounts" that explain and remove culpability for an untoward act after it has been committed. *Excuses* admit the act was bad or inappropriate but deny full responsibility, often through appeals to accident, or biological drive, or through scapegoating. In contrast, *justifications* accept responsibility for the act but deny that it was wrong—that is, they show in this situation the act was appropriate. *Accounts* are socially approved vocabularies that neutralize an act or its consequences and are always a manifestation of an underlying negotiation of identity.

Stokes and Hewitt (1976:837) use the term "aligning actions" to refer to those tactics and techniques used by actors when some feature of a situation is problematic. Stated simply, the concept refers to an actor's attempt, through various means, to bring his or her conduct into alignment with culture. Culture in this sense is conceptualized as a "set of cognitive constraints—objects—to which people must relate as they form lines of conduct" (1976:837), and includes physical constraints, expectations and definitions of others, and personal biography. Carrying out aligning actions implies both awareness of those elements of normative culture that are applicable to the deviant act and, in addition, an actual effort to bring the act into line with this awareness. The result is that deviant behavior is legitimized.

This paper presents an analysis of interviews we conducted with a sample of 114 convicted, incarcerated rapists. We use the concept of accounts (Scott and Lyman, 1968) as a tool to organize and analyze the vocabularies of motive which this group of rapists used to explain themselves and their actions. An analysis of their accounts demonstrates how it was possible for 83 percent (n = 114)[1] of these convicted rapists to view themselves as non-rapists.

When rapists' accounts are examined, a typology emerges that consists of admitters and deniers. Admitters (n = 47) acknowledged that they had forced sexual acts on their victims and defined the behavior as rape. In contrast, deniers[2] either eschewed sexual contact or all association with the victim (n = 35),[3] or admitted to sexual acts but did not define their behavior as rape (n = 32) . . .

Justifying Rape

Deniers attempted to justify their behavior by presenting the victim in a light that made her appear culpable, regardless of their own actions. Five themes run through attempts to justify their rapes: (1) women as seductresses; (2) women mean "yes" when they say "no"; (3) most women eventually relax and enjoy it; (4) nice girls don't get raped; and (5) guilty of a minor wrongdoing.

(1) Women as Seductresses

Men who rape need not search far for cultural language which supports the premise that women provoke or are responsible for rape. In addition to common cultural stereotypes, the fields of psychiatry and criminology (particularly the subfield of victimology) have traditionally provided justifications for rape, often by portraying raped women as the victims of their own seduction (Albin, 1977; Marolla and Scully, 1979) . . .

Since women are supposed to be coy about their sexual availability, refusal to comply with a man's sexual demands lacks meaning and rape appears normal. The fact that violence and, often, a weapon are used to accomplish the rape is not considered.

Like Peer Gynt, the deniers we interviewed tried to demonstrate that their victims were willing and, in some cases, enthusiastic participants. In these accounts, the rape became more dependent upon the victim's behavior than upon their own actions.

Thirty-one percent (n = 10) of the deniers presented an extreme view of the victim. Not only willing, she was the aggressor, a seductress who lured them, unsuspecting, into sexual action. Typical was a denier convicted of his first rape and accompanying crimes of burglary, sodomy, and abduction. According to the pre-sentence reports, he had broken into the victim's house and raped her at knife point. While he admitted to the breaking and entry, which he claimed was for altruistic purposes ("to pay for the prenatal care of a friend's girlfriend"), he also argued that when the victim discovered him, he had tried to leave but she had asked him to stay. Telling him that she cheated on her husband, she had voluntarily removed her clothes and seduced him. She was, according to him, an exemplary sex partner who "enjoyed it very much and asked for oral sex."[4] "Can I have it now?" he reported her as saying. He claimed they had spent hours in bed, after which the victim had told him he was good-looking and asked to see him again. "Who would believe I'd meet a fellow like this?" he reported her as saying.

In addition to this extreme group, 25 percent (n = 8) of the deniers said the victim was willing and had made some sexual advances. An additional 9 percent (n = 3) said the victim was willing to have sex for money or drugs. In two of these three cases, the victim had been either an acquaintance or picked up, which the rapists said led them to expect sex.

(2) Women Mean "Yes" When they Say "No"

Thirty-four percent (n = 11) of the deniers described their victim as unwilling, at least initially, indicating either that she had resisted or that she had said no. Despite this, and even though (according to pre-sentence reports) a weapon had been present in 64 percent (n = 7) of these 11 cases, the rapists justified their behavior by arguing that either the victim had not resisted enough or that her "no" had really meant "yes." For example, one denier who was serving time for a previous rape was subsequently convicted of attempting to rape a prison hospital nurse. He insisted he had actually completed the second rape, and said of his victim: "She semi-struggled but deep down inside I think she felt it was a fantasy come true." The nurse, according to him, had asked a question about his conviction for rape, which he interpreted as teasing. "It was like she was saying, 'rape me.'" Further, he stated that she had helped him along with oral sex and "from her actions, she was enjoying it." In another case, a 34-year-old man convicted of abducting and raping a 15-year-old teenager at knife point as she walked on the beach, claimed it was a pickup. This rapist said women like to be overpowered before sex, but to dominate after it begins.

> A man's body is like a coke bottle, shake it up, put your thumb over the opening and feel the tension. When you take a woman out, woo her, then she says "no, I'm a nice girl," you have to use force. All men do this. She said "no" but it was a societal no, she wanted to be coaxed. All women say "no" when they mean "yes" but it's a societal "no," so they won't have to feel responsible later.

Claims that the victim didn't resist or, if she did, didn't resist enough, were also used by 24 percent (n = 11) of admitters to explain why, during the incident, they believed the victim was willing and that they were not raping. These rapists didn't redefine their acts until some time after the crime. For example, an admitter who used

a bayonet to threaten his victim, an employee of the store he had been robbing, stated:

> At the time I didn't think it was rape. I just asked her nicely and she didn't resist. I never considered prison. I just felt like I had met a friend. It took about five years of reading and going to school to change my mind about whether it was rape. I became familiar with the subtlety of violence. But at the time, I believed that as long as I didn't hurt anyone it wasn't wrong. At the time, I didn't think I would go to prison. I thought I would beat it.

Another typical case involved a gang rape in which the victim was abducted at knife point as she walked home about midnight. According to two of the rapists, both of whom were interviewed, at the time they had thought the victim had willingly accepted a ride from the third rapist (who was not interviewed). They claimed the victim didn't resist and one reported her as saying she would do anything if they would take her home. In this rapist's view, "She acted like she enjoyed it, but maybe she was just acting. She wasn't crying, she was engaging in it." He reported that she had been friendly to the rapist who abducted her and, claiming not to have a home phone, she gave him her office number—a tactic eventually used to catch the three. In retrospect, this young man had decided, "She was scared and just relaxed and enjoyed it to avoid getting hurt." Note, however, that while he had redefined the act as rape, he continued to believe she enjoyed it.

Men who claimed to have been unaware that they were raping viewed sexual aggression as a man's prerogative at the time of the rape. Thus they regarded their act as little more than a minor wrongdoing even though most possessed or used a weapon. As long as the victim survived without major physical injury, from their perspective, a rape had not taken place. Indeed, even U.S. courts have often taken the position that physical injury is a necessary ingredient for a rape conviction.

(3) Most Women Eventually Relax and Enjoy it

Many of the rapists expected us to accept the image, drawn from cultural stereotype, that once the rape began, the victim relaxed and enjoyed it.[5] Indeed, 69 percent (n = 22) of deniers justified their behavior by claiming not only that the victim was willing, but also that she enjoyed herself, in some cases to an immense degree. Several men suggested that they had fulfilled their victims' dreams. Additionally, while most admitters used adjectives such as "dirty," "humiliated," and "disgusted," to describe how they thought rape made women feel, 20 percent (n = 9) believed that their victim enjoyed herself. For example, one denier had posed as a salesman to gain entry to his victim's house. But he claimed he had had a previous sexual relationship with the victim, that she agreed to have sex for drugs, and that the opportunity to have sex with him produced "a glow, because she was really into oral stuff and fascinated by the idea of sex with a black man. She felt satisfied, fulfilled, wanted me to stay, but I didn't want her." In another case, a denier who had broken into his victim's house but who insisted the victim was his lover and let him in voluntarily, declared "She felt good, kept kissing me and wanted me to stay the night. She felt proud after sex with me." And another denier, who had hid in his victim's closet and later attacked her while she slept, argued that while she was scared at first, "once we got into it, she was OK." He continued to believe he hadn't committed rape because "she enjoyed it and it was like she consented."

(4) Nice Girls Don't Get Raped

The belief that "nice girls don't get raped" affects perception of fault. The victim's reputation, as well as characteristics or behavior which violate normative sex role expectations, are perceived as contributing to the commission of the crime. For example, Nelson and Amir (1975) defined hitchhike rape as a victim-precipitated offense.

In our study, 69 percent (n = 22) of deniers and 22 percent (n = 10) of admitters referred to their victims' sexual reputation, thereby evoking the stereotype that "nice girls don't get raped." They claimed that the victim was known to have been a prostitute, or a "loose" woman, or to have had a lot of affairs, or to have given birth to a child out of wedlock. For example, a denier who claimed he had picked up his victim while she was hitchhiking stated, "To be honest, we [his family] knew she was a damn whore and whether she screwed one or 50 guys didn't matter." According to pre-sentence reports this victim didn't know her attacker and he abducted her at knife point from the street. In another case, a denier who claimed to have known his victim by reputation stated:

> If you wanted drugs or a quick piece of ass, she would do it. In court she said she was a virgin, but I could tell during sex [rape] that she was very experienced.

When other types of discrediting biographical information were added to these sexual slurs, a total of 78 percent (n = 25) of the deniers used the victim's reputation to substantiate their accounts. Most frequently, they referred to the victim's emotional state or drug use. For example, one denier claimed his victim had been known to be loose and, additionally, had turned state's evidence against her husband to put him in prison and save herself from a burglary conviction. Further, he asserted that she had met her current boyfriend, who was himself in and out of prison, in a drug rehabilitation center where they were both clients.

Evoking the stereotype that women provoke rape by the way they dress, a description of the victim as seductively attired appeared in the accounts of 22 percent (n = 7) of deniers and 17 percent (n = 8) of admitters. Typically, these descriptions were used to substantiate their claims about the victim's reputation. Some men went to extremes to paint a tarnished picture of the victim, describing her as dressed in tight black clothes and without a bra; in one case, the victim was portrayed as sexually provocative in dress and carriage. Not only did she wear short skirts, but she was observed to "spread her legs while getting out of cars." Not all of the men attempted to assassinate their victim's reputation with equal vengeance. Numerous times they made subtle and offhand remarks like, "She was a waitress and you know how they are."

The intent of these discrediting statements is clear. Deniers argued that the woman was a "legitimate" victim who got what she deserved. For example, one denier stated that all of his victims had been prostitutes; pre-sentence reports indicated they were not. Several times during his interview, he referred to them as "dirty sluts," and argued "anything I did to them was justified." Deniers also claimed their victim had wrongly accused them and was the type of woman who would perjure herself in court.

(5) Only a Minor Wrongdoing

The majority of deniers did not claim to be completely innocent and they also accepted some accountability for their actions. Only 16 percent (n = 5) of deniers argued that they were totally free of blame. Instead, the majority of deniers pleaded guilty to a lesser charge. That is, they obfuscated the rape by pleading guilty to a less serious, more acceptable charge. They accepted being over-sexed, accused of poor judgment or trickery, even some violence, or guilty of adultery or contributing to the delinquency of a minor, charges that are hardly the equivalent of rape.

Typical of this reasoning is a denier who met his victim in a bar when the bartender asked him if he would try to repair her stalled car. After attempting unsuccessfully, he claimed the victim drank with him and later accepted a ride. Out riding, he pulled into a deserted area "to see how my luck would go." When the victim resisted his advances, he beat her and he stated:

> I did something stupid. I pulled a knife on her and I hit her as hard as I would hit a man. But I shouldn't be in prison for what I did. I shouldn't have all this time [sentence] for going to bed with a broad.

This rapist continued to believe that while the knife was wrong, his sexual behavior was justified . . .

In sum, deniers argued that, while their behavior may not have been completely proper, it should not have been considered rape. To accomplish this, they attempted to discredit and blame the victim while presenting their own actions as justified in the context. Not surprisingly, none of the deniers thought of himself as a rapist. A minority of the admitters attempted to lessen the impact of their crime by claiming the victim enjoyed being raped. But despite this similarity, the nature and tone of admitters' and deniers' accounts were essentially different.

Excusing Rape

In stark contrast to deniers, admitters regarded their behavior as morally wrong and beyond justification. They blamed themselves rather than the victim, although some continued to cling to the belief that the victim had contributed to the crime somewhat, for example, by not resisting enough.

Several of the admitters expressed the view that rape was an act of such moral outrage that it was unforgivable. Several admitters broke into tears at intervals during their interviews. A typical sentiment was,

> I equate rape with someone throwing you up against a wall and tearing your liver and guts out of you. . . . Rape is worse than murder . . . and I'm disgusting.

Another young admitter frequently referred to himself as repulsive and confided:

> I'm in here for rape and in my own mind, it's the most disgusting crime, sickening. When people see me and know, I get sick.

Admitters tried to explain their crime in a way that allowed them to retain a semblance of moral integrity. Thus, in contrast to deniers' justifications, admitters used excuses to explain how they were compelled to rape. These excuses appealed to the existence of forces outside of the rapists' control. Through the use of excuses, they attempted to demonstrate that either intent was absent or responsibility was diminished. This allowed them to admit rape while reducing the threat to their identity as a moral person. Excuses also permitted them to view their behavior as idiosyncratic rather than typical and, thus, to believe they were not "really" rapists. Three themes run through these accounts: (1) the use of alcohol and drugs; (2) emotional problems; and (3) nice guy image.

(1) The Use of Alcohol and Drugs

A number of studies have noted a high incidence of alcohol and drug consumption by convicted rapists prior to their crime (Groth, 1979; Queen's Bench Foundation, 1976). However, more recent research has tentatively concluded that the connection between substance use and crime is not as direct as previously thought (Ladouceur, 1983). Another facet of alcohol and drug use mentioned in the literature is its utility in disavowing deviance. McCaghy (1968) found that child molesters used alcohol as a technique for neutralizing their deviant identity. Marolla and Scully (1979), in a review of psychiatric literature, demonstrated how alcohol consumption is applied differently as a vocabulary of motive. Rapists can use alcohol both as an excuse for their behavior and to discredit the victim and make her more responsible. We found the former common among admitters and the latter common among deniers.

Alcohol and/or drugs were mentioned in the accounts of 77 percent (n = 30) of admitters and 84 percent (n = 21) of deniers and both groups were equally likely to have acknowledged consuming a substance—admitters, 77 percent (n = 30); deniers, 72 percent (n = 18). However, admitters said they had been affected by the substance; if not the cause of their behavior, it was at least a contributing factor. For example, an admitter who estimated his consumption to have been eight beers and four "hits of acid" reported:

> Straight, I don't have the guts to rape. I could fight a man but not that. To say, "I'm going to do it to a woman," knowing it will scare and hurt her, takes guts or you have to be sick . . .

In contrast, deniers' justifications required that they not be substantially impaired. To say that they had been drunk or high would cast doubt on their ability to control themselves or to remember events as they actually happened. Consistent with this, when we asked if the alcohol and/or drugs had had an effect on their behavior, 69 percent (n = 27) of admitters, but only 40 percent (n = 10) of deniers, said they had been affected.

Even more interesting were references to the victim's alcohol and/or drug use. Since admitters had already relieved themselves of responsibility through claims of being drunk or high, they had nothing to gain from the assertion that the victim had used or been affected by alcohol and/or drugs. On the other hand, it was very much in the interest of deniers to declare that their victim had been intoxicated or high: That fact lessened her credibility and made her more responsible for the act. Reflecting these observations, 72 percent (n = 18) of deniers and 26 percent (n = 10) of admitters maintained that alcohol or drugs had been consumed by the victim. Further, while 56 percent (n = 14) of deniers declared she had been affected by this use, only 15 percent (n = 6) of admitters made a similar claim. Typically, deniers argued that the alcohol and drugs had sexually aroused their victim or rendered her out of control. For example, one denier insisted that his victim had become hysterical from drugs, not from being raped, and it was because of the drugs that she had reported him to the police. In addition, 40 percent (n = 10) of deniers argued that while the victim had been drunk or high, they themselves either hadn't ingested or weren't affected by alcohol and/or drugs. None of the admitters made this claim. In fact, in all of the 15 percent (n = 6) of cases where an admitter said the victim was drunk or high, he also admitted to being similarly affected.

These data strongly suggest that whatever role alcohol and drugs play in sexual and other types of violent crime, rapists have learned the advantage to be gained from using alcohol and drugs as an account. Our sample was aware that their victim would be discredited and their own behavior excused or justified by referring to alcohol and/or drugs.

(2) Emotional Problems

Admitters frequently attributed their acts to emotional problems. Forty percent (n = 19) of admitters said they believe an emotional problem had been at the root of their rape behavior, and 33 percent (n = 15) specifically related the problem to an unhappy, unstable childhood or a marital-domestic situation. Still others claimed to have been in a general state of unease. For example, one admitter said that at the time of the rape he had been depressed, feeling he couldn't do anything right, and that something had been missing from his life. But he also added, "being a rapist is not part of my personality . . ."

Our data do indicate that a precipitating event, involving an upsetting problem of everyday living, appeared in the accounts of 80 percent (n = 38) of admitters and 25 percent (n = 8) of deniers. Of those experiencing a precipitating event, including deniers, 76 percent (n = 35) involved a wife or girlfriend. Over and over, these men described themselves as having been in a rage because of an incident involving a woman with whom they believed they were in love.

Frequently, the upsetting event was related to a rigid and unrealistic double standard for sexual conduct and virtue which they applied to "their" woman but which they didn't expect from men, didn't apply to themselves, and, obviously, didn't honor in other women. To discover that the "pedestal" didn't apply to their wife or girlfriend sent them into a fury. One especially articulate and typical admitter described his feeling as follows. After serving a short prison term for auto theft, he married his "childhood sweetheart" and secured a well-paying job. Between his job and the volunteer work he was doing with an ex-offender group, he was spending long hours away from home, a situation that had bothered his wife. In response to her request, he gave up his volunteer work, though it was clearly meaningful to him. Then, one day, he discovered his wife with her former boyfriend "and my life fell apart." During the next several days, he said his anger had made him withdraw into himself and, after three days of drinking in a motel room, he abducted and raped a stranger . . .

As with alcohol and drug intoxication, a claim of emotional problems works differently depending upon whether the behavior in question is being justified or excused. It would have been counterproductive for deniers to have claimed to have had emotional problems at the time of the rape. Admitters used psychological explanations to portray themselves as having been temporarily "sick" at the time of the rape. Sick people are usually blamed for neither the cause of their illness nor for acts committed while in that state of diminished capacity. Thus, adopting the sick role removed responsibility by excusing the behavior as having been beyond the ability of the individual to control . . .

(3) Nice Guy Image

Admitters attempted to further neutralize their crime and negotiate a non-rapist identity by painting an image of themselves as a "nice guy." Admitters projected the image of someone who had made a serious mistake but, in every other respect, was a decent person. Fifty-seven percent (n = 27) expressed regret and sorrow for their victim indicating that they wished there were a way to apologize for or amend their behavior. For example, a participant in a rape-murder, who insisted his partner did the murder, confided, "I wish there was something I could do besides saying 'I'm sorry, I'm sorry.' I live with it 24 hours a day and, some-times, I wake up crying in the middle of the night because of it . . ."

The "nice guy" statements of the admitters reflected an attempt to communicate a message consistent with Schlenker's and Darby's analysis of apologies. It was an attempt to convey that rape was not a representation of their "true" self. For example,

> It's different from anything else I've ever done. I feel more guilt about this. It's not consistent with me. When I talk about it, it's like being assaulted myself. I don't know why I did it, but once I started, I got into it. Armed robbery was a way of life for me, but not rape. I feel like I wasn't being myself.

Admitters also used "nice guy" statements to register their moral opposition to violence and harming women, even though, in some cases, they had seriously injured their victims . . .

Finally, a number of admitters attempted to improve their self-image by demonstrating that, while they had raped, it could have been worse if they had not been a "nice guy." For example, one admitter professed to being especially gentle with his victim after she told him she had just had a baby. Others claimed to have given the victim money to get home or make a phone call, or to have made sure the victim's children were not in the room . . .

Even a young man, who raped his five victims at gun point and then stabbed them to death, attempted to improve his image by stating:

> Physically they enjoyed the sex [rape]. Once they got involved, it would be difficult to resist. I was always gentle and kind until I started to kill them. And the killing was always sudden, so they wouldn't know it was coming.

Summary and Conclusions

Convicted rapists' accounts of their crimes include both excuses and justifications. Those who deny what they did was rape justify their actions; those who admit it was rape attempt to excuse it or themselves. This study does not address why some men admit while others deny, but future research might address this question. This paper does provide insight on how men who are sexually aggressive or violent construct reality, describing the different strategies of admitters and deniers.

Admitters expressed the belief that rape was morally reprehensible. But they explained themselves and their acts by appealing to forces beyond their control, forces which reduced their capacity to act rationally and thus compelled them to rape. Two types of excuses predominated: alcohol/drug intoxication and emotional problems. Admitters used these excuses to negotiate a moral identity for themselves by viewing rape as idiosyncratic rather than typical behavior. This allowed them to reconceptualize themselves as recovered or "ex-rapists," someone who had made a serious mistake which did not represent their "true" self.

In contrast, deniers' accounts indicate that these men raped because their value system provided no compelling reason not to do so. When sex is viewed as a male entitlement, rape is no longer seen as criminal. However, the deniers had been convicted of rape, and like the admitters, they attempted to negotiate an identity. Through justifications, they constructed a "controversial" rape and attempted to demonstrate how their behavior, even if not quite right, was appropriate in the situation. Their denials, drawn from common cultural rape stereotypes, took two forms, both of which ultimately denied the existence of a victim.

The first form of denial was buttressed by the cultural view of men as sexually masterful and women as coy but seductive. Injury was denied by portraying the victim as willing, even enthusiastic, or as politely resistant at first but eventually yielding to "relax and enjoy it." In these accounts, force appeared merely as a seductive technique. Rape was disclaimed: Rather than harm the woman, the rapist had fulfilled her dreams. In the second form of denial, the victim was portrayed as the type of woman who "got what she deserved." Through attacks on the victim's sexual reputation and, to a lesser degree, her emotional state, deniers attempted to demonstrate that since the victim wasn't a "nice girl," they were not rapists. Consistent with both forms of denial was the self-interested use of alcohol and drugs as a justification. Thus, in contrast to admitters, who accentuated their own use as an excuse, deniers emphasized the victim's consumption in an effort to both discredit her and make her appear more responsible for the rape. It is important to remember that deniers did not invent these justifications. Rather, they reflect a belief system which has historically victimized women by promulgating the myth that women both enjoy and are responsible for their own rape.

While admitters and deniers present an essentially contrasting view of men who rape, there were some shared characteristics. Justifications particularly, but also excuses, are buttressed by the cultural view of women as sexual commodities, dehumanized and devoid of autonomy and dignity. In this sense, the sexual objectification of women must be understood as an important factor contributing to an environment that trivializes, neutralizes, and, perhaps, facilitates rape.

Finally, we must comment on the consequences of allowing one perspective to dominate thought on a social problem. Rape, like any complex continuum of behavior, has multiple causes and is influenced by a number of social factors. Yet, dominated by psychiatry and the medical model, the underlying assumption that rapists are "sick" has pervaded research. Although methodologically unsound, conclusions have been based almost exclusively on small clinical populations of rapists—that extreme group of rapists who seek counseling in prison and are the most likely to exhibit psychopathology. From this small, atypical group of men, psychiatric findings have been generalized to all men who rape. Our research, however, based on volunteers from the entire prison population, indicates that some rapists, like deniers, viewed and understood their behavior from a popular cultural perspective. This strongly suggests that cultural perspectives, and not an idiosyncratic illness, motivated their behavior. Indeed, we can argue that the psychiatric perspective has contributed to the vocabulary of motive that rapists use to excuse and justify their behavior (Scully and Marolla, 1984).

Efforts to arrive at a general explanation for rape have been retarded by the narrow focus of the medical model and the preoccupation with clinical populations. The continued reduction of such complex behavior to a singular cause hinders, rather than enhances, our understanding of rape.

NOTES

1. These numbers include pretest interviews. When the analysis involves either questions that were not asked in the pretest or that were changed, they are excluded and thus the number changes.

2. There is, of course, the possibility that some of these men really were innocent of rape. However, while the U.S. criminal justice system is not without flaw, we assume that it is highly unlikely that this many men could have been unjustly convicted of rape, especially since rape is a crime with traditionally low conviction rates. Instead, for purposes of this research, we assume that these men were guilty as charged and that their attempt to maintain an image of non-rapist springs from some psychologically or sociologically interpretable mechanism.

3. Because of their outright denial, interviews with this group of rapists did not contain the data being analyzed here and, consequently, they are not included in this paper.

4. It is worth noting that a number of deniers specifically mentioned the victim's alleged interest in oral sex. Since our interview questions about sexual history indicated that the rapists themselves found oral sex marginally acceptable, the frequent mention is probably another attempt to discredit the victim. However, since a tape recorder could not be used for the interviews and the importance of these claims didn't emerge until the data was being coded and analyzed, it is possible that it was mentioned even more frequently but not recorded.

5. Research shows clearly that women do not enjoy rape. Holmstrom and Burgess (1978) asked 93 adult rape victims, "How did it feel sexually?" Not one said they enjoyed it. Further, the trauma of rape is so great that it disrupts sexual functioning (both frequency and satisfaction) for the overwhelming majority of victims, at least during the period immediately following the rape and, in fewer cases, for an extended period of time (Burgess and Holmstrom, 1979; Feldman-Summers et al., 1979). In addition, a number of studies have shown that rape victims experience adverse consequences prompting some to move, change jobs, or drop out of school (Burgess and Holmstrom, 1974; Kilpatrick et al., 1979; Ruch et al., 1980; Shore, 1979).

REFERENCES

Abel, Gene, Judith Becker, and Linda Skinner. 1980. "Aggressive behavior and sex." *Psychiatric Clinics of North America* 3(2):133–151.

Abrahamsen, David. 1960. *The Psychology of Crime.* New York: John Wiley.

Albin, Rochelle. 1977. "Psychological studies of rape." *Signs* 3(2):423–435.

Athens, Lonnie. 1977. "Violent crimes: A symbolic interactionist study." *Symbolic Interaction* 1(1): 56–71.

Burgess, Ann Wolbert, and Lynda Lytle Holmstrom. 1974. *Rape: Victims of Crisis.* Bowie: Robert J. Brady.

———, 1979 "Rape: Sexual disruption and recovery." *American Journal of Orthopsychiatry* 49(4): 648–657.

Burt, Martha. 1980. "Cultural myths and supports for rape." *Journal of Personality and Social Psychology* 38(2):217–230.

Burt, Martha, and Rochelle Albin. 1981. "Rape myths, rape definitions, and probability of conviction." *Journal of Applied Psychology* 11(3): 212–230.

Feldman-Summers, Shirley, Patricia E. Gordon, and Jeanette R. Meagher. 1979. "The impact of rape on sexual satisfaction." *Journal of Abnormal Psychology* 88(1):101–105.

Glueck, Sheldon. 1925. *Mental Disorders and the Criminal Law.* New York: Little Brown.

Groth, Nicholas A. 1979. *Men Who Rape.* New York: Plenum Press.

Hall, Peter M., and John P. Hewitt. 1970. "The quasi-theory of communication and the management of dissent." *Social Problems* 18(1):17–27.

Hewitt, John P., and Peter M. Hall. 1973. "Social problems, problematic situations, and quasi-theories." *American Journal of Sociology* 38(3): 367–374.

Hewitt, John P., and Randall Stokes. 1975. "Disclaimers." *American Sociological Review* 40(1): 1–11.

Hollander, Bernard. 1924. *The Psychology of Misconduct, Vice, and Crime.* New York: Macmillan.

Holmstrom, Lynda Lytle, and Ann Wolbert Burgess. 1978. "Sexual behavior of assailant and victim during rape." Paper presented at the annual meetings of the American Sociological Association, San Francisco, September 2–8.

Kilpatrick, Dean G., Lois Veronen, and Patricia A. Resnick. 1979. "The aftermath of rape: Recent empirical findings." *American Journal of Orthopsychiatry* 49(4):658–669.

Ladouceur, Patricia. 1983. "The relative impact of drugs and alcohol on serious felons." Paper presented at the annual meetings of the American Society of Criminology, Denver, November 9–12.

Luckenbill, David. 1977. "Criminal homicide as a situated transaction." *Social Problems* 25(2): 176–187.

Marolla, Joseph, and Diana Scully. 1979. "Rape and psychiatric vocabularies of motive." Pp. 301–318 in Edith S. Gomberg and Violet Franks (eds.), *Gender and Disordered Behavior: Sex Differences in Psychopathology.* New York: Brunner/Mazel.

McCaghy, Charles. 1968. "Drinking and deviance disavowal: The case of child molesters." *Social Problems* 16(1):43–49.

Mills, C. Wright. 1940. "Situated actions and vocabularies of motive." *American Sociological Review* 5(6):904–913.

Nelson, Steve, and Menachem Amir. 1975. "The hitchhike victim of rape: A research report." Pp. 47–65 in Israel Drapkin and Emilio Viano (eds.), *Victimology: A New Focus.* Lexington, KY: Lexington Books.

Queen's Bench Foundation. 1976. *Rape: Prevention and Resistance.* San Francisco: Queen's Bench Foundation.

Ruch, Libby O., Susan Meyers Chandler, and Richard A. Harter. 1980. "Life change and rape impact." *Journal of Health and Social Behavior* 21(3):248–260.

Schlenker, Barry R., and Bruce W. Darby. 1981. "The use of apologies in social predicaments." *Social Psychology Quarterly* 44(3):271–278.

Scott, Marvin, and Stanford Lyman. 1968. "Accounts." *American Sociological Review* 33(1) 46–62.

Scully, Diana, and Joseph Marolla. 1984. "Rape and psychiatric vocabularies of motive: Alternative perspectives." In Ann Wolbert Burgess (ed.), *Handbook on Rape and Sexual Assault.* New York: Garland Publishing.

Shore, Barbara K. 1979. "An examination of critical process and outcome factors in rape." Rockville, MD: National Institute of Mental Health.

Stokes, Randall, and John P. Hewitt. 1976. "Aligning actions." *American Sociological Review* 41(5):837–849.

Sykes, Gresham M., and David Matza. 1957. "Techniques of neutralization." *American Sociological Review* 22(6):664–670.

Williams, Joyce. 1979. "Sex role stereotypes, women's liberation, and rape: A cross-cultural analysis of attitude." *Sociological Symposium* 25 (Winter):61–97.

Think Critically

1. Describe the concept of "vocabulary of motive." How does it relate to the behavior of rapists specifically, and to other deviants more generally? Provide some examples.

2. Discuss the excuses and justifications given for rape by the perpetrators. Do you think that these have changed over time, and if so, in what ways, and to what degree? Do you feel that reactions to these justifications by authorities and/or the public have changed? Explain.

Learning to Strip: The Socialization Experiences of Exotic Dancers

Jacqueline Lewis

Acknowledgement

I would like to acknowledge the contributions of my four research assistants to this project: Jocalyn Clark, June Oakes, Shelley Young, and Jennifer Zubick. I would also like to thank all the women who took time away from their lives to speak with me. This study was funded by the National Health Research Development Program, Health Canada, Ottawa, Canada.

Introduction

Entering any new job or social role requires a process of socialization where the individual acquires the necessary values, attitudes, interests, skills and knowledge in order to be competent at her/his job. As with any new job or social role, becoming an exotic dancer requires a process of socialization. For exotic dancers, achieving job competence involves getting accustomed to working in a sex-related occupation, and the practice of taking their clothes off in public for money. In addition, in order to be a successful exotic dancer, women must also learn how to manipulate clientele and to rationalize such behaviour and their involvement in a deviant occupation.(1) For some dancers, the socialization process is partially anticipatory in nature, although dancers reported that most of their socialization occurred once they had made their decision to dance and found themselves actually working in the strip club environment. In this paper, I explore the factors influencing entry into exotic dancing, the socialization experiences of exotic dancers and the process of obtaining job competence.

Background

Since the late 1960s, exotic dancing and the experiences of exotic dancers have been the focus of academic inquiry (Boles & Garbin, 1974a, 1974b, 1974c; Carey, Peterson & Sharpe, 1974; Dressel & Petersen, 1982a, 1982b; Enck & Preston, 1988; Forsyth & Deshotels, 1997; McCaghy & Skipper, 1969, 1972; Petersen & Dressel, 1982; Prus, 1980; Reid, Epstein & Benson, 1994; Ronai & Ellis, 1989, Ronai, 1992; Skipper & McCaghy, 1971; Thompson & Harred, 1992). The relevance of some of the available literature to the present study is, however, limited by the focus of the articles. Within this literature on exotic dancers, only the articles by Boles and Garbin (1974b, 1974c), Carey et al., (1974), Dressel and Petersen (1982b), McCaghy and Skipper (1972), Prus (1980), Skipper and McCaghy (1971), and Thompson and Harred (1992) address the socialization experiences of dancers in any detail. Dressel and Petersen's (1982b) focus on the socialization of male exotic dancers makes their work of limited applicability to the present study.

Although much of this research was conducted over 15 to 20 years ago, some of it remains relevant to the work reported here. For example, the findings of Boles and Garbin (1974b, 1974c), Carey et al. (1974), McCaghy and Skipper (1972), Prus (1980) and Skipper and McCaghy (1971) provide an historical point of comparison that indicates some consistency between past and current research findings on the occupational socialization of exotic dancers.

The literature on occupational socialization of exotic dancers emphasizes two basic themes: (1) the factors that influence entry into dancing; and (2) anticipatory and on-the-job socialization experiences. Two types of models have been advanced to explain entry into exotic dancing: (1) career contingency models (Skipper & McCaghy, 1971; Carey et al., 1974; Thompson & Harred, 1992); and (2) conversion models (Boles & Garbin, 1974b; Carey et al., 1974; Thompson & Harred, 1992). In some research reports, these models are used on their own (e.g., Skipper & McCaghy, 1971; Boles & Garbin, 1974b), and in others they are used in combination (Carey et al., 1974; Thompson & Harred, 1992). Although a variety of singular and combined models have been used to explain entry into exotic dancing, there are several common factors that are identified across the studies: (1) knowledge and accessibility of an opportunity structure that makes exotic dancing an occupational alternative (Carey et al., 1974; Skipper & McCaghy, 1971; Prus, 1980; Thompson & Harred, 1992); (2) an awareness of the economic rewards associated with being an exotic dancer (Boles & Garbin, 1974b; Carey et al., 1974; Dressel & Petersen, 1982b; Skipper & McCaghy, 1971; Prus, 1980; Thompson & Harred, 1992); (3) a recruitment process involving personal networks (Boles & Garbin, 1974b; Dressel & Petersen, 1982b; Thompson & Harred, 1992); and (4) financial need or a need for employment (Boles & Garbin, 1974b, 1974c; Carey et al., 1974; Prus, 1980; Thompson & Harred, 1992).

With respect to the anticipatory and on-the-job socialization experiences of dancers (Boles & Garbin, 1974c; Dressel & Petersen, 1982b; Thompson & Harred, 1992), early research found that most female dancers had either professional training in dance, music or theatre, had been previously employed in the entertainment industry, or received extensive training in stripping prior to dancing before an audience (Boles & Garbin, 1974c; McCaghy & Skipper, 1972, Prus, 1980). However, despite their advanced (anticipatory) preparation, a large part of the occupational socialization dancers experienced occurred through informal channels after they had entered the occupation. Through observing and interacting with other subcultural members, dancers learned the tricks of the trade, such as how to: interact with customers for profit; manage their deviant lifestyle; and be successful at their job (Boles & Garbin, 1974c; Dressel & Petersen, 1982; McCaghy & Skipper, 1972; Thompson & Harred, 1992).

Method

This study used a combination of field observations inside strip clubs, and interviews with exotic dancers and other club staff to identify issues associated with the work and careers of exotic dancers. Observations were conducted at clubs in several cities in southern Ontario. Observational data were collected primarily to supplement interview data and to assist us in describing the work environment of exotic dancers including: physical setting; contacts between those present in the club (employees and clients); and the atmosphere of different clubs.

Thirty semi-structured, in-depth interviews were conducted with female exotic dancers, club staff and key informants. Participants were recruited either by the research team during field trips to the clubs or by dancers who had participated in the study. Each interview was audio taped and took place in a location chosen by the respondent (e.g., respondent's home, a research team member's office, a private space at a strip club, a local coffee shop). Interviews lasted anywhere from one to three hours, with the majority taking approximately one and half hours. All interviews were conducted informally to allow participants to freely express themselves, and to allow for exploration of new or unanticipated topics that arose in the interview.

The interviews explored each woman's work history, her perception of her future in the occupation, a description of her work, the various forms of interaction engaged in with clients, use of drugs and alcohol, current sexual practices, perception of risk for HIV and other STDs associated with dancing, sexual health-maintaining strategies, factors influencing risk and ability to maintain sexual health, and the presence and/or possibility of a community among exotic dancers. Interviews with other club employees were designed to tap their experiences in, and impressions of, club-related activities.

As interviews were collected and transcribed, it became increasingly apparent that there was a variety of recurrent themes that ran throughout the interviews (e.g., motivations for entry, socialization process, health and safety concerns, relationships between club employees, impact of dancing on dancers' lives, etc.). Coding categories were developed to fit with these emerging themes. All interviews were then coded in Nud*ist, a qualitative analysis software package, by members of the research team. As noted by Glaser and Strauss (1967), "[. . .] in discovering theory, one generates conceptual categories or their properties from evidence; then the evidence from which the category emerged is used to illustrate the concept" (p. 23). The quotes that appear in this paper were selected as examples of the responses provided by the women interviewed that fit the various conceptual categories that emerged during data analysis.

Becoming an Exotic Dancer

Unlike other more conventional occupations with formally structured socialization programs, the socialization experiences of the women we spoke with were informal in nature. Dancers reported that they acquired the requisite skills for the job through informal socialization processes that were either: (1) anticipatory in nature, occurring prior to dancing; and/or (2) that occured on the job, once they were employed to dance in a strip club.

Anticipatory Socialization

Early studies of female exotic dancers (see Boles & Garbin, 1974; McCaghy & Skipper, 1972) found that most dancers had fairly broad anticipatory socialization experiences, having been previously employed in an entertainment-related job, having some type of professional training in dance, music or theatre, or having an agent who helped prepare them for the career of exotic dancing. In this study, we, however, found little indication of the latter two types of anticipatory socialization experiences. Although one woman had a background in drama, she talked about how it actually did little to prepare her for the job:

> I thought you know, OK being in drama, ya, I'm kind of a freer person, whatever. But, like, actually taking off your clothes—nothing, nothing prepares you for it. Nothing. Seconds before I went up to go dance [for the first time], I'm thinking, oh my God, I can't do this, I can't do this. I can't do this. Then my music started playing and I'm like, I guess I have to now. And you know, your stomach's all in knots and you just do it. There's no way to describe it. You just do it.

Even the few women who indicated that they began dancing with the help of an agent talked about how they received little job preparation. For example, one woman said:

> I responded to an ad in the local paper and there was a number and you phoned the number and then you met with this guy and he made you sign a contract and then he kind of talked to you about what goes on. There was no training. Then he just took me to the bar later that evening and that was it.

Although the experiences dancers reported during their interviews varied, the women we spoke with who reported engaging in anticipatory socialization talked about spending time in strip clubs before deciding to dance. In recalling their entry into exotic dancing, some of the dancers we interviewed spoke of being curious about dancing, and wanting to find out if it was something they could do. These women reported that they sussed out and gained familiarity with dancing by going out to strip clubs on their own

and talking to dancers or by going out to the clubs with friends who hung out at or worked in strip clubs.

> So, I read some more about it. I read a couple of books on the sex industry and strippers in particular and burlesque dancers. Um, and then I visited a lot of the clubs and tried to talk to the dancers about how they got interested in it and how they get paid and what the job entails. They were pretty open to talking to me about it.
>
> I had a girlfriend who was a pretty promiscuous person, you know . . . We used to get together and like just hang out in dance clubs. Not strip clubs, but just normal clubs . . . She's a pretty cool person, you know, she's my best friend and my daughter's godmother and she told me that she was working in a club as a waitress. So I said, great, you know, "What kind of club is it?" Then she said, "It's a strip bar." And, I'm kind of like, "What? You're working in a strip bar?" And, she's like, "Yeah, I make really good money being a waitress there." I'm like, "OK whatever," you know. Then eventually she came out with it, and she's like, "I'm not really just waitressing, I'm dancing too." And I'm like, "Wow, oh, how much money are you making doing that?" And she's like, "Well, really good and you know if you want to help make your daughter's life better, why don't you come with me one night?" And I'm like, "Oh, man, I don't know if I could do that, you know." I got real scared and everything, but we set a date for the next Friday.

The other women who had anticipatory socialization experiences reported experiencing a more gradual drift into dancing (Matza, 1992)(2). Instead of purposefully going to strip clubs and talking to people in the industry with the intention of sussing it out, these women drifted into dancing through associations they had with people in the industry or by working as a waitress in one of the clubs.

> I didn't start out dancing. First I was a waitress. Eventually, I quit waitressing and I went and started dancing at a strip club.
>
> I waitressed for about a year at the Maverick, and then I started to dance. I've been dancing for 7 years, just over 7 years.
>
> I used to date this guy and some of his friends worked in the clubs, so we could go and hang out. He used to try to get me to try it [dancing], but I wouldn't. But, once we broke up, I decided to try it.
>
> This one woman I sort of knew, she had danced a few years before and it just came up in discussion that she used to be a dancer. So she kind of gave me a little information and where to go and what to do. So that is how I got started.

According to Ritzer and Walczak (1986), "[. . .] deviant occupational skills may be learned through involvement in different but related occupations or through nonoccupational activities" (p. 144). Through hanging out with people associated with the industry or by working in a strip club in some other capacity, these women experienced a form of anticipatory socialization that enabled them to view dancing as a viable job option. As noted by Matza (1992), "some learning is truly a discovery [for the individual], for until they have experimented with the forbidden, [. . . they] are largely unaware that infraction is feasible behavior" (p. 184).

> A lot of my friends and a lot of the group that I used to hang around with while I was waitressing were uh, we were all in the same circles with the guys from a strip club for women and uh, the two clubs were connected, and so they kept saying "try it" and, you know, "go to this bar, start there" and that's just how I ended up there.

> I lived with a guy when I was at [high] school . . . I was still a virgin. I slept with him on my seventeenth birthday and he blew my mind. The first thing he asked me was if I masturbated. And, like I'm a hick town girl, naive as shit and it was like wow. This guy's cool. And, I moved in with him the next day . . . We moved right into the city, downtown Toronto and he was hanging out with strippers . . . And I used to threaten him, you know, if you keep hanging out with these girls, I'm gonna become one. And I did. I used to waitress at a saloon and then I was hanging out with some of the girls and then dating guys from a dance club for women, heaven forbid, and it just went from there, I guess that's how I got into dancing.

> I started out waitressing in one of the local clubs. Watching the girls and the money they were making back then, I thought well, I'll try it [referring to dancing].

The experiences of the women who drifted into dancing can be viewed as a form of recruitment or conversion process whereby the individual is gradually introduced/exposed to the inner world of a new role or career and gives up one view of that role, or one world view, for another (see Becker, 1964; Lofland & Stark, 1965; Prus, 1977). According to Lofland and Stark (1965), the reinforcement and encouragement made available through intensive interaction with subgroup members is necessary if the recruit is to experience a complete conversion process.

Regardless of how they began their process of occupational socialization, in providing themselves with time to think things through, and to learn to identify with the norms, values and beliefs of the dancing subculture prior to entering it, these women were engaging in a form of role rehearsal and anticipatory socialization. Such efforts provided them with the opportunity to prepare themselves for the eventual reality of their new status, thereby easing the difficulties associated with the transition. Through engaging in anticipatory socialization, the women interviewed became accustomed to the strip club environment and the idea of taking their clothes off in public for money, thereby facilitating their entry into dancing.

On-the-Job Socialization

Similar to the socialization experiences of individuals in other occupations, novice dancers learn through interaction and observation while on the job. Since exotic dancers, however, have little, if any, formal training, learning through observation and interaction is crucial for attaining job competence (see Sanders, 1974). Although some of this learning may be anticipatory in nature and occur prior to the initial dancing experience, it takes some time and experience to move from being a novice dancer to a seasoned pro. Since there is no formal certification structure, peers play an important role in this transformation process. During this period, novices can continue to acquire knowledge from those around them about how to be successful at their job. Experienced strip club staff can therefore play an important role in the socialization process of the novice dancer. As one woman noted:

> You learn as you go. Other people in the club give you advice. And, you know, you gradually learn about how to make more money and who to talk to and that kind of stuff as you go.

Through talking to and receiving advice about the job from other staff members, novice dancers learn how to handle situations that may arise while working in the club, and how to dance for profit.

> The DJ at the first club I danced at was very good. On my first night he was like, "Don't worry about it . . . You know, just go up there and do your thing and you know, don't worry about it." And the other girls were kind of supportive, like, "Oh, you'll get used to it, it's not that bad after a while." You know, some of them kind of take you under their wing and sort of show you the ropes so to speak.

I had just gone to the DJ booth and given him my music for when I was going to go onstage and he said it would be after a few girls, because he already had a few on the list . . . I had no idea what to do with myself after I had given the music to him. He said, "Just hang out and, you know, talk to people, be friendly, you know." So I was just walking back to put my CDs back in my bag, the ones I wasn't going to use, and three guys called me over to their table.

I learned a lot just watching the other women. Some of them had been dancing for a while and they were really good at handling customers when they tried to break the rules.

Other dancers play a particularly important role in the socialization process. As the following quotes illustrate, novices can learn how to dress, dance and interact with customers for profit, through observing and interacting with dancers more experienced than themselves.

Most of the dancers are really nice, like, they're really understanding. They knew, you know, I hadn't danced for very long. Everybody was offering me advice. There were a few that were kind of like, stay away from me and I'll stay away form you sort of thing.

I get ideas for my show from watching, you know, the ones that have been doing this [dancing] for a while. There were these three other dancers that were there [at the club she had begun working]. Normally they have six on at a time. But, there were these three other dancers there that were amazing. Like, they couldn't have helped me more. And you know, they knew, like, at that time I'd only been dancing for about a week and you know, they were offering me advice left, right and centre. And you know, they were just so nice.

They couldn't be more helpful.

One woman explained how a friend of hers, who was an experienced dancer, helped teach her how to table dance.

[Talking about her first table dance] So, she comes up beside me and the next thing I know, both our tops are off and she's like all rubbing close to me and I'm like going, "Oh my God." I never thought of her that way before, you know. Cuz we've always just been friends, you know. So, it was kind of a funny experience. But, he ended up spending like a hundred dollars on songs. So, I'm thinking, hey, this is great, you know. I mean, this is awesome. I've got money to come home with, you know, it wasn't a wasted night. I thought, OK, I can deal with this a couple nights a week.

She went on to describe how her friend, along with a few other dancers, also helped her with her first stage performance:

The only thing that was really scary after my first night in the club was the stage, because I had never been on a stage before, and I'm thinking, "Oh my God, I don't have big breasts, I'm not like toned and tanned and blonde" or whatever. So, my friend's like, "Well, we can do like the dance that we did with that guy. We should do a dance on stage together." And, I'm like, "But I'm not gay and I'm not going to be able to make them think that I am." She's like, "Well, don't worry, just follow my lead [. . .]" The stage show actually went well because two other girls came up, so there was four girls on stage. So it made everybody kind of, you know, sort of stare at the stage and everyone was happy, so I was like, "OK, this isn't so bad", you know? And then after doing that a few times I decided that, you know, I wanted to try it on my own. So I did, and I didn't like it as much because, you know, you sort of feel really centred out. But eventually I got used to it and I was able to do it, you know. Now I've got the hang of it.

Rationalizing Participation in a Deviant Occupation

Since exotic dancing is viewed as a deviant occupation in our society, if novice dancers are to retain a valued sense of self, they must learn ways to justify their involvement in the strip club subculture. According to Sykes and Matza (1957), in order to deviate, people must have access to a set of rationalizations or neutralizations that allow them to reduce the guilt they feel about violating social norms. Neutralization makes norm violations "morally feasible since it serves to obliterate, or put out of mind, the dereliction implicit in it" (Matza, 1992, p. 182).

During interviews with dancers, it became apparent that dancers typically rely on several "techniques of neutralization" (Sykes& Matza, 1957) to justify their involvement in deviant behaviour. Similar to Thompson and Harred's (1992) research on topless dancers, we found that the dancers we interviewed tended to rely primarily on three of Sykes and Matza's (1957) techniques of neutralization. They denied injury or harm:

Ya well, we pretend [that they like the customers], but what do they really expect. Do they really think we are there because we like them, that we like to dance for men—no. And really, who are we hurting? We may take their money, and although sometimes it may be a lot, but, they are adults, they should know better. And besides, it's just money.

They condemned the condemners:

People may judge us and say that dancing is bad, but they seem to forget who it is we are dancing for—doctors, lawyers, sports figures. If it wasn't for them there would be no dancing—so maybe the focus is on the wrong people [the dancers rather than the customers]. As soon as you tell people you dance, it's "Oh." It's a totally different idea of what kind of person you are, or however you are is a put-on. I just think what is the big deal. We are all the same here.

So I take my clothes off for a living. Doesn't make you any different. You all go there smoking dope and drinking beer anyway so. I mean I don't know how many people I know that work at a car plant and say, "I go to work, have a couple beers, smoke a doobie and go to work." And I said, "Where'd you guys get the beer." "Aw the guys in the parking lot sell it." And I'm laughing my guts out thinking are you guys serious? I think Jesus, these are people that build our motor vehicles and people are driving around in these things.

A guy friend of mine, known him for years, government employee, a very high job, used to smoke crack in the parking lot before he went to work. He has this home in the city, a historical home, I don't know, a four or five hundred thousand dollar home . . . perfect job, normal job like everybody else, a wife and three kids at home, but smokes crack in the parking lot before he goes to work in the morning. Like how is he any better than me? I would just think you guys have the nerve to judge me and think you are a bit of a weirdo cuz you take your clothes off, wow how smart could you be? At least I'm not hooked on crack or anything. That's what I'm saying, some people that I know really well, you'd be shocked to hear what they do. So like I think what I do is just a drop in the bucket. At least I have an excuse, I'm a stripper. Like what is your excuse? You are a government employee, got a good job and you're the head of what? So I'm kinda laughing who are you to judge me.

And they appealed to higher loyalties:

Well, they say that you're not supposed to show your body to lustful men and that that's a sin. So I assume that like, obviously God wasn't gonna be very happy that I was doing something like this. But, the other way

I looked at it was, I have a daughter who is two years old and the government really doesn't give you enough to survive, so I had to do something. And I figured that if it's a sin to take off your clothes and it's a sin to let your child starve, definitely, I would take care of the second one, and it's probably more normal.

I had all these bills and I needed to feed my kids and well, what was I going to do. I do what I have to do to get by. If you need to feed your kids, what are you going to do?

In addition to using some of Sykes and Matza's (1957) techniques of neutralization to justify their involvement in exotic dancing, we found that dancers used the technique of normalization. As the following quote illustrates, some women attempted to justify or neutralize their involvement in exotic dancing by refuting the deviancy associated with it.

And I looked at the salaries these people were making and it was, you know, a thousand dollars a night, some nights, and it was really, really substantially helping with their tuition. And these were people working on master's degrees and doctorates and all kinds of things and I thought, "Wow, if they can do this, hey, maybe I can."

Despite the deviancy associated with being an exotic dancer and the negative aspects of the job, most of the women we spoke with seemed to be able to rationalize or justify their involvement in exotic dancing. In summarizing the use of justifications by exotic dancers, one woman said:

You can justify it because you bring home money and at the end of the night that feels great. You don't reflect on, you know, how you were degraded, the leering and the other bad stuff. You know, you don't think about it because you've got a big wad of money in your hand.

In other words, the major incentive for entering dancing, money, is also used as the main justification or rationale for continuing to do it. As with Hong and Duff's (1977) study of taxi-dancers, the neutralization techniques or rationalizations used by exotic dancers to downplay the norm-violating nature of their behaviour, soothe guilt feelings, and cope with the unpleasant aspects of their jobs, were learned during the informal socialization processes that occur on the job.

Putting on a Show

Beyond acquiring the courage to take off one's clothes in public and learning how to justify one's actions, obtaining competence as an exotic dancer also requires learning to be good at the job. In order to become a successful exotic dancer, the novice dancer must learn how to put on a good show or performance. As with any successful performer, dancers need to learn how to use impression management skills to create an illusion that will allow them to control/manipulate their audience in order to achieve some specified goal, in this case the acquisition of money. In their interviews, the women talked about how their job required they put on a skilful performance that would lure men in and get them to spend their money on dancers.

> A dance is not just dancing, it is the way you present yourself, the way you talk to the customer, the way you introduce yourself . . . If you gonna have a smile, right away it's gonna be easy [to make money].
>
> Just turn the guys on, make them think that we are like, you know, licking each other [when performing with another woman]. But we weren't, it's all show. I mean, you don't have to do anything, you know, that's real. You just have to make it look real. So, you know, you would lift up the girl's leg, put your head down, you know, pretend that you're like, oh, you know, that kind of stuff. You know, like men are kind of stupid, so they buy it, right. Sometimes you just look at a customer, the way he reacts . . . I can tell what they like. I'm always doing things that flatter my body. I touch my boobs all the time. I touch myself all the time. It's kind of masturbation but in front of people . . . It gets the men going and keeps them coming back.

As dancers reported in their interviews, learning how to control or manipulate an audience is acquired through observation and interaction with subcultural members within the club setting.

> I was really glad I waitressed before dancing. I got to overhear a lot of the conversations between the dancers and the customers. It was that way that I figured out how to operate and ways to play the men for their money. Some of the girls that have been dancing awhile here were really nice to me. They gave me advice on how to keep the guys interested so they will buy several table dances in a row.

Skill development, improvement and job competence more generally were affirmed by coworkers through praise, and by customers through applause, requests for table dances, the development of a regular clientele, and increased take home pay.

Typology of Dancers

Although the women interviewed reported that they experienced a process of adjustment in becoming a dancer, this process differed somewhat according to the type of dancer each woman could be classified as. Based on the interview data collected, there appear to be two types of dancers: the career dancer and the goal-oriented dancer. Both types of dancers report money as the primary motivating factor for entry into dancing; however, they differ in the types of future they envision for themselves. Despite the fact that most of the women we spoke with told us that they never intended on making dancing a career, some ended up staying in the industry for many years, essentially making it one. Other women reported that they entered the world of dancing with the expectation that dancing would be their career for a while. Whether they intended on making dancing a career or not, the career dancers we spoke with tended to possess limited skill training and education. As a result, they saw dancing as an employment opportunity that enabled them to make a decent living that would otherwise be unavailable to them through other channels.

> This, as a career for me, it's seventeen years. I don't want to stop this now. And besides, what other job could I get where I can earn this kind of money? There really are no jobs for women like me who have little education. At least none where I could make this much money.
>
> You know I'm not educated . . . uh, it's hard to, hard to get back out into the real world once you're in there, it's like I feel like, what else can I do? I've been a stripper for seven years, what else am I gonna be able to do? You know, even if I try I'm always gonna be a dancer, I'm always gonna be labeled. I make good money, so why go work for minimum wage.

In contrast with the career dancer, the goal-oriented dancer enters dancing with a specific goal in mind.

> I don't look at it like a career so it's kind of like a means to an end. You know how you put yourself on a program, like a five-year program. Get in there and make a whack of cash and then go on to something else. Like that can't be the only thing that I want to do for the rest of my life.
>
> There's aspects of the job I like, I mean, I do like some of the girls that work there, some of the bar staff. You know, they're fun to be around at work. And the guys, if they're nice, I can, you know, have had some

good conversations. But, I do not like taking my clothes off, you know? And I don't want to make this a career. It is a means to an end.

Some dancers report being motivated to enter dancing in order to make the money they needed to get or stay out of debt.

I'm getting my Honours Bachelor of Arts in Drama and I want to eventually open my own Drama Therapy Clinic. So, this is just a means of getting there because the money is really good and I'd like to start saving. You know, I've spent all my money on my education and I haven't put any aside for my future, so this would be a quick way to do it, cuz the money's really good and it's really fast.

The bills kept coming in and coming in and I couldn't keep my head above water and everybody was threatening to take me to court and I had all these debts and I just needed money fast. So, I thought I could dance for a bit until I got on top of things.

I don't want to do it, but you have to, I have to do it, I don't have a choice. I have a car payment, I have to pay my rent, I can't not do it. Nothing else will pay my bills. So that's it.

One specific group of goal-oriented dancers are the students. These women report that for them dancing is a short-term job that pays well and that can fit in with their class schedule.

It's ideal when you're going to school because you just you make your own schedules. When I have exam week I don't go at all. So, it fits in with school. So, I guess, I mean, I don't think I would work [as a dancer] once I finish school, unless I couldn't find a job or something.

I have two hundred from my Child Tax and a hundred from my support. And then I was given eleven thousand from OSAP [Ontario Student Assistance Program] to do me 'til January. But then I have tuition and daycare costs and they have gone up, and prescriptions that I have to cover. I'm really down and out right now. So, I really have no choice except to dance—there really is no other way to pay the bills and keep from getting farther in debt while I'm in school.

The commonality among goal-oriented dancers is that dancing is seen as a short-term thing, a means to an end, once the end is achieved (e.g., they graduate from university, pay off their debts, etc.), the plan is to leave dancing. It is important to note, though, that although many goal-oriented dancers reported planning on leaving,

some spoke of difficulties exiting once they got used to the money they could earn.

It's kinda hard once you get used to the money to leave [dancing]. I mean, like, I always said I would leave when I got out of debt, but the money draws you back.

I've wanted out for so many years now and just didn't know how. You get so trapped in there and I didn't know what to do or what I could do.

I started dancing to help pay off the mortgage on my house and get rid of some debts. I thought it was a one shot deal, but I seem to fall back on it whenever I need money.

How a dancer identifies herself as has implications for the socialization experiences of dancers. Women who see dancing as a career, rather than as a temporary job, tend to be more inclined to get involved in the "dancer life," develop relationships with other dancers and club employees, and become immersed in the strip club subculture. As a result, they are likely to experience a more complete socialization process than goal-oriented dancers. Goal-oriented dancers, in contrast, tend to limit their ties to others in the business. As the following quotes illustrate, they try to keep dancing and their private lives separate.

I don't hang out with other dancers. When I leave here I go back to my other life.

Although I try to be friendly to everyone here [at the club] I stick to myself as much as possible and when I leave [work], I try to leave it and everybody associated with it behind.

The implication of keeping the two aspects of their lives separate is that goal-oriented dancers have to contend with the stigma associated with dancing on their own and, as a result, often live very closeted/secretive lives.

I work really hard at keeping this [dancing] a secret from my family. It is hard cuz I still live at home with my parents. So, I keep my costumes in the trunk of my car and I make sure I am the only one with a key.

And I went home to visit and my mom's like, "So, how's your summer going?" And she's asking me all these questions and I had to lie and say that I was working for a security company. I hate it [lying], cuz my mom and I just started to get really close again and here I was suddenly back to the way I was when I was a teenager, the lying and you know, staying out all hours of the night and all this stuff, and you know, it hurt to lie to her. It scares the hell out of me that if they found out, you know, especially my dad, the man my mom's with right now. Like, he's been around since I was a real little kid and he's been married a couple of times. He has eleven children altogether. I'm the only girl—the only one to go to university, so, I'm just like the apple of his eye, you know. He's so proud of me. And when I made honours, he was just, like, he couldn't have been prouder. He goes to the office and you know, he had a mechanic's shop, and he'd walk in and he'd tell all the boys, you know, "This is my daughter. She's an honours student." And he's you know, strict Irish Catholic, and he would just be crushed.

It's really hard because, you know, you're lying to your parents. Well, I am. And I'm close to my family. And I was lying to my friends and to my boyfriend at the time.

Without a community of supportive others, these women have limited access to competing definitions of reality and are therefore more likely to feel some sort of guilt and shame for choosing to dance. Since it is through interacting with other subcultural members that people learn rationalizations for their behaviour, these women are likely to have limited access to the techniques of neutralization used by other dancers that are important for the maintenance of a positive sense of self.

Limitations of the Dancer's Socialization Process

Although both career and goal-oriented dancers felt they were able to experience successful occupational socialization that enabled them to achieve competence as exotic dancers, most of the women interviewed talked about how the socialization process inadequately prepared them for some of the realities of the life of an exotic dancer. *A Stripper's Handbook* (1997), a booklet written by several dancers in the Toronto region, nicely illustrates the benefits and limitations of learning about exotic dancing through informal channels. Although the booklet contains helpful information and advice about the job (e.g., where to get a licence, how much a license costs, how to save money on costumes, stage show rules, DJ fees, fines, freelancing vs. working on schedule, etc.), it also glosses over some of the negative effects the job can have on women's lives (e.g., relationship problems, inhibition of heterosexual desire, etc.). The tendency to overlook the negative is typical of the advice women reported being given by subcultural members, especially the women with limited ties to the subculture.

When discussing the limitations of their socialization experiences, the women we spoke with reported having little knowledge of, and therefore being unprepared for the impact of, dancing on their private lives. The area of impact most often mentioned was relationships. In terms of relationships, women spoke of the difficulties of having and sustaining heterosexual relationships with males outside of the industry. For some women, relationship difficulties were tied to the problems men they date tend to have with their occupation (see Prus, 1980):

I'd suggest to any girl that ever dances, unless your boyfriend's a male dancer, don't date someone when you're stripping. Most guys say they can handle it. They can't and then they start coming into clubs and causing bullshit.

My ex didn't like it. It wasn't because he didn't trust me, he just didn't like the whole idea. He didn't want me dancing not because he was jealous or anything, just because I think he knows it's stressful and it's just not good for you psychologically. None of the guys I dated ever were worried or anything, they knew that I don't really like it . . . They know I would never go out with anyone else that I met at work. My current boyfriend, he dances at a gay bar so he knows what it's all about.

Other women reported that the difficulty of developing or sustaining heterosexual relationships was tied to the nature of their job (i.e., they usually work at night, in a bar, in a job that requires them be around and constantly interacting with customers, many of whom they don't like).

Relationshipwise it's very hard. I think it's hard for someone to take a dancer seriously, it takes a certain type of guy that can look beyond that and ah, if I'm involved I have a really hard time doing my job. If I'm single I'm better with my job. It's hard to meet people cuz I work nights all the time. When I was working full time I was there a good 5 nights a week. On my night off I don't want to go to a bar or anything, I'm in one every day, so you never get a chance to meet people. It's pretty much taboo to date someone you meet at work, cuz you don't know who they are outside of there and they've been giving you money to strip in front of them all night, and they are like, "Ooh yeah, I want to take you on a date." And you are thinking, "Yeah, sure you do. For what, why?" So that's hard. And it's hard if you have a boyfriend, it's hard for them to deal with it.

Most of the time in the afternoon I like to spend my time alone. My boyfriend works and I like this. It's probably to do with my job. It's not because I don't love my boyfriend, but sometimes, he gets on my nerves. Like,

I work an eight-hour shift and all night long everybody is bugging me. At least, I'm there for that. I bug people and people bug me. But, when you get out of there, it's just like you want to have silence everywhere.

Right now, my boyfriend doesn't live with me. We tried it and it didn't work. I'm not patient. I like to be by myself; I really love to be by myself most of the time. And sometimes I think I would like to be with my boyfriend because I miss him, but as soon as he is here he gets on my nerves. Even if you have a boyfriend, sometimes you don't even want to talk with him . . . When I'm finished work, I really don't want to talk with anybody.

Despite the difficulties exotic dancers confront in terms of developing and sustaining relationships, some of the women interviewed expressed an interest/desire to have a stable intimate heterosexual relationship. Others, however, talked about being disinterested in men.

I'm kind of sick of, you know the men and, I just, I've always been a, you know, a big chested person. So, I always gotten the yee-haw's and stuff walking down the street and I just kinda had it after a while, you know? I hate to be looked at. I don't like to be looked at by men. I don't like men very much.

One solution identified by dancers to the relationship difficulties and inhibited heterosexual desire dancers experience, is pursuing relationships with other women. According to the women we interviewed, it is not uncommon for female exotic dancers to develop lesbian relationships, either because of a disinterest in heterosexual relationships stemming from dancing, or because relationships with women are just easier to develop and sustain while they are working as exotic dancers (see Carey et al., 1974; McCaghy & Skipper, 1969; Prus, 1980).

I think a lot of girls end up bi . . . I think it's convenient because it's easier to go out with another dancer, another girl than go out with a guy. You know what I mean? They understand your likes and a lot of guys that date dancers are assholes. So why deal with the hassle of going out? Why not just date a girl? I would have [dated women] if I met a nice girl.

It's a lot easier to date a girl than to bother with going out. But I just happened to meet Paul who dances as well and fits into my lifestyle. But, if I wouldn't have met him I probably would date women. But I just never, I just never met any girl that I had enough in common with. A lot of the girls are [lesbian]. But a lot of people stereotype you. You know what I mean?

As noted by McCaghy and Skipper (1969), three conditions associated with the occupation are supportive of same-sex relationships: "(1) isolation from affective social relationships; (2) unsatisfactory relationships with males; and (3) an opportunity structure allowing a wide range of sexual behavior" (p. 266).

Conclusion

As other studies of exotic dancers have found, there are various factors influencing occupational entry into exotic dancing. This study provides support for a combined career contingency/conversion model. According to this model, four factors influence entry into the exotic dancing: (1) knowledge and accessibility of an opportunity structure that makes exotic dancing an occupational alternative; (2) an awareness of the economic rewards associated with being an exotic dancer; (3) a recruitment process involving personal networks; and (4) financial need or a need for employment. For the women interviewed, these factors played a significant role in their anticipatory socialization process and their movement in the direction of exotic dancing.

Although similar to earlier studies of exotic dancers (this study found evidence of a combined career contingency/conversion model for entry into exotic dancing), there were also some differences between the findings of this study and that of previous research in the area. For example, contrary to earlier studies, we found little indication of dancers having pre-job formal socialization experiences that involved professional training in entertainment-related fields, prior to entering dancing. This difference, however, may be tied to the evolution of stripping. Over the past 25 years or so, stripping has gone from a form of theatre or burlesque stage show, where complete nudity was rare and touching was prohibited, to the more raunchy table and lap dances performed today that often involve complete nudity, and sometimes physical and sexual contact between the dancer and the customer.

Despite some different findings in terms of the anticipatory socialization experiences of dancers, similar to other research in the area we found that once the decision to dance was made and they were employed as dancers, the women we interviewed continued to experience a socialization process through interacting with and observing other subcultural members. The on-the-job, informal occupational socialization the women reported experiencing enabled them to achieve job competence, even in a deviant occupation.

As social learning theories of deviance suggest, although most of us learn the norms and values of society, some of us also learn techniques for committing deviance and the specific motives, drives, rationalizations, and attitudes that allow us to neutralize our violation of normative codes. The socialization experiences of dancers fit with this framework. Learning occurs through observing and interacting with strip club employees, especially more experienced dancers. Through such observations and interactions, novice dancers learn techniques for rationalizing their involvement in the occupation, a process which enables them to stay in the job and succeed, while retaining a valued sense of self.

Although exotic dancers can experience socialization processes that result in job competence, their occupational socialization often inadequately prepares them for the potential impact of their job on their lives outside of the club. The most often mentioned area of concern was intimate relationships, due to the difficulties exotic dancers reported on developing and sustaining heterosexual relationships and desire.

1. According to Ritzer and Walczak (1986, p. 374), "an occupation will be treated as deviant if it meets one or more of the following criteria: (1) it is illegal; (2) one or more of the central activities of the occupation is a violation of nonlegalized norms and values; and (3) the culture, lifestyle, or setting associated with the occupation is popularly presumed to involve rule-breaking behaviour."

2. According to Matza (1992, p. 29), "drift is motion guided gently by underlying influences. The guidance is gentle and not constraining. The drift may be initiated or deflected by events so numerous as to defy codification. But underlying influences are operative nonetheless in that they make initiation to . . . [deviant behaviour] more probable, and they reduce the chances that an event will deflect the drifter from his [/her deviant] . . . path. Drift is a gradual process of movement, unperceived by the actor, in which the first stage may be accidental or unpredictable."

3. Appeal to higher loyalties involves rationalizing deviant behaviour by couching it within an altruistic framework.

4. Although money is part of the motivation for anyone seeking employment, for dancers, it was the amount of money that could be earned dancing, compared with the amount that could be earned in more legitimate jobs, that motivated them to try dancing.

REFERENCES

Boles, Jacqueline M. and Garbin, A.P. (1974a). "The strip club and stripper-customer patterns of interaction." *Sociology and Social Research,* 58, 136–144.

Boles, Jacqueline M. and Garbin, A.P. (1974b). "The choice of stripping for a living: An empirical and theoretical explanation." *Sociology of Work and Occupations,* 1, 110–123.

Boles, Jacqueline M. and Garbin, A.P. (1974c). "Stripping for a living: An occupational study of the night club stripper." In C.D. Bryant (Ed.), *Deviant Behavior: Occupational and Organizational Bases,* (pp. 312–335). Chicago: Rand McNally.

Carey, S.H., Peterson, R.A., and Sharpe, L.K. (1974). "A study of recruitment and socialization into two deviant female occupations." *Sociological Symposium,* 8, 11–24.

Dressel, P.L. and Petersen, D.M. (1982a). "Gender roles, sexuality, and the male strip show: The structuring of sexual opportunity." *Sociological Focus,* 15, 151–162.

Dressel, P.L. and Petersen, D.M. (1982b). "Becoming a male stripper: Recruitment, socialization and ideological development." *Work and Occupations,* 9, 387–406.

Enck, G.E. and Preston, J.D. (1988). "Counterfeit intimacy: A dramaturgical analysis of an erotic performance." *Deviant Behavior,* 9, 369–381.

Forsyth, C.J. and Deshotels, T.H. (1997). "The occupational milieu of the nude dancer." *Deviant Behavior,* 18, 125–142.

Hong, L.K. and Duff, R.W. (1977). "Becoming a taxi-dancer: The significance of neutralization in a semi-deviant occupation." *Sociology of Work and Occupations,* 4, 327–342.

Lofland, J. and Stark, R. (1965). "Becoming a world-saver: A theory of conversion to a deviant perspective." *American Sociological Association,* 30, 862–875.

McCaghy, C.H. and Skipper, J.K. (1969). "Lesbian behavior as an adaptation to the occupation of stripping." *Social Problems,* 17, 262–270.

McCaghy, C.H. and Skipper, J.K. (1972). "Stripping: Anatomy of a deviant life style". In S. D. Feldman and G. W. Thielbar (Eds.), *Life Styles: Diversity in American Society,* (pp. 362–373). Boston: Little Brown.

Petersen, D. and Dressel, P.L. (1982). "Equal time for women: Social notes on the male strip show." *Urban Life,* 11, 185–208.

Prus, R. C. and Sharper, C.R.D. (1977). *Road Hustler: The Career Contingencies of Professional Card and Dice Hustlers.* Toronto: Lexington Books.

Prus, R.C. and Styllianoss, I. (1980). *Hookers, Rounders, and Desk Clerks: The Social Organization of the Hotel Community.* Toronto: Gage Publishing Limited.

Reid, S.A., Epstein, J.S., and Benson, D. E. (1994). "Role identity in a devalued occupation: The case of female exotic dancers." *Sociological Focus,* 27, 1–16.

Ronai, C.R. and Ellis, C. (1989). "Turn-ons for money: Interactional strategies of the table dancer." *Journal of Contemporary Ethnography,* 118, 271–298.

Ronai, C.R. (1992). "The reflexive self through narrative: A night in the life of an erotic dancer/researcher." In C. Ellis and M. G. Flaherty (eds.), *Investigating Subjectivity: Research on Lived Experience,* (pp. 102–124). Newbury Park, CA: Sage Publications.

Sanders, C.R. (1974). "Psyching out the crowd: Folk performers and their audiences." *Urban Life and Culture,* 3, 264–282.

Skipper, J.K. and McCaghy, C.H. (1971). "Stripteasing: A sex-oriented occupation." In James M. Henslin (Ed.), *Studies in the Sociology of Sex,* (pp. 275–296). New York: Appleton-Century-Crofts.

Sykes, G. M. and Matza, D. (1957). "Techniques of neutralization: A theory of delinquency." *American Sociological Review,* 22, 664–670.

Thompson, W.E. and Harred, J.L. (1992). "Topless dancers: Managing stigma in a deviant occupation." *Deviant Behavior,* 13, 291–311.

Think Critically

1. What do you think about the experiences of exotic dancers in learning their trade, and how do they appear to differ from the socialization experiences in more conventional occupations? Explain with examples.

2. How are neutralization techniques employed in allowing women to enter the world of exotic dancing? What other deviant occupations can you think of where such neutralizations would become relevant for potential participants?

From Sex as Sin to Sex as Work
COYOTE and the Reorganization of Prostitution as a Social Problem*

Valerie Jenness**

WHILE PROSTITUTION HAS NEVER BEEN accepted as a legitimate activity, during the 1970s and 1980s a new image of prostitution has emerged to challenge traditional views of prostitutes as social misfits, sexual slaves, victims of pimps and drug addiction, and tools of organized crime (Bullough and Bullough 1978; Lerner 1986; Otis 1985; Schur 1984; Tannahill 1980). This new image of prostitutes is championed by a social movement with roots both in feminism and in the world of prostitution. The leading prostitutes rights organization in the United States is COYOTE (an acronym for "Call Off Your Old Tired Ethics"). Founded in 1973 in San Francisco by ex-prostitute Margo St. James, COYOTE has vocal and persuasive leaders. It has gained legitimacy both in the mass media and in the world of government grants, foundation support, the academy, social science disciplines, and non-profit organizations.

As the first and best-known prostitutes' rights groups in United States, COYOTE was originally founded to provide a "loose union of women"—a coalition of housewives,

*Copyright © 1990 by The Society for the Study of Social Problems. Reprinted from *Social Problems* 37:3 (August 1990), pp. 403–420, by permission of the publisher.

**I thank Alex Chisolm, Diane Hamer, and Patricia King of the Schlesinger Library at Radcliffe College for their assistance with data collection for this research; and Naomi Abrahams, Robin Lloyd, Wayne Mellinger, and Malcolm Spector for comments on earlier drafts of this paper. Special thanks to Beth E. Schneider for her generous assistance with clarifying the substance and form of this paper, as well as with the larger project from which it derives.

lawyers, feminists, and prostitutes—to expose laws and law enforcement procedures that make prostitution problematic (*San Francisco Magazine* 1973:23). COYOTE has grown into a national organization with national and international affiliates.[1] These organizations continue to act as the leading voice in the prostitutes' rights movement in the United States and abroad (Delacoste and Alexander 1987; Hobson 1987; Pheterson 1989).

COYOTE advocates the repeal of all existing prostitution laws, the reconstitution of prostitution as a credible service occupation, and the protection of prostitutes' rights as legitimate workers. While acknowledging a number of abuses against women associated with prostitution (e.g., drug abuse among prostitutes, violence against prostitutes, and juvenile prostitution), COYOTE claims that most of the problems associated with prostitution are directly related to the prohibition of prostitution and the stigma attached to sex and especially sex work.

COYOTE is an organization vying for control of the definition of a social problem. In Spector and Kitsuse's (1977) language, it is a "claims-making" organization attempting to participate in the social construction of prostitution as a social problem. COYOTE has attempted to change the discourse surrounding prostitution by severing prostitution from its historical roots with sin, crime, and illicit sex. COYOTE locates the social problem of prostitution firmly in the discourse of work, choice, and civil rights.

My analysis shows that COYOTE has participated in three separate arenas of discourse, each of which has made distinct contributions to the growth and direction of the prostitutes' rights movement. By engaging law enforcement and municipal government officials in debate over selective enforcement and discrimination of the criminal law, COYOTE recruited prostitutes and others to support its cause. In challenging the contemporary women's movement not to ignore their sisters (i.e., prostitutes), COYOTE linked the problems of prostitutes to dilemmas of women elsewhere in society. As the AIDS epidemic reached alarming proportions, prostitutes' rights organizations became a link between public health agencies and sex workers, as well as a watchdog organization to counter assertions that prostitutes were spreading the disease. After discussing my methods of research and the sources of data for this project, I present the core of COYOTE's position. Then I analyze each of the three arenas of discourse through which COYOTE's position has evolved.

Methods and Data

This work is based on historical documents housed in the archives of The Schlesinger Library at Radcliffe College in Cambridge, Massachusetts. These documents were given to the library by the founder of COYOTE, Margo St. James, and cover the years 1973–1984.[2] These holdings include newsletters of prostitutes' rights organizations, interviews with organizational members and opponents, meeting minutes and notes, questionnaires and reports, position statements, public and personal correspondence, resolutions, grant abstracts and proposals, membership lists, newspaper clippings reporting on COYOTE's political activities, phone logs, budgets, contracts, news releases, conference agendas and charters, and videotapes of four talk shows in which COYOTE representatives were guests, including *The Phil Donahue Show*.

In addition to the material obtained from The Schlesinger Library, I have interviewed and remain in contact with St. James and Priscilla Alexander (the former Co-Director of COYOTE and Executive Director of The National Task Force on Prostitution). Alexander allowed me to consult material in her San Francisco office dated 1984–90. Finally, I relied upon a variety of other sources of information, including published works on COYOTE and the prostitutes' rights movement.

These materials provided me with information on COYOTE's activities, ideology and political strategies. As such, my approach to these data was interpretive and historical. I viewed these documents as the by-products of interested actors playing important roles in definitional processes (Kitsuse and Cicourel 1963). Throughout this work, I was concerned with the evolution of COYOTE's claims, as well as the political context in which these activities were embedded. My goal was to examine the viability, rather than the validity, of COYOTE's claims. Viable claims were understood as definitions and assertions that "live" and that claimants can "get away with" (Spector and Kitsuse 1977). Viability was evident when prostitutes and their advocates, critics, and constituencies gave credibility to claims and definitions by responding to them and/or by offering counterclaims.

A New Image of Prostitution

Three propositions underly COYOTE's crusade to reconstruct the social problem of prostitution. First, prostitution is work and the master concept of work should replace the master concept of crime as the fundamental stance of society toward prostitution. Second, most women who work as prostitutes choose to do so, even in a society where prostitution is, for the most part, illegal. Finally, prostitution is work that people should have the right to choose and that should be respected and protected like work in legitimate service occupations.

Prostitution as "Voluntarily Chosen Service Work"

The notion of work is central to COYOTE's position. To challenge historically developed images of prostitution, COYOTE's crusade relies upon two accessible and powerful linguistic devices to present an alternative image of prostitutes. One of these is the focus on the "work of prostitution," while the other is the focus on the "civil rights" of prostitutes as service workers. The image of prostitution as work is made evident by COYOTE leaders St. James and Alexander. In an editorial they express their strong reaction to traditional views of prostitution:

> A rather profound misconception that people have about prostitution is that it is "sex for sale," or that a prostitute is selling her body. In reality, a prostitute is being paid for her time and skill, the price being rather dependent on both variables. To make a great distinction between being paid for an hour's sexual services, or an hour's typing or an hour's acting on a stage is to make a distinction that is not there (St. James and Alexander 1977;n.p.).

Dolores French, a self-proclaimed prostitute, author, president of the Florida COYOTE, president of HIRE (Hooking Is Real Employment), and an appointee on Atlanta Mayor Andrew Young's Task Force on Prostitution, argues that the work of prostitution resembles other kinds of work women do:

> A women has the right to sell sexual services just as much as she has the right to sell her brains to a law firm where she works as a lawyer, or to sell her creative work to a museum when she works as an artist, or to sell her image to a photographer when she works as a model or to sell her body when she works as a ballerina. Since most people can have sex without going to jail, there is no reason except old-fashioned prudery to make sex for money illegal (quoted in Henkin 1988:3).

The vocabulary of work is especially pronounced in a testimony on prostitution given to the New York State Bar Association by the leaders of COYOTE:

> The laws against pimping (living off the earnings of a prostitute) and pandering (encouraging someone to work as a prostitute) should be repealed, to be replaced with labor laws dealing with working conditions in third-party owned and managed prostitution businesses. Commissions, a majority of whose members should be prostitutes or ex-prostitutes, including individuals who have worked on the street, in massage parlors and brothels, and for escort services, should develop guidelines for the operation of third-party owned and managed businesses, including but not limited to health and safety issues, commissions, and employer/employee relationships. . . . Because prostitution is illegal, women and men who work in third-party run prostitution businesses have no legal status as workers. Therefore, they are unlikely to have their income and social security taxes withheld, or to be provided with health, disability, and worker's compensation insurance, sick leave, vacation pay (St. James and Alexander 1985:1).

COYOTE insists that most prostitution is voluntary. For COYOTE, "most women who work as prostitutes have made a conscious decision to do so, having looked at a number of work alternatives" (*COYOTE Howls* 1988:1). Accordingly, "we need to demand the right of these women to opt for prostitution if that's their choice. We can't deny women a choice" (St. James quoted on "The Phil Donahue Show" 1980). COYOTE does distinguish between those who choose prostitution as work and those who are forced into prostitution to survive. COYOTE claims that "only 15 percent of prostitutes are coerced by third parties" (*COYOTE Howls* 1988:1), and that the problems associated with "forced prostitution cannot be addressed until voluntary prostitution is legitimate" (Delacoste and Alexander 1987:200–201).

Prostitution as a Civil Rights Issue

COYOTE relies upon claims that prostitution is legitimate and voluntarily chosen work as a foundation for claims about prostitutes' civil rights as workers. In 1982, the National Organization for Women (NOW) adopted a COYOTE resolution, which:

> . . . affirms its support of the right of women not to be forced into prostitution, as well as affirms the right of women to choose to work as prostitutes when it is

their own choice and, California NOW shall support legislation to decriminalize the voluntary aspects of adult prostitution (Alexander 1983:19).

A public statement submitted to California NOW by COYOTE elaborated on the above declaration in the following assertion:

> Whatever one thinks of prostitution, women have the right to make up their own minds about whether or not to work as prostitutes, and under what terms. They have the right to work as freelance workers, just as do nurses, typists, writers, doctors, and so on. They also have the right to work for an employer, a third party who can take care of administration and management problems. . . . They have the right to a full human existence (Alexander 1983:15).

Finally, a 1988 COYOTE newsletter claims that:

> prostitutes have the right to work independently, to work in small collectives, or to work for agents, they should be covered by enlightened employment policies providing paid sick leave and vacation, disability, health, and workers compensation insurance, and social security, like other employed workers (*COYOTE Howls* 1988:1).

COYOTE argues that along with the right to choose prostitution as an occupation, prostitutes must have the right not to be subject to public harassment, such as stigma, rape, violence, denial of health care, denial of protection by and under the law, and denial of alternative job opportunities. From COYOTE's perspective as workers, prostitutes should be afforded equal protection under the law and should be free of violations of their civil rights, especially in the form of legal repression.

COYOTE has made its position felt by pressing claims cloaked in the vocabulary of work, choice, and civil rights in three arenas of discourse: the discourse of law enforcement, the feminist discourse, and AIDS discourse. COYOTE entered the arena of feminist discourse through its national and international campaign to decriminalize prostitution; thus that campaign provided a link between the discourse of law enforcement and the feminist discourse.

The Discourse with Law Enforcement

In 1973, The Point Foundation at Glide Memorial Church provided St. James with a $5000 grant to organize a prostitutes' union in San Francisco. She recruited an advisory board of 50 influential San Franciscans, as well as local prostitutes to advocate reform.[3] In addition, anyone could become a member of COYOTE by paying a small fee. Within the first year of its formation. COYOTE claimed a membership of over 1000, ten percent of whom were active prostitutes (Ritter 1973).

As a grassroots advocacy and service organization, COYOTE originally formed to protest a number of abuses of local prostitutes. In the early and mid-seventies, COYOTE's activities centered around: 1) protesting legal discrimination against prostitution, especially police harassment and entrapment; 2) opposing the quarantining of arrested prostitutes for venereal disease; and 3) convincing the community that law enforcement's response to prostitution is a waste of taxpayers' money. COYOTE also provided numerous services for prostitutes, including a hotline for prostitutes called SLIP (Survival Line for Independent Prostitutes), immediate legal assistance for prostitutes who had been arrested, suitable clothing for prostitutes making court appearances, and classes on survival skills for prostitutes in jail.

With slogans such as "Hookers Unite, You Have Nothing to Lose But Cop Harassment," "No More Jive in '75," and "My Ass Is Mine," COYOTE claimed police harassment of prostitutes, not illicit sex, makes prostitution problematic. It is not surprising that police harassment was one of the most immediate concerns of COYOTE. Prior to the formation of COYOTE, the gay community in San Francisco had successfully organized to protest police harassment. As St. James explained, "it's well past time for whores to organize. The homosexuals organized and now the cops are afraid to harass them anymore" (Bryan 1973a:2).

COYOTE members and supporters protested the use of downtown hotels by police to entrap prostitutes. As a San Francisco paper described:

> The hookers and their friends were members of COYOTE. They had come to San Francisco's futuristic new Hyatt Regency Hotel to picket the place for being finky and providing vice-coppers with free rooms to entrap their sisters. . . . It was noon and the first day of a week long picketing campaign to bring public attention (and hopefully indignation) to bear on the increasingly frequent use of free rooms in fancy downtown hotels as "lurid setups" to which the vice-coppers bring suspected hookers. Once there, COYOTE says the cops entrap the girls into "soliciting" an act of prostitution. Most notorious of the

hotels which give the cops their free entrapment rooms is the San Francisco Hilton which COYOTE picketed Oct. 23. Also picketed was the Bellevue Hotel on Oct. 24 and the Stanford Court on Oct. 25. So, COYOTE's campaign got underway in a light drizzle with at least 20 pickets, half a dozen vice cops and six or eight newspaper and television reporters on hand. The signs said: "OFF THE PUSSY PATROL," "MY ASS IS MY OWN." "STOP ENTRAPMENT," "DOES IT HAVE TO BE BAD TO BE GOOD?," and a lot more. COYOTE also participated prominently in the October 24th Board of Supervisors hearing on the question of issuing citations against those accused in 'victimless crimes' rather than hauling them down to jail for booking (Bryan 1973b:1).

Despite denials by the Board of Supervisors, COYOTE's proposal to issue citations for prostitution rather than arresting prostitutes attracted considerable media attention. It was also the source of a heated debate in at least three Board of Supervisors' meetings (Bryan 1974).

COYOTE instigated and/or sponsored at least 26 law suits on behalf of prostitutes. For example, with the support of the American Civil Liberties Union (ACLU), COYOTE filed numerous class action suits challenging the constitutionality of a California statute directed against anyone who solicits or engages in any act of solicitation. Suits were filed on the grounds that

> it is an invasion of privacy, overly vague, and restricts freedom of expression, and that the state has no compelling interest in regulating sexual behavior between consenting adults, and therefore, that its selective enforcement violates the right to equal protection (M. Anderson 1975:41).

COYOTE was successful in lifting a mandatory three-day venereal disease quarantine imposed by the San Francisco Police Department on prostitutes by pressing the claim that the incidence of VD is at least as high among people 20 to 24 years old as among whores and "only women are arrested and forced to have regular checks for VD" (St. James quoted in Metzger 1975:8).

With the slogan "The Trick Is Not Getting Caught," COYOTE's early campaign attempted to bring attention to unequal enforcement of the law. Although solicitation is a crime for both the prostitute and the customer, only prostitutes are arrested. As *The Washington Post* reported:

> Margo meets her interviewers with xeroxed copies of papers by psychiatrists, sociologists and lawyers,

all tending to demonstrate the laws on the subject are indefensibly biased in favor of the hooker's customers who never gets arrested and against the hooker who often does (von Hoffman 1974:n.p.).

Partially in response to claims such as these, one San Francisco judge dismissed prostitution charges against 37 women whose male customers were not arrested. She charged the police with an "intentional purposeful, selective enforcement policy" (Mydans 1976:n.p.). COYOTE was also central in convincing three female judges in San Francisco to participate in the women's political caucus and in peer counseling for prostitutes.

Finally, COYOTE argued that "the real victim of victimless crime [such as prostitution] is the taxpayer" (Terzian 1974:n.p). For COYOTE, it is a waste of law enforcement's time and resources to arrest prostitutes. As St. James claimed at a hotel protest, "The police have their hands full dealing with real crime and they should not be distracted into pursuits concerning what consenting adults do" (Carib 1973:2). She argued further that "while this city continues to be plagued by crimes against life and property, these overpaid officers are wasting their time and harassing people on non-victim charges (St. James quoted in Bryan 1973a:2).

COYOTE instigated and supported at least two taxpayers' suits in San Francisco and Alameda Counties to decriminalize prostitution on the grounds that it is a waste of taxpayers' money (Ashley 1974). City officials, especially law enforcement officials, responded publicly to COYOTE by suggesting that the use of taxpayers' money to control of prostitution is well-spent. A San Francisco Deputy District Attorney publicly argued, "vice-squad officers look at it the way I do. That there is something sort of subterranean [about vice crime] which if left to grow and fester would overwhelm certain parts of the city" (Butler 1974:6). The Inspector for the San Francisco vice-squad argued that "there's no such thing as a victimless crime. The prostitute is the victim in these crimes. She is usually the victim of a brutal pimp" (Bryan 1973a:n.p.).

COYOTE's campaign against law enforcement generated local controversy. For example, Gloria Steinem sent a letter of support to COYOTE and canceled a luncheon engagement with City Supervisor Feinstein in protest of Feinstein's failure to support COYOTE's campaign. Only seven months after COYOTE's inception, a San Francisco paper reported that "Margo St. James is overwhelmed with speaking engagements, particularly before groups of law and medical students. . . . Sheriff Dick Hongisto has attended COYOTE meetings" (Ritter 1973:4).

Beginning in 1974, and ending in 1978. COYOTE staged a number of media events designed to raise funds, draw attention to the organization, and legitimate its campaigns.[4] Most notably, COYOTE staged two media events each year to generate revenue and public attention: the Annual Hookers' Convention and the Hookers' Ball. With the slogan "74, Year of the Whore," the first National Hookers' Convention was held in June of 1974 in San Francisco's Glide Memorial Church. The church was packed with prostitutes, plainclothes policemen, city officials, news reporters and interested spectators. National networks and news magazines covered this event where the "Trick of the Year" award was given out and a giant keyhole was awarded to the "Vice Cop of the Year."

The first Hookers' Ball was held in October 1974 at the San Francisco Longshoreman's Hall. In attendance were such VIPs as state legislator Willie Brown and San Francisco County Sheriff Hongisto. Like the Hookers' Convention, the Hookers' Ball drew attention to COYOTE and its cause, especially from the press. As *The Chicago Tribune* reported, "for the press it was an orgy. They filmed, photographed, and interviewed anyone who was generous with her eyeshadow" (Keegan 1974:1).

The second Hookers' Convention, held in June 1975, featured panels of experts who discussed the decriminalization of prostitution. Over 1,200 people attended, including activists, lawyers, celebrities, and prostitutes. Between these annual events, COYOTE sent out information, attracted the press, provided speakers, organized lawyers, fought hypocrisy in government and the courts, and supported prostitutes in trouble. Each year from 1974 to 1978 the Hookers' Ball drew larger crowds and generated more funds than the previous Ball. The 1977 Hookers' Ball grossed over $93,000. According to the Bay Area Seating Service (BASS), an event promotion company used by COYOTE, over 1,160 publications around the world covered the 1977 Hookers' Ball held in San Francisco.

By 1978 COYOTE had succeeded on a number of fronts in San Francisco: the quarantining of arrested prostitutes was discontinued, public defenders began to make more serious attempts to defend women arrested for prostitution, and arrested prostitutes became eligible to take advantage of the pre-trial diversion program to be released on their own recognizance. Following COYOTE's early political gains, "streetwalkers and call girls began to take notice, and COYOTE began to branch out" (Kellog 1974:23). Two COYOTE affiliates had also emerged—the Associated Seattle Prostitutes (ASP) and the Prostitutes of New York (PONY). In addition, COYOTE chapters were in the process of organizing in San Diego, New Orleans, Des Moines, and Miami.

COYOTE gained support for its cause from prostitutes and reform minded liberals through its discourse with law enforcement. Supported by local protests and media attention, COYOTE's campaign against law enforcement projected an image of the prostitute as a victim of laws prohibiting prostitution and of the discriminatory enforcement of such laws, rather than a victim of illicit sex. Further, COYOTE suggested that it is simply a waste of taxpayers' money to enforce laws that create and perpetuate rather than eliminate the victimization of prostitutes.

However, it was COYOTE's national and international campaign that solidified a genuinely alternative conception of prostitution. By undertaking these campaigns, COYOTE and its affiliates found a home in the feminist discourse of the late 1970s and early 1980s; especially the feminist discourse that defined rape, pornography and violence against women as social problems (Brownmiller 1975; Dworkin 1981; Griffin 1981; Lederer 1980; Linden et al. 1982; MacKinnon 1983). Through these debates COYOTE developed ties with the contemporary women's movement, and found another forum to press their claims about prostitution.

COYOTE's National and International Crusade

In the late 1970s COYOTE began a national and then international crusade to decriminalize prostitution.[5] In order to kick off a national campaign, in 1976 COYOTE held its Third Annual National Hookers' Convention, also referred to as The First World Meeting of Prostitutes, in Washington, D.C. At this meeting, the first Hookers' Lobby was formed and went to Capitol Hill to promote a resolution calling for the decriminalization of prostitution (Palmer 1976; Volz 1976). Formulated by COYOTE, this resolution was presented in Brussels earlier the same year at the International Tribunal on Crimes Against Women and was supported by NOW, the ACLU, and other civil rights and women's groups. Sponsored by COYOTE, the Feminist Party, and the First International Hookers' Film Festival, this lobbying effort included delegates from 14 states and Canada, several hundred prostitutes from the East and West coasts, and a chartered planeload of prostitutes and ex-prostitutes from Europe. After lobbying the Capitol, delegates visited political conventions in Kansas City and New York, where they engaged in "loiter-ins" to protest the illegality of prostitution.

In another move to nationalize its campaign, COYOTE declared itself The National Task Force on Prostitution (NTFP) in 1979. With the formation of the National Task Force on Prostitution, the COYOTE newsletter (*COYOTE Howls*) became the *NTFP NEWS,* but bears the logo of COYOTE as well as the subtitle *COYOTE Howls.* Similarly, most National Task Force on Prostitution letterhead bears the trademark of COYOTE, and recent COYOTE letterhead bears the trademark of the National Task Force on Prostitution. In short, COYOTE and the National Task Force on prostitution are essentially the same organization. The NTFP formed in order to promote legitimacy for COYOTE. As Diamant (1981:15) reported, "mail sent on COYOTE stationary wasn't getting responses from the likes of the State Department. So COYOTE has become the more official-sounding National Task Force on Prostitution." The National Task Force on Prostitution was also formed to establish an umbrella organization responsible for developing a network of prostitutes' rights advocacy organizations in the United States.

COYOTE's crusade became international when representatives were sent to the United Nations Conference on Women held in Copenhagen in 1980. A week before the 1984 Democratic National in San Francisco, COYOTE sponsored the Second Annual International Hookers' Convention, which was billed as a "Women's Forum on Prostitutes' Rights" (Dorgan 1984). This event capitalized on the media personnel in town for the Democratic Convention. Participants in the hookers' convention also drafted a prostitutes' right platform calling for the repeal of all laws against prostitution, protection and health care for prostitutes, taxation for prostitutes, and a code of ethics.

In 1985 COYOTE's international crusade continued with the formation of the International Committee for Prostitutes' Rights (ICPR) based in The Netherlands. The International Committee on Prostitutes' Rights sponsored the World Whores' Congress in Amsterdam in 1985 and in Brussels in 1986. Founders, representatives, and members of prostitutes' rights organizations from all over the world attended these conferences. Two hundred sex workers and their invited advocates from 16 countries attended the 1986 meeting and were provided with security guards, translators, and considerable media coverage. The activities and claims from the conference were eventually published in two editions of the newsletter *World Wide Whores' News (WWWN)* and in a book entitled *The Vindication of the Rights of Whores* (Pheterson 1989).

As COYOTE extended its crusade to the national and the international scenes, it developed close ties with contemporary feminism.

The Feminist Discourse

Although the contemporary women's movement addresses a broad set of concerns, sexuality has loomed especially large on its agenda (D'Emilio and Freedman 1988; Ferree and Hess 1985). Subsumed in the feminist discourse on sexuality are discussions of the social control of women's sexuality, women's rights to control their bodies, and institutionalized violence against women. Central to these discussions is a concern for liberating women from the sexual and social double standard.

The centrality these concerns within the contemporary women's movement provided COYOTE with a fertile ground for the development and public presentation of analyses of prostitution and its relationship to the status of women. By entering and shaping contemporary feminist discourse, COYOTE cemented ties with the women's movement and ensured that prostitution represented a difficult dilemma for feminists (Alexander 1987; Hobson 1987; Pheterson 1989; Snider 1976; St. James and Alexander 1977). Although NOW adopted a resolution to decriminalize prostitution in 1973, it wasn't until the late 1970s that NOW recognized prostitution as a legitimate issue. Nonetheless, the women's movement in the United States has been slow to support prostitute women (Jaget 1980).

One of the first significant alliances COYOTE established with a nationally recognized women's organization was with the Wages for Housework Campaign. *The Chicago Tribune* reported that:

strumpets and housewives both need the power money brings . . . [and] many prostitutes are also mothers with second jobs. Last September in a Chicago suburb, the FBI arrested three women who were part of a $100-a-night call girl operation. Many of the hookers were house-wives supplementing family incomes (Gorner 1977:2).

The Los Angeles Wages for Housework chapter also formed an alliance with COYOTE to put government and business on trial for "pimping off prostitution and pimping off all the work women do." The coalition claimed that "an attack against prostitutes is an attack on all women" (Wages for Housework 1977:8).

Boasting a membership of 20,000, in 1979 COYOTE aligned itself with NOW to promote a "Kiss and Tell" Campaign designed to strengthen lobbying efforts for the passage of the Equal Rights Amendment (ERA).[6] During this time, the immediate goal of COYOTE became the passage of the ERA and securing public funding for abortions (Castonia 1979:B14). A 1979 COYOTE newsletter reported:

> COYOTE has called on all prostitutes to join the international "Kiss and Tell" campaign to convince legislators that it is in their best interest to support the decriminalization of prostitution, the Equal Rights Amendment, abortion funding, lesbian and gay rights, and all other issues of importance to women. The organizers of the campaign are urging that the names of legislators who have consistently voted against those issues, yet are regular patrons of prostitutes, be turned over to feminist organizations for their use (*COYOTE Howls* 1979:1).

COYOTE also secured affiliations with such organizations as the ACLU, NOW, The California Democratic Council, the California Corrections and Parole Officers Association, the Northern California Business and Professional Women's Organization. The Feminist Party, Wages for Housework, lesbian and gay advocacy organizations, CAL-PEP (California Prostitutes' Education Program), the American Bar Association, many state bar associations and various Barristers' Clubs.

While focusing on coalition building and establishing recognition as a legitimate national civil rights organization. COYOTE also entered the feminist discourse on violence against women. COYOTE's central claim was that "outlawing of prostitution promotes rape and violence against women" (St. James quoted in Nielson 1979:105).

Combining claims about prostitution and rape, St. James argued in a speech delivered at Western Washington University that:

> Prohibition [of prostitution] promotes disrespect for women, promotes violence and promotes rape. . . .

If we had legalized porn and prostitution at the same time, we wouldn't be sitting on the powder keg of sex and violence we're sitting on in this country (quoted in Reiper 1982:3).

This argument was pressed further by St. James and Alexander in an editorial:

> what the decriminalization of pornography has done is to allow an entire industry to develop that is based on a taunting and baiting, "look, but don't touch" philosophy that is compounded by the prohibition of prostitution. . . . Should a woman offer to put on a private, pornographic show for an undercover officer, she would be arrested for soliciting an act of prostitution. (Alexander and St. James 1981:n.p.).

Finally, while addressing an Episcopal church congregation in Alameda County, California, St. James claimed that prostitution should not be isolated from pornography because present laws allow "white males to sell women's bodies, but do not allow women to sell their bodies themselves" (Anderson 1984:14).

Alexander, a former member of the California and National Boards of Directors of NOW and a founding member of Women Against Violence in Pornography and Media (WAVPM), has been central in making public COYOTE's fight against violence against women. She has consistently argued that the decriminalization of prostitution would help reduce violence against women, especially rape and pornography:

> The NTFP is calling on the National Organization for Women to implement its 1973 resolution calling for decriminalization by establishing a prostitution task force to put pressure on the legislature. It is important that other feminist organizations, the National Women's Political Caucus and the League of Women Voters, for example, make the issue a priority alongside of the Equal Rights Amendment, abortion, domestic violence, rape, and lesbian and gay rights. Only when women are treated equally in this society, both sexually and economically, will the tremendous abuse that women face be eliminated (Alexander 1979b:3).

Through contemporary feminist discourse on violence against women, COYOTE's crusade responded to feminist analyses of prostitutes as sexual slaves who are victimized by impersonal and commercialized sex.

WHISPER and the Emergence of an Organized Nemesis

Along with the emergence of COYOTE's crusade, competing images of prostitution began to surface within the feminist discourse on violence against women. Most prominent among these was the image of the prostitute described by Kathleen Barry (1979) in her book *Sexual Slavery*. In this book, Barry describes women who are abducted or sold for sexual purposes and transported to the United States, West Germany, Saudi Arabia, and other countries. The book, which has been translated into four languages, served as the basis for a 1983 United Nations report that said "prostitution is slavery" and a grave cause for international concern (Klemesrud 1985:C16). Barry founded the International Feminist Network Against Female Sexual Slavery in 1983 in Rotterdam. Financed by grants from the Dutch Government and the Ford Foundation, this network included women who worked with grassroots women's organizations from 24 countries.

WHISPER (Women Hurt in Systems of Prostitution Engaged in Revolt) emerged in the early 1980s. With its headquarters in New York City, WHISPER is an organization made up of volunteers, feminist scholars, and clergy who are concerned with saving prostitutes from the life of prostitution. WHISPER argues that prostitution must be understood as an institution created by patriarchy to control and abuse women. WHISPER claims that no women *chooses* prostitution and that all prostitutes are victims. As Sarah Wynter, editor of the WHISPER newsletter, argued:

> Prostitution isn't like anything else. Rather everything else is like prostitution, because it is a model for women's condition, for gender stratification and its logical extension, sex discrimination. Prostitution is founded on enforced sexual abuse under a system of male supremacy that is itself built along a continuum of coercion. . . . We, the women of WHISPER, reject the lie that women freely choose prostitution (quoted in Delacoste and Alexander 1987:268–269).

The primary objective of WHISPER is the abolition of prostitution, not just laws prohibiting prostitution.

In the early 1980s a schism developed between COYOTE's campaign and feminist analyses of prostitution such as those exemplified by WHISPER. This schism centered on the tension between COYOTE's crusade to empower prostitutes and legitimate prostitution as work, and WHISPER's attempts to rescue prostitutes from what they see as an inherently powerless position. A story covering a pornography and prostitution conference in which St. James was a panelist reported:

> What she's [St. James] selling, which some parts of the women's movement are having trouble buying, is the vision of prostitution as a viable career option. In St. James' vision, the crass marketplace sexuality of the female skin trade is not the problem. An advocate of decriminalization, she sees prostitution as a labour issue with poor working conditions, an absence of collective bargaining rights and hostile legislators as its key determinants. And while many anti-porn feminists are sympathetic to their hooker sisters and offer resources from the women's community to fight laws which hound them, they are having trouble swallowing COYOTE's appeal to artisanal pride in the craft of commercial sex. . . . The historic feminist identity with women of the night has traditionally been constructed out of empathy for the desperate victims of harsh socio-economic realities. But increasingly, voices in the sex industry are offering an alternative perspective— one that sees prostitutes as active agents in their vocation choice (Kirzner 1985:n.p.).

After attending a conference supported by the Dutch Government on sexual slavery, St. James located COYOTE's claims in its conflict with WHISPER:

> I recently travelled to the Netherlands to participate in a conference on sexual slavery by the Dutch Government—since the U.S. would never fund such a thing. It was organized by Kathy Barry, author of *Female Sexual Slavery,* a book which borders on equating slavery with prostitution. Although she gives lip service to decriminalization, she finds it impossible to grant it a professional status equal to her own (St. James 1980:7).

Moreover, COYOTE's 1984–85 charter stressed that "all prostitutes are *not* inert, helpless objects to whom men do an endless number of things." Gail Pheterson, the Co-Director of the International Committee on Prostitutes' Rights (ICPR), asserted that "in trying to stop abuses in prostitution, one should not try to put the women out of work" (quoted in Henkin 1989:5).

The emergence of an organized ideological nemesis fueled COYOTE's crusade by generating controversy. *The New York Times* reported that:

> Miss Barry said one of the biggest problems she faces in her work is "the happy hooker" image, which she believes

tends to glorify prostitution and makes it seem like an alternative work experience. "The Xaviera Hollanders of the world only represent about 5 percent of the prostitute population," she said, quoting from her research. "More often, prostitutes are runaways who become pimp-controlled, and pimp-controlled prostitution is female sexual slavery." . . . Asked about Margo St. James, who heads Coyote, a San Francisco-based organization that defends prostitutes' rights, she replied, Margo was very helpful in providing information about women being victimized and exploited by police. But we basically disagree, because I want to end prostitution, and she regards it as a viable profession (Klemserud 1985:C16).

The emergence of organized opposition such as this suggests that COYOTE's claims have not only generated an audience, but have also been taken seriously enough to warrant counterclaims.

Through national and international campaigns, COYOTE participated in debates within contemporary feminist discourse. In the process COYOTE reached beyond the technical aspect of the enforcement of criminal laws governing prostitution. Using feminist discourse on violence against women as a forum, COYOTE put forth images of prostitutes that challenge both traditional images of prostitution and recent feminist analyses of prostitution as a social problem. Through coalition building and the development of ties with the contemporary women's movement, COYOTE pressed their claims about the rights of women to choose prostitution as a viable service occupation. The emergence of an organized nemesis, WHISPER, led to a crystallization of COYOTE's views, both within the women's movement and before a wide public audience.

The Discourse on AIDS

The AIDS epidemic represents the most recent and the most dramatic change in the political environment of prostitutes' rights organizations. In addition to posing a health threat to prostitutes, the AIDS epidemic represents a social and legal threat to prostitutes as well. Accordingly, when prostitutes met at the Second Annual International Hookers' Convention in 1984, "AIDS was very much on their minds" (Mitchell 1984: 10). By the end of the Second World Whores Congress in 1986, "the AIDS epidemic had reached alarming proportions and prostitutes were being scapegoated for spreading the disease" (Pheterson 1989:28).

Many governmental and medical establishments reacted to AIDS with calls for increased regulation of prostitution in the form of registration, mandatory AIDS testing, and prison sentences for those carrying antibodies to the virus. With the spread of AIDS well-documented, and without a viable cure in sight, the introduction of legislation calling for mandatory AIDS testing of prostitutes has been introduced across the nation.[7] In short, the AIDS epidemic has led to increased social control of prostitutes, especially in the form of legal sanctions.

COYOTE and other prostitutes' rights organizations have recently devoted considerable activity to the threats that AIDS poses to prostitutes. In 1986 St. James moved to France to work through the International Committee on Prostitutes' Rights (ICPR). *The San Francisco Chronicle* reported a change in the leadership of COYOTE and the organization's emerging concern for the scapegoating of prostitutes for AIDS:

> When Margo St. James moves to Europe at the end of March, she will leave behind her Rolodex. . . . [She] will turn everything over to Priscilla Alexander, a feminist educator, and Gloria Lockett, a former prostitute. . . . The teaming of feminist and hooker pleases St. James. . . . Alexander's main concern is educating the public about prostitution and AIDS. Prostitutes are always linked in the public's mind with the spread of disease, she said. "But there isn't any documented evidence of a customer getting AIDS from a prostitute." (Rubin 1986:n.p.)

Consistent with this change in leadership, COYOTE's immediate goal became combatting the scapegoating of prostitutes through public education. As a 1988 COYOTE charter stated:

> COYOTE is working to prevent the scapegoating of prostitutes for AIDS and other sexually transmitted diseases, and to educate prostitutes, their clients, and the general public about prevention of these diseases (*COYOTE Howls* 1988:1).

Many of COYOTE's activities from the mid eighties to the present respond to the notion that prostitutes represent a pool of contagion. Exprostitute and COYOTE Co-Director Gloria Lockett claimed at a press conference in San Francisco in 1988:

> Prostitutes test no higher for exposure to HIV than other women—when studies take into consideration IV drug use—and since prostitutes use condoms,

they should not be targeted for measures which so patently violate our civil rights (quoted in Winklebleck 1988:2).

COYOTE has distributed public announcements, attended conferences, issued press releases, and staged protests to oppose legislation requiring the mandatory testing of prostitutes for the AIDS virus.

COYOTE also has protested AIDS testing on the grounds that selective testing is discriminatory and a violation of prostitutes' civil rights:

> Outraged members of COYOTE, a national organization concerned with the rights of male and female prostitutes, sent up a howl in San Francisco last week at the recent passage of two state bills aimed at putting prostitutes who test HIV positive behind bars. . . . Earlier this year COYOTE joined ranks with AIDS activists ACT UP and the US Prostitutes Collective to protest the proposed legislation before Speaker of the House Willie Brown and other politicians and lobbyists in Sacramento. They argued that the proposals singled out and unfairly punished a group which tests HIV positive no more frequently than do other sexually active women in the United States. "Prostitutes haven't been transmitting AIDS," asserted Carol Leigh (a.k.a. Scarlet Harlot), COYOTE legislative media coordinator. "Most of the prostitutes I know are getting tested on their own. They use condoms. Obviously we're being used as a symbol" (Everett 1988:n.p.).

The primacy of AIDS related activity is also evident in COYOTE's January 1989 newsletter which offered exclusive coverage of the AIDS epidemic, including AIDS laws affecting prostitutes which were passed in California in 1989 (*COYOTE Howls* 1989). In short, the AIDS epidemic has potentially circumvented COYOTE's original primary goal of decriminalization. As Alexander (personal communication 21 September 1988) explained, "we [COYOTE] don't have time for focusing a concerted effort on decriminalization, we're worried about quarantining [of prostitutes]."

The AIDS epidemic has prompted government agencies, such as Centers for Disease Control (CDC) in Atlanta and the State of California Department of Health, to invite prostitutes' rights organizations to assist them in investigating the role of prostitution in the spread of the disease. For example, in 1987 COYOTE was asked by the AIDS Activity Office of the California Department of Health to submit a proposal for an AIDS prevention project for prostitutes. As a result, the California Prostitutes' Education Program (CAL-PEP), which operates out of COYOTE's office in San Francisco and bears COYOTE's letterhead and logo, was awarded a $40,000 grant for the purpose of educating street prostitutes about safer sex practices and intravenous hygiene. CAL-PEP has also received funding from the Robert Wood Johnson Foundation, the Centers for Disease Control, the Alameda County Health Department, and the San Francisco District Attorney's Office.

The AIDS epidemic has altered the politics of prostitution, as well the political environment of prostitutes' rights organizations such as COYOTE. Key individuals, constituencies, and organizations in COYOTE's environment have become increasingly dependent upon prostitutes' rights organizations for resources. Prostitutes' organizations such as COYOTE are in a position to provide access to prostitutes who may need AIDS education, and knowledge about how to effectively educate prostitutes. This gives prostitutes' rights organizations a legitimate purpose, an opportunity to work within the system, and an institutionalized forum for pressing claims.

Discussion

Although prostitution has existed in every society for which there are written records (Bullough and Bullough 1978; Otis 1985; Tannahill 1980), prostitutes' rights organizations such as COYOTE are a fairly recent development in the history of prostitution in particular and sexual politics more generally. Never before have prostitutes acted as their own advocates, both challenging commonly held notions about prostitution and offering proposals for reform. COYOTE consists of and represents individuals who have been socially and culturally stigmatized, degraded, and segregated. As Kitsuse (1980:2) remarked in 1980, "Who would have thought that prostitutes would lobby the halls of legislative bodies to denounce 'your old tired ethics.'"

Shielded by a small but vocal movement that views prostitution as legitimate work, prostitutes' rights organizations such as COYOTE have emerged from the "lunatic fringe" into public attention (DeYoung 1984). Their arrival has been greeted with ambivalence, support, criticism, and organized opposition (Hobson 1987; Jaget 1980; Pheterson 1989; Weitzer 1989). Viewing themselves as a beleaguered minority group whose time to advocate reform has come, COYOTE and its affiliates have permanently affected the rhetorical landscape surrounding prostitution as a social problem:

> Margo St. James and COYOTE are not to be dismissed as kooky California phenomes. She is internationally respected by a global network of whores, ex-whores, and people who support the hooker's right to work (Diamant 1981:16).

Due to increased visibility and the development of a support base through coalition building, COYOTE's grassroots campaign flourished as a national and then an international crusade. Focusing on discriminatory law enforcement practices against prostitutes, the feminist discourse on violence against women, and AIDS, COYOTE's campaign of the early and mid-seventies moved beyond specific reforms and service provisions to challenge existing images of prostitutes as social misfits, deviant actors, victimized women, and sexual slaves.

While the identification and acknowledgement of "problematic conditions" and/or "undesirable conditions" is a necessary element in the process of *re*defining social phenomena as problematic, it is not a sufficient element. Klapp (1972:340) has noted, "The symbolic task [of any] movement is to construct new meanings and values." Unlike Gusfield's (1967) repentant deviant, COYOTE has developed a radical critique of popular views of prostitution by substituting a new ethic that affirms their behavior as sensible and moral. In Kitsuse's (1980) terms, COYOTE represents an instance of deviants "coming out all over" not in acts of confession, but rather to profess and advocate the lives they live, along with the worth and values those lives express. COYOTE's crusade has made public a lengthy list of grievances. At the same time, COYOTE's campaign has offered new definitions, explanations, and understandings of prostitution and prostitutes by putting forth numerous claims that *re*define prostitution as a social problem.

At the heart of COYOTE's crusade are three primary claims. First, COYOTE claims that not all prostitution is forced prostitution; in fact, often prostitution is voluntarily chosen. Second, COYOTE claims that prostitution is work and should be respected (i.e., destigmatized) as work like any other type of service work. Finally, COYOTE claims that to deny a woman the option to work as a prostitute under conditions of her own choosing is a civil rights violation. Combined, these claims define prostitution as problematic because of its relationship to something our culture purports to abhor; namely, the violation of individuals' civil rights and social rights based on membership in a particular group.

COYOTE redefines the social problem of prostitution by declaring its presence openly and without apology in order to claim prostitutes' rights of citizenship, especially their right to work under conditions of their own choosing. In framing the social problem of prostitution in this manner, COYOTE's activities threaten to take ownership of the "problem" of prostitution away from traditional experts by disavowing prostitutes' deviant status and legitimating the work of prostitutes.

By invoking and institutionalizing a vocabulary of sex as work, prostitutes as sex workers, and prostitutes' civil rights as workers, COYOTE's claims sever the social problem of prostitution from its historical association with sin, criminality and illicit sex. The social problem of prostitution is firmly placed in the rhetoric of work and civil rights. When terminologies change, when new terms are invented, or existing terms given new meanings, these signal actions that something important has happened to the career of a social problem. After all, the categories and meanings that they have created have direct consequences for the ways such phenomena are conceived, evaluated, and treated. To the degree that COYOTE's vocabulary is adopted and institutionalized (e.g., "sex work" and "voluntary prostitution"), concepts of the opposing groups fall into obscurity (e.g., prostitutes as sexual slaves and as victims).

In view of the historically developed and deeply ingrained views on prostitution, redefining prostitution as a social problem is a difficult task. Indeed, prostitutes' rights organizations must operate under a "heavy yoke of disreputability" (Weitzer 1989). Nonetheless, COYOTE, as well as its track record and social remnants, still exists in a field where many have failed. COYOTE's crusade and the degree to which COYOTE's claims have been or will be adopted by the public is important in at least two respects. First, in part it will determine the degree to which the activities of COYOTE have fundamentally altered prostitutes' political as well as cultural situation. Second, the impact of COYOTE's claims will help determine the future of the prostitutes' rights movement currently underway in the United States and abroad, as well as the future of prostitution as a social problem.

NOTES

1. COYOTE is based in San Francisco, with branches in Los Angeles, Seattle, Boulder, Sacramento, Fort Lauderdale, Atlanta, Boston, St. Paul, Miami, San Diego, Des Moines, New Orleans, and New York. COYOTE affiliates include FLOP (Friends and Lovers of Prostitutes), CAT (California Advocates for Trollops), DOLPHIN (Dump Obsolete Laws; Prove Hypocrisy Isn't Necessary), 80s Ladies and Friends, HIRE (Hooking Is Real Employment), Hooker's Hookup, HUM (Hooker's Union of Maryland), PASSION (Professional Association Seeking Sexual Identification Observant of Nature), and PUMA (Prostitute Union of Massachusetts Association). COYOTE leaders and supporters formed COYOTE's national and international affiliates: The National Task Force on Prostitution (NTFP) in the United States and the International Committee for Prostitute's Rights (ICPR) in Amsterdam.

2. These holdings are officially "closed" to the public until the death of the founder of COYOTE. However, authorization from St. James enabled me to gain access to the documents. Complete citations for the documents were not always possible since COYOTE did not always attend to preserving that information.

3. In COYOTE's formative years, the COYOTE letterhead carried the names of novelist Herb Gold, feminist writer Kate Millet, feminist lawyer Florence Kennedy, Zen philosopher Alan Watts, actor Peter Boyle, entertainer Tom Smothers, feminist Betty Dodson, San Francisco's liberal sheriff Richard Hongisto, one time San Francisco art commissioner and noted city maverick Jeremy Ets-Hokin, and labor leader David Jenkins.

4. The 1978 Hookers' Ball, which was attended by San Francisco Police Chief Gain, proved to be the final Hookers' Ball. After lengthy litigation, COYOTE lost rights to the Hookers' Ball, for reasons too complicated to detail here.

5. Prostitute's organizations emerged internationally, including the International Prostitution Documentation Center and ASPASIE in Geneva; PLAN (Prostitution Laws are Nonsense) and the English Collective of Prostitutes (ECP), both of Great Britain; the Comitato Per I Diritti Civili Delle Prostitute (Committee for the Civil Rights of Prostitutes) in Italy; Germany's HYDRA in Berlin, HWG in Frankfurt, Solidarietaet Hamburger Huren (Solidarity of Hamburg Whores) in Hamburg, Messalina in Munich, Kassandra in Nuremberg, Lysistrata in Cologne, and Nitribitt in Bremen; CORP (Canadian Organization for Prostitutes) in Canada; the Australian Prostitutes Collective in Australia; the Austrian Association of Prostitutes in Austria; De Rode Draad (The Red Thread) and De Roze Draad (The Pink Thread) in the Netherlands; and The National Association of Prostitutes in Brazil.

6. The "Kiss and Tell" idea originated in Europe, particularly Spain and Portugal, where it had some success. In Spain this tactic was used to rid the country of its adultery laws, which had been enforced only against women. In Portugal, this tactic was used to keep abortion and prostitution laws out of the new legal code. The Kiss and Tell campaign required that prostitutes violate their own code of ethics. As *COYOTE Howls* reported, "one of the points in the prostitute's code of ethics is that the prostitute will never divulge the name of the client" (Alexander 1979a:4).

7. As of 1988, many states had introduced legislation requiring mandatory testing of arrested prostitutes. Georgia, Florida, Utah, and Nevada now forcibly test arrested prostitutes.

REFERENCES

Alexander, Priscilla. 1979a. "Kiss and tell campaign: A question of ethics." *Coyote Howls* 3(2):4.

———. 1979b. "National decriminalization a must as hypocritical, sexist vigilante groups spring to action across the U.S." *NTFP News* (September/October), 1, 3.

———. 1983. "Working on Prostitution." A paper prepared for California NOW, Inc.

———. 1987. "Prostitution: a difficult issue for feminists." In *Sex Work: Writing by Women in the Sex Industry,* ed. Frederique Delacose and Priscilla Alexander, 184–214. Pittsburgh, Penn.: Clets Press.

Alexander, Priscilla and Margo St. James. 1981. "Prostitutes question porno's legitimacy." *Womenews* 6(1).

Anderson, Els. 1984. "What better place to discuss sin and sex?" *Alameda Times-Star,* February 10, 14.

Anderson, Maurica. 1975. "Hookers arise." *Human Behavior: The Newsmagazine of the Social Sciences,* January, 40–42.

Ashley, Beth. 1974. "Unusual prostitute with a set of unusual ideas." *Marin County Examiner.* October 25.

Barry, Kathleen. 1979. *Female Sexual Slavery,* New York: Basic Books.

Brownmiller, Susan. 1975. *Against Our Will: Men, Women, and Rape.* New York: Simon and Schuster.

Bryan, John. 1973a. "Hookers resist clean-up: COYOTE campaign could expose Alioto's motive." *San Francisco Phoenix,* September, 1, 2.

———. 1973b. "Hookers picket 4 hotels." *San Francisco Phoenix,* November 8.

———. 1974. "Will supervisors screw whores?" *San Francisco Phoenix,* June 27, 1, 2, 9.

Bullough, Vern and Bonnie Bullough. 1978. *Prostitution: An Illustrated Social History.* New York: Crown Publishers.

Butler, Katy. 1974. "On the trail of vice: the crusade against sin on the streets of San Francisco." *San Francisco Bay Guardian,* April 13–26, 6, 7.

Carib, Ralph. 1973. "Hookers of the world unite." *San Francisco Chronicle,* May 29.

Castonia, Don. 1979. "U.S. run for the pleasure of men, founder of prostitute organization says." *Post-Crescent,* Nov. 16, B14.

Coyote Howls. 1979. "Kiss and tell campaign." 3(2): 1.

———. 1988. "What COYOTE wants." March 26, 1.

———. 1989. "Awful new prostitution laws." January, 1.

D'Emilio, John and Estelle B. Freedman. 1988. *Intimate Matters: A History of Sexuality in America.* New York: Harper and Row.

Delacoste, Frederique and Priscilla Alexander, ed. 1987. *Sex Work: Writings by Women in the Sex Industry.* San Francisco: Cleis Press.

DeYoung, Mary. 1984. "Ethics and the 'lunatic fringe': the case of pedophile organizations." *Human Organization* 43:72–74.

Diamant, Anita. 1981. "Women's work: Margo St. James on prostitution." *Boston Phoenix,* April 21, 8, 15–17.

Donahue, Phil. 1980. *The Phil Donahue Show.* P.O. Box 211, Cincinnati, Ohio 45201.

Dorgan, Michael. 1984. "Oldest profession' holds its own S.F. convention." *San Jose Mercury News,* July 13.

Dworkin, Andrea. 1981. *Pornography: Men Possessing Women.* New York: Perigree.

Everett, Karen. 1988. "State bills outrage prostitutes." *San Francisco Sentinel* 16(3).

Ferree, Myra Marx and Beth B. Hess. 1985. *Controversy and Coalition: The New Feminist Movement.* Boston: Twayne Publishers.

Gorner, Peter. 1977. "Prostitutes and housewives unite, forming a surprising sisterhood." *Chicago Tribune,* April 18.

Griffin, Susan. 1981. *Pornography and Silence: Culture's Revenge Against Nature.* New York: Harper and Row.

Gusfield, Joseph R. 1967. "Moral passage: the symbolic process in public designations of deviance." *Social Problems* 15:175–88.

Henkin, William. 1988. "What's a nice girl like you doing in a book like this?" *Spectator,* October, 3.

———. 1989. "Whores are people too." *Spectator,* August 18–24, 4–5, 18.

Hobson, Barbara. 1987. *Uneasy Virtue: The Politics of Prostitution and the American Reform Tradition.* New York: Basic Books.

Jaget, Claude, Ed. 1980. *Prostitutes: Our Life.* Bristol, England: Falling Wall Press.

Keegan, Anne. 1974. "World's oldest profession has the night off." *Chicago Tribune,* July 10.

Kellog, Mary Alice. 1974. "Solidarity sweetheart: can hookers be happy and militant?" *Chicago Sun Times,* October 6.

Kirzner, Ellie. 1985. "Margo St. James selling sex work." *Now Magazine / Toronto Weekly,* n.d.

Kitsuse, John I. 1980. "Coming out all over: deviants and the politics of social problems." *Social Problems* 28:1–13.

Kitsuse, John I. and Aaron Cicourel. 1963. "A note on the official use of statistics." *Social Problems* 11:121–39.

Klapp, Orrin. 1972. *Currents of Unrest: An Introduction to Collective Behavior.* New York: Holt, Rinehart and Winston.

Klemesrud, Judy. 1985. "A personal crusade against prostitution." *New York Times,* June 24.

Lederer, Laura, Ed. 1980. *Take Back the Night: Women on Pornography.* New York: William and Morrow.

Lerner, Gerda. 1986. *The Creation of Patriarchy.* New York: Oxford University Press.

Linden, Robin, Darlene R. Pagano, Diana E.H. Russell, and Susan Leigh Star, Ed. 1982. *Against Sadomasochism: A Radical Feminist Analysis.* San Francisco: Frog in the Well.

MacKinnon, Catherine. 1983. "Marxism, feminism, method and the state: toward feminist jurisprudence." *Signs* 8:635–58.

Metzger, Peter H. 1975. "COYOTE head promotes the image of a healthy hooker." *Rocky Mountain News,* August 3.

Mitchell, Cynthia. 1984. "Inside the hookers' convention." *Point Reyes Light,* July 19, 10.

Mydans, Seth. 1976. "Attitudes on prostitution changing." *New Times,* February 15.

Nielson, Gary. 1979. "Screwing the system: local power structure should be held accountable for their role in prostitution, says ex-hooker activist." *Valley Advocate* 11:13, 105, 125.

Otis, Leah Lydia. 1985. *Prostitution in Medieval Society: The History of an Urban Institution in Languedoc.* Chicago: University of Chicago Press.

Palmer, Barbara. 1976. "Hookers cashing in on the 'Liz Ray Thing.'" *Washington Star,* n.d.

Pheterson, Gail, Ed. 1989. *A Vindication of the Rights of Whores.* Seattle, Washington: Seal Press.

Reiper, Donna. 1982. "Legal prostitution said key to stopping rape." *Western Front,* May 7, 3.

Ritter, Jess. 1973. "COYOTE: society's underdogs begin biting back." *Pacific Sun,* December 20–26, 4–5.

Rubin, Sylvia. 1986. "COYOTE's new leadership." *San Francisco Chronicle,* February 25.

San Francisco Magazine. 1973. "COYOTE: A loose woman's organization." June, 23.

Schur, Edwin. 1984. *Labeling Women Deviant: Gender, Stigma, and Social Control.* New York: Random House.

Snider, Burr. 1976. "The gospel of sex according to Margo St. James." *OUI* 5(2): 159–162.

Spector, Malcolm and John I. Kitsuse. 1977. *Constructing Social Problems.* Menlo Park, Calif: Cummings Publishing Press.

St. James, Margo. 1980. "COYOTE Howls: Margo visits Netherlands, finds 'Sexual Slavery' author bigoted." *San Francisco's Appeal to Reason,* n.d., 7.

St. James, Margo and Priscilla Alexander. 1977. "Prostitution: the feminist dilemma." *City Magazine,* October/November.

———. 1985. "Testimony on prostitution." Given to the New York State Bar Association, October 30.

Tannahill, Ray. 1980. *The History of Sex.* New York: Stein and Day.

Terzian, Sandra. 1974. "The real victim." *COYOTE Howls,* October/November.

Von Hoffman, Nicholas. 1974. "COYOTE, ASP, PONY and other such in the nut capital." *Washington Post,* May 27.

Volz, Joseph. 1976. "Hookers' Lobbyist Aims Her Legal Hustle at D.C." *Daily News,* June 22, 14.

Wages for Housework. 1977. *Newsletter,* Spring, 8.

Weitzer, Ronald. 1989. "Failure of an 'immoral crusade': prostitutes' rights in the United States." Paper presented at the annual meetings of the Society for the Study of Social Problems in Berkeley, California.

Winklebleck, Layne. 1988. "COYOTE howls over new law!" *Spectator,* September 30–October 6, 2.

Think Critically

1. Why is it important, from a sociological perspective, to view prostitution as "work" rather than simply as "crime," and how does this afford a better understanding of prostitution as a social problem?

2. Pick one discourse that Jenness describes and discuss how it affected the political process regarding the efforts of COYOTE. Give some examples of other social movements to which this same discourse was applied, and how it was used in these particular cases.

Bodies, Borders, and Sex Tourism in a Globalized World

A Tale of Two Cities—Amsterdam and Havana*

Nancy A. Wonders and Raymond Michalowski**

THE GREAT DRAMA OF THE LAST QUARTER of the 20th century was the collapse of socialism and the subsequent attempt to refashion the world into a single capitalist system managed and controlled from a small core of "global cities" scattered around the world (Amin 1990, 1997; Greider 1997; Hoogvelt 1997; Mander and Goldsmith 1996; Sassen 1996, 1998, 2000a). This process of integrating the world into a single capitalist system—typically termed "globalization"—is often cast as an unprecedented political-economic development (Karliner 1997; Korten 1995). Others suggest that today's "globalization" is essentially a contemporary expression of the historical project of creating a worldwide capitalist system, a project that extends roughly from the rise of mercantile capitalism in the 1400s to the present (Friedman 1999; Hirst 1996). Whether it represents a novel form of political-economy or is just a resumption of the pre-socialist urge of capitalism to command the globe, the current era of globalization is characterized by unprecedented movement of material, information, finance, and bodies across borders.

In this article, we examine how globalization facilitates the growth of sex tourism, as well as the particular character of sex tourism in different locales. As others have already detailed (Opperman 1998), "sex tourism" is a protean term that attempts to capture varieties of leisure travel that have as a part of their purpose the purchase of

*Copyright © 2001 by The Society for the Study of Social Problems. Reprinted from *Social Problems* 48:4 (November 2001), pp. 545–571, by permission of the publisher.

**An earlier version was presented at the annual meeting of the American Sociological Association in Chicago, Illinois, in August, 1999.

sexual services. Clearly the concepts of "prostitution" and "tourism" are both central to an analysis of sex tourism, but neither term captures the full meaning of sex tourism. "Sex tourism" highlights the convergence between prostitution and tourism, links the global and the local, and draws attention to both the production and consumption of sexual services. The growth in sex tourism over the last two decades is well established (Kempadoo and Doezema 1998; Opperman 1998). In this article, we focus specifically on how the global forces shaping this growth connect the practice of sex work in two disparate cities with globalized sex tourism.

Our analysis of sex tourism has two closely related goals. First, we explore the *global forces* that shape the production and consumption of sex tourism. We argue that global forces influence the production of globalized sex tourism via the increased movement of bodies associated with migration and tourism. Global forces also shape the consumption of sexual services by fostering tourism as an industry aimed at those who have the resources to travel and purchase what they desire, thus facilitating the commodification of both male desire and women's bodies within the global capitalist economy.

By examining sex tourism as a product of global forces, we hope to shift attention from individual "prostitutes" as social problems to "sex tourism" as a form of global commerce that is transforming sex work, cities, and human relationships. Most writings on the sex trade take prostitutes as the starting point for analysis of sex work. This leads to an overemphasis on individuals, particularly women, as deviant or pathological for their participation in the sex trade.[1] It is our view that an adequate analysis of contemporary sex tourism must consider how the meshing of the supply and demand curves for sex creates a transnational business like any other.

A second goal of our analysis is to foreground cities as strategic sites of globalization and, further, to identify some of the mediating institutions that connect cities to the global forces shaping sex tourism. As Sassen (2000a:143) points out, "Large cities in the highly developed world are the places where globalization processes assume concrete, localized forms. These localized forms are, in good part, what globalization is about." The exchanges of money, ideas, and commands that comprise globalization must always take place *somewhere,* and the modern city is that somewhere, the place where "key global processes ranging

from international finance to immigration" are constituted (Sassen 1996:131). When analyzing a single city, however, it can be difficult to assess the extent to which the local is shaped by larger, global forces. Comparative work such as ours, makes it possible to observe the way that global forces serve to create *global connections* between practices in disparate places. In this article, we explore the global connections between sex tourism and two cities with very different histories: Amsterdam and Havana. As our analysis will evidence, although sex tourism differs in each city, the impact of globalization is evident in the changing character of a variety of common mediating institutions that link each city to the global economy and to globalized sex tourism. Because sex work always occurs in a localized context, it is typically treated as an individual adjustment to local economies and local cultures. We contend, however, that in some places global forces increasingly overdetermine the localized experience of sex work.

In pursuing the goals outlined above, our approach to sex tourism is both theoretical and ethnographic. Employing political—economic, feminist, and postmodern theoretical perspectives, we seek to further understand the relationship between sex tourism and the emerging, global capitalist order. We do this by utilizing the methodology of "global ethnography," as outlined by Burawoy, et al. (2000). Global ethnography combines traditional ethnography with ethno-historical information as a strategy to analyze the impact of globalization.[2] Because globalization operates across time and space, traditional ethnographic methods, which tend to be place-bound, must be supplemented with information linking the particular research moment to the broader historical context, and the particular research site to the broader transnational forces and processes that constitute the global. Global ethnography describes a set of strategies for combining abstract, theoretical insights about globalization with concrete, historically contextualized, geographically situated practices . . .

Global Forces: The Production and Consumption of Globalized Sex Tourism

Globalization has wrought many changes, but two are particularly salient for understanding the emergence of sex tourism as a significant form of economic activity.

One significant global force shaping sex tourism is the worldwide movement of bodies across borders, whether for business, war, or pleasure. The movement of bodies takes many forms, but two of the most significant are migration and tourism. Migration typically involves bodies from less developed or less stable nations moving across borders into more developed or stable ones in an attempt to improve economic options, or to escape life-threatening conflicts including genocide, war, and famine. Cross-border tourism typically reverses this pattern as privileged bodies from industrialized nations cross into less developed ones in search of exotic pleasures and a little (highly controlled) danger. These increases in tourism and migration have fostered heightened opportunities for sex work as these global forces expand the pools of both potential sex consumers and potential sex workers.

The second global force affecting sex tourism is the shift from a worldwide economic system based on expanding production to one whose central engine of growth is expanding *consumption* (Lury 1996). Globalized capitalism demands the continual development of new commodity forms. The consequence is that many elements of social life that once remained outside the realm of commodity exchange must now be commodified in order to create new markets and to protect or expand profits (Friedman 1999). This, in turn, introduces new forms of labor and new forms of consumption into the global marketplace, of which the expansion of sex tourism is but one example. In the analysis that follows, we argue that sex tourism both fosters and is fostered by the global commodification of (primarily male) desire and (primarily women's) bodies as new markets in ways that transcend and shape local institutions and discourses.

The Production of Sex Tourism: Global Inequality, Bodies, and Border Crossings

A great deal has been written in recent years detailing the economic, social, and physical dislocation of people caught in the tide of globalization. Some emphasize that this movement of humanity is largely a response to profound inequality between countries due to the growing concentration and centralization of wealth under globalization (Burbach, Núñez and Kargarlitsky 1997; Dougherty and Holthouse 1998). Others suggest that this heightened transnational flow of bodies is not necessarily

negative, since people often move in search of higher standards of living, work, or just to enjoy travel and white sandy beaches (Davidow and Malone 1992; Friedman 1999). What is not in dispute, however, is that two of the most significant waves of human movement today are migrants and tourists. While their immediate motivations differ, both tourists and migrants travel because they desire something better than what their current home has to offer.

The intersection of tourism and migration in the globalized world system facilitates the production of sex tourism by bringing together mobile sex workers with mobile sex consumers. This increased mobility has two vectors. On the one hand, increased concentrations of wealth within industrialized nations means that more people—mostly men, but also some women—can afford to travel as tourists in foreign lands where they can enjoy "exotic" sights, sounds, and in some cases, "otherly" bodies. On the other hand, as global capital disrupts established patterns of economic survival in less developed nations, unemployment, urban migration, and national out-migration rise (Wonders and Danner 2002). This push toward migration was clearly visible in the International Labor Organization's (ILO) estimate that around *thirty percent* of the world's labor force is "unemployed and unable to sustain a minimum standard of living" (Chomsky 1994:188, emphasis added).

Not all social groups are affected equally by economic displacement. Wonders and Danner (1999:3) make the point that "globalization has engendered profound change because it is itself gendered." As a 1996 ILO report noted, "the feminization" of international labor migration is "one of the most striking economic and social phenomena of recent times" (Kempadoo and Doezema 1998:17). Among other consequences, the feminization of migration brings growing numbers of women into geographical and social environments where their best (and in some cases, only) option for economic survival and social advancement is sex work. This is true not only in developing countries where economic options are bleak for the majority, but it is increasingly so in industrialized countries that have thrown up employment barriers to intentionally discourage migration. As Wijers (1998:72) points out, such restrictions on employment create a situation where "almost the only work migrant women are allowed to do is in the entertainment section or sex industry, whether this is the official policy, as in Switzerland, or just everyday practice, as in the Netherlands."

The growth of tourism as a result of the expanding global economy constitutes one of the most significant engines fueling the increase in commercial sex. As an area of employment, tourism is both large and growing. The World Trade and Tourism Council (WTTC) estimates that between 1989 and 1992 employment in all tourism—international and internal—grew by 20 percent (ILO 1998). In 1996, "the industry's gross output was estimated to be U.S. $3.6 trillion, 10 percent of all consumer spending. The travel and tourism industry is the world's largest employer, with 255 million jobs, or almost 11 percent of all employees. This industry is the world's leading industrial contributor, producing over 10 percent of the world gross domestic product . . ." (Theobald 1998:4). While most of this tourism does not involve the production or consumption of sexual services, an important and growing proportion does. Pietila and Vickers (1994:121) argue that "prostitution has become big business, and 'traffic in persons' has taken on new and more sophisticated forms and extended on an unforeseen scale to become an international trade . . . massive expansion of intercontinental tourism, coupled with the deteriorating situation of women in many developing countries, has made sex holidays an ever flourishing phenomenon." Echoing this perspective, Herman (1995:5) calls sex tourism "one of the booming markets in the New World Order—a multibillion dollar industry with finders, brokers, syndicate operations and pimp 'managers' at the scene of action." Even conservative business publications have noted the growing strength and globalization of the sex "industry"; *The Economist* (1998:23) estimates that the global sex industry is worth "at least $20 billion a year and probably many times that."

Although sex tourism can take many forms, sex tourists are overwhelmingly men with resources, while sex workers are overwhelmingly poor women of color (Richter 1998). This has led many researchers to contend that most global sex tourism—both North–South and North–North—arises from the linkage between the political economic advantage enjoyed by affluent men from developed countries and the widespread cultural fantasy in those nations that dusky-skinned "others" from exotic southern lands are liberated from the sexual/emotional inhibitions characteristic of women (and/or men) in their own societies

(Kempadoo and Doezema 1998; Sanchez Taylor 2000). For advantaged men from the developed world, sex tourism provides an opportunity, not only to experience fantasized sexual freedom with imagined uninhibited women, but also the opportunity to experience—in their bodies—their own privilege. As Skrobanek, et al. (1997:viii) write of sex tourism in Thailand, "Thailand is like a stage where men from around the world come to perform their role of male supremacy over women and their white supremacy over Thai people." The gendered and racialized patterns of sex tourism characterized by Skrobanek, and found in the ILO case studies in Southeast Asia are not unique to these countries. Rather, as our case studies of Amsterdam and Havana will show, they are local patterns that are structured by broader global forces.

The Consumption of Globalized Sex Tourism: Commodification of Bodies and Desire

Global economic forces not only facilitate the production of sex tourism, they also facilitate its consumption. In the global economic search for new markets, the process of commodification has gone beyond material goods to all social life. One book title—*Consuming People* (Firat and Dholakia 1998)—plays out a double entendre that accurately reflects the contemporary global situation. Today people are constantly consuming not only material goods, but other people as well, via the purchase of human services, relational experiences, and sexual encounters. Indeed, "consumption . . . may be the most important force that unites the contemporary world" (Firat and Dholakia 1998:103).

The recognition that consumption is an important engine of global and local economic growth requires that we analyze the production of sex tourism in terms of the behavior and preferences of sex consumers, not just sex providers. In the global capitalist marketplace, the desires of those with resources, particularly privileged male consumers, have become prime targets for producers and retailers of all types of goods and services. As a number of researchers on gender and leisure note, white male desire has itself been commodified in the global production of leisure services, including sex tourism (Adkins 1995; Craik 1997). In their quest for markets and money, creative entrepreneurs develop products and services designed to both fulfill and shape male desire. Thus, male desire facilitates the production of commodified services at the same time as service providers in leisure industries seek to commodify male desire. This interrelationship is necessitated, in part, because of the close proximity of the production of leisure services to their consumption; "This proximity is thought to mean that cultural practices, especially the cultural expectations of consumers, act to significantly determine the social relations of production" (Adkins 1995:7). As primary providers of a range of leisure activities, including sex work, women are expected to tailor the services they provide to consumer expectations, particularly the expectations of their primarily male clientele. In a study of leisure services in England, Adkins (1995), for example, notes that all of the female service workers in two major hotel and entertainment parks were expected to undertake emotional and sensual work as a regular part of their jobs. As primarily male customers voiced their desires, female service workers were expected to immediately respond to expectations. Thus, customers shaped the services they received in a relational fashion.

This relational understanding of work in the service sector is taken to an extreme in sex work, since the sexual services sold by prostitutes are largely shaped in the moment, as customers express their desires (Zatz 1997). Thus, the particular form of sex work provided both reflects and (re)constitutes (primarily) male desire. For example, some research shows that the desire expressed by some male sex consumers for emotional and sensual labor to accompany sexual labor shapes the character of sex work for some prostitutes (see the growing body of writings by female sex workers on this point; e.g., Chapkis 1997; Nagle 1997). In this regard, it is crucial to point out that sex tourism is similar to other forms of tourism in that "the cultural experiences offered by tourism are consumed in terms of prior knowledge, expectations, fantasies and mythologies generated in the tourist's origin culture, rather than by the cultural offerings of the destination" (Craik 1997: 118). The expectations and desires of those with resources influences what "others" try to sell to them; in essence, privileged desire influences what options "others" have as they seek wages in the globalized economy (O'Connell Davidson 1998; Richter 1998).

The objectification of bodies, particularly women's bodies, is well documented as a primary source of the commodification of bodies under capitalism (Bordo 1993). But to fully understand the commodification of bodies under globalization, we need to link the process of objectification to the more general disembodiment of workers within the capitalist economy. For Marx, all workers under capitalism are alienated; they are symbolically disembodied as they sell their labor power to employers for a wage in order to survive (Marx 1887/1958:207–208). For women in both industrialized and developing countries, however, reasonably remunerative wage labor associated with commodity production is increasingly difficult to secure. This is particularly true for migrant women of color. Under these circumstances, some women do not sell their bodily labor to produce a commodity; instead, their *bodies* become commodities. It is important to emphasize here that we are not positing sex itself as inherently exploitative or problematic, but we do problematize the commodification of bodies in order to make a living wage. As newly industrializing countries struggle to find commodity niches in the globalized economy, they frequently find many of the best product niches taken. As a consequence, in some countries, sex tourism becomes a significant market fostering of both national economic development and international capital accumulation (Enloe 1989; Kempadoo and Doezema 1998; Lean Lim 1998; Truong 1990). In these countries and in many other parts of the globalized world, sex work is a tolerated "choice" for women for whom it appears the best option for supporting themselves and their families (see selections in Chapkis 1997 or Nagle 1997). In this way, sex work reveals "the gendered organization of the 'economic': of the ways in which social identities available to men and women in the workplace, for instance, relate to the gendered nature of the very fabric of society—to (gendered) economic relations" (Adkins 1995:52).

As we noted above, the rise of mass tourism is one of the major transformations of the contemporary period. Although other scholars have already made the point, we wish to join the voices emphasizing the gendered character of tourism (Craig-Smith and French 1994; Craik 1997; Richter 1998). As Richter (1998:392) argues, "Travel has had a different *contextual* meaning for men than for women. . . ." For men, tourism and travel are more often defined as adventure and constant change, as distance and escape from the routine and familiar. This sense of tourism, along with the idea that leisure for the tourist takes place beyond (some might say "against") the home reflects a historically male interpretation of pleasure. While selling sexual services is an old commerce, and leisure travel has long been common for the wealthy, both have changed in ways that increasingly parallel the globalized economy and the desires of privileged male tourists. Increasingly, women are themselves viewed as a tourist destination. Sex and bodies are viewed as commodities that can be packaged, advertised, displayed, and sold on a global scale. Rojec and Urry (1997:17) argue that "Travel and tourism can be thought of as a search for difference. . . . Women are the embodiment of difference . . . the act of leaving home to travel involves, for men, sexual adventure, finding a woman." Craik (1997:116) emphasizes "the manufacture of simulacra (or 'as if' experiences) as the basis of the contemporary tourist experience." Whether prostitutes are displayed in windows (like clothes on mannequins) or appear in hotel lobbies (as though they are complementary beverages), bodies increasingly are used as simulacra to represent "something else" to the leisure tourist; prostitutes appear as "minor wives," "girlfriends," "exotic others" or "sex toys"—whatever the tourist needs them to be to achieve the experience he desires. In this sense, both tourists and tourist sites engage in a kind of performance where each pretends to meet the "other's" expectations as a way to simulate the desired experience (see Chapkis 1997; Nagle 1997; Rojec and Urry 1997).

Not only is the desire for new experiences commodified in the globalized economy, but so, too, is the desire to experiment with different identities. Increasingly scholars have come to understand all identities as fluid, changeable, social constructions (Ferrante and Brown 1998; Wonders 2000). Much of the tourist and consumer experience involves buying products, services, and experiences that create the illusion of becoming someone else. MacCannell (1999) suggests that this opportunity to become someone else is an important reason why many tourists travel in the first place. Travel to other countries facilitates the fluidity of identity because we typically leave behind the signposts and people associated with our present identity, making it easier to adopt new ones. Similarly, tourists feel free to experience the identity of "others" by sampling cultural products, experiences, bodies, and identities. But this sampling is rarely without judgment, since the tourist brings along cultural assumptions and biases on every trip. In the case of sex tourism, expectations and assumptions about other cultures and racial groups often result in racist payment schedules for sexual services; this serves to perpetuate racial hierarchies among sex workers (Kempadoo and Doezema 1998; Pettman 1997), as well as racist laws and regulatory policies directed at particular categories of prostitutes (Bell 1994). Our own ethnographic research confirms that reality.

In this section, we have outlined some of the key global forces shaping the growth and character of sex tourism. Specifically, we suggest the production of sex tourism is facilitated by the worldwide movement of bodies across borders as a result of expanding migration and tourism, while its consumption is facilitated by the commodification of bodies and desire. In the next section, we investigate the ways that these seemingly abstract global forces come to ground in two diverse cities: Amsterdam and Havana.

Global Connections: A Tale of Two Cities

Research provides compelling evidence that cities are strategic sites for observing the effects of globalization (Sassen 1998, 2000a, 2000b; Sassen and Roost 1997). In our analysis, we detail the way that the global forces shaping the production and consumption of sex tourism impact two very different cities: Amsterdam and Havana. We explore the global connections that link sex work in these two cities with the forces associated with globalized sex tourism. Specifically, we argue that global forces impact sex work in both cities through four mediating institutions: 1) the tourism industry, 2) labor markets, 3) the localized sex industry, and 4) law and policy. As mediating institutions in these cities adjusted to the impact of global forces, they created opportunities for sex tourism to flourish.

It is important to our analysis that Amsterdam and Havana are very different cities. Many argue that global forces are easily discerned in "global cities" like Amsterdam (Sassen 2000a, 1998). Global cities are strategically positioned at the center of the global capitalist system as command points, key locations, and marketplaces for leading industries, and major sites of production; they are "strategic sites for the management of the global economy and the production of the most advanced services and financial operations" (Sassen 2000a:21). Within these cities, the impact of globalization has been documented to be far-reaching (Sassen 1998, 2000a; Sassen and Roost 1997).

In contrast, Havana is located in Cuba, one of the last self-identified socialist states in the world. Cuba is a developing island nation struggling to find a foothold in the new global capitalist economy that will enable it to grow economically, while preserving its socialist accomplishments in health, education, and social welfare (Dello Buono and Lara 1997). Within Cuba, Havana occupies a central role and is best characterized as a "primate city"; that is, one which accounts "for a disproportionate share of population, employment, and gross national product (GNP)" within a country (Sassen 2000a:34). Not surprisingly, "the Caribbean has a long history of urban primacy" (Sassen 2000a:39). Rarely viewed as a central site of globalization, primate cities are affected by globalization nevertheless, since global forces first come to ground in a country with a primate urban system by impacting these cities (Sassen 2000a).

Despite their differences, we illustrate that globalization's reach is evident in both Amsterdam and Havana. The specific responses to global forces differ, but comparison between these two cities reveals the impact of significant global connections on sex work in both locations.[3]

Shopping for Bodies in Amsterdam

In Amsterdam, the commodification of bodies has been perfected to the level of an art form. The red light district resembles the modern open-air shopping mall in the United States. Relatively clean streets, little crime, a neon atmosphere, and windows and windows of women to choose from—every size, shape, and color (though not in equal amounts). The red light district seems designed to be a sex tourist's Mecca. The range of services for the leisure traveler includes sex clubs, sex shows, lingerie and S&M clothing shops, condomories, and a sprinkling of porno stores. But the character of Amsterdam's red light district is different from most other sex tourist locations because it is centered in an historic district between the Oude Kerk (Old Church) and de Waag (an old weighing station)—two of the most spectacular cultural tourist sites in the city—and it is surrounded by an old, well-established residential neighborhood. Indeed, walking through the red light district in the daytime is not so different from walking down any other shopping street in the city, though the area takes on a festival atmosphere at night. Crowds of men walk the street, stopping to gaze at

the living merchandise in the window. The routine among men is much like the routine observed among women shopping for clothes, with plentiful commentary on the size, shape, color, and cost of the women on display. The smorgasbord of languages rising through the air reveals the international character of those shopping for bodies.

In describing the Amsterdam scene, it is important to make clear that women sex workers are far from passive in the shopping interaction. On quieter evenings and in the daytime, it is common for women to hover near the doorways of their small window booths, hooting and calling at men to "come here!" in a number of different languages. In an odd role reversal, one male friend commented to me after a walk through the district that: "I've never felt so objectified in my life. I felt like a piece of meat walking through there."

Historical and Cultural Background: Dutch Tolerance and Sex "Work". Like other Western industrialized cities, prostitution has a long history in Amsterdam. Indeed, in the Netherlands, "it has never been forbidden to prostitute oneself" (Boutellier 1991:209). Although most citizens stigmatize prostitutes, the Dutch have long viewed prostitution as one among many social problems to be minimized, but not criminalized. The goal of Dutch policy toward sex work primarily focuses on reducing the adverse impact of prostitution on local citizens and neighborhoods, what one writer calls "regulated tolerance" (Brants 1998). Thus, officially, there is no national policy toward sex work; rather, each municipality controls policies toward prostitution.

The concept of tolerance plays an important role in preventing and managing conflict in this small, heavily populated country built on religious and cultural difference (Rochon 1999). The Netherlands is often regarded as a liberal country politically, primarily because of its extensive social welfare system and its progressive, "tolerant" attitude toward social problems that other countries tend to criminalize, such as prostitution and drug use. What is little known to outsiders is that much of the country's apparently liberal policy emerges from compromise, particularly among relatively conservative religious groups, rather than broad consensus (Cox 1993). This is the foundation of Dutch pragmatism and tolerance. In practice, tolerance has historically meant that the law is rarely used to regulate social problems, such as prostitution, since compromise is difficult to reach around controversial moral questions (Brants 1998; Marshall 1993). Instead, until recently, local responses to prostitution typically reflected a complex and shifting interplay between prostitutes, authorities and the concerns of local citizens . . .

Tourism: Amsterdam as a Tourist Destination. It has been well established that tourism, as a global force, has affected all of Western Europe. As Williams and Shaw (1998:20) note, "Europe dominates international movements of tourists. . . . Between 1950 and 1990, the number of international tourists in Europe increased 16 times." There is strong competition among European countries for international tourists, since they tend to spend more money than domestic tourists; additionally, starting in the 1970s, "international tourism income grew considerably faster than international merchandise trade" making it a market worth pursuing (Williams and Shaw 1998:36).

The Netherlands as a country has not fared particularly well in the race for tourists; tourism receipts to GDP as a result of international tourism are 1.4% in contrast to Spain, Portugal, and Greece, which run closer to 4%, and Austria, where international tourism contributes 6% to GDP. Indeed, given the expenditures the country makes to attract international tourists, the Netherlands is running a deficit with respect to international tourism (Pinder 1998).

But the situation is quite different when cities are the point of comparison. Amsterdam was among the top ten most popular European cities for tourism throughout the 1990s, currently ranking seventh (Dahles 1998). Amsterdam's positioning as a major tourist destination may be surprising to some. Although the city is filled with tree-studded canals and quaint narrow buildings, it lacks the tourist attractions characteristic of other tourist destinations in Europe; there is no cathedral, tower, or monument to draw visitors to the city. Yet, as one writer has noted, "foreign tourists have been attracted to the Netherlands in increasing numbers" and, within the country, "Amsterdam is overwhelmingly the dominant target for visitors from abroad. 1.7 million foreigners stayed in the city in 1995, one-third of them from outside Europe" (Pinder 1998:307). Dahles (1998:55) argues that: "The image of Amsterdam as a tourism destination is based on two major themes. The first is the image of the city as being dominated by the urban town design of the early modern period. . . . The second is the current popular image of Amsterdam, which was formed in the late 60s and is based

on a youth culture of sexual liberation and narcotic indulgence." Pinder (1998:310) agrees with this assessment and adds that, "The city is renowned for the ready availability of soft drugs, and tolerance has also underpinned the rise of sex tourism as a niche market." He goes on to detail that, ". . . visitor attractions based on the sex industry have gained a firm foothold. Almost half a million people visited the *Venustempel* sex museum in 1995, and 158,000 the Erotic Gallery. Both figures had risen by one-fifth in just two years" (Pinder 1998:310). The increase in sex tourism and the sex industry as a share of Amsterdam's tourist market is related, in part, to declines in tourism dollars from more traditional tourist sites. As tourism directed toward Amsterdam's cultural heritage stagnates, sex tourism plays an increasingly important role in keeping tourism dollars—and related tourism industry jobs—within the city. It is not the case that the Dutch government or Amsterdam city officials openly embrace the marketing of sex tourism or Amsterdam's image as a liberal city, but a variety of mediating institutions, including the tourism industry, have adjusted to global forces in ways that create opportunities for sex tourism to expand.

Labor Markets: Globalization and Migration. By the late 1970s and 1980s, the reach of globalization became evident within the Netherlands in other ways as well, particularly in Amsterdam. Clearly, one of the most important global forces affecting sex work in the country was migration. Migration to the Netherlands during this period came from several sources. First, there was an influx of migrants from former Dutch colonies, particularly from Suriname and the Caribbean Islands. Additionally, like many other European countries, the Netherlands was affected by a surge of migrant guest workers from the Mediterranean area, most of whom were directed toward employment in undesirable, low-paying service sector jobs. Later in the 1980s and 1990s, another group of migrants arrived, including those escaping economic hardship in South America and Africa and the former Soviet bloc countries (Bruinsma and Meershoek 1999; de Haan 1997). Importantly, most of these migrant populations settled in the major Dutch cities, including Amsterdam. Almost half of the population of Amsterdam now consists of non-native Dutch residents making it, literally, a global city.

The presence of relatively large numbers of migrants within the city plays an important role in shaping local labor markets and the current character of the sex trade.

For many female migrants, sex work is virtually the only employment available, particularly given the relatively high unemployment rate for ethnic minorities within the Netherlands (de Haan 1997). As Visser (1997b) notes, ". . . the numbers are beginning to get so big that these migrant prostitutes can no longer be considered as a detail." One estimate put the current number of foreign prostitutes to be approximately 60 percent of all sex workers in the city (Marshall 1993), and a "repeated count by the Amsterdam police in 1994 and 1995 indicated that about 75 percent of all prostitutes behind windows in the Red Light District, De Wallen, are foreigners and that 80 percent of all foreign prostitutes are in the country illegally" (Bruinsma and Meershoek 1999:107).

Although prostitution in the Netherlands preceded this mass migration, it is apparent that migration has both increased the number of sex workers and changed the character of the sex industry. According to the Mr. A. de Graaf Foundation (1997:2), "in the Netherlands, the total number of professional prostitutes is estimated at 20,000." However, this is clearly a low estimate given the large number of sex workers who are not considered "professional," including a large number of illegal immigrants. Another source puts the number closer to 25,000 and notes that survey research by the Dutch Foundation against Trafficking has found that female sex workers represent at least 32 different countries of origin (Hughes 2000). In the last two decades, the growth of sex workers accompanying the rise of migration spawned a more complex sex industry within the city (Brants 1998; Marshall 1993). While the window brothels are the most visible form of prostitution in Amsterdam, and according to some sources, workers here are among the most highly paid (see Reiland 1996), this form of prostitution is only one version of sex work in the city. Other forms of sex work include clubs, private houses, escort services, and street prostitution (Meulenbelt 1993). In the majority of these forms of sex work, however, bodies are highly commodified. *Sexed* bodies are put on display for purchase. Even in the case of sexual services that are delivered to your door, advertisements in local papers hawk the physical characteristics of the bodies for sale. Although emotional labor can be purchased in the Netherlands for those willing to pay the price, many sex workers prefer to simply sell their bodies and keep their emotions for themselves (Chapkis 1997).

Localized Sex Work: The Shift to a Sex "Industry." Over the last two decades there has been an important shift within the city from a focus on the individual providers of sexual services, "prostitutes," to a focus on the sex "industry." Although this shift is partly due to local circumstances, it is also partly a response to the global forces associated with the production and consumption of sex tourism. This shift is reflected in two areas: 1) organizational changes that reflect the growth of sex tourism as an industry and 2) the globalized character of sex tourists and sex workers.

In her analysis of prostitution policy in Amsterdam, Brants (1998:627) describes these changes in some detail:

> As conditions changed and opportunities for making money from the sex industry increased, ever more power became concentrated in the hands of a few not particularly law-abiding citizens. Some of the pimps who had once controlled part of traditional window prostitution now also owned highly lucrative sex clubs and sex theaters. Prostitution had become big business with a huge and partly invisible turnover that was reinvested in gambling halls, sex tourism and more sex clubs.

This concentration of economic interests combined with consumer interest to create several organizations devoted to supporting sex tourism. Interestingly, some Dutch customers developed an organization to support the interests of the clients of prostitution; this organization is called the Men/Women and Prostitution Foundation. Although the number of active members in this organization is small (personal conversation with a member), it is symbolically important in legitimizing the sex industry as an important "industry" serving consumer desires. Members write articles that articulate client interests and the social benefits of prostitution (Ten Kate 1995) and collaborate with other organizations interested in greater acceptance of prostitution . . .

A second global force shaping the sex industry in Amsterdam is the wide variety of sex tourists visiting the city. Currently, the sex industry is amazingly global in character; not just in terms of the providers of sexual services, but also in terms of the consumers. Sex tourists come to Amsterdam from around the world and vary depending, in part, on national holidays. The local *Pleasure Guide* notes, for example, that Italians are common in August. Although Dutch men are common customers, it appears that the Red Light District exists primarily to fulfill the desires of foreign, male, leisure travelers, often executives conducting business in this global city. Unlike tourists, Dutch consumers of the sex trade can frequent the mostly white women in window brothels down less known side streets, or they can utilize the listings in the paper and obtain door-to-door service. It is important to appreciate that foreign tourists do not just pay for sex, they pay for accommodations, to eat at nice restaurants, and to attend cultural events. Indeed, the consumer behavior of sex tourists visiting this city helps to ensure that there will be many organized interests facilitating the continuation of sex tourism within the city.

Public Policy and Law; Facilitating Sex Tourism and Stratification of Sex Workers. As might be expected, policies within Amsterdam are also changing in ways that reflect broader global forces associated with the production and consumption of sex tourism. Despite the growth of organized business interests in the sex industry, the city's economic benefit from sex tourists, and the greater legitimacy accorded sex work, current policy does not appear to be strengthening the hand of sex workers. It appears that the full package of worker's rights are withheld from prostitutes for a variety of reasons (Brants 1998; van der Poel 1995).

The presence of drug-addicted prostitutes makes it difficult for those advocating rights for prostitutes to argue for respectability. Perhaps, more importantly, the large and growing presence of non-native Dutch sex workers leads to local hostility toward sex work. One consequence of Dutch participation in the global economy is the inability of the state to continue to provide the extensive social welfare benefits it has provided to its citizens since the 1960s (de Haan 1997). As welfare rights are restricted for citizens, social services continue to be extended to migrants, creating substantial anger toward immigration. Restrictive policies are creeping up everywhere, including in the sex industry. At least one motivation for this greater regulation is to restrict migrant women from engaging in sexual labor. As Raymond (1998:5) points out, "Third World and Eastern European immigrant women in the Netherlands, Germany, and other regulationist countries lower the prostitution market value of local Dutch and German women. The price of immigrant prostitution is so low that local women's prices go down, reducing the pimps' and brothels' cuts. . . ." To the extent that

regulation is designed to keep non-native Dutch women out of sex work, it fosters a two-tiered hierarchy of sex work within the city that leads to even greater impoverishment and risk for migrant women.

Thus, the twin forces of greater organization among sex industry owners and clients, and the reduced power of sex workers as a result of the growing hostility toward migrant and drug dependent sex workers have led to efforts to define sex tourism as a "business," rather than as a form of individual self-employment. Significantly, legislation legalizing brothels was approved by the Dutch Parliament and Senate in 1999 (Brewis and Linstead 2000); this is a radical move in the Netherlands, where sex workers were historically only considered "workers" when "self-employed." Until recently, third party involvement in sex work was considered a crime resulting in the oppression and even enslavement of sex workers. Some argue that the legalization of brothels is a first step toward their ultimate regulation, a situation that could improve the working conditions for some sex workers (Brants 1998; Visser 1997a). However, it seems that the focus of regulation is increasingly on improving the "merchandising" environment for the sex industry and for consumers, and reducing disruption to local citizens. Currently local officials are attempting to identify who owns the buildings that house window brothels and sex clubs so that some standards can be imposed on facilities where sex is sold. Brothels that pass government inspection would receive special certification, serving as a kind of quality control for sex tourists (Visser 1997a). Regulations are growing and include strange new guidelines that limit how long clients can be tied up during purchased sadomasochistic acts. A new "red light district manager" will facilitate the implementation of the new regulations. To many, including de Rode Draad, the rights of sex workers have taken a back burner (Visser 1997a). The proliferation of new regulations has caused some to argue that the red light district is becoming "the red tape district" (Reiland 1996:29) . . .

At least one Dutch scholar, Chrisje Brants (1998) believes that the new rules and restrictions, including the legalization of brothels, will continue to facilitate the creation of sex tourism as an industry, since small brothel owners and individual prostitutes are unlikely to be able to compete with the resources of organized crime and proprietors of large sex clubs. As she puts it, "the prostitution business will be professionalized, but with the greater scale that is the inevitable result, will come greater concentrations of power and money." In the end "prostitutes who find themselves unable to compete economically, will simply disappear into illegality. . . ." (Brants 1998:633).

In this description of sex tourism and current policy trends in Amsterdam, it is important not to lose sight of the enormously positive public health consequences of current Dutch policy as compared with most other countries. HIV rates are extremely low among prostitutes in the Netherlands and sex workers clearly have more rights than in most countries worldwide. Still, it is also evident that globalization has changed and will continue to change the character of sex tourism in this global city. It is important to appreciate that the Netherlands is not unique in this regard. As Raymond (1998:5) writes:

> The reality is that during the 1980s, as the sex industry in several European countries underwent notable development, commercialization, *and* legitimation through regulationist legislation, it also became an international business . . .

Globalization and the Commodification of Emotional Labor in Havana

Havana, like so many other places in the Caribbean, is a sensuous and social city. Warm nights, humid sea breezes laden with the complex perfume of flowers, diesel exhaust, and restaurant odors, music everywhere, bodies unencumbered by layers of cold-weather clothing, and a culture of public interaction that brings tourists and locals into easy contact. This is the context for Havana's particular soft-sell sex trade. Since the reemergence of sex tourism in the 1990s, the following scene has become relatively common in Havana's tourist districts: A woman, usually decades younger than the object of her immediate interest, approaches a foreign tourist. Brandishing a cigarette, she asks for a light, or maybe points to her wrist and asks for the time. The opening gambit leads to other questions: Where are you from? Where are you going? For a walk? Would you like me to walk with you? Have you been to such-and-such disco? Would you like me to take you there? If the mark seems interested, the woman turns the subject to sex, describing the pleasures she can give, often with no mention of price unless the man asks. If they agree to go off to a disco or for a drink, the subject of

sex may not even be openly discussed. Instead, both the *jinetera* and her mark proceed as if they are on a date. Who knows? Maybe this one will be around for a few days, a week, even a month, providing steady work and freedom from having to continually find new customers. Whether the liaison lasts for a night or a month, the tourist will leave something to be remembered by—maybe money or a few nice new dresses, perhaps some jewelry—something that makes the sex and the attention provided worth the effort. This is not the hard sell of commodified bodies typical of sex tourism in Amsterdam. This is a more subtle trade. A trade where local, rather than immigrant women, make themselves available as sex partners and companions to privileged men from North America and Europe who can give them access to the currency of globalization, U.S. dollars.

Historical and Cultural Background. In recent years, the visible presence of sex workers in Havana who are willing to provide tourists with sexual access for material compensation in the form of cash, gifts, or other benefits has received considerable attention from social analysts.[4] This is not because the sex trade in Havana is comparable in size to what can be found in major international sex tourist destinations such as Amsterdam or Bangkok (Kempadoo and Dozeman 1998). Rather, many analysts see sex tourism in Havana as a demonstration that the forces of globalization are so far-reaching that they are being felt even in a socialist society that was once able to claim the elimination of prostitution and the reorientation of prostitutes to non-sexual labor as one of its earliest revolutionary accomplishments (Elizalde 1996:19). Or, as Aleida Guevara (1998:A5), Cuban pediatrician and daughter of Che Guevara, commented, "Just a few prostitutes in a country that had none before have created quite a scandal." Nor is it only a "scandal" in the eyes of foreign observers. Cuban sociologist Aurelio Alonso (1998:1) notes that prostitution is "shocking for us, because we were used to seeing a society without prostitutes on the street."

Cuban tourism has always centered on Havana, and the relationship between globalization and the reemergence of sex tourism in that city cannot be appreciated without placing Cuba in the context of its pre-revolutionary, and revolutionary history. In the 1950s, Cuba led the first wave of mass tourism in the Caribbean. The number of hotel rooms in Havana grew from 3,000 in 1952 to 5,500 in 1958, making it the single largest tourist destination in the region. In 1957, Havana accounted for 21 percent of *all* visitors to the Caribbean, with 86 percent of these visitors coming from the United States. By comparison, the next two largest tourist destinations, the Bahamas and Puerto Rico, accounted for 15 percent of all Caribbean tourism each (Villalba 1993).

This growth in tourism had its destructive side, however. Reflecting on Havana of the 1950s, Arthur Schlesinger Jr. (1996:323–324) described it as a "lovely city . . . being debased into a great casino and brothel for U.S. businessmen over for a big weekend from Miami." There was certainly much more to Havana in the 1950s than the hotel/casino district serving foreign tourists. Nevertheless, in the eyes of many potential tourists in the 1950s, the estimated 270 brothels and as many as 100,000 prostitutes who operated there, defined Havana (Elizade 1996).[5]

The Cuban Revolution that triumphed on January 1, 1959, was not initially committed to ending Havana's role as a tourist center for Americans. To the contrary, in 1959, Fidel Castro told the American Society of Tourist Agents annual convention in Havana that the Revolution hoped to establish Cuba as "the best and most important tourist center in the world" (Castro 1993:262). Soon, however, the unwillingness of revolutionary leaders to enter into corrupt relationships with casino owners, deteriorating U.S—Cuban relations, and the U.S. embargo of Cuba initiated by President Eisenhower at the end of 1960, began to take its toll. Cuban tourism dropped from a pre-Revolutionary high of 272,491 visitors in 1957 to 86,491 by 1960. In 1963, President John F. Kennedy invoked the Trading with the Enemy Act against Cuba, prohibiting U.S. citizens or businesses from engaging in commercial exchanges there, and thus bringing to an end Havana's role as a freewheeling tourist destination (Thomas 1998).

The Tourism Industry: Cuba in the Caribbean. In the late 1960s, the emergence of relatively affordable jet service created a new era of Caribbean island vacations (Patullo 1996:16). Between 1970 and 1994, the number of stay-over visits to Caribbean islands increased six-fold (Caribbean Tourism Organization 1995). Just as this boom in Caribbean tourism was beginning, the U.S. embargo against Cuba sent Cuban tourism into a steep decline that bottomed out with a mere 15,000 visitors in 1974. From that point forward, however, Cuba began to reorient its development plans to include investments in the

tourist industry. (Mesa-Lago 1981). Although some development was focused on internal tourism by Cubans, by 1979, foreign tourism had grown to 130,000 stay-over visits. A decade later, 300,000 foreign tourists visited the island, more than in any year prior to the Revolution (Triana 1995). Moreover, only 18 percent of these tourists were from Sovietbloc countries. Forty percent came from Canada, 15 percent from Western Europe, 15 percent from Latin America, and—despite the embargo—another 12 percent from the United States (Miller and Henthorne 1997:8) . . .

Some of Cuba's tourism growth has taken place in tourist-oriented beach resorts such as varadero and Cayo Largo. As Cuba's primate city, however, Havana remains the centerpiece of Cuban tourism, accounting for 75 to 80 percent of all stay-over visits (Miller and Henthorne 1997). As Sassen (2000a) notes, primate cities such as Havana are linked to "cross-border circuits" in ways that differentiate them from the rest of their country. Thus, while tourist sections of Havana are significantly shaped by the need to meet the desires of foreign tourists, daily life in much of the rest of the city and country is less affected by these global forces and continues to be more nationally than internationally oriented.

Labor Markets: Cuban Tourism in a Globalized World Order. Many Habaneros today look back on the 1980s as the "good old days" of growth and development. During the early 1980s, the Cuban Gross Domestic Product (GDP) *grew* by almost 23 percent at a time when the combined GDP of Latin America *fell* by 9 percent under the impact of accumulating foreign debt and structural adjustments mandated by the IMF and the World Bank (Budhoo 1994). As the 1980s continued, however, economic development in Cuba began to slow, and by the decade's end, growth had stalled. As the socialist world crumbled between 1989 and 1993, Cuba underwent a dramatic reversal of fortune that forced a radical reorganization of economic life (Azicri 1992; Landau and Starratt 1994). The disappearance of Cuba's socialist trading partners created what Cuban sociologist Elena Diaz González (1997a) characterized as the worst crisis in the history of Cuban socialism. Between 1989 and 1993, the Cuban GDP fell between 35 and 50 percent, importation of Soviet oil declined by 62 percent, overall imports fell by 75 percent, and the domestic manufacture of consumer goods fell by 83 percent (Diaz González 1997a; Espinosa 1999).

As Cuba struggled to reconstruct its trade and financial relations to meet the hard-currency demands of the new capitalist world order, many Cubans found themselves facing a significantly altered labor market (Eckstein 1997). As in other former socialist bloc countries, the Cuban government could no longer provide the extensive employment and social-welfare package it once sought to establish as a universal birthright for all Cubans (Koont 1998; Verdery 1996). By 1999, although Cubans continued to benefit from state subsidies in the areas of food, housing, transportation, health care, and education, many desired goods could increasingly only be purchased in dollar stores for prices roughly equivalent to those found in the United States for the same goods (Michalowski 1998). It was at this very moment that international tourism to Havana began to increase significantly, with a concomitant growth in tourist-sector jobs—jobs where it was possible to earn at least some portion of one's salary in hard currency. As a consequence, a growing number of high school and college students in Havana began orienting themselves toward tourist-sector employment rather than state-sector jobs, while some Habaneros already employed in professional careers abandoned them to work in tourism as well (Randall 1996) . . .

Public Policy and Law: The Contradictions of Market Freedom. Although Cuba has had a significant number of foreign tourists since the late 1970s, the state-centered structure of life in Havana was not well suited to serving them. The array of small private restaurants and shops many European and North American tourists expect when they travel was absent in a city where most retail transactions took place in standardized, state-run enterprises. There was also concern that lively trade between Cubans and affluent foreigners might weaken public commitment to the collective pursuit of social equality. As a result, international tourism in Cuba during the 1980s was organized around self-contained hotels filled with consumer amenities for foreign visitors, but normally off-limits to Cubans. It proved impossible, however, to maintain a sharp divide between tourists and Cubans, particularly in Havana. It was soon breached by an energetic currency black market offering tourists exchange rates four to five times the official one, and by a domestic commodity black market where Cubans sold goods that were purchased illegally (or in some cases stolen) from tourist shops (Michalowski 1995; Michalowski and Zatz 1989). After attempts to suppress

these emerging illegal markets during the 1980s and early 1990s, the Cuban government reversed course, and rather than increasing the penalization of these offenses, began legalizing, controlling, and taxing the developing linkages between tourists and Cubans.

In 1993, the government legalized the possession of foreign currency, and began allowing citizens to legally exchange dollars for *pesos* at banks and government-run street kiosks known as *cadecas*. Between 1992 and 1994, the Cuban government promulgated a number of other legal changes that would indirectly help create an infrastructure for sex tourism in Havana. These included: 1) permitting the private rental of rooms, apartments, and houses; 2) expanding the arena of self-employment; 3) legalizing the establishment of privately-owned restaurants, colloquially known as *paladares;* 4) expanding the licensing of private vehicles as taxicabs; and 5) opening "dollar" stores where Cubans could purchase a broad range of items including food, appliances, furniture, clothes, jewelry, and many other items for U.S. currency (Gordon 1997).

Structurally, these changes facilitated sex-tourism in several ways. The legalization of the U.S. dollar meant that sex workers could obtain hard currency payment from foreign clients without violation of currency laws, and the opening of dollar stores meant they could spend their earnings without having to enter into black market exchanges. Legalizing the rental of private rooms and houses created new opportunities for commercial sexual transaction by eliminating the rules that required tourists to stay in hotels, while prohibiting Cubans from visiting foreigners in their hotel rooms. The legalization of private restaurants provided places where sex workers and tourists could meet and spend non-sex time. Meanwhile, the legalization of private taxis became an important conduit through which some cab drivers could help sex tourists find their way to prime locations for meeting sex workers, or work as pimps by directing their fares to specific sex workers.

Sex Work in Havana: Commodifying Bodies and Emotions. Although the growth of Havana's tourist industry resulted in a subsidiary increase in sex tourism to the island, so far, this sex trade has not become the province of the organized syndicates—whether legal or illegal—that typically control sex work in many other nations. During her fieldwork in Cuba in 1995, O'Connell Davidson (1996:40) observed that there was "no network of brothels, no organized system of bar prostitution: in fact, third party involvement in the organization of prostitution is rare. . . . Most women and girls are prostituting themselves independently and have no contractual obligations to a third party." What O'Connell Davidson saw in 1995 was still in evidence in 1999. While some Habaneros serving sex tourists, particularly younger girls or recent migrants to Havana, were fronted by pimps, and some relied on more fluid third-party arrangements with landlords or taxicab drivers, the predominant form of tourist-oriented sex work in Havana involved women and girls engaging in a variety of independent approaches to male tourists on streets and in clubs . . .

One Italian sex tourist summarized his attraction to Cuban *jineteras* by saying he came to Cuba because "the women here are really sweet. They make you feel like they really care. They are always trying to do whatever makes you feel good, not just sex, but everything else too." A pair of ex-patriot American men currently living in Costa Rica echoed this sentiment: "The Cuban women don't act like professional whores, 'here's the sex, now give me the money.' They are really kind. They want to spend time with you, be your friend." As experienced sexual tourists, they bemoaned the growth of sex tourism in Costa Rica because it "ruined" Costa Rican sex workers: "Now they act just like whores in the States. They just do it for the money and when it's over, they want to move on to the next customer. It wasn't like that in the 60s when there were hardly any tourists. Then they were really nice like the Cuban women are today. Things will probably change here [in Cuba], too. So we thought we'd enjoy it while it lasts."[6] In the complicated world of emotional simulacra, sex tourists like these experience the consumption of emotions that sex workers are rarely actually providing. Yet as long as sex workers give their customers the time and kind of attention that sex tourists in Cuba believe to be signifiers of "caring," the desires that brought them to the island are met.

Another appeal of sex tourism in Havana is its price. In 1999, a sex tourist could spend as little as ten dollars for a quick sexual encounter, and between thirty and forty dollars for a companion for the entire evening. This means that for between one hundred and two hundred dollars a day, including the meals, the tours, and other "gifts." European, Canadian, and American men in Havana can spend days or even weeks in the company of young,

seemingly-exotic women who appear to be providing them with loving attention, all at a price they can afford. In this way, for a short time, they can enjoy a level of class privilege available only to wealthier men in their home countries . . .

Sex Tourism in a Globalized World

Policy-makers, scholars, and ordinary citizens tend to see prostitution as a problem caused by prostitutes. Similarly, there is a tendency to view sex tourism as a problem belonging to other nations, a problem that originates primarily with poor Third World women who choose to deviate from "good" women by selling their sexuality. But prostitutes do not cause prostitution any more than poor people cause poverty, or poor nations cause global inequality. We contend that the contemporary growth and character of sex tourism is intimately linked to significant global forces.

These global forces, which include tourism, migration, and commodification, are not just abstract concepts; they can be observed within grounded contexts as a variety of local mediating institutions respond to global pressures. In the cases of Amsterdam and Havana, our research suggests that global forces have altered particular institutions in these cities in ways that expand the possibilities for sex tourism. Our work supports Sassen's (1998) view of cities as strategic sites for globalization. Furthermore, in the cases we studied, this is true regardless of whether the city is a global city, like Amsterdam, or a primate city, like Havana. At a theoretical level, we contend that the global forces of tourism and migration stimulate the production of sex workers, while the increasing commodification of bodies ensures a steady stream of clients who desire to consume sexual services. Within the cities we analyzed, these global forces find concrete expression at the institutional level, specifically in the changing character of the tourism industries, labor markets, sex work, and laws and policies.

As we have described in some detail, in both Amsterdam and Havana, the tourism industry has become a noticeable sector of the local economy as a by-product of efforts by these cities to secure a share of the burgeoning market created by global tourism. This competition is necessitated by a world in which global markets dominate and determine local fortunes for countries and cities.

Additionally, in both of the cities we analyzed, labor markets changed in ways that increased the attractiveness and, for some women, the necessity of sex work. This is particularly true among certain populations of women, such as immigrants in Amsterdam seeking jobs in an environment hostile to migrant workers, or young Cuban women in Havana for whom the globalization has meant that they can earn more dollars and go to more exciting places by selling sex and companionship than they can through more routine employment. Although sex work existed in both cities prior to the current period of globalization, it is evident that the global forces associated with consumption shaped the character of sex work in each city in significant ways. In Amsterdam, sex work became more organized, more stratified, and more like an "industry," while in Havana, tourist-oriented sex work not only reemerged, but reconstituted in ways that reflect tourist desires for emotional labor and "otherly" bodies. Consumption practices alone do not cause these changes, but the desires of privileged consumers do shape the particular expression and organization of sex work in each city. Finally, in both cities, laws and policies affecting sex tourism increasingly reflect local accommodation to global forces originating outside of the country. In Havana, efforts to find a political-economic niche in a globalized world economy shaped numerous laws and policies, ranging from changing currency regulations to more freedom for local taxicab drivers. In Amsterdam, efforts to make the city more attractive for privileged consumers and to deal with the problem of migration have led to laws and policies ranging from the legalization of brothels to regulating S&M practices. Despite the efforts of these cities to maintain internal control, their mediating institutions evolved in response to global forces, creating the foundation for globally structured, though geographically localized, sex tourism. What is new and noteworthy about global sex tourism is not "sex," "sex work," or even the commodification of bodies, but the extent to which sex work in specific locales is over-determined by broader global forces. This is what has changed significantly in the contemporary period. Thus, local infrastructures that shape the possibilities for sex tourism in Amsterdam and Havana increasingly reflect global, rather than local forces. To the extent that local institutions are increasingly responsive to global forces, city and national governments find it increasingly difficult to exert control over localized practices of sex

work (Boyer and Drache 1996). Like most consequences of globalization, sex tourism is a global social problem, even though its expression is locally constituted within cities.

Although sex tourism is growing and changing as a result of the impact of global forces on local structures, it is important to also note that our research reveals that the actual practice of sex work reflects the positionality of each city within the global economy. Amsterdam, a highly developed global city in an advanced capitalist nation, manifests a highly organized and stratified form of sex tourism based on the commodification of the "otherly" bodies of migrant women. In Cuba, the pattern is more characteristic of a developing nation as a primary producer. That is, sex tourism in Cuba involves the exploitation and consumption by foreigners of a local resource, in this case, Cuban women. Thus, although we theorize that global forces affect most major cities, our research also demonstrated that they would be affected differently depending upon their position in the global economic order and the unique character of local infrastructures and cultural histories.

Our analysis suggests that the forces subsumed under the term globalization are reshaping local contexts, whether their histories are capitalist or socialist, and often doing so in ways that cannot be anticipated. In the cities we analyzed, there is a high probability that local institutions will increasingly privilege the economic interests associated with "tourism" as a way to ensure one more niche in the global marketplace. Whether intentionally or as a by-product of local responses to global forces, the growth of tourism will likely increase tourist-oriented commercial sex, often at the expense of the health and welfare of those who provide the sexual services that wealthy tourists demand. In their struggle to stay afloat as the global tide comes their way, cities and nations need not embrace or endorse sex tourism in order to become the beneficiaries of the consumer dollars it generates. Thus, sex tourism in Amsterdam and Havana and, presumably, in many other cities, is increasingly structured by global forces, connecting sex work in cities around the world with the broader, more abstract phenomena of globalized sex tourism. Imagining localized sex tourism as a consequence of global forces and connections is an important first step toward understanding and responding to this social problem.

NOTES

1. This focus on "prostitutes" has led to lengthy debates over the character of prostitution. Because these debates are covered in detail elsewhere (e.g., Chapkis 1997), we do not reproduce them here. Our goal, instead, is to transcend the dichotomy between sex work as a form of oppression versus an employment choice. Our ethnographic work indicates that for many women it is *both*.

2. For more detailed discussions of the ethnographic methods we employ, see also, Aggar (1986), Clifford and Marcus (1986), Dubisch (1996), Michalowski (1996), and Van Maanen (1988).

3. The ethnographic knowledge of sex tourism in Amsterdam was gathered by Nancy Wonders and spans a six-year time period; however, the primary fieldwork for this project was conducted during a six-month period in 1997 while she was a Visiting Scholar at the University of Amsterdam. Her fieldwork involved in-depth conversations and interviews with sex workers, sex consumers, public officials associated with advocating for sex workers, academic faculty, and ordinary citizens about sex tourism, as well as extensive research in local libraries, bookstores, and government offices. The ethnographic information reported for Cuba is part of a larger study of social adaptations to the intersection of political-economy and law in a transforming Cuba that has been ongoing since 1985 (Michalowski 1996). The data on current patterns of sex tourism and *jineterismo* are based on fieldwork in 1998 and 1999. During these trips, Ray Michalowski discussed the changing face of social life in Havana with state-sector professionals, faculty from the University of Havana, members of the Cuban legal community, and professionals working in Cuba's emerging private-sector economy. The information acquired from these exchanges was cross-compiled with that obtained from unscheduled interviews with an opportunity sample of male sex tourists, *jineteras*, longterm professional prostitutes, pimps, and taxi drivers encountered in hotels and other tourist sites in the city. All conversations and interviews were conducted with full disclosure of the research nature of the exchange. As ethnographers, we spent significant time just living in these locales in order to understand and know the cultural context, however imperfectly. As gendered researchers, however, our access to information was also gendered. Ray could more easily fall into conversation with male sex tourists, and could enter into conversations with sex workers and pimps as a result of their initial interest in him as a possible customer. Nancy could more easily interact with formal associations linked to sex work without being questioned as a voyeur or potential client. Although we note

these differences as an important statement of reflexivity about our work, we found that our fieldwork yielded roughly comparable case studies, particularly when our ethnographic knowledge was combined with available ethnohistorical literature about each city.

4. See for example, Cabezas (1998); Diaz González (1997b); Elizalde (1996); Fernandez (1999); Fusco (1996); Hodge and Abiodun (2001); O'Connell Davidson (1996, 1998); Paternostro (2000); Randall (1996); Sanchez Taylor (2000); Strout (1995).

5. An estimate of 100,000 prostitutes operating in Havana is often quoted in discussions of pre-Revolutionary sex tourism. This figure, however, includes a significant proportion of prostitutes who served Cuban men. Even at the height of pre-Revolutionary tourism in Cuba there were only 270,000 tourists visiting the island, far too few to account for 100,000 prostitutes.

6. See Contreras (2001) for a similar description of the sex trade in Costa Rica.

7. During a January, 1999 speech commemorating the founding of the National Revolutionary Police, Fidel Castro called for a crackdown on uses of Cuba's emerging private sector to facilitate sex tourism. By February of that year, *jineteras* had become less visible and more subtle in marketing their services, a trend which continued into the following year (see Paternostro 2000).

REFERENCES

Adkins, Lisa. 1995. *Gendered Work: Sexuality, Family, and the Labour Market*. Philadelphia: Open University Press.

Aggar, Michael. 1986. *Speaking of Ethnography*. Beverly Hills: Sage Publications.

Alonso, Aurelio. 1998. Quoted in Patricia Grogg. "Prostitution re-emerges on the heels of economic crisis." *Interpress Service: Havana*, October 30.

Amin, Samir. 1990. *Maldevelopment: Anatomy of a Global Failure*. Tokyo: United Nations University Press.

———. 1997. *Empire of Chaos*. New York: Monthly Review Press.

Association of Caribbean States. 2001. "Statistical database." Available at www.acs.aec.org/Trade/DBase/DBase_eng/dbaseindex_eng.htm

Azicri, Max. 1992. "The rectification process revisited: Cuba's defense of traditional Marxism-Leninism." In *Cuba in Transition: Crisis and Transformation*, Sandor Halebsky and John M. Kirk, eds., 37–54. Boulder, CO: Westview.

Bell, Lara, Jose Pulido Escandell, and Clara Pulido Escandell. 1997. Visión desde leuba. Madrid: SODePAZ.

Bell, Shannon. 1994. *Reading, Writing, and Rewriting the Prostitute Body*. Bloomington: Indiana University Press.

Bordo, Susan. 1993. *Unbearable Weight: Feminism, Western Culture and the Body.* LA: University of California Press.

Boutellier, Johannes C. J. 1991. "Prostitution, criminal law and morality in The Netherlands." *Crime, Law and Social Change* 15:201–211.

Boyer, Robert, and Daniel, Drache; eds. 1996. *States against Markets: The Limits of Globalization.* NY: Routledge.

Brants, Chrisje. 1998. "The fine art of regulated tolerance: Prostitution in Amsterdam." *Journal of Law and Society* 25, 4:6211–6235.

Brewis, Joanna, and Stephen Linstead. 2000. *Sex, Work and Sex Work: Eroticizing Organization.* London: Routledge.

Bruinsma, Gerben J. N., and Guus Meershoek. 1999. "Organized crime and trafficking in women from Eastern Europe in The Netherlands." In *Illegal Immigration and Commercial Sex: The New Slave Trade,* Phil Williams, ed., 105–118. London: Frank Cass.

Budhoo, Davison. 1994. "IMF/World Bank wreaks havoc on the Third World." In *50 Years is Enough: The Case against the World Bank and the International Monetary Fund,* K. Danaher, ed., 20–23. Boston: South End Press.

Burawoy, Michael, Joseph A. Blum, Sheba George, Zsuzsa Gille, Teresa Gowan, Lynne Haney, Maren Klawiter, Steven H. Lopez, Seán Ó Riain, and Millie Thayer. 2000. *Global Ethnography: Forces, Connections and Imaginations in a Postmodern World.* Berkeley: University of California Press.

Burbach, Roger, Orlando Núñez, and Boris Kagarlitsky. 1997. *Globalization and its Discontents: The Rise of Postmodern Socialisms.* Chicago: Pluto Press.

Cabezas, Amalia Lucia. 1998. "Discourses of prostitution: The case of Cuba." In *Global Sex Workers: Rights, Resistance and Redefinition,* Kamala Kempadoo and Jo Doezema, eds., 79–86. London: Routledge.

Caribbean Tourism Organization. 1995. "Statistical report: 1994 edition." Barbados, WI: Caribbean Tourism Organization.

Castro, Fidel. 1993. Quoted in "Villalba." *Cuba y el Turismo.* Havana: Editorial de Ciencias Sociales.

———. 1999. *Neoliberal Globalization and the Global Economic Crisis.* Havana: Publications Office of the Council of State.

Chapkis, Wendy. 1997. *Live Sex Acts: Women Performing Erotic Labor.* NY: Routledge.

Chomsky, Noam. 1994. *World Orders Old and New.* NY: Columbia University Press.

Clifford, James, and George E. Marcus. 1986. *Writing Culture: The Poetics and Politics of Ethnography.* Berkeley: University of California Press.

Contreras, Joseph. 2001. "The dark tourists." *Newsweek International,* April 30:20.

Cox, Robert H. 1993. *The Development of the Dutch Welfare State: From Workers' Insurance to Universal Entitlement.* Pittsburgh: University of Pittsburgh Press.

Craig-Smith, S., and C. French. 1994. *Learning to Live with Tourism.* Melbourne: Pitman Publishing.

Craik, Jennifer. 1997. "The Culture of Tourism." In *Touring Cultures: Transformations of Travel and Theory,* Chris Rojec and John Urry, eds., 113–136. London: Routledge.

Dahles, Heidi. 1998. "Redefining Amsterdam as a tourist destination." *Annals of Tourism Research* 25:55–69.

Davidow, William H., and Michael Malone. 1992. *The Virtual Corporation: Structuring and Revitalizing the Corporation for the 21st Century.* New York: Harper Collins.

DeHaan, Willem. 1997. "Minorities, crime and criminal justice in The Netherlands." In *Minorities, Migrants and Crime: Diversity and Similarity across Europe and the United States,* Ineke Haen Marshall, ed., 198–223. Thousand Oaks, CA: Sage.

Dello Buono, Richard A., and Jose Bell Lara, eds. 1997. *Carta Cuba: Essays on the Potential and Contradictions of Cuban Development.* La Habana: FLACSO-Programa Cuba.

Diaz González, Elena. 1997a. "Introduction." In *Cuba, Impacto de las Crises en Grupos Vulnerables: Mujer, Familia, Infancia,* Elena Diaz, Tania Carmen León, Esperanza Fernández Zegueira, Sofía Perro Mendoza, and María del Carmen Abala Argüeller, eds., 3–8, Habana: Universidad de La Habana.

———. 1997b. "Turismo y Prostitución en Cuba. In *Cuba. Impacto de las Crises en Grupos Vulnerables,: Mujer, Familia, Infancia,* Elena Diaz, Tania Carmen León, Esperanza Fernández Zegueira. Sofía Perro Mendoza, and María del Carmen Abala Argüeller, eds., 3–8. Habana: Universidad de La Habana.

Dougherty, John, and David Holthouse. 1998. "Nogales nightmare: Life in the Maquiladora industry borders on exploitation." *Tucson Weekly,* November 19.

Dubisch, Jill. 1996. *In a Different Place: Sex, Gender and Fieldwork at a Greek Shrine.* Princeton: Princeton University Press.

Eckstein, Susan. 1997. "The limits of socialism in a capitalist world economy: Cuba since the collapse of the Soviet bloc." In *Toward a New Cuba?: Legacies of a Revolution.* Centeno and Font. eds., 135–150. Boulder, CO: Lynne Rienner Publishers.

Elizalde, Rosa Miriam. 1996. *Flores Desechables: ¿Prostitución en Cuba?* Havana: Casa Editoria, Abril.

Enloe, Cynthia. 1989. *Bananas, Beaches and Bases: Making Feminist Sense of International Politics.* LA: University of California Press.

Espinosa, Luis Eugenio. 1999. "Globalización y la economia de Cuba." Interview, Havana, January 23.

Fernandez, Nadine. 1999. "Back to the future: Women, race and tourism in Cuba." In *Sun, Sex, and Gold: Tourism and Sex Work in the Caribbean,* Kamala Kempadoo, ed., 81–92. Lanham, MD: Rowman and Littlefield Publishers.

Ferrante, Joan, and Prince Brown, Jr. 1998. *The Social Construction of Race and Ethnicity in the United States.* NY: Longman.

Firat, A. Fuat, and Nikhilesh Dholakia. 1998. *Consuming People: From Political Economy to Theaters of Consumption.* London: Routledge.

Forbes, Magazine. 1996. "A letter from the Tipplezone." 157, 12:120.

Friedman, David. 1999. *The Lexus and the Olive Tree.* New York: Farrar, Straus, Giroux.

Fusco, Coco. 1996. "Hustling for dollars." *Ms. Magazine* 7, 2:62–70.

Geertz, Clifford. 1983. *Local knowledge: Further essays in interpretive anthropology.* New York: Basic Books.

Gordon, Joy. 1997. "Cuba's entrepreneurial Socialism." *The Atlantic Monthly* 279, 1:18–30.

Greider, William. 1997. *One World, Ready or Not: The Manic Logic of Global Capitalism.* New York: Simon and Schuster.

Guevara, Aleida. 1998. Quoted in Irwin Block. "Much work to be done: Cuban revolution hasn't brought full emancipation of women." *Montreal Gazetter,* March 24:A5.

Herman, Edward S. 1995. *Triumph of the Market: Essays on Economics, Politics and the Media.* Boston: South End Press.

Hirst, Paul Q. 1996. *Globalization in Question: The International Economy and The Possibilities of Governance.* Cambridge, MA: Blackwell Publishers.

Hochschild, Arlie Russell. 1983. *The Managed Heart: Commercialization of Human Feeling.* Berkeley: University of California Press.

Hodge, Derrick G., and Hehanda Abiodun. 2001. "The colonization of the Cuban body." *NACLA Report on the Americas,* March/April: 34, 15:20–30.

Hoogvelt, Ankie. 1997. *Globalization and the Postcolonial World: The New Political Economy of Development.* Houndmills, Basingstoke, Hampshire: Macmillan.

Hughes, Donna. 2000. "The transnational shadow market of trafficking in women." *Journal of International Affairs* 53, 3:625.

International Labor Organization (ILO). 1998. "Sex Industry assuming massive proportions in Southeast Asia." *ILO Press Release,* August 19. Geneva: International Labor Organization.

Karliner, Joshua. 1997. *The Corporate Planet: Ecology and Politics in the Age of Globalization.* San Francisco, CA: Sierra Club Books.

Kempadoo, Kamala, and Jo Doezema, eds. 1998. *Global Sex Workers: Rights, Resistance and Redefinition.* London: Routledge.

Koont, Sinan. 1998. "Cuba's unique structural adjustment." Unpublished paper presented at the Latin American Studies Association annual meeting, Chicago, IL.

Korten, David C. 1995. *When Corporations Rule the World.* West Hartford, CT: Kumerian Press.

Landau, Saul, and Dana Starratt. 1994. "Cuba's economic slide." *Multinational Monitor* (November, 15), 10:7–13.

Lean Lim, Lin. 1998. *The Sex Sector: The Economic and Social Bases of Prostitution in Southeast Asia,* Geneva: International Labour Office.

Lury, Celila. 1996. *Consumer Culture.* New Brunswick, NJ: Rutgers University Press.

MacCannell, Dean. 1999. *The Tourist: A New Theory of the Leisure Class,* 2nd edition. Berkeley: University of California Press.

Mander, Jerry, and Edward Goldsmith. 1996. *The Case against the Global Economy and for a Turn toward the Local.* San Francisco, CA: Sierra Club Books.

Marshall, Ineke Haen. 1993. "Prostitution in the Netherlands: It's just another job!" In *Female Criminality,* Concetta C. Cullive and Chris E. Marshall, eds., 225–248. NY: Garland.

Marx, Karl. 1958 [1887]. *Capital,* Vol. 1, Moore and Aveling, trans. Moscow: Progress Publishers.

Mesa-Lago, Carmelo. 1981. *The Economy of Socialist Cuba.* Albuquerque: University of New Mexico Press.

Meulenbelt, E. B. 1993. De Verdiensten van Prostitutie. Doctoraal Scriptie Sociologie, Amsterdam.

Michalowski, Raymond. 1995. "Between citizens and the Socialist state: The negotiation of legal practice in Socialist Cuba." *Law and Society Review* 29, 1:65–101.

———. 1996. "Ethnography and anxiety: Fieldwork and reflexivity in the vortex of U.S. Cuban relations." *Qualitative Sociology* 19, 1:59–82.

———. 1998. "Market spaces and socialist places: Cubans talk about life in the post-Soviet world." Unpublished paper presented at the Latin American Studies Association, Chicago.

Michalowski, Raymond, and Marjorie Zatz. 1989. "The second economy in Cuba: Nothing fails like success." In *Second Economies in Marxist States,* eds., 101–121. London: MacMillan.

Miller, Mark M., and Tony L. Henthorne. 1997. *Investment in the New Cuban Tourist Industry: A Guide to Entrepreneurial Opportunities.* Westport, CT: Quorum Books.

Mr. A. De Graaf Foundation. 1997. Between the Lines. *Newsletter of the Mr. A. de Graaf Foundation, Institute for Prostitution Issues.* Amsterdam, The Netherlands.

Nagle, Jill. 1997. *Whores and Other Feminists.* NY: Routledge.

O'Connell Davidson, Julia. 1996. "Sex tourism in Cuba." *Race and Class* 38, 1:39–48.

———. 1998. *Prostitution, Power and Freedom.* Ann Arbor, MI: University of Michigan Press.

O'Connell Davidson, Julia, and Jacqueline Sanchez Taylor. 1998. "Fantasy islands: Exploring the demand for sex tourism." In *Sun, Sex, and Gold: Tourism and Sex Work in the Caribbean.* Kamala Kempadoo, ed., 37–54. Lanham, MD: Rowman and Littlefield Publishers.

Opperman, Martin. 1998. *Sex Tourism and Prostitution: Aspects of Leisure, Recreation, and Work.* NY: Cognizant Communication Corporation.

Paternostro, Silvana. 2000. "Communism vs. prostitution." *The New Republic,* July 10:18–22.

Patullo, Polly. 1996. *Last Resorts: The Cost of Tourism in the Caribbean.* London: Cassell.

Pettman, Jan Jindy. 1997. "Body politics: International sex tourism." *Third World Quarterly* 18, 1:93–108.

Pietila, Hilkka, and Jeanne Vickers. 1994. *Making Women Matter: The Role of the United Nations.* London: Zed Books.

Pinder, David. 1998. "Tourism in The Netherlands: Resource development, regional impacts and issues." In *Tourism and Economic Development: European Experiences.* Allan M. Williams and Gareth Shaw, eds., 301–323. NY: John Wiley and Sons.

Randall, Margaret. 1996. "Cuban women and the U.S. blockade." *Sojourner* 22, 3:10–11.

Raymond, Janice G. 1998. "Violence against women: NGO stonewalling in Beijing and elsewhere." *Women's Studies International Forum* 21, 1:1–9.

Reiland, Ralph. 1996. "Amsterdam's taxing issue: Wages of sin." *Insight on the News* (June) 12, 21:29.

Richter, Linda K. 1998. "Exploring the political role of gender in tourism research." In *Global Tourism,* William F. Theobald, ed., 391–404. Oxford: Butterworth-Heinemann.

Robinson, Linda. 1998. "Castro gives tourism a try: The Pope and 1.4 million other people are expected to visit Cuba this year." *U.S. News and World Report* (Jan, 12) 124, 1:32–36.

Rochon, Thomas R. 1999. *The Netherlands: Negotiating Sovereignty in an Interdependent World.* Boulder, CO: Westview Press.

Rojec, Chris, and John Urry. 1997. *Touring Cultures: Transformations of Travel and Theory.* London: Routledge.

Sanchez Taylor, Jaqueline. 2000. "Tourism and 'embodied' commodities: Sex tourism in the Caribbean." In *Tourism and Sex: Culture, Commerce, and Coercion,* Stephen Clift and Simon Carter, eds., 41–53. New York: Pinter.

Sassen, Saskia. 1996. "Identity in the global city: Economic and cultural encasements." In *The Geography of Identity,* Patricia Yaeger, ed., 131–151. Ann Arbor, MI: University of Michigan Press.

———. 1998. *Globalization and its Discontents: Essays on the New Mobility of People and Money.* NY: The New Press.

———. 2000a. *Cities in a World Economy.* Thousand Oaks, CA: Pine Forge Press.

———. 2000b. "Women's burden: Counter-geographies of globalization and the feminization of survival." *Journal of International Affairs* 53, 2:503.

Sassen, Saskia, and Frank Roost. 1997. "The city: Strategic site for the global entertainment industry." In *The Tourist City,* Dennis R. Judd and Susan S. Fainstein, eds., 143–154. New Haven, CT: Yale University Press.

Schlesinger, Arthur Jr. 1996. Quoted in Robert E. Quirk, *Fidel Castro,* 323–324. New York: W. W. Norton.

Skrobanck, Siriporn, Nataya Boonpakdee, and Chutima Jantateero. 1997. *The Traffic in Women: Human Realities of the International Sex Trade.* London: Zed Books.

Strout, Jan. 1995. "Women, the politics of sexuality, and Cuba's economic crisis." *Socialist Review* 25, 1:5–16.

Ten Kate, Niel. 1995. "Prostitution: a really valuable asset." Paper distributed by the Mr. A. de Graaf Stichting, Amsterdam: The Netherlands.

The Economist. 1998. "The sex industry: Giving the customer what he wants." February 14:23–25.

Theobald, William E. 1998. *Global Tourism.* Oxford: Butterworth-Heinemann.

Thomas, Hugh. 1998. *Cuba: Or, The Pursuit of Freedom,* Updated. New York: Da Capo Press.

Triana, Juan C. 1995. "Consolidation of the economic reanimation." *Cuban Foreign Trade* 1:17–24.

Truong, Thanh-Dam. 1990. *Sex, Money and Morality: Prostitution and Tourism in Southeast Asia.* London: Zed Books.

Van Der Poel, Sari. 1995. "Solidarity as boomerang: The fiasco of prostitutes' rights movements in the Netherlands." *Crime, Law, and Social Change* 23: 41–65.

Van Maanen, John. 1988. *Tales of the Field: On Writing Ethnography.* Chicago: University of Chicago Press.

Verdery, Katherine. 1996. *What Was Socialism, and What Comes Next?* Princeton, NJ: Princeton University Press.

Villalba, Garrido, Evaristo. 1993. *Cuba y el Turismo.* Havana: Editorial de Ciencias Sociales.

Visser, Jan. 1997a. "Dutch preparations for a different prostitution policy." Mr. A. de Graaf Foundation: Institute for Prostitution Research, Amsterdam, The Netherlands (January).

———. 1997b. "The Dutch law proposal on prostitution. Text and explanation." Mr. A. de Graaf Foundation: Institute for Prostitution Research, Amsterdam, The Netherlands (July).

Wijers, Marjan. 1998. "Women, labor, migration: The position of trafficked women and strategies for support." In *Global Sex Workers: Rights, Resistance and Redefinition,* Kamala Kempadoo and Jo Doezema, eds., 69–78. London: Routledge.

Williams, Allan M., and Gareth Shaw. 1998. *Tourism and Economic Development: European Experiences.* NY: John Wiley and Sons.

Wonders, Nancy. 2000. "Conceptualizing Difference." In *Investigating Difference: Human and Cultural Relations in Criminal Justice,* The Criminal Justice Collective of Northern Arizona, eds., 11–26. Boston: Allyn and Bacon.

Wonders, Nancy, and Mona Danner. 1999. "(En)gendering globalization: International women's rights and criminology" Unpublished paper presented at the annual meeting of the American Society of Criminology (November), Toronto, Canada.

————. 2002. "Globalization, state-corporate crime, and women: The strategic role of women's NGOs in the New World Order." In *Controversies in White Collar Crime,* Gary W. Potter, ed. Cincinnati, OH: Anderson.

Zatz, Noah D. 1997. "Sex work/sex act: Law, labor, and desire in constructions of prostitution." *Signs* (Winter) 22, 21:277–308.

Think Critically

1. According to the authors, how is globalization related to the sex tourism industry? Discuss three major ways.

2. Describe some of the pressures that globalization has placed on local cultures to adapt in terms of sex tourism and other social institutions. How might localities respond in order to reduce these demands for change?

COMMON CRIME AND SOCIAL CONTROL

IN AN EXCERPT FROM A LONGER ARTICLE entitled, "Incarceration as a Deviant Form of Social Control," Wayne Welsh and I analyze the problems resulting from societal over-incarceration, including overcrowded jails and state and federal court orders levied against government entities that administer them. A significant irony in crime control policy is presented. By touting incarceration as the major response to crime, the state inevitably fails to keep the "public promise" of more certain, swift, and severe punishments. Formal social control mechanisms are thwarted by the massive influx of persons brought into the criminal justice system. Given this situation, which has led to horrid jail conditions and crumbling prison systems in many jurisdictions, the law has turned on itself, labeling the use of incarceration as "deviant" when punishment practices become so extreme (i.e., violate Constitutional standards) that they threaten the legitimacy of the criminal justice system.

Edwin Lemert's classic work, "The Behavior of the Systematic Check Forger" examines the "behavior system" that allows persons to engage in check forging. Using Sutherland's framework developed in his research on the professional thief, Lemert studies convicted check forgers as well as those who were serving sentences for writing checks with insufficient funds. As in any business, complex planning is necessary, specific technical skill are required, and mobility and association issues must be addressed. Unlike other forms of professional theft, the systematic forger tends to work alone, avoiding contact with other criminals whenever possible. Lemert explains how his findings are at odds with Sutherland's earlier statement that it was necessary for forgers to work in cooperative arrangements with others and concludes that check forgery is not "a professional behavior

system acquired or maintained through associations with other criminals."

David Sudnow's "Normal Crimes" is a classic work in the sociology of deviance and social control. Sudnow attempts to make sense of the ways in which crimes are categorized by enforcers. He seeks to answer the question of how the penal code is employed in the everyday activity of legal administrators in order to assess the utility of the labeling perspective on deviance. "Normal crimes" are those occurrences seen as "typical" and whose perpetrators and victims have characteristics that fit common circumstances of such acts. Sudnow's examination of the "law in action" shows how the socially constructed categorization of crime by public defenders and prosecutors affects legal decision making. He argues that categories of crime are not simply defined by statutes, but must be studied sociologically in order to make empirical sense of the processing of deviance by formal institutions of social control. Moreover, the study suggests that the smooth operation of the criminal justice system is dependent upon such "normal crimes."

In "Computer Crime," which is a chapter from the book, *Profit Without Honor: White-Collar Crime and the Looting of America,* Stephen Rosoff, Robert Tillman, and I review relatively new and technologically sophisticated forms of deviance that are enacted through computers. Among the deviant behaviors presented are embezzlement and financial theft, hacking, espionage, and "phone phreaking." The piece employs numerous case histories and ties their relevant themes to theories of deviance. Among other things, we find that improved security technology is often met with better criminal technology by these sophisticated deviants, making it extraordinarily difficult to maintain effective social control mechanisms for very long.

Incarceration as a Deviant Form of Social Control*

Henry N. Pontell and Wayne N. Welsh**

OVER THE PAST DECADE, THE USE OF incarceration has increased dramatically as witnessed by population explosions in the nation's prisons and jails. The average daily jail population rose from 157,930 inmates in 1978 to 395,553 in 1989 (U.S. Department of Justice 1990), whereas the number of inmates in state and federal prisons increased from 329,821 in 1980 to 771,243 in 1990 (Associated Press 1991). Much attention typically focuses on burgeoning prison populations that house society's most serious criminals. Until their recent overcrowding problems, less attention has been given to jails, which are more numerous than prisons and more local in nature. In many jurisdictions, jails have become such brutal places to house people that judges have ordered, among other things, that they not be allowed to exceed a set population capacity. Moreover, in an effort to keep pace with what is perceived as the public's desire to equate punishment with incarceration, legislatures have approved massive funds for constructing additional facilities, despite the fact that projections show that such construction will not alleviate crowding if past trends in incarcerative policies and crime rates continue.

Overcrowded jails create a host of problems for formal social control efforts that are not easily dealt with by correctional administrators, legislators, or criminal justice officials. As Briar (1983) has pointed out:

> Considered bastions of community neglect, these overcrowded, understaffed maximum security structures subject both those confined—as well as their keepers—to an array of personal indignities and life-threatening conditions unparalleled in other institutions in this country. Described as "scandalous" and "ultimate ghettos," conditions in many of these institutions are generally forced upon public purview only with the occurrence of suicides, strangulations, gang rapes, fires, escapes, and lawsuits. Yet once official assurances have been issued that crises have abated, concern subsides and previous patterns of operation may ensue. (p. 387)

A "crisis mentality" on the part of administrators and policy makers is not likely to produce effective solutions to problems in criminal justice (Feeley 1983; Sherman and Hawkins 1983). Yet the system continues its movement from one crisis to the next, and a more recent one is that of overincarceration and the resulting severe strain on penal resources.

The rise of the prisoners' rights movement in the 1970s has been accompanied by numerous court orders against prison and jail systems throughout the country. Such orders have mandated population "caps" or limits, as well as improvements in conditions of confinement, including specific changes in the internal environments of these institutions. In 1989, 31% of the nation's large jails were under court order to improve conditions of confinement (U.S. Department of Justice 1990), whereas one or more state prisons in 41 states experienced court intervention (National Prison Project 1990). These developments, coupled with scarce resources to build enough facilities have created a major roadblock for legislative efforts designed to punish with more certainty and severity. In fact it could

*From Henry N. Pontell and Wayne N. Welsh, *Crime and Delinquency,* vol. 40, no. 1, pp. 18–36, copyright © 1994 by Sage Publications, Inc. Reprinted by permission of Sage Publications, Inc.

**This research was supported by grants from the Committee on Research, Academic Senate, University of California, Irvine, the Guggenheim Program in Criminal Justice, Boalt Hall School of Law, University of California, Berkeley, and by a fellowship from the Social Sciences and Humanities Research Council of Canada. The authors thank Matt Leone, Patrick Kinkade, and Jack Pederson for their research assistance.

be reasonably argued that a latent function of the "get tough movement" (Cullen, Clark, and Wozniak 1985) has been to quicken the pace by which it becomes apparent that the capacity of the criminal justice system to punish violators is limited by a range of political, economic, social, and legal forces that cannot be easily manipulated or fully anticipated by legislative changes (Pontell 1984).

Moreover, research suggests a direct connection between prison and jail overcrowding and that progressive reforms have been used primarily as "safety-valve institutions," relieving the pressure created by legislative actions designed to enhance the severity and certainty of punishment (Rothman 1980; Sutton 1987). For example, Rothman (1980) has argued that the reforms of probation, parole, and indeterminate sentencing arose through the interplay between "conscience and convenience." Conscience was evident in the ideology of progressive reformers who believed that criminals could be rehabilitated into productive members of society. The specific reforms adopted, however, were largely a reflection of administrative convenience, as they functioned to increase official discretion in handling offenders and supplemented efficient processing and control of inmates. Similarly, as Sutton (1987) points out in his empirical study of imprisonment in the United States, incarceration rates were most closely tied to the manner in which officials used their discretionary authority to control flows of inmates through institutions. His analysis suggests that reforms were used to give authorities increased discretion to release inmates where prison and jail systems were expanding the fastest. He notes:

> Jail capacities were influenced by probation legislation, which increased discretion over rates of admission, and by indeterminate sentencing, which probably encouraged faster releases. The effect of indeterminate sentencing was also strongest where jails were most expansive. It appears that reforms were used to contain explosive growth and relieve overcrowding. . . . In particular, the findings of this study imply that local jails supplemented the limited capacity of centralized prison systems, especially in urban areas. (Sutton 1987, pp. 626–27)

Research on jails has concentrated on a number of areas including the evolution of jails (Flynn 1983; Goldfarb 1975; Irwin 1985), problems such as overcrowding (Advisory Commission 1984; Flynn 1983; Pontell, Welsh, Leone, and Kinkade 1989; Welsh, Pontell, Leone, and

Kinkade 1990; Welsh, Leone, Kinkade and Pontell 1991) and litigation issues (Feeley and Hanson 1986; Taft 1983; Welsh and Pontell 1991). Little systematic research exists, however, regarding the detailed accounting of the number and types of violations alleged in complaints against jail facilities and how courts have responded to them.

Overcrowded jails and subsequent court orders against them can involve broad consequences, far beyond the boundaries of these institutions themselves. For example, the large proportion of county and state budgets that needs to be devoted to corrections negatively impacts funds available for health, education, and welfare (California Legislative Analyst 1987). At the same time, the "common knowledge" that crime is increasing, or that our need to punish is increasing, is at best questionable (Clear and Harris 1987). Further, strong signals by the courts that overcrowded and inhumane conditions of incarceration will not be tolerated, combined with fiscal realities, inevitably limit the potential effectiveness of simple "get tough" legislative proposals calling for harsher punishments in response to increased crime (Austin and McVey 1989). In short, court intervention in corrections may have far-reaching impacts that result in structural limits on the ability to employ punishment as a major solution to the crime problem and, more specifically, on the use of incarceration as a major form of punishment.

Jail overcrowding has already resulted in a relatively "elite" criminal being detained prior to trial, and both pretrial and sentenced-prisoner release options are extremely limited in many jurisdictions. Given the reluctance of communities to accept new jail construction in their midst (Welsh, Leone, Kinkade, and Pontell 1991), as well as severely limited local financial resources (Welsh 1990), jail administrators will be increasingly hard-pressed to regulate jail populations by simply building new facilities.

One major difficulty in fostering changes and producing less costly alternatives to overincarceration and expensive court suits is the fact that the public is not wont to support anything but victims' rights and that any support for the rights of criminals (or in the case of pretrial detainees, the rights of suspected criminals) would only be met by political disaster for legislators and other elected officials. Thus it is extraordinarily difficult to ensure decent conditions, especially under the conservative and mostly reactionary vision of the role of criminal justice and criminal punishment over the past decade (Advisory Commission 1984; Busher 1983; Cullen, Clark, and Wozniak

1985). The legislative-political process is proving itself to be impotent if not ultimately destructive, with the possible exception of approving funds for new construction.

There are, however, serious difficulties with approaches that rely on constructing new facilities, which render them extremely problematic. The costs of construction are extremely high, as are the operating costs of jails once they are built. The extremely high cost necessarily means that other social programs will suffer. There also is a long time lag between current problems and the potential opening of new facilities. There is also no guarantee, nor any body of systematic scientific evidence, that shows that when such new facilities are opened they will solve the overcrowding problem.

Nonetheless, many observers seem to agree that there is a great ability to expand the capacity to punish. Indeed, through the passage of laws that alter sentences and allocate or create new public funds, legislatures can manipulate schemes that attempt to control and to punish. It is perhaps stating the obvious, however, to say that forms of punishment are in fact limited by political, legal, economic, and cultural restraints (Newman 1978). There is some threshold at which it becomes necessary for changes to occur in forms of punishment when its use rises above manageable proportions, and when resulting crises in legitimacy require new social control practices. Foucault (1979) argues a similar idea when he notes that penal ceremonies, public tortures, and corporal punishments diminished in Europe 200 years ago because civilization had reached a point where these forms were considered too brutal to send the proper message to the public. Punishment then took on a more ideological function, with its form changing to that of incarceration. Legislatures have not yet dropped incarceration as a major means of punishment, but their desire to expand its certainty and severity is thwarted by fiscal realities that face the state. A latent result is that selectivity in the use of incarceration increases as the state wrestles with problems associated with limited resources, and with what constitutes "legitimate punishment." As a consequence, the state inevitably fails to keep the public "promise" of more certain, swift, and severe criminal sanctions.

The manner in which this actually occurs in the criminal justice system is through the use of discretion, an institutional element that is essential to the functioning of the justice system itself. "Law" mandates that discretion exist in the criminal justice system, whereas "laws" designed to limit or do

away with it, simply dislodge it to other parts of the system. For example, determinate sentencing laws aimed at reducing judicial discretion may simply result in an increase in the discretionary power of district attorneys (McCoy 1984) or move it from prison and parole authorities to judges and prosecutors (Casper, Brereton, and Neal 1981). As Sutton (1987) among others has suggested, criminal justice reforms may serve multiple manifest and latent functions. The analysis presented here has attempted to explicate the role of jails in responding to various legal changes regarding the manner in which formal social control takes place.

The "production of social control" is not a process that is merely dictated by the state. The overall ability of the state to expand its punishment capacity may vary over time, but the forms by which it attempts to accomplish this are limited by political, legal, and economic restraints. A study of the repression of ghetto riots by Balbus (1977), for example, showed that short-term expansions of local criminal justice system capacity were possible to restore public order, but that the vast majority of those arrested in police sweeps were released soon thereafter to avoid further exacerbation of already strained conditions in city courts and jails. Punishment theorists such as Rusche and Kirchheimer (1939) and Foucault (1979), as well as many legal authorities today, have viewed the "production of punishment" as a result of factors external to the legal system itself. The more we rely on the criminal justice system to control the population, the more resources it will attract, and the more unwieldy it is likely to become as it is pressured by the very social problems it was meant to control. In short, it appears that the use of imprisonment as an instrument of "normalization" is limited (Foucault 1979). That social control agents are held in contempt of court orders epitomizes the futility in responding to complex social problems through attempts to increase imprisonment. Over time, the legal system has turned on itself, labeling its own use of incarceration as "deviant" when punishment practices become so extreme as to threaten the very legitimacy of the punishment system itself.

Essential research in the area of correctional overcrowding includes much more than merely focusing on emergency plans to reduce inmate populations. In the current stampede toward nonincarcerative intermediate sanctions, policy makers have lost sight of the very factors that precipitated their widespread adoption in the first place. Such factors include an overreliance on incarceration as a means of social control, and recognition by the courts of deviant institutional conditions that resulted from short-sighted, politically motivated correctional policy. Continued failure to factor the jail overcrowding problem into valid causes and corresponding policy choices is likely to lead to more poorly planned and ineffective solutions (Welsh et al. 1990) that supplement official discretion but leave underlying social problems and their causes untouched (Irwin 1985).

As Feeley (1983) has noted in regard to court reform:

> There is little incentive for those engaged in day-to-day administration of criminal courts to think about systemwide changes or, when they do, to pursue them vigorously. But when change comes, as we have seen, it is often initiated by "dramatic events" and offered as a "bold solution" that is promoted as a panacea. Such conditions do not give rise to serious thinking or realistic expectations. (p. 192)

Feeley (1983) outlines the reasons for this dilemma in what he identifies as the problems of crisis thinking, lack of historical perspective, the inevitability of crisis thinking, and the fallacy of formalism. What Feeley notes for courts is likely to hold true for correctional institutions as well. Building more facilities and adopting a variety of intermediate sanctions have been offered as bold solutions to what has been interpreted as a major crisis in incarceration. Whether this can alter the present growth of deviant punishment systems is something that remains to be seen.

REFERENCES

Advisory Commission. 1984. *Jails: Intergovernmental Dimensions of a Local Problem.* Washington, DC: Advisory Commission on Intergovernmental Relations.

Associated Press. 1991. "U.S. Prison Population Up 8.2 Percent to 771,243." *Philadelphia Inquirer,* May 16, p. 19B.

Austin, James and Aaron David McVey. 1989. *The 1989 NCCD Prison Population Forecast: The Impact of the War on Drugs.* San Francisco: National Council on Crime and Delinquency.

Balbus, Isaac D. 1977. *The Dialectics of Legal Repression: Black Rebels before the American Criminal Courts.* New York: Transaction Books.

Briar, Katherine Hooper. 1983. "Jails: Neglected Asylums." *Social Casework* 64:387–93.

Busher, Walter. 1983. *Jail Overcrowding: Identifying Causes and Planning for Solutions.* Washington, DC: Office of Justice Assistance, Research and Statistics.

California Legislative Analyst. 1987. *Analysis of the 1987–88 Budget Bill.* Report to the Joint Legislative Budget Committee. Sacramento: State of California.

Casper, Jonathan D., David Brereton, and David Neal. 1981. *The Implementation of the California Determinate Sentence Law.* Washington, DC: National Institute of Justice.

Clear, Todd R. and Patricia M. Harris. 1987 "The Costs of Incarceration." Pp. 37–55 in *America's Correctional Crisis,* edited by D. Gottfredson and S. McConville. Westport, CT: Greenwood.

Cullen, Francis T., Gregory A. Clark, and John F. Wozniak. 1985. "Explaining the Get Tough Movement: Can the Public Be Blamed?" *Federal Probation* 49:16–24.

Feeley, Malcolm M. 1983. *Court Reform on Trial: Why Simple Solutions Fail.* New York: Basic Books.

Feeley, Malcolm M. and Roger P. Hanson. 1986. "What We Know, Think We Know and Would Like to Know about the Impact of Court Orders on Prison Conditions and Jail Crowding." Presented at the Meeting of the Working Group on Jail and Prison Crowding, Committee on Research on Law Enforcement and the Administration of Justice, National Academy of Sciences, Chicago, IL.

Flynn, Edith E. 1983. "Jails." Pp. 915–22 in *Encyclopedia of Crime and Justice,* edited by S. H. Kadish. New York: Macmillan.

Foucault, Michel. 1979. *Discipline and Punish: The Birth of the Prison.* New York: Vintage.

Goldfarb, Ronald. 1975. *Jails.* Garden City, NY: Anchor.

Irwin, John. 1985. *The Jail: Managing the Underclass in American Society.* Berkeley: University of California Press.

McCoy, Candace. 1984. "Determinate Sentencing, Plea Bargaining Bans, and Hydraulic Discretion in California." *Justice System Journal* 9:256–75.

National Prison Project. 1990. "Status Report: State Prisons and the Courts." *Journal of the National Prison Project* 22:7–8, 14–17, 20.

Newman, Graeme. 1978. *The Punishment Response.* Philadelphia: J. B. Lippincott.

Orange County Administrative Office. 1986. *Systems Approach to Jail Crowding in Orange County.* Prepared for the Board of Supervisors, Orange County, CA.

Pontell, Henry N. 1984. *A Capacity to Punish: The Ecology of Crime and Punishment.* Bloomington: Indiana University Press.

Pontell, Henry N., Wayne N. Welsh, Matthew Leone, and Patrick Kinkade. 1989. "Prescriptions for Punishment: Official Ideologies and Jail Overcrowding." *American Journal of Criminal Justice* 14:43–70.

Rothman, David J. 1980. *Conscience and Convenience: The Asylum and Its Alternatives in Progressive America.* Boston: Little, Brown.

Rusche, Georg and Otto Kirchheimer. 1939. *Punishment and Social Structure.* New York: Russell and Russell.

Sherman, Michael and Gordon Hawkins. 1983. *Imprisonment in America.* Chicago: University of Chicago Press.

Sutton, John R. 1987. "Doing Time: The Dynamics of Imprisonment in the Reformist State." *American Sociological Review* 52:612–30.

Taft, Philip B., Jr. 1983. "Jail Litigation: Winning in Court Is Only Half the Battle." *Corrections Magazine* 9:22–27, 30–31.

U.S. Department of Justice, Bureau of Justice Statistics. 1990. *Jail Inmates 1989.* Bulletin NCJ-123264. Washington, DC: U.S. Department of Justice.

Welsh, Wayne N. 1990. "The Impact of Jail Litigation on County Financial Expenditures." Paper presented at the Annual Meeting of the American Society of Criminology, November, Baltimore.

Welsh, Wayne N., Matthew C. Leone, Patrick T. Kinkade, and Henry N. Pontell. 1991. "The Politics of Jail Overcrowding: Public Attitudes and Official Policies." Pp. 131–47 in *American Jails: Public Policy Issues,* edited by J. Thompson and G. L. Mays. Chicago: Nelson-Hall.

Welsh, Wayne N. and Henry N. Pontell. 1991. "Counties in Court: Interorganizational Adaptations to Jail Litigation in California." *Law and Society Review* 25:73–101.

Welsh, Wayne N., Henry N. Pontell, Matthew C. Leone, and Patrick T. Kinkade. 1990. "Jail Overcrowding: An Analysis of Policymaker Perceptions." *Justice Quarterly* 7:341–70.

Think Critically

1. Explain the irony of social control that the authors present regarding incarceration in America. What general implications does it have for crime control policy?
2. Give two examples of other social institutions where a "crisis mentality" has led to a "bold solution" that, rather than actually solving the original problem, has in fact, made it worse.

The Behavior of the Systematic Check Forger*

Edwin M. Lemert

THE CONCEPT OF BEHAVIOR SYSTEMS IN crime was first approximated in this country in Hall's analysis of several types of larceny in terms of their historical, legal, and social contexts. (Hall, 1952) Later the concept was made explicit and formulated into a typology by Sutherland and by Sutherland and Cressey. (Sutherland, 1937; Sutherland and Cressey, 1955; Lindesmith and Dunham, 1941; Piubaraud, 1893; Gruhle and Wetzel, 1916; Bonger, 1916, pp. 579–589)

Although this has hitherto inspired only a few monographic studies, there seems to be a growing consensus that focusing attention on specific orders of crime or making behavior systems the unit of study holds considerable promise for criminological research. (Reckless, 1955)

Because this paper proposes to assess the usefulness of Sutherland's formulation of the behavior system in analyzing or understanding the behavior of the systematic check forger, the typology outlined in his study of the professional thief will be employed. The five elements of the behavior system of the thief are as follows: (1) stealing is made a regular business; (2) every act is carefully planned,

*© 1958 by The Society for the Study of Social Problems. Reprinted from *Social Problems,* 6, (Fall, 1958), pp. 141–149 by permission of the author and the publisher.

including the use of the "fix"; (3) technical skills are used, chiefly those of manipulating people; this differentiates the thief from other professional criminals; (4) the thief is migratory but uses a specific city as a headquarters; (5) the thief has criminal associations involving acquaintances, congeniality, sympathy, understandings, rules, codes of behavior, and a special language. (Sutherland, 1937; 1937B; Clinard, 1957, pp. 256–262; Reckless, 1955; Cavan, 1948, Ch. 5; Elliott, 1942, Ch. 4; Maurer, 1955; Von Hentig, 1943)

Altogether seventy-two persons currently serving sentences for check forgery and writing checks with insufficient funds were studied. Three additional check offenders were contacted and interviewed outside of prison. The sample included eight women and sixty-seven men, all of whom served time in California correctional institutions.

Thirty of the seventy-five check criminals could be classified as systematic in the sense that they (1) thought of themselves as check men; (2) had worked out or regularly employed a special technique of passing checks; (3) had more or less organized their lives around the exigencies or imperatives of living by means of fraudulent checks. The remaining forty-five cases represented a wide variety of contexts in which bogus check passing was interspersed with periods of stable employment and family life, or was simply an aspect of alcoholism, gambling, or one of a series of criminal offenses having little or no consistency.

Findings

Projected against the typology of professional theft, the behavior of the person falling into the systematic check forgery category qualified only in a very general way as professional crime. In other words, although it is possible to describe these forgeries as *systematic,* it is questionable whether more than a small portion of them can be subsumed as *professional* under the more general classification of professional theft. A point-by-point comparison will serve to bring out the numerous significant differences between systematic forgery and professional theft.

1. *Forgery as a "regular business."* It is questionable whether check men look upon their crimes as a "regular business" in the same way as do members of "other occupational groups" who "wish to make money in safety."

(Sutherland and Cressey, 1955, p. 240) In virtually all cases the motivation proved to be exceedingly complex. This fact was self-consciously recognized and expressed in different ways but all informants revealed an essential perplexity or conflict about their criminal behavior . . .

The conflicts expressed involved not merely the rightness or wrongness of behavior; they also disclosed a confusion and uncertainty as to the possibility of living successfully or safely by issuing false checks. All of the cases, even the few who had a history of professional thieving, admitted that arrest and imprisonment are inevitable. None knew of exceptions to this, although one case speculated that "It might be done by an otherwise respected businessman who made one big spread and then quit and retired . . ."

Many of the check men depicted their periods of check writing as continuous sprees during which they lived "fast" and luxuriously. Many spoke of experiencing considerable tension during these periods, and two cases developed stomach ulcers which caused them to "lay off at resorts . . ."

In general the picture of the cool, calculating professional with prosaic, matter-of-fact attitudes towards his crimes as a trade or occupation supported by rationalizations of a subculture was not valid for the cases in question.

2. *Planning as an aspect of forgery.* In regard to the second element of professional theft—planning—the behavior of check forgers is again divergent. Actually the present techniques of check passing either preclude precise planning or make it unnecessary. Although systematic check passers undeniably pay careful attention to such things as banking hours, the places at which checks are presented, and the kinds of "fronts" they employ, these considerations serve only as generalized guides for their crimes. Most informants held that situations have to be *exploited as they arise* with variation and flexibility being the key to success. What stands in the behavior of systematic check forgers is the rapid tempo—almost impulsiveness—with which they work . . .

3. *Technical skills.* Although the systematic check man relies upon technical skills—those of manipulating others—these are usually not of a high order, nor do they require a long learning period to master. From

the standpoint of the appearance of the check or the behavior involved at the time of its passing, there need, of course, be no great difference between passing a bad check and passing a good check. This is particularly true of personal checks, which are at least as favored as payroll checks by check men . . .

4. *Mobility.* Like the thief, the systematic forger is migratory. Only one check man interviewed spoke of identifying himself with one community, and even he was reluctant to call it a headquarters. Generally check men are migratory within regions.

5. *Associations.* The sharpest and most categorical difference between professional theft and systematic forgery lies in the realm of associations. In contrast to pickpockets, shoplifters, and con men, whose criminal techniques are implicitly cooperative, most check men with highly developed systems work alone, carefully avoiding contacts and interaction with other criminals. Moreover, their preference for solitude and their secretiveness gives every appearance of a highly generalized reaction; they avoid not only cooperative crime but also any other kinds of association with criminals. They are equally selective and cautious in their contacts and associations with the noncriminal population, preferring not to become involved in any enduring personal relationships.

A descriptive breakdown of the thirty check forgers classified as systematic bears out this point. Only four of the thirty had worked in check-passing gangs. Two of these had acted as "fences" who organized the operations. Both were close to seventy years old and had long prison records, one having been a receiver of stolen property, the other having worked as a forger. Both had turned to using gangs of passers because they were too well known to detectives either to pass checks themselves or to permit their handwriting to appear on the checks. The other two forgers who had worked in gangs were female drug addicts who had teamed up with other female addicts.[1]

Three other systematic check forgers did not work directly with other criminals but had criminal associations of a *contractual* nature. One old-time forger familiar with the now little-used methods for forging signatures and raising checks usually sold checks to passers but never had uttered (passed) any of his own forgeries. Two men were

passers who purchased either payroll checks from a "hot printer" or stolen checks from burglars. Apart from the minimal contacts necessary to sell or obtain a supply of checks, all three men were lone operators and very seclusive in their behavior.

Six of the thirty systematic forgers worked exclusively with one other person, usually a girl or "broad."[2] The check men seemed to agree that working with a girl was equivalent to working alone. These pairs ordinarily consisted of the check man and some girl not ordinarily of criminal background with whom he had struck up a living arrangement and for whom he felt genuine affection. The girl was used either to make out the checks or to pass them. In some cases she was simply used as a front to distract attention. Some men picked up girls in bars or hotels and employed them as fronts without their knowledge.

The remaining seventeen of the thirty systematic check forgers operated on a solitary basis. The majority of these argued that contact with others is unnecessary to obtain and pass a supply of checks. Most of them uttered personal checks. However, even where they made use of payroll or corporation checks they contrived to manufacture or obtain them without resorting to interaction with criminal associates or intermediaries. For example, one Nisei check man arranged with a printer to make up checks for a fraternal organization of which he represented himself as secretary-treasurer. Another man frequented business offices at noontime, and when the clerk left the office, helped himself to a supply of company checks, in one instance stealing a check-writing machine for his purposes.

It was difficult to find evidence of anything more than rudimentary congeniality, sympathy, understandings, and shared rules of behavior among the check forgers, including those who had worked in gangs. Rather the opposite seemed true, suspicion and distrust marking their relationships with one another. One organizer of a gang, for example, kept careful account of all the checks he issued to his passers and made them return torn off corners of checks in case they were in danger of arrest and had to get rid of them. Only two of the thirty forgers indicated that they had at times engaged in recreational activities with other criminals. Both of these men were lone wolves in their work. One other lone wolf stated that he had on occasion had dinner with another check man he happened to know well and that he had once or twice entered into a rivalry with him to see who could pass a check in the most difficult place.

The two men who had organized gangs of check passers worked with a set of rules, but they were largely improvised and laid down by the fence rather than voluntarily recognized and obeyed by the passers. The other check men with varying degrees of explicitness recognized rules for passing checks—rules learned almost entirely on an individual trial-and-error basis. The informants insisted that "you learn as you go" and that one of the rules was "never use another man's stunt . . ."

Interpretation

How can these findings be reconciled with the specific statement of Sutherland's informant. (Sutherland, 1937, p. 77)[3] that "laying paper" is a form of professional theft most often worked in mobs? The answer to this apparent contradiction requires that a distinction be made between forgery of *the nineteenth and early twentieth centuries and that of the present day*. In the past, forgery was a much more complex procedure in which a variety of false instruments such as bank notes, drafts, bills of exchange, letters of credit, registered bonds, and post office money orders as well as checks were manufactured or altered and foisted off. A knowledge of chemicals, papers, inks, engraving, etching, lithography, and penmanship as well as detailed knowledge of bank operations were prime requisites for success. The amounts of money sought were comparatively large, and often they had to be obtained through complex monetary transactions. (Adam, 1908) The technological characteristics of this kind of forgery made planning, timing, specialization, differentiation of roles, morale, and organization imperative. Capital was necessary for living expenses during the period when preparations for the forgeries were being made. (Pinkerton, 1905; Pinkerton, 1884, pp. 338–441; Dilnet, 1929) Intermediates between the skilled forger and the passers were necessary so that the latter could swear that the handwriting on the false negotiable instruments was not theirs and so that the forger himself was not exposed to arrest. A "shadow" was often used for protection against the passer's temptation to abscond with the money and in order to alert the others of trouble at the bank.[4] "Fall" money was accumulated and supplied to assist the passer when arrested. Inasmuch as forgery gangs worked

together for a considerable length of time, understandings, congeniality, and rules of behavior, especially with regard to the division of money, could and did develop. In short, professional forgery was based upon the technology of the period.

Although precise dating is difficult, the heyday of professional forgery in this country probably began after the Civil War and lasted through the 1920s. (Speare, 1927) It seems to have corresponded with the early phases of industrialization and commercial development before business and law-enforcement agencies developed methods and organization for preventing forgery and apprehending the offenders. Gradually, technological developments in inks, papers, protectographs, and check-writing machines made the forging of signatures and the manufacture of false negotiable instruments more difficult. According to one source, for example, raised drafts have been virtually nonexistent since 1905. (Speare, 1927) Similarly, at the present time raising of checks is quite rare. The establishment of a protective committee by the American Bankers Association in 1894, related merchants' protective agencies, and improvements in police methods have made the risks of organized professional forgery exceedingly great. (Pinkerton, 1905; Maurer, 1941) . . .

A factor of equal importance in explaining the decline of professional organized forgery has been the increasingly widespread use of business and payroll checks as well as personal checks. Whereas in the past the use of checks was confined to certain kinds of business transactions, mostly involving banks, today it is ubiquitous. Attitudes of business people and their clerical employees have undergone great change, and only the most perfunctory identification is necessary to cash many kinds of checks. Check men recognize this in frequent unsolicited comments that passing checks is "easy." Some argue that the form of the check is now relatively unimportant to passing it, that "you can pass a candy bar wrapper nowadays with the right front and story."[5] It is for this reason that the systematic check man does not have to resort to criminal associates or employ the more complex professional procedures used in decades past.

These facts may also account for the presence among lone-wolf check forgers of occasional persons with the identification, orientation, skills, codes, and argot of the thief. Case histories as well as the observations of informants show that older professional criminals in recent decades have turned to check passing because they face long sentences for additional crimes or sentencing under habitual criminal legislation. They regard checks as an "easy racket" because in many states conviction makes them subject to jail sentences rather than imprisonment. Check passing may be a last resort for the older criminal . . .

The Check Forger as an Isolate

The preference of many systematic check forgers for solitary lives and their avoidance of primary-group associations among criminals may also be explicable in terms of their educational characteristics and class origins. The history of forgery reveals that in medieval times it was considered to be the special crime of the clerical class, as indeed it had to be inasmuch as the members of this class monopolized writing skills. (Tout, 1919, pp. 5–31) It also seems to be true from the later history of the crime that it has held a special attraction for more highly educated persons, for those of higher socioeconomic status and those of "refined" or artistic tastes.[6] The basic method of organized forgery is stated to have been invented and perfected in England, not by criminals but by a practicing barrister of established reputation in 1840. (Rhodes, 1934; Dilnet, 1929) An early gang of forgers organized by a practicing physician is also described by Felstead. (Felstead, 1926) A number of studies directed to the differentiating characteristics of check criminals point to an "above-average" intelligence and formal education. This refers to the general population as well as to the criminal populations with which they have been compared. (Berg, 1944; Fox, 1946; Hooton, 1939, p. 87; Lawes, 1938, p. 40)

All of this is not to say that less-educated persons do not frequently pass bad checks but rather that the persons who persist in the behavior and develop behavior systems of forgery seem much more likely than other criminals to be drawn from a segment of the population distinguished by a higher socioeconomic status. Generally this was true of the systematic forgers in this study. Eight of the thirty had completed two or more years of college. Fourteen of the thirty had fathers who were or had been in the professions and business, including a juvenile court judge, a minister, a postmaster of a large city, and three very wealthy ranch owners. One woman came from a nationally famous family of farm implement manufacturers. Four others had siblings well established in business and the professions, one of whom was an attorney general in another state. Two of the men had been successful businessmen themselves before becoming check men.

The most important implication of these data is that systematic check forgers do not seem to have had criminal antecedents or early criminal associations. (Lemert, 1953; 1956) For this reason, as well as for technical reasons, they are not likely to seek out or to be comfortable in informal associations with other criminals who have been products of early and lengthy socialization and learning in a criminal subculture. It also follows that their morality and values remain essentially "middle" or "upper" class and that they seldom integrate these with the morality of the professional criminal. This is reflected in self-attitudes in which many refer to themselves as "black sheep" or as a kind of Dr. Jekyll–Mr. Hyde person. Further support for this interpretation comes from their status in prison where, according to observations of themselves and others, they are marginal so far as participation in the primary groups of the prison is concerned.

Conclusion

The cases and data presented suggest that present-day check forgery exists in systematic form but does not appear to be a professional behavior system acquired or maintained through associations with other criminals. The technical demands of contemporary check forgery preclude efficient operation on an organized, cooperative basis. In addition to these factors the class characteristics and backgrounds of systematic forgers incline them to avoid intimate association with other criminals.

NOTES

1. One may question whether they were systematic check forgers in a true sense; other informants state that "such people are not real check men; they are just supporting a habit." Their self-definitions and the organization of their lives centers around drug addiction rather than forgery.

2. One of the "pair" workers consisted of two homosexual females. The other non-man-woman pair was made up of two brothers, both of whom had substantial prison records. They worked up and down the West Coast, alternating in making out checks and playing the part of passer.

3. Maurer refers to check forgery as a branch of the "grift," and also speaks of professional forgers without, however, defining the term. Yet he recognizes that check forgers are usually lone wolves. (Maurer, 1941)

4. Pinkerton enumerates the following roles of the forgery gang: (1) backer, (2) forger, (3) middleman, (4) presenter, (5) shadow; Maurer (Maurer, 1941) without specifying the historical period to which his description applies, distinguishes the following as check forger roles: (1) connection, (2) fence, (3) passer. (Pinkerton, 1905)

5. Detectives in Santa Monica, California showed the writer a collection of checks successfully passed with such signatures as: "I. M. A. Fool," "U. R. Stuck," and others not printable. For a discussion of the crudeness of bogus checks accepted by business people see (Sternitzky, 1955).

6. This is the thesis of Rhodes (1934); two of the four participants in the famous Bank of England forgery in 1873 were college educated, one being a Harvard graduate. See Dilnet (1929); forgers coming from "good" families are described by Adam (1908); fourteen of the nineteen persons tried for forgery at Newgate Prison in England during the later eighteenth and early nineteenth centuries were what can be termed "middle" and "upper" class, including three army or navy officers (one who commanded the royal yacht of Queen Caroline, consort of George IV), one banker, one physician Cambridge graduate, one prosecuting attorney, two engravers (one by appointment to George III), three "gentlemen" of good connections; and three bank clerks. Two of the three men who had "poor parents" had married women of "good means." Tegg (1841) and Bonger (1916, pp. 429, 430, 437) give data from France and Italy which support this idea. A number of writers have commented on the fact that forgery has been quite common among the educated classes of India, particularly the "wily Brahmins." (Adam, 1908; Edwards, 1924, pp. 3–6, 16)

REFERENCES

Adam, H. L., *Oriental Crime*. London: T. Werner Laurie, 1908.

Berg, I., "A Comparative Study of Forgery," *Journal of Applied Psychology,* 28, June, 1944: 232–238.

Bonger, W. A., *Criminality and Economic Conditions*. Boston: Little, Brown, 1916.

Cavan, R. S., *Criminology*. New York: Crowell, 1948.

Clinard, M. B., *Sociology of Deviant Behavior*. New York: Rinehart, 1957.

Dilnet, G., *The Bank of England Forgery*. New York: Scribners, 1929.

———. *The Trial of Jim the Penman*. London: Geoffrey Bles, 1930.

Edwards, S. M., *Crime in India*. London: Oxford University Press, 1924.

Elliott, M., *Crime in Modern Society*. New York: Harper and Bros., 1942.

Felstead, T. S., in *Famous Criminals and Their Trials*. New York: Doran, 1926.

Fox, V., "Intelligence, Race and Age as Selective Factors in Crime," *Journal of Criminal Law and Criminology,* 37 July–August, 1946: 141–152.

Gruhle, H. W. and L. Wetzel, Eds. "Verbrechentype," in Bonger, W. A., *op. cit.,* p. 581.

Hall, Jerome, *Theft, Law and Society,* 2nd. Ed. Indianapolis: Bobbs-Merrill, 1952.

Hooton, E. A., *The American Criminal,* Vol. I. Cambridge: Harvard University, 1939.

Lawes, L., *Life and Death in Sing Sing*. New York: Sun Dial Press, 1938.

Lemert, E., "An Isolation and Closure Theory of Naive Check Forgery," *Journal of Criminal Law and Criminology,* 44: September–October, 1953, 296–307.

———. "Generality and Specificity in Criminal Behavior: Check Forgery Considered," paper read before American Sociological Society, September, 1956.

Lindesmith, A. R. and H. W. Dunham, "Some Principles of Criminal Typology," *Social Forces,* 19: March, 1941, 307–314.

Maurer, D. W., "The Argot of Check Forgery," *American Speech,* 16: December, 1941, 243–250.

Maurer, D. W., *Whiz Mob* (Gainesville, Florida: American Dialect Society, No. 24, 1955).

Pinkerton, W. A., "Forgery," paper read before Annual Convention of the International Association of Chiefs of Police, Washington D. C., 1905.

———. *Thirty Years a Detective*. New York: G. W. Carleton, 1884.

Puibaraud, L., *Les Malfaiteurs de Profession*. Paris: E. Flammarion, 1893.

Reckless, W. C., *The Crime Problem,* 2nd Ed. New York: Appleton Century, 1955.

Rhodes, H. T. F., in *The Craft of Forgery*. London: J. Murray, 1934.

Speare, J. W., *Protecting the Nation's Money*. Rochester: Todd Protectograph Co., 1927.

Sternitsky, J. L., *Forgery and Fictitious Checks.* Springfield: Charles C. Thomas, 1955.

Sutherland, E. H., *The Professional Thief.* Chicago: University of Chicago, 1937.

————. "The Professional Thief," *Journal of Criminal Law and Criminology,* 28: July–August, 1937, 161–163.

Sutherland, E. H. and D. Cressey, *Principles of Criminology,* 5th Ed. New York: Lippincott, 1955.

Tegg, T., *The Chronicles of Crime,* Vols. I, II. London: Camden Pelham, 1841.

Tout, T. F., *Medieval Forgers and Forgeries,* Bulletin of the John Rylands Library, 5, 3, 4, 1919.

Von Hentig, H., "The Pickpocket: Psychology, Tactics and Technique," *Journal of Criminal Law and Criminology,* 34: May–June, 1943, pp. 11–16.

Think Critically

1. Explain how Lemert's analysis of the systematic check forger differs substantially from the propositions put forth by Sutherland. What implications does this have for theorizing?

2. How might Lemert's description of the check forger relate to the financial criminals of today given technological changes that can facilitate such crimes? Give some examples.

Normal Crimes
Sociological Features of the Penal Code in a Public Defender Office*

David Sudnow**

TWO STANCES TOWARD THE UTILITY OF official classificatory schema for criminological research have been debated for years. One position, which might be termed that of the "revisionist" school, has it that the categories of the criminal law, e.g., "burglary," "petty theft," "homicide," etc., are not "homogeneous in respect to causation."[1] From an inspection of penal code descriptions of crimes, it is argued that the way persons seem to be assembled under the auspices of criminal law procedure is such as to produce classes of criminals who are, at least on theoretical grounds, as dissimilar in their social backgrounds and styles of activity as they are similar. The entries in the penal code, this school argues, require revision if sociological use is to be made of categories of crime and a classificatory scheme of etiological relevance is to be developed. Common attempts at such revision have included notions such as "*white collar* crime," and "*systematic* check forger," these conceptions constituting attempts to institute sociologically meaningful specifications which the operations of criminal law procedure and statutory legislation "fail" to achieve.

The other major perspective toward the sociologist's use of official categories and the criminal statistics compiled under their heading derives less from a concern with etiologically useful schema than from an interest in understanding the actual operations of the administrative legal system. Here, the categories of the criminal law are not regarded as useful or not, as objects to be either adopted, adapted, or ignored; rather, they are seen as constituting the basic conceptual equipment with which such people as judges, lawyers,

*© 1965 by the Society for the Study of Social Problems. Reprinted from *Social Problems,* 12, (Winter, 1965) pp. 255–76 by permission of the publisher.

**This investigation is based on field observations of a Public Defender Office in a metropolitan California community. The research was conducted while the author was associated with the Center for the Study of Law and Society, University of California, Berkeley. I am grateful to the Center for financial support. Erving Goffman, Sheldon Messinger, Harvey Sacks, and Emanual Schegloff contributed valuable suggestions and criticisms to an earlier draft.

policemen, and probation workers organize their everyday activities. The study of the actual use of official classification systems by actually employed administrative personnel regards the penal code as data, to be preserved intact; its use, both in organizing the work of legal representation, accusation, adjudication, and prognostication, and in compiling tallies of legal occurrences, is to be examined as one would examine any social activity. By sociologically regarding, rather than criticizing, rates of statistics and the categories employed to assemble them, one learns, it is promised, about the "rate producing agencies" and the assembling process.[2]

While the former perspective, the "revisionist" position, has yielded several fruitful products, the latter stance (commonly identified with what is rather loosely known as the "labeling" perspective), has been on the whole more promissory than productive, more programmatic than empirical. The present report will examine the operations of a Public Defender system in an effort to assess the warrant for the continued theoretical and empirical development of the position argued by Kitsuse and Cicourel. It will address the question: what of import for the sociological analysis of legal administration can be learned by describing the actual way the penal code is employed in the daily activities of legal representation? . . .

Guilty Pleas, Inclusion, and Normal Crimes

It is a commonly noted fact about the criminal court system generally, that the greatest proportion of cases are "settled" by a guilty plea.[3] In the county from which the following material is drawn, over 80 percent of all cases "never go to trial." To describe the method of obtaining a guilty plea disposition, essential for the discussion to follow, I must distinguish between what shall be termed "necessarily-included-lesser-offenses" and "situationally-included-lesser-offenses." Of two offenses designated in the penal code, the lesser is considered to be that for which the length of required incarceration is the shorter period of time . . .

I shall call *lesser* offenses that are not necessarily but "only" *actually* included, "situationally-included-lesser-offenses." By statutory definition, necessarily-included-offenses are "actually" included. By actual here, I refer to the "way it occurs" as irrelevant. With situational inclusion, the "way it occurs" is definitive. In the former case, no particular course of action is referred to. In the latter, the scene and progress of the criminal activity would be analyzed . . .

If a murder occurs, the defendant cannot be charged and/or convicted of both "homicide" and "intent to commit a murder," the latter of which is necessarily included in first degree murder. If, however, a defendant "intends to commit a homicide" against one person and commits a "homicide" against another, both offenses may be properly charged. While it is an extremely complex question as to the scope and definition of "in the course of," in most instances the rule is easily applied . . .

Complaint alterations are made when a defendant agrees to plead guilty to an offense and thereby avoid a trial. The alteration occurs in the context of a "deal" consisting of an offer from the district attorney to alter the original charge in such a fashion that a lighter sentence will be incurred with a guilty plea than would be the case if the defendant were sentenced on the original charge. In return for this manipulation, the defendant agrees to plead guilty. The arrangement is proposed in the following format: "If you plead guilty to this new lesser offense, you will get less time in prison than if you plead not guilty to the original, greater charge and lose the trial." The decision must then be made whether or not the chances of obtaining complete acquittal at trial are great enough to warrant the risk of a loss and higher sentence if found guilty on the original charge. As we shall see below, it is a major job of the public defender, who mediates between the district attorney and the defendant, to convince his "client" that the chances of acquittal are too slight to warrant this risk.

If a man is charged with "drunkenness" and the public defender and public prosecutor (hereafter P.D. and D.A.) prefer not to have a trial, they seek to have the defendant agree to plead guilty. While it is occasionally possible, particularly with first offenders, for the P.D. to convince the defendant to plead guilty to the originally charged offense, most often it is felt that some "exchange" or "consideration" should be offered, i.e., a lesser offense charged . . .

If a man is charged with "molesting a minor," there are not any necessarily included lesser offenses with which to charge him. Yet an alternative charge—"loitering around a schoolyard"—is often used as a reduction. As above, and central to our analysis the question is: What would the defendant's behavior be such that "loitering around a schoolyard" would constitute an appropriate alternative? . . .

Offenses are regularly reduced to other offenses, the latter of which are not necessarily or situationally included in the former. As I have already said, the determination of whether or not offense X was situationally included in Y involves an analysis of the course of action that constitutes the criminal behavior. I must now turn to examine this mode of behavioral analysis.

When encountering a defendant who is charged with "assault with a deadly weapon," the P.D. asks: "What can this offense be reduced to so as to arrange for a guilty plea?" As the reduction is only to be proposed by the P.D. and accepted or not by the D.A., his question becomes "what reduction will be allowable?" (As shall be seen below, the P.D. and D.A. have institutionalized a common orientation to allowable reductions.) The method of reduction involves, as a general feature, the fact that the particular case in question is scrutinized to decide its membership in a class of similar cases. But *the penal code does not provide the reference for deciding the correspondence between the instant event and the general case; that is, it does not define the classes of offense types.* To decide, for purposes of finding a suitable reduction, if the instant case involves a "burglary," reference is not made to the statutory definition of "burglary." To decide what the situationally included offenses are in the instant case, the instant case is not analyzed as a *statutorily* referable course of action; rather, reference is made to a *non-statutorily* conceived class "burglary" and offenses that are typically situationally included in it, taken as a class of behavioral events. Stated again: in searching an instant case to decide what to *reduce it to,* there is no analysis of the statutorily referable elements of the instant case; instead, its membership in a class of events, the features of which cannot be described by the penal code, must be decided. An example will be useful. If a defendant is charged with burglary and the P.D. is concerned to propose a reduction to a lesser offense, he might search the elements of the burglary at hand to decide what other offenses were committed. The other offenses he might "discover" would be of two sorts: those necessarily and those situationally included. In attempting to decide those other offenses situationally included in the instant event, the instant event might be analyzed as a statutorily referable course of action. Or, as is the case with the P.D., the instant case might be analyzed to decide if it is a "burglary" in common with other "burglaries" conceived of in terms other than those provided by the statute.

Burglaries are routinely reduced to petty theft. If we were to analyze the way burglaries typically occur, petty theft is neither situationally or necessarily included; when a burglary is committed, money or other goods are seldom illegally removed from some person's body. If we therefore analyzed burglaries, employing the penal code as our reference, and then searched the P.D.'s records to see how burglaries are reduced in the guilty plea, we could not establish a rule that would describe the transformation between the burglary cases statutorily described and the reductions routinely made (i.e., to "petty theft"). The rule must be sought elsewhere, in the character of the non-statutorily defined class of "burglaries," which I shall term *normal burglaries.*

Normal Crimes

In the course of routinely encountering persons charged with "petty theft," "burglary," "assault with a deadly weapon," "rape," "possession of marijuana," etc., the P.D. gains knowledge of the typical manner in which offenses of given classes are committed, the social characteristics of the persons who regularly commit them, the features of the settings in which they occur, the types of victims often involved, and the like. He learns to speak knowledgeably of "burglars," "petty thieves," "drunks," "rapists," "narcos," etc., and to attribute to them personal biographies, modes of usual criminal activity, criminal histories, psychological characteristics, and social backgrounds. The following characterizations are illustrative:

> Most ADWs (assault with deadly weapon) start with fights over some girl.
>
> These sex fiends (child molestation cases) usually hang around parks or schoolyards. But we often get fathers charged with these crimes. Usually the old man is out of work and stays at home when the wife goes to work and he plays around with his little daughter or something. A lot of these cases start when there is some marital trouble and the woman gets mad.
>
> I don't know why most of them don't rob the big stores. They usually break into some cheap department store and steal some crummy item like a $9.95 record player, you know.
>
> Kids who start taking this stuff (narcotics) usually start out when some buddy gives them a cigarette and they smoke it for kicks. For some reason they always get caught in their cars, for speeding or something.

They can anticipate that point when persons are likely to get into trouble:

> Dope addicts do OK until they lose a job or something and get back on the streets and, you know, meet the old boys. Someone tells them where to get some and there they are.

> In the springtime, that's when we get all these sex crimes. You know, these kids play out in the schoolyard all day and these old men sit around and watch them jumping up and down. They get their ideas.

The P.D. learns that some kinds of offenders are likely to repeat the same offense while others are not repeat violators or, if they do commit crimes frequently, the crimes vary from occasion to occasion:

> You almost never see a check man get caught for anything but checks—only an occasional drunk charge.
>
> Burglars are usually multiple offenders, most times just burglaries or petty thefts.
>
> Petty thefts get started for almost anything—joy riding, drinking, all kinds of little things.
>
> These narcos are usually through after the second violation or so. After the first time some stop, but when they start on the heavy stuff, they've had it.

I shall call *normal crimes* those occurrences whose typical features, e.g., the ways they usually occur and the characteristics of persons who commit them (as well as the typical victims and typical scenes), are known and attended to by the P.D. For any of a series of offense types the P.D. can provide some form of proverbial characterization. For example, *burglary* is seen as involving regular violators, no weapons, low-priced items, little property damage, lower class establishments, largely Negro defendants, independent operators, and a non-professional orientation to the crime. *Child molesting* is seen as typically entailing middle-aged strangers or lower class, middle-aged fathers (few women), no actual physical penetration or severe tissue damage, mild fondling, petting, and stimulation, bad marriage circumstances, multiple offenders with the same offense repeatedly committed, a child complainant, via the mother, etc. *Narcotics* defendants are usually Negroes, not syndicated, persons who start by using small stuff, hostile with police officers, caught by some form of entrapment technique, etc. *Petty thefts* are about 50–50 Negro-white, unplanned offenses, generally committed on lower class persons and don't get much money, don't often employ weapons, don't make living from thievery, usually younger defendants with long juvenile assaultive records, etc. *Drunkenness* offenders are lower class white and Negro, get drunk on wine and beer, have long histories of repeated drunkenness, don't hold down jobs, are usually arrested on the streets, seldom violate other penal code sections, etc.

Some general features of the normal crime as a way of attending to a category of persons and events may be mentioned:

1. The focus, in these characterizations, is not on particular individuals, but offense types. If asked "What are burglars like?" or "How are burglaries usually committed?," the P.D. does not feel obliged to refer to particular burglars and burglaries as the material for his answer.

2. The features attributed to offenders and offenses are often not of import for the statutory conception. In burglary, it is "irrelevant" for the statutory determination whether or not much damage was done to the premises (except where, for example, explosives were employed and a new statute could be invoked). Whether a defendant breaks a window or not, destroys property within the house or not, etc., does not affect his statutory classification as a burglar. While for robbery the presence or absence of a weapon sets the degree, whether the weapon is a machine gun or pocket knife is "immaterial." Whether the residence or business establishment in a burglary is located in a higher-income area of the city is of no issue for the code requirements. And, generally, the defendant's race, class position, criminal history (in most offenses), personal attributes, and particular style of committing offenses are features specifically not definitive of crimes under the auspices of the penal code. For deciding "Is this a "burglary" case I have before me" however, the P.D.'s reference to this range of non-statutorily referable personal and social attributes, modes of operation, etc., is crucial for the arrangement of a guilty plea bargain.

3. The features attributed to offenders and offenses are, in their content, specific to the community in which the P.D. works. In other communities and historical periods the lists would presumably differ. Narcotics violators in certain areas, for example, are syndicated in dope rackets or engage in systematic robbery as professional criminals, features which are not commonly encountered (or, at least, evidence for which is not systematically sought) in this community. Burglary in some cities will more often occur at large industrial plants, banking establishments, warehouses, etc. The P.D. refers to the population of defendants in

the county as "our defendants" and qualifies his pro-totypical portrayals and knowledge of the typically operative social structures, "for our county." An older P.D., remembering the "old days," commented:

> We used to have a lot more rapes than we do now, and they used to be much more violent. Things are duller now in. . . .

4. Offenses whose normal features are readily attended to are those which are routinely encountered in the courtroom. This feature is related to the last point. For embezzlement, bank robbery, gambling, prostitution, murder, arson, and some other uncommon offenses, the P.D. cannot readily supply anecdotal and prover-bial characterizations. While there is some change in the frequencies of offense-type convictions over time, certain offenses are continually more common and others remain stably infrequent. The troubles created for the P.D. when offenses whose features are not readily known occur, and whose typicality is not easily constructed, will be discussed in some detail below.

5. Offenses are ecologically specified and attended to as normal or not according to the locales within which they are committed. The P.D. learns that burglaries usually occur in such and such areas of the city, petty thefts around this or that park, ADWs in these bars. Ecological patterns are seen as related to socioeco-nomic variables and these in turn to typical modes of criminal and non-criminal activities. Knowing where an offense took place is thus, for the P.D., knowledge of the likely persons involved, the kind of scene in which the offense occurred, and the pattern of activity characteristic of such a place:

> Almost all of our ADWs are in the same half a dozen bars. These places are Negro bars where laborers come after hanging around the union halls trying to get some work. Nobody has any money and they drink too much. Tempers are high and almost anything can start happening.

6. One further important feature can be noted at this point. . . . Knowledge of the properties of offense types of offenders, i.e, their normal, typical, or famil-iar attributes, constitutes the mark of any given attor-ney's competence. A major task in socializing the new P.D. deputy attorney consists in teaching him to rec-ognize these attributes and to come to do so naturally.

The achievement of competence as a P.D. is signalled by the gradual acquisition of professional command not simply of local penal code peculiarities and courtroom folklore, but, as importantly, of relevant features of the social structure and criminological wisdom. His grasp of that knowledge over the course of time is a key indication of his expertise . . .

Over the course of their interaction and repeated "bargaining" discussions, the P.D. and D.A. have developed a set of unstated recipes for reducing original charges to lesser offenses. These recipes are specifically appropriate for use in instances of normal crimes and in such instances alone. "Typical" burglaries are reduced to petty theft, "typical" ADWs to simple assault, "typical" child molesta-tion to loitering around a schoolyard, etc. The character of these recipes deserves attention . . .

Both P.D. and D.A. are concerned to obtain a guilty plea wherever possible and thereby avoid a trial. At the same time, each party is concerned that the defendant "receive his due." The reduc-tion of offense X to Y must be of such a character that the new sentence will depart from the anticipated sentence for the origi-nal charge to such a degree that the defendant is likely to plead guilty to the new charge and, at the same time, not so great that the defendant does not "get his due". . .

Having outlined the formal mechanics of the guilty plea disposition, I shall now turn to depict the routine of representation that the categories of crime, imbued with elaborate knowledge of the delinquent social structure, provide for. This will entail a brief examination of perti-nent organizational features of the P.D. system.

Public "Defense"

Recently, in many communities, the burden of secur-ing counsel has been taken from the defendant.[4] As the accused is, by law, entitled to the aid of counsel, and as his pocket book is often empty, numerous cities have felt obliged to establish a public defender system. There has been little resistance to this development by private attor-neys among whom it is widely felt that the less time they need spend in the criminal courts, where practice is least prestigious and lucrative, the better.[5]

Whatever the reasons for its development, we now find, in many urban places, a public defender occupying a place alongside judge and prosecutor as a regular court employee. In the county studied, the P.D. mans a daily station, like the public prosecutor, and "defends" all who come before him. He appears in court when court begins and his "clientele," composed without regard for his preferences, consists of that residual category of persons who cannot afford to bring their own spokesmen to court. In this county, the "residual" category approximates 65 percent of the total number of criminal cases. In a given year, the twelve attorneys who comprise the P.D. Office "represent" about 3,000 defendants in the municipal and superior courts of the county . . .

While the central focus of the private attorney's attention is his client, the courtroom and affairs of court constitute the locus of involvements for the P.D. The public defender and public prosecutor, each representatives of their respective offices, jointly handle the greatest bulk of the court's daily activity.

The P.D. office, rather than assign its attorneys to clients, employs the arrangement of stationing attorneys in different courts to "represent" all those who come before that station. As defendants are moved about from courtroom to courtroom throughout the course of their proceedings (both from municipal to superior courtrooms for felony cases, and from one municipal courtroom to another when there is a specialization of courts, e.g., jury, non-jury, arraignment, etc.), the P.D. sees defendants only at those places in their paths when they appear in the court he is manning. A given defendant may be "represented" by one P.D. at arraignment, another at preliminary hearing, a third at trial and a fourth when sentenced.

At the first interview with a client (initial interviews occur in the jail where attorneys go, *en masse,* to "pick up new defendants" in the afternoons), a file is prepared on the defendant. In each file is recorded the charge brought against the defendant and, among other things, his next court date. Each evening attorneys return new files to the central office where secretaries prepare court books for each courtroom that list the defendants due to appear in a given court on a given day. In the mornings, attorneys take the court books from the office and remove from the central file the files of those defendants due to appear in "their court" that day.

There is little communication between P.D. and client. After the first interview, the defendant's encounters with the P.D. are primarily in court. Only under special circumstances (to be discussed below) are there contacts between lawyers and defendants in the jail before and after appearances in court. The bulk of "preparation for court" (either trials or non-trial matters) occurs at the first interview.

The attorney on station, the "attending attorney," is thus a stranger to "his client," and vice versa. Over the course of his proceedings, a defendant will have several attorneys (in one instance a man was "represented" by eight P.D.s on a charge of simple assault). Defendants who come to court find a lawyer they don't know conducting their trials, entering their motions, making their pleas, and the rest . . .

P.D.s seldom talk about particular defendants among themselves. When they converse about trials, the facts of cases, etc., they do so not so much for briefing, e.g., "This is what I think you should do when you get him," but rather as small talk, as "What have you got going today?" The P.D. does not rely on the information about a case he receives from a previous attending attorney in order to know how to manage his "representation." Rather, the file is relied upon to furnish all the information essential for making an "appearance." These appearances range from morning calendar work (e.g., arraignments, motions, continuances, etc.) to trials on offenses from drunkenness to assault with a deadly weapon. In the course of a routine day, the P.D. will receive his batch of files in the morning and, seeing them for the first time that day, conduct numerous trials, preliminary hearings, calendar appearances, sentencing proceedings, etc. They do not study files overnight. Attorneys will often only look over a file a half hour or so before the jury trial begins.

The First Interview

. . . When a P.D. puts questions to the defendant, he is less concerned with recording nuances of the instant event (e.g., How many feet from the bar were you when the cops came in? Did you break into the back gate or the front door?), than with establishing its similarity with "events of this sort." That similarity is established, not by discovering statutorily relevant events of the present case, but by locating the event in a sociologically constructed class of "such cases." The first questions directed to the defendant are of the character that answers to them either confirm or throw into question the assumed typicality. First questions with ADWs are of the order: "How long had you been drinking before this all started?"; with child molestation cases: "How long were you hanging around before this began?"; with forgery cases: "Was this the second or third check you cashed in the same place?" . . .

For most cases that come before their courts, the P.D. and D.A. are able to employ reductions that are formulated for handling typical cases. While some burglaries, rapes, narcotics violations and petty thefts are instigated in strange ways and involve atypical facts, some manipulation in the way the initial charge is made can be used to set up a procedure to replace the simple charge-alteration form of reducing.

Recalcitrant Defendants

Most of the P.D.'s cases that "have to go to trial" are those where the P.D. is not able to sell the defendant on the "bargain." These are cases for which reductions are available, reductions that are constructed on the basis of the typicality of the offense and allowable by the D.A. These are normal crimes committed by "stubborn" defendants.

So-called "stubborn" defendants will be distinguished from a second class of offenders, those who commit *crimes which are atypical in their character (for this community, at this time, etc.) or who commit crimes which, while typical (recurrent for this community, this time, etc.), are committed atypically.* The manner in which the P.D. and D.A. must conduct the representation and prosecution of these defendants is radically different. To characterize the special problems the P.D. has with each class of defendants, it is first necessary to point out a general feature of the P.D.'s orientation to the work of the courts that has hitherto not been made explicit. This orientation will be merely sketched here.

As we noticed, the defendant's guilt is not attended to. That is to say, the presupposition of guilt, as a *presupposition,* does not say "You are guilty" with a pointing, accusatory finger, but, "You are guilty; you know it, I know it, so let's get down to the business of deciding what to do with you." When a defendant agrees to plead guilty, he is not *admitting* his guilt; when asked to plead guilty, he is not being asked, "Come on, admit it, you know you were *wrong,*" but rather, "Why don't you be sensible about this thing?" What is sought is not a *confession,* but reasonableness.

The presupposition of guilt as a way of attending to the treatment of defendants has its counterpart in the way the P.D. attends to the entire court process, prosecuting machinery, law enforcement techniques, and the community . . .

A Note on Special Cases

To conduct trials with "stubborn" defendants (so-called) is no special trouble. Here trials are viewed as a "waste of time." Murders, embezzlements, multiple rape cases (several defendants with one victim), large scale robberies, dope ring operations, those cases that arouse public attention and receive special notice in the papers—these are cases whose normal features are not constructed and for which, even were a guilty plea available, both parties feel uncomfortably obliged to bring issues of moral character into the courtroom. The privacy of the P.D.-D.A. conviction machinery through the use of the guilty plea can no longer be preserved. Only "normal defendants" are accorded this privacy. The pressure for a public hearing, in the sense of "bringing the public in to see and monitor the character of the proceedings," must be allowed to culminate in a full-blown jury trial. There is a general preference in the P.D. office to handle routine cases without a jury, if it must go to trial at all. In the special case the jury must be employed and with them a large audience of onlookers, newspapermen, and daily paper coverage must be tolerated . . .

Some Conclusions

An examination of the use of the penal code by actually practicing attorneys has revealed that categories of crime, rather than being "unsuited" to sociological analysis, are so employed as to make their analysis crucial to empirical understanding. What categories of crime are, i.e., who is assembled under this one or that, what constitutes the behaviors inspected for deciding such matters, what "etiologically significant" matters are incorporated within their scope, is not, the present findings indicate, to be decided on the basis of an *a priori* inspection of their formally available definitions. The sociologist who regards the category "theft" with penal code in hand and proposes necessary, "theoretically relevant" revisions, is constructing an imagined use of the penal code as the basis for his criticism. For in their actual use, categories of crime, as we have reiterated continuously above, are, at least for this legal establishment, the shorthand reference terms for that knowledge of the social structure and its criminal events upon which the task of practically organizing the work of "representation" is premised. That knowledge includes, embodied within what burglary, petty theft, narcotics violations, child molestation and the rest *actually stand for,* knowledge of modes of criminal activity, ecological characteristics of the community, patterns of daily slum life, psychological and social biographies of offenders, criminal histories and futures; in sum, practically tested criminological wisdom.

The operations of the public defender system, and it is clear that upon comparative analysis with other legal "firms" it would be somewhat distinctive in character, are routinely maintained via the proper use of categories of crime for everyday decision making . . .

NOTES

1. D. R. Cressey, "Criminological Research and the Definition of Crimes," *American Journal of Sociology,* Vol. 61 (No. 6), 1951, p. 548. See also, J. Hall, *Theft, Law and Society,* second edition, Indianapolis: Bobbs-Merrill, 1952; and E. Sutherland, *Principles of Criminology,* review, New York: Lippincott, 1947, p. 218. An extensive review of "typological developments" is available in D. C. Gibbons and D. L. Garrity, "Some Suggestions for the Development of Etiological and Treatment Theory in Criminology," *Social Forces,* Vol. 38 (No. 1) 1959.

2. The most thorough statement of this position, borrowing from the writings of Harold Garfinkel, can be found in the recent critical article by J. I. Kitsuse and A. V. Cicourel, "A Note on the Official Use of Statistics," *Social Problems,* Vol. 11, No. 2 (Fall, 1963) pp. 131–139.

3. See D. J. Newman, "Pleading Guilty for Considerations," 46 J. Crim. L. C. and P. S. Also, M. Schwartz, *Cases and Materials on Professional Responsibility and the Administration of Criminal Justice,* San Francisco: Matthew Bender and Co., 1961, esp. pp. 79–105.

4. For general histories of indigent defender systems in the United States, see The Association of the Bar of the City of New York, *Equal Justice for the Accused,* Garden City, New York: 1959; and E. A. Brownell, *Legal Aid in the United States,* Rochester, New York: The Lawyers Cooperative Publishing Company, 1951.

5. The experience of the Public Defender system is distinctly different in this regard from that of the Legal Aid Societies, which, I am told, have continually met very strong opposition to their establishment by local bar associations.

Think Critically

1. What does Sudnow mean by the term "normal crimes," and what specific criminal justice practices does he provide to support this idea?

2. From a more general sociological perspective, why is it important to distinguish between legal statutes and the way that the law is applied? That is, why is the distinction between the written law and the "law in action" important in revealing various social phenomena that might not be obvious to the casual observer? Give two examples to support your answer.

Computer Crime*

Stephen M. Rosoff, Henry N. Pontell, and Robert H. Tillman

IN THE LATE 19TH CENTURY, THE FRENCH social theorist Gabriel Tarde constructed his *law of insertion,* which noted how newer criminal modes are superimposed on older ones through imitative learning and technological innovation.[1] Thus, for example, the European highwayman of the 18th century prepared the way for the American stagecoach bandit of the 19th century. Likewise, the train robber of the 19th century was the progenitor of the 20th century truck hijacker. As the 21st century looms, Tarde's insight is being

*Excerpted from Chapter 12 ("Computer Crime") of *Profit Without Honor: White-Collar Crime and the Looting of America* (5th ed.). Upper Saddle River, NJ: Pearson Prentice Hall, 2010. pp. 533–88.

validated again—this time in ways Tarde himself scarcely could have imagined.

Today, the falsified ledger, long the traditional instrument of the embezzler, is being replaced by corrupted software programs. The classic weapons of the bank robber as well can now be drawn from a far more sophisticated arsenal containing such modern tools as automatic teller machines and electronic fund transfers. In short, white-collar crime has entered the computer age.

Computer crime has been defined broadly as "the destruction, theft, or unauthorized or illegal use, modification, or copying of information, programs, services, equipment, or communication networks."[2] Donn B. Parker, one of the country's leading computer crime researchers, offers a less formal definition of computer crime as any intentional act associated with computers where a victim suffers a loss and a perpetrator makes a gain.[3] Under these definitional guidelines, the following offenses all could be classified as computer crimes: (1) electronic embezzlement and financial theft; (2) computer hacking; (3) malicious sabotage, including the creation, installation, or dissemination of computer viruses; (4) utilization of computers and computer networks for purposes of espionage; (5) use of electronic devices and computer codes for making unauthorized long-distance telephone calls. Each of these offenses will be examined in this chapter; however, it would be instructive to consider first just how sizable this problem has become and how fast it has grown.

For obvious reasons, computer crime has a short history. Its most immediate precursor was probably the invention of the so-called "blue box" in the early 1960s. The blue box was an illegal electronic device capable of duplicating the multifrequency dialing system developed by AT&T. The telephone company had described its new direct-dialing technology in its technical journals, apparently confident that no one in the general public would ever read or at least understand such esoteric information. How wrong they were. "Ma Bell" became the first casualty of the first law of electronic crime: *If it can be done, someone will do it.* Motivated by a curious blend of mischievousness and greed, a cadre of young wizards tape-recorded piccolos and other high-pitched sounds, and thus created the blue box, which gave them unauthorized access to the entire Bell network. They called themselves "phone phreaks." One ingenious phreak even discovered that a giveaway whistle packaged in Cap'n Crunch cereal produced a perfect 2600-cycle tone that allowed him to place overseas telephone calls without paying charges.

Although occasional arrests were made, phone phreaking was more or less hidden from the public—both by the phreaks themselves who feared exposure *and* by the telephone company which feared an epidemic. But in 1971, a popular magazine "blew the whistle" (appropriately enough!) with the publication of an explosive article entitled "Secrets of the Little Blue Box."[4]

At about this same time, the fledgling computer industry had graduated from the self-contained mainframe to interactive linkage and primitive networks. Once again, the first law of electronic crime was activated, as computer buffs now could use terminals to explore powerful mainframes previously off-limits. A new term entered the public lexicon: hacker. In the 1970s, the early hackers began using school computers for a variety of misdeeds—most notably the alteration of grades. However, since few schools even had computers then, hacking was still a relatively minor nuisance.

However, by the end of the decade, modems (devices linking computers with telephones) and computerized bulletin board services (BBSs) appeared. By the early 1980s, the home PC (personal computer) had become increasingly common. To the hackers this was the missing ingredient—a high-tech skeleton key that could open a myriad of locked doors. For example, in 1985 twenty-three teenagers broke into a Chase Manhattan Bank computer by telephone, destroying accounting records and changing passwords. No money was stolen, but customers effectively were denied access to their own files.[5]

Predictably, the first generation of hackers, for all their mischief, were only setting the stage for far more insidious types of computer crime; for what may have begun as a questionable hobby shared by a network of adolescent misfits has been co-opted by a more malevolent class of white-collar criminal. Some individuals began employing the basic hacker methodology to break into systems, not as a vandalic prank or simply to do it, but to steal. "Computers have created opportunities for career criminals, an increasing number of whom are becoming computer literate."[6] An early (and ongoing) example involves the planting of an unauthorized program known as a Trojan Horse. A Trojan Horse program can transfer money automatically to an illegal account whenever a legal transaction is made.[7] To many skilled thieves and embezzlers, this was akin to striking the mother lode.

How common and how costly has computer crime become? It is believed to be the fastest-growing type of crime in America.[8] A 1986 survey asked respondents if they believed that their companies were being victimized by computer crime. Only 7 percent said yes.[9] A 1993 survey reported that *70 percent* of the more than 400 companies responding admitted to at least one security infringement in the previous twelve months; 24 percent put the loss per incident at more than $100,000.[10] The head of the organization which conducted the latter survey noted: "The problem is much more serious than expected."[11] Of the 150 large companies surveyed by Michigan State University in 1995, 148 said they had suffered from computer crime; 43 percent said they had been victimized 25 times or more.[12]

Moreover, computer crime is no longer just an American problem. It has been uncovered in both Canada[13] and Mexico[14], as well as Western European nations, such as the United Kingdom,[15] Sweden[16], The Netherlands[17], Germany[18], Switzerland[19] and Italy[20]. Viruses have been created in such distant places as Bulgaria and South Africa[21]. Hackers reportedly have proliferated in France and Israel,[22] India and Singapore,[23] and Russia (where they are called *chackers*).[24] Likewise, computer security has become a major concern in Japan[25], Hong Kong[26], Australia[27], and New Zealand.[28] In one especially malignant use of computer technology, an Argentine kidnapping ring illegally accessed financial records to determine how much ransom victims could pay.[29]

Regarding cost, estimates of annual losses due to computer crime range from $550 million (National Center for Computer Crime Data) to $15 billion (Inter-Pact computer security organization)[30] or even more. This remarkably wide range of estimates no doubt reflects the substantial variation which exists in defining what qualifies as computer crime. Thieves can steal anything from entire systems[31] to transportable laptop and notebook computers[32] to integrated circuits, semiconductors, or memory chips[33]—all of which can be resold for their illicit "street value." Is hardware theft computer crime? About 14 million federal tax returns are now filed electronically. In 1989, IRS agents arrested a Boston bookkeeper for electronically filing $325,000 worth of phony tax refund claims.[34] A 1993 report by the General Accounting Office warns the IRS of its potential vulnerability to a number of new electronic schemes.[35] Should this be classified as tax fraud or computer crime? The Internet offers sociopathic young malcontents an opportunity to download "The School Stopper's Textbook," which instructs students on how to blow up toilets and how to "break into your school at night and burn it down."[36] Is this criminal incitement or free speech? Dealers in child pornography utilize the Internet and computer bulletin board services to advertise materials and exchange information.[37] Pedophiles also use the Internet to "troll" for potential victims—usually adolescent boys.[38] This is obviously felonious conduct of the most offensive sort, but can it really be considered computer crime? Computer systems have assisted the daily operations of prostitution rings.[39] Illegal gambling records are now routinely computerized.[40] Organized crime uses computers in many of its operations, from bribery to hijacking[41], and illegal drug cartels employ computers to describe clients and distribution networks.[42] The computer has also become an indispensable tool for "laundering" drug money[43] and other organized crime revenues. Money laundering is now a $100 billion-a-year industry in the United States.[44] Should all those billions of dollars be considered part of the cost of computer crime?

The truth is that there is little consensus in these matters. In fact, some experts have adopted an "agnostic" position that the true cost is unknowable. To further complicate estimation, it has been suggested that by the year 2000 virtually *all* business crime will conform to what now is considered computer crime.[45]

Some varieties of telemarketing fraud described in Chapter 2 have already spread to the Internet. A state securities commissioner has warned: "Don't believe that just because it's on a computer, that it's true. Computers don't lie, but the people who put messages on computers lie."[46] In 1995, for example, a 15-year-old Utah boy was charged with bilking $10,000 out of Internet users by posting phony advertisements for computer parts.[47] Penny stock swindlers post messages on "investor's" bulletin boards about supposedly major developments at small companies. The object is to build interest in and increase the buying of the stock so that the price will shoot up. The people behind the fabricated messages then sell their shares at a hefty profit and leave other stockholders with near-worthless paper. This technique is known in penny stock parlance as "pump and dump." An Oklahoma con artist pumped and dumped to drive up the shares of Bagels and Buns, a publicly traded company with no assets, from 38 cents to $7.50 in just four months.[48]

Other crooks have masqueraded as financial advisers or licensed brokers on the Internet and solicited investments in fictitious mutual funds. One Michigan scam artist talked a New York investor into sending him $91,000 and cheated a Texas victim out of $10,000. Six months later, the Texan ruefully acknowledged his gullibility: "I was terribly embarrassed. I knew I'd been screwed."[49] Cyberspace is also stuffed with hundreds of more "exotic" investment scams—everything from wireless cable television to ostrich farming.[50]

Another gray area in estimating the losses from computer crime is software piracy. No one knows the actual cost of this offense, but a study conducted by the Software Publishers Association (SPA) claims that $7.4 billion worth of business application software was counterfeited in 1993—a figure nearly equal to the total legitimate revenues for the entire industry in that same year.[51] In addition to business applications, piracy also entails the illegal copying of software for personal use—known as "softlifting."[52] A Massachusetts bulletin board service, recently raided by the FBI, had subscribers from 36 states and 11 countries, who paid $99 a year to download illegally copied personal software.[53]

Foreign piracy of American software is an extremely costly problem. Some countries provide no copyright protection at all for software, and many that do have copyright laws choose not to enforce them.[54] Computer software is predominantly an American asset (American companies control about 80 percent of the world market); so other nations "tend to be slow to provide protection for goods they don't produce themselves."[55] In 1993, just seven countries—South Korea, Spain, France, Germany, Taiwan, Thailand, and Poland—reportedly cost American software companies more than $2 billion. In each of these countries, pirated American software was said to account for between 75 and 90 percent of the total software in use.[56] The former chairman of the International Trade Subcommittee of the U.S. Senate has stated that the elimination of piracy would significantly shrink the American trade deficit.[57] An overseas dealer, for example, was selling pirated copies of the popular *Lotus 1-2-3* spreadsheet software (which usually retails for around $200) for $1.50![58] To put it in perspective, this means that for every $100 in pirated Lotus sales generated by this dealer, MicroPro, the manufacturer of Lotus, lost nearly $15,000 in legitimate sales. Similarly, in China a pirated CD-ROM containing

70 popular software programs is available for just $100. The legitimate price is $10,000 in the United States, where millions of dollars were spent to develop it.[59]

When one considers as well the vast amount of undetected software piracy certain to exist, guessing the bottom line jolts the imagination. Indeed, based on their survey of 45,000 American households, McGraw-Hill Information Systems conservatively estimates that there is one pirated copy of software for every authorized copy.[60] The Software Publishers Association places the ratio at *seven to one.*[61]

A newer form of piracy involves Internet sites known as WAREZ. WAREZ sites are subterranean—though often "conspicuously subterranean"—Web sites which provide copyrighted programs for downloading. With a little bit of expertise and a couple of quick clicks of a mouse, one can download thousands of dollars worth of commercial software, copyrighted computer games, even the latest movies. Most computer games are available illegally on WAREZ sites before they're even available for public release. And, some recent movies, such as *Star Wars: The Phantom Menace* and *Austin Powers: The Spy Who Shagged Me,* were on the Internet before they were released to theaters.[62]

People who create WAREZ sites are known as "crackers" because they "crack" copy protection codes. Most of them are teenage boys, who trade WAREZ like baseball cards. They use a program called a machine code monitor, which allows them to read protected disks one byte at a time—an operation known as "boot tracing." At critical points in the sequence they insert new instructions and "liberate" the disk. Groups such as the Inner Circle, Addiction, and the Phrozen Crew pass gigabytes of pirated software through cyberspace. WAREZ groups have even created their own brazenly illegal, "in your face" Web sites.[63]

As with traditional sofware piracy, it is difficult to put a price tag on WAREZ piracy because no one can determine how many people are downloading illegal WAREZ and how many of them would otherwise buy legal versions. But the figure is certainly high and growing rapidly.

The ultimate cost of computer crime is further clouded because there is a huge "dark figure" of unreported cases. "Because of public humiliation, liability issues, and security inadequacies, many corporations do not report computer crime losses, especially large ones."[64] Businesses often hire so-called "cyber-posses," private security firms that monitor for intrusions and identify system flaws that gave unauthorized entry, instead of reporting hacker assaults to law enforcement authorities.[65] The reason for bypassing the law is that many victims believe they stand to lose more by revealing their vulnerabilities to customers and clients than from the crimes themselves.[66] The fear of "copycat" incidents also probably discourages the reporting of security breaches.[67] Furthermore, when it is information that is stolen, rather than money, the loss may be incalculable in terms of dollars. A survey of major corporations conducted by Computer Security Institute, released in 1996, found that only 17 percent of those suffering electronic intrusions notified authorities.[68]

Finally, the estimation of computer crime losses perhaps is most complicated by the clandestine nature of the crimes themselves. The most proficient electronic thieves are able to cover up all traces that a crime has been committed.[69] As the president of a major computer security consulting firm has noted: "We only read about the failed computer criminals. The really successful ones are never detected in the first place."[70]

However, even if the actual computer crime loss figure can only be guessed, no one questions that the losses are enormous. A survey by ComSec, an organization of computer security professionals, reports that 36 of 300 companies responding (12 percent) acknowledged losses of $100,000 or more in just the first three months of 1993, with another 42 (14 percent) losing between $10,000 and $100,000. For the preceding year, 69 percent of respondents admitted security problems, with 53 percent of those problems resulting in losses of at least $10,000.[71] Once more, the findings far exceeded the predictions of the startled investigators.

But survey data and raw numbers, however robust, are an undramatic way to tell a dramatic story. To understand the dimensions and the dangers of computer crime, we must examine the crimes themselves. So let us now consider in more detail the five categories of computer crime suggested earlier.

Embezzlement and Financial Theft

According to recent FBI statistics, the average armed bank robbery nets $3177.[72] The Data Processing Management Association reports that the average computer crime loss may be as high as $500,000.[73] This great disparity reveals that while there are physical limitations to the potential payoff available to the blue-collar robber—large amounts of money have weight and take up space—the white-collar thief who can access the appropriate computer can steal a fortune without moving anything heavier than some decimal points. As if to demonstrate this lack of physical limitations, millions of gallons of heating oil from Exxon's Bayview refinery were misappropriated by altering computer files.[74] A gang of rogue employees in a major railroad's computerized inventory center once "stole" 200 30-ton boxcars.[75] Without a doubt, the modern thief can steal more with a computer than with a gun.[76] In addition, bank robbers must face the prospect of getting shot at; not so the computer criminal. Dillinger never had it so good.

One of the most famous bank-related computer crimes, however, did involve the physical movement of hard cash. For three years, beginning in 1970, the chief teller at the Park Avenue branch of New York's Union Dime Savings Bank embezzled over $1.5 million from hundreds of accounts. Despite having no formal computer training, he was able to shift nonexistent money around from account to account, falsifying quarterly interest payments and satisfying visiting auditors with remarkable ease. So slick were his manipulations that, reportedly, he had difficulty explaining the intricacies of his crime to the bank's executives after his arrest.[77] He eventually served 15 months of a 20 month sentence. At last report, he was driving a taxicab in New Jersey. None of his pilfered funds has ever been recovered.

His eventual downfall happened almost by accident—as a by-product of an entirely different case. A routine police raid on a "bookie joint" revealed that he had been betting as much as $30,000 a day on sporting events. "If his indiscreet bookmakers had not kept his name in their files, he might well have kept up his embezzlement for quite a while longer than he did."[78]

It is interesting to note that the Union Dime Savings case serves as a perfect model of criminologist Donald Cressey's earlier research on the social psychology of embezzlement. According to Cressey, embezzlers typically go through a three-stage process. In stage one, they are faced with what they perceive to be an unshareable financial problem—that is, a need for money which they cannot share with spouses, relatives, or friends. A $30,000 a day gambling habit on an $11,000 a year salary[79] would certainly seem to qualify in this regard. In stage two, they recognize an opportunity to solve their problem secretly. This opportunity rests in the positions of trust which they hold. A position of chief teller, of course, would provide just such an opportunity. Finally, in stage three, they manage to avoid internalizing a criminal identity by rationalizing their acts as borrowing rather than stealing.[80] It is the curse of compulsive gamblers like the Union Dime teller to continue expecting a financial recovery, even as the debts keep mounting. As we shall see, such labored rationalization is a recurring theme among computer criminals.

Embezzlement is a traditional crime, but computers have done for it what the microwave did for popcorn. It is no coincidence that between 1983 and 1992—the pubescent years of the computer revolution—arrests for embezzlement rose 56 percent.[81] As one state official has observed: "All scams are old, it's merely the technology that's changing."[82] In 1991, someone, believed to be an employee, used the computer in the payroll department of a prestigious New York bank to steal $25 million without leaving a trace. As of this writing, the case remains unsolved—not because there are no suspects, but because there are too many. "[H]undreds of employees had access to the same data that appear to have made at least one of them very rich."[83] This case underscores the findings of numerous major studies which report that most computerized theft is committed by authorized users, trusted insiders, skilled employees.[84] "The easiest way into a computer is usually the front door."[85]

Hacking

In its original sense, the word "hacker," coined at MIT in the 1960s, simply connoted a computer virtuoso. "However, beginning in the 1970s, hackers also came to describe people who hungered to know off-limits details about big computer systems—and who were willing to use devious and even illegal means to satisfy this curiosity."[86] The pioneer hackers of the 1960s and 1970s probably exemplified sociologist Edwin Lemert's classic concept of primary deviance[87]—that is, their conduct would have been described by observers as norm-violating. Of course, computers were so new then, there may have been few clear norms to violate. If their intent was not to destroy private files, could they be considered vandals? If their intent was not to steal data, could they be considered thieves? Perhaps the least ambiguous way to characterize them was as trespassers.

On the other hand, there was likely little, if any, of Lemert's notion of secondary deviance[88]—that is, no deviant self-identity on the parts of the hackers themselves. Indeed, their mastery of skills that may have seemed more magic than science to the general public endowed them with a sense of intellectual elitism. "[A]mong these young computer outlaws was a sense of superiority to the bureaucrats whose systems they could so easily infiltrate."[89] As one author, commenting on the first generation of hackers, has observed: "[T]o be a computer hacker was to wear a badge of honor."[90]

Most hackers display what Jay "Buck" Bloombecker, director of the National Center for Computer Crime Data, terms a "playpen mentality."[91] They see breaking into a system as a goal, not a means to some larcenous end.

> Sipping cola and munching pizza, they work through the night, often alone, their computers linked to the outside world by modems. They share their successes with confidants whom they often know only through voice or electronic messages. Many are teenagers whose parents don't know a modem from a keyboard.[92]

At least two categories of "playpen" hackers have been identified: creative "showoffs," who break into data bases for fun, rather than profit; and "cookbook hackers," the most common category, defined as computer buffs who coast along the global Internet computer network without any specific target, twisting electronic door knobs to see what systems fly open.[93] The "recipes" used by the "cookbook" hackers generally are those that have been developed by the more knowledgeable "showoffs." Many of these recipes apparently are of gourmet quality. A security analyst for AT&T has estimated that less than 5 percent of intrusions into computer systems by outsiders are even detected, let alone traced.[94]

Hackers might be thought of as a deviant subculture. They ascribe to a set of norms, which apparently they take very seriously, but which often conflicts with the norms of the dominant society. They have their own peculiar code of ethics, known as the "cyberpunk imperatives."[95] For instance, they believe computerized data are public property and that passwords and other security features are only hurdles to be jumped in pursuit of these communal data.[96] A famous hacker known as The Knightmare has summed up this haughty creed: "Whatever one mind can hide, another can discover."[97] There is even an ultimate proscription: "Hackers will do just about anything to break into a computer except crashing a system. That's the only taboo."[98]

Another way of looking at young hackers is from the perspective of Sykes and Matza's well known "drift" theory of delinquency.[99] Hackers might be viewed in this manner as fundamentally conforming youths who drift into occasionally deviant behavior through the use of such "neutralizations" as the claim that they are only trying to expose lax security systems[100] or merely learn more about computers.[101] These may seem like lame rationalizations, but more than one young hacker has justified his misconduct on those very grounds.

Beyond the "playpen mentality," however, there is a dark side to hacking, personified by a very different species of "stunt hacker" whose motivations are undeniably malicious. One such individual revealed this dark side in an article he wrote under the ominous pen name Mr. X:

> I can turn off your electricity or phone, destroy your credit rating—even take money out of your bank account—without ever leaving the keyboard of my home computer. And you would never know I was the one ruining your life![102]

If one doubts the plausibility of Mr. X's frightening boast, consider that in 1985 seven New Jersey teenagers were arrested for stealing $30,000 worth of computer equipment, which they had billed to total strangers on "hacked" credit card numbers.[103] Hackers have also invaded credit files[104]—including those at TRW, the nation's largest credit information storage system.[105] In 1985, a Houston loan officer utilized the bank's credit-checking computer terminal to steal the records of a Fort Worth couple. He used that information to open twenty-one bogus accounts in their name and ran up bills of $50,000.[106] Anyone who has ever been victimized in this manner has experienced the living hell of the credit pariah. If one's credit rating is sabotaged, one can no longer apply for a mortgage or loans of any kind. Even renting an apartment may become impossible.[107] As one victim has lamented: "There's only one problem with having good credit. Someone may steal it."[108]

Viruses

Another reason for so much congressional anxiety is the threat of pernicious computer viruses—once a rare phenomenon, now, some claim, approaching epidemic proportions.[109] A virus is an instructional code lodged in a computer's disk operating system that is designed to copy itself over and over. A virus may have four different phases: (1) *dormancy,* in which the virus does not destroy files, thus establishing a false sense of trust and complacency on the user's part; (2) *propagation,* in which the virus begins to replicate; (3) *triggering,* in which the virus is launched by some occurrence, such as a particular date; (4) *damaging,* in which the virus carries out the actual harm intended by its author.[110]

A computer can be infected with a virus for months or even years without the user's knowledge.[111] When an infected computer comes in contact with an uninfected piece of software, the virus is transmitted. Computerized bulletin boards are major targets for infection.[112] Viruses can also be hidden on diskettes.[113] "In today's computer culture, in which everybody from video gamesters to businessmen trades computer disks like baseball cards, the potential for widespread contagion is enormous."[114]

Some viruses are relatively innocuous, such as the so-called Peace virus. Designed by a 23-year-old Arizona programmer, it showed up on the screens of thousands of Macintosh computers in 1987, flashed a single peace message, then erased itself and disappeared.[115] The Peace virus, like most American computer viruses, is derived from the first-generation Stoned virus, which announces its presence by printing the message "Your PC is now stoned," followed by a demand to legalize marijuana.[116]

Like Stoned, certain viruses might be described as playful:

> A rogue program that made the rounds of Ivy League schools featured a creature inspired by *Sesame Street* called the Cookie Monster. Students trying to do useful work would be interrupted by persistent messages saying: "I want a cookie." In one variation, the message would be repeated with greater and greater frequency until users typed the letters C-O-O-K-I-E on their terminal keyboards.[117]

Far less playful, however, is the Rock Video virus that entertains unsuspecting users with an animated image of Madonna—then erases all their files and displays the ignominious taunt, YOU'RE STUPID.[118]

Some viruses appear deceptively benign. In December, 1987, a seemingly harmless Christmas Tree virus, designed by a German student, was loosed on the worldwide IBM network. Instructions to type the word "Christmas" would flash on a terminal screen. Users who complied with this innocent-sounding request tripped a virus that ultimately infected 350,000 terminals in 130 countries. IBM had to shut down its entire electronic mail system for two days to contain the spread.[119] According to a 1993 survey of corporations conducted by the national Computer Security Association, viruses cost American businesses $2 billion a year.[120] A quarter of the attacks require more than five days to correct.[121]

Viruses are sometimes placed in so-called "logic bombs." In other words, the virus program contains delayed instructions to trigger at some future date or when certain pre-set conditions are met, such as a specific number of program executions.[122] An early example was the Jerusalem virus, so named because it was discovered at Hebrew University. This virus, which had the potential to cause a computer to lose all its files instantly, was set to go off on the 40th anniversary of the State of Israel. Fortunately, the virus was eradicated well before that date.[123] Additional examples are the Joshi virus, which instructed the user to type "Happy Birthday Joshi" and was set to activate on January 5, 1993, and the Casino virus, set to activate on January 15, April 15, and August 15, 1993. Casino is a particularly mischievous virus which challenges the user to a slot-machine game and damages files if the user loses.[124]

Newer "stealth" viruses are much more complex than the earlier generations just described, hiding inside the computer memory whenever an antivirus scanning program searches the hard drive.[125] One of the worst of this new breed is the Mutating Engine virus. Unleashed by a Bulgarian known as the Dark Avenger, Mutating Engine can change form every time it replicates.[126]

According to the U.S. Department of Energy, so-called "macro" viruses now pose a significant threat to computers. An early macro strain, Concept, became the world's number one virus in just six months: "Faster than any in history,"[127] according to the head of the National Computer Security Association. Concept does not destroy data—it repeatedly flashes an annoying numeral onscreen—but it is very expensive to eradicate. "Other strains overseas, notably one called Hot, are more sinister,

says William Orvis of CIAC [Computer Incident Advisory Capability]. 'How much do you want to bet that they'll come here?'"[128]

Macro viruses are actually "worms." They spread so fast because they can be transmitted through e-mail and because they infect documents, rather than programs. The Melissa virus has shut down thousands of e-mail servers. It is sent in the form of a Microsoft Word e-mail attachment. It copies itself, then sends out a list of Internet porn sites to the first 50 names in the victim's e-mail address book. The original virus has been traced to a posting in the Internet news group alt.sex. Melissa's victims include Merrill Lynch, Paine Webber, Intel, Compaq, Lockheed Martin, Indiana University, the state government of North Dakota, the U.S. Department of Energy, the daily show-business newspaper *Variety,* and even *Security* magazine.[129]

Espionage

While computer viruses generally receive substantial media attention, statistics reveal that the misuse of computers as tools for industrial, political, and international espionage may be a cause for greater concern. A major FBI sting operation in 1982, for instance, targeted more than twenty employees of the Hitachi and Mitsubishi corporations of Japan, who were suspected of stealing data from IBM.[130] Since then, industrial espionage by means of computer has exploded, increasing by a reported 260 percent between 1985 and 1993.[131]

In 1992, American companies suffered losses from computer-related industrial espionage exceeding $1 billion. It is estimated that more than 85 percent of these crimes were committed or aided by employees. Sometimes the motive is to settle a grudge. An NBC employee embarrassed *Today* show host Bryant Gumbel by breaking into confidential computer files and publicly releasing a nasty memo Gumbel had written about his jovial colleague, weatherman Willard Scott.[132] Sometimes the motive is simply to make some money.[133] For example, employees with access to equipment and passwords can download strategic data or client lists and sell them to unscrupulous competitors. Because of the number of company insiders with such access, as well as the number of mercenary outsiders capable of breaking through passwords and cracking data encryption, many computer networks have proven vulnerable to spying and data theft.[134]

Occasionally, industrial espionage and virus infection are melded into a single computer crime. Consider the plight of the head of a British technology company whose latest product was sabotaged with a software virus by a rival exhibitor during a 1993 trade show for potential customers. In an open letter to an industry journal, this embittered executive writes in a tone more suggestive of a street crime victim:

> There is a fair chance that whoever planted the virus is reading this . . . Whoever you are, I understand why your bosses told you to do it. Nevertheless, it was vandalism, you tried to wreck something which is very valuable to me, and I won't stand for it. I'm going to pursue this with the full weight of the law, and if I ever find out who you are, may God help you.[135]

Computers have also been used illegally to obtain confidential information "that can help or hinder political candidates at all levels of government."[136] A dramatic example of political espionage occurred in New York in 1992. The medical records of a Congressional candidate were hacked from a hospital computer by an unknown party and sent to a newspaper. Those records revealed that the candidate once had attempted suicide, and this information soon was published in a front-page story. The candidate won the election, despite the publicity regarding her medical history, but the personal aftermath of this electronic invasion of her privacy serves as a reminder of why this book is as much about victims as villains. "It caused me a lot of pain," she would later say, "Especially since my parents didn't know."[137]

Computer crime in the area of international espionage is more difficult to assess. The covert nature of spying makes it hard to determine the actual number of incidents.[138] Moreover, since by definition this brand of white-collar crime often involves material classified as secret by the government, details of certain cases probably have been concealed from public scrutiny. A few stories, however, have been reported by the media. An arrest warrant was issued in 1996 for a 22-year-old former Harvard student who allegedly used stolen university passwords to break into American military computers from his home in Argentina.[139] When a young Washington-area hacker was arrested for breaking into a Pentagon computer system, he demonstrated his proficiency to investigators by cracking an Air Force system as they looked on. It took him 15 seconds.[140]

The most widely chronicled computer espionage case is that of the so-called "Hanover Hackers" in 1989. A group of young West German men were arrested for selling American military data to the Soviet KGB in exchange for cash and cocaine. This spy ring consisted of five members of West Germany's notorious Chaos Computer Club, which had achieved European hacking stardom in 1987 by breaking into two NASA computers.[141] The most proficient member of the Hanover group, 24 year-old Markus Hess, had illegally accessed a computer at the Lawrence Berkeley Laboratory on the University of California campus at Berkeley and had used that computer as a launchpad to access U.S. military computers at sites such as the Pentagon, the White Sands Missile Range, and the Redstone Missile Base.[142]

International computer espionage in the United States appears to be taken more seriously than in Europe. Indeed, it has been called the single most important security issue of the 1990s.[143] This concern may have originated in the early 1980s, when the Reagan administration withdrew funding for an international research center in Vienna, because its computers were tied to other research centers in both the United States and the Soviet Union. A fear was expressed that this connection might have allowed the Russians to log in to American computers and scan for classified data.[144]

Under the Computer Fraud and Abuse Act of 1986, it is illegal to tamper with any computer system used by the federal government or by government contractors. The act empowers the FBI to investigate the damage, destruction, or alteration of any data stored in such systems.[145] A representative case occurred in 1990 when personal computers at NASA and the EPA were infected with the Scores virus—although the FBI ultimately turned this case over to local police because of difficulty in proving the suspect's intent to contaminate government computers.[146]

As equipment becomes increasingly sophisticated, the threat of computer espionage gets more serious. Compression technology has already reached a level where an ordinary digital audio tape (which can hold text as easily as music), purchased at Kmart for under $10, can hold about 10,000 books in digital form. With current encryption technology, the entire computerized files of the stealth bomber, for example, could be completely and imperceptibly hidden on an ordinary music cassette.[147] Science may never be able to answer the venerable conundrum about how many angels can fit on the head of a pin, but it may be on the verge of discovering just how many classified documents can fit on an 8-track cassette of Pearl Jam's greatest hits.

Phone Phreaking

As noted earlier in this chapter, phreaking is the oldest and most durable form of electronic crime. Among the first generation of phone phreaks, some achieved legendary status: Jerry Schneider, the shameless self-promoter who appeared on the *60 Minutes* television program in 1976 and used his telephone to raise the overdraw limit on Dan Rather's personal checking account from $500 to $10,000, as millions of viewers looked on—including a stunned Rather;[148] Joe the Whistler, blind since birth but possessing perfect musical pitch and an uncanny ability to call anywhere in the world by whistling into a receiver;[149] the six-member gang—dubbed the "Gay Phone Phreaks" by the tabloid press—who placed an untraceable $19,000 twelve-hour call to Indonesia;[150] and rising above them all was the king of the phreakers—Captain Crunch.

Captain Crunch (John Draper) took his "nom de phreak," of course, from the breakfast cereal with the direct-dialing whistle. At the time of the famous *Esquire* article,[151] Crunch was a 28-year-old walking encyclopedia of telephony. Despite three convictions, he has never considered himself a criminal and utilizes the same neutralization techniques as his hacker brethren, claiming he performs a valuable public service by exposing weaknesses in communication systems. Captain Crunch's early ambition was to phreak legally in the employ of the phone company. Reportedly, he was quite dismayed when AT&T hired his old friend Joe the Whistler, but not him.[152]

As a devoted member of the '60s counterculture, Captain Crunch's favorite activity was spying electronically on the government. While he was serving a 4-month prison sentence in 1977, "he tweaked the coil of an FM radio with a nail file to listen in on guards' [telephone] conversations."[153]

It is not difficult to find a perverse charm in the exploits of Captain Crunch—or those of his co-legends. Even the austere Donn Parker acknowledges personal affection for the Captain.[154] But the blend of social immaturity and grand egotism that gave the pioneer phone phreaks their "Robin Hood" images also gives them the potential to teach their extraordinary skills (intentionally or otherwise) to career criminals. Thus, Parker argues, despite their individual charms, Captain Crunch and his crew are "dangerous."[155]

Furthermore, there now exists a second generation of phone phreaks, more dangerous—and less charming—than the first. A 1993 survey by TAI (Telecommunications Advisors, Inc.) reveals that 70 percent of respondents report that they have been victims of telephone toll fraud.[156] TAI interprets this finding as an indication that toll fraud may be a greater risk than previously believed. As the report observes: "[I]n 1990, 70 percent of respondents probably did not even know what toll fraud was, but it is now a thriving underground business."[157]

A 1992 published interview with a young phone phreak reveals once more that the familiar litany of neutralization techniques continues to be recited by members of the hacker subculture. This phreak insists that fraudulent calls are of no consequence to multi-million dollar corporations[158] (denial of victim again). He further asserts that his actions express his anti-capitalist political beliefs. This latter claim seems to flirt with hypocrisy, since he admittedly is making a considerable profit from his crimes.

And how much money can an ambitious anti-capitalist make? A 1992 Congressional committee estimated that toll fraud costs $2.3 billion annually.[159] In 1993, the International Communications Association complained to the FCC that over a five-year period, 550 incidents of toll fraud had cost its members alone $73.5 million.[160] Long-distance carriers are reluctant to reveal how much they lose each year to computer fraud, but one expert has estimated that losses now approach $4 billion, which is of course passed on to consumers as a covert "fraud tax."[161] In 1994, an MCI employee was arrested and charged with stealing more than 100,000 calling card numbers that were used to make $50 million worth of long-distance calls. Fifty million dollars was roughly 9 percent of MCI's net profits for the entire year.[162]

The rapidly-growing cellular telephone industry has been hit particularly hard by illegally accessed calls; losses industrywide are now at $300 million a year and climbing.[163] The drawback to cellular phones is that they can be scanned easily using an inexpensive Radio Shack scanner.[164] The numbers can then be programmed into another cellular phone, making it a "clone" of the original phone.[165] Bills in the hundreds of thousands of dollars can be run up on unsuspecting victims.[166] Cordless telephones are also considered easy prey.[167]

In response to the issue of liability, American insurance firms and long-distance carriers now are providing coverage against toll fraud.[168] In 1992, for example, The Travelers Corporation offered $1 million in protection for $49,000 with a $100,000 deductible. At the lowest end, a $50,000 policy was available for $2500 with a $5,000 deductible.[169] These steep premiums exemplify some of the substantial indirect costs of phone phreaking.

Another cause for concern is the movement of phone phreaks into the area of industrial espionage. The proliferation of fax machines has created one of the easiest ways to steal corporate information. Computer criminals can now break into a phone line and produce a "shadow" version of the faxes received.[170] According to security experts, most corporations currently are vulnerable to data leaks resulting from telephone espionage.[171]

Finally, a common toll fraud scheme involves sidewalk "call-sell operators," who buy stolen outdialing access codes and use them to make or sell long-distance calls, often overseas. The charges for these calls, which can run into huge amounts of money, later show up on the victimized party's telephone bill.[172] Some of the stolen codes are purchased from "shoulder surfers"—persons who hang out at airports using their eyes and ears to steal access numbers from careless business travelers making long-distance calls.[173] Most of the access codes, however, are peddled by hackers who simply program their computers to "war dial"—that is, to dial "800" numbers randomly and rapidly.[174] They are able to call tens of thousands of "800" numbers in a single night and record all those answered by the "unique carrier tone of computers."[175] "Call-sell operators" then offer customers long-distance calls via the victim's phone system. These customers are often recent immigrants, too poor to afford telephones of their own, who wish to speak to relatives and friends in their native countries. In New York City, throngs of homesick foreigners reportedly line up in front of designated phone booths where well-dressed "call-sell operators" charge them $30 to talk for 10 minutes.[176]

Anti-fraud systems, such as voice-recognition spectographs, now are appearing on the market.[177] Similarly, unauthorized computer access can be obstructed through biometric technology, including retina scanners, hand print readers,[178] and DNA identification devices,[179] as

well as by the development of highly sophisticated "firewall" software that shields private information from hackers and thieves.[180] But computer criminals, as Gabriel Tarde might well have predicted, respond consistently to improved security technology with improved criminal technology,[181] and they will no doubt in time find a way to keep apace. This, in turn, will encourage still more advances in security and continue a never ending cycle of thrust and parry.

NOTES

1. Tarde, Gabriel. *The Laws of Imitation.* Gloucester, Massachusetts: Peter Smith, 1962. This book was published originally in 1903.

2. Perry, Robert L. *Computer Crime.* New York: Franklin Watts, 1986.

3. Parker, Donn B. *Fighting Computer Crime.* New York: Scribners, 1983.

4. Rosenbaum, Ron. "Secrets of the Little Blue Box." *Esquire* 76, October, 1979: 222–226.

5. Francis, Dorothy B. *Computer Crime.* New York: Dutton, 1987.

6. Parker, Donn B. "Computer Crimes, Viruses, and Other Criminoids." *Executive Speeches* 3, 1989: 15–19.

7. Perry, *op. cit.*

8. Meyer, Michael. "Stop! Cyberthief!" *Newsweek,* February 6, 1995: 36–38.

9. McEwen, J. Thomas. "The Growing Threat of Computer Crime." *Detective,* Summer 1990: 6–11.

10. *PC User.* "Security Survey Reveals Huge Financial Losses," April 21, 1993: p. 20. As testimony to how fast computer crime had grown, surveys conducted just five years earlier had reported the cost of most computer crimes to be less than $10,000 (Gilbert, Jerome. "Computer Crime: Detection and Prevention." *Property Management* 54, March/April 1989: 64–66).

11. *Ibid.*

12. Anthes, Gary H. "Security Plans Lag Computer Crime Rate." *Computerworld* 29, November 6, 1995: p. 20.

13. Wood, Chris. "Crime in the Computer Age," *Maclean's* 101, January 25, 1988: 28–30.

14. Sherizen, Sanford. "The Globalization of Computer Crime and Information Security." *Computer Security Journal* 8, 1992: 13–19.

15. Sykes, John. "Computer Crime: A Spanner in the Works." *Management Accounting* 70, 1992: p. 55. This article notes the exploits of England's "Mad Hacker." See also: Hearnden,

Keith. "Computer Crime: Multi-Million Pound Problem?" *Long Range Planning* 19, 1986: 18–26; and Evans, Paul. "Computer Fraud—The Situation, Detection and Training." *Computers & Security* 10, 1991: 325–327.

16. Saari, Juhani. "Computer Crime—Numbers Lie." *Computers & Security* 6, 1987: 111–117.

17. Norman, Adrian R. D. *Computer Insecurity*. London: Chapman and Hall, 1989.

18. Hafner, Katie and Markoff, John. *Cyberpunk*. New York: Touchstone, 1991.

19. Bird, Jane. "Hunting Down the Hackers." *Management Today,* July, 1994: 64–66.

20. Rockwell, Robin. "The Advent of Computer Related Crimes." *Secured Lender* 46, 1990: pp. 40, 42.

21. Sherizen, *op. cit.*

22. Major, Michael J. "Taking the Byte out of Crime: Computer Crime Statistics Vary as Much as the Types of Offenses Committed." *Midrange Systems* 6, 1993: 25–28.

23. Gold, Steve. "Two Hackers Get Six Months Jail in UK." *Newsbytes,* May 24, 1993: 1–2.

24. Sherizen, *op. cit.* See also: McHugh, David. "Hackers, Pirates Thrive in Russia's Tech Underworld." *USA Today.* June 1, 2000: p. 17A.

25. *Ibid.*

26. McGrath, Neal. "A Cleft in the Armour." *Asian Business* 31, 1995: p. 26.

27. Hooper, Narelle. "Tackling the Techno-Crimes." *Rydge's,* September, 1987: 112–119.

28. Ceramalus, Nobilangelo. "Software Security." *Management-Aukland* 41, 1994: 26–27.

29. Sherizen, *op. cit.*

30. Major, *op. cit.*

31. McLeod, Ken. "Combatting Computer Crime." *Information Age* 9, January, 1987: 32–35.

32. Daly, James. "Out to Get You." *Computerworld* 27, March 22, 1993: 77–79.

33. Bloombecker, J. J. "Computer Ethics: An Antidote to Despair." *Mid-Atlantic Journal of Business* 27, 1991: 33–34.

34. Flanagan, William G. and McMenamin, Brigid. "The Playground Bullies Are Learning How to Type." *Forbes* 150, December 21, 1992: 184–189.

35. Quindlen, Terry H. "IRS Computer Systems Are Catching More Fishy Tax Returns: GAO Praises Agency for Reeling in Electronic Cheaters But Urges Tighter Controls." *Government Computer News* 12, 1993: p. 67.

36. Diamond, Edwin and Bates, Stephen. "Law and Order Comes to Cyberspace." *Technology Review* 98, October, 1995: p. 29.

37. Torres, Vicki. "New Puzzle: High-Tech Pedophilia." *Los Angeles Times,* March 5, 1993: p. B3. Also: Snider, Mike. "On-Line Users Cheer Arrests for Child Porn." *USA Today,* September 15, 1995: p. 1D.

38. Wickham, Shawne K. "Crimes in Cyberspace Posing New Challenges for Law Enforcement." *New Hampshire News,* March 6, 1994: p. 1A. See also: *Bay Area Advertiser* (Clear Lake, Texas). "Cyberspace Porn Figures in Assault Case of Two Teens." December 6, 1995: 1–2. Villafranca, Armando. "Ex-Guard Jailed in Computer Porn Case." *Houston Chronicle.* December 6, 1995: pp. 25A, 33A. *aol.com.* "Disgrace Follows Child Porn Bust." November 7, 1998. Rather, Dan. "Cybercrime: Oh, What a Wicked Web We Weave." *Houston Chronicle.* January 28, 2001: p. 6C.

39. McEwen, *op. cit.*

40. McEwen, J. Thomas. "Computer Ethics." *National Institute of Justice Reports* (U.S. Department of Justice), January/February 1991: 8–11.

41. Chester, Jeffrey A. "The Mob Breaks into the Information Age." *Infosystems* 33, March, 1986: 40–44.

42. *Ibid.*

43. Moore, Richter H., Jr. "Wiseguys: Smarter Criminals and Smarter Crime in the 21st Century." *Futurist,* September/October 1994: 33–37.

44. Kerry, John. "Where Is the S&L Money?" *USA Today Magazine,* September, 1991: 20–21.

45. Major, *op. cit.*

46. Flaum, *op. cit.*

47. Anthes, Gary H. "Juvenile Charged with Internet Crimes." *Computerworld* 29, May 8, 1995: p. 12.

48. Spears, Gregory. "Cops and Robbers on the Net." *Kiplinger's Personal Finance Magazine,* February 1995: 56–59.

49. *Ibid.,* p. 56

50. *Consumers' Research.* "On-Line Investment Schemes: Fraud in Cyberspace." Vol. 77, August, 1994: 19–22.

51. *Houston Post.* " 'Pirates' Cheat Computer Software Industry out of Billions by Illegal Copying', Study Says," July 5, 1994: p. C9.

52. Simpson, Penny M., Banerjee, Debasish, and Simpson, Claude L. Jr. "Softlifting: A Model of Motivating Factors." *Business Ethics* 13, 1994: 431–438.

53. Marshall, Patrick G. "Software Piracy." *CQ Researcher,* May 21, 1993: 435–448.

54. Taft, Darryl K. "Software Piracy Rates Tied to Cultural Factors." *Computer Reseller News* 585, July 4, 1994d: pp. 69, 72.

55. *Ibid.,* p. 437. Copyright protection is one of the most complicated areas of international law. Some nations take a very territorial approach, usually providing protection only for

works first published in that country (Forscht, Karen A. and Pierson, Joan. "New Technologies and Future Trends in Computer Security." *Industrial Management & Data Systems* 94, 1994: 30–36).

56. *Ibid.*

57. *Ibid.*

58. Elmer-DeWitt, Phillip. "Invasion of the Data Snatchers." *Time* 132, September 26, 1988: 62–67.

59. *USA Today.* "Punishment for Pirates." February 6, 1995: p. 10A.

60. Francis, *op. cit.*

61. Marshall, *op. cit.*

62. Rosoff, Stephen M. "Who Carez About WAREZ?: The 'Other' Software Piracy." Paper presented to the Western Society of Criminology. Hawaii, May 2000. Presumably, the cracker subculture contains moles at game producers and within the technical side of the movie industry.

63. *Ibid.*

64. *Ibid.,* p. 25.

65. Zuckerman, M. J. "Businesses Bypass Law to Fend off Hackers." *USA Today,* June 6, 1996: p. 3A.

66. Parker, Donn. "Computer Crime." *Financial Executive* 2, December, 1986: 31–33. Fields, Gary. "Reno Seeks Increased Cybercrime Reporting." *USA Today.* June 19, 2000: p. 3A.

67. Didio, Laura. "Security Deteriorates as LAN Usage Grows." *LAN Times* 7, 1993: 1–2.

68. Zuckerman, *op. cit.*

69. Roufaiel, Nazik S. "White-Collar Computer Crimes: A Threat to Auditors and Organization." *Managerial Auditing* 9, 1994: 3–12.

70. Quoted in Schuyten, Peter J. "Computers and Criminals." *New York Times,* September 27, 1979: p. D2.

71. Didio, *op. cit.*

72. U.S. Department of Justice. "FBI Uniform Crime Reports 1991" in *Crime in the United States 1991,* 1992: p. 13.

73. Nawrocki, Jay. "There Are too Many Loopholes: Current Computer Crime Laws Require Clearer Definition." *Data Management* 25, 1987: 14–15.

74. Prasad, Jyoti N., Kathawala, Yunus, Bocker, Hans J., and Sprague, David. "The Global Problem of Computer Crimes and the Need for Security." *Industrial Management* 33, July/August 1991: 24–28.

75. Brandt, Allen. "Embezzler's Guide to the Computer." *Harvard Business Review* 53, 1975: 79–89.

76. For a detailed consideration of electronic bank robbery, see: Radigan, Joseph. "The Growing Problem of Electronic Theft." *United States Banker* 103, June, 1993: 37–38; Radigan, Joseph. "Info Highway Robbers Try Cracking

the Vault." *United States Banker* 105, May, 1995: 66–69; Sherizen, Sanford. "Criminologist Looks into Mind of High-Tech Thief." *Bank Systems & Equipment* 25, November, 1988: 80–81; Sherizen, Sanford. "Future Bank Crimes." *Bank Systems & Technology* 26, October, 1989: pp. 60, 62; Sherizen, Sanford. "Warning: Computer Crime Is Hazardous to Corporate Health." *Corporate Controller* 4, 1991: 21–24; Sobol, Michael I. "Computer Crime Trends: A Brief Guide for Banks." *Bank Administration* 63, June, 1987: p. 52.

77. Whiteside, Thomas. *Computer Capers: Tales of Electronic Thievery, Embezzlement, and Fraud.* New York: Thomas Y. Crowell, 1978.

78. *Ibid.*

79. Conklin, John E. *"Illegal But Not Criminal": Business Crime in America.* Englewood Cliffs, New Jersey: Prentice-Hall, 1977.

80. Cressey, Donald R. *Other People's Money: A Study in the Social Psychology of Embezzlement.* Belmont, California: Wadsworth, 1971.

81. Touby, Laurel. "In the Company of Thieves." *Journal of Business Strategy* 15, 1994: 24–35.

82. Quoted in Flaum, David. "Scams Remain the Same Except Cons Now Use Newest Toys in Thievery." *Memphis Commercial Appeal,* August 14, 1994: p. C3.

83. Violino, Bob. "Are Your Networks Secure?" *Information Week,* April 12, 1993: p. 30.

84. Alexander, Michael. "The Real Security Threat: The Enemy Within." *Datamation* 41, July 15, 1995: 30–33. See also: Alexander, Michael. "Computer Crime: Ugly Secret for Business" (Part I). *Computerworld* 24, March 12, 1990: pp. 1, 104; Ubois, Jeff. "Risky Business." *Midrange Systems* 8, July 14, 1995: 21–22; Stuller, Jay. "Computer Cops and Robbers." *Across the Board* 26, June, 1989: 13–19; Carter, Roy. "The Psychology of Computer Crime." *Accountancy* 101, April, 1988: 150–151; Clemons, Keith. "Computer Security: A Growing Concern." *Computerdata* 12, January, 1987: p. 7; Lewis, Mike. "Computer Crimes: Theft in Bits and Bytes." *Nations Business* 73, February, 1985: 57–58.

85. Cheswick, William R. and Bellovin, Steven M. "Secure Your Network: Keep the Riffraff Out." *Computer Reseller News* 609, December 12, 1994: p. 161.

86. Roush, Wade. "Hackers Taking a Byte out of Computer Crime." *Technology Review* 98, April, 1995: p. 34.

87. Lemert, Edwin M. *Human Deviance, Social Problems, and Social Control.* Englewood Cliffs, New Jersey: Prentice-Hall, 1967.

88. *Ibid.*

89. Roush, *op. cit.,* p. 34

90. Hafner and Markoff, *op. cit.,* p. 11

91. Quoted in Beyers, Becky. "Are You Vulnerable to Cybercrime: Hackers Tap in for Fun, Profit." *USA Today,* February 20, 1995: p. 3B.

92. Carr, O. Casey. "Their Call Is to Steal Over the Phone, So Beware of Hackers." *Seattle Times-Post Intelligence,* September 8, 1991: p. E1.

93. *Houston Post.* " 'Billy the Kid' Hacker Was not a Threat to Networks." February 17, 1995: p. 15.

94. *Ibid.*

95. Stephens, Gene. "Crime in Cyberspace." *Futurist* 29, September, 1995: p. 25.

96. McEwen, J. Thomas. "Computer Ethics." *National Institute of Justice Reports,* January/February 1991: 8–11.

97. Quoted in Cizmadia, Robert A. "Secrets of a Super Hacker" (Book Review). *Security Management* 38, September, 1994: p. 197.

98. *Ibid.,* p. 9

99. Sykes, Gresham M. and Matza, David. "Techniques of Neu-tralization: A Theory of Delinquency." *American Sociological Review* 22, 1957: 664–666.

100. Kabay, Mich. "Computer Hackers Are No Vigilantes." *Computing Canada* 18, 1992: p. 36. The claim of helping to expose lax security is not limited to juvenile hackers. Recently, a 41-year-old man, using a so-called "John the Ripper" Internet password-cracking tool, broke into com-puters at NASA's Sonny Carter Training Facility in Hous-ton. His lawyer argued that he had performed a service for his country by calling attention to security deficiencies. The prosecutor scoffed at this claim: "Patriots don't use 'John the Ripper' to hack into government computers." (Brewer, Steve. "Man Pleads No Contest to Computer Hacking." *Houston Chronicle.* October 9, 1999: p. 36A.)

101. Keefe, Patricia. "Portraits of Hackers as Young Adventurers Not Convincing." *Computerworld* 26, 1992: p. 33.

102. quoted in Francis, *op. cit.,* p. 35

103. *Ibid.*

104. Van Brussel, Carolyn. "Arrest of N.Y.C. Hackers Hailed as 'Breakthrough.' " *Computing Canada* 18, 1992: p. 1.

105. Benedetto, Richard. "Computer Crooks Spy on Our Credit." *USA Today,* July 22–24, 1984: p. 1A.

106. Boyd, Robert S. "In Cyberspace, Private Files Are Becoming an Open Book." *Houston Chronicle,* December 8, 1995: p. 3G.

107. Kirvan, Paul. "Is a Hacker Hovering in Your Horoscope?" *Communications News* 29, 1992: p. 48.

108. Shaw, Stephen J. "Credit Crime." *St. Petersburg Times,* August 23, 1992: p. 1D.

109. Powell, Douglas. "Mopping Up After Michelangelo." *Toronto Globe and Mail,* March 7, 1992: p. D8.

110. Greenberg, Ross M. "Know Thy Viral Enemy." *Byte,* June, 1989: 175–180.

111. Hancock, *op. cit.*

112. *Credit Union Management.* "Operations: A Viral Epidemic." Vol. 12, May, 1989: p. 28.

113. Hancock, Wayland. "Computer Viruses" (Part 2). *American Agent & Broker* 60, September, 1988: 14–18.

114. Elmer-DeWitt, Phillip. "Invasion of the Data Snatchers." *Time* 132, September 26, 1988: p. 63.

115. *Ibid.*

116. Powell, *op. cit.*

117. *Ibid.,* p. 66

118. *Ibid.*

119. Bloombecker, *op. cit.*

120. Daly, July 12, 1993, *op. cit.*

121. *Ibid.*

122. Adams, Tony. "Of Viruses and Logic Bombs" (Part I). *Australian Accountant* 58, May, 1988: 83–85.

123. Elmer-DeWitt, *op. cit.*

124. Daly, James. "Viruses Ringing in the New Year." *Computer-world* 27, 1992: p. 79.

125. Hyatt, Josh. "Computer Killers." *Boston Globe,* March 3, 1992: p. 35.

126. Powell, *op. cit.*

127. Kim, James. "Virus Strain New 'Hazard' to Computers." *USA Today,* March 1–3, 1996: p, 1A.

128. Quoted in *Ibid.,* p. 1A

129. Kornblum, Janet. "Widespread Melissa Virus Snarls E-Mail Servers." *USA Today.* March 30, 1999: p. 1B.

130. Parker, 1983, *op. cit.*

131. Lee, Moon. "The Rise of the Company Spy." *Christian Sci-ence Monitor,* January 12, 1993: p. 7.

132. Lopez, Ed. "Can Your Computer Keep Secrets?" *Miami Her-ald,* March 13, 1989: Business Section, p. 1.

133. Rothfeder, Jeffrey. "Holes in the Net." *Corporate Computing* 2, 1993: 114–118.

134. Violino, *op. cit.*

135. "Jules." "On the Use of Weapons." *EXE* 10, 1993: 52–53.

136. Forcht and Pierson, *op. cit.,* p. 32

137. Hasson, Judi. "Access to Medical Files Reform Issue." *USA Today,* July 27, 1993: 1A–2A. In 1995, legislation was introduced in the United States Senate aimed at protecting the privacy of patients' health records. The senator who sponsored the bill argued: "Doctors and nurses and phar-macists may know things about us we don't even tell our spouses or friends" (Quoted in Boyd, *op. cit.,* p. 3G).

138. Lee, *op. cit.*

139. Rosenberg, Carol. "Argentine Unmasked as Computer Hacker." *Houston Chronicle,* March 30, 1996: p. 8A.

140. Roush, *op. cit.*

141. Hafner and Markoff, *op. cit.*

142. Stoll, Clifford. *The Cuckoo's Egg.* New York: Doubleday, 1989.

143. *Ibid.*

144. Hafner and Markoff, *op. cit.*

145. Belts, Mitch. "Recovering From Hacker Invasion." *Computerworld* 27, 1993: p. 45.

146. *Houston Post.* "Dallas Police Investigate Suspect in Spreading of Computer Virus." December 29, 1990: p. 19.

147. Kelly, Kevin. "Cyberpunks, E-Money, and the Technologies of Disconnection." *Whole Earth Review,* Summer 1993: 40–59.

148. Bloombecker, *op. cit.*

149. Parker, 1983, *op. cit.*

150. *Ibid.*

151. Rosenbaum, *op. cit.*

152. Parker, 1983, *op. cit.*

153. *Ibid.*

154. *Ibid.*

155. *Ibid.*, p. 180

156. Daly, James. "Toll Fraud Growing." *Computerworld* 27, 1993: 47–48.

157. *Ibid.*, p. 47.

158. Herman, Barbara. "Yacking with a Hack: Phone Phreaking for Fun, Profit, & Politics." *Teleconnect* 10, 1992: 60–62.

159. Quinn, Brian. "$2.3 Billion: That's About How Much Toll Fraud is Costing Us a Year (Maybe More)." *Teleconnect* 10, 1992: 47–49. See also Taff, Anita. "Users Call for Toll Fraud Laws to Distribute Losses." *Network World* 9, 1992: 27–28.

160. Dodd, Annabel. "When Going the Extra Mile Is Not Enough." *Network World* 10, 1993: 49–50.

161. Titch, Steven. "Get Real About Fraud." *Telephony* 227, October 17, 1994: p. 5.

162. *Ibid.*

163. McMenamin, Brigid. "Why Cybercrooks Love Cellular." *Forbes* 150, 1993: p. 189.

164. Panettieri, Joseph C. "Weak Links: For Corporate Spies, Low-Tech Communications Are Easy Marks." *Information Week,* August 10, 1992: 26–29.

165. Flaum, *op. cit.*

166. Kapor, Mitchell. "A Little Perspective, Please." *Forbes* 15, June 21, 1993: p. 106,

167. *Ibid.*

168. Daly, James. "Get Thee Some Security." *Computerworld* 27, 1993: 31–32. See also Daly, James. "Out to Get You." *Computerworld* 27, 1993: 77–79.

169. Brown, Bob. "Insurer Adds Phone Fraud Protection." *NetworkWorld* 9, 1992: 1–2.

170. Panettieri, *op. cit.*

171. *Ibid.*

172. Urbois, Jeff. "Saving Your Company From Telephone Fraud." *MACweek* 6, 1992: p. 22.

173. Marvin, Mary Jo. "Swindles in the 1990s: Con Artists Are Thriving." *USA Today Magazine,* September 1994: 80–84.

174. Colby, Richard. "Anatomy of a Toll Fraud." *Portland Oregonian,* July 5, 1992: p. 1.

175. Jahnke, Art. "The Cops Come to Cyberspace." *Boston Magazine,* November 1990: p. 90.

176. *Ibid.*

177. Quinn, *op. cit.*

178. Falconer, *op. cit.*

179. Stephens, *op. cit.*

180. Cheswick, William R. and Bellovin, Steven M. *Firewalls and Internet Security: Repelling theWily Hacker.* Reading, MA: Addison-Wesley, 1994.

181. For example, criminologist Gene Stephens has warned that the development of virtual-reality technology portends fantastic new varieties of computer fraud: "In the future, a virtual-reality expert could create a hologram in the form of a respected stockbroker or real estate broker, then advise clients in cyberspace to buy certain stocks, bonds, or real estate. Unsuspecting victims acting on the advice might later find that they had enlarged the coffers of the virtual-reality expert, while buying worthless or nonexistent properties" (Stephens, *op. cit.*, p. 27).

Think Critically

1. Which general category of computer crime discussed by the authors do you find most important and/or interesting? Explain your reasoning, and provide specific examples.

2. Find two examples of computer crime on the Internet and relate them to the ideas presented in this reading. What aspects of the cases fit or do not fit with the descriptions and explanations of computer crime more generally?

ORGANIZED CRIME

ORGANIZED CRIME PRESENTS UNIQUE challenges to society in terms of practical issues of prevention and control, and to scholars in terms of appropriate definition and study. Depictions of organized crime have traditionally relied on various ethnic groups and families, where strong bonds of allegiance were essential to the success of illegal enterprises. Such characterizations are fading in modern times, and the sophistication of organized crime has increased, along with the types of crimes that may fall under the general rubric of "organized" crime. For example, many corporate and white-collar crimes are organized, and have networks of actors whose coordination is necessary for the commission of crimes. In other words, while there is a tendency to locate organized crime within specific ethnic groups with strong familial bonds (e.g., "the Sopranos syndrome"), organized crime today exists in numerous areas of society, and in many forms, which may or may not be tied to ethnicity or family structures. Most importantly perhaps, organized crime could not exist without the influence and cooperation of politicians and otherwise legitimate businesspersons and enterprises.

Donald Cressey's book, *Theft of the Nation,* provides a major sociological account of the phenomenon of organized crime as it existed in early- to-mid-twentieth-century America. The selection from this work, "From Mafia to Cosa Nostra," discusses the labeling of the "criminal fraternity" of Italian roots that had long been influential in the underworld of crime. Cressey points out that the vast majority of Italian-Americans have nothing to do with this underworld, and many immigrants came to America precisely to *escape* from Mafia despotism in the old country. He also discusses the role that power struggles have in organized crime groups, and how convenient it has been to scapegoat groups within society for social ills connected with organized crime, rather than to sociologically examine the structural roots of such problems which extend far past ethnic identity. He concludes that public demand for protection from Sicilian bandits, and for other services not provided by the legitimate government, created an illicit government which has then exploited and ruled the same public that created it. In other words, the American demand for illicit goods and services has created an illicit government where organized crime can flourish.

Peter Lupsha's article, "Individual Choice, Material Culture and Organized Crime," follows up Cressey's analysis and examines both the roots of organized crime and its place in American culture. Arguing that organized crime is "as American as McDonald's," Lupsha critically explores the ideas of ethnic succession and limited mobility, including Daniel Bell's classic formulation of the "queer ladder of mobility." He finds that these do not fully account for the place and persistence of organized crime, and argues instead that among other topics, those of "choice" as well as the role of distinct American values and attitudes need to be brought to bear on understanding the phenomenon.

From Mafia to Cosa Nostra

Donald R. Cressey

The extraordinary thing about organized crime is that America has tolerated it for so long.

President's Crime Commission

The threat which organized crime poses to traditional American economic and political freedoms can, interestingly enough, be determined by looking at Sicily as well as by looking at America. Because the Sicilian Mafia has been the subject of discussion and investigation, if not study, for almost a century, Americans can readily learn more about it than they can about the activities of organized criminals in their own country. While we are confident that American organized crime is not merely the Sicilian Mafia transplanted, the similarities between the two organizations are direct and too great to be ignored.

For at least a century, a pervasive organization of criminals called the Mafia has dominated almost all aspects of life—economic, political, religious, and social—in the western part of the island of Sicily. This organization also has been influential, but not dominating, in the remainder of Sicily and in southern Italy. In the early part of this century, thousands of Sicilians and southern Italians became American immigrants. The immigrants brought with them the customs of their homeland, and included in those customs are psychological attitudes toward a wide variety of social relationships. At the same time, the immigration established an obvious and direct route for further diffusion of the customs of Sicily to the United States. Because the American farm land had been more or less settled by the time the Sicilians and Italians arrived, they tended to settle in the large cities of the Eastern seaboard, where they lived together in neighborhoods. The fact that they lived together enabled them to retain for some time many of the customs of the old country, unlike, say, the Scandinavians who scattered through the upper Midwest. A certain "clannishness" contributed to the retention of the custom of "clannishness." Further, the custom of "clannishness" probably was accentuated by the move to a strange land.

In these early Sicilian and Italian neighborhoods, discussion of the workings of the Mafia and "The Black Hand" was commonplace. Violence was attributed to these organizations, and people feared the names. Men were shot on the streets but, out of fear, obvious witnesses refused to come forward. In Brooklyn, it became customary for housewives to say to each other, on the occasion of hearing the sounds of a murderer's pistol, "It is sad that someone's injured horse had to be destroyed." Fear was present, just as it had been in Italy and Sicily. No one can be sure that this fear was a product of the Old World Mafia, rather than merely the work of hoodlums who capitalized on the fear of the Mafia that existed back home.

During national Prohibition in the 1920s and early 1930s, the various bootlegging gangs across the nation were made up of immigrants and the descendants of immigrants from many countries. There were Irish gangs, Jewish gangs, Polish gangs, German gangs, Italian gangs, and many others. An organization known as "Unione Siciliana" was involved. Near the end of Prohibition, the basic framework of the current structure of American organized crime, to be described later, was established as the final product of a series of "gangland wars" in which an alliance of Italians and Sicilians first conquered other groups and then fought each other. During these conflicts the Italian-Sicilian alliance was called "the Mafia," among other things. There is no sound information about whether this "Mafia" was a branch of the Sicilian Mafia.

The Italian-Sicilian apparatus set up as a result of a 1930–1931 war between Italian and Sicilian criminals continues to dominate organized crime in America, and it is still called "the Mafia" in many quarters. The Federal Bureau of Narcotics has called it "Mafia" since the early 1930s, but the Federal Bureau of Investigation has denied the existence of an organization going by that name. While the Kefauver Committee in 1950 concluded that "there is a nationwide crime syndicate known as the Mafia," the Director of the FBI as recently as 1962 stated that "no single individual or coalition of racketeers dominates organized crime across the nation." Now the Director uses "Cosa Nostra" to refer to the "criminal fraternity" which others call "the Mafia":

> La Cosa Nostra is a criminal fraternity whose membership is Italian either by birth or national origin, and it has been found to control major racket activities in many of our larger metropolitan areas, often working in concert with criminals representing other ethnic backgrounds. It operates on a nationwide basis, with international implications, and until recent years it carried on its activities with almost complete secrecy. It functions as a criminal cartel, adhering to its own body of "law" and "justice" and, in so doing, thwarts and usurps the authority of legally constituted judicial bodies.

We shall later discuss the various names given to the organization controlling organized crime. Whatever the "criminal fraternity" be called, there remains the question of whether it is the Mafia of Sicily and southern Italy transplanted to this country or whether it has arisen principally as the result of the response to a new cultural setting by hoodlum immigrants, some of whom happened to be Italian or Sicilian and thus knowledgeable about how to set up and control, by fear, an illicit organization. There are several reasons why this question is important.

First, it is a fact that almost all Italian and Sicilian immigrants, and their descendants, have been both fine and law-abiding citizens. They have unwittingly let criminals who are Italians or Sicilians, or Americans of Italian or Sicilian descent, be identified with them. Criminals of Italian or Sicilian descent are called "Italians" or "Sicilians," while bankers, lawyers, and professors of Italian or Sicilian descent are called "Americans." More Americans know the name "Luciano" than know the name "Fermi."

In early 1965 a group of New Yorkers formed an "American-Italian Anti-Defamation League," presumably to protect citizens of Italian descent from unwarranted attacks. From the beginning, however, it looked as though this association was designed to encourage respectable Italian-Americans to assist Italian-American criminals. A law suit brought by the Anti-Defamation League of B'nai B'rith caused the association to change its name first to "American-Italian Anti-Defamation Council," then to

"Americans of Italian Descent." In early 1968, the group decided to stress the constructive contributions of Italian-Americans, rather than to pursue its campaign of opposition to "ethnic slurs." However, Mrs. Mary Sansone, President of the Congress of Italian-American Organizations, was skeptical that the group's shift in official policy would help matters much. She said, "It's going to take them quite a while to clean up the mess of the group's first two years of existence."

Part of "the mess" arose because members of the association's Board of Directors made speeches on "How Italians Are Persecuted" and used the Organized Crime Report prepared by the President's Commission as an exhibit. The "mess" also arose in part from the selection, in 1966, of Frank Sinatra as National Chairman of the original group. This singer, actor, and entrepreneur was to help conduct "a campaign to discourage identification of gangsters in ethnic terms." Charles Grutzner, writing in *The New York Times,* pointed out that in 1963 the Nevada Gaming Control Board revoked Mr. Sinatra's license to operate a gambling casino because he had allowed a member of "the Mafia's national commission" to participate. This was Sam Giancana of Chicago. Mr. Grutzner also referred to a 1947 Havana meeting between Mr. Sinatra and Charles Luciano, whose organizational genius, and guns, helped create the current form of organized crime in America.

Ralph Salerno, an Italian-American, was formerly with the Criminal Investigation Bureau of the New York City Police Department, and in all his twenty years of police work he specialized in the detection of the affairs of the organization sometimes called the Mafia. In commenting on the American-Italian Anti-Defamation League and, more specifically, on the appointment of Sinatra, Mr. Salerno said:

> I think the Italio-American community has been following the ostrich principle of putting its head in the sand and hoping the problem will go away. These twenty million fine, decent people have failed to disassociate themselves from about 10,000 wrongdoers who enjoy a blending in with the 20 million, so that when anyone points a finger at the wrongdoers they are able to say, "You are unfairly maligning 20 million good Americans."

Because his police work led to the arrest and public exposure of many criminals with Italian names and Mafia or Cosa Nostra membership, Salerno was frequently and severely criticized by Italian-American criminals. He was rarely defended by respectable, law-abiding Italian-Americans. On one occasion the brother of a defendant in a murder case against whom Salerno was testifying came up to him in a court corridor and said, "Why does it have to be one of your own kind that hurts you?" Salerno responded,

> I'm not your kind and you're not my kind. My manners, morals and mores are not yours. The only thing we have in common is that we both spring from an Italian heritage and culture—and you are the traitor to that heritage and culture which I am proud to be part of.

If the American criminal organization, which is at once a criminal cartel and a confederation of criminals, is an importation from Sicily and Italy, it should be disowned by all Italian-Americans and Sicilian-Americans because it does not represent the real cultural contribution of Italy and Sicily to America. If it is an American innovation, the men of Italian and Sicilian descent who have positions in it should be disowned by the respectable Italian-American and Sicilian-American community on the ground that they are participating in an extremely undesirable aspect of American culture. This position was taken in 1963 by Paul P. Rao, Jr., the national President of the United Italian-American League, Inc. A few years later, Rao changed his position—apparently for personal reasons—and became a Director of the American-Italian Anti-Defamation League. But when the McClellan Committee received the usual complaints that its hearings were casting reflections on Americans of Italian ancestry, Mr. Rao, who was then New York City Tax Commissioner and a former Assistant District Attorney for New York County, came forward and said:

> We regret that there have been some who have irresponsibly accused the Justice Department and the U.S. Senate subcommittee of maintaining a political smear against the Italo-Americans. . . . They who consider an exposé of racketeers dealing in narcotics, illegal gambling, prostitution, and murder as being ethnically prejudicial are either arguing illogically or are selfishly being motivated by their desire for personal publicity. We should not peremptorily dismiss the functions of the committee with diversionary cries of persecution and thereby mislead the millions of decent Americans of Italian origin who sincerely feel a personal obligation over the recent revelations, because of the coincidence of racial identification. We welcome the efforts of the committee to eliminate gangsterism, especially when

involving individuals of Italian extraction. The public, however, fully realizes that other notorious names in the annals of the underworld clearly indicate that no ethnic group has a monopoly on crime. How can we eliminate criminal elements from our society if we are unenlightened as to their evil activities?

Second, many of the Sicilian and Italian peasants who emigrated to America did so precisely to escape Mafia despotism. During the early part of the current century, the Mafia dominated the economic, political, and social affairs of western Sicily, as it does today. Persons who defied the organization's leaders were injured, killed, or ruined financially. Some victims fled to the United States. These persons certainly did not bring the Mafia with them. Were they once more dominated? Are any of them, or their descendants, now members of an illicit crime syndicate?

Third, the Sicilian Mafia, like the American organization, was, and is, characterized by power struggles between individuals and factions. These struggles are most apparent when a top leadership position becomes vacant. Some of the losers in such struggles occurring in the early part of the century unquestionably fled to America. Further, in the late 1920s, Benito Mussolini, Fascist Premier of Italy, had the Mafia of southern Italy and Sicily hounded to the point where some of the members found it necessary to migrate, either to avoid official prosecution or to avoid "unofficial" liquidations and executions by the police. The number entering the United States, legally or illegally, is unknown. The rulers of the principal units of the American organization are now in their late sixties or early seventies. Many of them came to this country from Sicily or southern Italy early in the 1930s, and Burton B. Turkus, once an Assistant District Attorney in Brooklyn, has pointed out that the major business of one New York "Mafia" leader at the time "was in smuggling alien criminals who had been chased from Sicily and lower Italy." However, it might be a mere coincidence that the Italian-Sicilian domination of American illicit syndicates and the confederation integrating them began shortly after Mussolini's eradication campaign. The American "gangland war" and peace settlement which determined the present order of things also occurred in the early 1930s.

Fourth, if the American cartel and confederation is an importation from Italy and Sicily, and if it has retained its connections with the old country, then the strategy for eradicating it must be different from the strategy for eradicating a relatively new American organization. In other words, if "Cosa Nostra" is but a branch of the Sicilian-Italian Mafia, then its "home office" abroad must be eliminated before control will be effective. Some of the amateurs and independents now selling marijuana and LSD to American college students let it be known that their work is backed by a ruthless "Cosa Nostra" or "the syndicate." This myth gives power to persons having only a very slight relationship, if any, with Cosa Nostra. By the same token, some members of the American confederation propagate the legend that their organization is a branch of the old Sicilian Mafia. This legend also confers power on the persons who cultivate it. The legend helps perpetuate the notion that the current conspiracy is ancient and therefore quite impregnable.

Fifth, there is a tendency for members of any society or group to look outside itself for the cause whenever it finds itself confronted with a serious problem or, especially, with an evil. Any analysis of organized crime in America is affected, directly or indirectly, by this tendency. Even if all the evidence were to point to the conclusion that the American organization is merely a branch of a foreign organization, the person drawing the conclusion would in all probability be accused of "scapegoatism." As our discussion above indicated, even concluding that organized crime is dominated by Sicilians, Italians, and persons of Sicilian-Italian descent brings the accusation that the troubles of America are being tied to the back of an ethnic group, the scapegoat. Further, one who insists, as we did in Chapter I, that there *is* an organization of criminals in America risks being accused of assigning an assortment of evils and ills to a hidden, mysterious scapegoat. One who writes about organized crime risks being placed in the same category as flying-saucer fanatics and communist-conspiracy zealots, who know "they" are out there creating evils in our society even if we can't see them.

In some cases, "looking outside" means attributing problems to the characteristics of individuals rather than to the characteristics of the society or group itself. Our society tends, both popularly and scientifically, to view the criminal's behavior as a problem of individual maladjustment, not as a consequence of his participation in social systems. It is common to maintain, for example, that criminality is strictly an individual disorder which, therefore, can be treated in a clinic, just as anemia or syphilis can be treated in a clinic. An extreme position is that criminality actually is a biological disorder, treatable by modification of the physiology or anatomy of the individual through lobotomy, castration, interference with glandular functioning, or something else. The much more popular view is that criminality is an individual psychological disorder which may or may not have a strictly biological basis. The criminal may be considered as a person who is unable to canalize or sublimate his "primitive," antisocial impulses or tendencies; or he may be considered as expressing in criminal behavior some unconscious wish or urge created by an early traumatic emotional experience; or he may be considered as possessing some other kind of defective personality component. In any event, the implication is that crime and criminality are matters of the faults and defects of individuals, not of the society or group.

It is possible that attributing criminality to individual disorders is mere scapegoatism, permitting us to denounce the origins of crime without challenging any existing social conditions which we hold dear, and without assigning any blame to ourselves. James G. March and Herbert A. Simon have suggested, for example, that business managers tend to perceive conflict as if it were an individual matter, rather than an organizational matter, because perceiving it as an organizational problem would acknowledge a diversity of goals in the organization, thereby placing strain on the status and power systems. Similarly, in a family which has inadvertently but nevertheless inexorably produced a son's delinquency, it is convenient for the father to attribute the delinquency to "bad blood on the mother's side." For the same reason, the behavior of cold-blooded hired killers, and of the enforcers and rulers who order the killings, is likely to be accounted for solely in terms of the depravity or viciousness of the personnel involved, rather than in terms of organizational roles, including the roles of the victims. But during the last decade criminologists everywhere have been increasingly shifting to the position that criminality is "owned" by groups rather than by individuals and that, therefore, attributing it to individual disorders is either mistake of fact or scapegoatism.

In other cases, looking outside the society or group for the cause of an evil means looking to another society or group and heaping our sins on it. As Gus Tyler has said, "When such a scapegoat can be found, the culture is not only relieved of sin but can indulge itself in an orgy of righteous indignation." Recent work in the sociology of deviance has shown the great contribution to delinquency, alcoholism, homosexuality, and mental disorder made by the very agencies which attempt to deal with these phenomena. We will later discuss the fact that American society supports organized crime by demanding the right to purchase illicit goods and services. But if the Italian and Sicilian Mafia is responsible for organized crime in the United States, then documenting that fact and identifying the Mafia as the cause of our troubles is more science than scapegoatism. On the other hand, if the American cartel and confederation is a response to conditions of American life, documenting that fact is the critical problem. In a very real sense, then, deciding whether or not the American organization is a branch of the Sicilian one is a problem of deciding whether organized crime is "owned" by American society . . .

While the members of Cosa Nostra, and its affiliates, have learned a thing or two from the Sicilian Mafia, this organization is indigenous to the United States. It does things "the American way." But because the objectives of Cosa Nostra are similar to those of the Sicilian Mafia, certain similarities between the two organizations become obvious. The potential danger of Cosa Nostra to the citizens of the United States can be observed by examining the tremendous degree of control the Mafia exercises in western Sicily. The Sicilian organization originated in peasant society, where face-to-face relations between neighbors predominated. It adapted, and it continues to adapt, as Sicily has become more industrialized and urbanized. At first it provided law and order where the official government failed to do so. It collected taxes, which were payments for protection against bandits. In the latter part of the nineteenth century, for example, one Mafia group governed a cluster of eleven mountain villages; the head and his assistants had a private police force of about 130 armed men. The leaders were well-established citizens, landowners and farmers, who supervised all aspects of local life, including agricultural and economic activities, family relations, and public administration.

Like contemporary rulers of Cosa Nostra units in the United States, the despots soon demanded absolute power. No one dared offend the chief's sense of honor. The lines between tax and extortion and between peace enforcement and murder became blurred, as they always do under despots. Today, "an overall inventory of Mafia activities leaves no doubt that it is a criminal organization, serving the interests of its membership at the expense of the larger population." Norman Lewis, among others,

has shown that it has extended its influence from farms and peasant villages to the cities of western Sicily, where it now dominates commerce and government. It has a monopoly on almost all aspects of life. Mafia doctors get patients when other doctors do not, and only Mafia doctors can find vacant beds in overcrowded hospitals. Mafia lawyers have all the clients they can handle, and they have uncanny luck in winning cases. Mafia contractors get all the government contracts, even when their bids are higher than those of non-Mafia men, and despite the fact that they pay wages lower than the trade-union minimums. Mafia members, by tradition, do not run for seats in Parliament, but no man can get elected to Parliament—or anything else—without the support of "men of respect," also known as "men of honor."

Such corruption is not like "the bite" put on anyone doing business with Latin American civil servants. It is an *organized* bite, a feast by a society of cannibals. Sicily has given the Mafia a place. Both Luigi Barzini, a keen observer of the Italian scene, and Norman Lewis, a student of Mafia history, have given indications of the extent to which all economic, professional, political, and social life is dominated:

> There are the cattle and pasture Mafie; citrus grove Mafie; water Mafie (who control scarce springs, wells, irrigation canals); building Mafie (if the builder does not pay, his scaffolding collapses and his bricklayers fall to their death); commerce Mafie; public works Mafie (who award contracts); wholesale fruit, vegetable, flower, and fish markets Mafie, and so forth. They all function more or less in the same way. They establish order, they prevent pilfering, each in its own territory, and provide protection from all sorts of threats, including the legal authorities, competitors, criminals, revenue agents, and rival Mafia organizations. They fix prices. They arrange contracts. They can see to it, in an emergency, that violators of their own laws are surely punished with death. This is rarely necessary. Most of the time the fact that they can condemn any man to death is enough to keep everybody toeing the line.
>
> [By 1945] a great gathering of vulturine chiefs had collected to wet their beaks at the expense of farmers, whose produce they bought dirt cheap on the spot and carried to market in the Mafia's own beautifully decorated carts—or later, trucks. In the

market only those whose place had been "guaranteed" by the Mafia were allowed to buy or sell at prices the Mafia fixed. The Mafia wetted its beak in the meat, fish, beer, and fruit businesses. It moved into the sulphur mines, controlled the output of rock salt, took over building contracts, "organized labor," cornered the plots in Sicily's cemeteries, put tobacco smuggling on a new and profitable basis through its domination of the Sicilian fishing fleets, and went in for tomb robbing in the ruins of the Greek settlement of Selinunte. . . . The Mafia gave monopolies to shopkeepers in different trades and then invited them to put up their prices—at the same time, of course, increasing their Mafia contribution. . . . The most obvious of the Mafia's criminal functions—and one that had been noted by the Bourbon attorney general back in the twenties of the last century—now became the normally accepted thing. The Mafia virtually replaced the police force, offering a form of arrangement with crime as a substitute for its suppression. When a theft, for instance, took place, whether of a mule, a jeweled pendant, or a motorcar, a Mafia intermediary was soon on the scene, offering reasonable terms for the recovery of the stolen object. . . .

The Mafia intermediary, of course, wetted his beak at the expense of both parties. The situation was and is an everyday one in Sicily.

The public demand for protection against Sicilian bandits, and for other services not provided by the established government, created an illicit government which, in the long run, exploited all its members and ruled the very public that created it. The American demand for illicit goods and services has created an illicit government.

Individual Choice, Material Culture, and Organized Crime

Peter A. Lupsha

THE AMERICAN PHENOMENON OF ORGANIZED crime has been examined from a variety of perspectives. Donald Cressey (1972) tended to stress organization, hierarchy and structure; Francis Ianni (1972) kinship and familial cultural adaptation; Schelling's (1967) and Annelise Anderson's (1979) work stresses economic variables; Daniel Bell (1953) has emphasized social mobility. The major theoretical construct that flows through most of these works is the "ethnic succession thesis." This formulation sees organized crime as simply the adaptation of a deprived group to limitations on upward mobility and

opportunities for social status. Immigrant groups accepted crime as an alternative status ladder and rose on it. Or, as Balzac aptly said: "Behind every great fortune is a crime."

In this article we dispute this thesis, and present an alternative perspective on the emergence of organized crime in twentieth-century America. Our thesis is that organized crime as we know it is not based on either (a) a narrow or limited status or mobility ladder for early twentieth-century immigrants; or (b) frustration or anger at thwarting of mobility desires of immigrants by the dominant culture. These are the root arguments of the ethnic succession thesis. Instead we suggest that entrance to organized crime life styles was a self-choice based on individual skills and a personal rationalization which perverts traditional American values and culture. In our view the organized criminal does not seek, and has not sought, traditional status and respect values because he has his own world view of our culture which makes him right and the rest of us suckers (Lupsha, 1980). The very openness of our values permits this and supports the rise of different views. From his perspective the organized criminal is correct, and success has replaced respect or deference as a value. Power wealth and the fear it can generate replaces the positive deference of any "good society." Yet organized crime is a true product of American values and American culture. It is an American crime. It has simply taken the very openness of those values and placed them in a "fun house" perspective of its own . . .

By organized crime, we refer to those crimes involving ongoing criminal conspiracies and interactions over time, which therefore may be thought of as organized or syndicated. While there are many ways to define organized crime, this broad definition should be suitable for this article.[1]

Organized criminal groups have operated in the United States from its very beginnings. Whenever there is an opportunity to enhance profit, or create wealth; whenever there are imbalances in the market system or government has through its actions created scarcity and "black markets"; or whenever local culture and mores make for illicit actions or behaviors against which there are no universal taboos, enterprising individuals will appear to take advantage of the opportunity and risk possible sanction in order to accrue potential windfall profits. The boundaries of such fields of illicit action are delineated only by culture, precedent, opportunity, and the swiftness and certainty of sanction. If the balance of this behavioral equation swings in the direction of large profits from criminal action and relatively little certain, or immediate, sanction, the potential for criminal enterprise and entrepreneurship is enhanced.

To say organized crime is rooted in the "Jungle" quality of American business traditions is not new. Daniel Bell (1953) said it in his classic, "Crime as an American Way of Life," in the *Antioch Review*. To say that organized crime is based in "a frontier ethic which justifies an individual taking the law into his own hands," or in "the struggle under our value system of every ethnic group to achieve greater social and economic status" is not new. Gus Tyler (1971)

said that in his "Sociodynamics of Organized Crime," in the *Journal of Public Law*. Along with Bell's theme of organized crime as a "queer ladder of social mobility," this notion of "ethnic succession" is repeated as orthodoxy by every student in the field (Ianni, 1972) . . .

Daniel Bell (1953), Dwight Smith (1975), and others (Hawkins, 1969) are properly skeptical of the existence of a tightly organized, singular conspiratorial group called the "Mafia." Yet, it is equally foolish to be so close-minded as to fail to recognize that loose interactions, and associational and goal commonalities do exist among organized criminals and organized criminal groups. Certainly changes are taking place among the different organized crime groups, but this does not constitute "ethnic succession," nor a loss of the preeminent position of the Italian-American leadership among these groups. This is an area in need of long-term research. The typical law enforcement conceptualizations of the major changes in LCN (La Cosa Nostra) groups are: (a) the increased diversification into legitimate business areas, complex crime schemes, and political corruption matrices; (b) the use of multiple individual and corporate "fronts" and "buffers" staffed by non-Italian associates; (c) a shift away from "line" activities in some of the traditional crime matrices, such as drug trafficking and bookmaking, while maintaining a financing, franchising, and licensing role; (d) dispersion of blood relatives into widely diverse career paths, but always maintaining a controlling family influence in the crime side of the business; (e) increased age, death, and retirement among well-known LCN leadership; but their replacement by kin, relatives, and "greenies" from Sicily; (f) increasing use of non-Italian nonmember associates in management, professional, and high-risk line activities.[2] Such changes may suggest to some that ethnic succession is taking place, but close examination of control and paper flow, particularly profits, shows the continuing premier influence of the Italian-American LCN groups.

To focus in on this we must first look to the Bell (1953) article, "The American Way of Crime," which, while dated, still represents the classic formulation of the "queer ladder of mobility" thesis. Bell (1953: 141–143) presents the argument for the Italian-American groups as follows:

> The Italian community has achieved wealth and political influence much later and in a harder way than previous immigrant groups. The Italians found the more obvious big city paths from rags to riches preempted. . . .

The children of the [Italian] immigrants, the second and third generations became wise in the ways of the urban slums. Excluded from the political ladder . . . finding few open routes to wealth, some turned to illicit ways.

Here we have the basic tenets of the "queer ladder" thesis. The second half of the argument, "ethnic succession," comes about as one group replaces another on the "queer ladder" of crime, and the earlier group moves on to respectability, and legitimate status and livelihood. Thus, according to the argument, Jews replaced the Irish in crime, Italians replaced the Jews, and now the Blacks, Cubans, Puerto Ricans, and Mexicans are replacing the Italians.

This argument seems neat and facile and superficially sound, but Bell presents no hard data. Were the legitimate avenues of mobility and advancement blocked for the Italian-American immigrants? Did their "slum-wise" children, frustrated by "finding few open routes to wealth," thus turn to crime?

We do not find the picture as bleak as the thesis presents, and most importantly, we do not find that those who chose the "queer ladder" did so because of frustration or because few legitimate routes to wealth were open to them. They did it because they—Luciano, Teresa, Lansky, and the others—saw in American values and culture an alternative easy, exciting, and romantic route to wealth: Namely, "something-for-nothing, there's-a-sucker-born-every-minute" lawlessness. Plus, they were good at crime and depersonalized violence, and received peer and material reinforcement from it. Equally important, they arrived at adulthood as Prohibition began. Thus, serendipity provided opportunity, capital, and organization to routinize nationwide syndicated crime. At the time of the enactment of national Prohibition legislation, "Lucky" Luciano was 20, Vito Genovese 19, Carlo Gambino 17, Joseph Profaci 20, Al Capone 18, Thomas Lucchese 18, Frank Costello 26. By the time it went into effect, on January 16, 1920, other teenagers were becoming of an age to make a name in crime: Meyer Lansky 17, Peter Licavoli 16, Jerry Catena 17, Joe Adonis 17, Albert Anastasia 15. By March 1933, when legislation repealing Prohibition was enacted, these teenagers had grown to manhood, and had capital, organizational skills, and influence. Prohibition and personal choice, not career blockage or frustration with legitimate mobility paths, provided the opportunity structure

to move these small-time hoodlums into nationally syndicated confederations of crime.

Let's look at other data. Nelli (1976: 129) cites a 1909 study which showed:

> Today in New York City alone the estimated material value of the property in the Italian colonies is $120,000,000, aside from $100,000,000 invested by Italians in commerce, $50,000,000 in real estate, and $20,000,000 on deposit in the banks.

While comparative data with other groups is called for, these data do suggest that there was considerable wealth in the Italian colonies at that time. It is unlikely that this wealth was brought into the United States, and so suggests that the ladder of socio-economic opportunity for an ambitious, hardworking immigrant was not as narrow or blocked as has been suggested.

When discussing the occurrence of the Mano Nera (Black Hand), Nelli (1976) notes that between 1901 and 1903, extortion gangs "reaped a harvest from hundreds of wealthy Italians," and gives the estimated wealth of one victim, Nicola Cappiello, a Brooklyn contractor, at $100,000. He also cites a New York *Herald* article which "recounts that prominent Italian bankers, merchants, and physicians have corroborated accounts of blackmail." Given that this was 1903, it shows the Italian colonies had their own elite and professional leadership and suggests exaggeration when Bell (1953) says, "the Italian community achieved wealth much later" or "the more obvious paths from rags to riches were preempted." Nelli's (1976) analysis of Italian colonies in the first decade of the twentieth century clearly shows that while there was much poverty and crime, the bulk of the Italian community was hardworking, seeking both education and opportunity. Nelli (1976: 105) also notes:

> To slum area youngsters like Salvatore Lucania (Charles "Lucky" Luciano), John Torrio and Alphonse Caponi (Al Capone), excitement and economic opportunity seemed to be out in the streets rather than in the classroom. As soon as they reached the legal withdrawal age of fourteen, they left school.

As this was a period when "education began to emerge as an increasingly important qualification for . . . employment," we can only interpret "economic opportunity" to mean criminal or delinquent activity. Lucky Luciano worked at a "straight" job approximately one week before deciding work was for "crumbs" and chose life in the pool halls and street gangs, taking and pushing drugs instead. As Nelli (1976: 106) states:

> Unlike most of their contemporaries, who also belonged to street gangs and were involved in occasional mischief-making, the criminals-in-the-making had little or nothing to do with legitimate labor, which they believed was only for "suckers," men who worked long hours for low play and lived in overcrowded tenements with their families.

This picture of the opportunity pattern and choices sounds somewhat different than the "queer ladder" thesis. Yes, some turned to crime, but not from frustration, or any long struggle of being excluded from the political ladder, or blocked from avenues for advancement. They turned to crime because they felt the legitimate opportunity structure was for "suckers."

They were "wiseguys"—a term still used to denote organized crime soldiers—and could make an easy buck without working. They could have economic mobility without ever climbing the status ladder. Their choice was an individual decision, a self-choice, reinforced by peers, experience, and a talent for violence. They were not more frustrated, nor deprived (relatively or absolutely), than their classroom peers and fellow street gang members who chose to be "straights" and "suckers," following the legitimate socioeconomic mobility ladder, narrow and crowded as it may have been.

Meyer Lansky, for example, graduated from eighth grade, and was a promising apprentice tool and die maker, running crap games on the side. He then decided to become an automobile mechanic, stealing and altering cars and trucks for thieves, and, with Prohibition, entered the alcohol hauling and hijacking business. His opportunity path in the legitimate world was never blocked or frustrated, he simply preferred the "fast track" of crime (Messick, 1971) to the less exciting and, for him, less remunerative legitimate world of work.

The second half of the thesis is the concept of "ethnic succession." In order for this to take place, the group that has been successful in crime must leave it and be replaced by some new immigrant group that is lower on the status ladder. The model assumes that with increased wealth, the organized criminal will move into the legitimate sector of the economy and his children will live lives of honesty

and respectability. The basic assumption (Bell, 1953: 147–150) is that the organized criminal desired respectability all along:

> Yet it was, oddly enough, the quondam racketeer, seeking to become respectable, who provided one of the major supports for a drive to win a political voice for Italians. . . .
>
> The early Italian gangsters were hoodlums—rough unlettered and young (Al Capone was only twenty-nine at the height of his power). Those who survived learned to adapt. By now they are men of middle age or older. They learned to dress conservatively. Their homes were in respectable suburbs. They sent their children to good schools and had sought to avoid publicity.
>
> As happens with all "new" money in American society the . . . racketeers polished up their manners and sought recognition and respectability in their own ethnic community.
>
> Many of the top "crime" figures long ago had foresworn violence, and even their income, in large part, was derived from legitimate investments . . . or from such quasi-legitimate but socially acceptable sources as gambling casinos.

These statements are all from Bell's classic article, yet today they seem naive.

Of course organized criminals bought homes in respectable suburbs and sent their children to good schools. Such actions are common to anyone of affluence in our society, criminal or college professor. That they dressed conservatively and avoided publicity likewise tells us nothing about either their respectability or having left crime. Such comments focus on the trappings and appearance of a noncriminal lifestyle, they show nothing of the substance. These comments also seem to reflect little understanding of the use of "fronts," "buffers," and political connections for criminal purposes . . .

The use of business "fronts" as laundries to wash illegally gained wealth, and for purposes of creating a basis for taxable income, as well as the penetration of legitimate business by organized crime has been well documented (Bers, 1970; Kwitny, 1979). The use of gambling casinos to skim millions of dollars in cash, as well as fronts for acts of corruption and blackmail is also well documented and is a common reason for organized crime's interest and hidden ownership in such enterprises (Reid and Demaris, 1963; Messick, 1971). Perhaps these facts were not widely known in 1953, but they are today, and they suggest goals other than respectability.

If the ethnic succession thesis is to stand the test of evidence, we must find: (a) Italian organized crime figures who, once they had economic status, sought social status by getting out of the business of crime; or (b) that intergenerationally the sons, nephews, and relations of organized crime figures are not entering the business of crime; or (c) that the new ethnic groups—Black, Mexican, Puerto Rican—are succeeding not only to control crime markets that the LCN groups have discarded as having poor risk-to-profit ratios, such as prostitution or street level narcotics dealing and bookmaking, but that they are moving up to positions of real influence. In short, if the ethnic succession model is working, we must be able to show that Italian-American organized criminals are leaving the business of crime, and not simply using their capital and influence to buffer themselves while they license and franchise the new ethnics in the high risk-lower profit aspects of the business.

To do a proper empirical study to prove, or disprove, this is very difficult. The needed data is hard to collect; it is scattered and fragmentary. A proper study will take years of effort, but the initial work is underway. In the meantime, enough bits and pieces of data are around to suggest that ethnic succession is not taking place. New elites are emerging, particularly in the high risk crime markets (Ianni, 1974b). New ethnics are forming successful crime elites within their own ethnic communities, and in the street level retailing of crime. The part of the proposition that remains to be proven is that the Italian organized criminal families who chose the business of crime early in this century are giving up their premier positions and choosing legitimate lifestyles and revenue sources—not as fronts and laundries—instead of crime. We do not find that ethnic succession has been proven on this latter point.

One can show the increased age of Italian organized crime figures, the problems of recruitment, and promotion of "the best and the brightest" of relatives in the family (Lupsha, 1979). Yet, disturbing contrary evidence and data remains, and suggests that the Italian groups are not giving up control, they are simply engaging in wider use of non-Italian criminal associates, entering new and more complex crime matrices, and licensing the new ethnics to operate the more traditional, more risky, and lower profit organized crime markets. Let us briefly turn to this, before concluding.

First, what evidence is there that any of the major leaders of Italian-American organized crime have made an obvious break with the past, to live a life outside of crime? There appears to be very little. Frank Costello retired after being shot, but simply lived off the proceeds of his earlier life, as did John Torrio. Meyer Lansky and Joseph Bonanno claim to be in retirement, yet information regularly surfaces to suggest they are still active in controlling their interests in criminal enterprises. Recent FBI searches of Bonanno's Tucson home confirm this. Meanwhile, a 1978 New Jersey Department of Law and Public Safety report cites Lansky interests in the development of Resorts International Inc., the Atlantic City Casino Company (New Jersey Department of Law and Public Safety, 1978). Tony Accardo lives in retirement in Palm Springs, as Moe Dalitz does at "La Costa" in California; both, however, maintain active contacts with Las Vegas, Chicago, the Teamster pension fund, and other organized crime interests and personalities. In all we find little evidence of people leaving successful careers in organized crime except when death intervenes. Second, what evidence is there that children and relatives of Italian-American organized crime figures are getting out of the business? While there is evidence that some of the children and relatives choose not to follow the criminal side of family business, there appears to be equal evidence that a sufficient number of family members and relatives do stay in the business that family control is maintained.

The Kansas City "Family" of Nick Civella, which in 1980 is an active and aggressive organized crime family, for example, has the ongoing participation of a brother, Carl "Corky" Civella; a nephew, Anthony Civella; relatives by marriage; and another nephew, Anthony Chiavola, a Chicago police lieutenant who hosted meetings for Chicago crime boss Joseph Aiuppa and Nick Civella (Federal Bureau of Investigation, 1979). This was not a social meeting; it involved organized crime group interests in Las Vegas, Teamster pension fund loans, and skimming of casinos. Joseph Bonanno's sons Salvatore (Bill) and Joe, Jr., both currently in prison, appear to be following in the family tradition. Carmine Galante was chauffeured by his nephew, James, the day he was murdered in Brooklyn (July 12, 1979). Johnny Dio was the nephew of James "Jimmy Doyle" Plumeri, and Dio's brother, Thomas, is still active in the business. Carlo Gambino's relatives, Paul Castellano and Joseph Gambino, Jr., have not separated themselves from the family's past activities; nor has Anthony Zerrilli, son of the late Detroit Don, who in 1972 was convicted in a Las Vegas skim and hidden ownership. So where are we? There is evidence that some of the children leave the family business. There is other evidence that enough remain in the business to maintain, manage, and control it. The answer is we need more data and more research. However, for now we can say there is no clear empirical evidence that the Italian families who became active in organized crime early in this century have left the business. Perhaps one reason for this has to do with our material culture and the way we handle inheritance of legitimate versus illegitimate fortunes. Annelise Anderson (1979) suggests this as a proposition relating to organized crime penetrations of legitimate economic sectors and organizational continuity. It deserves further thought and research.

What is American about American organized crime? Precisely that it is such a reflection of American economic and political institutions. Bell (1953) has noted the parallel between the "robber barons" of business and the early organized crime entrepreneurs, and the way organized crime, like business, has moved from production to consumer services, although one could argue the specifics of this point. He did note that, like the corporation—moving from direct family participation in all phases of the enterprise to indirect, diversified manager control—organized crime has evolved into a similar buffered position where the organized crime family can sit on the Board and still control the company, without dirtying their hands in the line tasks. Are the Italian-Americans, or the members of any other ethnic group who have made millions in organized crime, going to abandon this queer, but successful, ladder of economic success? Given our thesis that organized crime in America is deeply imbedded in our Lockeian values and beliefs, we can predict this will occur when the Rockefellers give up their interest in banking and Standard Oil; the Mellons their interest in Gulf Oil; and all others who have gained a dominant place in our socioeconomic system willing to step aside for new elites. The new ethnics have a rung of the "queer ladder of crime" to stand on. They have the dirty, dangerous line jobs in crime, the less profitable and higher risk crime markets, they even have some limited autonomy within their own communities and enclaves, but it is doubtful that the old elites of organized crime will simply give them their empire.

In making these observations about the implications of the general American culture, its values, and attitudes, we do not mean to ignore or deny that ethnic, racial, and religious factors also influence organized crime groups. These groups depend on trust and loyalty to operate and survive. Cultural bases for that trust are usually in the primary "blood" culture, not the overall social, political, and economic culture. Thus for Italian-American, Mexican-American, and Chinese-American organized crime groups, kinship patterns, place of family origin, and birth are important factors. For Black-Americans and WASP-Americans engaged in organized crime, racial ties, prison association, neighborhood and cohort associations are important. These cultural factors affect organizational life, as does the overall social, economic, and political values of the culture. By choosing to emphasize the latter in this article, we in no way intended to dismiss the former.

To sum up, in this essay we have attempted to look at what is American about American crime by focusing on the evolution of organized crime, and particularly Italian-American organized crime groups. We have argued that organized crime is rooted in our values and culture, and that its development mirrors our economic and political institutions. Rather than being a forced option because of limited choice or opportunities for mobility, it is a chosen career path, a rational choice, rooted in one perverse aspect of our values: namely, that only "suckers" work, and that in our society, one is at liberty to take "suckers" and seek easy money, just as one is at liberty to be one. Like American values, organized crime is flexible, practical, and adaptive. It is an American institution, not a Sicilian by-product. It has moved from prostitution to pornography in film and home video cassettes as smoothly as our technology and corporations. Like corporate evolution it has evolved into a diversified multinational conglomerate, franchising criminal markets and firms. In a society that has always had a place for lawlessness, sharp practice, easy money, a disdain for suckers, and an idolatry of mammon and lucre, organized crime is as American as McDonald's.

NOTES

1. Definitions of organized crime range widely from Frank Hogan's dictum that organized crime consists "of two or more persons engaged in criminal activity," to the State of California's inclusion of prison gangs and terrorist groups. The author's own working definition is as follows: Organized

crime consists of activity by a group of individuals who consciously develop roles and specializations, patterns of interaction, spheres of responsibility and accountability, and who, with continuity over time, engage in a variety of illegal and illicit endeavors (enterprises) involving the use of large amounts of capital, nonmember associates, and the corruption of public officials and their agents, directed toward the achievement of greater capital accumulation in the form of untaxed monies and goods of value which are then processed through legitimate "fronts" and "buffers" to "launder" this black income into white (legitimate economic) earnings.

2. It is important to recognize that these statements are, for the most part, propositions that have only fragmentary verification, and badly need empirical testing on a large enough data base as to allow hard confirmation.

REFERENCES

Anderson, A. G. (1979) *The Business of Organized Crime.* Stanford, CA: Hoover Institution Press.

Bell, D. (1953) "Crime as an American way of life." *Antioch Rev.* 13 (Summer): 131–154.

Bers, M. (1970) *The Penetration of Legitimate Business by Organized Crime.* Washington, DC: U.S. Government Printing Office.

Cressey, D. (1972) *Criminal Organization: Its Elementary Forms.* New York: Harper & Row.

Federal Bureau of Investigation (1979) Affidavits for Kansas City wiretaps—23 volumes transcript. Released Kansas City, MO. (Xerox)

Hawkins, G. (1969) "God and the Mafia." *Public Interest* 14 (Winter): 24–51.

Ianni, F.A.J. (1978) Ethnic Succession in Organized Crime: Summary Report. Washington, DC: National Institute of Law Enforcement and Criminal Justice.

———. (1974a) *Black Mafia: Ethnic Succession in Organized Crime.* New York: Simon & Schuster.

———. (1972) *A Family Business.* New York: Russell Sage.

Kwitny, J. (1979) *Vicious Circles: The Mafia in the Marketplace.* New York: Norton.

Lupsha, P. (1980) "American values and organized crime: suckers and wiseguys," in S. Girgus (ed.) *Myth, Popular Culture and American Ideology.* Albuquerque: Univ. of New Mexico Press.

———. (1979) "Mobs and myths: a requiem for La Cosa Nostra?" Presented at the Western Social Science Association, Lake Tahoe, CA.

Messick, H. (1971) *Lansky.* New York: G. P. Putnam.

Nelli, H. (1976) *The Business of Crime.* New York: Oxford Univ. Press.

New Jersey Department of Law and Public Safety (1978) Report to the Casino Control Commission with Reference to the Casino License Application of Resorts International Hotel, Inc. Trenton, NJ: Division of Gaming Enforcement.

Reid, E. and O. Demaris (1963) *The Green Felt Jungle.* New York: Trident Press.

Schelling, T. (1967) "Economic analysis of organized crime." Appendix D. Organized Crime Task Force Report. Washington, DC: President's Commission on Law Enforcement and Organized Crime.

Smith, D. C., Jr. (forthcoming) "Paragons, pariahs, and pirates: A spectrum-based theory of enterprise." Crime and Delinquency.

———. (1978) "Organized crime and entrepreneurship." *J. of Criminology and Penology* 6 (May): 161–177.

———. (1975) *The Mafia Mystique.* New York: Basic Books.

Tyler, G. (1971) "Sociodynamics of organized crime." *Journal of Public Law 20,* 3: 487–498.

———. (ed.) (1962) *Organized Crime in America.* Ann Arbor: Univ. of Michigan Press.

U.S. Senate (1965) Organized Crime and the Illicit Traffic in Narcotics. 89th Congress, 1st Session. Washington, DC: U.S. Government Printing Office.

Think Critically

1. Describe the major theoretical construct of "ethnic succession," which Lupsha identifies as part of many mainstream studies of organized crime. Do you agree with his critique of this model? Why or why not?

2. Daniel Bell coined the term "queer ladder of mobility" in his classic work, "Crime as an American Way of Life." Explain what he meant by this, and how it relates to understanding organized crime.

WHITE-COLLAR
AND CORPORATE CRIME

WHITE-COLLAR AND CORPORATE CRIME have only more recently been incorporated into the general area of deviance theory, even though they clearly account for (at least according to many persons) widespread and serious physical, fiscal and social harm. Over a half-century ago, Edwin Sutherland, the progenitor of the term "white-collar crime," considers the question which still exists in many quarters today regarding more complex illegalities, of whether it is really "crime" in the excerpt "Is 'White-Collar Crime' Crime?" which is taken from his classic book, *White-Collar Crime*. Sutherland examines various laws relating to business practices and their differential implementation. He finds that white-collar crime fits the general criteria of criminal behavior, as contained in the legal definition of social injury and criminal punishment. He also notes that criminologists have not seen these deviant behaviors as crimes because they are treated differently by the legal system, and that lack of resentment toward such acts on the part of the public is explained by their lenient treatment by authorities.

In "Medical Criminals," which is a chapter from the book, *Prescription for Profit: How Doctors Defraud Medicaid*, Paul Jesilow, Gilbert Geis, and I describe the criminal and abusive behavior of physicians in the government health insurance program, Medicaid. Four basic categories of deviance are examined, including billing schemes, poor quality of care, illegal distribution of controlled substances, and sex with patients. Opportunities for dishonesty are discussed along with actual case histories and punishments meted out by authorities. Doctors rarely lose their licenses for Medicaid fraud, and the penalties for such acts are relatively lenient given the fiscal damage and abuse of patients involved in such cases.

Over a decade before the corporate and accounting scandals involving Enron, Worldcom and a host of other major American businesses, the single most costly set of white-collar crimes in history involved the savings and loan debacle in the 1980s. Fraud was responsible for a significant portion of the money lost by failed savings and loans, over $150 billion of which was eventually paid by American taxpayers. As of this writing in 2009, that amount now seems exceedingly small given the global financial crisis that was set in motion by problems in the home mortgage industry and Wall Street, as well as the clear lack of adequate regulatory provisions to protect the economy and citizenry from what is now seen as (by far) the largest financial debacle in world history. One cannot help but ponder the lessons never learned about white-collar crime from "smaller" past scandals.

In "White-Collar Crime in the Savings and Loan Scandal," Kitty Calavita and I use government reports to examine fraud in the savings and loan industry and trace savings and loan crime to the perverse incentives created by government deregulation in the early 1980s. The study discusses a typology of crimes that include "unlawful risk taking, covering up, and collective embezzlement," which refers to the deliberate looting of funds by top-level bank officials. Thrift crime and the response of law enforcement are discussed in light of the government's limited capacity to deal with the sheer magnitude of the savings and loan crisis and new and widespread forms of fraud that were a significant part of it.

In "Denying the Guilty Mind," Michael Benson examines how white-collar criminals deny criminal intent when they are caught in acts of deviance. Benson studies the reactions of offenders, including anti-trust and tax violators, those violating financial trust, and those convicted of fraud and false statements. He shows how offenders attempt to deflect blame and defeat the process of status degradation during their criminal cases. "Denying the guilty mind" helps to defeat the success of the degradation ceremony and allows for minimal identity transformation of the white-collar offender.

Is "White-Collar Crime" Crime?*

Edwin H. Sutherland

[A S OF THE WRITING OF THIS CHAPTER, WHICH was published in 1949], 980 decisions have been made against the 70 largest industrial and mercantile corporations, with an average of 14.0 decisions per corporation. Although all of these [were] decisions that the corporations have acted unlawfully, only 158, or 16 percent, of them were made by criminal courts and were ipso facto decisions that the behavior was criminal. Since not all unlawful behavior is criminal behavior, these decisions can be used as a measure of criminal behavior only insofar as the other 822 decisions can be shown to be decisions that the behavior was criminal as well as unlawful.

This is a problem in the definition of crime and involves two types of questions: First, may the word "crime" be applied to the behavior regarding which these decisions were made? Second, if so, why is it not generally applied and why have not criminologists regarded white-collar crime as cognate with other crime? The first question involves semantics, the second explanation or interpretation. The following analysis will be limited almost entirely to the laws regarding restraint of trade, misrepresentation in advertising, infringements of patents and analogous rights, and unfair labor practices in violation of the National Labor Relations Law. Little attention is devoted to the other laws, in part because some of the other laws are explicit criminal laws, such as those relating to rebates or adulteration of foods and drugs, and in part because so many different laws are involved in the miscellaneous group of offenses that the analysis would be unduly extended if each of those laws was given specific attention.

The definition of crime, from the point of view of the present analysis, is important only as a means of determining whether the behavior should be included within the scope of a theory of criminal behavior. More specifically, the problem is: From the point of view of a theory of criminal behavior, are the illegal acts of corporations which have been tabulated above cognate with the burglaries, robberies, and other crimes which are customarily included within the scope of theories of criminal behavior? Some writers have argued that an act is criminal only if a criminal court has officially determined that the person accused of that act has committed a crime. This limitation in the definition of crime may be made properly if a writer is interested primarily in administrative questions. The warden of a prison would not be justified in receiving an offender in the penal institution unless that offender had been officially convicted and sentenced to serve a term of imprisonment in that institution. Similarly, public authorities would not be justified in denying civil rights to offenders who had not been convicted of crimes. In contrast, the criminologist who is interested in a theory of criminal behavior needs to know only that a certain class of acts is legally defined as crime and that a particular person has committed an act of this class. The criminologist needs to have certain knowledge on both of these points, but for this purpose a decision of a court is no more essential than it is for certain knowledge in chemistry or biology. However, . . . decisions of courts and commissions have been used as proof that prohibited acts have been committed.

The essential characteristic of crime is that it is behavior which is prohibited by the State as an injury to the State and against which the State may react, at least as a last resort, by punishment. The two abstract criteria generally regarded by legal scholars as necessary elements in a definition of crime are legal description of an act as socially harmful and legal provision of a penalty for the act.[1]

The first of these criteria—legal definition of a social harm—applies to all of the classes of acts which are included in the 980 decisions [referred to] above. This can be readily determined by the words in the statutes— "crime" or "misdemeanor" in some, and "unfair," "discrimination," or "infringement" in all the others. The person injured may be divided into two groups: first, a relatively small number of persons engaged in the same occupation as the offenders or in related occupations, and second, the general public, either as consumers or as constituents of the general social institutions which are affected by the violations of the laws.

The antitrust laws are designed to protect competitors and also to protect the institution of free competition as the regulator of the economic system and thereby to protect consumers against arbitrary prices, and to protect the institution of democracy against the dangers of great concentration of wealth in the hands of monopolies. Laws against false advertising are designed to protect competitors against unfair competition and also to protect consumers against fraud. The National Labor Relations Law is designed to protect employees against coercion by employers and also to protect the general public against interferences with commerce due to strikes and lockouts. The laws against infringements are designed to protect the owners of patents, copyrights, and trademarks against deprivation of their property and against unfair competition, and also to protect the institution of patents and copyrights which was established in order to "promote the progress of science and the useful arts." Violations of these laws are legally defined as injuries to the parties specified.

Each of these laws has a logical basis in the common law and is an adaptation of the common law to modern social organization. False advertising is related to common law fraud, and infringement to larceny. The National Labor Relations Law, as an attempt to prevent coercion, is related to the common law prohibition of restrictions on freedom in the form of assault, false imprisonment, and extortion. For at least two centuries prior to the enactment of the modern antitrust laws, the common law was moving against restraint of trade, monopoly, and unfair competition.

Each of the four types of laws under consideration, with the possible exception of the laws regarding infringements, grew primarily out of considerations of the welfare of the organized society. In this respect, they are analogous to the laws of the earliest societies, where crimes were largely limited to injuries such as treason, in which the organized society was the victim and particular persons suffered only as they were members of the organized society. Subsequent criminal laws have been concerned principally with person-to-person injuries, as in larceny, and the State has taken jurisdiction over the procedures principally in order to bring private vengeance under public control. The interest of the State in such behavior is secondary or derivative. In this sense, the four laws under consideration may properly be regarded as criminal laws in a more fundamental sense than the laws regarding larceny.

Each of the four laws provides a penal sanction and thus meets the second criterion in the definition of crime, and each of the adverse decisions under these four laws, except certain decisions under the infringement laws to be discussed later, is a decision that a crime was committed. This conclusion will be made more specific by analysis of the penal sanctions provided in the four laws.

The Sherman Antitrust Act states explicitly that a violation of the law is a misdemeanor. Three methods of enforcement of this law are provided, each of them involving procedures regarding misdemeanors. First, it may be enforced by the usual criminal prosecution, resulting in the imposition of fine or imprisonment. Second, the attorney general of the United States and the several district attorneys are given the "duty" of "repressing and preventing" violations of the law by petitions for injunctions, and violations of the injunctions are punishable as contempt of court. This method of enforcing a criminal law was an invention and, as will be described later, is the key to the interpretation of the differential implementation of the criminal law as applied to white collar criminals. Third, parties who are injured by violations of the law are authorized to sue for damages, with a mandatory provision that the damages awarded be three times the injuries suffered. These damages in excess of reparation are penalties for violation of the law. They are payable to the injured party in order to induce him to take the initiative in the enforcement of the criminal law and in this respect are similar to the earlier methods of private prosecutions under the criminal law. All three of these methods of enforcement are based on decisions that a criminal law was violated and therefore that a crime was committed; the decisions of a civil court or a court of equity as to these violations are as good evidence of criminal behavior as is the decision of a criminal court. . . .

The differential implementation of the law as it applies to large corporations may be explained by three factors: Namely, the status of the businessman, the trend away from punishment, and the relatively unorganized resentment of the public against white-collar crimes. Each of these will be described.

First, the methods used in the enforcement of any law are an adaptation to the characteristics of the prospective violators of the law, as appraised by the legislators and the judicial and administrative personnel. The appraisals regarding businessmen, who are the prospective violators of the laws which are now under consideration, include a combination of fear and admiration. Those who are responsible for the system of criminal justice are afraid to antagonize businessmen; among other consequences, such antagonism may result in a reduction in contributions to the campaign funds needed to win the next election. The amendment to the Pure Food and Drug Law of 1938 explicitly excludes from the penal provisions of that law the advertising agencies and media (that is, principally, newspapers and journals) which participate in the misrepresentation. Accessories to crimes are customarily included within the scope of the criminal law, but these accessories are very powerful and influential in the determination of public opinion and they are made immune. Probably much more important than fear, however, is the cultural homogeneity of legislators, judges, and administrators with businessmen. Legislators admire and respect businessmen and cannot conceive of them as criminals; businessmen do not conform to the popular stereotype of "the criminal." The legislators are confident that these respectable gentlemen will conform to the law as the result of very mild pressures. The most powerful group in medieval society secured relative immunity by "benefit of clergy," and now our most powerful group secures relative immunity by "benefit of business," or more generally "high social status." The statement of Daniel Drew, a pious old fraud, describes the working of the criminal law with accuracy,

"Law is like a cobweb: it's made for flies and the smaller kind of insects, so to speak, but lets the big bumblebee break through. When technicalities of the law stood in my way, I have always been able to brush them aside easy as anything."

This interpretation meets with considerable opposition from persons who insist that this is an egalitarian society in which all men are equal in the eyes of the law. It is not possible to give a complete demonstration of the validity of this interpretation, but four types of evidence are presented in the following paragraphs as partial demonstration.

The Department of Justice is authorized to use both criminal prosecutions and petitions in equity to enforce the Sherman Antitrust Act. The department has selected the method of criminal prosecution in a larger proportion of cases against trade unions than of cases against corporations, although the law was enacted primarily because of fear of the corporations. From 1890 to 1929 the Department of Justice initiated 438 actions under the this law with decisions favorable to the United States. Of the actions against business firms, 27 percent were criminal prosecutions, while of the actions against trade unions 71 percent were criminal prosecutions.[2] This shows that the Department of Justice has been comparatively reluctant to use a method against business firms which carries with it the stigma of crime.

The method of criminal prosecution in enforcement of the Sherman Antitrust Act has varied from one presidential administration to another. It was seldom used in the administrations of the presidents who were popularly appraised as friendly toward business, namely, McKinley, Harding, Coolidge, and Hoover.

Businessmen suffered their greatest loss of prestige in the depression which began in 1929. It was precisely in this period of low status of businessmen that the most strenuous efforts were made to enforce the old laws and enact new laws for the regulation of businessmen. The appropriations for this purpose were multiplied several times and persons were selected for their vigor in administration of the law, with the result that the number of decisions against the 70 corporations was quadrupled in the next decade.

The Federal Trade Commission Law states that a violation of the law by a corporation shall be deemed to be also a violation by the officers and directors of the corporation. Businessmen, however, are seldom convicted in criminal courts, and several cases have been reported, like the 6 percent case of the automobile industry, in which corporations were convicted and the persons who directed the corporation were all acquitted. Executives of corporations are convicted in criminal courts principally when they use methods of crime similar to the methods of the lower socioeconomic class.

A second factor in the explanation of the differential implementation of the law as applied to white collar criminals is the trend away from penal methods. This trend advanced more rapidly in the area of white collar crimes than of other crimes. The trend is seen in general in the almost complete abandonment of the extreme penalties of death and physical torture; in the supplanting of conventional penal methods by nonpenal methods such as probation and the casework methods which accompany probation; and in the supplementing of penal methods by nonpenal methods, as in the development of casework and educational policies in prisons. These decreases in penal methods are explained by a series of social changes: the increased power of the lower socioeconomic class upon which previously most of the penalties were inflicted; the inclusion within the scope of the penal laws of a large part of the upper socioeconomic class as illustrated by traffic regulations; the increased social interaction among the classes, which has resulted in increased understanding and sympathy; the failure of penal methods to make substantial reductions in crime rates; and the weakening hold on the legal profession and others of the individualistic and hedonistic psychology which had placed great emphasis on pain in the control of behavior. To some extent overlapping those just mentioned is the fact that punishment, which was previously the chief reliance for control in the home, the school, and the church, has tended to disappear from those institutions, leaving the State without cultural support for its own penal methods.[3]

The third factor in the differential implementation of the law in the area of white collar crime is the relatively unorganized resentment of the public toward white collar crimes. Three reasons for the different relation between law and mores in this area may be given. (a) The violations of law by businessmen are complex and their effects diffused. They are not a simple and direct attack by one person on another person, as is assault and battery. Many of the white collar crimes can be appreciated only by persons who are experts in the occupations in which they occur. A corporation often violates a law for a decade or longer before the administrative agencies or the public becomes aware of the violation. The effects of these crimes may be diffused over a long period of time and affect perhaps millions of people, with no particular person suffering much at a particular time. (b) The public agencies of communication do not express the organized moral sentiments of the community as to white collar crimes, in part because the crimes are complicated and not easily presented as news, but probably in greater part because these agencies of communication are owned or controlled by businessmen and because these agencies are themselves involved in the violations of many of these laws. Public opinion in regard to picking pockets would not be well organized if most of the information regarding this crime came to the public directly from the pickpockets themselves. This failure of the public agencies of communication may be illustrated by the almost complete lack of attention by newspapers to the evidence presented in the trial of A. B. Dick and other mimeographing companies that these companies maintained a sabotage school in Chicago in which their employees were trained to sabotage the machines of rival companies, and even their own machines if the supplies of rival companies are being used.[4]

Analogous behavior of trade unions, with features as spectacular as in this case, would have been described in hundreds of newspapers with large headlines on the front page, while many newspapers did not even mention this decision, and those which did mention it placed a brief paragraph on an inner page. (c) These laws for the regulation of business belong to a relatively new and specialized part of the statues. The old common law crimes, as continued in the regular penal codes, were generally limited to person-to-person attacks, which might be committed by any person in any society. In the more complex society of the present day, legislatures have felt compelled to regulate many special occupations and other special groups. The penal code of California, for instance, contains an index of penal provisions in the statutes outside of the penal code which are designed to regulate barbers, plumbers, farmers, corporations, and many other special groups. This index occupies 46 pages, and the complete statutes to which reference is made in the index would occupy many hundreds of pages. This illustrates the great expansion of penal provisions beyond the simple requirements of the earlier societies. The teachers of criminal law, who generally confine their attention to the old penal code, are missing the larger part of the penal law of the modern state. Similarly, the general public is not generally aware of many of these specialized provisions and the resentment of the public is not organized.

For the three reasons which have been presented, the public does not have the same organized resentment toward white-collar crimes as toward certain of the serious felonies. The relation between the law and mores, finally, tends to be circular. The laws, to a considerable extent, are crystallizations of the mores, and each act of enforcement of the laws tends to reenforce the mores. The laws regarding white-collar crimes, which conceal the criminality of the behavior, have been less effective than other criminal laws in re-enforcing the mores.

The answers to the questions posed at the beginning of this chapter may be given in the following propositions: First, the white-collar crimes which are discussed in this [chapter] have the general criteria of criminal behavior, namely, legal definition of social injuries and penal sanctions, and are therefore cognate with other crimes. Second, these white-collar crimes have generally not been regarded by criminologists as cognate with other crimes and as within the scope of theories of criminal behavior because the administrative and judicial procedures have been different for these violations of criminal law than for other violations of criminal law. Third, this differential implementation of the criminal law as applied to businessmen is explained by the status of the businessman, the trend away from reliance on punitive methods, and the relatively unorganized resentment of the public toward white collar crimes.

Since this analysis is concerned with violations of laws by corporations, a brief description of the relation of the corporation to the criminal law is necessary. Three or four generations ago the courts with unanimity decided that corporations could not commit crimes. These decisions were based on one or more of the following principles. First, since the corporation is a legislative artifact and does not have a mind or soul, it cannot have criminal intent and therefore cannot commit a crime. Second,

since a corporation is not authorized to do unlawful acts, the agents of a corporation are not authorized to do unlawful acts. If those agents commit unlawful acts, they do so in their personal capacity and not in their capacity as agents. They may be punished, therefore, as persons but not as agents. Third, with a few exceptions the only penalties that can be imposed on corporations, if found guilty of crimes, are fines. These fines are injurious to stockholders, and consequently, as a matter of policy, should not be imposed.

These principles have now been reversed by the courts and corporations are now frequently convicted of crimes. Corporations have been convicted of larceny, manslaughter, keeping disorderly houses, breaking the Sabbath, destruction of property and a great variety of other crimes.[5] Such decisions involved reversal of the three principles on which the earlier decisions were based. First, the corporation is not merely a legislative artifact. Associations of persons existed prior to the law and some of these associations have been recognized as entities by legislatures. These corporations and other associations are instrumental in influencing legislation. Consequently legislation is in part an artifact of corporations, just as corporations are in part an artifact of legislatures.[6] Second, the requirement that criminal intent be demonstrated has been eliminated from an increasing number of criminal laws, as was described above. Third, the location of responsibility has been extremely difficult in many parts of modern society, and responsibility is certainly a much more complicated concept than is ordinarily believed. The old employers' liability laws, which were based on the principle of individual responsibility, broke down because responsibility for industrial accidents could not be located. Workmen's compensation laws were substituted, with their principle that the industrial establishment should bear the cost of industrial accidents. Some attention has been given to the location of responsibility for decisions in the large corporations.[7] Although responsibility for actions of particular types may be located, power to modify such actions lies also at various other points. Due largely to the complexity of this concept, the question of individual responsibility is frequently waived and penalties are imposed on corporations. This does, to be sure, affect the stockholder who may have almost no power in making decisions as to policy, but the same thing is true of other penalties which have been suggested as substitutes for fines on corporations, namely, dissolution of the corporation, suspension of business for a specified period, restriction of sphere of action of the corporation, confiscation of goods, publicity, surety for good behavior, and supervision by the court.

Two questions may be raised regarding the responsibility of corporations from the point of view of the statistical tabulation of violations of law. The first is whether a corporation should be held responsible for the action of a special department of the corporation. The advertising department, for instance, may prepare and distribute advertising copy which violates the law. The customary plea of the executives of the corporation is that they were ignorant of and not responsible for the action of the special department. This plea is akin to the alibi of the ordinary criminal and need not to be taken seriously. The departments of a corporation know that their recognition by the executives of the corporation depends on results and that few questions will be asked if results are achieved. In the rare case in which the executives are not only unaware of but sincerely opposed to the policy of a particular department, the corporation is customarily held responsible by the court. That is the only question of interest in the present connection. Consequently, an illegal act is reported as the act of the corporation, without consideration of the location of responsibility within the corporation.

The second question is concerned with the relation between the parent corporation and the subsidiaries. This relationship varies widely from one corporation to another and even within one corporate system. When subsidiaries are prosecuted for violations of law, the parent company generally pleads ignorance of the methods which have been used. This, again, is customarily an alibi, although it may be true in some cases. For instance, the automobile corporations generally insist that the labor policy of each subsidiary is determined by that subsidiary and is not within the control of the parent company. However, when a labor controversy arose in a plant in Texas and a settlement was proposed by the labor leaders, the personnel department of that plant replied, "We must consult Detroit." They reported the following morning, "Detroit says 'No'." For the present purpose, the corporation and its subsidiaries are treated as a unit, without regard to the location of responsibility within that unit.

NOTES

1. The most thorough analysis of crime from the point of view of the legal definition is Jerome Hall, *Principles of Criminal Law* (Indianapolis, 1947). He lists seven criteria of crime: "(1) certain external consequences ("harms"), (2) which are legally forbidden (principle of legality); (3) conduct; (4) *mens rea*; (5) the fusion, "concurrence," of *mens rea* and conduct; (6) a "causal" relationship between the legally forbidden harms and the voluntary misconduct; and (7) (legally prescribed) punishment" (p. 11). The position taken in the present chapter is in most respects consistent with Hall's definition; certain differences will be considered later.

2. Percentages complied from cases listed in the report of the Department of Justice "Federal Antitrust Laws, 1938."

3. The trend away from penal methods suggests that the penal sanction may not be a completely adequate criterion in the definition of crime.

4. *New York Times,* March 26, 1948, pp. 31, 37.

5. George F. Canfield, "Corporate Responsibility for Crime," *Columbia Law Rev.,* 14:469–81, June 1941; Frederic P. Lee, "Corporate Criminal Liability," ibid., 28:1–28, February 1928; Max Radin, "Endless Problem of Corporate Personality," Ibid., 32:643–67, April 1932.

6. For a summary of classical theories of corporate personality, see Frederick Hallis, *Corporate Personality* (London, 1930). See also Henri Levy-Bruhl, "Collective Personality in the Law," *Annales Sociologique,* ser. C, fasc. 3, 1938.

7. Robert A. Gordon, *Business Leadership in the Large Corporation* (Washington, D.C., 1945).

Think Critically

1. According to Sutherland, how does white-collar crime fulfill the criteria of criminal behavior?

2. How does the fact that white-collar crimes are often treated in different ways by the legal system affect the way they are treated by the public? Scholars? Policy makers? Give some examples.

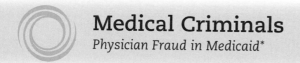

Medical Criminals
*Physician Fraud in Medicaid**

Paul Jesilow, Henry N. Pontell, and Gilbert Geis

ORGANIZED MEDICINE CLAIMS THAT IT CAN police itself, but the record of Medicaid fraud and abuse indicates that the profession is unable to ferret out and punish errant doctors. If doctors who cheat are, as the profession's elite argue, only "the few rotten apples" in an otherwise pristine barrel, one would expect the medical associations to have an efficient control mechanism to spot and remove them quickly. However, few errant doctors are brought to enforcement's attention through professional channels. Rather, most physician offenses are uncovered by government fraud-control activities or are reported by former employees or current patients. And most of these offenses are committed by physicians in private practice, illustrating that Medicaid abuse is not exclusively the domain of doctors at work in inner-city Medicaid mills.

In this chapter we use case file material to tell the story of physicians' criminality. We also discuss the demographics of physicians sanctioned for violations of the Medicaid laws. We have removed all references to physicians' names . . .

Like most statistics on lawbreakers, these cases tell us at least as much about enforcement patterns and priorities as about the actual distribution of crimes. Enforcement resources tend to be allocated to cases in which the dollar amounts are high, the aberrancies identified by computer checks are striking, the intent to commit fraud is reasonably clear, and the case seems relatively simple to prosecute successfully—all matters that recommend action to a prosecutor who has great discretion about which cases to accept. Cases involving unnecessary tests and proce-

dures, for instance, receive much less attention than those in which bills are submitted for services never rendered, because the former are apt to involve a labyrinthine "paper chase" in which intent is extremely difficult to establish. How careful a physician is in defrauding Medicaid also influences the probability of discovery. The sloppiest and least clever crooks are most likely to be snared. Such matters influence the aggregate characteristics of physician violators who comprise the "official record" of known Medicaid fraud cases.

Demographics

To obtain a general picture of physician violators and their offenses during the early years of enforcement, we obtained lists of providers suspended from participation in Medicare or Medicaid between 1977 and 1982. Federal law now requires that any physician or other health care professional convicted of a crime related to participation in Medicaid, Medicare, or other social service programs be suspended from participation in Medicare. Medicare suspension usually prompts Medicaid suspension, although a state can elect to continue to pay a provider who has been suspended from the federal program.

Of the 358 medical providers suspended during the period in question, 147 were physicians. Of the 138 physicians for whom we were able to obtain background information, 50 (36 percent) were graduates of overseas medical schools. Six of the 43 schools mentioned had more than one graduate among the sanctioned doctors. Three physicians had graduated from the University of Havana, and two came from each of the following schools: Central University of Manila; Far Eastern Institute of Medicine, Manila; University of Innsbruck; University of Bologna; and the Medical University of Nuevo León in Mexico.

*© 1993 The Regents of the University of California. Selections from *Prescription For Profit: How Doctors Defraud Medicaid*, pp. 102–147. Reprinted by permission of the University of California Press.

Among the 88 domestically trained doctors, six had trained at Meharry Medical College, followed by the University of California, Irvine (five); Loma Linda in California (four); and the University of Louisville (three). Among the fifteen other schools that logged two graduates on the government list were such preeminent institutions as Johns Hopkins, the University of Wisconsin, UCLA, Tulane, New York University, and Columbia.

The disproportionate number of foreign graduates among the violators is striking. They constituted approximately 25 percent of doctors at work in the United States and 31 percent of the known violators. Also unexpected was the number of sanctioned doctors from Meharry Medical College, whose student body is predominantly black; black doctors made up only about 3 percent of the 400,000 physicians practicing in the United States at the time of our research. These results seem to reflect the heavier concentrations of black and foreign graduates in inner-city work, where enforcement resources are aimed against large providers and where practitioners may be most apt to feel the need—and possess the self-excusatory rationalizations—for cheating in order to compensate for the lower fees offered by Medicaid. Black physicians and foreign medical graduates may be more vulnerable to fraud detection because greater enforcement resources are focused on the communities in which they work.

Nationally, California accounted for 41 sanctioned doctors (28 percent of the total), followed by New York with 25 (17 percent). Thereafter came Maryland with eight, Florida and Pennsylvania with seven each, Texas with six, and Michigan with five. These states have the largest Medicaid budgets, so their share of violators is not disproportionate.

Family or general practitioners accounted for the greatest percentage of violators (27 percent), followed by psychiatrists (18 percent), general surgeons (11 percent), internists (8 percent), and obstetricians and gynecologists (7 percent). The "other" category includes specialties with only one or two offenders. General practitioners, the largest category of sanctioned physicians, also represent the largest specialty in the profession. In contrast, psychiatrists were overrepresented among sanctioned physicians, partly because of their vulnerability to enforcement. Psychiatrists' bills are based on the time actually spent with patients. It is difficult for them to bill for extra services or

interventions, but it is easy to "inflate" the time they spend with patients. The "time game" proves to be irresistible to some members of the profession, and the relative ease of catching them often induces enforcement authorities to focus resources on psychiatrists' Medicaid fraud. Anesthesiologists can also play the time game, but the time they are engaged with patients before, during, and after surgery is much more difficult to monitor. The disproportionate number of psychiatrists sanctioned for Medicaid offenses, however, cannot be laid solely at the doorstep of enforcement idiosyncrasies. Psychiatrists, as we shall see, have also been convicted of numerous other forms of illegal behavior.

We were also curious about whether women doctors were suspended from Medicaid in proportion to their presence in the profession. In the late 1970s and early 1980s about 10 percent of all physicians were women, and among the suspended doctors in our sample for whom we could ascertain gender, fourteen (about 10 percent) were women.

The Crimes

There are four basic categories of crimes committed by physicians caught violating Medicaid programs: (1) billing schemes, which include billing for services not rendered, charging for nonexistent office visits, or receiving or giving kickbacks; (2) poor quality of care, which includes unnecessary tests, treatments, and surgeries as well as inadequate record keeping; (3) illegal distribution of controlled substances, which includes drug prescriptions and sales; and (4) sex with patients whereby physicians, under the guise of "therapy," received payments for sexual liaisons with their patients. These categories are not mutually exclusive, and the latter two can also be regarded as subsets of poor quality of care.

Opportunities for Dishonesty

Opportunity is often the hallmark of white-collar crime by professional persons—a theme echoed by health care providers testifying before congressional committees. Two chiropractors convicted of Medicaid fraud maintained before a Senate subcommittee that the system was "so bad that it virtually invites" criminal activity.[1] A physician convicted of stealing several hundred thousand dollars from Medicaid and other government programs told a joint hearing of Senate committees that his criminal behavior was so flagrant that only a seriously flawed system could have permitted him to get away with what he did for so long. He testified that the forms he sent into the programs for payment were so "arrogant and outrageous" that the services could not possibly have been performed as he alleged they had been. He pointed out that the diagnoses he put down "didn't relate to either the services or to other diagnoses that were submitted at the same time."[2]

The fee-for-service nature of Medicaid payments provides dishonest doctors with ample opportunities to bill for services never rendered or rendered by others and to bill for unnecessary tests and procedures. At first, some Medicaid providers stumbled upon these possibilities. One physician, for example, tired of waiting for Medicaid payment, worried that the government might have lost his bills. He sent in duplicates and, in time, was paid twice. When such stories spread in the medical community, some doctors were convinced that "nobody was minding the store."

For other physicians, the opportunity to provide medical care without concern about the cost proved attractive bait for illegal behaviors. Under Medicaid's lax scrutiny, these physicians had only to convince themselves that certain services would benefit their patients, a conclusion made more appealing when the services also benefited the physicians' pocketbooks.

In the case files, we found numerous examples of reimbursements for patients who were never seen, double-billing for the same patient, billing for phantom services and lab tests, billing for fictitious visits to disguise illegal prescriptions for controlled substances, and "upgrading" services. Another scam, though one rarely treated as criminal fraud because of problems in proving intent, is billing for unnecessary services. Even surgeons who perform unneeded operations, which can be regarded as equivalent to assault, are rarely prosecuted unless the abuses are wanton, again largely because of the difficulty in second-guessing medical opinions and demonstrating recklessness or culpable intent . . .

Some billing schemes go undetected because government agencies fail to communicate with each other. One case involved a doctor who had graduated from Havana Institute just before Castro took power. On seven attempts she failed the Foreign Licensing Examination, so Illinois, where she was then living, decided to revoke her

temporary license. Undaunted, she continued to practice and to bill Medicaid, which continued to pay her, unaware of the revocation of her license. Medicaid had reimbursed this doctor more than $180,000 before agents, investigating a pharmacy scam, discovered her because she also was involved in a scheme with the pharmacy owner. She diagnosed virtually all her patients as having an upper respiratory infection and prescribed an average of five to seven items. Most, such as soaps and shampoo, were medically unnecessary but were prescribed to benefit the pharmacy. The doctor cooperated with the Medicaid agents against the pharmacy owner and was allowed to plead guilty to one count of practicing medicine without a license. She was put on probation for a year . . .

Fake Laboratory Tests

Some physicians' employees accepted their bosses' illegal conduct in order to keep their jobs. The employee, in this regard, resembles the corporate criminal whose conduct mainly benefits the company. A deputy attorney general explained how he saw one such case:

> The employee's conduct was inexcusable. However, her culpability is certainly not of the same character as the doctor's. It was the doctor whose orders she followed. As a physician and her employer, he occupied a position of leadership and dominance. Since the employee's only financial gain from this conduct was the job security that came from pleasing her employer, it is likely that the doctor's dominance was a significant factor in inducing her to participate in these misrepresentations.

This doctor had directed his employee of ten years to bill Medicaid for expensive office laboratory tests, although his patients actually received inexpensive tests performed by an outside laboratory. The doctor, a graduate of Harvard Medical School, had previously been in trouble: A decade earlier the state licensing board, citing his gross negligence in the treatment of pre- and postoperative patients and nursing home patients, had placed him on two years' probation and banned him from performing any major surgical procedures. Nine years later the board once again put him on probation, charging that he was excessively prescribing amphetamines and diuretics to patients with weight-control problems. The doctor pled guilty to grand theft from the Medicaid program; he still faced trial on charges that he had bypassed his home gas meter and unlawfully obtained $4,000 in gas to heat his swimming pool and spa.

The supervising deputy attorney general who prosecuted the case clearly wanted jail time for the doctor. He argued that the doctor's blatant criminal behavior had diverted funds from needy indigents and had contributed to the public's growing lack of confidence in the medical assistance programs . . .

The judge agreed that the doctor should make full restitution but did not fine him, instead ordering one hundred hours of community service. There also was a sixty-day jail sentence . . .

Medicaid and Murder

One of the most shocking Medicaid cases involved a physician living in Miami, Florida. She had arrived in the United States from Cuba in 1960 and claims to have graduated from medical school at the University of Havana. She began practicing medicine in Miami in 1967 while she completed her state licensing requirements. By 1980, five years after she began treating Medicaid patients, she had become the second largest provider of such services in Florida and was operating two clinics. According to official reports, she received $184,000 in state monies in 1980.

The doctor came to the attention of investigators when two women complained that her "acne treatments" had left them disfigured. In March 1981 the doctor was arrested on racketeering charges, which alleged that she had billed Medicaid for more than $97,000 for treatments never performed. During the jury trial, the prosecutor asked a witness if he had ever been treated by the doctor for acne, tonsillitis, viral fever, an ingrown toenail, depression, asthma, or diaper rash. The spectators and jurors laughed. The witness was a 19-year-old, 220-pound college football player who had visited the doctor twice, complaining of a cold. But the doctor had billed the state for 51 visits and received payments of $1,885. Another of the ten witnesses testified that she had never even met the doctor, although the physician had used her Medicaid number to bill the state for 165 visits, totaling $1,638.

The jury took only one hour to convict the doctor on 24 counts of filing false claims and 24 counts of receiving payments to which she was not entitled. The judge sentenced her to twenty years in prison, saying, "This so-called white-collar crime is also stealing money allocated to the poor." A state attorney said that the money paid to the physician could have gone to treat more than 10,000 poor patients. The sentence was the most severe punishment yet given to a physician for Medicaid violations.

But the Miami doctor's story does not end here. Shortly after she was sentenced, she became a prime suspect in the murder of her former partner, who had been gunned down outside a Miami hospital a few weeks before the fraud indictment was announced. She was accused of having paid $10,000 for a contract killing to prevent her former partner from testifying against her in the fraud case.

During the murder trial, the prosecution produced a "hit list" containing the murdered partner's name and the name of the investigator heading up the case against the doctor. The doctor testified that the list was to be delivered to a *Santería* practitioner (*Santería* is a Caribbean religion) who had requested that she furnish names of people she might be involved with in future legal disputes. She did not believe in *Santería,* she said, but her accountant had recommended she try it to ease her mind.

The doctor was sentenced to life imprisonment with a 25-year minimum sentence on the murder charge and another 30 years for conspiracy. The new sentences were to run consecutively with the 20-year sentence she had already received for her Medicaid fraud conviction.

The convictions for conspiracy and murder were upheld in a district court of appeal, but on April 27, 1989, the Florida Supreme Court overturned the murder conviction and ordered a new trial. The court ruled that the circumstantial and hearsay evidence presented at the trial may have prejudiced the jury's decision . . .

Doctors in Large Clinics

The case files we reviewed included relatively few cases of doctors who used their corporate medical clinics to perpetrate fraud. The most likely explanation is that illegal billings can be hidden in a high-volume organization. Large-scale business not only provides dishonest individuals with camouflage for larceny but also allows them to place barriers between themselves and proof of their criminal culpabilities.

A Los Angeles physician who owned and operated a medical group billed Medicaid for his corporation's activities by using its Medi-Cal provider number. An investigation showed he routinely padded the bill by adding minutes to his group's charges for anesthesia services. A Los Angeles grand jury indicted the doctor on 20 counts of wrongdoing, but the prosecution ran into trouble when the district attorney's office realized that no law prohibited the doctor's behavior—a common oversight in the first decade of the benefit program. An agent wrote:

> The whole case for fraud hangs on the doctor's misuse of time modifiers under the RVS [relative value scales—an insurance billing mechanism]. The problem is somewhat surprisingly that the RVS, although in common usage at the time, had never been adopted as a regulation of the Department of Health when the conduct in this case was occurring. Without undue elaborations, suffice it to say, there were serious legal problems of a due-process nature connected with penalizing anyone for breach of standards which are not a matter of written law. . . . If taken to trial, this case would be quite time-consuming, and the result would be difficult to predict.

Following heated pretrial arguments, the defense and prosecution struck a deal. A year and a half after the indictment, the doctor appeared in court to plead no contest to an amended charge of receiving stolen property. By agreement, his practice of medicine was put on probation for two years and he was ordered to provide 384 hours of community service during that period. In addition, the state's health department suspended him (and his corporation) from billing Medi-Cal for five years. An agent in the case wrote to the state's medical licensing board urging them to acquiesce in the agreement: "It is as tough a penalty as we would likely be able to achieve, even if we tried the case; it deters the doctor, it gives the board supervisory power over him for two years, and it will serve as a warning to other doctors."

Interjurisdictional Problems

Like many enforcement and regulatory officials, those concerned with Medicaid investigation and administration often feel frustrated by what they regard as judicial leniency and indulgence. Enforcement problems are multiplied in instances where suspect doctors move from one state to another. For example, a New York physician was convicted of stealing approximately $20,000 from the state's Medicaid program by billing for services he never performed. The court fined him $5,000, placed him on probation for three years, and ordered him to complete a one-year obligation as a VISTA volunteer. After the New York conviction, California routinely revoked this physician's license to practice medicine in that state. (Doctors frequently hold licenses in more than one state.) The doctor's request for reinstatement tried to dispel his criminal image:

> He is a board-certified pediatrician, and is employed as a pediatrician on the poverty program operated in New York City by the neighborhood health services program. Throughout his medical career, the doctor has demonstrated a continuing interest in, and commitment to, the development and implementation of community health care programs. He provides medical supervision to . . . a settlement house in New York City founded in 1889 which serves preschool children, adolescents, and senior citizens primarily from minority, low-income families living in Manhattan. He has served as a VISTA volunteer and worked with the federal Headstart Health Care Program. He also serves as a pediatrics lecturer for the Stony Brook Physician Assistant Program operated by the State University of New York. He is aware of the serious nature of his misconduct and is contrite. There is no evidence of any other criminal activity before or since the conduct in question, which occurred approximately seven years ago. The doctor appears to have rehabilitated himself. He is in compliance with all terms and conditions of the orders of probation.

One member of California's licensing board was dismayed by the doctor's dossier and commented, "He can stay in New York. I cannot believe the double standard concerning physicians. If some middle-class or poor person had committed the same crime, they would be in prison. Are the judges protecting doctors? Maybe we should do something. I realize this happened in New York, but we have had similar cases here—$20,000 stolen, $5,000 returned. Question: Is this rehabilitation?" Doctors convicted of serious offenses can often resurrect their practices elsewhere. This doctor was not relicensed in California. However, other states are not so strict in preventing errant physicians from practicing within their boundaries.

The Punishments

The Judicial Response

The records we reviewed do not enable us to draw definitive conclusions about judges' attitudes toward errant doctors. But it appears that judges do make an effort to tailor sentences to fit what they perceive as the special conditions of convicted doctors. For example, a psychiatrist who routinely billed the government for services either not rendered or rendered by others could have been held to account for up to $360,000—$260,000 for overcharges, $37,000 in interest, and $62,000 for government investigative costs. When the psychiatrist pleaded guilty to one felony count of grand theft, the court placed him on eight years' probation, ordered him to pay a $5,000 fine and to make restitution of $160,000, and sentenced him to six months in a county work furlough program that allowed him to work during the day but spend his nights in jail. The judge also offered the doctor the opportunity to reduce the restitution by up to $50,000 by providing a thousand hours of community service—a pay scale, $50 an hour, far higher than Medi-Cal rates at the time.

The psychiatrist probably did not deserve such special treatment. Only one month before his sentencing, he was still cheating the government. When he told a patient that "he was going to get his money one way or another," the patient complained to the government. Fifteen months later, the state Medicaid agency forwarded to the MFCU (Medical Fraud Control Unit) a file its agents had compiled on the doctor based on this complaint. The chief of the MFCU was shocked to find the new information unattached to the main case file. A few phone calls revealed the cause. A "computer misplaced the civil case," she was told.

Medical Mercy

Another case that illustrates the leniency accorded to high-status offenders is that of a 50-year-old Brooklyn internist who had been paid $250,000 by Medicaid. This doctor had consistently billed for office visits, injections, and electrocardiograms he never performed. Before fraud charges could be brought, a federal grand jury indicted him on fifteen felony counts of narcotics distribution and sales. He consented to plead guilty to two counts and went to jail for four months; his medical license was revoked.

When he was released from jail, the state charged him with 137 acts of Medicaid theft; he pled guilty to three. The judge, in sentencing him to a conditional discharge, noted the doctor's recent incarceration on the unrelated offenses and his loss of license. The fact that the doctor was nearly destitute also contributed to the judge's decision to be merciful. It is unlikely that a poor person with a previous conviction for narcotics sales would have been treated so indulgently.

Revoking Licenses

It is unusual for physicians to lose their medical licenses for Medicaid violations. During the first eight years of the program, California routinely lifted the California licenses of doctors sanctioned in New York but pulled the license of only one of its own Medicaid violators. The case of that doctor, a psychiatrist, illustrates how only the most egregious violations get a doctor booted out of medicine.

The psychiatrist first ran into trouble with the Medicaid program over hundreds of bills for psychiatric treatments she never rendered. The case relied heavily on the testimony of owners and administrators of nursing homes. After a year's delay, however, some witnesses were not as sure as they originally had been about the doctor's failure to provide psychiatric care.

Because of the ambiguities in the witnesses' testimony, the state's licensing board concluded it was best to seek a negotiated penalty. An agreement was reached by which the psychiatrist received five years' probation and a nine-month suspension of her license. She also was required to provide eight hours of free community service a week for the first year and four hours a week for the remaining four years of probation. Even during the nine-month suspension, she was allowed to practice medicine as long as her work was limited to community service. The board noted, "The variation in the standard form of this condition seems justified as the public will derive some benefit from her activities. We have no evidence that she is unqualified, from a clinical standpoint, to practice medicine."

Less than a year later, the board acted to revoke the psychiatrist's license permanently. During a few morning hours over 80 days of working at a clinic in a building she and her husband owned, she had written 2800 prescriptions, most of them for controlled substances such as Ritalin, Valium, and codeine, which she would prescribe without examinations. She also failed to fulfill most of the conditions of her probation.

In contrast to California's board, which automatically revokes the license of any doctor convicted of a crime in another state lest California become a retreat for wayward doctors, Georgia's board appears less willing to issue revocations or suspensions. A Georgia doctor convicted of 23 felonies for filing false claims was suspended from practice for three months and given five years' probation. In several states, including California, New York, and New Jersey, doctors can expect major license troubles if convicted of even one felony.

Georgia's judiciary also seems to be lenient with doctors who file false claims. One physician fraudulently billed the state's Medicaid program for $13,000. He was allowed to plead no contest to a misdemeanor. The court fined him $1,000 to be paid, with interest at 7.5 percent, at $85 a month. He was put on probation until he finished paying the fine. The state licensing board also placed him on probation for three months.

Judges are not inclined to send doctors to prison for billing for services never rendered. Again and again they assign probation and community service in lieu of suspended prison terms. The files we saw did not indicate the judges' sentencing criteria. The two rationales that seem most likely are that stealing funds from a government program is deemed similar to a property offense (first-time thieves are rarely sent to prison) or that physicians are too valuable a community resource to waste in prison.

Consider a New Jersey physician who pled guilty to a 20-count indictment of Medicaid fraud. The behaviors charged represented only the tip of the doctor's criminal activities, evidenced by his repayment to the state of $60,000 in addition to a $30,500 fine. The judge sentenced the doctor to 20 years in prison but immediately suspended the prison term in favor of "two days per week gratuitous service at a hospital." The president of the New Jersey Medical Licensing Board, which revoked the doctor's license, took a firmer stand:

> The illegal conduct was a systematic pattern which persisted over a three-year period. . . . Further, while letters on behalf of the doctor describe him as the only dermatologist serving a poor population in Newark, it is notable that the conduct for which he was convicted arose out of treating that same population which he

now argues could benefit by his continued licensure. His crime shook public confidence in the Medicaid system as well as having attempted to divert public dollars. Despite attempts to characterize defendant's conduct as a mere digression from an otherwise virtuous life, there exists a wide gap between this individual's conduct and that which the public has a right to expect from a physician.

In another case, the New Jersey Medical Licensing Board also rejected a doctor's appeal for leniency based on his long list of good deeds: "That those anti-social activities continued concurrently with respondent's charitable work in no way lessens the breach of public trust committed by respondent under the privileged mantle of his medical licensure. Clearly, he utilized the privilege of his title to perpetrate the fraud and hoped to elude detection by the well-publicized acts of good works."

Negotiated Administrative Settlements

Sanctioned physicians face punishments from Medicaid administrators (suspensions and restitution), criminal courts (jail, fines, restitution), and physician licensing boards (license suspensions, revocations, fines). So at times physicians choose to negotiate settlements with enforcement officials and thereby possibly avoid criminal and licensure actions. Negotiations often result in voluntary, permanent suspensions from Medicaid and large restitutions. New York's Medicaid agency, for example, charged a physician with negligence and incompetence and ordered him to repay $32,000. The doctor agreed to withdraw voluntarily from the state's assistance program, and the Medicaid agency agreed to "withdraw its allegations of unacceptable practices" and to stipulate that the doctor "in no way admits to any wrongful intent or unlawful acts nor shall there be deemed such wrongful intent or unlawful acts in connection with such withdrawal from the program." After such an agreement, neither the state medical board nor a criminal court could use the administrative settlement as a basis for further action.

Such negotiated agreements between crooked doctors and the state's Medicaid agency were common in New York, probably because the agency appeared to be lenient, particularly when a physician compared the proposed administrative sanctions to the potential sentence for a criminal conviction.

New York State routinely audits its highest-billing Medicaid providers, believing that a doctor can see only so many Medicaid patients in a year and those who greatly exceed the norm are most likely to be using fraudulent tactics. Besides, only a big biller can be stealing a substantial sum; a physician who has a small Medicaid practice could not be cheating on a large scale.

For each of these high-billing doctors, the department selects a statistically valid sample of patient case files. In one instance, 100 cases were chosen from 3,327 Medicaid patients and a $157,000 billing to represent 26 months of a physician's practice. When this doctor was unable to produce charts for 36 of the cases, investigators discovered numerous deficiencies in his records and quality of care. Extrapolating from the sample to the doctor's full caseload, the auditors estimated that the doctor owed Medicaid $72,000 plus $6,000 interest. The agency and the doctor negotiated a settlement that included restitution of part of the estimated theft and a delayed voluntary permanent withdrawal from the state's welfare programs.

The files of negotiated settlements contain some agreements that seem unsettling given the scope and seriousness of the physicians' crimes. One audit, for example, concluded that half of one doctor's $240,000 Medicaid payments were illegally obtained. Further, it revealed:

> (a) the consistent failure to provide adequate histories (e.g., presenting symptoms, complaints) to pursue diagnosis; (b) physical examinations, necessary for information indispensable to good medical care, which are incomplete, illegible or absent and are never directed by historical findings; (c) radiographs and electrocardiographs which are not interpreted or are inadequately interpreted; (d) diagnoses which are inconsistent with history, examination or lab findings, or which are not stated at all; (e) the consistent failure to record dates, treatment plans or dispositions; (f) the prescription of medications inappropriate or without regimes; and (g) the overutilization of psychotropic drugs.

Yet the state agency negotiated an agreement in which the total claim against the doctor was $77,000, and the agency agreed to accept $59,000 to be paid over two years with interest. The doctor's voluntary permanent suspension was delayed six weeks, during which time he was paid half of any Medicaid funds he earned, with the other half credited to his restitution.

Doctors who faced criminal procedures prior to Medicaid administrative actions fared worse than those who took their Medicaid lumps first. The criminal procedures usually resulted in lower restitution orders, but the doctors were suspended from Medicaid and faced licensure actions as well as adverse publicity—penalties avoided by doctors who agreed to negotiated settlements.

Some physicians convicted of crimes fight subsequent civil and administrative actions. A plea of no contest in a criminal action, for example, was later used by a doctor at an administrative hearing to try to block further action. At the hearing to bar him from Medicaid, he argued that he had no criminal intent and that his no contest plea was entered to avoid the possible adversities of going to trial. The prosecutor noted that a plea of no contest, according to court decisions, was to be accepted only when there was a "strong factual basis for the plea." The doctor also contested his permanent suspension from Medicaid on the grounds that he had cooperated with prosecutors and because "he previously enjoyed a good reputation in his community and profession." The prosecutor, in rebuttal, stated the government's position on suspension from Medicaid:

> Appellant's cooperation and previous good reputation do not relieve the State of its obligation to exclude from participation in the Medical Assistance program providers whose conduct constitutes an unacceptable practice. Appellant knowingly and repeatedly defrauded the Medical Assistance program and can no longer be trusted as a provider in that program. Furthermore, it should be remembered that participation in the Medical Assistance program is voluntary and contractual in nature. No vested right is being denied the provider, as would be the case if an unacceptable practice hearing could result in a criminal conviction or in the revocation of the provider's license to practice his profession. Since the relationship between provider and government agency is a voluntary and contractual one, that government agency should have wide latitude in deciding which providers it will do business with.

Drugs, Sex, and Psychiatrists

Fraud by Psychiatrists. As noted earlier, psychiatrists were overrepresented in our sample of doctors who committed Medicaid fraud. The most common offense was inflating the amount of time spent with patients. There are also cases of billings for fictitious patients and for therapy administered by someone other than the psychiatrist. Psychiatrists have also been caught dispensing drugs to patients and charging the government for therapy time. They have also become involved sexually with patients or former patients and have billed the benefit program for such dalliances.

As discussed earlier, what is known and believed about fraud against government medical benefit programs by psychiatrists reflects particularly unfavorably on them. But there is extenuating evidence suggesting that the high rate of fraud by psychiatrists, compared with that of physicians in other specialties, may be a function of their particular susceptibility to discovery and successful prosecution. Consider, for example, the differences between psychiatrists and anesthesiologists, specialists who also bill for the time spent with patients rather than for specific procedures. Unlike the psychiatrist's patients, the anesthesiologist's patients are in no condition during treatment to remember the duration of the physician's activities. Nor do anesthesiologists have much opportunity to become familiar with patients or to exchange drugs for payment or sex. Investigators must rely almost entirely on checking hospital records concerning the times of surgeries as well as established billing norms of anesthesiologists in order to convince a prosecutor to bring charges. As a result, the behavior of an anesthesiologist who inflates his record may surface only during a routine audit and investigation—a rare occurrence.

As to the issue of billing for work done by others, one must consider that various professionals bill for services performed by their staffs. Lawyers, for instance, often charge their clients high hourly fees for work performed by low-paid clerks. Medicaid, however, views such activities by doctors as an abuse of the program. And overwhelmingly it is psychiatrists who are caught billing for others' work, although various physicians have been sanctioned for such billing. For example, two doctors got into trouble when they submitted bills for supervising hearing exams at which they were not present, and another physician billed Medi-Cal for X-rays he claimed were taken in his office under his supervision, though they were actually taken by unauthorized personnel in a different city.

When psychiatrists have had sex with patients and charged the government for therapy, the sexual misconduct has overshadowed the issue of fraud, which was usually viewed as a minor aspect of the case. All but one of the sex cases in the files we analyzed involved psychiatrists. The intense intimacy that can develop between doctor and patient is unlikely to occur nearly as readily in other specialties. A case that involved an osteopath seems almost childlike compared to the instances of psychiatric sexual abuse. The osteopath admitted to having felt the breasts of four female patients and having kissed three of the four without their consent. He pled guilty to four counts of sexual abuse in the third degree and was disqualified from the state's Medicaid program.

Psychiatrists often got into trouble with Medicaid because the autonomy they enjoy as independent providers of service runs afoul of Medicaid regulations. One clinician, for example, was suspended from Medi-Cal because he had charged the program for group psychotherapy sessions at which he was not present and that were led by his wife, a psychiatric nurse. He said the patients were told that his wife was a psychiatric nurse and not a physician, and that he and his wife discussed the cases after the sessions. Since his wife was a psychiatric nurse and provided the group psychotherapy under his supervision, he felt that he qualified as the provider for billing Medi-Cal . . .

Dishonest psychiatrists have victimized employees as well as patients and the government. One psychiatrist who charged the government for sessions provided by psychologists and nurses repeatedly promised his employees a percentage of the payments but often failed to make good. He promised a nurse 50 percent of what Medi-Cal offered, but she quit after repeated problems in collecting her salary. Another nurse left because the psychiatrist was using the payroll money for a Hawaii vacation—something he had done before. The nurse and others turned him in to the labor board and collected what was owed them. As if this were not enough, the psychiatrist was receiving a 10 percent kickback from another psychiatrist to whom he was referring cases.

Apparently, some doctors believed that even the most blatant cheating would go undetected. As early as 1969, one psychiatrist had habitually billed Medi-Cal for one-hour psychotherapy sessions that were at most half-hour visits or totally nonexistent encounters. Between

May 1977 and July 1977, he billed Medi-Cal for 24 to 28 individual one-hour sessions on each of eight separate days. On one "26-hour day," he billed an additional ten hours for private patients, producing a 36-hour billing day. It was simple for the investigators to choose a couple of the doctor's more astonishing days (27 and 28 hours billed) and to interview the beneficiaries the doctor claimed to have treated.

When the investigator went to the psychiatrist's office with a search warrant to seize records, the psychiatrist's lawyer was there and refused to allow the investigator to question his client. The lawyer argued that it was common for doctors to inflate time "to receive comparable payments as they receive from private patients," and he attempted to derail criminal prosecution by offering to have the doctor repay any illegal bills. "Hypothetically speaking," the lawyer offered, "if 40 percent of the total amount the doctor received from Medi-Cal were returned, would this stop any criminal action?" At his jury trial, the psychiatrist was represented by a different lawyer, but the 40 percent estimate of overpayment his first attorney had suggested came back to haunt him when the government used that figure to estimate restitution at about $125,000 . . .

Another psychiatrist billed for patients he never saw. He would tell a mother that he needed Medi-Cal stickers for all her children even though he provided therapy for only one. He also obtained Medi-Cal stickers for canceled appointments. Investigators were tipped off by a patient who received a notification of benefits and observed that the doctor had billed for services rendered while the patient was in jail. An undercover operation and interviews with other beneficiaries quickly unearthed additional fraudulent bills. The doctor's billing clerk explained that if patients saw the doctor more than eight times in four months (Medi-Cal's limit without prior authorization), the billings were spread over a longer period to meet the legal requirement. When the investigator stated that such practices were illegal, the clerk replied that the procedure was intended only to help the patients.

In another case, a computer review revealed that a psychiatrist billed for eighteen patients in one day, all of whom he diagnosed as suffering from "anxiety neurosis." Investigator interviews with the doctor's patients indicated that he was billing for psychotherapy on patients whom he treated for general medical disorders such as diabetes and arthritis. The psychiatrist had billed Medi-Cal for scores of therapy sessions that he had not provided and that he claimed were performed in a health center where he was a salaried employee.

This doctor learned he was under investigation when one of his patients informed him that she had been interviewed by the fraud unit. He contacted a lawyer friend and asked him to intercede. The lawyer met with the fraud unit investigator and stated that the doctor wished to repay the $29,000 he had stolen. But the investigator continued his inquiries, noting that the doctor's provider number was "littered with fraud." These ongoing interviews prompted a phone call from the psychiatrist's attorney, who said he was worried that the investigation "was creating a potential problem" for the doctor with regard to his patients.

The doctor's admission of guilt and desire to repay the government probably did not work to his advantage. The government investigator had decided to end the investigation after uncovering $3,500 in fraudulent payments. The judge who sentenced the doctor, however, ordered him to make restitution of $29,000—the figure first supplied by the doctor—and fined him $5,000. The doctor's admission of guilt prior to any plea agreement made it easier for the prosecutor to obtain a 90-day jail sentence.

The Medicaid fraud files show several other cases in which psychiatrists attempted to use the "patients' health" to deter further investigation. One psychiatrist's attorney wrote the head of the state fraud unit about the doctor's concern that "the mental health of the patient can be impaired by heavy-handed examination by your staff." The psychiatrist had informed his attorney "that the psychological condition of a number of his patients has deteriorated as a direct result of the contacts."

He suggested to the chief enforcement agent "that any further contact between his patients in your office either be supervised by [me] or be made by a board-certified psychiatrist with sufficient experience in handling chronic psychotic patients to minimize the potential for damage". . .

Oral Copulation as Therapy. In the case files we also found reports of psychiatrists who had sexual contact with patients. How prevalent is sexual misconduct? In a survey answered by 1,314 psychiatrists in

1986, seven percent of the male psychiatrists and three percent of the female psychiatrists said they had had sexual contact with a patient. Moreover, 65 percent of these psychiatrists said they had seen at least one patient who reported sexual contact with a previous therapist; only eight percent had reported these cases to authorities.[3]

When investigators suspect a doctor of patient abuse, they cannot rely on a paper trail that can be introduced at a trial to convince jurors of a defendant's guilt. Instead, they typically must stage an undercover operation. The following case illustrates some of the difficulties they encounter.

A psychiatrist came under investigation when a patient turned first to health administrators and then to the local police. She said she had begun to see the doctor seven years earlier because she had been depressed over her recent divorce. The doctor gave her tranquilizers and sleeping aids on the first visit. By her third session, she felt she was becoming dependent on the drugs, and she acquiesced to the doctor's request that she have oral sex with him. For the next seven years, she continued to see him on a monthly basis: she would perform fellatio, and he would write drug prescriptions for her.

The state licensing board's review unearthed two other patients who claimed similar experiences. The board assigned an investigator and an undercover operative to run a "sting" on the psychiatrist. The agent, equipped with a hidden microphone, saw the doctor and complained that she was depressed over her separation from her husband. What follows are excerpts from the investigator's report:

> He repeatedly returned to the subject of conversation regarding the patient's sexual activity, asking her such questions as whether or not she masturbated or whether she has ever had a climax while she was sleeping. The doctor ultimately stated that one of her problems was that she had a cold, unemotional relationship with her father and, subsequently, married her husband subconsciously looking for a father figure. After approximately forty minutes, the doctor gave the agent a capsule which he wanted her to take. He stated the capsule would relieve the tension in her stomach. When the doctor turned his back, the agent dropped the capsule into her purse.
>
> [At the end of the session] the psychiatrist gave her prescriptions for an antianxiety and antitension

pill as well as one for an antidepressant. A week later the agent returned. The conversation, which lasted approximately one hour, dealt mainly with the agent's marital and sexual problems. The doctor stated the agent subconsciously wanted to have a sexual relationship with her father. During the conversation the doctor continually changed all subjects back to sex and, on a couple of occasions, asked the agent if she had sexual fantasies about him. The doctor stated, this feeling for a doctor by a patient does occasionally happen. The doctor persistently talked about whether or not the agent could have a sexual relationship with him and, at one point, asked if she felt that if she had sex with him it would be a gratifying experience.

Shortly thereafter, the agent returned to the office to take two personality tests, but she did not see the psychiatrist. Two days later she came back for another session.

> The doctor began the conversation by asking if she had taken her medication, did she sleep better, and was she any less depressed. The agent told the doctor she had spoken to her husband on the phone the previous day and after the conversation she felt very depressed. The doctor asked if she had felt like calling him after her conversation with her husband. She told him she had just imagined talking to him. The doctor then changed the subject to a dream she had made reference to in a prior session wherein she remembered waking up and having a climax. The agent told the doctor about another dream which had nothing to do with sex. The doctor then brought the subject back to the sexual dream. He asked the agent if she would like her psychiatrist to be nice to her and if she wanted to please him. She stated she wanted him to think OK of her. He asked the agent why her husband wanted a divorce. She stated he feels she is a lousy wife, mother, and lover. She stated this was not true, she was good at all these things. The doctor asked if she liked oral sex and if her sex partners enjoyed it also. He also asked if any of her sex partners had ever stimulated her orally and, if so, could she have an orgasm this way. She advised she had, after which he made a comment relative to the fact she could have a climax orally but not with penetration. The doctor then stated, most men like oral sex and asked if she had not yet discovered that.
>
> The doctor then changed the subject and asked the agent if she had gained any weight. She advised she had gained several pounds. He had her stand up and turn

around so that he could look at her. He stated she had a nice figure. The agent sat down and picked up a book which was on the doctor's desk and advised she was nervous and he should have something in his office for people to hold on to. The doctor stated, it wasn't the book she needed to hold, but his hands instead. At that point the agent began repeating the doctor's statements because he was speaking very softly. The investigator could overhear the agent repeat that the doctor wanted her to sit on his lap. Also overheard was a statement by the agent that she could feel his penis moving. Also overheard was a statement by the agent that the doctor wanted her to kneel down in front of him. There were several minutes of unintelligible conversations after which I heard the agent say, "Why are you doing this to me?" At that point I left my vehicle and went into the office, identified myself and effected the arrest. The doctor resisted being placed in handcuffs, stating he was going to telephone his attorney before he went anywhere. The doctor was handcuffed and placed in the rear of my vehicle. At that time I advised him he was being arrested . . . and of his rights per the *Miranda* decision.

The state medical board forwarded to the county's district attorney the evidence it had collected against the psychiatrist, but the chief deputy district attorney felt there was "insufficient evidence to pursue filing charges." In his opinion, "the language of the statute prescribing conduct which is unprofessional or gross immorality is so big and uncertain that the law is probably defective." Although the investigators had compiled the testimony of former patients and a reconstruction (but not a tape recording) of the events that took place during the undercover operation, the vagueness of the statute, the doctor's subsequent strong denials of wrongdoing, and the legal difficulties of proving that the situation was not entrapment but attempted rape, all contributed to the prosecutor's reluctance to go forward.

Sexual Exploitation of the Sick. Taped confrontations involving patients did help bring about the conviction of a psychiatrist on charges of Medi-Cal fraud and his subsequent dismissal from the program. The case was initiated when two female patients reported through a university professor that the doctor billed Medi-Cal for psychotherapy sessions that in fact consisted only of sexual activity with them. Both women had been diagnosed as manic-depressive, and both were said to be suicidal. One of the women first became a patient of the psychiatrist when she was hospitalized after an attempted suicide. She reported that he became romantic with her and allowed her to leave the hospital for a day, when he had intercourse with her at his home. He released her from the hospital about a week later. She then went to his office for treatment three times a week for the first month, and once a week thereafter. The doctor billed Medi-Cal for these visits, which, according to the patient, consisted almost entirely of sexual intercourse.

The patients helped the police by secretly taping meetings with the psychiatrist in which he acknowledged his sexual involvement with them. One of the patients asked him how he felt about getting paid to have sex with her. He told her he didn't feel very good about it. He said he regretted his behavior, was depressed at the time, and was looking for intimacy. He told her that sex with her "was an expression of our being close, of getting involved emotionally, and of my not making the boundaries clear."

This psychiatrist told another patient that "the next time she was making love to imagine it was him she was having sex with." He also had sexual intercourse with her during a camping trip. According to the investigative report:

> He persuaded her to go camping when he told her that a friend of his, who was also a therapist, would also be with them along with some of his patients. He reassured her that "nothing would happen." He also told her, "You have nothing to worry about, chaperones will be around." The suspect picked her up in the evening. They then drove to pick up his friend and the others. While en route he unzipped his pants and took out his penis, and said, "I don't care about Bill or anyone else, I'm going to stick this thing in you tonight." He then took her hand and tried to hold it on his penis. She kept trying to pull her hand away, but he kept pulling it back on to his penis.

They met his friend Bill in a parking lot. But he was alone, saying the others couldn't make it. While Bill drove, the doctor again unzipped his pants and removed his penis. He took her hand and put it on his penis. She told him she didn't want to do this and kept pulling back. He told her that she "owed" it to him because Medi-Cal didn't pay him enough for his services treating her.

A few days after they returned from camping, he telephoned her before a group session. He told her to be "discreet" about the camping trip, especially around his wife, who would be at the group. That night after the group meeting, she went home and attempted suicide by taking more than forty lithium pills. She said she was feeling depressed and confused by the sexual relationship. Later he advised her how to commit suicide with lithium by taking smaller doses of ten pills at a time. She was scared that she would do it and thought she had to keep receiving treatment from him. He told her that he would keep her as a patient and that sometimes they would talk and sometimes they would have sex.

In this case, the MFCU filed criminal charges against the doctor for charging Medi-Cal for his liaisons. The district attorney declined to file sexual assault charges because "the sexual conduct was not the result of force in the usual sense." At the sentencing the defendant's attorney argued that the doctor had already been punished, suffering "public humiliation and other ancillary consequences of criminal acts." The prosecutor rebutted this view: "It is important to remember that the ancillary losses suffered by a white-collar criminal are of advantages not enjoyed by many other defendants coming before the court for sentencing. Neither the legislature nor the judicial counsel in enacting the rules of court suggested that the loss of professional privileges, public humiliation, and dissolution of marriage are factors to be considered in mitigation of punishment."

The court placed the psychiatrist on three years' probation, ordered him to pay $2,000 restitution, fined him a paltry $10, and ordered a six-month jail term and continuing psychiatric counseling. The state licensing board placed the psychiatrist on ten years' probation, which allowed the doctor to practice only in a supervised setting. One of the patients sued and settled for $200,000 . . .

Conclusion

In sentencing physicians, the courts look beyond the offenses committed. As one federal judge explains:

> I didn't want to send him to jail because I felt that it would deprive him and his family of the livelihood he could make as a doctor and it would deprive the

neighborhood of his services. So what I was trying to accomplish was to see that to some extent he could repay society. In this particular case there was a strong enough reason to overcome whatever good would be done for society by imposing a sentence for general deterrence, which is the only justification that exists for [prison] sentences in these cases.[4]

The relative leniency expressed by judges and colleagues with respect to physician criminality most certainly contributes to the extent of the behaviors. Lacking censure, errant physicians practice without proper parameters of behavior. They are unlikely to perceive their own acts as criminal when others do not.

NOTES

1. Subcommittee on Long-Term Care, Special Committee on Aging, U.S. Senate, *Fraud and Abuse Among Practitioners Participating in the Medicaid Program* (Washington, D.C.: U.S. Government Printing Office, 1976), 81.
2. Committee on Finance and Special Committee on Aging, U.S. Senate, *Oversight of HHS Inspector General's Effort to Combat Fraud, Waste, and Abuse* (Washington, D.C.: U.S. Government Printing Office, 1982), 34–40, quote at 36.
3. Nanette Gartrell et al., "Psychiatrist-Patient Sexual Contact: Results of a National Survey, I: Prevalence," *American Journal of Psychiatry* 143 (Sept. 1986): 1126–31.
4. Stanton Wheeler, Kenneth Mann, and Austin Sarat, *Sitting in Judgment: The Sentencing of White-Collar Criminals* (New Haven: Yale University Press, 1988), 155.

Think Critically

1. What do you think the stories of fraud and abuse by physicians reveal about crime in the professions in general? Explain.
2. Discuss some of the reasons for the relatively light sanctioning of physicians for fraud and abuse. Locate one story of physician fraud on the Internet, and relate it to the discussion by Jesilow, Pontell and Geis.

White-Collar Crime in the Savings and Loan Scandal*

Henry N. Pontell and Kitty Calavita

THE COLLAPSE OF THE SAVINGS AND LOAN industry was in no small part due to what may be the costliest set of white-collar crimes in history. Accounting for the eventual cost to taxpayers is no easy task, but reports of the expenses have continued to rise dramatically since the mid-1980s . . .

There is abundant evidence that white-collar crime was a central factor in 70 to 80 percent of thrift failures.[1] A Resolution Trust Corporation (RTC) study estimates that about 51 percent of RTC-controlled thrifts—insolvent institutions—have had suspected criminal misconduct referred to the FBI and that "fraud and potentially criminal conduct by insiders contributed to the failure of about 41 percent of RTC thrifts."[2] In addition, the RTC reports that (1) 138 of the 392 thrifts that were under RTC conservatorship had had criminal misconduct referred to the FBI; (2) in about 50 percent of failed thrifts, insider abuse and misconduct contributed significantly to the failure; and (3) in 15 percent of the insolvencies, possible fraudulent transactions involved the participation of other financial institutions.[3]

The amount of thrift crime officially uncovered and prosecuted largely depends on the response of regulators and law enforcement officials. White-collar crimes are often well hidden by intricate paper trails and require extensive documentation before the cases can even be brought to a prosecutor. As Katz has noted, the investigative and prosecutorial functions in white-collar crimes are often one and the same.[4] Thus a central determinant of the extent of white-collar crime in the savings and loan crisis is the capacity and willingness of enforcers and other state officials to define what could be regarded as illegal behavior . . .

*From *Annals of the American Academy of Political and Social Science,* vol. 525, pp. 31–45, copyright © 1993 by Sage Publications, Inc. Reprinted by permission of Sage Publications, Inc.

Industry Structure and Origins of the Crisis

The federally insured savings and loan system was put into place in the 1930s, primarily to encourage the construction and sale of new homes during the Depression and to protect savings institutions from the kind of disaster that followed the 1929 depression. The Federal Home Loan Bank Act of 1932[5] established the Federal Home Loan Bank Board, designed to provide a credit system to ensure the availability of mortgage money for home financing and to oversee federally chartered savings and loans (S&Ls, also known as "thrifts"). Two years later, the National Housing Act[6] created the Federal Savings and Loan Insurance Corporation (FSLIC) to insure thrift deposits. Until the broad reforms enacted by the Financial Institutions Reform, Recovery and Enforcement Act of 1989, the Federal Home Loan Bank Board was the primary regulatory agency responsible for federally chartered savings and loans.

Economic conditions of the 1970s substantially undermined the health of the S&L industry and contributed to the dismantling of the traditional boundaries within which they had operated for decades. Perhaps most important, high interest rates and slow growth squeezed the industry at both ends. Locked into low-interest mortgages from previous eras, prohibited by regulation from paying more than 5.5 percent interest on new deposits, and with inflation reaching 13.3 percent by 1979, the industry suffered steep losses. As inflation outpaced the small return on their deposits, savings and loan institutions found it increasingly difficult to attract new funds. Compounding their problems, the development of money market mutual funds by Wall Street allowed middle-income investors to buy shares in large-denomination securities at high money-market rates, which triggered disintermediation, or massive withdrawals of deposits from savings and loans.

Along with these economic forces a new ideological era had begun. Though policymakers had been considering further loosening the restraints on savings and loans since the early 1970s, it was not until the deregulatory fervor of the early Reagan administration years that this approach gained widespread political acceptance as a solution to the rapidly escalating savings and loan crisis. Referring to the new deregulatory mentality and the conviction and enthusiasm with which deregulation was pursued, a senior thrift regulator said, "I always describe it as a freight train. I mean it was just the direction, and everybody got on board."[7] In a few bold strokes, policymakers dismantled most of the regulatory infrastructure that had kept the thrift industry together for four decades.[8] The deregulators were convinced that the free enterprise system worked best if left alone, unhampered by perhaps well-meaning but ultimately counterproductive government regulations. In 1980, the Depository Institutions Deregulation and Monetary Control Act[9] phased out restrictions on interest rates paid by savings and loans. But the move to the free-market model was incomplete and accompanied by a decisive move in the opposite direction. At the same time that the new law unleashed savings and loans to compete for new money, it bolstered the federal protection accorded these private enterprise institutions, increasing FSLIC insurance from a maximum of $40,000 to $100,000 per deposit.

In 1982, the Garn-St. Germain Depository Institutions Act[10] accelerated the phase-out on interest rate ceilings initiated in 1980. More important, however, it expanded the investment powers of thrifts, authorizing them to make consumer loans up to a total of 30 percent of their assets; make commercial, corporate, or business loans; and invest in nonresidential real estate worth up to 40 percent of their assets. In addition, the new law allowed for 100 percent financing, requiring no down payment from the borrower. At the same time, federal regulators dropped the requirement that thrifts have at least 400 stockholders, opening the door for a single entrepreneur to own and operate a federally insured savings and loan.

Federal and state governments—whose state-chartered thrifts' deposits were, by and large, insured by federal funds—had created an industry environment that was ripe for widespread lawbreaking. Martin Mayer, a former member of the President's Commission on Housing under the Reagan administration, describes these deregulatory years:

> What happened to create the disgusting and expensive spectacle of a diseased industry was that the government, confronted with a difficult problem, found a false solution that made the problem worse. This false solution then acquired a supportive constituency that remained vigorous and effective for almost five years after everybody with the slightest expertise in the subject knew that terrible things were happening everywhere. Some of the supporters were true believers, some were simply lazy, and most were making money—lots of money—from the government's mistake.[11]

With their new-found wealth and freedom from effective regulation, thrift operators were encouraged—indeed, were impelled by their addiction to high-interest brokered deposits—to make risky investments in junk bonds, stocks, commercial real estate projects, anything that had the potential to reap windfall profits. The magic was that every deposit up to $100,000 was federally insured, and therefore these high-risk investments were, from the depositors' and bankers' perspective, essentially risk free. Some of the transactions were legitimate, if foolhardy, attempts to raise capital; others were outright scams involving insiders, borrowers, Wall Street brokers, and developers. This scenario was created by an organizational environment altered by the deregulation of the 1980s, which transformed the industry virtually overnight and precipitated its demise . . .

The Violations

The Federal Home Loan Bank Board describes fraud as it relates to the savings and loan industry as follows:

> . . . individuals in a position of trust in the institution or closely affiliated with it have, in general terms, breached their fiduciary duties; traded on inside information; usurped opportunities or profits; engaged in self-dealing; or otherwise used the institution for personal advantage. Specific examples of insider abuse include loans to insiders in excess of that allowed by regulation; high risk speculative ventures; payment of exorbitant dividends at times when the institution is at or near insolvency; payment from institution funds for personal vacations, automobiles, clothing, and art;

payment of unwarranted commissions and fees to companies owned by the shareholder; payment of "consulting fees" to insiders or their companies; use of insiders' companies for association business; and putting friends and relatives on the payroll of the institutions.[12]

. . . The list of frauds carried out by thrift operators and related outsiders is a long one. The misconduct can be separated into three analytically distinct categories of white-collar crime. These are (1) unlawful risk taking, (2) collective embezzlement, and (3) covering up.[13] The categories often overlap in actual cases, both because at times one individual committed several types of fraud and because the same business transaction sometimes involved more than one type.

Unlawful Risk Taking

In its study of savings and loan insolvencies, the GAO concluded, "All of the 26 failed thrifts made non-traditional, higher-risk investments and in doing so . . . violated laws and regulations and engaged in unsafe practices."[14] While deregulation made it legal for thrifts to invest in "non-traditional, higher-risk" activities, loans frequently were extended beyond permissible levels of risk—for example, by concentrating investment in one area, particularly construction loans. These high-risk levels often were accompanied by inadequate marketability studies and poor supervision of loan disbursement, both of which constitute violations of regulatory standards.

The factors that triggered this unlawful risk taking are similar in some ways to those described in other white-collar crime studies. Sutherland, Geis, Farberman, and Hagan, for example, note the importance of competition, the desire to maximize profit, and corporate subcultures as major determinants of corporate crime.[15] Analyses of Medicaid fraud have documented how the conflict between government regulation and the norms of the medical profession results in an environment where fraud is likely to occur.[16]

The opportunity structure is often cited as a facilitating factor in the commission of corporate crime. Some analyses emphasize the ease with which corporate crime can be committed as a complement to the profit motive in the generation of such crime.[17] The infamous electrical company conspiracy of the 1940s and 1950s, which involved price fixing in government contract bids,

provides an excellent example.[18] In that case, the small number of very large corporations that dominated the industry offered an ideal opportunity structure and facilitated the criminal conspiracy among the nation's largest electrical manufacturing companies.

The unlawful risk taking in the savings and loan industry, however, is distinct in a number of ways from such traditional corporate crimes. While successful corporate crime traditionally results in increased profits and long-term liquidity for the company, unlawful risk taking in the thrift industry is a gamble involving very bad odds. Unlike more traditional corporate and white-collar crimes in the industrial sector, S&L crimes often resulted in the bankruptcy of the institution.

Collective Embezzlement

As the Commissioner of the California Department of Savings and Loans stated in 1987, "The best way to rob a bank is to own one."[19] "Collective embezzlement," also referred to here as "looting," refers to the siphoning off of funds from a savings and loan institution for personal gain at the expense of the institution itself and with the implicit or explicit endorsement of its management. This form of illegality is estimated to have been the most costly category of thrift crime, having precipitated a significant number of the largest insolvencies to date.[20]

Discussing various forms of white-collar lawbreaking, Sutherland noted that "the ordinary case of embezzlement is a crime by a single individual in a subordinate position against a strong corporation."[21] Cressey, in his landmark study *Other People's Money,* examined the motivations of such a lone embezzler.[22] The collective embezzlement in the S&L fraud differs in important ways from this individual model. Traditional embezzlement is clearly an example of deviance in an organization, insofar as it is perpetrated by an individual stealing from the institution and thereby jeopardizing its organizational goals. Collective embezzlement, however, not only is deviance in an organization—in the sense that the misconduct harms the viability of the institution—but also constitutes deviance by the organization.[23] Not only are the perpetrators themselves in management positions, but the very goals of the institution are precisely to provide a money machine for its owners and other insiders; the S&L can be discarded after serving this purpose. This form of thrift crime utilizes what Wheeler and Rothman have called "the organization as weapon": ". . . the organization . . . is for white-collar criminals what the gun or knife is for the common criminal—a tool to obtain money from victims."[24] The principal difference between Wheeler and Rothman's profile of the organization as weapon and the collective embezzlement in the S&L industry is that the latter is an organizational crime against the organization's own best interests. That is, the organization is both weapon and victim . . .

The most expensive S&L failure to date has been that of Charles Keating's Lincoln Savings and Loan in Irvine, California. Keating contributed heavily to political campaigns at both the state and federal levels and to both political parties. When Lincoln Savings came under fire from the Federal Home Loan Bank in 1987, five Senators intervened on Keating's behalf. The investigation of Lincoln was soon moved from the San Francisco regional office of the Federal Home Loan Bank, which was widely known for its rigorous regulatory approach, to the central office in Washington, D.C. The move is said to have postponed by two years the closing of Lincoln and the indictment of Keating, a delay that is estimated to have cost taxpayers about $2 billion.[25] While the case of the Keating Five, as the Senators who came to Keating's rescue are called, is the most well publicized instance of influence peddling to save off scrutiny of thrift activities, it is only part of a larger pattern, the repercussions of which go far beyond one or two institutions.

Covering Up

A considerable proportion of the criminal charges leveled against fraudulent savings and loans involve attempts to hide both the thrift's insolvency and the fraud that contributed to that insolvency. The cover-up is usually accomplished through a manipulation of S&L books and records; this form of fraud may be the most pervasive criminal activity of thrift operators. Of the alleged 179 violations of criminal law reported in the 26 failed thrifts studied by the GAO, 42 were for covering up, constituting the single largest category.[26] The same GAO study found that every one of the thrifts had been cited by regulatory examiners for "deficiencies in accounting."[27]

Covering up is employed for a variety of purposes by S&L operators. First, it is used to produce a misleading picture of the institution's state of health, or, more specifically, to misrepresent the thrift's capital reserves as well as its capital-to-assets ratio. Second, deals may be arranged that include covering up as part of the scheme. In cases of risky or "reciprocal" loans, for example, a reserve account may be created to pay off the first few months or years of a development loan to make it look current, whether or not the project has failed or was phony in the first place. Third, covering up may be used after the fact to disguise actual investment activity . . .

In their unlawful risk taking, collective embezzlement, and covering up, thrift officers often were joined by outsiders from various occupations and professional groups, whose roles were essential for perpetrating the criminal transactions. Real estate developers and deposit brokers, among others, were coconspirators in numerous cases of thrift fraud. In some instances, innocent savings and loan institutions were victimized by less virtuous counterparts. Lewis, for example, describes how Wall Street brokerage firms enriched themselves through fraud against their clients, many of whom were thrifts which had invested in stock market schemes and related securities and junk bond deals.[28]

According to many experts, the hired guns of the industry, including appraisers, lawyers, and accountants, are among the most egregious outside offenders; their well-paid services made many of the S&L frauds possible. Perhaps most important was the role of accountants, whose audits of savings and loan records allowed many scam transactions to go unnoticed, while disguising the state of the financial institution's health. Although some of their activities technically were not criminal, a number of the largest accounting firms in the country are now being sued by government regulators for their negligence in reporting potential and actual malfeasance.

Enforcement

Cases of savings and loan malfeasance move through a complex web of enforcement jurisdictions before they are finally closed. Regulatory agencies, such as the Office of Thrift Supervision, the Resolution Trust Corporation, and the Federal Deposit Insurance Corporation (FDIC), have a number of administrative and civil remedies at their disposal. Serious cases are turned over to the FBI and the U.S. Attorney's offices for potential criminal prosecution.

As the receiver of failed institutions, the federal government, primarily through the FDIC and RTC, can become involved in civil fraud litigation. When the RTC seizes a thrift, it receives certain assets of the institution—usually real estate—and investigates the possibility of filing legal claims against former officers, directors, and outsiders . . .

Within the RTC, the Professional Liability Section of the Legal Division is responsible for litigating such cases. Lawsuits may target directors and officers, attorneys, accountants, commodity and securities brokers, and/or appraisers. The lawyers of this division work with RTC investigators and outside fee counsel to pursue civil recoveries for the RTC . . .

The criminal justice system becomes involved in thrift cases when a financial institution or regulator refers a suspected criminal violation to the Department of Justice. Once a criminal referral is made, the FBI or, as of January 1991, the Secret Service in the Department of the Treasury investigates to determine if criminal charges can be brought. FBI and Secret Service investigators usually work with a U.S. Attorney's office in the early stages, both to determine if the investigation should proceed and to set expectations regarding what evidence will be needed to prosecute successfully.

Prosecutorial task forces provide a useful enforcement tool in many areas of the country, bringing together a variety of agency experts to work on particularly complex financial institution fraud cases. These task forces combine the resources of the U.S. Attorney's Office, the Criminal, Tax, and Civil divisions of the Justice Department, the FBI, the Internal Revenue Service, the FDIC, the Office of Thrift Supervision, the RTC, and other agencies . . .

Detecting and prosecuting S&L fraud constitute one of the most challenging tasks in the history of American law enforcement. First, the nature of the crimes and the complex financial transactions within which they are usually embedded make it extraordinarily difficult to detect the acts in the first place and then to uncover adequate evidence to prosecute them successfully. Second, the magnitude of the workloads resulting from this epidemic of financial fraud ensures that a substantial number of cases will fall through the cracks . . .

In the absence of other information regarding the nature of criminal referrals, investigative strategies, and enforcement resources, as well as in the face of the difficulty of detecting crime in transactions in which criminal intent can be disguised by ordinary occupational and organizational routines, such official processing data are largely ceremonial. That is, as production figures they may function to legitimate the activities of the organization reporting them.[29] The data reveal at least as much about organizational activities as they do about patterns of financial crime. Despite such limitations of official data, the reported figures speak to the sheer volume of financial fraud prosecutions and to the widespread participation of insiders in the looting of their institutions.

Conclusion

The financial losses incurred in the savings and loan crisis are in part the result of deliberate and widespread criminal activity. The combination of deregulation, increased government deposit insurance, and the lack of effective oversight mechanisms provided a "criminogenic environment" in the thrift industry.[30] Financial fraud of the kind described here, of course, is not new. What is new is its magnitude and scope and that it occurs at a time when the economic structure of the United States, and to a lesser extent that of other Western democracies, is increasingly focused on financial transactions rather than on the manufacturing enterprises of the industrial era. Further research, focused on the thrift and banking industries as well as other comparable financial institutions, is vital to advancing a theoretical understanding of the dynamics of white-collar crime in the postindustrial period.

NOTES

1. U.S., General Accounting Office, *Failed Thrifts: Internal Control Weaknesses Create an Environment Conducive to Fraud, Insider Abuse and Related Unsafe Practices,* Statement of Frederick D. Wolf, Assistant Comptroller General, before the Subcommittee on Criminal Justice, Committee on the Judiciary, House of Representatives, GAO/T-AFMD-89-4, 22 Mar. 1989; U.S., Congress, House, Committee on Government Operations, *Combatting Fraud, Abuse and Misconduct in the Nation's Financial Institutions: Current Federal Reports Are Inadequate,* 72d report by the Committee on Government Operations, 13 Oct. 1989.

2. Resolution Trust Corporation, Office of Investigations, Resolutions and Operations Division, *Report on Investigations to Date,* 31 Dec. 1989.

3. James R. Dudine, *The Extent of Misconduct in Insolvent Thrift Associations,* Testimony before the Commerce, Consumer and Monetary Affairs Subcommittee, Committee on Government Operations, U.S. House of Representatives, 15 Mar. 1990.

4. Jack Katz, "Legality and Equality: Plea Bargaining in the Prosecution of White-Collar and Common Crimes," *Law and Society Review,* 17(3):431 (Winter 1979).

5. 12 U.S.C. 1421 et seq.

6. 12 U.S.C. 1724 et seq.

7. Personal interview.

8. Martin Mayer, *The Greatest-Ever Bank Robbery: The Collapse of the Savings and Loan Industry* (New York: Charles Scribner's Sons, 1990).

9. Pub. L. 96–221.

10. Pub. L. 97–320.

11. Mayer, *Greatest-Ever Bank Robbery,* p. 8.

12. U.S., General Accounting Office, *Failed Thrifts: Internal Control Weaknesses,* p. 8.

13. Kitty Calavita and Henry N. Pontell, "'Heads I Win, Tails You Lose': Deregulation, Crime and Crisis in the Savings and Loan Industry," *Crime & Delinquency,* 36(3):309 (July 1990).

14. U.S., General Accounting Office, *Failed Thrifts: Costly Failures,* p. 17.

15. Edwin H. Sutherland, *White Collar Crime* (New York: Dryden, 1949); Gilbert Geis, "The Heavy Electrical Equipment Antitrust Cases of 1961," in *Criminal Behavior Systems: A Typology,* ed. by M. B. Clinard and R. Quinney (New York: Holt, Rinehart & Winston, 1967); Harvey A. Farberman, "A Criminogenic Market Structure: The Automobile Industry," *Sociological Quarterly* 16(4):438 (Autumn 1975); John Hagan, *Modern Criminology: Crime, Criminal Behavior, and Its Control* (New York: McGraw-Hill, 1985).

16. Henry N. Pontell, Paul D. Jesilow, and Gilbert Geis, "Policing Physicians: Practitioner Fraud and Abuse in a Government Benefit Program," *Social Problems,* 30(1):117 (Oct. 1982); idem, "Practitioner Fraud and Abuse in Medical Benefit Programs: Government Regulation and Professional White-Collar Crime," *Law and Policy,* 6:405 (Oct. 1984); Paul Jesilow, Henry N. Pontell, and Gilbert Geis, *Prescription for Profit: How Doctors Defraud Medicaid* (Berkeley: University of California Press, 1993).

17. Stanton Wheeler and Mitchell Lewis Rothman, "The Organization as Weapon in White Collar Crime," *Michigan Law Review,* 80(7):1403 (June 1982).

18. Geis, "Heavy Electrical Equipment Antitrust Cases."

19. U.S., Congress, House, Committee on Government Operations, *Combatting Fraud, Abuse and Misconduct.*

20. Ibid.

21. Sutherland, *White Collar Crime,* p. 231.

22. Donald R. Cressey, *Other People's Money: A Study of the Social Psychology of Embezzlement* (Glencoe, IL: Free Press, 1953).

23. Lawrence Sherman, *Scandal and Reform* (Berkeley: University of California Press, 1978).

24. Wheeler and Rothman note the distinction between embezzlement and corporate crime in pointing out that "either the individual gains at the organization's expense, as in embezzlement, or the organization profits regardless of individual advantage, as in price-fixing." They argue that this separation ignores cases where both organization and individual may benefit, as when an individual's career is advanced by crime perpetrated on behalf of the organization. Wheeler and Rothman, "Organization as Weapon," p. 1405. What they neglect to note, however, is the possibility of organizational crime in which the organization is a weapon for perpetrating crime against itself.

25. Committee on Standards of Official Conduct, *Report in the Matter of Wright;* Mayer, *Greatest-Ever Bank Robbery.*

26. General Accounting Office, *Failed Thrifts: Costly Failures,* p. 51.

27. Ibid., p. 40.

28. Michael Lewis, *Liar's Poker* (New York: Penguin Books, 1989).

29. John W. Meyer and Brian Rowan, "Institutionalized Organizations: Formal Structure as Myth and Ceremony," *American Journal of Sociology,* 83(2):340 (Sept. 1977).

30. Martin Needleman and Carolyn Needleman, "Organizational Crime: Two Models of Criminogenesis." *Sociological Quarterly,* 20(4):517 (Autumn 1979).

Think Critically

1. Given limited government capacity issues regarding the policing and punishment of financial fraud discussed by the authors, what policies might best help reduce these costly criminal acts? Explain.

2. Relate the concept of "collective embezzlement" to two examples of financial fraud, naming both the specific crimes and the perpetrators. In your answer, discuss how these crimes comprise forms of collective embezzlement.

Denying the Guilty Mind
*Accounting for Involvement in a White-Collar Crime**

Michael L. Benson

ADJUDICATION AS A CRIMINAL IS, TO USE Garfinkel's (1956) classic term, a degradation ceremony. The focus of this article is on how offenders attempt to defeat the success of this ceremony and deny their own criminality through the use of accounts. However, in the interest of showing in as much detail as possible all sides of the experience undergone by these offenders, it is necessary to treat first the guilt and inner anguish that is felt by many white-collar offenders even though they deny being criminals. This is best accomplished by beginning with a description of a unique feature of the prosecution of white-collar crimes.

In white-collar criminal cases, the issue is likely to be *why* something was done, rather than *who* did it (Edelhertz, 1970:47). There is often relatively little disagreement as to what happened . . .

If the prosecution is to proceed past the investigatory stages, the prosecutor must infer from the pattern of events that conscious criminal intent was present and believe that sufficient evidence exists to convince a jury of this interpretation of the situation. As Katz (1979:445–446) has noted, making this inference can be difficult because of the way in which white-collar illegalities are integrated into ordinary occupational routines. Thus, prosecutors in conducting trials, grand jury hearings, or plea negotiations spend a great deal of effort establishing that the defendant did indeed have the necessary criminal intent. By concentrating on the offender's motives, the prosecutor attacks the very essence of the white-collar offender's public and personal image as an upstanding member of the community. The offender is portrayed as someone with a guilty mind.

Not surprisingly, therefore, the most consistent and recurrent pattern in the interviews, though not present in all of them, was denial of criminal intent, as opposed to the outright denial of any criminal behavior whatsoever. Most offenders acknowledged that their behavior probably could be construed as falling within the conduct proscribed by stature, but they uniformly denied that their actions were motivated by a guilty mind. This is not to say, however, that offenders *felt* no guilt or shame as a result of conviction. On the contrary, indictment, prosecution, and conviction provoke a variety of emotions among offenders . . .

The traumatic nature of this moment lies, in part, in the offender's feeling that only one aspect of his life is being considered. From the offender's point of view his crime represents only one small part of his life. It does not typify his inner self, and to judge him solely on the basis of this one event seems an atrocious injustice to the offender.

For some the memory of the event is so painful that they want to obliterate it entirely, as the two following quotations illustrate.

> I want quiet. I want to forget. I want to cut with the past.
>
> I've already divorced myself from the problem. I don't even want to hear the names of certain people ever again. It brings me pain.

For others, rage rather than embarrassment seemed to be the dominant emotion.

> I never really felt any embarrassment over the whole thing. I felt rage and it wasn't false or self-serving. It was really (something) to see this thing in action and recognize what the whole legal system has come to through its development, and the abuse of the grand jury system and the abuse of the indictment system. . . .

*Reprinted from *Criminology*, 23:4, (Nov., 1985), pp. 589–599 by permission of the author and the American Society of Criminology.

The role of the news media in the process of punishment and stigmatization should not be overlooked. All offenders whose cases were reported on by the news media were either embarrassed or embittered or both by the public exposure.

> The only one I am bitter at is the newspapers, as many people are. They are unfair because you can't get even. They can say things that are untrue, and let me say this to you. They wrote an article on me that was so blasphemous, that was so horrible. They painted me as an insidious, miserable creature, wringing out the last penny. . . .

Offenders whose cases were not reported on by the news media expressed relief at having avoided that kind of embarrassment, sometimes saying that greater publicity would have been worse than any sentence they could have received.

In court, defense lawyers are fond of presenting white-collar offenders as having suffered enough by virtue of the humiliation of public adjudication as criminals. On the other hand, prosecutors present them as cavalier individuals who arrogantly ignore the law and brush off its weak efforts to stigmatize them as criminals. Neither of these stereotypes is entirely accurate. The subjective effects of conviction on white-collar offenders are varied and complex. One suspects that this is true of all offenders, not only white-collar offenders.

The emotional responses of offenders to conviction have not been the subject of extensive research. However, insofar as an individual's emotional response to adjudication may influence the deterrent or crime-reinforcing impact of punishment on him or her, further study might reveal why some offenders stop their criminal behavior while others go on to careers in crime (Casper, 1978:80).

Although the offenders displayed a variety of different emotions with respect to their experiences, they were nearly unanimous in denying basic criminality. To see how white-collar offenders justify and excuse their crimes, we turn to their accounts. The small number of cases rules out the use of any elaborate classification techniques. Nonetheless, it is useful to group offenders by offense when presenting their interpretations.

Antitrust Violators

Four of the offenders had been convicted of antitrust violations, all in the same case involving the building and contracting industry. Four major themes characterized their accounts. First, antitrust offenders focused on the everyday character and historical continuity of their offenses.

> It was a way of doing business before we even got into the business. So it was like why do you brush your teeth in the morning or something. . . . It was part of the everyday. . . . It was a method of survival.

The offenders argued that they were merely following established and necessary industry practices. These practices were presented as being necessary for the well-being of the industry as a whole, not to mention their own companies. Further, they argued that cooperation among competitors was either allowed or actively promoted by the government in other industries and professions.

The second theme emphasized by the offenders was the characterization of their actions as blameless. They admitted talking to competitors and admitted submitting intentionally noncompetitive bids. However, they presented these practices as being done not for the purpose of rigging prices nor to make exorbitant profits. Rather, the everyday practices of the industry required them to occasionally submit bids on projects they really did not want to have. To avoid the effort and expense of preparing full-fledged bids, they would call a competitor to get a price to use. Such a situation might arise, for example, when a company already had enough work for the time being, but was asked by a valued customer to submit a bid anyway . . .

Managed in this way, an action that appears on the surface to be a straightforward and conscious violation of antitrust regulations becomes merely a harmless business practice that happens to be a "technical violation." The offender can then refer to his personal history to verify his claim that, despite technical violations, he is in reality a law-abiding person . . .

Third, offenders were very critical of the motives and tactics of prosecutors. Prosecutors were accused of being motivated solely by the opportunity for personal advancement presented by winning a big case. Further, they were accused of employing prosecution selectively and using tactics that allowed the most culpable offenders to go free . . .

The fourth theme emphasized by the antitrust offenders involved a comparison between their crimes and the crimes of street criminals. Antitrust offenses differ in their mechanics from street crimes in that they are not committed in one place and at one time. Rather, they are spatially and temporally diffuse and are intermingled with legitimate behavior . . .

A consistent thread running through all of the interviews was the necessity for antitrust-like practices, given the realities of the business world. Offenders seemed to define the situation in such a manner that two sets of rules could be seen to apply. On the one hand, there are the legislatively determined rules—laws—which govern how one is to conduct one's business affairs. On the other hand, there is a higher set of rules based on the concepts of profit and survival, which are taken to define what it means to be in business in a capitalistic society. These rules do not just regulate behavior; rather, they constitute or create the behavior in question . . .

One might suggest, following Denzin (1977), that for businessmen in the building and contracting industry, an informal structure exists below the articulated legal structure, one which frequently supersedes the legal structure. The informal structure may define as moral and "legal" certain actions that the formal legal structure defines as immoral and "illegal."

Tax Violators

Six of the offenders interviewed were convicted of income tax violations. Like antitrust violators, tax violators can rely upon the complexity of the tax laws and an historical tradition in which cheating on taxes is not really criminal. Tax offenders would claim that everybody cheats somehow on their taxes and present themselves as victims of an unlucky break, because they got caught . . .

The widespread belief that cheating on taxes is endemic helps to lend credence to the offender's claim to have been singled out and to be no more guilty than most people.

Tax offenders were more likely to have acted as individuals rather than as part of a group and, as a result, were more prone to account for their offenses by referring to them as either mistakes or the product of special circumstances. Violations were presented as simple errors which resulted from ignorance and poor recordkeeping. Deliberate intention to steal from the government for personal benefit was denied.

> I didn't take the money. I have no bank account to show for all this money, where all this money is at that I was supposed to have. They never found the money, ever. There is no Swiss bank account, believe me.

My records were strictly one big mess. That's all it was. If only I had an accountant, this wouldn't even of happened. No way in God's creation would this ever have happened.

Other offenders would justify their actions by admitting that they were wrong while painting their motives as altruistic rather than criminal. Criminality was denied because they did not set out to deliberately cheat the government for their own personal gain . . .

All of the tax violators pointed out that they had no intention of deliberately victimizing the government. None of them denied the legitimacy of the tax laws, nor did they claim that they cheated because the government is not representative of the people (Conklin, 1977:99). Rather, as a result of ignorance or for altruistic reasons, they made decisions which turned out to be criminal when viewed from the perspective of the law. While they acknowledged the technical criminality of their actions, they tried to show that what they did was not criminally motivated.

Violations of Financial Trust

Four offenders were involved in violations of financial trust. Three were bank officers who embezzled or misapplied funds, and the fourth was a union official who embezzled from a union pension fund. Perhaps because embezzlement is one crime in this sample that can be considered *mala in se,* these offenders were much more forthright about their crimes. Like the other offenders, the embezzlers would not go so far as to say "I am a criminal," but they did say "What I did was wrong, was criminal, and I knew it was." Thus, the embezzlers were unusual in that they explicitly admitted responsibility for their crimes. Two of the offenders clearly fit Cressey's scheme as persons with financial problems who used their positions to convert other people's money to their own use.

Unlike tax evasion, which can be excused by reference to the complex nature of tax regulations or antitrust violations, which can be justified as for the good of the organization as a whole, embezzlement requires deliberate action on the part of the offender and is almost inevitably committed for personal reasons. The crime of embezzlement, therefore, cannot be accounted for by using the same techniques that tax violators or antitrust violators do. The act itself can only be explained by showing that one was under extraordinary circumstances which explain one's uncharacteristic behavior. Three of the offenders referred explicitly to extraordinary circumstances and presented the offense as an aberration in their life history. For example, one offender described his situation in this manner:

> As a kid, I never even—you know kids will sometimes shoplift from the dime store—I never even did that. I had never stolen a thing in my life and that was what was so unbelievable about the whole thing, but there were some psychological and personal questions that I wasn't dealing with very well. I wasn't terribly happily married. I was married to a very strong-willed woman and it just wasn't working out.

The offender in this instance goes on to explain how, in an effort to impress his wife, he lived beyond his means and fell into debt.

A structural characteristic of embezzlement also helps the offender demonstrate his essential lack of criminality. Embezzlement is integrated into ordinary occupational routines. The illegal action does not stand out clearly against the surrounding set of legal actions . . . The embezzler must be discrete in his stealing; he cannot take all of the money available to him without at the same time revealing the crime. Once exposed, the offender can point to this restraint on his part as evidence that he is not really a criminal. That is, he can compare what happened with what could have happened in order to show how much more serious the offense could have been if he was really a criminal at heart . . .

Even though the offender is forthright about admitting his guilt, he makes a distinction between himself and someone with a truly "devious criminal mind."

Contrary to Cressey's (1953:57–66) findings, none of the embezzlers claimed that their offenses were justified because they were underpaid or badly treated by their employers. Rather, attention was focused on the unusual circumstances surrounding the offense and its atypical character when compared to the rest of the offender's life. This strategy is for the most part determined by the mechanics and organizational format of the offense itself. Embezzlement occurs within the organization but not for the organization. It cannot be committed accidentally or out of ignorance. It can be accounted for only by showing that the actor "was not himself" at the time of the offense or was under such extraordinary circumstances that embezzlement was an understandable response to an unfortunate situation . . .

Fraud and False Statements

Ten offenders were convicted of some form of fraud or false statements charge. Unlike embezzlers, tax violators, or antitrust violators, these offenders were much more likely to deny committing any crime at all. Seven of the ten claimed that they, personally, were innocent of any crime, although each admitted that fraud had occurred. Typically, they claimed to have been set up by associates and to have been wrongfully convicted by the U.S. Attorney handling the case. One might call this the scapegoat strategy. Rather than admitting technical wrongdoing and then justifying or excusing it, the offender attempts to paint himself as a victim by shifting the blame entirely to another party. Prosecutors were presented as being either ignorant or politically motivated.

The outright denial of any crime whatsoever is unusual compared to the other types of offenders studied here. It may result from the nature of the crime of fraud. By definition, fraud involves a conscious attempt on the part of one or more persons to mislead others. While it is theoretically possible to accidentally violate the antitrust and tax laws, or to violate them for altruistic reasons, it is difficult to imagine how one could accidentally mislead someone else for his or her own good. Furthermore, in many instances, fraud is an aggressively acquisitive crime . . . Thus, those involved in large-scale frauds do not have the option open to most embezzlers of presenting themselves as persons responding defensively to difficult personal circumstances.

Furthermore, because fraud involves a deliberate attempt to mislead another, the offender who fails to remove himself from the scheme runs the risk of being shown to have a guilty mind. That is, he is shown to possess the most essential element of modern conceptions of criminality: an intent to harm another. His inner self would in this case be exposed as something other than what it has been presented as, and all of his previous actions would be subject to reinterpretation in light of this new perspective. For this reason, defrauders are most prone to denying any crime at all. The cooperative and conspiratorial nature of many fraudulent schemes makes it possible to put the blame on someone else and to present oneself as a scapegoat. Typically, this is done by claiming to have been duped by others.

Two illustrations of this strategy are presented below.

I figured I wasn't guilty, so it wouldn't be that hard to disprove it, until, as I say, I went to court and all of a sudden they start bringing in these guys out of the woodwork implicating me that I never saw. Lot of it could be proved that I never saw. Inwardly, I personally felt that the only crime that I committed was not telling on these guys. Not that I deliberately, intentionally committed a crime against the system. My only crime was that I should have had the guts to tell on these guys, what they were doing, rather than putting up with it and then trying to gradually get out of the system without hurting them or without them thinking I was going to snitch on them.

Discussion: Offenses, Accounts, and Degradation Ceremonies

The investigation, prosecution, and conviction of a white-collar offender involves him in a very undesirable status passage (Glaser and Strauss, 1971). The entire process can be viewed as a long and drawn-out degradation ceremony with the prosecutor as the chief denouncer and the offender's family and friends as the chief witnesses. The offender is moved from the status of law-abiding citizen to that of convicted felon. Accounts are developed to defeat the process of identity transformation that is the object of a degradation ceremony. They represent the offender's attempt to diminish the effect of his legal transformation and to prevent its becoming a publicly validated label. It can be suggested that the accounts developed by white-collar offenders take the forms that they do for two reasons: (1) the forms are required to defeat the success of the degradation ceremony, and (2) the specific forms used are the ones available given the mechanics, history, and organizational context of the offenses.

Three general patterns in accounting strategies stand out in the data. Each can be characterized by the subject matter on which it focuses: the event (offense), the perpetrator (offender), or reduced. Although there are overlaps in the accounting strategies used by the various types of offenders, and while any given offender may use more than one strategy, it appears that accounting strategies and offenses correlate.

REFERENCES

Casper, Jonathan D. 1978. *Criminal Courts: The Defendant's Perspective.* Washington, D.C.: U.S. Department of Justice.

Conklin, John E. 1977. *Illegal But Not Criminal: Business Crime in America.* Englewood Cliffs, N.J.: Prentice Hall.

Cressey, Donald. 1953. *Other People's Money.* New York: Free Press.

Denzin, Norman K. 1977. "Notes on the criminogenic hypothesis: A case study of the American liquor industry." *American Sociological Review* 42:905–920.

Edelhertz, Herbert. 1970. *The Nature, Impact, and Prosecution of White Collar Crime.* Washington, D.C.: U.S. Government Printing Office.

Garfinkel, Harold. 1956. "Conditions of successful degradation ceremonies." *American Journal of Sociology* 61:420–424.

Glaser, Barney G. and Anselm L. Strauss. 1971. *Status Passage.* Chicago: Aldine.

Katz, Jack. 1979. "Legality and equality: Plea bargaining," in the prosecution of white-collar crimes." *Law and Society Review* 13:431–460.

Think Critically

1. Compare two types of white-collar criminals studied by Benson and discuss how their neutralizations varied with their offenses.
2. Why do you think that those convicted of fraud and false statements were much more likely to deny doing anything wrong at all? Explain.

MENTAL DISORDER

IN HIS CLASSIC WORK, "ON BEING SANE IN Insane Places," D.L. Rosenhan explores the question of how sanity exists by having people be "pseudo-patients" in twelve different hospitals. The experiment raises questions as to the definitions of what is considered "normal" and "abnormal," but does not challenge the notion that some behaviors may be odd or deviant. The study finds that diagnoses of sanity and insanity are less substantive and more subjective than previously realized. Rosenhan concludes that given the special environment of psychiatric hospitals, which he describes in detail, it is not possible to distinguish the sane from the insane.

Along similar lines of thought, Erving Goffman presents the path leading to institutionalization, and the changes in identity that occur once one is admitted, in his work, "The Moral Career of the Mental Patient." Goffman describes the ways in which persons are admitted to hospitals ("prepatient phase"), and the "betrayal funnel" that can be part of this process. The "inpatient phase" of the patient career involves a full range of mortifying experiences that involve the transformation of self in response to the hospital environment. In time, the patient's views become discredited, and he or she is forced to actually take, or pretend to take, the hospital's view in order to best survive his or her institutionalization.

Ronny Turner and Charles Edgley's work, "From Witchcraft to Drugcraft," questions the biochemical etiology of mental illness. The authors argue that explanations of deviant behavior focusing on the witch, the curse, and the sin, have been supplanted by the terminology of medicine, psychiatry, and biochemistry. Evidence is presented to show that diagnoses of mental illness are not and cannot be based on chemical analyses, but rather are social judgments that result in the labeling of deviance.

Finally, the classic work of Edwin Lemert, "Paranoia and the Dynamics of Exclusion" provides a forceful and brilliant sociological analysis of what, to almost all observers, would appear to fully be a psychological phenomenon: paranoia. Lemert provides a fascinating and precise analysis of the reciprocal relationship between the mentally ill person and those they interact with. Writing well within the labeling perspective, he explains that many paranoids are so labeled as a product of strained interactions with others. Rather than simply "imagining" that they are the objects of social exclusion, the individual often properly realizes this. Distorted communication and lack of feedback are interactional elements that amplify the labeling process by intensifying the perceptions of others, which leads to further exclusion and greater feelings of paranoia by the person.

On Being Sane in Insane Places*

D. L. Rosenhan**

IF SANITY AND INSANITY EXIST, HOW SHALL WE know them?

The question is neither capricious nor itself insane. However much we may be personally convinced that we can tell the normal from the abnormal, the evidence is simply not compelling. It is commonplace, for example, to read about murder trials wherein eminent psychiatrists for the defense are contradicted by equally eminent psychiatrists for the prosecution on the matter of the defendant's sanity. More generally, there are a great deal of conflicting data on the reliability, utility, and meaning of such terms as "sanity," "insanity," "mental illness," and "schizophrenia".[1] Finally, as early as 1934, Benedict suggested that normality and abnormality are not universal.[2] What is viewed as normal in one culture may be seen as quite aberrant in another. Thus, notions of normality and abnormality may not be quite as accurate as people believe they are.

To raise questions regarding normality and abnormality is in no way to question the fact that some behaviors are deviant or odd. Murder is deviant. So, too, are hallucinations. Nor does raising such questions deny the existence of the personal anguish that is often associated with "mental illness." Anxiety and depression exist. Psychological suffering exists. But normality and abnormality, sanity and insanity, and the diagnoses that flow from them may be less substantive than many believe them to be.

At its heart, the question of whether the sane can be distinguished from the insane (and whether degrees of insanity can be distinguished from each other) is a simple matter: Do the salient characteristics that lead to diagnoses reside in the patients themselves or in the environments and contexts in which observers find them? From Bleuler, through Kretchmer, through the formulators of the recently revised *Diagnostic and Statistical Manual* of the American Psychiatric Association, the belief has been strong that patients present symptoms, that those symptoms can be categorized, and, implicitly, that the sane are distinguishable from the insane. More recently, however, this belief has been questioned. Based in part on theoretical and anthropological considerations, but also on philosophical, legal, and therapeutic ones, the view has grown that psychological categorization of mental illness is useless at best and downright harmful, misleading, and pejorative at worst. Psychiatric diagnoses, in this view, are in the minds of the observers and are not valid summaries of characteristics displayed by the observed.[3–5]

Gains can be made in deciding which of these is more nearly accurate by getting normal people (that is, people who do not have, and have never suffered, symptoms of serious psychiatric disorders) admitted to psychiatric hospitals and then determining whether they were discovered to be sane and, if so, how. If the sanity of such pseudopatients were always detected, there would be prima facie evidence that a sane individual can be distinguished from the insane context in which he is found. Normality (and presumably abnormality) is distinct enough that it can be recognized wherever it occurs, for it is carried within the person. If, on the other hand, the sanity of the pseudopatients were never discovered, serious difficulties would arise for those who support traditional modes of psychiatric diagnosis. Given that the hospital staff was not incompetent, that the pseudopatient had been behaving as sanely as he had been outside of the hospital, and that it had never been previously suggested that he belonged in a

*Reprinted from *Science,* Vol. 179, 4070, (Jan. 19, 1973), pp. 250–258, by permission of the American Association for the Advancement of Science, Copyright © 1973 by the AAAS.
**Portions of these data were presented to colloquiums of the psychology departments at the University of California at Berkeley and at Santa Barbara; University of Arizona, Tucson; and Harvard University, Cambridge, Massachusetts.

psychiatric hospital, such an unlikely outcome would support the view that psychiatric diagnosis betrays little about the patient but much about the environment in which an observer finds him.

This article describes such an experiment. Eight sane people gained secret admission to 12 different hospitals.[6] Their diagnostic experiences constitute the data of the first part of this article; the remainder is devoted to a description of their experiences in psychiatric institutions. Too few psychiatrists and psychologists, even those who have worked in such hospitals, know what the experience is like. They rarely talk about it with former patients, perhaps because they distrust information coming from the previously insane. Those who have worked in psychiatric hospitals are likely to have adapted so thoroughly to the settings that they are insensitive to the impact of that experience. And while there have been occasional reports of researchers who submitted themselves to psychiatric hospitalization,[7] these researchers have commonly remained in the hospitals for short periods of time, often with the knowledge of the hospital staff. It is difficult to know the extent to which they were treated like patients or like research colleagues. Nevertheless, their reports about the inside of the psychiatric hospital have been valuable. This article extends those efforts.

Pseudopatients and Their Settings

The eight pseudopatients were a varied group. One was a psychology graduate student in his twenties. The remaining seven were older and "established." Among them were three psychologists, a pediatrician, a psychiatrist, a painter, and a housewife. Three pseudopatients were women, five were men. All of them employed pseudonyms, lest their alleged diagnoses embarrass them later. Those who were in mental health professions alleged another occupation in order to avoid the special attentions that might be accorded by staff, as a matter of courtesy or caution, to ailing colleagues.[8] With the exception of myself (I was the first pseudopatient and my presence was known to the hospital administrator and chief psychologist and, so far as I can tell, to them alone), the presence of pseudopatients and the nature of the research program was not known to the hospital staffs.[9]

The settings were similarly varied. In order to generalize the findings, admission into a variety of hospitals was sought. The 12 hospitals in the sample were located in five different states on the East and West Coasts. Some were old and shabby, some were quite new. Some were research-oriented, others not. Some had good staff-patient ratios, others were quite understaffed. Only one was a strictly private hospital. All of the others were supported by state or federal funds or, in one instance, by university funds.

After calling the hospital for an appointment, the pseudopatient arrived at the admissions office complaining that he had been hearing voices. Asked what the voices said, he replied that they were often unclear, but as far as he could tell they said "empty," "hollow," and "thud." The voices were unfamiliar and were of the same sex as the pseudopatient. The choice of these symptoms was occasioned by their apparent similarity to existential symptoms. Such symptoms are alleged to arise from painful concerns about the perceived meaninglessness of one's life. It is as if the hallucinating person were saying, "My life is empty and hollow." The choice of these symptoms was also determined by the *absence* of a single report of existential psychoses in the literature.

Beyond alleging the symptoms and falsifying name, vocation, and employment, no further alterations of person, history, or circumstances were made. The significant events of the pseudopatient's life history were presented as they had actually occurred. Relationships with parents and siblings, with spouse and children, with people at work and in school, consistent with the aforementioned exceptions, were described as they were or had been. Frustrations and upsets were described along with joys and satisfactions. These facts are important to remember. If anything, they strongly biased the subsequent results in favor of detecting sanity, since none of their histories or current behaviors were seriously pathological in any way.

Immediately upon admission to the psychiatric ward, the pseudopatient ceased simulating *any* symptoms of abnormality. In some cases, there was a brief period of mild nervousness and anxiety, since none of the pseudopatients really believed that they would be admitted so easily. Indeed, their shared fear was that they would be immediately exposed as frauds and greatly embarrassed. Moreover, many of them had never visited a psychiatric ward; even those who had, nevertheless had some genuine fears about what might happen to them. Their nervousness, then, was quite appropriate to the novelty of the hospital setting, and it abated rapidly.

Apart from that short-lived nervousness, the pseudopatient behaved on the ward as he "normally" behaved. The pseudopatient spoke to patients and staff as he might ordinarily. Because there is uncommonly little to do on a psychiatric ward, he attempted to engage others in conversation. When asked by staff how he was feeling, he indicated that he was fine, that he no longer experienced symptoms. He responded to instructions from attendants, to calls for medication (which was not swallowed), and to dining-hall instructions. Beyond such activities as were available to him on the admissions ward, he spent his time writing down his observations about the ward, its patients, and the staff. Initially these notes were written "secretly," but as it soon became clear that no one much cared, they were subsequently written on standard tablets of paper in such public places as the dayroom. No secret was made of these activities.

The pseudopatient, very much as a true psychiatric patient, entered a hospital with no foreknowledge of when he would be discharged. Each was told that he would have to get out by his own devices, essentially by convincing the staff that he was sane. The psychological stresses associated with hospitalization were considerable, and all but one of the pseudopatients desired to be discharged almost immediately after being admitted. They were, therefore, motivated not only to behave sanely, but to be paragons of cooperation. That their behavior was in no way disruptive is confirmed by nursing reports, which have been obtained on most of the patients. These reports uniformly indicate that the patients were "friendly," "cooperative," and "exhibited no abnormal indications."

The Normal are not Detectably Sane

Despite their public "show" of sanity, the pseudopatients were never detected. Admitted, except in one case, with a diagnosis of schizophrenia,[10] each was discharged with a diagnosis of schizophrenia "in remission." The label "in remission" should in no way be dismissed as a formality, for at no time during any hospitalization had any question been raised about any pseudopatient's simulation. Nor are there any indications in the hospital records that the pseudopatient's status was suspect. Rather the evidence is strong that, once labeled schizophrenic, the pseudopatient was stuck with that label. If the pseudopatient was to be discharged, he must naturally be "in remission"; but he was not sane, nor, in the institution's view, had he ever been sane.

The uniform failure to recognize sanity cannot be attributed to the quality of the hospitals, for, although there were considerable variations among them, several are considered excellent. Nor can it be alleged that there was simply not enough time to observe the pseudopatients. Length of hospitalization ranged from 7 to 52 days, with an average of 19 days. The pseudopatients were not, in fact, carefully observed, but this failure clearly speaks more to traditions within psychiatric hospitals than to lack of opportunity.

Finally, it cannot be said that the failure to recognize the pseudopatients' sanity was due to the fact that they were not behaving sanely. While there was clearly some tension present in all of them, their daily visitors could detect no serious behavioral consequences—nor, indeed, could other patients. It was quite common for the patients to "detect" the pseudopatients' sanity. During the first three hospitalizations, when accurate counts were kept, 35 of a total of 118 patients on the admissions ward voiced their suspicions, some vigorously. "You're not crazy. You're a journalist, or a professor [referring to the continual note-taking]. You're checking up on the hospital." While most of the patients were reassured by the pseudopatient's insistence that he had been sick before he came in but was fine now, some continued to believe that the pseudopatient was sane throughout his hospitalization.[11] The fact that the patients often recognized normality when staff did not raises important questions.

Failure to detect sanity during the course of hospitalization may be due to the fact that physicians operate with a strong bias toward what statisticians call the type 2 error. This is to say that physicians are more inclined to call a healthy person sick (a false positive, type 2) than a sick person healthy (a false negative, type 1). The reasons for this are not hard to find: It is clearly more dangerous to misdiagnose illness than health. Better to err on the side of caution, to suspect illness even among the healthy.

But what holds for medicine does not hold equally well for psychiatry. Medical illnesses, while unfortunate, are not commonly pejorative. Psychiatric diagnoses, on the contrary, carry with them personal, legal, and social stigmas.[12] It was therefore important to see whether the tendency toward diagnosing the sane insane could be reversed. The following experiment was arranged at a research and teaching hospital whose staff had heard these findings but doubted that such an error could occur in their hospital. The staff was informed that at some time during the following three months, one or more pseudopatients would attempt to be admitted into the psychiatric hospital. Each staff member was asked to rate each patient who presented himself at admissions or on the ward according to the likelihood that the patient was a pseudopatient. A 10-point scale was used, with a 1 and 2 reflecting high confidence that the patient was a pseudopatient.

Judgments were obtained on 193 patients who were admitted for psychiatric treatment. All staff who had had sustained contact with or primary responsibility for the patient—attendants, nurses, psychiatrists, physicians, and psychologists—were asked to make judgments. Forty-one patients were alleged, with high confidence, to be pseudopatients by at least one member of the staff. Twenty-three were considered suspect by at least one psychiatrist. Nineteen were suspected by one psychiatrist *and* one other staff member. Actually, no genuine pseudopatient (at least from my group) presented himself during this period.

The experiment is instructive. It indicates that the tendency to designate sane people as insane can be reversed when the stakes (in this case, prestige and diagnostic acumen) are high. But what can be said of the 19 people who were suspected of being "sane" by one psychiatrist and another staff member? Were these people truly "sane," or was it rather the case that in the course of avoiding the type 2 error the staff tended to make more errors of the first sort—calling the crazy "sane"? There is no way of knowing. But one thing is certain: Any diagnostic process that lends itself so readily to massive errors of this sort cannot be a very reliable one.

The Stickiness of Psychodiagnostic Labels

Beyond the tendency to call the healthy sick—a tendency that accounts better for diagnostic behavior on admission than it does for such behavior after a lengthy period of exposure—the data speak to the massive role of labeling in psychiatric assessment. Having once been labeled schizophrenic, there is nothing the pseudopatient can do to overcome the tag. The tag profoundly colors others' perceptions of him and his behavior.

From one viewpoint, these data are hardly surprising, for it has long been known that elements are given meaning by the context in which they occur. Gestalt

psychology made this point vigorously, and Asch[13] demonstrated that there are "central" personality traits (such as "warm" versus "cold") which are so powerful that they markedly color the meaning of other information in forming an impression of a given personality.[14] "Insane," "schizophrenic," "manic-depressive," and "crazy" are probably among the most powerful of such central traits. Once a person is designated abnormal, all of his other behaviors and characteristics are colored by that label. Indeed, that label is so powerful that many of the pseudopatients' normal behaviors were overlooked entirely or profoundly misinterpreted.

All pseudopatients took extensive notes publicly. Under ordinary circumstances, such behavior would have raised questions in the minds of observers, as, in fact, it did among patients. Indeed, it seemed so certain that the notes would elicit suspicion that elaborate precautions were taken to remove them from the ward each day. But the precautions proved needless. The closest any staff member came to questioning these notes occurred when one pseudopatient asked his physician what kind of medication he was receiving and began to write down the response. "You needn't write it," he was told gently. "If you have trouble remembering, just ask me again."

If no questions were asked of the pseudopatients, how was their writing interpreted? Nursing records for three patients indicate that the writing was seen as an aspect of their pathological behavior. "Patient engages in writing behavior" was the daily nursing comment on one of the pseudopatients who was never questioned about his writing. Given that the patient is in the hospital, he must be psychologically disturbed. And given that he is a disturbed, continuous writing must be a behavioral manifestation of that disturbance, perhaps a subset of the compulsive behaviors that are sometimes correlated with schizophrenia.

One tacit characteristic of psychiatric diagnosis is that it locates the sources of aberration within the individual and only rarely within the complex of stimuli that surrounds him. Consequently, behaviors that are stimulated by the environment are commonly misattributed to the patient's disorder. For example, one kindly nurse found a pseudopatient pacing the long hospital corridors. "Nervous, Mr. X?" she asked. "No, bored," he said.

The notes kept by pseudopatients are full of patient behaviors that were misinterpreted by well-intentioned staff. Often enough, a patient would go "berserk" because he had, wittingly or unwittingly, been mistreated by, say, an attendant. A nurse coming upon the scene would rarely inquire even cursorily into the environmental stimuli of the patient's behavior. Rather, she assumed that his upset derived from his pathology, not from his present interactions with other staff members. Occasionally, the staff might assume that the patient's family (especially when they had recently visited) or other patients had stimulated the outburst. But never were the staff found to assume that one of themselves or the structure of the hospital had anything to do with a patient's behavior. One psychiatrist pointed to a group of patients who were sitting outside the cafeteria entrance half an hour before lunchtime. To a group of young residents he indicated that such behavior was characteristic of the oral-acquisitive nature of the syndrome. It seemed not to occur to him that there were very few things to anticipate in a psychiatric hospital besides eating . . .

Powerlessness and Depersonalization

Eye contact and verbal contact reflect concern and individuation; their absence, avoidance and depersonalization. The data I have presented do not do justice to the rich daily encounters that grew up around matters of depersonalization and avoidance. I have records of patients who were beaten by staff for the sin of having initiated verbal contact. During my own experience, for example, one patient was beaten in the presence of other patients for having approached an attendant and told him, "I like you." Occasionally, punishment meted out to patients for misdemeanors seemed so excessive that it could not be justified by the most radical interpretations of psychiatric canon. Nevertheless, they appeared to go unquestioned. Tempers were often short. A patient who had not heard a call for medication would be roundly excoriated, and the morning attendants would often wake patients with, "Come on, you m - - - - - f - - - - - s, out of bed!"

Neither anecdotal nor "hard" data can convey the overwhelming sense of powerlessness which invades the individual as he is continually exposed to the depersonalization of the psychiatric hospital. It hardly matters *which* psychiatric hospital the excellent public ones and the very plush private hospital were better than the rural and shabby ones in this regard, but, again, the features that

psychiatric hospitals had in common overwhelmed by far their apparent differences.

Powerlessness was evident everywhere. The patient is deprived of many of his legal rights by dint of his psychiatric commitment.[15] He is shorn of credibility by virtue of his psychiatric label. His freedom of movement is restricted. He cannot initiate contact with the staff, but may only respond to such overtures as they make. Personal privacy is minimal. Patient quarters and possessions can be entered and examined by any staff member, for whatever reason. His personal history and anguish is available to any staff member (often including the "gray lady" and "candy striper" volunteer) who chooses to read his folder, regardless of their therapeutic relationship to him. His personal hygiene and waste evacuation are often monitored. The water closets may have no doors.

At times, depersonalization reached such proportions that pseudopatients had the sense that they were invisible, or at least unworthy of account. Upon being admitted, I and other pseudopatients took the initial physical examinations in a semipublic room, where staff members went about their own business as if we were not there.

On the ward, attendants delivered verbal and occasionally serious physical abuse to patients in the presence of other observing patients, some of whom (the pseudopatients) were writing it all down. Abusive behavior, on the other hand, terminated quite abruptly when other staff members were known to be coming. Staff are credible witnesses. Patients are not.

A nurse unbuttoned her uniform to adjust her brassiere in the presence of an entire ward of viewing men. One did not have the sense that she was being seductive. Rather, she didn't notice us. A group of staff persons might point to a patient in the dayroom and discuss him animatedly, as if he were not there.

One illuminating instance of depersonalization and invisibility occurred with regard to medications. All told, the pseudopatients were administered nearly 2,100 pills, including Elavil, Stelazine, Compazine, and Thorazine, to name but a few. (That such a variety of medications should have been administered to patients presenting identical symptoms is itself worthy of note.) Only two were swallowed. The rest were either pocketed or deposited in the toilet. The pseudopatients were not alone in this. Although I have no precise records on how many patients rejected their medications, the pseudopatients frequently found the medications of other patients in the toilet before they deposited their own. As long as they were cooperative, their behavior and the pseudopatients' own in this matter, as in other important matters, went unnoticed throughout.

Reactions to such depersonalization among pseudopatients were intense. Although they had come to the hospital as participant observers and were fully aware that they did not "belong," they nevertheless found themselves caught up in and fighting the process of depersonalization. Some examples: A graduate student in psychology asked his wife to bring his textbooks to the hospital so he could "catch up on his homework"—this despite the elaborate precautions taken to conceal his professional association. The same student, who had trained for quite some time to get into the hospital, and who had looked forward to the experience, "remembered" some drag races that he had wanted to see on the weekend and insisted that he be discharged by that time. Another pseudopatient attempted a romance with a nurse. Subsequently, he informed the staff that he was applying for admission to graduate school in psychology and was very likely to be admitted, since a graduate professor was one of his regular hospital visitors. The same person began to engage in psychotherapy with other patients—all of this as a way of becoming a person in an impersonal environment.

The Sources of Depersonalization

What are the origins of depersonalization? I have already mentioned two. First are attitudes held by all of us toward the mentally ill—including those who treat them—attitudes characterized by fear, distrust, and horrible expectations on the one hand, and benevolent intentions on the other. Our ambivalence leads, in this instance as in others, to avoidance.

Second, and not entirely separate, the hierarchical structure of the psychiatric hospital facilitates depersonalization. Those who are at the top have least to do with patients, and their behavior inspires the rest of the staff. Average daily contact with psychiatrists, psychologists, residents, and physicians combined ranged from 3.9 to 25.1 minutes, with an overall mean of 6.8 (six pseudopatients over a total of 129 days of hospitalization). Included in this average are time spent in the admissions interview, ward meetings in the presence of a senior staff member, group and individual psychotherapy contacts, case

presentation conferences, and discharge meetings. Clearly, patients do not spend much time in interpersonal contact with doctoral staff. And doctoral staff serve as models for nurses and attendants.

There are probably other sources. Psychiatric installations are presently in serious financial straits. Staff shortages are pervasive, staff time at a premium. Something has to give, and that something is patient contact. Yet, while financial stresses are realities, too much can be made of them. I have the impression that the psychological forces that result in depersonalization are much stronger than the fiscal ones and that the addition of more staff would not correspondingly improve patient care in this regard. The incidence of staff meetings and the enormous amount of record-keeping on patients, for example, have not been as substantially reduced as has patient contact. Priorities exist, even during hard times. Patient contact is not a significant priority in the traditional psychiatric hospital, and fiscal pressures do not account for this. Avoidance and depersonalization may.

Heavy reliance upon psychotropic medication tacitly contributes to depersonalization by convincing staff that treatment is indeed being conducted and that further patient contact may not be necessary. Even here, however, caution needs to be exercised in understanding the role of psychotropic drugs. If patients were powerful rather than powerless, if they were viewed as interesting individuals rather than diagnostic entities, if they were socially significant rather than social lepers, if their anguish truly and wholly compelled our sympathies and concerns, would we not *seek* contact with them, despite the availability of medications? Perhaps for the pleasure of it all?

The Consequences of Labeling and Depersonalization

Whenever the ratio of what is known to what needs to be known approaches zero, we tend to invent "knowledge" and assume that we understand more than we actually do. We seem unable to acknowledge that we simply don't know. The needs for diagnosis and remediation of behavioral and emotional problems are enormous. But rather than acknowledge that we are just embarking on understanding, we continue to label patients "schizophrenic," "manic-depressive," and "insane," as if in those words we had captured the essence of understanding. The facts of the matter are that we have known for a long time that diagnoses are often not useful or reliable, but we have nevertheless continued to use them. We now know that we cannot distinguish insanity from sanity. It is depressing to consider how that information will be used.

Not merely depressing, but frightening. How many people, one wonders, are sane but not recognized as such in our psychiatric institutions? How many have been needlessly stripped of their privileges of citizenship, from the right to vote and drive to that of handling their own accounts? How many have feigned insanity in order to avoid the criminal consequences of their behavior, and, conversely, how many would rather stand trial than live interminably in a psychiatric hospital—but are wrongly thought to be mentally ill? How many have been stigmatized by well-intentioned, but nevertheless erroneous, diagnoses? On the last point, recall again that a "type 2 error" in psychiatric diagnosis does not have the same consequences it does in medical diagnosis. A diagnosis of cancer that has been found to be in error is cause for celebration. But psychiatric diagnoses are rarely found to be in error. The label sticks, a mark of inadequacy forever.

Finally, how many patients might be "sane" outside the psychiatric hospital but seem insane in it—not because craziness resides in them, as it were, but because they are responding to a bizarre setting, one that may be unique to institutions which harbor nether people? Goffman calls the process of socialization to such institutions "mortification"—an apt metaphor that includes the processes of depersonalization that have been described here. And while it is impossible to know whether the pseudopatients' responses to these processes are characteristic of all inmates—they were, after all, not real patients—it is difficult to believe that these processes of socialization to a psychiatric hospital provide useful attitudes or habits of response for living in the "real world."

Summary and Conclusions

It is clear that we cannot distinguish the sane from the insane in psychiatric hospitals. The hospital itself imposes a special environment in which the meanings of behavior can easily be misunderstood. The consequences to patients hospitalized in such an environment—the powerlessness, depersonalization, segregation, mortification, and self-labeling—seem undoubtedly counter-therapeutic.

I do not, even now, understand this problem well enough to perceive solutions. But two matters seem to have some promise. The first concerns the proliferation of community mental health facilities, of crisis intervention centers, of the human potential movement, and of behavior therapies that, for all of their own problems, tend to avoid psychiatric labels, to focus on specific problems and behaviors, and to retain the individual in a relatively non-pejorative environment. Clearly, to the extent that we refrain from sending the distressed to insane places, our impressions of them are less likely to be distorted. (The risk of distorted perceptions, it seems to me, is always present, since we are much more sensitive to an individual's behaviors and verbalizations than we are to the subtle contextual stimuli that often promote them. At issue here is a matter of magnitude. And, as I have shown, the magnitude of distortion is exceedingly high in the extreme context that is a psychiatric hospital.)

The second matter that might prove promising speaks to the need to increase the sensitivity of mental health workers and researchers to the *Catch-22* position of psychiatric patients. Simply reading materials in this area will be of help to some such workers and researchers. For others, directly experiencing the impact of psychiatric hospitalization will be of enormous use. Clearly, further research into the social psychology of such total institutions will both facilitate treatment and deepen understanding . . .

NOTES

1. P. Ash, *J. Abnorm. Soc. Psychol.* 44, 272 (1949); A. T. Beck, *Amer. J. Psychiat.* 119, 210 (1962); A. T. Boisen, *Psychiatry* 2, 233 (1938); N. Kreitman, *J. Ment. Sci.* 107, 876 (1961); N. Kreitman, P. Sainsbury, J. Morrisey, J. Towers, J. Scrivener, *ibid.*, p. 887; H. O. Schmitt and C. P. Fonda, *J. Abnorm. Soc. Psychol.* 52, 262 (1956); W. Seeman, *J. Nerv. Ment. Dis.* 118, 541 (1953). For an analysis of these artifacts and summaries of the disputes, see J. Zubin, *Annu. Rev. Psychol.* 18, 373 (1967); L. Phillips and J. G. Draguns, *ibid.* 22, 447 (1971).

2. R. Benedict, *J. Gen. Psychol.* 10, 59 (1934).

3. See in this regard H. Becker, *Outsiders: Studies in the Sociology of Deviance* (Free Press, New York, 1963); B. M. Braginsky, D. D. Braginsky, K. Ring, *Methods of Madness: The Mental Hospital as a Last Resort* (Holt, Rinehart & Winston, New York, 1969); G. M. Crocetti and P. V. Lemkau, *Amer. Sociol. Rev.* 30, 577 (1965); E. Goffman, *Behavior in Public Places* (Free Press, New York, 1964); R. D. Laing, *The Divided Self: A Study of Sanity and Madness* (Quadrangle, Chicago, 1960);

D. L. Phillips, *Amer. Sociol. Rev.* 28, (1963); T. R. Sarbin, *Psychol. Today* 6, 18 (1972); E. Schur, *Amer. J. Sociol.* 75, 309 (1969); T. Szasz, *Law, Liberty and Psychiatry* (Macmillan, New York, 1963); *The Myth of Mental Illness: Foundations of a Theory of Mental Illness* (Hoeber-Harper, New York, 1963). For a critique of some of these views, see W. R. Gove, *Amer. Sociol. Rev.* 35, 873 (1970).

4. E. Goffman, *Asylums* (Doubleday, Garden City, N.Y., 1961).

5. T. J. Scheff, *Being Mentally Ill: A Sociological Theory* (Aldine, Chicago, 1966).

6. Data from a ninth pseudopatient are not incorporated in this report because, although his sanity went undetected, he falsified aspects of his personal history, including his marital status and parental relationships. His experimental behaviors therefore were not identical to those of the other pseudopatients.

7. A. Barry, *Bellevue Is a State of Mind* (Harcourt Brace Jovanovich, New York, 1971); I. Belknap, *Human Problems of a State Mental Hospital* (McGraw-Hill, New York, 1956); W. Caudill, F. C. Redlich, H. R. Gilmore, E. B. Brody, *Amer. J. Orthopsychiat.* 22, 314 (1952); A. R. Goldman, R. H. Bohr, T. A. Steinberg, *Prof. Psychol.* 1, 427 (1970); unauthored, *Roche Report* 1 (No. 13), 8 (1971).

8. Beyond the personal difficulties that the pseudopatient is likely to experience in the hospital, there are legal and social ones that, combined, require considerable attention before entry. For example, once admitted to a psychiatric institution, it is difficult, if not impossible, to be discharged on short notice, state law to the contrary notwithstanding. I was not sensitive to these difficulties at the outset of the project, nor to the personal and situational emergencies that can arise, but later a writ of habeas corpus was prepared for each of the entering pseudopatients and an attorney was kept "on call" during every hospitalization. I am grateful to John Kaplan and Robert Bartels for legal advice and assistance in these matters.

9. However distasteful such concealment is, it was a necessary first step to examining these questions. Without concealment, there would have been no way to know how valid these experiences were; nor was there any way of knowing whether whatever detections occurred were a tribute to the diagnostic acumen of the staff or to the hospital's rumor network. Obviously, since my concerns are general ones that cut across individual hospitals and staffs, I have respected their anonymity and have eliminated clues that might lead to their identification.

10. Interestingly, of the 12 admissions, 11 were diagnosed as schizophrenic and one, with the identical symptomatology, as manic-depressive psychosis. This diagnosis has a more favorable prognosis, and it was given by the only private hospital in our sample. On the relations between social class and psychiatric diagnosis, see A. deB. Hollingshead and F. C. Redlich, *Social Class and Mental Illness: A Community Study* (Wiley, New York, 1958).

11. It is possible, of course, that patients have quite broad latitudes in diagnosis and therefore are inclined to call many people sane, even those whose behavior is patently aberrant. However, although we have no hard data on this matter, it was our distinct impression that this was not the case. In many instances, patients not only singled us out for attention, but came to imitate our behaviors and styles.

12. J. Cumming and E. Cumming, *Community Ment. Health* 1, 135 (1965); A. Farina and K. Ring, *J. Abnorm. Psychol.* 70, 47 (1965); H. E. Freeman and O. G. Simmons, *The Mental Patient Comes Home* (Wiley, New York, 1963); W. J. Johannsen, *Ment. Hygiene* 53, 218 (1969); A. S. Linsky, *Soc. Psychiat.* 5, 166 (1970).

13. S. E. Asch, *J. Abnorm. Soc. Psychol.* 41, 258 (1946); *Social Psychology* (Prentice Hall, New York, 1952).

14. See also I. N. Mensh and J. Wishner, *J. Personality* 16, 188 (1947); J. Wishner, *Psychol. Rev.* 67, 96 (1960); J. S. Bruner and R. Tagiuri, in *Handbook of Social Psychology,* G. Lindzey, Ed. (Addison-Wesley, Cambridge, Mass., 1954), vol. 2, pp. 634–654; J. S. Bruner, D. Shapiro, R. Tagiuri, in *Person Perception and Interpersonal Behavior,* R. Tagiuri and L. Petrullo, Eds. (Stanford Univ. Press, Stanford, Calif., 1958), pp. 277–288.

15. D. B. Wexler and S. E. Scoville, *Ariz. Law Rev.* 13, 1 (1971). *I thank W. Mischel, E. Orne, and M. S. Rosenhan for comments on an earlier draft of this manuscript.

Think Critically

1. Do you feel that Rosenhan's "experiment" would be able to pass the requirements of human subject committees at universities today? Explain the reasons you feel this way.

2. The dramatic conclusions of this study have been questioned by others. Find some critiques of this study and discuss some specific points of contention. Do you agree with the critics? Why or why not? Explain.

The Moral Career of the Mental Patient*

Erving Goffman

TRADITIONALLY THE TERM *CAREER* HAS BEEN reserved for those who expect to enjoy the rises laid out within a respectable profession. The term is coming to be used, however, in a broadened sense to refer to any social strand of any person's course through life. The perspective of natural history is taken: Unique outcomes are neglected in favor of such changes over time as are basic and common to the members of a social category, although occurring independently to each of them. Such a career is not a thing that can be brilliant or disappointing; it can no more be a success than a failure. In this light, I want to consider the mental patient, drawing mainly upon data collected during a year's participant observation of patient social life in a public mental hospital,[1] wherein an attempt was made to take the patient's point of view.

One value of the concept of career is its two-sidedness. One side is linked to internal matters held dearly and closely, such as image of self and felt identity; the other side concerns official position, jural relations, and style of life, and is part of a publicly accessible institutional complex. The concept of career, then, allows one to move back and forth between the personal and the public, between the self and its significant society, without having overly to rely for data upon what the person says he thinks he imagines himself to be.

This paper, then, is an exercise in the institutional approach to the study of self. The main concern will be with the *moral* aspects of career—that is, the regular sequence of changes that career entails in the person's self and in his framework of imagery for judging himself and others.[2]

The category "mental patient" itself will be understood in one strictly sociological sense. In this perspective,

the psychiatric view of a person becomes significant only in so far as this view itself alters his social fate—an alteration which seems to become fundamental in our society when, and only when, the person is put through the process of hospitalization.[3] I therefore exclude certain neighboring categories: the undiscovered candidates who would be judged "sick" by psychiatric standards but who never come to be viewed as such by themselves or others, although they may cause everyone a great deal of trouble;[4] the office patient whom a psychiatrist feels he can handle with drugs or shock on the outside; the mental client who engages in psychotherapeutic relationships . . .

This general sociological perspective is heavily reinforced by one key finding of sociologically oriented students in mental hospital research. As has been repeatedly shown in the study of nonliterate societies, the awesomeness, distastefulness, and barbarity of a foreign culture can decrease in the degree that the student becomes familiar with the point of view to life that is taken by his subjects. Similarly, the student of mental hospitals can discover that the craziness or "sick behavior" claimed for the mental patient is by and large a product of the claimant's social distance from the situation that the patient is in, and is not primarily a product of mental illness . . .

The career of the mental patient falls popularly and naturalistically into three main phases: the period prior to entering the hospital, which I shall call the *prepatient phase;* the period in the hospital, the *inpatient phase;* the period after discharge from the hospital, should this occur, namely, the *ex-patient phase.*[5] This paper will deal only with the first two phases.

The Prepatient Phase

A relatively small group of prepatients come into the mental hospital willingly, because of their own idea of what will be good for them, or because of wholehearted

*From *Psychiatry, 22* (1959), pp. 123–142. Used by permission of William Alanson White Psychiatric Foundation, Inc., © 1959. Copyright renewed 1987.

agreement with the relevant members of their family. Presumably these recruits have found themselves acting in a way which is evidence to them that they are losing their minds or losing control of themselves. This view of oneself would seem to be one of the most pervasively threatening things that can happen to the self in our society, especially since it is likely to occur at a time when the person is in any case sufficiently troubled to exhibit the kind of symptom which he himself can see. As Sullivan described it,

> What we discover in the self-system of a person undergoing schizophrenic changes or schizophrenic processes, is then, in its simplest form, an extremely fear-marked puzzlement, consisting of the use of rather generalized and anything but exquisitely refined referential processes in an attempt to cope with what is essentially a failure at being human—a failure at being anything that one could respect as worth being.[6]

Coupled with the person's disintegrative re-evaluation of himself will be the new, almost equally pervasive circumstance of attempting to conceal from others what he takes to be the new fundamental facts about himself, and attempting to discover whether others too have discovered them.[7] Here I want to stress that perception of losing one's mind is based on culturally derived and socially ingrained stereotypes as to the significance of symptoms such as hearing voices, losing temporal and spatial orientation, and sensing that one is being followed, and that many of the most spectacular and convincing of these symptoms in some instances psychiatrically signify merely a temporary emotional upset in a stressful situation, however terrifying to the person at the time . . . Interestingly, subcultures in American society apparently differ in the amount of ready imagery and encouragement they supply for such self views, leading to differential rates of *self-referral*; the capacity to take this disintegrative view of oneself without psychiatric prompting seems to be one of the questionable cultural privileges of the upper classes.[8]

For the person who has come to see himself—with whatever justification—as mentally unbalanced, entrance to the mental hospital can sometimes bring relief, perhaps in part because of the sudden transformation in the structure of his basic social situations; instead of being, to himself, a questionable person trying to maintain a role as a full one, he can become an officially questioned person known to himself to be not so questionable as that.

In other cases, hospitalization can make matters worse for the willing patient, confirming by the objective situation what has theretofore been a matter of the private experience of self.

Once the willing prepatient enters the hospital, he may go through the same routine of experiences as do those who enter unwillingly. In any case, it is the latter that I mainly want to consider, since in America at present these are by far the more numerous kind.[9] Their approach to the institution takes one of three classic forms: They come because they have been implored by their family or threatened with the abrogation of family ties unless they go "willingly"; they come by force under police escort; they come under misapprehension purposely induced by others, this last restricted mainly to youthful prepatients.

The prepatient's career may be seen in terms of an extrusory model; he starts out with relationships and rights, and ends up, at the beginning of his hospital stay, with hardly any of either. The moral aspects of this career, then, typically begin with the experience of abandonment, disloyalty, and embitterment. This is the case even though to others it may be obvious that he was in need of treatment, and even though in the hospital he may soon come to agree.

The case histories of most mental patients document offense against some arrangement for face-to-face living—a domestic establishment, a workplace, a semi-public organization such as a church or store, a public region such as a street or park. Often there is also a record of some *complainant,* some figure who takes that action against the offender which eventually leads to his hospitalization. This may not be the person who makes the first move, but it is the person who makes what turns out to be the first effective move. Here is the *social* beginning of the patient's career, regardless of where one might locate the psychological beginning of his mental illness . . .

Career contingencies occur in conjunction with a second feature of the prepatient's career—the *circuit of agents*—and agencies—that participate fatefully in his passage from civilian to patient status.[10] Here is an instance of that increasingly important class of social system whose elements are agents and agencies, which are brought into systemic connection through having to take up and send on the same persons. Some of these agent-roles will be cited now, with the understanding that in any concrete circuit a role may be filled more than once, and a single person may fill more than one of them.

First is the *next-of-relation*—the person whom the prepatient sees as the most available of those upon whom he should be able to most depend in times of trouble; in this instance the last to doubt his sanity and the first to have done everything to save him from the fate which, it transpires, he has been approaching. The patient's next-of-relation is usually his next of kin; the special term is introduced because he need not be. Second is the *complainant,* the person who retrospectively appears to have started the person on his way to the hospital. Third are the *mediators*—the sequence of agents and agencies to which the prepatient is referred and through which he is relayed and processed on his way to the hospital. Here are included police, clergy, general medical practitioners, office psychiatrists, personnel in public clinics, lawyers, social service workers, school teachers, and so on. One of these agents will have the legal mandate to sanction commitment and will exercise it, and so those agents who precede him in the process will be involved in something whose outcome is not yet settled. When the mediators retire from the scene, the prepatient has become an inpatient, and the significant agent has become the hospital administrator . . .

In the prepatient's progress from home to the hospital he may participate as a third person in what he may come to experience as a kind of *alienative coalition.* His next-of-relation presses him into coming to "talk things over" with a medical practitioner, an office psychiatrist, or some other counselor. Disinclination on his part may be met by threatening him with desertion, disownment, or other legal action, or by stressing the joint and explorative nature of the interview. But typically the next-of-relation will have set the interview up, in the sense of selecting the professional, arranging for time, telling the professional something about the case, and so on. This move effectively tends to establish the next-of-relation as the responsible person to whom pertinent findings can be divulged, while effectively establishing the other as the patient. The prepatient often goes to the interview with the understanding that he is going as an equal of someone who is so bound together with him that a third person could not come between them in fundamental matters; this, after all, is one way in which close relationships are defined in our society. Upon arrival at the office the prepatient

suddenly finds that he and his next-of-relation have not been accorded the same roles, and apparently that a prior understanding between the professional and the next-of-relation has been put in operation against him. In the extreme but common case the professional first sees the prepatient alone, in the role of examiner and diagnostician, and then sees the next-of-relation alone, in the role of advisor, while carefully avoiding talking things over seriously with them both together.[11] And even in those nonconsultative cases where public officials must forcibly extract a person from a family that wants to tolerate him, the next-of-relation is likely to be induced to "go along" with the official action, so that even here the prepatient may feel that an alienative coalition has been formed against him.

The moral experience of being third man in such a coalition is likely to embitter the prepatient, especially since his troubles have already probably led to some estrangement from his next-of-relation. After he enters the hospital, continued visits by his next-of-relation can give the patient the "insight" that his own best interests were being served. But the initial visits may temporarily strengthen his feeling of abandonment; he is likely to beg his visitor to get him out or at least to get him more privileges and to sympathize with the monstrousness of his plight—to which the visitor ordinarily can respond only by trying to maintain a hopeful note, by not "hearing" the requests, or by assuring the patient that the medical authorities know about these things and are doing what is medically best. The visitor then nonchalantly goes back into a world that the patient has learned is incredibly thick with freedom and privileges, causing the patient to feel that his next-of-relation is merely adding a pious gloss to a clear case of traitorous desertion.

The depth to which the patient may feel betrayed by his next-of-relation seems to be increased by the fact that another witnesses his betrayal—a factor which is apparently significant in many three-party situations. An offended person may well act forbearantly and accommodatively toward an offender when the two are alone, choosing peace ahead of justice. The presence of a witness, however, seems to add something to the implications of the offense. For then it is beyond the power of the offended and offender to forget about, erase, or suppress what has happened; the offense has become a public social fact[12] . . .

Two other aspects of sensed betrayal should be mentioned. First, those who suggest the possibility of another's entering a mental hospital are not likely to provide a realistic picture of how in fact it may strike him when he arrives. Often he is told that he will get required medical treatment and a rest, and may well be out in a few months or so. In some cases they may thus be concealing what they know, but I think, in general, they will be telling what they see as the truth. For here there is a quite relevant difference between patients and mediating professionals; mediators, more so than the public at large, may conceive of mental hospitals as short-term medical establishments where required rest and attention can be voluntarily obtained, and not as places of coerced exile. When the prepatient finally arrives he is likely to learn quite quickly, quite differently. He then finds that the information given him about life in the hospital has had the effect of his having put up less resistance to entering than he now sees he would have put up had he known the facts. Whatever the intentions of those who participated in his transition from person to patient, he may sense they have in effect "conned" him into his present predicament.

I am suggesting that the prepatient starts out with at least a portion of the rights, liberties, and satisfactions of the civilian and ends up on a psychiatric ward stripped of almost everything. The question here is *how* this stripping is managed. This is the second aspect of betrayal I want to consider.

As the prepatient may see it, the circuit of significant figures can function as a kind of *betrayal funnel*. Passage from person to patient may be effected through a series of linked stages, each managed by a different agent. While each stage tends to bring a sharp decrease in adult free status, each agent may try to maintain the fiction that no further decrease will occur. He may even manage to turn the prepatient over to the next agent while sustaining this note. Further, through words, cues, and gestures, the prepatient is implicitly asked by the current agent to join with him in sustaining a running line of polite small talk that tactfully avoids the administrative facts of the situation, becoming, with each stage, progressively more at odds with these facts. The spouse would rather not have to cry to get the prepatient to visit a psychiatrist; psychiatrists would rather not have a scene when the prepatient learns that he and his spouse are being seen separately and in different ways; the police infrequently bring a prepatient to the hospital in a straitjacket, finding it much easier all around to give him a cigarette, some kindly words, and freedom to relax in the back seat of the patrol car; and finally, the admitting psychiatrist finds he can do his work better in the relative quiet and luxury of the "admission suite" where, as an incidental consequence, the notion can survive that a mental hospital is indeed a comforting place. If the prepatient heeds all of these implied requests and is reasonably decent about the whole thing, he can travel the whole circuit from home to hospital without forcing anyone to look directly at what is happening or to deal with the raw emotion that his situation might well cause him to express. His showing consideration for those who are moving him toward the hospital allows them to show consideration for him, with the joint result that these interactions can be sustained with some of the protective harmony characteristic of ordinary face-to-face dealings. But should the new patient cast his mind back over the sequence of steps leading to hospitalization, he may feel that everyone's *current* comfort was being busily sustained while his long-range welfare was being undermined. This realization may constitute a moral experience that further separates him for the time from the people on the outside[13] . . .

The final point I want to consider about the prepatient's moral career is its peculiarly *retroactive* character. Until a person actually arrives at the hospital there usually seems no way of knowing for sure that he is destined to do so, given the determinative role of career contingencies. And until the point of hospitalization is reached, he or others may not conceive of him as a person who is becoming a mental patient. However, since he will be held against his will in the hospital, his next-of-relation and the hospital staff will be in great need of a rationale for the hardships they are sponsoring. The medical elements of the staff will also need evidence that they are still in the trade they were trained for. These problems are eased, no doubt unintentionally, by the case-history construction that is placed on the patient's past life, this having the effect of demonstrating that all along he had been becoming sick, that he finally became very sick, and that if he had not been hospitalized much worse things would have happened to him—all of which, of course, may be true. Incidentally, if the patient wants to make sense out of his stay in the hospital, and, as already suggested, keep alive the possibility of once again conceiving of his next-of-relation as a decent, well-meaning person, then he too will have reason to believe some of this psychiatric work-up of his past.

Here is a very ticklish point for the sociology of careers. An important aspect of every career is the view the person constructs when he looks backward over his progress; in a sense, however, the whole of the prepatient career derives from this reconstruction. The fact of having had a prepatient career, starting with an effective complaint, becomes an important part of the mental patient's orientation, but this part can begin to be played only after hospitalization proves that what he had been having, but no longer has, is a career as a prepatient.

The Inpatient Phase

The last step in the prepatient's career can involve his realization—justified or not—that he has been deserted by society and turned out of relationships by those closest to him. Interestingly enough, the patient, especially a first admission, may manage to keep himself from coming to the end of this trail, even though in fact he is now in a locked mental hospital ward. On entering the hospital, he may very strongly feel the desire not to be known to anyone as a person who could possibly be reduced to these present circumstances, or as a person who conducted himself in the way he did prior to commitment. Consequently, he may avoid talking to anyone, may stay by himself when possible, and may even be "out of contact" or "manic" so as to avoid ratifying any interaction that presses a politely reciprocal role upon him and opens him up to what he has become in the eyes of others. When the next-of-relation makes an effort to visit, he may be rejected by mutism, or by the patient's refusal to enter the visiting room, these strategies sometimes suggesting that the patient still clings to a remnant of relatedness to those who made up his past, and is protecting this remnant from the final destructiveness of dealing with the new people that they have become.[14]

Usually the patient comes to give up his taxing effort at anonymity, at not-hereness, and begins to present himself for conventional social interaction to the hospital community. Thereafter he withdraws only in special ways— by always using his nickname, by signing his contribution to the patient weekly with his initial only, or by using the innocuous "cover" address tactfully provided by

some hospitals; or he withdraws only at special times, when, say, a flock of nursing students makes a passing tour of the ward, or when, paroled to the hospital grounds, he suddenly sees he is about to cross the path of a civilian he happens to know from home. Sometimes this making of oneself available is called "settling down" by the attendants. It marks a new stand openly taken and supported by the patient, and resembles the "coming out" process that occurs in other groupings.[15]

Once the prepatient begins to settle down, the main outlines of his fate tend to follow those of a whole class of segregated establishments—jails, concentration camps, monasteries, work camps, and so on—in which the inmate spends the whole round of life on the grounds, and marches through his regimented day in the immediate company of a group of persons of his own institutional status.[16]

Like the neophyte in many of these "total institutions," the new inpatient finds himself cleanly stripped of many of his accustomed affirmations, satisfactions, and defenses, and is subjected to a rather full set of mortifying experiences: restriction of free movement; communal living; diffuse authority of a whole echelon of people; and so on. Here one begins to learn about the limited extent to which a conception of oneself can be sustained when the usual setting of supports for it are suddenly removed.

While undergoing these humbling moral experiences, the inpatient learns to orient himself in terms of the "ward system."[17] In public mental hospitals this usually consists of a series of graded living arrangements built around wards, administrative units called services, and parole statuses. The "worst" level involves often nothing but wooden benches to sit on, some quite indifferent food, and a small piece of room to sleep in. The "best" level may involve a room of one's own, ground and town privileges, contacts with staff that are relatively undamaging, and what is seen as good food and ample recreational facilities. For disobeying the pervasive house rules, the inmate will receive stringent punishments expressed in terms of loss of privileges; for obedience he will eventually be allowed to reacquire some of the minor satisfactions he took for granted on the outside.

The institutionalization of these radically different levels of living throws light on the implications for self of social settings. And this in turn affirms that the self arises not merely out of its possessor's interactions with significant others, but also out of the arrangements that are evolved in an organization for its members . . .

Once lodged on a given ward, the patient is firmly instructed that the restrictions and deprivations he encounters are not due to such things as tradition or economy—and hence dissociable from self—but are intentional parts of his treatment, part of his need at the time, and therefore an expression of the state that his self has fallen to. Having every reason to initiate requests for better conditions, he is told that when the staff feels he is "able to manage" or will be "comfortable with" a higher ward level, then appropriate action will be taken. In short, assignment to a given ward is presented not as a reward or punishment, but as an expression of his general level of social functioning, his status as a person. Given the fact that the worst ward levels provide a round of life that inpatients with organic brain damage can easily manage, and that these quite limited human beings are present to prove it, one can appreciate some of the mirroring effects of the hospital.[18]

The ward system, then, is an extreme instance of how the physical facts of an establishment can be explicitly employed to frame the conception a person takes of himself. In addition, the official psychiatric mandate of mental hospitals gives rise to even more direct, even more blatant, attacks upon the inmate's view of himself. The more "medical" and the more progressive a mental hospital is—the more it attempts to be therapeutic and not merely custodial—the more he may be confronted by high-ranking staff arguing that his past has been a failure, that the cause of this has been within himself, that his attitude to life is wrong, and that if he wants to be a person he will have to change his way of dealing with people and his conceptions of himself. Often the moral value of these verbal assaults will be brought home to him by requiring him to practice taking this psychiatric view of himself in arranged confessional periods, whether in private sessions or group psychotherapy . . .

If the person can manage to present a view of his current situation which shows the operation of favorable personal qualities in the past and a favorable destiny awaiting him, it may be called a *success story*. If the facts of a person's past and present are extremely dismal, then about the best he can do is to show that he is not responsible for what has become of him, and the term *sad tale* is appropriate . . .

In the mental hospital, the setting and the house rules press home to the patient that he is, after all, a mental case who has suffered some kind of social collapse on the outside, having failed in some overall way, and that here he is of little social weight, being hardly capable of acting like a full-fledged person at all. These humiliations are likely to be most keenly felt by middle-class patients, since their previous condition of life little immunizes them against such affronts; but all patients feel some downgrading. Just as any normal member of his outside subculture would do, the patient often responds to this situation by attempting to assert a sad tale proving that he is not "sick," that the "little trouble" he did get into was really somebody else's fault, that his past life course had some honor and rectitude, and that the hospital is therefore unjust in forcing the status of mental patient upon him. This self-respecting tendency is heavily institutionalized within the patient society where opening social contacts typically involve the participants' volunteering information about their current ward location and length of stay so far, but not the reasons for their stay—such interaction being conducted in the manner of small talk on the outside.[19] With greater familiarity, each patient usually volunteers relatively acceptable reasons for his hospitalization, at the same time accepting without open immediate question the lines offered by other patients. Such stories as the following are given and overtly accepted.

> I was going to night school to get a M.A. degree, and holding down a job in addition, and the load got too much for me.
>
> The others here are sick mentally but I'm suffering from a bad nervous system and that is what is giving me these phobias.

. . . A whole social role in the patient community may be constructed on the basis of these reciprocally sustained fictions. For these face-to-face niceties tend to be qualified by behind-the-back gossip that comes only a degree closer to the "objective" facts. Here, of course, one can see a classic social function of informal networks of equals: They serve as one another's audience for self-supporting tales—tales that are somewhat more solid than pure fantasy and somewhat thinner than the facts . . .

Certainly the degrading conditions of the hospital setting belie many of the self-stories that are presented by patients; and the very fact of being in the mental hospital is evidence against these tales . . .

The mental hospital setting, however, is more treacherous still. Staff has much to gain through discreditings of the patient's story—whatever the felt reason for such discreditings. If the custodial faction in the hospital is to succeed in managing his daily round without complaint or trouble from him, then it will prove useful to be able to point out to him that the claims about himself upon which he rationalizes his demands are false, that he is not what he is claiming to be, and that in fact he is a failure as a person. If the psychiatric faction is to impress upon him its views about his personal make-up, then they must be able to show in detail how their version of his past and their version of his character hold up much better than his own.[20] If both the custodial and psychiatric factions are to get him to cooperate in the various psychiatric treatments, then it will prove useful to disabuse him of *his* view of their purposes, and cause him to appreciate that they know what they are doing, and are doing what is best for him. In brief, the difficulties caused by a patient are closely tied to his version of what has been happening to him, and if cooperation is to be secured, it helps if this version is discredited. The patient must "insightfully" come to take, or affect to take, the hospital's view of himself.

NOTES

1. The study was conducted during 1955–56 under the auspices of the Laboratory of Socio-environmental Studies of the National Institute of Mental Health. I am grateful to the Laboratory Chief, John A. Clausen, and to Dr. Winfred Overholser, Superintendent, and the late Dr. Jay Hoffman, then First Assistant Physician of Saint Elizabeth's Hospital, Washington, D.C., for the ideal cooperation they freely provided. A preliminary report is contained in Goffman, "Interpersonal Persuasion," pp. 117–193; in *Group Processes: Transactions of the Third Conference,* edited by Bertram Schaffner: New York, Josiah Macy, Jr. Foundation, 1957. A shorter version of this paper was presented at the Annual Meeting of the American Sociological Society, Washington, D.C., August 1957.

2. Material on moral career can be found in early social anthropological work on ceremonies of status transition, and in classic social psychological descriptions of those spectacular changes in one's view of self that can accompany participation in social movements and sects. Recently new kinds of relevant data have been suggested by psychiatric interest in

the problem of "identity" and sociological studies of work careers and "adult socialization."

3. This point has recently been made by Elaine and John Cumming, *Closed Ranks;* Cambridge, Commonwealth Fund, Harvard Univ. Press, 1957; pp. 101–102. "Clinical experience supports the impression that many people define mental illness as 'That condition for which a person is treated in a mental hospital.'... Mental illness, it seems, is a condition which afflicts people who must go to a mental institution, but until they do almost anything they do is normal." Leila Deasy has pointed out to me the correspondence here with the situation in white collar crime. Of those who are detected in this activity, only the ones who do not manage to avoid going to prison find themselves accorded the social role of the criminal.

4. Case records in mental hospitals are just now coming to be exploited to show the incredible amount of trouble a person may cause for himself and others before anyone begins to think about him psychiatrically, let alone take psychiatric action against him. See John A. Clausen and Marian Radke Yarrow, "Paths to the Mental Hospital," *J. Social Issues* (1955) 11:25–32; August B. Hollingshead and Fredrick C. Redlich, *Social Class and Mental Illness;* New York, Wiley, 1958: pp. 173–174.

5. This simple picture is complicated by the somewhat special experience of roughly a third of ex-patients—namely, readmission to the hospital, this being the recidivist or "repatient" phase.

6. Harry Stack Sullivan, *Clinical Studies in Psychiatry;* edited by Helen Swick Perry, Mary Ladd Gawel, and Martha Gibbon; New York, Norton, 1956; pp. 184–185.

7. This moral experience can be contrasted with that of a person learning to become a marihuana addict, whose discovery that he can be "high" and still "op" effectively without being detected apparently leads to a new level of use. See Howard S. Becker, "Marihuana Use and Social Control." *Social Problems* (1955) 3:35–44; see especially pp. 40–41.

8. See footnote 4: Hollingshead and Redlich, p. 187, Table 6, where relative frequency is given of self-referral by social class grouping.

9. The distinction employed here between willing and unwilling patients cuts across the legal one, of voluntary and committed, since some persons who are glad to come to the mental hospital may be legally committed, and of those who come only because of strong familial pressure, some may sign themselves in as voluntary patients.

10. For one circuit of agents and its bearing on career contingencies, see Oswald Hall, "The Stages of a Medical Career," *Amer. J. Sociology* (1948) 53:227–336.

11. I have one case record of a man who claims he thought *he* was taking his wife to see the psychiatrist, not realizing until too late that his wife had made the arrangements.

12. A paraphrase from Kurt Riezler, "The Social Psychology of Shame," *Amer. J. Sociology* (1943) 48:458.

13. Concentration camp practices provide a good example of the function of the betrayal funnel in inducing cooperation and reducing struggle and fuss, although here the mediators could not be said to be acting in the best interests of the inmates. Police picking up persons from their homes would sometimes joke good-naturedly and offer to wait while coffee was being served. Gas chambers were fitted out like delousing rooms, and victims taking off their clothes were told to note where they were leaving them. The sick, aged, weak, or insane who were selected for extermination were sometimes driven away in Red Cross ambulances to camps referred to by terms such as "observation hospital." See David Boder, *I Did Not Interview the Dead;* Urbana, Univ. of Illinois Press, 1949; p. 81; and Elie A. Cohen, *Human Behavior in the Concentration Camp;* London, Cape, 1954; pp. 32, 37, 107.

14. The inmate's initial strategy of holding himself aloof from ratifying contact may partly account for the relative lack of group-formation among inmates in public mental hospitals, a connection that has been suggested to me by William R. Smith. The desire to avoid personal bonds that would give license to the asking of biographical questions could also be a factor. In mental hospitals, of course, as in prisoner camps, the staff may consciously break up incipient group-formation in order to avoid collective rebellious action and other ward disturbances.

15. A comparable coming out occurs in the homosexual world, when a person finally comes frankly to present himself to a "gay" gathering not as a tourist but as someone who is "available." See Evelyn Hooker, "A Preliminary Examination of Group Behavior of Homosexuals," *J. Psychology* (1956) 42:217–225; especially p. 221. A good fictionalized treatment may be found in James Baldwin's *Giovanni's Room;* New York, Dial, 1956; pp. 41–63. A familiar instance of the coming out process is no doubt to be found among prepubertal children at the moment one of these actors sidles *back* into a room that had been left in an angered huff and injured *amour-propre.* The phrase itself presumably derives from a *rite-de-passage* ceremony once arranged by upperclass mothers for their daughters. Interestingly enough, in large mental hospitals the patient sometimes symbolizes a complete coming out by his first active participation in the hospital-wide patient dance.

16. See Goffman, "Characteristics of Total Institutions," pp. 43–84; in *Proceedings of the Symposium of Preventive and Social Psychiatry;* Washington, D.C., Walter Reed Army Institute of Research, 1958.

17. A good description of the ward system may be found in Ivan Belknap, *Human Problems of a State Mental Hospital;* New York, McGraw-Hill, 1956; see especially p. 164.

18. Here is one way in which mental hospitals can be worse than concentration camps and prisons as places in which to "do" time: in the latter, self-insulation from the symbolic implications of the settings may be easier. In fact, self-insulation from hospital settings may be so difficult that patients have to employ devices for this which staff interpret as psychotic symptoms.

19. A similar self-protecting rule has been observed in prisons. Thus, Hassler, in describing a conversation with a fellow-prisoner: "He didn't say much about why he was sentenced, and I didn't ask him, that being the accepted behavior in prison" (p. 76). A novelistic version for the mental hospital may be found in J. Kerkhoff, *How Thin the Veil: A Newspaperman's Story of His Own Mental Crack-up and Recovery;* New York, Greenberg, 1952; p. 27.

20. The process of examining a person psychiatrically and then altering or reducing his status in consequence is known in hospital and prison parlance as *bugging,* the assumption being that once you come to the attention of the testers you either will automatically be labeled crazy or the process of testing itself will make you crazy. Thus psychiatric staff are sometimes seen not as *discovering* whether you are sick, but as *making* you sick; and "Don't bug me, man," can mean, "Don't pester me to the point where I'll get upset." Sheldom Messenger has suggested to me that this meaning of bugging is related to the other colloquial meaning, of wiring a room with a secret microphone to collect information usable for discrediting the speaker.

Think Critically

1. Explain what Goffman means by the "moral career" of the mental patient? How is the concept tied to the symbolic interaction approach to deviance?

2. How might some of the experiences by mental patients relate to others who are confined in "total institutions?" How might these experiences relate to behaviors in institutions in general? Give examples.

From Witchcraft to Drugcraft
*Biochemistry as Mythology**

Ronny E. Turner and Charles Edgley**

FROM THE FOURTEENTH THROUGH THE seventeenth century, continental Europeans executed more than 500,000 witches. This ideology or theodicy enabled and justified inquisitors (witchprickers) to persecute thousands of people over a longer period of time than the centuries mentioned above. Witchcraft was the legitimized and acceptable explanation for deviance, therapeutic welfare, and exploitation; it was the "cause" of the black plague, heresy, crime, poor harvests, women stepping out of traditional roles, and any or all maladies affecting the individual or society.[1]

Likewise, the nineteenth century saw another problem, masturbation, so ubiquitous as to cause virtually every form of deviance. Masturbation caused masturbatory insanity which produced more masturbation in a continuous confusion of concepts of cause and effect. This "self abuse" of the nineteenth century, which has become a therapy in today's medical nomenclature, was seen as the etiology of suicide, neurasthenia, dementia, brain damage, neuroses, homosexuality, hypochondria, and epilepsy; it led to physical, mental, moral, and intellectual degeneracy. Like witchcraft earlier, masturbation threatened to destroy society.[2]

The condition, craft, and curse of the witch, used by humanity for centuries to explain aberrant behavior, no longer hold sway in the Western world. They have been replaced by the languages of medicine, psychiatry, and biochemistry. With the increasing medicalization of our rhetoric[3] the witch, the curse, sin, and the devil have all given way to the errant chemical—a chemical pathology of the brain. The primary political implication of this shift, of course, has been to cast chemotherapy into the role of preserver of the status quo of social conduct, now called "mental health," by curing or mitigating deviance in its various forms by subsuming it under the rubric of "mental illness." The biochemical specialist, psychobiologist, psychiatrist dispensing antipsychotic drugs, medical doctors prescribing a vast chemical arsenal—these representatives of science have replaced the witchpricker. In short, drugcraft has replaced witchcraft.

The Brain as a Chemical Factory

That there are chemical and neurological processes and components involved in all of the activities of the brain goes without saying; the brain is in large measure a chemical machine that functions with an infinitely complex interplay of chemical processes. Chemicals transmit impulses among the brain cells; dopamine, secreted by nerve cells, crosses synapses as neurotransmitters "communicate" to neuroreceptors. Through this process it is believed that thought, mood, and behavior are either created or activated.

Organic-biochemical theories assume that imbalances in these chemical processes are responsible for a wide variety of mental illnesses—especially schizophrenia and chronic depression . . .

Many other eminent scientists could be cited to show the current unanimity of this view[4] . . .

How does all of this work? In acute schizophrenia, the receptors are believed to be too sensitive to an excessive amount of released dopamine or else the neurotransmitters reabsorb their manufactured dopamine too slowly after transmission. The problem of a surplus of dopamine or overly sensitive receptors is addressed by administering antischizophrenic drugs to either block or blunt the absorption of the dopamine receptors[5] . . .

*Reprinted from *Social Science Journal,* 20:4 (October 1983), pp. 1–12, by permission of JAI Press, Inc.
**Revised version of a paper originally presented at the meetings of the Western Social Science Association, Denver, Colorado, April 1982.

Although none of these claims has ever been demonstrated to be true and the biochemical mechanisms postulated are not well understood even by their advocates, a veritable parade of chemical substances have been used in the attempt to find what Don Jackson once derisively called a "Salk Vaccine for the mind."[6] Introduced over a quarter of a century ago, Chlorpromazine was believed to be an effective drug in reversing the symptoms of schizophrenia by biochemically blocking the release of dopamine from certain submicroscopic sacs in the brain cells. Nevertheless, "there are over 330,000 institutionalized psychotics (many of whom are diagnosed as schizophrenic) who have proven wholly unresponsive to dopamine blockage therapies."[7] Similarly, a host of antidepressant drugs such as Elavil, Tofranil, Sinequan, Marplan, and Nardil have been pumped into the systems of depressives, the most common category of mental patient, because they are believed somehow to increase or inhibit neurotransmitter action. Hyperactive children, adolescents with extreme fluctuations in mood, and adults facing the anxieties of everyday life are among others who have been served this chemical pharmacopoeia.[8]

Furthermore, the futures market in drugs looks bright, at least judging from the statements of those who speculate on such matters. Drugs are seen in the not-too-distant future as improving the performance of "normal" people by increasing memory and intellectual acuity. The need for sleep could be lessened, thereby allowing more waking hours for other activities. Although drugcraft has been developing rapidly since World War II, research in brain chemistry is in its infancy. "We're on the verge of a new era."[9] Some neuroscientists even foresee the day when it "would become possible to diagnose mental illness from a simple blood, urine, or spinal fluid sample."[10] Doctors would then give appropriate drugs "once the imbalances in blood chemistry are determined"[11] . . .

Treated throughout organic/biochemical theories of deviance is the largely taken-for-granted assumption that a person's social acts are governed (or at least affected) by the neurochemical functioning of the brain. Conversely, these arguments assert that a person's conduct, the social context of his acts, and many other factors affect the chemical composition of the brain. "Many schizophrenic patients are under extreme emotional stress which is known to cause profound biochemical changes in man."[12] An environment loaded with stress might "trigger" chemical reactions which produce mental illness in certain persons. In other words, the organic assumption at work here is that brains secrete mental illness just as the kidneys secrete urine.

This line of reasoning flounders at several crucial points. First, it is difficult, if not impossible, to differentiate between a person's internal brain chemistry and his or her external conduct in terms of which precedes the other, since persons are inherently active[13] . . . Distinguishing the mentally healthy from the mentally ill is part of a social process of defining who is deviant and who is normal; the identification of chemical compositions in the brain *is not* and *cannot* be *prima facie* evidence for the diagnosis of mental illness.

The Myths of Chemical Mental Illness

. . . The decision to identify a person as mentally ill is obviously not now based on chemical or blood analysis. The promise of drugcraft is that this procedure could some day be used to diagnose mental illness and lead to chemical cures. But how can this happen if the physical "symptoms" are not systematically differentiated from the meaningful behavior out of which the symptomatic inference is drawn? Moreover, the prior symptomotology on which patients might be differentiated for chemical analysis and research is inexact, unsystematic, ambiguous, and lacks a creditable consensus even among psychiatrists. How could such a chaotic nosology be a basis for establishing variables in the testing of brain chemistry? Even if one conceded that the mentally ill could somehow be differentiated from the mentally healthy by using some measure of social consensus (not an easy task either), the identification of chemical differences in the brain (if they *were* ever substantiated) would rest on prior social labeling anyway . . .

Paranoid Schizophrenia

If schizophrenia is a "disorder in thinking," to whom is the thinking incomprehensible? What chemical evidence distinguishes ordered from disordered thinking? It would seem quite inconceivable that chemical analysis of two different brains could, in a double-blind experiment, distinguish normal thinking and conceptions of reality from abnormal and unrealistic ones . . .

Lemert[14] has demonstrated that those persons diagnosed as paranoid schizophrenics *do* have people out to get them. The "dynamics of exclusion" that often result from paranoid performances are quite real so that eventually, if not initially, the paranoid comes to have enemies. Labeling a person as paranoid, with all the implications of that designation, obviously reinforces the person's paranoia. Could chemistry distinguish unwarranted paranoia from the warranted variety? Original paranoia from the socially reinforced kind?

Questions such as these pose problems similar to trying to distinguish tap water from Holy Water. There is a real difference, but the difference that exists exists solely by social definition. To understand the difference necessitates an understanding of the Catholic Church, not chemical processes. Are there chemical differences in the brains of Republicans, Democrats, and anarchists? Or is Thomas Szasz's rendering of the problem more to the point?

> If you believe that you are Jesus, or have discovered a cure for cancer (and you have not), or the Communists are after you (and they are not)—then your beliefs are likely to be regarded as symptoms of schizophrenia. But if you believe that the Jews are the Chosen People, or that Jesus was the Son of God, or that Communism is the only scientifically and morally correct form of government—then your beliefs are likely to be regarded as a reflection of who you are: Jew, Christian, Communist. This is why we will discover the chemical cause of schizophrenia when we discover the chemical cause of Judaism, Christianity, and Communism. No sooner and no later.[15]

There is probably as much chemical difference in diagnosed schizophrenics and normal people as between liberals and conservatives, though in the latter case the definitions are sharper and the behavior more predictable.

The Delusional Schizophrenic

Supposedly, the neurochemical analysis could differentiate between the person who hears legitimate, nonexistent voices from those who hear illegitimate, nonexistent voices. Again, Thomas Szasz states, "If you talk to God, you are praying; if God talks to you, you have schizophrenia. If the dead talk to you, you are a spiritualist; if God talks to you, you are schizophrenic."[16]

Even setting aside Szasz's acerbic sarcasm, we can still appreciate his point. Many Christians talk to God daily, yet they are not usually seen as schizophrenic.[17] Even if God talks to you, the right identity and vocabulary of motives can be mobilized to legitimize the experience. For example, the Reverend Jerry Falwell, spokesman for the Moral Majority, claims that God told him to oppose the Equal Rights Amendment. Evangelist Oral Roberts claims to have seen Christ standing 900 feet tall, and talked with him personally one evening. Christ assured him that his new hospital in Tulsa, Oklahoma, delayed by debt and politics, would be completed. After Roberts reported this experience, an extra $5 million was received in contributions. Are the brains of Falwell and Roberts the chemical equivalent of a dopamine-disordered schizophrenic who claims to have conversed with Plato?

Person A converses daily with God and hears voices from a deity. These voices are nonexistent by scientific standards. If he is Pentecostal, he may claim to be a vessel through which the Holy Spirit speaks to others in "tongues." If one follows the logic of neurochemistry, would not person A have a similar brain chemistry to person B who claims to hear voices from some being residing in another galaxy?

These rhetorical questions show a highly relative and heavily nuanced social process in which persons in society have defined normal and abnormal from the standpoint of their own values. It is not *hearing* voices that constitutes psychiatric disease, it is *whose* voices are being heard. Given these examples, it is difficult to see how chemistry could address itself to deviance because of its socially constructed nature. "If Christianity or Communism[18] were called diseases, would they [neurochemists] then look for the chemical and genetic 'causes' of these 'conditions'?"

Extending the arguments of the psychobiologists: If Christianity were considered a disease and research done on the brains of Christians as is now done with schizophrenics, should we not expect to find the chemical complex that makes Christians Christian? Furthermore, if these substances could be identified and extracted or manufactured, could not the recruitment of potential Christians be medicalized? Injections of this "Christian chemical complex" could then be given producing "chemo-Christians," thereby considerably reducing the workload of the clergy.

Presumably there would be slightly different chemical formulas to produce Christians of various denominations: Baptists, Methodists, and Catholics . . .

Conclusion: The Two Meanings of Biochemistry as Mythology

Our inquiry into the mythologies of biochemistry has been conducted primarily along one line in this paper. By showing how biochemistry fails to account for what it purports to explain, much of the paper has had a debunking and satiric tone. In other words, we have explored the mythology of biochemistry according to the common sense view of myth as "falsehood." However, there is another meaning of the term "myth" which must be explored. This is the more intellectually traditional view, born in anthropology and folklore, that a myth is a narrative tale conducted for certain social purposes. Since myths are usually associated with primitive cultures, the dominant mythologies of our own time and place, especially scientific ones, are often overlooked either because they blatantly bill themselves as the "truth," or because our immersion in them obscures our vision; it is most difficult to question the myths by which we live. The medicalization of deviance may be viewed in this second context as a change in the narrative tales of our society. It is this second meaning of mythology—a story told for social purposes—with which we wish to conclude our analysis.

Science has been able to replace other forms of explanation primarily by producing and claiming certain "facts" as its own. Just as witchcraft claimed to account for certain aberrations in human conduct, drugcraft makes such claims today. But neither, strictly speaking, deals with "facts," because all facts are paradigm-dependent and therefore integrally tied to interpretation.[19] Drugcraft is an attempt, like many before it, to provide objective, value-free standards for assessing social conduct . . .

The best single analytical variant of mythology for sociological purposes is the idea of "vocabularies of motive."[20]

The extraordinary success of biological science in establishing itself as the dominant vocabulary of motives of the twentieth century should not divert us from a close examination of the problems to which such explanations inevitably lead. Every mythology has social consequences (indeed, that is what myths are for). But the biochemical version is fraught with some very negative ones,[21] not the least of which is that it diverts our attention away from the existential burdens that we all share as human and social beings. In all these things we must resist the compelling temptation to look for lost possessions (in this case the meanings of a person's life) under lampposts simply because the light is better there.

NOTES

1. See Nachman Ben-Yehuda, "The European Witch Craze of the 14th to 17th Centuries," *American Journal of Sociology*, vol. 86, no. 1 (July 1980), pp. 1–31 for an extensive sociological analysis of variables related to the development of witchcraft.

2. A concise and succinct statement of how badness became madness is insightfully presented by Peter Conrad and Joseph Schneider, in *Deviance and Medicalization* (St. Louis: C. V. Mosby, 1980).

3. Thomas Szasz, *The Myth of Mental Illness* (New York: Perennial Library, 1961); Paul Chalfant, "Sinners, Suckers and Sickees: The Medicalization of Practically Everything," in H. Paul Chalfant (ed.), *Sociological Stuff* (Dubuque: Kendall-Hunt Publishing Co., 1977), pp. 239–245; Peter Conrad, "Implications of Changing Social Policy for the Medicalization of Deviance," *Contemporary Crises*, vol. 4 (1982), pp. 195–205; Eliot Friedson, *Profession of Medicine* (New York: Dodd Mead, 1970).

4. Richard Haier, "The Diagnosis of Schizophrenia: A Review of Recent Developments," *Schizophrenia 1980* (Washington, D.C.: National Institute of Mental Health, 1981), pp. 2–13; Malcolm Bowers, "Biochemical Process in Schizophrenia: An Update," *Schizophrenia 1980* (Washington, D.C.: National Institute of Mental Health, 1981), pp. 27–37.

5. Bowers, *op. cit.*, pp. 27–37. We are well aware of the intricacies of the mind/brain debate; it is not our purpose to enter into such a discussion here. Our inquiry centers instead on the claim that the social conduct called "mental illness" can be accounted for biochemically as well as the meaning and significance of such claims. Those who wish to immerse themselves in a full treatment of the complexity of the mind/brain problem should consult C. V. Borst, *The Mind/Brain Identity Theory* (London: St. Martin's Press, 1973).

6. Don Jackson, *Myths of Madness* (New York: Macmillan, 1964).

7. Barbara Villet, "Opiates of the Mind," *Atlantic Monthly* (June 1978), p. 83.

8. Peter Conrad, "The Discovery of Hyperkinesis: Notes on the Medicalization of Deviant Behavior," *Social Problems,* vol. 23 (October 1975), pp. 12–25.

9. Matt Clark, et al., "Drugs and Psychiatry: A New Era," *Newsweek* (November 12, 1979), p. 104.

10. Hedley Donovan, "Psychiatry on the Couch," *Time,* vol. 113, no. 14 (April 2, 1979), p. 77.

11. *Ibid.,* p. 77.

12. Amerigo Farina, *Schizophrenia* (Morristown, NJ: General Learning Press, 1972).

13. John Dewey, *Human Nature and Conduct* (New York: Henry Holt and Co., 1922), pp. 112–113.

14. Edwin Lemert, "Paranoia and the Dynamics of Exclusion," *Sociometry,* vol. 25, no. 1 (March 1962), pp. 2–20.

15. Thomas Szasz, *The Second Sin* (Garden City: Anchor, 1974), pp. 113–114.

16. *Ibid.,* p. 113.

17. We must be careful here. Psychiatric nosology has made suspect many conventional religious interpretations, especially those which literally interpret spiritual relationships, and it is quite possible that there are psychiatrists, as well as many educated lay persons, who regard such practices as evidence of mental illness.

18. Should such a blatantly political view as "communism" seem a far-fetched example of the lengths to which the rhetoric of organic psychiatry could be extended, one only has to look to the conservative use of such arguments in the so-called "Twinkie" defense constructed for San Francisco policeman Dan White after he killed Mayor George Moscone and Supervisor Harvey Milk in a fit of anti-homosexual rage. For a full account of the trial and the role played by biochemical arguments in it, see Thomas Szasz, "How Dan White Got Away with Murder and How American Psychiatry Helped Him Do It," *Inquiry* (August 6 and 20, 1979).

19. Thomas Kuhn, *The Structure of Scientific Revolution* (Chicago: University of Chicago Press, 1962); and Harold Garfinkel, *Studies in Ethnomethodology* (Englewood Cliffs: Prentice Hall, 1967).

20. C. W. Mills, *op. cit.;* Kenneth Burke, *A Rhetoric of Motives* (Berkeley: University of California Press, 1950); and Edgley and Turner, "Masks and Social Relations," *op. cit.*

21. The liabilities of the drug revolution have only begun to surface. See George E. Crane, "Clinical Psychopharmacology in the Twentieth Century," *Science,* vol. 181 (July 13, 1973), pp. 124–128; D. F. Klein and J. M. David, *Diagnosis and Drug Treatment of Psychiatric Disorders* (Baltimore: Williams and Wilkins, 1969); and L. A. Scrouffe and M. A. Stewart, "Treating Problem Children with Stimulant Drugs," *New England Journal of Medicine,* vol. 289 (August 23, 1973), pp. 407–412. The "side effects" of therapeutic drugs have been downplayed by the pharmaceutical industry; there is little discussion of the 40–50 percent of schizophrenics who develop tartive dyskinesia after long-term use of drugs analogized as insulin for the diabetic. Furthermore, well-designed research studies have shown "no quantitative correlation between the percentage of patients receiving drug therapy . . . and the amount of improvement or releases." Andrew Scull, *Decarceration* (Englewood Cliffs, N.J.: Prentice Hall, 1977), p. 84. Compared to placebo patients, schizophrenics treated with Chlorpromazine were more susceptible to deterioration when released from the hospital. See Maurice Rappaport, et al., *Schizophrenics for Whom Phenothiazines May Be Contraindicated or Unnecessary* (University of California: Langley Porter Neuropsychiatric Institute, 1975). Although in some cases there were temporary improvements, in the long run the patients not receiving the drugs did better. The touting of drugs as causative agents in reducing staff loads in mental hospitals or the deinstitutionalization of the mentally ill now seems at best fiction, perhaps designed to justify massive uses of psychotropic chemicals. There are simply too many social correlates of discharge to regard it as a purely clinical phenomenon. See G. W. Brown, "Length of Hospital Stay and Schizophrenia," *Acta Psychiatrica et Neurologica Scandinavia,* vol. 35 (1960), pp. 414–430; J. R. Greenly, "Exit from a Mental Hospital," Ph.D. dissertation, Yale University, 1970; Greenly, "Alternative Views of the Psychiatrist's Role," *Social Problems,* vol. 20 (1972), pp. 252–262; and D. Watt and D. Buglass, "The Effects of Clinical and Social Factors on the Discharge of Chronic Psychiatric Patients," *Social Psychiatry,* vol. 1 (1966), pp. 57–63.

Think Critically

1. What do the authors mean by "biochemistry as mythology?"

2. Do you agree with Turner and Edgley's thesis that diagnoses of mental illness cannot be based upon chemical analyses, but rather are subjective judgments? Why, or why not? Explain your answer using some examples.

Paranoia and the Dynamics of Exclusion*

Edwin M. Lemert

ONE OF THE FEW GENERALIZATIONS ABOUT psychotic behavior which sociologists have been able to make with a modicum of agreement and assurance is that such behavior is a result or manifestation of a disorder in communication between the individual and society. The generalization, of course, is a large one, and, while it can be illustrated easily with case history materials, the need for its conceptual refinement and detailing of the process by which disruption of communication occurs in the dynamics of mental disorder has for some time been apparent. Among the more carefully reasoned attacks upon this problem is Cameron's formulation of the paranoid pseudocommunity (Cameron, 1943).[1]

In essence, the conception of the paranoid pseudocommunity can be stated as follows:[†]

> Paranoid persons are those whose inadequate social learning leads them in situations of unusual stress to incompetent social reactions. Out of the fragments of the social behavior of others the paranoid person symbolically organizes a pseudocommunity whose functions he perceives as focused on him. His reactions to this *supposed community* of response which he sees loaded with threat to himself bring him into open conflict with the actual community and lead to his temporary or permanent isolation from its affairs. The "real" community, which is unable to share in his attitudes and reactions, takes action through forcible restraint or retaliation *after* the paranoid person "bursts into defensive or vengeful activity" (Cameron, 1943).

That the community to which the paranoid reacts is "pseudo" or without existential reality is made unequivocal by Cameron when he says:

> As he (the paranoid person) begins attributing to others the attitudes which he has towards himself, he unintentionally organizes these others into a functional community, a group unified in their supposed reactions, attitudes and plans with respect to him. He in this way organizes individuals, some of whom are actual persons and some only inferred or imagined, into a whole which satisfies for the time being his immediate need for explanation but which brings no assurance with it, and usually serves to increase his tensions. The community he forms not only fails to correspond to any organization shared by others but actually contradicts this consensus. More than this, the actions ascribed by him to its personnel are not actually performed or maintained by them; *they are united in no common undertaking against him* (Cameron, 1943). (Italics ours.)

The general insightfulness of Cameron's analysis cannot be gainsaid and the usefulness of some of his concepts is easily granted. Yet a serious question must be raised, based upon empirical inquiry, as to whether in actuality the insidious qualities of the community to which the paranoid reacts are pseudo or a symbolic fabrication. There is an alternative point of view, which is the burden of this paper, namely that, while the paranoid person reacts differentially to his social environment, it is also true that "others" react differentially to him and this reaction commonly if not typically involves covertly organized action and conspiratorial behavior in a very real sense. A further extension of our thesis is that these differential reactions are reciprocals of one another, being interwoven and concatenated at each and all phases of a process of exclusion which arises in a special kind of relationship. Delusions and associated behavior must be understood in a context

*The research for this paper was in part supported by a grant from the California State Department of Mental Hygiene, arranged with the assistance of Dr. W. A. Oliver, Associate Superintendent of Napa State Hospital, who also helped as a critical consultant and made the facilities of the hospital available.
[†]In a subsequent article Cameron (Cameron, 1959)[2] modified his original conception, but not of the social aspects of paranoia, which mainly concern us.

of exclusion which attenuates this relationship and disrupts communication.

By thus shifting the clinical spotlight away from the individual to a relationship and a process, we make an explicit break with the conception of paranoia as a disease, a state, a condition, or a syndrome of symptoms. Furthermore, we find it unnecessary to postulate trauma of early childhood or arrested psychosexual development to account for the main features of paranoia—although we grant that these and other factors may condition its expression.

This conception of paranoia is neither simple *a priori* theory nor is it a proprietary product of sociology. There is a substantial body of writings and empirical researches in psychiatry and psychology which question the sufficiency of the individual as primary datum for the study of paranoia. Tyhurst, for example, concludes from his survey of this literature that reliance upon intrapsychic mechanisms and the "isolated organism" have been among the chief obstacles to fruitful discoveries about this disorder (Tyhurst, 1957).[3] Significantly, as Milner points out, the more complete the investigation of the cases the more frequently do unendurable external circumstances make their appearance (Milner, 1949).[4] More precisely, a number of studies have ended with the conclusions that external circumstances—changes in norms and values, displacement, strange environments, isolation, and linguistic separation—may create a paranoid disposition in the absence of any special character structure (Pederson, 1946).[5] The recognition of paranoid reactions in elderly persons, alcoholics, and the deaf adds to the data generally consistent with our thesis. The finding that displaced persons who withstood a high degree of stress during war and captivity subsequently developed paranoid reactions when they were isolated in a foreign environment commands special attention among data requiring explanation in other than organic or psychodynamic terms (Kline, 1951; Listivan, 1956).[6,7]

From what has been said thus far, it should be clear that our formulation and analysis will deal primarily with what Tyhurst (Tyhurst, 1957) calls paranoid patterns of behavior rather than with a clinical entity in the classical Kraepelinian sense. Paranoid reactions, paranoid states, paranoid personality disturbances, as well as the seldom-diagnosed "true paranoia," which are found superimposed or associated with a wide variety of individual behavior

or "symptoms," all provide a body of data for study so long as they assume priority over other behavior in meaningful social interaction. The elements of behavior upon which paranoid diagnoses are based—delusions, hostility, aggressiveness, suspicion, envy, stubbornness, jealousy, and ideas of reference—are readily comprehended and to some extent empathized by others as social reactions, in contrast to the bizarre, manneristic behavior of schizophrenia or the tempo and affect changes stressed in manic-depressive diagnoses. It is for this reason that paranoia suggests, more than any other forms of mental disorder, the possibility of fruitful sociological analysis.

Data and Procedure

The first tentative conclusions which are presented here were drawn from a study of factors influencing decisions to commit mentally disordered persons to hospitals, undertaken with the cooperation of the Los Angeles County Department of Health in 1952. This included interviews by means of schedules with members of 44 families in Los Angeles County who were active petitioners in commitment proceedings and the study of 35 case records of public health officer commitments. In 16 of the former cases and in seven of the latter, paranoid symptoms were conspicuously present. In these cases family members and others had plainly accepted or "normalized" paranoid behavior, in some instances longstanding, until other kinds of behavior or exigencies led to critical judgments that "there was something wrong" with the person in question, and, later, that hospitalization was necessary. Furthermore, these critical judgments seemed to signal changes in the family attitudes and behavior towards the affected persons which could be interpreted as contributing in different ways to the form and intensity of the paranoid symptoms.

In 1958 a more refined and hypothesis-directed study was made of eight cases of persons with prominent paranoid characteristics. Four of these had been admitted to the state hospital at Napa, California, where they were diagnosed as paranoid schizophrenic. Two other cases were located and investigated with the assistance of the district attorney in Martinez, California. One of the persons had previously been committed to a California state hospital, and the other had been held on an insanity petition but was freed after a jury trial. Added to these was one so-called

"White House case," which had involved threats to a President of the United States, resulting in the person's commitment to St. Elizabeth's Hospital in Washington, D. C. A final case was that of a professional person with a history of chronic job difficulties, who was designated and regarded by his associates as "brash," "queer," "irritating," "hypercritical," and "thoroughly unlikeable."

In a very rough way the cases made up a continuum ranging from one with very elaborate delusions, through those in which fact and misinterpretation were difficult to separate, down to the last case, which comes closer to what some would call paranoid personality disturbance. A requirement for the selection of the cases was that there be no history or evidence of hallucinations and also that the persons be intellectually unimpaired. Seven of the cases were of males, five of whom were over 40 years of age. Three of the persons had been involved in repeated litigations. One man published a small, independent paper devoted to exposures of psychiatry and mental hospitals. Five of the men had been or were associated with organizations, as follows: a small-town high school, a government research bureau, an association of agricultural producers, a university, and a contracting business.

The investigations of the cases were as exhaustive as it was possible to make them, reaching relatives, work associates, employers, attorneys, police, physicans, public officials and any others who played significant roles in the lives of the persons involved. As many as 200 hours each were given to collecting data on some of the cases. Written materials, legal documents, publications and psychiatric histories were studied in addition to the interview data. Our procedure in the large was to adopt an interactional perspective which sensitized us to sociologically relevant behavior underlying or associated with the more apparent and formal contexts of mental disorder. In particular we were concerned to establish the order in which delusions and social exclusion occur and to determine whether exclusion takes conspiratorial form.

The Relevant Behavior

In another paper (Lemert, 1946)[8] we have shown that psychotic symptoms as described in formal psychiatry are not relevant bases for predictions about changes in social status and social participation of persons in whom they appear. Apathy, hallucinations, hyperactivity, mood swings, tics, tremors, functional paralysis or tachychardias have no intrinsic social meanings. By the same token, neither do such imputed attributes as "lack of insight," "social incompetence" or "defective role-taking ability" favored by some sociologists as generic starting points for the analysis of mental disorders. Rather, it is behavior which puts strain on social relationships that leads to status changes: informal or formal exclusion from groups, definition as a "crank," or adjudication as insane and commitment to a mental hospital (Lemert, 1946). This is true even where the grandiose and highly bizarre delusions of paranoia are present. Definition of the socially stressful aspects of this disorder is a minimum essential, if we are to account for its frequent occurrence in partially compensated or benign form in society, as well as account for its more familiar presence as an official psychiatric problem in a hospital setting.

It is necessary, however, to go beyond these elementary observations to make it pre-eminently clear that strain is an emergent product of a relationship in which the behaviors of two or more persons are relevant factors, and in which the strain is felt both by ego and *alter* or *alters*. The paranoid relationship includes reciprocating behaviors with attached emotions and meanings which, to be fully understood, must be described cubistically from at least two of its perspectives. On one hand the behavior of the individual must be seen from the perspective of others or that of a group, and conversely the behavior of others must be seen from the perspective of the involved individual.

From the vantage of others the individual in the paranoid relationship shows:

1. A disregard for the values and norms of the primary group, revealed by giving priority to verbally definable values over those which are implicit, a lack of loyalty in return for confidences, and victimizing and intimidating persons in positions of weakness.
2. A disregard for the implicit structure of groups, revealed by presuming to privileges not accorded him, and the threat or actual resort to formal means for achieving his goals.

The second items have a higher degree of relevancy than the first in an analysis of exclusion. Stated more simply, they mean that, to the group, the individual is an ambiguous figure whose behavior is uncertain, whose loyalty can't be counted on. In short, he is a person who can't be trusted because he threatens to expose informal power structures. This, we believe, is the essential reason for the frequently encountered idea that the paranoid person is "dangerous" (Cameron, 1959).[9]

If we adopt the perceptual set of ego and see others or groups through his eyes, the following aspects of their behavior become relevant:

1. the spurious quality of the interaction between others and himself or between others interacting in his presence;
2. the overt avoidance of himself by others;
3. the structured exclusion of himself from interaction.

The items we have described thus far—playing fast and loose with the primary group values by the individual, and his exclusion from interaction—do not alone generate and maintain paranoia. It is additionally necessary that they emerge in an interdependent relationship which requires trust for its fulfillment. The relationship is a type in which the goals of the individual can be reached only through cooperation from particular others, and in which the ends held by others are realizable if cooperation is forthcoming from ego. This is deduced from the general proposition that cooperation rests upon perceived trust, which in turn is a function of communication (Loomis, 1959).[10] When communication is disrupted by exclusion, there is a lack of mutually perceived trust and the relationship becomes dilapidated or paranoid. We will now consider the process of exclusion by which this kind of relationship develops.

The Generic Process of Exclusion

The paranoid process begins with persistent interpersonal difficulties between the individual and his family, or his work associates and superiors, or neighbors, or other persons in the community. These frequently or even typically arise out of bona fide or recognizable issues centering upon some actual or threatened loss of status for the individual. This is related to such things as the death of relatives, loss of a position, loss of professional certification, failure to be promoted, age and physiological life cycle changes, mutilations, and changes in family and marital relationships. The status changes are distinguished by the fact that they leave no alternative acceptable to the individual, whence comes

their "intolerable" or "unendurable" quality. For example: the man trained to be a teacher who loses his certificate, which means he can never teach; or the man of 50 years of age who is faced with loss of a promotion which is a regular order of upward mobility in an organization, who knows that he can't "start over"; or the wife undergoing hysterectomy, which mutilates her image as a woman.

In cases where no dramatic status loss can be discovered, a series of failures often is present, failures which may have been accepted or adjusted to, but with progressive tension as each new status situation is entered. The unendurability of the current status loss, which may appear unimportant to others, is a function of an intensified commitment, in some cases born of an awareness that there is a quota placed on failures in our society. Under some such circumstances, failures have followed the person, and his reputation as a "difficult person" has preceded him. This means that he often has the status of a stranger on trial in each new group he enters, and that the groups or organizations willing to take a chance on him are marginal from the standpoint of their probable tolerance for his actions.

The behavior of the individual—arrogance, insults, presumption of privilege and exploitation of weaknesses in others—initially has a segmental or checkered pattern in that it is confined to status-committing interactions. Outside of these, the person's behavior may be quite acceptable—courteous, considerate, kind, even indulgent. Likewise, other persons and members of groups vary considerably in their tolerance for the relevant behavior, depending on the extent to which it threatens individual and organizational values, impedes functions, or sets in motion embarrassing sequences of social actions. In the early generic period, tolerance by others for the individual's aggressive behavior generally speaking is broad, and it is very likely to be interpreted as a variation of normal behavior, particularly in the absence of biographical knowledge of the person. At most, people observe that "there is something odd about him," or "he must be upset," "or he is just ornery," or "I don't quite understand him" (Cumming, 1957).[11]

At some point in the chain of interactions, a new configuration takes place in perceptions others have of the individual, with shifts in figure-ground relations. The individual, as we have already indicated, is an ambiguous figure, comparable to textbook figures of stairs or outlined cubes which reverse themselves when studied intently. From a normal variant the person becomes "unreliable," "untrustworthy," "dangerous," or someone with whom others "do not wish to be involved." An illustration nicely apropos of this came out in the reaction of the head of a music department in a university when he granted an interview to a man who had worked for years on a theory to compose music mathematically:

> When he asked to be placed on the staff so that he could use the electronic computers of the University *I shifted my ground* . . . when I offered an objection to his theory, he became disturbed, so I changed my reaction to "yes and no."

As is clear from this, once the perceptual reorientation takes place, either as the outcome of continuous interaction or through the receipt of biographical information, interaction changes qualitatively. In our words it becomes *spurious,* distinguished by patronizing, evasion, "humoring," guiding conversation onto selected topics, underreaction, and silence, all calculated either to prevent intense interaction or to protect individual and group values by restricting access to them. When the interaction is between two or more persons in the individual's presence it is cued by a whole repertoire of subtle expressive signs which are meaningful only to them.

The net effects of spurious interaction are to:

1. stop the flow of information to ego;
2. create a discrepancy between expressed ideas and affect among those with whom he interacts;
3. make the situation or the group image an ambiguous one for ego, much as he is for others.

Needless to say this kind of spurious interaction is one of the most difficult for an adult in our society to cope with, because it complicates or makes decisions impossible for him and also because it is morally invidious.*

The process from inclusion to exclusion is by no means an even one. Both individuals and members of groups change their perceptions and reactions, and vacillation is common, depending upon the interplay of values, anxieties and guilt on both sides. Members of an excluding group may decide they have been unfair and seek to bring the individual back into their confidence. This overture may be rejected or used by ego as a means of further attack. We

have also found that ego may capitulate, sometimes abjectly, to others and seek group re-entry, only to be rejected. In some cases compromises are struck and a partial reintegration of ego into informal social relations is achieved. The direction which informal exclusion takes depends upon ego's reactions, the degree of communication between his interactors, the composition and structure of the informal groups, and the perceptions of "key others" at points of interaction which directly affect ego's status.

Organizational Crisis and Formal Exclusion

Thus far we have discussed exclusion as an informal process. Informal exclusion may take place but leave ego's formal status in an organization intact. So long as this status is preserved and rewards are sufficient to validate it on his terms, an uneasy peace between him and others may prevail. Yet ego's social isolation and his strong commitments make him an unpredictable factor; furthermore the rate of change and internal power struggles, especially in large and complex organizations, means that preconditions of stability may be short-lived.

Organizational crises involving a paranoid relationship arise in several ways. The individual may act in ways which arouse intolerable anxieties in others, who demand that "something be done." Again, by going to higher authority or making appeals outside the organization, he may set in motion procedures which leave those in power no other choice than to take action. In some situations ego remains relatively quiescent and does not openly attack the organization. Action against him is set off by growing anxieties or calculated motives of associates—in some cases his immediate superiors. Finally, regular organizational procedures incidental to promotion, retirement or reassignment may precipitate the crisis.

Assuming a critical situation in which the conflict between the individual and members of the organization leads to action to formally exclude him, several possibilities exist. One is the transfer of ego from one department, branch or division of the organization to another, a device frequently resorted to in the armed services or in large corporations. This requires that the individual be persuaded to make the change and that some department will accept him. While this may be accomplished in different ways, not infrequently artifice, withholding information, bribery, or thinly disguised threats figure conspicuously among the means by

---

*The interaction in some ways is similar to that used with children, particularly the *"enfant terrible."* The function of language in such interaction was studied by Sapir (1915)[12] years ago.

which the transfer is brought about. Needless to say, there is a limit to which transfers can be employed as a solution to the problem, contingent upon the size of the organization and the previous diffusion of knowledge about the transferee.

Solution number two we call encapsulation, which, in brief, is a reorganization and redefinition of ego's status. This has the effect of isolating him from the organization and making him directly responsible to one or two superiors who act as his intermediaries. The change is often made palatable to ego by enhancing some of the material rewards of his status. He may be nominally promoted or "kicked upstairs," given a larger office, or a separate secretary, or relieved of onerous duties. Sometimes a special status is created for him.

This type of solution often works because it is a kind of formal recognition by the organization of ego's intense commitment to his status and in part a victory for him over his enemies. It bypasses them and puts him into direct communication with higher authority who may communicate with him in a more direct manner. It also relieves his associates of further need to connive against him. This solution is sometimes used to dispose of troublesome corporation executives, high-ranking military officers, and academic *personae non gratae* in universities.

A third variety of solutions to the problem of paranoia in an organization is outright discharge, forced resignation or non-renewal of appointment. Finally, there may be an organized move to have the individual in the paranoid relationship placed on sick leave, or to compel him to take psychiatric treatment. The extreme expression of this is pressure (as on the family) or direct action to have the person committed to a mental hospital.

The order of the enumerated solutions to the paranoid problem in a rough way reflects the amount of risk associated with the alternatives, both as to the probabilities of failure and of damaging repercussions to the organization. Generally, organizations seem to show a good deal of resistance to making or carrying out decisions which require expulsion of the individual or forcing hospitalization, regardless of his mental condition. One reason for this is that the person may have power within the organization, based upon his position, or monopolized skills and information,* and unless there is a strong coalition against him the general conservatism

of administrative judgments will run in his favor. Herman Wouk's novel of *The Caine Mutiny* dramatizes some of the difficulties of cashiering a person from a position of power in an essentially conservative military organization. An extreme of this conservatism is illustrated by one case in which we found a department head retained in his position in an organization even though he was actively hallucinating as well as expressing paranoid delusions.[†] Another factor working on the individual's side is that discharge of a person in a position of power reflects unfavorably upon those who placed him there. Ingroup solidarity of administrators may be involved, and the methods of the opposition may create sympathy for ego at higher levels.

Even when the person is almost totally excluded and informally isolated within an organization, he may have power outside. This weighs heavily when the external power can be invoked in some way, or when it automatically leads to raising questions as to the internal workings of the organization. This touches upon the more salient reason for reluctance to eject an uncooperative and retaliatory person, even when he is relatively unimportant to the organization. We refer to a kind of negative power derived from the vulnerability of organizations to unfavorable publicity and exposure of their private lives that are likely if the crisis proceeds to formal hearings, case review or litigation. This is an imminent possibility where paranoia exists. If hospital commitment is attempted, there is a possibility that a jury trial will be demanded, which will force leaders of the organization to defend their actions. If the crisis turns into a legal contest of this sort, it is not easy to prove insanity, and there may be damage suits. Even if the facts heavily support the petitioners, such contests can only throw unfavorable light upon the organization.

The Conspiratorial Nature of Exclusion

A conclusion from the foregoing is that organizational vulnerability as well as anticipations of retaliations from the paranoid person lay a functional basis for conspiracy among those seeking to contain or oust him. Probabilities are strong that a coalition will appear within the organization, integrated by a common commitment to oppose the paranoid person. This, the exclusionist group, demands

---

*For a systematic analysis of the organizational difficulties in removing an "unpromotable" person from a position see (Levenson, 1961).[13]

[†]One of the cases in the first study.

loyalty, solidarity and secrecy from its members; it acts in accord with a common scheme and in varying degrees utilizes techniques of manipulation and misrepresentation.

Conspiracy in rudimentary form can be detected in informal exclusion apart from an organizational crisis. This was illustrated in an office research team in which staff members huddled around a water cooler to discuss the unwanted associate. They also used office telephones to arrange coffee breaks without him and employed symbolic cues in his presence, such as humming the Dragnet theme song when he approached the group. An office rule against extraneous conversation was introduced with the collusion of supervisors, ostensibly for everyone, actually to restrict the behavior of the isolated worker. In another case an interview schedule designed by a researcher was changed at a conference arranged without him. When he sought an explanation at a subsequent conference, his associates pretended to have no knowledge of the changes.

Conspiratorial behavior comes into sharpest focus during organizational crises in which the exclusionists who initiate action become an embattled group. There is a concerted effort to gain consensus for this view, to solidify the group and to halt close interaction with those unwilling to completely join the coalition. Efforts are also made to neutralize those who remain uncommitted but who can't be kept ignorant of the plans afoot. Thus an external appearance of unanimity is given even if it doesn't exist.

Much of the behavior of the group at this time is strategic in nature, with determined calculations as to "what we will do if he does this or that." In one of our cases, a member on a board of trustees spoke of the "game being played" with the person in controversy with them. Planned action may be carried to the length of agreeing upon the exact words to be used when confronted or challenged by the paranoid individual. Above all there is continuous, precise communication among exclusionists, exemplified in one case by mutual exchanging of copies of all letters sent and received from ego.

Concern about secrecy in such groups is revealed by such things as carefully closing doors and lowering of voices when ego is brought under discussion. Meeting places and times may be varied from normal procedures; documents may be filed in unusual places and certain telephones may not be used during a paranoid crisis.

The visibility of the individual's behavior is greatly magnified during this period; often he is the main topic of conversation among the exclusionists, while rumors of the difficulties spread to other groups, which in some cases may be drawn into the controversy. At a certain juncture steps are taken to keep the members of the ingroup continually informed of the individual's movements and, if possible, of his plans. In effect, if not in form, this amounts to spying. Members of one embattled group, for example, hired an outside person unknown to their accuser to take notes on a speech he delivered to enlist a community organization on his side. In another case, a person having an office opening onto that of a department head was persuaded to act as an informant for the nucleus of persons working to depose the head from his position of authority. This group also seriously debated placing an all-night watch in front of their perceived malefactor's house.

Concomitant with the magnified visibility of the paranoid individual, come distortions of his image, most pronounced in the inner coterie of exclusionists. His size, physical strength, cunning, and anecdotes of his outrages are exaggerated, with a central thematic emphasis on the fact that he is dangerous. Some individuals give cause for such beliefs in that previously they have engaged in violence or threats, others do not. One encounters characteristic contradictions in interviews on this point, such as: "No, he has never struck anyone around here—just fought with the policemen at the State Capitol," or "No, I am not afraid of him, but one of these days he will explode."

It can be said parenthetically that the alleged dangerousness of paranoid persons storied in fiction and drama has never been systematically demonstrated. As a matter of fact, the only substantial data on this, from a study of delayed admissions, largely paranoid, to a mental hospital in Norway, disclosed that "neither the paranoiacs nor paranoids have been dangerous, and most not particularly troublesome" (Ödegard, 1958).[14] Our interpretation of this, as suggested earlier, is that the imputed dangerousness of the paranoid individual does not come from physical fear but from the organizational threat he presents and the need to justify collective action against him.*

However, this is not entirely tactical behavior—as is demonstrated by anxieties and tensions which mount among those in the coalition during the more critical phases of their interaction. Participants may develop fears quite analogous to those of classic conspirators. One leader

Supra, p. 3.

in such a group spoke of the period of the paranoid crisis as a "week of terror," during which he was wracked with insomnia and "had to take his stomach pills." Projection was revealed by a trustee who, during a school crisis occasioned by discharge of an aggressive teacher, stated that he "watched his shadows," and "wondered if all would be well when he returned home at night." Such tensional states, working along with a kind of closure of communication within the group, are both a cause and an effect of amplified group interaction which distorts or symbolically rearranges the image of the person against whom they act.

Once the battle is won by the exclusionists, their version of the individual as dangerous becomes a crystallized rationale for official action. At this point misrepresentation becomes part of a more deliberate manipulation of ego. Gross misstatements, most frequently called "pretexts," become justifiable ways of getting his cooperation, for example, to get him to submit to psychiatric examination or detention preliminary to hospital commitment. This aspect of the process has been effectively detailed by Goffman, with his concept of a "betrayal funnel" through which a patient enters a hospital (Jaco, 1957).[15] We need not elaborate on this, other than to confirm its occurrence in the exclusion process, complicated in our cases by legal strictures and the ubiquitous risk of litigation.

The Growth of Delusion

The general idea that the paranoid person symbolically fabricates the conspiracy against him is in our estimation incorrect or incomplete. Nor can we agree that he lacks insight, as is so frequently claimed. To the contrary, many paranoid persons properly realize that they are being isolated and excluded by concerted interaction, or that they are being manipulated. However, they are at a loss to estimate accurately or realistically the dimensions and form of the coalition arrayed against them.

As channels of communication are closed to the paranoid person, he has no means of getting feedback on consequences of his behavior, which is essential for correcting his interpretations of the social relationships and organization which he must rely on to define his status and give him identity. He can only read overt behavior without the informal context. Although he may properly infer that people are organized against him, he can only use confrontation or formal inquisitorial procedures to try to prove this. The paranoid person must provoke strong feelings in order to receive any kind of meaningful communication from others—hence his accusations, his bluntness, his insults. Ordinarily this is non-deliberate; nevertheless, in one complex case we found the person consciously provoking discussions to get readings from others on his behavior. This man said of himself: "Some people would describe me as very perceptive, others would describe me as very imperceptive."

The need for communication and the identity which goes with it does a good deal to explain the preference of paranoid persons for formal, legalistic, written communications, and the care with which many of them preserve records of their contracts with others. In some ways the resort to litigation is best interpreted as the effort of the individual to compel selected others to interact directly with him as equals, to engineer a situation in which evasion is impossible. The fact that the person is seldom satisfied with the outcome of his letters, his petitions, complaints and writs testifies to their function as devices for establishing contact and interaction with others, as well as "setting the record straight." The wide professional tolerance of lawyers for aggressive behavior in court and the nature of Anglo-Saxon legal institutions, which grew out of a revolt against conspiratorial or star-chamber justice, mean that the individual will be heard. Furthermore his charges must be answered; otherwise he wins by default. Sometimes he wins small victories, even if he loses the big ones. He may earn grudging respect as an adversary, and sometimes shares a kind of legal camaraderie with others in the courts. He gains an identity through notoriety.

Reinforcement of Delusion

The accepted psychiatric view is that prognosis for paranoia is poor, that recoveries from "true" paranoia are rare, with the implication that the individual's delusions more or less express an unalterable pathological condition. Granting that the individual's needs and dispositions and his self-imposed isolation are significant factors in perpetuating his delusional reactions, nevertheless there is an important social context of delusions through which they are reinforced or strengthened. This context is readily identifiable in the fixed ideas and institutionalized procedures of protective, custodial, and treatment organizations in our society. They stand out in sharpest relief where paranoid persons have come into contact with law enforcement agencies or have been hospitalized. The cumulative and interlocking impacts of such agencies work strongly to nurture and sustain the massive sense of injustice and need for identity which underlie the delusions and aggressive behavior of the paranoid individual.

Police in most communities have a well-defined concept of cranks, as they call them, although the exact criteria by which persons are so judged are not clear. Their patience is short with such persons: in some cases they investigate their original complaints and if they conclude that the person in question is a crank they tend to ignore him thereafter. His letters may be thrown away unanswered, or phone calls answered with patronizing reassurance or vague promises to take steps which never materialize.

Like the police, offices of district attorneys are frequently forced to deal with persons they refer to as cranks or soreheads. Some offices delegate a special deputy to handle these cases, quaintly referred to in one office as the "insane deputy." Some deputies say they can spot letters of cranks immediately, which means that they are unanswered or discarded. However, family or neighborhood quarrels offer almost insoluble difficulties in this respect, because often it is impossible to determine which of two parties is delusional. In one office some complainants are called "fifty-fifty," which is jargon meaning that it is impossible to say whether they are mentally stable. If one person seems to be persistently causing trouble, deputies may threaten to have him investigated, which, however, is seldom if ever done.

Both police and district attorney staffs operate continuously in situations in which their actions can have damaging legal or political repercussions. They tend to be tightly ingrouped and their initial reaction to outsiders or strangers is one of suspicion or distrust until they are proved harmless or friendly. Many of their office procedures and general manner reflect this—such as carefully recording in a log book names, time, and reason for calling of those who seek official interviews. In some instances a complainant is actually investigated before any business will be transacted with him.

When the paranoid person goes beyond local police and courts to seek redress through appeals to state or national authorities, he may meet with polite evasion, perfunctory treatment of his case or formalized distrust. Letters to administrative people may beget replies up to a certain point, but thereafter they are ignored. If letters

to a highly placed authority carry threats, they may lead to an investigation by security agencies, motivated by the knowledge that assassinations are not unknown in American life. Sometimes redress is sought in legislatures, where private bills may be introduced, bills which by their nature can only be empty gestures.

In general, the contacts which the delusional person makes with formal organizations frequently disclose the same elements of shallow response, evasion or distrust which played a part in the generic process of exclusion. They become part of a selective or selected pattern of interaction which creates a social environment of uncertainty and ambiguity for the individual. They do little to correct and much to confirm his suspicion, distrust and delusional interpretations. Moreover, even the environment of treatment agencies may contribute to the furtherance of paranoid delusion, as Stanton and Schwartz have shown in their comments on communication within the mental hospital. They speak pointedly of the "pathology of communication" brought about by staff practices of ignoring explicit meanings in statements or actions of patients and reacting to inferred or imputed meanings, thereby creating a type of environment in which "the paranoid feels quite at home" (Stanton and Schwartz, 1954).[16]

Some paranoid or paranoid-like persons become well known locally or even throughout larger areas to some organizations. Persons and groups in the community are found to assume a characteristic stance towards such people—a stance of expectancy and preparedness. In one such case, police continually checked the whereabouts of the man and, when the governor came to speak on the courthouse steps, two officers were assigned the special task of watching the man as he stood in the crowd. Later, whenever he went to the state capitol, a number of state police were delegated to accompany him when he attended committee hearings or sought interviews with state officials.* The notoriety this man acquired because of his reputed great strength in tossing officers around like tenpins was an obvious source of pleasure to him, despite the implications of distrust conveyed by their presence.

It is arguable that occupying the role of the mistrusted person becomes a way of life for these paranoids, providing

---

*This technique in even more systematic form is sometimes used in protecting the President of the United States in "White House cases."

them with an identity not otherwise possible. Their volatile contentions with public officials, their issuance of writings, publications, litigations in *persona propria,* their overriding tendency to contest issues which other people dismiss as unimportant or as "too much bother" become a central theme for their lives, without which they would probably deteriorate.

If paranoia becomes a way of life for some people, it is also true that the difficult person with grandiose and persecutory ideas may fulfill certain marginal functions in organizations and communities. One is his scapegoat function, being made the subject of humorous by-play or conjectural gossip as people "wonder what he will be up to next." In his scapegoat role, the person may help integrate primary groups within larger organizations by directing aggressions and blame towards him and thus strengthening feelings of homogeneity and consensus of group members.

There are also instances in which the broad, grapeshot charges and accusations of the paranoid person function to articulate dissatisfactions of those who fear openly to criticize the leadership of the community, organization, or state, or of the informal power structures within these. Sometimes the paranoid person is the only one who openly espouses values of inarticulate and politically unrepresented segments of the population (Marmor, 1958).[17] The "plots" which attract the paranoid person's attention—dope rings, international communism, monopolistic "interests," popery, Jewry, or "psychopoliticians"—often reflect the vague and ill-formed fears and concerns of peripheral groups, which tend to validate his self-chosen role as a "protector." At times in organizational power plays and community conflicts his role may even be put to canny use by more representative groups as a means of embarrassing their opposition.

The Larger Socio-Cultural Context

Our comments draw to a close on the same polemic note with which they were begun, namely, that members of communities and organizations do unite in common effort against the paranoid person prior to or apart from any vindictive behavior on his part. The paranoid community is real rather than pseudo in that it is composed of reciprocal relationships and processes whose net results are informal and formal exclusion and attenuated communication.

The dynamics of exclusion of the paranoid person are made understandable in larger perspective by recognizing that decision-making in American social organization is carried out in small, informal groups through casual and often subtle male interaction. Entree into such groups is ordinarily treated as a privilege rather than a right, and this privilege tends to be jealously guarded. Crucial decisions, including those to eject persons or to reorganize their status in larger formal organizations, are made secretly. The legal concept of "privileged communication" in part is a formal recognition of the necessity for making secret decisions within organizations.

Added to this is the emphasis placed upon conformity in our organization-oriented society and the growing tendency of organization elites to rely upon direct power for their purposes. This is commonly exercised to isolate and neutralize groups and individuals who oppose their policies both inside and outside of the organization. Formal structures may be manipulated or deliberately reorganized so that resistant groups and individuals are denied or removed from access to power or the available means to promote their deviant goals and values. One of the most readily effective ways of doing this is to interrupt, delay or stop the flow of information.

It is the necessity to rationalize and justify such procedures on a democratic basis which leads to concealment of certain actions, misrepresentation of their underlying meaning and even the resort to unethical or illegal means. The difficulty of securing sociological knowledge about these techniques, which we might call the "controls behind the controls," and the denials by those who use them that they exist are logical consequences of the perceived threat such knowledge and admissions become to informal power structures. The epiphenomena of power thus become a kind of shadowy world of our culture, inviting conjecture and condemnation.

Concluding Comment

We have been concerned with a process of social exclusion and with the ways in which it contributes to the development of paranoid patterns of behavior. While the data emphasize the organizational forms of exclusion, we nevertheless believe that these are expressions of a generic process whose correlates will emerge from the study of paranoia in the family and other groups. The differential responses of the individual to the exigencies of organized exclusion are significant in the development of paranoid reactions only insofar as they partially determine the "intolerable" or "unendurable" quality of the status changes confronting him. Idiosyncratic life history factors of the sort stressed in more conventional psychiatric analyses may be involved, but equally important in our estimation are those which inhere in the status changes themselves, age being one of the more salient of these. In either case, once situational intolerability appears, the stage is set for the interactional process we have described.

Our cases, it will be noted, were all people who remained undeteriorated, in contact with others and carrying on militant activities oriented towards recognizable social values and institutions. Generalized suspiciousness in public places and unprovoked aggression against strangers were absent from their experiences. These facts, plus the relative absence of "true paranoia" among mental-hospital populations, leads us to conclude that the "pseudo-community" associated with random aggression (in Cameron's sense) is a sequel rather than an integral part of paranoid patterns. They are likely products of deterioration and fragmentation of personality appearing, when and if they do, in the paranoid person after long or intense periods of stress and complete social isolation.

REFERENCES

1. Cameron, N., "The Paranoid Pseudocommunity," *American Journal of Sociology,* 1943, 46, 33–38.

2. Cameron, N., "The Paranoid Pseudocommunity Revisited," *American Journal of Sociology,* 1959, 65, 52–58.

3. Tyhurst, J. S., "Paranoid Patterns," in A. H. Leighton, J. A. Clausen, and R. Wilson, (eds.), *Exploration in Social Psychiatry,* New York: Basic Books, 1957, Ch. II.

4. Milner, K. O., "The Environment as a Factor in the Etiology of Criminal Paranoia," *Journal of Mental Science,* 1949, 95, 124–132.

5. Pederson, S., "Psychological Reactions to Extreme Social Displacement (Refugee Neuroses)," *Psychoanalytic Review,* 1946, 36, 344–354.

6. Kine, F. F., "Aliens' Paranoid Reaction," *Journal of Mental Science,* 1951, 98, 589–594.

7. Listivan, I., "Paranoid States: Social and Cultural Aspects," *Medical Journal of Australia,* 1956, 776–778.

8. Lemert, E., "Legal Commitment and Social Control," *Sociology and Social Research,* 1946, 30, 33–338.

9. Dentler, R. A., and K. T. Erikson, "The Functions of Deviance in Groups," *Social Problems,* 1959, 7, 102.

10. Loomis, J. L., "Communications, The Development of Trust, and Cooperative Behavior," *Human Relations,* 1959, 12, 305–315.

11. Cumming, E., and J. Cumming, *Closed Ranks,* Cambridge, Mass.: Harvard Press, 1957, Ch. VI.

12. Sapir, E., "Abnormal Types of Speech in Nootka," *Canada Department of Mines, Memoir 62,* 1915, No. 5.

13. Levenson, B., "Bureaucratic Succession," in *Complex Organizations,* A. Etzioni, (ed.), New York: Holt, Rinehart and Winston, 1961, 362–395.

14. Ödegard, Ö., "A Clinical Study of Delayed Admissions to a Mental Hospital," *Mental Hygiene,* 1958, 42, 66–77.

15. Goffman, E., "The Moral Career of the Mental Patient," *Psychiatry,* 1959, 22, 127 ff.

16. Stanton, A. H., and M. S. Schwartz, *The Mental Hospital,* New York: Basic Books, 1954, 200–210.

17. Marmor, J., "Science, Health and Group Opposition" (mimeographed paper), 1958.

Think Critically

1. How are reactions of others important in understanding the phenomenon of paranoia according to Lemert? Explain using main concepts from the reading.

2. Discuss what this analysis may say about other forms of mental illness. Give some examples.

APPEARANCE NORMS WITHIN A CULTURE AND physical characteristics of individuals play an important role in deviance defining. The conditions themselves, however, cannot fully explain the responses of others to them. A person's physical characteristics can come into play *socially* in interaction with others and in forming a self-identity. When these characteristics deviate from cultural standards, they can have a significant impact on social relationships. Goffman's research on the concept of stigma is a major example of the contribution of the interactionist or labeling approach to the understanding of how and why certain physical attributes may focus interactions in such a way that individuals who possess them may be labeled as deviants by others.

In the selection, "Marks of Mischief: Becoming and Being Tatooed," Clinton Sanders provides an in-depth examination of body alteration, the history of tattooing in Western culture, and both the process by which a person decides to be tattooed and how this affects the tatooee's self-definition and social experience. Drawing from data from over six years of field research and almost 200 subjects, Sanders finds that the tattoo is considered as a "mark of disaffiliation" from conventional society, and, at the same time, a symbolic affirmation of personal identity.

Michael Petrunik and Clifford Shearing provide a penetrating analysis of how persons cope with disability in the piece, "Fragile Facades: Stuttering and the Strategic Manipulation of Awareness." The authors elaborate upon and extend the work of Goffman, Schneider, Conrad, and others on the strategic manipulation of awareness to manage potential stigma. They examine strategies used by stutterers to manage interactions and identity by concealing, revealing, or disavowing stuttering. Their analysis offers insights into the ways people manage their disabilities, and how management strategies shape, and are shaped by, the experience of disability.

In "Legitimating the First Tattoo: Moral Passage Through Informal Interaction," Katherine Irwin examines how deviance is negotiated in everyday contexts. Her study of first-time tatooees in the 1990s shows the interpretive processes involved in the destigmatization of deviance. Using participant observation data, Irwin documents the legitimation techniques used by persons to overcome the negative meanings associated with tattoos. The process of legitimation she identifies shows how everyday interactions contribute to much larger cultural shifts.

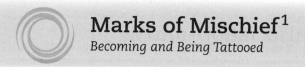

Marks of Mischief[1]
Becoming and Being Tattooed

Clinton R. Sanders

A PERSON'S PHYSICAL APPEARANCE IS A central element affecting his or her self-definition, identity, and interaction with others (Cooley, 1964: 97–104, 175–178, 183; Stone, 1970; Zurcher, 1977: 44–45, 175–178). People use appearance to place each other into categories which aid in the anticipation and interpretation of behavior and to make decisions about how best to coordinate social activities (Goffman, 1959: 24–25; McCall and Simmons, 1982: 214–216; Ruesch and Kees, 1972: 40–41, 57–65).

How closely one meets the cultural criteria for beauty is an appearance factor of key social and personal import. Being defined as attractive has considerable impact on our social relationships. We think about attractive people more often, define them as being more healthy, express greater appreciation for their work, and find them to be more appealing interactants (Jones et al., 1984:53–56). Attractive people are more adept at establishing relationships (Brislin and Lewis, 1968) and enjoy more extensive and pleasant sexual interactions than do those who are not as physically appealing (Hatfield and Sprecher, 1986). Their chances of economic success are greater (Feldman, 1975), and they are consistently defined by others as being of high moral character (Needleman and Weiner, 1977).

Enjoying more frequent positive interactions, attractive people have correspondingly more positive self-definitions. In general, they express more feelings of general happiness (Berscheid et al., 1973), have higher levels of self-esteem and are less likely than the relatively unattractive to expect that they will suffer from mental illness in the future (Napoleon et al., 1980).

AUTHOR'S NOTE: I appreciate the support and criticism (especially the former) provided by Patricia Adler, Peter Adler, Eleanor Lyon, Stephen Markson, Priscilla Warner, and three anonymous reviewers.

Clothing, cosmetics, and hair styling are mechanisms for altering appearance that have in common the relative ease with which one can change one's social "vocabulary" if the message communicated becomes outdated, undesirably stigmatizing or otherwise worthy of reconsideration. In general, the cross-cultural literature on adornment and body alteration indicates that nonpermanent decorative forms (principally costume and body paint) are most commonly associated with transitional statuses or specific and limited social situations. The major forms of permanent alteration—body sculpture, infibulation (piercing), cicatrization (scarification) and tattooing—are, on the other hand, connected to permanent statuses (e.g., gender, maturity), life-long social connections (e.g., clan or tribal membership) or conceptions of beauty that show considerable continuity from generation to generation (see Polhemus, 1978: 149–173).

Those who choose to permanently modify their bodies in ways that violate prevailing appearance norms—or who reject culturally prescribed alterations—risk being defined as socially or morally inferior. Public display of voluntarily acquired, symbolic physical deviance effectively communicates a wealth of information that shapes the social situation in which interaction takes place (Goffman, 1963a; Lofland, 1973: 79–87).

This article focuses on tattooing as a form of permanent body alteration in contemporary society. Choosing to mark one's body in this way changes the tattooee's experience of his or her physical self and has significant potential for altering social interaction. Because of the historical course of tattooing in the West the tattoo is conventionally defined as an indication of the bearer's alienation from mainstream norms and social networks. It is *voluntary stigma* that symbolically isolates the bearer from "normals." Since tattooees are deemed to be responsible for their "deviant" physical condition, the mark is especially discrediting (Jones et al., 1984: 56–65).

Like most stigmatizing conditions, however, tattooing also has an affiliative effect; it identifies the bearer as a member of a select group. When publically displayed the tattoo may act as a source of mutual accessibility (Goffman, 1963b: 131–139). Fellow tattooees commonly recognize and acknowledge their shared experience, decorative tastes and relationship to conventional society. Tattooing also has affiliative impact in that it is routinely employed to demonstrate one's indelible connection to primary associates (e.g., name tattoos) or groups whose members share specialized interests and activities (e.g., motorcycling, use of illegal drugs, or involvement with a specific youth gang) . . .

The History of Western Tattooing

The modern history of western tattooing begins with the exploratory voyages of Captain James Cook and his encounters with tribal tattooing in the South Pacific in the mid-18th century. The decorative practice became popular among sailors, who frequently wore tattoos as exotic commemorations of their world travels and as magical symbols intended to protect the wearer from drowning or other forms of harm. Given tattooing's association with seafarers and the less savory social elements with whom they associated, the practice was generally frowned upon in "polite" society in both Europe and the United States. In the mid to late 19th century, however, tattooing enjoyed a short period of faddish popularity among European nobility (Bruchett and Leighton, 1958; Paine, 1979; Parry, 1971).

By the mid-20th century tattooing was established firmly as a definedly deviant practice in the public mind. Despite the short-lived flirtation of European and American elites with tattooing, members of the middle class saw it as a decorative cultural product dispensed by largely unskilled and unhygienic practitioners from dingy shops in urban slums. Tattoo consumers, in turn, usually were seen as being drawn from marginal, rootless, and dangerously unconventional social groups. The tattoo was a symbol of disaffiliation directed at those who were law abiding, hard working, family oriented, and stable.

Since the mid-1960's, however, tattooing has undergone what some (e.g., Hill, 1972; Rubin, 1983; Tucker, 1981) have called a "renaissance." Although a commercially oriented craft structure continues to dominate contemporary tattooing and the general public continues to define it as a deviant activity, significant changes have been occurring during the last two decades. Younger tattooists, frequently with university or art-school backgrounds and experience in traditional artistic media, have begun to explore tattooing as a form of expression. Unlike the traditional tattooist, the younger artists emphasize creative over economic values, specialize in custom designed—commonly large-scale—tattoos, and are selective about the images they create and the clients with/on whom they will work. Consistent with their backgrounds and aesthetic orientations, the new tattoo artists draw images from diverse artistic sources. Fantasy/science fiction illustrations, traditional Japanese styles, tribal designs, portraiture, and abstract expressionism are major influences on contemporary fine-art tattooing (see Morse, 1977; Richter, 1985; Sanders, 1985b, 1986; Wroblewski, 1981).

In line with the movement into tattooing of practitioners who define themselves as "artists" and present their products as "art," the larger art world has begun to take notice of the medium. Tattooing is vying for legitimation as the work is shown in museums and gallery shows and is subjected to critical discussion by academics and critics/agents of the traditional art world. The tattooists, as a consequence, profit as their work comes to look like art, is displayed like art, is discussed like art, and is bought and sold as art. Their social and occupational status is enhanced, they enjoy greater control over their work lives, and they encounter a new client pool of individuals with more sophisticated aesthetic tastes and sufficient disposable income to purchase extensive custom-designed art products.

The Process of Becoming a Tattooed Person

Initial Motives

Becoming tattooed is a highly social act. The decision to acquire a tattoo (and, as we will see in a later section, the image that is chosen), like most major consumer products is motivated by how the recipient defines him- or herself. The tattoo becomes an item in the tattooee's personal "identity kit" (Facetti and Fletcher, 1971; Goffman, 1961: 20–21), and in turn it is used by those with whom the individual interacts to place him or her into a particular, interaction-shaping social category (see Csikszentmihalyi and Rochberg-Halton, 1981; Solomon, 1983).

When asked to describe how they decided to get a tattoo, the vast majority of respondents made reference to another person or group. Family members, friends, business associates, and other people with whom they regularly interacted were described as being tattooed. Statements such as "Everyone I knew was really into tattoos. It was a peer decision. Everyone had one, so I wanted one" and "My father got one when he was in the war and I always wanted one, too" were typical. Entrance into the actual tattooing "event," however, has all of the characteristics of an impulse purchase. It typically is based on very little information or previous experience (58% of the questionnaire respondents reported *never* having been in a studio prior to the time they received their first tattoo). While tattooees commonly reported having "thought about getting (a tattoo) for a long time," they usually drifted into the actual experience when they "didn't have anything better to do," had sufficient money to devote to a nonessential purchase, and were, most importantly, in the general vicinity of a tattoo establishment. The following accounts were fairly typical.

> We were up in Maine and a bunch of us were just talking about getting tattoos—me and my friends and my cousins. One time my cousin came back from the service with one and I liked it. . . . The only place I knew about was _____'s down in Providence. We were going right by there on our way back home, so we stopped and all got them.
>
> My friends were goin' down there to get some work, you know. That was the only place I knew about, anyway. My friends said there was a tattoo parlor down by the beach. Let's go! I checked it out and seen something I liked. I had some money on me so I said, "I'll get this little thing and check it out and see how it sticks." I thought if I got a tatty it might fade, you know. You never know what's goin' to happen. I don't want anything on my body that is goin' to look fucked up.

. . . The tattoo event frequently involves a ritual commemoration of a significant transition in the life of the recipient (compare Brain, 1979: 174–184; Ebin, 1979: 39–56; Van-Gennep, 1960). The tattooee conceives of the mark as symbolizing change—especially achieving maturity and symbolically separating the self from individuals or groups (parents, husbands, wives, employers, etc.) who have been exercising control over the individual's personal choices.

A tattoo artist related his understanding of his clients' motivations in this way:

> I do see that many people get tattooed to find out again . . . to say, "Who was I before I got into this lost position?" It's almost like a tattoo pulls you back to a certain kind of reality about who you are as an individual. Either that or it transfers you to the next step in your life—the next plateau. A woman will come in and say, "Well, I just went through a really ugly divorce. My husband had control of my fucking body and now I have it again. I want a tattoo. I want a tattoo that says that I have the courage to get this, that I have the courage to take on the rest of my life. I'm going to do what I want to do and do what I have to do to survive as a person." That's a motivation that comes through the door a lot.

Locating a Tattooist

. . . Like the initial decision to get a tattoo, the tattooist one decides to patronize commonly is chosen through information provided by members of the individual's personal networks. The shop in which they received their first tattoo was located by 58% of the questionnaire respondents through a recommendation provided by a friend or family member. Since in most areas establishments that dispense tattoos are not especially numerous, many first-time tattooees choose a studio on a very practical basis—it is the only one they know about or it is the studio which is closest to where they live (20% of the questionnaire sample chose the shop on the basis of location, 28% because it was the only one they knew about) . . .

Most first-time tattooees enter the tattoo setting with little information about the process or even the relative skill of the artist. Rarely do recipients spend as much time and effort acquiring information about a process that is going to indelibly mark their bodies as they would were they preparing to purchase a TV set or other far less significant consumer item.

Consequently, tattooees usually enter the tattoo setting ill-informed and experiencing a considerable degree of anxiety. Their fears center around the anticipated pain of the process and the permanence of the tattoo . . .

For the most part, tattooists are quite patient about answering the questions clients ask with numbing regularity (pain, price, and permanence). This helps to put the recipient more at ease, smooths the service delivery interaction, and increases the chances that a satisfied customer—who will recommend the shop to his/her friends and perhaps return again for additional work—will leave the establishment (for extended discussions of in-shop interaction see Becker and Clark, 1979; Govenar, 1977; St. Clair and Govenar, 1981; and Sanders, 1983 and 1985b) . . .

Choosing a Design and Body Location

. . . One of the most common responses which tattoo clients gave to my routine question, "How did you go about deciding on this particular tattoo?" was to make reference to a personal association with whom they had a close emotional relationship. Some chose a particular tattoo because it was like that worn by a close friend or a member of their family. Others chose a design which incorporated the name of their boy/girl friend, spouse or child or a design associated with that person (e.g., zodiac signs):

> I had this homemade cross and skull here and I needed a coverup. [The tattooist] couldn't just do anything, so I thought to myself, "My daughter was born in May, and that's the Bull." I'm leaving the rest of this arm clean because it is just for my daughter. If I ever get married, I'll put something here [on the other arm]. I'll get a rose or something for my wife.
>
> This tattoo is a symbol of friendship. Me and my best friend—I've known him since I could walk—came in together and we both got bluebirds to have a symbol that when we do part we will remember each other by it.

The ongoing popularity of "vow tattoos," such as the traditional heart with "MOM" or flowers with a ribbon on which the loved one's name is written, attests to the importance of tattooing as a way of symbolically expressing love and commitment (see Anonymous, 1982).

Similarly, tattoos are used to demonstrate connection and commitment to a group. For example, military personnel pick tattoos which relate to their particular service, motorcycle gang members choose club insignia, and members of sports teams enter a shop en masse and all receive the same design.

Tattoos are also employed as symbolic representations of how one conceives of the self or interests and activities which are key features of self definition. Tattooees commonly choose their birth sign or have their name or nickname inscribed on their bodies. Others choose more abstract symbols of the self.

> I put a lot of thought into this tattoo. I'm an English lit major, and I thought that the medieval castle had a lot of significance. I'm an idealist, and I thought that that was well expressed by a castle with clouds. Plus, I'm blond and I wanted something blue.
>
> [Quote from field notes] Two guys in their twenties come in and look at the flash. After looking around for a while one of the guys comes over to me and asks if we have any bees. I tell him to look through the book [of small designs] because I have seen some bees in there. I ask, "Why do you want a bee? I don't think I have ever seen anyone come in here for one." He replies, "I'm allergic to bees. If I get stung by one again I'm going to die. So I thought I'd come in here and have a big, mean looking bee put on. I want one that has this long stinger and these long teeth and is coming in to land. With that, any bee would think twice about messing with me."

Tattooees commonly represent the self by choosing designs which symbolize important personal involvements, hobbies, occupational activities, and so forth. In most street shops, the winged insignia of Harley-Davidson motorcycles and variants on that theme are the most frequently requested images. During one particularly busy week in the major shop in which I was observing, a rabbit breeder acquired a rabbit tattoo, a young man requested a cartoon frog because the Little League team he coached was named the "Frogs," a fireman received a fire fighter's cross insignia surrounded by flame, and an optician chose a flaming eye.

No matter what the associational or self-definitional meaning of the chosen tattoo, the recipient is commonly aware of the decorative-aesthetic function of the design. When I asked tattooees to explain how they went about choosing a particular design, they routinely made reference to aesthetic criteria—they "liked the colors" or they "thought it was pretty" . . .

On their part, tattooists tend to recognize the aesthetic importance of their work as seen by their clients. One tattooist, for example, observed:

> If you ask most people why they got [a particular tattoo] they aren't going to have any deep Freudian answers for you. The most obvious reason that someone gets a tattoo is because they like it for some reason and just want it. I mean, why do people wear rings on their fingers or any sort of nonfunctional decorative stuff—put

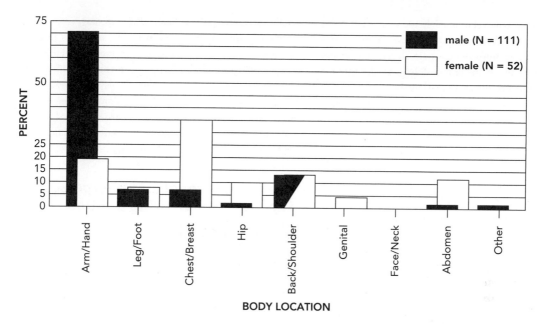

FIGURE 1   **Body Location of First Tattoo (N = 163)**

on makeup or dye their hair? People have the motivation to decorate themselves and be different and unique . . . Tattooing is really the most intimate art form. You carry it on your body. The people that come in here are really mostly just "working bumpkins." They just want to have some art they can understand. This stuff in museums is bullshit. Nobody ever really sees it. It doesn't get to "the people" like tattoo art.[2]

A number of factors determine a tattooee's decision about where on the body the tattoo will be located. The vast majority of male tattooees choose to have their work placed on the arm. In his study of the tattoos carried by 2,000 members of the Royal Navy, Scutt found that 98% had received their tattoo(s) on the arm (Scutt and Gotch, 1974: 96). In my own research, 55% of the questionnaire respondents received their first tattoo on the arm or hand (71% of the males and 19% of the females. The 16 interviewees had, all together, 35 tattoos, 27 of which were carried by the 10 males. Eighty-one percent (22) of the men's tattoos were on their arms (of the remainder 2 were on hips, one was on the back, one on the face and one on the recipient's chest). The six women interviewees possessed eight tattoos—three on the back or the shoulder area,

three on the breast, one on an arm and one on the lower back. Thirty-five percent of female questionnaire respondents received their first tattoo on the breast, 13% on the back or shoulder and 10% on the hip (see Figure 1).

Clearly, there is a definite convention affecting the decision to place the tattoo on a particular part of the body—men, for the most part, choose the arm while women choose the breast, hip, lower abdomen or back/shoulder. To some degree the tendency for male tattooees to have the tattoo placed on the arm is determined by technical features of the tattoo process. Tattooing is a two-handed operation. The tattooist must stretch the skin with one hand while inscribing the design with the other. This operation is most easily accomplished when the tattoo is being applied to an extremity. Tattooing the torso is more difficult and, commonly, tattooists have an assistant who stretches the client's skin when work is being done on that area of the body. Technical difficulty, in turn, affects price. Most tattooists charge 10 to 25% more for tattoos placed on body parts other than the arm or leg. The additional cost factor probably has some effect on the client's choice of body location.

Pain is another factor shaping the tattooee's decision. The tattoo machine contains needle groups which superficially pierce the skin at high speed, leaving small amounts of pigment in the tiny punctures. Obviously, this process will cause more or less pain depending on the sensitivity of the area being tattooed. In general, tattooing arms or legs is less painful than marking body areas with a higher concentration of nerve endings or parts of the body where the bones are not cushioned with muscle tissue.[3]

The different symbolic functions of the tattoo for males versus females appears to be a major issue affecting the sex-based conventions regarding choice of body site. Women tend to regard the tattoo (commonly a small, delicate design) as a permanent body decoration primarily intended for personal pleasure and the enjoyment of those with whom they are most intimate. The chosen tattoos are, therefore, placed on parts of the body most commonly seen by those with whom women have primary relationships. Since tattoos on women are especially stigmatizing, placement on private parts of the body allows women to retain unsullied identities when in contact with casual associates or strangers (see Goffman, 1963a: 53–55, 73–91). Here, for example, is a portion of a brief conversation with a young woman who carried an unconventional design (a snake coiled around a large rose) on what is, for women, an unconventional body location (her right bicep).

Sanders—How did you decide on that particular design?

Woman—I wanted something really different and I'd never seen a tattoo like this on a woman before. I really like it, but sometimes I look at it and wish I didn't have it.

S—That's interesting. When do you wish you didn't have it?

W—When I'm getting real dressed up in a sleeveless dress and I want to look . . . uh, prissy and feminine. People look at a tattoo and think you're real bad . . . a loose person. But I'm not.

. . . Men, on the other hand, typically are less inclined than women to define the tattoo primarily as a decorative and intimate addition to the body. Instead, the male tattoo is an identity symbol—a more public display of interests, associations, separation from the normative constraints of conventional society and, most generally, masculinity. The designs chosen by men are usually larger than those favored by women and, rather than employing the gentle imagery of nature and mythology (flowers, birds, butterflies, unicorns and so forth), they frequently symbolize

more violent impulses. Snakes, bloody daggers, skulls, dragons, grim reapers, black panthers and birds of prey are dominant images in the conventional repertoire of tattoo designs chosen by men. Placement of the image on the arm allows both casual public display and, should the male tattooee anticipate a critical judgment from someone whose negative reaction could have untoward consequences (mostly commonly, an employer), the tattooed arm can be easily hidden with clothing . . .

The Intrapersonal and Interpersonal Experience of Wearing a Tattoo

Impact on Self-Definition

As indicated in the foregoing presentation of the initial motives which prompt the decision to acquire a tattoo, tattooees consistently conceive of the tattoo as having impact on their definition of self and demonstrating to others information about their unique interests and social connections. Interviewees commonly expressed liking their tattoo(s) because it (they) made him or her "different" or "special" (see Goffman, 1963a: 56–62):

> Having a tattoo changes how you see yourself. It is a way of choosing to change your body. I enjoy that. I enjoy having a tattoo because it makes me different from other people. There is no one in the whole world who has a right arm that looks anything like mine. I've always valued being different from other people. Tattooing is a way of expressing that difference. It is a way of saying, "I am unique."

Interactional Consequences

. . . In general, tattooees' observations concerning the effect of having a tattoo and the process of being tattooed on their self-definitions were rather basic and off-hand. In contrast, all interviewees spoke at some length about their social experiences with others and how the tattoo affected their identities and interactions. Some stressed the affiliational consequences of being tattooed—the mark identified them as belonging to a special group.

> I got tattooed because I had an interest in it. My husband is a chef and our friends tend to be bikers, so it gets me accepted more into that community. They all think of me as "the college girl" and I'm really not. So this [tattoo] kind of brings the door open more . . . The

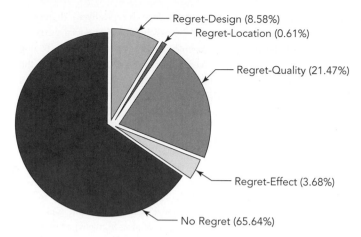

Regret-Design (8.58%)
Regret-Location (0.61%)
Regret-Quality (21.47%)
Regret-Effect (3.68%)
No Regret (65.64%)

FIGURE 2   **Extent and Source of Tattooee Regret (N = 163)**

typical biker would tell you that you almost have to have tattoos to be part of the group.

Most took pleasure in the way the tattoo enhanced their identities by demonstrating their affiliation with a somewhat more diverse group—tattooed people . . .

Given the symbolic meaning carried by tattoos in conventional social circles, all tattooees have the experience of being the focus of attention because of the mark they carry. The positive responses of others are, of course, the source of the most direct pleasure . . .

Revelation of the tattoo is also the source of negative attention when defined by others as a stigmatizing mark.

> Sometimes at these parties the conversation will turn to tattoos and I'll mention that I have some. A lot of people don't believe it, but if I'm feeling loose enough I'll roll up my sleeve and show my work. What really aggravates me is that there will almost always be someone who reacts with a show of disgust. "How could you do that to yourself?" No wonder I usually feel more relaxed and at home with bikers and other tattooed people.

> I think tattoos look sharp. I walk down the beach and people look at my tattoos. Usually they don't say anything. [When they do] I wish they would say it to my face . . . like, "Tattoos are ugly." But, when they say something behind my back . . . "Isn't that gross." Hey, keep your comments to yourself! If you don't like it, you don't like it. I went to the beach with my father and I said, "Hey, let's walk down the beach," and he said, "No, I don't feel like it." What are you, embarrassed to walk with me?

Given the negative responses that tattooees encounter with some frequency when casual associations or strangers become aware of their body decorations, most are selective about to whom they reveal their tattoos. This is particularly the case when the "other" is in a position to exercise control over the tattooee . . .

Tattooees commonly use the reactions of casual associates or relative strangers as a means of categorizing them. A positive reaction to the tattoo indicates social and cultural compatability, while a negatively judgmental response is seen as signifying a narrow and convention-bound perspective.

> It seems as though I can actually tell how I'm going to get along with people and vice-versa by the way they react to my tattoo. It's more or less expressive of the unconventional side of my character right up front. Most of the people who seem to like me really dig the tattoo too [quoted in Hill, 1972: 249].

. . . Given the negative social reaction often precipitated by tattoos, it would be reasonable to expect that tattooees who regretted their decision would have emphasized the unpleasant interactional consequences of the tattoo. Interviewees and questionnaire respondents rarely expressed any doubts about their decision to acquire a tattoo. Those that did indicate regret, however, usually did not focus on the stigmatizing effect of the tattoo. Instead, regretful tattooees most commonly were dissatisfied with the *technical quality* of the tattoo they purchased.[4] (Figure 2; see also Sanders, 1985a).

Summary and Conclusion: Tattooing, Stigma, Self, and Identity

Potential tattooees typically begin to think about altering their bodies in this manner and to devise an understanding of what the tattoo will signify to themselves and others through contact with tattooed associates or by attending media presentations of tattooing and tattooed people (compare Cohen, 1973; Matza, 1969). In general, they define the tattoo as a mark of affiliation—demonstrating connection to significant groups, primary associates, or those who share specific interests—or as an isolative symbol of unconventionality or unique personal decoration. Having come to conceive of themselves as tattooed, potential recipients locate a tattoo establishment and acquire the mark.

When revealed to others, the newly acquired corporeal embellishment affects interactions and relationships. Positive responses from co-interactants tend to reinforce social connections, certify tattooees' positive evaluations of self and the tattoo acquisition decision, and increase the likelihood that tattooees will expand the universe of situations in which they choose to reveal their unconventional body decorations.

If being tattooed leads to negative social and self-definitional consequences, regretful tattooees are faced with various alternatives. When met with disapproval, tattooees may respond by negatively evaluating the disapproving other and becoming more selective in disclosing the fact that they bear a tattoo (see Goffman, 1963a: 11). If regretful, tattooees focus the responsibility for the negative consequences of having acquired the tattoo upon themselves; they can deny responsibility for the decision or take steps to obliterate the tattoo. Since negative evaluations of the tattoo decision are most commonly due to the perceived inferior quality of the work, regretful tattooees often have the offending mark covered or reworked by another, hopefully more skilled, tattooist (see Figure 3).

The central factor shaping this process—from initial stages of interest through dealing with the consequences of being a tattooed person—is that the tattoo is conventionally regarded as a stigma symbol (Goffman, 1963a: 43). The decision to acquire a tattoo is a decision not only to alter one's physical appearance. It is a choice to change how the person experiences his or her self and, in turn, how he or she will be defined and treated by others.

Definitions of tattoos and tattooees, contained within both the general culture and the "scientific community,"

are predominantly negative. Tattoos typically are defined as being symptomatic of the psychological or social deviance of the bearer.[5] Conventional repulsion imbues tattooing with significant power and appeal. For some tattooees the act of acquiring a tattoo marks them as being involved in an exotic social world centered on the pleasurable flaunting of authority and convention (compare Lofland, 1969: 106).

> [Why do you think you initially wanted to put the tattoo someplace that is well hidden?] I guess I thought that someone would think it was creepy. It would have connotations of loose women or being foolish. Like kids don't think through the consequences of stuff. They do things impetuously. I thought that people might think I just ran down there in a fit of glee. [Actually] a tattoo is not serious. I think that is part of the pleasure of it. When I was first thinking about it it was, "Oh boy, let's do this!" It was sort of a gleeful thing. It is like being a little bit bad.
>
> I can't think of one nice compact reason [I got a tattoo]. They are pretty. But most of all they are a poke in the eye to people who don't have them—people who are straights or whatever.

The tattoo acts as more than simply a "mark of disaffiliation" (Goffman, 1963a: 143–147). It may also demonstrate connection to unconventional social groups. In some cases it symbolizes membership in subcultures (e.g., outlaw motorcyclists, youth gang) centered around socially disvalued or law-violating interests and activities.[6]

The stigmatized social definition of tattooing and the negative response tattooees commonly experience when "normals" are aware of their stigma may also precipitate identification with a subculture in which the tattoo is of primary significance. Within the informal "tattoo community" consisting of those tattooees who positively define their unconventional mark, the tattoo acts as a source of "mutual openness" (Goffman,, 1963b: 131–139), providing opportunities for spontaneous appreciative interaction with others who are also tattooed (Goffman, 1963a:23–25; Pfuhl, 1986: 168–188).[7]

As is commonly the case with subcultural groups bound together by the problems associated with possession of a physical stigma, the tattoo world has developed an organized core. More or less formal groups such as the National Tattoo Association hold regular meetings and provide practitioners with technical information, legal assistance, access to the latest equipment and supplies,

Decisional Antecedents
1. Contact w/lattooed other (as model or source of overt pressure)
2. Contact with/exposure to tattoo setting (exotic place/culture)
3. Media contact (learn "meaning" of tattoo and nature of tattooees)

Locate Tattoo Site
1. Social/personal contact
2. Media information, advertisements, Yellow Pages
3. Encountering physical site

Tattoo Meaning
A. Affiliative
  1. Masculinity
  2. Connection to significant other (eg., vow)
  3. Symbolization of group connection
  4. Symbolization of shared interest/activity

B. Isolative/individuating
  1. Display of unconventionality
  2. Personal decoration/beauty accessory

Acquire Tattoo
1. Pleasure of place (exotic contact, new experience)
2. Ritual (social display of courage, self-assertion, control, etc.)
3. After self-definition (self as more beautiful, courageous, unique, connected, belonging, etc.)

Revelation

Social/Personal Response
A. Positive Response (admiration, praise, etc.)
  1. Reinforce connection to positive responder and/or symbolized other (eg., vow)
  2. Reinforce positive self definition
  3. Increase likelihood of acquiring additional tattoos
  4. Increase likelihood of further tattoo display/disclosure

Increase likelihood of negative response

B. Negative Response (disgust, avoidance, etc.)
  1. Negatively define source of negative response
  2. Negatively define self
  3. Avoid future disclosure (secrecy, selectivity)
  4. Obliteration (self or surgical removal)
  5. Cover or rework tattoo (if regret due to technical dissatisfaction)

Avoidance

Reestablish positive self definition (disavowal of responsibility/intent — eg., drunkenness, excessive peer pressure)

Passing

Regain non-deviant self

Regain positive sense of choice, appearance (decrease cognitive dissonance)

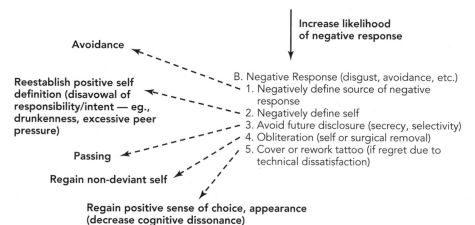

FIGURE 3   **The Tattoo as Social Symbol: Acquisitional Process and Self-Definitional/Identity Consequences**

and other essential occupational resources. Serious tattoo "enthusiasts" and collectors are also active in this organized world. Tattoo conventions provide them with an opportunity to display their work, enlarge their collections, and associate with other tattooees in situations in which *they* are "normal." Understandably, a major focus of organizational activity is the public redefinition of tattooing as a legitimate form of artistic production.

Tattooists have the most immediate and practical interest in the organized destigmatization of tattooing.

Stigma decreases the size of the potential client pool and generates both legal and informal social control efforts. The redefinition of tattooing as an art form expands the tattoo market while providing the tattooist with an opportunity to assume the honorific role of "artist." This role offers tattooists enhanced social status and increases the control they can exercise over their work life (see Sanders, 1985b).

Contemporary commercial culture provides a variety of products (t-shirts, bumper stickers, buttons, and so forth) by which people may announce their perspectives, personal interests, and social attachments. Clothing, jewelry, hairstyle, and other aspects of personal decoration are used to demonstrate aesthetic taste. These modes of self symbolization are, however, relatively safe and transitory expressions. For some, these conventional mechanisms are inadequate. Typically impelled by personal association with others who have chosen a more drastic and symbolically powerful approach, tattooees purchase what is, as yet, a "tarnished" cultural product (Shover, 1975). In so doing, tattooed people voluntarily shape their social identities and enhance their definitions of self. Drawn by the affiliational and individuating consequences of their choice and despite the potential for disrupted interactions, tattooees choose to mark their bodies with indelible symbols of what they see themselves to be.

NOTES

1. I've been strung along with my eyes open and strung along with them closed, but the dime-a-dozen holy joes are the ones I hate the most. Give me rogues with golden earrings, rogues with slick-backed hair. It's the mark of mischief that they wear. Comes down to me like a breath of fresh air. Is it sin or insanity, balance or profanity?

   Rascals

   The Albion Band *Under the Rose.*

2. Of the 35 tattoos worn by the 16 interviewees, 14% (5) represented birds, 6% (2) represented mammals, 14% (5) represented mythical animals, 9% (3) represented insects, 3% (1) represented a human female, 17% (6) represented human males, 14% (5) were noncommercial symbols (hearts, crosses, military insignia, etc.), 14% (5) were floral, 3% (1) were names or vow tattoos, and 6% (2) were some other image. Questionnaire respondents were asked to indicate the design of their first tattoo. They were: 14% (23) bird, 11% (18) mammal, 12% (19) mythical animal,

10% (17) insect, 1% (2) human female, 6% (10) human male, 4% (6) commercial symbols, 8% (13) noncommercial symbols, 21% (34) floral/arborial, 4% (7) name/vow, and 9% (14) other.

3. The painfulness of the tattoo process is the most unpleasant element of the tattoo event. Only 33% [54] of the questionnaire respondents maintained that there was something about the tattoo experience that they disliked. One third of these [18] said that the pain was what they found most unpleasant. Fourteen of the 16 interviewees mentioned pain as a troublesome factor. Numerous observations of groups of young men discussing pain or stoically expressing little regard for the pain as they were receiving tattoos made it difficult not to see the tattoo event as having ritualized initiatory aspects. In some cases the tattoo process provides a situation in which the male tattooee can demonstrate his "manliness" to his peers. Here, for example, is a description of an incident in which five members of a local college football team acquired identical tattoos on their hips:

   I asked the guy nearest to me if they are all getting work done. "Yeah. He (indicates friend) was so hot for it he would have done it himself if we couldn't get it done today." (You all getting hip shots?) "Yeah, that's where all jocks get them. The coach would shit if he found out." The conversation among the jocks turns to the issue of pain. They laugh as the guy being worked on grimaces as W (artist) finishes the outline and wipes the piece down with alcohol. The client observes that this experience isn't bad compared to the time "I fucked up my hand in a game and had to have steel pins put in the knuckles. One of them got bent and the doctor had to cut it out. That was *bad.* I got the cold sweats." Some of the others join in by telling their "worst pain I ever experienced" stories. The guy being worked on is something of a bleeder and the others kid him about this. As W begins shading one of them shouts, "Come on, really grind it in there."

   The cross-cultural literature on body alteration indicates that the pain of the process is an important factor. Ebin (1979: 88–89), for example, in discussing tattooing in the Marquesas Islands, states:

   The tattoo was not only an artistic achievement: it also demonstrated that its recipient could bear pain. On one island, the word to describe a person who was completely covered with tattoos is *ne'one'o*, based on a word meaning either 'to cry for a long time' or 'horrific'. One observer in the Marquesas noted that whenever people discussed the tattoo design, they emphasized the pain with which it was acquired.

See also Becker and Clark, 1979: 10, 19; Brain, 1979: 183–184; Ross and McKay, 1979: 44–49, 67–69; St. Clair and Govenar, 1981: 100–135.

4. Other than simply accepting the regretted mark, there are a few avenues of resolution open to dissatisfied tattooees. At the most extreme, the tattooee may try to obliterate the offending mark with acid or attempt to cut it off. A somewhat more reasoned (and considerably less painful) approach entails seeking the aid of a dermatologist or plastic surgeon who will medically remove the tattoo. However, the most common alternative chosen by regretful tattooees is to have the technically inferior piece redone or covered with another tattoo created by a more skilled practitioner. Tattooists estimate that 40 to 50% of their work entails reworking or applying cover-ups to poor-quality tattoos. See Goldstein et al., 1979 and Hardy, 1983.

5. Analysts variously see tattooees as suffering from masochism (Measy, 1972), sexual immaturity, or immorality (Brain, 1979: 124; Parry, 1971; see also Scutt and Gotch, 1974: 15–88), mental retardation (von Hentig, 1979: 102–109), and other psychopathological conditions (e.g., Briggs, 1958; Kurtzberg, et al., 1967; Zimmerman, 1979). The wearing of a tattoo has long been associated with criminality. Lombroso (1911: xiv), for example, specifically identified tattooing as an indicator of atavism. Other criminological writers (e.g., Burma, 1965; Stebbins, 1971: 129–130) have stressed that choosing to become tattooed indicates the desire (or, at least, functions) to label one's self as being isolated from law-abiding society.

Some psychological writers present the tattoo rather distinctly from the dominant view that it is related to the wearer's pathology. Hamburger (1966) and Popplestone (1963), for example, maintain that the tattoo is one of a variety of "exoskeletal defense" mechanisms by which the the tattooed person protects his or her "psychological integrity" in the face of perceived external threat. Grumet (1983) has recently presented the tattoo as having therapeutic utility as a general indicator of the wearer's internal states and perceptions.

6. One traditional use of tattooing has been to mark indelibly social outcasts or defined deviants so that they can be easily identified and/or avoided by officials and "normals." In sixth-century Japan, for example, criminals and social outcasts were tattooed on the face or arms as a form of negative public identification and punishment (Richie and Burma, 1980: 12–13). Similarly, in the nineteenth century, inmates of the Massachusetts prison system had "Mass S.P." and the date of their release tattooed on their left arms (Ebensten, 1953:20). More recently, the Nazis tattooed identification numbers on the arms of concentration camp inmates. In April of 1986 conservative columnist William Buckley suggested that victims of AIDS (Acquired Immune Difficiency Syndrome) be tattooed on the buttocks in order to limit the spread of the disease among homosexuals (*Hartford Courant,* April 19, 1986, p. C6).

7. The literature directed at the fan world surrounding tattooing consistently makes reference to the "tattoo community." For example:

The choice of the artist and the image are of paramount importance. The collector is not only making a statement about himself, but is also visually displaying the art of tattooing. The collector has an obligation that goes far beyond commitment to oneself. The tattoo community as a whole is dependent on the critical abilities of those who look upon tattooing as a serious art form. . . . Like any other area of the arts that has a large following, tattooing creates for both the artist and the patron a culture that is familiar and appreciated. The tattooing community has a close bond between the artist and the collector, a bond much closer than in most artistic communities because of the intimate nature of a tattoo. Everyone who is part of the community shares in the responsibilities involved in keeping the art form alive and responsive [Brachfeld, 1982: 24–25].

REFERENCES

Anonymous (1982) "The name game," *Tattootime 1:* 50–54.

Becker, N. and R. Clark (1979) "Born to raise hell: an ethnography of tattoo parlors." Presented at the meetings of the Southwestern Sociological Association, March.

Bell, G. (1967) "Self-confidence, persuasability and cognitive dissonance among automobile buyers," pp. 442–468 in D. Cox (ed.) *Risk-Taking and Information Handling in Consumer Behavior.* Boston: Harvard University Graduate School of Business Administration.

Berscheid, E. et al. (1973) "Body image, physical appearance and self-esteem." Presented at the annual meetings of the American Sociological Association.

Brachfeld, T. (1982) "Tattoos and the collector." *Tattootime 1* (Fall): 24–25.

Briggs, J. (1958) "Tattooing," *Medical Times* 87: 1030–1039.

Brislin, R. and S. Lewis (1968) "Dating and physical attractiveness: a replication." *Psych. Reports* 22: 976–984.

Burchett, G. and P. Leighton (1958) *Memoirs of a Tattooist*. London: Oldbourne.

Burma, J. (1965) "Self-tattooing among delinquents: a research note," pp. 271–276 in M. Roach and J. Eicher (eds.) *Dress, Adornment and the Social Order*. New York: John Wiley.

Cohen, S. (1973) "Mods and rockers: the inventory as manufactured news," pp. 226–241 in S. Cohen and J. Young (eds.) *The Manufacture of News: A Reader*. Newbury Park, CA: Sage.

Cooley, C.H. (1964 [1902]) *Human Nature and the Social Order*. New York: Schocken.

Csikszentmihalyi, M. and E. Rochberg-Halton (1981) *The Meaning of Things*. Cambridge: Cambridge Univ. Press.

Ebensten, H. (1953) *Pierced Hearts and True Love*. London: Derek Verschoyle.

Ebin, V. (1979) *The Body Decorated*. London: Thames & Hudson.

Facetti, G. and A. Fletcher (1971) *Identity Kits: A Pictorial Survey of Visual Signals*. New York: Van Nostrand Reinhold.

Feldman, S. (1975) "The presentation of shortness in everyday life," pp. 437–442 in S. Feldman and G. Thielbar (eds.) *Life Styles*. Boston: Little, Brown.

Goffman, E. (1959) *Presentation of Self in Everyday Life*. Garden City, NY: Doubleday.

Goffman, E. (1961) *Asylums*. Garden City, NY: Doubleday.

Goffman, E. (1963a) *Stigma*. Englewood Cliffs, NJ: Prentice-Hall.

Goffman, E. (1963b) *Behavior in Public Places*. New York: Free Press.

Goldstein, N. et al. (1979) "Techniques of removal of tattoos." *J. of Dermatological Surgery and Oncology* 5: 901–910.

Govenar, A. (1977) "The acquisition of tattooing competence: an introduction." *Folklore Annual of the University Folklore Association 7 and 8*: 43–63.

Grumet, G. (1983) "Psychodynamic implications of tattoos." *Amer. J. of Orthopsychiatry* 53: 482–492.

Hamburger, E. (1966) "Tattooing as psychic defense mechanisms." *Int. J. of Social Psychiatry* 12: 60–62.

Hatfield, E. and S. Sprecher (1986) *Mirror, Mirror. . . .* Albany: State Univ. of New York Press.

Hardy, D. (1983) "Inventive cover work." *Tattootime 2:* 12–17.

Hill, A. (1972) "Tattoo renaissance," pp. 245–249 in G. Lewis (ed.) *Side-Saddle on the Golden Calif.* Pacific Palisades, CA: Goodyear.

Jones, E. et al. (1984) *Social Stigma: The Psychology of Marked Relationships*. New York: Freeman.

Kurtzberg, R. et al. (1967) "Psychologic screening of inmates requesting cosmetic operations: a preliminary report." *Plastic and Reconstructive Surgery 39*: 387–396.

Lofland, J. (1969) *Deviance and Identity*. Englewood Cliffs, NJ: Prentice-Hall.

Lofland, L. (1973) *A World of Strangers*. New York: Basic Books.

Lombroso, C. (1911) "Introduction," in G. L. Ferrara, *Criminal Man According to the Classification of Cesare Lombroso*. New York: G. P. Putnam.

McCall, G. and J. Simmons (1982) *Social Psychology*. New York: Free Press.

Matza, D. (1969) *Becoming Deviant*. Englewood Cliffs, NJ: Prentice-Hall.

Measly, L. (1972) "The psychiatric and social relevance of tattoos in Royal Navy detainees." *British J. of Criminology 12:* 182–186.

Morse, A. (1977) *The Tattooists*. San Francisco: Albert A. Morse.

Napoleon, T. et al. (1980) "A replication and extension of 'physical attractiveness and mental illness'." *J. of Abnormal Psychology* 89: 250–253.

Needleman, B. and N. Weiner (1977) "Appearance and moral status in the arts." Presented at the annual meetings of the Popular Culture Association.

Nichols, M. (1985) "The piercing profile evaluated." *Piercing Fans Int. Q. 24:* 14–15.

Parry, A. (1971 [1933]) *Tattoo: Secrets of a Strange Art Practiced by the Natives of the United States*. New York: Collier.

Paine, J. (1979) "Skin deep: a brief history of tattooing." *Mankind 6:* 18ff.

Pfuhl, E. (1986) *The Deviance Process* (second edition). Belmont, CA: Wadsworth.

Polhemus, T. (ed.) (1978) *The Body Reader*. New York: Pantheon.

Popplestone, J. (1963) "A syllabus of exoskeletal defenses." *Psych. Record 13:* 15–25.

Richter, S. (1985) *Tattoo*. London: Quartet.

Ross, R. and H. McKay (1979) *Self-Mutilation*. Lexington, MA: Lexington Books.

Rubin, A. (1983) "Prologues to a history of the tattoo renaissance." Presented at the Art of the Body Symposium, UCLA.

Ruesch, J. and W. Kees (1972) *Nonverbal Communication*. Berkeley: Univ. of California Press.

St. Clair, L. and A. Governar (1981) *Stoney Knows How: Life as a Tattoo Artist*. Lexington: Univ. Press of Kentucky.

Sanders, C. (1986) "Tattooing as fine art and client work: the art work of Carl (Shotsie) Gorman." *Appearances 12:* 12–13.

Sanders, C. (1985a) "Tattoo consumption: risk and regret in the purchase of a socially marginal service," pp. 17–22 in E. Hirshman and M. Holbrook (eds.) *Advances in Consumer Research, Vol. XII*. New York: Association for Consumer Research.

Sanders, C. (1985b) "Selling deviant pictures: the tattooist's career and occupational experience." Presented at the Conference on Social Theory, Politics and the Arts, Adelphi University, October.

Sanders, C. (1983) "Drill and fill: client choice, client typologies and interactional control in commercial tattoo settings." Presented at the Art of the Body Symposium, UCLA.

Scutt, R. and R. Gotch (1974) *Art, Sex and Symbol.* New York: Barnes.

Shover, N. (1975) "Tarnished goods and services in the market place." *Urban Life and Culture 3:* 471–488.

Solomon, M. (1983) "The role of products as social stimuli: a symbolic interactionist perspective." *J. of Consumer Research 10 (December):* 319–329.

Stebbins, R. (1971) *Commitment to Deviance.* Westport, CT: Greenwood.

Stone, G. (1970) "Appearance and the self," pp. 394–414 in G. Stone and H. Farberman (eds.) *Social Psychology Through Symbolic Interaction.* Waltham, MA: Xerox.

Tucker, M. (1981) "Tattoo: the state of the art." *Artforum (May):* 42–47.

Van Gennep, A. (1960) *The Rites of Passage.* Chicago: Univ. of Chicago Press.

von Hetig, H. (1979) *The Criminal and His Victim.* New York: Schocken.

Wroblewski, C. (1981) *Skin Show: The Art and Craft of Tattoo.* New York: Dragon's Dream.

Zimmerman, M. (1979) "Suits for malpractice based on alleged unsightly scars resulting from removal of tattoos." *J. of Dermatologic Surgery and Oncology 5:* 911–912.

Zurcher, L. (1977) *The Mutable Self.* Newbury Park, CA: Sage.

Think Critically

1. Identify the factors Sanders cites as having contributed to the "renaissance" of tattooing. Based on his discussion and findings, what do you feel are the most important elements that lead a person to become tattooed? Why?

2. In what way(s) does the study of tattooing reveal important information about stigma, the self, and identity? Explain your response.

Fragile Facades: Stuttering and the Strategic Manipulation of Awareness*

Michael Petrunik and Clifford D. Shearing

STUTTERING IS A PUZZLING DISORDER OF human communication which has defied explanation and cure for thousands of years (Van Riper, 1971:2). According to survey estimates in Europe and North America, stutterers constitute about 1 percent of the school-age population, regardless of language or dialect (Bloodstein, 1981:79; Van Riper, 1971:39). Although systematic data are not available—there are only impressionistic accounts from anthropologists—stuttering appears to be less common in non-western, non-industrial societies.[1] Stuttering typically appears between two and nine years of age. There is some evidence that stuttering has a genetic basis; it tends to appear in successive generations of the same family and frequently in identical twins (Bloodstein, 1981:94). Stuttering is more common among males than females, by a ratio of three or four to one

*An earlier version of this paper was presented by Petrunik at the annual meetings of the Society for the Study of Social Problems, Toronto, August, 1981. The authors thank John Gilmore and the anonymous *Social Problems* reviewers for their comments. Correspondence to: Petrunik, 53 Westfield Crescent, Nepean, Ontario K2G, OT6, Canada, or Shearing, Centre of Criminology, University of Toronto, Toronto, Ontario M5S 1A1, Canada.

(Bloodstein, 1981:86). Only about one fifth of those who stutter in early childhood continue to stutter into adulthood (Bloodstein, 1981:86; Van Riper, 1971:45).

Stuttering, as visible behavior, refers to interruptions in speech involving the prolongation or repetition of sounds or words, pauses between words or syllables, and "blocking" on words, sometimes accompanied by extraneous sounds such as grunts, facial grimaces, body movements, and postural freezing as the person struggles to "get the word out." These speech difficulties can range from a split second to, in the worst cases, about a minute (Bloodstein, 1981:3).

Like other perceived impairments, stuttering interferes with "the etiquette and mechanisms of communication" (Goffman, 1963:103) and disrupts the "feedback mechanics of spoken interaction" (1963:49). Depending on the social context, the culture, and the health and social status of the speakers (Petrunik, 1977:37), persons who unintentionally and chronically deviate from fluency standards are likely to be defined as stutterers and subjected to various penalizing social reactions, including pity, condescension, embarrassment, amusement, ridicule, and impatience (Johnson, 1959:239; Lemert, 1967:135).

The extent and frequency of stuttering varies. No one stutters all the time. Indeed, there are some situations in which virtually all stutterers are fluent, for example, when singing, speaking in unison with others (including other stutterers), and speaking to themselves, animals, and infants. In addition, stutterers are often more fluent when speaking with a drawl, accent, or different pitch (Petrunik, 1977:34, 71). Some individuals stutter on some words or sounds but not others. ("I can never say 'g's'." "I always stutter on the word 'coffee'.") Setting is also important. Many stutter more during telephone conversations than they do in face-to-face conversation; others find speaking to strangers particularly difficult; still others are more fluent in formal than informal situations, or vice versa. Stutterers have good periods and bad periods. ("Some days I wake up and I'm fine, other days I'm in for hell all day.") There are even some actors and entertainers who stutter but who are fluent when playing a role or facing an audience.

Studying the ways stutterers cope with their stuttering offers valuable insights into how people manage perceived disabilities (Freidson, 1965) and the potential stigma associated with them by highlighting processes that are usually taken for granted, and thus obscured (Davis, 1961). This strategy of using the specific to identify the general has recently been employed by Kitsuse (1980) who has used the "coming out of the closet" metaphor to examine the processes which establish new and legitimate identities. Schneider and Conrad (1980) have developed Kitsuse's analysis by using epilepsy to examine how persons manage discreditable information where there is "no clear identity to move to or from" (1980:32) and where "no 'new' readily available supportive . . . subculture exists" (1980:33).

Both Kitsuse, and Schneider and Conrad, focus on identity rather than interactional order, and on calculated and planned management rather than moment-to-moment strategies. We broaden this analysis by examining: (1) how people coordinate the requirements of creating acceptable identities *and* orderly interaction; (2) how they integrate management strategies thought out in advance with those selected on a moment-to-moment basis; and (3) how the subjective experience of disability together with the reactions of others, shape the management process (Higgins, 1980; Petrunik, 1983). Stuttering has three features which facilitate an examination of these issues. First, stuttering is a potentially stigmatizing disability that disrupts interaction. Second, because stutterers experience speech as a function over which they exercise partial but precarious control, their management of speech is both spontaneous and premeditated. Third, the experience of stuttering is critical for how stutterers, and others, define and manage stuttering.

After briefly describing our research, we examine the central importance of stuttering as a reality experienced by the stutterer. We then examine a variety of strategies which stutterers use to manipulate awareness of their stuttering and present the fragile facade of normal speech. Although we refer throughout to Goffman's (1963) analysis of stigma management as a benchmark in demonstrating how an understanding of stuttering contributes to a more general understanding of stigma, we go beyond Goffman and those who have extended his work, such as Conrad and Schneider, in emphasizing the importance of the experiential domain for sociological analysis.

The Research

This paper is based upon both our personal experience with stuttering and a variety of stuttering therapies, and field studies which we conducted between 1970 and

1983 in clinical and everyday settings. We used qualitative methods, including participant observation, life histories, and focussed interviews.

The major research setting was a speech pathology clinic associated with a psychiatric institute in a large Canadian city. Between 1970 and 1972 we were participant observers (Petrunik for the entire period, Shearing for the first year) taking part in weekly therapy groups which used an approach based on the non-avoidance of stuttering (Van Riper, 1971). A total of 25 individuals took part during this period, with the numbers present at group sessions ranging from three to 10. Most participants underwent therapy for less than a year (Petrunik, 1977, 1980). A year earlier Shearing had participated, with about 10 others, in a similar program, involving weekly sessions arranged through a private clinic for a year.

A second setting was the Webster Precision Fluency Shaping Program, a three-week intensive course based on operant conditioning principles (Webster, 1975), in which Shearing participated with four others in 1980 and Petrunik with two others in 1983.

In addition, both authors participated in a course conducted by the late William Kerr, a roving unlicensed speech therapist from the Isle of Jersey. This course was based largely on changing the rhythm of speech. Shearing participated in a three-week, intensive live-in session as an adolescent in Durban, South Africa, in 1954, with about 20 others. Petrunik took a two-week intensive course with nine others in Canada in 1970. Petrunik kept a research diary and collected news clippings, correspondence, and other documents related to the course. He attended several meetings either to introduce or advertise the course or to protest against it. He also maintained contact with six of the nine other stutterers who had participated in the course for at least a year afterwards (Petrunik, 1974:204, 215; 1977:27).

Petrunik examined the clinical literature of speech pathology, biographies and autobiographies of stutterers, works of fiction, the journal of the National Council of Stuttering, a voluntary association of stutterers in Washington, D.C., records from the speech pathology clinic and—with the consent of subjects—personal correspondence and diaries. A few subjects provided detailed written life histories. Petrunik conducted lengthy, formal interviews with 20 stutterers and numerous informal interviews with stutterers,[2] their families and friends, speech therapists, and medical and para-medical practitioners.

Since stuttering varies with situation, circumstance and mood, we tried to see our subjects in as many different settings and for as long as possible. All quotes, unless otherwise attributed, are from our interviews and field notes.

The Experience of Stuttering

> I suppose that the hope of every stutterer is to awaken some morning and find that his disability has vanished. There is just enough promise of this in his experience to make it seem possible. There are days when, for some reason, the entangled web of words trips him only occasionally. In such periods of relief, he may peer back into his other condition and puzzle over the nature of the oppressive "presence" . . . [hoping that it] is a transitory aberration which might fade and vanish. . . . One feels that only an added will-power, some accretion of psychic rather than physical strength, should be necessary for its conquest. Yet, try as I might, I could not take the final step. I had come up against some invisible power which no strength of will seemed to surmount (Gustavson, 1944:466).

Like normal speakers, stutterers believe speech is something that should be intentionally controlled. Yet, somehow their words are mysteriously blocked or interrupted. Stutterers experience stuttering as the work of an alien inner force (often referred to in the third person as "it") which takes control of their speech mechanism. Stuttering is something which stutterers feel happens *to* them, not something they do: "somebody else is in charge of my mouth and I can't do anything about it" (Van Riper, 1971:158).

In coping with this subjective reality, stutterers use three general strategies: concealment, openness, and disavowal. Concealment strategies involve three principal tactics: avoidance, circumvention, and camouflage. These tactics allow most stutterers to avoid being seen as stutterers part of the time and a few to become secret stutterers. Openness tactics include: treating stuttering as unproblematic, struggle with the "it," and voluntary disclosure. Disavowal—which often calls for the tacit co-operation of others—involves the pretense that stuttering is not occurring when it is obvious that it is. We discuss in turn each of these strategies and their tactics.

Concealment

Avoidance

The simplest way to conceal stuttering is to avoid speaking. Many stutterers select occupations they think will minimize speaking. Others avoid situations in which they fear stuttering will embarrass them.

> I never went to the dances at school because I was afraid of stuttering and looking silly. Because I didn't go, I didn't learn to dance or mix socially. I always felt bad when people would ask me if I was going to a dance or party. I would make up some excuse or say that I didn't want to go. I felt that people thought I was some sort of creep because I didn't go. Each time I wouldn't go because of my fears, I felt even weirder.

Stutterers avoid specific types of encounter. Instead of using the telephone they will write a letter, "drop in on someone," or go to a store to see if it has the item they want. Stutterers avoid particular words, substituting "easy" words for "hard" ones. Word substitution sometimes results in convoluted phrasing in which nothing seems to be addressed directly.

> If I didn't dodge and duck, I wouldn't be able to carry on a conversation. If I didn't circumlocute, I wouldn't be able to get certain words out at all. Unless I'm coming in through the back door and taking a run at it, I'd never get it out.

Where this tactic proves difficult or impossible, stutterers may structure conversations so others say the troublesome words for them. One way of doing this is by feigning forgetfulness:

> You know what I mean, what was it we were talking about this morning, you know, John has one, it's ah, this is annoying, it's right on the tip of my tongue. . . .

Another tactic is to structure the situation so that someone else will be called upon to do the talking. For example, most stutterers fear they will stutter on their name (Petrunik, 1982:306). To avoid introducing themselves when they meet strangers, stutterers sometimes arrange their entry so that someone who knows them will proceed them into the situation. They then rely on the social conventions governing introductions to compel the other person to introduce them. Similarly, stutterers often fear placing orders in restaurants because here, too, word substitution is difficult. To cope with this situation, stutterers may encourage others to order before them; as soon as an item they would like—or at least find acceptable—is mentioned, they can use words they feel more confident with to duplicate the other person's order: "me too" or "same here." With close associates such cooperation may take on the character of finely tuned team work.

> When we were visiting friends of ours and I was having blocks, my wife would sometimes get what seemed to be a slightly anxious look and would quietly supply the word. She did this in a way that seemed so natural to me that I wondered if the others noticed it.

While the willing cooperation of others, especially intimates, has been well documented (Goffman, 1963:55, 97) a study of stuttering draws attention to how others may unknowingly be coopted to conceal a potential stigma.

Circumvention and Camouflage

Stutterers sometimes use tactics based on timing and rhythm to outsmart the "it." Using these tactics requires a knowledge of both the etiquette of conversation and the patterns of one's own stuttering. Some speak quickly, for example, "building up" momentum to get "past" or "over" "difficult words." Others rhythmically pace their speech with the aid of coordinated hand and/or leg movements. Some arrange their sentences so that "easy" words precede "hard" ones, to establish a "flow" which carries them uneventfully over "trouble spots." Others arrange their speech so that "difficult" sounds are said on falling (or rising) pitches. Still others find that changing their tone of voice, or speaking in dialect or with an accent, is helpful.

A similar tactic involves delaying saying a troublesome word until the stutterer feels "it" no longer threatens to control speech and the word is ready to "come out." One way of doing this is to introduce starters and fillers (well, like, er, ah, um) into speech, to postpone troublesome words until the moment when they can be said. One stutterer, for example, was walking along a street when a stranger asked him for directions: "Where is the Borden Building?" A sudden panic gripped the stutterer. He knew exactly where the building was but, to permit him to wait for a moment when "it" could be caught off guard, he responded: "Well, let me see [pause with quizzical expression] oh, ah, near . . . let me see . . . near, I think Spadina and, ah, College." A variant of this tactic involves rearranging words. The late

British humorist and stutterer, Patrick Campbell, gave an example of this in a television interview. While travelling on a London bus, he feared he would not be able to say, "May I have a ticket to Marble Arch?" without stuttering. So, when the conductor approached, he said instead, "May I have a ticket to that arch which is of marble made?"—which he executed fluently.

Where stutterers fail to outwit the "it" they may attempt to camouflage their problem by, for example, visually isolating others from evidence of their stuttering. A teacher who stutters accomplished this by writing on the blackboard just as he was about to stutter, thereby disguising a "block" as a pause to write.

Secret Stutterers

Most stutterers avoid detection only part of the time. However, some stutterers manage to maintain the identity of a "normal speaker" virtually all the time. They define themselves as stutterers not because they stutter in secret, like Becker's (1963:11) "secret deviants," but because they confront and respond to an inner propensity to stutter. Some stutterers report going for years without overtly stuttering. This fact—that a deviant identity can exist in the absence of visible deviant behavior—adds weight to Jack Katz's (1972) critique of those conceptions of labeling which focus exclusively on deviance as behavior and ignore deviance as an inner essence imputed to individuals. Goffman's (1963:56) refusal to recognize that stigmatized people may define themselves in terms of an inner essence and "that what distinguishes an individual from others is the core of his being" has limited his ability to comprehend how both stigmatized and "normal" people perceive their differences and the consequences of this for defining their "real" or "natural" groupings (1963:112). Some speech pathologists, on the other hand, have long recognized that stigmatized people define themselves on the basis of their subjective experience. They refer to secret stutterers as interiorized, indicating that stuttering can be an internal experience as well as an external appearance (Douglass and Quarrington, 1952:378).

Interiorized stutterers place great importance on preserving a social identity and will go to extraordinary lengths to preserve it. For example, a self-employed businessman in his early forties concealed his stuttering from his first wife. He confided in his second wife, but continued to conceal his stuttering from his children. At work, he had his secretary handle potentially troublesome situations. He would, for example, have her make certain phone calls for him. He claimed he would lose business if his stuttering became known. At one time he fired a secretary who had been working with him for a number of years because he thought her facial expressions showed that she had noticed him stuttering. He took great care not to drink too much or become fatigued so that he would not lose control over his speech. He preferred to entertain at home rather than to go out because he felt he could better regulate his drinking at home.

Successful interiorized stutterers develop a particular sensitivity to the intricacies of syntax. They "become 'situation conscious' [and display] special aliveness to the contingencies of acceptance and disclosure, contingencies to which normals will be less alive" (Goffman, 1963:111).

Avoiding stuttering has many costs. Some tactics exclude the stutterer from fully participating in social life as a "normal person," infringing on the very status the stutterer wishes to preserve. The interactional costs may be relatively trivial (not eating what one really wants in a restaurant, or saying something quite different from what one intended), or far more consequential (depriving onself of a social life or not pursuing a desired occupation).

> Because I wasn't normal I thought I couldn't do normal things like get married. I avoided going to parties, because I didn't want to feel bad, and then I felt bad because I didn't go and wasn't meeting people and having a good social life.

Similarly, the consequences for social identity may be relatively benign (being defined as "quiet" or "shy") or even somewhat flattering (being a "good listener" or a "strong silent type"). On the other hand, avoiding interaction may result in derogatory characterizations ("nervous," "odd," "rude," "affected," "silly," "strange," or "retarded").[3] A border crossing incident illustrates how avoidance can be interpreted as evidence of impropriety:

> The border guard asked me where I was born. Because I was afraid I would stutter on "Nova Scotia," I hesitated and started to "ah" and "um" to him. "Let me see now . . . it's the . . . uh, Maritimes . . . uh . . ." and so on. The outcome of all this evasion was that they made a thorough search of my car and even threatened to slit my seat covers.

The importance which stutterers give to the costs of concealment determines the tactics they use. Some people will do almost anything to avoid stuttering; others prefer to stutter in some situations rather than face the consequences of concealment.

> On the first day [of the Kerr course] we were gathering at the motel and going through the ritual of introductions. One man put his hand out to me and said, "May name is . . . uh . . . actually . . . my name is Jim." Afterwards one of the other men in the group who had a highly noticeable stutter shook his head and said, in an aside to me, "What a fool! I'd rather stammer my head off than avoid like that. It looks ridiculous. People must think he's crazy!"

Openness

Unproblematic Stuttering

Unlike interiorized stutterers, those with visible and audible speech disruptions find that some audiences become so familiar with their stuttering that they no longer have anything to conceal. ("All my friends know I stutter. I can't hide my stuttering long enough.") These stutterers simply go ahead and speak without thinking about the consequences. As a result, particularly when speaking with persons who know their problem, they can be barely conscious of their stuttering.

> With Evelyn, if you asked me, I never stutter. If there was a tape recorder going it might show that I was stuttering. But I don't notice it and it doesn't bother me. I don't have any trouble talking to her on the phone unless others are there.

At the same time those who know stutterers well seem less conscious of their stuttering. Spouses and friends remarked:

> You know, since I've got to know you well, I hardly ever notice your stuttering.
> You know, sometimes I forget he stutters.
> I notice his stuttering only when others are present.
> I'm more conscious of it. At other times, I don't care.

Goffman (1963:81) argues that friends are less aware of a stigmatized person's problem because they are more familiar with the stigma. In the case of stuttering, however, what is critical is its obtrusiveness—"how much it interferes with the flow of interaction" (Goffman, 1963:49)—rather

than mere visibility. When stutterers are with friends they feel less constrained to meet the exacting requirements which talk requires in other circumstances, because both parties develop idiosyncratic rules which enable them to become less dependent on such things as precise timing. For example, in telephone conversations between stutterers and their friends silences can cease to be interpreted as cues indicating the end of a speaking turn or a break in the telephone connection.

Once such understandings are developed stutterers feel less pressure to account for their problems or to work at concealing and controlling the "it"; thus, the sense of stuttering as a subjective presence wanes. For stutterers who learn to speak fluently by meticulously learning a new set of speech behaviors (Webster, 1975), the experience of stuttering as an "it" may fade away because with their speech under control there is no longer any need to account for stuttering.[4]

Struggling with the "It"

Stutterers who find it difficult to conceal their stuttering face the additional problem of how to converse with people who take interruptions in the speech of stutterers as a signal to resume talking themselves. Stutterers attempt to avoid this by making two claims: first, that they are competent persons who understand the conventions of talk; and second, that they have not relinquished their speaking turn—even though they are lapsing into unusually long silences—and should be permitted to continue speaking uninterrupted. These claims are important to the stutterer because together they provide the basis for participation in conversation and for maintaining an acceptable identity. One way stutterers make these claims is by confronting a block "head on" and trying to force out the word or sound: a typical pattern is a deep breath followed by muscle tension and visible strain as the stutterer attempts to "break through" the interruption and regain control of speech. The late Japanese novelist Yukio Mishima (1959:5) vividly described this phenomenon: "When a stutterer is struggling desperately to utter his first sound he is like a little bird that is trying to extricate itself from thick lime."

By making visible the "I/it" conflict through struggle, stutterers demonstrate to those they are conversing with that they have not given up their speaking turn and are doing their utmost to limit the interruption in their speech. This process of externalizing stuttering enables stutterers to share with others their experience of stuttering as a mysterious intrusive force. By demonstrating that their deviation from the conventions of speech is not intentional (Blum and McHugh, 1971; Goffman, 1963:128, 143; Mills, 1940) they hope to persuade others to bear with them and not to regard them as outsiders who reject, or do not understand, the norms others adhere to. The struggle that stutterers engage in is the "stigma symbol" (Goffman, 1963:46) that others recognize as stuttering. Struggle feeds into the troubles stutterers are trying to remedy in a classic vicious circle: stuttering is in part a product of attachment to the very social conventions that stutterers struggle to avoid breaking.

This analysis is supported by evidence that some members of the British upper classes view stuttering (or stammering as it is referred to in Britain) as a mark of distinction (Kazin, 1978:124; Shenker, 1970:112). They openly cultivate stuttering as a display of their superior social status and expect others to wait at their convenience. These persons make no apology for their stuttering and accordingly do not struggle with it to demonstrate its involuntary character. Consequently, their stuttering typically takes the form of a "slight stammer" characterized by relaxed repetitions and hesitations without any of the facial distortions associated with struggle.

Voluntary Disclosure

Like concealment, struggle also involves costs. Stuttering presents the listener with the problem of knowing how to sustain an interaction punctuated with silences, prolongations, and facial contortions. As one observer noted:

> What am I supposed to do when a stutterer is struggling to say something? Should I help him by saying the word—because I usually know what he is trying to say—or am I supposed to wait? Then if you wait, what do you do? Am I supposed to watch him struggling? It can be awful. And then there is just no knowing what to do with the time. It can be a long wait. It's embarrassing.

One way stutterers deal with this, and with the fear of exposure in the case of concealment, is by voluntarily disclosing their stuttering (Van Riper, 1971:211) in much the same manner as epileptics (Schneider and Conrad, 1980).

The person who has an unapparent, negatively valued attribute often finds it expedient to begin an encounter with an unobtrusive admission of his own failing, especially with persons who are uninformed about him (Goffman, 1967:29).

Stutterers who make public speeches may begin by referring to their problem so their audiences won't be unduly shocked. One university professor started off each term by talking about his stuttering and inviting students to ask questions about it. Another began his courses by deliberately stuttering, so that he would not create expectations of fluency that he might later fail to meet.

Stutterers sometimes indicate the involuntary nature of their disability by apologizing or by noting that their present stuttering is worse than usual. Through such tactics they, in effect, argue that the stigmatized and normal categories represent poles of a continuum, and that they are much further toward the normal end of this continuum than their present behavior would suggest. In doing so, stutterers typically take advantage of the fact that while struggling with some sound or word they can often make fluent asides which display their relative normality.

> We went to the shh— shh— (s's always give me trouble) shh— show last night.
> I was talking to K— K— en (Wow! I had a hard time on that one) and he was saying. . . .

Other stutterers put listeners at ease with retrospective accounts such as, "Boy, I'm having a hard time today. I must be really tired."

Sometimes humor is used to anticipate and defuse confusion or embarrassment. One stutterer told people at informal gatherings to "go ahead and talk amongst yourselves if I take too long about saying anything." A teacher attempted to put his students at ease by inviting them to "take advantage of my stuttering to catch up on your note-taking."

Other stutterers use humor to claim more desirable identities for themselves.

> I use humor a lot now. If I'm having a problem, I'll make a comment like, "Boy, it's a problem having a big mouth like mine and not being able to use it." When I'm having a hard time getting out a word in a store I'll say something like, "Three tries for a quarter." Once a waitress started guessing when I blocked giving my order and kept on guessing and guessing wrong.

Every so often, I would smile and say, "You just keep guessing." Everyone was laughing but they were laughing at her, not me.

Stutterers may also take a more aggressive stance. By pitting themselves against the listener, they indicate that they refuse to allow others to use their stuttering to belittle them. One of our respondents referred to this as the "fuck you, Mac" approach.

I challenge the listener. I can make a game out of it. I look them straight in the eye and in my mind tell them to "fuck off." I might stutter like hell, but so what. It doesn't make them any better than me.

In using this strategy stutterers attempt to disavow the implications that they suspect others will draw about their lack of control over speech by displaying "cool." This strategy draws its impetus from the fear that many stutterers have that they will be seen as nervous and easily ruffled persons when they perceive themselves as normal persons in every respect other than their inability to control speech.

Another non-apologetic, but less aggressive, strategy that is occasionally used is one in which the stutterer systematically attempts to redefine stuttering as a "new and proud identity" (Schneider and Conrad, 1980:32) and to use this new identity as a means of getting stuttering "out of the closet" (M. Katz, 1968; Lambidakis, 1972). Some of our respondents reported that talking about their problem to new acquaintances proved to be a good way of gaining rapport. Revealing one's weakness to another can be a way of appearing honest, frank, and "more human." Others claimed that their efforts to overcome their "handicap" had strengthened their character. A few (e.g., Van Riper, Sheehan, and Douglass) have even used their personal experience of stuttering professionally, in therapy and research, to gain knowledge and rapport with patients and/or subjects. Even in occupations such as sales or journalism, where stuttering might ordinarily be seen to be a great handicap, some stutterers have used stuttering to their advantage. A Canadian journalist was said to have "disarmed" those he interviewed with his stuttering so that they were sympathetic toward him and unusually frank. A salesman had his business cards printed: "B-B-Bob G-G-Goldman the stuttering Toyota salesman."

Public figures sometimes use their stuttering as a trademark and a means to success. Some examples are the comedian "Stuttering Joe" Frisco, the humorist Patrick

Campbell, and the country and western singer Mel Tillis. In his autobiography, Campbell (1967:212) reports how his stuttering on British television made him famous:

While making the ginger ale commercials I looked upon my stammer as a nuisance that would have to be played down as much as possible if we weren't to have endless takes. . . . Although I didn't care to think about this aspect of it too much I did realize that my stammer fitted rather neatly into their campaign, the essence of which was never to mention the word 'Schweppes', but merely to mention the first syllable 'sch—', and that was quite enough for me in every way.

It wasn't until nearly a year later [when asked to advertise butter] that I realized my mistake. [Again Campbell tried to control his stuttering. The producer called him aside and said] "I don't know quite how to put this—but could we have a little more of your trademark on the word 'butter'?" . . . I'd been trying to suppress the very thing it seemed that everyone wanted.

Reflecting on his "asset," Campbell claimed that while he tried to put the best possible light on it, he never really became proud of his identity as a stutterer. The frequent and fleeting gains did not offset the losses that recurred day after day.

If I was offered by some miraculous overnight cure the opportunity never to stammer again, I'd accept it without hesitation, even though it meant the end for me of television (1967:213).

Disavowal

While stutterers sometimes try to put listeners at their ease by drawing attention to themselves, there are often circumstances in which they prefer to define their stuttering out of existence. To do this successfully, they need the tacit cooperation of their listeners. Both parties must share the assumption that the embarrassment and awkwardness associated with stuttering and attempts to control it are best dealt with by acting as if the stuttering were not happening. This provides a "phantom normalcy" (Goffman, 1963:122). By overlooking stuttering, both parties act as if "nothing unusual is happening" (Emerson, 1970) rather than acknowledge something which would require a response for which no shared guidelines exist. This tactic leaves intact the stutterer's status as a normal and competent person and the other's as a decent and tactful person who avoids needlessly embarrassing others.

Tactful overlooking, as Safilios-Rothschild (1970:129) has suggested, is normatively prescribed:

> Regardless of any degree of aversion felt toward the disabled, the non-disabled are normatively not permitted to show these negative feelings in any way and their fear of making a verbal or a non-verbal "slip" indicating their emotions renders the interaction quite formal and rigid.

The importance of tacit disavowal of stuttering is indicated by the anxiety some stutterers feel when they enter a situation where they know it cannot, or will not, be ignored. Conversations with little children are one example.

> Children give me the hardest time. They know something is wrong and they don't hide it. My little nephew embarrassed me terribly in front of the family. He said "your mouth moves funny." I tried to explain to him that I had something wrong with my mouth just like other people had something wrong with their ears or their eyes.

Another example is where stutterers are forced to watch and listen to themselves or others stuttering. Just as many fat people avoid scales and mirrors (Himelfarb and Evans, 1974:222), many stutterers shun mirrors and audio and video tape recorders. Similarly, stutterers are often uncomfortable watching others stutter. We witnessed stutterers in the speech clinic cover their faces with their hands or even walk out of the room rather than witness another person stutter. These attempts to distance themselves from stuttering appeared in some cases to be experienced as a disassociation of the body and the self through a loss or blurring of self-awareness. Stutterers talked of "slipping out of the situation" at the moment of stuttering and not being aware of what they or others were doing when they "returned." During these periods, stutterers experience a "time out" (Goffman, 1967:30; Scott and Lyman, 1968) from the situation. Time appears to stop so that when speech resumes it is as if the block did not occur. This sense of time having stopped, and of stuttering occurring outside the situation, is symbolized by the frozen poses stutterers sometimes adopt at the moment of stuttering: gestures are stopped, only to be resumed once speech continues. For example, one stutterer regularly "blocked" on a word just as he was about to tap the ash off his cigarette with his finger. During the few seconds he was "caught" in his block, his finger remained poised, frozen an inch or so above his cigarette.

When he released the sound, the finger would simultaneously tap the ash into the ashtray.

Stutterers and their listeners manage time-outs cooperatively by severing eye contact. Normally, people who are conversing indicate their attentiveness by facial expressions and eye contact, thereby reaffirming that they are listening and involved in the interaction. By breaking eye contact at the moment of stuttering, stutterers and their listeners jointly disengage from the conversation and exclude stuttering from the interaction. The moment fluent speech returns engagement is reestablished through a renewal of eye contact; the participants confirm their mutual subterfuge by acting as if nothing had happened. During time outs listeners may also confirm their disengagement by doing something unrealted, such as assuming an air of nonchalance, shuffling papers, glancing through a magazine or a book, fiddling with an object, or surveying the immediate surroundings. These signals indicate that the participants are not "in" the conversation.

While struggling to "get a word out" stutterers may avert their faces or hide their mouths with their hands. This phenomenon reveals an apparent difference in the social significance of sight and hearing. During this obscuring of the sight of stuttering, as with the time out, both parties are presumably aware that stuttering is taking place, and indeed that the stutterer is doing her or his best to "get past the block" and resume the conversation. Yet, at the same time, stuttering is denied. It is as if through the "thin disguises" (Goffman, 1963:81) which contradictory appearances provide it is possible to establish opposing social claims and thus "have one's cake and eat it too."

Time out, besides resolving the interactional problem of how to respond to stuttering, protects or hides one's vulnerability; it's much like the common response of averting your eyes when you accidentally see someone naked. Stutterers are, in a sense, "naked" at the moment of stuttering; they are without a mask, their front is crumbling and their "raw self" exposed (Goffman, 1963:16). Averting their eyes is a cue to the other to look away from the stutterer's "nakedness," thus saving both from embarrassment. The stutterers we interviewed expressed this sense of "nakedness" or vulnerability with descriptions such as "weak," "helpless," "like a little kid," and "with my shell removed." Some even said that at the point of stuttering they felt transparent. This can be related to the saying that the eyes are the mirror of the soul, which stems from the belief that the eyes reflect one's true feelings even though the rest of one's face may camouflage them.

Loss of eye contact gives stutterers time to recover their composure, manage the "unsatisfactory" image that has emerged, and, if possible, project a new image. Listeners have their own self to consider. Because they too may be held partly responsible for the stutterer's embarrassment, they can use loss of eye contact to indicate that they did not intend the embarrassment to happen and, above all, that they are not amused or uncomfortable.

While the tactic of mutual disavowal is usually a situational one the comment of one stutterer we interviewed indicates that in some cases it can be much more pervasive:

> Ever since I was a young child I can't remember my parents ever directly mentioning stuttering. It seemed obvious that they saw me stuttering, and they knew I stuttered, but they never said anything. The only incident I can remember is my father singing "K-K-Katy" a couple of times. I felt badly about that. Nothing direct was ever said, even by my brothers. My younger brother always gave me a lot of trouble. But he never mentioned stuttering once. I wondered if my parents told them not to say anything. My parents did make lots of references to me as nervous, sensitive, or different, and were always saying they were going to take me to the doctor for my nerves. But except for brief references on very few occasions, they never mentioned anything about stuttering.

In such cases, the disavowal of stigma is extended across entire situations. This requires others to tacitly agree to ignore the stigma in all encounters with the stigmatized person.

Discussion

Our study of stuttering provides a vehicle to elaborate upon and extend the work of Davis, Goffman, Schneider and Conrad, and others on the strategic manipulation of awareness to manage potential stigma. The implications of our analysis also extend beyond stigma management to a consideration of the importance of the experiential dimension for the construction of social order. Because the stutterer finds problematic what others take for granted, the stutterer's social world is the world of everyman writ large.

In our consideration of stuttering we have developed three major lines of argument. First, our analysis shows the importance of considering subjective experience as well as behavior when studying the management of identity and the construction of interactional order. Stutterers engage in the ongoing creation of a subjective reality which at once shapes, and is shaped by, the management strategies they employ to regulate awareness of their disability and claim or disown identities. This consideration of the subjective experience of stuttering supports Jack Katz's (1972) argument that deviance theory should recognize that people sometimes perceive deviance as an inner essence independent of behavior. In addition, our analysis extends rather than simply elaborates upon Goffman's work, for though he writes of "ego" or "felt" identity, which he defines as "the subjective sense of [the stigmatized person's] own situation" (1963:105), he does not develop this concept.

Second, we have shown that the management of potential stigma can involve strategies conceived of, and executed, on a moment-to-moment basis, in addition to the premeditated strategies that have attracted most sociologists' attention. Advance planning was usually necessary where stutterers tried to conceal their problem through role avoidance. In speaking situations, management became more spontaneous: stutterers selected strategies in the light of opportunities and difficulties which arose in the course of interaction. In both cases, concealment strategies were marked by a high level of self-consciousness. When stutterers used openness or disavowal, however, only voluntary disclosure was consciously employed. Both struggling to overcome the "it" and time outs were non-calculated, though, especially in the latter case, stutterers were quick to recognize these tactics as coping and "restorative measures" (Goffman, 1963:128) once they were brought to their attention.

Finally, we have called attention to the fact that stutterers, like other stigmatized persons, seek to manage two interrelated, yet analytically distinguishable, problems. They are concerned both with preserving an acceptable identity and with preserving orderly interaction so that they can get on with the business of living. In exploring this issue we have shown how stutterers sometimes find themselves in situations in which it is not possible to simultaneously achieve both these objectives and thus are required to choose between them. The repertoire of tactics stutterers develop, and by implication the limits they place on their involvement in social life, depend on the importance they attach to these objectives.

NOTES

1. A good summary is provided in Bloodstein (1981:103). Some observers have reported an absence of stuttering among certain North American Midwest Indian tribes such as the Utes, the Shoshone, and the Bannock (Johnson, 1944, 1944b; Snidecor, 1947). Other studies (Clifford, 1965; Lemert, 1967: 135; Sapir, 1915; Stewart, 1959; Van Riper, 1946) have noted that this is by no means true for all North American Indian tribes. Both Lemert and Stewart found that tribes (particularly those on the Pacific Northwest coast of Canada) which encouraged competition and stricter child-rearing practices, and which placed more emphasis on self-control, reported more instances of stuttering. Lemert (1967:146) also offered a similar explanation for a higher incidence of stuttering among Japanese than Polynesians.

2. While we make no claims of representativeness, we interviewed or observed stutterers of both sexes, ranging in age from adolescence to middle age and in occupations from blue-collar workers to professionals. We studied persons from a variety of racial, ethnic, and cultural backgrounds in addition to English-speaking Canadians, including a French Canadian, a Brazilian Jew, several Italians, an East Indian, a Trinidadian of East Indian descent, a white South African, a South African of mixed descent and a Jamaican of mixed descent, a Dutchman, and a Chinese man.

3. See Goffman (1963:94) for a parallel between stutterers and the hard of hearing.

4. While fluency can be achieved and the sense of stuttering as an "it" can disappear, the continued maintenance of fluency is quite another matter. Time and again those who have achieved fluency—through whatever means—find themselves relapsing, even years later (Perkins, 1979; Sheehan, 1979, 1983).

REFERENCES

Becker, Howard S. 1963. *Outsiders,* New York: The Free Press.

Bloodstein, Oliver. 1981. *A Handbook on Stuttering,* Chicago: National Easter Seal Society.

Blum, Alan, and Peter McHugh. 1971. "The social ascription of motives," *American Sociological Review 36 (February),* 98–109.

Campbell, Patrick. 1967. *My Life and Easy Times,* London: Anthony Blond.

Clifford, S. 1965. "Stuttering in South Dakota Indians," *Central States Speech Association Journal 26 (February),* 59–60.

Davis, Fred. 1961. "Deviance disavowal: The management of strained interaction by the visibly handicapped," *Social Problems 9 (Fall),* 120–132.

Emerson, Joan. 1970. "Nothing unusual is happening," in Thomas Shibutani, (ed.), *Human Nature and Collective Behavior,* Englewood Cliffs: N.J.: Prentice Hall, 208–223.

Freidson, Elliot. 1965. "Disability as social deviance," in Marvin Sussman, (ed.), *Sociology and Rehabilitation,* Washington, D.C.: American Sociological Association, 71–99.

Goffman, Erving. 1963. *Stigma.* Englewood Cliffs, N.J.: Prentice-Hall.

———. 1967. *Interaction Ritual.* Garden City, N.Y.: Doubleday-Anchor.

Gustavson, Carl. 1944. "A talisman and a convalescence," *Quarterly Journal of Speech 30 (1),* 465–471.

Higgins, Paul C. 1980. "Social reaction and the physically disabled: Bringing the impairment back in," *Symbolic Interaction 3 (Spring):* 139–156.

Himelfarb, Alex, and John Evans. 1974. "Deviance disavowal and stigma management: A study of obesity," in Jack Haas and Bill Shaffir (eds.), *Decency and Deviance,* Toronto: McClelland and Stewart.

Johnston, Wendell. 1944a. "The Indian has no word for it: Part 1, Stuttering in children," *Quarterly Journal of Speech 30 (October),* 330–337.

———. 1944b. "The Indian has no word for it: Part 2, Stuttering in adults," *Quarterly Journal of Speech 30 (December),* 456–465.

———. 1959. *The Onset of Stuttering,* Minneapolis: University of Minneapolis Press.

Katz, Jack. 1972. "Deviance, charisma, and rule-defined behavior," *Social Problems 20(2),* 186–202.

Katz, Murray. 1968. "Stuttering power," *Journal of the Council of Adult Stutterers (January):* 5.

Kazin, Alfred. 1978. *New York Jew,* New York: Random House.

Kitsuse, John I. 1980. "Coming out all over: Deviants and the politics of social problems," *Social Problems 28 (October),* 1–13.

Lambidakis, Elenore. 1972. "Stutterers' lib," *Journal of the Council of Adult Stutterers (Winter):* 4–6.

Lemert, Edwin. 1967. *Human Deviance, Social Problems and Social Control.* Englewood Cliffs, N.J.: Prentice-Hall.

Mills, C. Wright. 1940. "Situated action and vocabularies of motives," *American Sociological Review 5 (December):* 904–913.

Mishima, Yukio. 1959. *The Temple of the Golden Pavilion,* New York: A.A. Knopf.

Perkins, William. 1979. "From psychoanalysis to discoordination," in Hugo Gregory (eds.), *Decency and Deviance,* Toronto: McClelland and Stewart, 97–129.

Petrunik, Michael. 1974. "The quest for fluency: Fluency variations and the identity problems and management strategies of stutterers," in Jack Haas and Bill Shaffir (eds.), *Decency and Deviance,* Toronto: McClelland and Stewart, 201–220.

———. 1977. "The quest for fluency: A study of the identity problems and management strategies for adult stutterers and some suggestions for an approach to deviance management," unpublished Ph.D. dissertation, University of Toronto.

————. 1980. "Stutterers' adaptations to non-avoidance therapy: Primary/secondary deviance theory as a professional treatment ideology," paper presented at the annual meetings of the Society for the Study of Social Problems, New York, August.

————. 1982. "Telephone troubles: Interactional breakdown and its management by stutterers and their listeners," *Symbolic Interaction 5 (Fall)*, 299–310.

————. 1983. "Being deviant: A critique of the neglect of the experiential dimension in sociological constructions of deviance," paper presented at the annual meetings of the Society for the Study of Social Problems, Detroit.

Safilios-Rothschild, Constantina. 1970. *The Sociology and Social Psychology of Disability and Rehabilitation,* New York: Random House.

Sapir, Edward. 1915. "Abnormal types of speech in Nootka," Canadian Geological Survey, Memoir 62, Anthropological Series No. 5, Ottawa: Government Printing Bureau.

Schneider, Joseph W., and Peter Conrad. 1980. "In the closet with illness: Epilepsy, stigma potential, and information control," *Social Problems 28 (October)*, 32–44.

Scott, Marvin B., and Stanford Lyman. 1968. "Accounts," *American Sociological Review 33 (February)*, 44–62.

Sheehan, Joseph. 1979. "Current issues on stuttering recovery," in Hugo Gregory (ed.), *Controversies about Stuttering Therapy,* Baltimore: University Park Press.

————. 1983. "Invitation to relapse," *The Journal, National Council on Stuttering (Summer)*, 16–20.

Shenker, Israel. 1970. "Stammer becomes fashionable," *Globe and Mail* (Toronto), November 12, 12.

Snidecor, John. 1947. "Why the Indian does not stutter," *Quarterly Journal of Speech 33 (December)*, 493–495.

Stewart, Joseph. 1959. "The problem of stuttering in certain North American Societies," *Journal of Speech and Hearing Disorders* (Monograph Supplement 6), 1–87.

Van Riper, Charles. 1946. "Speech defects among the Kalabash," *Marquette County Historical Society 8 (December)*, 308–322.

————. 1971. *The Nature of Stuttering,* Englewood Cliffs, N.J.: Prentice-Hall.

Webster, Ronald. 1975. *The Precision Fluency Shaping Program: Speech Reconstruction for Stutterers,* Roanoke, Virginia: Communication Development Corporation.

Think Critically

1. Explain how the authors' analysis of stuttering offers insights into how people manage disabilities.

2. Describe how the coping strategies of openness and disavowal are used in social situations. What situational elements do you regard as crucial for their success? Give some examples.

Legitimating the First Tattoo: Moral Passage through Informal Interaction

Katherine Irwin

ONCE CONSIDERED AN ARTIFACT OF criminals, gangs, sailors, and social outcasts, tattoos careened into the American mainstream in the 1990s. If the increased numbers of college students, young urbanites, and business professionals wearing tattoos have not adequately articulated the idea that tattoos have reached mainstream status, the media have driven the message home. Print journalists have claimed that tattoos are "edging into the mainstream" (*Milwaukee Journal Sentinel,* November 29, 1998, p. 1), that they are so "thoroughly middle class" that the only rebellious thing about them "may be the decision not to get one" (*Providence Journal-Bulletin,* July 15, 1999, p. 6B), and that "7 million adults now have tattoos" (Telvin 1999:1A). Celebrities such as

Cher and Johnny Depp who openly sport tattoos have reinforced the message that tattoos are moving "from being a symbol of the outcast to that of the rock star, model, and postmodern youth" (DeMello 1995:49).

Periodically throughout American history, tattoos have undergone dramatic redefinition. In the late 1800s elite social crowds adopted small, easily concealed tattoos and made them a fad among European aristocracy and the American upper class (Parry 1933; Sanders 1989; Vale and Juno 1989). After the turn of the century, especially after World War I (Steward 1990), tattoos became associated primarily with deviant characters. Rubin (1988) has argued that since the 1960s the practice, structure, and patronage of tattooing experienced a "renaissance" that included an influx of fine artists to the profession of tattooing. By the 1980s and 1990s the renaissance in the tattoo profession was met with a dramatic moral passage (Gusfield 1967) as tattoos entered popular culture.[1]

In this article I look at the phenomenon of becoming tattooed from the perspective of individuals contemplating their first tattoos in the late 1990s. Although media images in the 1990s often defined tattoos as hip and trendy, many individuals suggested that older definitions associating tattoos with dangerous outcasts continued to shroud this form of body modification. To reconcile their desires for tattoos with their fears of being associated with low-status groups, the middle-class tattooees often employed a set of legitimation techniques to help maintain their social status. I argue that these techniques went beyond stigma management maneuvers designed to repair identities during face-to-face interactions. Instead, they framed tattoos within core mainstream norms and values. In the end, individuals' identities and their tattoos were rescued from ill repute . . .

Setting and Methods

I collected data for this article during a four-year participant observation at the Blue Mosque, a tattoo shop located in a middle-class university town in the western United States.[2] Falling within the opportunistic research tradition (Riemer 1977), this study had a serendipitous beginning. I first walked into the Blue Mosque in spring 1996, when I accompanied a friend who was getting her first tattoo. Before entering the clean, comfortable, and friendly shop, I had never thought about getting permanent body art

myself. In fact, I had specifically promised my family that I would never get a tattoo. After watching my friend go through the experience, I changed my mind and began wondering what forms of body modification I could sport. The shop's congenial atmosphere made it easy to return several times while choosing my own piercings and eventually my own tattoos. During my visits, I formed friendships with all the artists and started dating and eventually married the shop's owner, Lefty Blue. Our home became a stopping ground for tattooists traveling through town and a social center for the shop . . .

My tattoo recreational life became a research interest after Lefty and I took a vacation to California. We rented a car and roamed the California coastline, visiting a score of tattoo shops and discussing the meaning of tattoos in society. At the end of one of these conversations, Lefty mentioned that someone should do a study chronicling the changes in attitudes toward tattoos. As a graduate student in sociology looking for a dissertation topic, I quickly stepped up to the research task and Lefty willingly assumed the responsibility of key informant.

Because the other tattooists had already met me in the context of my relationship with Lefty, my research role became "the girlfriend" and eventually "the wife."[3] More accurately, because many of the tattooists had girlfriends during my research, I became just one among a group of these women and a peripheral member of the setting (Adler and Adler 1987). Romantic partners were part of a larger social group called "shop regulars" that included cherished tattoo clients and friends who hung out at the shop and frequently attended informal social functions such as barbecues, dinners, picnics, brunches, bowling parties, and snowboarding excursions. From the beginning of our relationship, Lefty and I hosted many of these events.

As a tattooist's wife and a shop regular, I gained a unique view of this social world. Over the four-year participant observation study, I visited the shop hundreds of times and was present during thousands of conversations among tattoo artists both at home and at social occasions. Similar to Sanders's (1989) role as a shop regular, I also had many chances to talk with tattoo clients. Occasionally, I was asked to take over for the shop manager while he ran errands. I chatted with clients as they thumbed through books and asked numerous questions about the nuances of getting tattooed. At first I documented all my interactions by taking copious field notes after I returned home from a shop visit or after a conversation with an artist. Soon I began to see that first-time tattooees were a unique group in this world. I noticed that they were much more concerned about the societal reactions than were more experienced clients. I began to focus my interactions at the shop and my field notes on this novice tattoo group. During informal interactions, I inquired about novice clients' motivations, fears, and reasons for choosing particular designs.

Men and women received their first tattoos at the Blue Mosque in equal numbers. Ages of novice clients ranged from eighteen to sixty, although most were in their twenties or thirties. In addition, first-time clients at the Blue Mosque were usually residents of the predominantly white, middle-class town in which the shop was located. Many were students at the nearby university, which was known for attracting a middle- to upper-middle-class student body. Therefore, my observations reflect the middle-class experience of getting a first tattoo. I resembled the clients in age, class, race, and ethnicity, which made developing rapport an easy task. In addition, as a woman with only one visible tattoo, I was seen by first-time female clients as more approachable than the heavily tattooed men at the shop. This initial rapport made it easy for me to recruit clients for in-depth interviews. From early interviews and conversations with clients, I began to gather that they feared the negative images associated with tattoos. Thinking that my alliance with the tattoo artists and other heavily tattooed shop regulars might dissuade interviewees from speaking openly about their fears, I began to recruit interviewees by asking my friends on and off campus to refer individuals to me who were thinking about getting or who had gotten a single tattoo. I conducted these interviews outside of my home and the shop.

Combining in-shop and out-of-shop recruitment methods, I completed forty-three interviews with a collection of people involved in various aspects of the tattoo scene, including people who had only one or two tattoos, clients who were heavily tattooed, people who decided not to get tattooed, and professional tattooists. During casual conversations and interviews, I asked about their initial impression of tattoos, what first made them want to become tattooed, what their tattoos meant to them, what made their tattoos special, and what their concerns were regarding getting and having a tattoo.[4] Since most clients primarily feared that getting a tattoo might hurt their relationship with their parents, I interviewed ten parents of tattooees and potential tattooees using the same out-of-shop recruitment methods I used for first-time tattooees. I asked questions regarding parents' impression of tattoos, how they felt about their children getting tattoos, and what would help them feel better about their children's tattoos. As the wife of a tattooist and a member of the shop, I was especially interested in individuals' impressions of tattooists, how clients negotiated their ideal tattoos with tattooists, and what environment individuals felt would be best for acquiring a tattoo. . . .

Negotiating the Tattoo Status

In the 1990s tattoos quickly became a visible feature of middle-class life as they were seen in advertisements, on charismatic athletes, and even on such well-known American icons as Barbie (Kuntzman 1999). Despite the increasing popularity of this form of body art, many mainstream moralists continued to see tattoos as markers of "alienation from mainstream norms and social networks" (Sanders 1989:41). The result was the creation of a sort of cultural war (Moynihan 1993) over the definitions and meanings of tattoos in society.

Reflecting the competing definitions associated with tattoos in the 1990s, middleclass individuals were plagued by confusion, conflict, and multiple challenges as they obtained their first tattoo. Like the establishment of rules in a police department (Manning 1977), treatment of psychiatric patients (Strauss et al. 1963), or development of institutional identities (Kleinman 1982, 1996), obtaining a tattoo became a negotiated process. Although some negotiated orders are marked by cooperation and mutual dependence, the moral climate surrounding tattoos in the 1990s injected conflict into the tattoo journey. Individuals often felt attracted to becoming tattooed after interacting in the deviant, hip, or trendy worlds they shared with their friends. Conversely, after interacting in the conventional worlds they shared with their families, individuals often experienced several tattoo aversions. Potential tattooees developed a set of legitimation techniques to maximize what they saw as the positive benefits of becoming tattooed (independence and autonomy from authority) and minimize the negative meanings associated with tattoos (low class, criminal, dangerous).

Deviant Attractions

Becoming tattooed proved an extremely provocative prospect for many people, especially youth, in the 1990s. The idea that individuals are drawn to deviant lifestyles has remained a well-established assumption among deviance and criminology researchers. The deviant life offers several attractive perquisites, including the chance to bond with peers (Akers et al. 1979; Elliott and Menard 1996; Erickson and Empey 1965; Hirschi 1969; Warr 1993), rebel from or defy conventionality (Hebdige 1979; Jankowski 1991; Merton 1968), and, for men, construct a masculine identity (Messerschmidt 1993). In the example of tattooees, many suggested that an intoxicating deviant mystique surrounded this form of body modification. Some felt that tattoos connoted freedom from conventionality and used their tattoos to escape conventional constraints. Others saw tattoos as a way to become more enmeshed in fringe social groups (Sanders 1989; Vail 1999). In this way tattoo attractions played on individuals' desire for particular identity and interactional opportunities.

Freedom from Constraints

Building on older, deviant meanings associated with tattoos, many respondents suggested that becoming tattooed symbolized liberation, independence, and freedom. This was especially true for individuals who felt inhibited by the conventional social opportunities available to them. Several tattooees first contemplated becoming tattooed while in high school or college. Some suggested that their peers in conventional high school and college crowds were cruel, petty, and shallow and began to see getting tattoos as a way to step outside of the dominant peer politics surrounding them (Adler and Adler 1998) . . .

Women especially saw tattoos as a sign of liberation and freedom and became tattooed to construct a sense of self outside of conventional ideals of femininity and female beauty (DeMello 1995; Mifflin 1997; Sanders 1991). Contrary to traditional images of women as soft, vulnerable, and physically weak, they described becoming tattooed as an act of toughness and strength. Tattooed women were considered those who "did not take shit," and were forceful, resilient, and had control over their lives. Emphasizing the issue of strength and control, Judy, a college professor, commented:

> It is so traditionally unfeminine. It is a strength sign for women to go out and get something like that. It shows that they are not wimpy, but then some of them go out

and get these really wimpy tattoos. I think that that is even a strength sign, even if they want to express that strength in a traditionally feminine design. . . . It means something for a woman to be making a decision to permanently mark her body without having to get permission from her father or her boyfriend or something like that. It's a big empowerment thing.

For some men and women, becoming tattooed marked a passage from one life phase to another. Potential tattooees often saw this passage as representing movement out of an oppressive phase and entrance into a freer and more independent one. This passage included such activities as moving out of their parents' houses, graduating from college, or ending unsavory relationships. Because they saw having tattoos as a violation of female beauty norms, many women used their tattoos to symbolically "take back their bodies" from their husbands' or boyfriends' control . . .

Deviant Associations

While tattoos represented a sign of independence and freedom from constraints for some individuals, others saw them as a way to increase their attachment to alternative social groups (Sanders 1989; Vail 1999). Research participants reported turning their backs on popular social sets when they were in high school. Instead, they enmeshed themselves in fringe social groups such as punk rockers, straight edge groups, dead heads, and skate punks. Members of these crowds often wore tattoos, as well as other forms of appearance deviance, as a way to mark their disassociation from mainstream culture (see Hebdige 1979). While interacting with individuals in these groups, many became eager for tattoos . . .

Some participants became tattooed before interacting in unconventional circles. Feeling dissatisfied with mainstream life, many used their tattoos to gain entrée into fringe social worlds. Lefty described his former girlfriend's reasons for becoming tattooed: "She was a San Francisco funky woman. She wanted to get the jobs at the cool places. She wanted to be able to waitress at the neat restaurants with tattooed people. She went right ahead and got tattooed on her forearm before I got tattooed on my forearm" . . .

Deviant Aversions

One of the major constraints that prevents individuals from engaging in deviance is their relationship with mainstream individuals. Those with a high stake in conventional life

(Waldorf et al. 1991), who have strong bonds to conventional individuals (Hirschi 1969), or who have strong external social support (Garmezy 1985; Werner 1989, 1992) are often thought to be protected from deviance or delinquency. In the example of potential tattooees, aversions to deviance included the fear of damaging relationships with parents and the desire to maintain legitimate statuses. While interacting with family members, conservative friends, and employers, many learned that important people in their lives disliked tattoos and looked down on tattooed people. No matter how much these young men and women wanted to use tattoos to establish independence from authority, most could not separate themselves from wanting to secure approval from parents and appear successful in conventional society. Like tattoo attractions, tattoo aversions played on key aspects of individuals' identities and social networks.

Conservative Reactions

Middle-class tattooees circulated in several social worlds. While at school and with friends, they often learned that tattoos symbolized independence and freedom from conventional society. However, with family, at work, or hanging out with conventional individuals, potential tattooees learned that many continued to see getting tattoos as outrageous and unacceptable behavior. Through their interactions with tattoo critics, potential tattooees studied the many ways a tattoo might change their interactions in conservative social worlds.

Strangers and acquaintances may have judged tattoos implicitly, but parents spoke openly about their dislike for them. Interviews with parents revealed many dimensions of their disapproval of tattoos. They often mentioned that tattoos communicated dirtiness and poor hygiene. They saw tattooists as unconcerned about sterilization and thought of tattoo shops as smoke-filled, unclean places. Parents expressed particular concern that their children might contract diseases or infections when getting tattoos[5] . . .

Parents also saw tattoos as serious status risks. Many parents feared that their children would be looked down on because tattoos signified association with undesirable social groups. Frank; a father of four, discussed some of the reasons he disliked tattoos:

> My initial fears were that I associated tattoos with people who are not my favorite: Hells Angels, sailors, and convicts. . . . I didn't like what the tattoos meant to

them. . . . With Hells Angels and the convict world, I didn't like their willingness to scar themselves It was pitiful and shameful. These tattoos were obtrusive and really damaged their future possibilities. I associated [tattoos] with self-destruction . . . like their obsessive use of drugs and alcohol, petty crime, and just generally stupid behavior which got them into trouble.

Parents had usually spent considerable time attempting to steer their children toward successful, happy lives in conventional society. The idea of their children getting tattoos cast a shadow over their hopes and dreams for their children's future. Nedra, a mother of two, described her worries: "No matter how old your kids get you want to protect them. From the tattoo, you want to protect them from being ostracized, from being laughed at, from being put down. I don't want that to happen to my kids." Children's tattoos also threatened their parents' social status. Parents of children who became tattooed were seen as "too permissive" and as "poor moral guides." Among the most pressing concerns for parents was maintaining the image of being a "proper parent". . .

Status Anxiety

After interacting with friends and parents, potential tattooees began to see that tattoos held many different meanings. Potential tattooees experienced status anxiety when they imagined how the negative meanings associated with tattoos might change their interactions with important individuals in their lives. Younger tattooees especially expressed a common concern that receiving a tattoo would threaten emotional ties with family and their parents' regard for them. Larry, a college freshman, was determined to get a tattoo. He described his experience with his father after experimenting with deviant body modification in high school:

> He hit the roof when I got my ear pierced and when I dyed my hair. I didn't do it to rebel against him or to hurt him. . . . I was crushed. I hated it. My dad and I had a pretty strong relationship so it really bothered me. That really hurt him. Of course I want my dad's approval and my dad's love. I wasn't doing it to hurt him.

Reflecting on his father's reactions to his ear piercing and hair dying, Larry braced himself for emotional turmoil and the loss of his father's esteem after getting a tattoo.

Some feared serious financial losses if they became tattooed. Melody, a college junior, had received four tattoos while in college. She explained her concerns about revealing her tattoos to her parents:

> My parents are completely against tattoos. They believe they are for bikers and sailors and that anyone who has one is scum. They threatened to cut me off from college and kick me out of their house if I ever got one. . . . They are paying for college and my apartment. Unless I want to get cut off, my tattoos will have to remain a secret until I'm twenty-two.

Potential tattooees often internalized their parents' worries that tattoos might threaten their future opportunities. Stew, a senior in college, suggested that his parents' prohibitions did not deter him from getting a tattoo. However, he understood and agreed with the cause of his parents' concerns. He explained: "I believe that they want you to make the right decision and to not have regrets later in life. It may be so important now, to get a tattoo, but you may be stuck and branded for life. I think that it is important that parents try to encourage their children to think it over". . .

Aside from losing status in family and professional spheres, some potential tattooees acknowledged that tattoos might threaten important aspects of their self-presentations in the larger society. Addison, a twenty-nine-year-old graduate student, explained:

> I went through this weird little period of grief after getting my ankle tattoo. Although I had thought about and wanted a tattoo for two years and was completely dedicated to having a tattoo, I experienced this unexpected sadness. It started when I was watching this old movie with Lauren Bacall. She was standing behind a billboard with only her ankles showing. Humphrey Bogart let out this terrific whistle, like isn't she beautiful. I realized that my ankle would never evoke that same sense of femininity. Sure, in some alterna-crowd it might say "cool, deviant chick," but it would never universally communicate "beauty."

Once they realized the status consequences of having tattoos, individuals lost their initial tattoo zeal. Many discussed worries about others' reactions as forces that "competed with" or "muddied" their enthusiasm. Meg, who decided not to get a tattoo, described the competition between tattoo attractions and aversions as a battle between good and evil. She remarked:

> I think that in the back of my mind that I want one [a tattoo]. But even from the moment that I started to want one, there is the fear of . . . the consequences.

Kind of like the little angel on one shoulder and a little devil on the other shoulder. One telling you to do something and one telling you all the consequences of what would happen. I guess my little angel is stronger than my little devil.

Through a series of interactions, individuals learned ways to reconcile their desires for tattoos with their fears of losing social status. While interacting with parents and other conventional individuals, potential tattooees collected detailed information about the nature and dimensions of the anti-tattoo sentiments surrounding them. This information prompted many respondents to pursue body art in ways that complemented mainstream norms and values. Potential tattooees also interacted with and watched others embark on the journey of becoming tattooed. Their observations allowed them to pick up on techniques used by those facing the same dilemma.

Legitimation Techniques

At its core, the competition between attractions to and aversions from deviance involved a legitimation process. Working within a Weberian framework, some scholars have looked at legitimation as having authority and power over others (Thomas, Walker, and Zelditch 1986; Walker, Thomas, and Zelditch 1986; Walker and Zelditch 1993; Wolf 1986). Legitimation among tattooees remained a subtle expression of power and prestige; it was not located in the power dynamics between subordinates and superiors working in formal organizations. Like many deviants who find themselves subjected to informal sanctions, potential tattooees worried about losing status in interaction contexts. Similar to those who use accounts (Scott and Lyman 1968), neutralizations (Sykes and Matza 1957), and other stigma management techniques (Goffman 1963), tattooees expressed concern about how they would be defined during face-to-face interactions. To maintain their middle-class status, and all its advantages, tattooees employed four legitimation maneuvers to define their actions and their tattoos within core mainstream norms and values. Like accounts, verbal neutralizations, and stigma management techniques, legitimation techniques often rescued individuals from negative sanctions during face-to-face interactions. However, unlike stigma management maneuvers, legitimation techniques worked by changing the meanings associated with the deviant activity.

Using Mainstream Motivations

Throughout the process of becoming tattooed, individuals attempted to frame their desires for tattoos within mainstream definitions of success and achievement. Like deviant and criminal individuals with tattoos (Phelan and Hunt 1998), middle-class tattooees in the 1990s used their tattoos to announce their passage through particular moral careers. Whereas prison gang members wanted to chronicle their passage through deviant careers, middle-class tattooees used their tattoos to mark conventional aspects of themselves.

Many tattooees explained that they wanted tattoos to commemorate special times in their lives. Their celebrations usually centered on a set of conventional achievements such as graduation from college or graduate school, finishing major exams, or the birth of children. As rites of passage, getting tattoos at major life transitions served as permanent reminders of lessons learned, milestones accomplished, and personal growth gained . . .

Potential tattooees also explained that tattoos helped them to celebrate their favorite personality traits. They chose designs with symbolic meanings, for example, to foster their sense of humor (comic book characters), their artistic nature (nonfigurative designs), their gentleness (flowers, birds, dolphins, hearts), or their personal power (lions and jaguars). Judy described why she was drawn to her tattoo:

> I liked it right off the bat. I started thinking about it and why I liked it. The design is kind of round, kind of strong, it flowed from one half into the other without stopping and separating. . . . It reinforces and says "me." I felt that I didn't want a flower or a bird or one of the really femmy designs. It didn't fit my personality. I felt that I was a forceful woman and I needed a forceful tattoo. I needed something strong.

Interestingly, the life transitions, skills, achievements, and personality traits that individuals celebrated with tattoos were those that were also celebrated and rewarded in conventional society. By casting their motivations for tattoos within conventional frameworks, individuals were marking their passage through mainstream moral careers.

Using mainstream motivations quelled parents' concerns about tattoos. Parents who initially suggested that they did not approve of tattoos sometimes changed their minds when they heard the reasons that others became tattooed . . .

Committing to Conventional Behavior

Responding to conventional individuals' beliefs that tattoos accompanied a host of undesirable behaviors, tattooees became dedicated to proving that they could get a tattoo while remaining active in a variety of conventional pursuits, including school, family, and professional careers. Some tattooees suggested that their involvement in conventional activities outweighed the negative meanings associated with their tattoos. Addison explained why she felt that her tattoo was not a serious threat to her social status:

> My dad said something negative about [my tattoo] the other day. He made this little joke about me having a little bit of dirt on my ankle. However, I don't think that he really means anything by it. How could he really oppose? Look at me, I'm everything he could want a kid to be. I'm a serious student. I get great grades. I am doing well in a career that I love and he loves. I'm married. Someday soon I will give him plenty of grandchildren. With all that, what difference is a tattoo going to make?

Others attempted to demonstrate how getting tattoos was part of their commitment to conventionality. Potential tattooees often noted how they carefully planned their tattoos and attempted to show how they were conforming to conventional standards of self-control and rationality . . .

Contrary to the image of first tattoos as the product of reckless, impulsive, and drunken decisions, tattoos at the Blue Mosque resulted from careful planning. Adopting their parents' concerns about safety, hygiene, and cleanliness, first-time clients at the Blue Mosque often searched for clean shops that employed experienced, professional artists who conformed to rigorous sterilization procedures and artistic goals . . .

Tattooees' behaviors before, during, and after becoming tattooed demonstrated their continued involvement in conventional activities. By carefully studying their tattooists, their (tattoo) environments, and their designs, tattooees demonstrated that they did not make spontaneous decisions. Instead, tattooees showed that getting tattoos, like conventional activities, required hard work, restraint, and much forethought. In this way tattooees placed getting tattoos within a repertoire of conventional behaviors.

The technique of committing to conventional behavior resembled the destigmatization technique of transcendence (Warren 1980). Unlike those engaging in the technique of transcendence, however, tattooees did not attempt to "insulate, hide or encapsulate [their] negative essence by superior performances" (Warren 1980:65). Rather, they attempted to demonstrate how their tattoos were part of their conventionality. Commitment to conventional behavior thus helped the stigmatized behavior itself, not just the stigmatized person, to transcend a deviant status.

Tattooees were often pleased to find that their commitment to conventionality worked to appease their parents and helped others to overcome their worries about tattoos. Many tattooees' parents, who initially feared the idea of their children getting tattoos, admitted feeling that the tattoo did not detract from their children's other conventional attributes. Nedra, who was concerned that her child would be negatively labeled, described why she did not oppose her daughter's tattoo: "The only thing I worry about [with my daughter's tattoo], is that she will continue to get more. The one that she has, I'm not so worried about. . . . I think that being in the field that she is, having the education that she does, the tattoo is not going to label her as a counterculture person."

Other parents suggested that they approved of the way their children pursued becoming tattooed. The following is an excerpt from my field notes describing my conversation with a parent of an eighteen-year-old:

> I just got off the phone with a friend of mine. She told me that her daughter was thinking about getting a tattoo. My friend is from an upper-class family and I am assuming that this family will not like one of their own getting a tattoo. However, instead of being worried, my friend sounded excited. She told me that her daughter went to every tattoo shop in town, asked about their sterilization procedures, and looked at all their portfolios of artwork before deciding to get a tattoo. She also said that her daughter found a very clean and professional shop in town. At the end of the conversation, my friend suggested that the care with which her daughter selected the shop showed that her daughter was thinking wisely and being very adult in her tattoo decision.

Conforming to Conventional Aesthetics

. . . Because tattooees worried that others thought of tattoos as unsightly emblems of outcast culture, they wanted artwork that departed as much as possible from images of "ugly," antisocial tattoos. In contrast to members of deviant groups such as bikers, punk rockers, and skinheads, middle-class tattooees primarily wanted small, discreet tattoos with conventional themes. For women, this often meant getting images that associated with femininity. Grace said: "To me, up until I got one, and to her [her mother], tattoos were ugly. They were macho and white trash. I got one and mine is not like that. Mine is very feminine. Mine is very unique. . . . I think that when girls get tattoos it should be soft." Size was as important as imagery and themes. First-time tattooees often preferred to get small designs and suggested that small tattoos were the least likely to offend others . . .

Individuals' attempts to create discreet, pleasant, fine art-inspired tattoos worked to sway some critics' opinions of tattoos. Frank initially did not want his children to get tattoos for fear that they would be stigmatized. After looking at two of his children's tattoos, as well as tattoos worn by their contemporaries Frank changed his mind. He explained: "It is clear that tattoos have become much more artistic. They are crossing lines and it has erased the stigma. Some of these tattoos on the shoulders, I find artistic."

While individuals initially reported being attracted to the deviant mystique surrounding tattoos, their motivations for tattoos, their repertoire of behaviors before, during, and after getting a tattoo, and the types of tattoos they acquired usually demonstrated their conventionality. In the end, their tattoos did more to announce their connection to rather than their independence from conventionality.

The techniques of legitimation employed by tattooees played an important part in changing conventional individuals' opinions of tattoos. Conservative parents, friends, and partners reported liking some aspect of others' tattoos. Tattooees' behaviors, their motivations, and the aesthetic quality of their tattoos were among the more powerful forces that softened conventional individuals' stances. In fact, after seeing their children, friends, or partners become tattooed, a few critics suggested that they were interested in becoming tattooed themselves . . .

Conclusion

I have shown how middle-class tattooees take up a once-deviant behavior and help to reduce or remove the stigma associated with it through a series of legitimation maneuvers. Interaction rested at the core of the development, use, and success of these legitimation techniques practiced by middle-class tattooees in the 1990s. Potential tattooees initially felt that tattoos connoted freedom and independence from adult constraints. However, after interacting with the conventional individuals in their lives, potential tattooees learned the different ways that tattoos threatened core conventional values and norms regarding hygiene, beauty, decision making, and self-presentation. These young adults became concerned that the negative associations attached to tattoos would vitiate the positive connotations of becoming tattooed. Through interaction with others (tattooees, parents, tattooists), potential tattooees learned different ways to negotiate their tattoo status. This network of informal, everyday interactions eventually led tattooees to develop, refine, and use a set of similar responses to maintain their status after getting tattoos.

These data suggest not only that tattooees pursued becoming tattooed in common ways but that their efforts to maintain legitimacy were largely successful. When tattooees braced themselves to hear criticisms and complaints from others, they were often pleased to find themselves the recipients of acceptance and praise. Over time, many tattooees found that their standing in conventional society remained unchanged. Legitimation techniques not only worked to mitigate the negative associations with tattoos, but they worked to conventionalize many aspects of the tattoo experience. In an ironic twist, tattooees ended up confirming many of the norms and values they were initially trying to escape. My findings suggest the need for a model of moral passage that places everyday interactions at the center of its explanations.

In fact, those working within the two dominant interaction models of social change, the moral entrepreneurial (Becker 1963; Best 1990; Spector and Kitsuse 1977) and the diffusion (Adler and Adler 1978; Goode 1970; Winick 1977), tend to gloss over the importance of everyday interactions. Those working within the moral entrepreneurial model have put such forces as moral campaigns, political protests, and media coverage at the center of their theoretical discussions. Within this model, social construction has become equated with formal, political, or institutional action. Those working within the diffusion model have not looked at the interactional mechanisms that cause association with mainstream individuals to end

in the legitimation of a behavior. At best, the diffusion model suggests that legitimation occurs through imitation. My research goes beyond suggesting that mainstream individuals imitate the activities of deviants. It suggests that middle-class individuals are conscious, self-reflective actors who interpret the social meanings of their activities and the consequences these meanings have for their identities. It also demonstrates how deviants develop a set of patterned techniques to negotiate for more conventional statuses of particular behaviors.

These findings point to a general inability of our theories to explain how interactions are tied to social change. The dominant image provided by moral passage theories is that informal, everyday interactions can only serve as stigma management techniques (Davis 1961; Goffman 1963; Hewitt and Stokes 1975; Lyman 1970; Scott and Lyman 1968) and that changing social definitions of deviance are the result of larger social forces, formal political behavior, or population shifts. However, I argue that informal interactions occur alongside larger, more formal forces and contribute to moral passage. Given the common social constructionist argument that everyday, symbolic interaction remains at the core of how objects and behaviors are constructed (Best 1998; Blumer 1969; Mead 1934), I argue that our theories need to offer a specific explanation of the way interactions contribute to cultural shifts. To date, the most forceful statement explaining this process comes from Stokes and Hewitt, who have argued:

> Members of a society facing altered circumstances but still cognizant of culture, may use aligning actions to square their altered conduct with those prevailing standards. Over longer periods of time, the presumption we make is that culture follows conduct, and that the evolutionary drift is toward the adjustment of culture to actual conduct. (1976:848)

. . . The context of tattoo legitimation in the 1990s sheds some light on when legitimation is mostly likely to occur. During the 1990s, people attributed conflicting meanings to tattoos as the older deviant meanings coexisted with newer, more progressive ones. Given the varied tattoo images circulating in different social groups, individuals with contacts in many social worlds were likely to experience attractions to and aversions from this form of deviance. Lacking a clear consensus regarding the meaning of becoming tattooed, individuals who experience conflict were likely to use their everyday interactions to tip the general moral balance toward acceptance of this activity. This suggests that individuals might be more likely to use legitimation techniques with activities that lack a unified symbolic meaning. Those engaged in commonly denounced activities (i.e., pedophilia, incest, devil worship) might be more likely to distance themselves from or hide their deviance by using stigma management techniques. The occurrence of legitimation techniques might also indicate the level of moral consensus on particular activities. If individuals tend to rely on legitimation more often than stigma management techniques, then society might be experiencing a time of moral indecision regarding certain deviant acts.

Becoming tattooed in the 1990s demonstrates some of the informal means through which a behavior becomes more tolerated. This study implies that informal interaction processes might be an important force not only when behaviors become normalized but also when deviance is created and tolerance for an activity is decreased. Future research needs to identify how such formal behaviors as moral entrepreneurial campaign building (Becker 1963), claims making (Best 1990; Spector and Kitsuse 1977), public arena competition (Hilgartner and Bosk 1988), and formal political behavior combine with informal interactions in everyday contexts to create deviance.

Acknowledgments

I want to offer special thanks to the following for their guidance and helpful suggestions: Patricia Adler and Peter Adler, Alice Fothergill, Kathryn Fox, Jennifer Lois, Adina Nack, Dmitri Shalin, Lance Talon, Angus Vail, and the anonymous reviewers for *Symbolic Interaction*.

NOTES

1. Throughout history, tattooists have reported working with middle-class clients (Steward 1990). However, the numbers of middle-class tattoo clients during the 1980s and 1990s increased so dramatically that many tattooists relied almost exclusively on a middle-class clientele.

2. Warren (1988:36) notes that sexual relationships with subjects in the field is a "prevalent" theme in fieldwork but not one about which "researchers like to elaborate." Nevertheless, sexual relationships in the field are a documented reality (Davis 1986; Golde 1986; Goode 1999; Kulick and Wilson 1995; Newton 1993; Styles 1979).

3. Interestingly, among all the concerns inherent in the first tattoo, price was usually not an issue. First tattoos were usually small and cost between $100 and $200. This did not prove an economic hardship for the middle-class individuals in this subculture.

4. According to tattooists, larger work was less likely to blur and lose distinction over time. In addition, tattooists were able to use more of their fine art skills while working on large designs.

5. The history of tattooing in America reveals several popular panics over the connection between tattoos and diseases. Steward (1990:190) notes that "by 1968 over 47 major cities . . . had special ordinances against tattooing." Many of these ordinances, especially those in New York City in 1964, were to control the spread of such diseases as hepatitis B. While some medical literature has implicated tattooing in the spread of diseases (Jones, Maloney, and Helm 1997; Limentani et al. 1979), McCabe (1995) suggests that the outlawing of tattooing in New York City came more from moral concerns than from attempts to stem the spread of hepatitis B.

REFERENCES

Adler, Patricia and Peter Adler. 1978. "Tinydopers: A Case Study of Deviant Socialization." *Symbolic Interaction* 1:90–105.

———. 1987. *Membership Roles in Field Research.* Newbury Park, CA: Sage.

———. 1998. *Peer Power: Preadolescent Culture and Identity.* New Brunswick, NJ: Rutgers University Press.

Akers, Ronald L., Marvin D. Krohn, Lonn Lanza-Kaduce, and Marcia Radosevich. 1979. "Social Learning and Deviant Behavior: A Specific Test of a General Theory." *American Sociological Review* 44:636–55.

Becker, Howard. 1953. "Becoming a Marijuana User." *American Journal of Sociology* 59:235–42.

———. 1963. *Outsiders.* New York: Free Press.

Best, Joel. 1990. *Threatened Children: Rhetoric and Concern about Child-Victims.* Chicago: University of Chicago Press.

———. 1998. "Too Much Fun: Toys as Social Problems and the Interpretation of Culture." *Symbolic Interaction* 21:197–212.

Blumer, Herbert. 1969. *Symbolic Interactionism: Perspective and Method.* Berkeley: University of California Press.

Davis, Donna. 1986. "Changing Self-Image: Studying Menopausal Women in a Newfoundland Fishing Village." Pp. 240–61 in *Self, Sex and Gender in Cross Cultural Fieldwork,* edited by T. L. Whitehead and M. E. Conaway. Urbana: University of Illinois Press.

Davis, Fred. 1961. "Deviance Disavowal: The Management of Strained Interaction by the Visibly Handicapped." *Social Problems* 9:120–32.

DeMello, Margo. 1995. "Not Just for Bikers Anymore: Popular Representations of American Tattooing." *Journal of Popular Culture* 29:37–52.

Elliott, Delbert S. and Scott Menard. 1996. "Delinquent Friends and Delinquent Behavior: Temporal and Developmental Patterns." Pp. 28–67 in *Delinquency and Crime: Current Theories,* edited by J. D. Hawkins. Cambridge: Cambridge University Press.

Erickson, Maynard and LaMar Empey. 1965. "Class Position, Peers and Delinquency." *Sociology and Social Research* 49:268–82.

Garmezy, Norman. 1985. "Stress Resistant Children: The Search for Protective Factors." Pp. 213–33 in *Recent Research in Developmental Psychopathology,* edited by J. E. Stevenson. New York: Pergamon.

Goffman, Erving. 1963. *Stigma.* Englewood Cliffs, NJ: Prentice-Hall.

Golde, Peggy. 1986. "Odyssey of Encounter." Pp. 67–93 in *Women in the Field: Anthropological Experiences,* edited by P. Golde. Berkeley: University of California Press.

Goode, Erich. 1970. *The Marijuana Smokers.* New York: Basic Books.

———. 1999. "Sex with Informants as Deviant Behavior: An Account and Commentary." *Deviant Behavior* 20:301–24.

Hebdige, Dick. 1979. *Subculture, the Meaning of Style.* London: Methuen.

Hewitt, John P. and Randall Stokes. 1975. "Disclaimers." *American Sociological Review* 40:1–11.

Hilgartner, Stephen and Charles L. Bosk. 1988. "The Rise and Fall of Social Problems: A Public Arenas Model." *American Journal of Sociology* 94:53–78.

Hirschi, Travis. 1969. *Causes of Delinquency.* Berkeley: University of California Press.

Jankowski, Martin Sanchez. 1991. *Islands in the Street: Gangs and American Urban Society.* Berkeley: University of California Press.

Jones, M. S., M. E. Maloney, and K. F. Helm. 1997. "Systemic Sarcoidosis Presenting in the Black Dye of a Tattoo. *Cutis* 59:113–15.

Kleinman, Sheryl. 1982. "Actors' Conflicting Theories of Negotiation: The Case of a Holistic Health Center." *Urban Life* 11:312–27.

———. 1996. *Opposing Ambitions: Gender and Identity in an Alternative Organization.* Chicago: University of Chicago Press.

Kulick, Don and Margaret Wilson. 1995. *Taboo: Sex, Identity, and Erotic Subjectivity in Anthropological Fieldwork.* New York: Routledge.

Kuntzman, Gersh. 1999. "It's Been 40 Years Coming and Now . . . Barbie's New, Improved and Tattooed." *New York Post,* 4, 61–62.

Limentani, A. E., L. M. Elliott, N. D. Noah, and J. K. Lamborn. 1979. "An Outbreak of Hepatitis B from Tattooing." *Lancet* 2(8133):86–88.

Lyman, Stanford M. 1970. *The Asian in the West.* Reno/Las Vegas, NV: Western Studies Center, Desert Research Institute.

Manning, Peter K. 1977. "Rules in Organizational Context: Narcotics Law Enforcement in Two Settings." *Sociological Quarterly* 18:44–61.

McCabe, Michael. 1995. "Coney Island Tattoo: The Growth of Inclusive Culture in the Age of the Machine." Pp. 48–55 in *Pierced Hearts and True Love,* edited by D. E. Hardy. New York: Drawing Center.

Mead, George H. 1934. *Mind, Self and Society.* Chicago: University of Chicago Press.

Merton, Robert K. 1968. *Social Theory and Social Structure.* New York: Free Press.

Messerschmidt, James W. 1993. *Masculinities and Crime.* Lanham, MD: Rowman and Littlefield.

Mifflin, Margo. 1997. *Bodies of Subversion.* New York: Juno Books.

Milwaukee Journal Sentinel. 1998. "Beauty Marks." November 29, p. 1.

Moynihan, Daniel Patrick. 1993. "Defining Deviance Down." *American Scholar* 62:17–30.

Newton, Esther. 1993. "My Best Informant's Dress: The Erotic Equation in Fieldwork." *Cultural Anthropology* 8:3–23.

Parry, Albert. 1933. *Tattoo: Secrets of a Strange Art Practiced by the Natives of the United States.* New York: Collier.

Phelan, Michael P. and Scott A. Hunt. 1998. "Prison Gang Members' Tattoos as Identity Work: The Visual Communication of Moral Careers." *Symbolic Interaction* 21:277–98.

Providence Journal-Bulletin. 1999. "The Bay State Tattoo Crisis." July 15, p. 6B.

Riemer, Jeffrey W. 1977. "Varieties of Opportunistic Research." *Urban Life* 5:467–77.

Rubin, Arnold. 1988. "The Tattoo Renaissance." Pp. 233–62 in *Marks of Civilization,* edited by A. Rubin. Los Angeles: Museum of Cultural History, University of California, Los Angeles.

Sanders, Clinton. 1989. *Customizing the Body: The Art and Culture of Tattooing.* Philadelphia: Temple University Press.

———. 1991. "Memorial Decoration: Women, Tattooing, and the Meanings of Body Alteration." *Michigan Quarterly Review* 30:146–57.

Scott, Marvin B. and Stanford M. Lyman. 1968. "Accounts." *American Sociological Review* 33:46–62.

Spector, Malcolm and John I. Kitsuse. 1977. *Constructing Social Problems.* Menlo Park, CA: Cummings.

Steward, Samuel M. 1990. *Bad Boys and Tough Tattoos: A Social History of the Tattoo with Gangs, Sailors, and Street-Corner Punks 1950–1965.* New York: Haworth Press.

Stokes, Randall and John P. Hewitt. 1976. "Aligning Actions." *American Sociological Review* 41:838–49.

Strauss, Anselm, Leonard Schatzman, Danuta Ehrlich, Rue Bucher, and Melvin Sabshin. 1963. "The Hospital and Its

Negotiated Order." Pp. 147–69 in *The Hospital in Modern Society,* edited by E. Freidson. New York: Free Press.

Styles, Joseph. 1979. "Outsider/Insider: Researching Gay Baths." *Urban Life* 2:135–52.

Sykes, Gresham M. and David Matza. 1957. "Techniques of Neutralization: A Theory of Delinquency." *American Sociological Review* 22:664–70.

Telvin, Jon. 1999. "Body Art Uninspiring in Today's Job Market." *Star Tribune,* August 6, p. 1A.

Thomas, George M., Henry A. Walker, and Morris Zelditch, Jr. 1986. "Legitimacy and Collective Action." *Social Forces* 65:378–404.

Thornton, Arland. 1985. "Changing Attitudes towards Separation and Divorce: Causes and Consequences." *American Journal of Sociology* 90:856–72.

Vail, D. Angus. 1999. "Tattoos Are Like Potato Chips . . . You Can't Have Just One: The Process of Becoming and Being a Collector." *Deviant Behavior* 20:253–73.

Vale, V. and Andrea Juno. 1989. *Modern Primitives: An Investigation of Contemporary Adornment and Ritual.* San Francisco: Re/Search Publications.

Waldorf, Dan, Craig Reinarman, and Sheigla Murphy. 1991. *Cocaine Changes: The Experience of Using and Quitting.* Philadelphia: Temple University Press.

Walker, Henry A. and Morris Zelditch, Jr. 1993. "Power, Legitimacy, and the Stability of Authority: A Theoretical Research Program." Pp. 364–81 in *Theoretical Research Programs: Studies in the Growth of Theory,* edited by J. Berger and M. Zelditch, Jr. Stanford: Stanford University Press.

Walker, Henry A., George M. Thomas, and Morris Zelditch, Jr. 1986. "Legitimation, Endorsement, and Stability." *Social Forces* 64:620–43.

Warr, Mark. 1993. "Age, Peers, and Delinquency." *Criminology* 31:17–40.

Warren, Carol A. B. 1980. "Destigmatization of Identity: From Deviant to Charismatic." *Qualitative Sociology* 3:57–72.

———. 1988. *Gender Issues in Field Research.* Newbury Park: Sage.

Werner, Emmy E. 1989. "High Risk Children in Young Adulthood." *American Journal of Orthopsychiatry* 59:72–81.

———. 1992. *Overcoming the Odds: High Risk Children from Birth to Adulthood.* Ithaca, NY: Cornell University Press.

Winick, Charles. 1977. "From Deviant to Normative: Changes in the Social Acceptability of Sexually Explicit Material." Pp. 219–46 in *Deviance and Social Change,* edited by E. Sagarin. Beverly Hills, CA: Sage.

Wolf, Charlotte. 1986. "Legitimation of Oppression: Response and Reflexivity." *Symbolic Interaction* 9:217–34.

Think Critically

1. Which "negotiations" analyzed by Irwin do you feel are most important in determining whether or not a person becomes tattooed?
2. Do you feel that Irwin's insider status in the tattoo world provided extra insights that would not ordinarily be available to outsiders? Explain your answer.

Index